BUSINESS ORGANISATION AND MANAGEMENT

EIGHTEENTH REVISED EDITION

M.C. SHUKLA
B.A. B.Com (Birmingham), Bar-at-Law,
Retired Professor of Commerce and
Director of Correspondence Course
University of Delhi
Delhi

S.CHAND
PUBLISHING

S Chand And Company Limited
(ISO 9001 Certified Company)

S. CHAND
PUBLISHING

S Chand And Company Limited

(ISO 9001 Certified Company)

Head Office: D-92, Sector–2, Noida – 201301, U.P. (India), Ph. 91-120-4682700

Registered Office: A-27, 2nd Floor, Mohan Co-operative Industrial Estate, New Delhi – 110 044, Phone: 011-49731800

www.**schandpublishing.com;** e-mail: **info@schandpublishing.com**

Marketing Offices:

Chennai : Ph: 23632120; chennai@schandpublishing.com
Guwahati : Ph: 2738811, 2735640; guwahati@schandpublishing.com
Hyderabad : Ph: 40186018; hyderabad@schandpublishing.com
Jalandhar : Ph: 4645630; jalandhar@schandpublishing.com
Kolkata : Ph: 23357458, 23353914; kolkata@schandpublishing.com
Lucknow : Ph: 4003633; lucknow@schandpublishing.com
Mumbai : Ph: 25000297; mumbai@schandpublishing.com
Patna : Ph: 2260011; patna@schandpublishing.com

First Edition 1953
Subsequent Editions and Reprints 1954, 56, 58, 60, 62, 64, 65, 67, 68, 70, 71, 72, 74, 75, 76, 78, 80, 81, 82, 83, 85, 86, 88, 91, 93, 94, 95, 97, 98, 99, 2000, 2001, 2003, 2006, 2007, 2008, 2009, 2010, 2011, 2013, 2014 (Twice), 2017 (Thrice), 2018, 2021
Reprint 2024

ISBN: 978-81-219-0813-9 **Product Code:** H8ORM48BMGT10ENAR0XR

PRINTED IN INDIA

By Vikas Publishing House Private Limited, Plot 20/4, Site-IV, Industrial Area Sahibabad, Ghaziabad – 201 010 and Published by S Chand And Company Limited, A-27, 2nd Floor, Mohan Co-operative Industrial Estate, New Delhi – 110 044.

PREFACE TO THE EIGHTEENTH EDITION

Many changes that have taken place since the publication of the Seventeenth Edition have necessitated thorough and exhaustive revisions and updating of several chapters, as well as re-writing of some of them. More particularly, chapters dealing with Company Management, Principal of Management, Government and Business, Public Enterprises, Financial Function of Management and Advertising have been re-written either in part or in full with a view to incorporating new ideas and developments. As a result, the book should prove of greater utility to the student and the practising manager.

A book such as this one owes much to the ideas of many people — writers, teachers and managers — most of them unnamed. The author offers, as in previous editions, his sincere thanks for the valuable suggestions which have been adopted wherever practicable.

I must, of course, continue to offer my grateful thanks to my late wife, Blanche Sheila Shukla, who saw the first twelve editions of the book through the press. But for her sacrifices and patience those editions of the book could not have been brought out. She was indeed the best helpmate and communicator.

NEW DELHI M.C. SHUKLA

PREFACE TO THE FIRST EDITION

I have endeavoured in the present volume to set forth the principles of Business Organisation and Management with as much precision, cohesion, and system as the subject admits of and with as much detailed consideration as is necessay to make the work one of practical utility. While the book is written chiefly as a text book for students preparing for the B. Com and M. Com. Examinations of the various Indian Universities, it is not intended to be merely a 'cram book' for examinations. Apart from supplying the requisite information in a logical and convenient manner the book aims to encourage the student to augment his knowledge by reading some of the many monographs on various aspects of the subject; indeed, it is hoped that the reading of this book will stimulate him to read more widely, and for this purpose a list of books is appended at the end.

It is not claimed that the present work contains an exhaustive treatment of all the topics dealt with in it; this is almost an impossibility in the case of such a vast subject. An attempt has, however, been made to make it as comprehensive and up-to-date as possible with regard to its objects, which are mainly to meet in full measure the requirements of Commerce students. It is also hoped that businessmen who are concerned, directly or indirectly, with the organisation, conduct and management of commercial and industrial undertakings will find this exposition, in moderate compass, of considerable use; for in writing the following pages I have amply drawn upon my practical experience as an executive in two cotton textile mills and also as liquidator of companies.

Many cross-references in the text enable any particular subject to be quickly traced. A selection of examples is also given, some of the these are descriptive, others are calculations. Another important feature of the book is numerous charts and diagrams, designed specially to illuminate the subject. A number of tables give up-to-date list of contents, and cross-Indian conditions. To further facilitate the use of the book, the page headings have been selected to form a running list of contents, and cross-references are given in the exhaustive index to link up different aspects of the same subject. A considerable variety of questions have been set at the end of the book, some of which have been composed by the author and the others are based upon the various examination papers.

The nature of the present work does not permit me to acknowledge my indebtedness, individually, to all the authorities of the world from whom I have drawn materials as well as inspiration in preparing the treatise. All the authorities mentioned at the end of the book have been consulted. I express my sense of gratitude to them.

In the onerous task of preparing this book, I have received helpful assistance from my friends, and colleagues, Messrs, A.B. Ghosh, M.A., and T.S. Grewal, M.A., which I hasten to acknowledge.

I feel particularly indebted to Prof. V.K.R.V. Rao, M.A. Ph.D., D.Litt., Director, Delhi School of Economics, and Professor of Economics, University of Delhi, for his very kindly writing an introduction to this book.

Before placing this volume in the hands of the readers, I must extend my grateful thanks to my wife for co-operation and encouragement in various ways and for careful reading of the manuscript in its different stages of preparation.

July 17, 1952

M.C. SHUKLA

CONTENTS

PART ONE — BUSINESS SYSTEM

PART TWO — LEGAL OWNERSHIP AND SIZE OF FIRM

PART THREE — COMPANY MANAGEMENT

PART FOUR — HORIZONS OF BUSINESS

PART FIVE — PRINCIPLES OF MANAGEMENT

PART SIX — PRODUCTION FUNCTION OF MANAGEMENT

PART ONE
Business System

CHAPTER I
THE NATURE OF BUSINESS

Introduction. The subject of this book is business enterprise system and how it is organised and managed. The book also deals with the factors which influence the operation of the enterprise as an efficient and progressive concern. An enterprise is also influenced, directly and indirectly, by its environment, for it cannot function in isolation. There are, however, many forms of enterprise in India; and economic activities are performed by sole traders, partnerships, incorporated companies and cooperatives. In the earlier portion of the book, therefore, the enterprise will be studied as a system and the factors which constitute it.

Economic Activities. Man is a wanting being : he always wants, and wants more. The journey of an individual through life can take almost infinite number of paths: yet at every point in the journey—infancy to old age—each individual seeks to fulfil his unique set of needs and wants. Many of these desires, such as the biological drives and the instinct for sustaining life, are inherent; there are others which are ever expanding. Man must work, and work to satisfy these wants through the use of scarce resources of production. Economic activities of man, therefore, deal with the business of living and making a living. To make a living, every person follows an occupation according to his inkling and training. He may follow a profession, or seek employment or set up a business, which may be organised on personal level or may be conducted through a joint stock company. A brief description of each type of human occupation is in point.

Professions. By profession is meant an occupation which renders specialised, expert and personal service. A lawyer, a doctor, a chartered accountant, or an engineer renders specialised services in respective of his field in return for payment. For example, a doctor provides health services by preventing illness from arising and by treating when it has arisen. A doctor's or lawyer's work is purely and essentially of personal character. He comes into personal and intimate contact with his patient or client and uses his expert knowledge to deal with his patients' or clients' problems. Since a doctor or a lawyer or any other practitioner of a profession has to be an expert in his own special activity, he must possess the minimum academic and other qualifications prescribed by law, before he can practise his profession.

Employment. In this type of activity, a person undertakes to work for another according to the terms of a service agreement in return for a salary or wage, or even commission. A relation of master and servant is created under a contract of service, and the servant acts under the control and supervision of his master and is bound to conform to all reasonable orders given to him in the course of his work. A person may be appointed a manager, a secretary. or even a professionally qualified person, e.g., a chartered accountant, may be appointed to look after the finances of the company.

Business. Literally, 'business' means *busyness* or the state of being busy—any activity a man is busy about. Accordingly, a person may become busy in reading, writing, painting, playing, because any of these activities may bring him money, prestige, power or any other kinds of satisfaction known only to him. But in economic sense, the word "Business" means work, efforts and acts of people which are connected with the production of wealth.

Functionally, by business, we mean those human activities which involve production or purchase of goods with the object of selling them at a profit. In the words of Urwick and Hunt,* a "Business is any enterprise which makes, distributes or provides any article or service which other members of the community need and are able and willing to pay for." In essence, therefore, business concerns with producing and selling for profit.

Characteristics of Business. The activities termed "Business" possess the following characteristics :

(a) *Production or acquisition of goods.* Since it is the business of "business" to provide goods to people for a price, it is necessary that there are goods to be supplied. They must therefore be either manufactured or produced or they must be procured so that they can be sold and supplied.

(b) *Sale or transfer of title.* Goods which have been produced or procured for sale in return for price enter the realm of business. This activity of selling results in the production and acquisition of wealth. Goods produced or acquired for personal consumption, however, do not fall within the scope of business.

(c) *Dealings in goods and services.* Business means dealing in goods and services. The goods may be consumers' goods, such as cloth, bread, jams, shoes, watches, etc., or producers' goods, such as machinery and tools. Services consist of those items which are not stored by consumers, such as transport services.

(d) *Regularity of dealings.* Regularity and recurring nature of buying and selling which ensures continuity of transactions is a characteristic of business. A single transaction involving buying and selling does not become business. For instance, if a person sells his motor car and makes a profit, it does not amount to business. On the other hand, if he keeps a stock of cars and sells them to customers, he carries on a business.

(e) *Profits as reward for service rendered.* Business is an activity by which men make their living, or earn profit. Making profit is an essential characteristic of business. Profit is the biggest stimulus for maintaining the continuity of business. In other words, profit is essential for survival

---

***Hand book of Business Administration*

and development. The hope of making a good profit attracts men of ability to business. In fact, profit is, in a sense, a reward for the individual ability or efficiency of the enterpriser and also for the service that he renders to the community.

(f) *Uncertainty or risk about future.* Economic activity, because it is activity focuses on the future; and one thing certain about the future is its uncertainty, its risk. It is through risk-taking that any businessman earns his profit. The conduct of industry or business always involves a certain amount of risk and uncertainty of return to the entrepreneur.

OBJECTIVES OF BUSINESS

Every human activity has some objective or objectives, and business, as one of the important human activities, must have objectives.

There is a common belief that money making is the objective of business. Maximisation of profits is the prevailing norm among businessmen themselves. Money-chasing to them seems to be the primary economic objective of business. So a company must earn profit if it is to continue to exist. It is necessary to make earnings if additional capital is to be attracted and reserves are to be built up for meeting risk inherent in business activity. But to say that the sole purpose of any business is to make profit, is like saying that eating is the sole purpose of living, or that blood circulation is of supreme importance for human survival and breathing, digestion, or proper functioning of the nervous system count for nothing.

Obviously, a company must make profit for survival, but for survival it is also necessary that it produces goods or renders services that customers want. Its conditions of employment must be so good as to attract competent employees, and it should be an acceptable firm to the community in which it operates. Remove any of these essentials and the enterprise collapses. It is therefore important to recognise the fact that profit is the legitimate reward for honest endeavour, something the entrepreneur gets for rendering service to the community.

Viewed in this light, profit plays a vital role as a measure of efficiency, and must be watched constantly. After all, profits provide not only the most accurate test of business efficiency, but also a sure check against failure. Over a course of time, profits are the measures of how well a company has met the needs of labour, consumers, shareholders, and the general public.

Besides economic objectives, a business has social objectives. In fact, the two objectives are intimately related. The primary objective of business therefore should be satisfaction of human wants through supply of quality goods at reasonable prices. Another objective is to provide a fair return to the investor and to have sufficient amount to cover future risks and to ensure future expansion. The third objective is to 'create customers' and meet their needs and wants, and also provide fair wages to the workers.

A detailed discussion of the subject will be found in the Chapter on Social Responsibilities of Business. Suffice it to state here that business has economic as well as social objectives. Its economic objectives relate to earning a satisfactory profit, creating customers and making innovation. Its social objectives comprise supply of quality goods in sufficient quantity at reasonable prices, fair deal to workers, fair returns to investors, and fair dealings with suppliers of materials. The following table gives in a summary form the objectives of business :

BUSINESS OBJECTIVES

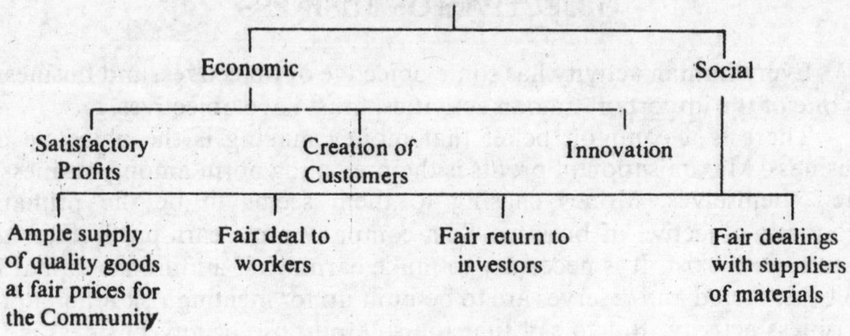

To sum up, "business" may be said to be any enterprise which makes, distributes, or provides any article or service which other members of the community need. And business transactions are essentially measured in terms of money. These measurements must show profit to the enterprise, if it is to remain in business. But money and profit are measuring devices; yet a measuring device is not a purpose. To realize a profit may be, and usually, is the motive or purpose of some of the individuals who engage in business. But "the only valid definition of business purpose is to create a customer",* that is, to provide goods or services which someone needs.

The Enterprise or Business Firm. Business enterprises are frequently called "firms". Romesh Bansal, merchant and sole owner and manager of his retail store, is the head of his firm. Tata Iron and Steel Company with its many ramifications is also a firm. Hindustan Steel Company is a firm with steel mills in different places. The important characteristic of the business firm is that it is owned and controlled essentially as a unit, however diverse its parts. Thus, business enterprise or firm is the unit within which productive resources are combined to turn out goods and services for sale. It comes into being when an individual or a body of individuals co-ordinate their efforts and combine their resources or "agents of production" to conduct business activity. The function of making fundamental decisions in an enterprise is generally called the

*Peter F. Drucker, *The Practice of Management*, p. 19

function of "entrepreneurship" on the part of one or more persons. Since it is the entrepreneur who combines the productive resources and makes fundamental policy decisions, a firm is a business unit under one co-ordinated "entrepreneurship"

Entrepreneur or Businessman. The businessman is at the centre of all business activity. As an entrepreneur, he decides as to how productive agents will be combined, what shall be produced, and how much. He decides how many employees to hire and how much he is willing to pay them. It is he who decides how the concern will be financed and the consumer demand met. The entrepreneur formulates the business plans and sees to their execution. In short, he is essentially a person who, "through his foresight and ability, directs the application of human energy in the shape of labour-power and capital-saving to the exploitation of the opportunities afforded by nature." As an entrepreneur, he guarantees wages to his employees and interest to those who have lent him capital. He undertakes to supply any of the numerous wants of consumers for goods. But business is a game of skill, and every player cannot hope to succeed. Ability required, service performed, and the risk borne are great and go together. Therefore, ability of the highest order is required to make the more successful businessman.

Qualities of a Successful Businessman. To make a success of the enterprise, the business leader should possess, broadly speaking, the following basic qualities :

1. *Accuracy.* The first main quality in the businessman is that he knows what he is talking about, and what he means. Precision in regard to orders and their execution is imperative. Accurate action depends upon accurate thinking. The good businessman must be able to grasp his problems by treating them quantitatively.

2. *Time Sense and Foresight.* Modern business, subject to fast changes, requires a businessman to appreciate time. He must always think in terms of time. There is a chain of actions which must fit in with the rapidly changing desires of the ultimate consumer. He must be able to forecast with foresight, and look into the future. Having detected the wants, he must proceed intelligently to utilise his property to satisfy them. In this way he will have a well-established business long before others who are still groping in the dark.

3. *Alertness.* A businessman keen on success must keep in touch with the world, and not keep himself. He must be up and doing in order not only to satisfy existing wants but to create fresh wants.

4. *Honesty or Business Morality.* In order to adequately satisfy consumer demand, the businessman must be honest. He must use all his ability to provide precisely what is wanted, if he wishes to make goodwill for himself and the organisation he conducts. The honesty and optimism which goes with it are attributes of the businessman at his best. Honesty with him is not only the best policy but also the best practice.

5. *Ability to Co-operate.* Another notable quality of the businessman is ability to co-operate with a large number of others. He must be

able to compromise, adjust, adapt and be willing to admit that his judgment may on occasions be wrong. Besides he must be temperamentally fitted to exercise a divided authority. Understanding others today is viewed as a perquisite par excellence—as a most expedient stepping-stone to success.

6. *Consistency and Dependability.* The businessman must have consistent mind so as to be able to exercise firmness in his dealings with others. He should hold the organisation constant and hence dependable, because it does not fluctuate from day to day. A dependable businessman has satisfied co-workers who are inevitably loyal to him and the unit directed by him. Thus, a businessman who wants results should avoid inconsistency, and its inevitable result, unfairness.

7. *Initiative and Capacity to make Decisions.* Success in any human activity depends in large measure on initiative and capacity to make decision. Indecision very often results in missing business opportunities which have a tendency to wriggle away if not captured promptly. Decision-making is the basic ingredient of executing any task. Therefore, it is but essential for a successful businessman to make quick and correct decisions.

8. *Energy.* A bountiful endowment of physical and nervous energy is another requisite without which other qualities are hardly of any value. Infinite capacity for taking pains is essential. In addition to abundant energy, he should possess forcefulness enough to put across his ideas and suggestions which he believes to be right.

9. *Personal qualities.* Additionally, a businessman should possess all or at least some of the qualities common to all leaders. He should have a better than average intelligence; or mental alertnss, constructive imagination, knowledge of human nature, enthusiasm, a sense of humour, self-confidence, self-control, pleasing personality, concentration, tolerance and sympathy.

Requisites of a Successful Business. In order to be successful or to avoid failure, a business must render a worthwhile service or make a worthwhile product that can be sold at a profit, and it must sell that product consistently and continuously. To do this an enterprise must conform to the following requisites of success in business.

Company Objectives. The most important and fundamental essential of a successful business is the establishment of definite and clear objectives; for without purpose no organisation can be effective. To avoid failure, both long-range and short-range objectives should be established. They must be so definite that they can be clearly described and so realistic that they can be achieved.

Planning. Planning is another corner-stone upon which successful enterprise depends. Planning is the analysis of a problem, thinking out the forward solutions to that problem, and then outlining the steps that must be taken to reach the objective defined in the solution. To plan is to propose a forward programme for guiding the future affairs of an enterprise. Planning assumes that the future will be different from the present, and it attempts to determine how the enterprise can make use of that difference. It enables business enterprise to meet the contingencies of the future and thus saves it from floundering.

Research. In these days of expanding technology, increasing competition, new methods of buying and selling and of dealing with people, business success depends on improved methods of production, selling and ability to manage men by getting along with them. One way of doing all this is by getting and making use of new and up-to-date facts. Research supplies these new facts.

Research may be defined as 'the systematic search for new knowledge.' If it is conducted solely to probe the unknown, it is called *Pure Research,* i.e., an investigation in the quest of knowledge for the sake of knowledge itself, as in the fields of basic science. If research is made for immediately practical or commercial purposes, it is known as *Applied Research.* The distinction between the two is not sufficiently clear, and applied research is often the result of pure research. For example, the theories of nuclear fission have resulted in useful atom-powered engines, or experiments with coal, air and water have led to the manufacture of nylon. We are, however, concerned more with applied research, as it involves the study of some particular problem, the solution of which will benefit the business enterprise. Applied research in industry is designated *Industrial Research* and is usually concerned with (1) marketing, (2) materials, (3) product, and (4) equipment and processes.

Market Research is the study of the consumers and tne market with a view to testing consumer acceptance of products and to developing data for production schedules and prices.

Materials Research is linked with product development. For example, research in metals, coal, oil and chemicals has played a big part in recent years in bringing forth new alloys, synthetic rubbers, plastics, resins, fibres, etc.

Product Research involves creation of new product and improvement of the existing one.

Equipment and Processes Research is usually directed towards the development of methods of manufacture, tools, and equipment, as well as handling devices that tend to increase productivity.

In addition to Industrial Research, Industrial Relation Research and Research in Indusrial Psychology have proved of great advantage to business enterprise in man-power management. Industrial relations research may relate to general social and economic relationships in employment or it may take up specific problems, such as absenteeism, labour turn-over, employee grievances and frustrations. Research in industrial psychology attempts to study individual differences as a basis for selection, placement and promotion.

Sound Organisation. For the success of any business enterprise it is essential that it has a well-defined organisation, manned with competent personnel, whose duties are delimited. The authority of each man is perfectly clear as well as his responsibility to his superiors.

Adequate Finance. Finance is said to be the life-blood of a business enterprise. It is, therefore, imperative for the success of any business that adequate provision for long-term and short-term finance is made.

Proper location of the Plant, its lay out and size also contribute substantially to the success of a business unit.

Effective and Efficient Management is probably the most important requisite of a successful business; for it is through management that the economic forces are utilised to the best advantage. It is necessary that the ship of enterprise is put under the control of intelligent and enlightened executives or managers. To succeed in their objective to run the business enterprise successfully they must be endowed with at least some of the qualities of a businessman already discussed.

All these essentials of a successful business will be discussed at appropriate places in the later chapters. Suffice it to say at this stage that ability to buy right, to manufacture correctly, to keep costs down, to sell, to keep records, to conserve resources and to get along with others will go a long way to make a business successful.

COMPONENTS OF BUSINESS

Being an all-embracing term, business includes trade, commerce and industry. **Business** may, therefore, be classified into two broad categories; (a) *Industry*, (b) *Commerce* (including trade). **Industry** is concerned with the production of goods, and commerce with the distribution of what is produced. A brief description of each is in point.

Industry. The processes of extraction, production, conversion, processing or fabrication of products are described as industry. These products of industry are sold either for further transformation into finished goods or for ultimate consumption. Goods used by final consumers are called consumers' goods, and those used in the production of other goods are described as producers' goods. An enterprise manufacturing motor cars, cloth, jams, edible oils produces consumers' goods. A steel mill may make steel for further fabrication into variety of articles, such as surgical instruments, blades, etc., or an engineering concern may manufacture machine tools and machinery to be used for manufacturing other products. These are producers' goods or capital goods.

Types of Industry. Broadly, an industry is either *Primary* or *Secondary*. Primary industry may be either extractive or genetic, and secondary industry is either manufacturing or construction.

Extractive Industries. These industries are engaged in supplying commodities which are extracted or raised from the earth, sea and air with comparatively little help from man. The products of such industries are generally used by manufacturing and construction industries for fabricating finished goods. Fishing, mining, fruit gathering, agriculture and afforestation are some of the examples of extractive industries.

Genetic Industries. These are industries which, though dependent upon nature, require a greater application of human skill in their production. The enterprises engaged in agriculture, forestry and fish culture are examples of genetic industries. Though agriculture is dependent upon the nature and quality of the soil and climatic conditions, yet success in this line will very much depend upon the application of human skill and knowledge. Intensive cultivation is possible with greater amount of capital and larger number of workers. Similarly, cultivation of forests is necessary for securing supply of timber for various purposes.

Manufacturing Industries. Manufacturing industries are concerned with the working of raw materials or partly finished materials into finished products. Manufacturing processes are carried on chiefly in factory enterprises and constitute a very large part of the total business activities. Among the manufacturing industries we may mention iron and steel works, spinning and weaving mills, flour mills, the making of machinery, etc.

Construction Industries. These are concerned with the making or constructing of buildings, bridges, dams, roads, canals, etc. The process of laying out, fitting and connecting materials which have been already prepared is involved in these industries.

Service Enterprises. Business provides not only goods but also services. At every point in the economic system an infinite variety of services are furnished, e.g., domestic services, financial and aesthetic services to individuals and to business enterprises. When a person goes to a cinema, or takes out an insurance policy on his life, he receives nothing material in return for his money but a piece of paper. A cinema house or an insurance company is nonetheless a business concern. What each of them provides cannot be classified as goods; they are rather opportunities—an opportunity to save money and make provision for a wife and family after death. Generally, such things are termed services. Hotels provide accommodation, railways and aeroplanes means of getting from one place to another. Shipping companies also cater for health by means of holiday cruises. All of them provide services. The diagram (page 14) gives the components of business.

Classification of Manufacturing Industries. Manufacturing industries may be either a continuous or an Assembly type. A continuous industry may be either analytical or synthetic. Assembly industries are also of two types. One with similar components and the other with dissimilar components. A brief account of each type is given below.

1. *Continuous Industry.* It is an industry in which all the material is received at one point, from which successive operations turn it into a finished product. Yarn spinning, paper and pottery manufacture are examples.

2. *Assembly Industry.* In an assembly industry the finished product can be produced only after various components have been made and then brought together for final operations, such as manufacture of shoes and automobiles.

3. *Analytical Industry.* In this type of continuous industry, the basic material is analysed and separated into several parts so that the final product emerges separate and distinct from the mass of original material. All refining industries, such as oil and by-products of coke, are of this nature. The crude mineral oil is analysed and separated into kerosene, diesel oil, lubricating oil, and the final product petrol.

4. *Synthetical Industry.* In this type of continuous industry various ingredients are brought together and combined in the manufacturing process to produce a new product. Paper manufacture, yarn spinning, paint making and soap making are example of this type.

5. *Assembly Industries with Similar Components.* Here the components are similar and go through similar operations, as in clothing industry.

6. *Assembly Industries with Dissimilar Components.* In this type the components are dissimilar and go through unlike processes, as in automobile industry.

Commerce. The process of buying and selling, and all those activities which facilitate trade. such as storing, grading, packaging, financing, insuring, transporting, are called commerce. The principal function of commerce is to remove the hindrances of person, place, time, exchange and knowledge, in connection with the distribution of commodities until they reach the consumers. By removing these hindrances commerce ensures a free and smooth flow of goods from producers to consumers. The hindrances referred to above are discussed below.

Hindrances of persons. Buyers and sellers of goods are not always situated at the same place so that contact between them is hindered by distance. Commerce helps to remove this hindrance between persons by means of trade. Trade as part of commerce therefore plays a major role in establishing contact between the producers as sellers of their products and the consumers as buyers of those goods to satisfy their wants.

Hindrances of exchange. With money as the medium of exchange, payment for goods and services is made possible through institutions such as the banks. In this way, banks, as part of commerce, act to remove the hindrance of exchange and enable buyers to procure goods, especially by extending their own credit. The banks very often finance trade in various ways.

Hindrances of place. The goods may be produced at one place and the demand for them may be the greatest at a different place, because they are not produced there. This barrier of distance is removed by commerce through the different means of transport, and goods are carried from one place to another. Added to the direct movement of goods from the point of production to the point of consumption or use, are the services of insurance to cover the risk of loss and packing to protect goods against damage and pilferage.

Hindrances of time. Goods, especially in modern times, are produced in anticipation of demand. They must therefore be stored in a safe place to be released as and when demanded. The function of storing and preservation is performed by warehouses. In other words, warehouse remove the hindrances of time by balancing the time lag between production and consumption, and so create time utility. Insurance comes into play even where goods are stored in warehouses and removes the risk of loss or damage through theft or fire.

Hindrances of information. Selling of products is today the most important problem that a manufacturer has to solve. His products may be the best, but how are the prospective buyers to know about them. This lack of information about the products and the company is a great hindrance in the way of consumers buying them. Advertising and salesmanship help to remove the hindrances of the lack of information by bringing to the notice of the people the advantages of buying the goods and services offered.

To conclude, commerce may be said to be that branch of business which facilitates exchange of goods by removing the various hindrances, namely, those of persons through trade, of exchange through banking, of place through transport, as well as insurance and packing, of time through warehousing as well as insurance, and of lack of information through salesmanship and advertising. Hence, Stephenson defines commerce as "the sum total of those processes which are engaged in the removal of the hindrances of persons (trade), place (transport and insurance) and time (warehousing) in the exchange (banking) of commodities."

Trade. Trade is the final state of business activity and involves sale and purchase of products. It is to facilitate the transfer of goods from the seller to the buyer (trade) that all the other activities are undertaken.

Types of Trade. Trade has been classified in many ways. The normal classification of trade is (a) Internal Trade, and (b) Foreign or International Trade. Internal trade, in turn, may be either wholesale trade or retail trade; and foreign trade may be import trade or export trade.

Internal trade, also known as home trade or domestic trade, comprises buying and selling of goods within the bounds of a country. All transactions connected with it, such as payment and transporting, are national, and no external agency is involved.

Foreign or International trade refers to buying goods from, or selling commodities to, traders doing business in foreign lands. This type of trade involves payment for goods in the currency of the country of the supplier of goods and the use of international means of transport.

Wholesale trade relates to purchase of goods in large quantities from producers and growers and their resales to retailers in small lots. It serves as a link between the manufacturers or producers and the retailers who sell them to the ultimate consumers.

Retail trade is the last link in the economic chain whereby human wants are satisfied. The retailer assembles at a convenient place various types of products from numerous sources and supplies in small quantities to consumers.

International trade is normally wholesale trade and takes the form

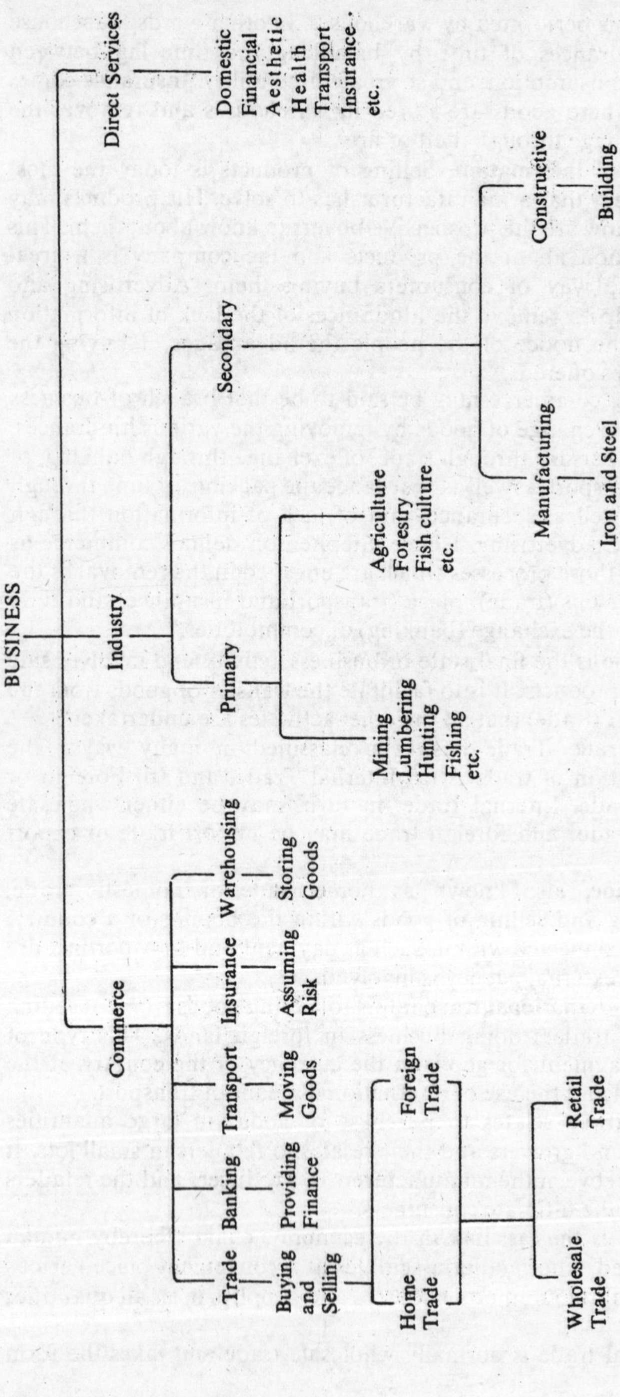
BUSINESS
Commerce
Industry
Direct Services
Trade
Banking
Transport
Insurance
Warehousing
Buying and Selling
Providing Finance
Moving Goods
Assuming Risk
Storing Goods
Home Trade
Foreign Trade
Wholesale Trade
Retail Trade
Primary
Secondary
Mining
Lumbering
Hunting
Fishing
etc.
Agriculture
Forestry
Fish culture
etc.
Manufacturing
Iron and Steel
Spinning and Weaving
Machine Making
Flour Milling etc.
Constructive
Building
Bridges
Dams
Canals
etc.
Domestic
Financial
Aesthetic
Health
Transport
Insurance
etc.

of import or export, or it may be entrepot trade. By import trade is meant buying goods from suppliers in foreign lands and by export trade selling to buyers in foreign countries. Entrepot trade consists of importing of foreign produced goods with the object of re-exporting them.

BUSINESS ORGANISATION AND MANAGEMENT

Since we are concerned with the organisation and management of a business enterprise, we may, with profit, start with working definitions of the two terms.

Business Organisation. "Organisation," says Sir Ian Hamilton, "is the art or science of building up a systematical whole by a number of parts, just as the human frame is built up by heart, liver, brain, legs, etc." J.W. Schulze defines organisation as "a combination of necessary beings, materials, tools, equipment, working space and appurtenances brought together in a systematic and effective correlation, to accomplish some desired object." It is the systematic arrangement of parts for a defined purpose.

A business enterprise consists of manpower, machines, materials, money and management. Organisation brings these assets into the position of greatest effectiveness and productivity. It is in effect the harmonious inter-relation of functions and staff for the attainment of a common purpose.

Management. Management of a business enterprise is a process by which man attempts to give order, direction and control to the various operations to achieve its objectives, the most important of the same being the production of quality goods at the lowest possible cost, and enabling the consumers to have them at the lowest possible price and yet earning adequate profits. For achieving these objectives and others, management makes use of human and material resources.

To sum up, the purpose of business enterprise is to serve the general welfare. The function of management is to see that the enterprise fulfils this objective through meeting the needs of its owners, its customers, its employees, and the general public. In the following pages effort has been made to explain the various facets of business organisation and management.

CHAPTER II

ENVIRONMENT OF BUSINESS SYSTEM

A business organisation does not exist in a vacuum. It exists in a world of concrete places and things, natural resources, important abstractions, and living persons. The sum of all these factors and forces is called the organisation's environment. In fact, environment is a suprasystem of which organisations are subsystems, each having identifiable boundaries that separate a business organisation from its environment, which is external and beyond the control of the organisation. A business organisation receives inputs from the environment, transforms them, and returns outputs.

Environmental forces have a direct impact on the way the organisation structures its activities. It is usually necessary to establish functional departments within the organisation to deal with environmental inputs and outputs. For example, purchasing activity receives materials inputs; personnel departments recruit and select employees; market research sections obtain information from the environment. On the output side, sales departments perform the major function of distribution. Public relations department is concerned with providing informational outputs to the environment that will enhance the reputation and prestige of the organisation. It is important, therefore, that all managers must take into account the element and forces of their external environment. They must identify, evaluate and react to the forces external to the enterprise that may affect its operations.

External environment may be classified in various ways, such as, local, national and international, or past, present and future, or economic and non-economic. We are concerned with economic and non-economic environments and will confine our discussion to these environments. The determinants of economic environment are fiscal policy, monetary policy, industrial policy, physical controls of prices, incomes, the nature of economic system-capitalist, socialist, communist or mixed as in India—the tempo of economic development, the national economic plan, competition and customers. Non-economic environment refers to social, political, legal, educational, cultural, physical and technological factors affecting business operation. It should be noted at the very outset that, although the economic and non-economic environments comprise different factors, there is an interaction between them. The economic environment has non-economic implications and the non-economic environment is affected by the economic environment. A brief description of each type of environment follows.

ECONOMIC ENVIRONMENT

A business organisation exists in three types of economic environment: *first* in the total economy; *second*, in a particular industry, and *third*, in a specific geography area. In each of these types of environment, the company will want to consider its position in relation to its competition and its customers or potential customers.

The Economy. As regards the total economy, the enterprise will have to consider a broad range of business indicators, such as, industrial production, wholesale and consumer prices, nature and extent of employment and unemployment, average work week, and average earnings, personal incomes, sales and inventories, gross national product, disposition of personal income, and corporate profits.

Every enterprise, as a system, imports various things from the economic environment and export a product or service to it. Since the objective of business is essentially economic, an organisation must introduce a number of elements as inputs from the economic environment. For instance, every type of organisation must procure capital—machinery, buildings, inventories of goods, office equipment, tools of all kinds, and cash. Another extremely important element of the input side of the economic environment is the availability, quality and price of labour of all kinds—skilled and unskilled, trained and untrained. Price level changes also affect the input side of the enterprise. Inflation, for example, not only upsets business but has highly disturbing influences on every kind of organisation. Again, productivity of labour and capital has considerable impact on enterprises. Another major economic input is the availability of high-quality entrepreneurs and managers. This input is, of course, likely to have correlation with the social environment, particularly in the area of education, individual freedoms and cultural development. Furthermore, the nature of Government fiscal and tax policies affect the economic inputs, even though these are more correctly, aspects of political environment.

Competition. Competition is a major part of the enterprise's environment. It is, therefore, important to find out (1) in what position of the total market is each competitor a significant factor, and with what products ? (2) What are his business policies—credit terms, delivery schedules, discount practices. (3) What is his product line—is it a single product or a diversified line ? (4) What is his financial structure ? and so on.

Customers. On the output side of any business organisation, there are also important economic considerations in the environment, the most important of which are customers, both direct and indirect. Without customers a business could not exist. To succeed in capturing customers a business must try its best to know what people want and will buy. The frailties of consumer acceptance impose a constant challenge, because non-economic factors in the environment, such as, attitudes, desires, and expectations of people also, influence consumer behaviour.

NON-ECONOMIC ENVIRONMENT

The non-economic environment that has direct impact on business organisations comprise socio-cultural, educational, legal, political, physical, historical and technological. An over-view of these factors of non-economic environment follows.

SOCIOCULTURAL

Sociological factors give content and form to the system of values and culture. The culture prescribes and teaches what an individual learns and accepts. All language, customs, habits, values, and attitudes are culturally derived. In some ways, the culture overwhelms the individual. Therefore, the importance of understanding the role that sociocultural environment plays can never be underestimated. Every society depends on its culture to instill normative behaviour into the populace so that it can be maintained and survive. Thus, the sociocultural environment that impacts on business is made up of the attitudes, desires, expectations, degrees of intelligence and education, beliefs, customs, of people in a given group or society. To these may be added idealogies and norms of the society, views on authority relationships, leadership patterns, inter-personal relationships and rationalism.

EDUCATIONAL

In this category may be listed the general literacy level of the population, the degree of specialisation in the education system, attitude towards education and acquisition of knowledge, the proportion of the people with a high level of professional and specialised training which may meet the requirements of industry. These and other factors constituting educational cultural environment exercise a strong influence on business activity and management skills.

POLITICAL

The political environment is primarily that complex of laws, regulations and Government agencies and their actions which affects all kinds of organisations. Furthermore, general political climate of society; the degree of concentration of political power and the political party system have major effect on business organisation.

LEGAL

The nature of legal system, jurisdictions of various government units and constitutional considerations impinge on business. Specific laws concerning formation, management, taxation and control of organisations have considerable impact on business.

HISTORICAL

The historical background of the country also influences the current environment of business. Historical events and ideologies leave a strong impact on the current state of business. Societal change has occurred throughout human history, bringing about a differing set of values for the people growing up during different periods thus producing current environment.

ETHICAL

The ethical environment includes sets of generally accepted and practised standards of personal conduct. All over the world certain standards of personal conduct are recognised and accepted. Management ethics is a study of what is right and good in the moral decisions managers make. In relation to business, ethical environment is doing the right thing towards every one and win public confidence.

PHYSICAL

Climate, terrain, resources, and population density are some of the variables in the physical environment, which affect human behaviour and even, in some cases, physical make up. There is some evidence that climate may affect behaviour. For example, the average level of achievement motivation is very high in societies that live in temperatures with a mean between 40 and 60°F. Resources, both natural and human-made have effect on behaviour. Food, water, housing and medical care influence a persons well being. These resources, along with many others, are needed to sustain physical activity and life itself. Population is another very important environmental factor, for population explosion inevitably contributes to the limited resources problem.

TECHNOLOGICAL

Technological environment has considerable impact on management and organisations. For our purpose, technology is defined as the mechanical techniques and abstract knowledge that are employed by humans to help attain organisational objectives. Therefore, the state of technology at any one time is an extremely important factor affecting the success of any business. It is a truism that any business that wishes to survive in a changing world must keep abreast of the technology applicable to its products and services and to its methods of operations.

In sum, it may be stated that the list of factors in non-economic environment is not exhaustive but is only illustrative. But what is important to note is that the environment is becoming more dynamic and uncertain, Each of the environmental factors involves and accelerating rate of change. For example technological conditions are changing rapidly; cultural and social changes are underway, and so on. An important problem in the study of organisations and organisational changes is that the environment in which organisations function is itself changing, and at an increasing rate as well as towards increasing complexity. There is "an increasing turbulence in modern societies and organisations are moving from "placid" fields to "turbulent" fields: Consequently, organisations of the future will be even more subject to external forces and must be prepared to adapt.

BUSINESS ORGANISATIONS INFLUENCE THEIR ENVIRONMENT

So far we have looked at organisations as being impacted by their environment as if they were passive and external forces alone were active. But in many cases the organisation selects the environment within which it will operate and continually attempts to shape that environment to accomplish its goals. The organisation selects the environments it will inhabit, and it subjectively defines the environment it has selected. This two-way process between environment and organisation is evident in many situations. The business firm determines a market niche for its products or services. It may diversify into new product markets or expand into new geographic regions. Furthermore, once established, the organisation tries to manipulate its environment in order to accomplish its purposes.

INTERACTION OF ENVIRONMENTAL FACTORS

As hinted earlier, the environmental factors interact with each other. Since we started out major classification as economic and non-economic environment, we will make economic environment as the pivot and see how factors in non-economic environment interact with it.

Interaction between Sociological Environment and Economic Environment of Business. The social attitude towards business and management determines how many people would enter business. If business is regarded as respectable occupation, commerce and industry will develop at a rapid pace and professional managers will emerge to manage different business enterprises. Again if there is confrontation between labour and management rather than cooperation, a repressive economic system may be, needed to cope with industrial unrest. If, on the other hand, the aim is the attainment of highest productivity, the management will pay more attention to incentives to workers rather than maximisation of profits.

Interaction between Educational-Cultural Environment and Economic Environment. The stage of economic development is a decisive factor for the available system of education. The system of education, on the other hand, may bring about a certain economic environment. For instance, emphasis on liberal arts education and the neglect of vocational training may militate against ready employment opportunities.

Interaction between Political-Legal Environment and Economic Environment. There is a direct relationship between political environment and economic environment. When there is political stability, business men are willing to venture into new economic activity. The reverse will be the case if there is political instability. The ideology of the ruler will determine whether private enterprise will have its away or public enterprise will be the outcome-socialist system. Thus, the stage of political environment decides the pattern of economic legislation, and the stage of economic environment decides the continuity or discontinuity of a particular political administration.

Interaction between Historical Environment and Economic Environment. The historical and economic environments are quite interdependent. The present economic environment of business can be treated as a legacy of its past or historical environment. Every business has a history, and every historical phenomenon has a lesson. As such, the present is the reflection of the past, and the present can also be handled in terms of the experience of the past. For example, the economic environment of business in the newly independent countries is the outcome of the colonial states which those countries had in the past. Also, the past history, as a storehouse of lessons, can provide guidelines for present economic policy decisions. The implementation of the past five year plans, for instance, can provide direction to the formulation and implementation of the present five year plan, which, in turn can act as a guide for the future plan, thus setting a course of history.

Interaction between Physical Environment and Economic Environment.* There is a growing concern today over the deterioration of the natural environment. Water and air pollution, creation of radioactive materials, oil spills and many cases of poisoning of humans, other animals and plant life are clearly evident. Traditionally, we have viewed nature as available for human exploitation: resources to be used for our betterment. Now, however, steps are being taken to bring about a balance between people and nature. This obviously raises major question about economic, materialistic and social progress. Every industrialised society is facing problems of environmental deterioration. There is a growing evidence that our traditional demands for greater industrialisation, a higher standard of living, and more resource utilisation have a disastrous affect on the environment.

To meet these environmental issues, we will have to re-evaluate our priorities and concepts. New ideologies, legal and structural arrangement, and management skills will be necessary to utilize organisational resources, both public and private, to deal with environmental problems and conservation of resources.

ENVIRONMENT AND MANAGEMENT

From what is stated above it follows that there is a "linkage" between the organisations' environment and its internal subsystems—the technology utilized in the transformation process, the relationships among people performing various tasks, and the managerial system of planning, organising, directing, motivating and control. An organisation, as an open system, receives support from its environment, which has an important impact on its internal structure. Organisations establish departments to deal with inputs from and outputs to specific sectors of its environment. As stated earlier, in business enterprises many departments interact directly with specific sectors of environment. Consequently, internal structure of the organisation is very largely influenced by environmental factors and forces. For example, the technology that the

*Kast and Rasenzweig, Organisation and Management, P.108.

organisation utilises has an impact on internal structure, as the technical system determines the structure of product line and the machine shop. Movement into new environment through product diversification or geographic dispersion would result in restructuring. Similarly, psycholocial system both affects and is strongly influenced by the structure, for instance, people with different educational and work experiences will often respond differently to various structural arrangements. The professional or technical specialist may seek autonomy and freedom from tight structure.

Taken together, environmental influences, technological requirements, and psycholocial factors are key determinants of structure. The management should design the organisation in response to these internal factors. Managers very often decide which environment will be relevant. In fact, environment and management go together.

Finally, the modern manager has to balance the interests of all his constituents—himself, his employees, his customers, his shareholders and the Government. His own economic aspirations may come in conflict with

(a) the economic needs of his employees,
(b) the economic decisions of his customers,
(c) the economic demands of his shareholders, and
(d) the economic policies of his Government.

If the manager is able to resolve these conflicts, he gets the better of the environment. If he perpetuates these conflicts, the environment gets the better of him.

BUSINESS SYSTEM

Almost all life is a system. Our bodies, our homes, our universities and our businesses are. Those, in turn, are inter-connected with various other systems, and each has within it a number of sub-systems. In dealing with the environment of business organisations, we observed that environment is a supra system of which business organisation is a sub system. We also noted that an organisation is an energetic input-output system which is open in its interaction with the environment. It is in the fitness of things, therefore, that we begin with analysing the "Business System".

Meaning of System.

The *Oxford English Dictionary* defines a system as "a set or assemblage of things connected or interdependent, so as to form a complex unit; a whole composed of parts in orderly arrangement according to some scheme or plan". System conveys the idea that everything is inter related and interdependent. Thus, a system is composed of elements that are related and dependent upon one another but, when in interaction, form a unitary whole. Stated conversely, a system is a whole entity consisting of functionally related, inter-acting or interdependent parts, known as sub-systems. The human body can be said to be the best example of a system. If consists of a number of body organs or parts or subsystems which *act together* as a system to perform a bodily function. Our body possesses a nervous system., a circulatory system, a digestive system, and so on. Each of these systems is a part of, or a subsystem of, one large unified organic system which we call the human being. Thus, the body is a whole system consisting of subsystems each of which performs its functions in a unified and balanced manner. One system provides oxygen; another the sense of touch; and so on. Each system, however, is not an *independent* system in the body but rather is depèndent or orderly-functioning of the other subsystems for its harmonious and continuous action.

Business System and its Subsystems

Business as a whole may be regarded as a super-system with industry and commerce as its major subsystems. A company has, many subsystems and, in turn, is a subsystem of a larger system, such as an industry. Being a social system, it is a complex and human contrived system for fulfilling particular purposes and satisfying particular needs. Thus, by definition every company is a system, and the subsystems are the people, machines that perform the operations and the procedures that define the operations. Let us view an operating firm as a total organic whole, consisting of various subsystems which operate in a balanced coordinated and integrated manner to make the whole what it is.

Every business enterprise needs money or capital to operate. This is accomplished by the finance function, or subsystem, as it supplies funds in the appropriate amount to various departments or activities. A product must be produced, and this is accomplished by the production function, or the production subsystem. Again, the product must be sold and distributed, and the marketing subsystem performs this function. Each of these subsystems, inturn, is composed of subsystems. It is the wheel within a wheel, within a wheel concept. For example, the marketing subsystem would have advertising, consumer satisfaction, research, sales, inventory, customer relations subsystems. Each of these subsystems goes to make up the whole subsystem of marketing which is an integrated and necessary part of the total overall system of the operating firm. For a firm to function successfully, each of its subsystems must operate in a coordinated, balanced, integrated fashion. If any of the subsystems does not operate in a balanced and integrated manner, the whole system suffers.

A company can also be looked at as a technological system with important characteristics of plant layout, equipment design, process integration and materials flow. This is particularly the case in enterprises, like steel works, assembly plants and oil refineries. Again, the company may be seen as a socio-technical system with emphasis on system of communications and information flows, and on system for making and implementing decisions. It is also both a political and a status system The political system embraces different interest groups of shareholders, directors, managers, and workers which exert pressure on each other and often make conflicting demands. The satisfaction derived from work is to some extent positively correlated with status and the prestige conferred by the performance of certain kinds of work.

An Integrated System's View of Organisation

An organisation receives inputs of energy, information, and materials from the environment, transforms these and returns outputs to the environment. Under this view, an organisation is not simply a technical or social system. It is indeed a structuring and integrating of human activities around various technologies. The technologies affect the types of inputs into the organisation, the nature of the transformation processes, and the outputs from the system. However, the social system determines the effectiveness and efficiency of the utilisation of the technology. The internal organisation, as seen earlier, is composed of several major subsystems. The organisational goals and values are one of the more important of these subsystems. The organisation takes many of its values from the broader sociocultural environment. As a subsystem of the society the organisation must accomplish certain goals that are determined by the broader system. Therefore, an organisation must conform to social requirements, if it is to be successful in receiving inputs.

The technical subsystem refers to the knowledge required for the performance of tasks, including the techniques used in the transformation of inputs into outputs. It is determined by the task requirements of the organisation and varies with the particular activities. This subsystem is shaped by the specialisation of knowledge and skills required, the types of machinery and equipment involved, and the layout of facilities. The technology affects the organisations structure as well as its psychological subsystem.

The psychosocial subsystem of an organisation is composed of individuals and groups in interaction. It consists of individual behaviour and motivation, status and role relationships and influence systems. It is also affected by sentiments, values, attitudes, expectations and aspirations of the people in the organisation. This subsystem is affected by external environmental forces as well as by the tasks, technology and structure of the internal organisation. These forces set the organisational climate within which the human participants perform their roles and activities.

Structure involves the ways in which the tasks of the organisation are divided and coordinated. The organisation chart sets forth positions and functions. It is also concerned with the patterns of authority, communication, and work flow.

The managerial subsystem spans the entire organisation by relating the organisation to its environment, setting the goals, developing comprehensive, strategic and operational plans, designing the structure and establishing control processes.

In conclusion, it may be pointed out that systems theory stresses the dynamic character of business enterprise, and the interdependence of activities. It treats the enterprise as a living organisation and directs attention to the relationships between the enterprise and its environment, and between the parts of the system—the enterprise. Although a system has subsystems and sub-systems are interrelated and interdependent, the system has to be viewed as a totality. The whole is not just a sum of the parts. In fact, as pointed out by Aristotle, "the whole is more than the sum of the parts". With the exception of the entire universe, all systems are subsystems, although they have, inturn, subsystems. Stating it in another way, systems have subsystems and are also a part of a supra-system; they are hierarchical.

BUSINESS AND ECONOMIC SYSTEMS

Business system is essentially an organised economic activity. Economics and business management are inter-twined. Both deal with business and the way business operates in the economic scene. It is true that economics is the study of the whole economic system and how it operates in satisfying the wants of society. It is also true that business management is the study of how to operate a business concern most effectively. But it is also important to business management to know how the economy behaves, because the economic system prevailing in any area has a big impact on any business. It is, therefore, desirable to briefly study the various economic systems.

The Functions of every Economic System. Every economic system, no matter what it is called or what political arrangements go with it, has to do three main jobs:

1. It must decide what is to be produced.
2. It must decide how it is to be produced.
3. It must decide how the products are to be distributed among the people.

Implied in these three is a fourth job, which may be kept in mind as a separate point:

4. It must decide between the present and the future —how many of society's resources should be devoted to growth and how many to current consumption.

How does each of the "system" get these job done ? A systematic comparison needs to ask the same four questions about each.

The Test of Good Economic System. All the systems get the job done somehow, as a primitive economy does. So by answering these four questions we will have only a comparative picture. If we want to evaluate the different systems, we need to set up our criteria for judging each. The tentative four criteria could be:

1. Does the system provide a progressively higher standard of living for all ?
2. Does it provide economic freedom and security for the individual ?
3. Does it produce the goods and services consumers indicate they want ?
4. Does it provide an equitable distribution of income ?

As economic activity takes place under each system, but the forms, methods and policies differ we shall turn, therefore, to a description of the different economic systems and conditions which prevail under each. We will begin with capitalist system.

Capitalist System

Freedom of enterprise, ownership of private property, economic motivation and competition are the important institutions of capitalist system.

Freedom of Enterprise. Freedom of enterprise is one of the basic institutions of a capitalistic economy. It refers to the general right which each individual has to engage in any line of economic activity that appears desirable to him. He has the freedom to choose his own line of work and also to move to any part of the country. However, it should be noted that this freedom to choose one's occupation or business and freedom of action therein does not guarantee success in the chosen line of activity, nor does it promise all individuals an equal chance to succeed from the economic point of view. No matter what the politician say, a capitalistic system offers only freedom of entry into occupations and industries and not genuine equality of opportunity therein.

Restrictions on Freedom of Enterprise. The social-welfare theory in connection with freedom of enterprise, assumes that social welfare will be maximised if we can induce each individual to produce commodities and services which will have the greatest possible value on the market. This assumption by no means is always justified. Since an individual, in selecting the field of activity most profitable to himself might well choose something which would be antisocial. In such cases, the Government may impose restrictions in public interest or to ensure social welfare.

Economic Motivation. Economic motivation is a second important institution of a capitalist system. It means that individuals, in this system, are usually motivated by the desire for economic or pecuniary gain in their economic activities. They are strongly inclined to seek their own welfare, as they conceive it, rather than that of other people. Besides profit motive, people also work to acquire power, or to gain admiration and respect of their fellow men, or by the desire to serve their fellow men, or by family affections, there are, of course exceptions. Normally, the desire for economic gain make people work harder in a capitalist system.

Restrictions on Economic Self-Interest. It very often happens that individuals, in following their economic self-interest, obtain an unjust advantage at the cost of the society. For example, a manufacturer, instead of increasing the efficiency of his organisation, might try to obtain the large income he desires by forming a monopoly and charging high prices, by "Sweating" his labour, or by cheapening his product through adulteration. In such cases, the State is bound to intervene with laws designed to control the growth of monopolies, to regulate working conditions, or to prohibit the sale of impure food. However, restrictions of these kinds must be regarded as departure from the norm of capitalistic operation.

Private Property. Economic motivation and freedom of enterprise would not in themselves be adequate to insure the operation of a capitalist economy if individuals were not protected in the use of the economic goods which they acquired through economic activity. Thus in a capitalist system there exists the institution of private property. An individual can own, possess, buy and sell property as he desires. The system also recognises the freedom of contract.

Restrictions on Private Property. Since property rights are conferred by society as a whole upon its individual members, these rights can be modified and limited by social action. In practice, even under capitalism, property rights are often restricted by Governments. For example, no individual can acquire a piece of land in a residential area and set up and operate a slaughter house or a factory. Again, an individual cannot with impunity use his automobile or other object of wealth in such a way as to damage or destroy the wealth of other people. Moreover, if society decides that too great inequality in the distribution of income is undesirable, the rights of individuals to use their money incomes may be limited by a progressive tax applicable to these incomes.

Competition. The efforts of individuals to advance their economic self interest, under the protection of the institutions of private property and freedom of enterprise, results in competition, which is another fundamental characteristic of a capitalistic economic system. Like economic motivation, competition is a way of reacting in economic situations. A capitalist economy is supposed to be free market economy. Prices of goods are supposed to be determined by the joint action of the forces of demand and supply. However, the market for a given economic good can be freely competitive only if several general conditions are fulfilled. There must be a large number of both buyers and sellers in the market for the good. There must be no agreements or conspiracies among sellers with regard to the production, sale, or price of the good. The buyers and sellers must be reasonably intelligent and reasonly well informed concerning market conditions affecting the good in question. But the fact is that competition in the economic sense hardly ever prevails. Monopolistic competition is more common than competition, and the consumer is hardly ever "the King".

Fascism

Fascism of pre-War-II Germany and Italy was essentially a political system; it glorified the state above the individual. Otherwise, it was very much like the capitalist system, so far as the ownership of productive wealth was concerned. But under fascism, the private owners of productive wealth were not supposed to think that they had any sacred property rights, for they held their wealth only on the sufferance of the "leader", Hitler in Germany and Mussolini in Italy. The uses which could be made of productive wealth were closely controlled, and private wealth was even expropriated on occasion. As such, facism appeared to be different from capitalism, because an all-powerful central Government interferred with and controlled economic and other activities to an enormous degree.

Socialist Economic System

In contrast to free enterprise under capitalist system, the planned socialist economic system is characterised by social ownership of means of production, central planning and social welfare objectives. The distribution of what is centrally produced is also centrally controlled in some cases, as in Soviet Russia.

Social Ownership. Under this system the wealth belongs to the people. The state owns all productive resources and there is complete regimentation of economic activity. The Government decides what shall be produced and in what quantities and does not allow the amount of production to be determined by price movements. Thus, the State owns not only the agents of production, but also the commodities produced. Under communism, the highest stage of socialism, the consumption is also controlled. The distribution of consumer goods is on the basis of one's needs without regard to producing ability. Communism does not depend upon individual economic motivation, but upon non-economic, social stimulus for the productive efforts.

Central Planning. Planning, and often centralised planning is a *sene quo non* of socialism. The state enterprises have to function in accordance with the directives of the Planning Body. As the socialist plan is centralised planning, it is planning from the top—from the national level to the regional level, to the local level, to the industry level, to the corporate level, to the individual level. Each unit of economic system has to adjust individual activity as per the requirement of national plan. Thus, individuals are expected to work for the good of the society as a whole.

Social Welfare. The underlying motive is not economic but social welfare. One of the means of ensuring social welfare is through distributive justice. To this may be added moderate differentials in wages. For instance, the highest wage paid to anyone would not be more than 10 to 15 times the lowest wage paid to any one. In addition to economic growth for social justice, other determinants of social welfare are health, education, diet, and old age security, and so on.

Competition. A great reduction in the importance of competition in economic life is one of the features of an ideal socialist system. Individual workers would presumably compete to get into the better-paying and more pleasant occupations of the system, but in economic and other respects the governing influence of competitions would be replaced by the dictates of economic planning. A socialistic economy is in general, intended to be a single great co-operative enterprise.

DEMOCRATIVE SOCIALIST OR MIXED ECONOMIC SYSTEM

Somewhere between the extremes of substantially free enterprise and complete government regimentation lies another plan, viz., 'democratic Socialism' or *laissez collectives faire.* The underlying philosophy in this system is to flatten the social pyramid, in so far as economic possessions are concerned, and to shorten the distance between the very high and the very low in terms of ability to consume economic goods, but by democratic means. Both private and public enterprise are encouraged, keeping in view the social welfare. The institutional features of this "middle way" are co-existence of private and public sectors, combination of planning with price system, and co-ordination between economic motivation and social welfare.

Private and Public Sectors. In mixed economic system, the elements of private capitalism and state socialism are sought to be combined. Both private and public sectors co-exist, and are required to contribute to the general welfare. Under this system, several public enterprise have been set up in areas in which private enterprise would not enter either because they were unprofitable or because profits were likely to be long delayed. In India, particularly, the two sectors are expected to function as partners rather than partisans, as the utimate aim is to secure the greatest happiness of the greatest number. As was emphasised by the late Prime Minister, Jawahar Lal Nehru, "there is no private sector and public sector; there is only a National Sector.........We have, by consensus of opinion, decided upon planned development in a mixed economy."

Planning and Pricing. To ensure cooperative co-existence of private and public sectors, it is essential that centralised planning is justaposed with the system of market pricing. The Planning Commission lays down the basic socio economic objectives, fixes the physical targets, specify the sources and instruments of mobilising financial resources and lays down the procedures for implementing the national economic plan. The private and public sectors are then expected to act as per the plan. In guiding the resource allocation, the market mechanism plays a crucial role. As in a mixed economy, planning and pricing must go together, some statutory controls and regulation of free market forces of demand and supply are necessary for a planned functioning of the system.

Conclusion

Since the beginning of recorded history, men have sought the perfect society. Economists have tried to suggest plans to achieve an "ideal" democratic socialist society. Different economic systems have been tried in different countries, with more or less success. We may conclude by emphasising that the economic system should be our servant, not out master. In a working, democratic society all must win and all must have prizes.

PART TWO
Legal Ownership and Size of Firm

CHAPTER III

FORMS OF LEGAL OWNERSHIP (PRIVATE SECTOR)

The processes of production and distribution are carried out by lakhs of establishments at work. These business units differ in form of ownership and in the way they are organised for operation. A person, who wishes to start a new business, has many forms of organisation to choose from. From the point of view of *ownership,* there are. in the private sector, four main forms of organisation to run a business unit. They are as follows :

(a) Individual or sole proprietorship;
(b) Partnership;
(c) Joint stock company; and
(d) Cooperative undertaking.

To these may be added Joint Hindu Family Firm, although this form is fast losing ground as a form of business organisation.

In the Public Sector an enterprise may be owned and managed by Government Department Organisation, Public Corporation, Company or Commission. The following chart gives the forms of ownership organisation both in the private and public sectors :

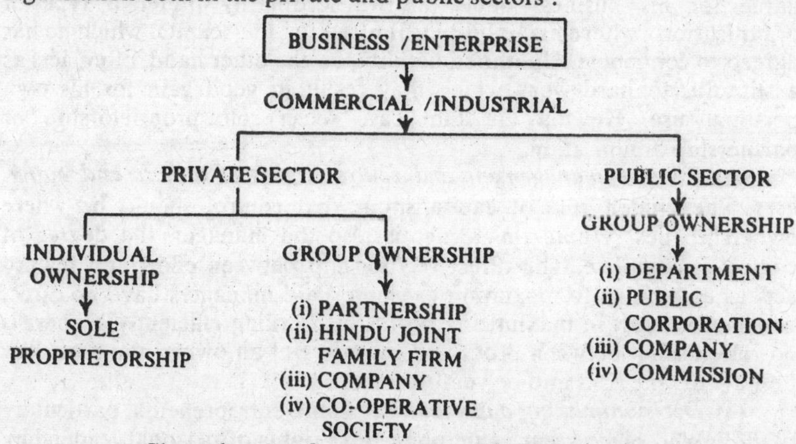

Chart showing forms of ownership organisation

A business enterprise in the private sector may be owned by anyone of the above, but usually one form is more suitable than others for a particular enterprise because of its distinguishing characteristics. Therefore, the choice in this sector will depend to a large measure on the consideration of the special characteristics of each type of organisation. A brief account of these factors is given on the next page.

FACTORS AFFECTING CHOICE OF ORGANISATION

(a) *Ease of formation.* One of the primary considerations in making the choice of the most suitable form of organisation is the ease with which it can be set up. Facility of formation, minimum or no legal requirements, freedom from payment of any fees to the state or attorneys are the ideal conditions favouring the choice of an ideal form of organisation to own and run a business.

(b) *Ease of raising capital.* Another important factor that contributes to the suitability of an organisation is the ease with which the requisite amount of capital can be raised. Small amount of capital can be invested by the entrepreneur himself and he would be content to set up his own business, and individual proprietorship form of organisation would serve his purpose effectively. If a large business, requiring huge amount of capital, is to be set up, company form may be necessary which will entail certain formalities to be followed for raising the necessary amount.

(c) *Extent of liability.* By liability is meant the extent to which a person can be made to account at law. He is either fully liable, i.e., he can be made to pay the full amount of the debts owed. or he is liable only to a limited extent, i.e., he can be made to pay towards those debts only up to a certain limit, but not beyond it. In the former case his liability is said to be unlimited and in the latter case it is limited. Since, where the liability of the owner is unlimited, his personal or private estate will be liable for his business debts, he will ordinarily prefer a type of organisation where his liability is limited to the capital which he has agreed to contribute. Unlimited liability, on the other hand, often acts as a stimulus to hard work which may result in good gain for his own personal use. He may in that case select sole proprietorship or partnership organisation.

(d) *Relative management and control rights of owners and managers.* The golden rule of capitalism is that control should be where ownership lies. Where the owner is also the manager, the degree of control is complete. The direct relationship between effort and reward acts as a stimulus to maximum exertion. Paid managers have no direct personal interest in maximizing profits by working efficiently as there is no relationship between profit and reward. But an owner manager may hesitate to take risks and be venturesome.

(e) *Decision-making opportunities.* Some entrepreneurs, particularly those who place great value upon their rights of personal leadership, would prefer sole proprietorship as the form of organisation. If a very high level of leadership is required which he may not possess, he will then be compelled to form a company in order to attract able leadership to assume responsibility for the operation of the enterprise.

(f) *Flexibility of operation.* A good form of organisation lends itself to maximum flexibility, as changes can be introduced promptly without let and hindrance. Individual proprietorship, for example, enjoys to the maximum degree this characteristic of flexibility of operation.

(g) *Maintenance of secrecy.* Secrecy, especially in the case of small business concerns, is of supreme importance. For that purpose the entrepreneur would most probably prefer sole proprietorship. In case, he has to take other persons as partners, he shall have to exercise great care in choosing his partners.

(h) *Continuity of existence.* Continuity of existence and stability are factors which make an organisation superior in status as against those which lack continuity. Company, as a legal person, may outlive many generations of individual producers. The life span of a sole proprietorship is often limited to the life span of the proprietor, and in case of partnership to the life span of the partners.

(i) *Freedom from government regulation.* Different forms of organisation are subject to varying degrees of government regulation and control. In sole proprietorship the government regulation is minimum but a partnership is exposed to more legal complications, particularly regarding ownership and sharing of profits. A company is created by the process of law and the Government reserves the right to control its actions more closely than of the other two types of organisation.

(j) *Impact of taxation.* The basis of taxation is different in case of each of the forms of organisation. Some of the business taxes affect all forms of enterprise alike, and need not affect the choice, such as excise duties, sales tax, property tax and customs duties. But individual income tax has an important bearing upon the choice of the form of business organisation.

Making a choice of proper Form of Organisation. In making the choice of a suitable form of organisation, the factors mentioned above will have to be weighed against each other. This will ensure the best realization of the result. Of the various factors discussed above, facility in formation, ease in raising the requisite amount of capital are the most important. Limited liability, especially if the capital requirements are large and relationship between ownership and management is not direct, is another important factor. There should also be available flexibility of operation, continuity, secrecy, freedom from government regulation and minimum tax liability.

These factors are inter-related and cannot be taken into account singly. The entrepreneur will make his choice after weighing all of them. The capital will, of course, influence him most and then the limitation of liability. Some other factors, such as the type of the product to be manufactured and sold, competitive conditions in the chosen industry and so on. All of these factors will be considered in relation to each of the forms of organisation. In the following sections are discussed the distinguishing features of each form of organisation.

SOLE PROPRIETORSHIP BUSINESS

Meaning and Leading Features. A sole proprietorship or one-man business is a form of organisation in which an individual produces independently with his own capital, skill and intelligence and is entitled to receive all the profits and assumes all the risks of ownership. As this simple definition indicates, where a business undertaking is owned, and controlled by one man, with or without the help of his family members or a few employees, we have one-man business and the owner is commonly called the Sole Proprietor or Sole Trader. It is also known as Individual Proprietorship or Individual Entrepreneurship.

Historically, this form of organisation is the oldest form of business ownership. It is also the simplest and the most natural. Its leading feature is that the individual carries on business exclusively by and for himself. He invests his own capital and is his own manager. The full control of the business rests in him. He is the supreme judge of all matters pertaining to it, as he makes his own decisions. He bears the entire risk and derives the total benefit. He has almost unlimited freedom of action. He may engage in any business he chooses without any legal formalities, unless he wishes to engage in certain types of business requiring licences. For example, if a man wishes to open a shoes shop, a grocery store, he may do so, if he can find a suitable location and can furnish money to produce a supply of merchandise. On the other hand, to open a restaurant, he will have to obtain a license from the Health Department of the Municipal Corporation.

As his capital is limited and his liability unlimited, a sole trader must confine his activities to small undertakings. It is also difficult, if not impossible, for him to enter into new enterprise or experiment.

To sum up, individual or sole proprietorship form of organisation possesses the following characteristic features :

1. One-man ownership.
2. Personal control.
3. Total or undivided risk.
4. Unlimited liability.
5. Free from government regulation.
6. Proprietor and the firm identical.

Suitability. Because of its peculiar features, sole proprietorship form of organisation is suitable for, and is adopted by, enterprises :

(a) which are small in size;
(b) which require little capital;
(c) which lend themselves readily to control and management by one man;
(d) where risk involved is not heavy;
(e) where personal attention to customers' needs and tastes is important.

The main types of businesses that take the form of sole proprietorship are retailers, hawkers, small grocery stores, bakers, confectioners, launderers, small printing houses, small machine shops, and thousands of similar enterprises, and professional firms, such as solicitors, attorneys, accountants, photographers, hairdressers, etc.

Advantages of Sole Proprietorship. The principal advantages of sole proprietorship organisation are as follows :

1. *Ease of formation.* An individual enterprise is easy to form and simple to run. No legal formalities like registration are required to set it up. Any person can engage in such a business at will. The only restriction is where he wishes to start certain specified types of business. In that case, he will have to obtain a licence, as where he wants to start a restaurant, or sell opium or liquor.

2. *Direct motivation.* The proprietor has a direct personal interest in the business which makes for efficiency and economy. Indeed, the direct relationship between effort and reward acts as a stimulus to maximum exertion for a sole proprietor.

3. *Complete degree of control.* As the sole proprietor is the sole master of his business, his control over it is complete. He is responsible to no one else. Actually, no problem of coordination arises; his own decisions will make for reconciliation of the various interests of the firm. As he knows all his employees personally, he is in a position to encourage team work. This helps to eliminate waste. The golden rule of capitalism that 'where the risk lies, control must lie', is admirably satisfied in this form of organisation.

4. *Promptness in decision-making.* Promptness in taking decisions makes for efficiency. A sole trader, being the supreme and sole master, can make a prompt decision, and thereby take advantage of an opportunity for gain before it slips away. Since there is no one else to dispute his judgment, he can also maintain a decision made by him.

5. *Flexibility in operation.* As the proprietor has the full control over his business and is the supreme judge in all matters, he can introduce changes as the exigencies of occasion demand, and without any delay. Hence, there is a great deal of flexibility in policy-making in this type of organisation.

6. *Maintenance of secrecy.* Secrecy is of vital importance for the success of a small business; and a sole trader is in an eminent position to keep his affairs to himself. As there is no legal obligation to supply any information regarding his business to any one, he can maintain utmost secrecy in all matters.

7. *Catering for individual tastes.* A sole trader is in a position to be in close touch with his customers and to cater for their individual tastes. This helps him to build up goodwill for himself. The individual owner flourishes in all enterprises where the "personal element" is important.

8. *Credit standing.* The fact of large goodwill and wide clientele, coupled with unlimited liability are likely to prompt creditors to grant him liberal credit. The assets of the firm along with his resources outside the firm (i.e., his private property and investments) will all help to build up his credit-worthiness with the result that the suppliers and other institutions will readily extend him credit.

9. *Minimum government regulation.* The activities of a sole trader are regulated by government and law to the minimum extent. In fact, his

rights and obligations are the same as of any other citizen. It is true that a sole proprietor has to comply with tax and labour laws, but otherwise interference is minimum. The formation and dissolution of the business are not subject to any government regulation in this form of organisation.

Social Advantages of Individual Proprietorship. The sociological significance of individual proprietorship in the form of a small shop consists in rendering some important, nay, indispensable services to the community and at the same time providing the basis of an independent livelihood for many.

1. *Independent way of life.* This form of organisation provides a way of life for those who take pride in ownership and control of what they own. Such persons are obviously of independent spirit and would not care to serve under others. It gives him an opportunity to utilize his capacity to the maximum and to enjoy freedom of action. The sole proprietor is his own master and manager, and this fact generates the greatest possible satisfaction.

2. *Generation of social virtues.* It affords a form of life and work which permits a high degree of self-determination, the enjoyment of purposeful work, the warmth of social contact, and a well-integrated family and respectable life. It also develops the qualities of self-reliance, responsibility, and initiative, which are of great social importance.

3. *Diffusion of business ownership.* As under this form of organisation, a very large number of people must own and manage vast number of small business units, it makes for diffusion of business ownership as against concentration of power in a few hands offered by a joint stock company.

Disadvantages or Limitations. Despite so many advantages, both economic and social, one-man business, suffers from some very serious limitations. The limitations of individual proprietorship are as follows :

1. *Limited amount of capital.* The first limitation is as to capital. The amount of capital that a sole proprietor can get together must of necessity be limited. Save for a few exceptions, no one would be rich enough or even inclined to supply considerable amount of money for his business. Since the sole trader determines his business policy, investors cannot readily be induced to give their funds into his hands. He is therefore limited to such funds as he may own or raise from friends and relatives. As a result, he cannot expand his business when it may be found necessary to take advantage of economies of large-scale operation.

2. *Limited managerial ability.* An individual, however capable. cannot be expected to possess full knowledge of all branches of a business and is bound to fritter away his energies in doing things which could best be left to others in a partnership or a company. Since, being alone, he must keep his fingers on everything, he carries a staggering load of responsibility, which may crush him under its weight unless he is a giant in judgment, intelligence and intellect. He may, therefore, at times make wrong decisions which would increase the cost of production and

decrease his profits. After all, two heads are better than one, unless the one is the best.

3. *Unlimited liability.* The liability of the proprietor is unlimited. It is not only the assets of the business that are liable, but also his entire personal fortune for the debts of the business. The advantage of personal control is counterbalanced by personal risk which might turn out to be very great.

Limited capital and managerial ability and unlimited liability of the owner act as brakes to the development and expansion of business.

4. *Uncertainty of continuity.* Permanence or continuity of business is difficult to maintain. When the proprietor dies or is no longer able to run the business, the business may come to an end, if there is no one capable enough to take his place. Very often the heirs lack the requisite ability or inclination to carry on the business. If it falls into weak hands, it will fail causing loss not only to the owner but also to society. The closure of the business, which has been rendering a useful service to the community, would be a social loss.

In conclusion, it may be safely stated that one-man control is the best from the point of view of efficiency and profitability, provided that one man is big enough to manage everything indefinitely.

Scope and Prospects of Sole Proprietorship Business. It is a commonplace that single proprietorship businesses are the most numerous in India as everywhere else, in spite of the fact that large corporations and companies owning giant business have entered the field. It is also almost certain that individual proprietorship is in no danger of being crowded out by large corporations, because of the opportunities it offers to a vast number of people.

It is true that large corporate enterprises have certain advantages inherent in large-scale operation, namely, economic viability, operational efficiency and limited liability of the investors. Yet, a small entrepreneur possesses advantages which in some circumstances will allow him to compete successfully against a large manufacturer or trader. The following factors show that single proprietorship business will continue to hold intact its position in the business world in face of large corporations :

1. Normally, a business is started as a one-man venture, because of the many advantages it offers. As the proprietor makes a success of it and is faced with the problem of expansion, he resorts to the formation of a company. If his capital needs are not vast and he wishes to preserve secrecy and family character of his business he will form a private company.

2. Because the proprietor is closely in touch with details, and because results are quickly known, the advantages of economic viability, direct motivation, personal contact inherent in individual proprietorship sustain one-man businesses along with giant concerns. As a result, in the field of distribution in particular this form of organisation continues to flourish all over the world.

3. In the field of production, too, there are certain industries which can be run successfully only on a small scale. For instance, industries whose products cannot be standardized and establishments which attempt to make products to suit the different tastes of consumers can best be owned and run by individual proprietors. Such industries produce 'tailored' suits, high-grade furniture, art goods, handicrafts, finely bound books, etc.

4. In India, the government has been encouraging individual owners to take up small manufacturing activities by setting up industrial estates and by providing training facilities, as well as by granting financial assistance. The National Small Industries Corporation has been rendering a useful service in this direction.

5. The vast majority of the service enterprises like transport and warehousing are normally organised as individual proprietorships. Professionals, such as chartered accountants, lawyers can function only as sole proprietors or partnerships.

JOINT HINDU FAMILY BUSINESS

In India, we have family businesses in the form of Joint Hindu Family Firms, which are in essence individual entrepreneurs possessing almost all the merits and limitations discussed above. A short consideration of this type of business is called for, although it is not so common now.

There are two schools of Hindu Law: *Dayabhaga*, which is applicable in Bengal and Assam, and *Mitakshara*, which is current in the rest of India. According to the *Mitakshara* law, an undivided family is the normal condition of Hindu society, and the Joint Hindu Family consists of all persons lineally descended from a common ancestor and includes their wives and unmarried daughters. Within this joint family there is a narrower body which includes only those persons who acquire by birth an interest in the joint or coparcenary property. The business belonging to a joint family is ordinarily managed by the father or other senior member for the time being of the family. He is called *Karta* or manager. The *Karta*, as head of the family, has control over the income and expenditure and he is the custodian of the surplus, if any. The other members cannot question his judgment in running the business : their only remedy is to demand partition. On the other hand, he is liable to make good to them their shares of all sums which he has misappropriated or which he has spent for purposes other than those in which the joint family is interested. The manager has an implied authority to borrow money for family business, but the other members will be liable only to the extent of their share in the joint family property. He has general power to carry on the business or shut it down as an individual proprietor may do.

PARTNERSHIP ORGANISATION[1]

In an individual proprietorship, the work is carried on in cramped circumstances, each man is for himself, and the administration of the business is purely a process of each man minding his own business. The organisation is nothing more than a mere extension of the proprietor. If he possesses the various qualities of a good businessman, he makes good profit. But it is not always possible that an individual is endowed with all the requisite qualities or even enough capital to run a successful business which must of necessity grow in size for better results. Therefore, very often men of ability combine their resources, and from this combination of capital, labour and skill, partnership organisation results.

Historically, partnership organisation has grown out of the need for more capital to produce for the ever-growing market, more effective supervision and control, greater specialisation and division of work between proprietors, and for spreading of risk. It is indeed the simplest method of extending the size of a business and at the same time relieving the sole proprietor of part of the burden. Yet partnership organisation is not always free from pitfalls. Its successful working depends upon mutual confidence and good faith. As each partner is the agent of the others and binds them to the fullest extent of their fortunes, it is necessary to be careful when selecting a partner. When you are considering a partner, do not be in too great a hurry—give yourself time to test him. Choosing a partner is like choosing a wife; marry in haste and repent at leisure—in either case there is need for second thought and sure knowledge.

Meaning of Partnership. An association of individuals competent to contract who agree to carry on a lawful business in common with the object of sharing profit is a partnership. Section 4 of the Partnership Act, 1932 defines Partnership as "The relation between persons who have agreed to share profits of a business carried on by all or any of them acting for all." This definition brings out the following five characteristics of partnership :

1. *Contractual relationship.* The partnership results only from a contract between a certain number of persons called partners. As a result only persons competent to enter into a contract can be partners, so that a minor cannot be a partner. A Hindu Joint Family firm which results from status is not a partnership.

2. *Plurality of persons.* As partnership results from a contract, there must be at least two partners, although there must not be more than twenty.

3. *Existence of business.* Partnership implies business, and where there is no business there is no partnership. Thus, the persons must form an association by contract to carry on some business.

4. *Sharing of profits.* The agreement to carry on business must be

1. For detailed information regarding the legal aspects of Partnership, see the author's *Manual of Mercantile Law.*

with the object of making profit and sharing it among all the partners. A piece of philanthropy, though it may involve a good deal of business, is not a partnership.

5. *Mutual agency.* The business must be carried on by all the partners or any one or more of them acting for all the partners. In result, each partner is both an agent and a principal—agent for other partners and principal for himself.

Legal Implications. The definition of partnership, as explained above, brings out some important legal implications which deserve to be kept in mind while forming a partnership and conducting partnership business.

1. *Legal position.* Legally a partnership firm is not a legal entity nor a person with any separate right distinct from the partners constituting it. It is only an association of persons who are called individually partners and collectively "a firm". "Firm" is only a convenient phrase to describle the partners and has no legal existence apart from them.

2. *Extent of liability.* The liability of each partner for the debts of the firm is unlimited. The creditors have a right to recover the firm's debts from the private property of any or all partners, where the firm's assets are insufficient.

3. *Nature of partners' liability.* It follows that, while the acts of partnership are in the name of the firm, the responsibility created is joint and several resting upon each of the partners. No agreement between the partners to limit this liability only to some of them has any validity as against the claims of any uninformed parties.

4. *Utmost good faith.* The relation of partners is founded on mutual confidence and trust. Each partner must, therefore, be just and honest towards the other partners. In other words, he owes a duty to act towards the other partners with the utmost good faith. He must not make any secret profits, and must keep and render true accounts and disclose all facts relating to the business of the firm.

5. *Implied authority.* Each partner is an agent able to bind the others with respect to all regular acts done by him on behalf and in the name of the firm, such as the buying and selling of stock in trade, the hiring and firing of employees, the borrowing of money, or the issuing of negotiable instruments. Such an act of the partner is deemed to be the act of the firm (i.e., the act of all the partners), and the authority so exercised by a partner is known as the partner's implied authority to bind all the partners.

6. *Unanimity of consent.* In matters of importance and those affecting policy and nature of the business, or relating to an alteration in the partnership constitution, unanimous decision by all the partners is necessary. A majority cannot effect any change. In fact, majority principle does not apply in all such matters.

7. *Non-transferability of share or interest.* No partner can assign or transfer his partnership interest to any other person, so as to make him a partner in the business. This may, however, he done with the consent of

all the other partners.

8. *Dissolution.* Unless there is an agreement to the contrary, the death or insolvency of a partner dissolves the firm. If, however, all the partners, or all the partners but one are adjudicated as insolvent, or the business of the firm becomes unlawful, the firm is compulsorily and automatically dissolved.

CHIEF FEATURES OF PARTNERSHIP

1. *Formation.* Although a partnership is constituted by means of a contract between the partners, no legal formalities are required for its formation. An oral contract is sufficient to bring it into being. But it is advisable to reduce the agreement to writing, and prepare a properly drafted Deed of Partnership or Articles of Partnership laying down the terms and conditions of partnership and the rights, obligations and duties of partners.

Registration of a partnership firm is not compulsory under our law. nor is any penalty provided for non-registration. The law, however, introduces certain disabilities, which make registration necessary at one time or other. In fact, the law has effectively ensured registration of firms without making it compulsory. The first disability is that an unregistered firm cannot file a suit, or take other legal proceedings, to enforce a right arising from a contract. Secondly, a partner cannot sue the the firm or other partners arising under a contract or conferred by the Partnership Act. But an outsider can sue an unregistered firm and its partners.

2. *Finance.* Normally, the capital of a partnership firm consists of the amounts contributed by the various partners. The capital contributions by all the partners need not be equal, and one or more may not put in any capital at all. This will happen where such partners bring in special skills and abilities. The initial capital may be augmented or more for expansion of business may be obtained, by borrowing on the security of the firm's property and also on the strength of the private estates of partners.

3. *Control.* As partnership results from a contract, the control will depend upon its terms. Where all the partners take active part in the conduct of the partnership business, the control rests with all of them. All major decisions, as observed earlier, must be made by the unanimous consent of all the partners. There may, however, be some partners who do not take active part in the conduct of the business. They are known as sleeping or dormant or secret partners. In a word, the control is ordinarily shared by the active or ostensible partners.

4. *Management of Affairs.* In law, every partner has a right to take part in the conduct and management of the business of the firm. In practice, partnership agreement provides for the division of work among the different partners according to their experience and knowledge. It is not unusual to have one of them as the senior partner who would be in the position of the chief executive, exercising overall supervision.

5. *Duration of Partnership.* The partners are at liberty to fix the duration of the partnership or say nothing about it. Where they agree to carry on business for a definite period of time, it is called a *partnership for a fixed term.* When the term is over, the partnership comes to an end; but if the business is continued after the expiry of the period originally fixed, the renewed partnership will become a *partnership at will.* Where a partnership is formed for a particular adventure, it is called *Particular partnership* which would presumably last until the business is finished. If the partners say nothing about the duration, or agree to carry on the business as long as they wish to do so, the partnership will be one *at will.* It can dissolved at the will of any partner, on his giving notice. Where partners cannot agree on the dissolution of the firm, the court may, on application, order its dissolution.

6. *Taxation.* A partnership firm is liable to pay income tax and other taxes as an individual is liable to pay. But there is a slight difference with regard to the rate of tax according as whether the firm is registered under the Income Tax Act or not. If it is so registered (apart from registration under the Partnership Act), the income will be divided among partners and each partner will be assessed separately. If the firm is not registered, the firm will be required to pay tax on its total profit as distinct from the incomes of the individual partners.

7. *Joint ownership.* Every partner is a joint owner of the partnership property, and has an equal share in it, unless different shares are provided by agreement. The property of the firm is required to be used exclusively for the purposes of the partnership.

PARTNERSHIP PROPERTY

It is open to the partners to agree among themselves as to what is to be treated as the property of the firm, and what is to be the separate property of one or more partners, although employed or used for the purposes of the firm. In the absence of any such agreement, all property, rights and interests brought by the partners into the common stock, all property acquired in the course of business with money belonging to the firm, and the goodwill of the business will be deemed to be firm's property, and must be used only for the purposes of the firm.

REQUISITES OF AN IDEAL PARTNERSHIP

Partnership business grows out of the need for combining resources, both human and material. Some persons may contribute capital, others their business ability and experience and still others may bring in technical skill. The faithful contribution by each partner of his gift will make it successful. An ideal partnership will satisfy the following conditions or requisites :

1. *Common purpose.* All partners must act with zealous cooperation

and the greatest common advantage. Each partner should make his contribution to the success of the business according to one's capital, skill, knowledge, influence and personality.

2. *Good faith.* Honesty of purpose and fairness in dealings are the fundamental principles of partnership, each partner should create mutual trust and confidence among themselves. For this purpose, care must be exercised in selecting a partner, as the wrong selection may bring ruin to the firm. The number of partners should be as small as will bring in the requisite resources, human as well as material.

3. *Sufficient capital.* The necessary funds, both for short-term and long-term use should be available in sufficient amount. Long-term funds would normally be supplied by the partners as capital, and others may be obtained by loans. To maintain sound financial position of the firm, drawings by the partners should be kept as low as possible. Part of the profits should be ploughed back into the business of the firm for further development.

4. *Long duration.* The duration of partnership should be long. Only long-term partnerships can properly set up businesses and consolidate them effectively for success. Therefore, it should be a constant endeavour of all the partners to extend firm's life over a long period by working honestly and skilfully and by avoiding disputes.

5. *Written agreement.* In order to avoid misunderstanding and future disputes it is desirable that the mutual rights and obligations of partners be incorporated into a partnership deed. It should contain full details about capital, sharing of profit, extent of the authority of each partner and so on.

6. *Registration.* The partnership should be registered with the Registrar of Firms as soon after formation as possible. As indicated earlier, an unregistered partnership firm cannot sue outsiders, although the outsiders can sue it. In case it is not registered soon after its formation, the firm can be registered any time before filing a suit.

PARTNERSHIP DEED

While to constitute a partnership there must be an agreement between the parties, it need not necessarily be in writing. It may be of the most informal character, even oral, though the business of partnership may involve lakhs of rupees, or on the other hand, it may be an elaborate written document called the Deed of Partnership or Articles of Partnership, and drafted by a lawyer. Where the partners have decided to enter into a deed of partnership, it should be stamped according to the provisions of the Stamp Act. The partnership deed is not a public document like a Memorandum of Association of a Company and only binds third parties so far as they have notice of it. A properly drawn up deed of partnership should ordinarily cover the following points :—

1. The name of the firm together with the names of the partners composing it.

2. The nature of business and the duration of partnership.
3. The amount of capital each partner undertakes to contribute and the manner of its contribution.
4. The ratio for sharing profits and losses.
5. Salaries, commissions, etc., if any, payable to partners; and also any drawings which may be allowed.
6. Interest on partners' capital, partners' loans, drawings by partners and interest, if any, to be charged on overdrawn accounts.
7. The division of work among the partners for the management of the firm.
8. Matters relating to retirement, death and admission of partners, and valuation of goodwill and share of profits available to such partners; and any restraint on business by a retiring partner.
9. Settlement of accounts at the dissolution of the firm.
10. Arbitration clause to settle disputes which may arise among the partners without recourse to a court of law.
11. Any other clause or clauses which may be found necessary in any particular kind of business.

DISTINCTION BETWEEN PARTNERSHIP AND JOINT HINDU FAMILY FIRM

The following are the points of distinction between a partnership and a joint Hindu family firm :

1. A partnership can only arise as a result of a contract between partners, while a Joint Hindu Familv Firm is created by the operation of law.

2. A Joint Hindu Family Firm is not dissolved by the death or insolvency of a co-parcener, but a partnership is ordinarily so dissolved.

3. A co-parcener is not entitled, on severing his connection with the family firm, to ask for accounts of past profits and losses. It is otherwise in the case of a partner.

4. In a joint family firm it is only the manager, and no other co-parcener, who has an implied authority to contract debts and pledge the credit and property of the firm for the ordinary purposes of the family business. In the case of partnership, any partner can bind his co-partners by debts incurred in the ordinary course of business.

5. The liability of partners is joint and several, that is, it is not only the share of each partner in the partnership property which is liable for the payment of partnership debts, but also the separate property of each partner. In the case of debts contracted by a *Karta,* in pursuance of his implied authority in the ordinary course of the family business, there is a distinction between the liability of the manager and the liability of his co-parceners. The manager is liable not only to the extent of his share in the joint family property, but, being a party to the contract, he is liable

personally, that is to say, his separate property is also liable. The other co-parceners are liable only to the extent of their interest in the family property, unless, in the case of adult co-parceners the contract was virtually entered into by them also, or subsequently ratified; and in the case of minors, unless ratified on attaining majority.

6. In a partnership, both males and females can be partners, but in a Hindu co-parcenary only males are members. No female can be a co-parcener under *Mitakshara* law, not even a wife, who has interest in it to the extent of maintenance, but under *Dayabhaga* law, both males and females can be members of a co-parcenary under certain circumstances.

7. In a partnership, a minor cannot become a partner nor is he one of the group of persons called firm, though he may be admitted to the benefit of partnership. In a Joint Hindu Family Firm a minor is a co-parcener.

8. A partnership is expected to be registered in order that partners may enforce their rights between themselves or against strangers, but no such registration is necessary in the Joint Hindu Family Firm.

9. Subject to any agreement to the contrary, partners have equal interest in the partnership property and share its profits equally. A member of the Joint Hindu Family Firm, on the other hand, cannot predict at any given moment what his share in the joint business is. His interest is subject to fluctuations, as it would enlarge by deaths and be curtailed by births, for he does not inherit through his father but of his own right through birth. His share becomes defined only when partition takes place. Also, no member is entitled to any definite share of the profits of the business.

10. When a partner dies, his interest in the partnership devolves on his heirs, although they cannot demand to become partners if other partners do not so desire, but where a co-parcener dies before partition of the co-parcenary business, his undivided share devolves, not by succession upon his heirs, but by survivorship upon the surviving co-parceners.

11. A partnership firm, not being a person, cannot (nor can a partner on behalf of the firm) enter into partnership with a stranger. A partner may in his own personal right become a member of any number of partnership firms. The manager of a joint family business, acting on behalf of the family firm, is competent to enter into partnership with a stranger.

LIMITED PARTNERSHIP

Some of the limitations such as unlimited liability and the limited amount of capital of an ordinary partnership can be obviated by resorting to the "Limited Partnership Organisation". We have seen before that the successful working of a partnership depends upon mutual confidence and trust, and that, therefore, strangers may be wary to invest funds in a partnership. The limited partnership form of organisation permits of the admission of "special partners" with limited liability along with the "general partners" whose liability is unlimited. We have no such device in India, but in the Western countries this form of organisation is quite common. The principle underlying all the Statutes creating such partnerships being the same, we will outline the important provisions of the English Limited Partnership Act, 1907.

The object of the Act is to allow some of the partners to be responsible only for capital actually found by them thus limiting the liability of those partners, and having the others fully liable for the debts of the firm. The important features of a limited partnership are :—

1. It must consist of one or more persons called "general partners", who shall be liable for all debts and obligations of the firm.
2. It must also contain one or more persons, to be called "limited partners", who shall contribute a certain amount of capital and be liable only to the extent of that capital and no more. The limited partner is in fact in the nature of a fully paid shareholder, whose capital cannot be returned as long as the partnership continues.
3. A limited partner cannot take part in the management of the partnership business, nor can he bind the firm; but he can inspect its books, etc.
4. If he takes part in the management of the business, he shall be liable to the full extent for all debts and obligations incurred when he so acted.
5. A limited partner may, with the consent of the general partners, assign his share in the partnership, so as to make the assignee a limited partner in his place.
6. Every limited partnership must be registered.

As compared with the ordinary partnership, the limited partnership has certain advantages. While retaining the direct motivation in management, it furnishes a single direction of management which may act with greater unity and promptness. Also, it provides impetus to the investing public to supply funds in large quantities, thus affording an industrial leader with little capital to put his genius and energy at the service of society. The general partner can secure additional capital without any loss of control. The limited partnership will usually be found advantageous "where a highly concentrated and responsible management is desired at the same time with considerable capital, especially if incorporation is not desirable either because of expense or regulatory provisions."

EVALUATION

Partnership organisation is admirably suitable for medium-size undertakings, where personal efforts of the owners are essential. It possesses some of the characteristics of the individual proprietorship organisation, and consequently most of its advantages and limitations.

Advantages. Partnership organisation enjoys the following advantages :

1. *Facility of formation.* Like individual enterprise partnership can be formed without legal formality and much expense, and can be dissolved in the same way. No formal documents are required to be drawn up as in the case of joint stock companies. Partnership taxes are relatively small.

2. *Benefits of larger resources.* Partnership enjoys larger resources than a sole trader, so that the scale of operation can be enlarged to reap the benefits of important economies. There is always scope for the introduction of new partners to augment resources

3. *Flexibility.* The business is abundantly mobile and elastic, being almost free from legal restrictions on its activities. The partners can introduce any changes they consider desirable to meet the changed circumstances.

4. *Personal element.* The personal element in the business and the corresponding care, efficiency and economy are ensured. There is thus an effective motivation to production. The supervision of the staff can also be carried out effectively, as the partners personally act in the management of the affairs of the firm.

5. *Benefits of combined ability.* Partnership enjoys the benefits of combined ability of its partners possessing varying degrees of talent and skills. This is a distinct advantage over sole proprietorship. Two heads are better than one is an old saying.

6. *Prompt decisions.* The partners exercise joint responsibility and meet frequently. This enables them to make decisions promptly, which is conducive to taking advantage of sudden business opportunities.

7. *Sharing of risk.* Any losses sustained by the firm will be shared by all the partners with the result that the burden borne by each partner will be much less than what a sole proprietor may have to bear.

8. *Wholesome effect of unlimited liability.* The fact that the liability of the partners is unlimited and each one is liable to the full extent of his private fortune acts as a great check against dangerous speculation. This is a great safeguard against recklessness. Secondly, unlimited liability also enhances the credit of the firm in the eyes of the lending public and thus enables it to borrow easily and at low rate of interest.

9. *Protection of minority interests.* The minority interest in a partnership is effectively protected by law. In matters of policy all partners must agree; and even in ordinary affairs of routine nature a dissatisfied partner may withdraw and dissolve the firm. Thus in all important matters, the minority enjoys the right of veto. In fact, the law gives each partner the right to be heard and consulted. In consequence, each partner is as important as the others.

Disadvantages. Despite several advantages, the partnership form of organisation suffers from the following limitations :

1. *Lack of harmony.* There is always likelihood of friction within

the firm. Difference of opinion very often results in disharmony and lack of united management. Generally, differences crop up and each partner tries to vie with the others in dishonest dealings. This frequently results in disruption and ultimate dissolution.

2. *Limited resources.* The limit of 20 on the number of partners, limits the amount of capital that can be raised. Actually, in order to secure harmony among the partners, the number has to be kept much smaller than the maximum allowed by the law. This further limits the resources, with the result that large-scale business cannot be run by partnership. Though superior to one-man business in this respect, it is inferior to more highly developed form of joint stock company.

3. *Restricted enterprise.* As unlimited liability extends to the entire fortune of each partner, the partners tend to be overcautious. This restricts enterprise. In fact, the liability of individual partners may be regarded as excessive for most purposes. Therefore, the partnership organisation tends to be useful only for comparatively small businesses, such as retail trade, a moderate-sized mercantile houses or a very small manufacturing business.

4. *Instability.* The business may come to an abrupt end on the death or insolvency of any partner. The business may also be closed where a partner signifies his intention to dissolve the partnership or gets it dissolved by order of court on account of a wrongful act of another partner.

5. *Social loss.* Such an abrupt closure of business is harmful not only to its owners, but also to society particularly if it has been successful and contributing to the well-being of the community.

6. *Lack of public confidence.* The absence of legal regulations, and the fact that there is no publicity in regard to a partnership's affairs reduces to some extent public confidence.

7. *Heavy burden through implied authority.* Each partner is an agent able to bind the others by his acts and omissions in the ordinary and usual course of the business of the firm. When, therefore, one partner is negligent, or commits a wrong, or is guilty of a fraud, within the scope of his authority, his partners are equally liable financially and without limit. This may put a very heavy financial burden on the partners, which may, in some cases, result in the ruin of a person.

Conclusion. On balance, partnership form of organisation is most suitable where the size of the business is relatively small, and so the capital can be contributed to meet its needs by the partners themselves. It is an organisation that can be usefully adopted by men of equal wealth and ability who combine their resources—capital, labour and skill,—and run it for the common advantage of all the partners. But the very success of the business would create problems relating to expansion for coping with the increased demand for the goods. In such a case, it would be necessary to convert the business into a limited company and collect funds from the public and take advantage of limited liability.

CHAPTER IV

COMPANY FORM OF ORGANISATION

The power over enterprise having passed to capital, individual proprietorship or partnership could not supply sufficient capital. Nor could technology needed by large-scale business be handled by either of the forms of organisation. Therefore, it became necessary to have another form of organisation through which large sums of money could be amassed from large number of people who are either not capable of running business enterprises or have no time to do so. They are, however, willing to invest their savings in a business provided they are assured that their money is safe and they will not be called upon to pay anything more than what they undertake to invest. The form suitable to serve these purposes was found to be a limited company. This form enables the entrepreneurs to get the necessary capital from the general public, retaining at the same time, the control and management in their own hands. As a matter of fact, most of the shortcomings of the partnership form of organisation can be overcome by organising a business as a joint stock company with limited liability.

Fundamental Principle of Company Organisation. The fundamental principle of joint stock organisation is that the capital of the undertaking is contributed by a large group of people, the shareholders, who have very restricted powers and have hardly any voice in the management of the business. This is entrusted by them to a committee of management called the Board of Directors, who exercise their control through General and Departmental Managers. The system of joint stock organisation is very useful for large undertakings for which large capital is required, which can be obtained from a large number of people, who are certain that whole fortunes are not exposed to danger as in the case of partnerships. Hence, joint stock enterprise is today the recognised medium for the supply of capital to trade and industry, and as a powerful and efficient engine of production.

Company—Its Meaning and Characteristics. A company is a voluntary association of persons, recognised by law, having a distinctive name, a common seal, formed to carry on business for profit, with capital divisible into transferable shares, limited liability, a corporate body and perpetual succession. An analysis of this definition will bring out the distinctive characteristics of a company.

1. *Creature of law.* A company is a creation of law, and is sometimes called artificial person. It exists only in contemplation of law and therefore has no physical shape or form. Although invisible and intangible, as a legal person, it enjoys almost all the rights of natural person. It has a right to enter into contracts and own property. It can sue and can be sued. The legal personality is one of its distinctive features.

2. *Distinct legal entity.* Being a creature of law, a company is a legal entity, something distinct from the persons who are its members. A shareholder is not liable for the acts of the company, even though he holds almost all the shares. Also the shareholders cannot bind the company by their acts. They are not its agents. As the company is an artificial creature of the law, distinct and separate from its members, a shareholder can both own its shares and be its creditor. The life of the company is independent of the lives of its members. Even if all the members die, the company does not come to an end because of their demise.

3. *Limited liability of members.* The limited liability is another important feature of a company. A person, by buying shares in a company, acquires an interest in the company, and is at liberty to dispose of these shares whenever he likes. If anything goes wrong with the company, his liability is limited by the nominal amount of the shares held by him. In other words, while he stands to lose the money he has invested, he cannot be called upon to pay a paisa out of his private property in order to help meet the company's obligations.

4. *Perpetual Succession.* The incorporation process brings into being a corporate body distinct and separate from the members who constitute it. The right given to the shareholders to transfer their shares without in any manner affecting the position of the company gives the company continuity. As a natural consequence of incorporation and transferability of shares, the company has perpetual succession or uninterrupted existence. As we have noted above, the life of the company being independent of the lives of its members, its life expectancy is not limited to that of the various founders. Members may come and members may go, but the company goes on uninterrupted (until, of course, wound up according to law). The law creates the company and the law brings it to an end.

5. *Common Seal.* The law requires every company to have a seal with its name engraved on it. As the company has no physical form, it cannot sign its name on a contract. Therefore, originally all documents and contracts required the affixing of the seal. But now most of the transactions are signed by the directors who act as its agents. When it is affixed on any document, two directors must witness its affixation.

6. *Divorce between Ownership and Management.* The personality of the company is separate and distinct from those humans who compose it—the shareholders. Therefore, the shareholders cannot bind the company by their acts. Since the investors of capital are a heterogeneous group of people residing far and wide, they cannot manage the affairs of the company. They leave this task to their representatives—the Board of Directors. This characteristic of a company militates against the Golden Rule of Capitalism, which will be discussed later.

The chief implications of the above analytical description of the company may be summed up as follows :

1. It is a voluntary association

2. of mutually agreeing persons, natural or legal;
3. it is an autonomous legal unit,
4. distinct from its associating members
5. in name, in the duration of its life, and its liability to creditors;
6. it exists because the State has by statute enabled it to exist.

In all these respects company organisation differes radically from a partnership business.

CHIEF FEATURE OF COMPANY FORM OF ORGANISATION

The principal and distinguishing features of a company organisation may be detailed as follows :

1. *Formation.* A company is an artificial legal person created by process of law which makes it an entity separate and distinct from its members that constitute it. Since corporate life and form cannot exist without the permission of the State, a company, having corporate personality, can be brought into being by following certain legal formalities. The formation of a company passes through two stages: Promotion and Incorporation. Both of these processes will be discussed in the following section.

2. *Financing.* Where the capital needs are not vast and it is desired to preserve secrecy and family character of the business, but enjoy the benefit of limited liability, a private limited company is formed. A private company raises its capital by private arrangement from friends and relatives. It cannot invite the general public to buy its shares. Where huge capital is required for production and distribution of what has been produced, a public limited company is formed and the general public is invited to supply the capital. For this purpose, a prospectus has to be issued inviting the general public to take up the shares of the company. This is an elaborate document required to disclose detailed information, the preparation and issue of which involves good deal of expenditure. But it enables the company to collect funds from far and wide and in amount which is far beyond the powers of partnerships.

3. *Control.* In law and theory, the members of the company, who contribute the share capital, have the ultimate control of company's affairs. Every company is required to hold an annual general meeting at which the shareholders are supposed to exercise their power of control. In practice, the control lies with the Board of Directors or the 'inside group'. But the Board is required to publish and present to the shareholders at the annual general meeting the accounts and the results of the working of the company.

4. *Management.* Since the risk-bearing shareholders are widely scattered, and do not, in most cases, have the time, or knowledge of business, especially where they are engaged in their own occupations and professions, the management of the company has to be entrusted to the Board of Directors. The Companies Act also states that the Board is entitled to exercise all such powers as the company is authorised to

exercise in general meeting. Thus, the directors are the exclusive representatives of the company, and are charged with the administration of its internal affairs and the management and use of its assets. The shareholders are the risk-bearers, but the directors are the risk-takers.

5. *Duration.* A company comes into being by a process other than natural birth, and so possesses the property of immortality. Its life is not measured by the lives of its members. It continues to exist even if all the members constituting it die or are adjudicated insolvent. This capacity of perpetual succession ensures its continutiy. Members may come and members may go, but the company goes on undisturbed until dissolved by a process of law. Also, a shareholder cannot get back his money from the company and so be a cuase of its disintegration. In all these respects the company is superior to partnership or sole proprietorship.

6. *Taxation.* In a large number of situations the tax burdens on companies are heavier than on partnerships. For example a company's profits are taxed at a flat rate as against slab rates in case of un-incorporated associations, e.g., partnerships. This means that the rate of income-tax does not rise with the rise in profits or fall with the fall in profits; it remains constant regardless whether the profits are low or high. In the case of a sole proprietor or a partnership firm the rate is progressive, going up with the increase in the amount of assessable income.

Distinction between a Company and a Partnership Firm

1. *Registration.* A company is formed by registration under the Companies Act. A partnership need not be registered.

2. *Legal Person.* A company, being a legal entity, is a person distinct from its members. It acts in its own name. A partnership has no legal existence apart from the partners. The firm and the partners are one and the same.

3. *Limited liability.* The liability of shareholders is invariably limited, while that of partners is unlimited.

4. *Number of Members.* A private company can have a maximum number of 50 members and a public company has no limit. A partnership firm cannot have more than 20 partners.

5. *Transferability of shares.* The shares in a company are transferable, with the result that shareholders can go on changing. A partner cannot transfer his share and interest in the partnership business without the consent of all the other partners.

6. *Continuity of existence.* A company has perpetual succession. The death or insolvency of any or all the shareholders does not affect the life of the company, as it is distinct and separate from their lives. The partnership comes to an end by the death or insolvency of a partner.

7. *Capital requirements.* A company raises its financial resources from the savings of a large number of people, usually in small amounts. A partnership has to depend upon the resources of the partners. It may

borrow from banks or individuals, but it cannot issue debentures to the general public, as can a company.

8. *Management.* The shareholders, who supply the capital, cannot as shareholders, manage the affairs of the company. They entrust it to the Board of Directors. In a partnership, every partner is entitled to take part in the management of the firm's business.

9. *Compulsory audit.* A company is required by law to have its accounts audited once a year by a Chartered Accountant in practice. No such obligation is placed upon a partnership firm.

10. *Change of objects.* A company can change its objects and powers only with the permission of the Court. The partners can, by mutual agreement, change them as and when they like.

11. *Government control.* The Government that creates a company reserves the right to regulate its actions more closelv than those of partnerships.

12. *Majority rule.* In a company, the right of the majority to decide is the cardinal rule. In partnership the majority rule does not apply in all important matters. Unity in partnership being the rule, all partners must concur in matters of policy.

CLASSES OF COMPANIES

Companies may be classified from different points of view, namely ;—

1. From the point of view of incorporation;
2. From the viewpoint of liability;
3. From a functional standpoint.

1. *As regards incorporation.* There are three ways in which companies may be incorporated, namely, by Charter, by Statute or by Registration.

(a) *Chartered Companies.* A company created by the grant of a charter by the Crown is called a Chartered Company, and is regulated by that Charter. The East India Company and the Chartered Bank of India, Australia and China are examples of this type. Such companies have no place in India since Independence. Even in England charters are rarely granted these days.

(b) *Statutory Companies.* These are created by Special Act of Parliament or State legislature. A statutory company is governed by the provisions of the special Act creating it. The Companies Act does not apply to it. Examples are Reserve Bank of India, State Bank of India, Life Insurance Corporation of India, etc.

(c) *Registered Companies.* The companies which are incorporated under the Companies Acts by registration with the Registrar of Companies, by far the largest number of companies are incorporated by registration, and all references to companies in this book are to registered companies.

2. *From the viewpoint of liability.* Companies which may be

registered under the Companies Act are : Companies with unlimited liability, companies with liability by guarantee and companies with liability limited by shares.

(a) *Unlimited Companies.* In an unlimited company, the members are liable, each in proportion to the extent of his interest in the company, to contribute the sum necessary to discharge in full the debts and liabilities of the company if it is wound up. The liability is similar to the one under individual proprietorship or partnership. Such companies are now almost non-existent.

(b) *Guarantee Companies.* A company limited by guarantee is a registered company having the liability of its members limited by its memorandum to such an amount as the members may respectively thereby undertake to contribute to the assets of the company in the event of its being wound up. The members of a guarantee company are, in effect, placed in the position of guarantors of the company's debts up to the agreed amount. Guarantee companies are also of rare occurrence these days.

(c) *Companies limited by shares.* A company limited by shares is a registered company having the liability of its members or shareholders limited by its memorandum to the amount, if any, unpaid on the shares respectively held by them. Thus, a member can be called upon to pay only the balance due on the shares held by him. For example, a shareholder, who has paid Rs. 75 on a Rs. 100 share, can be called upon to pay the balance of Rs. 25, and nothing more. Most of the companies formed are of this class.

3. *Functional Division of Companies.* From a functional point of view there are Private or Public Companies. A public or a private company may be a Government company.

(a) *Private Company.* A private company is a company, which by its articles—

(i) restricts the right to transfer its shares;
(ii) limits the number of members to 50, excluding employee members and ex-employee members;
(iii) prohibits any invitation to the public for subscription to its shares or debentures.

A private company must always comply with all the three restrictions. If it fails to comply with any of these restrictions it will be treated as a public company. Under Section 43A, a private company which employs public money, though indirectly, to an appreciable extent will be subject to the same restrictions as apply to a public company even if its articles continue to contain the restrictions required under the Act. Section 43A states that a private company will automatically become a public company as soon as not less than 25 per cent of its paid-up capital is held by one or more bodies corporate. But it will again become private company, if its paid up capital held by another body corporate falls below 25 per cent.

The minimum number of members to form a private company is

two. By definition, a company which is not private is public. The minimum for a public company is seven, but there is no limit to the maximum number.

A private company suits the needs of those who wish to take advantage of limited liability and at the same time keep the business as private as possible. It is in some respects like a partnership. The shares are not freely transferable nor can share warrants be issued. In this way the members of a private company like partners are in a position to maintain personal contact. *A private company, therefore, combines the advantage of limited liability and the facilities of the partnership organisation.*

Because of the special feature of a private company and many privileges and exemptions enjoyed by it, it is a common practice with businessmen to convert their family businesses into private limited companies, and enjoy the double advantage of retaining privacy as regards internal affairs and limiting their liabilities. Then, as and when the need arises, they convert the private company into a public company by simply altering the Articles of Association by special resolution.

Advantages that a private company enjoys over a public company. These advantages may be listed as follows :

1. A private company is simpler to form than a public company. Only two signatories are enough to form it, and it need have only two directors.

2. It can commence business immediately after incorporation; no certificate to commence business, which is compulsory for a public company, is required to be obtained.

3. Since it collects the requisite capital by private arrangement and does not invite the general public to buy its shares by the issue of a prospectus, it may allot shares without following the formalities laid down for a public company.

4. As no 'outsiders' are its shareholders, it is not required to hold a statutory meeting or file a statutory report.

5. Unlike a public company, it may pay remuneration to directors and managerial personnel or appoint any one to an office of profit without any restrictions.

6. It may grant loans to directors without obtaining consent or approval of the Central Government.

7. Its balance sheet and profit and loss account are not open to inspection by the public, although three copies of each are required to be filed with the Registrar.

8. The control and management is generally in the hands of the owners of capital which is not the case in a public company.

9. There is greater flexibility in regard to management and conduct of the business than in the case of a public company.

(b) *Public Company.* According to the Companies Act, a public company is one which is not a private company. Since this is a negative definition and does not tell us much, we may define it as follows :

A public company is a company the membership of which is open to the general public under the provisions of its Articles. The minimum number required to form it is seven, but there is no limit to the maximum number. It offers its shares to the public by advertising such offer in a prospectus. A public company does not impose any of the restrictions necessary in the case of a private company, and any person competent to contract can become its member, no matter whether he is an Indian or a foreigner. It must allot its shares within 120 days of the issue of the prospectus, but only if the "Minimum Subscription" has been subscribed or applied for. It must have at least three directors and can commence business only after it receives from the Registrar a Certificate to Commence Business.

Private Company becomes Public Company

Section 43A of the Companies Act provides that a private company becomes public company –

(a) where not less than 25 per cent of its paid up share capital is held by one or more public companies or deemed public companies; or

(b) where the average annual turnover during three preceding years of a private company, having share capital, is Rs. 5 crores or more, irrespective of its paid up capital; or

(c) where not less than 25 per cent of the paid up share capital of a public company, having share capital, is held by a private company; or

(d) where a private company accepts, after invitation by advertisement, or renews, deposits from the public, other than members, directors or their relatives.

However, after a private company has become a deemed public company, its articles may include provisions relating to matters specified in section 3(i)(iii) and the number of its members may be less than seven, and it may have only two directors.

(c) *Government Company.* A government company is a company, in which not less than 51 per cent of the paid up share capital is held by the Central Government, or by any State Government or Governments, or partly by the Central Government and partly by one or more State Governments. Up to 49 per cent of the paid up share capital may therefore be held by private individuals or financial institutions. A Government company may be either private or public company. Most of the government companies in India are private limited companies, and the entire share capital in almost all of them is held by the government.

The following chart gives the classification of companies :

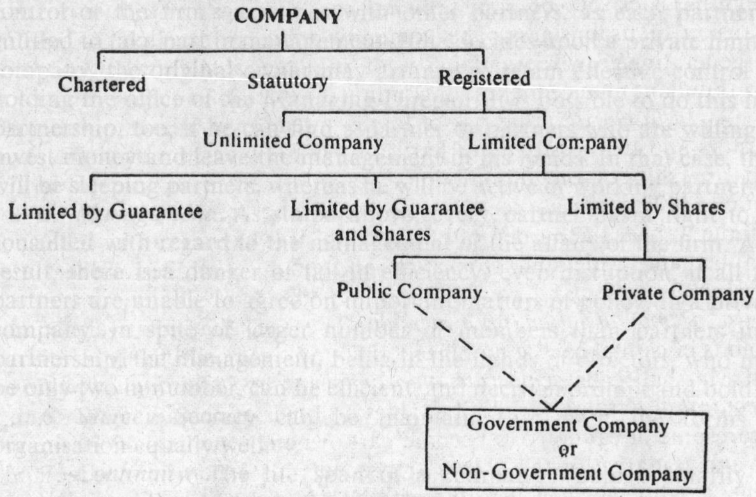

EVALUATION

The company is the most effective vehicle yet discovered to manage and control modern business enterprise. Other forms of organisation may outnumber it, but most business is transacted by companies. In fact, the company pervades the economic and social life all over the world, because of so many advantages it enjoys over other forms of organisation. Some of the inherent advantages of company form of organisation have been touched upon while dealing with its nature and characteristics. The other important merits are stated below.

Advantages. The principal advantages of the company form of organisation are as follows :

1. *Vast amount of capital.* The outstanding advantage of the company is that it allows the mobilization for production purposes of a vast amount of capital that would otherwise have little chance of being used. In a public company there is no limit to the maximum number of its members. Very large number of people who are otherwise busy may, by buying shares in a company, acquire interest in it without giving up their own vocations. As the shares can be bought in small amounts, investors can divide their savings amongst a number of companies, and thus reduce the overall risk. The fact that the shares are readily transferable gives joint stock companies an added advnatage in attracting capital. Thus method of collecting capital from many people, each of whom may have only a comparatively small amount, gives the company the use of much larger total than can easily be collected by private business which must depend on what the proprietors possess or can borrow. Actually, no business form is so well adapted to raising large amounts of capital as the joint stock company.

2. *Greater scope for expansion.* Vast aggregation of capital and ploughing back of company's own. large earnings contribute to the expansion of its business. The company offers an excellent scope for self-generating growth. Availability of managerial talent when coupled with abundant finance makes for continued expansion and growth.

3. *Diffused risk.* The risk of loss is spread over a large number of investors and the possibility of hardship on a few persons as in the case of partnership or on an individual as in the case of sole trader is minimised. There is no need now for men who are already wealthy to continue to bear the burden of business, as large capital can be collected from far and wide and from rich and poor, controlled under one management.

4. *Democratisation of ownership.* The fact that relatively small amounts of capital can be mobilized and employed collectively results in what Marshall calls *democratisation of ownership as distinguished from the control of business.* While it enables all types of people, big or small, venturesome or cautious, to become part owners, it permits of the use of skill and initiative of the able entrepreneur, his expert knowledge and business ability which would otherwise be lost to the community.

5. *Transferability of shares.* A shareholder can any time without let or hindrance transfer his shares to any person who is willing to take them. The stock exchanges assist in the sale and purchase of the shares. As shares are ordinarily freely transferable, a shareholder can easily convert his holdings into cash. The facility coupled with the limited liability has an encouraging investment by the general public.

6. *Stability.* The organisation is a legal entity with perpetual succession: it may outlive many generations of private producers. A private firm without tremendous amount of vigour is sure to die. A large company has many advantages many of which do not materially dwindle with age. In fact, its greater endurance, perhaps permanence arising out of incorporation which makes for stability on account of continuity of succession and unit of action, is a great advantage, as it encourages experimentation for efficiency. This continuity of a company is not seriously affected by a change either in the management or the owners. In fact, enterprises which are really individually owned are often incorporated as "one-man" companies the owner giving a few shares to friends and relatives so that business may be organised in such a manner as to ensure its continuance after his death.

7. *Organised intelligence.* The power of capital is supplemented by organised intelligence which makes for increased efficiency of direction and management. The skill and flexibility of administration is increased as a result of limited liability and the entity idea. The wisest and the most skilful directors may be chosen; and any one found indifferent or inefficient may be removed. The company being independent of any single man, the organised intelligence of the Board of Directors and other top managers is available for sound and bold policies.

8. *Dominant financial advantage.* The salaries which the company pays to its managing director and chief managers are much less in the aggregate than the excess of the profits of successful private business over the mere interest on its capital, which is required to induce rich people to continue to shoulder the burden of their business.

9. *Definite standing.* The company gives a definite standing and facilitates binding actions through its agents. An outsider is ever willing to deal with a company because he knows the exact scope of its business and legal limits of its powers.

10. *Limited liability.* The liability of the members of a company is limited. He cannot be called upon to pay anything more than the nominal value of the shares held by him. When buying shares in a company, he knows the maximum loss he may suffer if the company fails. This encourages people, even those with relatively small savings, to invest money in a company, thus providing ample capital for initial outlay and expansion.

11. *Social advantage.* The great advantage to society of the company organisation is to be found in its added encouragement of investment and the possibility it affords of efficient direction of large-scale industry. The element of stability is notably well cared for by the company. The compulsory publicity and other regulations of companies are beneficial to the community, especially with regard to banking and public utility companies.

12. *Tax relief.* A company pays income-tax as a separate legal person at a flat rate fixed by the Finance Act from year to year. In case of higher incomes, this rate is lower than that charged in the case of sole traders and partners.

DISADVANTAGES OF COMPANY ORGANISATION

In spite of so many advantages of the company form of organisation, there are several drawbacks. Of course, most of the advantages are connected with the people who form and manage companies. The principal disadvantages of company form of organisation are as follows :

1. *Difficulty and cost of formation.* The legal formalities and procedures required in the formation of a company are many and irksome. The cost involved is quite heavy. It has to approach large number of people for its capital, and it cannot commence business unless it has obtained a certificate of incorporation and a certificate to commence business. These will be granted only after legal formalities have been observed and requisite documents have been filed with the Registrar.

2. *Incapable or fraudulent management.* The company form of organisation can be used by unscrupulous promoters and fraudulent directors to fleece the ignorant public. The company law has, of course, gone a long way in curbing the flotation of fradulent companies. But the danger is there.

3. *Reckless speculation encouraged.* The company form of organisation encourages reckless speculation on the stock exchange. This is an evil of great magnitude in our country because in many cases the stock exchanges act as "hush agencies" rather than an aid to sound investment or stability.

4. *Waste and inefficiency associated with indirect management.* Lack of personal interest on the part of salaried managers leads to inefficiency and waste, there being little individual initiative and personal responsibility. Motivation is less direct than in sole proprietorship. The spur to zeal and fidelity is not so sharp as in the case of an owner manager. An individual producer can act quickly; the joint stock company moves ponderously and only after the agreement of diverse interests.

5. *Clash of interests between members and management.* The company form of organisation does not promote or safeguard the interests of the shareholders. Because of the separation of management from ownership, it is not the owners who govern but a few who control and manage a company's affairs. In other words, a few govern but let the shareholders believe that they themselves do it. Thus, in theory, the company is a democracy, but in practice, it is an oligarchy. The interests of the minority shareholders are often in jeopardy. This lack of identity of interests between the company and its management encourages manipulation, speculation, and in many cases ruin.

6. *Bureaucratic approach.* The bureaucratic habit of the company officials to shirk troublesome initiative because they get no direct benefit from it often retards growth. It has had social effect, too, for it leads to classification of the social organism and levelling down the character. The company organisation does not enjoy the same flexibility and promptness in decision making as the sole proprietorship or partnership firms do. Decisions are further delayed, at least to some extent, wher they have to be taken at meetings. which are often few and far between.

7. *Excessive regulation by law.* The state that creates a company regulates its activities much more closely than those of non-corporate associations. A company and its management have to function well within the law, and the provisions of the Companies Act are quite elaborate and complex. At every step, it is necessary to comply with its provisions lest the company and management might be penalised. The penalties are quite heavy, and in several cases, officers in default can be punished with imprisonment. This often detracts from the main objectives for which the company has been formed.

8. *Social ill-effects of a large company.* There are the notable failings of big business which necessarily flow from company organisation. They may be summed up as follows :

(a) The absence of responsibility of the shareholder for work done with his wealth frequently leads to abuse, e.g., sweating, unsatisfactory working conditions and exploitation of labour.

(b) In a big business, each department must be full and precise which involves a system of checks and counter-checks. Such a system is necessarily wasteful of effort and represses elasticity and initiative and encourages men to do work in mechanical manner.

(c) There is generally a tendency for company organisations to form themselves into combinations exercising monopolistic powers which may react detrimentally to other producers in the same line or to consumers of the commodity produced.

Conclusion. From the social point of view, the effects of company organisation upon the distribution of wealth are highly important. It has great potentialities both for good and evil. On the one hand, it might tend to diffuse wealth by encouraging widespread investment in small amounts and the distribution of the profits and interests of industry accordingly. On the other hand, it might result in vicious and undemocratic concentration of wealth in the hands of a few industrial dictators. Inequality in wealth distribution has been encouraged by joint-stock organisation. To permit companies to grow to large sizes and at the same time to ensure the return to the common people of the benefits so derived seems to be no easy task.

On balance, taking good and bad in the history of business units, no finer instrument exists with which to meet the complex problems of modern enterprise. The company is the most effective vehicle yet discovered to manage and control modern business enterprise. To the large unit it offers an easier way to finance itself by means of dividing its ownership into many small portions that can be sold to a wide range of purchasers, including those with only small savings to invest. In fact, the social wonder, the giant company, is no longer simply a device for doing business; it is a vast, sprawling immeasurable force. Its impact has been so great upon us that without the products and services of corporate bodies it is just inconceivable to think of the smooth functioning of the economic life of any country. Other forms may outnumber it, but most business is transacted by units of this type.

FORMATION OF A COMPANY

The whole process of company formation may be divided into three distinct stages, namely :—

1. Promotion. 2. Incorporation. 3. Floatation.

PROMOTION

The process of conceiving an idea and developing it into a concrete proposition or project to be accomplished by the incorporation and floatation of a company is called promotion. The person or persons who take the necessary steps to accomplish these objectives is known as a promoter.

The promoter discovers the opportunities to make money, investigates such propositions, assembles and finances them and thereby produces a going concern. A promoter may be an individual, firm, syndicate, association or even a company, as long as it takes all the necessary steps to create, and mould a company and set it going. Thus, the promoters have in their hands the power of defining how, and when, and in what manner, and under what supervision, it shall come into existence and begin to act as a trading company. This being the case, they stand in a fiduciary position to the company. As a result, the promoters are accountable to the company just like agents or trustees. They must not make secret profits and must disclose all receipts from the company in whatever form. The company, until in the hands of its own Board of Directors, is but the creature of the promoters, unable to consider its own interest or act on its own behalf, the promoters must, therefore, be extra-cautious and always act honestly and in good faith.

Stages in Promotion. There are four main stages in the promotion of a company. A brief description of each is given below.

Discovery of idea. A person conceiving an idea has a boundless enthusiasm for the creation of his own mind. He is partial to it. For example, an inventor is a man of mechanical skill, cleverness, and originality, but he cannot test the work of his invention by determining its economic value. It is for this reason that an inventor is called "an impractical genius." He has no "business head" nor the "gift for organising" that the trained promoter possesses. It is in his interest to turn over his idea to the impartial investigator, the trained promoter, who can weigh the elements of success and failure. Promoter's preliminary investigation will consist in making a rough estimate of whether or not it will pay or make a detailed investigation. He estimates probable revenues and expenditures, and then compares this estimate with actual figures of going concerns. He may then patent the invention for its commercialisation.

Detailed Investigation. The second stage in promotion is detailed investigation of the idea and the plan or proposition to discover hidden weaknesses of the plan, to determine the amount of funds needed, and to estimate the operating expenses and probable income. When this investigation is completed, the findings are put in a type-written report, giving the data collected, estimates on costs and incomes, and opinions of experts in particular fields, e.g., engineering. During the course of this investigation, an exhaustive research into important problems shall have to be made. These include the production problem, settled by the engineer or chemist; discovery of demand and the proper method to reach is settled by a market analysis expert; the question of proper patents, settled by an expert lawyer; the problem of the proper location of the plant, taking into consideration such factors as transport, nearness to raw materials and to markets, satisfactory labour supply and favourable climate, etc., settled in consultation with a management consultant; the question of whether the capitalisation is sufficient or the proposed company is over-capitalised or the reverse, is settled by a financial expert. In short, what is determined by this detailed investigation is whether the estimated income will be large enough to take care of the estimated operating costs, interest on capital invested, and compensation to owners for risks and services.

Assembling. After a thorough investigation of the proposition has been made, the promoter decides whether he wants to take the risk of promotion and decides upon a plan of capitalisation. After this, he starts to assemble the proposition. By "assembling" we mean protecting the fundamental idea, securing all the property needed by the enterprise, and making contracts with all the men that are selected to fill the chief managerial positions.

Financing the Proposition. An idea has been conceived, investigated and assembled; now the promoter has what is known as the "proposition". This proposition is presented to the public and underwriters in the form of a well-organised report known as "the Prospectus" in order to persuade them that the proposition is worthy of their financing. The prospectus contains a detailed discussion of the whole proposition and is supported by copies of the reports by the various experts consulted during investigation. This process is also called the Capitalisation of the opportunity. This step is composed of two parts, the first being the formation of the company to take over property, and the second being the actual taking over of the property.

INCORPORATION

The promoters select a few suitable names in order of preference indicating as far as possible the main object of the proposed company. Then they apply to the Registrar of Companies to ascertain as to which of the names selected by them is available for adoption by the company. The application form is supplied by the Registrar's office and a fee of Rs. 10 is payable with the application. After obtaining the approval of a name, the promoters get the Memorandum and Articles of Association drafted and printed and get the same stamped as per the Stamp Act. Thereafter they file the following documents with the Registrar of Companies of the state in which the registered office of the company is to be situated :

1. The Memorandum of Association to which at least seven persons (two persons in the case of a private company) have subscribed their names and each one of them has taken at least one share.
2. The Articles of Association, similarly signed.
3. A statement of nominal capital, and where it exceeds Rs. one crore, a Certificate from the Controller of Capital Issue permitting the issue of capital.
4. The agreement, if any, which the company proposes to enter into with any individual for appointment as its managing or whole-time director or manager.
5. A statutory declaration by an advocate, an attorney, or a secretary or a chartered accountant practising in India.

engaged in the formation of the company, or by a director or any other officer of the company that all requirements of the Act and Rules thereunder in respect of registration have been complied with.

6. A list of directors and their consent to act signed by each.
7. The address of the registered office.

The Registrar will scrutinise the documents, and, when satisfied that everything is in order, will enter the name of the company on the Register of Companies maintained in his office. He will issue a Certificate of Incorporation, which gives the company legal existence from the date given on it.

Memorandum of Association

The Memorandum of Association is the most important document of the company. It is its charter which contains the fundamental conditions upon which alone the company can be incorporated. It defines the limitations of the powers of the company; the area beyond which the actions of the company cannot go. Its purpose is to enable shareholders and creditors and those who deal with the company to know what is its permitted range of enterprise and powers. The memorandum of a company limited by shares must contain the following particulars or clauses :

1. The name of the company with the word "Limited" as the last word of its name in the case of a public company, and the words "Private Limited" as the last words of the name in case of a private company.

2. Every company must have a registered office. But it is enough to mention in the memorandum the name of the State in which the registered office is to be situated.

3. The statement of the objects in the memorandum is of supreme importance, as it indicates the sphere of its activities and the extent of its powers. The 'main' objects and other 'objects' must distinctly and separately be stated in the memorandum.

4. A declaration that the liability of the shareholders is limited to amounts unpaid on their respective shares must be made in the memorandum.

5. The capital clause must contain a statement as to the amount of capital with which it is proposed to register the company, and the division thereof into shares of a certain fixed amount.

6. The subscription clause precedes the names of the signatories to the memorandum and reads something like this : We, the several persons whose names, occupations and addresses are subscribed, are desirous of being formed into a company in pursuance of the Memorandum of Association and we respectively agree to take the number of shares in the capital of the company set opposite our respective names.

Alteration of Memorandum. Any clause in the memorandum may be altered by following the procedure laid down in the Companies Act.

1. The name of the company may be changed by a special resolution in general meeting and with the approval of the Central Government.

2. A company may, by special resolution and with the sanction of the Company Law Board change (i) the registered office from one State to another, (ii) the objects clause, if such change is rendered necessary—

(a) to carry on its business more economically and more efficiently;
(b) to attain its main purpose by new or improved means;
(c) to enlarge or change the local area of operations;
(d) to carry on some business which under existing circumstances may advantageously be combined with the business of the company;
(e) to restrict or abandon any of the objects specified in the Memorandum;
(f) to sell or dispose of the whole or any part of the undertaking, or any of the undertakings, of the company; or
(g) to amalgamate with any other company or body of persons.

3. If the articles authorise, a company limited by shares may, by an ordinary resolution in general meeting, alter its share capital so as to (i) increase it by issue of new shares, (ii) consolidate and divide its capital into shares of large amount, (iii) sub-divide its shares into shares of smaller amount, (iv) convert its fully paid-up shares into stock or reconvert the stock into fully paid-up shares, or (v) cancel shares which have not been taken or promised to be taken at the time of the resolution.

4. If the articles authorise, a company by special resolution confirmed by the court may reduce its share capital in any way and in particular by (i) reducing or extinguishing the liability of members for uncalled capital, (ii) writing off lost capital, (iii) paying off capital which is in excess of the company's requirements.

Articles of Association

The Articles of Association are the regulations or bye-laws which govern the internal management and conduct of the affairs of the company. They embody the powers of the directors and officers and of the shareholders as to voting, etc., the mode and form in which the business of the company is to be carried on and the mode and form in which changes in the internal regulation of the company may be made. The articles are subordinate to the memorandum. The memorandum lays down what is to be done, and the articles state how it is to be done.

The articles being the regulations for the internal management of the company can be altered any time by a Special Resolution, provided that the alteration is made bona fide and in the best interest of the company. If an alteration is unfair or inequitable between the members, the court will, on application, interfere and disallow it. For example, an alteration will be disallowed if it constitutes an oppression or fraud on the minority, or increases the liability of members, or is made for committing a breach of contracts.

Effect of Memorandum and Articles. The Memorandum and Articles, when registered, bind the company and its members as if they had been signed by each member and contained covenants by members to observe all the provisions of the same. The members are thus bound to the company and the company to the members as members and not in any other capacity; and also members inter se. The memorandum and articles are public documents and a person contracting with the company is presumed to have knowledge of the contents. But he has a right to assume that the provisions of the articles have been observed by the company's officers. This is known as the "doctrine of indoor management."

FLOATATION

When a company has been incorporated, it is ready for floatation. It has to raise capital sufficient to commence business and carry it on satisfactorily. A private company must obtain the requisite amount of capital from friends and relatives by private arrangement. A public company may also, if its needs are not vast, raise it by private arrangement. In practice, the promoters invariably raise the greater part of the capital from the general public and issue an invitation in the form of a prospectus to the public to subscribe or purchase shares in the company.

Prospectus

Section 2(36) defines a prospectus as "any document described or issued as a prospectus and includes a notice, circular, advertisement or other document inviting offers from the public for the subscription or purchase of any shares in, or debentures of, a body corporate". In short

Section 2(36) defines a prospectus as "any document described or issued as a prospectus and includes a notice, circular, advertisement or other document inviting deposits from the public or inviting offers from the public for the subscription or purchase of any shares in, or debentures of, a body corporate". In short, a prospectus is an invitation to the members of the public—anyone who brings his money and applies in due form—to buy shares or debentures of the company. *The object of a prospectus is four-fold:*

1. to bring to the notice of the public that a new company has been formed;
2. to convince those who have savings to invest that the proposed company having secured the services of honest and able directors, as also of other factors which make for success, offers the best opportunity for gainful investment;
3. to preserve an authentic record of the terms and allotments on which the public have been invited to buy its shares or debentures; and

4. to secure that the directors of the company accept responsibility for the statements in the prospectus.

The intending shareholders are entitled to all true disclosures in the prospectus. It may be presented in the rosiest possible invitation, but everything must be stated with strict and scrupulous accuracy. It must not conceal any material fact. For this purpose, the Act requires certain information relating to the directors and their interests in the company, expenses of formation of the company, business and property of the company and matters of interest to investors such as minimum subscription, amounts payable on application and allotment, etc., to be given in the prospectus.

Misleading Prospectus. As stated above, the prospectus must tell the truth, the whole truth and nothing but the truth, nor must it conceal or keep back what must be told. It must not mislead. But if a prospectus is misleading or fraudulent, because it contains false statements or there are misleading omissions of material facts, any person who applies for shares on the faith of such a false prospectus is entitled to the following remedies :

(a) he may rescind the contract, give up the shares and get back his money with interest, getting his name removed from the register of members;
(b) he may claim damages from the company;
(c) he may claim compensation from the persons who authorised the issue of the misleading prospectus.

The directors and other persons who had authorised the issue of the false prospectus are, in addition, criminally liable for untrue statements.

Safeguards for Investors. The law is jealous for the public. In order to ensure that a company starts business with adequate capital and also to check it from fixing at random an arbitrary amount such as ten shares as its minimum capital requirement, the Act lays down a minimum basis, called the "Minimum Subscription." This amount must be stated in the prospectus for the information of the prospective buyers of shares. The minimum subscription must be fixed at an amount to be raised by issue on cash basis and sufficient to provide for—

(a) the purchase price of any property bought or to be bought out of the proceeds of the issue of shares;
(b) preliminary expenses and commission payable by the company;
(c) the repayment of sums borrowed to provide for the foregoing;
(d) the working capital.

The amount payable on application must not be less than 5 per cent of the nominal amount of the share, nor must the commission, including underwriting commission, be more than 5 per cent of the issue price. The application money must be deposited in a scheduled bank and no part of it must be utilized before the receipt from the Registrar of Certificate to Commence Business.

Subscriber Beware !

In spite of the safeguards provided by the Act, there is always a danger of an ignorant but over-zealous investor being trapped by reckless directors and promoters through subtle and apparently reasoned statements in the prospectus. Very often the investor is ignorant but does not know it, and falls an easy prey to the optimisic and boastful prospectus, whereby the promoters can obtain funds for inefficient investment. It is therefore necessary for an intending buyer of shares or a lender of money on debentures to carefully study the prospectus before he parts with his money. If he is not in a position to understand the intricacies of the various matters put in the prospectus, he should consult his broker or banker before he allows himself to be lured by promise of quick and easy profits.

The investor should first of all examine the nature of the business and its prospects in the light of factors that make for success, such as the general business outlook, availability of the various factors of production, transport and marketing facilities and the attitude of the State. In the second place, he should find out all about the people who are at the helm of the enterprise. The success of any enterprise depends upon the quality of this small group of directors and the extent of their interests. Thirdly, the capital plan of the company should be studied in order to find out whether the capital proposed to be raised is likely to be adequate for the success of the venture. It should be seen whether the shares have been underwritten and what commissions are being paid. The company's bankers, legal advisers, auditors, brokers and other consultants are a good index of its position. These persons and institutions enjoying good reputation would not ordinarily associate themselves with dubious business.

Application for Shares

An intending investor will be supplied with an abridged prospectus along with an application form for shares but a copy of the full prospectus must be supplied on request before the closing of the subscription list. He will apply for a certain number of shares by inserting the number in the blank space for the purpose and by putting his signature. The Board of Directors will then allot the shares to him and enter his name on the register of members. The Act provides that any person applying for shares in a fictitious name, or otherwise inducing the company to allot any shares to him or any other person is liable to be imprisoned for a period not exceeding 5 years. This provision must be inserted in the prospectus at a prominent place.

Allotment of Shares. The allotment of shares by the Board is in effect an acceptance by the company of the offer to take shares. Like any other acceptance, it must be communicated. Communication is complete as soon as the notice of allotment is posted. An allotment can be made only after the following conditions have been fulfilled :

1. A prospectus or statement in lieu of prospectus has been filed with the Registrar before making the *first* allotment.

2. The minimum subscription, as provided in the prospectus, has been subscribed or applied for, before the *first* allotment.

3. The company has received in cash the application money amounting to at least 5 per cent of the nominal value of the share, and the moneys so received have been deposited in a scheduled bank before making any allotment.

Irregular allotment. If a company without complying with any of the above conditions makes an allotment, the applicant may avoid the allotment within 2 months after the Statutory Meeting, and if the allotment is made after this meeting, then within 2 months of such allotment he can claim the refund of his money even if the company is being wound up. The directors are liable to compensate the company or the allottee for any loss suffered by either through such allotment.

Subscription list. Section 72 of the Act requires that the subscription must be kept open for 5 days after the issue of the prospectus. An applicant cannot withdraw his application until after the expiry of the 5th day after the opening of the subscription list. These provisions are expected to prove of advantage to the investing public as well as to the undertaking.

Inability to allot. If a company for want of the minimum subscription, or for the non-fulfilment of any of the other conditions, is unable to allot any shares within 120 days after the first issue of the prospectus, it must refund without interest all moneys received from the applicants within the next ten days. Thereafter, the directors shall be jointly and severally liable to repay all moneys with interest at 6 per cent per annum.

With effect from June 15, 1988, listing of shares in a public company which issues a prospectus has been made compulsory. Every such company must make an application to one or more recognised stock exchanges before issuing the prospectus. If no application is made or the application has been rejected by the Stock Exchange no allotment of shares can be made. If it is made, it shall be void. All moneys received must be refunded forthwith and if it is not refunded then the directors shall be personally liable to pay with interest ranging between 4% and 15% according to period of delay in refunding.

CERTIFICATE TO COMMENCE BUSINESS

The company is now in a position to apply to the Registrar for a grant of the Certificate to Commence Business, which will be issued if all the formalities and legal requirements have been complied with. The Registrar will grant this certificate only if—

(i) the Minimum Subscription has been allotted;

(ii) the directors have taken up and paid for their qualification shares, as provided in the articles;

(iii) the prospectus or the statement in lieu of prospectus has been filed as also a statutory declaration that the aforesaid conditions have been complied with.

A company cannot commence business under "other objects" without obtaining the prior approval of the shareholders by a special resolution passed at a general meeting.

CHAPTER V

THE CO-OPERATIVE ORGANISATION

Philosophy of Co-operation. The philosophy of co-operative organisation is to serve the common man and to liberate him from the oppression of the economically strong people and organisations. Mutual assistance and service is the objective as distinguished from the aim of the other forms of organisation which is primarily making of profit. It aims at encouraging self-help on the part of economically weaker sections of the society by looking after their own affairs in co-operation with one another. The principal theory of true co-operative organisation is the elimination of profit and provision of goods and services to members at cost. As a form of organisation it is an enterprise ordinarily set up by "economically weak" individuals to further their common economic and social interests to eradicate capitalist exploitation, to eliminate middle men, and to bring the consumer and producer together.

With these objectives in view, the consumers, belonging to working and lower middle class strata of society, combine either to produce goods themselves or to purchase them collectively thus retaining for themselves some of the benefits usually derived from business by capitalists. This joint effort on the part of economically weak enables them to protect themselves against the economically strong. In form, co-operative organisation is democratic, because the consumers are at once the owners and managers.

Definition. A co-operative organisation is a voluntary association with unrestricted membership, and collectively owned funds, organised on democratic principle of equality by persons of moderate means and incomes, who join together to supply their needs and wants through mutual action, in which the motive of production and distribution is service rather than profit.

Principles and Characteristics. As a form of business organisation, the co-operative association possesses the following special characteristics :

1. *A co-operative society is a voluntary association.* The membership of the society is voluntary and open to all persons having a common interest. In other words, there is no compulsion for any one to become a member, nor can any person be denied the right to become a member of the society. A member is at liberty, by giving due notice, to leave the society and withdraw his capital. He may not, however, transfer his shares to another person.

2. *Its members enjoy equal voting rights.* A co-operative society is a democratic organisation and so all its members have equal voice in the management of its affairs. The rule is one member, one vote. Therefore each member has one vote irrespective of the number of shares held by

him. This rule is based upon the principles of co-operation and equality which states that a rich man cannot be allowed to exercise control because he is rich and can easily afford to buy large number of shares.

3. *Its management is democratic.* As a necessary result of the principle of equality, the management of a co-operative society is essentially democratic. In general, co-operative societies work on local bases, which enable almost all the members to attend the meetings and elect their managing committees. Since each member exercises an equal right with others, the managing committee is in the real sense an elected body and must pay attention to the wishes of all members and not only to a section of them.

4. *A co-operative society is organised to render service to its members and not to make profit.* If, for instance, society produces a product, it is mainly to supply to its members at a reasonable price. A consumer society is expected to supply goods first to its members and then to outsiders at a profit.

5. *Payment of surplus as bonus to members onpurchases made by them.* The surplus at the end of the year is not distributed as dividend among shareholders in proportion to the share capital provided by them, as is done in the case of a company. The share capital is virtually treated as loan capital on which a very moderate rate of interest is allowed out of the net surplus. A portion of the balance is utilised for the general benefit of the members. A portion may be paid as bonus to employees and workers. The rest of the net surplus is distributed among the members in proportion to their individual purchases from the society. The non-members are not usually paid anything out of the surplus, although there is no bar.

6. *Trading on cash basis.* As a rule, co-operative societies conduct business on cash basis, and allow no credit. A member in need of money can get back part of his capital, and reinvest when he can afford to do so. Since the members are persons of small means, this principle helps both the member-buyers and the society. The members do not incur debts and the society does not face the danger of bad debts.

7. *State control and corporate status.* A co-operative society is required to be registered under the Co-operative Societies Act, 1912. On registration, it becomes a corporate body like an incorporated company enjoying certain privileges, and subject to control and supervision of the Government.

How Cooperatives And Companies Differ

Although in some respects companies and cooperatives are similar, there are many points of distinction between the two types of organisations. They differ in the following ways :

1. In the case of cooperatives, the control is vested in the members equally, as each member has only one vote regardless of his investment in the enterprise. In a company, the amount of investment determines the number of votes.

2. A cooperative is thus an economic democracy, since its members having equal right to vote can effectively exercise their power. In a company, since the votes vary with the capital holding, only a few rich people can control it.

3. A cooperative society operates within a limited area and so all the members can attend its meetings and exercise their control. This is not possible in a company as shareholders are scattered all over the country; only the inner group is able to control the affairs of company.

4. In a company, the shareholder earns the profit and receives a dividend, and often at the cost of the consumer. But in a cooperative store the consumer is the one who is looked after. The major part of the surplus of the cooperative store is divided among the members in proportion to the amount of their purchases from the store. The share capital is virtually treated as loan capital on which a very moderate rate of interest is allowed out of the net surplus. A company looks after the shareholder, whereas a cooperative society functions for the benefit of the member-consumer.

5. A shareholder in a company can transfer his shares to another person, but he cannot take back his capital from the company by surrendering his shares. A member of a cooperative cannot transfer his shares to another person, but he can, by giving reasonable notice, withdraw his capital and cease to be a member at will.

6. In a cooperative society, there is no limit to the number of members which usually exist in the case of a company by means of a limit to shares. In fact, in a cooperative, efforts are made to limit the number of shares a person may hold in order that the number of members should be large.

Furthermore, if in a company, capital is increased, the further shares must be offered to existing shareholders; while in a cooperative, the capital is increased mainly for admitting new members.

7. In a joint-stock enterprise there is a great divorce between ownership and control and often a clash of interests, but the cooperative enterprise makes for oneness of interest.

8. The joint stock companies are not directly interested in the promotion of welfare or efficiency of their shareholders; but in the case of cooperatives, it is a part of their creed to take such interest in their members.

9. In a joint stock enterprise, the dominant, if not the only motive is profit or gain, while the cooperative functions to meet the needs of the consumers who are happily the owners and share in the surplus.

10. Cooperatives receive certain special concessions from the law and the Government, in order to encourage healthy development of cooperatives. Some of the privileges extended to them are exemption from stamp duty and registration fees as well as exemption from income-tax up to a certain limit. Companies, which function for profit, do not get such exemptions.

CLASSES OF CO-OPERATIVE SOCIETIES

Cooperatives as a form of business organisation may be classified as follows :—

1. Producers' Cooperatives.
2. Marketing or Sales Societies.
3. Consumers' Cooperative Societies.
4. Housing Cooperative Societies.
5. Cooperative Farming Societies.
6. Cooperative Credit Societies.
7. Others.

Producers' Cooperatives. Producers' Cooperative Societies are formed by small producers with the object of eliminating the capitalist from the control of production. Here, the workers and consumers participate in the manufacture of goods and share the management and profits of the enterprise. These co-operatives are organisations for collective production of goods for own consumption and for sale at a profit, in order to retain the gain which would otherwise go to the capitalist. Such cooperatives may be set up either as member consumer cooperatives or member-employee cooperatives. In the case of the first type, each member contributes a certain minimum share of the capital, agrees to sell his produce to the society and profits are divided in proportion to the business done. Membership is open to all artisans of the locality and one man has one vote. In the case of the second type the member producers are treated as employees and are paid wages for their labour. The society in both cases supplies raw materials, tools and equipment to the producers and takes up the output for sale or distribution among mambers or outsiders. Where workers are employed, part of the profits is divided among them, and the part is set aside for education and other social amenities.

Marketing or Sales Societies. In the sphere of agriculture, there is great scope for such societies. They can also be usefully employed to market goods produced by small producers and artisans. The marketing or sales cooperatives are voluntary associations of small independent producers organised for two-fold purpose, namely, to secure a remunerative price and to make available a permanent and ready market for the produce of members. The marketing society collects the produce of its members, grades them and then sells at remunerative price to the wholesale market. The proceeds are then distributed among the members according to the quantity pooled.

Consumers' Cooperative Societies. These societies are set up by consumers, usually with low incomes, for the distribution of fundamental consumption goods, primarily among the member-consumers, and sometimes to outsiders. Normally these stores buy goods from the wholesale market and sell them at retail market prices. At the end of the working period, normally a year, a percentage of the surplus is set aside as a reserve, and the balance is distributed among the members in proportion to the amount of their purchase from the store during the working period. This is the oldest form of cooperative organisation and the most successful.

Housing Cooperatives. Housing cooperative societies are associations of the persons who are interested in owning a house. Such societies are normally formed in urban areas. Intending builders of houses get together and form such a society. The membership is open to such persons, each member buying at least one share. The cooperative society can secure for the members the economies of collective purchase of buildings, building materials, and loans at low rates of interest.

Cooperative Farming Societies. These societies are formed by agriculturists to derive the benefits of large-scale farming for maximising output and gain. Such societies are very useful in countries like India, where the holdings are rather small as a result of fragmentation. Membership is usually confined to small holders.

Cooperative Credit Societies. Such societies were the very first cooperatives. The aim of these societies was to enable farmers to escape from the clutches of the money-lenders. Thus, a cooperative credit society may be said to be an association of persons with moderate means formed with the object of granting short-term loans to them and encouraging the habit of thrift among its members. The funds of the society consist of the share capital contributed by the members. The liability of members is normally unlimited. This enables the society to raise funds from outside agencies and also encourages members to take keen interest in the working of the society.

Miscellaneous Societies. In addition to the main types of cooperatives discussed above there are some others, such as Processing Cooperatives, Labour and Construction Cooperatives, Sugar Cooperatives and so on.

EVALUATION

As a form of business organisation, the cooperative society yields the following advantages :

1. The consumer controls his own supplies, and cuts out the middleman's profits.

2. He is saved the loss common to retail trade, on speculative buying. The ordinary shop has to rely on itself to judge whether there is a market for an article. The cooperative store knows what is required by the members.

3. There is no need to have surplus stock at hand, as the demand is constant and regular.

4. Some of the expenses of management are saved by the voluntary service of the controlling committees. It is possible to get even a paid manager at a lower salary, as a result of the ideal of cooperation.

5. There is a complete integration between the manufacturer, the wholesaler and the retailer, and thus, they have clear advantage over capitalistic enterprise.

6. A cooperative store has its customers and therefore does not have to incur expenses on publicity, which is a big item in the budget of a capitalist manufacturer.

7. There is no profit for special class of investors which factor tends to equalise the distribution of wealth.

8. The payment of part of the profits as bonus on purchases is an ingeneous method and ties the consumers to the organisation. The capitalists have tried to copy this system by issuing gift coupons or giving away small items with certain amount of purchases.

9. Above all, the cooperative societies are more than a mere device for getting necessaries cheaper. They have a social value of increasing weight. They provide a school of self-government for a class that has difficulty in getting it elsewhere. The movement has done a great service to the weaker section of society by giving it an opportunity to walk out of the capitalist arena.

10. Since the development of cooperation is an important instrument of Government's economic policy, the State extends several kinds of assistance, such as financial aid, exemption from stamp duty, registration fees and income-tax upto a certain limit.

Drawbacks and Limitations. In spite of so many advantages the cooperative form of business enterprise has some drawbacks and limitations. These are as follows :—

1. Because of the limitation of capital, cooperatives can run business on small scale. The members come from a limited area and have limited means. Hence, their activites cannot be expanded beyond a certain limit.

2. The factor that its market is more or less guaranteed becomes a source of inefficiency in management and slackness in organisation.

3. Again, the management of a cooperative society vests in the managing committee which is frequently manned by persons who lack technical or professional knowledge. It is often difficult to get the services of experienced and efficient officers, because of the inability of the society to pay adequate remuneration.

4. The movement has still to develop the entrepreneurial functions.

5. The cooperatives suffer from lack of secrecy, as their affairs are exposed to all the members.

6. Cooperatives also suffer from the internal intrigues and bickering among their members. It has been often seen that once the first wave of enthusiasm about the ideals of cooperation is dampened faction develops among the members. This militates against the efficient working of the societies.

7. Since the rate of return to the members is limited by law, there is very little motivation on the part of the managing committee to make a success of the enterprise.

It follows from the foregoing evaluation that cooperatives are suitable mainly for small and medium size enterprises. At any rate they cannot succeed in the following three types of industrial enterprise, namely :—

1. Those in which there is a large element of speculation;

2. Those involving the production of finer and individualised commodities in which high qualities of skill and adaption are called for; and

3. Those industries which require high centralised production but whose customers are scattered over wide areas, and where demand is not regular.

CO-OPERATION IN INDIA

In spite of tremendous efforts both on the part of the people and the Government ever since 1904 when the first Act was passed, the progress has been rather disappointing in general, although some of the cooperative societies have shown good results.

Of the total volume of production, distribution and consumption in the wealth of the country, the share of the co-operatives even after a considerable growth during the Plan periods, is negligible. A substantial momentum was gained by the movement after 1954 when the Rural Credit Survey Committee set up by the Reserve Bank of India submitted its Report and made its recommendations for far-reaching reforms. Since then the number of all types of societies has been rising steadily. For example, at the beginning of the First Five-Year Plan the total of all kinds of societies was 1,81,000. It rose to 2,40,000 at the beginning of Second Plan and to 3,32,000 at the commencement of the Third Plan. The Third Plan placed a greater emphasis so that the number has gone up to about 4,00,000 by now.

Causes for the Slow Growth of Co-operatives in India. In absolute terms the co-operative organisation has made considerable progress, particularly since 1954. But in relation to population and in spite of the encouragement given by the Government the progress cannot be said to be satisfactory. Some of the causes of this slow progress are as follows :

1. *Lack of spontaneity.* The co-operative movement in India was Government sponsored and did not spring from the people themselves. In reality, the movement in the past was a department of the Government and therefore the people did not take much interest in it. In the words of M.B. Nanavati, the movement was "breast-fed, bottle-fed and spoon-fed" with the inevitable result that it took an official form out of which it was not able to grow.

2. *Illiteracy and ignorance of people.* The illiteracy, ignorance and conservatism of the rural populace stood in the way of the development of co-operatives. The movement was meant to help them to help themselves, but they did not understand the significance of co-operation and what it meant to them. The result has been that they have failed to run the societies successfully.

3. *Unlimited liability.* The liability in the case of a credit society the majority of members of which are agriculturists is unlimited. As a result of this unlimited liability better class of farmers did not join the credit society. Hence, there was lacking a complete and willing co-operation on the part of the people.

4. *Poor management and leadership.* An inherent defect of co-operatives which stems from the very philosophy of the movement is that great stress is laid on the principle of co-operation and hardly any attention is paid to the management aspect. No doubt its social purpose is extremely important, yet the business and management functions have to be kept in view if a co-operative society has to succeed. Very little attention has been paid to the management side of the movement. Furthermore, there has been an absence of leadership so that the movement has suffered as a result of nepotism, favouritism and partiality.

5. *Casteism and party-politics.* In recent years, with political awakening in the country, politics have entered the co-operative movement too. Different groups vie with each other to get their nominees elected to the management committee with a view to securing control of the organisation for sectional gains instead of looking after the interests of all the members. In the result, the needy fail to get any assistance, which works against the spirit of co-operation.

6. *Provision of credit only.* There has been complete failure to recognise that there is an organic connection between credit, marketing and processing. Consequently, co-operative societies confined their activities to the granting of loans to the farmers, but failed to help them in other ways, e.g., marketing of their produce. Fortunately, after 1954, efforts have been made to link credit with marketing and encourage the formation of multi-purpose co-operative societies.

7. *Competition from vested interests.* One of the powerful opponents of the co-operative movement has been the vested interests. The small traders and money-lenders worked for the failure of the rural societies. In urban areas, consumer societies have had to face strong opposition and hostility of traders and speculators. The weak financial position of the societies and indifference of the people who should take advantage of the movement have combined to make the position still worse.

Achievements of co-operation. In spite of its weaknesses and slow progress, co-operation has been in a position to shower some benefits on the people.

1. The farmers have been able to secure credit at a cheap rate, and they have to a very large extent got out of the clutches of the money-lenders.

2. In general, the farmers have benefited from the principles of thrift and self-help. They have given up, or at least reduced considerably wasteful expenditures and resorted to saving.

3. The Co-operatives have encouraged the use of better farming methods, by helping the procurement of better manures and improved

seeds. Similarly, the marketing societies have enabled the farmers to buy their requirements at fair prices and sell their produce at reasonably good prices.

4. The co-operative movement has contributed to the improvement of rural life. Undesirable social customs have been given up, and the general social and moral climate in rural areas has improved.

5. The non-credit societies have helped their members to improve their economic condition and saved them from the exploitation of powerful groups. For example, in many urban areas, housing co-operatives have enabled middle-income groups to buy plots of land at reasonable rate and construct their houses. Similarly, consumers' co-operative societies have rendered a great service to the community by supplying goods of short supply equitably and in selling goods at reasonable prices.

Thus, whatever the position of the movement might have been in the past, the future is not so gloomy. On the contrary, the movement has a bright future. The quicksand of officialdom has been replaced by the bed-rock of the spirit of co-operation, enthusiasm for self-help and comradeship for building the future co-operatives.

Cooperative Marketing Societies have made substantial progress in marketing agricultural produce. For example, the value of the agricultural produce marketed by them increased from Rs. 921 crores during 1972–73 to Rs. 1,100 crores in 1973–74 and is estimated to have reached the level of Rs. 1,200 crores in 1974–75. The number of primary marketing societies stood at 3,262 with a membership of 30 lakhs as on June, 1973.

The number of cooperative sugar factories (as component of cooperative Processing Societies) stood, at end of December, 1974, at 178 with installed licensed capacity of 36.9 lakh tonnes constituting 53.5 per cent of the total licensed capacity. There were in all 1856 agricultural processing units in March, 1974, including, apart from sugar factories, rice mills, oil mills, cotton ginning, cotton growers, spinning mills and jute baling units.

The National Cooperative Development Corporation has been rendering substantial assistance to cooperative societies. For instance, during 1974–75, the Corporation provided total assistance of Rs. 1100 crores under various schemes.

Consumer Co-operatives. At the end of June, 1974, there were 14 State Federations, 400 Central/Wholesale Consumer Cooperative Stores and about 13,150 primary consumer cooperatives with the National Cooperative Consumers' Federation at the apex. Total sales were estimated to be around Rs. 325 crores in 1973–74 as against a target of Rs. 400 crores. The scheme of guarantee from the Government of India for securing adequate working capital on reduced margins to these stores, through banking channels was extended further from April 1, 1974 to March 31, 1979.

CHAPTER VI

ENTREPRENEURIAL DECISIONS

A community satisfies its wants by using its productive resources, namely, land, labour and capital. This the community does through the fourth factor of production—the *uncertainty-bearing.* The person who supplies this fourth factor, and then co-ordinates all the factors of production is called an *entrepreneur.* His reward is profit. Since the uncertainty is bound up with policy-making, the entrepreneur is frequently defined as the person responsible for policy, who organises and co-ordinates the work of the other three factors and takes the decisions which are necessary to set up a firm and keep it in line with the changing patterns of demand.

He is the king-pin of the business world, either as a manufacturer of some product, or as the distributor of the products made by others. Whatever activity he chooses, he will be confronted with numerous problems, and his ultimate success will depend upon his ability and foresight to handle them. To begin with his problems will relate to the very launching of his enterprise. Secondly, he will have to tackle the recurring problems in the course of running it. Thirdly, he will have to take decision with regard to alternative forms of organisation, especially when he is faced with the problem of expansion of his business. We will deal with the various considerations first with respect to the launching of the enterprise and then relating to its expansion.

LAUNCHING A NEW ENTERPRISE

The entrepreneurial decisions in connection with the setting up of a new business will have to be as follows :

1. *Objectives.* The very first decision will relate to the determination of the objectives. For, in setting objectives, he is concerned with the future, and clearly defined objectives provide the guiding, unifying care of company planning.

2. *The Idea.* The other step in the inauguration of an enterprise is the development of the idea that there is a specific business opportunity. The idea may arise from the knowledge of an unused supply of raw materials, from the observation of the inferiority of some article or service now holding the field, or from the knowledge that certain firms are making large profits, or from the knowledge that suitable opportunity has at last arrived for utilizing the knowledge one has gained of a particular branch of business.

3. *The Product.* He will then decide what to produce. He will obviously enter that branch of industry or commerce which offers the best chance of profit. His decision will also depend upon his own ability and preferences as well as the preferences of consumers. In addition to

the chance of making profit, he will also be guided by his own background and temperament, his technical knowledge (if any), his personal interests, his estimate of the differing degrees of risk in different industries, the amount of capital required, and his estimate of his own ability. Before choosing the product, he will have to ascertain the potential market. For this purpose marketing research will be necessary.

4. *The Marketing Research.* Since the first business of every business is to get customers and keep customers, he will have to ask these questions : Will the customers buy the product offered ? Will they buy at the price asked ? Will they buy at the places it will be available ? Will they buy in the package it comes in ? Will they buy it again and again ? The answer to these questions will vary from product to product. The potential success of a product depends upon its ability to satisfy the values that customers attach to any product. Product analysis should precede the actual market research or the study of the whole market and customer behaviour. In studying the market, you have to find out whether there is a market for your product, and if so, where is it, and what is its character, and what is its approximate size ? Such research helps to reduce risks in making wrong decisions regarding production and sales.

5. *The Form of Organisation.* Next he must decide what legal form of organisation to adopt for his business. Is it to be one-man firm or a partnership, or should he form a company, and if so should it be a private or a public company ? In some instances in which new business enterprises are launched, no real choice of legal form of ownership is available to the founder of the firm. Such would be the case if the organisation being considered were to be a bank or insurance business, which must, by law, be an incorporated company. In other instances, the enterprise contemplated may be so mammoth in scale, and involve so many people, that a company would be the only feasible form of organisation from an operational point of view. In the great majority of instances the entrepreneurs have to study a number of major factors before deciding upon the form of organisation. The decision regarding choice of the form of organisation needs detailed consideration, and is postponed to the end of the chapter, after all the other factors have been discussed.

Scale of operation and size of the Unit or Plant. The proper scale for initial operations will, in some measure, depend upon the degree of certainty of ultimate success. Where experienced persons, backed with ample capital, enter upon the production of a staple article, the first objective may be the attainment of economies of large-scale production. But where the establishment of a new enterprise involves the trying out of a number of experiments as to processes or selling plan, the initial scale of operations should be as small as will yield the desired experimental knowledge. Where there is a strong element of uncertainty, investment of permanent nature, such as that for buildings, machinery and manufactured stock should be kept at the minimum. The small beginning has many advantages. The proprietors are closely in touch with details. Results are quickly known. If there is success, the particular line of effort can be followed up promptly. If there is failure, a quick change will keep losses within small figures. In a few months or years the proprietors will have learnt so many new things in relation to managing the business. They can then expand their operations with confidence and run them skilfully. Long-term and short-term forecasts of sales will help any entrepreneur to decide upon the size of the establishment.

Plant Location. The next problem relates to the location of the plant or factory. This divides itself into determining the area and the specific site in the area. The choice should be based upon careful consideration of all factors relating to the business of the particular enterprise. Very often the very success of the operation of a plant depends upon the right choice of the location for it. The following factors usually influence the selection of a location of a manufacturing plant; market for the product, transport facilities, availability of raw materials and dependable labour, cost of location and political aspects of location. The entrepreneur will, however, remember that all of these are not of equal importance. He will have to sort out the factors and weigh the advantages of different factors against one another before arriving at the location and choose that site which gives him the maximum economy in operation.

Plant Buildings and Equipment. The next step is to make a preliminary study of the manufacturing processes to be followed and the equipment to be used. The exact determination of the nature and sequence of manufacturing processes will help decision regarding the character of the buildings, machinery, yard spaces, and general layout of an establishment. There are two difficulties with reference to equipment to be purchased by new entrants who are more or less inexperienced. The first difficulty is that certain suppliers may take advantage of their ignorance. The second difficulty is that the new equipment must be tried out by workers not quite seasoned to their duties, with the result that the speeds will be low and wear and tear heavy, spoiled work and numerous accidents. The first difficulty can be got over by employing an expert agency to buy or advise purchase of equipment. The advice of men of experience is against the purchase of second-hand plant or machinery.

Plant Layout. The next problem deals with the layout of machinery and equipment for good performance of work. Layout is important because efficient layout of plants can minimise production costs and faulty arrangement of machinery and equipment may slow down the work and raise the cost of production and cause dislocation of work. Before a layout plan is finalised, information about the product to be manufactured, the quantity to be made in a period of time, the machines needed, the building, the routing of work, the spacing of machines, the aisle space, the material storage place, and the method of handling materials should be obtained. Layout will depend upon the nature of the work to be done and the sequence to be followed.

Financial Planning. Many an enterprise with a brilliant idea has failed to come into existence for want of adequate finance and at the proper time. Before it is a going concern a business enterprise will require land, buildings, machinery, tools and equipment. This is the fixed capital to be invested in the firm for a long period of time. The enterprise will also require working capital to finance materials, labour, supplies, light and power and other current costs. Where is the money to come from for financing the new business enterprise ? New concerns of small size will usually depend upon the individual entrepreneurs or partners, or upon local capital. For large-scale operation funds are collected from far and wide through joint stock companies. Whatever the source, it is imperative to the success of the enterprise that adequate funds are available to meet its initial needs and future requirements. For this purpose the entrepreneur will prepare or have a professional agency to prepare a financial plan, which will state the financial requirements, the profitable use of the funds, the capital structure and the appropriate time to finance the enterprise.

Labour Force—Skilled and Unskilled. A new business, having no men of its own training, must face the problem of gathering rapidly a complement of skilled workmen and capable foremen, as well as a dependable force of unskilled workers. Men who come from different plants bring with them different ideas as to speed and methods of work, and have to be brought into harmony with the new unit's policy. It is necessary to be careful in recruiting men coming from other concerns, for they are likely to be the least efficient and rejects of the original concern, unless very tempting terms of service are offered to induce good and efficient workers to join the new unit.

Managerial Staff or Creating the Organisation Structure. Business activities do not run automatically. A group of unarranged machines, a body of unorganised workers, and a pile of unassembled materials do not make a factory. Someone must plan what is to be produced with the machines, and must direct the arrangement of those machines as well as the uses to which the materials are to be put. Furthermore, someone must control the activities of the workers. In other words, there must be someone to direct the activities of the enterprise in achieving its purposes, and that someone is the Manager or the Chief Executive. The wisdom with which he acts will well decide the future of the enterprise. He must, to ensure success of the unit, build an organisation structure, entrusting different functions to efficient functional managers. He should take steps to define clearly the various classes of executive duties, such as those relating to production, sales, finance, etc., and arrange them in such a way that each person performs a specific function, and all these persons are bound together in a well-balanced administrative hierarchy. It is an advantage to record the administrative functions on a chart of authority as they are allotted, to ensure that every necessary duty has been assigned, but no one is overloaded. Of course, an individual proprietor supplies his own managerial skill—planning, directing, staffing and controlling. In large enterprises, the management function becomes of much greater importance because of the impersonal nature of the owner—the company. The problems of organisation structure stated above assume importance when individuals with special knowledge in different areas of management perform their respective functions and the chief executive co-ordinates their activities for good results.

Each of the afore-mentioned problems is dependent on each of the others. Therefore, all the problems must be handled and solutions to them found by putting them in proper perspective. Having done that the entrepreneur can proceed to launch the enterprise. Another factor of supreme importance, which we have not touched upon here, but which will be taken up at appropriate places, should never be forgotten while tackling the various problems. This is the human factor which always looms large in business administration. All the various problems relating to the launching of a new enterprise have been stated at this stage merely to provide a background for their consideration in the following parts of the book, when a detailed study of each one will be made.

Before any unit can be actually launched, certain legal requirements have to be complied with. For instance, if the industry to be set up falls under the Scheduled industries under the Industries (Development and Regulation) Act, 1951, a licence has to be obtained from the Government. Then for building a factory, approval of the site, the plan of the building must be obtained from the State Government. Before occupying the factory, the occupier must register it with the Chief Factory Inspector and also obtain a licence to run it. If the capital of the company is to be more than Rs. 50 lakhs, then permission to issue capital must be obtained from the Controller of Capital Issues under the Capital Issues (Control) Act, 1947.

OWNERSHIP ORGANISATION DECISION

Choice of the Legal Form. A review of the legal form of organisation is important, because the power and responsibility for making decisions for an enterprise are affected by the form of organisation used. The entrepreneur's choice of the type of the organisation will primarily depend upon the nature of the business to be started and his own preferences together with the amount of capital he can contribute as compared with the total amount required and the scale of operation, as well as some other considerations. His initial decision with regard to the choice of the form of organisation will normally be governed by the following factors :

1. Nature of business—manufacturing, trading, service.
2. Scale of operation—small, medium, large.
3. Capital requirements—small amount, large, vast.
4. Ownership rights and responsibilities.
   (a) Control and decision-making opportunity.

(b) degree of risk and liability.
(c) sharing of gains.

5. Internal organisation.
6. Impact of taxation.

It is important to remember that all these factors are inter-related and have bearing on one another. For example, the capital requirements will be governed by the nature of the business and the scale of operation. His decision to enter one industry rather than another will depend not merely on a comparison of the monetary rewards he can expect from each, but also on such things as his own background and temperament, his technical knowledge, his personal interests, his estimate of the differing degrees of risk in different industries, the amount of capital required, and his estimate of his own ability. A man brought up in the grocery trade will be attracted to that trade if he goes into business on his own account, even though he knows that bigger profits are being made by others in other trades. A tailor may see the advantages to be gained by mass production of ready-made garments, but he doubts his ability to manage a large enterprise, so he contents himself with a small tailoring business. The passionate devotee of total abstinence (staunch teetotaller) is hardly likely to go in for liquor retailing or distilling. Subject to such qualifications as these, the intending entrepreneur will choose the trade which seems most profitable.

In a small business, e.g., retailing, service trades, capital requirements are small, and the entrepreneur can usually invest his own savings. The degree of risk and liability, though unlimited, will be small. There is complete union of ownership and control. As he does not have to consult anyone else while taking decisions, he enjoys all the gains which come from shrewd policy-making. As regards internal organisation, there will be hardly any problems : There will be very few employees (if any), and organisation will remain very simple.

If the type of business and the scale of operation, which are the basic determining factors in the choice of the form of organisation, is to be different from what a small man can handle, he will seek out other people willing to join him as partners. In this way, more capital and new ability will be brought into the business. The risk will be shared and so will be the management. Partnerships are very common in commercial businesses and professions. A partnership which works smoothly and harmoniously can be highly profitable for the owners, but disagreement or lack of trust between them can spell ruin. As a partnership is not a legal entity, the partners are personally responsible for all acts done in the name of the firm. As a result, though shared, the risk is greater, as any partner can be held liable to the full extent of his fortune for the debts of the firm.

Larger amount of capital can be brought into business, and the risks associated with unlimited liability can be avoided by forming a limited company. If the capital requirements are not very large, a private limited company may be formed, while to meet the needs of vast amount of capital to run a very large business, a public company will have to be formed. If expansion of the existing business is the object, then it can be sold to the company. If new business has to be started on a large-scale, a public limited company can be formed. In either case, it will be clear, the public company possesses the virtue of facilitating growth and large-scale production. It enables the business man to tap wide sources of capital. It is also superior to one-man business or partnership, and to most private companies, in that it is not dependent on a particular group of people, e.g., one family—for its supply of managerial ability, any more than for its capital.

EXPANSION OF EXISTING BUSINESS

Where an individual has made a success of his business he has to expand it to meet much larger demand. Since his own capital and ability are limited, he will have to take another look at the existing form of ownership organisation and see whether a change-over to another form will enable him to carry out the necessary expansion. The problems that an expanding firm will have to tackle usually are :

1. Larger capital and other financial requirements.
2. Need for internal re-organisation.
3. Need for the use of the services of outside expertise.
4. Increase or decrease in risks and personal liability of the owners.
5. Retention of control.
6. Tax liability.

The nature and extent of the problems will depend upon the starting point of ownership. In order to trace the full course of growth and development of a business enterprise we will start with sole proprietorship. The sole proprietor has to choose between taking a partner or partners or appointing a paid manager, or even converting his business into a limited company. In case the present organisation is a partnership, the choice is between increasing the number of partners (up to 20) or converting it into a private limited company. If it is a private company, it may become necessary to consider whether or not to convert it into a public company. The factors that will influence the choice one way or the other are the same as were discussed in connection with the forms of legal ownership in Chapter III, namely :—

Formation; Finance; Liability; Management and Control; Flexibility; Secrecy; Continuity; State Regulation; Impact of taxation.

Manager or Partners. When an individual proprietor has made a success of his business, the need for its expansion becomes urgent. To accomplish this, he must have more capital and some one to help him in management. Two courses are open to him. He may either appoint a paid manager or assistant, or take one or more partners. His decision will depend upon the considerations as detailed below.

1. *Re-organisation.* The appointment of a suitable person as a

manager does not require any adjustment in the ownership of the business. All that is needed is the settlement of the terms of employment and his remuneration by contract of service. On the contrary, the taking in of a partner will involve the settlement of the terms and conditions of the partnership. Even the deed of partnership may have to be drafted by a lawyer, and registration of the firm will be necessary. All this will mean some additional cost. Again, no suitable person may be available to join him as a partner, while a manager or an assistant may not be so difficult to find.

2. *Capital.* The appointment of a manager will leave the proprietor with the full responsibility of arranging for the additional capital himself. He may do this by borrowing from a bank on giving some tangible security or from his friends and relatives. The merit of this method is that he can repay the principal together with interest out of the increased earnings, and continue to enjoy the full benefit of all the profits. If he takes a partner or partners, additional capital will be brought in by them. The proprietor will be saved from the burden of paying interest and giving security for the loan. But the partners will have to be given shares in the future profits of the firm.

3. *Control.* The appointment of a manager will leave the control of business affairs with the proprietor. The policy-making function continues to be with him and he enjoys all the gains after payment of the salary to the manager. This union of ownership and control makes for the strength of one-man business. If he takes a partner or partners he will have to share the control of the business with them. All major and policy decisions can be made by the unanimous consent of all the partners. With the sharing of the control, the partners share profits. The sole proprietor may, of course, retain full control in his own hands by admitting 'sleeping partners', who take no active part in the business at all. They merely help to finance the business in return for a share of the profits.

4. *Management.* The quality of management with a manager to assist the sole proprietor will depend upon the ability, competence and business acumen of the manager. The lack of direct personal gain as a result of successful working, and of financial stake in the business is likely to militate against complete devotion to duty. If he selects his partners with due care, he gets the advantage of a wider range of ability. Their personal interest and day-to-day control of the firm will add to the flexibility and vigour of the management.

5. *Secrecy.* With a manager, the sole proprietor will be in a position to keep all important business secrets to himself. In a partnership, business secrets have to be shared with partners. So long as partners act with good faith and harmoniously the secrets are safe with them but if they fall out, secrets may become public.

6. *Business Risks.* Where the sole proprietor employs a manager, he has to bear all the risks of the business. He pays interest on loans taken and salaries and wages to employees. It may be that there is no profit

after meeting all the charges. In a partnership, business risks are shared by all the partners, so are the losses. The partners will have brought in capital and no loans will have been taken which means saving of interest payment. On the other hand, the individual proprietor, who has all the authority, can keep good control over the risks. In a partnership, an act of one partner done in the name of the firm renders all the partners personally liable.

7. *State Regulation.* Appointment of an assistant involves no compliance with any legal regulation. In a partnership also the state regulation is minimal, so that both methods are almost at par on this count.

8. *Impact of Taxation.* The salary paid to the manager is a charge against profits and is an admitted deduction for tax purposes. Again, the firm does not have to pay the tax on the manager's income. The share of profit payable to partners is liable to tax in the hands of the firm, in case it has not been registered under the Income Tax Act.

The foregoing considerations appear to suggest that it will be more feasible for the sole proprietor to appoint a manager than take a partner. He may, at a later stage, consider the possibility of converting his business into partnership in order to take advantage of new capital and new ability which the partners will contribute.

Partnership or Private Company. With the further expansion of his business, the sole proprietor is confronted afresh with the alternatives of the forms of organisation. Before taking the final decision as to whether he should bring in new ability and new capital into the business by taking in partners, or convert his business into a private limited company, he will weigh the two alternatives of partnership and private company after considering the following factors :

1. *Re-organisation.* The partnership enjoys a distinct advantage over a private company on this count. No legal formalities necessary for the registration of a company are required to be complied with while forming a partnership. Even an oral contract is sufficient to bring it into existence.

2. *Capital Requirements.* If the expansion of business does not go beyond the medium scale of operation, the necessary capital can be raised either by adopting the partnership form of organisation or by converting the business into a private company. As long as the amount of capital required for this new level of operations can be supplied by the partners, partnership organisation is superior to a private company. Then, the fact the partners' liability is not only unlimited but it is also joint and several, gives them an added advantage to secure additional capital by means of loans.

3. *Liability.* For a medium size business the suitable choice would be partnership, particularly if it is stable. If the scale has to be rather large necessitating the raising of capital from larger number of people, all of whom may not be able to participate in the management, a private limited company will be preferable.

4. *Control.* In a partnership, the original owner would have to share control of the firm's activities with other partners, as each partner is entitled to take part in management. If he decides upon a private limited company, the original owner may arrange to retain effective control by holding the office of the Managing Director. It is possible to do this in a partnership, too, if he can find a partner or partners who are willing to invest money and leave the management in his hands. In that case, they will be sleeping partners, whereas he will be active or working partner.

5. *Management.* As stated above, every partner has a right to be consulted with regard to the management of the affairs of the firm. As a result, there is a danger of fall in efficiency, even disruption, if all the partners are unable to agree on important matters of policy. In a private company, in spite of larger number of members than partners in a partnership, the management, being in the hands of directors, who may be only two in number, can be efficient, and decision prompt and bold.

6. *Secrecy.* Secrecy can be maintained in both the forms of organisation equally well.

7. *Continuity.* The life span of a company would ordinarily go much beyond that of the partners, so that a private company may last for generations. A partnership, on the other hand, may come to an end on the death or insolvency of a partner and at a most inconvenient time.

Regarding dissolution, unless all the partners agree to dissolve the firm, there is not much difference between the two. A private company can be dissolved through voluntary winding up, and in case of partnership, an order of the court will be necessary where a partner proves troublesome or incapable.

8. *State Regulation.* The State regulates the activities of a private company much more than it regulates activities carried on by partners. For instance, audit of the partnership accounts is not compulsory, while it is so in the case of a private company.

9. *Impact of Taxation.* The tax burden is lighter in the case of a partnership business than in case of a private limited company, more so where the scale of operation is small or medium and the share of profit of each part in a year is less than Rs. one lakh. Where the incomes fall within the higher levels, private company would be preferable.

Private Company or Public Company. We have seen in the previous discussion that for a medium size business either a partnership or a private company may be adopted. Very often, the sole proprietor will convert his business into a private limited company to take advantage of limited liability, particularly where expansion of his business has resulted from diversification thereby increasing business risks. He may have reached that higher level of income where it is advantageous to enjoy the benefits of flat rate of income tax as a private company. It may also happen that the private company has reached that stage of expansion which necessitates the raising of vast amount of capital. In that event it may have to be decided whether or not to convert the private company into a public limited company. The decision will depend upon the consideration of the following factors :

1. *Re-organisation.* There are many advantages of initially forming a private company and then converting it into a public company as and when need arises. The double advantage of privacy and limited liability that a private company enjoys prompts business men to convert their family businesses into private limited companies. A private company can commence business immediately on incorporation and does not have to raise the minimum subscription compulsory for a public company. When business expands, a private company can be converted into a public company by altering the Articles of Association with respect to number of members, offer of shares to the public and their transferability.

2. *Capital.* The financial resources of a private company will be rather small as compared with a public company, because of a limit on the maximum number of shareholders to fifty. The limited liability puts a limit on its borrowing power. A public company, on the other hand, can raise limitless amount of money from the public, provided that the promoters enjoy good reputation and business to be conducted shows good prospects. Additional funds can be procured by a public company by the issue of debentures and by borrowing from the Development Corporations, such as Industrial Finance Corporation, Industrial Credit and Investment Corporation, National Development Corporation and Industrial Development Bank.

3. *Control.* A private company enables the sole trader to expand his business, and enjoy the advantages of limited liability and wider ownership, without loss of control. After conversion into a public company, control may have to be shared with others. As now the finance institutions like the IFC, IDB, LIC, etc., are permitted to convert their loans into equity shares in public companies, the control could pass into their hands. Happily, however, these institutions do not invest for control, treating the shares held in companies as mere commodities for earning returns.

4. *Management.* The management of both the types is in the hands of the Board of Directors. In the case of a private company, however, the entrepreneur himself and one or two members of his own family will constitute the Board, the entrepreneur retaining almost all the powers in his own hands by getting himself appointed as the Managing Director. In the case of a public company, most of the directors are "policy-making directors" and one or two functional directors." As a result, the management of a private company is in the hands of an entrepreneur-manager and of a public company it rests in the policy-making directors and "professional" managers.

5. *Secrecy.* A private company enjoys a great deal of secrecy in the conduct of its business affairs. Although it is required to file annual accounts with the Registrar, they are not open to public inspection. A public company is not in a position to maintain secrecy as all its documents and papers when filed with the Registrar become public documents and open to public inspection on payment of a nominal fee.

6. *Government Regulation.* Since the business in the case of a private company remains in the hands of a small circle of acquaintances and relatives, very little government regulation and supervision is exercised. The public company, being composed of members from far and wide, is subject to numerous regulations with regard to its management. The regulatory provisions very often prove cumbersome and costly, if not irksome.

It follows from the discussion of various alternative choices, that the entrepreneur would try to retain his control of the enterprise by one way or the other. He would also try to escape governmental regulation as much as possible. He would therefore carry the expansion of his business through the stages of partnership and private limited company. When, however, the financial needs of the business reach a stage which a private company cannot meet, it is converted into a public company. Even in this case the "inner group" can and does exercise effective control because of the indifference of the shareholders.

CHAPTER VII

THE SCALE OF OPERATION AND SIZE OF FIRM

One of the most striking features of modern industrial organisation is the increase in the size of industrial undertakings resulting in large-scale production. The growth has been in two general directions :

1. the growth in the size of industrial establishments; and
2. **growth by the centralisation or consolidation of like or unlike establishments under some form of common control.**

This two-fold development has at times caused considerable confusion with regard to the "size" of the business unit or scale of operation. When talking of size or scale of operation, even economists are not always clear as to whether they mean "firm" or "plant" or, perhaps, neither. It is therefore necessary to clearly define the various terms used in connection with the size of a business unit. There are three such terms, namely : *Plant or establishment, firm, industry,* which should be explained clearly in order that we may have a full understanding of the concept of size.

The Plant or the Establishment. Any place where goods are produced or distributed or service provided is a Plant or an Establishment. It includes the machinery and equipment as well as the workers employed for the production of goods and the supply of services. The establishment may be a shop, a warehouse, a farm or a factory, a transport depot or an office and so on. Sometimes one establishment carries out all processes of manufacture or distribution—as, for example, the woollen mill which turns out raw wool into finished cloth ready for the tailor, or the department store which buys direct from manufacturer and sells to the consumer. Thus, in the ordinary usage a plant means a factory, a mill, a shop, an establishment.

The Firm. Establishments are controlled and directed by firms. A firm is essentially a unit of ownership and of control and administration. The firm usually owns the land on which the plant or establishment is situated, the building, the capital equipment which it employs, and the raw materials it uses. In simple words, a firm is a unit which owns, controls and manages the plant or plants. Sometimes a firm may own only one plant so that the plant and the firm are identical. A firm may, on the other hand, own several plants. If the one or more establishments engaged in different processes in the chain of production are owned by one firm, production is said to be organised vertically. If they are owned by different firms, any one of which may have a number of establishments, all concerned with the *same stage* of production, then production is said to be organised horizontally.

Industry. An industry is an aggregation of firms owning and managing plants which turn out similar products. Thus, we have the cotton textile industry, sugar industry, iron and steel industry and so on. The cotton mill industry, for instance, would comprise the total of all the firms owning and controlling cotton mills (plants) turning out the total supply of cotton yarn and cloth.

Measures of Size

Business units vary in sizes. Some are small, others big and many more are giant. But what standard or standards can be applied to adequately measure the size ? The difficulty arises because there is no set standard which can provide a precise measure. All standards can only be approximate; and each one has limited applicability. Then again, measures may vary from industry to industry on the basis of the nature of industry or the character of its output.

Despite want of preciseness one or more of the following measures are generally adopted to determine the size of a business unit :

1. *Capital investment.* One measure of size usually adopted is the capital investment. The larger the capital investment, the bigger will normally be the size of the business unit. But the difficulty of this measure is non-availability of the accurate data concerning capitalisation. This is so because the capital requirements of the individual units and the methods of financing them vary widely. As a result the figures of paid up capital or the total capital invested do not provide an adequate measure of size.

2. *Volume of output.* This is an important measure of size of industries with uniform or homogeneous product like cement, sugar, or coal, etc. But in industries like the cotton textile which produce wide varieties of goods, the volume of output will fail to reflect the differences in the size of the industrial unit.

3. *Plant capacity.* This is a fairly good measure of size. For example, number of spindles and looms together with their capacity in cotton mills may be a good measure of size. Similarly, in industries like paper, chemicals, glass or iron and steel, the number of plants with their production capacity may be a reliable index of size.

4. *Value of products.* The value of products in terms of rupees provides a good basis of size, particularly where outputs of various types of products are not comparable. If the value is of fluctuating nature, it may be difficult to get accurate results. It will not be appropriate to apply this measure to compare size at two different periods of time, one during depression and the other during boom.

5. *Number of wage-earners employed.* This is another measure commonly employed and is useful for comparing units producing similar type of goods and in the same stage of development. But when there are vast differences in the technique of production and also in the character and variety of output, the results are likely to be misleading.

6. *Amount of raw materials consumed.* The annual consumption of raw materials by an establishment also provides a good standard where the units are self-sufficing and where the differences in the character of

the output are not very great.

7. *The amount of power used.* The amount of power used for a business unit is another index of the size and growth of manufacturing plants.

Very often the combination of the value of product, the number of workers employed and the amount of raw material consumed reveals the dominance of the same tendencies in the size of units.

Factors determining size of business units. It follows from the above that the size of a business unit does not depend upon the arbitrary decision of the entrepreneurs. Certain economic and non-economic factors govern and determine the size of business unit. *In general, the size or scale will depend on the type of the industry and the nature of its products.* Subject to this overriding principle, the following factors determine the size of a business unit :

1. *Demand for the Product.* Where the product is perishable and cannot be carried to distant markets or where it has limited local market or a small market, e.g., high grade furniture, art goods, etc., or where it is subject to changes in fashion, or where it caters to the individual tastes of customers, or where the nature of the product is such as requires skilled labour, e.g., engraving, job printing, etc., the tendency will be for small units to prevail. Where the product is standardized and lends to mass production, or is of large size, e.g., locomotive, ship building, or of complex character, e.g., typewriters, adding machines, automobiles, etc., units of large size are necessary to produce it.

2. *Capital requirements.* Industries which require large capital investment, e.g., sugar refining, tend towards large scale. But business units requiring small capital and more labour and a few tools and machines can be started on a small scale.

3. *Cost of transport.* Where the transport costs for carrying raw materials to the plant and of finished goods from the plant to the market are heavy, it is advisable to start on a small scale depending on the local supply of raw materials and the local market for finished goods.

4. *Laws of returns.* Where an industry or its product is subject to decreasing returns, the increased production will mean higher cost. Such industries cannot grow beyond a certain size to become large. But where increasing returns apply, larger production will result in lower cost, so that the firms can keep on growing larger in size, provided of course the demand for the product is elastic.

5. *Entrepreneurial ability and efficiency.* The ability and managerial efficiency of the entrepreneur is an important factor which may affect the size of a business unit. As the firm continues to expand, the tasks of organisation and coordination become progressively more difficult. The entrepreneur is gradually overloaded with decisions which only he can take, so that he is unable to give enough time and thought to any one problem. The resulting inefficiency is reflected in rising costs. The inability of the entrepreneur to successfully coordinate and supervise large unit is a factor that may check the expansion of the firm.

6. *Market.* Market is another factor which affects the size of a business unit. If the market for the product is limited, the size will be small. If the market is national or international in dimension, the size of the firm shall have to be large.

7. *Government regulation.* Large-scale firms are subject to much more rigorous state regulation than small ones. Licences have to be obtained, and they have to conform to a certain standard size. It is often desirable to start on small scale to take advantage of low taxes and then expand at a gradual pace.

8. *Concentration and early start.* The momentum of an early start at a particular place attracts more and more units to that place, and there is a tendency for the firms to grow in size. For example, the industrial units in Bombay are bigger than those in Ahmedabad, and in other centres of the country. On the other hand, the average Bombay mill is smaller than an average Manchester mill. Thus, it is possible to achieve efficiency in units of varying sizes.

OPTIMUM FIRM OR OPTIMUM BUSINESS UNIT

"In every industry, and for every method of production within each industry, there is more or less a fixed minimum size of plants below which production is technically impossible or economically unprofitable,"[1] and is known as the minimum "technical" or "economic" size. The small beginning has many advantages, and many a business unit is started on a larger than the minimum economic size. No business unit, however, is likely to be satisfied with this minimum, and is bound to expand to a size which will yield the advantages of large-scale production, but no further. There is a point beyond which it will not be possible to enlarge with profit, and this is an important point in the scale of operation and is known as the optimum size.

"By the optimum firm", says Robinson,[2] "we must mean that firm which in existing conditions of technique and organising ability has the lowest average cost of production per unit, when all those costs which must be covered in the long run are included." For any industry, during a given period of time, there is a particular-sized business unit which functions a little more efficiently than it would if it were slightly enlarged or, on the other hand, slightly curtailed. The unit is called the optimum unit or optimum firm, and so long as conditions remain constant, to take the producer's point of view, this firm will produce its products at the minimum average cost per unit, i.e., if we include all the expenses that must be covered in the long period. It is the best firm with exactly the right size, neither too large nor too small.

The optimum is not a fixed point, except over a short period. It is always changing; if the conditions of technique, knowledge, and

1. Lokanathan, *Indusrial Organisation in India,* p. 132.
2. Robinson, *The Structure of Competitive Industry,* p 15

organising ability improve, the optimum grows. Therefore, optimum is a relative and not an absolute concept. What is the optimum in relation to a given set of resources, changes with every modification in one or more of those factors. Technical progress, improvements in the art of marketing, and new facilities for the acquisition of capital, may change the size of the optimum unit very considerably in an upward direction; on the other hand, new difficulties in the way of obtaining command over one or more types of resources may move the optimum in a reverse direction.

Passimum Firm. As a firm continues to expand towards the optimum size, the tasks of organisation and coordination become progressively more difficult. Individual management is replaced by group management and local market extends to national market. In the initial stages of this expansion, it may not be possible to reap the benefits of the technical economies of large scale. This temporary phase of growth in the life of a firm has been designated by Robinson as "Passimum Firm". He defines it as "a size of firm which combines the technical disadvantages of smallness with the managerial disadvantages of being too large for individual control."[3] This is a critical stage in the growth of a firm, but can be overcome by expanding with speed and dynamism, as if by "jumping over or rushing through the passimum size towards the optimum scale."

Representative Firm. Before discussing the forces which determine the optimum size of the firm, it is necessary to draw a clear distinction between the "optimum firm" and what Marshall called the "Representative Firm." A representative firm is one which is typical of an industry, a firm which can be used as a standard of reference, and which is working under average conditions and at average efficiency. It is neither a new firm just struggling into business, nor a firm which by exceptionally long-sustained ability and good fortune has got together a vast business which gives it superiority over almost all its rivals. But a representative firm, to use Marshall's own words, is "one which has had a fairly long life, and fair success, which is managed with normal ability, and which has normal access to the economies, external and internal, which belong to that aggregate volume of production; account being taken of the class of goods produced, the conditions of marketing them and the economic environment generally."[4]

The representative firm, as stated by Marshall, is in a sense an average firm which has been running with normal success over a sufficiently long period of time. Such a firm can be located only after a broad survey of the firms under different patterns of management.

The concept of representative firm is too abstract and far removed from reality to have much practical utility. In fact, it will be impractica-

---

3. *Ibid.*, p. 122.
4. Alfred Marshal, *Principles of Economics*, p. 265.

ble to pin-point a firm which could be regarded as the average firm. There are many firms which are from the very beginning of large size, which may be the optimum size. Similarly, many small firms may, even after a long life, find it profitable not to expand. Thus a representative firm need not necessarily be an optimum firm. The representative firm is a long period concept and a long period average firm. The optimum firm is 'least cost' or the 'most efficient' firm.

Equilibrium Firm. Pigou has introduced another concept in the "Equilibrium Firm". An equilibrium firm is one which has reached a stage in its growth where there is no stimulus to expand in size and to increase its output any further. A firm will be in equilibrium when the industry as a whole will be in equilibrium. A firm is in equilibrium when it has reached its most profitable position and the entrepreneur, being satisfied, has no urge to reduce or expand the size of the firm. In the language of the economist, a firm, is in equilibrium where marginal revenue is equal to marginal cost.

The concept of the equilibrium firm is also far from reality, and of little practical utility. No producer can be expected to make experiments with the size of his firm. Under conditions of perfect competition, equilibrium size is equal to optimum size. This means that optimum firm and equilibrium firm can be found under conditions of perfect competition, but the actual position in the present-day economy is that of the absence of perfect competition. But, since precise calculation regarding size in case of equilibrium firms is impossible, the optimum firm is a concrete possibility, and we discuss the forces which determine this size.

FORCES DETERMINING OPTIMUM OR BEST SIZE

The forces which determine the size of the optimum firm or business unit have been classified by Robinson into the following five categories :[5]

(a) The technical forces, making for an *optimum technical unit;*
(b) The managerial forces, making for an *optimum managerial unit;*
(c) The financial forces, making for an *optimum financial unit;*
(d) The marketing forces, making for an *optimum marketing unit;*
(e) The forces of risks and fluctuations, making for an *optimum survival unit,* i.e., a unit possessing the greatest power of survival in the face of industrial vicissitudes.

The final size of the business unit as a whole will depend on the reconciliation of the different optima, where all the five forces are at equilibrium. It is a point where the diseconomies from further growth are offset fully by the economies. Thus, Robinson compares an optimum firm in equilibrium to the motionless tug-of-war rope and observes : "The equilibrium may be similar either to that of the tug-of-war rope, which is motionless because no one is yet pulling in either direction, or to

5. Robinson, E.A.G. : *Structure of Competitive Industry,* pp. 16-17.

the tug-of-war rope which is motionless because the two teams are for the moment equally matched."

The Optimum Technical Unit

(a) *Technical forces.* The optimum technical unit results from the technical forces of *division of labour* and *integration of processes.* The division of labour increases dexterity in every workman, saves time which is commonly lost in passing from one kind of work to another, and facilitates the invention of machines which reduces labour and enables one man to do the work of many. The maximum benefit of division of labour can be derived by a sufficiently large firm. The i tegration of processes means bringing together of many processes to reduce them to fewer in number. This can be done by designing a large machine to take over what has hitherto been by a series of manual, or less completely mechanical operations. This is the exact opposite of division of labour, because few rather than more processes of manufacture are required to complete a job. Such a large machine, however, can be used only by a large firm, because a small firm cannot afford its high cost. The integration of processes results in economies in form of reduction of fixed costs and increase of costs of construction and operation less than in proportion to increase of output. The technical optimum unit is fixed by a balance of the processes. With the expansion a stage may arrive when economies cease but diseconomies do not begin. This is the *optimum technical unit;* and at this point the technical cost of production remains constant and the optimum size varies between certain limits. Hence, the technical optimum unit fixes a minimum scale but not the maximum which is fixed by other forces. Any increase beyond this maximum will attract diseconomies, so that the cost of further addition to size will not bring corresponding gain.

The Optimum Managerial Unit

(b) *Managerial forces.* An optimum managerial unit is also the result of the economies and diseconomies of division of work and integration of processes in the managerial functions. A big establishment or firm has more opportunities for securing the economies arising from specialisation, not only in the technical sphere but also in the managerial. As the firm grows specialisation and division of labour will spread to the administrative side of its work. Some of the tasks which the owner of a small firm has to do for himself can be delegated to specialists—designing, buying and selling, day-to-day supervision of the office, maintaining a smooth flow of production, personnel relations, etc. New departments can be established for research, publicity, etc. Each job is done by a specialist in it. The example of integration of processes here is machine book-keeping. Unlike the technical forces the diseconomies in this case begin as soon as the economies are exhausted. But the problem of coordination sets a limit to the increase of size beyond a certain point. Thus, the difficulties of co-ordination beyond a certain size lay down a lower as well as an upper limit to the size of the optimum managerial units.

The Optimum Financial Unit

(c) *Financial forces.* Financial forces also act in favour of large firms. The task of raising capital exerts important influences both upon the size and upon the structure of firms. A large firm can raise funds easily at relatively low rate of interest. This encourages it to grow further, which enables it to secure finance still cheaper. The result of all this is that the financial costs go on falling as more and more output is produced. Financial forces thus do not prescrible either a minimum or a maximum size of the business unit.

The Optimum Marketing Unit

(d) *Marketing forces.* Buying and selling play an important part in the total expenditure of a firm, and have considerable influence upon the optimum firm and the structure of industry. The optimum marketing unit is the result of the economies and diseconomies of large-scale buying and selling. A large firm when buying large amounts can do so at a lower price. It has a strong bargaining position. It can employ expert buyers, and can secure large orders with the help of good advertising and aggressive salesmanship. Bulk purchasing enables it to save transport costs. Large-scale selling results in economies in travellers' expenses, in smaller stocks and therefore less interest charges. There is also an economy in the capacity to keep larger variety of stocks. A firm, by growing in size, can secure economies in sales even when the technical optimum or the managerial optimum has been reached. In conditions of perfect competition, the equilibrium will result from a balancing of the forces of ecnomies in sales against the diseconomies of managing a large output. In imperfect competition, however, the firm is not likely to reach the sales optimum, not for that matter, any other optimum.

There are two difficulties, which may even develop into serious dangers, that a large firm may encounter, and a small firm does not have to face. Mistakes committed by large firms are likely to be big and costly. The larger the firm, the more difficult will it be to rectify the mistakes. A large firm may have bought large quantities of raw materials which cannot be used, their disposal will bring down the price for them below the normal level, causing heavy loss.

The Optimum Survival Unit

(e) *Forces of risks and fluctuations.* So far we have proceeded on the assumption that there is steady demand for the output. In practice, however, changes in demand are more frequent than this assumption warrants. The possibility of change in demand introduces an uncertainty and the producer has to take account of such changes when planning the size of his firm. Now, the demand may change due to changes in tastes and fashions, or it may change due to inventions and technological improvements. To meet these situations high degree of ability in the entrepreneur is necessary.

When the demand is steady, the producer will try to secure the most efficient size of the firm and use the most specialised machinery. A large firm can reap all the benefits of large scale production. If, however, demand changes, the specialised machinery, and therefore very costly, cannot be adapted to the production of another type of commodity demanded in the market. A small firm has an advantage in this regard, as it can easily adapt itself to the production of a new type of product. Thus the forces of risks and fluctuations and changes in demand make for a smaller optimum survival unit.

Reconciliation of Optima

To what extent any particular firm has reached the optimum depends upon the nature of its business. It may happen (though a rare chance) that when a firm has reached the optimum size with respect to one set of forces, e.g., technical or managerial, it has also reached the optimum in respect of all other sets of forces. Some industries have greater advantages in this respect than others, for in their case the various optima lend to the same rate of output, and there is hardly any problem for the entrepreneur. But experience shows that different forces favour a different optimum size. For example, the optimum technical unit may be 15,000 units, optimum managerial unit only 12,000, or optimum marketing unit may be 20,000 units and so on. The final optimum unit is determined at that rate of output at which the total economies are just balanced by the total diseconomies. In other words, it will be those units of production which give the lowest cost of production per unit. Confronted with the situation of finding a solution to his problem, the entrepreneur will endeavour to reconcile the various optima. For this purpose, he will have to calculate long-term average cost of production of all the levels of production and fix the size at the level which yields the lowest average cost of production. Some of the ways to reconcile the various optima are summarised below :

(1) Where the technical optimum unit is greater than the managerial optimum unit steps may be taken to increase the efficiency of management by separating the two distinct activities of coordination and supervision. The firm can be divided into departments for supervision and each department put in charge of an expert, and made autonomous. Steps may also be taken to employ professional managers experienced in handling problems of large enterprises. Another step would be to split the firm up into separate establishments, giving each a large measure of independence and autonomy. For example, a manufacturer of office equipment might have one factory making type-writers, another making filing cabinets, another making calculating machines and so on. Decentralisation reduces burden on the top management.

(2) Where the technical optimum size is smaller than the managerial optimum size, it will pay the firm to add to the technical productive

facilities. In other words, it will be profitable to have three or four factories rather than the original one. Vertical integration is another course open to the firm. That is to say, it may acquire control over the raw material, or use its products to manufacture other goods. A sugar mill may either grow its own sugarcane or take up the manufacture of sweets and toffees or syrups.

(3) Where the financial optimum unit is larger than the managerial optimum unit, steps similar to (1) above should be taken.

(4) Where, perchance, the financial optimum is smaller than the managerial optimum, steps similar to (2) above may be taken.

(5) Where the marketing optimum unit is larger than the managerial or technical optimum unit, the firm will attempt to sell allied goods produced by others in addition to its own goods. This will take care of the market which is larger than production.

(6) Where the marketing optimum is smaller than in technical or managerial optimum, the product may be utilized to produce a product of higher value, or the marketing may be handed over to an outside agency, e.g., sole distributor or wholesaler.

The question of reconciliation is quite complicated and requires a good deal of patience on the part of the management, and a good deal of trial and experiment. Since competition is never perfect, we can seldom have optimum firms. Optimum firms for us, imperfect beings, is an unattainable ideal.

The Tendency Towards Large Size

Industrial Revolution ushered in an era of factory system. Machines replaced crude manpower. With the passage of time sophisticated technology has brought in new innovations and more powerful machines. All these require heavy investment of capital, and a large business organisation. Large firms predominate in today's industrial world. Says Sargant Florence : "There are logical reasons for supposing that, granting the advantages of mechanical and human specialisation, large-scale production, especially when conducted in large-scale firms and plants, results in maximum efficiency."[1] Large-scale operation is used to denote large-scale production when conducted within one organisation. Large-scale operation has many advantages because of the various economies that arise from it. These economies are considered in the following groups :

I. ECONOMIES IN PRODUCTION

(a) *Bulk Transactions.* A large firm buys raw material and fuel in great quantities directly from producers or wholesalers. Bulk purchases are normally cheaper, so that a large firm saves in prices.

(b) *Economy in freight.* Goods transported in great bulk require full

1. *The Logic of British and American Industry*, p. 48.

ship or wagons. The freight rates for ship-loads or wagon-loads are much lower than for small lots.

(c) *Economies arising from specialisation.* The bigger the establishment or firm, the more opportunities there are of securing the economies arising from specialisation. This can be done in the following ways :

(i) *Division of labour.* A large firm can enjoy the maximum advantages of division of labour. In big firms, the operations can be broken down, thus allowing workers to specialise, with consequent economies of time and skill.

(ii) *Continuous use of specialised machines.* Only a big firm can afford to install specialised automatic machines. And continuous full-time use of these machines reduces costs. Replacement of old machinery by new and up-to-date machines can conveniently be made by a large firm; thus bringing down the cost of production still further.

(d) *Research and development.* A large firm is in a happy position to set up a new department for research. A research section must be of a certain size to do any effective work, and the cost of fitting out and staffing any worthwhile research department would be prohibitive for a small firm. But the large firm, spending only the same proportion of its revenue, can set up fully equipped laboratories and testing sheds and hire the services of expert scientists.

(e) *Utilisation of waste products.* Only when the flow of waste products reaches a certain size does it become worthwhile to try to make use of them. A large firm can have large quantities of scraps and waste products to justify their utilisation for producing by-products. A small firm is not in a position to do this.

(f) *Timely repairs.* A large firm can maintain its own service department, and carry out repairs promptly. This makes for saving of time and cost.

(g) *Economies of increased dimensions.* Costs do not increase in proportion to the size. 'The capacity of a boat increases as the cube of its dimensions; the water resistance increases only as the square'. Every building has one roof, no matter how many floors. A double-decker bus does not cost twice as much as a single-decker, nor does it use twice as much petrol; it requires only one driver and one conductor. A thousand copies of a poster or advertising leaflet cost very little more than a hundred. A purchasing agent will spend no more effort in negotiating a Rs. 10,000 order for a given article, or a clerk in booking and filing it, than in the case of a Rs. 10 order. For this alone, a big firm can usually produce, buy, and sell, more cheaply than a small firm.

(h) *Acquisition or control of patents, etc.* A large firm can acquire more readily patent rights of new inventions, and be the leader in the market. It may also control many patents, trade marks and secret devices, and can give the advantages of those to other plants, by combining different firms and best patents, thereby enjoying the "economy of firms" or monopoly.

The afore-mentioned economies help a large firm produce goods at a lower cost per unit than a small one. We have seen earlier that average cost (i.e., cost per unit) of production is not constant, but varies with output. The average cost will almost certainly fall as output increases. This happens because of *the law of non-proportional returns.* Every firm has two kinds of costs—fixed and variable. The fixed costs or overheads are capital equipment or machinery, interest and depreciation on capital, contractual payments like rent and rates and agreements with service trades, salaries of permanent staff, etc. These costs remain almost constant from year to year. The variations in output do not affect them proportionately and directly; each unit of output bears a smaller and smaller proportion of the fixed cost as total output increases. The variable costs vary in direct proportion to the volume of output. These costs relate to the purchase of raw materials and the hiring of labour. As it is only the variable cost that increases with increased output and the fixed costs increase very slightly, a large firm is in a position to economise on the cost of production per unit.

II. ECONOMIES IN MANAGEMENT

(a) *Use of organised knowledge.* With the coming into use of technology modern business has become more complex. Technology requires specialised man-power. Organised knowledge is possessed by specialists in different branches of technology. Only large-scale firms can afford specialists. When business becomes big, planning becomes essential. A higher degree of talent is necessary to foresee the future in all its dimensions. Ability to organize and to employ information for coordination is required. Men with such high talent are expensive and can be employed by large firms.

(b) *Lower overheads.* As we have seen in the previous section, the overhead cost per unit of product, particularly the salaries of the permanent staff, will not increase proportionate to the production. Doubling the capacity or doubling the sales does not involve doubling the number of works manager or sales-manager.

(c) *Economy of organisation.* A large firm can achieve the economy of organisation. More skilful organisation of labour and adaptation to ways and means are possible. The bigger the concern the more neatly it can fit the suitable man to the right job. It can use special abilities to the full.

(d) *Use of mechanical equipment.* A large firm can easily afford to make use of the various calculating and computing machines for better management.

III. ECONOMIES IN FINANCIAL ADMINISTRATION

(a) *Facility of raising capital at lower cost.* A large firm can obtain capital at cheaper rates, as it can offer greater security. Financial institutions readily buy shares and debentures of successful large companies.

(b) *Re-investment of earnings.* As the earnings of large firms are large, they can re-invest part of them to augment their financial resources. This is not only an economical method of supplying capital, but also there is high certainty as to its availability.

(c) *Survival in times of depression.* A large firm has a distinct advantage as compared to small units during periods of slump and depression. During such periods, both large and small firms sustain losses, but the large firm can fall back on large reserves that it has been able to build up during boom periods. Also, it can borrow more easily than a small concern. As a result, a large firm can survive long periods of depression, while a small firm is more likely to fail.

(d) *Business insurance.* A large company tends to balance its profits and losses. It is carrying its own business insurance, which a small firm cannot afford to do. A large concern produces several lines of products. If one line fails, the other may make up the losses. Or, the unsuccessful product can be given up, and another introduced.

(e) *Elimination of bad debts.* If the large firm is a market leader or a monopolist, the customer cannot afford to refuse payment lest he should fail to get further supplies. Thus, there is a greater possibility of the elimination of bad debts.

(f) *Stability of income.* The large firm shows a greater stability of income than that enjoyed by the small firm. This is possible because large firms tend to have rates of profit or loss which fall within a narrow range, while in the case of a small firm, the extremes of profits and losses are great.

IV. ECONOMIES IN MARKETING

(a) *Economy in selling.* A large firm is able to sell in large quantities, and can therefore save in selling expenses. For example, goods transported in great bulk will enable the firm to make a saving per unit transported. The lower marketing cost per unit of sale augments its competitive power.

(b) *Vigorous advertising.* As the advertising costs will represent a small burden on each unit of output it would be possible for a large firm to spend more on advertising for intensive as well as extensive publicity and sales promotion. Salesmen can follow aggressive salesmanship.

(c) *Prompt service.* A large firm can meet all orders promptly, whatever the quantity. This will add to the goodwill of the firm which may be already quite great.

(d) *Economy in sales effort.* A large firm can gainfully maintain distributing and selling agencies. They can push all varieties of products. Further, salesmen will not have to exert effort for the firm producing a number of allied articles.

(e) *Economies of risk-bearing.* Large firms are usually better equipped than small firms to meet some of the risks of trading. The law of averages benefits the large firm. The wider the area over which events occur, the more uniform, and hence the more predictable, does their occurrence become. It is, for example, easier to predict annual rainfall over ten years than over two years, easier to predict birth-rates and death-rates over a year than over a particular week within the year. In much the same way, calamities which occur at random in industry, e.g., the spoiling of a batch of products, can come as a ruinous shock to the small firm, while the large firm can use the law of averages to predict them, and allow for them in their calculations of cost.

(f) *The Principle of Massed Reserves.* If the orders from individual customers fluctuate widely from week to week, but in no regular pattern, the more customers one has the more likely is it that these random individual fluctuations will cancel each other out. Hence a large firm usually needs smaller stocks, in proportion to total sales, than a small firm.

All these advantages ignore the structural situation. The result is that appraisals are often contradictory. For example, saving of cross-freights and specialization of plants do not always go together as results of large-scale operation. Professor Sargant Florence[1] has therefore classified the economies of large-scale operation under different structural patterns.

Economies of the large firm under different patterns of its structure

1. *Economies of the large firm with a single plant and single line of product.* (a) Increased specialization and division of labour; (b) increased use of specialised machiney; (c) decreased expenses for administration per unit of output.

2. *Economies of the large firm with several (not so large) plants making the same lines of product on a large scale.* (a) Production at least costly locations for dispersed markets or from dispersed resources. Saving cross freights. (b) comparative accounting. Exchange of cost information between plants. (c) During business depressions selection of the more efficient plants to run full and closing down less efficient.

3. *Economies of the large firm making large line of product.* (a) Saving in selling expense; (b) filling all orders promptly whatever the quantity; (c) supplies bought to greater advantage.

4. *Economies of the large firm with several (not so large) plants making different lines of product.* (a) A large order for different classes of goods could be distributed among the different mills each one adapted for the manufacture of a particular class (and, presumably, adapted for its procurement and distribution too). (b) Requirements of demand and supply readily met by vertical integration.

5. *Economies of the large firm making a number of products (on not so large a scale)*—(Lateral Integration). (a) Can supply all leading

1. *The Logic of British and American Industry, pp. 58-61.*

qualities of goods. (b) Insurance against risks. In a very great enterprise, the success may be expected in the long run to outweigh the failures.

6. *Economies of the large firm, whatever its substructure of plants and products.* (a) Reduction of bad debts; (b) common use of patents, trade marks, brands and similar business devices; (c) can command big brains. The first class man is cheap at almost any price but only a large firm can pay the price and use his capacity to the full; (d) can distribute subordinate management and skill among a variety of jobs according to capacity.

7. *Economies of large plant whatever the firm, superstructure, or product superstructure.* (a) Co-ordination on the spot. Specialisation of men and machinery often compels their congregation at one point and place. A single big plant is more localised than any localization of separate plants can possibily be. (b) A very large establishment finds it profitable to manufacture some by-products from its waste material.

It follows from what has been stated above that the large firm has much greater strength than the small firm. It can produce goods at a lower cost of production per unit of goods produced than can a small firm. It is the large firm that, in this era of technological development, can command respect and power. No wonder that the size of the firms has tended to be larger and larger and ever larger.

WEAKNESS OF THE LARGE FIRM

The large firm, we have stated, enjoys numerous advantages over the small firm. But that does not mean that it has no weak points and the small firm has no strong points. The weakness of the large firm arises from increase in size. As explained earlier, as the firm continues to expand, the tasks of organisation and co-ordination become progressively more difficult. As management comprises two definite types of activity—taking decisions, and seeing to it that those decisions are carried out, the larger the firm the more difficult becomes the tasks of co-ordination and supervision. It is true that two heads are better than one, but too many cooks spoil the broth. Individual departments may do their respective work efficiently, but their activities may become difficult to be co-ordinated. In the final co-ordination of the firm's activities no division of labour is possible. What happens in one department affects, and is affected by, what happens in others. In a very large firm lack of co-ordination may cause loss which may be tremendous.

The bigger the firm, the greater will be a tendency for departmental heads, when in doubt, to avoid responsibility, by referring problems back to a higher level. There is always the danger of friction cropping up between departments. Then policies which have to be transmitted through subordinates and for which co-ordination between several people is required take time to change. "A mistake," says Professor Robinson,[1] by a platoon commander demands only an instantaneous 'as

1. *Op. cit., p. 45*

you were !' A mistake by an Army Commander may require days of labour to set right." Hence, beyond a certain point, efficiency may decrease with size. *Decisions are delayed, management becomes top heavy, and the firm grows less flexible, less able to adapt itself quickly to market changes.*

SOCIAL EVILS OF BIG BUSINESS

(a) Big business through specialisation produces atomization of society. As the firm becomes big the employer and employees become far apart from each other. What was a family group or a community when the firm was small is now all too often an anarchy of opposing interests.

(b) Large scale operation leads to proletarization of workers; they cease to be craftsmen.

(c) As a result of the above two situations, the workers are likely to be exploited by the employers.

(d) Big business is prone to exploit consumers.

(e) Big business tends towards monopoly and exploit consumers and crush small business.

(f) Failure of a big business may prove calamitous to the whole community around it.

(g) Big business encourages bureaucratisation of business leading to red-tapism.

Reasons for the Survival of the Small Firm

There are obvious advantages of large-scale production and therefore firms tend to grow larger and larger. Yet, small firms exist in nearly all industries and even prevail in some. How are they able to compete effectively against large manufacturers or traders ? The answer to this question can be traced to the following reasons, namely :—

1. *Fear of losing control.* Growth of the firm is hampered by lack of capital. The entrepreneur may be unwilling to hire capital in unlimited amounts, because of the fear of losing control. The provision of capital is usually linked with control. Secondly, he may not like to obtain 'outside' capital because of the principle of Increasing Risk. Interest on borrowed capital is a cost which must be paid before the entrepreneur receives anything for himself. Moreover, it is a fixed cost. Interest on loans must be paid whatever the revenue may be. Hence the entrepreneur will not enlarge the firm beyond his own capacity to provide funds.

2. *Entrepreneurial inertia.* The second reason for the small firm to remain small is the entrepreneur's inability or reluctance to expand. There are several reasons for this. One is fear of loss of control. Some entrepreneurs prefer to work alone, rather than as a member of a Board of Directors. Again, many entrepreneurs are content with a modest income; they would rather have ease or leisure than a fortune.

3. *Difficulties of co-ordination.* Large size creates problems relating to organisation and co-ordination. The entrepreneur, being overloaded

with decisions which only he can make, he is unable to give enough time and thought to any one problem. If he sub-divides the work and entrusts each sub-division to a department head, he creates for himself the problem of co-ordination. If there is no effective co-ordination, diseconomies of the large employer on the mercy of his under-managers, the entrepreneur tends to stay small.

4. *Gain from direct supervision.* A small employer can exercise personal supervision over all his employees, maintain personal contact with them and deal with all their problems personally. This results in better understanding between the two which is conducive to greater efficiency. In a large firm the relationships become impersonal because of the distance between the workers and the "boss". This leads to suspicion on both sides and disharmony.

5. *Personal Interest and greater motivation.* Since his gain or loss depends upon the vigilance he is able to show, a small man will definitely work hard to make his business a success. It is not likely that a paid manager will work as wholeheartedly as will the proprietor who is directly affected by gain or loss.

6. *Consideration of quality and variety.* As pointed out by Beecham [1] "where quality, variety, and attention to detail are important, the small firm often has the advantage over its larger competitor." Handlooms, with special quality and variety, are definitely superior to larger cotton textile mills.

7. *Special individual tastes.* One of the major reasons for the survival of the small firm is that it can meet the needs of special markets and special individual tastes and requirements. Suiting has not reached the ready-made stage as yet as has the shirting. People still want their suits to be tailor-made, and small traders do this business.

8. *Fast changes in fashions.* Industries whose products must change fast with changing fashions must be run by small firms. Womens' clothing, for instance, are subject to quicker changes of fashion than mens' and must be created in small firms.

9. *Market limitations.* Again, in the words of Beecham, market limitation of one kind or another provide the most important explanation of the continued survival of the small firm. In some industries the main productive operations (e.g., production of bricks) are necessarily dispersed over a very wide area. Since buildings are put up over vast areas, the kilns must be as near to the building centres as possible. otherwise transport costs will eat away the economies of large-scale operation.

10. *Fluctuating demand.* If the demand fluctuates very widely, the size of the firm will remain small, for only in such a case can the entrepreneur run his plant to full capacity. He will keep the size at a level where be can always meet the minimum demand.

11. *Unorganised labour.* Small firms often flourish where labour is

1. *Economics of Industrial Organisation*, p. 58.

unorganised or in small towns where alternative employment is difficult to find. Labour can therefore be obtained cheaply and pressure can be successfully exerted on wage-rates in difficult times.

12. *Cover for monopoly.* Beecham suggests that where an industry is dominated by a few large firms, the continued existence of small firms may be tolerated in that they do not threaten the monopolistic position of the large firms. On the contrary, they provide superficial evidence that monopoly does not exist, and afford some guarantee against the emergence of new competition.

13. *Greater flexibility.* Small units frequently display greater flexibility than large units. Their over-heads are lighter and therefore they are less likely to be affected by depression. Again, the remuneration of the entrepreneur of a small unit can be varied within wide limits. Mistakes in manufacture or the buying of raw material are less serious

14. *State assistance.* In welfare states, small units are regarded as a great check to the growth of monopolies. In developing countries, like India, the state provides all possible facilities and financial assistance to small firms. Small scale industry in our country has been allotted special role in the planned development of the country. The 1977 Industrial Policy statement shows the reservation of 504 industries for exclusive development in the small scale sector.

METHOD OF EFFECTING LARGE-SCALE OPERATION

Business undertakings, in general, grow in size in two ways, namely : (a) *through aggregation*, and (b) *through integration.*

1. *By Aggregation.* This takes place by the natural growth of an individual plant or establishment by accretion or aggregation without any change in its character as such. A business undertaking may have made a humble beginning with a small but economic size. Now, by using its earnings it may enlarge the size of the plant. For example, a cotton textile mill may commence production with only 1,000 spindles, but may add from time to time over a number of years, so that it reaches the maximum number of 50,000 spindles employed by the unit. The result will be that the production of yarn will increase manifold. Here the same product continues to be produced but in much larger quantity. The growth through aggregation will continue until optimum size is reached.

2. *By Integration.* The second method of growth is by the centralisation or consolidation of like or unlike establishments under some form of common control. Such growth takes place by the process of *Integration.* An integration may be (a) horizontal, (b) vertical, (c) lateral, (d) diagonal, or (e) circular.

The integration or combination of business units will be discussed in detail in the chapter on 'Business Combinations' in Part Four of the book.

PART THREE
Company Management

CHAPTER VIII

STRUCTURE OF COMPANY MANAGEMENT

The company is an instrument that unites the efforts of great number of people—shareholders, directors, members of the top management team and the functional or departmental managers and their subordinates. The shareholders who provide the funds for the company are commonly regarded as the 'owner' of the company and its business and property. Legally, they are not the owners; they have been given some rights and privileges of exercising control over the affairs of the company in the same manner as has an individual proprietor over his own business or partners over the partnership business. In practice, shareholders do not and, in most cases, cannot exercise control and carry out management of the business. They delegate their powers and authority to their elected representatives—the members of Board of Directors. The Board of Directors is thus entrusted with the task of direction and management. Usually, the Board appoints one of their members to be the Chairman, and one to the position of the Managing Director. In theory, therefore, the control of a company's affairs is in the hands of the shareholders; but, in practice, it is in varying degrees in the hands of the Board, Managing Director or any other chief executive, specially qualified for the task.

Divorce between ownership and management. The divorce between ownership and management or separation of ownership from direction and management is inherent in the company form of organisation for the following reasons :—

1. The company as a legal entity is distinct and separate from its shareholders so that the shareholders can, if they so desire, carry on a competing business with the company. As such it is not in the interest of the company as a whole to allow the competitor shareholder to manage its affairs and have access to its business secrets which he might use for his own private gain.

2. The number of shareholders is generally so large that it would not be feasible for them to carry on day-to-day work of management.

3. The shareholder are a heterogeneous body of people belonging to different walks of life and none of them may be able or interested to handle the complex problems of business.

It will be noticed that the position of a shareholder is that of an entrepreneur and proprietor who bears the risk and provides the funds, but leaves the management to the directors and managing director or other chief executives. In theory, he is the master, in actual practice, he is often only a sleeping partner. The extensive diffusion of ownership makes for an almost complete divorce between ownership and control of business.

Patterns of Company Management. A distinguishing feature of company law in India is the statutory recognition of various types of managerial personnel. Before the Companies Act of 1956, the pattern could be.

The Board of Directors
The Managing Agents
The Secretaries and Treasurers
The Managing Director
The Manager.

After the coming into force of the Companies Act 1956, a company could have in addition to the Board of Directors, the following managerial personnel :

Managing Agents or Secretaries and Treasurers
Managing Director
Manager

This meant that a company could have, in addition to the Board, either managing agents or secretaries and treasurers; and additionally a managing director and/or manager.

The employment of all types of managerial personnel at the same time was, however, needless and too expensive. By the Amendment Act of 1960, therefore, a new Section 197 A was added which provided that no company could henceforth employ more than one of the four following categories of managerial personnel, namely, managing agent, secretaries and treasurers, managing director and manager. As a result, after December 28, 1960, a company was prohibited from appointing or employing at the same time, more than *one* of the following categories of managerial personnel;

(a) managing director,
(b) managing agent,
(c) secretaries and treasurers, and
(d) manager.

The Companies (Amendment) Act, 1969, abolished the managing agency system and the category of secretaries and treasurers with effect from April 3, 1970. As a result of this abolition only two forms of managerial personnel are now available to choose from, namely,—managing director and manager.

Existing forms of management. The alternative forms of management out of which a company may now choose *one* are limited to *three* which can be :

(a) The Board of Directors.
(b) The Board of Directors with a Managing Director.
(c) The Board of Directors with a Manager.

As stated earlier, the shareholders, as investors, are in the position of proprietors, but they are not managers. The actual direction and management of the company is in the hands of their elected representatives—the Board of Directors. The Board may sometimes appoint an executive committee. For executing the policies laid down by it, the

Board appoints the chief executive, who may be either the managing director or manager. Under him is a small group of top managers, then a larger group of middle managers, still larger group of first line supervisors, and finally the employees. The structure of company management is depicted through the following chart :

Structure of Company Management

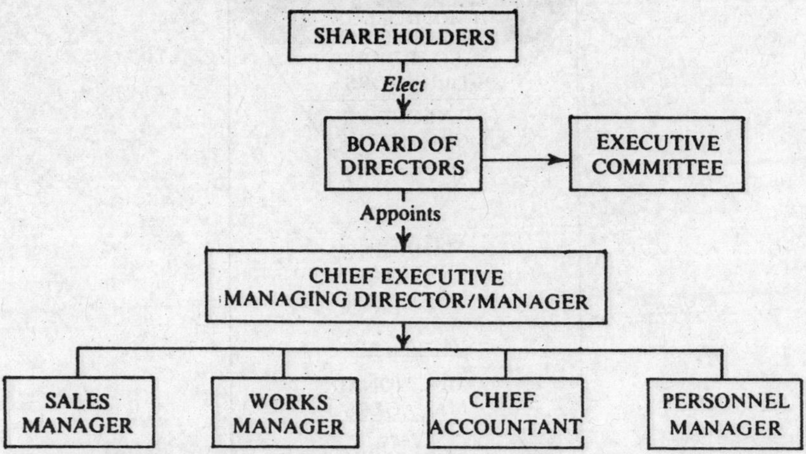

The government of a company whose shares are widely held may be pictured as proceeding like the sand in an hourglass. At the top are the thousands of shareholders. Then the government narrows down to a dozen or so directors, then still further to the Board's executive committee. The waist represents the chief executive, often the managing director or general manager. Under him are the functional managers, and then a larger group of first-line supervisors or foremen. Finally, at the base, we have as many workers perhaps as the shareholders. The figure on page 114 depicts the picture.

It follows that at present the control and management rests with the shareholders, the Board of Directors and either of the two executives mentioned above. Many companies are managed by the Board of Directors alone and no managing director or manager is appointed. The role of the controllers of the company's affairs is discussed in the following pages of this chapter.

SHAREHOLDERS

Rights of shareholders. Since the shareholders furnish the funds and bear the risk, they have been given certain rights, both in their individual capacity and as a group. It is as a group, when attending general meetings of the company, that shareholders enjoy the privilege of exercising control over the policy in relation to the working of the company.

Individual Rights. The individual rights of a shareholder include the right (i) to receive notice of general meetings of the company and to attend those meetings and vote at them either in person or by proxy; (ii)

Figure depicting Government of the Company

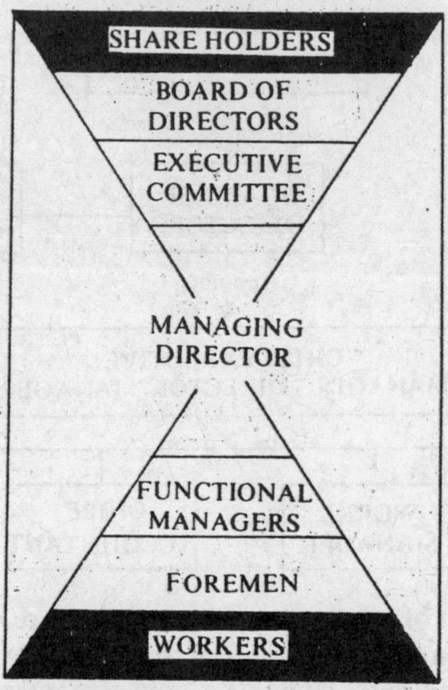

to receive dividends, when declared; (iii) to transfer his shares, subject to restrictions, if any, imposed by the articles; (iv) to inspect registers and records of the company and obtain extracts; (v) to apply to the court to have any variation or abrogation of his rights set aside by the court; (vi) to share in the assets of the company on its dissolution.

Group Rights. The group rights of the shareholders are of importance from the point of view of the management of the company. Every year at the *annual general meeting,* the shareholders as a group determine the broad policy of the company. This is actually done when they consider the report of the Board of Directors and approve or disapprove of the policies pursued by the Board. They are entitled to discuss the profit and loss account and the balance sheet of the company and give their approval to the same. These accounts have already been audited by the auditors appointed by the shareholders at the annual general meeting. They elect directors and declare dividend at a rate as recommended by the Board. They cannot, however, increase the rate.

Where the shareholders feel that there are certain urgent and special matters requiring immediate attention and cannot be left over till he next annual general meeting, they have a right to requisition an raordinary general meeting. If the Board fail to hold the meeting, the hareholders may hold it and transact the special business.

Ordinarily, the management of the company is left to the directors and whole-time officers, but the law requires that the following things can be done only with the consent of the shareholders in a meeting: —

(a) commencement of any new business (as stated in the memorandum under 'other objects').
(b) sale, lease or disposal of the whole, or substantially the whole of the undertaking of the company;
(c) remission of, or granting time for, the repayment of any debt due by a director;
(d) investment of any compensation received by the company for the compulsory acquisition of its undertaking (such consent is not required if the investment is made in trust securities):
(e) borrowing of moneys in excess of the aggregate paid-up capital and its free reserves;
(f) contribution in any year to outside charitable and other funds of amounts exceeding Rs. 25,000 or 5 per cent of the average net profits during the past three financial years, whichever is greater;
(g) appointment of sole selling agents by the Board;
(h) issue of bonus shares;
(i) reorganisation of the capital;
(j) amendment of the memorandum and articles;
(k) voluntary winding up of the company.

It should be remembered in this connection that these powers of the shareholders are the minimum and cannot be taken away or reduced, although they can be enlarged by making suitable provisions in the articles. Furthermore, enhanced powers are given to the shareholders in a meeting in certain important matters inasmuch as they can be transacted only by a special resolution.

BOARD OF DIRECTORS

Since a company cannot act in its own person, for it has no physical form or shape nor has it intelligence or will, it must act through the agency of natural persons. Basically, the ultimate authority of a company is vested in its shareholders acting through a general meeting. But by their nature, general meetings are few and far between. Therefore, the overall right to manage the affairs of a company is conferred on the Board of Directors, the supreme executive.

It is open to the Board to carry out such management by itself through company executives. This form of management is very common these days in our country. The Board may also entrust the day-to-day management to managerial personnel, e.g., managing director or manager, subject to their own control, direction and superintendence.

Disqualification of Directors. With a view to ensuring that the

1. Sections 149, 293, 293-A, 294.

management of companies does not fall into the hands of undesirable persons, the Companies Act provides for a blanket prohibition on insolvents, insane persons, or persons who have been guilty of fraud, etc., from associating with the management of companies.

Number of Directors. Every public company is required by law to have at least three directors, and every private company to have at least two directors. A private company which becomes public under Section 43A is also required to have only two directors.

Subject to this minimum, the articles usually fix the minimum and maximum number of directors for the Board. Within the limits fixed by the articles, the company may by ordinary resolution increase or reduce the number of the directors. An increase beyond the maximum can be made only with the approval of the Central Government, unless the increased number does not go above twelve. Of the total number of directors, two-thirds must be subject to retirement by rotation. One-third of these two-thirds must retire at every annual general meeting. It follows that of the total number of directors one-third can be permanent. But the articles may provide that all the directors will retire by rotation. The retiring directors are usually eligible for re-election and they are almost always re-elected.

Appointment of Directors. The first directors are either appointed by the promoters or are named in the articles, in which case it is essential to file with the Registrar consent to act as directors. If neither of the above procedures is adopted the subscribers to the memorandum (who are individuals) are deemed to be first directors. The first directors, however, appointed must retire at the first general meeting of the company. The members then elect directors at this meeting. Each director must be elected by a separate resolution; and only an individual can be a director.

The Board may fill a casual vacancy, or appoint additional or alternate directors, provided the total number remains within the maximum laid down in the articles. The Central Government is also authorised to appoint directors under Section 408. The articles sometimes authorise financial institutions or debenture holders to nominate directors on the Board.

Share Qualification. The Companies Act does not lay down any academic, technical or professional qualifications for directors. It does not even provide for any share qualification, so that a director need not be a member of the company. But the articles usually provide for a minimum share qualification. Where such qualification is laid down, the Act provides that the nominal value of the qualification shares must not exceed Rs. 5,000, or the nominal value of one share where it exceeds Rs. 5,000. Directors must obtain their share qualification within two months after appointment.

Number of Directorships. Multiple directorships was a normal feature of company management in India before the Companies Act of 1956. This very often led to inefficient management of companies, for no one, however smart he may be, can be expected to look after numerous companies at the same time. It is true that small companies were able to get the benefit of their knowledge and experience, but the large ones suffered. As a compromise measure, therefore, a limit on the maximum number of directorships a person may hold at the same time is laid at *twenty*.

The Monopolies and Restrictive Trade Practices Act, 1969, lays down further restrictions on multiple directorships or interlocking of directorships. Under this Act, a person cannot be appointed a director in more than *ten* inter-connected companies without the previous approval of the Central Government, if at the time of his appointment, he is a director of (i) an undertaking having assets worth Rs. 100 crores or more, or (ii) of a dominant undertaking[1] having assets worth Rs. one crore. The result of these provisions is that *in very large companies or dominant undertakings, a person cannot hold more than 10 directorships and in others not more than 20 directorships.* It is suggested that 10 directorships should be fixed for all public companies, big or small.

The Directors must act as a Board meeting. Individual directors have no powers. They must act as a Board by passing resolutions at Board meetings. *Prima facie,* the directors cannot delegate their powers. But this rule may be controlled by an express authority to delegate provided by the articles. The articles usually provide and the Act now lays down that the Board may appoint servants and agents and determine their powers, and further that the Board may delegate to any one or more of their number some of their powers.

In companies controlling large undertakings it is customary to divide the Board into committees for looking after specific functions, such as finance, production, distribution, appointments, transfers, etc. The specific work is generally entrusted to directors specially qualified for the task, thereby securing the advantage of expert opinion and advice. Also division of work makes for economy in time, money and effort. But no director is permitted to assign his office.

Board meetings. A meeting of the Board of Directors of every company must be held in every three months and at least four such meetings must be held in every year.[2] A notice of every Board meeting

---

1. Sec. 2(d) defines a dominant undertaking as to mean an undertaking which either by itself or along with inter-connected undertakings,—

(i) produces, supplies, distributes or otherwise controls not less than one-fourth of the total goods of any description that are produced, supplied or distributed in India or any substantial part thereof, or

(ii) provides or otherwise controls not less than one-fourth of any services that are rendered in India or any substantial part thereof.

2. According to the interpretation by the Company Law Board, so long as four meetings of the Board are held in a year, the interval between two meetings may be more than three months. For instance, if a meeting is held on January 1, the next meeting may be held any time not later than the 30the June.

must be given to every director, unless all the directors have been informed that the meetings would be held on certain fixed days, e.g., first Saturday of every month. The quorum for the Board's meetings is one-third of the total number of directors, or two directors, whichever is greater. The directors interested in any matter to be decided at the Board's meeting are not allowed to vote, nor is their presence counted for purposes of quorum. Normally, the Board would try to arrive at decisions unanimously. But if a decision is taken by majority vote, it is compulsory to record in the minutes the names of the directors who voted against the resolution.

POWERS AND FUNCTIONS OF DIRECTORS

As the supreme executive of the company the directors have all the powers that the company has, and are required to perform all the functions which are necessary for giving direction to the affairs of the company. These may be studied under two heads : (i) Statutory functions, and (ii) Managerial functions.

I. *Statutory Functions.* The Companies Act confers powers on the directors specially, and empowers the Board of Directors generally to exercise all powers of the company other than those reserved for the company in general meeting. The powers of the Board as given by the Companies Act may be considered, under four heads :

(a) *Powers which must be exercised at Board meetings and cannot be delegated to a committee or a managerial personnel.* The following powers must be exercised or functions performed by the Board, by means of resolutions passed at its meetings :

(i) to make calls on shareholders for payment of unpaid balance on their shares;
(ii) to issue debentures;
(iii) to fill up casual vacancy in office of directors;
(iv) to accord sanction for certain contracts in which some directors are interested;
(v) to appoint *unanimously* a person as managing director if he is already a managing director or manager of another company:
(vi) to invest by *unanimous* resolution in any shares or debentures of any other body corporate under Section 372.

(b) *Powers which should normally be exercised at Board meeting but may be delegated by a resolution passed at a Board meeting to any committee of directors, or any managerial personnel.*

(i) to borrow moneys otherwise than by issue of debentures;
(ii) to invest the funds of the company; and
(iii) to make loans.

The Board should specify the total amount up to which the delegate may borrow under clause (i), invest funds under clause (ii) and make loans and the purposes of the loan under clause (iii)

(c) *Powers which can be exercised by the Board only with the consent of the shareholders given by a resolution passed at a general meeting.*[1]

(d) *Powers which can be exercised with the approval of the Central Government.*

(i) to appoint or reappoint any person as a managing director or manager;

(ii) to amend any provision for the appointment or re-appointment of the above;

(iii) to increase the remuneration of any managerial personnel;

(iv) to grant loan to a director;

(v) to invest in the shares of another body corporate in excess of the percentage specified in Section 372.

2. *Managerial Functions.* Directors carry specific managerial responsibilities in addition to their legal responsibilities. The managerial function of directors is to give a sense of direction to the activities of their company. For this, they must always have in mind the primary purpose of the company and use it as a standard by which to judge the future plans and day-to-day decisions of the Board and those under them. The managerial functions normally exercised by the Board are :

(a) *To establish long-term objectives and basic methods of attainment.* In the highly competitive world conditions today it is essential for every company to have clearly defined objectives for its long term growth and return on capital, and clear strategies for achieving them. And it is a basic responsibility of the Board, which it cannot delegate or abdicate, to decide what these corporate objectives and strategies should be.

(b) *To define specific policies to be followed.* Most Boards think they are performing this function fairly well for any Board decision is ded as a 'policy' decision. But policy is really a statement of general principles and specific rules to be used as guidelines for future decisions and actions of management at all levels of the organisation.

(c) *To maintain the management organisation.* It is necessary constantly to review the organisation structure and make it more suited to the present and future needs. This helps to avoid the making of major changes when the structure becomes out-of-date and cannot cope with the increased responsibilities.

(d) *To maintain effective planning, information and control systems.* A common deficiency in many large companies is the lack of an effective system of management planning, information, and control. As a result, many boards simply do not know enough about the present and past actions of their executive managements to have effective control over the companies' results. As the legal liabilities of Boards is great, it is necessary to remove this deficiency. The Board must have (i) adequate knowledge in advance of what management proposes to do; (ii) timely and accurate information on management's progress to carry out its plan, and the actual results that are being achieved compared with

---

[1] For these powers see p. 115. *ante*.

planned results; and (iii) the will and ability to challenge deviations from the plan; to find out by what action management proposes to get the plan back on course.

(e) *To decide certain legal matters reserved to the Board.* The fifth function of the Board involves making decisions that they either cannot legally, or do not wish, to delegate. On the whole this function is better understood and more consistently performed than the preceding four. The decision may relate to payment of dividends, disposal of company's assets, appointments to the Board.

(f) *To enter into contracts.* The Board of Directors are invariably authorised to enter into contracts on behalf of the company, such as purchase of machinery, land or patents, and erection of buildings and so on. All their contracts *intra vires* the company and themselves bind the company.

(g) *To issue additional securities.* The Board first considers the desirability of fresh shares and debentures to augment company's resources. It then recommends it to the company in general meeting. After the shareholders in general meeting have decided to issue further securities, the Board decides the time, amount and terms of issue.

Composition of the Board and its Structure. We have seen above that the management responsibilities of the Board, as the topmost organ of the company, are those of control, policy determination and supervision. It is necessary that, to perform its managerial functions effectively, the Board must be properly constituted or structured. True, it is difficult to say what constitutes an 'optimum' Board-room structure, but the following points are important concerning the structure of a Board :

1. **The size, i.e., the total number of directors;**
2. **The age distribution;**
3. **The ratio between inside directors and outside directors;**
4. **Active and dummy directors;**
5. **Balance in Board membership;**
6. **Nominee directors.**

1. *Size of the Board.* It is not possible to lay down a definite limit to the size of the Board of Directors. The number of members of the Board will obviously vary according to the nature of the business, subject to the minimum laid down by the law—3 in the case of a public company and 2 in the case of a private company. A company carrying on small business will naturally have a small Board, while a large company will need a larger Board. Clearly, the Board should be big enough to do its job; and as far as possible different groups of shareholders should be represented on it. It should also include some persons with special business knowledge and experience.

2. *Age Distribution.* It is conducive to good management to so constitute the Board as to include in it both young and old directors. The young, say, below the age of 45 years bring freshness of vision and knowledge of new techniques and methods, as well as wider outlook. The old should be included in order to benefit from their experience and maturity.

approval of the central government. However, the cases of appointments covered by section 269 read with Schedule XIII are nc affected by this provision, nor does it affect the fees paid to directors for attending Board meetings or the committee meetings.

In addition to sitting fee, a director who is neither in the whole-time employment of the company nor a managing director may be paid remuneration by way of a monthly, quarterly or annual payment with the approval of the Central Government, or by way of Commission if the company by special resolution authorises such payment. But the remuneration in either case paid to such a director, or where there is more than one director, to all of them together shall not exceed (i) one per cent of the net profits of the company, if the company has managing director or whole-time director or manager; three per cent in any other case.

A whole-time director or managing director cannot be paid (either on a monthly basis or as a percentage of net profits) more than 5 per cent of the net profits for one such director and more than 10 per cent for all of them together. If any director receives as remuneration any sum in excess of the percentages stated above, he shall have to refund it to the company. The company cannot waive the recovery of any sum refundable to it. Any increase in the remuneration of any director can be made only with the approval of the Central Government.

Section 637AA of the Companies Act, 1974, empowers the Centr: Government to fix, while according approval to any appointment or to any remuneration, where such approval is required at such amount or percentage of profits of the company, within the maximum limit fixed by the Act, as it deems fit. But while fixing the remuneration the Central Government shall have regard to—

(a) the financial position of the company;
(b) the remuneration or commission drawn by the individual concerned in any other capacity, including the capacity as a sole selling agent;
(c) the remuneration or commission drawn by him from any other company;
(d) professional qualifications and experience of the individual concerned;
(e) public policy relating to the removal of disparities in income.

CHIEF EXECUTIVE

The Board of Directors stands between the shareholders and the management group. It does not, and is not expected to, direct the business in any detail. It is required to exercise a broad supervision. The Board is specially concerned with policy formulation, broad planning and a philosophy of action. The executive functions are usually delegated by the Board to the management group or chief executives. Even in the development of policies relating to changes in capital structure, new products, expansion, price policies, labour relations, etc., the initiative is taken by the chief executives. The Board only considers them and gives its approval, remaining all the time responsible for the acts of the executives done on behalf of the company. The usual practice is for the Board to appoint one of its members to head the management group and so work as the chief executive of the company. The person so appointed is designated the Managing Director. In his dual role, the managing director, as a director, is a member of the Board and shares its responsibilities, and, as the chief manager, he is responsible for the effective management of the organisation in pursuance of the policies laid down or approved by the Board.

Sometimes a General Manager is appointed to perform the functions of the chief executive. He may or may not be a member of the Board, but he generally attends the Board meetings as a special invitee, if he is not a director. In India, the law restricts the choice to any one of the following categories to act as the chief executive, namely,—managing director, or general manager.

Functions of the Chief Executive. The chief executive, by whatever name designated, is the top executive of the management group of an enterprise. He is an individual who is delegated the task of running the entire business effectively. The total task of management consists of organising, planning, leading and controlling. As each of these is vital to the success of any business, a detailed treatment will have to wait till we consider principles of management. At this stage, we will outline the functions of the chief executive.

The major functions of the chief executive, who may be the managing director or general manager are as follows :

1. Formulation of basic operating policies within established company policy.
2. Formulation of basic organisation structure.
3. Formulation of basic employment and compensation plans within established company policies.
4. Administering company finances and financial controls.
5. Preparing operating budgets and submitting the same to the Board of Directors for approval.
6. Administering company production and sales activities.
7. Administering procurement activities and traffic and movement services.
8. Establishing pricing schedules within established company policies.
9. Authorising acquisitions, additions, alterations, replacements, maintenance, construction, expansion, and disposal of properties within designated amounts.
10. Planning company growth and extension of business.
11. Selection of subordinate company officers.
12. Maintaining contact with Government departments, trade associations, trade unions and other bodies in connection with the formulation and execution of company policies and plans.

MANAGING DIRECTOR

As a common practice, the Board of Directors appoints one of its members to manage the affairs of the company as a whole-time officer and designates him as Managing Director. As the name indicates, he occupies a position of dual authority and responsibility. As a director, he attends the Board Meetings and, as manager, he performs the management functions. In law, he is an individual entrusted with 'substantial powers of management' which are usually specified in the terms of his appointment and are exercised by him subject to the control, direction and superintendence of the Board of Directors. It is usual for the directors at the time of his appointment to specify the powers which the managing director is to exercise, provided that the powers so delegated do not include those which can be exercised only by the Board at a meeting.

A person cannot be a managing director of more than 2 companies at the same time. In the case of the second company, if it is a public company, the appointment must be made with the unanimous approval of the Board. The Central Government may, if satisfied that the companies should have a common managing director for their common management, permit a person to be the managing director of more than 2 companies.

A managing director can be appointed for a period of 5 years at a time, which can be extended by 5 years. The extension can be made only within the last 2 years of his term. The Central Government may, however, approve the appointment for less than 5 years, in cases where approval of that Government is required. The maximum remuneration that a managing director can be paid is 5 per cent of the net profits.

Section 269, which provides for the appointment of a managing director, whole-time director and manager has been recast by the Companies (Amendment) Act, 1988. It now provides as follows:

1. On and from June 15, 1988, every public company, or a private company which is a subsidiary of a public company having a paid-up share capital of Rs. one crore or more must have a managing director or whole-time director or a manager.

2. No approval of the Central Government is necessary for the appointment of a managing or whole-time director or a manager, if such appointment is made in accordance with the conditions specified in Part I, remuneration is paid within the monetary ceilings specified in Part [illegible]

---

1. Sec. 2(26) defines a managing director as "a director w[illegible] [illegible]rtue of agreement with the company or of a resolution passed by the company in general meeting or by its Board of directors or by virtue of its Memorandum or Articles of Association, is entrusted with substantial powers of management which would not otherwise be exercisable by him, and includes a director occupying the position of a managing director, by whatever name called."

and shareholders' resolutions are passed in general meeting as specified in Part III of Schedule XIII.

3. If the conditions specified in Schedule XIII are not complied with, then an application must be made to the Central Government within 90 days of the appointment for the approval of the Central Government of such appointment.

4. The Central Government shall not accord approval to an application for the appointment of a managing director or whole-time director or manager, if it is satisfied that —

(a) the person appointed is, in its opinion, not a fit and proper person to be appointed as a managing director or whole-time director or a manager, or such appointment is not in the public interest; or

(b) the terms of the appointment are not fair and reasonable.

5. The Central Government may accord approval for a period lesser than the period for which the appointment is made.

6. Where the Central Government is of opinion that any appointment is made without approval in contravention of Schedule XIII, it may refer the matter to the Company Law Board. If the Company Law Board, after giving an opportunity to the company, the incumbent of the post, the director or other officer responsible for complying with the requirements of the Schedule to be heard comes to the conclusion that the appointment has been made in contravention of Schedule XIII, it will make an order to that effect.

In that case the company will be liable to a fine upto Rs. 5,000, every officer in default shall be liable to a fine of Rs. 10,000 and the appointment shall be deemed to have come to an end. The person so appointed shall, in addition to being liable to pay a fine of Rs. 10,000 refund to the company the entire amount of salaries, commission and perquisites, received or enjoyed by him between the date of appointment and the passing of the order.

7. If the company does not comply with the aforesaid provision or any direction given by the Company Law Board, every officer of the company who is in default and the managing or whole-time director or the manager, as the case may be, shall be punishable with imprisonment upto 3 years and fine upto Rs. 50 for every day of default.

8. However, all acts done by a managing or whole-time director or the manager, whose appointment has been terminated, shall, if the acts so done are valid otherwise, be valid.

Schedule XIII

PART 1

Appointments — No person shall be eligible for appointment as a managing director or whole-time director or manager (hereinafter referred to as managerial person) of a company unless he satisfies the following conditions, namely : –

(a) he had not been sentenced to imprisonment for any period, or to a fine exceeding Rs. 1,000, for the conviction of an offence under any of the following Acts :

(i) the Indian Stamps Act, 1899
(ii) the Central Excise and Salt Act, 1944
(iii) the Industries (Development and Regulation) Act, 1951
(iv) the Prevention of Food Adultration Act, 1954
(v) the Essential Commodities Act, 1955
(vi) the Companies Act, 1956
(vii) the Securities Contracts (Regulation) Act, 1956
(viii) the Wealth Tax Act, 1957
(ix) the Income Tax Act, 1961
(x) the Customs Act, 1962
(xi) the Monopolies and Restrictive Trade Practices Act, 1969
(xii) the Foreign Exchange Regulation Act, 1973
(xiii) the Sick Industrial Companies (Special Provisions) Act, 1985
(xiv) the Securities and Exchange Board of India Act, 1992
(xv) the Foreign Trade (Development and Regulation) Act, 1992

(b) he had not been detained for any period under the Conservation of Foreign Exchange and Prevention of Smuggling Activities Act, 1974.

(c) he had completed the age of 25 years and has not attained the age of 70 years or the age of retirement, if any, specified by the company, whichever is earlier.

(d) where he is managerial person in more than one company, he opts to draw remuneration from only one company.

(e) he is resident in India.

Explanation. For the purpose of this Schedule resident in India includes a person who has been staying in India for a continuous period of not less than twelve months immediately preceding the date of his appointment as a managerial person and who has come to stay in India

(i) for taking up employment in India; or

(ii) for carrying on a business or vocation in India.

PART II

Remuneration

Section I. Remuneration payable by companies having profits —

Subject to the provisions of Section 198 and Section 309, a company having profits in a financial year may pay any remuneration by way of salary, dearness allowance, perquisites, commission and other allowances which shall not exceed 5 per cent of the net profits for one such managerial person or 10 per cent for all of them together.

Section II. Remuneration payable by companies having no profits or inadequate profits —

1. Notwithstanding anything contained in this PART, where in any financial year during the currency of tenure of the managerial person, a company has no profits or its profits are inadequate, it may pay remuneration to a managerial person, by way of salary, dearness allowance, perquisites and any other allowances not exceeding ceiling limit of Rs. 10, 50,000 per annum or Rs. 87, 500 per month calculated on the following Scale :

	Where the effective Capital of Company is	Monthly Remuneration Payable shall not exceed
(i)	less than Rs. one crore	Rs. 40,000
(ii)	Rs. one crore or more but less than Rs. 5 crores	Rs. 57,000
(iii)	Rs. 5 crores or more but less than Rs. 15 crores	Rs. 72,000
(iv)	Rs. 15 crores or more	Rs. 87,500

2. **Perquisites.** A managerial personal shall also be eligible to the following perquisites which shall not be included in the computation of the ceiling on remuneration specified in paragraph-1 of this Section :

(a) contribution to Provident Fund, Superannuation Fund, or Annuity Fund to the extent these either singly or put together are not taxable under the Income-Tax Act, 1961 ;

(b) gratuity payable at a rate not exceeding half a month's salary for each completed year of service, and

(c) encashment of leave at the end of the tenure.

3. In addition to the perquisites specified in paragraph 2 of this Section, an expartriate managerial person (including a non-resident Indian) shall be eligible to the following perquisites which shall not be included in the computation of the ceiling on remuneration specified paragraph 1 of this Section.

(a) Children's education allowance in case of children studying in or outside India, an allowance limited to a maximum of Rs. 5000 per month per child or actual expenses incurred whichever is less. Such allowance is admissible up to a maximum of two children.

(b) Holiday passage for children studying outside India family staying abroad. Return holiday passage once in a year by economy class or once in two years by first class to children and to the members of the family from the place of their study or stay abroad to India if they are not residing in India with the managerial person.

(c) **Leave travel concession** : Return passage for self and family in accordance with the rules specified by the company where it is proposed, that the leave be spent in home country instead of any where in India.

PART III

1. The appointment and remuneration shall be subject to approval by a resolution of the shareholders in general meeting.

2. The auditor or Secretary of the Company or where the company has not appointed a Secretary, a Secretary in whole-time practice shall certify that the requirements of the Schedule have been complied with and such certificate shall be incorporated in the return filed with the Registrar under sub-section (2) of Section 269.

Note : The remuneration paid with reference to effective capital is *Minimum Remuneration* for the purpose of Section 198 of the Companies Act, 1956, which would be admissible in the event of absence or inadequacy of net profit in any financial year, without the approval of the Central Government in individual cases.

MANAGER

Like a managing director, a manager must be an individual, who is expected to devote his undivided attention to the affairs of a company and does not permit him to divide his energies between more than two companies. By virtue of Section 2(24), manager means "*an individual* (not being the managing agent) who, subject to the superintendence, control and direction of the Board of Directors, has the management of the whole, or substantially the whole, of the affairs of a company, and includes a director or any other person occupying the position of a manager, by whatever name called, and whether under a contract of service or not". To be deemed a manager of a company the individual must be incharge of the whole business of the company, e.g., General Manager. A mere head of a department or a branch manager would not be a manager.

Disqualifications. The Companies Act lays down the following restrictions on the appointment of a manager :—

1. A firm, company or association cannot be appointed as manager of a company. In result, only an individual can be a manager;
2. A person who is an undischarged insolvent, or one who has been adjudged insolvent within the preceding 5 years cannot be appointed a manager.
3. A person who suspends, or has suspended within the preceding 5 years, payment to his creditors cannot be a manager;
4. A person who makes, or has at any time within the preceding 5 years made, composition with his creditor cannot be a manager;
5. A person who is, or has at any time within the preceding 5 years been, convicted by a Court in India of an offence involving moral turpitude cannot be appointed a manager of a company.

As regards remuneration, number of managerships, appointment and re-appointment, term of office, the same provisions and conditions apply in case of manager as are applicable to the managing director.

CHAPTER IX

PATTERN AND PROBLEMS OF COMPANY MANAGEMENT

We saw in the last chapter that the company is governed by two main organs, the shareholders in general meeting and the directors acting as a Board. The Board must rely on executives and staff to carry on the day to day business of the company. Theoretically, the general meeting could direct the affairs of the company, but apart from very small companies, this obviously would not be practicable. Therefore, the law vests the executive authority in a Board of Directors, leaving only the ultimate authority to the general meeting. In practice, even the ultimate authority over the directors is not exercised by the general meeting because of the large number of shareholders spread over wide areas and having relatively small individual shareholdings. This obviously raises the problem of good or bad corporate management. The problem may be tackled by discussing it under the following heads :

1. Company Management oligarchic or democratic.
2. How effective is the Board of Directors.
3. Managing agency system: its rise and fall.
4. The emerging pattern of company management.

COMPANY MANAGEMENT OLIGARCHIC & NOT DEMOCRATIC

The law gives shareholders wide powers but they are not able to exercise effective control of the company's affairs. At every annual general meeting the shareholders are supposed to exercise their powers of control. We say 'supposed to exercise their powers of control' because it is only in law and theory that the risk-bearing shareholders are also considered to be the risk-takers, top-rulers and policy-makers, when they meet in a meeting. In practice, however, all decisions are taken by the Board or the 'inside group'. The shareholders simply approve, as if by a rubber stamp, the decisions made by the Board. Here lies the difference between decision-making and ratification. The Board makes the decisions and shareholders merely ratify them. Thus, in theory, the company management is a democracy, but in reality it is an oligarchy. Says Hobson, "In form an economic democracy....the joint stock company is in most instances a close oligarchy". The management is the close preserve of a few business leaders who constitute the 'inner group' and who wield the full power of management and control, in whom vests the decision-making powers. With the control concentrated in their hands, they are able to manipulate the working of the company to their own advantage and ignore the interests of the shareholders.

Causes of Oligarchy in Company Management. The management of companies is oligarchic because of the following reasons :

1. *Passivity and indifference of shareholders.* In theory, we have observed earlier, the shareholders are the masters, but in actual practice they are often only sleeping partners who hardly ever stir in sleep. Believing in the sound principle of spreading their risk, the majority of shareholders hold shares in a number of different undertakings. They have neither the time, nor the knowledge, nor, in most cases, do they desire to bother with the management of the concern, as long as they get their dividends, and as long as the management continues to be in the hands of capable and honest directors and executives. Furthermore, many shareholders, such as those engaged in other business and professions transient speculators, and corporate institutions, regard their shares as a commodity rather than a true investment in an enterprise. They hold shares for profit and not for control over management. Their association with the company is rather 'loose'.

2. *Absence of unity among and organised effort on the part of shareholders.* The practice of fragmentation and scattering of savings in a wide variety of companies results in small holdings by individual shareholders in several companies. As a result of this fragmentation, the vast majority of shareholders usually hold very small share in the total voting capital, and are thus unable to influence decisions. Again, this vast number of small shareholders, being too widely dispersed, are unable to organise themselves for concerted action. The 'inner group', on the other hand, is well-knit, comprising persons who are well-informed and can easily manage to get their decisions approved.

3. *Ineffectiveness of shareholders at meetings.* The Companies Act requires the holding of an *annual general meeting* of the company and gives the shareholders the power to exercise their rights at the meeting. In practice, the vast majority of small shareholders are unable to unite for effective exercise of their powers at the meetings. The shareholders, scattered as they are, and individually having very little stake, are very reluctant to attend meetings. Even where they attend the meeting, they find it almost impossible to rally to their support a simple, let alone a three-fourths majority of the voting power exercised at any given meeting. The smallness of the quorum normally required makes it possible for the directors to carry the day. The ineffectiveness of shareholders as a whole is also due to their quality. The great majority of persons holding shares are either ignorant, business-shy or too busy to take much interest in the affairs of the company and leave it all to the management. Therefore, an effective general meeting is almost impossible. "The annual meeting", says Galbraith, "is perhaps, our most elaborate exercise in popular illusion."[1]

4. *Election of directors who choose themselves.* In theory, the directors are the shareholders' appointees. But hardly more than in

1. *The New Industrial State, p. 84.*

theory. A contested election for a Board of Directors is an extreme rarity. In practice, the directors practically choose themselves, or they are the nominees of the managing agents or the 'inner group' with vitally important interests. *'The fact is that the shareholders elect the directors but they do not choose them.'* The shareholders merely confirm as though by rubber stamp the election of the directors. Again, once appointed they seldom go out. For, although the law provides for retirement by rotation, it permits the retiring directors to offer themselves for re-election. The retiring directors are invariably re-elected, and the control continues to be in the hands of the same persons. There is accordingly a sharp divergence between the theory and the practice of modern business organisation. In theory, the company is a democracy, but in practice, it is nothing of the sort. The shareholders are unable to make effective use of their normal voting power. Hence, G.D.H. Cole remarked : "While the ownership of modern industry has become widely diffused, its control is closely concentrated". So we say that there is "democratisation of ownership, and concentration of control", which is essentially oligarchical. The shareholders must take the personnel of the Board which is offered to them. Furthermore, the independent or 'outside' shareholders are not only unable to elect directors of their choice, but they cannot remove those whom they do not want, if such directors belong to the 'inside group'. In conclusion, it may be remarked that as in the case of political institutions, the form is democratic, but the essence is oligarchic. The few rule but they manage to make the many believe that they are ruling themselves.

5. *Misuse of proxies.* There is now provision in the Companies Act itself regarding proxies. The articles of companies invariably provide that shareholders may appoint any persons, whether members or not, as their proxies to vote in their place at the general meetings. Although the Act requires that proxy forms must be sent blank to all the members and no solicitation should be made at the expense of the company for the appointment of a particular person as proxy, the 'inner group' manage to get their own people appointed as proxies. An individual shareholder cannot easily get proxies and exercise his voting power.

6. *Withholding adequate information from members.* Many shareholders are relatively uninformed about the business of their company. And very often the Board and the members of the management group give out information which is either inadequate or incorrect. As a result, the management may report the working of the company in such a way that what is good is broadcast and that which is poor but vital to the shareholders is kept back.

7. *Closure of the register.* The law permits the closure of the register of members for limited periods, and the companies usually close them before the annual meeting. As a result, all transfers of shares remain unregistered so that the notice of the meeting goes to the transferor who is not now interested in the company's affairs. The transferee is thus deprived of his right to attend the meeting and vote at it.

8. *Concentration of power.* The concentration of economic power in the hands of a few business houses and industrial groups has brought some divergence and conflict of interests between passive owners or investors and the active managers, and led to many abuses. The managing agents exercised unfettered control over the company, and the unorganised shareholders were helpless against them. With the abolition of managing agency system, these industrial groups have, no doubt, lost an importance, but their stranglehold on companies continues unabated.

It is clear that there is a complete separation of ownership and control. The shareholders generally have no sense of responsibility for the conduct of corporate business. They have ceased to exercise any significant degree of supervision over corporate policy and personnel. Shareholding is no longer ownership, but a form of passive absentee profit-sharing contract. The management, the directors and officers, are in control of the corporate policy and affairs.

Evils of Oligarchic Management. Since the shareholders have no sense of responsibility, the control and management has passed into the hands of a few who wield full power unchecked and uncontrolled. This freedom of action very often leads to malpractices and abuse of power. Some of the evil effects of oligarchy may be summed up as follows :

1. It tends to militate against shareholders' democracy, encouraging autocratic attitude on the part of management.

2. It accelerates the divorce between financial interests and power of management, leading to nepotism and favouritism.

3. By keeping the power in the hands of the few, it stands in the way of professional management development.

4. Financial manipulation and misuse of the shareholders' money by the controlling group are direct consequences of oligarchy.

5. It not only facilitates but encourages concentration of economic power in a few hands, with the resultant ill-effects of such concentration.

Democratisation of Company Management. It follows from what has been discussed above that the so-called democracy in company management is illusory. It is suggested by some people that, in fairness to shareholders, the management of companies should be democratised, by giving them greater control over the working of their companies. The desirability of democratic control is laudable, but its possibility is rather remote. The law has already given tremendous power to the shareholders, but it has proved futile because the management is omnipotent and shareholdership impotent. Actually, the shareholder is not concerned or interested in control. His primary need is the security of investment and adequacy of return. More than 658 Sections of the Companies Act have not succeeded in satisfying this elementary need of the shareholder.

It is not democratisation of management or control that is required but Responsible Management. Where management is not responsible, indirect control through Shareholders' Associations and setting up of investor advisory institutions is called for.

The Role of Shareholders' Associations. It is said that the most disappointed people in the world are those who get what is coming to them. And they are adept at finding others to blame for their own disappointments. Since individual shareholders take what comes to them and are not able to command attention, it is necessary that they should organise themselves. It is a well-known fact that workers have well-organised Trade Unions and the company management have their Associations. The shareholders, who are the Kingpin of the corporate system, are not even loosely organised. It is true that there are about a dozen shareholders' associations, but excepting a couple, all the others have been moribund. It is incumbent on educated and enlightened shareholders to take the initiative and organise independent shareholders and form responsible associations.

In setting up these associations, certain points must be kept in mind if they have to perform their role effectively. In the *first* instance, the founder shareholders should be independent investors who are in no way associated with company management. They should be persons who are beyond the approach of the managements. *Secondly,* the officers of the association should be men of integrity whose only concern is safeguarding the interests of the shareholders, growth of the company to the common good of the investors and the community. *Thirdly,* the persons in the top management echelons of the companies should be discouraged from holding offices in the shareholders' associations. *Fourthly,* one man, one vote should be adopted as the principle for electing office-bearers. *Lastly,* the association will not, even in an indirect manner, accept any contributions from the corporate managements.

Functions of the Associations. Some of the important practical steps that the Shareholders' Associations might take to perform their functions effectively are listed below :

1. The association should function as an Advice Bureau to the member shareholders.
2. It should act as a processing centre for the complaints of the member shareholders.
3. It should act as a watch-dog and through informal arrangement with company managements, arrange to depute special representatives to the company meetings.
4. It should help the minority member-shareholders of companies in making their complaints specific and in order before they are forwarded to the Government.
5. It can very usefully fill up the gap in popular literature on investment matters in the country.
6. It can also help the minority shareholders in securing the requisite number of signatures, as are required in Section 399, for filing application in the court for seeking relief in cases of oppression and mismanagement.
7. It can also organise investment clubs to help the people with small savings to invest their money in shares of companies.

With the functions detailed above, the shareholders' associations would become effective and useful in the corporate sector. The Government department incharge of the administration of companies (The Company Law Board) can help these organisations by according them some kind of recognition. The Sachar Committee on Company Law Reform has also recommended such recognition.

Responsible Boards of Directors and Managers. Since the majority of shareholders are not knowledgeable and are remote from the managers, it is the duty of the management to discharge its responsibility to the shareholders honestly and faithfully. Management has a double responsibility to the share owners of the company. The first half is to manage the business effectively so as to produce the maximum profit possible for the owners. The second half is to see that share owners are aware of company's progress and are satisfied that the business is being effectively managed. Individual executives have recognised the importance of the shareholder in the overall corporate structure; and some have done an impressive job of keeping shareholders accurately informed about their companies' activities. Yet much more needs to be done if lakhs of investors are to function as an informed economic electorate and play an articulate role in economic affairs. The management can help by providing economic education for share owners and prospective investors. Broadly, the management can do much in this direction by—

1. promoting economic and investment education;
2. communicating more fully to owners and seeking their help and understanding more actively, as a means of getting fuller participation and support;
3. developing better employee share ownership plans;
4. establishing planned programmes of economic education for shareholders in every company;
5. encourage shareholders' associations;
6. taking positive action to encourage and stimulate individuals to participate much more broadly and directly in the risks and rewards of ownership of business;
7. making the annual general meeting an important and unique vehicle to enlist shareholders' interest in the economics of the enterprise and to create loyalty towards, and support for, the business in which the shareholder participates.

To conclude, it may be said that so long as management retains its stewardship of the company's business, it must give an accounting of itself to the owners. A constructive annual meeting is certainly one effective way to do this. The second way is to supply fuller information through an elaborate annual report and other literature.

EFFECTIVENESS OF THE BOARD OF DIRECTORS

Before the abolition of managing agency system neither the shareholders nor the directors had any say in the management and control of the affairs of the company. It was the managing agent who ruled more or les like a dictator. The shareholders were helpless and the Board of Directors a 'superfluity'. With the abolition of the managing agency system the responsibility of the Board to perform its function of direction has become greater and calls for greater skill and diligence in the discharge of its duties.

The Board of Directors of a company constitutes the executive of the company in whom the management of its affairs and control and direction of its policies is vested. Being the supreme authority in regard to imanagement, the Board may either carry out this function itself directly or through the company executives, e.g., the managing director, or even through executive committees of directors appointed by the Board. The most common pattern is the efecutive committee consisting of two or more directors to whom the Board delegates its managerial powers. In the U.S.A. and to some extent in the U.K., as a result of the emergence of what Galbraith calls the Technostructure, the Board of Directors relies more and more on the chief executives. The chief executives have first hand and constant knowledge of the day to day operations, and are therefore in a much better position to manage than are the directors who meet intermittently. In India, however, since April 3, 1970, the situation has become different. A large number of companies are managed by Board of Directors, assisted by their committees. But there are several companies which have managing directors. In either case, as the business cannot be conveniently carried on especially in large companies, by the whole body of directors, it is necessary to vest 'substantial powers of management" in one of the directors, called the Managing Director.

As long as the managing director functions within the powers delegated to him by the Board, the latter acts as "an organ of review, of appraisal, of appeal. Only in crisis it becomes an organ of action, and then only to remove existing executives that have failed....

It is true that modern business requires management by experts; but the directors must not allow the enterprise to get into the hands entirely of the bureaucrats.

THE MANAGING AGENCY SYSTEM

Although managing agency system has been abolished, it had played such an important role in the industrial development of India and in shaping the industrial structure in the country that a brief description of its rise and fall is necessary to complete the subject of company management.

Managing Agents. Modern industry in India owes its birth and development primarily to British merchants who had come out to represent British trading firms in India and to cotton merchants of Bombay and Ahmedabad. Being agents who managed business houses, on behalf of others they came to be known as Managing Agents. Managing agency system in its pure form was peculiar to India. It owed its birth to British enterprise, although later on it was adopted by Indian concerns too. The system emerged and grew in order to overcome shortages of entrepreneurial talent, managerial skill and financial resources. Some British business concerns took up the task of promoting new companies, arranging for their working finance and managing them.

Historically, managing agency was a system of company management which emerged and grew in the second half of the 19th century. Originally, the British managing agents confined their activities to Bengal, Bihar and Assam, developing jute, coal and tea plantations. Later on, they extended their activities to Madras and Northern India, particularly Delhi and Kanpur. Their lead was followed by Indian agency houses in Western India, specially Bombay and Ahmedabad. As pioneers, the managing agents rendered themselves indispensable; and during the various stages of industrial growth in India, they performed the triple role of promoting, financing and managing several industrial concerns. Indeed, the managing agents had assumed the responsibilities and performed the functions of the entrepreneur, the financier and the business manager.

The three functions—promotion, financing and management—were performed by managing agents in varying degrees throughout their sway over Indian industry and commerce. They began as promoters of industrial enterprises, and till the first quarter of the present century almost all the industrial enterprises were promoted by them. Their credit, drive, inititative and courage were responsible for the rise and growth of Indian industries. By the thirties of the present century, however, they began to lose ground as the only class of promoters.

The financing function of managing agents was the most criticised one. In the absence of an investing public and well-organised capital market, the managing agents and their friends and relatives supplied the necessary finance. The managing agents also assisted companies managed by them to raise loans from banks and financial institutions by giving their personal guarantee. They were, thus, at once the providers of capital and purveyors of advances to industry.

The third function is management of companies they formed and of which they became by agreement the managing agents. This function was expressly recognised by the Companies Act which defined a managing agent as "any individual, firm or body corporate entitled....to the management of the whole, or substantially the whole, of the affairs of a company by virtue of an agreement with the company...."

The taking up of the management of companies they formed and floated became necessary because of the paucity of managerial talent in the country. The British managing agency houses brought into the country the managerial ability and experience of the British who were the pioneers in industrial development as the result of Industrial

Revolution. This practice of the managing agents managing companies they floated resulted in what came to be known as 'Group Management' which produced the economies of large-scale operation and organisation. For example, the services of one expert could be utilized by many companies in the same group. The group management also resulted in a substantial measure of administrative integration, a feature of the managing agency system at its best.

Yet, the system was not an unmixed blessing. It grew out of the economic forces operating in the 19th century. While the economic conditions changed for the better, the working of the managing agency system became worse. Strangely enough, the Company Law lagged far behind, moving at a pace too slow to catch up with the abuses that cropped up as the system grew older. Prior to 1936 there was no provision in the Companies Act regulating the powers and functions of managing agents. Consequently, they wielded unfettered powers in the administration of companies. Some of these powers were sought to be curtailed by certain provisions incorporated into the Act by the Amendment Act of 1936. These restrictions, however, proved inadequate against the misuse of their powers by some of the managing agents. The prevailing circumstances also contributed to the continuation of the evils. Companies had earned enormous profits during and after World War II which enabled several managing agents to play with the funds of the companies under their management. They managed companies merely to advance their own interests in utter disregard of the interest of the shareholders.

Consequently, there arose a demand by a large section of the public for abolition of the managing agency system. The Companies Act, 1956 laid down a comprehensive code of conduct for the managing agents in the general context of the current economic and social policy of the country. The various provisions of the Act showed that the system should be abolished gradually. As a result of the severe restrictions laid down by the Act, managing agency system became quite unpopular. This was taken to mean that managing agency system, by the acts of the managing agents, had come to be shown as having outlived its utility and should be abolished altogether. The proponents of the system opposed its abolition. This raised a controversy. The appointment of the Managing Agency Enquiry Committee under the Chairmanship of Dr. I.G. Patel by the Government of India on January 4, 1965, further animated the controversy. The case for and against the abolition of the managing agency system is presented here as argued by its proponents and opponents.

The Case Against Abolition. The main advocates of the system and who argued for its retention were industrialists, businessmen and their associations. They asserted that the managing agency system was continuing to play a vital role in the economic development of the country and should be allowed to continue in existence. Their main arguments in support of their claim were as follows :

1. In view of the very low rate of industrial growth, industries needed the leadership of managing agents. The managing agents with their rich experience of managing companies and with their vast resources and organisation could accelerate the rate of growth.

2. Because of their continuing over long periods to manage companies they were able to give a stable government to the company. That enabled them to carry out long-term planning which added to the prosperity of the companies managed by them.

3. As there was paucity of managerial talent in the country and the compliance with complex provisions of the Companies Act required experienced people, managing agents alone could supply these.

4. A change over to some other forms of management at a time when expansion and consolidation was going on would create serious dislocation, and financial crisis in companies managed by them.

5. The last argument was a general statement that the managing agency system was not an evil but a very useful method of company management and should be encouraged rather than abolished.

The Case for Abolition. The critics of the managing agency system countered the above arguments by pointing out that despite so many checks the managing agents were continuing their exploitative activities without contributing much to the conduct and development of the corporate sector. Having lost its moorings, the tottering system had lost all its utility and should be abolished forthwith. Some of the arguments advanced for the abolition of the managing agency system are summarised below.

1. *As promoters.*. During the post-independence period the climate for company promotion has improved to such an extent through governmental act that the magic attached to the managing agency system has considerably disappeared. A person with sufficient business acumen and vision can easily promote and float a company and set up an industrial or commercial unit of reasonably good size.

2. *As financiers.* The managing agents did not supply any more substantial financial requirements of companies managed by them. The bulk of the finances raised by companies in recent years came from the accumulated profits (reserves), provisions and borrowings from banks and financial corporations. The portion of the paid up capital contributed by the managing agents was now insignificant. The I.G. Patel Committee also pointed out that the direct financial contribution of the managing agents was marginal and insignificant.

3. *Managerial skill.* The skill required to manage business concerns is no more the preserve of the managing agents. Many new entrants in the field of industry have given evidence of equal, if not superior, managerial skill in the efficient and economical working of their concerns. On the other hand, there has been continuous deterioration in the exercise of skill in the management of companies by the managing agents.

4. *Check on growth of professional management.* The top and policy

making positions have been reserved largely for members of the families of the managing agents and their close associates. The method put all the power in their hands and inhibited the growth of professional class of managers. Hardly any unattached person, however competent he might have been, was provided opportunity to reach any responsible position. The spread of managerial skill among large sections of the population has thus been denied and the best talents for this purpose not fully developed.

5. *Concentration of economic power.* It has been recognised by one and all that the managing agency system has been one of the major factors for the concentration of wealth and economic power in a few hands to the detriment of large public interest. This has resulted in a very big gap between a few extremely wealthy and powerful people and a mass of extremely poor people, with all the attendant evils of such a disparity. It has also led to the misdirection of investment. As a result, monopolies have been established, consumers exploited, competition stifled and economic growth stunted.

6. *Waning interest in managing agencies.* As a result of numerous restrictions placed on their powers by the Companies Act, 1956, managing agents started to give up their managing agencies, and retain control by other methods. Since their influence had considerably declined, as they were no more interested in managing companies as managing agents, there was no point in keeping a system alive which was fast decaying. For example, of the total working companies numbering about 28,000 only 720 companies with a paid-up capital of Rs. 494.64 crores were managed by 479 managing agents. What is more significant is the fact that of the 479 managing agents as many as 394 managed one company each, and another 35, two companies each. Only 2 managing agents managed 10 companies each, which was the maximum number allowed. The remaining 48 managing agents were managing 3 to 9 companies each. By March 31, 1969, only 594 companies were managed by 393 managing agents.

Management Trends Before Abolition. As the managing agency system became unpopular and the number of managing agents dwindled, a new pattern began to emerge. During the few years preceding the abolition of the system, management by Board of Directors with or without Managing Directors found favour with the newly registered companies. For example. during the three years 1964 to 1967, of the total of 3,684 companies registered, 2,622 adopted management by the Board of Directors alone, and 1,035 chose management by the Board with managing director. Only 17 companies decided to have managers or secretaries and treasurers. The trend continues, but after the abolition of managing agency system and the category of secretaries and treasurers, another pattern is emerging.

Emerging Pattern of Company Management. The abolition of managing agency system did not put an end to the control of the managing agents; they have appeared in a new garb. The managing agents developed new forms of business, popularly known as Consultancy Firms, or advisory and service companies. Mr. Fakhruddin Ali Ahmed, the then Minister for Industrial Development, Internal Trade and Company Affairs, stated on April 27, 1970 in Parliament that there had been instances where on the abolition of the managing agency system the managing agents had entered into agreements with the managed companies for consultancy services, financial and administrative services and other advisory services. Since there were no restrictions with regard to these types of institutions, the remuneration charged for such services could be fixed at any figure, even higher than what they were charging as managing agents.

Some companies had appointed the erstwhile managing agents as Secretaries. For example, Indian Iron Ltd. had appointed Martin Burn Ltd., who were the managing agents, as Secretaries. The appointment had been made on a monthly salary of Rs. 12,500 for a period of 5 years. Another company recently floated—Shree Synthetics Ltd.—had entered into an agreement with Messrs. Bangur Brothers, appointing them Secretaries for a period of 5 years with effect from April 1, 1970.

In some cases, members of the erstwhile managing agency firms have sought appointment as managing directors and whole-time directors. Normally, in a company managed by a Board and managing director, there would be only one managing director. But this would not take care of all the members of the managing agency firm. In several cases, therefore, as many as 5 managing directors had been proposed to be appointed in place of the erstwhile managing agents.

In some cases, whole-time paid directors have been proposed to be appointed in addition to managing directors. Although there are many sections equating the whole-time director with the managing director, especially with regard to appointment and remuneration, he is not included under Section 197A under the category of managerial personnel. As a result, whole-time directors once appointed with government approval can continue in employment *ad infinitum*. This is a serious lacuna.

All these trends were obviously undesirable. The new S.204A of the Companies Act therefore provides that during a period of 5 years from February 1, 1975, no erstwhile managing agents, secretaries and treasurers or their associates shall be appointed as secretary, consultant or adviser or to any other office, by whatever name called, without the prior approval of the company in general meeting and the Central Government. All existing appointments were to terminate within 6 months, unless approved as above.

Suggestions for Improvement. By and large, corporate managements are not performing their duties or discharging their economic and social responsibilities as they are expected to do. They are lagging behind the changing attitudes of the modern society. They must realise that the efficiency of corporate management is not a private concern but is a question of legitimate public interest. The following few suggestions are made to improve the present situation so that a better management pattern should emerge :

1. Corporate management should be increasingly professionalised. The Sachar Committee observes : "Professionalisation of management is not a mere concept but, in fact, an *inevitable necessity* for the well-being of the company itself."

2. With a view to incorporating changes in the Board of Directors in favour of professional management, West German pattern may be considered for application. For instance, there could be two tiers of management : one Executive Board, consisting of the departmental heads with one or two representatives of workers and presided over by the Chairman of the apex Policy Board. On the Policy Board, there would be representatives of (i) the shareholders, (ii) outside professional expertise, and (iii) whole-time executives of the enterprise.

3. The Boards of Directors of companies belonging to main industries may collectively elect a council of advisers from among the elder experienced persons who would meet regularly to give advice on important matters referred to them.

4. The recruitment and promotion procedures for middle level managers should be improved so that competent personnel is selected and retained in the enterprise instead of appointing favourites but incompetent persons as at present. An Industrial Service Commission could serve this purpose.

5. Genuine consultancy firms and companies with requisite professional know-how should be encouraged. Their remuneration, however, should be regulated.

6. Public accountability of the private sector, like the accountability of the public sector through Parliament, has been suggested by the Sachar Committee.

7. The Sachar Committee wants workers' representatives on the Board of directors.

8. The Companies must be required to make adequate disclosure in the form of a social report.

COMPANY SECRETARY

The secretary of a company is its most important officer with large responsibilities and great opportunities. Indeed, he is the first to appear in the formation of the company, and plays a dominant role throughout its existence. He in effect guides the management in the day-to-day work in matters of company law and in connection with administrative and ministerial functions. In many cases the functions of a secretary go beyond these and he is very often entrusted with managerial duties, too. He is incharge of the company office.

The companies (Amendment) Act, 1974 (S. 383A), now provides that every company having a paid-up share capital of Rs. 25 lakhs or more must have a whole time secretary, who must be an individual possessing the prescribed qualifications. He is not to hold office in more than one company having a paid-up share capital of Rs. 25 lakhs or more. Consequently, no firm or company can be appointed a secretary of a company. It is also provided that where the Board of Directors of any such company comprises only two directors, neither of them can be the secretary of the company.

The duties of a company secretary are various and varied. He is in many respects the brain and hands of the company, and guide to the management. For a detailed study of his duties, rights and liabilities the reader may refer to the author's book *"Secretarial Practice and Office Management."*

COMPANY LAW BOARD

As required under section 10 E as recast by the Companies (Amendment) Act, 1988 an autonomous Board has been constituted with much wider powers than the old Company Law Board. In addition to exercising the powers of the Central Government, it will act as Civil Court and decide numerous matters arising out of the working of the Companies Act and of the MRTP Act. Its orders are appealable to the High Court within 60 days of the communication of the order of the Company Law Board on questions of law.

CHAPTER X

COMPANY MEETINGS AND RESOLUTIONS

Kinds of Meetings. A substantial part of the administrative work of the company is transacted at its meetings. In fact many matters connected with the day-to-day working of the company are decided by resolutions passed either at shareholders' (i.e., General) Meetings or at the Board Meetings. A meeting may be defined as a gathering of some persons by previous notice for transacting some lawful business by passing resolutions.

The meetings of a company may be classified as follows :

(a) Meetings of the Board of Directors and its Committees.
(b) Meetings of its members, i.e., General Meetings.
(c) Meetings of debentureholders and creditors.

MEETINGS OF BOARD OF DIRECTORS

The affairs of a company are managed by the Board of Directors. It is therefore necessary that the directors should often meet to discuss various matters regarding the management and administration of the affairs of the company in the best interest of the company and the public interest. The Board of Directors is given powers by the Articles and the Memorandum and by the Act. Sections 285 to 290 deal with the holding and conduct of Board meetings as follows :

1. Section 285 provides that the Board must meet once in every three months and at least four meetings must be held in each year. Of course, the Board can meet more often. The Central Government is empowered to exempt any class of companies from these provisions.

2. Notice of every meeting of the Board must be sent in writing to every director who is in India at his usual address as lodged with the company. There is no provision in the Act about the length of the notice, but good company calls for sending such notices at least 21 days at the maximum and 10 days at the minimum.

3. The quorum at every Board meeting is one-third of its total strength or two directors whichever is higher. The quorum of the Board meeting must be a disinterested quorum. By disinterested quorum is meant that the number of directors making a quorum (i.e., one-third of the total strength) must be such who are not in any way interested in any matter which is under discussion at the Board meeting.

4. All meetings of the Board must be held during the business hours on a day which is not a public holiday. If any meeting could not be held for want of quorum, then the meeting would stand adjourned to the same day the next week and in case such a day is a public holiday, the next day and if that too is a public holiday, then on a subsequent working

day. If at the adjourned meeting the required quorum is not present, then the members (who are disinterested) present at the meeting would be the quorum and the business would be transacted.

The procedure for calling the meeting, the types of business transacted thereat, etc., are provided in the articles. There are certain powers which can be exercised by the Board at a meeting, viz., to issue debentures and to make calls, to borrow money, to invest funds of the company, and to grant loans, although the last three in this list can be delegated to a committee of the Board. It is therefore the duty of the company secretary to arrange for the Board meetings, prepare the agenda in consultation with the Chairman, issue the requisite notice and see that the meeting is held according to the provisions of the articles and the Act. He should also get the directors present at the meeting to sign the Attendance Book.

Form of Notice of a Board Meeting

........................Co., Ltd.

Dear Sir,

I beg to inform you that a meeting of Directors of the Company will be held at the Registered Office of the Company on ....the......... 197 , at .... (S.T.) when your presence is requested.

Yours faithfully,
Secretary.

....

....

The following business is to be transacted :

1. Confirmation of minutes of last meeting.
2. Consideration of list of accounts for payment.
3. Signing and sealing of ordinary share certificates.
4. Consideration of Report of Experts Committee for proposed extensions.
5. Next meeting.

Minutes of Board Meetings. After the meeting is over, the Secretary should proceed to draft the minutes of the meeting in the Minute Book, and they must not be written or typed on a separate sheet and the sheet pasted on the Minute Book. Each page of the Book must be consecutively numbered and initialled by the secretary. Each minute entered on the Minute Book should be consecutively numbered, abbreviated in the margin and indexed. The minutes must be recorded in the order in which the business was transacted at the meeting. Minutes may be recorded either in the form of Narration or as Conclusions. In the former case there is a brief narrative of what happened at the meeting, followed by the resolution. In the latter case, only conclusions in the form of resolutions passed are recorded. Minutes of each meeting must begin on a fresh page and should be headed with the number, date and nature of the meeting.

The minutes of a previous meeting must be presented at the meeting and after they have been confirmed, the Chairman of the meeting must sign them in the Minute Book. The Secretary is also to produce record of investments and to arrange for payment of fees to the directors. If some urgent business has to be transacted and the Board cannot meet, say for instance, an account has to be opened with a Bank or investment of the funds of the company has to be made in the shares of a certain company, then it is the duty of the secretary to draft a resolution and have it passed by circulation. However, any resolution passed by circulation, regarding investments of company's funds, must be confirmed at the next Board meeting.

Minutes

The fourteenth meeting of the Board of Directors was held at the Registered Office of the Company on Friday, the 30th May, 1979, at 4 p.m. (S. T.).

There were present :

..........(in the Chair).

....

Directors

In attendance

.... Secretary.

.........., Accountant/Manager.

The minutes of the last meeting held on 5th April, 1979, were read, approved as correct and signed.

31. Payments	List of accounts due for payment with their corresponding vouchers were submitted aggregating Rs. 21,751.75. The accounts were approved and cheques therefore were ordered to be signed.
32. Share Certificates signing and sealing.	Ordinary share certificates Nos. .... to .... inclusive in the names of allottees as given in the Allotment List were submitted and approved. It was resolved that the Company's Seal be accordingly affixed thereto and signed properly.
33. Report of Transfer Committee.	The report of the transfer committee, as recorded in that committee's minute book, was next considered. It was resolved that the report excepting the transfer of 100 shares from 5 shareholders be adopted in full.
34. Next Meeting.	The next meeting of the Board was fixed to be held at the Company's office on the 16th June, 1979.

Meetings of Committees of Directors. If the articles permit, a company can also have a Committee of Directors that may be given certain powers by the Board of Directors. But the powers to make calls and issue debentures cannot be delegated to a Committee, and must be exercised by the Board at a meeting. Such powers as investment of funds, lending of money, or borrowing otherwise than by the issue of debentures, can be delegated, but the Board must prescribe the maximum limit beyond which the Committee cannot act.

SHAREHOLDERS' MEETINGS

To enable members of the company to exercise some degree of control and to express their views on the working of the company, the law provides for holding their meetings. There are three kinds of meetings of the members and are known as General Meetings. They are : Statutory Meeting, Annual General Meeting, and Extraordinary General Meeting. Every general meeting requires 21 days' notice, and a private company is not required to hold a statutory meeting.

Statutory Meeting. It is the first general meeting which a public company is required to hold within a period of not less than one month nor more than six months from the date at which the company becomes entitled to commence business. The main purpose of this meeting is to give the members a general idea about the progress made by the company since its formation. At this meeting the directors must place before the members a statutory report duly certified as correct by at least two directors of the company. A copy of this report must be delivered to the Registrar immediately after it has been sent to the members of the company. At least 21 days before the day of the statutory meeting, the Board of Directors must forward to each member a copy of the statutory report, along with the notice calling the meeting. It must be stated in the notice that the meeting is a statutory meeting.

The statutory report must contain the following particulars, as required by S. 165(3) :

(a) The total number of shares allotted, distinguishing shares allotted as fully paid up or partly paid up otherwise than in cash, and the consideration for the allotment.

(b) The total amount of cash received by the company in respect of allotments.

(c) An abstract of the receipts and payments up to a date within 7 days of the report and the balance in hand.

(d) An account or estimate of the preliminary expenses and also of any commission or discount paid or to be paid on the issue or sale of shares or debentures must be shown separately.

(e) The names, addresses and occupations of directors, and auditors, and also of its manager and secretary.

(f) The particulars of any contract which or the modification of which is to be submitted to the meeting for its approval.

(g) The extent to which any underwriting contracts, if any, have not been carried out and the reason thereof.

(h) The arrears, if any, due on calls from every director and manager.

(i) The particulars of any commission or brokerage paid or to be paid in connection with the issue or sale of the shares or debentures to any directors or manager.

If the meeting is not held, the court may, on the application of the Registrar or a contributory, order the winding up of the company. Also, every director or other officer in default is punishable with fine up to Rs. 500.

The Secretary should prepare the statutory report carefully and see that all particulars mentioned above are incorporated into it. He should then get it certified as correct by at least two directors, one of whom shall be the managing director; if there is one. If the auditors have been appointed prior to the calling of the meeting, then all information regarding calls and allotment of shares must be certified by the auditors.

At the meeting the directors must at the outset produce a list of members and the number of shares held by them respectively. This list must be kept open and accessible to the members of the company during the continuance of the meeting. The Chairman will open the proceedings by asking the secretary to read the notice of the meeting, and after this the Chairman will commence the business in accordance with the items on the agenda. He will explain the progress made by the company since its incorporation and invite members to express their views on matters pertaining to the statutory report. The members are free to discuss any matters concerning the formation of the company or any matters arising out of the report. A discussion on these points can take place even if no previous notice has been given but no resolution can be passed for which a notice has not been given. After the meeting is over, it is the duty of the Secretary to prepare the minutes which will be signed and confirmed by the Chairman at the next general meeting of the company.

Notice of Statutory Meeting

.............Ltd.

Notice is hereby given that the Statutory Meeting of the Company, required to be held under Section 165 of the Companies Act, will be held at the Registered Office of the Company on the ......day of ....197 at ....p.m. (S.T.).

By order of the Board,
Secretary.

Agenda :

1. To read the notice convening the meeting, the Statutory Report circulated may be taken as read.
2. The Chairman to explain the purpose for which the meeting has been called under Section 165 of the Act.

3. Chairman's statement as to the general position of the company.

The members of the company present at the meeting are at liberty to discuss any matter relating to the formation of the company or arising out of the statutory Report. On the termination of the meeting, the Secretary will proceed to write the minutes of the proceedings of the meeting.

Minutes of the Statutory Meeting

Minutes of the Statutory Meeting of the ....Ltd., held at ....on the .... day of .... 197 at .... p.m. (S.T.).

Present :

1. Mr.____________ (in the Chair).
2. Mr.____________ In person/By Proxy.
3. Mr.____________. In person/By Proxy.
4.
5.

The Secretary of the company read out the notice convening the meeting and the Statutory Report having been duly circulated amongst the members of the company as contemplated by Section 165 of the Companies Act, was taken as read.

The Chairman informed the members present that a list showing the names, description and addresses of the members of the company and the number of shares held by them respectively was ready for their inspection and would remain open and accessible to any member of the company during the continuance of the meeting. He also explained to them the general position of the company as shown by the statutory report and pointed out to them that they were at liberty to discuss any matter relating to the formation of the company or arising out of the said statutory report irrespective of the fact whether notice thereof had or had not been previously given and invited the members to do so, whereupon some of the members asked questions on the aforesaid matters which were duly answered by the Secretary of the company to their entire satisfaction. The said statutory report was accordingly adopted after a brief discussion.

With a vote of thanks to the Chair, the meeting terminated.

CHAIRMAN

Annual General Meeting. It is a general meeting of the members of the company which must be held every year and not more than 15 months must elapse between the date of one annual general meeting and that of the next. But the first annual general meeting may be held within 18 months from the date of the incorporation of the company, and the company need not hold any annual general meeting in the year of its incorporation or in the following year. In case of difficulty in holding an annual general meeting (except the first annual general meeting), the Registrar may, for a speical reason, grant an extension in the time for holding the meeting by a period not exceeding 3 months.

Every annual general meeting must be held during business hours and must not be held on a public holiday. It must be held at the registered office of the company, or at some place within the city, town or village in which the registered office is situated. At least 21 days' clear notice must be given for calling the meeting. The notice should state that the meeting is an annual general meeting. The time, date and place of the meeting should also be indicated in the notice. The notice must be accompanied by a copy of the balance sheet at the close of the financial year, a profit and loss account for that year, directors' report on the company's position for the year and auditor's report on the accounts. The directors' report must also include a list showing the names of all the employees of the company who are in receipt of remuneration of Rs. 3,000 per mensem or more. It should also state whether any such employee is a relative of any director or manager of the company and if so, the name of such director. Companies having share capital should also state in the notice that a member entitled to attend and vote is entitled to appoint one or more persons as proxies (a private company only one proxy) and a proxy need not be a member. A proxy form should be enclosed with the notice. The proxy forms are required to be lodged with the company within 48 hours before the meeting.

If any default is made in holding the meeting, the Central Government may, on the application of a member of the company, call the meeting or direct that the meeting be called. Further, if default is made in holding an annual general meeting under S. 166, or in compliance with any directions of the Central Government, the company and every officer in default shall be punishable with fine up to Rs. 5,000 and in case of continuing default, with a further fine of Rs. 250 per day during default.

There are two kinds of business that may be transacted at an annual general meeting—Ordinary and Special. The Ordinary Business relates to the following matters :

(a) Consideration and adoption of annual accounts and directors' and auditors' reports;
(b) Declaration of dividend;
(c) Election of directors in place of those retiring; and
(d) Appointment of auditors and fixation of their remuneration.

All other business transacted at an annual general meeting will be deemed to be special business. In case any special business has to be transacted the nature of the business containing a draft resolution should be annexed to the notice of the meeting. If the said resolution is a special resolution, then an explanatory statement under S. 173 of the Act should accompany the notice. The notice should also give an idea as to the nature and extent of the interest of the directors or manager in the special business, as also the shareholding interest in the company of every such person. Where the business of the meeting includes approval of any document, the notice should also state that the document would be available for inspection at the Registered Office of the company during the particular dates and timings.

Transaction of Ordinary Business. At the meeting the notice of the meeting is read by the secretary or it is taken as read and the directors' and auditors' reports are put to vote. If any member queries, the same has to be answered to his satisfaction by the chairman or the auditors, if present at the meeting. Then the shareholders will pass a resolution declaring a dividend at a rate recommended by the Board of Directors. The directors are then elected in place of those retiring by rotation; but S. 263 of the Act requires a separate resolution to be passed for the election of each director.

In case of appointment of a whole-time director (an Executive Director) or Managing Director, or re-appointment of such persons, the approval of the Central Government is also required.

The item on the agenda is the appointment of auditors and the fixation of their remuneration, which is done by passing a resolution at the meeting. The Amendment Act, 1974, has made new provisions, and under those, a company, while appointing the auditor, has to obtain a certificate from the auditor to the effect that he is not already an auditor of 20 companies. This is because a person cannot be an auditor of more than 20 companies. Furthermore, in case of a company in which not less than 25 per cent of the subscribed share capital is held, whether singly or in combination, by any public financial institution or a Government Company or Central Government or any State Government or a nationalised bank or an insurance company carrying on general insurance business, the appointment and re-appointment at each annual general meeting of an auditor shall be made by *a special resolution;* and if no special resolution is passed at the annual general meeting, then the Central Government will appoint a person as an auditor of the company.

It may be mentioned here that to ensure that only members of the company attend the meeting an admission card is supplied to each member who is required to sign it and hand it over at the entrance. The card is duly checked by the secretarial staff with the register of members. It may also be noted that it is usual to keep the share transfer books closed for a period and give notice to the members of such closing.

Proxy Form

.... Co. Ltd.

I/we .... of .... in the district of .... being a member/members of the above named company, hereby appoint Shri .... of .... in the district of .... or failing him, Shri .... of .... in the district of .... as my/our proxy to vote for me/us on my/our behalf at the ....

general meeting of the company to be held on the .... day of .... 197 and at any adjourned meeting thereof.

Signed this .... day of .... 197 .

Signature on
Revenue Stamp
of 15 paise

NOTICE OF AN ANNUAL GENERAL MEETING

.... Co. Ltd.
Registered Office ....

To

The Shareholders of .... Co. Ltd.

Notice is hereby given that the Forty-fifth annual general meeting of the company will be held at the Registered Office of the Company on Tuesday, the 16th day of October, 1979, at 3 p.m. to transact the following business :

AGENDA

1. To receive and adopt the directors' report and the audited balance sheet and profit and loss account for the year ended 30th June, 1979.
2. To elect directors in place of those who are retiring by rotation :
   (a) To elect a director in place of Shri .... who is retiring by rotation and being eligible for re-election offers himself for re-election.
   (b) To elect a director in place of Shri .... who is retiring by rotation and being eligible for re-election offers himself for re-election.
3. To declare a dividend and sanction its payment.
4. To appoint auditors for the next year and fix their remuneration.

By Order of the Board

....

Dated.................. Secretary.

Notes : (1) A member entitled to attend and vote at the meeting is entitled to appoint a proxy to attend and vote in his place. A proxy need not be a member of the company.

(2) The Transfer Books and the Register of Members will be closed from 25th September, 1979, both days inclusive.

(3) The dividend, when declared and sanctioned for payment, will be payable on and from 30th October, 1979, to those shareholders whose names are on the Register of Members on 13th October, 1979.

Transaction of Special Business. If any special business is proposed to be transacted at the meeting, then an explanatory statement setting forth all material facts concerning each item of such business must be annexed to the notice of the meeting. The statement must in particular indicate the nature of the interest any director or manager may have in the proposed business.

EXPLANATORY STATEMENT
(as required by Sec. 173 of the Act)

Issue of Bonus Shares

As the shareholders had expressed a desire to capitalise a part of the amounts standing to the credit of the General Reserve Account and utilise it for the issue of Bonus Shares, an application was made to the Controller of Capital Issues, New Delhi, for his consent to the issuing of Bonus Shares. The Controller of Capital Issues by his letter No. R.575-CCI/75/71, dated March 20, 1979, has granted the necessary permission. The letter is open for inspection of the members at the Registered Office of the company at 59, Janpath, New Delhi.

It is necessary for the shareholders of the company to pass a resolution under Article 123 of the Articles of Association of the Company for capitalising out of the amount standing to the credit of General Reserve Account a sum of Rs. 50,00,000 and issue of 500,000 equity shares of Rs. 10 each to be allotted and distributed as fully paid equity shares in proportion and on terms mentioned in the Notice convening the meeting.

Secretary

Minutes of Annual General Meeting

The seventeenth annual general meeting of the company was held on ....at.......... at the ....

There were present :

1. Mr. .... (in the Chair).
2. Mr. ....
3. Mr. ....
4.
5.

Mr. ....Chairman of the Board of Directors who is entitled by Article No...........to take the Chair (or Mr. ....was voted to the Chair).

1. The notice convening the meeting was read by the Secretary.
2. The minutes of the last meeting were read, approved and signed.
3. The directors' report, accounts, duly certified by the company's auditors, were taken as read.
4. The report of the auditors was read.
5. It was proposed by the Chairman, seconded by Mr.......... and unanimously

Resolved "that the report and accounts, as audited and certified by the company's auditors now before the meeting, showing the positions of the company's affairs as on.......... be approved and adopted."

6. Mr................ proposed and Mr............ seconded and it was

Resolved that Mr.......... be re-elected a director of the company.

7. The Chairman proposed, Mr........... seconded and it was

Resolved that the dividend recommended to be paid by the directors in their annual report, viz., ... per cent on the ordinary shares for the year be approved. The dividends to be paid to such persons as appear on the register of members on the closing of the books on the ....

8. It was proposed by Mr. .... seconded by Mr. .... and

Resolved that Messrs......... ..., Chartered Accountants, be re-elected as the auditors of the company, and that their remuneration therefore be Rs...............

9. The meeting terminated with a vote of thanks to the Chair, moved by Mr..........., seconded by Mr.........., the Chairman suitably responding.

....

Secretary Chairman.

Extraordinary General Meeting. An extra-ordinary general meeting is a meeting of the company's members, usually called by the directors for transacting some special or urgent business which must be done before the next annual general meeting. For example, this meeting may be called when changes in the memorandum have to be made or share capital has to be increased or reduced.

The meeting may also be called by the directors on the requisition of the holders of not less than one-tenth of the paid-up share capital. If the Board of directors does not, within 21 days from the deposit of the requisition, proceed to call a meeting to consider the matters referred to in the requisition on a day not later than 45 days from the date of the requisition, the requisitionists, or majority of them may call such meeting to be held before the expiration of 3 months from the date of the deposit of the requisition. Any reasonable expense incurred by the requisitionists shall be paid by the company and the company may recover it from the directors.

Every member must be given a notice of the meeting at least 21 days before the holding thereof. The notice must state the object of the meeting and the particulars of the special business which is to be transacted at the meeting. If a special resolution is to be moved, it should accompany the notice. Only the special business for which the meeting has been called can be transacted at this meeting.

CONDUCT OF GENERAL MEETINGS

The procedure to be followed at general meetings is usually laid down in the articles of the company. But to curb undesirable practices, Sections 171 to 185 make detailed povisions relating to matters connected with meetings. Sections 171 and 172 deal with notice and its contents which we have already discussed. Section 173 states that all business transacted at any general meeting is special, except the consideration of annual accounts, election of directors, appointment of auditors and declaration of dividend at annual general meeting which fall under the category of ordinary business and have been dealt with earlier. Other matters are discussed below.

1. *Quorum.* A number of members of any body sufficient to transact business at a meeting is a quorum. The quorum for general meeting is at least two members in case of private company and at least five members in case of a public company. The articles may and usually do, provide for a larger quorum. The number of members to form this quorum must be personally present at the meeting.

If the quorum is not present within half-an-hour from the time appointed for the meeting, the meeting, if called upon the requisition of the members, shall stand dissolved; but in any other case, it shall stand adjourned to the same day in the next week at the same time and place. If the day of the adjourned meeting falls on a public holiday, then the next day and if that date is also a holiday, then the subsequent day. If at the adjourned meeting also the quorum is not present (within the half hour), the members present shall be a quorum. A resolution passed without a quorum is invalid, unless all the members, though smaller in number than the quorum, are personally present. It is also necessary that the quorum must be present throughout the meeting.

2. *Voting and Poll.* Section 87 gives every shareholder a right to vote (on a poll) in proportion to the equity share capital held by him. Where a company has no share capital, every member has one vote. At any general meeting all resolutions are decided in the first instance by a show of hands and every shareholder has one vote. But a poll may be ordered by the Chairman or demanded in the case of a public company having share capital, by any member or members has present in person or by proxy and holding shares in the company conferring one-tenth of the total voting power in respect of the resolution, or holding shares on which not less than Rs. 50,000 has been paid up. In case of a private company the poll can be demanded by one member where less than eight members are present and by two members where more than seven members are present.

Where poll is demanded, it must be taken at once, if it relates to the question of election of the Chairman or adjournment of the meeting; and in other cases it may be taken within 48 hours of the demand. The Chairman of the meeting may regulate the manner in which the poll should be taken. He will appoint two scrutineers to scrutinize the votes, and the Chairman then announces the decision.

It should be noted that a proxy is not allowed to vote by show of hands but he can vote only on a poll. He is also not permitted to speak at the meeting. The only right that he has is to cast his vote when there is a poll. In case of poll the proxy forms be required to be deposited not less than 24 hours before the time fixed for the poll. If a member or his proxy has more than one vote, he need use all votes on one side, he may cast some votes for the resolution and some against it.

3. *Chairman of the Meeting.* The Chairman is a necessary element of company's meetings and is usually appointed by the articles. But if he is not so appointed, each meeting elects its own Chairman He is always one of the members of the company. The chairman being the choice of the members they are construed to devolve on him certain powers to conduct them and the meeting. The chairman on his part performs his duties and exercises his powers *bona fide.*

Duties of the Chairman. The duties which the chairman performs in the exercise of his powers for guiding and controlling members' deliberations are as follows :

(a) It is the duty of the chairman to see that the meeting is properly convened through the requisite notice, that his own appointment is in order, and that the requisite quorum is present.

(b) Since a meeting begins with the reading of the minutes of the last meeting by the secretary, he must sign the minutes after obtaining their confirmation by members present.

(c) He should see that the business is taken in order set out in the agenda, unless the order is changed with the consent of the members.

(d) He should ensure that the business transacted is within the scope of the meeting.

(e) He must not permit any decision until a motion or proposition is duly proposed and seconded, nor must he permit any irrelevant discussion.

(f) He must see that every member gets a fair opportunity to express himself on the motion or amendment before the meeting.

(g) It is his duty to see that the majority do not refuse to hear the minority; but when the views of the minority have been heard, the chairman can, with the sanction of a vote of the meeting, declare the discussion closed and put the question to vote.

(h) He must preserve order, conduct proceedings properly and take care that the sense of the meeting is ascertained with regard to every question before it.

(i) He must act at all times *bona fide* in the interest of the company as a whole.

(j) He must ensure that the provisions of the Act and the articles are observed.

(k) He must exercise correctly his powers of adjournment and of demanding and ordering a poll.

(l) He must exercise his casting vote *bona fide* in the interest of the company.

Powers of the Chairman. The chairman has supreme authority in the conduct of business at a meeting as long as he is in the chair, provided he acts *bona fide.* To enable him to fulfil his duti s properly he has been given a number of powers as follows

(a) He can name a member and ask him to go out of the meeting in case the member concerned is found to be obstructing the business of the

(b) It is for the chairman of the meeting to decide whether any motions or questions can be put to vote and whether such motions and questions are within the scope of the meeting. He has the power to disallow any discussion which has no bearing on the business transacted.

(c) The chairman decides the points of order by giving his ruling.

(d) He has the power to declare the discussion closed. However, he should not abuse the power so as to prevent fair discussion of any questions.

(e) He has the power to adjourn the meeting, if in his opinion, it is necessary to do so to enable any question to be properly considered or for any other reason. However, he cannot use this power to adjourn or dissolve the meeting at his pleasure. If he does act in this manner or leave the meeting, the members may elect another chairman and continue with the meeting.

(f) The declaration of the chairman that the resolution has been passed is conclusive evidence of the fact, unless a poll is demanded.

4. *Motions.* After the minutes of the last meeting have been confirmed, the business on the agenda is taken up. For each item of business on the agenda a motion is put before the meeting and is seconded. A motion is a proposal moved by a member and is in writing. It becomes a resolution when passed by the required majority of votes cast in the meeting, after it has been discussed by the members present.

Amendments. An amendment is a revision of the original motion under discussion. An amendment may be made either by the addition of certain words, or an omission of some words, or modification in some other form. An amendment should be relevant to the original motion; must be formally moved before the motion is put to vote and must be within the scope of the notice. It must not altogether change the motion. After the chairman has allowed a reasonable discussion, he will put it to the meeting for vote. If it is carried, the original motion is modified accordingly, and then the revised motion becomes the substantive motion.

Procedural Motions. Every member legitimately present has a right to speak once on each motion or amendment, and the mover has a right of reply. When a motion has been moved and seconded, the debate on it may be interrupted by means of certain procedural motions which can be moved orally without any previous notice.

(i) *Previous Question.* Where the main motion is under discussion, a member, other than the mover or seconder of the motion, may feel that it is not desirable in the general interest to continue the discussion. He may accordingly move what is called the "Previous Question" by demanding "that the question be not now put." After it is seconded, the Chairman puts it to the meeting, when it may be discussed, but no amendment can be proposed. It takes precedence over all other business. If it is carried, then the original motion is shelved for good.

(ii) *Closure.* Where the discussion on the motion or amendments becomes usually lengthy, any member may move for closure by demanding that "the question be now put to vote." If seconded, the chairman puts it to vote, and if carried, the chairman will apply '*guillotine*' *or* '*gag*' and close the debate and put the question to vote. If it is not carried, then the discussion may be resumed.

(iii) *Next Business.* Sometimes it may become necessary to drop discussion in order to prevent a decision being taken on a motion. In that case, a member may move a motion "that the meeting do proceed to the next business." If seconded, it is put to the meeting without discussion; and if carried, the original motion is dropped, and if lost, the debate is resumed.

(iv) *Postponement.* If during discussion it appears that further information is necessary for the propoer disposal of the motion, any member, other than proposer or seconder of the motion under discussion, may move "that further consideration of the motion be postponed until......" If carried the debate is postponed. It should be noted that postponement is not the same thing as adjournment.

(v) *Adjournment.* An adjournment motion may be moved to adjourn the meeting for a stated period or *sine die*, i.e., for an indefinite period. The form of the resolution may be "that this meeting be now adjourned". A Statutory Meeting can be adjourned by the majority of the members present, but other meetings may be adjourned by the chairman, if so provided in the articles. A meeting may be adjourned for lack of quorum or the chairman may adjourn it for some time for restoration or order.

5. *Minutes*. Minutes are a record of business transacted at a meeting. Section 193 of the Act requires that every company must keep minutes containing a fair and correct summary of all proceedings of general meetings and Board meetings in books kept for that purpose. The minute books must have their pages consecutively numbered and minutes must be recorded therein within 30 days of meeting. They must be written directly on the numbered pages and typed minutes cannot be pasted to the minute book. Each page of every such book must be initialled or signed and the last page should be dated and signed (i) by the chairman of the Board meeting or of the succeeding meeting, and in case of a general meeting, by the chairman of the same meeting within 30 days of the said meeting or, in the event of the death or inability of that chairman within that period, by a director duly authorised by the Board for the purpose. In case of a meeting of the Board of Directors or its committee, the minutes must also state the names of the directors present at the meeting and the names of director, if any, dissenting from or not concurring in, a resolution passed at a meeting.

According to section 194, minutes of meetings kept in accordance with the provisions of section 193 described above (i.e., duly signed by the chairman in confirmation thereof) shall be evidence of the proceedings recorded therein. The minute books must be kept at the registered office of the company and must be open to inspection by members without charge at least for two hours every day. A member can also demand a copy of the minutes which must be supplied within 7 days of the demand on payment of 37 paise for hundred words or fraction thereof. As explained earlier, minutes may be either Minutes of Narration or Minutes of Resolution.

RESOLUTIONS

A resolution is a motion seconded and approved or adopted by the requisite majority of votes cast at a properly constituted meeting. Thus, when the chairman puts a motion to vote which is passed by the requisite majority, it becomes a resolution. Three kinds of resolutions are recognised by the Companies Act, namely :—Ordinary, Special, and a Resolution requiring Special Notice.

1. *Ordinary Resolution.* A resolution which is passed by a simple majority of votes cast by members is an ordinary resolution. Section 189 defines it as follows : A resolution shall be an ordinary resolution when the votes cast at a general meeting by members entitled to vote in its favour are more than the votes cast against it. The votes may be cast on a show of hands or on a poll in general meeting of which 21 days' clear notice has been given. If some special business has to be transacted by an ordinary resolution, the notice of the meeting must state such special business.

2. *Special Resolution.* A special resolution is one in regard to which the intention to propose it as a special resolution is specifically mentioned in the notice of the general meeting, and is passed by such a majority that the number of votes cast in favour of the resolution is three times the number of votes cast against it either by a show of hands or on a poll in person or by proxy. In other words, three-fourths majority of votes cast is necessary to pass a special resolution at a general meeting of which 21 days' clear notice is given.

Form of Notice Convening an Extraordinary General Meeting to Pass a Special Resolution

..............Co. Ltd.

Notice is hereby given that an Extraordinary General Meeting of the Company will be held at the Registered Office 59, Janpath, New Delhi, on Wednesday, the 18th day of July, 1979, at 3 p.m. to consider and if thought fit to pass the following resolution which will be proposed as a special resolution.

"Resolved that the equity share capital of the company be reduced from Rs. 10 lakhs to Rs. 5 lakhs writing down each fully-paid ten-rupee ordinary share to the value of Rs. 5 fully-paid and that a petition be made to the Court for an order confirming the reduction."

By Order of the Board

....

Dated, the 25th June, 1979. **Secretary**

NOTES 1. The share transfer register of the company will be closed from the 4th July, 1979, to 18th July, 1979, both days inclusive.

2. A member entitled to attend and vote at the meeting is entitled to appoint a proxy to attend and vote instead of himself and a proxy need not be a member of the company.

3. *Explanatory Statement.* At the Extraordinary General Meeting of the Company held on Monday the 2nd April, 1979, a Committee of Investigation was appointed to examine the extent of the loss of capital of the company and make its recommendation. The said committee has, on investigation, found that capital to the extend of Rs. 5 lakhs has been lost and has recommended that equity share be reduced to Rs. 5 lakhs by writing down each ten-rupee fully-paid share to the value of Rs. 5 fully-paid so as to re-introduce reality to the balance sheet.

Matters requiring Special Resolution. Special resolution is necessary in each of the following matters :

1. To alter the provisions of the memorandum so as to change the place of registered office from one state to another, or to change the objects of the company (confirmation by the Company Law Board is also necessary).

2. To change the name of the company (with the approval of the Central Government).

3. To alter or add to the articles of association.

4. To change the name by omitting "Limited" or "Private Limited," the Central Government by licence permitting the company with charitable object to do it.

5. To determine that any portion of the uncalled share capital shall not be called up except for the purpose of winding up.

6. To reduce the share capital (subject to the confirmation of the court).

7. To remove the registered office of the company outside the local limits of the city, town or village in which it is situated.

8. To pay interest out of capital in case of construction of works (with approval of the Central Government).

9. To enable the Central Government to appoint inspectors to investigate the affairs of the company.

10. To determine the remuneration payable to any director including managing director, if articles allow.

11. Enabling a director or other persons specified in S. 314 to hold office of profit under the company or its subsidiary.

12. To alter the memorandum so as to render unlimited the liability of its directors, or manager.

13. To authorise the making of a loan to, or giving of guarantee or providing security in connection with a loan made by any person to, or to any person by, another company under the same management.

14. To obtain an order from the court for the winding up of the company.

15. To wind up the company voluntarily.

16. To confer certain powers on the liquidator under Sections 494, 512 and 517.

17. To direct the manner of disposing of a company's books and papers when the affairs of the company have to be completely wound up in a voluntary liquidation.

18. To authorise the keeping of registers and indexes at a place other than the registered office.

Resolution Requiring Special Notice. The Act provides for a special notice to be given to the company for passing a resolution in respect to certain matters. The object of special notice is to give the members sufficient time to consider the proposed resolution and give the Board an opportunity to indicate their views. Accordingly, any member who wishes to move such a resolution must give a notice in writing at least 14 days before the date of the meeting. On receipt of such a notice the company must give to its members notice of resolution in the same manner as it gives notice of the meeting. In case that is not practicable, the company must give a minimum of 7 days notice to the members through advertisement in a newspaper of appropriate circulation or in any other manner allowed by the articles.

Matters Requiring Special Notice. Special notice is required to pass a resolution relating to the following matters :

1. For a resolution at an annual general meeting appointing an auditor a person other than a retiring auditor.

2. For a resolution at an annual general meeting to provide that the retiring auditor shall not be appointed.

3. For the appointment of a person other than a retiring director as director at any general meeting.

4. For a resolution to remove a director before the expiry of his period of office.

5. For a resolution to appoint another director in place of the other director.

6. For a resolution or a special resolution as required by the articles of association.

Class Meetings. These are the meetings of certain class of shareholder, such as preference shareholders, for transacting business relating to them. There should be a provision in the articles for holding of such meetings and for variation of rights of the class of shares.

Meetings of Debentureholders. When a company issues debentures it provides for the holding of meetings of debentureholders and gives them power to vary the terms of security or to alter their rights in certain cases. All matters connected with the holding, conduct and proceedings of the meetings of the debentureholders are given in the Debenture Bond. The decisions arrived at with the requisite majority are valid and binding upon the minority.

Meetings of Creditors. Sometimes a company, either as a running concern or in the course of winding up, has to make compromises with its creditors. The arrangement with creditors has to be worked out in meetings of creditors. Strictly speaking, meetings of creditors are not company meetings. Sections 391 to 393 of the Act authorise the company to compromise with the creditors with the sanction of the court. The court, on application, may order the holding of the creditors' meeting. If the scheme of arrangement is agreed to by majority in number holding debts to the value of three-fourths of the total value of the debts, the court may sanction the scheme. A certified copy of the court's order is then filed with the Registrar.

For the voluntary winding up of an insolvent company, a meeting of its creditors has to be called on the same day as that of its members or on the next following day for passing the necessary resolution to wind up the company voluntarily. At the same meeting a liquidator is also appointed. Such a voluntary winding up is called creditors' voluntary winding up.

CHAPTER XI

COMPANY OFFICE—ITS ORGANISATION AND MANAGEMENT

The office is an important department in the life of any business, and the study of its functions, organisation and management will repay all those who are concerned with the efficient and economical running of the business. It is the centre to which converge information from each part of the concern, and much useful knowledge goes out of its four walls. Even at the risk of offending the susceptibilities of those engaged purely on the buying and selling sides of a business, it can be stated with some justification that the office is in many respects the brains of a business organisation. Information about supplies and customers, purchases and sales, incomings and outgoings, and in fact about all matters in which the concern is interested is stored in the office, and is available for production and use whenever it is called upon. From this storehouse of facts and figures diverges information upon which the executive takes action in the control of the affairs of the business.

What is an Office ? An office is a place where the control mechanis ms for a business are located : where paper records for the purpose of control, information and efficient operation are prepared, handled, and serviced. Since paper handling activities may be found everywhere, it cannot be said that office work is done in one place within a business organisation. The point, however, at which the greatest concentration of paper work activity is found is popularly referred to as "the office".

As a function, office is concerned with the providing of a service of communication and record, coordination and standardisation. To communicate means to give and receive information, but in between there is usually recording and often arranging of the information in a form suitable to management. The arranging is often accompanied by analysing the information, as in costing and budgetary control.

Basic Functions of the Office. The basic functions of the office may be summarised as follows :

1. *Receiving information,* and the examples of the form in which information is normally received are letters, telephone calls, orders, invoices, and reports on the various activities of the business.
2. *Recording information.* The object of keeping records is to enable information to be made readily available to the management when rquired. Some records are required to be kept by law, but others are kept to meet the needs of the management in controlling the business. The records normally kept in a business office include financial and cost accounts,

orders, progress of work, hours worked by employees, price lists and correspondence.

3. *Arranging and analysing information.* The facts gathered together from different sources have to be arranged in a manner and in the form in which information will be most valuable to management. Examples of arranging information are preparing invoices, costings, statistical statements, financial statements and reports generally.
4. *Giving information.* The office gives out information from its records as and when the management requires it. Examples of information given out by the office are orders for materials, estimates, invoices and statements of account, progress reports, statistical and financial statements, and instructions to departments issued on behalf of the management.
5. *Safeguarding assets.* The duties of the office are not confined merely to receiving, recording, arranging and giving out information. There is in addition a responsibility to observe intelligently the affairs of the business as shown in the records and to warn the management of anything untoward which may take place. For example, in keeping stock records, deficiencies must be reported; in keeping the accounts, any bad or doubtful debts must be brought to the notice of the management before all hope of recovery is past.

Since, in a large organisation, the managing director or the General Manager cannot deal personally with all the communications in and out, he cannot remember all the facts relating to the business, nor can he exercise a detailed supervision over the handling of cash and other assets. The office is there to fulfil these functions on his behalf; the office is the servant of the management. In fact, the position of the office in business is threefold. *First,* it is subordinate to production or whatever the main purpose of the business happens to be. *Secondly,* it is complementary, and *thirdly,* it is controlling; e.g., production control, financial control and budgetary control.

Another very important function of the office is to aid management bring about coordination. In present-day industry and commerce there is a high degree of specialisation. It often requires hundreds of different firms to complete the production and distribution of a single article. Hand in hand with specialisation comes the need for proper co-ordination of individuals, departments, and firms so that they may work as a balanced team. This coordination is the task of management, and the decisions that the management makes must be based upon a proper knowledge of facts. The provision of those facts is one of the most important functions of the office, and a very real and essential contribution to production.

In order to perform its task of communication and controlling the office must maintain adequate and up-to-date records, such as factory records, personnel records, Board of Directors' records, sales records, finance records and so on. All these and other records are an integral part of the operations of an organisation and must be planned, organised and controlled to administer a business effectively. The office does this and many more things. It is indeed a paper-processing and memory centre for all departments of a business organisation, for office executives and clerical staff work together to accumulate facts and figures. Policies and ideas are recorded. Communication with suppliers, customers and technicians are prepared. Production records are accumulated. Market analyses, cost analyses and inventories are developed. An office houses all these records and makes them available when required by the management to make decisions. It is thus a control centre for a business.

Because all business transactions are presented by paper records or eventually result in paper records, the office becomes a nerve or brain centre for a business. The paper-records and reports are the tools used by the management to direct the activities of the business just as machines and appliances are the tools used by labour to manufacture a product.

Although paper work is extremely important in business and industry and office work is often described as paper work, there are many non-paper activities that are office work, such as telephone communications, receptionist activities and conferences. Office work therefore is not only paper handling but rather information handling. The office manager is functionally the "information officer".

It follows that the functions of the office and the office manager are specialised activities, whatever may be the main technical purpose served. A brief account of these functions will follow the problem of organisation of the office.

Organisation. Whenever a group of people work together, some kind of planned organisation is necessary. Relationships have to be established and identified. It has to be decided who does what, who reports to whom, who decides what should be done.

The absence of proper organisation brings undesirable results. Certain functions become dominant at the expense of others, because of the aggressiveness of a particular individual. As relationships are not clear, it leads to confusion and conflicts of authority. Individuals work as individuals, and not as members of a co-operative team. Activities which should be integrated or centralised are spread out and not supervised properly. Some individuals are overworked and others remain idle. Delays, errors and losses occur, expenses increase, profits decline and service to customers and to other departments of the business is poor. Individual initiative is lost because some people become confused and lose interest. They are the victims of disorganisation. A well-organised office will overcome all these shortcomings.

Centralisation or Decentralisation. The primary problem in office organisation is the decision regarding centralisation and how much of it should be there. In other words, the decision has to be made : how much should the office activities be brought under the direct control of the office manager. Centralisation is of two types : physical and functional. Complete physical centralisation of office activities would mean that all paper work would be done in one place. This is not possible, especially in large concerns. Complete decentralisation, on the other hand, would mean that it is performed by the department or function that originates. This arrangement results in much duplication and is costly.

Functional centralisation brings similar activities under the direction or supervision of one individual and his staff but leaves physical manifestation of the activity where it originates. For example, centralised functional control of office work within an enterprise would leave files at points of origin but make office management responsible for selecting and training filing clerks, for standardising equipment and procedures and for developing production standards. Functional centralisation of office work gives the office manager full responsibility for office work wherever it is done. Under such an organisational plan, it is possible to decrease office costs and increase office services by bringing the management of office work into each area where office work is done.[1]

Activities of the Office and of the Office Manager

The field of activities supervised by the office manager varies considerably with different companies, but in general he undertakes to touch upon a number of inter-related divisions of work in his office such as office accommodation and layout, office environment, office furniture and equipment, stationery and forms, office staff and office services.

The scope of modern office practices and management comprises the job of planning the office work and carrying out plans, together with effective control. The illustration gives a fairly comprehensive picture of the scope of office work as found in the average sized office today. The office manager has to plan the system of work, the layout and accommodation, and must take up the organisation of the personnel with skill. He should see to it that all the office services are performed most effectively and economically. Office management implements the performance of all other functions of a business; hence, it is a service and facilitating activity.

Office accommodation and layout. For the optimum use of the office work of the clerical force, the accommodation must be adequate. The layout of the office should be such that time and energy are not expended in overcoming unnecessary obstructions. There should be, as far as possible, straight line floor of work. The site must be carefully chosen so that the office is easily accessible, but not a thoroughfare for people working in other departments. Reasonably close proximity to Post Office, banking, transport and other services is also important. A large room properly planned is better than a number of small private rooms between which communication is difficult, though separate rooms should be provided for executives for secrecy.

Office environment. The office must be properly ventilated and each

1. Hicks and Place: *Office Management*, p. 52.

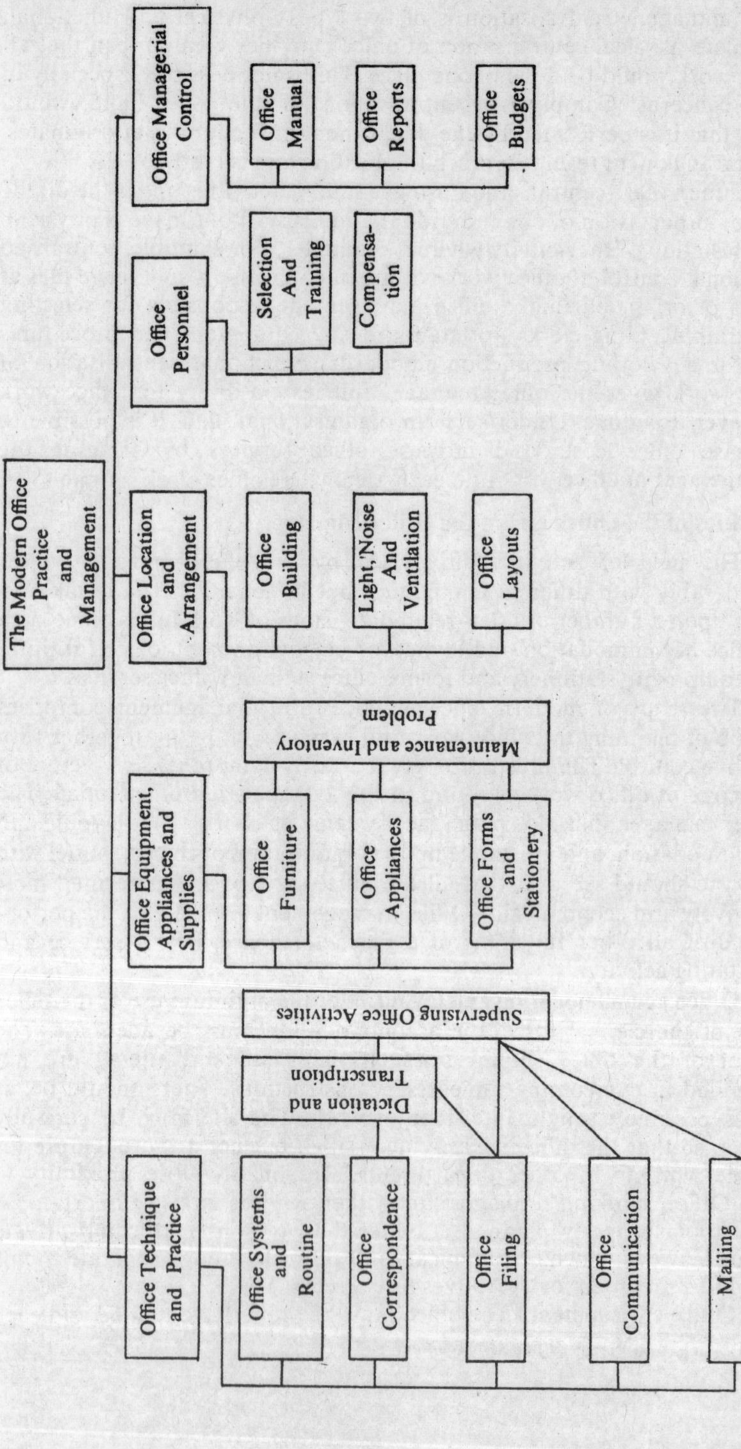
The Modern Office Practice and Management
Office Managerial Control
Office Manual
Office Reports
Office Budgets
Office Personnel
Selection And Training
Compensation
Office Location and Arrangement
Office Building
Light, Noise And Ventilation
Office Layouts
Office Equipment, Appliances and Supplies
Office Furniture
Office Appliances
Office Forms and Stationery
Maintenance and Inventory Problem
Office Technique and Practice
Office Systems and Routine
Office Correspondence
Office Filing
Office Communication
Mailing Activities
Dictation and Transcription
Supervising Office Activities

clerk must have adequate space, adequate light, preferably coming from his left hand downwards on to his work. Windows should be high, the walls should have light coloured lime washing or distemper. If artificial light is used, it should be sufficient, diffused and without glare. Too much noise produces tension, fatigue and difficulty of concentration. Efforts should be made to reduce noise. In connection with office lighting, special attention should be given to office equipment. For example, filing systems should not use cards with shiny surfaces.

Office furniture and equipment. Just as layout, ventilation and illumination have an important bearing on the health and efficiency of the clerical staff, so is there a close relation between furnishing of the office and the welfare of the staff. The selection of furniture deserves careful consideration. Broadly speaking, an office requires three classes. of furniture : (i) executive furniture; (ii) special purpose furniture; and (iii) clerical furniture. Of these the last group, because of its more regular and constant use by a large number of people, is vastly the most important. In India, however, it receives the least attention.

The executive and special purpose furniture is selected largely for its appearance. The clerical furniture should be standardised regarding material, finish, height, size and appearance. Face-to-face desks for clerks are undesirable partly on hygienic grounds, partly because they encourage conversation. Commensurate with the consideration of economy, the four major elements should be kept in mind : adaptability, simplicity, durability, and good taste.

Stationery and forms. Stationery and forms are effective tools of business to impress customers, simplify, speed up, and control work and thereby reduce costs. Stationery meant to go out of the business house must be of superior quality and well printed. Its purpose is two-fold : a means of communication and an instrument to impress customers. Forms, to be effective tools, must be properly designed from the point of view of accomplishing the purposes set, with a minimum of effort and the most economical (not cheap) materials. Sizes, rulings and types of forms should be standardised. Since properly designed form is convenient to use, easy to handle, and eliminates waste, the following points should be kept in mind while preparing a form, namely :—function, need, use, identification, instructions, spacing, colour, size, paper, filing and type faces.

Office Staff. An office is as effective as the people who work in it. The problem therefore, is to get the best possible person for each office job. By "best" is meant an employee who (i) wants and likes to work in an office; (ii) has interest, initiative and drive; (iii) is trained for office work; (iv) has good health; (v) gets along with people; (vi) has the special qualifications and attitudes needed for the job. The special qualifications of the various members will depend upon the nature of the work required to be done by a particular employee. The different type of tests used for the selection are proficiency tests, such as typewriting, shorthand, or book-keeping tests, and capacity test, including general adaptability tests and special tests. Academic qualifications are always taken into consideration.

Office Services

The principal purpose of office services is to help other departments to do their work well. Rendering of efficient and economical office services is therefore of extreme importance to every organisation. If mail is not delivered promptly to the various departments and executives, the work is delayed. If a good tactful letter does not go out of the company, its goodwill suffers. If letters and reports cannot be found in the files, costly delays on loss of business may result. Many customers judge a business by its telephone service, reception service, correspondence practices, and similar office activities because they are the major contacts the customers have with a business. The office manager should so organise, direct and control office activities that they act as lubricants to the smooth running of the entire organisation. All these office services may be grouped as follows :

1. Office Communication Service :
   (a) Correspondence;
   (b) Other means of communication, e.g., telephone.
2. Maintenance of Records, e.g., accounts, filing, etc.
3. Machines and Office Appliances.

Office Communications. Communication is one of the fundamental functions of the office and a process essential to all forms of business. It is, as we have seen earlier, the process of conveying information from one person to another through the post, by telephone, by messenger service, or by other means. The majority of business communications are received or originated by the office in the course of the day. The office manager has, therefore, the responsibility of maintaining a communication service as part of the office organisation. The selection of the means to be used is also important and should not be left to the junior clerk to decide, for instance, whether a letter should be sent by registered post instead of ordinary mail.

In arriving at a decision as to means of communication to be used in any circumstances, there are seven major factors to be considered[1]—

1. *Speed.* How soon after despatch must the communication reach the person for whom it is intended ?

2. *Accuracy.* Will the information be received accurately ? For instance, figures spoken on the telephone may be misheard.

3. *Safety.* What is the risk of losing the communication in transit ? If an important legal document is to be sent through the post, it may be prudent to send it by registered post.

4. *Secrecy.* Where secrecy is important, postcard should not be sent. Instead letters in covers will preserve secrecy.

5. *Record.* Written communication will be necessary where a record of the same has to be kept.

---

1. Mills and Standingford, *Office Organisation and Method*, p. 68.

6. *Impression.* Is the communication required to be in a form so as to produce a favourable reaction on the part of the person receiving it ?

7. *Cost.* In assessing the cost of any means of communication, all elements must be taken into consideration.

All communication systems may be divided into (1) written, (2) oral, and (3) mechanical. Written communication comprises letters by post and messenger service, postcards, telegrams, etc. Oral, including external telephone systems and internal telephone systems (and radio telephone service). Mechanical communication comprises teleprinter (and Telex), facsimile telegraphy, pneumatic tube, television.

Written Communication. Written communications may take the form of individually written letters, memoranda or reports, or may be formalised as in the case of orders, invoices or stereotyped letters. The majority of written messages are sent or received through the post and are termed correspondence.

Control of correspondence. In large offices, a central mail office or department is set up, through which incoming, outgoing and inter-office mail flows. The mail department should be organised and manned to ensure promptness, speed and accuracy. Responsibility for the mail function must be fixed. This is necessary in a small company as in a large one. As far as possible the mail rooms should be located in a central place. Mail procedures should concern both incoming and outgoing mail.

Incoming mail. Incoming mail starts most of the daily office activities and hence it is important that it be delivered promptly to the proper departments, desks and persons. Assuming there is a central mail office, the mail will be received there or picked up at the post office either at the delivery counter or from the Post Box, if the company has hired one. The mail is usually rough-sorted by class, important versus unimportant, or personal versus company.

It is opened; envelopes are checked to see that all contents have been removed and enclosures are pinned or stapled to the proper correspondence. Generally, mail addressed to specific individuals is not opened. Opened mail is sorted by content : orders, cheques, requests for information, credit information, sales information, etc. The officer incharge of the mail will indicate on each letter the section or person who has to attend to it so that, after being receipted, it should be sent to him. Letters containing remittances are marked with the amount received. The mail is then recorded in an Inward Letter Book, making brief notes of the date, the sender and the subject. Each letter is then rubber-stamped showing the date of receipt and its number on the Receipt Book is noted thereon. Thereafter, the mail is distributed by peon to the indicated sections or persons.

Outgoing mail. Outgoing mail comprises letters written during the day and business papers to be sent to customers and suppliers or to branch offices. Outgoing letters require great care, as they are the chief contacts with customers and suppliers. Letters represent the business and they can either build or destroy goodwill. Letters characterise a company as service oriented or careless, as progressive or out-of-date. A letter is really a salesman. It is a substitute for face-to-face conversation. Often it is the sole means of communicating with and impressing a customer or a creditor. A letter should, therefore, receive the utmost care before it leaves the office. In form and content the letter should convey impression of neatness, courtesy and friendliness. It must convey its message in simple, clear and precise language. Equally important with form and content is control and coordination. For example, one employee writes an aggressive sales letter to a customer, and another employee writes an antagonising collection letter to the same customer, the effect is bound to be harmful to the business.

When the correspondence is complete, it should be sent to the mailing office for despatch. The despatch clerk enters each letter in the despatch register, numbers it and hands it out to the mailing clerk. The copy of the letter duly numbered is sent to the filing department. When enclosures are included, it is essential to enclose all matters and notes made at the bottom left hand corner of the letter. Transparent and window envelopes are becoming very popular, as they are useful time-savers and also a check against letters being put into wrong envelopes. Routine mail to the same company or a branch is grouped and often accumulated for one mailing. This saves postage, cuts down on the job of addressing envelopes, and keeps items together. The mail, after it is properly stamped, is posted before the last clearance for the day.

Telegram is a fast, accurate and dependable means of written communication. Telegrams compel attention, assure a careful reading, and get quick action.

Oral Communication. Business uses the telephone much more than it uses the letters and telegrams. This enormous utilisation makes it necessary for employees in business organisation to understand how to use the telephone most effectively. As the voice makes all the difference in creating an impression on the listener on the other side of the line, it is but necessary to cultivate a 'voice with a smile'—the one which is pleasing, helpful, polite and distinct.

MAINTENANCE OF RECORDS

An office is a paper-processing and memory centre for all departments of a business concern. "Office" accumulates facts and figures. In the office will be found contracts, invoices, letters, reports, cheques, vouchers, statistics, costings, personnel reports, tax records, price lists, catalogues, and so on, and they should all be kept in the most convenient way, so that they can be located when required. This is done by "filing".

Filing

It has been said that the keystone of office organisation is the maintenance of comprehensive, simple, and efficient filing systems.

Nothing causes more chaos in an office than bad equipment and out-of-date systems, and when filing is treated as an unimportant task and entrusted to junior clerks. Modern records management involves not only filing, but also indexing, central filing, records retention and follow-up. We will start with filing.

Filing may be defined as the systematic arrangement of keeping business correspondence and records so that these may be found and delivered quickly when needed for reference in the future. It is an act of providing temporary or permanent storage space for letters and records so that they can be located easily and quickly when they are wanted.

Functions of filing. Filing performs four major functions, namely :—

1. It is a form of record keeping. The business document is history. It is evidence of what has taken place and be legal proof should occasion arise to submit it.

2. Filing performs the library function, especially in large companies under a centralised system. In addition to filing correspondence and records for its own business, the filing department may collect and preserve information relating to outside concerns but of prime importance to the company.

3. By preserving records of previous decisions, filing often aids business executives in the determination of business policies.

4. The final function of filing is to preserve in an orderly manner the important records of the progress of a business.

Advantages of good filing system. The following advantages follow from the above-mentioned functions of filing :

1. Correspondence can be handled systematically leading to the creation of goodwill.
2. It serves the purpose of ready reference. Very often customers give only the reference number of a previous letter, which can be traced if filing system is good.
3. It provides evidence in case of any dispute that may arise in the future.
4. Old files may give clue to opportunities for business by revealing the names of interested customers. They may also inform of the activities of competitors.
5. Filed material relating to past decisions may help in policy formulation in the future.
6. Decision-making is facilitated by good filing system.

Essentials of a Good Filing System. A good filing system is one that is adapted to the business, that can be depended upon for accuracy, and that will produce at once information required. Of course, there is no universal *best* system of filing. An office manager must analyse the problem of his own office, and adopt a filing system to suit his requirements. The basic requirements, or essential features or characteristics of a good filing system are as follows :

(a) *Compactness.* Space must not be taken up unnecessarily, for it is valuable. Much of the modern filing equipment is designed to assist this object.

(b) *Accessibility.* The records filed must be readily accessible so that they can be produced promptly when required.

(c) *Simplicity.* Whatever system is adopted it should be simple to understand and simple to operate. The classification chosen must not be liable to confuse or delay reference.

(d) *Economy.* The filing system should be economical as regards labour, consumable equipment and overhead. In other words, it should not be excessive in cost, either to install or to operate.

(e) *Suitability.* The system must be one which fits in with the requirements of the firm for which it is chosen; a centralised filing system might be just right for one firm, but entirely unsuitable for another.

(f) *Safety.* As the primary object of filing is to preserve letters and documents, the system should include some locking or other device to prevent unauthorised persons from tampering with them. The documents should also be protected against fire, rats, white ants, etc.

(g) *Protection* against dirt and dust should also be provided for.

(h) *Flexibility.* The system must be capable of being easily expanded with the expansion of the work of the concern.

(i) *Elasticity and Adaptability.* It must be sufficiently adaptable to meet changing circumstances and sufficiently elastic to cope with extension of the business.

(j) *Serviceability.* The system should be such that letters can be filed rapidly and can be traced and picked up speedily when required.

(k) *Ample* space should be provided, not only for the general filing system but also for the storage of transfer binders.

(l) *Classification.* The most suitable method of classification should be employed, without too many miscellaneous files. Too much bulk must be avoided.

The foregoing principles of filing should be followed as faithfully as possible, if it is desired to avoid filing on the principle of the "treasure hunt" game. Furthermore, the equipment must be built to preserve records as long as they are required. A good system of filing is no good without a good equipment. There are a number of different ways of filing, but before we deal with them, let us say a word with regard to the decision whether there should be central or departmental filing.

Central v. Departmental Filing

The manager has to decide whether there is to be central or departmental filing, or there is to be a compromise between the two. Before we compare the relative advantages of the two methods, it is well to bear in mind that "centralisation" may be physical concentration of all files and filing equipment in one central department, or it may mean control exercised from one central point while the files are allowed to be retained in different departments. In making the comparison, the former meaning has been adopted.

Advantages of Central Filing. The following advantages are claimed for central filing :

(a) *Control* is exercised more effectively, because responsibility is fixed and closer supervision is possible within the department.

(b) *Specialisation.* As the staff of the central department are able to specialise, they become more proficient in their work.

(c) *Uniformity of equipment* and of filing procedures is possible.

(d) *Duplication is eliminated,* as only one copy of each document is required for the central file.

(e) *Economy.* Various economies are effected in operating costs, equipment, space and overheads.

Disadvantages. The following are some of the criticisms of central filing :

(a) *Delay* in obtaining the required document or folder from the central department because of the distance involved or the frustrating rules of procedure to be followed.

(b) *Unsuitable classification.* The standard classification used by the central department may be entirely unsuitable for the documents received for filing from certain departments; e.g., correspondence from the sales department might be more suitably filed by *area* classification, whereas the central department's standard classification is an alphabetical one.

(c) *A "dead letter" repository.* The department often tends to become a repository for all the unwanted and unnecessary documents of all other departments. It is usually easier to pass *all* documents to the central department than to make a selection, even assuming that were permissible.

Advantages of departmental filing. The following are some of the advantages of departmental filing :

(a) *Convenience.* As each department has its own independent filing system—perhaps only a single filing cabinet—the staff have easy access to the documents.

(b) *Saving of time,* as there is no need to seek documents or folders from a central department.

(c) *Appropriate system and classification.* The filing system and classification adopted is the one best suited for each department.

Disadvantages of departmental filing. The departmental system of filing suffers from the following shortcomings :

(a) *Duplication of equipment.* As each department has its own filing cabinets, there is considerable duplication. This results in increased capital cost and waste of space. Moreover, as the filing equipment may vary from one department to another, the economies of bulk purchase cannot be effected.

(b) *Time is wasted* in each department by staff engaged in filing. In many cases, people are taken from more responsible work to attend to departmental filing for which they have no training.

(c) *Duplication of documents* often occurs, as several departments require copies of outgoing letters for their respective files, often quite unnecessarily.

Compromise. In many cases, a compromise may be quite profitable. A central filing department is used for all documents of a general nature, whilst other documents will be filed in the departments with which they are specially identifiable. But care should be taken to see that the central filing department does not become the "grave-yard" for dead letters.

Classification of Files

For quick and accurate location, the files are classified and sub-classified according to different methods. Although there are numerous methods of classification in use, each office adopts the particular one suitable for its own purposes. The most commonly used methods are discussed below.

Alphabetical. This method is most widely used in business offices for filing correspondence. It is suitable for both small and large offices and is of great significance where names of correspondents are important. Under this method, each folder bears the name of a correspondent. These folders are arranged in the strict alphabetical order of the surnames of the customers. Thus all folders of customers whose surnames begin with 'A' are placed together in one group, and those beginning with 'B' in another group and so on. In the simplest cases there will be 26 folders for the 26 letters of the alphabet. Where there are large number of names beginning with the same letter, each letter is again sub-divided into groups. In the sub-division also strict alphabetical order is followed.

Suppose there are a large number of names beginning with 'A', a strict Alphabetical order will be followed in the subsequent letters contained in the name. For example,

Ab, Ac.........Az.........Second letter;

Abb, Abc.........Abz.........Third letter;

Abb, Abbc, Abbd.........Abbz.........Fourth letter.

This is the simplest method and can be understood by every one, as most people are familiar with the arrangement followed in dictionaries. It is complete in itself and needs no index. It can be easily applied. It can be adapted to changes. It can be expanded up to a limit to accommodate more names. Beyond that limit it has to take the help of numerical method.

Numerical classification. Under this system of classification each customer is allotted a number. All papers relating to a particular customer or supplier or subject are placed in one folder bearing his distinctive number. These folders are arranged in the cabinet in the numerical sequence and guide cards are used to divide them suitably into groups of 10, 20, 30, etc. Thus, if a customer is allotted the number 17, all papers connected with him will be found in folder number 17. It is quite easy to locate this folder in the appropriate cabinet by the guide card.

This system is also extremely simple and easily understood by all. It is very useful, because it avoids the confusion which might arise when correspondents have the same, or nearly the same name. Numbered files can be easily located and less likely to be disarranged. The folder number can be used as a part of the reference number in correspondence, It automatically reveals certain useful information such as the total number of customers of the firm. It can be used for all kinds of papers and documents. The number of folders can be expanded indefinitely. It has one drawback. A numerical file can be used only with a separate index, for no filing clerk can remember every customer's or supplier's number. Accordingly, card index has to be used with this system of classification.

Alphabetic-Numerical System. This is a combination of the two systems, as its name suggests. Its special advantage lies in the fact that, while it has the exactness of the numerical system, it does not require a separate card index. Under this system the customer or subject folders are arranged in alphabetical groups. Within each group the individual folders are arranged numerically. Coloured tabs or guide cards are used to sub-divide the folders into groups to facilitate their speedy location.

Suppose all customers files are arranged alphabetically and the first alphabetic group is Aa-Ag. The folders of Ace Bros. and Agrawal Sons Ltd. are first and second in order within this group. The folder of Ace Bros. will bear the number A/1 and of Agrawal Sons Ltd. A/2 and so on.

This system enjoys all the advantages of the alphabetical and numerical methods. It is generally used by banks for filing specimen signatures of customers. It is also used by libraries and business offices for filing invoices, etc.

Geographical classification. This system is particularly useful in those lines of business where the territory or area, over which the activities of the firm are spread, is of paramount importance. Mail order houses, departmental stores, business houses with large number of branches, banks, advertising agencies usually conduct their operations over a wide area. The files are arranged according to geographical areas served, rather than by names of customers or subjects. The areas are divided into State, city or town.

Subject system. The subject system is adopted in offices, where the subject or content of a letter is more important than the name of the correspondent. All correspondence or records are filed together by certain subjects alphabetically arranged. Officers, contractors, lawyers, architects, local bodies and educational institutions usually adopt this method.

Chronological Order. The documents are put into a suitable container in the order of the date which they bear; e.g., newspapers, shipping lists, current prices, market reports, etc. It is a useful system if dates are known. It is good for orerall classification, e.g., correspondence in separate years.

FILING METHODS AND EQUIPMENT

The actual filing work needs proper equipment, trained personnel and suitable method. The equipment should be built to preserve records permanently, and it should be of uniform standard and interchangeable. For a good system of filing is no good without a good equipment. There are several methods of filing, some old and others modern, each having its merits and shortcomings.

Old Methods of filing. The old methods of filing which are still used in small business houses are as follows :

(a) *Guard book.* Letters and documents are held together by metal holders or are pasted in bound books in chronological order. The method is cumbersome and time consuming, and has been discarded in offices of size.

(b) *Wire or spike file.* A spike or wire is fixed to a small wooden stand which may be placed on the desk or table or hung on the wall. Letters, vouchers and all other papers are threaded into the metal spike as they are received. The system is simple and cheap. But reference is very difficult, because if a paper is right at the bottom, all the top papers have to be removed. The papers also collect dust and fade away through exposure.

(c) *Pigeon-hole or docket system.* The system requires a cabinet containing 24 compartments resembling pigeon-holes. The nest of pigeon-holes are labelled alphabetically, the last hole bearing the label 'X', 'Y' and 'Z'. All papers are sorted, folded and tied in neat bundles. Before putting the bundles in the appropriate holes they are docketed. Docketing refers to the writing on the outer top of each letter (i) the name of the correspondent, (ii) his place of residence, (iii) date of letter, and (iv) a brief note of its subject. The system is obviously crude and unsuitable for modern offices, and has been discarded. Professional and small commercial houses still use it; and the Post Office uses it for sorting letters.

(d) *Box file.* Card-board boxes, eight to ten cms. deep, are also used in some offices, especially for temporary storage. The boxes are fitted with spring clips to hold papers which having been sorted out, are placed under the clip. Although each document must be punched prior to filing, and is, therefore, time-wasting, the documents remain secured.

(e) *Press copy book.* This book is used in offices where modern methods are also followed. This is because the press copy book affords a useful evidence of the fact that a particular letter was written on a particular day in the regular course of business. All letters which are sent out are copied in this book. In the case of large firm press copy may be divided either on alphabetical or geographical basis. Thus, one press copy book may record letters written to persons whose surnames begin with letters A to E, others F to J, and so on. When the number of letters is not large and correspondents are scattered over different parts the press copy may be kept on geographical basis. An index has to be attached to each copy book.

Modern Methods of Filing. To meet the requirements of large offices, new and improved methods of filing have been devised. Basically, however, there are two systems : *Flat or Horizontal* and *Vertical.* Some of the features of each system are considered below :

(a) *Flat or Horizontal Filing.* In its earlier form, correspondence and other documents are filed in shallow trays or drawers and are held in position by means of springs or prongs. The trays or drawers may be wooden, steel or wire mesh. In its improved form covers of cardboard or thick paper are made with two metal hinges which are passed into the holes punched in the letters to be filed. Letters relating to a customer or subject are filed in one file in the order in which they are received or written. The files are arranged one on top of the other in a cupboard or in drawers of a filing cabinet. The files are numbered and a proper index is kept so that in case of need files are easily traced. The movement of the file from one person to another is recorded on a thick sheet of paper which stays in place of the file that has gone out of the cabinet.

The pilot or lever-arch files. These files are either made of card-boards or have filing cabinets. The cardboard type is opened by a lever, and "Era" file is an example. Of the cabinet type "Shannon" is the best known system. Where a letter is to be filed in a cardboard type, the lever is moved upwards which opens the springs or metal arches. If papers have to be inserted in the middle of those already on the file, the papers on the top of the file can be passed over the arches on to the standard at the back; then the arches are turned sideways, the new papers are placed on the front spikes, and the arches are turned back into position and the top part of the pile of letters is passed back over the arch into its proper position. Removal of any papers can be done in similar fashion. The Shannon system consists of a cabinet containing from four to sixty-four compartments or drawers. Each drawer contains index sheets below which letters are filed. From the bottom of the drawer project two spikes and the arches. The method of filing is the same as explained above.

Advantages of horizontal method of filing. For the small business particularly, it has possible advantages :

(i) *Simplicity.* The method of filing is simple and there are easy access to the documents.

(ii) *Safety.* There is very little risk of losing or mislaying the documents filed, as they can be referred to without being removed from the file.

(iii) *Compactness.* The letters cannot get out of order, as they are fixed on the arch, each in its place. Even if the file drawer is inverted or accidentally dropped, there is no danger of the letters getting mixed up, as the arches keep them in position.

Disadvantages. For the large business the system is usually impracticable for the following reasons :

(i) *Space is Wasted.* The system is generally wasteful of space as compared with vertical system.

(ii) *Lacks flexibility.* The system does not allow for expansion. There may be trouble in re-organising the cabinet if the drawers get filled with letters through increased volume of correspondence.

(iii) *Reference is difficult.* Unless a complete tray or drawer is kept for each classification, a "visible" system of indexing cannot be used.

(iv) *Relative slowness.* There is relative slowness in getting access to and removing a set of correspondence because the papers are filed over each other.

(b) *Vertical or Upright System of Filing.* To eliminate the limitations of horizontal filing system, vertical files are maintained by the use of folders which keep the papers in an upright position in alphabetical or numerical order in suitably designed drawers in cabinets. The folder is a folded sheet of heavy manilla paper with projecting tabs on the back fold. The tabs are used for writing the name, letter or number. The correspondence relating to each customer is put into separate folder. The folders are placed in drawers in the standing or upright position. Each drawer is fitted with an "expander" which slides backward or forward in the drawer and holds up the folders, however few or many the drawer may contain. A set of index or guide cards made of heavy manilla paper with projecting tabs divides the folders into sections. When a particular folder is removed from a drawer for reference, a memorandum card with the word "Out" printed on its tab is kept in place on the folder. The name of the person to whom the folder is sent is noted on the card and also the date.

Advantages of Vertical filing. Vertical filing is now almost universally adopted in modern offices because of its many advantages. Indeed, this method is considered as the best of all filling systems. Its principal advantages are as follows :

(i) *Easy accessibility.* The papers are kept in separate folders and are therefore easily accessible without waste of time. Even individual letters can be easily inserted or removed.

(ii) *Speed of location* is possible, as the system combines admirably with the visible system of indexing; that is, each folder is identified on a paper or visible plastic strip attached to the upper edge of the folder—or to the *outer* edge of the folder suspended in a lateral filing cabinet.

(iii) *Flexibility.* The system is flexible and easily extendable. The number of folders can be easily expanded to any limit within a drawer.

(iv) *Economy of space.* The application of vertical filing is comparatively economical of space, particularly when used in lateral (up-right) cabinets. One vertical drawer can hold a large number of folders.

(v) *Highly adaptable.* It is easily adaptable to several varieties of classification. Vertical filing has been adapted to filing cabinets of many different types—the steel (or wooden) cabinet with pull-out drawers, the lateral (upright) cabinet of later date, and in recent years, various "circular", mechanical filing equipments.

(vi) *Safety.* The papers are kept safe from dust and insects and secure from thieves as the drawers are locked.

(vii) *Less costly.* It is less costly as the folders are quite inexpensive.

INDEXING

An index is anything that "indicates" or "points out". Indexing is thus an important aid to filing. The principal purpose of an index is to facilitate the location of the requisite file. The main types of indexes are—

(1) Ordinary Page Index; (2) Vowel Index; (3) Card Index; (4) Visible Card Index.

1. *Ordinary Page Index.* It consists of a set of pages, each bearing one letter of the alphabet. Each page consists of a list of all the correspondents whose names begin with the letter to which that sheet is allotted. For example, all names beginning with 'A', such as Amar Chand, Anant Ram, Arshad Ahmed, Aziz Ali will be written on the first page which bears the letter 'A'. The page or folder number where correspondence relating to a particular correspondent appears is written against his name. The ordinary page index may be (i) fixed, i.e., bound in the front of a book, such as a letter book or ledger; (ii) it may be loose, i.e., bound as a separate volume, or when used with a loose leaf ledger, inserted in the ledger before each alphabetical section; (iii) it may be extended, i.e., bound in the book, but so arranged as to open outside the area of the book; (iv) it may be self-indexing, i.e., where the leaves of the book are cut to receive the indicative letter.

2. *Vowel Index.* The vowel index is an extension of the ordinary page index, in which each page is divided into six columns, headed A, E, I, O, U and Y, respectively. Each letter of the alphabet will have those vowels attached to it. For example, letter 'A' is subdivided into A, Ae, Ai, Ao, Au, Ay and a separate page is allotted to each subdivision. The names of the correspondents are entered on one page or other according to the letter with which his name begins and the first vowels in his name. This type is used when it is required to record many names, and when only one reference is required in respect of each.

The disadvantages of a page index are :

(i) the names are entered on each page in the order in which they first occur;

(ii) names need to be deleted as they cease to be of interest; and

(iii) there may not be sufficient room to add all new names, which may require the constant re-writing of the index.

3. *Card Index.* To overcome these difficulties, the loose or vertical card index was introduced. It is an improvement on the simple indexing system. It has been developed so scientifically that it can be used for recording correspondence, documents, books, quotations, stocks or stores, employees, in fact for anything. There are various ways of keeping card indexes; but the best of them is to have the cards in cabinets made

specially for the purpose. Each cabinet has a rod running from end of the drawer to the other for holding cards in their places. A card is used for each correspondent and on it are written the name, address and the number of folder, if index is used as an adjunct to the vertical filing, as already explained. If it is meant for subject index, then the subject and the number of the folder are written on the card. For facilitating the work of tracing a name card, 'guides' with the alphabetical letter are provided in the drawers. They subdivide the cards into suitable groups.

Advantages of Card Index. The card index system has many advantages, the principal of them being—

1. *Adaptability.* The cards can be arranged in any order, and the order can be changed at will. For instance, simple alphabetical order can be changed into a geographical order by re-arranging the cards.

2. *Flexibility.* It has great flexibility. The number of cards can be increased or decreased as desired. New cards can be inserted without disturbing the continuity of the arrangement. Similarly, when a customer ceases to be a customer, his card can be taken out and discarded or put into an out-of-date drawer as dead card.

3. *Accessibility.* The cards wanted for reference can be taken out without in any way holding up the work of recording of information as other cards are left behind.

4. *Facility of location.* It facilitates location of any name or subject with the minimum of searching, as the cards are arranged in alphabetical order.

5. *Capacity for expansion.* The system has an unlimited capacity for expansion, as the number of drawers can be increased as desired.

6. *Less costly.* In a big business house card indexing is cheaper than ordinary indexing as the expenses of having a bound book and its occasional renewal, with addition to existing correspondents, are saved or avoided.

7. *Neatness.* The system always remains neat and tidy. In the simple system, new names are unsystematically added and old ones cancelled so that there are additions, alterations and erasions everywhere. This is not so in card indexing.

8. *Suitable for any purpose.* The system can be adopted for any purpose. It can be used not only for indexing files, but also for maintaining particulars of customers, suppliers, employees, contracts, purchases or sales information and so on.

9. *Ease of reference.* For special purposes coloured cards can be used to facilitate easy classification of the customers or subjects into sub-groups. It avoids the necessity of keeping separate records for the purpose. Also, any number of persons can use the index at the same time.

Disadvantages. The card indexing has the following drawbacks :

1. If a card is misplaced, it is very difficult to trace it.

2. There is a danger of any card or cards being destroyed or mutilated, or substituted.

3. At any particular time only one card can be seen, so that several cards have to be consulted before the desired card can be handled.

4. It can be afforded only by large concerns because the equipment is very costly.

4 *Visible Card Index.* One of the defects of the card system is that a large number of cards cannot be seen at one glance. This defect is removed by the alternative method known as visible indexing. In this method the cards are held flat in transparent covers in a shallow metal tray. Each card overlaps its neigbour in such a way that a narrow strip at the bottom containing the name or title remains visible all the time. Each tray contains about 50 cards and the names or titles on all the cards are simultaneously visible, when the tray is pulled out. The trays may be fitted horizontally into cabinets or attached vertically to metal stands. A steel cabinet may contain six to twelve such trays. The arrangement or classification of the cards follows the usual alphabetical, numerical or mixed orders. Entries can be made in the cards without removing them from the tray.

Advantages. The main advantages of visible indexing are :

1. *Compactness.* It is very compact. The number of cards that can be kept in a tray is much larger than in other types of indexing.

2. *Speed.* Speedy reference is possible as the names of customers or subjects are all visible. Posting of cards is also very speedy. All this saves time.

3. *Control.* It is an aid to control. The management can control purchases, sales, production, or personnel matters by obtaining speedy and ready information.

4. *Simplicity.* It helps listing of customers or subjects as a photograph of the tray can provide a ready list with minimum effort and expense.

OFFICE MACHINES AND LABOUR-SAVING DEVICES

Office machines are being used more and more in modern offices, because they offer several benefits.

Advantages. Office machines and mechanical devices offer the following advantages :

1. First of all, they save labour and cost due to increased productivity and greater efficiency.

2. Secondly, they save time by increased productivity.

3. Thirdly, they promote accuracy in all types of work and particularly in calculations and statistical work.

4. Fourthly, they relieve monotony, by removing manual drudgery. To that extent machinery improves morale.

5. Fifthly, they lessen the chance of fraud. Sometimes machines will not save time or labour, but their intrinsic value is in lessening the opportunity to perpetrate fraud on the organisation. A good example is a cheque writing machine.

6. Finally, they make far better and quicker service and provision of faster information.

In addition to these, there are other subsidiary advantages which can be added. The larger type of accounting machines perform two or more operations simultaneously which is something far beyond human capabilities. Such machines will write figures, add them up at the same time and then move the paper ready for the next entry. Work performed by a machine is usually uniform in appearance, and is neat and more legible than when several different styles of handwriting appear in the books of account. Analysis can be obtained automatically at the time of entering in ledger accounts, stock records, or the like.

Kinds of Office Machinery. The machines and appliances may be classified into six main groups as follows :—

1. Communicational machinery.
2. Calculating machinery.
3. Copying and Duplicating machinery.
4. Recording and Tabulating machinery.
5. Sorting machines.
6. Miscellaneous.

Communicational Machinery

Communication is one of the fundamental functions of the office and a process essential to all forms of business. An efficient communication service is one in which the means selected is adequate. Telephone and dictaphone are the two most important communication instruments. The telephone system is *external* which connects the business houses with the outside world; and *internal* which is used for inter-communication within the office.

The *dictaphone* or *dictating-machine* is meant for recording the dictations given by an executive. This machine is later played on by the typist when he or she wishes to transcribe the message on the typewriter. The dictating machine has the advantages that (i) the dictator as well as the typist works at his own speed and time; (ii) shorthand notes are not necessary; (iii) work can be centralised and more evenly distributed; (iv) fewer typists are required; (v) telephone conversations can be recorded as they are going on; (vi) inspection and other reports can be prepared while the inspector is being driven from one location to another.

Calculating Machines

Calculating machines are those devices which either help in making calculations or actually do the calculating work. These machines are made to add, subtract, multiply, divide and even do problems of interest, exchange and discount and tabulating. These machines offer the following *advantages:* Speed of operation, simplicity of operation, simplicity of checking, accuracy and convenience. They also relieve strain and have great capacity.

Copying and Duplicating Machines

Duplicating processes may consist of making a single or a few copies of outgoing letters or they may involve making a very large number of copies. There are numerous methods of duplicating, and the principal ones are considered here.

(a) *The typewriter* is the most universally used duplicating machine for correspondence work. About eight copies can be taken out on an office typewriter. Electric typewriters are faster and produce much neater work, but they are costly and require specially trained personnel to operate them.

(b) *Automatic Typewriters* are designed to produce actual typewritten letters rapidly. The machine consists of a standard typewriter mounted on a stand and operated by an electric mechanism.

(c) *Press copying* is done in a letter book which contains a few hundred tissue sheets, numbered consecutively. The letter to be copied is either written by hand in copying ink or typed with a copying ribbon and is then placed at the back of the letter book page so that the writing or typed script can be seen through the tissue. On top is placed a specially prepared damp cloth, and the book is then closed. When pressure is applied to it by means of a hand-press, a copy is obtained. The system is slow and tends to smudge the original letter, but it has the advantage that the copy taken is an exact reproduction of the original, including the signature. The system is, however, going out of use.

(d) *Roneo Letter Copier* is an automatic copier designed to eliminate the messy process of damping sheets. The machine is worked either by hand or by electricity. The operator feeds the letters between the rollers, whereupon they are copied on a roll of paper fed through the machine and delivered on the other side in a collecting tray. Good many copies can be made by this process.

(e) *Stencil Duplicators* are used for reproducing exact copies of typewritten work as well as maps, charts, etc. A stencil is a waxed or composition sheet upon which is typed or traced the matter to be duplicated. The typing is done without the ribbon, and to make copies the stencil is fastened to the cylinder attached to the machine over the ink pad. A turn of the handle causes the cylinder to revolve, thus bringing the stencil in contact with the paper which has been fed into the machine. Gestetner is the principal type of duplicator used in India.

(f) *Photographic Duplicator or the Photostat* is a machine for the photographic reproduction of letters, maps, drawings, deeds, contracts, orders, invoices, testimonials, etc. It resembles a large camera, and is constructed to photograph direct upon sensitive paper which through a process of developing within the machine becomes the finished print.

(g) *Addressing Machine or Addressograph* is useful for addressing envelopes, wrappers or labels from prepared plates or stencil, and they save an enormous amount of time, when communications have to be sent regularly or frequently to the same persons. They can also be adapted for preparing inventory records, ledger pages, dividend warrants, shareholders' lists, or any other tabulation of names, such as lists of customers.

Recording and Tabulating Machine

Recording machines include all mechanical devices designed to record figures, or words, in connection with business operations. The following more important types fall under this category.

(a) *Book-keeping and Accounting Machine* is probably the most advanced mechanical device used in big business offices. It can post ledgers, make statements, add and subtract. Among the other records for which accounting machines may be used are purchase journal, distribution journal, sales journal, cost of sales journal, cash received journal, general journal, accounts receivable journal, customers' statements, accounts payable ledger, remittance advice, proof journal, cost sheets, store records, inventory records.

In addition to the usual advantages arising out of the use of proper office machinery, accounting machines have made one outstanding contribution to modern accounting and office management, namely, the virtual elimination of tedious hours of overtime at the end of the month and year on the part of accountants. These machines make it possible to keep all accounts posted up-to-date and constantly in balance which in turn enables the preparation of statements whenever they are required.

(b) *Invoicing Machine* does all the work connected with the preparation of invoices with great efficiency and speed.

(c) *The Billing Machine* is a combination typewriter and calculating machine. By the proper collation of forms as many as 18 copies may be made at one writing, thus saving much subsequent rewriting and copying which it is necessary to do if hand methods or typewriters are used for preparing bills. Calculations are known to be correct because they are mechanically performed. Billing machines have automatic devices which lock the machine when an error in posting has been made.

(d) *Cash Register* is a machine which keeps a duplicate record of all the cash memos. It is generally used in retail shops and successfully checks misappropriations on the part of the salesman.

(e) *The Tabulating Machines* are used to do tabulating work, and are used to prepare sales records, accounting and analysis work.

(f) *Time Recording Machine.* Time recorders are used for recording times of arrival and departure of an employee. These machines are most commonly used in big factories.

Sorting Machines

The devices used for sorting purposes save tremendous amount of time and labour. They may be used for sorting coins or cards. A coin sorter will sort out a mixture of all denominations of coins. After the coins have been separated into their respective drawers, they may then be poured into paper packets or other suitable containers.

The punched card sorting machine by sorting in succession the several columns in a particular field, cards are arranged into strict numerical order of the punching in that field. Another form of sorting machine is the Collator. The machine will collate cards of two packs, previously sorted in the same order, into one pack so as to bring together cards bearing the same punchings in a particular field.

Miscellaneous Machines

Under this category fall a large variety of different kinds of machines mostly small, inexpensive and used for diverse purposes. Among these machines may be mentioned the Gumming Machine which enables a strip of strongly gummed, tough paper, about three cms. wide and in any required length, to be neatly torn off and wetted, for attachment to the flaps and interslices of parcels. The Sealing Machine seals letters or parcels with wax neatly and speedily. The Stamp-affixing Machine counts and affixes stamps which are purchased in rolls for insertion therein. A Franking Machine is a useful time-saver, which prints stamps in ink on envelopes and other outgoing postage packages. Folding Machines are used for folding a large number of circulars or other papers of uniform size, and can fold four thousand documents per hour and can be adjusted to make many different kinds of folds. Stapling Machines are used for fastening together correspondence and other papers. Automatic Numbering Machines are very useful for numbering correspondence, invoices, dividend warrants, etc. They may be set to print one number continuously or to print consecutive numbers, or to repeat each number, and can be re-set to zero after each operation.

There are so many more devices, but space does not permit of anything more than a listing of them. They are Cheque Protectors, Writers, Certifiers, Credit Registers, Scales, Baling Presses, Calculation Rulers, Coupon Printing Machines, Eyelet Fasteners, Paper-cutting Machines, Perforating and Punching Machines, and so on. To these may be added some of the methods of inter-communication which are necessary in all but the smallest offices. The bell is the simplest device, and a mere pressing of the button informs the person that he is wanted. Internal telephone system for consultation is invariably used in a very big office to save valuable time of executives. For conveying documents to various parts of the building pneumatic tubes are frequently employed. Another modern device for communicating messages is the Creed Tele-writer or Teleprinter, whereby written or typed messages may be despatched almost simultaneously by telephone or telegraph lines, whichever is available.

PART FOUR

Horizons of Business

CHAPTER XII

BUSINESS COMBINATIONS

Anything that grows changes in growing. We have seen in Part three that over the past couple of centuries, the legal forms in which business firms have been organised have changed with the times. When small-scale business was the rule, the individual proprietorship was dominant. As the needs for larger capital funds increased with the expansion of organised business, partnerships became more popular. Then the Industrial Revolution ushered in the need for large-scale production. The modern joint stock company came into being to meet the needs of large-scale organisation and to avoid the drawbacks of its predecessors. Again, many of today's big companies are the result of combination of separate productive units. Those units are combined for some common purpose or purposes. The purpose may be the achievement of greater efficiency of operation, ensuring growth and survival, or it may be for mere perstige. It may also be for monopolistic control of the market.

In the evolutionary process of business organisations, therefore, combinations must be added to the partnership and the joint stock company. A combination is said to exist when two or more units are operated or controlled by one ownership interest. The combinations take numerous forms varying from the unwritten understanding amongst dealers to a highly integrated amalgamation or fusion of business houses covering a whole area of productive activity.

CAUSES OF COMBINATIONS

The forces which called the combination movement into being are involved and compex, and it is difficult to state them as clear-cut causes. There is an over-lapping of circumstances so that one natural or original cause appears to lead to the birth of another, the second preparing ground for the third. Attempts at analysis have been made by some authorities. For example, Haney has classified the causes of combinations into three broad categories, namely : (i) *original driving or impelling forces;* (ii) *beckoning forces,* and (iii) *facilitating forces.* According to him the original or driving forces include (a) the decrease in the opportunity for speculative gains, and (b) excessive competition. The beckoning conditions, in his opinion, were (a) opportunity for gain. (b) protection to industries, and (c) the possibilities of gain by over-capitalisation. The facilitating conditions, he said, were : (a) tariffs, (b) the development of the joint-stock company form of organisation, etc. These and some other important causes of combinations are discussed in the following paragraphs.

1. *Intensive* or *Wasteful competition.* In the earlier stages of Industrial Revolution, firms were comparatively small and correspondingly numerous in each industry. While competition among rivals was the normal condition, it was not intense. With the widening of markets, and the gorwth of large-scale production, which resulted from the great technical achievements, competition became intense and often wasteful. Unlike the artisan-producer who made to order, the large plant, in order to reap the benefits of large size, had to work for stock, i.e., produce for a market or in anticipation of demand. This involved locking up of huge capital. Each firm vied against the others to capture the market and used both fair means and foul. Industrial concerns and commercial houses indulged in successive orgies of price cutting and cut-throat irrational competition in order to capture the market, until all were on the verge of financial ruin. The only way to survive was to get together and cooperate to maintain prices. Thus, competition, by going too far, became a very powerful instrument for the inception and growth of combinations. In other words, the intensification of competition led to the formation of combinations.

2. *Influence of Tariffs.* The tariff policies of different countries facilitated the formation of combinations. The introduction of customs tariffs greatly increased the ability of protected industries to form cartels, etc., by making it possible for them to monopolise the market. With the elimination of foreign competition, new units come into existence to take advantage of high prices. This leads to competition among such units, and when it becomes too intensive, producers combine to reap the advantages of monopoly prices. The sugar industry of India and iron industry of Germany are examples. It should, however, be borne in mind that tariff is not an essential contributing factor to combinations, for combinations of different types have originated and developed without tariffs. At best, protection can only facilitate the rise and growth of a combination where the essential factors and forces for businesses combining effectively exist independently.

3. *Advantages of Large-Scale operation.* We have already discussed how large scale organisation and operation can effect big economies in production, management, financial administration and marketing.[1] Integration was resorted to for enjoying the benefi s of large-scale operation. It was not only to reduce current costs—"the cost of doing business"—but also to minimise future costs—"costs of staying in business," that industrialists turned to combinations. Large-scale operation in the shape of horizontal combination and vertical integration became an effective instrument to combat future uncertainty and risk. The impelling force is commonly believed to be "profit", but it is the "avoidance of loss" that mothers combinations. Combinations as successful enterprises provide not only for their own future costs, but they also contribute towards the risks of the less successful enterprises. As part

1. See pp. 100-105 ante.

of the whole (a combine) they carry a share of the losses other enterprises will sustain in the future.

4. *Trade Cycles.* Trade cycles or the "ups" and "downs" occur at regular intervals in capitalist economies. They in turn result in fluctuations in economic activity which enhance the movement towards concentration. Trade cycles, as is well known, consist of booms or the periods of highest prosperity and depressions or periods of minimum economic activity. Although combinations take place, both during boom and depression periods, the combination movement appears to be most active in periods of prosperity, risk prevention being the defensive weapon. During depression, there is weeding out of inefficient firms which are usually absorbed by the efficient ones. In times of boom, combination takes place on account of the expansion of existing units by means of horizontal, vertical or diagonal integration and also to prevent risk.

5. *Experimental Economic Policy.* An experimental and so vaccillating economic policy leads to instability. It is subject to continual changes in currency, trade, fiscal and wage policies, etc., which have in turn considerbly increased the element of uncertainty in the planning of individual firms. This instability of economic policy is another factor that has greatly encouraged economic concentration. The greater the risk, the greater the incentive to combine, especially concerns embracing different industries or different parts of the same industry or trade.

6. *Desire for Monopoly Power.* Monopoly usually leads to the control of the market and exploitation of the consumer through high prices. When business units amalgamate they find it much easier and simple to raise prices than to reorganise their methods of production. The consumer is the sufferer. Monopolies are generally successful in those units which produce articles of daily use for which the demand is inelastic. The monopolist can raise the prices of necessities of life without fear of much reduction in demand for them.

7. *Individual Organising Ability.* Shields[1] suggests that "great organising ability, strategic genius or personal ambition on the part of one or a number of men may account in part for the rise of certain business combinations. The scarcity of business talent became one of the causes of centralisation of power in fewer hands, endowed with business insight, business talent, and business courage". Thus the lag between technical and administrative development of industry became an additional factor encouraging combination movement.

8. *Cult of the Colossal or Respect for Bigness.* The mid-nineteenth century brought in its wake the cult of the colossal. Everything "big" began to enjoy respect and everything small was looked upon with contempt. Bigness today confers respectability; it gives power over fellow beings. The more one commands big things the more respectable he becomes. In the business world also "bigness" has become the vogue or

1. *The Evolution of Industrial Organisation*, p. 87.

fashion. Concentration of control over a large number of business by different means of integration or combination gives increased power, and so the race for combination.[2]

9. *Rationalisation.* Rationalisation is the movement to eliminate waste and inefficiency and one of the ways to do this is through business combination. For instance, amalgamation provides opportunity for unified control for the elimination of redundant designs. By reducing the number of designs each pattern can be repeated an enormous number of times so that the machine has long runs without re-setting, smaller quantities of spare parts are needed, and component processes can be carried out in bulk. Central control enables regulation of output and prices, planned utilisation of scarce materials and standardisation of products. Thus, combinations are an integral part of rationalisation.

10. *Joint-stock Enterprise.* Corporate form of organisation has also facilitated the growth of combinations. Companies usually run large businesses. It is easier to get working agreement amongst a few big businesses which share an industry between them than amongst a thousand small firms scattered all over the country. Again, a few persons can easily acquire controlling interest in a number of businesses owned by companies by merely acquiring shares in such companies.

11. *Patent Laws.* Concentration has been greatly fostered by patent laws. Patents give monopoly position to individual firm. Many times combinations are resorted to for enjoying the benefits of patent rights standing in the name of a particular unit.

12. *Possibility of Gain by over-capitalisation.* Very often promoters promoted combinations of business units with a view to reaping speculative profits. Periods of speculation and of steep-price rises normally encourage the formation of combinations.

13. *Under Pressure from Government.* Section 396 of the Companies Act, 1956 provides that where the Central Government is satisfied that it is essential in public interest that two or more companies should amalgamate, it may order such an amalgamation. The merger of Steel Corporation of Bengal with the Indian Iron and Steel Company Ltd. was ordered by the Government in 1953 with a view to making the unit of economic size.

14. *Emergence of International Markets.* To be able to compete in international markets the size of the unit must be very large. Combination of different units would reduce the risks involved in buying and selling in markets of international character.

TYPES OF COMBINATION

"To combine", says Haney, "is to become one of the parts of a whole, and combination is merely a union of persons to make a whole or group for the prosecution of some common purpose." Strictly, therefore, any association of coming together of two or more persons is a

2. Rope, *The Social Crisis of our Time*, p. 62.

combination. Taken in this light even a partnership which is formed to carry on business in common is a type of combination. We are, however, concerned with the industrial units as such, which join hands by simple association or by integration to achieve the common purpose, namely, the reduction of competition through "giant business." There are five chief divisions of combination according to the types of units intended to be brought together namely, horizontal, vertical, circular, lateral, and diagonal. As explained in an earlier chapter, this is brought about by the process of *integration*. In the following paragraphs we will deal with each of these integrations.

Horizontal or Parallel or Unit Integration. Where the units or industrial undertakings of similar character, engaged in producing similar products, such as automobiles, are brought under some single

Horizontal Integration

1.	Automobile	Automobile	Automobile	→	Market
2.	Spinning Mill	Spinning Mill	Spinning Mill	→	Market
3.	Sugar Mill	Sugar Mill	Sugar Mill	→	Market
4.	Local Coal Dealers	Local Coal Dealers	Local Coal Dealers	→	Market

Fig. 1.

form of management, horizontal integration takes place. Here two or more factories engaged in the same stage of production join together. Firms which compete on the same plane, or in the same trade, or which are in the same general line of business, reach out and unite. This has been the most frequent type of integration and one which has most heavily told against the consumer. It is the best example of establishing monopoly.

The economic advantages that accrue from horizontal integration are quite important. The advantages of centralised purchasing in quantity, and of centralised expert services, such as research and engineering, and of consolidated advertising are obvious. The re-arrangement of plants by consolidation is likely to result in production of the greatest quantity of the product in one place, as also the giving of line of work best suited to each plant. The greatest advantage is stronger competitive power, since the consolidation can more widely control market prices.

Vertical or Process Integration. Growth in size by vertical integration is very different from growth by horizontal integration. Vertical integration consists in coming together or integration of organisations which are on the different planes and which represent the successive stages or "trades" within an industry. It is the union of the successive stages or processes of manufacture of the finished article—beginning from the raw materials, passing through manufacture to the finished product and distribution. The organisations united are not competing side by side, but stand end to end, the one receiving the products of the other as its own raw material. Each unit of enterprise contributes a finished product, which becomes the raw material for the next process unitl the finished product is completed. The outstanding example of vertical integration is the iron ore, iron smelting and then the making of different products of iron and steel. Textile industry is another example where performance of consecutive processes of, say, carding, spinning and weaving, is carried out by one organisation. In this form, all stages, from the basic or extractive industry to the finished article, or even to marketing, are united. These stages are sometimes described as extractive (raw materials), analytical (fabrication of parts), assembling (putting the parts together to make the finished article), and marketing. We will take the example of automobile manufacture to illustrate this form of integration as also of textile.

Vertical Integration

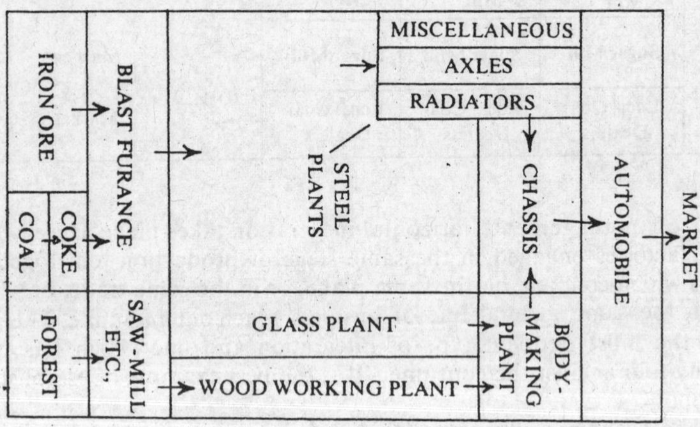

Fig. 2.

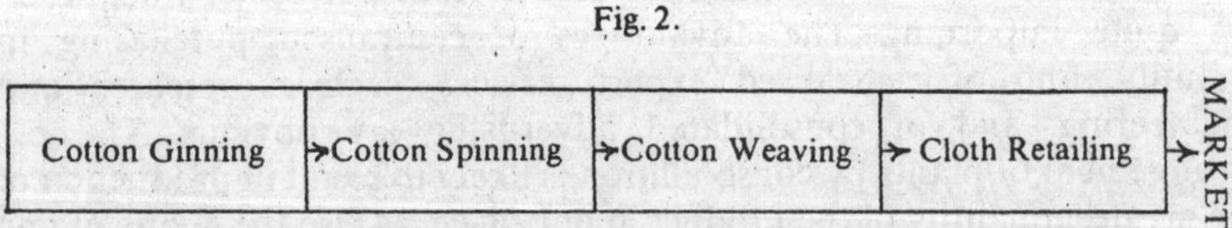

Fig. 2 A.

This is an integration of units that are normally independent or at least have been so until comparatively recently. It will be noted that it is an example of what may be described as a fully integrated group of establishments containing within itself all the processes necessary to produce the marketable product, an automobile, from the raw materials. Before integration, the raw materials, iron ore, coal, forest would be owned by three different firms and smelting, coking, sawing and glass making would be done by a number of others. The automobile maker would buy steel for making the chassis, but have axles and miscellaneous accessories made by still others. After completing the assembly work, he would have the body built by another establishment. When the product is ready for the market he would entrust the work of selling it to a distributing house. Now, after integration, all the successive processes, from the raw material stage to marketing, are in the hands of one organisation.

Integration may start from the manufacturer who desires control of supplies and markets; it may start with the merchandiser who wishes better control of the products that he is selling; it may emanate from the producer of raw materials who desires an outlet for them; or it may appear as a recognition of the mutuality of interest on the part of all concerned.[1] The industries which answer to the following characteristics tend to be vertically integrated.

1. Where quality of the product is important. Here the finished product determines the raw material, and therefore control over the raw materials becomes necessary.
2. Where the finished product of one industry can be used by the other as its raw material.
3. Where one process leads naturally to another.
4. Where "balanced production" is important, i.e., production of just the right amount at every stage of manufacture, e.g., spinning and weaving, can be done on the same scale.
5. Where the flow of supplies has to be regulated in point of time of delivery. Integration helps in the reduction to a minimum of the amount of stores that must be carried in each plant.

Broadly speaking, quality cases integrate and cheap ones tend to disintegrate or to remain apart. Obviously, the integration saves capital in storage, selling, buying, inspection, and transport of materials between the stages. But vertical integration can hardly make much progress except in very large-scale industries; and it is greatly facilitated by simplicity and uniformity in the product. But since the enterprise must necessarily be large, there is a great difficulty of effectively controlling it, particularly as it is made up of dissimilar units. Although modern methods of organisation and management have made it possible to control large enterprises more effectively than formally, yet this danger always exists. Highly integrated industries also tend to become inflexible and difficult to adapt to changes in production.

Lateral or Allied Integration. Where different sorts of articles, but nonetheless allied, are produced by one organisation, lateral integration takes place. That is to say, instead of a number of different firms making different articles after the analytical stage has been reached, they all come together and produce all these articles as one concern. For

1. Kimball. *op. cit. p. 63.*

example, pig iron is used in so many ways and in so many processes of fabricating iron and steel products after the analytical stage smelting, so that one firm may make needles, another scissors, third pins and the

LATERAL INTEGRATION

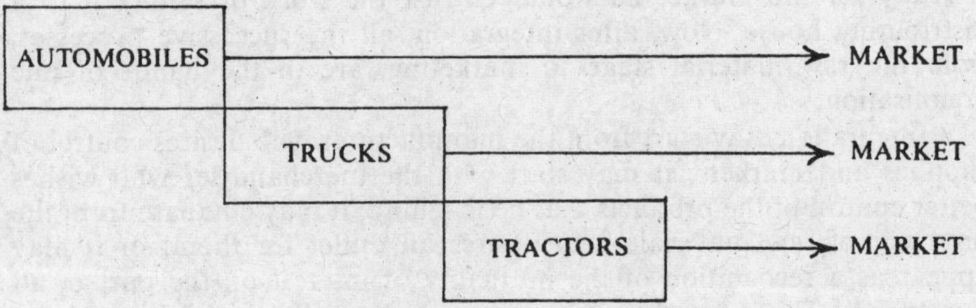

Fig.3.

fourth fish tackles and so on. When they come together, smelting is done at one place and all these articles and many others allied to them are manufactured by the same firm. Similarly, after leather has been tanned, saddles, harnesses, suit cases, bags, and other fancy goods, instead of being made by separate firms, are after lateral integration, made by one firm. By this integration, to use Professor Florence's expression, we "Broaden the Basis."

Lateral integration may be either "divergent" or "convergent". It is divergent where from one material are manufactured a number of articles, and it is convergent where different raw materials are brought together to make one article. In the former case, the products diverge from the same process or source, while in the latter, materials converge upon the same process or market.

Divergent Lateral Integration

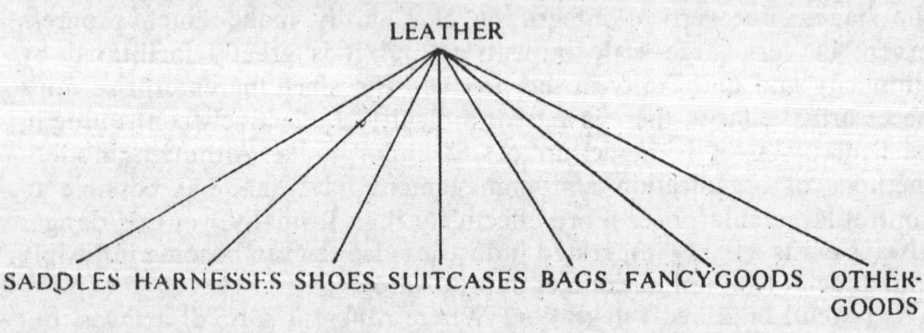

Fig. 4.

Leather is the source of raw material from which saddles, harnesses, shoes, suit cases, hand bags, fancy goods, etc., diverge. Since all these diverge from the same process and have the common raw material, the economy of "bulking" applies when one organisation buys common materials.

It may be noted that in convergent integration, the raw materials are many, e.g., feathers, gut, steel, wooden rod, for the manufacture of a fishing tackle for the use of the angler. Here they converge on the same market, and so have common marketing costs.

Lateral integration can be profitably made where a given special process can be used to capacity in one line of production, and a second or third line diverging from this process may be adopted to fill the gap.

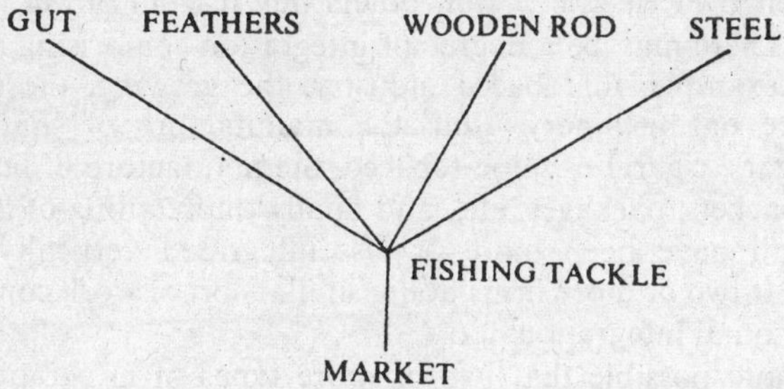

Fig. 5.

Also, where an organisation enlarges in this way, i.e., by engaging in several lines of transactions of given scale rather than by enlarging one line, "risks may be adopted to fill the gap." Also,where an organisation be formed by lateral integration along divergent lines for the reason that if demand fails or falls for one line, compensation may be found in increased demand for other lines. And larger firms may be formed by convergent integration to avoid the risk of failure or rising cost of one line of supply. Lateral integration is also described as the integration of materials and products.

Diagonal or Services Integration. Diagonal integration consists in the provision inside any one organisation of auxiliary goods or services required for the various main processes or lines of production of that organisation. An organisation may, for instance, provide its own designs or power, take its own tools and machines, or use its own carpenter's services for repairs. It may also make ancillary articles necessary for making the main product fit for sale. For example, cigarette makers may themselves make tin foils, cartons, containers, packets, etc., instead of buying them from different makers. Diagonal integration makes for economical transport, communication and supervision of execution, as consecutive processes and services are all carried on within one large plant.

Circular or Mixed Integration. When firms engaged in the manufacture of different products integrate or combine under a central agency, circular or mixed combination takes place. If a cement factory, a steel mill and a sugar mill combine, we will have a case of circular or mixed combination. The main object of such a combination is to derive the benefits of integrated administration. This method has been followed in India by the reverse method. The same house—Tatas, Birla or J.K.'s starting all kinds of business under this banner and exercising administrative control over them.

Conclusion. In conclusion, it may be observed that integration is a relative term, practically all industrial plants being integrated to some extent. Butthe precise degree of integration is not invariable. Some textile firms spin and weave, others merely spin, or merely weave. Some firms provide their own electric power, others buy it from power companies, and so on. There may be a degree of integration comprising all the four types. For example, in tobacco industry, the growing, the curing, the manufacture of machinery used, the manufacture of snuff, chewing tobacco, cigars, cigarettes, pipe tobacco, the maufacture of liquorice, tin foil, cans, packets, packages, etc., and finally the retailing of the finished products—all have been more or less integrated vertically, laterally, diagonally. If two or more firms doing similar sort of work come together we get horizontal integration, too.

It is quite possible that two or more types of integration may be combined to achieve the objective of combination. For example, there may be both horizontal and vertical integration at the same time. A brief description of each type of integration or combination is given below.

Forms of Combinations

The various devices for the reduction of competition, and/or for the realisation of the advantages of large-scale organisation may be stated in order of their development as—

1. Informal Agreements.
2. Formal Pooling Agreements.
3. Cartels.
4. The Trustee Device.
5. The Community of Interest Device.
6. The Holding Company Device.
7. Consolidation.
8. Trade Associations.

But a great deal of confusion is found in the use of these terms, and we may with advantage adopt a classification from the one given by Haney. He groups all the forms into two main categories : Simple Combinations and Compound Combinations. The first, being a direct combination or association of natural persons as in a partnership, is omitted from consideration, as it has already been fully discussed. The second group, i.e., compound combinations, includes all the 8 categories given above. According to this plan, therefore, the classification of combinations will be somewhat as follows :—

Simple Associations

1. Trade Associations.

2. Trade Unions.
3. Chambers of Commerce.
4. Informal Agreements.

Federation

1. Pools.
2. Cartels.

Consolidation

1. Partial Consolidation :
   (a) Trusts.
   (b) Community of Interest—(i) shareholding, (ii) interlocked directorate, (iii) group-interest, viz., managing agents.
   (c) Holding Company—(i) pure, (ii) operating, (iii) parent, (iv) offspring, (v) primary, (vi) intermediary.
2. Complete Consolidation :
   (a) Amalgamation.
   (b) Merger.

SIMPLE ASSOCIATIONS

Trade Associations. It is quite usual for industrialists, merchants or planters, having common purpose, to collaborate and form a trade association of their own. Trade associations are established to look after the interests of a particular trade or industry, and may be based on locality or community. The examples of these are Bombay Mill Owners' Association, Ahmedabad Textile Mill Owners' Association, East India Cotton Association, Bengal Silk and Art Silk Mill Owners' Association, United Planters' Association, Calcutta Trade Association, Madras Trades Association. In the national level, we have All-India Manufacturers' Organisation, Fertiliser Association of India, Federation of Associations of Small Industries of India and so on. Such associations meet frequently and discuss problems of their common interest such as raw materials, labour shortage, transport problems, State policy, etc. They aim at encouraging friendly communication among members, protection of their interests by means of representation, etc.

Trade Unions. The term Trade Union is commonly understood to mean a union or association of workers formed for looking after their interests by strengthening their bargaining power. But according to the Indian Trade Unions Act, a Trade Union is "a combination formed for the purpose of regulating the relations between workmen and employers, or between workmen and workmen, or between employers and employers or for imposing restrictive conditions on the conduct of any trade or business ...." The Indian Jute Mills Association is an example of a "Trade Union" of employers. Even merchants' associations, friendly societies and the like can register themselves as trade unions. Strictly speaking, a trade union is an organisation of employees, in which the workers find a powerful attack on their problems. The union bargains for higher wages to raise their income and establish working rules to make that income more secure. It seeks to protect them through seniority, regulation of innovation, benefits to unemployed members, the annual wage, work restriction, regulation of hours, etc. In all these tactics the union is insisting with some success that workers have right to income, that their wages must meet their needs, that the wage rate is something more than a price on a resource or a method of calculating costs.

CHAMBERS OF COMMERCE

Chambers of Commerce are voluntary non-profit associations of people engaged in trade, commerce and industry. Their members usually include merchants, industrialists, bankers, financiers, and brokers. They are formed for promoting and protecting the interests of their members and the business community in general. Chambers of Commerce are generally formed on a regional basis to foster the growth and development of business in their respective regions.

The principal functions of Chambers of Commerce are as follows :

1. The promotion of trade, commerce and industry of the country and looking after their interests generally.

2. The collection and dissemination of statistical and other information relating to trade, commerce and industry.

3. Acting as the spokesman of the business community by commenting on Government policies affecting business interests.

4. Communicating to the Government the views of Commercial community on proposed legislation concerning business.

5. Making suggestions and recommendations regarding legislation likely to foster trade and industry.

6. Providing a forum for the discussion of common problems and making them known to the Government.

7. Undertaking enquiries and conducting research in the interest of trade and industry.

8. Arranging for the amicable settlement of disputes between members by means of arbitration.

9. Organising industrial fairs and exhibitions and conducting seminars with a view to fostering the development of trade and industry.

10. Chambers of Commerce render useful service in the field of foreign trade. They provide detailed information to exporters and importers regarding availability of goods, procedures to be followed, shipping freight, etc.

It is clear that Chambers of Commerce zealously safeguard the interests of trade and industry and act as the mouthpiece of businessmen and keep the Government apprised from time to time of the problems affecting commercial and industrial development. They can elect representatives to various Central, State and Local Bodies. The Chambers of Commerce are also represented on quasi-government bodies such as

Port Trusts and Improvement Trusts. It is usual for the Government to obtain the views of the leading chambers and associations before embarking upon measures which are likely to affect trade, commerce and industry, and every consideration is given to any advice tendered.

CHAMBERS OF COMMERCE IN INDIA

These Chambers of Commerce are either Provincial or Local or they are General or All-India. The State Chambers and other associations are mainly concerned with the promotion and furtherance of commerce and industry of the State. Among the State Chambers of Commerce may be mentioned the Bengal Chamber of Commerce, Bengal National Chamber of Commerce, Marwari Chamber of Commerce, Bombay Chamber of Commerce. The All-India Chambers of Commerce are 15 in number. The Associated Chamber of Commerce of India, consisting of 15 chambers from the various parts of the country, was set up in 1920 with a view to promoting, protecting and more closely organising the European commercial interests throughout India. The Federation of Indian Chambers of Commerce and Industry, founded in 1926, is a Central organisation representing Indian commercial and industrial interests in India. The main objects of the Federation are to promote Indian business in matters of inland and foreign trade, transport, industry and manufactures and finance. The head office is in New Delhi and over 50 chambers and associations are its members. The All-India Organisation of Industrial Employers was established in 1942 and is a body allied to the above Federation. Its objects are to promote the industrial development, by encouraging or discouraging legislative or other measures affecting industry. In addition to the foregoing chambers and associations there are some other important bodies, namely, the Indian Chamber of Commerce, Calcutta; Indian Colliery Owners' Association, Calcutta; Indian Tea Association; Indian Central Cotton Committee; Indian Mining Association; Indian Mining Federation; Mining and Geological Institute of India; Wine, Spirit and Beer Association of India; All-India Manufacturers' Association.

International Chamber of Commerce. The chamber was established in 1920 at a meeting of the chief business interests of Belgium, France, Great Britain, Italy, and the U.S.A., and was subsequently joined by 40 other countries to promote the development of international trade, to remove or mitigate the effect of trade restrictions, and to foster harmonious commercial relations among the nations. The Chamber is governed by a Council to which representatives are elected by the National Committees in various countries. The Secretary-General carries out the decisions of the Council under the supervision of the President and a small Executive Committee. The Chamber has its head office in Paris. It holds biennially a congress in one of the affiliated countries, which is attended by delegates representing the different countries. In each country, which desires to participate in the membership, there is established a National Committee representing the industrial, commercial, financial and transport interests of the country. The National Committees are the administrative co-ordinating links between the Council on the one hand and the actual members in their respective countries on the other. The International Chamber has established a Court of Arbitration to facilitate the settlement of commercial disputes between the traders of different countries. Indian National Committee of the International Chamber of Commerce was established with its head office in New Delhi in 1928 to participate in the promotion of the objects for which the International Chamber of Commerce was established.

Informal Agreements. Another type of simple association took the form of understandings and agreements among competing enterprises for the purpose of directly controlling the prices of the products manufactured or services rendered. These simple agreements involve the exchange of promises of express understandings. They are sometimes called "working agreements", "gentlemen's agreements", "price combination", "open price associations", etc. All the persons or units party to the agreement, while retaining their individuality, are honour bound to obey and carry out their promises. Here, word of honour is more important than any written agreement. These agreements take four main forms: conditions of sale, price regulation, division of the market, and regulation of output. The first of these may deal with the terms of credit to be allowed to customers, the form of contract or discount. Price regulation may take the shape of fixing one price or a minimum level of price below which competitors are not to go. It may also restrict undercutting one another by prohibiting payment of discount. It achieves no real economy, either in manufacture or in marketing, for it is nothing more than an agreement not to sell below a stipulated price. The price fixed in the agreement is naturally higher than that price which would have emerged under competition, consequently it tends to preserve inefficient firms and to prevent the more efficient firms from gathering the fruits of their efficiency. Nevertheless, insofar as the agreement is carefully observed it may, in some cases, result in competition expressing itself in quality rather than in price. But the agreement does not often withstand the pressure of unfavourable circumstances. When demand falls short of producing capacity the signatories evade the agreement by offering higher discounts, or by selling cheaply articles not controlled by the agreement, or again by queer arithmetic processes exemplified in "Eggman's or Baker's dozen"—giving 13 eggs or loaves for a dozen. The difficulty to enforce the agreement on all the members is the greatest drawback of this form; for such an agreement cannot be enforced in Court, it being in restraint of trade.

The third form of agreement, the one by which the market is parcelled out among the producers, also fails to achieve economies of any significance. Each member undertakes not to raid the market of his ally. This allocation of markets may appear, at first, to reduce the cost of marketing the product, but it does not do so, for an efficient firm can sell in the market of the inefficient firm and so eliminate it. The territorial division of the market is not popular in manufacturing industry, as the market of the product is not localised. The fourth form of agreement provides for the regulation of output. The idea behind this is to put up the revenue, by keeping up prices through restriction of output. Output may be restricted by producing according to demand or by "short time" work.

FEDERATION

Pooling Agreement. The simple agreement, being loose and

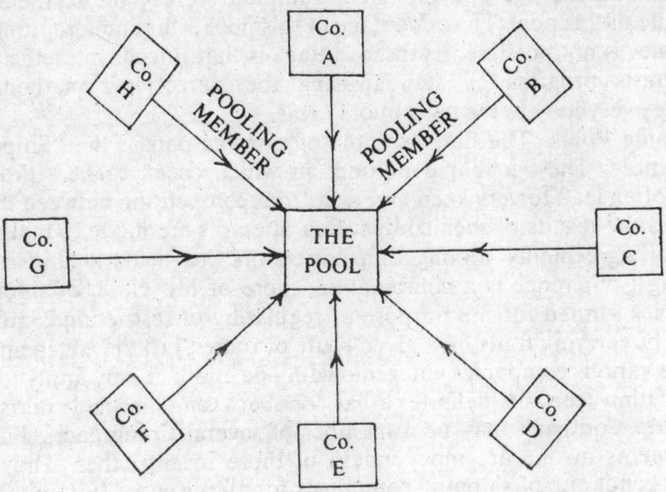

superficial, having failed, pooling agreements have been tried with some success. In a pool, some factors which determine price are pooled, without sacrificing the identity of the various organisations. Heney defines an industrial pool as "a form of business organisation established through federation of business units whose members seek a degree of control over price by combining some factor in the price-making process in a common aggregate and apportioning that aggregate among the units." Always some degree of control over supply is involved and is exerted more or less directly according to the type of pool. It seeks to maintain favourable prices, by only manipulating the price determining factors, such as the supply of the product or the market areas. The simple agreement merely names the price and seeks to maintain it by an agreement not to sell for less; but the pool undertakes to provide machinery for controlling price. A pooling agreement is always made by members producing and dealing in similar product. The above diagram illustrates relationship existing among the different pooling members, where members sign the agreement.

Pools may be divided into different types, such as output or traffic pools, market or territorial pools, income or profits pools, etc.

Output Pools. An output pool is formed by all or the principal manufacturers engaged in the same industry agreeing to combine to the extent of making their outputs form an imaginary aggregate fund or pool, and then divide that pool among themselves according to some agreed basis. Generally, quotas are fixed and each joining member is required not to produce more than that quota. This pool operates on the supply side of the market, seeking to control competition in producing quantities of goods. It is adopted mainly to avoid "over production". Each member is required to submit a monthly report of production which is checked up with the allotment. Any member found to produce more than the allotted quota is fined. Complete secrecy among members is the rule of this pool. The advantage of this pool is that undercutting for more sales is not possible. Its disadvantage is that it leads to inefficiency and arrests progress by standardising the stereotyped methods of bringing everybody to the level of old firms.

Traffic Pools. The best example of a traffic pool is the "Shipping Conference". The peculiar conditions in which ocean carriers provide service often lead to very keen and disastrous competition between them. To avoid the results of such competition attempts are made to maintain rates by agreements among ship operators, particularly Liners. A Shipping Conference is a combination, more or less close, of shipping companies formed for the purpose of regulating or restricting competition in the carrying trade on a given route or routes, i.e., the engagements that the various companies enter into with one another, only apply to the trade within certain definite areas or between specified ports. A Steamship Company may be a member of several Conferences, but its engagements in one are independent of those in any other. Thus the alliance is not one of shipping companies for all purposes, but only as to their operation within a specified area. The procedure followed is to fix uniform freight rates, and to apportion the traffic by either the allotment of ports of call or restriction of sailings or limitation of the volume which certain lines may carry. For example, open competition may be avoided, or at least minimised, between two or more lines operating from the same ports, by apportioning the sailing dates. In this way, two lines do not bid against each other for traffic on a certain day. In some cases total freight earnings, or a part of them, may be pooled and divided upon a pre-arranged basis. By this means, the strongest incentive for cutting rates is removed. Such an arrangement is sometimes described as a "money pool". One of the most effective methods of excluding new competitors from a trade is the Deferred Rebate System. By this system the shipping conferences turn themselves into practically monopolistic and generally anti-social organisations. It works as under : the companies issue a notice or circular to shippers informing them that, if at the end of a certain period (usually six months) they have not shipped goods by any vessels other than those dispatched by members of the Conference, they will be credited with a sum equivalent to a certain part (usually 10 per cent) of the aggregate freights paid in their shipments during that period, and that this sum will be paid over to them, and if at the end of a further period (usually six months) they have continued to confine their shipments to vessels belonging to the members of the Conference. A traffic pool in the case of railways may be formed by agreeing to pool the receipts from traffic between two or more competitive points, leaving members free to run services independently of the pooling agreement in territories where they do not compete. Before receipts are divided, each member is allowed a minimum amount for running expenses. The main object is to avoid duplicate services and eliminate wasteful competition.

Market Pools or Territorial Allotments. Another way of maintaining prices is to pool the market and divide it among the members of the combination. From one point of view this ensures a certain demand to each member, and so this form of pool may be thought of as seeking to influence the demand side of price determination. But a part of the object is to restrict the supply in certain sections by keeping the members from other sections in their own fields. The pooling of territory or market may be secured by direct specification or by indirect means. The prices fixed are above competitive level, so that highest net returns are made possible through selling large products in a market where the allottee has the greatest advantage. Such pools may extend into international spheres, and different countries may adopt similar methods for controlling competition among themselves. The market may be divided in any one of the three ways, namely, (a) by customers, (b) by products, or (c) by territories. The territory may be further divided into two subdivisions : "Pay Territory", i.e., territory covered by the pool, or "Free Territory", i.e., territory outside the ambit of the pool.The level of price to be charged in a territory within the pool is fixed as a "basic price" by fixing a place as a "basing point". The price so fixed aims to bring good profits. The price at any other point is fixed at a figure which equals the basic point price plus the freight rate from this point to that point.

Income and Profits Pools. Both the output and the market pools proved ineffective in two directions. There was over-production and hence temptation to disregard the pooling agreement; on the other hand, the customers resented it because that interfered with their freedom to buy according to their own choice. Income pools, intended to assure choice of goods to customers and some profits to everyone, were adopted. In this pool, the price charged on contracts for supplying to customers the requisite articles is fixed by a Central Board made up of representatives of the members making the article. To secure the contract each bids by an amount larger than the price set by the Board. The contract goes to the highest bidder. The difference between the price set by the Board and the higher price bid by the members getting the contract goes to the pool, to be distributed later among the parties to the pooling agreement, the share of each being determined by the productive capacity of each participant. A base price sufficient to cover expenses of production is retained by the members and the difference between this and the selling price is paid into the pool. In some cases, prices and output are fixed in advance, definite quotas are allotted to the various members and all income above a certain amount allowed for expenses is paid into the pool. Thus output or supply is the ultimate basis of control, even in income pools.

The advantages of pooling agreements are (a) facility of formation, (b) no danger of over-capitalisation, since the combination is loose and is sought only to manipulate price without permanent monopolistic organisation, and (c) saves cross freights, especially a territorial pool. The disadvantages may be stated as (a) reduction of output and manipulation of prices replace efficient management as a device to increase profits, thus reducing initiative, and (b) there is lack of stability due to unenforceability of contracts creating the pool or withdrawal of members or their unwillingness to co-operate.

Cartels or Sales Associations. In many cases pooling agreements proved ineffective because of their unenforceability. The members were often tempted to increase output beyond the allotted figures. To obviate this difficulty, various forms of sales associations or pools of rigid type were devised. The associations originated in Germany under the name of Cartels, although looser form of agreements on the lines of pools were also designated Cartels. It is because of this confusion that very often pooling agreements of the type described before are generally styled as Cartels by German writers, such as Von Beckereth, Robert Liefmann and H. Mullensiefen. Thus, these writers include in their definition of the term both cartel proper or the Syndicate and the loser agreements, when they say that a Cartel is a "voluntary agreement between, or association of, independent enterprises of similar type to secure a monopoly of the market."[1] The monopolisation or domination of the market is evidently the essential point in the definition. According to them the lower type of cartels takes the form of agreements for regional or zonal control, price fixing, production and quota fixing, tendering or quotation or profit distributing, and so on. In order to avoid confusion the term cartel is restricted here to the closer type of combination involving an organic change in the firm described below and frequently called a Syndicate.

A Cartel of this type or a Syndicate is essentially a selling agency acting on behalf of constituting manufacturing firms. A number of producers come together and form an association generally in the form of a joint-stock company for the purpose of selling their goods through it—the Cartel. All the members agree with the Cartel (the new company) that they would sell their entire product to it exclusively for a period. Then the Cartel sells the goods on the market. The individual producers are paid prices varying with the quality of the product, but bearing an agreed relation to a base price fixed for the standard quality. The Cartel, in turn, charges what the market will bear, and may charge different

1. See Liefmann, op. cit., p. 7.

prices in different zones. When the market can absorb all that the members are able to supply, the orders are rationed among the latter in the ratio of their producing capacities. It will be observed that the Cartel performs only the economic function of distribution and does not interfere with the internal management of the individual manufacturer. While the Cartel enjoying partial or complete monopoly performs all marketing functions including risks, it does not aim at a profit for itself.

Cartel or Syndicate

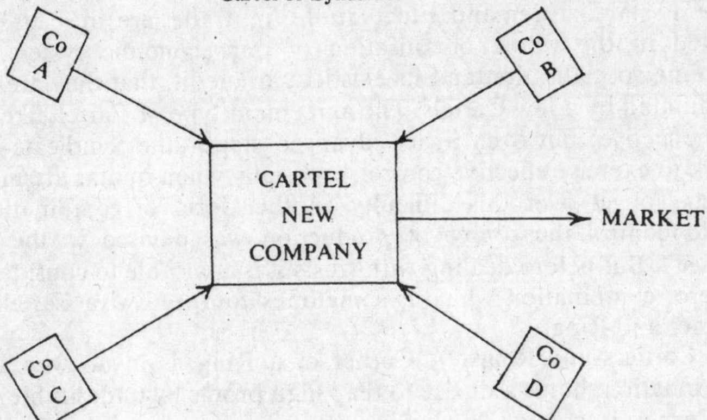

Any profit that is made is distributed among the members, who also share the losses, if any. The best example of such a Cartel or Syndicate in our country was the Indian Sugar Syndicate Limited, which has been dissolved. The Cement Marketing Company of India Limited is another example.

The Cartel as a form of organisation leads to some substantial economies and advantages to the members. The system guarantees minimum to cover cost of production. It does not directly limit the profit of the individual firms. If the market "bears" a high price the latter will be charged, and will lead either to high profits for distribution or to the payment of high base prices. Also, every successful effort to reduce manufacturing costs will be accompanied by a corresponding increase in the profit of the individual firms. Thus, under the Cartel system, the functions of making and selling are separated. and the manufacturer is enabled to concentrate attention upon the former. In this way, Cartels bring about a uniform market condition for the whole trade. Further, manufacture is carried on under semi-competitive conditions, while selling becomes the monopoly of the Cartel. Substantial economies in marketing the product are realised, for competitive advertising is no longer necessary, and constructive advertising is possible upon a scale far beyond the reach of firms competing with each other. The marketing of groups of allied products by a single agency is also more economical than separate marketing by individual firms. The collection and distribution of statistics relating to industry and its markets, actual and prospective react upon efficiency. In addition to these real economies, there are the usual advantages in selling due to monopoly. On the other hand, the Cartel system tends to stereotype an industry by retaining the less efficient firm, and also by affording it a chance of securing a sort of pension from some more efficient firm which desires to increase its own quota. It acts as a stimulus to unhealthy expansion in times of favourable trade, since its constituent members feel assured of its ability to provide them with work in less favourable times. Also, the Cartels have not been able to stabilize demand. Fluctuations in trade are, in fact, so deeply rooted in the whole organisation of our economic system, with its extreme specialisation and its elasticity of credit, that they are not to be eliminated by a few Cartels. The agreement type of Cartel, like the pool, is ineffective; but even in its advanced stage—the Syndicate—it is too weak to exercise effective control, especially when quotas are marketable asset. To get over this difficulty another form of combination which could control the source of production was devised in the shape of "Trust". But before dealing with trusts it is advisable to consider another type of combination which is sometimes confused with Cartel, namely, Corner and Ring.

Corners and Rings. A Corner or a Ring, is in no way a form of combination, but is a device to reap high profits by undesirable practices. A Corner is created by buying up, as far as possible, all the goods available on a given market with a view to monopolising them. It is not an association, but a trade manoeuvre which may be attempted by a single merchant. Corners are known to have been made in ancient times and in the Middle Ages, and they are common even these days. A Ring is an association of several persons with a view to forming a Corner in conjunction, although in popular language the word is often used as equivalent to Cartel. Thus a Ring is not an agreement between independent entrepreneurs, as in Cartel, but is a joint enterprise carrying out business in common. It aims, through the holding up of all available goods, at causing a scarcity and hence an increase of price, so that it can unload at the higher price and make a profit. A Ring is a highly speculative enterprise, and has nothing whatever to do with regulation of price, production and supply, which is the function of the cartels. The concentration of the entire or substantial stocks of a commodity in a single hand or a small group of persons and the withdrawal of them from the market is utterly at variance with the object of trade which is the distribution of goods. Further, since the Ring can only gain control of the entire volume of goods by outbidding all the other buyers and paying the producers the highest prices demanded, and since, in addition, it must make very high profits upon these high prices to compensate it for the very great risk it runs, it invariably makes the goods extremely expensive for the consumer. During periods of scarcity, e.g., war, cornering is resorted to by selfish businessmen to make very high profits. For all these reasons Corners and Rings are to be regarded with very great disfavour.

PARTIAL CONSOLIDATION

Trusts. Federation as a form of organisation, while possessing some advantages over closer combinations, suffered from the great weakness of instability and imperfect centralisation of direction and management. The remedy was discovered in consolidation, first partial and then complete, resulting in fusion. The first of such devices was a Trust, which originally appeared in the U.S.A. (though there are examples in other countries). It may be pointed out that in more popular views the term "trust" has come to be applied to all different kinds of big monopolistic combinations; but as a specific business form, it has a definite meaning and in the present discussion it is restricted to that special form. In its original and real sense therefore a combination trust has been defined as

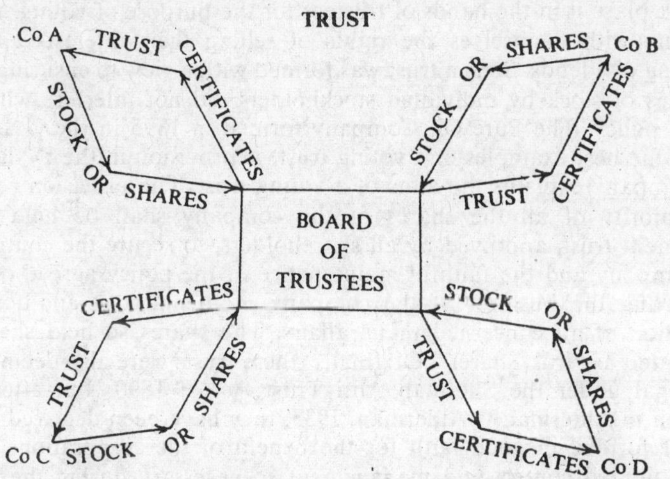

"a form of business organisation established through temporary consolidation, in which the stockholders (or shareholders) of the constituent organisations under a trust agreement transfer a controlling amount of their stock (or number of shares) to a Board of Trustees in exchange for trust certificates. These certificates show their equitable interest in the income of the combination". The definition is illustrated by the preceding diagram.

The diagram shows how by trustee device arrangement was made to establish a trust with a Board of Trustees, and all business enterprises joining the trust, if not already corporations (joint-stock companies), became incorporated. The shares owned by the shareholders of companies A,B,C, etc., were conveyed in trust to the Board of Trustees, which issued trust certificates in lieu thereof. Thereupon the Board of Trustees acquired the voting rights incident to the stock ownership and were compelled to carry on the business of member concerns in the interests of the real owners who received, as formerly, the distribution of profits through dividends. By making use of the control over the policies of the constituent companies through possession of voting power, and because of the transfer of title to the stock, the relationship became a binding one and thus accomplished the desired end of passing the nominal ownership and effective control into the hands of a small group of powerful trustees. The Standard Oil Interests were pioneers in the experimental use of the trust, and the Standard Oil Trust was organised by John D. Rockefeller in 1879 which came to control 95 per cent of the refining capacity of the United States. The success of this and Sugar and Whisky Trusts was so pronounced that a large number of trusts were formed, and trust system became an important method of combining business firms in the U.S.A., during the eighties of the last century.

The voting trust as a modified form of the ordinary trust came into being in the U.S.A. In this form of trust, at least the holders of a majority of stock place it in the hands of trustees for the purpose of voting, while retaining with themselves the rights of selling their interests and of receiving dividends. Such a trust was formed with a view to ensuring that the sales of stock by individual stockholders did not interfere with an agreed policy. The Pure Oil Company formed in 1895 in the U.S.A. is one of the best examples of a voting trust. A provision in the by-law of this company explains the aims of a voting trust. The provision reads: "A majority of all the shares of the company shall be held in a permanent trust, approved by all shareholders, to secure the control of the company and the faithful maintenance of the policy agreed on for conducting the business of the company in the interest and for the protection of all concerned in its affairs. The shares so held shall be designated as "trust shares". Originally, these trusts were also deemed to be illegal under the Sherman Anti-Trust Act of 1890; but after the decision in Alderman v. Alderman, 1935, they have been declared to be legal if formed in good faith for the benefit of the corporation. They secure unified control and management so necessary during the early years of the company.

The trust as a form of business organisation offered the advantages of stability and endurance and made for centralisation of direction and management, which gave it the advantages of large-scale operation. With a full control over output and marketing it was in a better position than cartels to regulate prices and output. Cross freights could be saved, as also managed and clerical expenses by locating them in one central establishment. Standardisation could be taken advantage of, and a system of comparative costs for judging efficiency of different units could be installed with advantage. Finally they "enabled the effective application of the largest aggregation of capital the world had yet known to the purposes of the combination."

The limitations of, and objections to, the trusts were many. The trust was more difficult to form, and it proved difficult in practice to satisfy members as to the valuation of their plants. Once formed, the trust could not readily be changed. The promoters were able at times to secure large gains for themselves by misrepresenting or concealing material facts. There was the added danger of over-capitalisation. They became anti-social by using the economic weapon of preferential prices to eliminate the competition of rivals in certain markets; while maintaining prices at higher levels at non-competitive points. The Courts did not recognise them as legal, and ultimately in 1890 they were declared illegal. As a result, many of the trusts were transformed into holding companies; in some cases the independent units were controlled by a system of interlocking directorate or communities of interest.

Community of Interest. When trusts were declared illegal and were forced to be dissolved some new form of organisation was called for to take their place to save the vast business which had been built up from disintegration and disruption. The solution was found in a type of combination or "aggregation" in what is called the Community of Interest, which may be defined as resting upon the personal undertaking among shareholders, or directors, or both, whereby the policies of several enterprises are determined for the good of all without any formal controlling mechanism. There are two classes of community of interest, one of which is community in ownership only, and the other community in ownership and direction. The latter type is more stable and effective than the former.

The first form of community of interest (community in ownership) is secured when stock or shares of several companies are held by members of any group of persons whose interests are closely related. Thus, the members of the group have some common interest which leads them to consult about and to agree upon directors of several companies—directors who are certain to act, for the most part, in harmony. Ahmedabad mill industry offers a very good example of this form of community of interest. The second form of community of interest (ownership and direction) is established by what is known as Interlocking Directorate. This kind of community of interests is found in an industry where there is no other sign of co-ordination, and it is especially common in a manufacturing business made up of many separately owned plants, usually confined to one geographical locality : e.g., where a dozen or more plants are engaged in one product. In such a case, a few prominent manufacturers, men recognised to be the leaders of the industry, will be found to be the directors in a number of competing factories. They have small holdings in these competing organisations so that their horizon extends to the welfare of the industry as a whole and is not confined to one factory. Through the influence of these men some kind of harmony among all the producers in the town or locality is obtained. In no sense can it be said that there is real consolidation of operating plants, but there is a real co-operative unity based on mutual financial interest in each other's business problems. Yet the management of each part is free and unhampered. As will be seen presently, in India, however, the scope of interlocking directorate organisation is much wider than elsewhere, as it extends to different industries located in different parts of the country.

The managing agency system was mainly responsible for the wider application of interlocking directorate plan.

Holding Company. As none of these devices of trustee or community of interest could properly meet the needs of combination in the real sense, another form was evolved, namely, the Holding Company. Thus, as a form of business organisation a holding company is created for the "purpose of combining other companies by owning a controlling amount of their stock." Legally, a holding company is one which holds directly or through a nominee a majority of the voting shares in the subsidiary companies or possesses the power to nominate the majority of the directors. Thus, if company H's assets consist in whole or in part of shares in company S, so that (i) the amount of the shares so held by company H is more than 50 per cent of the issued share capital of company S, or (ii) is such an amount as would entitle company H to more than 50 per cent of the voting power in company S, or (iii) company H has power to appoint the majority of the directors of company S, then company H is the holding company and company S is the subsidiary company. A holding company may have any number of subsidiary companies, and a subsidiary company may be holding company of another company or companies. A holding company may be freshly created to hold shares of other companies, or it may be in existence with power to hold shares in other companies, and may do so. The company acquires the shares by exchanging its own shares for them or by other means of purchase. The subsidiary companies retain their independence and legal entity by operating under their own names, but they are effectively managed by the officers of the holding company, whose directors vote their stock or shares, or a controlling part thereof, and so elect their directors. In this way, the combined plants are firmly bound together under the control of the holding company whose Board of Directors is virtually the same as for each of its subsidiaries. A holding company and its subsidiary companies may either carry on similar business or different types of business, or it may not do anything else but hold shares in its subsidiaries.

It follows that holding companies are of different kinds according as the conditions under which they are formed. Where a company is already in existence but proceeds to organise subsidiary companies and holds controlling shares it is called a Parent Holding Company. When a number of companies join together and start a new company which holds the majority of voting rights in these joining companies, Consolidated or Offspring Holding Company comes into existence. Holding companies may be pure or operating or mixed. A Pure Holding Company is that which does not engage in any of the technical processes of production directly, and merely holds the share of the operating companies. An Operating or Mixed Holding Company is that which holds shares of subsidiary companies, and also operates one plant. A Primary Holding Company is one which stands at the head of the combination organisation before or above it. An Intermediary Holding

Company is a holding company of a subsidiary, but is itself controlled by another holding company. All these holding companies are formed for the purpose of controlling subsidiary or affiliated concerns, and may therefore be described as "Control Holding Companies". They are the only holding companies proper; although some other similar organisations which do not aim at control at all, but desire to make profits by financing other concerns, are sometimes described as holding companies. For example, a company whose primary function is to earn profits by financing the operations of other companies through promotion, underwriting, or reorganisation is sometimes called a Finance Holding Company. Also a company which has as its purpose the holding of securities in other companies for the sake of income and "long-pull appreciation" is described as Investment Holding Company, although it may only be an investment company pure and simple, with no intention to exercise control but only to hold shares. In fact it seeks diversification of holdings to avoid risk of loss. The Companies Act, 1956, also lays down to the same effect that a finance or investment company, that is to say, a company whose principal business is to lend money and acquisition and holding of shares, stocks, debentures, or other securities, is not a holding company merely because part of its assets consists in 51 per cent or more of the shares of another company. The diagram below illustrates the different kinds of the aforesaid holding companies.

Where a company H already in existence decides to exercise control over companies, carrying on similar or different businesses, it buys

Holding Company

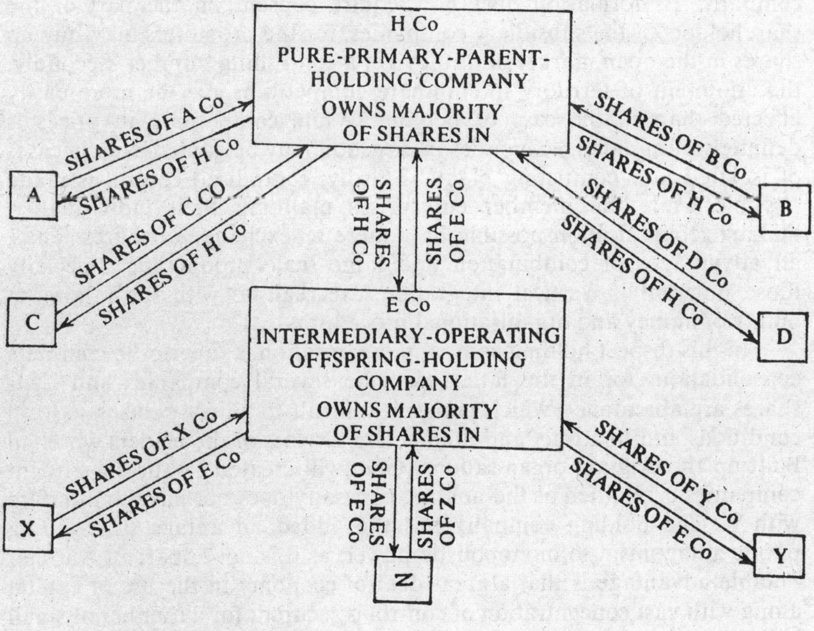

majority of shares of each company, A,B,C, and D, which become its subsidiaries. In this manner the H company becomes the shareholder of all the four companies, and its directors will elect their own nominees as directors of each of the subsidiary companies. Thus, though the subsidiary or controlled companies remain nominally independent and operate under their own names, they are effectively managed by the directors or officers of the holding company. The H company is a parent company because it is already there; it is primary, because there is no other company above it, and it is pure or simple, because it does not operate its subsidiary companies. Suppose there are three companies, X, Y, and Z, which compete with one another, and decide to organise a holding company E, which is also to operate. The same procedure as described above is then followed, and we get E as the offspring-operating-holding company of X, Y, and Z, subsidiaries. Thereafter, H company holds controlling shares in E company, with the result that E now becomes a subsidiary of H, and so an intermediary holding company. In consequence, A, B, C, D, E, X, Y, and Z companies are subsidiaries of H company. Thus, control by the holding company can be extended over any number of business concerns by a similar process of "Pyramiding."

The holding company device has many advantages over other forms. Of all the combinations of the consolidation type a holding company is organised most easily. Combination is facilitated by the fact that large control may be acquired by the purchase of only a small portion of the total amount of stock outstanding in each constituent company. Its formation does not require consent on the part of the shareholders of the subsidiary companies, for the promoters may buy up shares in the open market until they get a controlling number. Secondly, the allotment of territory to eliminate competition may be more easily effected than in the case of pooling. While competition in prices is definitely eliminated, economies in direction may be gained even in cases of isolated non-competing plants. Thirdly, centralised control is made possible while the member enterprises maintain their individuality, making reorganisation possible by a mere re-exchange of shares. Thus, all advantages of combination and large-scale production, especially those inherent in vertical integration, are realised with the minimum outlay of money and organisational procedure.

In this respect holding company organisation is superior to complete consolidation, for in the latter case the several companies and their shares are abandoned which makes it difficult to adjust policies to local conditions and to attract and hold active services of the leaders who had built up the original organisations. Goodwill created by the constituent companies is retained as the holding company does not have to interfere with it. The holding company has the added advantage of avoiding public antagonism to monopolistic power, as it is not apparent. Another notable advantage is that a great deal of economy in the use of capital along with vast concentration of control is secured; for a number of small holdings will control a relatively vast amount of capital.

From the point of view of the entrepreneur, a holding company in herits all the disadvantages of a joint-stock company. The greatest objection against the holding company is that it gives power without responsibility; and larger the number of combinations involved and more concentrated the control, the greater will be the power with little responsibility. Consequently, the dilution of liability and responsibility due to the pyramiding process, is liable to lead to fraud and inside manipulation of incorporated finances and policies. There is a danger of over-capitalisation, which tends to facilitate fraud. Financial manipulation and fraudulent practices detrimental to the subsidiaries have been noticed. Before January 15, 1937, it was common with holding companies to utilise for their benefit the profits of subsidiaries or to transfer to them their own losses.

To check these and similar questionable practices, a new section, 132-A, was added in 1936 which requires greater disclosures of the affairs of the subsidiary companies. It provides that the last audited balance sheet, profits and loss account and auditors' report of the subsidiaries must be attached to the balance sheet of the holding company, as also a statement signed by the persons by whom the balance sheet is signed and authenticated. This statement should show how the profits and losses of the subsidiary companies have been dealt with in or for the purpose of the accounts of the holding company, and, in particular, how and to what extent (i) provision has been made for the losses of a subsidiary company in the accounts of the subsidiary companies or of the holding company, or both, and (ii) how losses of the subsidiary company have been taken into account by the directors of the holding company in arriving at the profits and losses of the company as disclosed in its accounts. It is, however, not necessary to specify in any statement the acutal amount of any part of any such profits or losses which has been dealt with in any particular manner. The private companies which are subsidiaries of a public company do not enjoy any of the exemptions granted to a private company. They are in effect treated as public companics.

Trust and Holding Company Distinguished. Structurally, the holding company is similar to the trustee device, and functionally, it secures similar ends. Yet there are some notable differences between the two forms, which are :

1. That instead of a Board of Trustees, the holding company has directors of the joint-stock company, taking direct interest in the management of the concerns.
2. That instead of control of the enterprises by the trustees, which condition is effected by the nominal ownership of the shares transferred to them by the shareholders of the allied concerns, the shareholders of the holding company elect their directorate to manage the affairs of the combination.
3. In the trust, the shareholders surrender their shares to be held in trust for them by the trustees, thus becoming 'beneficiaries'

of the trust agreement. In the holding company, shares are secured by a legally authorised limited company which by virtue of its nature has the power to do so.

4. In the trust agreement, a federate relationship was involved, in which the parties maintained a nominally separate existence, whereas the holding company is a nominally responsible company, buying shares in the open market and doing what the State has authorised it to do.
5. In point of legality, the trust agreement is one between an association of individual trustees and a group of companies, which by implication give up their autonomy and so act ultra vires. With a holding company its practice of securing and disposing of stocks is entirely within its charter power, since it deals only with individual shareholders. Therefore, the trust is illegal and the holding is legal, so far as forms are concerned.

COMPLETE CONSOLIDATION

A complete consolidation is a total fusion by outright purchase of the properties of constituent companies into a single unit. It is a union in which the parts are fused and lose their identity, at least for operating purposes, and comes into being by sale. It may take the form of Amalgamation or Merger.

Amalgamation takes place where two or more companies organise a new company with which to consolidate. They lose their separate existence; e.g., two lines A and B combine under the name of C line and cease to exist as system A and B. The two companies may instead of giving the name C to the new company call it A & B Co., which will obviously be a new company with a new name. As a means for developing big into bigger business, ordinary firms into larger unified firms, amalgamation is of quite extraordinary influence. A Merger is a form of consolidation where one of the companies already in existence absorbs all the rest of the enterprise, each of the various companies losing its identity as a business unit, although the plants themselves may continue to operate. For example, the main line of a railway system may absorb branches and extension with the result that the branch companies cease to exist as separate organisations and the main line goes on as before. A merger is sometimes called a Concern. Indeed, a concern has been defined as a "merger of firms into a single unit for the purposes of productive technique, administration, trading, or (especially) finance." As already explained, these forms can be carried out by a special resolution and with the sanction of the Court under Section 394 of the Indian Companies Act. A consolidation scheme has to be submitted and when and as sanctioned by the Court to be adopted. Thereupon the shareholders of the constituent companies become shareholders in the new company on an agreed basis, and similarly their creditors become its creditors.

Holding Company and Complete Consolidation Distinguished. The holding company retains the separate existence of the combined companies and controls them by voting their shares. It cannot act formally and directly for them, but only through their directors. As seen before, it is only a partial or temporary consolidation. In a fusion or complete consolidation the combining units are no longer separate and independent, they fuse and become one. There is no question of controlling them, for they have now all become one.

In the case of a holding company, the relationship that is established by combination is between individual shareholders of the subsidiary companies and the holding company. Indeed, the holding company and subsidiary companies are relative terms and are used only in connection with the relation of two companies one of which holds a majority of the voting shares in the other company. In complete consolidation, the relationship is between the companies and therefore the interests of all the shareholders (including the dissenting shareholders who as a minority are compelled to transfer their shares) of all the combining companies are fused and are alike. There is, however, in the case of holding company organisation a danger of conflict of interests between two sets of shareholders, namely, those who join and those who are not in the combination. This does not happen in complete consolidation.

The advantages of complete consolidation over the holding company are: (i) that dilution of responsibility and liability of the latter is replaced by a unified and concentrated management, eliminating unnecessary official and other expenses incidental to maintaining a number of offices and independent plants; (ii) that the unity of interest resulting in greater confidence replaces the possibility of unfair manipulation of the affairs of the greater variety of constituent companies making up a holding company; (iii) that the legal position of complete consolidation, where properly effected, is more secure than that of the holding company; (iv) that as to responsibility to the public, or even to shareholders, it is decidedly superior to holding company, for in the holding company the total power is lodged in a few, while the total responsibility is spread among many; (v) that the holding company lends itself to undemocratic control more readily than fusion; (vi) that because complete consolidation is not so readily formed as is the holding company, it is not so apt to become a monopoly by embracing an entire industry. "Sound public policy will encourage complete consolidation by merger or amalgamation rather than by securities holding, and that, in the long run, legitimate individual interests lie in the same direction."

The complete consolidation surrenders some advantages inherent in the holding company form, viz., (i) a greater outlay of capital is necessary when purchasing outright, (ii) consent of a larger majority (three-fourths) of the shareholders of the constituent companies is necessary; (iii) goodwill built around firm names of the enterprises fused and patents acquired at great expenses, must be sacrificed where it could have been preserved in the holding company; (iv) the possibility of territorial allotment of business common to the holding company is lost in complete consolidation; (v) reorganisation is difficult where necessary because of the complete transfer of ownership instead of a mere exchange of one share of stock for another; (vi) unlike the holding company form which makes re-adjustment easier, fusion may first result in over-capitalisation due to excessive stock and bond payments, and then in the petrification of that capitalisation as the result of losing the identity of the several properties against which it was issued.

Consolidation versus Cartel. At the very outset it is necessary to bear in mind that the term consolidation is used here to include both partial consolidation and complete consolidation—trust, holding company, amalgamation and merger. Both cartels and consolidation aim at monopoly. Regarding method of organisation there is a similarity, for both are based on the mutual consent of the members. But here the likeness ends. The consolidation involves an organic change and, unlike a cartel, which is a mere federation, it is a fusion of interest. The cartel does not interfere with the internal management of the individual manufacturer; it is essentially a selling agency acting on behalf of the constituent manufacturing firms. In a trust, there is a common ownership of stock and direction of management of the various units by a few trustees who exercise complete control over them and their policies. The functions of making and selling are separated and it is possible to secure advantages of large-scale production and organisation. Further, cartels are contractual unions, while trusts, holding companies, amalgamations or mergers are financial capitalisation unions, resting upon the basis of ownership. The trustees are virtual owners of the shares held by them, and they act as principals and not as agents or servants.

On the other hand, the cartel is regarded as superior to the consolidation for three reasons. In the first place, the cartel is not exposed to the danger of over-capitalisation which may result in the case of the consolidation, if its capital is "watered". In the second place, the member firms of a cartel retain their individuality, and so management and financial independence. On the contrary, a consolidation is controlled from headquarters; the managers of factories are but subordinates who must obey their rulers. Thirdly, the fate of a cartel does not lie in the hands of one man or a small group of men, as it does in the case of a consolidation. Here, it is said, lies the chief weakness of a consolidation. It will be wrong to dogmatise on this subject, but it may be stated that to promote a consolidation is simpler than to control its destinies. Great businessmen may start a trust and manage it well, but their places may be, and are generally, taken by people trained in a different school and lacking perhaps, the outstanding qualities of pioneers who prove unequal to the task. This applies to all forms of consolidation, and greater the degree of centralisation of authority the greater the seriousness of error when it is made. In a trust, or in any like centralised organisation for that matter, the effects of an error at the top may reverberate through the entire organisation; a serious error may bring untold loss and suffering.

COMBINATIONS IN INDIA

Combination movement in India has lagged far behind the one in Western countries. Indeed, there has hardly been any movement in this direction, for there has not been any evolutionary development as in more industrialised countries, but only a merger here or an amalgamation there according to the exigencies of circumstances. The reasons for the slow growth of combinations and for the direction it has taken are as follows:

1. *Absence of Competition.* Before the First World War, the British companies operating in India enjoyed practically a monopoly in their lines of trade. There was no competition and so no combinations.

2. *Managing Agency System.* The managing agency system had led to financial and managerial integration in industry which resulted in concentration of control in a few hands. Since the economics of combinations were realised through such financial and managerial integration no need for formal combinations was felt.

3. *Individualistic Outlook.* The Indian businessmen by nature are prone to be individualistic so that this trait of theirs stood in the way of the growth of combination movement in India.

4. *Want of adequate impetus.* The need for combination usually arise with industrial development. As our industrial development was in its traditional stage, there was hardly any impetus towards combination movement.

5. *Larger Number of Units.* One of the facilitating forces for combinations is that the size of the business units should be large and their number should be small. In India, the number was too large and the size too small to make combination feasible.

In spite of the presence of these unfavourable factors acting as strong checks to any formal combination movement in India, the continued industrial hardship made our industrialists to recognise the usefulness of cooperation, with the result that a few combines came into being. A brief review of the different forms is given below.

TRADE ASSOCIATIONS AND CHAMBERS OF COMMERCE

There are a large number of trade associations and Chambers of Commerce. As we have observed in earlier pages, there are about 836 trade associations and 123 employers' associations. The more important associations are the Indian Jute Mills' Association, the Associated Cement Company, the Indian Paper Makers' Association, Indian Tea Association, United Planters' Association, Bombay Millowners' Association, All India Manufacturers' Organisation and so on. Similarly, there are numerous Chambers of Commerce, both regional and national which have been detailed earlier.

POOLS AND CARTELS

There are a few examples of pools and cartels which have proved effective. The first of these, Indian Jute Mills' Association, formed in 1886, is a curious mixture of a trade association, an output pool and a cartel. It is an association of jute mill owners, representing 95% of the trade, embracing 88% of the total number of mills. In cement industry Cement Marketing Company of India was formed in 1930 with the object of controlling the sale and distribution of cement produced by all the member companies. This cartel did not succeed in its aims, and so, in 1937 a complete consolidation of fusion took place in the shape of Associated Cement Companies Ltd. with the absorption of 11 cement companies. In sugar industry, Sugar Syndicate was formed in 1937, which acted as a cartel. It was, however, dissolved in 1950, and partial control over sugar was imposed. The agreement between the British India Steam Navigation Co. Ltd. and the Scindia Steam Navigation Co. Ltd. is an example of Shipping Ring or Conference.

HOLDING COMPANIES

There are a few instances of holding company organisations, some sample cases of which are given here. The Associated Cement Companies Ltd. holds a large number of shares in Patiala Cement Co. Ltd. and all the shares of the Cement Marketing Co. of India Ltd. Parry & Co. Ltd. owns the whole of the share capital in the Mofussil Warehouse and Trading Co. Ltd., Shaw Wallace & Co. Ltd. has 99% interest in some tea, cotton mills, flour mills and Atlas Fertilizers Ltd. The Tea Estates Ltd. is a subsidiary of Brooke Bond India Ltd. In the Public Sector, General Insurance Corporation of India is a holding company of various nationalised general insurance companies, such as Oriental Fire General Insurance Co. Ltd., Indian Mercantile Insurance Co. Ltd., New Great Insurance Co. of India Ltd., etc. The Steel Authority of India Ltd., (SAIL) is the holding company of the steel plants owned by the Hindustan Steel Ltd.

AMALGAMATION AND MERGER

There are not many cases of complete consolidation, and those which are notable have taken place either under the pressure of the Government or the managing agents before the system was abolished in 1970. For example, the British India Corporation was set up in 1920 to take over six separate companies engaged in manufacturing different products, namely, the Cawnpore Woollen Mills Ltd., the Cawnpore Cotton Mills Ltd., the New Egerton Woollen Mills Ltd., the North-West Tannery Co. Ltd., Copper Allen & Co. Ltd. and the Empire Engineering Co. Ltd. The Buckingham Carnatic Mills Ltd. is an amalgamation of three cotton mills. The absorption of the Bengal Iron Co. Ltd. by the Indian Iron & Steel Co. Ltd. and in 1953 the merger of the Steel Corporation of Bengal Ltd. into the Indian Iron & Steel Co. Ltd. is an example of complete consolidation in steel industry. The Indian Iron & Steel Co. Ltd. has since been taken over by the Government, as it was not being properly managed and operated. The Central Government has decided on the merger of sick textile and other units taken over by the Government with healthy units. Tax concessions are given in such cases.

COMMUNITY OF INTERESTS

This is the most widely employed form of combination in India, and has assumed two main forms, namely, (a) Interlocking of interests through managing agents or Financial and Managerial Integration, and (b) Interlocking through directors.

The managing agency system had been the greatest single force responsible for financial and managerial integration of business units. The Companies Act, 1956, however, laid down that no managing agent could manage more than ten public companies. In spite of this restriction the companies promoted and managed by them before the Act continued to be under their control and direction through indirect methods. But this kind of community of interest came to an end with the abolition of the managing agency system in 1970.

Interlocked or multiple directorships were also used to bring about community of interests. A person could be a director of any number of companies. For example, H.C. Waters and Purshotamdas Thakurdas held 50 directorships each. Leading families of Indian businessmen monopolised over 600 directorships in 1950–51. Even after the Companies Act, 1956 laying down the maximum of directorships at 20 a person could have, 14 Indian families held as many as 408 directorships, and 7 of them held 331 directorships among themselves. It was also found that in 1960–61, that 325 persons held multiple directorships in 631 companies. The study revealed that directors of large-sized companies tend to hold multiple directorships.[1]

A similar development of greater dimension and importance is the growth of "interlocutory" directorships in Indian industries. A large number of independent and anonymous Trusts are further interlinked by a group of common directors. The device of interlocutory directorships thus not only leads to concentration of ownership and control in still few

---

M.L. Kothari, *Industrial Combination in India,* p. 79.

hands, but also tends to secure greater collaboration and cooperation between the integrated units.

ALLIANCES

Soon after World War II, another development began, namely, the formation of alliances, or collaborations or working partnerships between Indian and foreign industrialists. In recent years, such collaborations have taken place even in the public sector. Some of the main collaborations are: the Hindustan Motors Ltd. as a result of Nuffield-Birla Motor Deal. Ashoka Motors Ltd.—linking with Austin Motors for the manufacture of cars and trucks; Telco.—Tata-Mercedez Benz joint deal for the manufacture of diesel trucks; Hindustan Pilkington is a collaboration between India and British Glass Manufacturers; Voltas Ltd. was formed by Tatas and Volkart Bros. collaborating for taking over the Volkart Bros. import and engineering activities.

Examples of public sector collaborations are: an agreement between the Government of India and Krupps and Demag of Germany for setting up of a steel plant at Rourkela, with a Swiss firm for Machine Tools Factory and British Steel syndicate for setting up a steel plant at Durgapur. Some State Governments have also entered into similar agreements with foreign firms. Orissa Government has started a tractor factory in collaboration with a British firm and Karnataka Government has entered into an agreement with an American firm for setting up a fertilizer factory.

ECONOMICS OF COMBINATION

In the earlier part of this chapter have been discussed the various reasons for effecting combinations. We have also noted the advantages that may follow from the different kinds of combines. We may now sum up the economies which can be achieved by combination. These economies are of two classes: (1) those due to the size of the business, and (2) those due to monopoly.

Economies due to Size. The economies of size consist, in the main, of internal and external economies, or the advantages of large-scale organisations, which we have already considered fully in Chapter VII. We may outline these economies which are—(i) economies in production, (ii) economies in management, (iii) economies in financial administration, and (iv) economies in marketing.

(i) *Economies in production*, such as economies of bulk purchasing of materials and fuel, of freight, of division of labour and specialisation, of operating costs due to the installation of costly automatic machinery and its fuller utilization and through research, of the utilization of materials more effectively either as by-product manufacture or disposal of waste in bulk, of independent arrangements for repairs and maintenance of plant.

(ii) *Economies in management,* for example, economy achieved through the reduction in the overhead costs per unit, through better management by best brains which big business can afford through fuller utilization of patents, etc., through economy of comparative accounting and production standards.

(iii) *Economies in Financial administration,* e.g., facility of raising finance at lower cost by offering greater security, ploughing back of reserves thus save interest payment and escape repayment obligations.

(iv) *Economies in marketing* through saving in selling expenses on account of larger sales, through elimination of cross freights, through extensive as well as intensive advertising campaign.

In addition to the above economies, combines are better able to face depressions. Combination is one of the methods of rationalisation which results in improved efficiency.

Economies due to monopoly. Combinations are also resorted to for gaining advantages of monopoly. A monopoly may assume any one of the three forms, namely it may be short-term monopoly, or a transitional monopoly, or again a long-term monopoly. A short-term monopoly may be achieved through informal types of organisation, such as gentlemen's agreements, associations for regulating output, pooling association, etc. A transitional monopoly, which is intermediate between the short-term terminable associations and the long-term forms is usually fairly longlived, but at the same time is terminable. Cartels and financial community of interests are examples. A long-term monopoly results from complete consolidation, such as trusts, mergers, amalgamations, etc.

1. Most of the economies indicated above for large-scale operations can be accomplished by a monopolist. For example, the economies in the sphere of marketing are partly due to size and partly to monopoly. The advantage of monopoly in this sphere is the *elimination of competitive advertising.*

2. Another economy of monopoly is *stability.* A monopoly is in a position to adjust supply to demand with greater success than a group of competing firms. Under competition an increase in demand which cannot quickly be met by increased supply leads to considerable rise in prices. Every producer revises his plans to cash in one the boom, so that there is all-round expansion. This would result in the phenomenon that supply exceeds demand at the new price. The price falls and the same mistake is made again, but in the opposite direction. Equilibrium price may be found after long time, and if demand is unstable, we may never reach anywhere near an equilibrium price. The industry can never settle down to a steady run of prosperity. All this results in wastage of resources. The monopolist, however, is not subject to such miscalculation since he is the sole producer.

3. A monopoly brought about by complete fusion of combining

firm can, by keeping its price steady, help to iron out trade cycles.

4. Long-term monopolies are in a position to secure the economies of specialisation and modernisation and so minimise cost, leading to the achievement of rationalisation.

5. A monopoly is the most efficient form of production where a single optimum firm can more than meet the total demand. For this reason public utilities lend themselves mostly to monopoly production.

6. A well co-ordinated monopoly can run its plant at fuller capacity and will more readily introduce new machinery to meet demand.

7. An important technical advantage to monopoly, particularly to long-term monopoly, is that it can make available to all plants the experience and knowledge of each.

8. There is an added advantage in the sphere of management. For example, it is possible to estimate total consumption of any commodity, but under competition, it is extremely difficult to forecast what part of the whole different competing firms will get. The monopolist is only concerned with the total demand, and very often he can control it, by dictating the rate of change of tastes and preferences. The task of management is further facilitated by receiving orders at one central office and then distributing them to different plants. This enables each plant to secure the greatest economies by working regularly and at fuller capacity.

9. Another advantage possessed exclusively by a monopoly relates to finance and capital raising. A monopoly makes possible ploughing back of profits for improvements and maintenance. Additional funds can be more easily raised by a monopoly for expansion and re-equipment. This will ultimately help to bring down costs and prices.

10. One of the greatest economies that a monopolist enjoys is on the side of buying. Since he is very likely to be the sole purchaser of some of the materials that he employs, he can obtain them at a relatively low price, as his bargaining power is likely to be greater than that of the suppliers.

Diseconomies of monopoly. As against these economies or advantages of monopoly, we must balance the losses which will accure because of growth beyond the capacity of management to control efficiently.

There is a danger of the organisation becoming rigid and inflexible because of its having become too big. Because of these factors, it may not be possible to continuously and successfully adapt its operations to changing conditions and circumstances.

A monopoly resulting from combination of different units will suffer from bureaucratic administration and red-tape which may slow down decision making.

Evils of Business Combinations. Combines and combinations have been censured by publicists and economists on account of so many evils which are associated with them. Combination, it is alleged, results in monopoly with all its evil consequences. But all combinations are not necessarily bad. A combination may be for the diminution of capital risk, which will inspire producers to try to produce more evenly and thus prove beneficial both to the consumer and producer. But monopoly organisations of producers by means of combination are on the whole in a position to damage the consumer, the new competitor and the community. We summarise the evils of combinations in the following paragraphs.

1. *Inefficiency.* A large combine may be so big that the law of diminishing returns robs it of efficiency. Inefficiency may also be generated by rigidities and inflexibilities which creep into large organisations. Some monopolies brought about by restriction of output or fixation of quotas may become subject to inefficiency because of the possibility of allowing the inefficient unit to continue functioning under the protection of the efficient one. Such units would be driven out of the market under competition.

2. *Exploitation of consumers.* When the combination is formed for the increase in profits by charging monopolistic prices which are invariably high, it is said to be a *conspiracy against consumers.* By eliminating the weaker producers (not necessarily inefficient), and so having built up monopolistic power, a combine may exploit the consumers ruthlessly causing them great hardships, especially if no substitutes are available to take place the monopoly products.

3. *Exploitation of producers.* The advantage of bulk buying at low price that results to the monopolist will prove damaging to the poor and unorganised producers of primary products or materials. Our cultivators who ordinarily produce in small lots suffer considerably because of their ignorance and lower bargaining power.

4. *Squeezing out of small businessman.* A combine, resulting in monopoly, is usually so big that it keeps new competitors out of the market and forces existing competitors out of the market. Through sheer bigness, it can squeeze every possible competitor into insolvency by using all kinds of unfair means.

5. *Hogs the market.* It is inherent in large combines to hog the market. That is to say, it uses its market power to beat down everyone who stands between the combine and high prices. As already mentioned a monopolistic combine charges high prices, chases after gigantic profits and by using its superior bargaining power, keeps competitors away.

6. *Concentration of wealth and economic and political power.* Business combination usually leads to concentration of wealth and economic as well as political power in the hands of a few persons. The appetite for expansion creates "tendency for accumulations," lust for power and "impersonal capitalism". This has happened in all countries in the world including India. According to a Study directed by Dr. R. K. Hazari, since 1951, the concentration has increased. For instance the four top groups, Tata, Birla, Martin Burn, Dalmia Sahu Jain, along with their outer circles and minority interests had nearly 30 per cent of the total share

capital of non-government companies under their control. The Tata and Birla complexes had nearly 20 per cent of the gross capital stock of all non-government public companies.[1] The managing agency system has been responsible to a very large extent for this concentration of wealth and economic power in the hands of a couple of dozen people. This economic power gives to these business magnates control over political life of the country. Political corruption is usually the outcome of this situation.

7. *Over-capitalisation.* Under long-term monopoly, brought about by mergers and amalgamation, there is always a danger of over-capitalisation which is undesirable from the point of view of the unit itself, the shareholders and the community.

8. *Enhancement of risk.* A combination of a number of units means the concentration of large resources and enhances the risk of failure and consequent loss not only to the combine and its owners and workers, but also to the community. A large unit is very often at the mercy of its under managers and their lack of loyalty and integrity may bring down the concern. Therefore, risk increases because of this factor as well as on account of public distrust of monopoly.

9. *Unfair tactics of monopolies.* Monopolistic firms have sometimes ordered dealers selling their products to refrain from handling the products of other firms, thus limiting the market, open to competitors. "Tying up contracts" have also been used to compel dealers to sell unremuneratives along with readily saleable goods. Sometimes monopolists "persuade" government officials to refuse or delay facilities such as grant of import licences to other firms and so keep out the competitors. These and similar other objectionable tactics obviously enable a monopolist to maintain high prices, keep the output low and thus injure the interests of society by producing less than what is socially required.

10. *Creating instability.* Monopolies also contribute to the instability of the economic system. In periods of good business they maintain stable prices for their products in the face of increasing production and favourable unit costs and without increasing the wages of labour significantly. Such policies are likely to lead to business breakdown and depression in the end. And in periods of depression, the monopolies are likely to hold their prices at about the customary level, taking losses by selling fewer units at the stable price rather than by selling more at a lower price. This policy results in laying off labour, curtailing purchases of materials and supplies, and reducing consumer purchasing power and eventually affects all industries and adds to the cumulative downward spiral of depression. As long as monopolies control large number of major industries trade cycles cannot be eliminated.

11. *Bar to economic progress.* Monopolies may also operate as a bar to economic progress. Long-term monopolies need not worry about developing new methods and processes or introducing innovations, for

1. Hazari, R.K., *The Corporate Private Sector-Concentration, Ownership and Control*, p. 305.

their profits do not depend upon continuous progress in production. Indeed, they may go to the other extreme and acquire control of new inventions by fair means or foul, only to put them on the Shelf for a long time so that they will not overturn existing conditions in the industry.

The Control of Monopoly. Since monopoly is less efficient than the Perfect Competition and less equitable, the public feels alarmed and disturbed by the ill-effects of monopoly. As a measure of combating the anti-social influences of monopoly, legislation and other measures are suggested. We shall consider here some of the effective measures to check monopoly power without destroying any of its advantages.

1. *Trust Busting or Anti-monopoly legislation.* Anti-monopoly legislation has been tried in many countries, but it has proved on the whole ineffective and futile. In our country, a Monopolies Act has been passed by Parliament. American experience over the last 65 years and the history of the British experience to break up the big German combines after 1945, seem to indicate that the chains which hold a monopoly together are very difficult to break once and for all. If one form of combination is prohibited, monopolies have a habit of reappearing in a different guise.

2. *Price Control.* Alternatively, socially useful combines or associations may be allowed to continue, but they should be prevented from using their power in anti-social ways. One method would be to fix a fair price for their products. But how are we to know what is a 'fair' price? Presumably it is one which is made up of the costs of an efficient firm plus a 'reasonable' profit margin. There are many difficulties in the way of adopting this method, but some kind of check can be introduced. In this is expected to restore condition of *free competition.* But we can hardly expect to ensure by this method that costs, profits, or prices will be identical with those which would prevail under Perfect Competition.

3. *Taxes and Subsidies.* It is also suggested that a system of taxes and subsidies could be used in relation to monopoly organisations. For example, if the value of the marginal product of labour is persistently higher in some industries than in others because of monopoly condition, society would benefit if labour were moved from the industries where its marginal product is relatively low to the industries where its marginal product is relatively high. The required shift of labour could be encouraged by a tax on wages in the first group of industries (to discourage them from taking on labour) and a subsidy on wages in the second group to induce them to expand their labour force. The taxes and subsidy shall have to be adjusted for making the value of marginal product of labour the same in all industries. Also, a monopolist or oligopolist whose output is less than the optimum could be encouraged to expand by offering him a subsidy based on output. This could be combined with a fixed tax—i.e., one which does not vary—to syphon off any excess profit. The subsidy should be adjusted until the firm is of optimum size and is receiving only normal profit. Neither policy has yet been tried, and there would be many practical difficulties.

4. *Publicity of undesirable activities of monopolists.* Professor Pigou and some other economists suggest that unfair practices followed by monopolists, should be publicised with a view to keeping the public alert. This method by itself is not potent enough to achieve the result, although it could be used as a supplementary mode.

5. *Nationalisation.* A more radical solution is the nationalisation of monopolies. To nationalise a monopoly does not, however, necessarily lead to better allocation of resources, nor is there any evidence that it has done so. One might argue that, even though nationalisation may not in practice succeed in producing the conditions of Perfect Competition it can at any rate be used to spread the profits from the monopoly over the whole community instead of leaving them in the hands of the monopolist entrepreneurs. So it can, but it does not follow that it *will.* No one has as yet discovered a method of control to ensure the efficient working of nationalised industries.

6. *Attacking the Roots of Monopoly.* All the above direct attacks on monopoly have their difficulties and weaknesses. They are not universally applicable at all times and in all cases, and nowhere are they certain to succeed. The alternative is to tackle monopoly at the roots : to try to create conditions which will stimulate competition.

We have noted that monopoly power depends on one or more of four factors—(i) the ignorance and irrationality of consumers, (ii) restrictions on entry into an industry, (iii) collective agreements between producers and/or distributors, and (iv) the power which comes from sheer size. These factors must be rooted out for successful handling of the problem of monopoly break up.

(a) *Consumers' Association.* To help consumers to make informed and rational choices of goods, they should be educated. This education can begin in the school which will help pupils to learn how to get the value for their money. For older customers an information service should supply useful details of the quality, composition and fitness for its purposes, of any article which they cannot judge by inspection. For this purpose Consumers' Association and Consumers' Advisory Service can be set up. They have been tried very successfully in Great Britain.

(b) *Freedom from restraint.* Everyone should have the freedom to enter into an industry, the freedom to buy where he wants, freedom to sell to anyone who will buy from him, and freedom to charge the price that he can command. But these freedoms can function within the following restrictions :

(i) Where monopoly is obviously superior to competition, e.g., in public utilities, the monopoly should be publicly owned and administered;

(ii) In times of acute shortage, when the rise in prices which would occur in a free market cannot bring forth an increased supply, e.g., during a major war—prices should be controlled by the State;

(iii) Where it is necessary to maintain certain standards of quality or service or technical competence, only persons or firms able to achieve these standards should be allowed to enter or remain in the trade concerned. Medicine and the food traders are probably the best examples;

(iv) The use of price-cutting as a means of unfair competition should be prohibited—if it can be proved !

To this end we need both *negative* and *positive* policies. The *negative policy* would consist of ban on restrictive practices, such as re-sale, price maintenance, loyalty rebates, black-listing and withholding of supplies, etc. Tariffs which make possible a monopoly of the domestic market should be rarely imposed and frequently reviewed.

On the positive side we need quality of educational opportunity. Technical and business education should be strengthened. New firms could be granted tax rebates if they employed adequately trained people. The patent laws might be revised so as to make it more difficult for firms to tie up patents for several years.

The imperfections, which arise from sheer size, or from concentration of control, are more difficult to deal with. It is useless to set a ceiling on the size of the firm, for the scale of operation required for maximum efficiency differs from industry to industry. Similarly, it is difficult to deal with concentration of control in an industry. A break up of the large groups is, legally, impossible and, on economic grounds, unwise, especially when our country lacks organisation more than it lacks capital.

Two long term remedies can be suggested to reduce concentrations of economic power. One is to encourage the growth of medium and small groups and the other is to further expand the public sector. Managing agency is going to be abolished. But we cannot expect any anti-monopoly policy to bring perfect results; we can only try for the best in public interest.

Monopolies in India

A commission, known as the Monopolies Inquiry Commission, was appointed by the Government of India in April, 1964, to enquire into the extent and effect of concentration of economic power in India and the prevalence of monopolistic and restrictive practices in important sectors of economic activity. The Commission submitted its report on the 31st October 1965 and made certain very important recommendations, including legislation to regulate concentration of restrictive practices. The Commission considered the problem of concentration of economic power on two bases : product-wise and country-wise. According to the Commission the product-wise concentration arises where one product is produced or controlled by a single or a few or closely knit and controlled large number of concerns in the production and distribution of a particular product or service. Country-wise concentration arises when the ownership or control of a large number of concerns engaged in the production and distribution of several commodities is in the hands of a single individual or a family or a group of persons closely connected by financial or other business interests. The Commission found that in both respects there was a good degree of concentration in the country.

In relation to product-wise concentration, the Commission found it in existence in a high degree. For 6 producers produce portable tools and Ralliwold Ltd. led with 80% production. Grinding wheels were produced by two companies to the extent of 80% of the total. In the case of 71 items of industrial machinery, 17 items were produced by a single producer; the top producer in the case of other items produced 90% of the total. For example, A.V.B. Ltd., Durgapur, produced 88% of water tube boilers. Three concerns produce motor cars, and Hindustan Motors account for 66.1% of the production, Standard 17.2% and Premier (Fiat) 16.7%. In terms of value, Hindustan totalled 76.6%. Dry batteries are produced by two companies—Union Carbide 82% and Estrela 18%.

In regard to country-wise concentration, 75 groups, having 1,536 companies command Rs. 2,605.95 crores assets and total paid up capital at Rs. 646.32 crores. Their share in the total paid up capital and assets was 44.1% and 46.9% respectively. The total paid up capital of the corporate sector, leaving out Government companies and banking companies, was Rs. 1,465.5 crores in 1963-64 and assets Rs. 5,552.14 crores in the same year.

Causes. The Commission found that emergence of corporations leading to large-scale production, managing agency system, inter-company investments, holding company method and the ability to secure licences for starting new ventures and getting of import licences and foreign exchange, produced concentration of economic power in the hands of a few persons.

Restrictive Practices. Referring to restrictive practices the Commission listed the following more important of such objectionable practices. (1) Traders hoarding in times of scarcity, especially in the case of consumer goods for which demand is inelastic. (2) Re-sale price maintenance, very widely prevalent practice, (3) Practice of exclusive dealing, by prohibiting a dealer to sell goods of others. (4). Tie-in or Tie-up practices where the supplier of a commodity refuses to supply it unless the dealer agrees also to take a certain other commodity stocked by the supplier; (5) Full-line forcing.

The Commission recommended *inter alia* the setting up of a permanent Commission to exercise vigilance and act to protect the country against the dangers arising out of concentration of wealth and economic power. The Commission also recommended the liberalisation of licensing policy, protection of consumers against exploitation by monopoly enterprises and encouragement to the establishment of Consumers' Co-operatives.

THE MONOPOLIES AND RESTRICTIVE TRADE PRACTICES ACT. 1969

The Monopolies Inquiry Commission had drafted a bill on the lines of their recommendation to be considered and passed by Parliament. The Government introduced in Parliament in 1967 a Bill structured mainly on the lines suggested by the Inquiry Commission. The bill, designed to ensure that the operation of the economic system does not result in the concentration of economic power to the common detriment and to prohibit such monopolistic and restrictive trade practices as are "prejudicial to public interest", was passed by Parliament in 1969.

A Commission known as the Monopolies and Restrictive Trade Practices Commission which is vested with mandatory powers in regard to cases of restrictive trade practices and advisory powers in respect of cases concerning monopolistic practices and concentration of economic power has been constituted under the Act. In the case of the latter category of cases, the final decision would lie with the Government.

The main provisions of the Act fall under the following heads :—

(i) Regulating expansions, mergers and amalgamation and appointment of directors in respect of "dominant undertakings" having assets of Rs. 1 crore and more and of undertakings which by themselves or with inter-connected undertakings have assets of not less than Rs. 20 crores in value.

(ii) Regulating the starting of new undertakings which would become inter-connected undertakings of such existing undertakings the total assets of which exceeded Rs. 20 crores.

(iii) Control over and prohibition of monopolistic and restrictive-trade practices as are found to be prejudical to public interest.

Resume of Various Types of Business Organisation. It is instructive to reflect that, in the sphere of private entrprise, complete consolidation completes the cycle in the evolution of business organisation. The chart exhibits in a summary form the whole field of the evolution of various types of business organisation.

Beginning with the individual entrepreneur, we come across various forms of associations such as Joint Hindu Family Firm and Partnership, culminating in the joint-stock company. The joint-stock company in turn led the way to various forms of combinations of companies, beginning with loose agreements to fusion, which seem likely to culminate again in the colossal company or corporation via rationalisation. This is a compound corporation built up through the consolidation of preceding organisation, which has a tendency to grow into a monopoly with its inherent danger of ruthless exploitation of workers and consumers. As a measure to combat the strong employer, the workers join together by forming trade unions. The unions aim at eliminating competition among wage earners by restricting the employers' monopoly power over wage-rates. This they are in a position to do by collective bargaining by meeting strength with strength. In the sphere of consumers' co-operation, which is nothing more than a combination of economically weak, it aims to meet the challenge of the strong. No doubt, co-operation cannot oust capitalist production and distribution

Chart showing the evolution of various types of Business organisation.

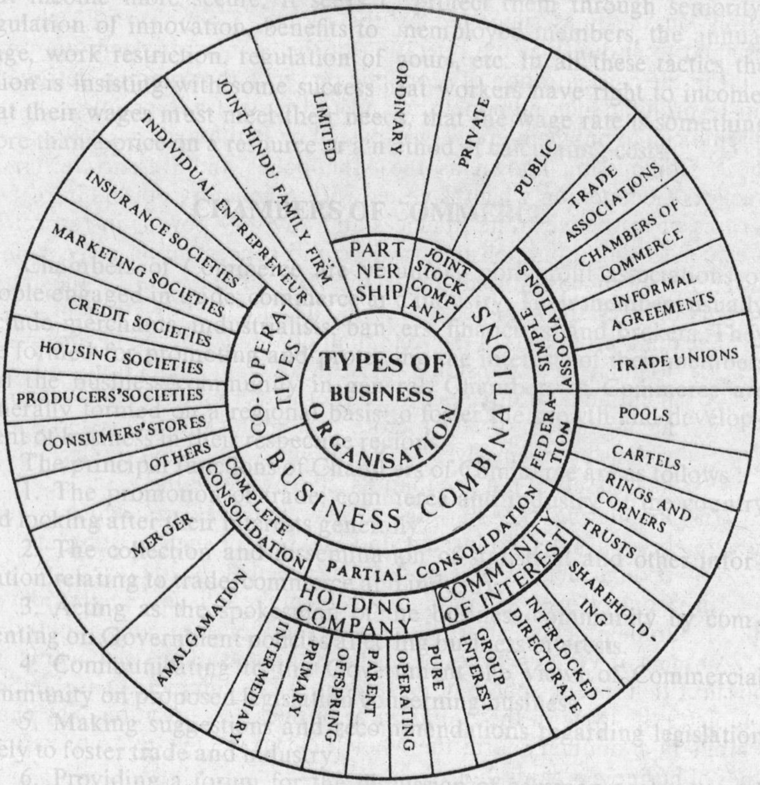

for a long time to come, yet it can be a stronghold against the onslaughts of the middle man and the capitalist producer.

CHAPTER XIII

RATIONALISATION

Rationalisation is a term used by economists and others to indicate the application of the most efficient methods in production, distribution, and transport. In its various uses, rationalisation would include ample modern equipment; mass production; co-operative effort; evenness and regularity of output; scientific organisation and management; and the elimination of unnecessary and wasteful competition. In its loose use, it is taken to mean combines to maintain prices, manipulation of shares to control markets, crushing out weak opponents by underselling, gaining special legal privileges for particular groups of traders, and other such acts commonly associated with trusts which are ordinarily of doubtful advantage to the community. Rationalisation has been carried to its greatest extreme in the U.S.A., especially in the great motor-car and steel plants. Next to the U.S.A., Germany carried rationalisation to the greatest extreme.

The word *rationalisation* derived its name from the German word *rationalisierung* which was first used in Germany at the end of World War I. In its original use the term was employed to describe a narrower and more specific aim of 'rationing' the output of certain establishments "to keep it within the limits of current market demands", and effecting, at the same time, a reduction of costs. But now, as stated in the previous paragraph, the term has come to be used for a far more comprehensive policy that is being followed by business magnates throughout the world. Since the term rationalisation essentially indicates rational thinking and scientific and logical methods in industry, the phrase has been differently interpreted. An attempt is made here to sort out some of the definitions with a view to get a clear idea of the meaning of the concept which has assumed much wider scope than its original meaning.

Meaning of Rationalisation. The various definitions of the term are as follows :

1. *The World Economic Conference, Geneva, 1927.* "Rationalisation means the methods and technique of organisation designed to secure the minimum waste of either effort or materials. It includes the scientific organisation of labour, simplification of processes, and improvements in the system of transport and marketing." Elimination of waste for greater efficiency is the core of this definition.

2. *Professor Sargant Florence.* The same idea of the reform of industry through the elimination of waste of labour, time and materials and by the reorganisation of industry scientifically is expressed by Prof. Florence. "Rationalisation", says he, "is the movement to eliminate waste and inefficiency 'scientifically and logically" by some sort of joint action between all the firms within one industry."

Professor Sargant Florence explains the science and logic involved in rationalisation, when he observes that the application of scientific management and vertical and horizontal integration of various firms eliminate waste and inefficiency. The emphasis primarily is on—

(a) elimination of waste and inefficiency (i) through the use of scientific techniques in every unit (internal aspect of rationalisation), and

(b) through business combination (external aspect of rationalisation).

3. *Professor E.A.G. Robinson.* Professor Robinson lays stress on the improvement of industrial structure through reorganisation. According to him, Rationalisation refers to the "reorganisation of the relationship of the individual firm to the industry as a whole." Besides the achievement of internal efficiency, he regards combination of firms as the means of achieving maximum economies of production and marketing.

4. *Mond in 'Industry* and *Politics'* sums up the scope by stating that "the rationalisation of industry, then, is an attempt to adjust the means of production to the probable means of consumption, and so to regulate prices, that instead of curves rising and falling like the contours of the Alps, there should be a fairly level roadway of prices along which trade and commerce could move."

The emphasis in this definition also is on reorganisation through loose association of firms for regulating prices, both for the benefit of the producer and the consumer.

5. *Advisory Committee on Management of the I.L.O. (1937)* spells out rationalisation in the following descriptions:

(a) Rationalisation, *in general*, is any reform tending to replace habitual, antiquated practices by means of methods based on systematic reasonings.

(b) Rationalisation, *in the narrowest sense*, is any reform of an undertaking, administration or other service, public or private, tending to replace habitual antiquated practices by means and methods based on systematic reasonings.

(c) Rationalisation, *in a wider sense,* is any reform which takes a group of business undertakings as a unit, and tends to reduce waste and loss due to unbridled competition by concerted action based on systematic reasoning.

(d) Rationalisation, *in the widest sense*, is a reform tending to apply means and methods based on systematic reasoning to the collective activities of large economic and social groups.

The central idea in this definition is two-fold: a conscious reorientation of the methods of production and those of distribution of what is produced in such a manner that it results in the maximum economic and social advantage, and the reduction of maladjustments and economic disequlibrium resulting in the restoration of economic and social order.

Aims and Objects of Rationalisation Movement. As stated earlier, rationalisation was originally employed as a remedy for the ills of German industry and as a scheme for its reconstruction. Its success attracted the attention of economists and industrialists in all the advanced countries of the world. The World Economic Conference held at Geneva in 1927 gave it a definite meaning and status. It defined the term and laid down its aims and objects. According to the Conference, Rationalisation aims at:—

"1. securing the maximum efficiency of labour with minimum effort;

2. eliminating waste of power and raw materials;

3. facilitating by reduction in the variety of patterns (where such variety offers no obvious advantage) research into the methods of manufacture and use of standardised parts;

4. simplifying distribution of products by eliminating unnecessary transport, burdensome financial charges and useless interposition of middlemen;

5. securing to the community greater stability and a higher standard of living;

6. ensuring to the consumer lower prices of goods more carefully adapted to general needs;

7. ensuring a higher and steadier remuneration to be equitably and fairly distributed among the various classes of producers."

According to the Bombay Textile Labour Inquiry Committee, 1941, rationalisation has 3 aims.

"(a) Increase in production per man and machine and its relation to wages;

(b) Improvement in the efficiency of workers and in working conditions, and

(c) Financial and Industrial re-organisation."

The fundamental aims may be summed up as—

(i) securing for each industry, considered as a whole, the maximum benefit of the most fruitful of all economic devices—the Division of Labour.

(ii) suppression of redundancy in all its forms, whether of plant, material, labour, or mechanical processes, and

(iii) bringing the whole of an industry under intelligent direction and management.

Major causes of wastage and inefficiency leading to Rationalisation. The need for joint action on the part of all the firms in an industry arose because of the following causes of wastage, inefficiency and low productivity;

1. *Scramble for scarce resources.* If some essential factor of production is not available in sufficient quantity, such a factor should be used in a planned manner in the interest of the entire industry. If all the firms

compete for the factor, prices will be high and, moreover, few firms may be in a position to get sufficient supply for profitable use. Suppose all the firms in India try to acquire foreign exchange by bidding for it, a good deal of it is bound to be wasted. Planned use is the only solution.

2. *Idle Capacity.* If the number of factories in an industry is too large the only effective remedy is the closing down of the most inefficient units. This alone will avoid unnecessary costs by way of depreciation, plant and maintenance, interest charge and so forth. But this remedy is not likely to be adequate unless there is a joint authority covering the whole industry. An independent firm will never think of closing down a part of its plant, unless it is suffering heavy losses in which case the firm will most probably become insolvent. The usual answer of an individual firm is heavier advertising and large number of varieties for increasing its sales and thus keeping its plant busy regardless of what happens to other firms. Obviously, this course of action raises costs still further. It is only when all firms are under the control of some one that a proper balance between productive capacity and demand for the product can be maintained. It is interesting to note that in theUnited Kingdom, a special company had to be set up to deal with idle capacity in the cotton textile industry before World War II. The task of the company was to buy up inefficient plants and scrap them.

3. *Unnecessary Varieties.* The size of units has an important influence on costs; and it is generally believed that the larger the size of the firm, the lower the cost of production per unit. But, as Prof. Florence has fully demonstrated, the large size of the firm does not necessarily contribute to the reduction of cost, but it is the output of an article on a large scale that makes for efficiency. If there are too many varieties, the output of each variety is likely to be small, even though the total output may be large. This raises costs not only of production but also of distribution. There shall have to be heavier expenditure on advertising. Large number of varieties militate against large sales, as the customer has to spend a good deal of his time in making a selection with the result that the retailer is able to handle a comparatively small number of customers. When we buy postage stamps, hardly any time is spent as no question of choice is involved. In buying, say handkerchiefs, we do spend some time in making our selection from the different varieties. If we want the cost of distribution to fall, we must cut down the number of varieties to a minimum. The possibilities are interesting to contemplate. In the U.S.A., after World War I, action was taken to remove unnecessary varieties from many industries. The result, to take a few examples, was as follows:

Product	*Number of varieties reduced*	
	From	*To*
Shovels, spades and scoops	4,460	384
Grinding Wheels	7,15,200	2,55,800
Brass toilet and sink taps	1,114	72
Milk bottles	49	9

Standardisation of products or removal of redundant varieties cannot be achieved if all firms operate in perfect freedom. This is because of the illogical behaviour of the consumer who gets tired of old things and wants at a fast rate new things with different shapes and shades, even though the price to be paid is high. To meet such demands the firms must keep on changing designs and shades of their products; and if one firm makes the change, the other must follow. In fact, one of the ways in which a new firm tries to find a place for itself in the market is to produce newer varieties of goods. This proliferation of varieties can be stopped and goods can be standardised only if a common authority pervades the whole industry.

4. *Obsolete Machinery.* Production with worn out and obsolete machinery is uneconomical, because it involves higher cost of repair and maintenance, higher operating expenses, greater strain on the worker and lower productivity per unit per worker. Efficiency can be increased only when steps are taken to modernise the plant and replace worn out machinery by up-to-date modern machinery. Automatic machinery taking the place of antiquated, hand-operated machinery surely leads towards rationalisation.

Stages in the Application of Rationalisation. The actual application of rationalisation involves three stages, namely:—

1. Planning, including combination;
2. Re-arrangement by standardisation and simplification;
3. Development through the extension of sectionalisation.

1. *Planning.* The first step in planning is to make an exact market survey which involves the review of the existing market, estimate of potential markets and the channels of distribution. From this survey it will be possible to decide what to produce and which of the various units of the combine should produce it, and what prices should be charged and what channels should be used. Once the integration of firms has taken place and the sales programme has been laid down, the planning of production in the rationalised units should present no great difficulty. Production, plant, labour, raw materials, power, supervision and inspection should be quantitatively determined and reduced into a common denominator of finance in order to check out and for comparison.

2. *Re-arrangement.* The second stage involves *Standardisation* and *Simplification.* It relates to the re-arrangement of equipment and machinery and their *Standardisation* for mass production. It also relates to *Simplification* and *reduction of varieties* of goods, in short, to *elimination of redundancy.* For the manufacturer, this means greater productivity and skill, less waste, and easier acquisition of proficiency of operatives, less capital is locked up in material and spare parts; simpler costing system results and the effects of seasonal variations are lessened. Neveretheless, rationalisation demands the planning of a unit as a marketing unit before it is planned as a producing unit. The opposite could be justified only in a completely socialised State, when production is for the State.

3. *Development.* The third stage deals with the development of the plan by means of the extension of *specialisation* or *Sectionalisation* which is really the logical sequence of *Standardisation.* These involve greater mechanisation so that machines can be used for the smallest processes of production. They perform the work with much greater speed and efficiency. Resources are actually made productive. Increased producti-vity releases productive resources. It operates not as a "return *on* capital", but as a "return *of* capital". It is genuine surplus. It can become economically effective in four ways.

1. The enterprise can use the released capital to turn out more of the same commodity.

2. The enterprise can lower price, with or without an increase in output.

3. It can raise wages.

4. It can show the released resources as if they were a profit and distribute them.

Rationalisation should not, however, be confused with greater and greater *mechanisation* nor should it be equated with *intensification.* Sometimes it may be possible to rationalise by employing more men than machines. Let it be noted that "intensification" is intrinsically different from rationalisation. Rationalisation means *modernisation* and guiding the machines and men *rationally*, while intensification involves the renovating of old machines and then attempting to achieve higher speed by means of "Speeding up" to the detriment of workers, and ultimately to that of the community.

Rationalisation in its true meaning, therefore, "demands the consideration of business not in its own purely selfish, technical and commercial aspects, but also in its wider economic, social, and generally human aspects; without all these aspects it will be pseudo-rationalisation of business affairs."[1] For the successful application of rationalisation, mass production must be balanced by mass consumption. Indeed, the principal purpose of rationalisation is the elimination of every form of waste in order that production may be cheapened, while supply and demand are kept in continual equilibrium.

Essential elements of rationalisation. The various elements involved in rationalisation as disclosed in the foregoing stages in its application are summed up below and may also be described as main characteristics or features of rationalisation.

1. *Combination*, through integration of different kinds, of small and inefficient units with large and efficient one for achieving all the economies of large-scale operation.

2. *Standardisation* of products or removal of redundant varieties and restricting production of a few varieties. This becomes possible because a common authority has been set up for the whole industry. The

1. Meyers, *op. cit.*, p. 22.

limitation of varieties makes for large-scale production of each variety and saving in cost of production and distribution.

3. *Specialisation* follows standardisation as a result of the elimination of redundant varieties. This leads to economies of production and minimisation of waste.

4. *Simplification* is the resultant of standardisation and specialisation leading to higher productivity and larger sales of each variety.

5. *Mechanisation* of functions which are being performed by manual labour before rationalisation increases the speed and efficiency of production.

6. *Modernisation of Plant* through replacement of worn-out and obsolete plant by modern machinery and equipment is another important feature of rationalisation.

7. *Management on Scientific lines on industry-wide scale.* This means that old traditional methods of management are given up and modern methods are adopted to manage various firms forming an industry. Efficiency of management is as important as efficiency of other factors for rationalisation to be achieved.

8. *Research.* Industrial research is another essential element on which rationalisation depends. Such a research helps in ascertaining the most economical processes of production. Marketing research enables large units to distribute on mass scale goods produced in large quantities.

9. *Social and human objectives.* Rationalisation is not intensification but guiding machines and men rationally. As stated earlier, rationalisation is concerned not only with mass production but with mass consumption, too. Therefore, attention is given not only to the economic aspects of industry but also to social and human aspects, too. The workers should receive their due share of prosperity resulting from rationalisation and the consumer should be supplied goods of good quality at a reasonably low price. The schemes should be applied at a speed which would cause the least unemployment.

Rationalisation and Scientific Management Distinguished. Both scientific management and rationalisation have similar aims. Both aim to employ scientific methods of organisation and work in place of outmoded methods with the objective of increasing efficiency and productivity as well as the utilisation of material and human resources to the maximum degree. Therefore at one time the word rationalisation was used to indicate the application of the principles of scientific management. Now, however, the distinction between the two terms has come to be appreciated.

1. Rationalisation has a much wider scope than scientific management. In fact, it embraces not only scientific management but many more things. Scientific management is employed by an individual business concern with a view to increase its efficiency. Rationalisation is concerned with the problems of industry as a whole and not with any particular units which constitute the industry. Thus scientific management seeks to eliminate causes of waste and inefficiency within an

individual unit, while rationalisation is concerned with the elimination of waste in an industry.

2. Scientific management is concerned primarily with increased efficiency of existing products whereas rationalisation is also and especially concerned with the simplification of the often needlessly numerous varieties of any particular products which have been already placed on the market. It is also concerned with the standardisation of materials, machines, products and their packing within the combine.

3. Scientific management is mainly concerned with the management and efficiency of workers while rationalisation covers all activities including financing production and distribution and the cost of transport, advertising and marketing generally.

4. Rationalisation necessarily involves integration of various units, but scientific management has nothing to do with it.

5. The most important object of rationalisation, with which scientific management in the independent firm cannot be concerned, is to reduce wasteful competition—

(i) by eliminating the weaker industrial firms through purchase and subsequent suppression,
(ii) by allocating or rationing the output of given product for each member of the combine.
(iii) by fixing their respective areas of the same or a given product, thus abolishing the waste of cross-sales,
(iv) by determining the price at which any common product of the combine is to be sold,
(v) by establishing common costing systems,
(vi) by effecting common arrangements for the purchase of raw materials and for the marketing of products of the concern,
(vii) by spreading over the whole combine any losses, and
(viii) by pooling the results of technical, commercial and economic research.

6. Scientific management is concerned with the integration, differentiation and co-ordination of functions within a single unit and its betterment. Rationalisation must do all these within a combine. It must also "consider the satisfaction and contentment of all grades of workers, the steadiness of employment, the needs of the consumer and ultimately of the whole community, securing to the former lower prices and goods more carefully adapted to his requirements, and to the latter greater economic stability and a higher standard in conditions of life."

To reiterate rationalisation covers the whole industry; scientific management covers only one firm. But the two are not exclusive. An industry may be rationalised and the individual plants must be run according to scientific management to achieve maximum efficiency. Thus, scientific management brings an individual unit under intelligent direction and management, while rationalisation brings the whole of an industry under such direction and management.

Rationalisation and Nationalisation. The two terms are entirely different in their scope and meaning. The points of distinction between rationalisation and nationalisation are as follows:

1. Rationalisation is a *process* by which the efficiency of an industry is attempted to be increased. Nationalisation is a *policy* of the State under which industries serving public interest are taken over and managed by the State. The action is taken with a view to cure economic ills, although it may not increase the efficiency of the nationalised units.

2. In the case of rationalisation the control and management remain with the private entrepreneurs. The aim is to improve the working of private enterprise. Nationalisation takes away the control and ownership of industry from private entrepreneurs; and the control and management of the nationalised units are placed in the hands of the Government.

3. Historically rationalisation has been employed in various countries to save private enterprise from ruin by eliminating wasteful competition and by organising industry on rational lines. The purpose of nationalisation is to eradicate exploitation of the community by private entrepreneurs and to run industry in public interest.

4. Rationalisation aims to cure the ills of private enterprise but nationalisation replaces it altogether—Private enterprise is converted into public enterprise. In fact nationalisation has been resorted to as a remedy against the abuse of power by private enterprise.

Despite these differences the two are not opposed to each other. As a matter of fact even nationalised industries must be run rationally. Both in private sector and in public sector large-scale management requires standardisation and science of management, the organisation of workers, and workers' informed participation in technical progress.

Rationalisation and Combination. Since it is necessary for rationalisation that all the firms in an industry be brought under a common authority, it has been contended by some that there is no difference between rationalisation and combination. Dr. T.E. Gregory termed rationalisation as a new fangled phrase to describe the old fashioned device of eliminating competition. There is, however, a difference between the two. If competition is eliminated in order to maintain and raise prices and maximize profits, it is combination. The now defunct Indian Sugar Syndicate is an example. But if competition is eliminated to cut dead wood and reduce costs and to benefit all concerned—employers, workers and consumers—it would be a case of rationalisation. The Associated Cement Companies Limited which was formed before World War II to save the cement industry from collapse is an outstanding example of rationalisation.

It must be acknowledged that rationalisation schemes started with the best of intentions are sometimes used to consolidate economic power in a few hands under the cloak of "higher organisation". It is for this reason that the Government must have a say in the formulation and execution of rationalisation schemes.

Advantages of Rationalisation. The advocates of rationalisation claim for it manifold advantages. The plausible economies resulting from rationalisation or its advantages may be stated as follows:

1. Rationalisation, by means of amalgamation, eliminates uneconomic competition and thus brings about stability in industry. It permits supply to be adapted to demand so as to mitigate the recurrent crises due to apparently inevitable fluctuations of the trade cycle.

2. It enables production to be concentrated as far as possible on the more efficient units, which are kept working continuously and makes for all the economies of large-scale operation. In a properly rationalised combine, the constituent individual concerns are no longer permitted to produce and sell how much and what they choose. Planned production avoids over-production and its resultant wastes.

3. A similar result follows the "sectionalisation" of manufacturing. For example, Mr. Ford not only makes Fords, he also makes the luxurious Lincoln cars and the humble tractor—but he makes them in different works, leaving his original plant at Highland Park, Detroit, to concentrate on Fords. Similarly, General Motors make a wide variety of models, but each is made at a separate plant. Thus, General Motors as a whole can offer the consumer all the variety of choice he requires, while at the same time the individual plants "combined" with General Motors can concentrate each on one or a few models. Sectionalisation and standardisation in production, and combination in marketing is here the watchword.

4. Another advantage follows from the "simplification" and "standardisation" of materials. "Only a limited number of types of product are thus made; useless or needless types are suppressed; the complex programme of production is reduced, improvements in technique, e.g., in construction of machines and in organisation, thus become possible; and once again methods of production are improved and costs are lowered. For the manufacturer, they mean greater productivity and skill, less waste and greater efficiency of the operator. The retailer benefits, because now he can carry smaller stock; his risks are reduced in respect to the perishing of stock or its passing out of date; selling becomes less complicated; a reduced capital outlay becomes possible. To the consumer, judicious simplification brings the advantages of improved quality, reduced selling price, and, hence, greater purchasing power."

5. Where different concerns within the combine produce identical goods (being horizontally integrated), rationalisation assigns different selling areas, and thus eliminates needless waste arising from cross-sales. There are common transport and advertising arrangements, which reduce cost of distribution. The market is also kept steady by rationalisation through regulative distribution and forecasts of variations in demand.

6. Allied to centralised and regulated selling is centralised buying. Very important savings can be effected by centralising the purchases of

materials, fuels, stores, etc., in a single agency. Central buying eliminates a large number of independent buying staff, and centralised selling excludes unnecessary middlemen. The savings possible under these headings can in many cases be very important.

7. Centralisation of finance, that is made possible by rationalisation, yields substantial advantages. The credit of one large unit is in the nature of things likely to be far stronger, other things being equal, than that of any of a large number of mutually conflicting units.

8. Another advantage of rationalisation is that it enables research to be centralised and endowed in a way which is hardly practicable under the small unit system. Research relates not merely to mechanical, chemical and physical problems but also to psychological enquires which lie at the base of all progress in scientific management. Market research is also enormously facilitated by the centralisation of information.

9. From the side of labour also rationalisation offers numerous advantages. It provides on an average better working conditions and larger opportunities for welfare work of all kinds, the economic value of which is tremendous. The application of principles of scientific management ensures these conditions which make for maximum labour efficiency, and encourages the adoption of progressive labour policy.

10. Apart from these advantages, rationalisation makes it possible for an industry to have a policy; it enables an industry to organise itself rationally and logically instead of blundering about fortuitously according to the various discordant dictates of hundreds of competing individuals.

The late Lord Melchett claimed for it a four-fold advantage—"that it allows of scientific allocation of capital expenditure and the financing of new plant and up-to-date equipment; that it encourages specialisation in the closing of inefficient concerns, and the concentration of management and of commercial propaganda, selling and other expenses; that it prevents waste and overlapping—e.g., duplication of stocks, unnecessary varieties in size and form of commodities, or overlapping of research; that it provides insurance against fluctuations of markets and prices and by promoting an orderly system of purchasing raw materials and marketing commodities facilitates a world review of economic needs and supplies."[1]

Dangers of Rationalisation. Rationalisation leads to numerous beneficial results to the manufacturers and business houses generally through elimination of competition, by control of prices and sales, or through mass production, by simplification and standardisation of output and by integration and specialisation in organisation. But when it is recognised that the financial success of those who direct the combine is not the only test of successful rationalisation, but the interests and welfare of the employee, the consumer and the general community must also be kept in the forefront, we are confronted by the danger of irrational application of rationalisation.

1. Quoted by Brown in *The Machine and the Worker* p. 158.

1. First of all the enlargement of the business unit, while to a large extent eliminating competition within a given area, may have the effect of intensifying competition on an international scale. The oil industry is a familiar example; where oil companies formed an international cartel, involving restrictions of exports by quotas.

2. The monopoly powers of combines and 'rings' have often led to restriction of output and artificial raising of prices. This policy has many a time reached its absurd stage in the burning of wheat and coffee or the destruction of rubber. It is to curb the increasing powers of combines that State supervision and ultimately international control in the interests alike of the workers and the consumer is essential.

3. Efficiency has not always followed from large combinations, owing to over-capitalisation, financial juggling, and lack of directive ability to control an unwieldy concern. Dr. Myers has made effective use of biological analogies to show the absurdity of supposing that huge business organisations are likely to be always the most suitable and that they should supplant the smaller concern entirely.

4. The policy of elimination of redundancy in regard to units of production may result in scrapping of surplus productive capacity at enormous cost, for the inefficient plants have to be bought at inflated prices. This very often results from the strong traditional opposition, and the protagonists must pay for it.

5. The reorganisation involved in rationalisation requires heavy initial expenditure in modernisation and in the reshuffling of production, and also in replacement of either worn out machinery, a necessary consequence of mass production, or of obsolete machinery. Such huge expenditures are likely to tell more heavily on rationalised industries than others during periods of slump, as was witnessed during the Depression of 1930's.

6. The "mixed business" complicates matters. Co-operation becomes difficult. The problems of organisation and management are enlarged rather than solved. It multiplies enormously the harm done by mistakes, and so tends to curb experimentation.

7. The greatest adverse effects of rationalisation are on the employees and that is why organised labour opposes it. The adverse effect is three-fold: (1) unemployment of all grades of workers, (2) exploitation of labour and 'speeding up', followed by increased fatigue and mental strain, (3) unfairness, as the increase in the earnings of the operative is not in keeping with the increase in productivity.

With regard to unemployment as a consequence of rationalisation it is argued that, due to reduction in price, increase in sales and output, rationalisation will expand employment, or at least maintain it, rather than curtail it. It is further contended that if employment contracts in one industry, say, cotton textiles, it will expand in others, e.g., in cotton textile machinery industry. Thus, there will only be a shift in employment, and not unemployment. It might be so in some cases, but there is bound to be a certain amount of technical unemployment, even if it is of temporary nature. Rationalisation reduces employment in three ways: (i) by closing down of unproductive undertakings and transferring production to other centres; (ii) by control of output and the modernisation of plant, (iii) by eliminating such staff and men as were rendered unnecessary solely by reason of the internal competition. The displacement, may however, arise either from a diminution of the total labour force or from the substitution of unskilled for skilled labour or female labour for male labour. For a short time at least the unemployment problem is to be increased, although the situation may remain fluid because of the different rates at which displacement and absorption of labour may go on over a considerable period of time. Moreover, even if labour is ultimately transferred and absorbed, it is frequently to a job which pays lower wages, and which is less satisfactory than the one which is left. This is a serious consequence of rationalisation, even where new demands for labour may come into being, apart from the obvious stimulation given to the constructional and equipment industries. Therefore, the victims of the "planned unemployment" should be treated in a generous spirit according to circumstances. Employment Exchanges are doing useful work in this direction, and unemployment insurance for making provision of a maximum living standard for all can be made a part of rationalisation programme. With regard to the other two objections, what was said in answer to the objections to scientific management applies here. Taylor always insisted that truly scientific management neither drove nor over-worked the worker; but the trouble is that the employers tend to neglect the human factor.

It follows that there is no quarrel with rationalisation or scientific management, but with their irrational and unscientific application. International Labour Organisation has declared itself as opposed "not to rationalisation as such, but to the abuses arising from it under the capitalist system", but a Joint Commission of the International Federation of Trade Unions and the Labour and Socialist International Federation agreed unanimously to a resolution outlining the safeguards under which rationalisation might be transformed "from a source of unemployment and overwork into a source of well-being". The resolution urges the following points: "(1) That rationalisation is not a matter for employers only since in its operation it may at any time bring about displacement of labour. For this reason the right of Trade Unions to be consulted regarding proposed changes in the methods or conditions of employment or in the distribution of labour should be recognised and machinery for this purpose should be provided, thereby safeguarding the interests of the workers and preventing any scheme of rationalisation from intensifying their exploitation. (2) That in order to mitigate as far as possible the effects of rationalisation upon employment and in order to facilitate the changes, the benefits arising from improved technique and organisation should be made immediately available for reducing the hours of work and increasing the real wages of the workers. (3) That provision should be made for paying adequate unemployment benefits through insurance systems or otherwise, without restriction of time, to persons thrown out of employment. (4) Industry considers it necessary to maintain and improve its plant and equipment. Many firms, therefore, create reserves not only for depreciation but also for the purpose of replacing plants by more modern types before it is worn out. It is necessary that industry should pay as much regard to the human element as to plant and equipment and that technical progress should not involve hardship to the workers concerned. Industry should take all financial responsibility possible for alleviation of the hardship caused by the substitution of machinery for human labour. (5) Finally governments should use to the fullest extent all means at their disposal to find employment for displaced workers under conditions at least equal to those previously enjoyed by them, or fit them for work in other employment."[1]

RATIONALISATION IN INDIAN INDUSTRY

The rationalisation movement has spread to almost all the Western countries, although its scope and shape differ in each case. In our country the process of rationalisation, involving re-orientation of methods of production and distribution for maximum economic and social advantage, has not so far been adopted except in a piecemeal and tentative fashion. Whenever attempted, rationalisation has mainly meant combination for maintaining high prices and exploitation of workers. According to a majority of employers the only other meaning of rationalisation is replacement of man by machine. Attempts at rationalisation have really meant the reduction of the number of workers and greater intensification of work. Since the industrialists have not made rational use of rationalisation, all the important trade unions such as INTUC, AITUC, UTUC and HMS have opposed rationalisation on the ground that it leads to unemployment of workers. It is essential, therefore, that rationalisation should be beneficially applied. The Union Ministry of Labour and Employment prepared in 1957 a model agreement to guide employers in regard to rationalisation. The agreement provided for mutual consultation and co-operation between management and labour and facilitated implementation of rationalisation schemes in various industries.

A brief description of what little has been done in this direction in different industries follows.

Cotton Textile Industry. The cotton textile industry is one of the oldest industries in India, offering employment to about five lakh workers. Being an old established industry, it has operated for the most part with antiquated machinery and traditional methods. It has been in great difficulties which have aggravated during the last few years; some

1. Reports and Proceedings of Fourth Congress of the Labour and Socialist International (Vienna, 1931).

mills have even been closed down. The need for rationalisation has been felt for quite some time and at present it has become unavoidable and imminent. An attempt was made in 1928 in Bombay mills in the E.D. Sassoon Group of Mills. The main emphasis of this scheme was on the saving of labour. The problems of the industry continued to grow more and more serious as the time passed. Committee after Committee has dealt with the problems and suggested measures to solve them. To mention a few, the Technical Sub Committee of the Working Party for Cotton Textile Industry (1950), The Kanungo Committee (1952), The Joshi Committee (1958), all stressed the need of rationalisation by specialisation of production, market research, systematic costing system, modernisation and scrapping of absolutely old and depleted machinery. In spite of all these recommendations nothing much has been done. The trade unions have also contributed to the troubles of the industry by resisting plans for modernisation in the late 'fifties on the ground that this would threaten future employment prospects. The failure to modernise when modernisation was overdue and could have been accomplished with available funds at relatively low cost has had disastrous results. The industry has stagnated and has become uncompetitive in world markets.

The industry closed the year 1968 with 90 mills shut down and 100,000 workers out of job. Everybody is now shouting aloud for modernisation; but the industry has no funds to do it. Yet there is no alternative to modernisation. Estimates vary as to how much this will cost. The Commerce Ministry's guess is about Rs. 375 crores of which Rs. 200 crores will go for modernisation and replacement and the remaining amount towards working capital requirements. The National Industrial Development Corporation has been advancing loans to mills. The Government has set up a Textile Corporation to divert funds to sick mills. Manubhai Shah Committee has in its second report recommended to the Gujarat Government that "the stronger units should be offered concessions and relief in taxes to induce them to take over the responsibility of reconstructing the weak units." Mergers are an excellent idea for an industry crying out for rationalisation. But budgetary assistance is also imperative in the form of some relief in excise duties and other tax concessions to release funds for modernisation. Both Japan and Britain are investing heavily in modern mills and many new countries are entering the world textile market. Unless the Indian Textile industry is modernised and rationalised the jobs of a lot more people are going to be threatened in the long run.

Jute Textile Industry. The jute industry suffered before the World War II from two serious ills which called for the adoption of rationalisation. One of these ills was overproduction and the other excessive productive capacity. Efforts were made to restrict production. After Independence the industry had to face other problems of raw material supply, loss of monopoly, extreme competition and substitution of other materials. The machinery used in the industry had become old and outmoded as a result of which production was becoming uneconomic. Rationalisation was, therefore, suggested as the remedy, especially because it has an importance in the export trade. The problem of modernisation has become very acute, as Pakistan, with up-to-date machinery and equipment, has been capturing foreign markets.

The Jute Inquiry Commission set up by the Government in 1953 recommended modernisation of plant, increasing efficiency and reducing costs to save the industry from permanent damage to it. In 1956 the industry began implementing modernisation programme. The Export Promotion Committee submitted its report in 1957. Its main recommendations were (i) that uneconomic units should be closed, and production should be concentrated in the modernised plants. (ii) efforts should be made to grow raw jute of the type which is now imported, and (iii) the mills should co-operate and pool profits for the common benefits of all the units.

The National Industrial Development Corporation has been granting loans to jute mills and the Indian Jute Manufacturers' Association has been working on the more efficient units without much adverse effects on labour. It is estimated that more than 50 per cent of the modernisation programme has been carried out, and the trend is continuing.

Sugar Industry. Sugar industry is also an old established industry and needs modernisation of plant. The modernisation and replacement outlay has been estimated at Rs. 78.05 crores. The resources available with the industry are meagre. As suggested by the Tariff Commission as early as 1959, the Government should make necessary arrangements for making available financial assistance to sugar mills on the same lines as provided to cotton and jute textile industries for modernisation and rehabilitation. The Industrial Finance Corporation is already giving assistance through loans for modernisation of mills. The cane development schemes have been intensified under the Three Plans and an outlay of Rs. 27 crores has been made.

Cement Industry. Avoidance of wasteful competition among the various units has been the main aspect of rationalisation of cement industry in India. In 1926 the Indian Cement Manufacturers Association was formed to eliminate competition within the industry. Next step with the process of combination was the formation of the Cement Marketing Company of India in 1930, to regulate and rationalise the marketing of cement produced by all the units. In 1936, ten out of the eleven cement producing units merged into one unit to form the Associated Cement Companies Limited. This was the beginning of the group system of organisation and management in the cement industry. The second group known as the Dalmia Cement Group came into being in 1937. The other aspects of rationalisation have not been found necessary.

Coal Industry. The coal industry in India has developed and is managed in an irrational manner and suffers from numerous maladies. Rationalisation is the crying need of the industry. Two aspects of rationalisation are urgently called for: mechanisation of coal mines and amalgamation of collieries into bigger units to make them of economic size.

Mechanisation of mines is necessary because (i) the rate of recovery of coal becomes larger and faster, (ii) quantity of coal raised increases output per man-shift which results in economy in overhead expenditure, (iii) underground transport equipments are not only fully utilised but the productivity of the haulage-workers is also increased, (iv) cost of production is reduced since in the long run manual labour proves to be costlier than machines, and (v) miner's energy is preserved which leads to increase in his productive potential.

A Committee on Amalgamation of Collieries was set up in 1955 to study the position of small coal-fields and work out definite proposals for their amalgamation. The Committee submitted its report in 1957. and recommended that the collieries unable to produce 10,000 tons per annum and having an area of less than 100 acres should be amalgamated with one or more collieries. The Government set up a Committee in 1958 to promote voluntary amalgamation, but by 1961 it was able to approve only 30 proposals. Voluntary amalgamation is bound to be slow. It is necessary to introduce compulsory amalgamation.

The Coal Productivity Team, sponsored by the National Productivity Council in collaboration with the U.S. Technical Co-operation Mission, after studying the complex problems, made the following recommendations in June, 1961 :

(1) The work of amalgamation already begun should be carried out with greater speed;

(2) The organisational structure in the public sector coal industry should be converted to the French pattern, which consists of a central policy-making body and autonomous coal-mining companies on regional basis. This would facilitate the exercise of effective administrative control contributing to higher productivity;

(3) A central co-ordinating body for rendering common technical services should be formed;

(4) Mechanisation may be restricted to machine cutting, blasting and shovelling on to conveyor;

(5) Efficient transport, which is the biggest single factor contributing to higher productivity, should be provided by removing bottlenecks;

(6) Wages should be paid to the productive workers on piece-rate basis wherever practicable.

Other Industries. Woollen industry is also burdened with old and obsolete machinery. But the working groups set up in 1960 by the NIDC for woollen and art silk industries have reported that these industries are capable of modernising their plants from their own resources. Measures of rationalisation have been taken in these and other industries such as iron and steel, matches and engineering. In iron and steel the Tata Iron and Steel Company has carried out schemes of modernisation of equipment

Government's Policy Regarding Rationalisation. The government, while encouraging rationalisation, has always emphasised the need of introducing it so that it does not cause unemployment. To safeguard the interests of labour, the government has suggested measures to avoid retrenchment, and to provide suitable employment to those who lose their jobs due to rationalisation. The Planning Commission also advised rationalisation only when it did not lead to unemployment. It further suggested that rationalisation should be introduced in consultation with workers after improving working conditions and guaranteeing a substantial share of gains to workers. In the light of these suggestions of the Planning Commission the Government of India evolved a "Model Agreement" which was adopted by the tripartite Indian Labour Conference in July, 1957, as a guide to employers in regard to rationalisation.

The Government has also provided financial assistance through the specialised financial institutions. Through the Indian Standards Institute it enables industry in the task of standardisation and simplification of products. A network of scientific and technological institutes set up by the government promote the cause of industrial research in the country. The government is doing its bit to help rationalisation. The employers and workers must co-operate to achieve the desired results. The employers should also provide efficient management, as management is the most important factor for efficiency. Rationalisation schemes should provide for professional management.

CHAPTER XIV

PUBLIC UTILITIES

Meaning and Scope. "Public Utilities" is a general name for those industries or services, such as the supply of gas, water, electricity, urban passenger transport, etc., which are "clothed with public interest" inasmuch as they are "necessary" or "indispensable" monopolies or semi-monopolies on whom is superimposed public regulation for "the common good", and special privileges or franchise to facilitate their proper functioning. Legally, public utility is a distinctive category of industry based upon the common law "doctrine of public interest". Early in the development of the common law, certain callings or occupations were singled out and impressed with special rights and duties. Especially were the duties stressed, which continued to persist even after the appearance of the *laissez-faire* philosophy and its emphasis upon non-regulation of business by government. The doctrine of public interest is so intimately connected with public utility that the two phrases are usually treated as synonymous. A public utility firm is readily distinguished from a non-utility business by the limitation that governments put on its freedom of treatment of buyers. But the restrictions are not without compensation, for utility companies are more likely to have exclusive markets for their commodities or services than the companies that do not have such a status. Being monopolies, these companies are subject to public regulation of their accounting, finances, earnings, prices, and service policies. Most of the regulatory action is directed towards prescriptions of reasonable earnings and prices. Neither the sellers nor the buyers obtain the prices that please them most; the sellers are denied full monopoly prices, and the buyers cannot insist on such low prices that the seller cannot survive. Output controls are used alongside the price controls. A utility company is required, for instance, to serve all buyers indiscriminately at the prescribed prices. Denied free exercise of its monopolistic power, a utility company is expected to serve up to the limits of its plant capacity, to take customers as they come, and to sell service at reasonable prices.[1]

ECONOMIC CHARACTERISTICS OF PUBLIC UTILITIES

Public utilities possess certain special characteristic features which distinguish them from non-utility industries. But it should be remembered that strict differentiation is not possible, nor is it attempted; for sometimes the non-utility industries seem to have all or nearly all the economic characteristics of public utilities. What is intended here is to

1. Troxel, *Economies of Public Utilities,* p. 3.

show that a public utility usually possesses these characteristics; while the other may or may not possess them. There are therefore two fundamental economic characteristics of public utilities, namely, (1) necessity, and (2) monopoly or tendency to monopoly or inadequate competition. To these may be added local nature of their activity, regulation and franchise, and general cost and demand characteristics.

Necessity. In the first place, public utilities provide necessary or indispensable products or services which must have an uninterrupted flow into the market. Any service or product is necessary or indispensable because it is regularly required and used by a very large section of the community, e.g., water, gas, electricity, urban transport.

Monopoly or Inadequate Competition. Public utilities commonly produce and sell their products and services under monopolistic or only nominally competitive conditions. There are several types of monopoly. The first is the natural monopoly, which is the common characteristic of utility industries. The term implies that the control of public utility service in market is somehow "naturally" or inherently monopolistic, that the rivalry between unregulated companies is inevitably eliminated by combination, and one company ultimately dominates the market which several companies once occupied. Monopoly therefore arises because of the grant of special franchise and the imposition of regulation under the doctrine of public interest. There is also a monopoly based on natural limitations in service; for example, a company or municipality controlling the only available source of water for a community has a monopoly of supply. So also has an electricity authority or urban transport corporation. Characteristically, the business is conducted in local plants with a market narrowly limited in area; and duplication of plants or of delivery service would be wasteful and ultimately burdensome to consumers. Some utilities deal in services that involve a limitation of time, such as telephones. The matter of speed and lack of time and danger of confusion arising out of possible competing communication services give each of them a genuine monopoly. More important than all these causes of monopoly is the condition of economic monopoly. The cost of construction, the low ratio of income to investment, the impossibility of ideal load factors, and the legal necessity of building in advance of needs, all tend together to make the utility operate under conditions of decreasing costs. Such a situation inevitably makes competition quite unstable and in the end, short of governmental interference, leads to combination and monopoly.

Regulation and Franchise. Since a public utility has a public interest status, and is consequently required to work for the maximum social advantage, it is subjected to more stringent regulation than a non-utility which may be a monopoly. On the one hand, public regulation is used to ensure regulary supply of good quality at reasonable price, and on the other, to regulate their right to interfere with public amenities, and to safeguard public life and property.

Another characteristic of a public utility is the special franchise that must be granted by the governmental authority before it can commence business, because, for the proper performance of its functions, it must interfere with public amenities like streets for laying tram lines, or pipelines for water, or conduit pipes for sewage: or with uninterrupted enjoyment of individual property. The control of price is made to enable all sections of the community to use the service. and also to check discrimination and undue preference which is possible in the case of unregulated utility service the demand for which is generally inelastic. Profits of public utilities are regulated so that they conform to specified reasonable return on certain capital figure and the surplus, if any, is returned to the consumers by reduction in subsequent prices. As long as a public utility is owned and managed by private enterprise its regulation and control in the interest of the community is essential: when nationalised it must be democratic in its working and effect.

Cost and Demand. Public utility industries have large fixed investments in plant and equipment and a low rate of capital turnover. Consequently, utility companies, like others with large plant investments, have low rates of capital substitution. Unwise investments are therefore ruinous to them. They have—indeed, are expected to have—sufficient plant capacity to serve all consumers who are willing to buy at the existing prices; but more than this they must have some unused capacity to meet 'peak demand' because utility service is non-storable. Since the demands of utility consumers have significant time dimensions, there must necessarily be some unused capacity during off-peak periods. In its very nature, the demand for utility service is both direct and derived, as it may be both elastic and inelastic. Direct demand means seeking the service for immediate consumption, e.g., electricity for lighting purposes, and water for daily use; indirect demand relates to the use of the service for further production. A derived demand will tend to be both elastic and inelastic. It will be elastic in so far as power substitutes are available, also where power costs are a major part of the total costs. The direct demands for utility tend to be inelastic, both in respect of price of the service and income of the buyers. Being unwilling to forego consumption of utility services to which they have got used, the buyers, as the prices rise or their incomes decline, are willing to reduce their expenditure on other non-essential things.

RIGHTS AND DUTIES OF PUBLIC UTILITIES[1]

Public utilities, unlike unregulated enterprises, have certain legal duties and privileges. The fulfilment of contractual obligations and the right to demand performance are generally the duties and rights of a merchant. So long as he does not deceive or conspire to limit competition, he may charge as little or as much as he can get, and whether he prospers or fails ordinarily is of no concern to society. The

1. Thompson and Smith—*Public Utility Economics*, pp. 70-72.

utility, however, in addition to those negative restrictions imposed on all business, has imposed upon it a group of positive duties and rights.

Duties. The first duty is to serve all who apply for service regardless of race, economic and social status, or other differences. Secondly, the utility or public interest occupation must use all its capacity to produce or service if the demand warrants. In other words, public utilities must stand ready to give instantaneous service. Thirdly, they must render safe and adequate service. With no satisfactory and immediately available substitute, users would be in a helpless position if utilities were permitted to render inadequate service. For this reason, there exist regulations of voltage requirements for electricity, but schedules for urban transport, and speed requirements for telephone connections, etc. And each of the services must be supplied by means of the safest equipment. Fourthly, there must not be unjust discrimination or undue preference. This does not, of course, mean that customer classification for rate making cannot be made. What it means is that the classification must be reasonable. Lastly, it may not demand more than a reasonale price for its service.

Rights. It is only fair that if utilities are bound to perform these duties, they should enjoy certain special rights not common to other business. Their first right is to charge a "reasonable rate". A reasonable rate is one that, under prudent and economical management, covers all operative expenses and also yields a fair rate of return on investment. On ethical as well as economic grounds such be the case, for if utilities cannot acquire monopoly profits, they must not be denied this minimum of a fair return. Finally, they enjoy the privilege of serving under reasonable rules and regulations. These generally include such items as office hours, prompt payment discounts, metre readings and investigations, service deposits, grant of "eminent domain" with power to use streets and buildings for fixing appliances. These regulations are meant to protect the utility service and thus the great majority of its customers.

PROBLEMS OF ORGANISATION

Broadly speaking, a business may be organised along one of the four traditional lines. It may be an individual proprietorship, a partnership, a joint-stock company, or the State. We have already discussed the suitability of different types for different sizes of business; but in the case of a public utility, the choice as to size is limited. Because of the extraordinarily heavy initial investment in plant and equipment, and because the entire area is to be served by one unit, the size of the utility undertaking must be large. The problem of plant location is rather more simple than in other industries, because this is mainly determined by the area to be served and also by regulation. Contrary to most business, utilities must secure huge amount of new capital, but the problem of finance raising, though most pressing, is extremely difficult. The reason for this is that the plant and equipment must be fully installed long before any business can be conducted with the result that large amounts must be spent without any hope of reasonable return during the early years of business.

The problems connected with the marketing for utility services are not many, for it is ordinarily assumed that the need for such services will sell itself. Though general principles of marketing apply to public utilities, yet there are few special problems in the field of utility marketing which are the result of the peculiar nature of the service. These special problems alone are tackled here. We have seen before that the utility service or service-product is non-storable except within limits, and one unit is identical with all other units. Secondly, the service or service product is delivered at or near the premises of the user. All except the bus and the telegraph concerns bring their services directly to the premises of the user by means of their appliances. Thus, utilities are of necessity engaged in direct, house-to-house selling, and the customer must accept this special relationship whether he likes it or not. This more frequent contact with customer requires greater courtesy and more efficient service. In the case of bus service the contact may be made several times a day. The quality of customer-employee contact is important. Yet, this particular utility has been the peculiarities, public utilities offer greater facilities in selling. Being monopolies, they foresee no danger of forced change in their selling methods and pricing policies. Also, their pricing is more closely related to costs. Decreasing costs make for fuller use of plant capacity, lowering of cost per unit and so transfer of part of this cost reduction to consumer in the shape of lower prices. Again, the sale being direct and standardised and on cash basis, the marketing process assumes routine character. Furthermore, there are no intermediaries between the producer and the consumer. The need for demand creation by means of advertising and salesmanship is the least.

OWNERSHIP AND MANAGEMENT

In the foregoing chapter an attempt was made to analyse private and public enterprise, and we came to the conclusion that, because nationalisation of industries substituted public service for private gain, public ownership should replace private ownership. Public utilities, clothed with public interest as they are, offer a stronger case for public ownership than other industries. They supply the basic and indispensable needs of the community and have a vital influence on its well-being—economic, social and political. As regards efficiency of service, the odds are as against efficient operation of the public as of the private establishment. But on social and ethical grounds it is not desirable to leave the necessity of life in the hands of a private company, however carefully its conduct may be watched. Regulation of utilities owned by private enterprise has proved ineffective; excessive profits have been reaped; and a few people have benefited at the cost of the many. In this way, the very foundation of the public utility concept that it is "clothed with public interest" and must work for the maximum social or common advantage is shaken. For these and many other reasons already discussed in the foregoing chapter, it is but necessary that utilities should be publicly owned.

Public ownership may be accomplished by three agencies or any combination of them : (1) the Central Government, (2) the State Governments, (3) the Municipalities. While public ownership of a public utility is conceded by all, its management and direction as a government department or by the municipal council through sub-committees is questioned. We have already examined the dangers of the first alternative, and shall outline the weak points of municipal direction.

During the last 50 years or more municipalities almost everywhere have started or taken over the developed public utilities, including water, electricity, gas and urban transport. Municipally-owned services are operated by the local authorities, generally through committees to whom the permanent officials answer for the conduct of the undertaking. Revenue derived from such services passes through municipal accounts, the surplus may be used in relief of rates and for development and improving the service to the consumer. Capital expenditure may be financed out of loans, but the general policy to redeem borrowings, through sinking funds chargeable on the undertakings, in order to reduce, and finally eliminate, indebtedness as soon as practicable. Many municipalities are free from debts, and from which the rate-payers benefit accordingly. The main handicap of municipal operation is its limitation to the area of the local authority. With modern technological development, restriction of public utilities to local authority area is often uneconomic, and prevents provison of the best possible service. Moreover, the lay committees are not fit and proper agencies for expert operation and supervision. Sometimes, for geographical or functional reasons, operation of an undertaking by a single municipality may prove difficult; and in such a case joint authorities or public boards are established. On the joint authority the local authorities are normally represented, but they are further removed from the electorate. In the words of Herbert Morrison, "The municipal joint committee or joint authority is one of the least democratic of our instruments of public administration. As often as not proceedings are private.....and sometimes it has unlimited power and again it cannot act freely....the joint authorities are often manned by second-rate and third rate counsellors or appointed persons,....and since the joint authority is joint, the members tend to think in terms of the needs and interests of their own municipalities rather than of the area of the joint authority as a whole."[1]

To escape the onslaughts of private enterprise, and the defects of public concerns, at the same time to steer clear of the direction and operation of the utility undertaking by government departments, as also to keep free from political interference, the public corporation as an administrative machinery for national and nationalised industries has already been discussed in the foregoing chapter, and all that was said there is equally applicable to public utilities.

1. Quoted by Davies in *National Enterprise*, pp. 20-22.

CHAPTER XV

GOVERNMENT AND BUSINESS

Doctrine of Laissez-faire and Government. More than a century ago the liberal school of political philosophy was under the influence of the doctrine of *laissez-faire*. Under this doctrine the Government was expected to leave business alone and confine its activities to the maintenance of law and order. The doctrine was obviously based on the assumption that every individual as a rational being would try to derive the greatest satisfaction from life for himself and the nation of such individuals would have the maximum satisfaction with a minimum pain. Competition would furnish the necessary control to safeguard the community against adverse effects of individual selfishness and greed. This, it was believed would lead to the greatest happiness of the greatest numbers.

The exponents of economic freedom did not visualize the evils of factory system ushered in by the Industrial Revolution, the development of the business corporation, or the effects of huge enterprises or great industrial combinations, upon public welfare. This shook the public faith in the doctrine of *laissez-faire*, for it tended to lead to the greatest good of a small number of people who owned or controlled vast business empires. The new industrial society performed miracles in production but seemed less successful in the task of equitable distribution. Hence, followed the dreadful paradox of poverty in the midst of plenty. The myth that unrestricted 'free enterprise' led to the 'greatest good to the greatest numbers' was exploded in the war of development of monopolies, exploitation of workers and consumers by industrial magnates and private gain rather than public good. The public opinion changed and expected the Government to give up "hands off" policy and take measures which would lead to more equitable distribution of wealth.

The 1917 Revolution had put an end to private enterprise in Russia. But in other countries also thought was being devoted to the need for more equitable distribution of wealth. Lord Keynes emphasised that equitable distribution of wealth was necessary to keep up full employment, for only then the 'propensity to consume' would be enough to call for the required investment. In 1924 he abandoned the doctrine of *laissez-faire* because the conditions for its success had disappeared. Laski declared in 1925 that "*laissez-faire* as a systematic principle ended with the outbreak of War in 1914." Hereafter. Government intervention in economic affairs became more pronounced. In England, in Scandanavia, and in India, mixed economy—a combination of evolutionary socialism and private enterprise—is firmly established. Even in the U.S.A. which is the stronghold of private enterprise, a similar system of mixed economy prevails.

REGULATION OF PRIVATE ENTERPRISE

Government regulation of private enterprise is exercised with a view to directing the economy towards maximum social good short of totally taking it over. Some of the methods used for regulating business activities are as follows :

1. Regulation of investment activity in private enterprise by means of planning.
2. Regulation of investment, location, size and expansion of undertakings through regulation and licensing.
3. Regulation of monopolies and restrictive trade practices through legislation.
4. Regulation of prices of commodities through legislation.
5. Regulation of wages, hours of work, payment of bonus and working conditions for good industrial relations.
6. Regulation of company management through legislation.
7. Regulation of specific kinds of business activity such as gambling in shares and commodities, etc.

ECONOMIC PLANNING

Totalitarian economies are highly planned and centrally controlled. The State owns all the productive resources and there is complete regimentation of economic activity. Not only is production planned but consumption is also planned by the State. The Government decides what shall be produced and in what quantities. and does not allow the amount and variety of production to be determined by consumer preferences. In fact all industrial undertakings and commercial units are owned and operated by the State and private enterprise has no place in this system of political and economic set-up.

Planning, however, is not the exclusive monopoly of totalitarian countries or communist nations. The idea has travelled far and wide. Since the end of World War II every country has formed a plan of some kind. Countries with democratic mixed economies (like India) have adopted planning as a major step forward for economic development and social justice.

Planning in India. The Karachi Session of the National Congress in 1931 may be said to have sown the seed of economic planning in India. In 1938, the National Planning Committee, with the late Jawaharlal Nehru as its President, was constituted, which produced some valuable reports. During the War the idea of planning attracted the attention of the people as well as of the Government. Before the close of War the Government of India set up a Planning Department. With the advent of Independence in 1947, planning became a live subject. A step of great importance was taken when a Planning Commission was set up in March 1950. The Planning

Commission was asked to make an assessment of the ·material, capital and human resources of the country and investigate the possibilities of adding to these resources from internal as well as external sources to meet the nation's requirements. It was further asked to formulate a Plan for the most effective and balanced utilization of country's resources.

First Three Five-Year Plans. The First Five-Year Plan (1951–52 to 1955– 56) had two-fold objective: (1) to correct disequilibrium in the economy caused by the Second World War and the partition of the country and (2) to initiate at the same time a process of allround balanced development which would ensure a rising national income and a steady improvement in the living standards over a period of time. The Plan accorded the highest priority to agriculture, including irrigation and power projects. About 44.6 per cent of the total outlay of Rs. 2,069 crores in the public sector (later raised to Rs. 2,356 crores) was allowed for their development. The Plan also aimed at increasing the rate of investment from the level of 5 per cent to about 7 per cent of the national income. The First Plan was completed satisfactorily; the economy responded well to the stimulus of the Plan. Both agricultural and industrial production recorded substantial increases.

In December I 954. Parliament declared that the broad objective of economic policy should be to achieve the 'socialist pattern of society' under which the basic criteria for determining lines of advance would be social gain and greater equality of incomes and wealth and not private profit.

The Second Five-Year Plan (1956–57 to 1960–61), therefore, sought to promote a pattern of development which would ultimately lead to the establishment of a socialistic society in India. In particular, it stressed that the benefits of economic development should accrue more to the relatively less privileged sections of society, and there should be a progressive reduction in the concentration of incomes, wealth, and economic power.

The main aims of the Plan were: (I) an increase of 25 per cent in the national income; (2) rapid industrialisation with particular emphasis on the development of basic and heavy industries; (3) large expansion of employment opportunities; and (4) reduction of inequalities in income and wealth and more even distribution of economic power. The Plan also aimed at increasing the rate of investment from 7 per cent of the national income to 11 per cent by 1960-61. With an outlay of Rs. 4,800 crores in the public sector and Rs. 3,100 crores in the private sector, the Plan laid special stress on industrialisation increased production of iron and steel, heavy chemicals including nitrogenous fertilizers and development of heavy engineering and machine building industry.

The Third Five-Year Plan (1961–62 to 1965–66) aimed at securing a marked advance towards self-sustaining growth. Its immediate objectives were to (I) secure an increase in the national income of over 5 per cent per annum, and at the same time ensure a pattern of investment which could sustain this rate of growth during subsequent Plan periods; (2) achieve self-sufficiency in food grains and increase agricultural production to meet the requirements of industry and exports; (3) expand basic industries like steel, chemicals, fuel and power and to establish machine building capacity, so that the requirements of further industrialisation could be met with a period of ten years or so mainly from the country's own resources (4) utilize fully the man-power resources of the country and ensure a substantial expansion in employment opportunities; and (5) establish progressively greater equality of opportunity and bring about reduction in disparities of income and wealth and a more even distribution of economic power. The national income was to increase by about 30 per cent from Rs. 14,500 crores in 1960–61 to about Rs. 19,000 crores by 1965–66 (at 1960–61 prices) and per capita income by about 17 per cent, from Rs. 330 to Rs. 385 during the same period.

Despite occasional setbacks, fifteen years of planned development resulted in all-round progress of the economy. There was a notable expansion in basic facilities like irrigation, power and transport. Agricultural production increased by about 41 per cent during the first two Plans. In the Third Plan, the performance of agriculture was not so satisfactory. Widespread drought in 1965-66 slowed down the rate of growth of the economy and led 10 increased imports of food and other items. During the Third Plan, 2.5 crore tonnes of food grains, 39 lakh bales of cotton and 15 lakh bales of jute were imported. The net output in organised manufacturing industries nearly doubled during the first two Plans. The share of the public sector industries went up from 1.5 per cent in 1951 to 8.4 per cent at the end of the Second Plan. Much of this increase was in the key industries such as steel, coal mining and heavy. chemicals. In the Third Plan, the production of organised industry increased by 8 to 10 per cent annually during the first four years but was only 5.3 per cent in the last year of the Plan because of the dislocation caused by the Indo-Pakistan conflict and disruption in the flow of foreign aid. Notwithstanding this, over the Third Plan period, the growth rate in organised industries was 8.2 per cent against the target of 11 per. cent. There was continuous increase and diversification of production capacity, specially in steel and aluminium, machine tools, industrial machinery, electrical and transport equipment, fertilizers, drugs, pharmaceuticals and petroleum products—all this contributed to strengthening of the industrial structure.

The situation created by the Indo-Pakistan conflict, two successive years of severe drought, devaluation of the currency, general rise in prices and erosion of resources available for Plan purposes delayed finalisation of the Fourth Plan. Instead, between 1966 and 1969, three Annual Plans were formulated within the framework of the Draft Outline of the Fourth Plan. They took into account the conditions prevailing at the time. The state of the economy and the non-availability of financial resources for Plan purposes kept down the size of development outlay during this period.

The Fourth Five-Year Plan (April 1969 to March 1974) was presented to Parliament on 18 May, 1970. It aimed at accelerating the tempo of development in conditions of stability, at reducing fluctuations in agricultural production as well as the uncertainties of foreign aid. The Fourth Plan envisaged a total outlay of Rs. 24,882 crores, comprising Rs. 15,902 cores in the public sector and an investment of Rs. 8,980 crores in private sector.

The Fifth Five-Year Plan (1974-1979) laid down the two major objectives, removal of poverty and the attainment of economic self-reliance. To achieve these objectives two-pronged attack was attempted : An increase in domestic product and decline in the growth of population. An investment of Rs. 45,315 crores was envisaged (Rs. 29,745 crores for the public sector and Rs. 15.570 crores for the private sector) at 1971–71 prices for the Fifth Plan. The National Development Council, however, increased it to Rs. 53,411 crores. But the situation deteriorated. prices rose sky high and the resource position became extremely difficult with the result that the Plan targets had to be revised. The situation was very grave, bordering on to economic crisis. In 1973–74, India had the highest rate of inflation of 27 per cent and immediately before the proclamation of emergency on 26th June, 1975, it had gone up to 32 per cent. The declaration of emergency followed by Prime Minister Mrs. Indira Gandhi's 20 point economic programme, helped to contain and curb inflation. Within one year of the declaration of emergency prices fell by 8 per cent, and there was an extensive economic progress. The investment went upto Rs. 64,000 crore, approximately. Industrial production went up, food grain yield and procurement surpassed targets. There was generally an upward swing in all directions. In 1977, however, a change of Government from Congress to Janata took place. The Planning Commission prepared the Sixth Five Year Plan (1978–83) and presented a draft of the Plan to the National Development Council. Since there is said to be a change in the strategy and thrust in this Plan as a result of a change in Government, it is appropriate to make a brief assessment of the five plans and their achievements and shortcomings.

Summary Evaluation of the Five Plans

As has been pointed out in the previous paragraphs, there was consistent step up in the Plan expenditure over the years, and a steady increase in investment over each successive plan. During the past 25 years, the country has made enormous progress in the fields of agriculture, industry and economic and social overheads. The National income is constant, prices increased during the period 1951–52 to 1976–77 from 9,303 crores to Rs. 22,210 crores. During the same period foodgrain output increased from just 55 million tonnes to 120 million tonnes. Industrial production increased four-fold. There has been a spectacular increase in exports revealing an eight-fold increase. The country has achieved tremendous success in its import substitution of a wide variety of items. In short, the economy has grown steadily and the industrial base has widened.

However, in spite of a steady increase in the net national product per capita income growth has been low, mainly because of a 2 per cent increase in population per year. This growth in the population has nullified to a great extent much of the benefits of the success of planned development.

The poor have continued to remain poor and even today 260 million people are below the poverty line.[1] Consequently, the fruits of planning have not percolated to the lower strata of society who live in abject poverty.

Another important shortcoming has been the wide difference between targets set and the actual achievements. Whereas in financial terms the investment targets and actual expenditures were more or less equal, the physical targets were not achieved except in the case of the First Plan. In the case of the First Plan the target fixed for the rate of growth was 2.3 per cent and the actual rate was 3.7 per cent. In all the subsequent plans the rate of growth was lower than the target.

In spite of increased investments and higher targets during the past 25 years, the economy grew at a rate of only 3.5 per cent on an average. Therefore, it was found necessary that factors which contributed to the gaps between targets and achievements should be located and remedial measures taken in the Sixth and subsequent plans.

The Sixth Five Year Plan (1980–85) The Sixth Plan began with the appreciation that "industrial development plays a crucial role in our development strategy, particularly with regard to the objectives of structural diversification, modernisation and self-reliance". The Sixth Plan therefore laid great stress on greater industrial investment and growth. The important features of this strategy and broad objectives of this plan were as follows:-

1. Substantial increase in manufacturing capacities;
2. Achieving a higher rate of growth of the economy than in the past–4.7 percent growth rate was aimed at;
3. Special attention to the growth of capital goods in general and electronics industry in particular;
4. Greater efforts to increase export of engineering and other industrial products;
5. Greater emphasis to be placed on development programmes;
6. Ensuring the country's continued progress towards self-reliance;
7. Moving towards a significant reduction in the disparities of income and wealth;
8. An appreciable rise in the standard of living, including that of the poorest section of the population;

1. Poverty Line is measured as a per capita consumption of Rs. 70 per cent.

9. Additionally, agricultural development had to be stepped up still further.

The total outlay in the Public Sector for industrial development was fixed at Rs. 22,187 crore, or nearly 23 per cent of the total outlay for the public sector. In the private sector, investment of Rs. 30,323 crore for industrial development was fixed.

INDUSTRIAL POLICY

The declared industrial policy of the Government is another instrument for regulating industry. Right up to the World War II private enterprise was almost fully immune from Government regulation. During the war, however, the need for regulating investment, production, distribution and prices became urgent, as it was necessary to make use of all the resources. In 1947, the country achieved independence and the national Government felt the need for developing the economy in a planned manner in the national interest. It was decided to establish public undertakings in certain fields, but also to allow private enterprise to continue and develop subject to certain regulations and controls.

Industrial Policy Resolution, 1948. The first step in this direction was the announcement of the Industrial Policy Resolution in 1948. This Resolution laid down that the manufacture of arms and ammunition, production and control of atomic energy and ownership and management of railways would be the exclusive responsibility of the public sector while in all other fields the private sector will be allowed to function. It was further stated that in the field of 6 industries, namely, coal, iron and steel, aircraft manufacture, ship -building, manufacture of telephone, telegraph and wireless apparatus excluding radio receiving sets and mineral oils, only the public enterprise will take the initiative of setting new undertakings. This provision, it will be noted, permitted the existing private units to expand their activities. But a great indirect control was exercised in this resolution by adding a Review Clause which gave the Government power to review and re-examine the matter regarding the existing units at the end of 10 years and the Government could nationalise them if found necessary.

Industrial Policy Resolution, 1956. The Review Clause militated against the expansion of existing undertakings and starting of new ones. As a result the Government had to re-state its Industrial Policy in 1956, and revise its policy concerning nationalisation. Under this resolution some more industries were included in this group and the "Review Clause" was deleted and it was stated that the existing units in the private sector would be allowed to expand with no fear of nationalisation. The more important features of the policy resolution, which continues to be in operation, are summarised below.

Objectives of the policy resolution. The 1956 policy resolution had as its objective the attainment of the socialist pattern of society through the reduction of economic inequalities and concentration of economic power and monopolisation.

Means to attain the objective. The means proposed to realise this objective were

(i) to accelerate the rate of economic growth and to speed up industrialisation;
(ii) to develop heavy and machine-making industries;
(iii) to expand the public sector;
(iv) to build up a large and growing co-operative sector; and
(v) to reduce disparities in income and wealth, and prevent private monopolies.

Classification of Industries. With a view to assuming direct responsibility for the future development of important industries, but leaving at the same time, some industries to the private sector, the industries were classified into 3 categories as follows :

(a) In the first category were those industries the future development of which was to be the exclusive responsibility of the state. This category contains 17 basic and key industries such as arms and ammunition, atomic energy, iron and steel, heavy machinery, coal and lignite, mineral oils, mining of ores, air and railway transport, shipbuilding, telephones and generation and distribution of electricity. The existing units in the private sector were to be allowed and encouraged to expand.

(b) The second category was to consist of industries which were to be progressively State-owned, and in which the State was generally to take initiative in establishing new undertakings, but in which private enterprise was also to be expected to supplement the effort of the State. Twelve industries mentioned in Schedule B of the Resolution fall in this category. They include some minerals, aluminium, machine tools, ferro-alloys, antibiotics, synthetic rubber, chemical pulp, road and sea transport, etc.

(c) The third category included all the remaining industries, and their future development was left to the initiative and enterprise of the private sector. The Government would help the private sector in this regard.

Public arid private sectors to be partners. The policy resolution, by categorising industries, did not seek to place them in water-tight compartment. Since the objective has been the economic development of the country, the resolution envisaged both sectors to play their roles to achieve the objective. As we have stated earlier, the two sectors are not partisans but they are partners in the grand venture.

Miscellaneous clauses of the resolution. The cottage and small-scale industries were to be encouraged and fostered. Every effort was to be made to bring about cordial industrial relations to ensure speedy growth. Facilities for the training and development of management and technical personnel were to be provided. The management of public enterprises was to be on business lines and to ensure speedy decisions and willingness to assume responsibility of authority was to be granted.

Appraisal of the Industrial Policy. The public reaction to the new Resolution was diversified. The main criticism came from the business community and ran something like this. The Resolution, it was claimed, greatly reduced the scope of private enterprise. Although flexibility was envisaged in the Resolution, yet it tended to operate primarily in favour of public sector, as the State could enter any trade or industry it chose. Industrial policy placed greater emphasis on public enterprise. The policy, if rigidly applied, could result in imposing heavy additional burdens on the already overstrained financial and administrative resources of the public sector and in restraining the rate of development in the vitally important fields. The competence of the Government to establish and run industries efficiently was questioned. The Resolution, however, charted a fresh course, permitting freedom of development in private sector, but with checks and balances to prevent detrimental concentration of economic power and wealth. The Resolution has been described by some observers as an "economic constitution" based upon its political counterpart, the Constitution of India. It is linked to the Constitution by re-stating the preamble of Justice, Liberty, Equality and Fraternity, and its Directive Principles of State Policy. Thus, the private enterprise has been given a new opportunity to justify its existence in socialistic state.

Review of Industrial Policy Resolution of 1956. A thorough overhaul of Industrial Policy Resolution was at one time contemplated in order to remove some of the inherent contradictions in the Resolution and bring it in line with the current needs. The main grounds for the revision of the Resolution were as follows:

(a) The objectives spelt out in the Resolution were self-contradictory and virtually tied the hands of the administration by stopping them from taking decisions calculated to accelerate the industrial development of the country.

(b) There was no firm statement of policy on foreign investments. It was suggested that clear enunciation of objectives and guidelines relating to foreign investment form part of the Resolution.

(c) There was a contradiction relating to the protection guaranteed by the Resolution to the small-scale and co-operative sectors. While more and more industries were being reserved for the small-scale sector, large units for the same products also existed side by side. In this situation, the small units which had to compete with large units were at a disadvantage.

(d) One of the objectives of the Resolution of 1956 was the prevention of undue concentration of wealth in a small section of the population. The Resolution failed in its avowed objective, since the concentration of wealth in a few hands has continued to increase.

The Industries (Development and Regulation) Act, 1951. With a view to implementing the Industrial Policy enunciated in the Industrial Policy Resolution of 1948 the Industries (Development and Regulation) Act was passed in 1951. It provides for control over production and distribution as well as balanced regional development, in order to ensure a well-regulated and desired expansion of industries in the private sector as part of development planning. The Act covers 38 groups of manufacturing and processing industries, each group having its component. For example, the Telecommunication group includes telephones; telegraph equipment; wireless communication apparatus; radio receivers, including amplifying and public address equipment; television sets and teleprinters. The important provisions of the Act are as follows :

1. *Regulation of Industries by Registration.* Every existing industrial undertaking was required to be registered after the Act came into force, provided it was included in the Schedule to the Act. The Central Government shall register the scheduled industries and issue to the owner of the undertaking so registered a certificate of registration containing the productive capacity of the industrial undertaking and other prescribed particulars.

2. *Control by licensing of Undertakings.* All new undertakings covered by the Schedule must obtain a licence from the Central Government before being established. The licence, when granted, may contain conditions regulating the site, location, the manufacturing programme, and expansion or addition of new product.

3. *Control by Investigation.* The Central Government enjoys wide powers of control by investigation into the scheduled industries or industrial undertakings. The Central Government may order investigation to be made in the case of any scheduled industry or industrial undertaking if it is of opinion that in the case of such undertaking there has been substantial fall in the volume of production, or a marked deterioration in the quality of any product, or any unjustifiable rise in price, or if the undertaking has been managed in a manner detrimental to the scheduled industry or to public interest.

On completion of the investigation, the Central Government may issue directions regulating the production, require the industrial undertaking to stimulate development of industry, prohibit the undertaking from reducing its production, capacity or economic value, or control the prices, or regulate the distribution of product or products. The Central Government is also empowered to revoke the registration or licence if it deems it necessary or justified in public interest.

4. *Taking over of industrial undertakings.* If the Central Government is of opinion that an industrial undertaking in respect of which directions were issued has failed to comply with such directions, or it is being managed in a manner highly detrimental to the scheduled industry concerned or to public interest, it may take over the management of such undertaking. It may also take over an industrial undertaking, if the persons incharge of such undertaking have, by reckless investments, or creation of encumbrances on the assets, or by the diversion of funds, brought about situation which is likely to affect the production, or if it has been closed for a period of

5. *Establishment of Central Advisory Council*. The Act requires the Central Government to establish a Central Advisory Council for the purpose of advising it, on matters concerning the development and regulation of scheduled industries. The Council is to consist of a Chairman and such other members not exceeding 30 in number, who are in the opinion of the Central Government capable of representing the interests of (a) owners of industrial undertakings in scheduled industries; (b) employees of such undertakings; (c) consumers of goods manufactured by these industries; (d) such other class of persons as the Central Government may consider suitable.

6. *Development Councils*. The Central Government may constitute for any scheduled industry or a group of scheduled industries a Development Council consisting of persons capable of representing the interests of the owners of industrial undertakings concerned, persons having special knowledge of matters relating to technical or other aspects of the industry, persons representing the interests of the employees and persons representing the interests of consumers.

The Development Councils are required to perform the following functions:

(i) recommend targets of production for securing fuller utilisation of installed capacity;

(ii) suggest norms of efficiency with a view to eliminating waste, obtaining maximum production, improving quality and reducing cost;

(iii) help in devising a system of distribution and sales which would satisfy the consumer;

(iv) promote standardisation of produce, training of employees, scientific and industrial research, etc.

(v) Investigate the possibilities of decentralisation of stages and processes of production;

(vi) promoting the adoption of measures for encouraging productivity or labour, etc.

Such Development Councils were set up by the Central Government. However, as pointed out by the Ramakrishna Study Group.[1] The functioning of these Development Councils over the past so many years has not been uniformly satisfactory. As the Development Councils provide a very vital link between the Government on one hand and the entrepreneurs, technical experts and consumers of goods manufactured on the other. the Government has accepted the recommendation of the Study Group to restructure these Councils so that they may perform their functions properly and more effectively.

Re-Structured Development Councils. The following structural and revitalising changes have been made in the Development Councils :

1. Study Group set up by the Central Government to study the working of the Industries (Development and Regulation) Act, 1951, and make recommendations.

1. The Councils will now be presided over by the Secretary or the Additional Secretary of the concerned Administrative Ministry.
2. In order that a Council may function as a compact body it shall have not more than 15 members including representatives of industry and consumers wherever appropriate, representatives of Department of Industrial Development Planning Commission, financial institutions, concerned national laboratories, Bureau of Industrial Costs and Prices and Director General, Technical Development.
3. The Development Councils will meet once every quarter and send a report to the Projects Approval Board functioning in the Ministry of Industry.
4. The Councils will organise their work through technical and economic sub-committees.
5. The recommendations of these councils will be taken into account in framing the annual guidelines for various industries and also for the purpose of determining the scope and extent of further licensing.

District Industries Centres. In keeping with the policy of exemption from licensing and decentralisation of powers the study group recommended the formation of a Bureau of Industrial Approvals under the aegis of the State Governments or the Directors of Industries in the states. The District Industries Centres which are being set up in the Districts will provide the requisite organisational frame work for this purpose. Government have accepted these recommendations and the State Governments have been requested to implement these recommendations.

The Act provides for the setting up of a Licensing Committee for granting licences for setting up new enterprises in the private sector after considering their capital, capital structure, location, plant capacity proposed to be installed, availability of transport capacity, technical and skilled personnel, and foreign collaboration,if any. Over a period since the enforcement of the Act in 1952, a number of changes have been made in the licensing procedures. An industrial unit having fixed assets of less than 3, crore rupees is not required to obtain a licence under the Act. An already licensed registered undertaking may expand or diversify without obtaining an additional licence. A brief description in the changes made in the licensing policy up to date is given below.

Industrial Licensing Policy. The basic framework for the Government's industrial licensing policy, designed to regulate indiscriminate entry and growth in the industrial sector, was provided in the Industrial Policy Resolution of 1948, as reiterated on April 30, 1956. Within the overall framework of the 1956 Resolution, the Government has effected changes, from time to time, in its industrial licensing policy, in order to fulfil the priority needs of the economy and to promote orderly growth of industries. But certain defects and shortcomings were found to be present in working of the licensing system and procedure. The Government, therefore appointed the Industrial Licensing Committee to look into the whole range or issues connected with the industrial licensing in India. The Committee made its report in 1969, making certain important recommendations.

Industrial Licensing Policy or 1970. In the light of the recommendation made by the Industrial Licensing Inquiry Committee (Dutt Committee), the Government announced in February, 1970 a new industrial licensing policy. Under the new policy emphasis was placed on expansion of the public sector in new directions as also on rapid growth of the small scale and medium sectors of industry. Besides, any further growth of the larger industrial groups, and foreign companies as also dominant undertakings was sought to be regulated into avenues of heavy investments, core sector industries, and backward areas. Another aspect of the policy was the stress laid on the development of the small scale sector in order to reduce regional imbalances and ensure greater employment-oriented industrial growth. No industrial undertaking with assets of over Rs. 10 lakhs in plant and machinery can normally take up or expand manufacture of items reserved for the small scale sector nor diversify into those items without a licence. The number of items reserved for the small-scale sector was also raised from 47 to 128.

In regard to the *medium sector*, that is the sector of industries involving the value of investment above Rs. 10 lakhs but not exceeding Rs. 5 crores in total assets, the issue of licences was liberalised to encourage entrepreneurs.

With regard to 'core sector' and 'Heavy Investment Sector' (investment in fixed assets exceeding Rs. 5 crores), licensing was to be used as a positive instrument for development and achievement of the detailed production plans drawn up for each of those items. In view of the large investment involved in this sector, Government would assume larger powers of direction and say in the management of undertakings, most of which involve substantial investment by public financial institutions. These financial institutions would also have the option to convert loans into equity.

The other important features of the 1970 policy were:

1. The area of exemption from licensing provision applicable to industries was extended up to Rs. One Crore;
2. The exemption was generally not applicable to larger industrial houses, foreign companies or branches or subsidiaries of branches of foreign companies.
3. In respect of agro-industries, particularly undertakings processing sugarcane, jute and other agricultural commodities, preference was to be given to applicants from the co-operative sector.1

Industrial Policy Statement of 1973. In February, 1973, the Government announced its decision on the industrial policy after reviewing

---

***Source :** Reserve Bank of India. Report on Currency and Finance, 1974-75.

the policies relating to industrial development in the light of experience gained in the implementation of the industrial licensing policy of 1970 and in the context of the Approach to the Fifth Plan. The Government reiterated that Industrial Policy Resolution of 1956 would continue to govern Government's policies for achieving the objectives of growth, social justice and self-reliance in the industrial sphere. The salient features of the new industrial policy were as follows :

Amending industrial licensing policy. The Government updated the Industrial Licensing Policy so that it should reflect the Approach to the Fifth Plan and take into account the legal and institutional arrangements that were available for the effective control of concentration of economic power.

Redefinition of larger houses. The industrial licensing policy of 1970 placed certain restrictions on undertakings with assets exceeding Rs. 35 crores. The new licensing policy reduced the value of the assets for an undertaking and of inter-connected undertakings at the same level as detained in the MRTP Act, 1969. The definition adopted in that Act is on the basis of a lower limit of assets, along with the assets of inter-connected undertakings, of not less than Rs. 20 crores. This would ensure more effective control on the concentration of economic power.

Consolidated list of Industries. Larger houses would be eligible to participate in and contribute to the establishment of industries provided the item of manufacture was not one reserved for production in the public sector or in the small scale sector. Larger houses would be excluded from this list except where production was predominantly for exports.

Policy towards foreign companies. Foreign companies may continue to invest in industries which produce primarily for export, but may not do so in industries not included in the list. Their investments will be subject, as hitherto,' to the guidelines on the dilution of foreign equity and will be examined with special reference to technological aspects, export possibilities and overall effect on the balance of payments.

Criteria for licensing. In granting licences preference would be given to medium entrepreneurs in all industries. Licensing policy would seek to promote production of ancillaries, wherever feasible and appropriate in medium and small scale sectors.

Co-operative sector. The policy of encouragement to the cooperative sector would receive special emphasis in industries which process critical raw materials such as fertilizers. Co-operatives would also be encouraged to participate in the production of mass consumption goods.

The changes proposed were designed to stimulate growth in all priority industries of importance to the Fifth Plan subject to a more effective enforcement of social objectives. The licensing approval procedure had been rationalised in order to reduce time-lag in processing applications for industrial licences. A Project Approval Board—an inter-ministerial committee of Secretaries—had been set up to see that the system was put to work. The following time limits had been prescribed for the disposal of various categories of applications : (1) 90 days for letters of intent, foreign collaboration approval and capital goods clearance; (2) 120 days for composite applications for industrial licences and foreign collaboration and capital goods clearance; (3) 150 days where clearance is sought under the MRTP Act.

Guidelines for Industries—1976–77. Another publication entitled "Guidelines for Industries—1976–77" spelt out the latest decisions on the scope and aims of industrial licensing policy. Although the framework for industrial policy remained the same the Government's determination to achieve growth with social justice and self-reliance in the industrial sector was re-iterated more specifically. The role of public sector was to be further enhanced and certain manufactures were to be continued and even extended in the small scale sector. Co-operatives and medium industries were to be given preference and encouraged to participate in mass consumption goods. Large industrial houses would be allowed as before to participate in the core industries, linked to core industries and industries with long term export potential provided that the items of manufacture were not reserved for production in the public sector or in the small scale sector. The large industrial units could also take up other industries, if they guaranteed a minimum export of 60 per cent of the new or additional capacities.

Foreign Companies having more than 50 per cent non-resident interest in paid-up equity capital were allowed to participate in the same manner as the larger industrial houses.

The policy regarding the joint sector remained unchanged. This sector was to play mainly a promotional role to guide small and medium industries in developing selected industries. But larger industrial houses and foreign companies were not allowed entry through joint-sector industries in which they were otherwise disqualified.

In the field of *Industrial Licensing* further changes had been made with a view to facilitating larger production. The provision for endorsement of licences on the basis of maximum utilisation of plant and machinery had been extended to units registered with technical authorities and the Directorate of Small Scale Industries under this provision. Speedy procedures were to be followed in considering requests for endorsement of licences seeking maximum utilisation of plant and machinery installed. Additionally, units which did not fall within the MRTP Act and/or FERA (Foreign Exchange Regulation Act) had been permitted to utilise their installed capacities without limit and in excess of their licensed capacities in 29 specified industries. This list was first announced on 25th October, 1975. This facility was, however, subject to the condition that the article of manufacture should not be reserved for the small scale sector. Industrial undertakings falling under MRTP Act or FERA could also avail of this facility provided the excess production was exported or sold in accordance with the directions of the Government.

By and large, through liberalisation of licensing provisions, automatic growth of capacity had been allowed to selected engineering industries. This facility was not available to dominant undertakings and undertakings having foreign collaborations. Furthermore, industrial research for commercial exploitation was being encouraged. Industrial undertakings other than those covered by the MRTP Act or FERA could set up capacity based on the results of their research and developmental works. As per a Press Note of 7th March. 1976, undertakings covered by the MRTP Act or the FERA could also engage in research and development work in their own spheres. Facilities were also available for diversification in industries without an industrial licence.

Foreign Collaborations and Joint Ventures. With a view to effective rapid industrialisation, the Government of India followed a policy of encouraging the participation of foreign capital and enterprise. The 1948 Industrial Policy Resolution "recognised foreign 'Capital as an important supplement to domestic savings for the development of the country and for securing scientific, technical and industrial know-how. Foreign enterprise was assured of non-discriminatory treatment at par with domestic enterprise in regard to industrial policy requirements, facilities for repatriation of profits and capital as well as payment of fair compensation in the event of compulsory acquisition of industrial units by the State." As a result of this encouragement, hundreds of agreements were entered into, assuming the forms of collaboration through subsidiaries or minority participation in joint ventures. The outflow of cash on account of dividend payments, royalty, technical service fees and meagre inflow of capital caused a drainage to the tune of Rs. 930 crores during 1964–70. The Government, therefore, imposed certain conditions with regard to Indianisation, only minority holdings by the foreign companies with a view to eliminating altogether foreign aid by 1980. Collaborations were permitted only in select fields of high priority.

The Guideline 1976-77 did not depart from the policy already followed. Collaboration would continue to be permitted in select fields of high priority, particularly in areas where the import of foreign collaboration resulted in substantial exports expansion or creation. Foreign equity participation was restricted to the ceiling of 40 per cent; and the equity capital was not to be tied to the import of machinery or payment for know how, trade marks, brand names. etc.

Balanced Regional Growth. Incentives to industries set up in backward areas have been in operation for some time with the avowed object of achieving balanced regional growth by encouraging entrepreneurs to move to those areas. The main incentive is in the form of a cash subsidy related to the fixed capital investment of the individual enterprise. The existing quantum of subsidy is at the rate of 15 per cent of the fixed capital investment or Rs. 15 lakhs, whichever is lower. This rate of subsidy has been in operation since 1973 without any change. It has also been decided that capital subsidy disbursed will not be taxable as income or revenue receipt. The other incentive is through extending confessional finance through the Industrial Development Bank of India, Industrial Finance Corporation of India and the Industrial Credit and Investment Corporation of India. The concessions take the form of low rate of interest, longer initial grace period and reduction of commitment charges. The small-scale units get this facility through State Financial Corporations.

The third incentive is transport subsidy. Recently, further concessions in the form of special tax rebates, liberalised import facilities and concessions on supply or machinery on hire-purchase have been introduced. The special tax rebate provides for exemption from income tax up to 20 per cent of the profits and gains realised by newly established industrial undertaking or total business in· backward area. The exemptions are available for the first 10 assessment years of the undertakings and the undertaking must be a factory.

The import policy for 1976–77 has allowed special facilities for the import of raw materials, components and spares in respect of small scale units set up in backward areas. These special facilities provided that—

(a) all units in the non-select list would be treated as select-units, i.e., small-scale units could set up any type of industry.

(b) the mode of financing in respect of these units would be 75 per cent in free foreign exchange and 25 per cent in U.K. credit; and

(c) import entitlements of these units up to Rs. 20,000 would be financed from free foreign exchange.

Furthermore, units in these areas would be eligible for preferential pricing in respect of canalised raw materials against release orders as if those units are exporting units.

Small-Scale Industries. The policy for encouraging .the growth of small scale units through special assistance, financial and technical, continues. Small entrepreneurs are allowed to operate in the reserve field without fear competition from large units. The items reserved for development in the small scale sector numbering 177 remain unchanged. A new scheme for guiding small units to adopt modern techniques in management and production so as to improve their competitive strength has been launched by the Small Industries Development Organisation. Under this scheme the industries to be modernised during 1976-77 are: Machine tools, automobile components and accessories, castings and forgings, domestic electrical appliances, hosiery and knit wears, bicycle and bicycle parts, leather and leather goods, handtools, scientific instruments and storage batteries. It is envisaged that every year 10 new industries will be selected for modernisation in the small-scale sector. The programme is designed to assist the small units by supplying machinery, equipment and raw materials both indigenous and imported, extending short-term and long-term credit facilities, and by arranging techno-managerial guidance, training, visits by foreign experts, etc.

The joint sector concept can also be utilised to further develop the under developed areas. In fact, new expansions and diversifications should be permitted to such units in backward areas only to Joint sector units, unless on techno-economic grounds it is totally non-feasible. The joint sector companies, being profit-oriented, should be directed to contribute to the balanced growth and welfare of backward areas.

Industrial Policy Statement of 1980

With the change in Government a new Industrial Policy Statement was made in July, 1980. This statement spelled out the following socio-economic objectives:

(a) Optimum utilization of installed capacity;
(b) Recognition of additional capacity arising out of replacement and modernisation of equipment, or labour productivity or technological improvement;
(c) Maximum production and achieving higher productivity;
(d) Higher employment generation;
(e) Correction of regional imbalances;
(f) Strengthening of agricultural base through agro-based industries and. promotion of .optimum inter-sectoral relationship;
(g) Promotion of export-oriented industries;
(h) Promotion of economic welfare through equitable spread of investment and disposal of returns;
(i) Consumer Protection against high prices and bad quality.

Investment limits for Small Scale and ancillary industries were raised to Rs. 20 lakh and Rs. 25 lakh, respectively. The limits were further raised to Rs. 35 lakh and 45 lakh respectively in 1985.

Installed capacities in excess of licensed/registered capacities in 34 selected industries were regularised. These include basic industries and those processing mass consumption goods not reserved for small-scale sector provided the units are non-MRTP or non-FERA.

Automatic growth was allowed to the extent of 5 per cent per annum or 25 per cent in five-year ·period in the registered or licensed capacity of 19 additional industries bringing the total to 34. Some relaxation in location policy was made with a view to provide for natural growth for export production.

Further liberalisation at a large scale started in 1985, and has continued at an accelerated rate so much so that by far the largest number of industries have been delicensed, and the process is going on. However, delicensed industries need to be registered.

Policy of liberalisation was also followed in case of industries which remain within the facility of "broad-banding" or "broad-categorisation" in respect of 25 industrial groups, so that those industries can make rapid changes in their products mix without seeking fresh licence. In 1987, industries in private sector were allowed to set up sugar mills in areas where the cooperatives or public sector undertakings did not come forward to establish sugar mills as a result of this liberalisation policy, in 1987–88, the industrial sector forged ahead by 12.4 per cent. An important point to note here is that the growth rate has shown consistent uptrend and the momentum has continued. If the drought had not intervened the industrial sector would have clocked its best ever performance since the inception of planning in this country.

Another effect of liberalisation is that it has introduced certain disproportionalities. A few sectors like the electronic, garments, grown disproportionately faster.

REGULATION AND CONTROL OF PRICES

The Government regulates and exercises control over prices by fixing prices of raw materials, semi-finished and finished goods. The general power is given by the Industries (Development and Regulation) Act, 1951. The Essential Commodities Act, 1955 gives special power to the Government to declare any commodity as essential in the public interest and exercise control over it. Prices are subject to two other controls, namely, the voluntary price control and control through executive orders. Voluntary price control is exercised under the Essential Commodities Act in which the Government only exercises persuasion on industries to adopt a rational price policy e.g., in case of cotton textiles, cotton yarn, jute and woollen yarn. The control through executive orders is exercised directly by issuing orders without making any reference to the above-mentioned two Acts with a view to avoiding the severity involved in recourse to these Acts. Prices of drugs are controlled like this.

Tariff Commission acts as the most important agency of the Government for fixing prices. The Commission acts primarily for granting protection to home industries against foreign competition. It enquires into claims for protection and also enquires into price of articular commodities whether protected or not. The Commission has since been abolished.

Regulation of company management is done through the Companies Act and has already been discussed in chapter on Company Management. Regulation of wages and working conditions of workers are discussed in chapters dealing with Management of Personnel.

REGULATION OF MONOPOLIES AND RESTRICTIVE TRADE PRACTICES

It is an established fact that unbridled monopolies lead to concentration of wealth and economic power to the detriment of public interest. Every Government, therefore, takes steps to curb monopolistic practices which prove prejudicial to common good. Our Constitution amply makes it clear that we should move towards building an equitable society. In addition to legislative measures, the Government had also embarked upon a massive programme of countervailing measures, such as enlarged role of public sector, protection of cottage industries development of modern small scale industries and co-operatives. Big commercial banks were nationalised. Managing agency system was abolished. Yet the concentration of economic power continued unabated. This led the late Prime Minister Jawaharlal Nehru to wonder where the wealth created since Independence had gone. Obviously, it had concentrated in the hands of owners of big business. Consequently, a number of Committees and Commissions were appointed during the 1960's, one of which was Monopolies Inquiry Commission (1965) which made a detailed analysis of product concentration and countrywide monopoly. It came to the conclusion that concentration had in both respects.

Prof. Hazari's and Industrial Licensing Policy Inquiry Committee's studies revealed that licensing regime had helped the larger houses to grow at a fast rate. According to the Monopolies Inquiry Commission in 1964, out of 1,170 products the manufacture was undertaken by units registered with the Directorate-General of Technical Development (DGTD) the production of 409 products or 35 per cent was concentrated in a single production unit. For 205 products or 17.5 per cent, production was concentrated in two units. The production of 1,120 products (out of 1,170 products) or 95.7 per cent was concentrated in 4 production units or less: The position has not changed since 1964. Country-wide concentration also showed similar concentration. Out of the aggregate paid-up capital of Rs. 1,376 crores owned by public limited companies (6.368 in number) the large public companies numbering 1,364 or 21.4' per cent of the total public companies accounted for 72.8 per cent of their paid-up capital.

It was under the background of these developments and on the basis of the recommendation of the MIC that the Monopolies and Restrictive Trade Practices Act was passed in 1969 and the MRTP Commission was established in 1970.

MONOPOLIES AND RESTRICTIVE TRADE PRACTICES ACT, 1969

Objects of the Act. The two main objects of the Act are: (1) Checking concentration of economic power which is detrimental to the community, and (2) controlling monopolistic and restrictive trade practices. It should be noted that the Act does not seek to strike at the concentration of economic power as such, but aims to check it when it becomes a menace to the best production (in quality and in quantity) or to fair distribution. The touchstone is the interest of the public and furtherance of common good.

MRTP Commission. For the attainment of these objectives, an administrative agency: Monopolies and Restrictive Trade Practices Commission has been set up to keep a constant watch that big business does not misuse its power. The Commission is to have a minimum of two and a maximum of eight members and its chairman is to be a person who is, or has been or is qualified to be a judge of the Supreme Court or of a High Court. The Commission may inquire into any monopolistic trade practice upon a reference made to it by the Central Government. All applications for expansion, establishing new undertakings, mergers, amalgamations and lake-overs are to be made to the Central Government. The Government, if it considers that an inquiry is needed before taking a decision, will refer the matters to the MRTP Commission. The Commission, after making the inquiry, will report back to the Government who will take the final decision. The Government's decision is subject to appeal to the Supreme Court. In this matter, the Commission acts only as consultants to the Government.

The other function of the Monopolies Commission pertains to these control of restrictive unfair trade practices. In these fields the Commission is autonomous and independent of the Government. It acts either on a reference by the Government or on a complaint by private parties or by the Director-General of Investigation and Registration or even on its own motion. It takes the final decision in the matter and its decision is subject to appeal to the Supreme Court.

Some Definitions. The operation of the provisions of the Act is directed to the specified economic activities of the undertakings. We, therefore, being with the definition of an undertaking.

"Undertaking" means an undertaking which is engaged in the production, supply, distribution or control of goods of any description or the provision of service of any kind.

"Dominant undertaking" is an undertaking whether within the purview of Industries Act or not, which has by itself or along with the inter-connected undertakings a licensed capacity for production of goods of not less than one-fourth of the total installed capacity in India for production of such goods, or produces, supplies, distributes or otherwise controls not less than one-fourth of total goods of any description that are produced, supplied, distributed in India or any substantial part thereof or provides or otherwise controls not less than one-fourth of any services that are rendered in India or any substantial part thereof, if it employs 50 or more workers and carries on a manufacturing process with the aid of power, or more than 100 workers where no power is used.

"Inter-connected undertakings" means two or more undertakings which are inter-connected with each other in any of the following manner, namely:—

(i) If one owns or controls the other,

(ii) where the undertakings are owned by firms, if such firms have one or more common partners,

(iii) where the undertakings are owned by bodies corporate,—

(a) if one manages the other, or

(b) if one is a subsidiary of the other, or

(c) if they are under the same management within the meaning of Section 370 of the Companies Act, 1956, or

(d) if one exercises control over the other in any other manner.

(iv) where one undertaking is owned by a body corporate and the other is owned by a firm, if one or more partners of the firm—

(a) hold, directly or indirectly, not less than 50 per cent of the shares, whether preference or equity, of the body corporate, or

(b) exercise control, directly or indirectly, whether as director or otherwise, over the body corporate.

(v) if one is owned by a body corporate and the other is owned by a firm having bodies corporate as its partners, if such bodies corporate are under the same management within the meaning of Section 370 of the Companies Act, 1956,

(vi) if the undertakings are owned or controlled by the same person or groups of persons,

(vii) if one is connected with the other either directly or through any number of undertakings which are Inter-connected undertakings within the meaning of one or more of the foregoing sub-clauses.

"Monopolistic Trade Practice" means a trade practice which has, or is likely to have, the effect of—

(i) maintaining prices at any unreasonable level by limiting, reducing or otherwise controlling the production, supply or distribution of goods of any description or the supply of any services or in any other manner,

(ii) unreasonably preventing or lessening competition in the production, supply or distribution of goods or in the supply of any services,

(iii) limiting technical development or capital investment to the common, detriment or allowing the quality or any goods produced, supplied, distributed, or any service rendered in India to deteriorate.

"Restrictive Trade Practice" means a trade practice which has, or may have, the effect of preventing, distorting or restricting competition in any manner and in particular—

(i) which tends to obstruct the flow of capital or resources into the stream of production, or

(ii) which tends to bring about manipulation of prices, or conditions of delivery or to affect the flow of supplies in the market relating to goods or services in such manner as to impose on the consumers unjustified costs or restrictions.

Registrable Agreement Relating to Restrictive Trade Practices. Section 33 of the Act requires the registration of the following categories of Restrictive Trade Agreements with the Registrar :

(a) any agreement between producers or as the case may be, wholesalers to restrict by any method the persons or classes of persons to whom they sell;

(b) any agreement between wholesalers or, as the case may be, retailers to restrict by any method the persons or classes of persons from whom they buy;

(c) any agreement between producers, wholesalers or retailers, as the case may be, to sell goods only at prices agreed -upon between themselves;

(d) any agreement requiring a purchaser of goods as a condition of such purchase to purchase some other goods of the seller;

(e) any agreement restricting in any manner the purchaser in the course of his trade from acquiring or otherwise dealing in any goods other than those of the seller;

(f) any agreement between producers, wholesalers or contractors, as the case may be, to purchase goods or tender for the sale or purchase of goods only at prices or on terms agreed upon between themselves;

(g) any agreement between producers and wholesalers or between wholesalers and retailers or any combination of them to grant or allow concessions or benefits, including allowances, discounts, rebates credit, in connection with or by reason of dealings;

(h) any agreement to sell goods on condition that the prices to be charged on resale by the purchaser shall be the prices stipulated by the seller unless it is clearly stated that prices lower than those prices may be charged;

(i) any agreement between producers and wholesalers or between a producer and any other person to limit, restrict or withhold the output or supply of any goods or allocate any area or market for the disposal of any goods;

(j) any agreement between producers not to employ or restrict the employment of any method, machinery or process in the manufacture of goods;

(k) any agreement for the unjustifiable exclusion from any trade association of any person carrying on, or intending to carry on, in good faith the trade in relation to which the trade association is formed;

(l) any agreement not herein before referred to in this section which the Central Government may notify specifying as being one relating to a restrictive trade practice;

(m) any agreement to enforce the carrying out of any such agreement as mentioned above.

The foregoing provisions will apply in relation to agreements making provision far services as they apply in relation to agreements connected with the production, supply or distribution of goods.

All Monopolistic activities are regulated. The Act has adapted three different methods for controlling or regulating these activities of the undertaking with the sole object of protecting public interest against any misuse of economic or market power and of controlling the concentration of economic power.

1. *Control of structural changes*. The first method seeks to control the structural changes that take place in the undertakings so that the undue concentration of economic power takes place to operate against public interest. For the purpose the Act has selected two types of undertakings :

(a) "Dominant undertaking" the total value of whose assets is not less than Rs. one crore; and

(b) Undertakings, other than dominant undertaking, the total value of whose assets is not less than Rs. 100 crores.

The direct and substantial beneficiaries of these provisions are the medium and small-scale industries. One of the structural changes in the undertakings that have been brought within the purview of the Act is the expansion (by issue of fresh capital, or installation of new machinery or in any other manner) or any existing dominant undertaking with not less than Rs. one crore assets or other undertakings with not less than Rs. 100 crores assets. It should be noted that the Act does not prohibit expansion, it only seeks to subject any proposal for expansion to scrutiny and prior approval of the Central Government. If the proposed expansion is not likely to be detrimental to the public interest, it will be approved.

2. *Division of undertaking*. The second method is to interfere with the structure of undertaking already in existence. This may be done by means of their division into various independent undertakings or division of any trade of these undertakings. But this method is to be used only—

(i) when the working of the undertaking is prejudicial to the public interest, or

(ii) when the working of the undertaking has led, or is leading, or is likely to lead to the adoption of any monopolistic trade practice, or

(iii) the working of the undertaking has led, or is leading, or is likely to lead to the adoption of any restrictive trade practice.

If any of the conditions mentioned above are satisfied the Central Government will refer to the Monopolies Commission for an inquiry as to whether it is expedient in the public interest to make an order for any such decision.

3. *Ensuring fair and free competition*. The third method is another variety of the second method. It deals with the consequences of or the mischiefs or abuse that are resorted to as a result of concentration of economic power. This method does not interfere with the structure of undertakings but interferes, controls or regulates the operational activities of the undertakings. For this purpose the Act has selected two concepts,

one monopolistic trade practice, and the other, restrictive trade practice, which terms have been explained above.

Unfair Trade Practices

"Unfair trade practice" means a practice which for the purpose of promoting the sale, use or supply of any goods or for the provision of any services, adopts one or more of the following practices and thereby causes loss or injury to the consumers of such goods or services whether by eliminating or restricting competition or otherwise, namely:—

(1) the making of any statement, whether orally or in writing or by visible representation in which—

(i) falsely represents that the goods are of a particular quality, standard or grade;

(ii) falsely represents that the services are of a particular quality, standard or grade;

(iii) falsely represents any rebuilt, second-hand, renovated reconditioned or old goods as new goods;

(iv) represents that goods or services have sponsorship, approval, performance, characteristics, accessories, uses or benefits which such goods or services do not have;

(v) represents that the seller or the supplier has a sponsorship or approval or affiliation which such seller or supplier does not have;

(vi) makes false or misleading representation concerning the need for, or the usefulness of, any goods or services:

(vii) gives to the public any warranty or guarantee of the performance, efficacy, or length of life of a product or any goods that is not based on any adequate or proper test thereof;

(viii) makes to the public a representation in a form that purports to be—

(a) a warranty or guarantee of a product or of any goods or services; or

(b) a promise to replace, maintain or repair on article or any part thereof or to repeat or continue a service until it has achieved a specified result of such purported warranty or guaranteed or promise ------------------------------- is materially misleading or if there is no reasonable prospect that such warranty, guarantee or promise will be carried out;

(ix) materially misleads the public concerning the price at which a product or like products or goods or services, have been or are ordinarily sold or provided, and, for this purpose, a representation as to price shall be deemed to refer to the price at which the product or goods or services has to have been sold by sellers or provided by suppliers generally in the relevant market.

(x) gives false or misleading facts disparaging the goods, services or trade of another person.

(2) permits the publication of any advertisement for the sale or supply at a bargain price of goods or services that are not intended to be offered for sale or supply at the bargain price, or for a period that is, and in quantities that are, reasonable, having regard to the nature of the advertisement;

(3) permits—

(a) the offering of gifts, prizes or other items with the intention of not providing them as offered or creating the impression that something is being given or offered free of charge when it is fully or falsely covered by the amount charged in the transaction as a whole:

(b) the conduct of any contest, lottery, game of chance or skill, for the purpose of promoting, directly or indirectly the sale, use or supply of any product or any business interest;

(4) permits the sale or supply of goods which he knows are sub-standard or likely to he injurious because they are not properly finished or packaged;

(5) permits the· hoarding or destruction of goods or refuses to sell the goods with the intention of raising the price of such goods.

The Commission may inquire into any unfair trade practice and issue injunction or pass a cease and desire order against the guilty party.

Evaluation of the MRTC Act. In making an assessment of the Act and the working or the MRTP Commission established under it the political and economic, background of the Act has to be kept in mind. One cannot look at the Act by itself. In fact, the genesis of the Act is to be found in the Directive Principles contained in Article 39 (b) and (c) of the Constitution. The Article provides that the State shall, in particular, direct its policy towards securing that (i) the ownership and control of the material resources of the community are so distributed as best to subserve the common good, and (ii) the operation of the economic system does not result in the concentration of wealth and means of production to the common detriment. The MRTP Act seeks to accomplish these aims and provides that the operation of economic system should not result in the concentration of economic power to the common detriment. It is required to control monopolies and prohibit monopolistic and restrictive trade practices, as ·well as unfairtrade practices.

The Act and the Monopolies Commission have been criticised by big businesses. One of the criticisms is that the effect of the Act has anti-growth (overkill legislation) of willing entrepreneurial initiative on the one hand and the consumer's buying capacity on the other.1 The Act has been in force for 20 years and very few applications have been handled. Again, its provisions are not against monopolies as such or even against concentration of economic power as such, but only where they prove detrimental to the common good. As regards the allegation that the Commission is a stumbling block in economic growth and investment it is pertinent to point out that only in a very small proportion of 10 per cent cases of industrial licences, clearance from the Monopolies Commission is required. The remaining 90 per cent are left free of the Commission. Only those cases of expansion, etc., which are likely to be detrimental to the common good are referred to the commission, which are not more than 10 per cent of the total number of applications field with the Government. Again, out of the cases referred to the Commission, not more than 17 or 18 per cent are on an average, rejected by the Commission.

The delay in deciding cases is another drawback. By the time the final orders are passed either by the Government or by the Commission, those who indulge in undesirable practices will have derived considerable benefits from the exploitations they have made. Furthermore, the Act does not provide any deterrence to persons practising any monopolistic or restrictive trade practices. The objectives of the Act cannot be accomplished unless the commission of these trade malpractices is made an offence punishable with imprisonment and heavy fine. Although there is a drastic remedy of division of undertaking provided in the Act, yet it comes at a much later stage when substantial mischief has already been done.

Again, the Act has not attempted to deal with the entire concentration of economic power that may conceivably have substantial impact on the public interest. For instance, it does not cover the public sector undertakings. Under the concept of mixed economy there is no justification in not dealing with the entire concentration of economic power.

The foregoing brief account shows that Because of the presence of some businessmen with anti-social attitude the government has had to intervene in the public interest. By discarding moral standards, a business minority, in its search for profits, brings on itself that government control which it abhors. In the present context the government exercises control over private enterprise in order to mould it into a whole pattern of a "Welfare State." The current policy is that private enterprise shall exist only if it benefits society. In a "mixed economy" there is room for private efforts but only as a loyal instrument of state economic policy. The private enterprise must accept not only the objective of social and economic policy but also its own obligations towards the workers and the consumers. A mixed economy requires enlightened liberal government as well as enlightened

1 Commerce. Bombay, July 6, 1974.

private enterprise; neither can do without the other. Planning is now the order of the day and both private and public enterprises have to exist side by side, each planning a well-defined role for the greatest good of the community. Nationalisation or State-ownership of agencies of production and the existence of private enterprise are merely instruments for the welfare of society and not as ends in themselves. At the same time, public enterprise is fast growing and thought is being devoted as to how public enterprise can best be run. The following chapter is therefore devoted to the discussion of the problem of organisation and management of public enterprises in India.

JOINT SECTOR

The joint sector is essentially an extension of the concept of mixed economy to the management of an undertaking where both public and private sectors exist. The growth of lndian industry in pre-independence era and immediately afterwards was largely due to the lead given by some "houses"· and individuals. After the independence, on account of the acceptance of the concept of planned development and its implementation through tile Five Year Plans, the role of the State began to increase as a partner in the industrial progress of the nation. With the emergence and fast expansion of the public sector and in view of the socio-economic thinking in the country, it soon began to be felt that it might be the only acceptable formula for future growth. But the disappointing performances by a large number of undertakings in the public sector showed that Government is not the proper institution to manage industrial undertakings.

The private sector also, in spite of notable record of achievement could not be accepted in view of its image ta tarnished by the misdeeds of many of its constituents as also due to the emerging anti-capitalist thinking in the country. Again, the Industrial Licensing Policy Inquiry Committee, which gave momentum to the thinking about joint sector, pointed out that 29 large industrial houses on an average received financial assistance from the public financial institutions to the extent of 54 per cent and a few labour 89 per cent of their entire project costs. The Committee observed that the large industrial undertakings in the private sector built their empires with the capital provided by the public financial institutions without the latter having any control over their management. It recommended the conversion of a few private sector undertakings into joint sector' enterprises as a means to curb the increasing concentration of economic power in the country.

The joint sector formula is very attractive and admirably suited to present position of the economy and the Government's thinking. It can harmoniously combine the efficiency, experience, financial acumen and dynamism of the private enterprise and the social objectives underlying the public sector. Such a system would enjoy more operational freedom and flexibility so as to be properly suited for on the spot decisions and result-oriented policies with the framework of the socio-economic policies of the Government in relation to industrial development. 'Growth with Welfare' can be achieved more readily through the agency of joint sector; for expansion and diversification in this sector will not generate concentration of economic power.

The joint sector, run and managed on business lines, with specific emphasis on welfare of the surrounding community can be the most useful formula. The licensing policy of the Government should be oriented towards supporting the joint sector.

The latest licensing policy regarding joint sector undertakings to be set up in future has been staled thus: Each proposal for setting up of a joint sector project will be judged and decided on merits, in the light of the Government's socio-economic objectives. The undertakings covered by the MRTP Act would not be permitted to use the joint sector as a device for entry into industries from which they are otherwise excluded.

Modes of establishing joint sector units. The joint sector undertakings may be established in three ways, namely :—

1. By converting loans or debentures of undertakings in private Sector held by public financial institutions into equity capital in that undertaking. As a first step in this direction, the Government of India has directed the public financial institutions to insert convertibility clause in all cases where the aggregate financial assistance to the concern exceeds Rs. 50 lakhs. Of course, the conversion can be made by the Central Government under Section 81 (4) of the Companies Act, 1956.

2. By offering minority ownership to private enterprise in new ventures to be set up by the Government.

3. By enlarging and utilising the equity holdings in the private undertakings by the public financial institutions in order to have participation in the management of the concerned undertakings.

Financial participation. The present formula of financial participation for new projects seems to be quite satisfactory. The formula is 26 per cent Government participation. 25 per cent private entrepreneurs, and 49 per cent public participation, the last including participation by public financial institutions. Such participation will allow only minority interest to private entrepreneurs in the joint sector undertaking so that the private sector will not be able to own or control it.

Management. One of the crucial factor for the success of projects in the joint sector is their proper management. It is therefore necessary that a suitable system of management for such project should be evolved on the basis of equality, confidence and trust between the major partners—the private and public sectors. Also, the management should have some freedom as is available to the management of a private undertaking so that the business principles can be followed in running the undertaking. Furthermore, an ideal joint sector should have people with real business acumen and professional expertise in various areas. It should be the underlying policy of such projects to encourage the development of professional managers from within and ultimately to utilise their services and abilities at the top management level.

The chief executive (Managing Director) who is to look after the day-to-day management, should be left to be selected by private sector so as to preserve efficiency, financial acumen and dynamism for positive results. However, the proposed Managing Director should be a professional man with adequate background. The Chairman of the Board of Directors should be the nominee of the Government, preferably from the public, whose ability and experience of business management should be the criterion for his appointment.

The Board of Directors should consist of representatives of the private party, Government, financial institutions and the public. In a joint sector company having financial participation of 25 per cent private party, 26 per cent Government, and 49 per cent public, the proportion of directors could be: 3 (including the Managing Director) for the private party, 4 (inclusive of the Chairman) 4 for the Government and 3 for the public. The public financial institution, which advances substantial funds, may be allowed to nominate not more than 2 directors who may be chosen from among professional people. The managing committees of the Board/ could supervise the working of the undertaking for better results.

In conclusion, it may be stated that the joint sector, if managed properly, can be a viable alternative to both State capitalism with its risk or bureaucratisation on the one hand and private capitalism with its acute inequality in the distribution of wealth and income.

INDUSTRIAL POLICY (1977)

The Industrial Policy Statement of the Janata Government laid before Parliament by Mr. George Fernandes, Minister of Industry on December 23, 1977 aims to lay greater stress on cottage and small scale industries and agriculture. It is stated that the new industrial policy should and will hereafter place man at the centre of planning and implementation of projects and schemes.

Small-Scale Industries. The emphasis of industrial policy so far has been mainly on large industries neglecting cottage industries completely relegating small industries to a minor role. The main thrust of the new industrial Policy will be on effective promotion of cottage and small industries widely dispersed in rural areas and small towns. Whatever can be produced by small and cottage industries must only be so produced. The industrial products which can be successfully produced in the small scale sector have been identified and the number of items has been increased from 180 to 504. Annual review will be made and new products and processes capable of being manufactured in the small scale sector will be identified and added to the list. The large-scale industries will not be allowed to enter these fields of manufacture.

While the existing definition of small scale industries will remain, within the small sector, special attention, will be given to units in the TINY SECTOR.[1] Schemes will be drawn up for making available margin money assistance especially to tiny units in the small scale sector as well as to cottage and household industries. The focal point of development for small scale and cottage industries will be taken away from the big cities and state capitals to the district headquarters. In each district there will be one agency, called the District Industries Centre to deal with the requirements of Small and village industries. Under the single roof of the District Industries Centre, all the services and support required by small scale and village entrepreneurs will be provided. These will include economic investigation of the district raw material and other resources; supply of machinery ·and equipment, provision of raw materials, arrangements for credit facilities, an effective set up for marketing and a cell · for quality control, research and extension.

The Centre will have a separate wing for looking after the special needs of cottage and household industries as distinct from small industries. The Centre will establish close linkages with the Development Blocks on the one hand and with specialised institutions like Small Industries Service Institutes on the other. Suitable financial and organisational support will be provided to the State Governments to achieve this objective.

The Industrial Development Bank of India has taken steps to set up a separate wing to deal exclusively with the credit requirements of this sector. It will coordinate, guide and monitor the entire range of credit facilities offered by other institutions for the small and cottage sector, for whom separate wings will be set up in these institutions particularly, nationalised banks.

The marketing of goods of these sector with its concomitant of product standardisation, quality control marketing surveys will receive special attention. The Government will provide the maximum support for these activities on a priority basis. Measures such as purchase preference and reservation for exclusive purchase by Government Departments and Public Sector Undertakings will. also be used to support the marketing of these products.

Role of Large-Scale Industries. In addition to small and village industries, there is also a clear role for large scale industry in India. However, the Government will not favour large scale industry merely for demonstration . of sophisticated skills or as monuments of irrelevant foreign technology. The role of large scale industry will be related to the

1 A unit with investment in machinery and equipment upto its one lakh and situated in towns with a population of less then 50,000 according to 1971 census is a unit in the Tiny Sector.

programme for meeting the basic minimum needs of the population through wider dispersal of small scale and village industries and strengthening of the agricultural sector. In general, areas for large scale industry will be :

(a) Basic industries which are essential for providing intra-structure as well as for development of small and village industries, such as steel, non-ferrous metals, cement, oil refineries;

(b) Capital goods industries for meeting the machinery requirements of basic industries as well as small scale industries;

(c) High technology industries which require large scale production, and which are related to agricultural and small scale industrial developments such as fertilizers, pesticides, and petro-chemicals etc:, and

(d) Other industries, which are outside the list of reserved items for the small scale sector, and which are considered essential for the development of the economy such as machine tools, organic and inorganic chemicals.

Large Houses. Past experience shows that Government policies have not succeeded in restraining the disproportionate growth of large houses. While a certain measure of growth of existing enterprises is inevitable and also necessary for continued health of these enterprises the growth of large houses has been disproportionate to the size of their internally generated resources and has been largely based on borrowed funds from public financial institutions and banks. This process must be reversed.

In future expansion of Large Houses will be guided by the following principles:

(a) The expansion of existing undertakings and establishment of new undertakings will continue to be subject to the provisions of the MRTP Act. The provisions of the Act relating to dominant undertakings would be effectively implemented;

(b) Except in the case of industries eligible for automatic growth out capacity, the expansion of existing undertakings into new lines and the establishment of new undertakings by large Houses will require specific approval of Government:

(c) Large Houses will have to rely on their own internally generated resources for financing new or expansion projects. While an appropriate debt equity ratio will be permitted in the case of industries like fertilizers, paper, cement, shipping, petro-chemicals, etc. which are relatively more capital intensive in nature, the debt equity ratio in the case of other less capital intensive or less sophisticated industries will be so fixed as to reflect the greater use of their own internally generated resources by the-large houses.

Public Sector. The public sector in India has come of age. Apart from socialising the means of production in strategic areas, public sector provides a counter-vailing power to the growth of large houses and large enterprises in the private sector. There will be an expanding role for the public sector in several fields. Not only will it be the producer of important and strategic goods of basic nature, but it will also be used effectively as a stabilizing force for maintaining essential supplies for the consumer. The public sector will be charged with the responsibility of encouraging the development of a wide range of ancillary industries, and contribute to the growth of decentralised production by making available its expertise in technology and management to small scale and cottage industry sectors. It will also be the endeavour of the Government to operate public sector enterprises on profitable and efficient lines in order to ensure that investment in these industries pays an adequate return to society.

Indigenous and Foreign Technology. Appropriate technology is advocated in the context of socio-economic conditions prevailing in developing countries. Future development of industries in India must be based on indigenous technology as far as possible. Full scope will be given to the development of indigenous technology. Suitable small and simple machines and devices must be developed and widely applied for improving the productivity and earning capacity of workers in Small and Village industries.

The Government also recognises the necessity for continued inflow of technology in sophisticated and high priority areas where Indian skills and technology are not adequately developed. In such areas, the Government's preference will be outright purchase of the best available technology and then adapting it to the country's needs.

Foreign Investment. So far as the existing foreign companies are concerned the provisions of the Foreign Exchange Regulation Act would be strictly enforced. After the process of dilution under this Act has been completed, companies with direct non-resident investment not exceeding 40 per cent will be treated on par with Indian companies, except in cases specifically notified, and their future expansion will be guided by the same principles as those applicable to Indian companies.

Foreign investment and acquisition of technology necessary for India's industrial development would be allowed on such terms as are determined by the Government of India to be in the national interest. In areas where foreign technological know-how is not needed existing collaborations will not be renewed and foreign companies operating in such fields will have to modify their character and activities in conformity with national priority within the framework of the Foreign Exchange Regulation Act. For all approved foreign investments, there will be complete freedom for remittance of profits, royalties, dividends as well as repatriation of capital subject of course to rules and regulations common to all.

Imports and Exports. The export and import policy 1990–93 was announced by the Government on March 30, 1990 with the following objectives.

(1) To encourage rapid and sustained export growth, including export of services, with special emphasis on exports on exports which generate foreign exchange earnings;

(2) To facilitate availability of necessary imported inputs for sustaining industrial growth including essential capital goods for modernisation and technological upgradation;

(3) To simplify and streamline procedure for import licensing and export promotion;

(4) To support recognised indigenous Research and Development Institutions for building their scientific and technological capability for technology absorption and development; and

(5) To promote efficient import substitution and self reliance.

Open General Licences have been issued with a validity upto 31st March, 1993. Eighty two capital goods have been added to the list of Capital Goods allowed to be imported under OGL. Blanket advance licensing scheme has been introduced for reputed manufacture exporters. Automatic licensing scheme has been introduced for actual users, and special import facility has been provided for recognised service. Centres to encourage employment of skilled persons are to be set up. Import of capitals goods at confessional duty of 25 per cent for export production has been allowed. Many other concessions and facilities have been extended with a view to encourage export for earning foreign exchange and for industrial development.

Location of Industries. Great-importance is attached to balanced regional development of the entire country so that disparities in the level of development between different regions are progressively removed. Most of the industrial development since independence has taken place around metropolitan areas and large cities. This has resulted in the deterioration in the living conditions especially for the working classes in the larger cities and attendant problems of slum and environmental pollution. Therefore, no more licences would be issued to new industrial units within certain limits of large metropolitan cities having a population of more than 5 lakhs as per 1971 census. Large existing industries will be provided assistance if and when they wish to shift from congested metropolitan cities to approved locations in backward areas.

Pricing Policy. A sound price policy has to aim at a reasonable degree of price stability and a fair parity between prices of agricultural and industrial products. It will be the policy of Government to ensure that in cases where there is price control, the controlled price will include an adequate return to the investor. Provided that the industry is operating at a fairly high utilisation of capacity and is conforming to the technologically attainable norms, it will be permitted to earn a sufficient return to provide for a reasonable dividend to the shareholders and also adequate funds to plough back into business for modernisation and growth. By the same token,

Government cannot permit exorbitant profits being made by industries which are operating well below their capacity or by units which operate in a monopolistic environment.

Workers' Participation in Equity. Human resources can be used effectively only, in an environment in which workers and managers develop a sense of personal involvement in the working of the enterprise. Family control of business particularly in the field of large scale industry is an anachronism, and it will be Governments' policy to insist on professionalisation of management. At the same time ways and means have to be found to create among workers, both in public and private sector industries, a stake in the efficient working of their units. The workers are to be encouraged to participate in the equity of industrial units without, in any way, adversely affecting their interests. Such equity participation together with an active association of workers in decision making from the shop floor level to the Board level will provide the necessary environment for meaningful participation by workers in the management at industry. It is proposed to make workers participation in decision making a statutory requirement.

Sickness of Industry. One of the disturbing features of the industrial scene in recent years has been the growing incidence of sickness of both large and small units. In some cases, such as cotton and jute textiles or sugar, a high proportion of the units in the industry have become sick with the result that in order to protect employment, Government has had to take over a number of such units. In many cases, very large amounts of public funds had to be pumped into the sick units which had been taken over but they continue to make losses. This process cannot continue indefinitely.

In future, take over of management of units would be resorted to selectively and only after careful examination of the steps required to revive the units. Quick steps will be taken to rehabilitate and reconstruct the units and to ensure professional management of such units. Government in cooperation with the Reserve Bank have also instituted arrangements for monitoring incipient sickness in industrial units so that corrective action can be initiated as soon as there is evidence of mismanagement or financial and technological weakness. Further more, the managers or owners who are responsible for mismanaging and turning their units sick will not be permitted to play any further part in the management of other units.

Conclusion. To achieve the objectives of the new industrial policy of accelerating the pace of industrial growth, rapid increase in levels of employment, productivity and income of industrial workers and a wide dispersal of small and village industries, the willing cooperation of industrial workers, trade unions, managers, entrepreneurs, financial institutions and various governmental authorities responsible for implementing schemes of assistance will be essential. The main brunt of the efforts has, however, to be borne by the industrial workers and managers. The Government on its part will try to remove irritants in the industrial approval procedures.

CHAPTER XVI

PUBLIC ENTERPRISE

GOVERNMENT IN BUSINESS

Basis of Government Ownership.

Since the greatest happiness of the greatest number failed to materialise under "free enterprise", and mere controls were not found sufficient to meet the needs of economic and social justice, the state was obliged to step in as the biggest entrepreneur. In almost all democracies, mixed economy is firmly established. In communist countries the State ownership of productive resources and of distribution of what is produced is complete. Under fascism there is a mixed form of controlled capitalism and socialism. Both fascism and communism are inseparably associated with political and economic dictatorship. It represents the complete extreme of both government ownership and government control. Theoretically, no private ownership is permitted. The wealth belongs to the people. Soviet Russia and China are the outstanding examples of the specific economic system called "Communism". The state owns not only the agents of production but also the commodities produced.

Somewhere between the extremes of substantially free enterprise and complete government regimentation lies another plan, namely, "*Democratic Socialism*". Under this system the means of production are controlled or owned by the State with a view to increasing the national income and distributing it more equitably. The aim of democratic socialism is to flatten the social pyramid, insofar as economic possessions are concerned and to reduce the existing inequality. Both public and private sectors work together for the common good of the community. The Government policy is democratic, relying on peaceful persuasion and the growth of social conscience. The wholesale nationalisation of all economic activity is rarely advocated. Both private and public sectors are expected to contribute to the well being of society as a whole. Freedom in business is curtailed only as a means of enlarging the liberty of the many and for meeting critical social and economic problems, rather than for strengthening the coercive power of the State.

Although nowhere in the world is to be found unfettered free enterprise, and although State ownership of at least some part of the economy will be found in almost all the countries, the controversy in relation to nationalisation or public ownership as against free enterprise is not finally settled. It is pertinent, therefore, to briefly examine the case for and against nationalisation or public ownership.

Case for Public Ownership or Nationalisation

Some of the more important advantages of public ownership or nationalisation are :

1. *Elimination of private monopolies.* Public ownership of enterprise breaks private monopolies and takes away, their power to exploit the public to their own advantage and at the cost of the happiness of the masses.

2. *Production for use and not for profit.* In private enterprise profit motive is the prime mover of business life, and individual urge to maximise profits the prime force in the economy as a whole. Public ownership becomes necessary to ensure that society gets all the basic necessities of life at reasonable prices and in reasonable quantities. Welfare of the community is the main purpose behind public ownership or nationalisation.

3. *Saving of consumer interest.* Since the supreme aim of the State is to serve the people in the best possible way, state-run industry will always try to maintain the quality of its products at a higher standard. As the objective is to serve and not to fill its coffers with high profits, high quality goods at reasonable price will be supplied to the consumer. Also no artifical shortages will be created by public enterprises which is a common practice in private enterprise.

4. *Balanced production and equitable distribution.* Public enterprises, under the control of a single authority, can conveniently arrange for balanced production of goods which are most needed by the people. The surplus earned by public entreprises can be used, for the well being of the people. The profits from private industries go to a few people, thus widening the disparity of income between the haves and havenots. The public entreprise, on the other hand, narrows the gap, by raising the levels of the poorer people.

5. *Economy of Operation.* Public ownership is conducive to greater coordination among the various industries brought under State control and ensure their harmonious functioning. This generates economies of unified control and large scale operation.

6. *Balanced regional development.* Although the government exercises control with regard to regional distribution of industries in the private sector, the task of balanced regional distribution becomes simpler when industries are set up by the State itself. Before locating a new plant, the government considers economic as well as social consequences and pays special attention to balanced development of different parts of the country.

7. *Long-term investment can be planned.* A public enterprise can plan its investment over a long period of time and maintain its stability whatever may temporarily happen to the demand for goods. In times of depression a privately owned industry will curtail production and investment because in that way it minimises its risk of incurring losses under the stress of falling prices. Public enterprise under such circum-

stances plays a vital role in checking unemployment and under-employment.

8. *Furtherance of economic development.* The surplus profits of public undertakings can be diverted to develop economic schemes of national importance. This has an indirect but welcome effect of keeping down the taxes which would be necessary otherwise for development of the country.

9. *Nationalisation aids sound rationalisation.* Public ownership is one of the methods of dealing with industries in which inefficiency persists and where the private owners lack either the will or the capacity to make improvements.

10. *Fuller employment possible.* According to the late Professor K.T. Shah *, "only under socialised production will the fullest possible employment to all adult workers, in accordance with the aptitude and training of each, be secured". The State owning a good number of industries can maintain a great part of its spending and investment programme stable from year to year and consequently prevent violent fluctuations in employment.

11. *Just and equitable deal to labour.* The State is essentially interested in giving a square deal to the workers and assisting them to raise their living standards. It will obviously not exploit the workers, and will offer just rates of wages, provide human conditions of work and generally devote itself to labour welfare.

Case Against Public Ownership or Nationalisation

The opponents of public ownership or nationalisation usually base their opposition on the following limitations and shortcomings of public undertakings:

1. *Lack of initiative and efficiency.* Public enterprises, as a rule, lack initiative and efficiency. Lack of profit motive is said to lead to inefficiency and sluggishness. Profit is said to be the key to efficiency, drive and initiative. A government official, it is argued, being devoid of profit motive, cannot display the same degree of initiative, drive and promptness in making decisions which an executive in private enterprise can show. It is also argued that the bureaucrats who manage public enterprises run them like government department resulting in red tapism and postponement of decision making. All these shortcomings lead to higher administrative and other costs.

2. *Regimentation.* Nationalisation is said to lead to regimentation. Under monopoly production by the State, the consumer loses his right of selection and choice of goods. There is some truth in this argument.

3. *Political interference.* There is a constant danger of undue interference in the working of public enterprises by politicians. Such interference militates against smooth and efficient working of these undertakings.

* K.T. Shah, Note in the Report of the Advisory Planning Board of the Government of India, P.47.

4. *Open to public criticism.* Public enterprises, because they are public or State owned are always, exposed to public criticism, which may not always be justified. As a result the men who manage public enterprises develop in them unadventurous and red-tapist frame of mind which is harmful to the running of business undertakings.

5. *Rigidity of public control.* Public accountability of public enterprises is very often stretched too far and the flexibility of private enterprise which is essential for the successful working of an industrial or commercial undertaking is denied to them.

Conclusion. In judging the various arguments against public enterprise, especially with respect to inefficiency and bureaucratic management, one has to apply the standard of welfare of the community. Both public and private sector industries must be organised, managed and operated to serve the widest interests of the community as a whole. A large business owned by a company in the private sector is bound to be as bureaucratic as any nationalised unit, and hence nationalisation on this score is not inferior to private ownership.

When we talk of efficiency, we usually mean only 'engineering' or 'physical efficiency'—'maximum output for minimum input'; and forget about 'Social efficiency'. The charge that public undertakings are, as a rule, less efficient than private undertakings loses its significance when we apply the test of social efficiency which is much greater in the case of public enterprise than in private enterprise. In terms of social costs, private enterprise is far inferior to public enterprise. Therefore, from the point of view of the general public, real efficiency should be judged by the application of the following criteria laid down by Professor Sargant Florence in his book : *The Logic of British and American Industry.*

1. Satisfaction of man's needs, wants and spontaneous demands in order of priority rather than his artificially stimulated demands.

2. Where it is demands that are supplied at a price, fullest satisfaction of consumers at lowest margin of profit.

3. Maximum spread of participation and satisfaction of the people, by the people, for the people. There should be co-ordinated use and direction of resources in the interest of the nation as a whole.

4. Efficiency measured in minimum cost per given output.

It will be noticed that the foregoing criteria are not all economic. *Economic Welfare* does not take into account the *'needs-first'* criterion nor social costs, nor the *'for and by the people'* test of democracy. These fall within *'general and total welfare'* of which economic welfare is only a *'part of a part'*.

There is no doubt that in terms of the aforementioned criteria public ownership scores over private ownership. Yet, it will not be quite true to say that nationalisation or public ownership is, by itself a cure of all the ills of enterprise or the saviour of workers and consumers. Public enterprises can succeed only if they are managed on business principles with sufficient operational autonomy granted to the managers so that the necessary flexibility is ensured. "Nationalisation", says Tawney[1], is not an end but a means to an end and when the question of ownership has been solved the question of administration remains for solution".

FORMS OF ORGANISATION

Public enterprise can adopt a variety of forms of organisation for its administration such as (1) Commissions—Oil & Natural Gas Commission, Khadi and Village Industries Commission; (2) Commodity Boards—Coffee Board, Tea Board; (3) Port Trusts—Bombay, Calcutta; (4) Departmental undertakings—Ordnance Factories, Integral Coach Factory, Railways; (5) Statutory Corporations—Air Corporations, Central Warehousing Corporations; (6) Limited Liability Companies—Hindustan Steel Ltd., Heavy Engineering Corporation.

Among the various types cited above the most preferred forms of organisation in India are :

1. Departmental Organisation.
2. Statutory or Public Corporation.
3. Government Company.

Departmental Organisation.

The oldest form of operating public enterprises is through government department. No distinction is made between public enterprises and traditional government functions.

The principal *characteristics* of departmental form of organisation are as follows :

1. The enterprise is managed by a government department, with a Minister at the top responsible to Parliament for its operation.

2. The enterprise is financed by annual appropriations from the Treasury and all, or major share, of its revenues are paid into the Treasury.

3. It is subject to the budget, accounting and audit controls applicable to other government activities.

4. Its permanent staff consists of civil servants, and their conditions of recruitment and service are the same as for other civil servants.

5. As the enterprise is a sub-division of a department of the government, it can be sued only by following the procedure prescribed for filing suits against the government.

Evaluation. The departmentally-operated enterprises, particularly manufacturing undertakings, have nothing much to commend themselves. In spite of a few merits, it suffers from multifarious disadvantages. The merits and demerits of this form of organisation are given below.

Merits of departmental organisation. The principal merits of departmentally-run manufacturing enterprises are :

(a) 'The accountability of departmental undertakings to Parlia-

1. R.H. Tawney, *The Acquisitive Society*, P. 149.

ment is complete, their management being under the Ministry concerned', or it assures the maximum degree of control by politically responsible officials.

(b) It provides a means of securing absolute government control.

(c) The State can make use of these undertakings as instruments of its economic and social policy.

(d) From the public point of view the department organisation has an advantage that if anything goes wrong or if the public is dissatisfied with the working of an undertaking the matter can be immediately raised in Parliament.

Shortcomings of departmental organisation. As against the forego-ing merits, the weaknesses of this type of organisation are many and varied. These are summarised below.

(i) The departmentally-managed undertakings are under the control of ministers and the political parties to which they belong and who hardly understand the problems of management of industry and trade. Furthermore, their policies suffer from instability because of the uncertainty attached to the tenure of political parties and ministers.

(ii) As the public enterprises are run on the same lines as the other government departments, the business principles necessary for their success are overlooked. In fact the government forgets that it is running business undertakings and must therefore deal with the public as a businessman rather than a sovereign.

(iii) Although it is the consumers who pay for the goods and services offered and not the tax-payers, the merging of the revenues of the department in general revenues results in either giving a subsidy to or charging too high a price from the consumer. Profits are likely to be used not for development but for giving tax relief, or losses are borne by the tax-payers.

(iv)) Government officials who are asked to manage these under-takings generally lack business acumen. They are selected and trained generally for a purpose quite different from running industries and services. They are used to working under a rigid system of set rules, and for every decision they look for a precedent. This causes delay in decision-making which is harmful in the case of a business undertaking.

(v) Under this form of organisation, public enterprises very often become synonymous with red tape, delays, inadequate service and insensitivity to consumer needs. Thus, government departments are traditionally too involved in red tape and routine to permit efficient conduct of commercial and industrial undertakings.

(vi) The department organisation fails to provide flexibility so essential to effective business operations.

(vii) Frequent transfers of officers and the annual nature of financial outlook of government departments runs counter to the continuous and long-term policy on the part of the business enterprise.

(viii) Since the officials of the department have to attend to different matters besides the problems of the enterprise placed in their charge, they lack the unity or homogeneity of purpose so essential to efficient working of an industrial undertaking, and so pronounced in private enterprise.

(ix) As the acts and decisions of the managements of public undertakings are ever open to public and Parliamentary criticism and questioning, this type of organisation provides no scope for initiative and skill. Actually this has the effect of training officials for giving good answers rather than take quick decisions on important matters.

(x) Some of the following things stand in the way of running public enterprises efficiently, namely,—(a) necessity for obtaining sanctions for expenditure and other matters in every single case; (b) inability to take out cash from the government account without prior sanction once cash receipts have been put into that account; (c) the application of the accounting and audit procedures; (d) purchase of raw materials and stores and the sale of products according to departmental system; and (e) the application of rules of promotion on seniority basis, which militates against promotion on merit or taking disciplinary action.

Since in many ways the departmental organisation is a negation of the requirements of autonomy and flexibility, it 'must be the rare exception, not the general rule.'

Public Corporation

A public corporation is a corporate body created by the legislature under a separate statute (hence, sometimes, called statutory corporation), which sets out its powers, purpose, duties and immunities. It is financially independent and has a clear-cut jurisdiction over a specified area or a particular type of industrial or commercial activity. It is administered by a Board of Directors appointed by the Government, to which it is answerable.

A public corporation is very much like a public company except in two respects. A company is incorporated by registration under the Companies Act, while a public corporation is *created* by an Act of Parliament or any State Legislature which sets out its powers, duties and functions. *Secondly*, the shareholders of a public corporation, where there are any, have no equity interests, *no* voting rights and no powers to appoint Directors.

Although the capital is usually provided by the government, in the case of a public corporation, its capital structure and financial operations are similar to those of a public company.

The leading *characteristics* of a *Public Corporation* are summed up as follows :

1. It is a corporate body created by a special law defining its objects, powers and privileges, and prescribing the form of management and its relationship with government departments and ministries.

2. It is owned wholly by the State. It has no shareholders in the ordinary sense of the term.

3. The public corporation is the combination of public ownership,

public accountability and business management for public ends.

4. It is a body corporate and can sue and be sued, enter into contracts, and acquire and own property in its own name.

5. Since it is a separate legal entity, the employees of a public corporation are not government servants and are not governed by Civil Service Rules. They are employed and remunerated independently by each public corporation.

6. Except for appropriations to provide capital or to cover losses, a public corporation is usually independently financed. It obtains funds by borrowing either from the government or, in some cases, from the public and through revenues derived from the sale of goods and services, and has the authority to use and re-use its revenue.

7. It is ordinarily not subject to the budget, accounting and audit law and procedures applicable to government departments.

8. It is generally exempted from most regulatory and prohibitory statutes applicable to expenditure of public funds.

9. It is, in a large measure, free from parliamentary inquiry into the internal management of the concern as distinct from its policy. It is, however, subject to ministerial control.

10. It is not expected to make profit, although it must work efficiently and show good results in the form of 'surplus' which must not be the result of exploitation. While it must pay its way, a public corporation should function to render service to the public and not with the motive of making profit.

The aforesaid features of the public corporation show that, despite varying structures of individual corporations, it is an administrative instrument of governmental functions rather than vesting its functions in government departments. The objective, of course, is flexibility and independence of management, subject only to a liberal concept of accountability. It is therefore "clothed with the power of government but is possessed of the flexibility of private entreprise", and has been tried over a period by the different countries as an administrative agency.

Evaluation. The public corporation is an administrative instrument which follows a middle course between the departmental organisation with its rigidity on the one side, and privately owned and managed companies on the other side. It attempts to ensure public accountability and flexibility and autonomy.

The comparative freedom from rigid and persistent control and regulation by the government is an important point in favour of the public corporation. As is clear from some of the characteristics enumerated above, it is free from restrictive laws and is in a position to follow the best commercial practice in carrying on its business. Unlike the departmental set-up in which all lines of authority must run to the Ministry's office in New Delhi, the public corporation can have in its main office its area of operation and its centre of gravity within the region it serves. This autonomy lends a great deal of flexibility to its operation and brings it quite close to private enterprise in matter of efficiency. Its accountability to Parliament ensures that it works to serve public interest and not merely to maximize profits. The third feature in our discussion sums it up which describes the public corporation as a 'combination of public accountability and business management for public ends'.

In theory, the public corporations possess all the above-mentioned advantages: in practice, however, it has not always been possible to let it have the full use of its merits. In practice, the autonomy or independence of management is somewhat limited. The Minister has power to issue instructions on matters of national interest, but sometimes this is stretched further than its legitimate field, and he meddles with matters concerning internal management, thereby defeating the fundamental objective—autonomy. It is essential, therefore, that for the efficient discharge of their duties by the managers, the government officials and ministers use their rights and powers judiciously and with restraint.

Government Company

The second form of corporate type of organisation is the limited liability company registered under the Companies Act, and known as a Government Company. Section 617 of the Companies Act, 1956, defines a Government Company as any company in which not less than 51 per cent of the Paid-up share capital is held by the Central Government, or by any State Government or Governments, or partly by the Central Government and partly by one or more State Governments.

The Act contemplates the formation of Government Company either with total capital furnished by the Government or with mixed capital furnished partly by the Government and partly by the members of the public. Where the public also subscribes to the share capital of a company in which the Government holds not less than 51 per cent of the paid up share capital it is also called a Mixed Ownership Corporation. The Government companies in India have mostly been registered as private limited companies though their control and regulation rests with the Government which is in most cases the sole holder of the share capital. This form of organisation combines the operating flexibility of privately operated company with the advantages of State regulation and control in public interest.

The chief *characteristics of a Government Company Organisation* are as follows :

1. It has most of the features of a private limited company organised in private sector.

2. The whole of the share capital, or 51 per cent or more of it, is held by the government.

3. All the Directors, or a majority of them, are appointed by the government depending upon the extent to which private capital is participating in the enterprise.

4. It is a body corporate, created under the Companies Act.

5. It can sue and be sued, enter into contracts, and acquire and hold property in its own name.

6. Unlike the Public Corporation, it is created by an executive decision of the government without Parliament's specific approval having been obtained and its Articles of Association, though conforming to the Companies Act, are drawn up and can be altered by the government.

7. Its funds are obtained from Government, and in some cases, from private shareholders, and through revenues derived from the sale of its goods and services.

8. It is generally exempt from the personnel, budget, accounting and audit laws and procedures applicable to government departments.

9. Its employees, excluding the officers taken from government departments on deputation, are not civil servants.

Evaluation of Company form : The strongest argument in support of government company is its flexibility, which may be operational or functional. Flexibility may also refer to the case with which the Articles are drawn up and altered. As the Ministry drafts the Articles, it can provide operational flexibility, which becomes more difficult in the case of a public corporation which is set up by an Act passed by the legislature. Similarly any modification or alteration of Articles can be made very easily by the Ministry, while in the case of a public corporation the procedure is lengthy and cumbersome.

The setting up of an enterprise takes hardly any time; and as a very large number of undertakings are being set up, it is very simple to form a company. To set up so many public corporations would have meant delay in setting up undertakings. Generally the provisions of the Acts creating public corporations are more rigid than the Articles of Government Companies and thus they militate against flexibility.

The advantage of autonomy is also greater in the case of a government company than with a public corporation.

The company form is very useful where foreign capital and know-how are invited to assist the setting up of huge public enterprises, such as the Hindustan Steel Limited, which is government company owning three steel plants and the assistance given by Great Britain, the U.S.A. and the U.S.S.R.

The company form may be, and is usually, adopted for any one of 3 reasons, namely :—

1. When the government may have to take over an existing enterprise in an emergency;
2. Where the State wishes to launch an enterprise in association with private (particularly foreign) capital; or
3. Where government wishes to start an enterprise with a view eventually to transferring it to private management.

Defects of Company form. The principal defects generally attributed to the government company are :—

(1) It evades the constitutional responsibilities which a State-owned enterprise should have to Government and Parliament.

This defect is no more present, because Section 639 of the Companies Act requires the Central Government to place before each

House of Parliament an annual report on the working and affairs of each government company together with a copy of the audit report. Hence, in India, there is no evasion of constitutional responsibility, and Parliament is given an opportunity to discuss the working affairs of the government company as much as shareholders of a company under private enterprise.

(2) There is an absence of government audit, for it is governed by the rules as laid down in its own Articles of Association, and so to constitute State-owned enterprises as private companies is to commit "a fraud on the Companies Act and on the Constitution".

After the passing of the Companies Act, 1956, this defect has been removed. Section 619 of the Act provides that the auditor of a Government Company shall be appointed by the Central Government on the advice of Comptroller and Auditor-General of India. Further the C.A.G. can direct the manner in which the audit is to be conducted and may conduct supplementary or test audit by person authorised by him. The auditor is required to send the audit report to C.A.G. who may comment upon or supplement the report. These reports, comments and supplements are placed before the Annual General Meeting of the Company and also before both Houses of Parliament.

(3) The law regulating limited companies became a mere fiction because all or most of the functions normally vested in the shareholders and in the management are reserved to government.

The government company is usually a private limited company and the President of India holds all the shares except one share which is held by a government official to complete the formality required by the Companies Act. There is therefore no meeting of shareholders because that would be meaningless. The Directors are also appointed by the Government. There is nothing wrong in this act. If the government is the shareholder, it should have the rights. In private sector one-man companies are common, and we tolerate them.

(4) In the case of a company in private sector the Directors are elected by shareholders who may be innumerable in number and their choice is made as a result of their joint judgement, while in the case of a government company, the government is the only shareholder and the judgment of a single shareholder is bound to be inferior.

The argument is not only illogical but fallacious. If the government is incapable of proper assessment and judgment in relation to its companies, it is not worth the name, it cannot run the country. If it is able to run the country democratically and generally in public interest, there is no reason why its judgments in regard to its companies and selection of Directors for them should not be sound. Moreover, the government is not one man and the judgment is not of a single person. It is the judgment of people constituting the government and is maturer and sounder than that of a heterogeneous body of shareholders.

(5) The extent of autonomy that it provides for can be materially affected or altered by executive agencies of the government.

This can happen, probably more, in the case of a public corporation, too.

Conclusion Regarding Choice of Organisation.

In selecting a suitable form of organisation for a particular enterprise several factors have to be considered, the more important of which are :

(i) the productive function of the enterprise;
(ii) its operational and financial requirements;
(iii) the nature and scale of its operation;
(iv) its effect on the life of the community and the country's economy;
(v) the bearing a particular form of organisation will have on the autonomy of the public undertaking and their accountability to Parliament and their control by the Minister concerned.

Of the three forms, it is now generally accepted that the form of departmental undertaking is unsuitable for running industrial and commercial undertakings. The choice is really between Public Corporation and Government Company, and it is a difficult choice. Both the public corporation and the Government company provide for autonomy and flexibility, though in a varying degree. It is not possible to prescribe one and leave out the other. The largest number of public enterprises are organised as Government companies and only about half a dozen being organised as public corporations.

It is significant to note that Government had originally intended to adopt public corporation as the form of organisation. The 1948 Industrial Policy Resolution had envisaged that the "management of State enterprise will, as a rule, be through the medium of public corporations under the Statutory control of the Central Government". Although this categorieal declaration has not been modified by the 1956 Policy Resolution and subsequent statement, including the recent Policy Statement made in December, 1977, Government has shown overwhelming preference to company form of organisation. This has been done in spite of the recommendations of the Estimates Committee and those of the Administrative Reforms Commission in favour of public corporation. The reason adduced is that the company form has greater flexibility. It is suggested that legislation and legislative amendment is a cumbersome process and each time any amendment is necessary it would raise political controversies about its performance which might result in lack of flexibility in matters of policy and operation of the industry.

The company is regarded as suitable for industrial and commercial undertakings or where the concerned is financial by more than one party. The public corporation is suitable for undertakings in which powers and functions of a company may be inadequate, such as (i) public utilities, (ii) enterprises which involve exercise of powers which can only be conferred by legislation, (iii) enterprises which may not be commercially self supporting and have to be financed by regular grants from the Government.

Administrative problems of Public Enterprises

A proper balance between independence and autonomy on the one hand, and ultimate control of the nation through Parliament on the other, must be established and maintained for successful administration of public enterprises. The management and administration of public enterprises which have increased in number during the last 30 years, raise some important problems. These are considered in brief in the following paragraphs.

Operational Freedom or Autonomy of Management.

It is universally recognised that if public enterprises are to be run successfully, they must have the flexibility and operational autonomy so that they can function independently on sound business principles. It is necessary, therefore, that they should not be subjected to the same treatment as is available to the Government Departments. Ministerial control is essential but it must be kept within bounds, if initiative and enterprise are to be encouraged. While retaining the reserve power for ministerial direction, the executive and functional powers should be delegated to the management so that they can carry on day-to-day administration without too much interference.

Board of Directors

The Government of a public corporation or a Government company is entrusted to a Board of Directors. The success of private enterprise depends a great deal on the ability, experience and enterprise of its Board of Directors. They function as a team of seasoned men with a variety of experience in the industrial field. They lay down the policy, the plans and programmes, direct the affairs and watch and evaluate the performance of the enterprise. In law and theory, they are elected by the shareholders.

In a public enterprise, it is the responsibility of the Minister to lay down the policy as well as appoint the top officials and nominate the members of the Board of Directors. The elective principle does not apply where the Government is the sole shareholder. The Board of Directors not being exactly a policy-making Board, occupies a position somewhat anomalous and somewhere between the Chief executive and the Minister. The powers it wields compare in no way with those of the Board of a company in private sector. The majority of the members of the Board are Government officials drawn from Ministries concerned. It is stated that these officials have not contributed very much to the efficiency or better performance of these enterprises. At best they could be said to have safeguarded the interests of the Ministry they represented The result is that when the Board is ineffective, the management get uidance from it, nor the Minister any effective assistance or advice.

Types of Board of Directors. Broadly speaking, there are 3 types of Boards that we come across in public undertakings. These are :—

1. *The Policy-making Board.* The members of such a Board are part-time except the chief executive who may be the full-time Chairman or Managing Director. Most of the public undertakings in India have this type of Boards at present.

2. *The functional Board.* The members of such a Board are full-time, and have specific responsibility for different subjects. The most notable example is that of the Railway Board.

3. *The Mixed Board.* This type has both part-time and full-time directors, the latter having specific responsibility for some of the subjects. The Boards of the Indian Oil Corporation and the State Trading Corporation are examples of this kind.

In India the Policy-making type of Board has been preferred to the functional kind. There are a few cases of mixed type having both full-time and part-time directors. In recent years, the Government has appointed non-officials in increasing numbers as directors of Government companies. In many cases, at least one-third are non-officials and in some there are more non-officials than officials.

Government or Ministerial Control

Control is an active function, a purposeful and positive activity. It means directing, restraining, stimulating a person or an organisation to a certain action or end. A public enterprise is normally set up by a Ministry. By virtue thereof it is under the administrative control of that Ministry or Minister.

An analysis of the relevant statutes creating public corporations and the articles of association of Government companies reveals that powers have been reserved to the Government in the following matters and the Minister exercises control over public enterprises by—

(a) dictating the policy of the enterprise;

(b) appointment and removal of top officials and members of the Board of Directors;

(c) issue of directives in conformity with the policy already laid down;

(d) requiring prior approval or sanction of expenditure in excess of 10 per cent in cases where Government had approved the detailed report;

(e) requiring prior approval of capital expenditure in other cases where it exceeds a ceiling fixed depending upon the size, complexity and type of management;

(f) requiring prior approval in all matters of borrowings, investment and distribution of profits;

(g) requiring prior approval of rules and regulations of public corporations;

(h) calling for information, reports and returns;

(i) requiring the corporation to submit a budget for approval of the Government when so provided in the statute;
(j) appointment of auditors in consultation with the Comptroller and Auditor General of India; and
(k) in a few cases, framing rules regarding terms and conditions of service of employees of the undertaking.

In addition to the formal powers, the Minister or Senior officials of the Ministry secure compliance with their wishes through informal means.

Parliamentary Accountability of Public Enterprises.

The public undertakings are under the *control* of the Ministry and both the Ministry and the Public undertakings in their turn are *accountable* to Parliament for their performance.

Whereas "control" as we have seen above, is an active function "accountability" is a passive function. It means and involves receiving accounts, reports, statistics etc. The person accountable has to give an account of how he has discharged his duties.

Under the Constitution, public enterprises as instruments of public policy and organs of the Government are clearly and ultimately accountable to Parliament.[1] Therefore, Parliamentary supervision is an essential feature of public accountability.

The main instruments that Parliament uses to secure accountability are :—

1. *Parliamentary Question.* Of all parliamentary devices the most commonly used to secure accountability is the Parliamentary Questions asked by the members. Under the Rules of Procedure and Conduct of Business in Lok Sabha, "unless the Speaker otherwise directs, the first hour of every sitting shall be available for asking and answering questions". Only policy matters or matters of public interest are required to be answered by the Minister. Questions which clearly relate to day-to-day administration are normally disallowed.

The question as an instrument of accountability is of little value. Questions about enterprises can only be meaningful when the members bring with them a certain knowledge of management and have kept themselves fairly well informed by going through the Annual Reports and Accounts.

2. *Parliamentary Debates.* The performance of public undertakings can form a subject of debate in Parliament in several ways, such as—

(i) in the shape of elaborate reference during the budget debate; or
(ii) the debate on the President's address; or
(iii) discussion on the Annual Reports and Annual Accounts; or
(iv) it can be raised as a subject-matter of half-hour discussion or even as adjournment motion;

The debate is definitely a better method to secure accountability

1. N.N. Mallya, Public Enterprises in India, P.124.

than the question. But a still better device is through Parliamentary Committee.

3. *Parliamentary Committee.* There is a great advantage in examination by a Committee of Parliament. In the case of debates and questions, it is the Minister who speaks on behalf of the public undertaking. But during the examination by a committee the Chairman and other officials of the undertaking get an opportunity to explain their point of view across the table. Previously, in addition to the Public Accounts Committee, the Estimates Committee examined the working of public undertakings. In May, 1964, a joint committee of both the houses, namely the Committee on Public Undertakings was constituted and it took over the work of examining public undertakings. The more important powers of this Committee are :

1. Power to send for persons, papers and records and to take oral and/or written evidence in connection with any matter under its consideration, examination, or investigation;

2. Power to make special reports on any matter that arises or comes to light in the course of its work;

3. Power to appoint one or more study groups for carrying out detailed examination of various subjects.

But matters of major Government policy or matters of day-to-day administration are expressly excluded from the purview of the Committee. The work of the Parliamentary Committee has been very useful, especially in the matter of the control of capital expenditure. The managements of public undertakings have welcomed it, since they can now appear before it and explain things.

BUREAU OF PUBLIC ENTERPRISES

With the rapid expansion of the public sector, the problem of gathering information, classifying it and communicating to different undertakings as well as coordinating became urgent. The Estimates Committee in their 52nd Report suggested the setting up an agency for performing the above-mentioned functions. The Government set up in March, 1965, the Bureau of Public Enterprises which has been entrusted with the following functions :

(i) to provide a central point of reference, consultation and advice on important aspects of management of public enterprises;

(ii) to explore all avenues of economy in the capital costs of the projects;

(iii) to devise steps to improve the productivity and profitability of the enterprises;

(iv) to review periodically the working of individual units as also to undertake examination of selected areas of their performance; and

(v) to present to Parliament or government agencies reports and reviews of their working.

Pricing Policy. Proper pricing policy in the case of public sector undertakings is an important aspect of their operation and attracted public attention from time to time. The main considerations for the framing of pricing policy for public enterprises are : (i) making products available to consumers as widely as possible, (ii) generation of surpluses for reinvestment, (iii) attainment of the optimum level of operation, (iv) meeting competition from private enterprises and foreign producers, and (v) Recovery of the total cost as far as possible. However, no fixed pricing policy can be laid down for all types of industries and undertakings. Some fix prices to make profit, others at non-profit and still others at no profit and no loss and so on.

1. Railways, Hindustan Steel, Hindustan Machine Tools, Sindri Fertilizers are examples of Profit-making undertakings.

2. No-Profit policy is followed by enterprises such as Hindustan Antibiotics.

3. Pricing even at a loss is adopted by enterprises which are established for promoting welfare schemes and plans for economic development, e.g., the State Bank of India's rural branch development scheme.

4. Import-parity pricing is adopted by enterprises whose products have to compete with products of foreign makers, e.g., Hindustan Shipyard.

5. Concessional pricing for long-term contracts or bulk purchases, e.g., Chittaranjan Locomotives long-term contract for the supply of locomotives and boilers and Hindustan Steel Limited for bulk purchases.

6. Differential rates on the basis of discriminating monopoly, so that higher prices are paid by well-to-do people and lower by poorer people. Levy rice and wheat and free market rice and wheat.

All undertakings, however, do not have autonomy in fixing prices. In some cases the Government fixes the prices. For example, the selling price and distribution of products is regulated and controlled by the Government, as in the case of fertilizers, drugs, coal, and petroleum products.

It was at one time believed and advocated that public enterprises should operate in public interest on a no-profit, no-loss basis. It is now accepted generally that public enterprises should operate to generate enough surpluses to take care of their requirements of growth, expansion, replacements and development and create new wealth to yield new wealth to finance Five-Year Plans.

Performance of Public Enterprises in India.

Some of the socio-economic objectives which the public sector is called upon to fulfil are :—

(a) To promote self-reliance in strategic sectors of the national economy;

(b) To provide infrastructural facilities for promoting a balanced and diversified economic structure in development;

(c) To prevent concentration of economic power;
(d) To reduce regional imbalances and to increase employment;
(e) To generate surplus for the investment; and
(f) To enforce social control on trade and industry for ensuring equitable distribution of goods and services.

It will be observed that public enterprises in India have been assigned the task of implementing the objectives of the Directive Principles of State Policy. The industrial development that has taken place during the last two decades has, to a large measure, been the result of the entrepreneurial effort of the state. From a bare investment of Rs. 290 crores in 1951, the figure reached Rs. 2,415 crores at the end of 1966. In the post '66 period, a much heavier additional investment of nearly Rs. 4,000 crores was made till the end of 1973-74, which became Rs. 7,261 in 1974-75 for 122 operating Central Government enterprises.

The country can justifiably feel proud that at last the policy of State intervention in economic development has been vindicated. After years of being in the red, the public enterprises emerged with a modest profit in 1972-73 of Rs. 18 crores. In 1973-74, the profit well-nigh quadrupled to Rs. 64 crores, and in 1974-75 it was Rs. 184 crores, almost thrice of the previous year. This represents a return of 8.4 per cent on capital employed. These figures are indeed heartening. They mean in effect that investments in the public sector are now beginning to pay off. The gestation periods are progressively being completed. The public sector will no longer be a drag on the national economy. Apart from being self-sufficient, it will generate resources for its own expansion and development and will make substantive contributions to the public exchequer to the relief of the tax-payer.

For a period of 20 years, public enterprises in general had failed to show good results. There was, therefore, all round criticism of their working, and general belief that state entreprise must inherently be inefficient. And that only private entreprise can run efficiently and profitably. There were certain very important causes of low productivity and poor performance of public enterprises which will be considered at the end of this discussion.

To continue the story of the progress made in recent years, at least by some of the enterprises, it may be stated that the achievements of such enterprises is all the more remarkable, when we remember that in India the State did not only nationalise existing entreprises, but set up new ones. This resulted in the building up an industrial infra-structure by developing coal, steel, petroleum, fertilizers, heavy engineering, non-ferrous metals, all requiring vast amount of capital and gestation period. Since everything was to be done from scratch we made mistakes, but now we have turned the corner in the case of a few enterprises

The public enterprises of the Central Government altogether earned a net profit after tax of Rs. 2,183 crores in 1987-88, although group wise results were not rosy in many cases, For example, in 1986-87, only 5 enterprises out of 12 manufacturing units showed profits. The

profit earners were engaged in petroleum, power, medium and light engineering, heavy engineering and minerals and metals. The losing sectors were textiles, coal, chemicals, fertilisers and pharmaceuticals, consumer goods, transport equipment, steel and agro based products.

The top profit makers include Oil and Natural Gas Commission, Indian Oil Corporation, National Thermal Power Corporation Ltd., Bharat Heavy Electricals Ltd., Mahanagar Telephone Nigam Ltd. However, ten enterprises have shown deterioration during the period. The important indicaters of growth of public sector are as follows :

The capital employed in 221 public enterprises in March, 1988 was Rs. 58,125 crores. The turnover in that year was Rs. 81,367 crores and the profit was Rs. 2,183 crores. The total contribution to the Central exchequer by way dividends, corporate tax, excise duty, customs and other duties was Rs. 13.38 crores in 1987-88.

Some of the important causes of low productivity and poor performance of almost all the undertakings are discussed below.

Causes of Poor Performance or Low Productivity

1. *Lack of clearly defined objectives.* Very often a public enterprise does not have a well defined objective. Whereas the primary objective of any undertaking in private sector is making ample profits, a public undertaking is not always intended to yield a positive return on investment. Many extraneous considerations also influence the establishment of a public sector project, even when it is found to be non-possible. This obviously leads to the laxity on the part of management.

2. *Poor Project Planning.* Most of the public enterprises suffer from poor project planning. This results, in undue time lag, over capitalisation and high rate of idle capacity. A public enterprise starts with a technical and economic feasibility report of the industry to be set up. The consultant cannot prepare an adequate report because the data or information given to him is meagre, incomplete, inaccurate, vague or even wrong. And when technical and economic studies are being made the consultant has no idea where the plant will ultimately be located. The consultant has no idea of the infra-structure facilities available nor of the cost of water, power and transportation.

3. *Poor man-power planning.* In many cases man-power requirements are assessed on the basis that so many workers would be required to carry on production even when production was to begin after a considerable time. Over-staffing is a common feature of all public enterprises. In case of Bhilai, for instance, the detailed project report envisaged 7,300 men for the Plant. But there are today 26, 812 men as against the standard force. Air India at one time employed 600 cleaners and chowkidars-a number almost unknown in any foreign airlines.

4. *Faulty production planning.* There is hardly any proper production targets or production planning, with the result that quite a few units

operate with under-utilised capacities. This becomes one of the causes of low productivity and inefficiency. Poor material management and lavish expenditure on inventories places a great strain on the financial resources of the undertakings. It is estimated that investment in inventory in India can be reduced by 50 per cent by scientific inventory management.

5. *Poor maintenance of Plant and Machinery.* The repair and maintenance of plant and machinery help to keep them at their maximum mechanical efficiency. Very little attention is paid in this direction. A good percentage of the imports are on account of damages and parts worn out earlier than their expected life would warrant.

6. *Poor labour management relations.* In most public sector undertakings labour relations are very low and morale of workers not at all high. This is so in spite of the large provision under social overheads.

7. *Heavy expenditure on social overheads.* The public sector undertakings have made excessive expenditure on townships to accomodate employees. It has been estimated that the average cost of townships range from 15 to 25 percent of the cost of the project. It is reported that they spend about Rs. 50 crores annually as recurring expenses on the maintenance and administration of townships and social overheads.

8. *Deficiencies in management.* Uptil 1972, management of most undertakings was entrusted to men on deputation from administrations cadres who did not have the feeling of belongingness towards the enterprises they served. Moreover, Managing Directors or Chief Executives lacked experience and knowledge of conducting productive enterprises. A good many were appointed to these posts merely because they were dealing with the enterprise at its early project stage. Bureaucratisation and labour intransigence born out of prescribed routines have contributed to inefficiency in management.

9. *Poor cost consciousness.* The prime need in management is for it to be cost conscious. Cost consciousness is not just an awareness of total cost. It means knowing the cost of each division, of each process or job and this must be known every month, every week, sometimes every day. This course needs a machinery geared upto supply this information. There is no indication that public enterprises have this machinery. On the other hand the examination of the financial arrangements reveal a sad story.

10. *No control over waste.* Management must keep track of waste and if possible eliminate it. But there is no one or no unit to keep track of them.

One other important contributing cause of public sector losses, is what A. N. Prabhu* calls the "Legacy of Takeovers". There are at present about 170 Central Government public enterprises. About 50 of them have come to the public sector by way of transfer from private sector and joint sectors. Of the 50 units, as many as 38 were effectively

* Economic Times, October 15,1978

transferred to the public sector after December, 1969—about 10 years ago. The key industries like coal, sick textile mills and copper mining (19 units in all) were nationalised. Six others such as IISCO, Braithwaite, Richardson & Crudas, Burn, Standard etc. were nationalised in public interest. Ten enterprises came into the hands of the Government through purchase of shares from private shareholders, and financial institutions as in the case of IBP, Balmer Lawrie, Jessop, Co., ESSO, Burmah Shell and Caltex. A fourth category is transfer from joint sector as in the case of the Indian Oil Blending Co.

An analysis of these units shows mounting losses year after year. Take for instance coal,—massive input of capital was necessary to step up production of coal essential for the economy. The Government injected a sum of Rs. 731.23 crores between 1972 and 1977 the result is a staggering loss of Rs. 163.48 crores during the same period. The story of the sick textile mills is no different. One hundred and three sick mills were nationalised in 1974. National Textile Corporation (NTC) was set up in 1968 to manage the affairs of sick units. A total sum of Rs. 90 crores had been sanctioned till March 31, 1977 for the modernisation of 106 sick mills. The operating results show a loss of Rs. 57.71 crores in 1975–76 and Rs. 35.74 crores in 1976–77.

Richardson & Crudas Ltd. taken over in 1972 has suffered a cumulative loss of Rs. 62 lakhs from 1972–73 to 1976–77. Braithwaite taken over in 1971 repeats the story the losses being Rs. 3.9 crores in 1975–76 and Rs. 2.87 crores in 1976–77. Burn & Co. Ltd. and Indian Standard Wagon Ltd. suffered losses of Rs. 4.33 crores in 1975–76 and Rs. 3.07 crores in 1976–77. Indian Iron & Steel Co.'s management was taken over in 1972 when its capacity utilisation had dropped to 13 per cent. In 1976 ownership was also taken over. The company showed a nominal profit of Rs. 1.05 crores in 1974–75, but losses amounting to Rs. 6.72 crores in 1975–76 and Rs. 14.75 crores in 1976–77. A sum of Rs. 61 crores had been sunk in replacement and rehabilitation of various old equipment. Jessop & Co. made a cumulative loss of Rs. 12.25 crores in 1976–77. Though paper was in great demand in the country, Mandya National Paper Mills Ltd. suffered a loss of Rs. 0.59 crores in 1976–77.

May be these units are facing some special problems leading to continuous losses. It is necessary for the Government to carry out performance studies and then take corrective steps to reduce losses.

With regard to the directly established enterprises, improvement have been noticed in recent years, as observed earlier in this chapter. The establishment of holding companies like the SAIL, to take over management of some public sector undertakings, like the Steel Plants, is one of the methods of improving management. The SAIL managing and administering the various steel mills in the public sector appears to have shown some good results.

Changing Role of Public Sector.–

Changing Role of Public Sector : It is becoming apparent every day that the role of the public sector is changing, and quite substantially. Private enterprise seems to be making inroads into the realm of public enterprise. Public sector investment under the five-year plans has dropped to 50 per cent of the total. Much of the public sector is commonly acknowledged as not pulling its weight. The public sector appears to have failed to "occupy the commanding position" in the economy. A new definition of the role of the public sector is called for; and the trends justify this demand. For example, in the sixth Plan, public sector investment was about 53 per cent of the total. By the time, the Seventh Plan was finalised, it was recognised that the private sector would have a higher level of investment than the public sectors investment of 48 per cent of the total Seventh Plan investments, well below the peak of 60 per cent reached in 1970.

The development of basic and infrastructural sector was left to the public sector by the 1956 Policy Statement. This also seems to have received a setback, because most of the major investments in steel, fertiliser, petrochemicals, oil refining, have been either in the private sector or the joint sector. Even in power generation the inability of the public sector to keep pace with the growing energy needs of the economy has prompted the Government to allow private sector participation in the power generation and distribution. Privatisation appears to have been encouraged in an indirect manner, namely, by setting up additional capacity in private and joint sectors, without of course, privatising invididual public sector units.

The factors which have weakened the base of the public sector in recent years and are likely to stand in the way of its future growth may be summarised as follows :

The principal contributing factor that has brought down the public sector from its commanding position before the 1980's is the "poisoned environment in which the public sector has to function today". The environment is poisoned by hostile public opinion because of the poor performance of some of the Central Government enterprises and almost all of the State enterprises resulting in huge losses. And the Government has failed to highlight the successful working of others, with the result that only the "dark" side of public enterprise is exposed. Had the Government not taken over sick textile mills, main l makers, and applied its mind seriously to remove obstacles and corrected its policies concerning public sector, the target set by the Planning Commission of an enterprise earning a surplus of 10 per cent could have been achieved.

The second cause is the setting up of enterprises in directions of industrial activity including consumer industries, and even in law investment areas without giving adequate attention to detailed scientific project planning.

The third factor is the induction of people having political clout into the management cadre in place of dynamic and competent as well as experienced managers. Further, the Boards of directors are packed with persons who are prone to create problems rather than solve them. On top of this, the top management posts are often left unfilled for long periods of time.

Another factor which is militating against the further growth of public sector is the strong lobby that is building up in favour of "privatisation"

CHAPTER XVII

SOCIAL RESPONSIBILITIES OF BUSINESS

Changing Philosophy of Business. Public demands on private business have expanded greatly in recent years. Business enterprise was once expected to devote its efforts to producing and distributing goods and services as efficiently as possible and to making innovations and improvements in products and processes with the ultimate objective of maximization of profits. Now, business is increasingly called upon to promote a variety of social purposes in addition to these long standing economic ones. The demands for "social responsibility" have provoked enthusiastic discussion and debate on what new roles, if any, business firms should play in the social system.

It is some times argued by economists as well as by business men accused of neglecting the public interest, that the business of business is just business. To their way of thinking end is all, means mean nothing, Maximization of profits seems to be the prevailing norm. Money-chasing continues to be the economic objective of business. Strangely enough, the idea of trusteeship has not had general acceptance in the land of its birth, in spite of the efforts on the part of Gandhiji to revive it. Despite the laws (partly because of court costs and inordinate delays) firms can often get by with false advertising, misleading information, and products that have lower quality and greater hazards than indicated to customers. There is hardly anything that is not adulterated. Most of these practices boil down to cheating and playing with the lives of people. The businessman in India, whose main aim is to make money, by fair means or foul, should take a leaf out of the biography of Henry Ford, who declared. "The best way to make money is not to think too much about making it". His company was organised to do "as much good as we can for every body". His philosophy and practice was "more and more goods for more and more people at lower and lower prices". But why should one do this ? For human betterment and self-improvement, for "service".

Social and Economic Objectives of Business. The purpose of business entreprise is to produce quality goods and distribute them and do it ethically so as to serve the general welfare. Since the economic and social objectives of business are not mutually exclusive, but are intertwined, the management has both social and economic responsibilities. In this context the function of management is to see that the business enterprise fulfils its purpose by paying investors a fair return on their capital, by paying workers a fair compensation for their effort, by paying vendors a fair price for the materials and supplies, and by "paying" the consumers in terms of reasonable price, quality and service and, above all, by helping our society to function in harmony as an organic whole.

This function imposes upon the business and its managers a higher responsibility than that arising out of private property and self-interest. Self-interest and public good cannot be kept apart. The manager must assume responsibility for public good, because management's responsibility to the enterprise and to society "is inextricably interwoven". This is based on the fact that the enterprise is an organ of society, and that its actions have a decisive impact on the social scene. If a business provide a product or service that is useful or otherwise of value to the community, then it is socially desirable that it continues to function.

The social responsibilities of business and its economic activities are so intermingled that so far we have discussed the two together. We will now attempt a summary discussion of the obligations of business separately to itself, to the shareholders, the workers, the consumers and the community.

Obligations of Business to Itself. The first task of business enterprise is to stay in business. This can be achieved by effective and profitable production. The next obligation is to grow bigger and constantly to grow better through innovation. To be able to discharge its social responsibilities an entreprise must work towards growth, expansion and stability. This can be accomplished by operating at a reasonable profit which will enable it to maintain as well as increase its wealth-creating and wealth-producing capacity and so the wealth of society.

Obligation of Business enterprise to Shareholders. As the company pervades almost all business activities, its shareholders who provide the necessary funds have certain expectations. Management has a double responsibility to the shareholders. The first half is to manage the business effectively so as to produce a reasonable profit for them, and the second is to see that the shareholders are aware of company's progress and are satisfied with its progress. So, in addition to giving a fair return on the capital invested and risk taken, the company should supply to its shareholders continuous, comprehensive and accurate reports giving full information about its working.

The shareholders have also certain obligations. They should support the management's efforts to balance the needs of the company for strong resources and continued development. They should not expect maximum possible dividends but ought to be satisfied with a fair return on their investment which should not exceed the risk and the cost of loans. Voluntary dividend restriction is desirable. This will enable the company to plough back ample profits for innovation and expansion.

Obligations to Workers. The business enterprise must provide security with fair wages to its workers, and an equal opportunity for growth and development within the company. The development of human potentiality is so important that it is not wrong to say that "management is the development of people and not the direction of things". In fact, business is people. It is incumbent on business enterprise through its management to give all possible assistance in the improvement of education, training and upgrading of skills so that every member of the enterprise has a chance to grow. Participation of workers in management is desirable but it can succeed only if workers are educated. Again, productivity ratio depends as much on education and training of workers as on economic factors. Collective bargaining is another right of workers and strike a sharp edged weapon. "Management should create such a work environment that the workers are not obliged to use their weapon."

Obligations to Consumers. Once the company is viable the consumers' claim on its profits is the greatest of all. After all consumer satisfaction is the primary and ultimate aim of business activity. This involves more than offering products at lowest possible price. Adulteration, poor quality, failure to give full measure, lack of service and courtesy to the customer, misleading or dishonest advertising, are all examples of violation by business enterprise of its obligation to the consumers of its products. Free competition provides good protection of consumers' interests in normal circumstances. Indeed, the principal reason for social irresponsibility is the failure of transactions to occur. Government regulation is one of the methods of protecting the interest of consumers. The management should encourage the establishment of Consumers' Advisory Councils and Consumers' Association should bring their complaints before these councils to be finally handled by the management.

Obligations to Society. In the words of Peter Drucker,* "the business enterprise should be so managed as to make the public good become the private good of the enterprise". Then only can it build its image of a responsible business enterprise and be esteemed. By producing goods and services efficiently and by fair means, business can contribute to the economic well-being of the community and its social uplift. Good management can directly advance social well-being by contributing to the advancement of local amenities of the particular locality and community where the enterprise functions. All managements also contribute indirectly to social welfare measures undertaken by the State by honestly paying the taxes out of which the State finances its welfare activities. Managements also, make a contribution to society as a whole by bringing about economic growth and increased prosperity to the nation.

As a good citizen, business enterprise should bear the social cost of its anti-social conduct, e.g., fouling the air, destruction of natural beauty of the surrounding landscape, creation of slums and congestion. It must also make a contribution to another social cost—the schools, the armament, medical aid, etc.—of society. Business can make a greater and more direct contribution to public weal. This can be done by establishing a corporation and endowing it with capital out of earnings and savings. The corporation is to earn no profits and pay no taxes, but its earnings are to be utilised for public weal. In this way great wealth can live up to its non-commercial responsibilities.

Business houses can make direct contribution by deputing their

* The Practice of Management, P.392

expert personnel to educational and technical training institutions on short assignments, thereby giving practical bias to teaching.

Business has a definite responsibility towards the community in areas from where people have been displaced as a result of its activities. Special training should be given to the displaced people apart from the cash compensation usually offered to them.

Business as an Agent of Government. There are certain matters of social policy which go with being in business. They involve the business firm as an agent of social policy or social reform. The business firm acts as a social instrument in respect to certain activities. Deducting tax at source (e.g., from salaries) represents a drafting of the firm into service of the Central Board of Revenue. Setting up of Provident Fund and Family Pension Schemes is another example of the firm being the "chosen instrument" for enabling workers to save for retirement. "Affirmative action programmes" in hiring and promotion of weaker sections of society is another example of business used as a social instrument. Health is another field in which business firms are uniquely convenient agents.

Conclusion. To conclude, it is suggested that business firms should act on the facts of business. They should seek their profits in a truly scientific way, and use them for public good. Let it be remembered, that every business individually and all businesses collectively to be profitable, must be organised to provide the greatest possible service to the masses of the population. Let our business enterprise combine public spirit and shrewd business sense and give up exploitation of the workers and consumers. As a businessman is as human as any other human being, he has to participate in human life, and human life is very largely social. The modern businessman should not tolerate a social order with so many economic corpses lying around. He should bury the dead and turn to building of a better world in which there will be no profits except the *earned* profits that come from real service and no privilege of participation in the upward march of human life.

If, however, business firms fail to move voluntarily very far their traditional economic role to assume new responsibilities for social problems, social costs, and social benefits, the government should step in. It should then assign social responsibilities to business enterprise through mixture of compulsion and inducement.

PART FIVE
Principles of Management

CHAPTER XVIII

NATURE AND IMPORTANCE OF MANAGEMENT

Importance of Management

Management is a universally necessary function. It is essential for all kinds of organisations, whether they be business organisations or non-business organisations. This is so because every organisation requires the making of decisions, the coordinating of activities, the handling of people, and evaluating the performance directed towards its objectives. This task for the organisation is performed by that responsible person called the *Manager.* He brings the principal resource—*human talent* into combination with non-human resources, viz., machines, materials and money. Every organisation, therefore has managers. They may be called supervisors, directors, superintendents, agency chiefs, or foremen, but managers, are present. In other words, management takes place at all levels in the organisational hierarchy. Every manager performs essentially the same functions whether he belongs to the top or middle or first-line management. The only difference is in the magnitude of the task and the scope and degree of the authority. Qualified managers, therefore, are important both to their firms and to the future of society. They are so important that high quality management is a firm's *single most important resource.*

Meaning of Management

In general usage, the word management identifies a special group of people who direct effort towards common objectives through the activities of other people. Simply stated, management "gets things done through other people". Hicks[1] defines management as "the process of getting things done by and through others. It is, for example, supervising the work of a group of typists rather than typing letters for oneself". Massie[2] defines management as "the process by which cooperative group directs actions toward common goals. This process involves techniques by which a distinguishable group of people (managers) co-ordinates activities of other people; managers seldom actually perform the activities themselves". Koontz and O'Donnell[3] state that "management means getting things done through and with people". Haimann[4] observes that "management is the function of getting things done through people and directing the efforts of individuals towards a common objective. All these definitions bring out the distinction between "doing" and "getting things done through others" We may define

1. Modern Business Management, p. 70
2. Essentials of Management, p. 4
3. Management, P.67
4. Professional Management, P.1

management as *a process by which responsible people (managers) in an organisation get things done through the efforts of other people in grouped activities.*

Lawrence Appley in his book. Management in Action—The Art of getting things done through people, emphasises the human relations aspect of management. In fact, "working satisfactorily with people", he says, "is the entire job of management". He, therefore, asserts that "management is the development of people and not the direction of things." It is the selection, the training, the supervision and the development of people. In essence, it means that management builds men: and men build products. Therefore, according to Appley, "management is the attainment of pre-established goals by the direction of human performance along pre-established lines."

ADMINISTRATION AND MANAGEMENT

The terms administration and management are widely used but have not been precisely defined. Very often they have been used interchangeably. Some use management as a broader term to include all the elements in the direction, guidance and control of all the business activities for achieving the desired goal. Some other writers regard all these activities as administration, and still others do not make any distinction between the two. This has led to a good deal of confusion. A few statements by eminent writers of different schools of thought are given here to enable the reader to form his own judgment.

1. *Oliver Sheldon.* [5] "Administration is the function in the industry concerned with the determination of the corporate policy, the coordination of finance, production and distribution, the settlement of the compass (structure) of the organisation, under the ultimate control of the executive." *Management,* according to him "is the function in industry concerned in the execution of policy, within the limits set up by the administration and the employment of the organisation for the particular objects before it."

Ordway Tead Schulze, Milward, Sargant Florence, Spriegal and LanasBurgh also hold the same view. According to them, administration determines the organisation, management uses it. Administration defines the goal; management strives to achieve it. Administration frames the policy; management executes it. Administration is, thus, legislative or determinative; management is essentially executive.

2. *Brech.* Brech regards management as an all-inclusive function involving "responsibility for the effective planning and regulation or guidance of the operation of an enterprise." In his view, "management is the total process of executive control" and administration is "that part of management which is concerned with the installation and carrying out of the procedures by which the progress of activities is regulated and checked against plans."

5. Philosophy of Management, p. 32.

3. *Fayol and Newman* do not make any distinction between administration and management. But when it is remembered that the two words are used to indicate different functions and not the persons who perform those functions, the distinction becomes important. Therefore administration and management, as function may be defined as follows.

Definitions of Administration and Management.

Administration means over-all determination of policies and major objectives. Functionally, it is the laying down of the general purpose of the entreprise, the framing of its major policies, the formulation of the general plan of procedure, the inauguration of the broad programme and approval of the specific major projects that fall within the general programme. It is, in a sense, the legislative function.

Management is essentially an executive function, the active direction of the human effort. It is the work that manager does as he seeks to get results through other people.

Although, as a function, administration is determinative and management is essentially executive, yet the same person may perform both the functions. In a large concern, the Chief Executive would devote a greater part of his time to the broader administrative responsibilities. But he will also participate (though, to a limited extent) in executing those policies. Similarly, many minor executives determine policies in a limited sphere and so perform administrative function. To repeat, top management devotes most of its time in administration, devoting some time to management. As we go down the hierarchical ladder, the administrative function becomes less and less and the management function more and more. The following figure clearly demonstrates this point:

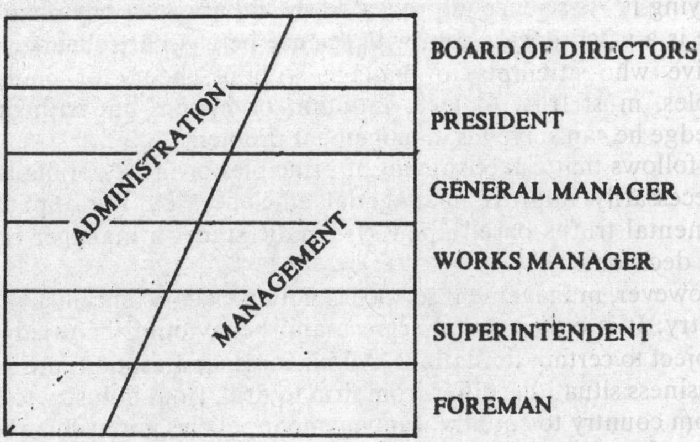

Is Management an Art, a Science or a Profession ?

Discussions about management usually raise the questions whether management is an art or a science or whether it is a profession. The answer to these questions will depend upon the clear understanding of these terms.

An art is practical skill and ingenuity, the way of doing specific things. It indicates how an objective is to be achieved. It means the know-how, and its application guided by certain principles. Science, on the other hand, is knowledge ascertained by observation and experiment, critically tested, systematised and brought under general principles.

When a carpenter shapes a log of wood into a piece of furniture, a goldsmith converts gold into a ring or bangles, or an electrician winds the armature of a fan, each one practices an art—a skill, an ingenuity. A surgeon or a physican without knowledge of medical science is a quack. Thus, behind all activities there are certain principles which the scientist unfolds and lays down in a systematic manner which are of universal application. These really become the working rules of an art. Examples of scientific principles are that two atoms of hydrogen and one atom of oxygen form one molecule of water; that if anything is thrown towards the sky, it will come down to the earth because of the law of gravitation and so on.

Management is both an art and a science. The management science provides a body of principles for guidance in the solution of specific management problems and objective evaluation of results. An analysis of basic management functions has led to the development of certain principles which can be applied as general guides for solving concrete problems. The art of management, on the other hand, deals with the application of skill and effort for producing desirable results. Thus, art and science are not mutually exclusive, but are complementary. The most productive art is always based on an understanding of the science underlying it. As science improves, so should art. As a physician without science is a witch doctor, and with science he is an artful surgeon, so an executive who attempts to manage without theory or management principles, must trust to luck, intuition or hunch, but with organised knowledge he can solve his management problems.

It follows that establishment of principles or theory of management will necessarily improve managerial efficiency. By the application of fundamental truths based upon systematic study, a manager can avoid chance decisions.

However, management science is not an exact science like physics or chemistry. It is only a social science and behavioural knowledge which are subject to certain limitations. All business organisations are not alike, and business situations differ from firm to firm, from industry to industry and from country to country. Management policies and techniques must, therefore, be adjusted to specific circumstances. Management theory and science do not advocate the "one best way" of doing things in the light of every situation. As a result, effective management is always situational management.

The question of whether management is a profession is complicated by the fact that management is a broad subject. Part of the subject may have characteristics of a profession and other parts may not. Profession should satisfy the following four criteria.[6]

1. A profession is a systematic body of knowledge and so requires intellectual training.
2. A profession maintains an experimental attitude towards information, and so requires a search for new ideas.
3. A profession emphasises service to others, and usually develops a code of conduct that requires that financial return not be the only motive.
4. Entrance into a profession is usually restricted by standards established by an association that requires its members be accepted by a group composed of people with common training and attitude.

Sachar Committee on Simplification and Modification of Company Law has advocated the professionalisation of management. It has recommended that a large public company with a paid-up capital of Rs. 50 lakhs and more must have a managing or whole-time director. It defines a managing director as a professional manager appointed as a whole-time director by the company in general meeting to manage the whole, or substantially the whole of the affairs of the company, or to exercise substantial powers of management.

Recognising some of the criteria mentioned above, the Committee defines Professional Manager thus: "Professional Manager is an individual who:—

(a) (i) belongs to the profession of law, accountancy, medicine, engineering or architecture; or

(ii) is a member of a recognised professional body or institution exercising supervisory jurisdiction over its members; or

(iii) is a holder of a degree or diploma in management from any recognised Institute of Management or from any recognised University; or

(iv) is a holder of a post-graduate degree from any recognised University;

and possesses not less than 5 years experience in an executive capacity in a company, corporation or a body corporate or in the Government; or

(b) possesses a minimum of 10 years experience in an executive capacity in a company, corporation or a body corporate or in the Government.

In the light of this requirement, educational institutions shall have

6. Massie, *Essentials of Management*, p. 10.

to prepare future managers who can manage business efficiently keeping in mind ethics of business and responsibilities to all sections of society.

Development of Management Thought

The study of management as a separate and distinct subject with different theories and techniques is a product of the twentieth century. Most writers agree that the origin of this discipline was the work of Frederick Winslow Taylor and his associates during the scientific management movement that developed around 1900. However, the problems of organising men to achieve the desired objectives is not new. It is as old as civilisation itself. As students of management we should trace the development of management thought.

Pre-scientific Management Era

Thousands of years ago, the Chinese, the Babylonians, the Egyptians, the Greeks, the Romans and Hindu philosophers wrote extremely interesting books and propounded theories which are followed even today. From the military come many examples of early management thought. With the advent of industrial revolution management of entreprises assumed an increasingly important role. Some of the persons who, before Taylor, made considerable contribution to the development of management thought were James Watt, Mathew R. Boulton, Robert Owen and Charles Babbage. Perhaps the most important contributor to management thought before Taylor was Henry Varnum Poor, editor of the American Railroad Journal in the latter half of the 19th century. In the words of Wren,* "Long before Frederick Taylor he (Poor) called for a system; long before Elton Mayo he called for recognition of the human factor; and long before Chris Argis he called for leadership to remove the rigidities of formal organisation."

Taylor's Scientific Management

Frederick Winslow Taylor (1856–1915), who is properly known as the father of scientific management, introduced the concept of management as a science. He studied the causes of low efficiency of workers. He was convinced that the management did not manage. He suggested that management should follow a *scientific approach* in their work and apply *scientific method* in tackling all problems relating to efficiency. He stated that "the best management is a true science, resting upon clearly defined laws, rules and principles as a foundation". Taylor's principal concern was that of increasing efficiency in production, with the object of lowering costs and raising profits, but also to make possible increased wages for workers. He suggested the fixation of standards which must be followed by the workers who have been trained. To this end he proposed the separation of planning functions from the doing functions; the management doing the planning and the workers performing the work as

* Daniel A. Wren, *The Evolution of Management Thought*, P.92

detailed in the instructions provided. The manager was given new functions in the form of principles, as follows:—

1. Following scientific methods in place of rule-of-thumb methods.
2. Scientific selection, placement and training of workers.
3. Cooperation of management and workers for harmony.
4. Maximum output by the application of scientific method.
5. Development of each worker to achieve maximum efficiency and prosperity.
6. Equitable division of work and responsibility between management and labour.
7. Complete mental revolution both on the part of workers and management.

Although Taylor's principles of scientific management were intended for broad application the actual emphasis was with the management at the shop level.[7]

No doubt, Taylor was a major contributor to scientific management, but by no means was be alone. Gantt devised a wage payment system, which stimulated foremen and workers to strive for improvement in work practices. Frank Gilbreth, alongwith his wife Lillian Gilbreth refined the techniques of time and motion study. In this way, they stressed the importance of giving attention minute details of work.

Universal Principle of Management

The approach of Taylor, Gilbreth, Gantt etc., has not been free from criticism. One of the criticisms is that the workers are not given proper recognition as human beings. It is pointed out that improvements only in the methods of doing the work will be of little avail unless the organisation itself is built on sound, rational principles. So the emphasis is not on the tasks to be performed by the organisation but on the structure of the organisation. One of the earliest important contribution came from Henry Fayol who pointed out that the principles of management and organisation are universal, regardless of whether the organisation is run for profit or for social purposes.

Henry Fayol (1841–1925) who was a mining engineer and became the Managing Director of a coal mining company in France. During his successful career he searched for sound management principles. In 1916, he published his famous work—*Administration Industrielle etc. generale*—"General and Industrial Management". Fayol divided all activities of industrial undertaking into six groups, namely:

1. Technical (production, manufacture, adaptation).
2. Commercial (buying, selling and exchange).
3. Financial (search for, and optimum use of, capital).
4. Security (protection of property and persons).
5. Accounting (stocktaking, balance sheet, costs, statistics).

---

* A detailed study of Taylor's *Scientific Management* is made in a later chapter in this book.

6. Managerial (planning, organisation, command, coordination and control).

Fayol devoted most of his discussion to an analysis of managerial activities. He recognised that for every activity there exists a corresponding ability. It may be technical, commercial or financial ability. According to him technical ability is required for most of the workers, and managerial ability is demanded mostly from higher managers. The higher the position on the scalar chain the lower the technical ability and higher the managerial ability is required.

Fayol's General Principles of Management

Fayol's principles of management are as follows:

1. *Division of Work.* This is the principle of specialisation so necessary for efficiency in all spheres of activity, technical as well as managerial.

2. *Authority and Responsibility.* These two are inter-related.

3. *Discipline.* It is respect for agreements which are directed at achieving obedience, application, energy, and outward marks of respect. Discipline requires good superiors at all levels. clear and fair agreements, and judicious application of penalties.

4. *Unity of Command* An employee should receive orders from one superior only.

5. *Unity of Direction.* Each group of activities having the same objective must have one head and one plan.

6. *Subordination of Individual Interest to General Interest.* In any group the interest of the group should supersede that of the individual. When these are found to differ, it is the duty of management to reconcile them.

7. *Remuneration.* Remuneration and methods of payment should be fair and afford the maximum satisfaction to employees and employers.

8. *Centralisation.* Individual circumstances should determine the degree of centralisation which will give the best overall yield.

9. *Scalar Chain or Line of Authority.* It is a chain of superiors from the highest to the lowest ranks. A subordinate should ordinarily follow the line of authority.

10. *Order.* This is essentially a principle of organisation in the arrangement of things.

11. *Equity.* This elicits loyalty and devotion from personnel by a combination of kindliness and justice on the part of managers when dealing with subordinates.

12. *Stability of Tenure of Personnel.* Unnecessary labour turnover should be avoided, for instability is both the cause and effect of bad management.

13. *Initiative.* Permit subordinates to exercise initiative.

14. *Esprit de corps.* This principle enunciates the well-known rule that "union is strength". The emphasis is on the need for team work and

the importance of communication in obtaining it.

Fayol regarded elements of management as its functions. He divided the functions into five categories—planning, organising, commanding, coordinating and controlling. He laid considerable emphasis on planning, (the French word for which is *prevoyance*—looking ahead), and said "to foresee ... means both to assess the future and make provision for it". According to him planning is at one and the same time, "the result envisaged, the line of action to be followed, the stages to go through, and methods to use."

The Human Relations Movement

As a reaction to Taylor and his followers' mechanical and physiological character of management, a movement grew in 1930's laying stress on human relations, largely under the leadership of Elton Mayo and F. J. Roethlishberger, whose work in the famous Hawthorne studies has been a major influence on management thought. The Hawthorne studies found that a business organisation does not consist of hands employed to perform certain tasks for which they are paid, but it goes much beyond that and takes cognisance of his feelings and emotions. Mayo pointed out that every organisation is essentially a social system which aims at not only the fulfilment of the economic functions but also the satisfaction of human needs. Since man is essentially at the centre of the organisation, his needs, aspirations, motivations, deserve far more attention than has been given so far. As a result of this new understanding, industrial relations programmes have been developed to deal with human relations problems. The slogans are "good human relations is plain good business" or "high morale leads to high profits" or, as Lawrence Appley asserts, "management is personnel management", or still further, management is the development of people and not the direction of things."

Application of Behavioural Sciences to Management

An early contributor to the psychology and sociology of management, Mary Parker Follett, attempted to interpret classical management principles in terms of human factors. According to her *a human group has a life as a group and is something more than the sum of so many individuals comprising it.* She proposed four principles as guides to management:

1. Coordination by direct contact of the responsible people concerned.
2. Coordination in the early stages.
3. Coordination as the reciprocal relating to all the factors in the situation.
4. Coordination as a continuing process.

The Central idea behind these principles was that management must continually adjust to the total situation. Follet observed that conflict is usually present in management situations and offered a process for resolving it. The manager must handle conflict by (1) domination,

(2) compromise, or (3) integration. The first two never satisfy every one but integration can achieve a new approach to the problem that will satisfy all parties. In order to achieve integration (i) the differences must be brought into the open; (ii) a re-evaluation must be made by all parties; (iii) all parties must anticipate the responses of the others and seek a new position that suits not only the parties but the relationship among the parties. In other words, each party should avoid the limitations of his own position and seek a new, integrated position acceptable to all. In this way, neither party scores a victory over the other; there is no compromise either.

The behavioural approach to management has been developed from the human relations approach which draws upon psychology, sociology, and cultural anthropology. Kurt Lewin developed theory and research under the heading of "group dynamics". Lewin and his associates generally concluded that "democratic" groups, in which there was active participation in decisions were more productive both of human satisfaction and of achievement of the group objective.

Among the professional management people Col. Lyndall Urwick stands out for his contribution to the science of management. Among the businessmen who have made substantial contribution to the theory of management are names of Henry Dennison, Mooney and Riley, Chester Barnard and Alvin Brown. Dennison developed concepts of motivation, leadership and team work. Mooney and Riley combined organisational principles into a logical pattern of principle, process and effect. Starting with the principle of coordination, they moved into the concept of Scalar organisation and functionalism, arriving by trials at a total nine principles of organisation. Barnard published his "Functions of the Executive" in 1938 which has had an important influence on the human relations movement. He placed considerable stress on informal organisation. He also emphasised the complexity of human motivation with strong views on the limitations of financial incentives.

Brown's *Organisation of Industry,* published in 1947, is an analysis the delegation of authority with an attempt to frame a theory of organisation and a division of the managerial functions into the phases of management of planning, doing and seeing.

Summing Up

To sum up, it may be noted that management has been defined by different writers according to the school of thought to which they belong. One school regards management as a process and is concerned with getting things done through others. The human relations school lays stress on the human element and the human relations aspect. The third school leans on sociological factors and considers organisation as a segment of society rather than hierarchical system. The fourth school attaches a great deal of importance to empirical experience, from which generalisations could be drawn. The fifth school looks at management as essentially a decision-making process. The sixth school believes that management problems can be converted into mathematical models which can be employed for problem solving, and that techniques play a great part ~~in~~ achieving managerial objectives. All these streams of thought have relevance to the study of management; and the modern manager must integrate and achieve his own balance in his own situation.

CHAPTER XIX

FUNCTIONS OF MANAGEMENT

Managerial Functions

As explained in the previous chapter, management is the process of getting things done through other people. The person who gets things done through other people is a 'manager', although he may be called a director, executive, supervisor, superintendent, or foreman. Now, the, question arises : How does the manager do that ? A useful way to answer this question is by looking at management functions. These functions are simply parts of a manager's job.

According to Fayol, functions of management include planning, organising, commanding, coordinating and controlling. Luther Gulick* coined the word POSDCORB from the initial letters of management functions: planning, organising, staffing, directing, coordinating, reporting, and budgeting. With some modifications we shall use this breakdown, and present managerial functions as :

Planning, Organising, Staffing, Directing, and Controlling, each one including its subsidiary functions. Co-ordination and decision-making take place in all the managerial functions. They will not, therefore, be discussed as subsidiaries of any function. Since they are important in the performance of all the managerial functions, they are dealt with as separate topics. Innovation or creating is also all pervasive and will be discussed separately.

Planning. Planning is deciding in advance what is to be done; how, when and where it is to be done; who is to do it and how results are to be evaluated. It consists of formulating the enterprise objectives, policies, programmes, procedures and other methods of attaining these objectives. Planning is thus looking ahead and preparing for the future.

Organising. Organising means the creation of a structure of functions and duties to be performed by a group of people for the attainment of the objectives and goals of the enterprise. The 'mechanics' of this is to identify activities and then group activities are assigned to groups, departments, and so on. Furthermore, necessary authority will be defined and delegated and the authority responsibility relationships will be established.

Staffing. By staffing we understand management's responsibility to recruit and make certain that there is enough executive personnel available to fill the various positions needed in the organisation. Staffing involves the selection and training of future managers. It also concerns

---

* Quoted by Ernest Dale in *Management*, P.5

promotions, appraisals, progressions, rotation and a wise system of compensation.

Directing. In this function of directing, the manager will guide, teach, coach and supervise subordinates, issuing directions for the accomplishment of objectives. It includes decision-making, guiding, issuing orders and instructions, supervising, communicating and motivating.

Controlling. The control function involves those activities which are essential in seeing to it that events proceed as planned. Controlling is thus laying down performance standards, measurement, interpretation and corrective action. Control consists in verifying whether everything occurs in conformity with the plan adopted, the instructions issued and principles established.

Universality of Management Functions

Managerial functions are performed in all types of organisation and at all levels of management in the organisation. This means that regardless of his level in the managerial hierarchy, the manager concerns himself with all the five functions. As stated earlier, the term "manager" includes all managers from the Chief Executive down to the first line supervisor. But the Chief Executive will obviously spend more time in planning and organising and less time in staffing, directing and controlling, whereas the superintendent on the floor probably will devote less time in planning and organising and more of his time will be spent in directing and controlling. Therefore, time and effort spent on different functions will be determined by the executives level in the managerial hierarchy. But the same five functions will be performed by every manager, regardless of his position in the organisation.

The sequence of a manager's functions will ordinarily be planning organising, staff, directing and controlling. However, because he is involved with projects in various stages of completion he performs all five functions simultaneously in a typical day. Again managerial functions have the quality of being interative. That is, they are contained within each other. For example, all the other functions occur within planning, in performing the organising function, planning and other functions would be involved and so on. Therefore, it is helpful to think of the managerial functions as a circular continuous movement. They flow into each other, as may be seen in the diagram on p. 340, and at times there is no clear line of demarcation when the one ends and the other one begins. It should also be remembered that although the "mix" of the functions will vary from task to task, they are all important and necessary in the accomplishment of any organisational goal.

DECISION MAKING

The life of manager is a perpetual decision-making activity. Executives at all levels have to make decisions everyday. Whatever a manager does, he does through decision-making. It is with the decisions and the power to make decisions that the manager rises or falls; and the outstanding executive is that who has the capacity to perceive a course and take it.

To come to a decision means to "cut off" or conclude deliberations and to come to a conclusion. Maissie * defines a decision as "a course of action consciously chosen from available alternatives for the purpose of achieving a desired result".

Basic Phases in Decision-Making

A decision involves both question of fact and of value. Questions of fact relate to "what is" and questions of value relate to "what ought to be". In short, a person makes decision based on his thinking of what ought to be. It is because:

1. The man does not have full knowledge of alternatives nor does he have full knowledge of the consequences of each alternative;
2. The future is uncertain and one has to necessarily imagine it. In doing so he is mostly affected by his value system, i.e., how he looks at things.
3. A decision maker just takes up a course of action which satisfies and meets his requirements.

Making decisions can either be time-wasting or it can be the manager's best means of solving the problem of time utilisation. To arrive at the best possible decision within a reasonable period of time, the manager should observe the following steps and follow them in the proper sequence.

1. *Diagnosing the problem and defining it.* Sound diagnosis is the crucial first phase of decision making. Proceed just like a doctor who must find out what the trouble is before he can prescribe the treatment. Defining or identifying the problem is no doubt time consuming, but it is time well spent. In definining the problem the manager should find the "critical strategic factor". This is the element in the situation that has to be changed before anything else can be changed, moved, acted upon.

There are three basic elements of sound diagnosis

(a) Identify the gap between the results desired and the existing or predicted state of affairs:

(b) Find out the direct root cause of the gap between the actual situation and the desired situation; and

(c) Analyse the overall situation and see whether it places any limits within which a satisfactory solution may be found out.

One of the ways to do the above is to identify the obstacles that must be overcome to reach the desired results. It is important to know what stands in the way of getting from where we are to where we would like to be.

2. *Analysing the problem.* After defining the problem, the manager

* Joseph L.Maissie, *Essentials of Management*, P. 52

can then set about analysing it: classifying it and finding facts. Drucker prescribes * principles of classification as follows:

(a) the futurity of the decision, i.e., to what length of time does the decision commit the business to a course of action, and at what speed the decision can be reversed;
(b) the impact of the decision on other areas and functions;
(c) the number of qualitative considerations which enter into it; and
(d) the uniqueness or periodicity of the decision.

This classification will enable the manager to take a comprehensive view of the business as a whole.

3. *Developing alternative solutions.* Once a problem has been well stated, the decision maker must find possible solutions. It is necessary to develop several alternative solutions for every problem. Otherwise there is the danger of falling into the trap of the false "either-or". Alternative solutions are the only means of bringing over basic assumptions upto the conscious level, forcing ourselves to examine several of them and testing their validity. Often good alternatives are quickly identified. Past experience, practice of competitors or other firms, suggestions by equipment manufacturers, employees, or customers, are normal and highly useful sources of ideas. But helpful as these ideas are, the manager who relies entirely on such sources is heading for trouble. He must be creative and adapt those proposals to the local situation. To be creative, he must search for new ideas, give up old ways of thought, and think differently and independently of other people. It is important to remember that the alternatives will vary with the problem, and at times taking no action may be the best solution of the problem.

4. *Projecting consequences of various alternatives.* After the several alternative solutions have been indentified, the decision maker must forecast the consequences of the following each alternative. This phase involves * :

(a) picking the crucial factors on which to concentrate attention in making projections;
(b) actually forecasting a set of consequences of each alternative; and
(c) since some uncertainty will inevitably exist, attaching subjective probabilities that the predicted consequences will occur.

From the practical point of view, the decision maker cannot attempt to forecast everything that bears on the desirability of each alternative. Also some alternatives may have effects which are not related to the stated objective. Then, too many factors can quickly push the analysis beyond human comprehension. Consequently, one must pick key factors and crucial aspects and concentrate on those. In making the actual forecast, we must think of both the operating conditions over which we

* The Practice of Management, P.357

* Newman, *Administrative Action,* P. 112.

have little or no influence, and the probable results of action we can initiate.

5. *Finding the best solution and making the choice.* The manager is now ready to try to determine the best solution or the optimum course of action. There are four criteria for picking the best from among the possible solutions:

(a) He must weigh the risks of each course of action against the expected gains.

(b) He should then determine which of the possible lines of action will give the greatest results with the least effort. Also find out which of the actions will cause least disturbance of the organisation.

(c) Timing of the decision is also important. If the situation is of great urgency, the better course of action which acts as a notice to the organisation that something important is happening. If, on the other hand, long consistent effort is needed, a slow start that gathers momentum may be preferable.

(d) Limitation of resources has great impact on decision making. The most important resource whose limitations have to be considered are the human beings who will carry out the decision. Their vision, competence, skill and understanding determine what they can and cannot do. No wrong decision should be made because there are no people to do the job. You may have to raise the ability and standard of the people or find new people who can do the job. No decision is worth the name which works on paper but fails in practice.

6. *Making the decision effective.* The final step is to make the solution effective in action. This means that the decision must be accepted by the organisation. The entire decision-making process is directed towards action. If others are affected the decision must be communicated to them. They must be motivated to implement the decision.

The following Flow Chart illustrates the decision process:

COORDINATION

Coordination is the essence of management or managership, for the achievement of harmony of individual effort towards the accomplishment of group goals is the purpose of management. It is a process by which the manager achieves harmonious group effort and unity of action in the pursuit of a common purpose. The manager brings about this process as he performs the basic managerial functions of planning, organising, staffing, directing and controlling. "In administration", says Newman,[1] "coordination deals with synchronizing and unifying the actions of a group of people. A coordinated operation is one in which the activities of the employees are harmonious, dovetailed, and integrated towards a common objective." McFarland defines co-ordination as "the

1. Ibid, P. 403

process whereby an executive develops an orderly pattern of group effort among his subordinates and secures unit of action in the pursuit of a common purpose."

Need for Coordination. Modern organisations depend upon specialisation of functions and activities delegated to different participating individuals. If each individual is allowed to perform his own function efficiently without taking note of the connected function performed by another individual, there will result a chaos in the organisation. It is essential that there be complete coordination, so that unity of action on the part of all is achieved. Also, conflict between the line executives and the staff poses the problem of coordination by the chief executive. Hence, the chief executive has to coordinate not only functions and activities but also individuals performing different functions. For example, to ensure harmonious functioning of the organisation, it is essential that the functions of purchasing, designing, production and sales departments are co-ordinated. If the sales manager procures a huge order to be executed within a specified period of time without reference to the production manager or the buyer, it may turn out that the goods cannot be produced in quantities ordered within the specified time. Or, even if they can be produced, the suitable raw material may not be available. Therefore, the inter-relationship between the purchasing department and production department as well as the sales department demands the establishment of coordination.

Principles of Coordination. Mary Parker Follet has enunciated the following fundamental principles of coordination.

1. *Direct contact.* Coordination can be achieved by direct contact among the individuals concerned. Direct personal communications bring about agreement on methods, actions and ultimate achievement. It also eliminates red-tapism and ensures prompt action.

2. *Early beginning.* Coordination can be achieved more readily in the early stages of planning and policy making. Therefore direct contact must begin in the very early stages of the process. If an order for the supply of a particular variety of the goods has been booked and the raw materials to produce them are not available, there will be trouble. Contact among the three functional managers at an earlier stage would have made it possible to know whether the order could be executed.

3. *Reciprocity.* All factors in a situation are reciprocally related and should be coordinated. For example, when A works with B and B in turn works with C and D, each of the four finds himself influenced by the others, influenced by all the persons in the total situation.

4. *Continuity.* Coordination is a continuing process, something which must go on all the time. It cannot be left to chance, but the manager must constantly work at it.

Attaining Coordination. Coordination is not easy to attain. No order to coordinate can achieve coordination. Each functional interest in the enterprise stresses its own opinion of how the purposes should be accomplished. Each of them tends to stress one or another different policy or method depending upon the experience of the department. Similar problem arises between functional managers at the same levels. The chief executive or the manager must secure harmonious action between different elements. He must synchronize the efforts of all the members of a group and see to it that there is willing cooperation of both managers and workers. An organisation is people. He must lead them by goals which they accept as justifiable, worthy, and fair to all concerned. This means *human relations,* and good human relations "pay off" through cooperative coordination. Good human relations, in turn, depend upon *understanding* of the goals of the organisation. In order that there be understanding among people, there must be effective means of *communication* among them.

The method of achieving coordination is largely horizontal, although vertical coordination in a large organisation cannot be ignored. *Vertical coordination* takes place between the various links of the different levels of the organisational unit. For example, take the case of production department, where we have the works manager, and under him the superintendent and then the foreman and last the workmen. In this situation, levels of authority are super-imposed upon each other, and the activities assigned to the several levels must be coordinated. This vertical coordination is secured by delegated authority, together with the means and manner of directing, supervising and controlling.

Horizontal coordination refers to coordination between horizontal departments on the same level in the managerial hierarchy. For example, coordination is necessary between the sales manager, the works manager, the finance manager and the buyer, so that when the sales department is ready to sell the new product, the production department will be in a position to fill the orders, and the financial arrangements have been made so that the necessary funds are available to have the suitable raw materials, etc. Coordination of various functions between independent managers calls for a greater understanding between the departmental managers so that they may cooperate. People cooperate as a result of understanding one another's tasks. Communication brings about good understanding. This may be illustrated as follows : *Communication—Understanding—Good human relations—Cooperation—Coordination.*

Techniques of Coordination. Newman [1] has suggested the following techniques or measures as tools for securing better coordination :—

1. Simplified organisation.
2. Harmonized programmes and policies.
3. Well-designed methods of communication.
4. Aids to voluntary coordination.
5. Coordination through personal guidance.

Simplified Organisation. In a large organisation, special functions are allotted to different heads of departments, each of whom is

1. Ibid, P. 404-415

concerned with only one phase of the total operation, and even bureaucratic in attitude. As for producing goods or rendering services each of these specialised units must contribute their share of the total operation, the need for co-ordination becomes imminent. Where coordination is lacking, re-arrangement of departments may be made in order to bring together activities which have been out of step. Furthermore, clear-cut organisation and procedures that are well-known to all persons concerned will ensure coordination. Since a business organisation is a network of formal and informal relations among people holding designated positions, horizontal and vertical coordination is called for. Coordination is greatly facilitated if the lines of authority and responsibility are clearly drawn. This is done by grouping various functions into homogeneous and non-overlapping units. The heads of these functional units will then know the exact limits of their authority and this will minimise the need for coordination. To ensure coordination, organisation should be kept as simple as possible.

Harmonised Programmes and Policies. The ideal time to bring about coordination is at the planning stage. The different plans can be re-examined and checked one against the other to ensure that they all fit together into an integrated, balanced whole. The coordinating executive should check plans developed by different individuals to bring about consistency, and to see that all the plans add up to a unified programme. Selection of one in preference to other or a compromise between all may have to be resorted to for effective coordination. Moreover, coordinated activities must not only be consistent with each other, but also be performed at the proper time. For example, one process must not hold back the next process in manufacturing processes. In an assembly line in an automobile plant, timing is one of the cardinal features. The various parts must arrive at the assembly line at just the right moment. Also, the speed of the assembly line itself and the assignment of work must be adjusted so that one group of employees is not idle for lack of something to do while others are finding it difficult to finish one job before the next job rolls along. Therefore, timing is vital in all operations.

Well-designed Methods of Communication. Good communication brings about coordination and helps members of a business organisation to work together. It helps to hold the organisation together by making it possible for members to influence one another and to react to one another. Flow of communication in all directions will facilitate coordination and smooth working of the enterprise. The use of formal tools like orders, reports and working papers and of informal devices like the *grapevine* will provide adequate information to all concerned. Continuous, clear and meaningful communication provides to every member a clear understanding of the nature and scope of his work as well as that of other persons whose responsibilities are related to him. This aids the executives in coordinating the efforts of the members of their teams.

The two tools of communication for bringing about coordination are : (i) *Committees,* and (ii) *Group Discussions.*

According to Ernest Dale, two types of committees can be helpful to coordination—the Executive Committee and Special Committees. The Executive Committee consists of top executives, permanently built into the organisation structure. This committee, according to Dale, (i) facilitates consultative supervision which contributes to uniformity of direction, (ii) makes possible coordination of long-term and short-term plans, (iii) offers a degree of flexibility in handling emergency situation, and (iv) provides greater opportunities for broader experience to executives thereby making possible a greater interchange of management personnel. Special Committees are set up with narrow and specific jurisdictions and help the executives in the task of coordination.

Group Discussion is the other tool for coordination. It provides opportunities for free and open exchange of views and interchange of ideas, problems, proposals and solutions. Face-to-face communication enables members to attain improved understanding of company-wide matters and leads to better coordination and unified achievement.

Aids to Voluntary Coordination. Ideally, coordination should take place through voluntary cooperation of the members of an enterprise. Each member should be ready and willing to adapt his work to secure unified action. In other words there is complete cooperation among all the members. According to Newman, voluntary coordination can be secured by (i) instilling dominant objectives among the members of the group, (ii) developing generally accepted customs and terms making it easy for people to work with one another, (iii) encouraging informal contacts to supplement formal communication, (iv) providing liaison officers to maintain close contact with various departments, or to work between the headquarters office and branches, and (v) using committees for direct personal contact and informal exchange of ideas and views.

Coordination Through Personal Guidance. The supervising executives have a dominant role to play in bringing about coordination of the tasks of their subordinates. They may do this by prodding, in some cases, restraining in others, providing supplementary help in another quarter, or arbitrating sincere difference of opinion among their subordinates. All this will ensure balance and unity in the total results. In the event of the work-load assigned to an executive being found too heavy to enable him to perform these coordinating duties effectively, he may rely upon one or more *staff* assistants.

INNOVATION AND CREATIVITY

An organisation needs new ideas to keep it healthy. John D. Rockefeller once said : "If you want to succeed you should strike new paths rather than travel the worn paths of accepted success". Managers must both be creative themselves and stimulate others to be creative. By increasing the flow of creative ideas, management can help ensure that the firm will survive and prosper. This sums up to the caption: "For lasting success, promote innovation."

To innovate successfully is a Fundamental requirement of both society and business if they are to remain dynamic. Innovation, in normal terms, is the introduction of something new—a new philosophy, idea, policy, or procedure. The first step in innovation, obviously, is the creation of a new idea, often in a flash of inspiration. The story of James Watt and his mother's tea kettle illustrates the way in which inspiration may come. Thousands of people had watched steam lift the lid of a Kettle, but it occurred to James Watt, seemingly in a flash, that there was a force that could be to useful work. Innovation promotion is a driving force on the whole managing process.

In the absence of prodding, many people tend to become satisfied with things as they are. They are content to settle into a comfortable rut and to go on doing things in the same old way, and the conditions within the company become static. But the conditions in the outside world go on changing. Therefore, if the company does not adjust itself to change it will soon become out of tune with the times. Its products will become obsolete, its methods will be slow and costly, its marketing approach will be outmoded, and so on. So it must keep up-to-date or die. This that a company should constantly respond to changes if it wants to keep going for a long time. A manager who wants his company to forge ahead must take the initiative and forcefully encourage innovation. He must never be satisfied with things as they are. He must constantly encourage people whom he directs to seek new products, better production methods, creative marketing approaches, sounder financial control, better personnel relations and better managing techniques.

Creating can be stimulated in the following ways: One important way is to have an atmosphere that encourages creativity. This means that management should always be ready to listen to new ideas from anyone in the firm. To encourage creative thought, a period of time should be set aside for people to be creative. If this cannot be done, then encourage people to plan their work to allow for some creative thought. One encouragement to creativity is a suggestion system. Suggestion boxes can for instances, be placed in each department. Cash award and a special citation should be given when a suggestion is accepted.

CHART SHOWING FUNCTIONS OF MANAGEMENT

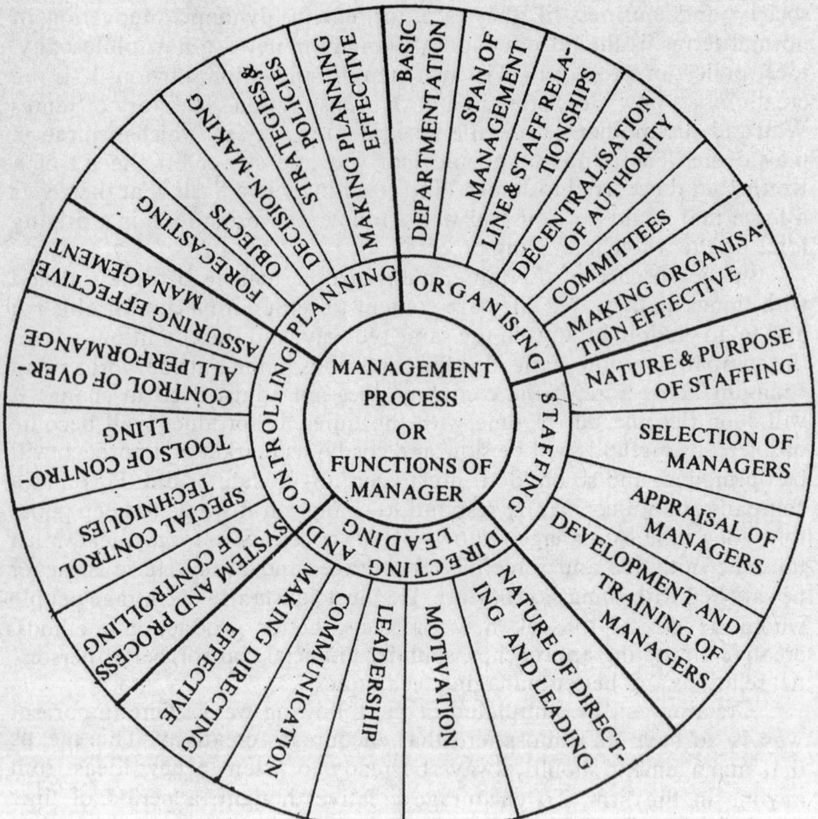

CHAPTER XX

PLANNING

Meaning of Planning

Speaking generally, planning is deciding in advance what is to be done; it is a projected course of action. To plan is to propose a forward programme for guiding the future affairs of an enterprise. Planning is the opposite of *improvising*. "It is organised foresight plus corrective hind sight." The planning process starts with the assumption that the future will be different from the present, and it attempts to determine how the enterprise can take advantage of that difference. Planning thus becomes a device for change to meet the future. If planning is ignored, there will be random behaviour and goal achievement will be almost impossible. As it is well said: "If you don't know where you are going no road will get you there". It is clear that individual activity and organisational activity without a plan will be ineffective.

Process of Planning

Planning is the essence of management. Conceived as a process, planning embraces a series of steps : (i) analysing factors affecting the future; (ii) forecasting the future environment; (iii) the determination of the objectives to be sought, and overall goals; (iv) policy-making and establishing programmes and procedures (v) decision-making and choosing between alternatives; (vi) preparing and installing plans. These and other elements are considered in the following paragraphs :

1. *Analysing factors affecting the future :* A plan provides a spring board from the present. The planner should start looking into the conditions which affect the company's future opportunity. These conditions are (1) the environment, (2) internal conditions, and (3) obligations of the enterprise.

The environment. The business organisation exists in three kinds of environment : first, in the total economy; second, in a particular industry; and third, in a specific geographic area.

If the enterprise is in a position to make its own independent appraisal of the total economy, it will want to consider a broad range of business indicators. The more important barometers are industrial production, wholesale prices, retail prices, employment and unemployment, personal incomes, sales and inventories, merchandise exports and imports, availability of credit, raw material prices, new incorporations, business failures, gross national product, corporate profits, central budget. In addition, further developments in the total economy, such as transport and communication developments.

Competition is also major part of the enterprise's environment. It is important to know as much about competition as possible. The business must also consider its direct and (in the case of capital goods industries) its indirect customers. The frailties of consumer acceptance impose constant challenge. The consumer is not concerned with the manufacturer's financial condition; he wants a product or service which fulfills his needs. The company must be willing and able to change the course of its business to meet customer demands and to find improved ways of service through better products, increased quality, and greater value.

2. *Forecasting.* Business forecasting is the calculation of probable events, to provide against the future. Thus, it is an estimate of a future condition. No one can really know what the future will bring. The only certain thing about the future is its uncertainty. It is possible, however, to visualise the future of events, on the basis of the study that has been made with respect to environment. The forecast could include a variety of elements, such as :

(a) estimates of general conditions in the total economy;
(b) estimates of specific conditions in the total economy, which affect the company's business;
(c) estimates of total demand for the products sold by the company;
(d) estimates of markets for the company's current and/or prospective product line;
(e) estimates of sales possibilities;
(f) estimates of activities at peak, normal and below-normal conditions and for short and long-range periods.

Methods of forecasting—direct and indirect : In direct method one can arrive at the requirements of the firm by summing up the estimates submitted by its different components or subordinate units. In the case of indirect method, first of all, requirements of the entire trade or industry are estimated and then the share of the particular unit is ascertained.

Empirical or Scientific forecasting. Empirical forecasting attempts to view the future in terms of the past. Previous experience properly organised and interpreted in terms of causal relationship is the basis of scientific forecasting.

3. *Establishing conditions and assumptions.* After the estimates based on forecasting have been made, logical development of assumptions from these known facts is the next step. The manager has to put together lists of information and fill in the gaps. Through necessary assumptions, he will picture the future.

4. *Establishing Objectives.* A plan is sometimes described as a statement of objectives to be attained in the future and an outline of the steps necessary to reach them. If plans have to ensure that objectives have to be achieved, they must be set. Objectives have to be established to give a sense of direction in which efforts are to be made. A goal is the end result towards which all management activities are directed. They constitute the purpose of the enterprise. But no one can accomplish an ambiguous goal. People must know what their goals are, what actions contribute to the attainment of those goals. Someone has said : "If you

don't know where you are going, no road will get you there". Hence. setting of objectives is necessary for each manager.

As the whole organisation must set goals and objectives, so must each department section or division. As a matter of fact, one of the recognised methods of managing business these days is managing by objectives or by results.

Hierarchy of Objectives. There is a hierarchy of objectives in an organisation. The structure of planning starts at the highest level. At the top, the entire organisation aims in a given direction. Each department, in turn, directs its efforts towards its own sets of goals. Each subdivision of each department has its own objectives. Each of the sub-goals should be consistent with and contribute towards, the goals of the next higher level in the hierarchy. Thus, the hierarchy can be built up by coordinating plans of different departments and with the overall company-wise programme. Any conflict between different departments should be reconciled.

Multiplicity of Objectives. In a business organisation the overall objective is to make the highest profit possible. But planning for profit will require planning for subsidiary goals as well. Such goals may include such things as company growth, diversification into entirely new types of business, development of new products, penetration in a new market, getting a larger share of the market that already exists for the products, or vertical integration for self-sufficiency. Companies may also have social objects : to pay good wages, to make their plants and offices good places to work in, to provide useful products at reasonable prices. Thus, even broad major objectives are normally multiple. A business might include among its overall objectives a certain rate of profit and return on investment, consumer satisfaction and rendering service to the community.

Management By Objectives. We have seen above that at each level of company's objectives, one level complements the next. The goals or ends of one level are the means of achieving other goals at the next higher level. It is important, therefore, to focus the attention of individual members of the organisation on the objectives that are meaningful to them. A useful approach, as suggested by Peter Drucker, is "*management by objectives,* in which objectives are supplied to every area where performance and results directly and vitally affect the survival and prosperity of business."

Management by objectives involves mutual goal-setting by managers at different levels right to the level of the worker. In this way, each person has a definite and measurable goal and each person then contributes towards company wide objectives. This requires each manager to develop and set the objectives of his unit himself. Higher management, of course, reserves the power to approve or disapprove these objectives. The overall objectives of a company generally are established by top management; yet, it is desirable for each subordinate manager to participate in the development of these objectives. This will not only give him a sense of participation, but he will clearly understand the relationship between his own objectives and the broader objectives of the company. He will accept such objectives as correct and strive in a joint effort for the attainment of the company's objectives. This generates the great advantage of management by objectives in that the manager can control his own performance. "Self-control means stronger motivation : a desire to do the best rather than just enough to get by".

Plans for Goal Achievement.

Once goals are set, other plans are made to carry them out. These plans can be divided into two groups : Standing plans and single-use plans.

Standing Plans are used more than once. They help solve repetitive problems. The most common forms of standing plans are policies, procedures, programmes and rules.

Policies. Policy-making is important in the process of planning. Policies are general statements that serve as guides for the actions of managers. They are indeed guidelines for actions which help subordinates to carry on their work in harmony with the overall goals of the business. Policies communicate top managements thinking to company employees and to suppliers, customers and the public. Policies set limits on activities, but do not tell someone exactly what to do. This gives the individual some "manoeuvering room" in making a decision.

The responsibility of determining policy rests with those who direct a business. The overall policies are made by top management and departmental managers may make policies for their respective department. Whether overall or departmental policies must come from above, they cannot well up from beneath. Policy making cannot be delegated to subordinates.

Procedures. Unlike policies, procedures state exactly what to do They reduce the judgment a person may use in problem solving; he must follow the procedure as laid down. Procedurers are useful where high degree of regularity is desired in frequently recurring event. When, for example, a department manager requisitions office supplies, he will have to follow a required procedure. An important advantage of establishing procedures is that a good procedure makes sure that the work will be done and can be done by a person who is not as skilled as the individuals laying down the procedure.

Rules. Rules are specific instructions in regard to what may or may not be done. "No smoking in the plant", "safety shoes must be worn in the plant" are examples of rules. Penalty may be provided for failure to observe the rule.

Programmes. A programme is a definite plan of work made in proper sequence and in conformity with the objectives, on the basis of policies and procedures laid down. Within the scope of policies, programmes aim at completion of the activities within a specific period

For example, a programme of modernisation of facilities might cover a year. Another example of a programme may be an automatic replacement of type-writers after they reach a certain age. Similarly, training programme, and management development programme are other examples.

Single-Use Plans. Some plans are used only once. They are needed for non-repetitive situations. Thus, single-use or single purpose plans are designed to accomplish specific objectives, usually within a relatively short period of time. Budgets, programmes and projects are examples of single-use plans. The overall budget might include sales budget, advertising budget, production budget, Raw Materials budget, personnel budget, equipment purchasing and maintenance budget, cost budget. cash flow budget and profit budget. All these budgets must be coordinated.

Plan standards and methods of measuring accomplishment. The executive deals with money, men, materials, machines, methods and time all at once. He must measure the hierarchy of objectives and possible action to be taken to reach them. Budgets help in numerical terms the requirements of the above resources. The quantification can be made as so many units of money to be spent on a programme or so many units of materials, so many man-hours or machine-hours to be utilised for the purpose.

Review and adjust plan in light of changing condition. Conditions are changing all the time. In some instances the rate of change is extremely rapid. Either there may not be time to plan, or the plan may become obsolete. It is a good idea to review policies and procedures periodically.

Who does the planning. Every manager plans, whether he belongs to the top or lower management group. By definition every executive in charge of his department is manager and every one of them plans. The importance and magnitude of the plan will depend upon the level on which it is performed. Planning at the top level of the managerial hierarchy is fundamental, broad, far reaching and basic. The various subordinate managers plan within their own particular area of authority. The scope, extent and importance of the nature of planning tend to decrease as we descend towards the lower levels of management and approach the point of execution of the plan. Hence all managers plan regardless of their rank in the managerial hierarchy.

Elements of Planning.

The following ten elements are included in some degree or other in any comprehensive planning activity.

1. *Organisation Planning* determines what functions an organisation requires, relates these functions in a systematic fashion, assigns responsibilities to individual positions, and installs and periodically reviews organisation plans.

2. *Product Planning* Coordinates the efforts of all departments in

maintaining and developing the most profitable product line. Product planning includes the addition of new products, addition of new product lines, and elimination of existing products.

3. *Facility Planning.* Facility planning is the determination of needed production facilities, their types, capacities, quantities and locations.

4. *Operations Planning* is concerned with production methods, standard practices, types and quantities of production equipment, and production capacities.

5. *Material Supply and Inventory Planning* is concerned with the type and quantity of stock to be acquired and placed in inventory and its systematic location, storage and control. Its purpose is to supply the desired quantity of product to the customer and to the various segments of the enterprise.

6. *Financial Planning* provides a central point for determining the organisations' future financial requirements and objectives, for developing plans and policies to fulfill those requirements and objectives and for developing controls to assure compliance with financial plans and goals. The financial plan outlines ways and means for meeting the companys' financial requirements within a prescribed course and within a specified time.

7. *Commercial Planning* is the estimation of future commercial conditions, the appraisal of these conditions and the preparation of plans to capitalise on them.

8. *Production Planning* deals with the effort for bringing together the necessary men, material, machinery and tools to create a product or service for offering in the market.

9. *Human Resource Planning* aims to see that the company is provided with the number and type of people it will need in the future. The human resource plan outlines ways and means of providing the entreprise with an adequate number of properly experienced and trained people when and as they are needed. It also provides a means for helping management achieve the maximum utilisation of human resources.

10. *Development Planning* investigates ways and means of securing opportunities for utilising the enterprise's total resources. The development plan outlines ways and means whereby the company's resources may be employed to the maximum advantage, taking into account all aspects of the company's capabilities and appraising the effect of possible changes in social, economic and political conditions.

In conclusion it may be re-iterated that planning is essential because it enables business enterprise to meet the contingencies of the future. But to be effective a plan must, as pointed out by Urwick, (i) be based on a clearly defined objective; (ii) be simple; (iii) provide for proper analysis and classification of actions, that is, which establishes standards; (iv) be flexible; (v) be balanced, and use available resources to the utmost before creating new authorities and new resources.

CHAPTER XXI

ORGANISATION

Ways of Looking at Organisations. Writers on organisation have looked at it from different points of view. Four groups can be distinguished. The oldest is the classical or traditional school, which has concentrated on stating how the formal organisation should be structured, and emphasising the application of principles in the process of organising. Writers in this school have stressed the need to classify authority and responsibilities. The human relations school has studied peoples' needs and reactions and sought to explain them. It has stressed the need to be aware of these reactions when designing the formal structure. It has shown how the formal organisation can affect peoples' behaviour, and also how people may develop their own informal organisation. The proponents of decision-making theory of organisation suggest that the structure be designed through an examination of the points at which decisions must be made and the persons from whom information must be required if decisions are to be satisfactory. The most recent way of looking at an organisation is as a system. The systems approach highlights the importance of the interactions between different parts of the organisation, and between it and its environment. Each group has made a contribution to understanding how organisations work. Each has its limitations. All can be helpful to the manager. We will, therefore, consider the view of these schools under different theories enunciated by them.

Theories of organisation.

The theories of, or approaches to, organisation may be classified as follows :

1. The classical or traditional theory.
2. The Human Relations or Neo-classical theory.
3. The decision-making theory.
4. The systems approach.

The Classical Theory.

The classical or traditional theory concentrates on the formal structure of organisation and leaves the human aspect of organisation to personnel specialists. The earliest writers on organisation, called the classical school, and their successors to the present day have discussed how to plan the formal organisation of work. They have been concerned with the best way of dividing up the tasks to be done, with how to group these tasks together into departments, and how to deal with the problems of coordination. They have paid particular attention to organisational relationships between line and staff. They have stressed the need for a clear definition of responsibilities and authority. They have sought to enunciate the principles, which should be used in designing this formal structure.

The chief contribution of the classical school is the definition and analysis of the tasks that have to be considered in building up an organisation. The emphasis is on structural frame work in which grouped activities are assigned to people. authority relations are established, individual efforts are properly coordinated and responsibilities fixed. The structure is built to help accomplish enterprise goals more effectively.

The theory has been criticised on many counts, especially by the behavioural scientists. The approach of the classical writers is too concerned with the formal structure, not sufficiently with the individuals who make the structure work. It is a static approach, paying too little attention to the many interactions that take place between different parts of an organisation. The principles of organisation are too broad to provide much help in the actual work of organising. Some of the principles are contradictory. Herbert A. Simon describes some of the principles as "no more than proverbs" and being simple generalisations devoid of predictive power. Since the classical theory ignores major facts of human nature, the newer theorists have developed some new approaches to the study of organisation.

The Human Relations Theory.

The human relations theory, also known as neo-classical theory, states that while designing an organisation structure, the people who are employed there and their behaviour should be taken into consideration. No manager can think solely of job descriptions, he has also to think of why people behave as they do and what influences their behaviour. The Hawthorne studies, and many subsequent ones, have shown that the way the people behave at work is affected by many other factors than monetary consideration. The organisation is composed of individuals with different needs that can be studied and of groups of people who develop their own ways of doing things and their own code of conduct. The proponents of the human relations school are research oriented. They try to find out what happens before seeking to explain it. This approach to the study of organisations has contributed much that can be of value to the manager : If he looks at a job only from the classical point of view, he will think of the tasks that have to be done. If he adopts the human relations approach, he will appreciate what it is like for the person who has to perform the tasks.

The human relations school has also its limitations. Some of its supporters have claimed too much for what can be achieved by thinking about peoples' needs and behaviour. Much bigger limitation is that although we have learnt a lot about people in organisations, there is still a great deal that we do not understand about human behaviour.

The Decision-Making Theory.

The next approach to organisation is known as the decision-making theory. Herbert A. Simon (who was awarded in the year 1978, the Nobel Prize mainly on the basis of this theory) regards organisation as a structure of decision makers. In an organisation, decisions are made at all levels, and important decisions tend to be made at higher levels. The decision making approach to organisation accepts the hierarchical form of organisation. Simon suggested that the organisation structure be designed through an examination of the points at which decisions must be made and the persons from whom information must be required if decisions are to be satisfactory.

The Systems Approach.

The systems approach looks at the organisation as a total system comprising a number of interacting variables. This approach emphasises that we should not deal with problems in isolation, but consider their interactions. In fact, the word system means a regularly interacting or interdependent group of items forming a "unified whole". Thus, the systems appraoch is concerned with the interaction between the different aspect of the organisation, people, technology, formal structure, the physical setting, and environment. The advantage of approaching any problem is that it enables us to see the critical variables and constraints and their interaction with one another. It keeps us alert and constantly aware that one single element, phenomenon, or problem should not be treated without regard to its interacting consequences with other elements. For example, the managerial functions of planning, organising, staffing, directing, leading and controlling are all interlocked, or contained within each other. All these functions can be conceived as sub-functions of each other.

It is also important to remember that the systems approach does not view organisation as a static arrangement of jobs but calls for identifying the functions required in terms of the decision areas involved in achieving goals. It calls for developing a pattern of inputs, outputs, feed backs, delays, and flows of materials and information. Frequent internal and external changes cause disturbances in the organisation. Consequently, for survival and growth of the enterprise the management must adjust different variables so that they should function in an orderly fashion and preserve organisational integrity. Organisation should be viewed as an open system, for neither objectives nor plans can possibly be set in the vaccum of a closed company system; Markets, government regulations, competitors, technology and many other elements of an enterprise environment affect plans and objectives and cannot be overlooked. Thus, the manager has to always bear in mind that the organisation exists within a wider system of its community, of the government and of the country, all of which may affect it. In other words, it is a part of a larger system with which it reacts.

All the aforementioned theories or approaches, the classical, the human relations, the decision-making and the systems, can be of help to the manager. One or two of them may be the most useful at a particular time, but an awareness of all of them is desirable. The classical principles are still widely used in organising, and the findings of the behavioural scientists are applied within a largely classical or formal structure. Similarly, the decision-making theory does not altogether reject the organisational hierarchy and the systems approach is being used in conjunction with the classical theory. In fact as pointed out by John Dearden[1], ... "the systems approach is precisely what every good manager has been using for centuries...."

Since most managers still think of an organisation in terms of its formal structure, and since we are discussing the managerial function, we discuss organisation as a process and a structure. This does not mean that the other approaches will be ignored, but, as stated earlier good managers take note of all the approaches at appropriate occasions.

Organising Functions.

Organising is the function performed after planning. Organising focuses attention on the structure and process of allocating jobs so that common objectives can be achieved. It is concerned with—

1. determining the specific activities that are necessary to accomplish the planned goals;
2. grouping the activities into logical pattern, framework, or structure; and
3. assigning the activities to specific positions and people.

The result of this process of organising is "the organisation", the people employed and the net work of relationships among them. Consequently, the term "organisation" is used in relation to the management of a business entreprise in two different senses—(i) as a *process*, and (ii) as a structure.

Organisation as a process. Organisation is a process of defining and grouping the activities of the enterprise and establishing the authority relationship, among them.[2] Considered as a process, then, organisation includes (i) breaking down the work necessary to achieve the objectives into individual jobs, and (ii) providing means of coordinating the efforts of the job holders.[3] Hence, organisation is the process by which the chief executive groups his men in order to get the work done. As a process, organisation is management's significant activity affecting human relations because it determines which people will have authority over others, what work people will do, and the type of contacts they will have.

Organisation structure. We create organisations to accomplish the goals and objectives conceived in planning. Hence, organisations have objectives or goals separate from the *individual or personal wants* of their members, such as food, shelter, security and status. It is necessary to integrate these personal wants with organisational objectives in a relationship of mutual interest so that personal wants and organisational

1. *MIS Is a Mirage*, Harward Business Review, Vol 50 no. 1, pp 90-99.
2. Theo. Haimann, *Professional Management*, p. 136.
3. Ernest Dale, *Management-Theory and Practice*, P. 178

objectives may be reached. The structure and relationships arising therefrom is known as *Formal Organisation.* One of the simplest ways of presenting a picture of an organisation is to draw up an organisation chart, which is simply a diagram of the formal authority structure. This shows by job titles who reports to whom, that is, the subordinate-superior relationships. More will be said about organisation charts at a later stage.

Traditional Principles of Organisation.

The formal structure of organisation is built to help accomplish enterprise goals more effectively. To ensure sound organisation, the following "Principles" have been suggested by the classical school in the form of guides for the organiser.

1. *Objectives.* Organisation structure enables us to accomplish goals. So organisation should have clearly defined objectives. Also each position should have an objective logically related to the overall objective or objectives in such a way that if each jobholder meets his goal, the goals of the entire organisation will be met. Once the objectives are clearly defined, the organiser can easily proceed to group activities, delegate authority to individuals to whom activities have been assigned and coordinate their efforts for better results.

2. *Specialisation.* Modern business has become a complex of specialised functions and activities. The primary step in organisation is to determine and to establish as separate entities, the smallest number of dissimilar functions into which the work of an enterprise may be divided. So far as possible, the work of each person should be confined to a single function, and related functions should be grouped together. Thus, the principle of specialisation enables the division of functions whereby different persons do different things at the same time. It makes for managerial efficiency by providing expertness (*expertise*) in an organisation and placing reliance on it.

3. *Definiteness.* Every necessary activity should contribute to the main objective of the business with a minimum effort and a maximum of effectiveness on the part of all job holders. Therefore, every employee must know of his place and purpose in the organisation and his responsibility for achieving that purpose.

4. *Scalar Principle.* We have seen earlier that the vertical dimension of organisation structure consists of levels of authority arranged in a hierarchy from the chief executive at the top (Top Management) through the Middle Management to the First Line supervisor at the bottom. According to Scalar principle, the organisation must have a supreme authority, and a clear line of authority should run from the person down through the hierarchy. For example, the authority should descend from the chief executive through the Froduction Manager, through the foreman to the rank-and-file production employees, thus establishing a "chain of command".

5. *Clear assignments of Responsibility.* Everyone should have a

clear understanding of the duties for which he is responsible. He must know what he is required to do.

6. *Authority commensurate with Responsibility.* As responsibility is assigned authority which is commensurate also should be delegated. When anyone is made responsible for achieving a given objective, he should be given enough authority to reach it. To assign a man responsibility without delegating him the requisite authority is to place the man in an impossible position.

7. *Unity of Command.* Each person should be accountable to only one superior. This will minimise conflict and ensure response. To subject a person to the authority of more than one immediate superior is to confuse his action and also to divide his loyalty.

8. *Unity of Assignment.* Functions of a like kind should be closely related within the structure. Functions assigned to each position should be compatible, and they should require reasonably equal demands of skill.

9. *Span of Control.* A manager should be expected to supervise a reasonable number of subordinates. What is reasonable depends upon a variety of factors and arbitrary limits are meaningless. If the span of control is narrow, there will be more organisational levels which in turn may impede communication. If the number of levels is reduced and the span of control widened, the supervisory load may become too great. Sound administration requires a balance between supervisory load and organisation levels.

10. *A Short Chain of Command.* There should be as few levels of supervision between the chief executive and the rank and file as possible. Obviously, if directions flow down from the top though the chain of command and reports on what is actually happening follows the same channel, the longer the chain, the greater the change that the directions and the reports will be distorted on the way.

11. *Balance.* Anorganisation is sound only if it is sound in every part. Conversely, it will be sound in every part if the whole is directed to the same end. Therefore, every branch of the business should be equally effective and conform to the plan of the whole. This is called "organisation balance". Consequently, the organisation must be continually surveyed to ensure that there is reasonable balance in the size of the various departments, between standardisation of procedures and flexibility, and between centralisation and decentralisation of decision making. Balance is also necessary between the principle of the span of control and the principle of the short chain of command, because shortening the span of control generally means lengthening the chain of command.

12. *Coordination.* The organisation should permit of complete coordination of every branch of its work. The performance of every unit, whether it be large or small, should be economically related to all allied units and the whole should comply with main policies. Therefore, the control of the organisation should be a "central control", achieved

by interlocking of all units.

13. *The Exception Principle.* This principle states that an executive attains best performance by delegating to his subordinates as much of the routine operations as possible. and leaves for himself only broad general problems and exceptions to routine. The subordinate is left to choose the means to accomplish, and the chief interferes only in exceptional circumstances.

14. *Principle of Decentralisation.* Decision should be made at the lowest competent level. Therefore, authority should be delegated as far down in the organisation as possible. Delegation of broad authority and decision-making power should also be made to semi-autonomous units.

15. *Simiplicity and Flexibility.* The organisation should be so planned that the objective can be attained with the lowest possible cost, which may mean either money costs or human costs or both. The organisation should also permit of growth and expansion without dislocation, regardless of changes in personnel and method. The organisation builder should make it so flexible that it can stand changes and stand through the years. The aim should be continuity.

ORGANISATION STRUCTURE

Organisation structure has two facets: *first*, the form of structure, and *second*, the functions which are to be performed. In the first we can apply the "principles" of organisation. In the second, we determine the activities that the enterprise needs and the degree of specialisation it can afford. Then we establish the functions and authorities within these activities, and relate these activities in a structure.

A typical organisation structure can be shown by a pyramid-shaped diagram as given below.

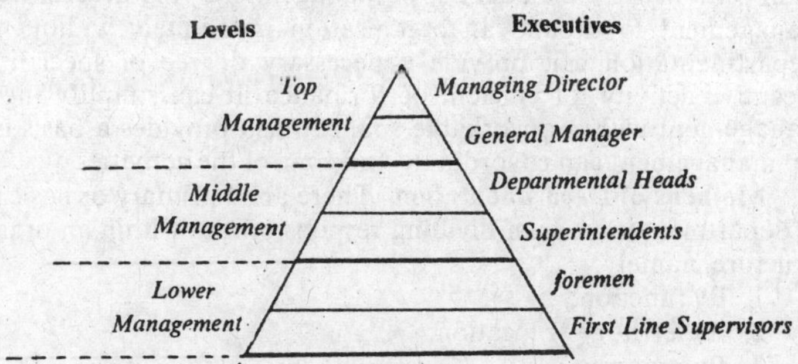

The diagram shows both the horizontal and vertical dimensions of the organisation structure. In other words, it gives the levels of management and the line executives in descending order. All the executives or officers from the Managing Director at the highest level down to the first line supervisors at the lowest level are designated 'Management'.

Levels of Management. In general practice, the management group comprises three distinct levels—(i) Top Management, (ii) Middle Management, and (iii) Lower Management.

The Top Management is represented by the chief executives, namely, the managing director or the general manager, who issues instructions on the basis of the policy formulated by the Board of Directors. The authority of the chief executives is "general" concerned as it is with the shaping of the general projects and the evaluation of general results. The heads of departments or functional managers and superintendents constitute the Middle Management. The Lower Management consists of foremen and first-line supervisors. They are in direct touch with the operative workers. It is these people who direct and guide the work people and act as the link between the middle management and the workers. So far as authority is concerned, as the subordinates, such as the department managers, superintendents, foremen and first line supervisors, follow in line the authority passes from general to special and so assumes greater detailed control.

DEPARTMENTATION

The process of organising an enterprise consists of (1) dividing and grouping the work to be done, and (2) assigning different duties and responsibilities to different people. *Departmentation* is the process which is used to group activities into units for purposes of administration at all levels. By this process, personnel and functions comprising an enterprise are departmentalised by division into separate sub-units and by arrangements of groupings so as to contribute to achievement of the organisation's purposes. Departments comprise a framework for an organisation and are an agency of management. This structuring enables management to expand an organisation indefinitely without collapse. Departmentation can provide a necessary degree of specialisation of executive activity for efficient performance. It can simplify the tasks of management within a workable span. It also provides a basis on which top management can co-ordinate and control the activities of sub-units.

Methods of Departmentation. There are 4 primary or basic methods of departmentation or of dividing responsibilities within an organisation structure, namely,

1. By function;
2. By territory or location;
3. By process;
4. By product or service.

Other methods exist, such as by *customers* or by *simple numbers* or by *time*, and are encountered under special circumstances. Departments may be set up on the basis of customers served. For example, Wenger's Restaurant serves regular meals in the big hall, and maintains an

Espresso Bar for serving snacks. Where 'shifts' become necessary because of rush of work, the division would be made on time basis—day shift, evening shift and night shift. Division by simple numbers occurs when a number of indistinguishable persons is involved in an uncomplicated situation, such as formation of squads among new recruits in an army camp. We will confine our discussion to the 4 basic methods prevalent in industry.

Functional Basis. The most commonly followed basis of departmentation is by functions. So the structure may build up by setting up departments by functions, such as sales, accounting, production, personnel, purchasing, etc.

Territorial Basis. Where organisations are large and geographically dispersed, departmentation on a territorial basis may be made, by having Northern division or Southern division and so on with a resident manager in charge of each division. Territorial departmentation enables an executive to become thoroughly familiar with Key details required of him, and facilitates on-the-scene management during emergencies. The branch plant or district sales office is also an excellent training situation for all-around managers needed in the future at higher levels.

Process Basis. Departmentation on a process basis is found both in manufacturing and in distribution activities. A job machine shop, for example, that is large enough for departmentation would probably establish process departments for lathe work, milling, shaping, drilling, and grinding. A large retail establishment might also have process departments for receiving goods, in-store transportation, wrapping and delivery.

Product Basis. Product departmentation, in which the major functional activities associated with a given product or commodity or service are organised under a single head, is a widely used basis for departmentation. Examples are plant, chemicals, machinery, etc. Within this form there may be 3 different types :

Each product made in separate plant and sold through separate sales unit.

Each product made in separate plant and sold through common sales unit.

Each product made in many plants and sold through common sales units but controlled by a central product division.

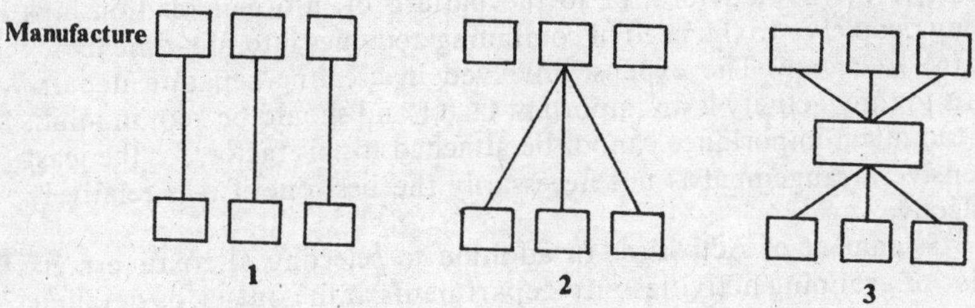

Product line grouping permits maximum use of specialised knowledge and skills, of specialised capital equipment, and of specialised production and sales methods. The grouping is part of the process of division of labour and of capital for increased productivity through specialization. It also limits the span of control for executives and facilitates co-ordination of effort by functional groups within the product cluster.

Factors in Departmentation. The following factors are to be taken into consideration in departmentation :

(1) *Specialisation.* Departmentation should be such as to yield the adventages of specialisation which is the most widely recognised characteristic of modern enterprise. Specialisation may be functional, as in the establishment of separate departments for sales, finance, etc., or by products.

(2) *Control.* Departmentation should simplify the executive's task of control. Departmentation may have a direct bearing on independence of checks, clear-cut accountability, telling comparison of results, or case of supervision. As a general rule one activity intended to serve as a check on another should be under a separate executive. For example, quality inspection should not be under the direction of a foreman who is being pressed for volume output. A clear cut division between the work of one department and that of another makes it easy to decide which executive is accountable for results. Territorial departments should be established in such a way that the performance of one can be checked by comparison with the other. Physical convenience of supervision should also be kept in mind as an aspect of control, when grouping activities.

(3) *Coordination.* Quite different activities may be grouped under a single executive because they need to be coordinated. The 'orphan' operations such as filing, or purchasing of supplies in a financial enterprise may be attached to a department where they are used most.

(4) *Securing attention.* An unusually important activity for the success of the enterprise should be given a special recognition in the organisation. For giving it greater attention than other activities, it may be placed in a separate division and also at a higher level in the administrative hierarchy according to its importance.

(5) *Recognition of local conditions.* The departmentation should take into consideration local conditions at the places concerned. For example, attention should be paid to the personalities of the people who will perform the activities, or to the pattern of informal relationships among people, or to the need of combining activities into full-time jobs.

(6) *Economy.* The expense involved in creating separate departments for any activity is an important factor and should be kept in mind. But too much importance cannot be attached to this factor, for the least expensive arrangement is not necessarily the best one if it is relatively ineffective.

Assignment of Activities. In addition to selecting alternative methods of grouping activities into departments at the outset, as detailed above, the executive is confronted from time to time with the problem of deciding where to fit in a new activity and where to shift an old one. The first need is usually that of *recognizing a function.* Once the purpose of an enterprise is defined, it is possible to deduce various activities that will contribute to the success of the primary production, marketing, and finance function. As an organisation develops more fully, engineering and purchasing functions achieve separate status and are allotted separate departments.

A second need is that of combining functions so as to realize efficient performance and balanced operation without increasing the number of management levels through creation of 'splinter' departments. Each major department consists of a combination of subsidiary activities narrower in scope. Essential activities of purchasing, inventory control, and production scheduling may well be combined under one individual in a simple organisation. Accounting, finance statistics, and business economics might all be grouped under a high level controller in a large organisation.

A third need is that of *developing principles* whereby activities may logically be combined. Two widely recognised principles underlying departmentation are : (i) similarity of function, and (ii) closeness of association. *Similarity of function* is useful primarily as a basis for classifying activities at the lower levels of the organisation structure where duties are not yet highly differentiated. Grouping of typists into a general typing pool is an example. Salesmen, machinists, and office workers are often grouped into their respective departments by reason of similarity of function.

The principle of similarity has narrow limitations, and diversity must be coped with in grouping most activities. We will touch upon the bases on which people involved in diverse activities are grouped in one department.

Bases of grouping diverse activities.[1] Diverse activities which are deemed so closely related or intimately associated in the achievement of enterprise purposes are grouped in one department unit on the following grounds or bases :—

1. *Most use.* The principle of 'most use' indicates that a given activity may well be placed in the major department that makes most use of it. For example, intraplant transportation, warehousing and the entire traffic management function might be placed within the production department.

2. *Most Interest.* The manager most interested in promoting a new activity may be assigned its supervision if he is also most willing and able to serve. Under this criterion, cost accounting sometimes turns up in the production department rather than in the general accounting department.

---

1. For detailed consideration, see L.C. Sorell, *"Organization of Industrial Traffic Activities"*, *Traffic World,* Vol. 16, 1930, Koontz and O'Donnell *op. cit.*, pp. 122-1·5.

3. *Competition.* In some instances, separation of activities is as important a consideration in departmentation as is association. The stimulus of competition between two departments within the organisation may be desired. For example, two distinct sales organisations may be developed to push two brands of tyres, one of which is sold through small dealers and the other of which is sold through wholesalers.

4. *Suppressed competition.* If two sister units begin to compete vigorously, to the detriment of the enterprise as a whole, both might be placed under the jurisdiction of a single executive so as to eliminate unnecessary managerial friction.

5. *Policy control.* An activity may be assigned to a particular department for development and enforcement of specific policies that are deemed in the interest of the unit to which the activity is allotted. For example, credits and collections functions may, as a matter of policy control, be placed in the finance department rather than in sales manager's department.

6. *No "Clean Break".* The absence of a "clean break" or division between two activities that logically could be placed in different departments may cause the two to be put together for adequate responsibility and orderly performance. For example, the close connection between purchasing of fashion goods and sales volume encourages stores management to place one person in charge of both activities to fix responsibility for results.

7. *Separation.* In some situations separation has to be attained in spite of considerable cost. For instance, if a function is checked upon for effectiveness and propriety by a second function, separation is mandatory for good results.

8. *Adequate attention.* Special attention needs to be given to certain activities to keep them from dying under adverse circumstances. If an auxiliary activity is assigned to an executive who does not consider it important, the performance will be disappointing. The activity should be shifted and the attention stepped up.

9. *Co-ordination.* The principle of co-ordination of activities requires proper timing plus integrated effort. The question arises as to where within the organisation structure activities should be integrated. If a business is decentralised, coordination may rest with the General Manager.

ORGANISATION CHARTS AND TITLES

An organisation chart is prepared to show formal organisational relationships which are intended to prevail. It shows who supervises whom and how the various units are related to each other. It also shows the main line of communication, the downward flow of authority and the upward flow of responsibility. It enables the top management to assign responsibilities by designating different persons entrusted with certain jobs. The assignment of responsibilities within a sound organisation structure serves several purposes :

(1) It acquaints all members of the enterprise with their own responsibilities and with the responsibilities of others with whom they must deal;
(2) It permits greater decisiveness of action by restricting duplication of effort;
(3) It eliminates frictions and the playing of politics;
(4) It eliminates unnecessary functions;
(5) It stimulates the execution of activities and the development of individual capacities by providing an understandable framework of authority within which to carry on the activities;
(6) It provides executives with more time for planning and policy formation by assuring them that all operating details are provided for; and
(7) It adopts the "principles of organisation" to individual company needs.

To accomplish those purposes it is necessary to define the titles of members and relate them to authority and responsibility. The titles may be such as Production Manager, Works Manager, Factory Manager, Plant Superintendent, General Foreman, Foreman, Supervisor and Department head, and should be defined and placed in their proper relationship to the whole. The title should not be changed very often. After all, titles are labels which define segment of work. They should be helpful to those outside the organisation and they should build an internal system of procedure. A title held by a person should be a badge of ability. It says the holder is capable of certain responsibilities and, therefore, possesses a given type of ability. Responsibility and ability go hand in hand, and subordinates have a right to expect that titles of persons above them mean that these persons deserve the recognition accorded to them.

Structure or People. Another very important problem has to be tackled when structuring an organisation. Should the organisation structure be built around people (i.e., to suit people), or should people be adapted to the structure ? Management specialists are generally, although not wholly, in agreement that the organisation structure should be determined on the organisational principles and then people fitted to it in the best possible way. This approach is useful as it recognises the fact that the organisation is definite and stable, while people enter and leave it. It is held by these experts that the key to organisational efficiency is sound organisation structure, more than design on the basis of personal interests and abilities.

Yet the fact remains that the people who perform the work must be considered at some point. Some companies go to the extreme and build all or part of their organisation structure around personalities. They do this in order to maximize potentialities of gifted executives or to use particular combinations of talents held by one person. Their philosophy is that people are paramount because they do the work. They argue that, as no two individuals will do a job alike, jobs should be redefined to fit people. This viewpoint is justifiable within the management group where jobs are quite flexible.

Which of the two approaches is most appropriate ? In answer to this question, it may be said that the question is really quite academic, because in nearly every case both approaches are necessary. Unless the organisation is entirely new, there is actually no alternative but to utilise existing personnel. It is also true, however, that existing personnel must adapt to the necessary change.

Assuming that the enterprise is already in existence, the preferred approach is first to develop an ideal organisation plan without regard to existing personalities. This approach would take into consideration—

(1) the activities needed to perform the unit's responsibilities;
(2) the authorities needed to carry them out; and
(3) proper relationships of the various units.

After the ideal plan is developed, it should be reviewed in consideration of available personnel. Does the enterprise have people capable of managing the proposed organisation ? In most cases, a few people will fit perfectly into the new structure; others, nearly so; and still others, not at all. The first group presents no problem. For a position into which some individual almost fits or into which no one fits, there are two alternatives. Either the positions should be modified to accommodate available people, or people should be brought in from outside.

If a person's experience in the company is close enough to the requirements of a new position, or if a measure of training will equip him for it, it may be preferable to modify the requirements and accommodate available personnel. If, on the other hand, no one's experience is adequate and if the function is so vital as to preclude modification, it may be necessary to bring in some one from outside the company.

As we have said earlier that jobs have to be performed by people, the job assignments should be consistent with the capacities of people. Based on this view it can be said that *the ideal organisation structure may be primarily designed on the basis of a logical grouping of functions, but that a practical, working structure is more effective when reasonably adjusted to fit the human resources available.* A sample organisation chart is given on page 361.

TYPES OF ORGANISATION

Organisation structure, as we have noted, is primarily concerned with the allocation of activities and delegation of authority. Three types of organisation are classified by the nature of authority :

1. Line organisation.
2. Functional organisation.
3. Line and staff organisation.

A SAMPLE ORGANISATION CHART

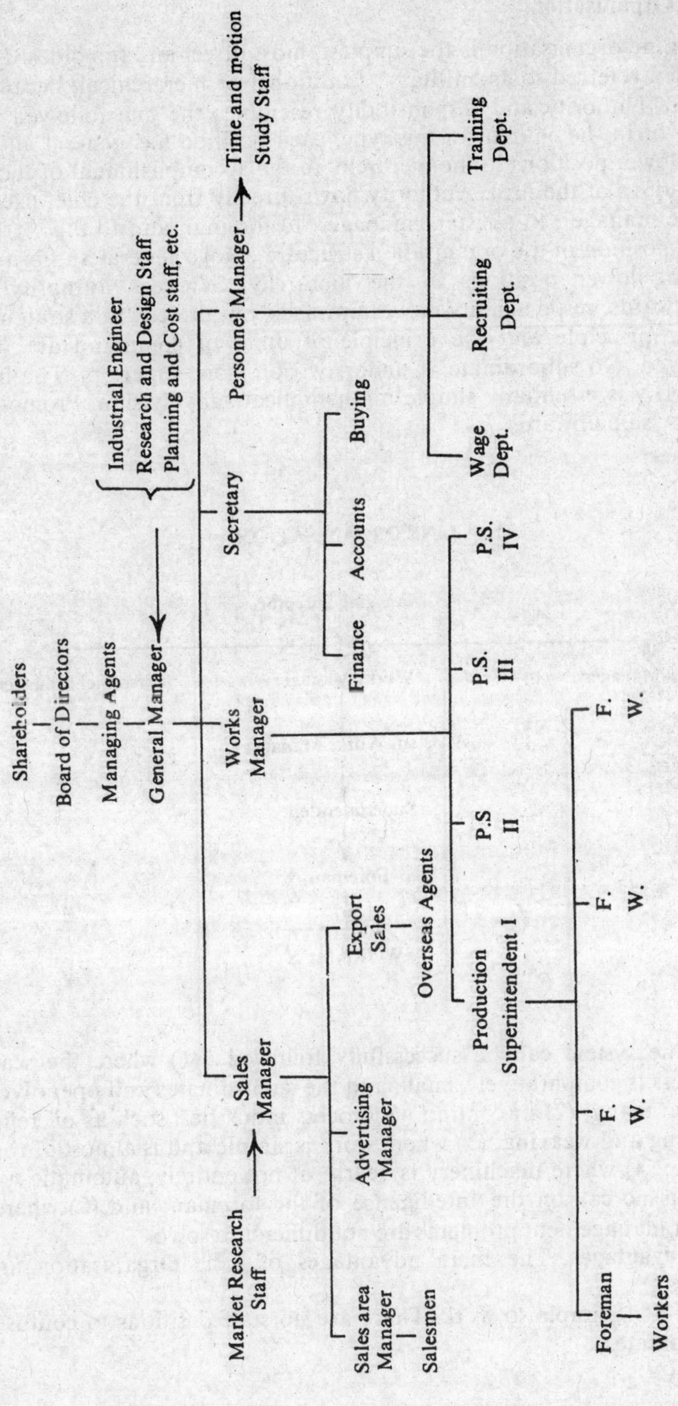

Line Organisation.

Line organisation is the simplest, most direct and the oldest type. It is often referred to as 'mititary', traditional or hierarchical, because the line of authority and responsibility resembles the one followed in the army or in the church. In this type, each position has general authority over lower positions in the hierarchy in the accomplishment of the main operations of the firm. Authority flows directly from the chief executive to the manager, to assistant manager, to foreman and to the workmen. Each position in the organisation structure enjoys general authority over all the lower positions in the hierarchy. Whereas authority flows downwards, responsibility moves upwards, but directly in a straight line. Scalar principle and the principle of unity of command are strictly followed. No subordinate is under two or more superiors. The line of authority is essentially simple mathematical sub-division. Promotion is step by step upwards.

LINE ORGANISATION

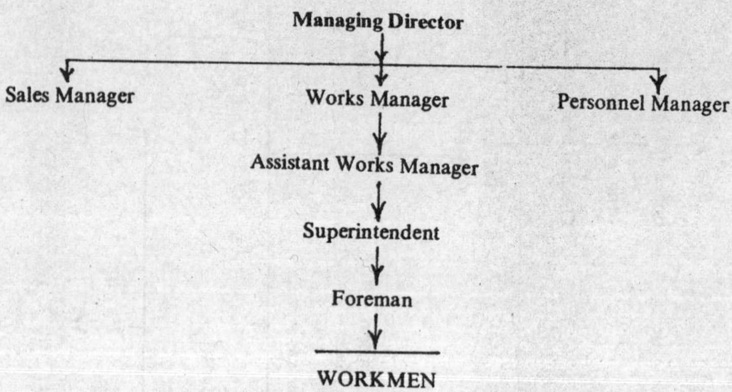

The system can be successfully followed : (1) where the scale of business is comparatively small, and the subordinates and operatives are not too many; (2) in continuous process industries, such as oil refining, spinning and weaving; (3) where work is simple and is almost of routine nature; (4) where machinery is nearly, if not entirely, automatic so that there is no call on the intelligence of the foreman; and (5) where the labour management problems are not difficult to solve.

Advantages. The main advantages of Line Organisation are as follows :

1. It is simple to work. There are no staff positions to confuse the subordinates.

2. It is economical and effective, for it permits of rapid decisions and effective coordination, as all the activities affecting the department are in the hands of one individual.

3. It makes for unity of command and also conforms to the scalar principle of organisation.

4. It fixes responsibility for the performance of tasks in a definite manner upon certain individuals.

5. It is stable and less expensive as no staff personnel or other specialists are involved.

6. It is conducive to positive discipline, the control being unified and loyalty undivided.

Disadvantages. The system has the following drawbacks :

1. It is based upon an autocratic system of management, and so business is subject to arbitrary decisions of one man.

2. The work may be divided according to the whims of the manager rather than according to any scientific plan.

3. It cramps progress and prevents effective working of the unit.

4. The foremen have so much to do that they cannot see to improvements as rapidly as is desirable.

5. It suffers from lack of specialisation. Each department manager has to buy his own materials, design his own product, engage his own labour, keep his own records, set his own standard of output and cost, Therefore, because of the lack of specialised skill each head of the department is inclined to be a jack of all trade and master of none.

6. The staggering responsibility on the shoulder of the manager can crush him under the load of too much work-load.

7. The system has no means of rewarding the good worker and punishing the loafer.

8. It is likely to encourage nepotism, and sycophancy.

9. Line organisation is rigid and inflexible. It is bureacratic and riddled with red-tape.

10. Above all, it cannot be employed without creating chaos in management in large concerns, and now-a-days, large-scale production is the rule.

Line and Staff Organisation.

As industrial firms grew in size, the managers who worked under departmental or line form of organisation found that they did not have time to give careful attention to every phase of management. Thus, a manager could not, under the pressure of growth, yield up time or find opportunity for investigational work and solid constructive enquiry and thought. The "staff" was, therefore, instituted to discharge this work, and to advise the manager on his problems. It is the formal recognition of the Specialist or Expert in industry. In its orign staff was added purely as adviser to the line structure, with no authority to place recommendations into action. Thus, staff refers to officers who are not in the line, but are more or less permanently detailed to special service, or to the study of some one phase of operations; and thus act as an advisory group adjunct to the line. The "staff idea" also first arose in the army, where it was found that with the growth of army, the commander could not look to the collection of information and its coordination for taking information and also to the actual fighting.

In the industrial world, too, the staff organisation came into being as the result of the inability of the departmental managers to investigate, think, and plan at the same time, as they were performing the ordinary tasks of production and selling. Consequently, the work of research, investigation, recording, standardising, and advising, i.e., the work of the expert, was wholly distinguished and separated from the direct processes of manufacturing and selling. As a result there arose a clear demarcation between "thinking" and "doing", the staff being the "thinkers and the line the doers". It is to be emphasised that the staff functions are co-ordinative and cooperative, but they do not stand to one another in any order of ascending or descending scale. The manager, simply as manager, ranks and commands the sub-manager, the latter in turn commands the superintendent, who commands the foreman under whose command the operators work. That is a "line" relation, as all of them stand in a line. But the cost accountant, the expert for research and designs, and the legal and financial advisers are the "Staff" who take no

LINE AND STAFF CHART

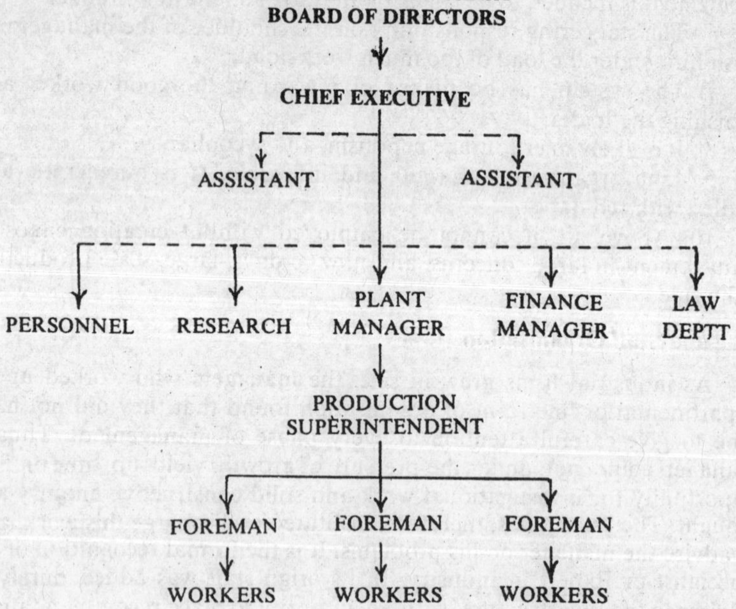

Unbroken lines show direct "line". Broken lines indicate "staff"

direct or executive share in carrying on the work of production and selling. The system is one of the great classifying factors between human beings: between men of action, leaders, managers, executives, i.e., the line; and the thinkers who are concerned more with the "why" and "how" and less with doing like scientists, planners, organisers, engineers, designers, accountants, i.e., the staff. To that extent the system is entirely sound.

A staff manager may act in one of the following roles :

1. Personal assistant to a senior manager.

2. Adviser on some particular aspect, although not directly responsible for the work done within the departments for which the advice is being given.

Advantages. The advantages of line and staff organisation are :

1. It adds the specialist to the line thus relieving the line manager of the subsidiary tasks of thinking and enabling him to concentrate on the main job of producing and selling.

2. It brings expert knowledge to bear upon management. The staff provide expert advice to the line managers on wide ranging matters.

3. It provides for better utilization of personnel and leads to more concerted skill development.

Drawbacks. The drawbacks of this type of organisation are :

1. The line and staff relationships often lead to friction and jealousy.

2. Line managers are likely to tend to depend too much on staff experts and thus lose much of their judgment and initiative.

3. There is the danger of the staff experts remaining ineffective because they do not have the authority to implement the recommendations.

The Functional Organisation

Functionalisation is a development of line and staff. Its basic concept is that part of the organisation should be based on functions and techniques. It is therefore the opposite of the departmental idea, as it disregards productions or areas. Taylor and others advocated it as a part of the scheme of Scientific Management. Under this plan, specific functions common to all or several departments are each placed in the hands of a man specially qualified for his particular function. Instead of giving attention to all factors in one department, he attends to one factor in all departments. The scheme is based on the theory of division of labour as applied to management. It splits up personnel according to managerial functions, such as accounting, cost control, budgeting, purchasing, research, manufacturing, production control, maintenance and transport. Under the line and staff organisation, the work of the staff is not regarded as a specific managerial function. Under functional plan, however, specialists become more than just advisers. They become executives incharge of single techniques which are common under several units of the work. The employee is no longer under one boss, but under as many bosses as his work requires. All related and similar work is done in one department under one executive. For example, the purchaser is responsible for all purchases of the company. The scope of the work is limited but the area of authority is unlimited.

The need for functional managers arises because of (i) the complexity of modern, large-scale organisation, (ii) the need to make the fullest use of the specialists, and (iii) the necessity to avoid burdening line managers with complex problems and making decisions on matters which are outside the direct process of producing and selling.

Taylor's Functional Organisation.

Recognising the limitations of the pure line organisation, and appreciating the fact that there could be greater productivity and improved efficiency through the use of specialised knowledge and skill, Frederick W. Taylor, the founder of Scientific Management developed the functional organisation, sometimes called Functional Foremanship organisation. He saw that one man, concentrating on a limited number of tasks, could become highly skilled. As part of his Scientific Management, he broke down the job of a single foreman into eight separate functions with a man incharge of each as follows :

Executive Functional Bosses. These were concerned with the supervision of the work on the shop floor. The titles given were :

(a) *Gang Boss.* whose function was preparing the work for the machine and getting it to the worker and also providing the tools, drawings and materials.

(b) *Speed Boss,* who supervised machine speeds and feeds and worker performance, so as to see that the job was done correctly and at the right speed.

(c) *Inspector,* who checked quality and provided guidance on drawings.

(d) *Repair Boss,* who was responsible for repairs and maintenance of machines.

Functional Bosses. These were located in the planning room and concerned with planning and control and were designated as :

(a) *Order of work or Route clerk,* whose duty was to determine how the job was to be done and to see that the production order was completed.

(b) *Instruction Card Clerk,* who made out instruction cards.

(c) *Time and cost clerk,* whose job concerned predetermination of times and costs and recording.

(d) *Shop Disciplinarian,* who was responsible for discipline throughout the works.

It will be noticed that under this system each workman had eight bosses or foremen.

Taylor sought to define the responsibilities of his functional bosses but to do that with exactness was a virtual impossibility. There was close

TAYLOR'S FUNCTIONAL FOREMANSHIP

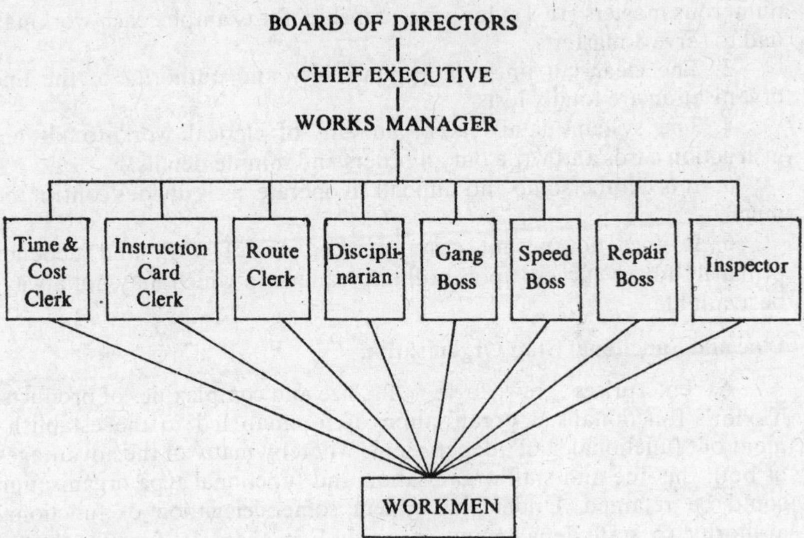

relationship between the duties performed by the eight foremen and the inevitable overlap of some of them. Taylor's functional foremanship system is seldom found in practice, at least under the present conditions. But functional organisation in the sense of the staff specialists enjoying functional authority relating to their respective areas of speciality over subordinate managers is quite popular.

Advantages. Functional organisation has the following advantages :

1. It ensures specialisation and efficiency, as one man devotes his entire time and energy in doing one thing.

2. Each person gives his best effort, because he develops according to his best abilities.

3. It allows the workman to study his work intensively and suggest improvements.

4. It does not hamper organisation growth, because each man grows in his own speciality. For example, it does not matter whether the buyer purchases 40 units or 40,000 units, he exercises one faculty and has one activity to control.

5. It helps mass production by standardisation and specialisation.

Disadvantages. Some of the drawbacks of the functional organisation are :

1. Because of the failure to define the exact nature of the functional authority, the system proves confusing from the point of view of procedures of control.

2. It is conducive to overlapping authority and lack of definiteness and fixed lines of responsibility, which often results in "buck passing". As in the case of Taylor's Functional Foremanship, each worker must serve numerous masters (In Taylor's foremanship, for example, each workman had to serve 8 masters).

3. The clear-cut lines of responsibility and authority of the line organisation are totally lost.

4. The system entails great amount of clerical work to fill out instruction cards and write out all orders and minute details.

5. It is cumbersome and difficult to operate, as it divides control too much.

6. It does not permit easy coordination of work and depends primarily for its success upon brilliant leadership which may not always be available.

Line and Functional Staff Organisation

As enterprises grew further in size and complexities of products, Taylor's functionalised organisation of foreman led to the establishment of "functional staff" departments whereby many of the advantages of both the line and staff organisation and functional type organisation could be retained. Under this system some delegation of functional authority to staff departments is given. For example, functional staff departments are given responsibility and authority over specialised activity such as inspection, time study, employment, purchasing, internal transport and shipping. It should be borne in mind that these are service functions performed by specialists (staff) who are different from the line people who are responsible to their line bosses and supervisors. Under this system it is possible to introduce functionalisation and maintain line as well as staff. The scheme is based upon the theory of division of labour as applied to management. It is really the Line and Staff type of organisation through functions. The specialists are more than mere advisers. They are executives incharge of single techniques which are common under several units of the works. The entire organisation is divided so that no activity is left out and there is no duplication in the allotment of activities to different departments. This eliminates the weakness of the pure functional plan and no employee is placed under more than one boss.

Line and Staff Authority Relationships

The phrase line and staff often causes confusion because it is used in different ways by different writers. It is most often used to distinguish between the departments called 'line' where the managers contribute directly to the objectives of the organisation either by producing a product or service or by selling it, and those departments, called 'staff' which contribute indirectly to promoting the objectives. In terms of functions, production and sales are commonly classified as line functions in manufacturing companies. But depending upon the importance of different activities and function to the enterprise, functions which are termed as line in one company need not be so in another company. In some companies research and development, and in others finance, would also be considered line.

According to these writers, staff refers to those elements of the organisation that help the line to work most effectively in accomplishing enterprise goals. Thus, staff is concerned with providing advice and service to the line.

Some writers argue that the distinction between 'line' and 'staff' should be based on the authority relationships. Line authority obeys the Scalar principle and falls in the direct line of command. Line authority runs from the top to the bottom through superior-subordinate relations in the organisation. Staff authority is auxilliary but adheres to the line as do sidings to the maintrack in the case of a railway. In other words, staff function exists in relation to some line function and not independent of it.

Urwick suggests that staff instead of being purely advisory, performs the following activities :

(a) frames procedures, regulations and some times policies to be issued to line personnel in the name of some top line superior;
(b) interprets plans and "sells" them to line personnel;
(c) renders help to line superiors and their subordinates by supplying them adequate information on the working of plans; and
(d) reports to superiors on the extent of compliance by line subordinates with staff advice.

Line and staff relations are distinguished on the basis of division of managerial functions. To *act* is said to be the line manager's function, and staff's function is to *think*. Frederick Taylor advocated separation of thinking and planning from doing. However, management represents the sum total of planning, organising, staffing, directing and controlling. Complete segregation of management into thinking and doing is neither desirable nor feasible.

It should be remembered that within a staff department, the relationships are line. The superior *tells* his subordinates and is accountable for their work, although he *sells* to other departments. Therefore, the authority relationship between line and staff is that 'line tells, staff sells'.

Conflict between Line and Staff

Although in many enterprises line and staff work together smoothly, there are others where much conflict between line and staff is found to exist. This certainly hurts the smooth functioning and productivity of the enterprise. What are the causes of this conflict ? Both line and staff offer their own causes.

Line's complaints. The line managers complain as follows :

1. The staff often goes beyond its sphere of activity and assumes

line authority. In this manner, staff elements encroach upon line managements' duties, responsibilities and prerogatives.

2. The advice given by the staff is not sound enough to be useful. It is, in line manager's view academic, theoretical and unrealistic.

3. Since staff is not responsible for the ultimate results, staff people have a tendencey to propose and suggest untried and untested new ideas.

4. The staff operates within the limited area of his speciality and fails to see the business as a whole. Line managment feels that the staff specialist is so involved with his own speciality he thinks only of the objectives of his own speciality instead of the objectives of the enterprise as a whole.

5. Another very common complaint against staff is that when a project has not worked out line management is blamed for its failure and that when a project has been successful staff tries to take the credit.

Staff's complaint. The staff gives different causes of conflict as follows :

1. The line management resists new ideas and is not willing to adopt the new speciality even though it is conducive to rapid progress.

2. The line does not make proper use of the available staff. It is felt that those line officers who are in most need of the specialised advice most often hesitate to ask for it.

3. Some line managers, after asking for advice, will reject the suggestions either because they really did not want to ask for advice or because they distrust the adviser.

4. Another complaint of staff is that they do not have enough authority. They often feel that if they have arrived at the best solution they should be able to put it into action. This of course, is defeating the staff concept completely.

How to make Line and Staff Relations Successful

For avoiding or at least minimizing conflict and friction between the two elements the following suggestions are offered, namely :—

1. Both line and staff should clearly understand, the nature of the relationship between them. Each must appreciate the role he has to play; the staff to advise and serve the line and the line to realise that the staff is there to help and not to undermine the role of the line executive. They should remember that the line tells and the staff sells.

2. Line should be encouraged to use staff effectively.

3. Properly qualified people should be selected for staff. They should be satisfied with tendering advice and counsel to the line executives and their feelings should not be hurt if the advice is not accepted.

4. Staff should appreciate the fact that it is human nature to resist change. He should use patience in persuading the line boss. He should "sell" the idea. One of the ways to do this is to encourage line executive to participate in the proposed scheme of change.

5. Staff must give full credit to the line elements for the results accomplished.

6. The line officer must also keep the staff elements well informed on decisions which will ultimatelv have an effect on their specialised activities.

7. The line manager should know that the more he calls upon staff the better acquainted the specialist would become with his problems and the more help would he be able to give him. In this way the line manager will save a great amount of his own time which he can devote to his managerial functions.

8. The final decision is line's prerogative and responsibility.

New Concept of Manager and Specialist Relation

Line and staff are useful concepts and contribute to some extent to organisational effectiveness. But confining our discussion to mere line and staff relationship touches only a part of the relationship, that exists between managers and specialists. Managers have to deal with an ever increasing number of specialities which develop out of new technology. Managers stand in many different kinds of relations to these varied specialists.

Relations Between Managers and Specialists *

The nature of the problems that arise between managers and specialists vary with their organisational relationships.

The specialist may be

1. On the staff of the manager, and has no other organisational link.
2. On the staff of the manager, but with a functional relationship to a more senior member of his speciality.
3. In a separate department. These departments can be distinguished by nature of their relationship with the other departments :
   - (a) They are purely service departments;
   - (b) Their task is solely to advise management;
   - (c) They have some authority to determine policy as well as to advise;
   - (d) They audit or inspect the work of other departments.
4. The specialist is outside the organisation and is employed as a consultant.

1. *Specialist on manager's staff.* The speeding up of technology has altered the situation in that new specialities have grown up and the old ones have to be subdivided. The older manager may not know anything about these, and a subordinate having specialist knowledge on the staff is likely to have more power because of this knowledge. A chief accountant for example, who has the computer manager reporting to him may find this different type of relationship from that which he has with his accounting staff. The manager, therefore, has more and more to work with subordinate whose speciality he knows little or nothing about. He

* Rosmary Stewart, *The Reality of Organisations*, pp. 97-106.

can create problems. One of the problems for the manager is how he can effectively manage something that he does not understand. The manager should not abdicate. He should train his staff to put forward proposals in as simple a way as possible and to describe the nature of the choice in language he can understand. He should learn to ask questions that can help him, and then to test this.

2. *Specialist on manager's staff, but reporting also to another superior specialist.* Here, the specialist, say a maintenance engineer, reports both to the line boss, who is responsible for what he does and when he does it, and also to a specialist superior outside the department, usually called the staff boss, who is responsible for how he does it. The task of the staff boss is to maintain professional standards as he is in a position to judge the professional competence. He may also lay down common procedures to be observed throughout the organisation. For example, the chief accountant may specify the form in which accounts are to be kept; the chief personnel officer may lay down policies for hiring and firing of employees; and the chief engineer may specify maintenance procedure.

This dual allegiance to line manager and staff boss is bound to create problems. The subordinate may be given conflicting instructions by his two bosses, or he may pay more attention to one boss than to the other. Such problems can be tackled and success ensured through the right attitude of the three people involved. The subordinate should have integrity and not play one boss against the other. The line and staff bosses should understand the demands of each other's work and seek to ensure that both contribute to the organisation's objectives, instead of playing politics or thinking too narrowly in terms of their own department.

3. *The specialist is in a separate department and not attached to the manager.* The simplest relationship with other departments is where the staff department provides a service that managers do not have to be persuaded to use. Catering is a good example; the typing pool can be another, although some managers may prefer to have the typists within their own departments. In these examples managers may grumble about the service that they get, but there will be none of the other difficulties that are found in relations between managers and specialists.

4. *The specialist employed from outside as consultant.* This type of relationship does not pose problems between the manager and the specialist. Outside specialist are used for a number of reasons. Small companies, or large companies that need highly specialist advice, may not have enough work to justify employing their own specialists. They may, therefore, find it more economical to make occasional or part-time use of outside specialists. The outsider may be able to contribute more because he has experience of other organisations than he could if he was employed by one company. Top management may want to have an outside opinion, and may also find it easier to talk to an outsider than to the subordinate specialist. Again, top management may be loathe to admit ignorance to a subordinate, and ask questions that may be foolish.

They may find it easier to do so to an outsider. Moreover, it may be easier to introduce, a change which the top management is desirous of introducing on the advice of an outside consultant, particularly if he is highly paid.

There are also dangers in the use of outside specialists. They may not be so responsible in their advice as their careers are less likely to be affected if their advice turns out to be poor. Management, too, tends to be less critical of the recommendations of outside experts. This may cause harm in the result if the advice is shown to be poor or irresponsible.

Specialist with functional authority. Sometimes a specialist does not only advise, but he is also given authority to issue instructions direct to line management on particular subjects. This authority of the staff department, called functional authority is usually concerned with how things should be done. Where specialists are given authority over particular policies or procedures the extent and nature of this authority should be clearly stated so as to try to prevent ambiguity about their power to issue instructions.

The danger of functional authority is that it reduces the scope of the manager's job. If many specialists are given such authority it would greatly diminish the manager's responsibility. Also there is a danger that the instructions issued by the manager and the specialist with functional authority may conflict.

COMMITTEES IN MANAGEMENT

A committee is a group of people who meet by plan to discuss or make decision for a particular subject. The need for committees stems from the growth of technology and specialisation in our commercial life and from the needs of people to participate. In business and industry, committees are appointed for a variety of reasons. Some committees undertake managerial functions and others do not. Some make decisions, others merely deliberate on problems without authority to decide. Some have authority to make recommendations to a manager, who may or may not accept them, while others are formed purely to receive information, without making recommendations or decisions.

Classification according to purposes. From the point of view of purposes for which committees may be created, they may be classified as—

1. Fact-finding Committees;
2. Problem-solving Committees;
3. Action Committees.

1. The fact-finding committee may be formed to collect information and report; or it may also be required to make recommendations, and this is a more common purpose.

2. The problem-solving objective would include fact-finding, an analysis of the possible solutions, and a recommendation of the solution

which the Committee feels is most wise. Usually, such recommendation is purely advisory.

3. The action objective is less common.

Why Committees

In a study of cross-section of managers in companies of different sizes, it was found that over 80 per cent of the organisations had regular committees. Two of the most important reasons for the use of committees were said to be the advantage of gaining group deliberations and judgment and inter-departmental co-ordination.

A group of people can bring to bear on a problem a wider range of experience than a single person. It is an old saying that "two heads are better than one". It is conceivable that results obtained by group judgment after due deliberation are likely to be superior to those obtained by individual judgment. Again, as every piece of work in each department in any enterprise has some connection with a piece of work in other departments, group participation is essential to ensure coordination and to promote cooperative relationships.

Another reason for the widespread use of committee is the fear of delegating too much authority to a single person. A committee may also be set up because the chief executive or the departmental head does not wish to take full responsibility for making a decision or to entrust the decision-making to a subordinate.

Committees have also been found useful for coordinating planning and the execution of programmes. They are also useful for transmission of information. All parties affected by a mutual problem or project can learn of it simultaneously. Committees are also valued as the best way to ensure informed decisions and because they promote creativity through the exchange of ideas.

Committees may also be appointed with a negative objective. The manager may appoint a committee when he does not want any action to ensue. One of the surest ways to delay the handling of a problem and even to postpone a decision indefinitely is to appoint a committee to study the matter, particularly if its membership is carefully selected with delay in mind.

Advantages of Committees. Committees have many potential advantages, and they are:

1. *Committees can improve decision-making by bringing together all those whose experience is necessary to the decision.* They are a means of coordinating the different view-points and knowledge of departments, and so ensuring that no relevant knowledge is overlooked.

2. *They can prevent decisions being taken too quickly.* Group judgment after due deliberation will produce superior decision to that made in a hurry by an individual.

3. *Committees have an educational value in keeping managers informed about the work of other parts of the company.* They encourage creativity.

4. *Decisions made by committees are likely to be more objective than those made by an individual.* A committee is impersonal in its actions, and its verdict is usually based on the facts presented. The very atmosphere of a committee tends to compel all to lay aside pettiness and personal prejudices or preconceived ideas and to act in accordance with the merits of the case.

5. *Committees act as motivators.* By participating in discussions or decisions in a committee, a member will likely be more highly motivated to accept a situation or implement decision than he would be if he did not involve himself in the subject matter through participation in committee deliberations.

6. *A committee can perform an excellent coordinating device.* It can bring together for agreement on a course of action all parties who will be involved in accomplishing an activity.

7. *Committees can be an excellent means of consolidating power and authority.* Often individual members do not have sufficient power and authority to make or implement a particular decision. A committee can then be used as a means of collecting and combining the authority and power of several individual members.

Disadvantages of Committees. Some of the more significant disadvantages of committees are:—

1. *High cost of committees.* Committee system is costly both in terms of time consumed and money involved. Committee work is time consuming for a number of people both in the actual meeting and in paper work before and after. For some, or all, of the people present at least part of the meeting may be a waste of time.

2. *Compromise and Watering down of decision.* It often happens that the committee decision is watered down, and is not the best from any one's point of view. Possibly no body is happy with a committee decision. Compromise might have been made to arrive at the decision. If the matter under consideration is so simple that differences of opinion do not exist, the use of committee time is wasteful. If differences of opinion exist, the point at which all or a majority of the committee members can agree will tend to be at the least common denominator of group agreement.

3. *Indecision.* Because of conflicting view points of members or poor leadership a committee is sometimes unable to reach needed decision.

4. *Tyranny or dominance of minority.* As committees tend to seek a consensus or unanimous agreement, it is easily possible for a minority of the committee to thwart committee action by refusing to accept the majority view-point.

5. *Splitting responsibility and accountability.* The Committees weaken accountability because no one may feel responsible for a decision taken by a committee. It is quite common for a member of a committee to say. "It was not my decision: the decision was made by the committee". This splitting of responsibility is probably one of the chief disadvantages of a committee.

How to make effective use of Committees

A manager can often use committees effectively by following the undernoted suggestions:

1. *Clear definition of purpose, authority and scope of committee.* The members of the committee should know the purpose of the committee, the exact scope of the subjects to be considered and the extent of authority. With authority and scope clear, committee members are better able to gauge whether they are meeting their responsibilities to the organisation.

2. *Proper size of the Committee.* The size that is appropriate will obviously vary with the purpose of the committee. Smaller groups are better for reaching conclusions. The number may be large if all interested parties have to participate in its deliberations.

3. *Composition of the Committee.* For a successful committee the members must be suitably representative of the interests they are intended to serve and possess the requisite authority, and they must be able to perform well in a group. The members should also have homogeneity of outlook so that they may be able to reach agreement, but heterogeneity of background so that each can make a distinctive contribution to the discussion. Strong personality clashes should be avoided as they are likely to inhibit constructive discussion.

4. *Careful selection of subject-matter.* Committee work should be limited to subject-matter that can be handled in group discussion. Certain kinds of subjects lend themselves to committee action, while others do not. Two groups of subjects are specially suitable for committees :

(a) problems that have many possible solutions;
(b) those that affect many aspects of the organisation.

5. *Importance of the Chairman.* Whatever the composition, size and purpose of the committee, good chairmanship will make a great difference to the speed and usefulness of the discussion. Efficient preparation of committee papers can also make a useful contribution.

It usually falls to the chairman to integrate committee deliberations. The chairman must also keep discussion from wandering. This often takes great skill, especially when a committee includes persons who enjoy the sound of their own voices or who lack ability to recognise essentials and to speak of them concisely.

6. *The Committee must be worth the cost.* Above all in measuring the success of committee operation, one must continually question whether the committees benefits are worth its cost. A committee can be justified only if the costs are definitely offset by tangible and intangible benefits.

7. *Follow-up action.* Merely making decision or recommendations is not enough. Follow up action must be taken. Minutes of the meetings should be promptly prepared and distributed to the members and also communicated to the line boss. The management should in turn inform the committee members as to the actions taken on the recommendation of the Committee.

Conclusion

Whatever the type or form of organisation, it is essential for good results to keep the following points in mind. The organisation structure should not be static. The people who man the organisation change; an enterprise grows and adopts new technology; the economic, political and social setting in which a company operates is continually in flux. The manager should keep his organisation adjusted to these changes. He should maintain flexibility in relation to duties and relationships. The most constant phenomenon is change. The successful manager is the master of change. Effective management creates a future; it does not wait for it. In approaching the future, management will have to find new ways of dealing with the accelerated rate of change. Not only must it respond to the external changes, but it must find new ways of planning, organising and motivating its internal human resources. We have already observed that a successful manager not only does a job well, but he knows how to get it done. One of the ways to accomplish this is by delegation of authority to subordinates, while assigning duties, which is discussed in the following chapter.

CHAPTER XXII

AUTHORITY AND RESPONSIBILITY

One of the purposes of an organisation chart is to show the structure of authority, power, accountability, and responsibility in an organisation. The chart represents channels or conduits through which authority, power and accountability flow. The authority and power flow downwards, through organisation structure, from the chief executive to the functional managers to the foremen, and accountability flows upwards from the foreman to the departmental manager to the chief executive.

Meaning of Authority

Authority is the right to do something or to tell someone else what to do. Authority is the key to the managerial job. It principally consists of the rights to decide and command subordinates. In an organisation therefore, the manager's authority consists of his right to do such things as :

(a) make decisions within the scope of his own authority;
(b) assign tasks to subordinates; and
(c) expect and require satisfactory performance from subordinates.

Sources of Authority. Authority can come either from above (i.e. from one's superiors) or below (i.e. from one's subordinates) For example, a department head gets his authority from the managing director. The managing director gets his authority from the Board of Directors, and the Board gets its authority from company's shareholders. Society has said that a firm's owners have the authority to manage their business. Thus "topdown" authority ultimately rests with society.

Authority also comes from one's subordinates. This is called "bottom up" authority because it starts at the worker level and moves upwards. How can a subordinate give his boss authority or even take away authority ? If the subordinate follows the instructions of the superior and carries out his orders, he gives authority to the boss. If he refuses to obey an order, or he follows it but does not really try to do a good job, he reduces his boss's authority.

Authority from the bottom up is sometimes called informal authority, because it is outside the formal organisation structure. It is not shown on the organisation chart. Individuals are willing to grant authority to superiors because of the following reasons :

A manager's personal qualities often cause subordinates to grant him informal authority. A manager's intelligence, wisdom, knowledge, appearance, or manner may affect how much acceptance his orders receive from subordinates. *Position or rank* may also result in subordinates granting informal authority. Simply because someone holds the position of managing director, others may respect his wishes and follow his direction. A person in an important position is often assumed to be someone to follow. *Basic beliefs in the firm's right to function* also result in the granting of authority. Workers may feel that the company has the right to operate and that the managers have the right to give orders. All these factors affect worker's and manager's decisions to grant authority to their superiors. The amount of informal authority they give reflects their support for a superior's decisions. Without their support the work will not be done as well, if it is done at all.

Power

Power is often confused with authority. Although power and authority are often found together, they are different. While authority is *the right to do something*, power is the *ability* to do it. In this role as a supervisor, a manager's power may be seen in his ability to cause subordinates to do what he wishes them to do. He exercises his power over others in diverse ways. They include: (1) promising rewards, (2) giving rewards, (3) threatening to withdraw current rewards, (4) withdrawing current rewards, (5) threatening punishment and (6) punishing.

Authority without power or power without authority will cause conflict in the organisation. Therefore, managers at all levels, must provide their subordinates with equal authority and power. That is, the subordinates should, for organisational stability, have means (power) equal to his right (authority) to do the things necessary to accomplish his part of the organisation's objectives.

Responsibility

Responsibility is the obligation to do something. In organisations, responsibility is the duty that one has to perform his organisational tasks, functions or assignments. Everyone in an organisation has responsibilities because everyone has a job or function to perform. It can best be described as a feeling one has regarding a task he is to do. It is created within the individual when he agrees to perform a task. Thus, responsibility is the obligation of a subordinate, to whom the superior has assigned a duty, to perform the service required. Authority and responsibility relationships, come into being where the superior-subordinate link exists. The superior has authority and the subordinate has responsibility.

Accountability

Besides his responsibility to himself, an employee or manager is accountable to higher authorities. A worker is accountable to his supervisor for his performance. The supervisor is in turn accountable to his department head, and so on to the top of the organisation. Ultimately the owners are accountable to society for the firm's performance.

Balance of Authority, Power, Responsibility and Accountability

Ideally, authority, power, responsibility and accountability should be equal to each other in every position in the firm. When any one is out of balance with the others, problems can arise. When authority in a position exceeds power, the person holding the job cannot be effective. He will be unable to use rewards and punishments to enfore authority. Even where authority and power are equal, they must be matched by responsibility and accountability. Otherwise the position holder may pass the buck to some one else when his actions cause problems.

DELEGATION OF AUTHORITY

Authority lodged in the manager gives him the power to get things done by others. Delegation of authority contributes to the creation of organisation. We have already noted that in any enterprise of size, establishment of departments is imperative, because no single executive can manage it alone. Creation of departments leads to delegation of authority to those who manage them. The principle of division of labour also applies to management, and the sub-division of duties also involves the sub-division and delegation of authority so that these duties may be accomplished. Since delegation means giving the subordinate authority to do something which the executive does not have the time to do, the subordinate gains by delegation, because he comes closer to his chief and is a true lieutenant, perhaps an understudy, ready for promotion. The superior gains also, because his mind is free from the anxiety of details. Delegation permits him to extend his influence beyond the limits of his own personal time, energy and knowledge. When the subordinate accepts the assignment through delegation of authority by the superior he becomes his superior's "delegate" and representative and assumes responsibility of performing the duties assigned to him.

Meaning and Elements of Delegation. Delegation is the assignment of work to a subordinate. Basically, it involves three elements or actions, either explicitly or implicitly :

1. *Assignment of duties* by the superior. Duties define the task which a person is to do. The manager indicates the work that the subordinate is required to do;
2. *Grant of authority* by the superior to the subordinate. This gives the subordinate the power and rights to use resources required to carry out the duties;
3. *Creation of obligation or responsibility* on the part of the subordinate to perform duties satisfactorily. The subordinate, by accepting the assignment, takes on an obligation to his superior to complete the job and do it well.

These three attributes or elements of delegation go together, and each depends on the others to support the whole and no two can stand alone. A clear understanding of each of these elements is necessary for mastering the process of delegation. A brief description of each is given below.

Assigning Duties. While allocating duties, an executive should know clearly what to delegate and what to retain. He should first consider the reasonable units of work and then select the most competent individual to be incharge of that work. He may express the duties either in the form of functions or in terms of goals and objectives or results. Expressing in terms of goals will probably result in more effective delegation, for the subordinate gets the mental satisfaction of being involved in fulfilling a mission through the performance of certain allotted activities.

Delegating Authority. In the process of delegating authority, the executive gives permission to the subordinate to use certain rights, such as the right to spend money, to direct the work of other people, to use raw materials, or to represent the company to outsiders. Effective delegation, however, requires that the limits of authority should be made clear to each subordinate. The superior and the subordinates should clearly understand the subordinate's right to act, to request others to act and to discipline. In short, they should clearly understand the limits of the authority, and it is never unlimited. Also, the superior, in delegating authority, does not "give away authority". He only delegates a part of it, retaining ultimate authority and responsibility.

There are various degrees of delegation, some giving the delegate or subordinate broad powers but others being rather limited. Each sets a different kind of relationship with the superior who delegates. Moreover, one person rarely receives one delegation. Instead, he gets different degrees of delegation for different duties. Keith Davis[1] mentions 5 distinctly different degrees of delegation :

1. Authority to which no prior notice, no approval, and no reporting required;
2. Authority to act, with reporting required, but no prior notice or approval;
3. Authority to act only with prior notice;
4. Authority to act only after consulting an appropriate staff adviser;
5. Authority to act only with prior approval.

Creating Responsibility or Obligation. The last step in the process of delegation is the creation of an obligation on the part of the subordinates for the competent or satisfactory performance of their duties. The creation of obligation is really "assumption" of responsibility by the subordinates. By accepting the authority and by responding to it, the subordinate becomes the superior's "delegate" and assumes the obligation or responsibility to carry out the assignment and to account to the superior for his performance. If he does not accept the assignment, delegation has been merely attempted and not made. A subordinate may accept the authority because of positive inducements or moral compulsion or coercion. By accepting exercise of authority, an individual is able thereby to contribute to the attainment of an enterprise purpose which

1. *Human Relation at Work*, p. 185.

he recognises as being good. By accepting an exercise of authority, he may thereby attain the approbation of his fellow workers, or obtain rewards from his superior. By accepting an exercise of authority, he may be acting in accordance with his own moral standards, or he may be responding to the qualities which he perceives in his superior. But there may be compulsion or coercion involved in this. For example, fear of losing the job, or demotion, or of social disapprobation.

If the last reason for acceptance prevails, delegation is poor. Therefore, it is necessary for the manager to remember that a subordinate will assume responsibility only if he receives authority to perform and take action. He should also bear in mind that when he assigns activities to his subordinates and therefore does not perform the work himself, he is still ultimately responsible for its performance. Since total responsibility remains even after delegation, we say that responsibility cannot be delegated.

Principles of Delegation. The following rules or principles are fundamental in relation to delegation of authority :

1. *Authority and Responsibility must be equal or co-terminus and co-extensive.* Orders are issued by virtue of authority and the recipients of orders are invested with responsibility. Therefore, there should be equality between authority and responsibility, otherwise many undesirable effects will be produced in the organisation. If, for example, authority exceeds responsibility, the subordinate may be tempted to misuse it. This will not be acceptable to those who are subject to it and will produce all sorts of resistances. On the other hand, if a subordinate accepts responsibility without authority to use resources, he will be unable to perform the task assigned to him. He will not be in a position to command co-operation for attaining desired goals. For example, it will be a waste of time to tell a machinist to get tools from the tool room unless he is given authority to require them of the person incharge of the tool room. Similarly it will create only problems and frustrations if a manager is told to perform a job which will require certain expenditures, but he is not authorised to make the expenditures. Therefore, an individual can be held strictly accountable only to the extent that the actions are really subject to his control. Although there are certain exceptions to equal authority and responsibility, yet if a man is assigned duties without responsibility, he will be *irresponsible;* but if he has duties and no authority to accomplish them, he is organisationally *impotent.*[1]

2. *Responsibility cannot be delegated.* When an executive delegates authority to a subordinate, he does not absolve himself from his responsibility, or does not abdicate responsibility. Therefore, by delegating duties, the executive does not free himself from his own obligations concerning them, for he must continue to guide, direct and hold responsible the subordinates to whom he has delegated authority. By delegating authority, the executive, in a manner, increases his responsibility. He will be now accountable to his superior for the acts of his

1. Keith Davis, *op. cit.*, p. 186.

subordinates also. The ultimate responsibility for the accomplishment of the task is his, even where it has been assigned to subordinates.

3. *Dual Subordination should be avoided.* No man can serve two masters properly. Therefore, dual command should be avoided, for it is a perpetual source of conflicts. It also violates the organisational principle of unit of command. Hence, an employee should receive orders from one superior only. For example, a department head should go through his foreman when giving orders and not go directly to the employees. "One boss for any one man" should be the rule.

4. *Duties should not overlap.* Duties of one person should not be permitted to overlap those of another. Overlapping duties put each person in an untenable position and are the surest way to develop clashes between the two. For example, A and B are jointly responsible for certain control functions. A fails to act (depending on B) and B fails to act (depending on A) and the job is not done. Both will have to face reprimand. The result of overlapping duties is that the joint workers find that co-operation is difficult.

5. *Organisational gaps should be avoided.* There are organisational gaps when certain duties need to be done but no one is responsible for them. As the duty which is "gapped" is necessary to the organisation, people become frustrated when they find that they have no person to depend on to get this necessary work performed and that their own work is being delayed or hindered because of this. Sometimes several persons step into the void to try to do the job, causing a *de facto* overlap, with all the problems described above.

6. *Improper use of Exception Principle should be avoided.* The *Exception Principle* states that an executive attains best performance by delegating to his subordinates as much of the routine operations as possible, and leaves for himself only broad general problems and exceptions to routine. Very often, however, this principle is misused by executives, because they do not understand its significance and overlook certain pre-requisites of its application. The exception principle assumes that the executive before delegating has worked out careful policies and procedures to guide those who will perform the delegated activities. Unless policies and procedures do exist, each employee may follow his own viewpoint, producing a number of unrelated activities. Therefore, the executive must, at the time of delegating authority and creating obligation, clearly express to each subordinate incharge of each unit the scope of the authority delegated. He must also establish controls so that he can assure that policies and procedures are being followed. The exception principle also requires an executive to know his subordinates—their strengths, weaknesses, needs, and temperaments. Also, he can delegate to the extent that persons are qualified. All this means that an executive should apply the exception principle only to the extent that he has pre-established policies and procedures, that he knows his people, that they are trained and equipped, and that he can control what he has delegated. To do otherwise is to invite conflict.

OBSTACLES TO DELEGATION

The foregoing comments show that delegation is not easy to accomplish. It runs into certain obstacles. The manager who recognises them is in a better position to overcome them. Some of the obstacles arise within the manager himself, and others through the attitude of the subordinates. Therefore, in spite of good intentions, the transfer of authority from the superior to the subordinate does not take place. Some of the obstacles in the way of delegation are summarised below.

Reluctance to Delegate. The reluctance on the part of the executive to delegate, although he pays 'lip service' to the need of delegation, depends on his personality. We shall list the reasons why superiors are reluctant to delegate authority.

1. *Perfectionism.* An executive may feel that he can do a job better himself. This is particularly true if he has done the job in the past and has developed a degree of skill which makes the initial efforts of a subordinate appear clumsy and inadequate. In such a situation, he may stick to the old cliche, "If you want a job done well, do it yourself". He is not a manager in the true sense. The longer the manager continues to do the job well, the longer the period until some one else is able to take over and he can then do some more important business. Therefore, he must accept the fact that someone else is capable of filling his shoes, and perhaps even of doing a better job of it.

2. *Autocratic Attitude.* An executive may be a power-worshipping autocrat, who believes in the least delegation of authority, and who interferes with the limited authority of his subordinates.

3. *Direction.* Many managers have difficulty in directing the efforts of other people. They may be impatient. Others may misinterpret the instructions which they give. Therefore, an executive who lacks ability to direct cannot direct however much he may wish to do so.

4. *Confidence.* Superiors often lack confidence in their subordinates for jobs they have not done before. So a manager who has no confidence in his subordinates does not delegate. But if delegations are not made, the future manager has no opportunity to gain experience. Confidence is built up gradually and on the basis of success.

5. *Controls.* One reason superiors resist delegation is the possibility that serious damage will be done before they find out about it. To prevent this controls are necessary.

6. *Temperamental aversion to take risk.* It is true that risk is involved in delegating a job to a subordinate. The manager may have temperamental aversion to taking a chance. Such a manager will be reluctant to delegate anything to anyone unless he adjusts himself emotionally as well as intellectually to the element of risk.

7. *Competition.* Some managers fear that if their subordinates learn too much they will become rivals. The obstacle is usually unexpressed and may be unconscious. It is very real nevertheless.

Reluctance on the part of Subordinates. Delegation is not always welcomed or carried through effectively by subordinates. A subordinate may shrink from accepting, even when the boss is ready and able to delegate authority, for the following reasons :

1. *Easier to ask.* Subordinates often find it easier to ask their superior for an answer than to figure it out for themselves. This is particularly true with some superiors : those who will accept only one answer to a problem—their own. In such a situation a subordinate may find that it does not pay to work out a problem. Rather, it is more effective to go to the superior for an answer.

2. *Fear of Criticism.* Subordinates sometimes fear criticism on the part of their superiors. This fear is often justified. In fact, some superiors tend to criticize any action taken by a subordinate. This discourages initiative, causes resentment and destroys a subordinate's self-confidence.

3. *Lack of Information or Resources.* A subordinate may hesitate to accept a new assignment if he believes that he lacks the necessary information and resources to do a good job.

4. *Overwork.* Subordinates may avoid delegation because they feel that they will not be able to do an additional task along with those which they presently have been assigned. This may be a perfectly legitimate reason. Unless the requirements for other tasks are relaxed or deadlines adjusted, the subordinate who avoids further delegation in this situation is wise.

5. *Lack of Self-confidence and Fear of Failure.* Lack of self-confidence also stands in the way of some people in accepting a delegation. Such subordinates often feel that they will fail, and so do not want additional responsibilities.

6. *Lack of Positive Incentive.* Subordinates need some system of reward for the acceptance and successful completion of delegated tasks. Such rewards are not always automatically provided. A successful completion of work is taken in stride and no mention is made of it. Some superiors systematically avoid praise. In such circumstances, positive inducements and incentives are lacking or are inadequate to prompt a subordinate to take an additional load. It is the responsibility of the superior to provide inducements in the form of pay increase, or improved opportunity for promotion, a fancy title, acknowledged status in the organisation, or personal recognition and approval by the boss.

All these obstacles show that the relationship between superior and subordinate is personal, and delegation works substantially as it is intended to work.

How to delegate more successfully. The following steps will aid more successful delegation of authority :

1. Developing a personal discipline for supervision: this requires a faith in the ability of subordinates and a tolerance of human mistakes. He must accept the position that someone else is capable of doing the job that he did before.
2. Reviewing the general concept with his own superior regarding

further delegation with a view to ascertaining whether it will be valuable to the organisation.

3. Establishment of clear and definite goals so that the subordinate knows why his work is necessary and important. This step is the key to successful delegation.
4. Determining what to delegate. This will involve appraisal of capacities of the people and needs of the job. After this authority and responsibility will be clearly defined to enable the subordinate to know the extent of his authority and the nature of the job.
5. Motivating subordinates by encouraging them in the effective carrying out of their delegated tasks. This can be achieved by providing positive inducements and incentives.
6. Delegating a complete job so that the subordinate completes the job and reports back to the superior the completion of that task. Only in this way the superior will be freed from this job to concentrate on other important ones, although he will be available for questions or discussion.
7. Developing subordinates through planned experience and training to accept delegation.
8. Setting up adequate controls which will act as selective checkpoints where measures will be made to see if any corrective action is needed. They will provide a warning before the damage is done. In this manner, the superior can protect his own responsibility for the results of the delegation as well as protect his subordinate from serious consequences.

Test of Effective Delegation. An organisation employing effective delegation would be characterised by :[1]

1. Members who have a clear understanding of their duties and authorities.

2. Members who have the information and facilities they need to accomplish their tasks.

3. Supervisors who concentrate on the results of subordinates' activities rather than on the details of how they get those results.

4. An easy flow of communication throughout the organisation.

5. A realization among subordinates that an outstanding performance will be recognised.

6. A pace in subordinates' activity which is at least as great as the supervisor's.

7. Subordinates who are kept informed on progress of work for which they share responsibility.

8. Subordinates who are encouraged to speak their minds freely and without apprehension of censure.

9. Supervisors who consult the subordinates most familiar with a problem upon what action must be taken.

---

1. Anderson, Richard C., *Management Practices*, p. 120

10. Contacts with other organisation units which are based upon needs of the task, not upon position or status.

11. Operating decisions which are made at the point of action.

12. Supervisors who have well-established and functioning controls

13. Members who are not expected to have all the details about their subordinates' activities in mind at all times.

14. Job instructions which are given by immediate supervisors—not by supervisors two or more levels removed.

15. Encouragement of innovation and originality through sympathetic reception of suggestions and new ideas.

SPAN OF CONTROL

Span of control (also called span of management/supervision) indicates the number of people directed or managed effectively by a single executive or supervisor. Stated differently, it refers to the number of subordinates reporting directly to a single manager who is accountable for their activities. Thus if a General Manager has 5 managers reporting to him directly in a firm employing 10,000 employees, the span of control of the General Manager is five, not 10,000. It is an accepted proposition that the larger the number of subordinates reporting directly to an executive, the more difficult it is for him to supervise and co-ordinate their activities effectively. On the other hand, if the number is too small, the task may not be performed efficiently. Generally speaking, for a sound organisation the span should be short, but care should be taken to see that the executive is not overloaded with too many subordinates.

The limits to the effective span of control arise from the following factors :

1. The capacity and skill of the executive, because all executives are not alike, limits the span of control.

2. The time at the disposal of the executive is limited.

3. With the increase in the number of activities to be supervised and controlled, the executive will have to lose a substantial part of his time in getting information.

The question of determining the proper span of control for a manager is a problem of great importance in relation to the organisation structure. Different opinions have been expressed by different writers; but the ratios between the superior and subordinates range from 1 : 5 in the higher executive positions and 1 : 25 in the lowest positions. Thus a foreman may have 25 men under him and manager may have 5 sub-managers and the latter may have 8 foremen. An important contribution to the theory of span of control has been made by V.A. Graicunas,[1] a management consultant. In his study, he analysed the nature of relationships that are brought into existence when an individual acquires subordinates. The acquisition of a new subordinate increases not only "direct single" relationships but also "direct group"

1. *The capacity and skill of the executive.*

relationships and "cross relationships". Graicunas showed that if a manager X supervises two subordinates, A and B, he will have four to six relationships within his span of control: two direct single relationships—X to A and X to B, two direct group relationships—X to A with B and X to B with A, and two cross relationships—A with B and B with A. After explaining the nature of multiple relationship, he calculated that the total number of relationships when an executive supervises two persons is six, with 4 subordinates it increases to 44. When a fifth subordinate is added, it rises to 100, and to 222 for a sixth and to 490 for the seventh subordinate added. By the time the tenth subordinate is reached, the number of relationships goes up to 5,210 and when we reach twelfth, the number jumps up to 24,708. These figures led him to conclude that as the number of subordinates increases, there is a more than proportionate increase in the total number of relationships and this imposes a heavier load on the mental capacity of the superior executive.

Factors determining Span of Control. The following factors determine the number of persons that one executive can effectively manage:

1. The capacity and skill of the executive.
2. Capacity and skill of the subordinates.
3. Stability of operations. A dynamic situation requires closer control and more time for co-ordination.
4. Type of operation. In general, a highly specialised mass production factory requires a smaller span in the management ranks than a retail store. In a factory each unit and department tends to be immediately dependent on other units for its work, which means that activities must be closely controlled and co-ordinated in order to keep all units busy. In this case, one superintendent directs only a few foremen.
5. The extent to which management activities, as distinguished from operative activities, are supervised. An executive who supervises other *managers* has a job different from the foreman who supervises operative workers. As a result, the optimum span varies from position to position. As the nature of the work performed by subordinates becomes increasingly routine, less subject to error, and less likely to involve complicated decision-making, direction or co-ordination, the span of control may be increased.

The Problem of Layering. Span of control determines whether an organisation structure shall be a "flat" or a "tall" one. If the supervisory responsibilities are such that each executive can direct a relatively small number of people, the organisation will be tall (also called deep); if a large number, the organisation will be flat. Therefore, a *tall structure* is one which has a small span of control. It typically results in a large number of levels in relation to the number of workers supervised. The *flat structure* has large span of control and tends to have fewer levels. The figures on next page exhibit the two types of structures. The flat structure has only two levels of supervision for 48 employees, whereas the tall structure requiries four levels to service the same number of employees.

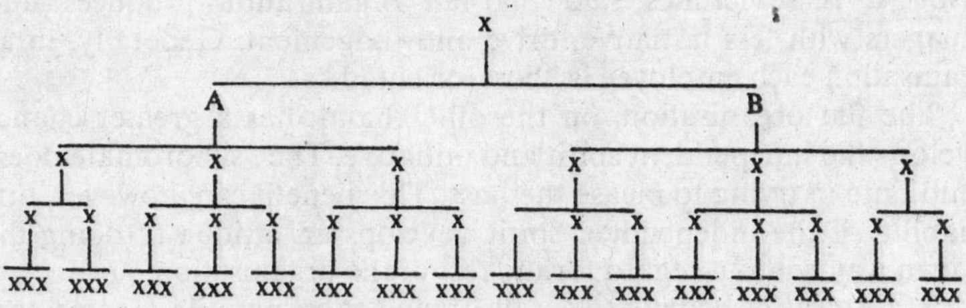

TALL ORGANISATION
(Maximum Span of Control : 3. Four levels of supervision)

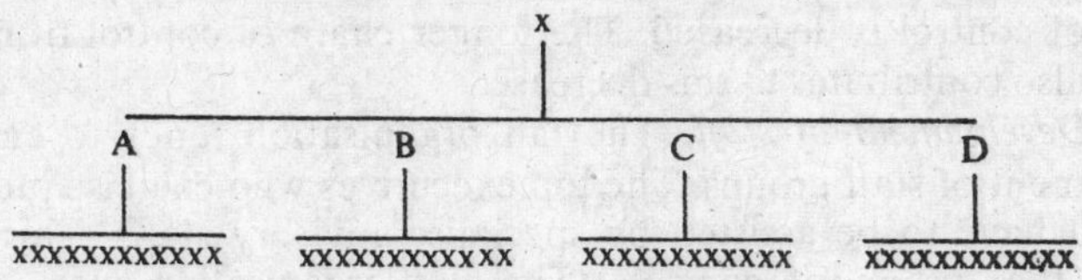

FLAT ORGANISATION
(Maximum Span of Control : 12. Two levels of supervision)

The flat organisation accomplishes its jobs with fewer supervisors. It will be noticed in the illustration that it uses only 5 supervisors as compared to the tall organisation's 25 supervisors. The result is that supervisory costs in the flat organisation tend to be consistently smaller.

Many of the differences between tall and flat organisations affect human relations. Davis enumerates some of these as:

1. Communication.
2. Relation of supervisor and his people.
3. Control of activities.
4. Development of staff.

1. *Communication.* The chain of communication upward or downward is much longer in the tall organisation. If a worker wishes to contact the chief executive he must go through 3 other levels of supervision before reaching him. Likewise communication within management is greatly complicated because there are more units to be informed. The longer the line of communication, the greater the chance for upward information to be filtered and edited. The flat organisation has a shorter and simpler communication chain, but supervisors have so many people to direct that they cannot spend much time face to face with any members of their group.

2. *Relation of supervisor and his people.* A tall organisation encourages frequent contact, mutuality and team work. These are important benefits. However, autocratic domination may develop along with these benefits. The chief executive who believes in close control and in making even minor decisions will prefer a tall type of structure and gather around him people who are ready to work under close control. For this

reason it is sometimes said that tall organisation produces middle managers with less initiative, drive and judgement. Generally, in a tall organisation each employee is "boss-oriented."

The flat organisation, on the other hand, has a greater chance to develop the independent spirit and initiative. The subordinate does not spend time in trying to please the boss. This benefit can, however, turn to a liability if the independent spirit develops an attidue of doing things his own way without regard for the rest of the organisation.

3. *Control of activities.* A tall organisation permits greater control of the performance of employees. Control requirements are one of the reasons for establishing a small span of supervision. But actually because of larger number of managers whose work has to be co-ordinated, the quality of control is decreased. The longer chain of control from top to bottom also contributes to this decrease.

4. *Development of staff.* The tall organisation tends to encourage development of staff groups. The top executives who exercise judgement and skill have to be assisted by specialist advisory staffs. This further extends the system of controls. The flat organisation may lack co-ordination so that time and effort are wasted. If staff specialists are not used the technical decisions made by line people may be of poorer quality and less uniform.

Both tall and flat organisation structures have their advantages. A flat organisation is strong if its managers are well trained and have sound judgement; it encourages initiative, independence and other human values. But an excessively flat structure will reduce both morale and efficiency, because executive cannot develop sufficient personal contact, communication and co-ordination.

DECENTRALISATION

The term "decentralisation" is commonly used in two senses in management field—(1) *Managerial Decentralisation,* and (2) *Geographical Decentralisation* or *Geographical Dispersion.*

Managerial decentralisation means wide delegation or distribution of authority from the superior to all the people right down to the lowest unit throughout the organisation. Although decentralisation is an advanced form of delegation to operating units and so delegation in large measure, the two are not the same and should be distinguished. Delegation can take place from one superior to one subordinate and be a complete process, but decentralisation, as its definition indicates, takes place only when the fullest possible delegation or distribution of authority is made to all, or most, of the people in the organisation, in respect of the specific function or activity or responsibility. It may, however, be remembered that managerial decentralisation does not necessarily mean distribution of authority in respect of all activities. One function may be decentralised and another may stay centralised. For example, in an automobile manufacturing concern, the sales function may be distributed or decentralised to product divisions, while labour relations may remain centralised because of company-wide bargaining. Similarly, purchasing of strategic materials may be centralised, but operating purchases may be decentralised to each factory.

Geographical decentralisation means geographical dispersion of the activities of a company. It is thus the physical decentralisation or dispersion of the production and service activities over several manufacturing plants or offices, each located in a different part of the country. The geographical dispersion is suitable in the case of industries and services which are big enough to admit of a network of units, spread far and wide in the country, such as the Life Insurance Corporation of India with divisional and unit offices all over the country.

Managerial decentralisation can take place without geographical dispersion and vice versa, but the two usually go together. In our discussion here, we are dealing with managerial decentralisation in the sense of diffusion of initiative and responsibility. It refers, as stated above, to systematic effort to delegate to the lowest appropriate levels all authority except that which can best be exercised at a central point. When no delegation is made, the authority, and hence, the responsibility is centralised. The detailed and comprehensive planning is done by the chief executive or by a small group of top-level managers. Too much centralisation, however, leads to over-loading of top executives, clogging of the line of communication and slowing down decision. But it may be emphasised at this stage that neither decentralisation nor centralisation is absolute. The extent to which decentralisation exists in any organisation depends on the extent to which clear cut decision-making authority is vested in levels below the top management level.

Managerial decentralisation is both a philosophy of management and a technique. As a philosophy it refers to top management's belief that *all managers,* and their personnel should have maximum opportunity to develop and use their talents as responsible people and, therefore, that managers should be given the necessary authority, personal development, plant facilities, and top-management guidance for maximum decision-making in their own area of operations. As a technique, decentralisation is a way of organising which distributes authority to semi-independent decision units, but which exercises carefully devised control to make sure that all separate decision units are working towards mutual goals. It increases the number of centres of initiative and gets rid of rigidity by permitting a dozen different independent decisions and, consequently, perhaps a dozen different approaches to a problem. This helps in the achievement of the popular management principle that "subject to policy guidance, each operating decision should be made as far from the central source of authority as the competence of the personnel permits." This is what is described by management experts as "centralised policy determination and decentralised management". It provides a clear balance between the central control needed to keep all parts working together and the freedom required to develop flexibility and small-group team work.

Bottom-up Management or Trickle-down Management. Junior executives' "freedom to make mistakes" underlies all decentralisation. William Given, President of American Brake Shoe Company, called it "freedom to fail" and devised, what he described "Bottom-up Management", based on this philosophy which is a combination of decentralisation and participation.

A typical chief executive regards all those who are below him in the organisation *as working for him* and servicing his needs. In assigning functions within the organisation structure, he follows the "Trickle-down" system. Under this system the assignment flows down from the top of the organisation; and the subordinates are deemed to exist to "help" the superior do his job. If we look at the division of work from the opposite end, i.e., from the "bottom up", we see that the functions necessary to operate the organisation are divided into parts and then grouped together for convenience of work performance. A supervisory element is then placed over these groups, beginning with the lowest level and moving upwards until we reach the apex of the pyramid at the top of the organisation. The purpose of these supervisory levels is to assist the work groups to carry out their tasks. When we view the organisation structure in this light, we see that *the superior becomes the helper;* that is, he is there to help and guide subordinates in the performance of their tasks. This is called by Given as Bottom-up Management. This reverses traditional thinking and views the executive as working for his men instead of the men working for him. His job is to service them so that they can perform their work more efficiently. In a sense, he is a service man to other managers, instead of a boss of them. In order that they may do their job, operations are decentralised into functional units, and authority is delegated as far as possible. Bottom-up concept appears to be more useful than Trickle-down system.

This pattern of organisation gives people all along the management line freedom to think, to plan to take calculated risks, to make decisions and—most important of all, says Given—*freedom to fail.* If men are to make decisions, they must have freedom to make mistakes occasionally without the feeling that their first mistake will cost them the job or ruin their chances of promotion. An executive who applies bottom-up management is as much a teacher as an order-giver. He helps his personnel learn how to lead and make effective decisions, and in doing this, he himself grows.

Circumstances that bring about decentralisation. The more important circumstances that bring about decentralisation are as follows :—

1. Mere growth and size may make decentralisation necessary; the organisation may become cumbersome; good direction is difficult; flexibility is lacking; and top executives become surrounded by assistants and committees.
2. The characteristics of the company's products or markets may make decentralisation desirable: can provide a special emphasis on a product line or concentrated attention to a particular market.

3. Physical separation of plants or facilities may call for some decentralised decision-making.
4. Technological developments may create the necessity for specific delegation of authority and responsibility.
5. If a company is diversified in products or processes, specialised knowledge in each dissimilar operating unit may make decentralisation mandatory.

Benefits of decentralisation. The benefits of decentralisation may be listed as follows :—

1. Decentralisation places decision-making authority, responsibility and accountability as near as possible to the place where the action takes place. Or stated another way it pinpoints responsibility for a product line or an area.
2. Delegating a decision further down the hierarchy may bring about internal and external economies. Internal economies of decentralisation include better and speedier decisions and communication, better utilisation of lower and middle management, greater incentive, more and improved training opportunities, insurance that some product will not be pushed at the expense of others. This type of economy makes possible the growth of the enterprise. External economies are reduction in the unit cost of production caused by factors outside the business.
3. Decentralisation permits the company to move quicker and with more flexibility in meeting competition.
4. Decentralisation of activities may cause a more widespread distribution of sales and purchases which may reduce proportionately the unavoidable impact of a decline.
5. Decentralisation provides a better means of developing future managers and executives. This is probably the most important benefit, particularly in our country where the short supply of competent managers is "the major limiting factor" on the rapid growth of our economy and of our principal industries.
6. Decentralisation allows the top management to concentrate on their primary job of policy formulation, long-range planning, and the devising of proper measurements of performance.

While decentralisation makes for an adequate number of managers commensurate with the delegation of authority, it does not follow that it is necessarily good and centralisation essentially bad. We should really find a balance between decentralisation of authority and responsibility on the one hand and centralisation of control on the other. Decentralised authority requires centralised control. The balance between the two can be found by appraising the advantages of delegation of decision-making powers to subordinates down the line in comparison with the disadvantages and difficulties which arise with regard to the necessity of single-mindedness in direction.

Communication. Top management needs to keep lower level supervisors and workers informed if the firm is to operate as an integrated organisation. By freely sharing information, the management takes the employees into its confidence, prepares them for changes, avoids the spread of misunderstanding and rumours, and makes them more intelligent on the problems and policies of the enterprise. Providing early and accurate information to line management for transmission to employees also helps to develop the prestige of the foreman. It is equally important that there be continuous communication from the employees to the management. This is called "two-way" communication. Most commonly, this refers to communication up and down the vertical dimension of the organisational hierarchy. Principles and policies flow through formal channels from the "big-boss" at the top of the pyramid *downwards* to the rank-and-file workers which form its base. Attitudes, feelings, and suggestions flow from the broad worker base *upwards* to the apex of the pyramid. Communication is also imperative *breadthwards*, i.e., communication among people at the *same* level in the hierarchy.

Vertically, there are three levels at which the interchange of understanding may take place : (1) between top management and supervisors; (2) between top management and employees; and (3) between supervisors and employees. Suggestions for the first level include :

1. Daily personal contacts by each member of management with his immediate subordinates in management, answering questions or complaints immediately.
2. Fact-finding surveys of supervisors' opinions and attitudes, valuable in revealing important information to management, stimulating supervisory morale and making supervisors management-minded, and shaping a pattern for improved management policy and practice.
3. Conferences with supervisors, achieved through such devices as round-table conferences, open forums, panel discussion, topical outlines for discussion, and periodic week-end meetings.
4. Supervisors' manuals and hand-books.

Suggestions for interchange between top management and employees include :—

1. Personal visits to various departments.
2. Talks to employees.
3. Letters to employees' homes.
4. Question-and-Answer Sessions.
5. Informal meetings.

Suggestions for interchange between supervisors and employees include day-to-day relationships, talks with individual employees, and group talks, which afford an easy and natural opportunity for the following :—

1. Giving credit promptly where it is due.
2. Seeking out and settling problems before they reach the grievance stage.
3. Encouraging the subordinate to look to his superior for information, help, and advice.
4. Discussing a mistake before the facts surrounding it have become vague, or before it is assumed that an error has been excused or overlooked.

5. Explaining promptly any change in policy that affects the employee, discussing the "why" as well as the "how".
6. Voicing the word of counsel or interest, and giving praise when due.
7. Giving periodic reviews and personal progress and problems.
8. Sounding out employees' opinions on certain business matters and reporting findings.

Laterally, communications at the same levels may take place through the medium of meetings of top-level staff members, plant managers, general foreman, line supervisors, or some other recognised layer in the company set-up. Here the conference and committee devices are used quite widely. With this concept of communication at the same level, we have "three-way" communication which covers the length and breadth of the organisation. To this may be added the most important dimension—the *depth*, which means action and reaction, the attitude of co-operation on the part of all concerned leading to high morale and complete harmony among the members of the organisation.

INFORMAL ORGANISATION

So far we have been dealing with formal organisation and its problems. But all organisations are not formal. Along with this formal organisation there exists what is called an informal organisation in an enterprise. A formal organisation, we have seen, is established by virtue of the power for sanctions, punishments or rewards. It includes passing down, through the line organisation, orders, directives, instructions and sanctions.

Nature and Characteristics of Informal Organisation. Informal organisation comprises the social inter-relationships of people within and without the enterprise, and is not established or required by formal organisation. It arises from the social interaction of people, which means it develops spontaneously as people associate with each other. Formal organisation emphasizes positions in terms of authority and function. Informal organisation lays emphasis on people and their relationships. As a result informal authority attaches to a *person*, while formal authority attaches to a *position* and a person wields it only by virtue of his position. Informal authority is personal, but formal authority is *institutional*.

Formal and informal organisation move together; the former is created and the latter comes into being or develops spontaneously. In every organisation it is found that several persons are in frequent contact with each other although their relationships are not necessitated by the formal organisation. And whenever people are associated, social relationships and groupings are bound to come about. This happens because human needs are satisfied in a way formal organisation does not and cannot satisfy. Informal organisations establish certain attitudes, understandings, customs, habits, and institutions and bring about the condition under which formal organisation may arise. Informal organisation is found on all levels within the managerial hierarchy from the bottom to the top. It exists as a necessary condition for collaboration. It can have constructive or destructive influence on formal organisation and the manager must not overlook its existence.

It is quite common to find in a working-group an individual who exercises a greater influence on his co-workers than is indicated by his rank or position in the organisation. He may be an old or senior employer whose advice, judgment or sympathy are readily sought. He may have a pleasant and responsive personality which make him popular so that his suggestions or requests are willingly accepted. If an executive can get such a person on his side and secure his interested co-operation, his group will achieve highly satisfactory results. It is, therefore essential for an executive to know not only the formal relationships between the members of his group but also the informal ones. When an informal leader is working against the management, his effect is far greater than his numerical proportion in the group.

Functions of Informal Groups. Informal groups arise, we have said earlier also, because they satisfy wants of their members. This function of informal organisation helps to preserve the group's integrity as a group.

The second function is the provision of social satisfaction. Informal organisations give a man recognition, status and further opportunity to relate to others. In a large office an employee may feel only a wage-earner, but his informal group gives him personal attachment and status. With them he is somebody, although in the formal structure he is one of a thousand clerks. His work may be uninteresting, and he may not look forward to doing it. When he can think of meeting his friends, sharing their jokes, and eating with them, his day takes a new dimension that makes easier any disagreeableness or routine in his work.

A third informal group function is communication. In order to meet wants and to keep its members informed of what is happening regarding want satisfaction, the group develops systems and channels of communication.

A fourth function is social control, by which the behaviour of others is influenced and regulated.

Some Areas of Danger. Each of the above four functions of informal organisation creates a major danger or difficulty which requires careful attention on the part of management.

1. *Resistance to Change.* With the persistence of certain culture, there develops a tendency to perpetuate the *status quo* and oppose change. What has been good, is good and shall be good is the attitude. Managers who are concerned with bringing about change must heed informal organisation and prepare their groups in advance for change.

2. *Role Conflict.* Quest for group satisfaction may lead members away from organisation objectives. What is good for the employee is not always good for his employer. Coffee break may be desirable, but if employees spend an extra 15 minutes socialising in the forenoon and afternoon, productivity may be reduced to the disadvantage of both employer and the public. Hence a role conflict occurs. Much of his role conflict can be avoided by carefully cultivating mutual interests within informal groups.

3. *Rumour.* The third function—Communication—leads to rumour. The whole informal communication system is known as the "Grapevine", and rumour is the untrue part of it. Rumour is a dangerous disease that sweeps through an organisation as fast as wild fire, and usually with as much damage. Rumour should be fought firmly and consistently. The best approach in dealing with rumour is to get at its causes, rather than try to kill

it after it has already started. A co-operative high-morale group does not indulge in rumour-mongering. Therefore, conditions to generate high morale should be created by the executive.

4. *Conformity*. The fourth function—social control—exerts strong pressures for conformity under formal organisation. But conformity is caused as much by informal organisation.

Benefits of Informal Organisation. (1) Informal organisations bring a number of benefits and advantage should be taken of their presence. Most important benefit is that they blend with formal systems to make a workable system for getting work done. Many requirements which cannot be met with formal organisation can be met better by informal relations. A good leader very often secures much greater co-operation through informal contacts.

(2) Another benefit is that an informal organisation lightens the workload of the formal manager. If the employees know that their manager has the support of the existing informal organisation, they are more likely to respond to his ideas, to be motivated to work efficiently. The manager in this situation feels more free to delegate and decentralise because he is confident that his group will co-operate.

(3) A significant benefit of informal organisation is that it gives satisfaction and stability to work group. It is the means by which workers achieve a sense of belonging and security.

(4) A well-known benefit of informal organisation is that it can be a useful channel of employee communication. Management, in fact, often depends on informal system to convey certain types of information. It also acts as a safety valve for the frustrations and other emotional problems. If a man is unhappy and feels he cannot talk to his supervisor, he will perhaps talk to a friend.

(5) A benefit which is not generally recognised is that the presence of informal organisation encourages a manager to plan and act more carefully than he would otherwise.

Informal Communication. One of the manifestations of informal organisation, we have seen earlier, is the informal 'grapevine' which carries authentic information as well as rumours with surprising rapidity and co-exists with the formal communication system. The term "grapevine" came into use during American Civil War days. Intelligence telegraph lines were strung loosely from tree to tree in the manner of a grapevine and the message thereon was often garbled. Hence, any rumour of informal communication was said to be from the grapevine. Now, the term applies to all informal information, whether truth or rumour.

Grapevine arises from the social interaction of people, which means that it is as fickle, dynamic and varied as people are. It is the expression of their natural motivation to communicate. It is the exercise of their freedom of speech, and is a natural, normal activity. It thus serves as the unofficial line of communication. It has both good and bad aspects and even if it were entirely undesirable, managers have no power to abolish it. It is here to stay and the managers must try to understand its good and bad qualities and then deal with it intelligently and use it to serve their purpose.

CHAPTER XXIII

STAFFING AND DIRECTING

Staffing

In an enterprise set up for the first-time, the staffing function follows the planning and organising functions. In a going concern, however, the staffing function is continuous. Staffing, like all other managerial functions, is a duty which the manager performs at all times. The staffing function pertains to the recruitment, selection, development, training, and compensation of subordinate managers.

Since management means getting things done through other people, it is obvious that in order to be successful an enterprise must ensure a constant supply of a sufficient number of capable executives. The future of any business depends more on the people in it than on any other single element. Therefore, keeping the jobs filled with right people is the staffing phase of the management job, and it includes several subfunctions :*

1. Recruitment, or getting applicants for the job;
2. Selection of the best qualified from those who seek the job;
3. Transfers and Promotions;
4. Training those who need further instruction to perform their work effectively or to qualify for promotion.

Sequence of Steps in staffing

The manager should perform his staffing function in the following sequence. First of all he must determine the different kinds of managers he needs to appoint. The organisation chart and the written job descriptions enumerating the various duties and responsibilities connected with each of the managerial position will help him in this task. The second step is to determine the number of executives the manager will need and when. In order to find out how many and how soon they are needed he must take an inventory of those executives he has available at this time. By looking at those who are available at the time, he can to some degree ascertain who will be available in three or five years hence.

The manager's next step is to determine how many of the incumbent managers will be capable and available to fill these vacancies as they occur. This will necessitate an appraisal of the incumbent personnel as to their effectiveness in their present jobs and as to whether or not they can be further developed and promoted to higher positions. In order to do this the manager makes use of executive appraisals. Also, it is managements' duty to provide the opportunity for further growth of subordinate managers. The next step in staffing, therefore, is to arrange for additional development of the incumbents. Such a development programme will in time enable executives to move into positions with higher responsibility. New persons will have to be recruited to fill these

* Dale, *Management*, p. 370.

positions. Training of young executives and devising a good plan of compensating executives will be the next steps.

Transfers and Promotions

A transfer is generally a change in position without a change in status or pay. Promotion, on the other hand, involves improvement of status and very often of pay. A transfer may some times be made to correct an original mistake in selection and placement. An executive may not be doing well where he is but his superior or the personnel department believes he has good possibilities and will do better at another type of work.

Making promotion has positive values relating to morale and reputation, as potentially fine managers are given a chance to go up the hierarchical ladder. Even though these positive values are important, their pursuit should not blind executives to the dangers of either over-emphasising this source or relying exclusively on it. The problem here is to ensure that the promotee will be able to operate effectively at a higher level. His past performance and potential based on adequate appraisal will, of course, be a good guide. In promoting a person, therefore, care should be taken to avoid the application of "Peter Principle", which says that managers tend to be promoted to the level of their incompetence.* In other words, according to Peter, if a manager succeeds in a position, this very success leads to promotion to a higher one until the person is ultimately "promoted over his head".

DIRECTING

In our earlier discussions, we have observed, that *management is the vocation of achieving desired results through other people.* To do that the manager plans, organises and staffs. Having done that he stimulates action by giving orders to subordinates and by supervising them as they go about their work or performs the managerial function of *Directing.*

Directing is the process around which all performance revolves. It is a managerial function performed by all managers at all levels of the organisation. Every manager, regardless of the number of subordinates, performs the directing function. The amount of time and effort an executive spends in directing, however, will vary depending on his level, the number of subordinates he has, and the other duties he is expected to perform. For example, a foreman supervising and directing operators will devote more time and effort to this function than the chief executive of the enterprise. Yet even the top chief executive must direct those subordinates, who report to him and who are there to help him carry out his responsibilities.

Directing embraces three essential activities:

(1) Issuing of orders and instructions to subordinates;
(2) Guiding or counselling and teaching the subordinates the proper way of doing work; and
(3) Supervising subordinates to ensure that the work done by them conforms to the plans.

Before dealing with each of the foregoing activities, it may be emphasised the superior manager should consider his directing function as the means of achieving of important objectives, namely :—

1. Getting the work done, and
2. Developing future managers.

His job is therefore, essentially one of human relations. His success will depend upon constant study of human nature, understanding its depths and limitations, and managing the many intangible traits, some good and some bad, that every individual possesses. It is true that fundamentals of human nature, do not change, but attitudes do. Attitudes of employees today are far different from those 50 years ago. Similarly, principles of management seldom change, but philosophies of management, like attitudes do change and so methods of management or getting work done through others. The day of driving manager is past; the manager of today is a leader, a planner, a guide and of necessity a student of motives of men at work.

Letus now turn to the three activities which directing embraces:

Issuing Orders

An instrument employed by managers in directing their immediate subordinates is the *order or command.* An order may be defined as "the expression of the will of a chief conveyed to subordinates". So giving of an order is of vital importance for good results. As all activities in an organisation must be in response to orders or instructions, it is imperative that managers give "good" orders. To be good, orders must be few in number, clear, brief but complete, prompt, in professional form, of proper tone, confined within legitimate scope, and adequately documented. The response mirrors the orders and tends to be of same quality. A few words about those characteristics of good orders are given below:

Few orders. Issue as few orders as possible, for then none will be wasted. No order should be issued for any thing which can be done by the subordinates without orders. Unnecessary orders kill initiative, independence and love of responsibility so valuable in subordinates.

Clear orders. The orders should be absolutely clear and unambiguous. An important virtue of a clear order is that the chance of misinterpretation is eliminated.

Brief but complete orders. Words, which add nothing to the sense of the clearness, diminish the force of the expression. Therefore, orders should be as brief as necessary to convey fully what is intended to be done.

Promptness, professional form, and proper tone in orders. Prompt orders are most economical, for the subordinates do not have to waste time 'waiting for the boss'. The form of the order or instructions should be professional, i.e., proper use of technical words and phrases be made.

Proper tone will depend upon rank. Between the highest executives there should prevail a deference to judgment, a free feeling as to the expression of opinion. In lower ranks there will necessarily be more specific expression and lessened latitude for independent judgment. Yet the tone of the order should be such that it does not rob the recipient of his self respect.

Legitimate scope of orders. The manager issuing the order should remain within his own domain. He must not encroach upon the proper sphere of initiative of the receiving executive. The sphere of the order-issuing superior is to outline the objective. The sphere of the order receiving executive is to determine upon the best means of using the agencies at his command for achieving it. Thus, when issuing orders, a manager should indicate *what* is to be done by each subordinate, but not *how* it is to be done.

Documentation of orders. In a small business, where there is a possibility of mutual adjustment because of close personal touch, oral orders may be feasible. But in large organisations, where orders may be many in number and the number of points may be too many to be remembered, it is necessary to give written orders. Also where considerable periods of time may elapse between the giving of the instructions and the completion of the task, or where instructions may have to pass through a number of persons, the instructions should be reduced to writing. This will give the management a permanent record.

Follow up orders. Another important principle of direction is that once orders or instructions are issued, they should be followed up to see that they are executed, or the instructions should be counter-manded or withdrawn, if they are no more found to be operative or efficacious.

Guiding, Counselling, and Coaching

A subordinate may understand clearly what is to be done, and he may agree wholeheartedly on why it should be done; but he may not know how it is to be done. If a man does not know how to do the job, he will not be as effective as he should be. The manager to guide such a worker, gives suggestions or teaches him how the objectives can be accomplished. If a man is floundering, the manager must direct, guide or counsel, lead or teach.

Supervising

This is the final step in directing. The manager has to see to it that the subordinates work effectively to accomplish the task that he has decided must be done. Thus, the function of supervision is to close the gap between desired performance and actual human performance. Supervision is necessary because the mere issuance of policies and instructions do not necessarily induce people to do what they are expected to do. Face-to-face contact between superior and subordinates. or management of subordinates at all levels is imperative to accomplish desired goals. The person, whether major executive, foreman, chief-clerk or section officer, exercises supervision, or directs and controls the activities of subordinates. His job is essentially one of human relations. It primarily is one of managing people, directing, controlling, guiding, leading and inspiring them into productive channels. In a word, it is making use of *super vision* which he is expected to possess. As part of this job he must understand the reasons why people work. What motivates them? This leads us to consider what is motivation and how a manager can motivate subordinates to perform their tasks effectively.

MOTIVATION

What is Motivation? Motivation is a mysterious force of life. It is the force that moves different people in different ways for different reasons. But what is motivation? In simple words, it is "the drive to achieve a goal". It is primarily a mental process, a mental attitude that incities or produces, a mental attitude that incities or produces physical action leading to the accomplishment of some practical result. It is indeed the action part of a need-satisfaction cycle.

Again, what give people the drive to achieve? Why does someone want to accomplish something? Very simply to derive some benefit from the result. That benefit is the reward; and a reward is something that helps an individual fulfill one or more of his tangible or intangible needs. Therefore, the reward for each individual must be as he defines it.

In business environment, motivation is "getting people to want to do, and do it well, what the manager wants them to do". Yet an employee's job behavior is always motivated by the benefits he seeks. Thus, the manager already has the motivation mechanism in place in every individual. It has to be triggered. To do that, the manager has to find out what his needs are. When we take action to satisfy these needs, we are motivated to achieve them. The sequence goes someting like this:

NEEDS **lead to** → MOTIVATION **leads to** → AETION

To be motivated, we must have one or more needs to satisfy. All of us have needs to satisfy; and no one has all his needs satisfied. When some needs are taken care of, others take their place. Thus everybody is motivated. To understand motivation, we must, therefore, understand needs. A great deal of research has been conducted on the subject, but the first *general theory* of human motivation was developed by Professor A.H. Maslow.*

Maslow on Human Motivation

Maslow advanced the following propositions about human behaviour:

1. *Man is a wanting being.* He always wants, and he wants more. But what he wants depends upon what he already has. As soon as one of man's needs is reasonably satisfied, another appears in its place.

2. *A satisfied need is not a motivator of behaviour.* Only unsatisfied needs motivate behaviour.

3. *Man's needs are arranged in a series of levels—a hierarchy of importance.* As soon as needs at a lower level are reasonably fulfilled, those on the next level will emerge and demand satisfaction.

Thus, Maslow regards an individual's motivation in terms of predetermined order of needs, each with its own rank. According to him

* A.H. Maslow: *Theory of Human Motivation in Psychological Review* vol. 50, 1943, pp. 370–396 and *Motivation and Personality,* 1954.

here is a need priority of 5 levels. These needs are:

1. Basic physiological needs
2. Safety needs
3. Social needs
4. Esteem and Self-respect needs
5. Self-realisation needs

The important point about needs levels is, as shown in the figure below, that they have a definite sequence of domination. Need Number 2 does not dominate until Need Number 1 is reasonably satisfied. Need Number 3 does not dominate until Needs Number 1 and 2 have been reasonably achieved, and so on.

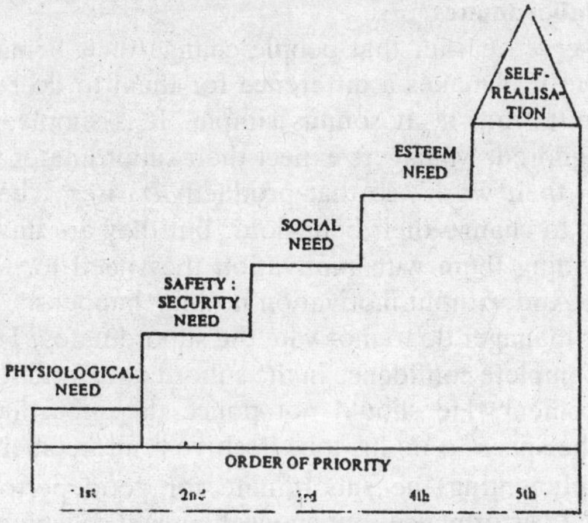

PRIORITY OF HUMAN NEEDS

Physiological Needs. At the lowest level of the hierarchy and at the starting point for motivation are the physiological needs for water, air, food, sex, sleep, shelter and clothing. Those needs are vital to life and must be satisfied to maintain life. These are also described as primary needs. But other needs are secondary.

Safety and Security Needs. After we satisfy our basic physical needs, we then want security. We want to be free from physical danger and free from the loss of job, property, food, clothing, and loss of livelihood.

Social Needs. When we have satisfied safety needs, we then get interested in social acceptance. Since people are social beings, they need to belong, to be accepted or approved by others.

Esteem Needs—Ego Satisfaction. Once we begin to satisfy our need to belong, we tend to want to be held in esteem both by ourselves and by others. This kind of need produces such satisfactions as power, prestige, status and self-confidence.

Self-realisation-accomplishment. Maslow regards this as the highest need in his hierarchy. This involves developing one's abilities to the fullest. It is the desire to become what one is capable of becoming to maximize one's potential and to accomplish something worthwhile.

However, some other studies show that needs do not necessarily follow hierarchy, especially when lower level needs are satisfied. What motivates individuals is often found to be a matter of personality, so that the same need will not lead to the same response in all individuals. Again, an act is seldom motivated by a single need; any act is more likely to be caused by several needs.

The effectiveness of motivation system depends on the ability of the supervisors to provide a PATH for the achievement of goals—individual's own goal and that of the enterprise. For this the manager should provide conditions of motivation, and satisfy needs through such actions as being fair and friendly and dispensing adequate information.

How to motivate subordinates?

We have observed earlier that people change their behaviour for better performance it it makes a difference for them to do so, if they derive some benefit from it. It sounds simple. It is simple, but it is constantly being ignored. Managers expect their subordinates to 'shape up' have 'pride in their work', so that productivity rises. They expect their subordinates to change their behaviour, but they are unwilling or incapable of providing them with motivation they need to make that necessary change. And without motivation nothing happens.

What can the manager do to motivate the subordinates? He should show that he has complete confidence in the subordinates and so provide positive re–inforcement. He should not police the subordinate, but should give him the space to do his job. Positive reinforcement can be achieved by complimenting the subordinate for good performance, criticise him for bad performance, but counselling and coaching him for better performance. Remember nothing succeeds like success, and the employee who achieves once is motivated to try again. However, while providing re-inforcement additional work should not be given.

As a manager, you should create an environment that breeds motivation in subordinates. Start by getting acquainted with each subordinate and give him a chance to get acquainted with you. Learn how to help him find satisfaction and sense of achievement in his job. Give him adequate compensation, too, but recognise that this alone will never achieve high motivation. What else does the subordinate want? He wants good working conditions, feelings of being involved in the business, full appreciation of work done, management loyalty to people, promotion and growth within the organisation, sympathetic understanding of personal problems, job security and interesting work. Additionally, you should give him real responsibility, and tell him about his on-the-job performance. Feed back serves as an ingredient for making people feel good about their progress. Positive feedback acts a form of nourishment needed by all winners. Your job is to work with your people and not have them work for you. Be responsive to their needs, and they will be responsible for doing the type of job that needs to be done. Remember, a manager who is not communicative and responsive to his subordinates invites suspicion and misunderstanding. Loyalty is reciprocal and commitment a two-way street. To repeat, recognition, appreciation and new challenges as well as involvement in those decisions which affect the subordinate are, among other factors, effective motivators.

How does a manager know when he is motivating a subordinate? He is motivating —

1. When the subordinate says *we, not you* or *I,* in discussing business matters;

2. When the subordinate is in complete agreement on objectives and works towards achieving them in the knowledge that these are attainable;

3. When the subordinate brings his problems to the manager without fear of criticism and knows that the manager will listen to him;

4. When the subordinate knows that the manager will attempt to correct his faulty behaviour and his personality.

COMMUNICATION

In simple terms communication means the process of passing information and understanding from one person to another. Two significant points by this definition are worth noting. First, communication always involves two people, a sender and a receiver. One person alone cannot communicate. Only a receiver can close the communication circuit. The second point is that effective communication involves both information and understanding. The receiver may hear a sender but still not understand what he means. If the idea received by the listener or reader is not the one which was intended, communication has not taken place. The sender has not communicated, he has merely spoken or written. The manager must "get through" to his subordinates. No subordinate can be expected to comply with a directive unless there is understanding on his part. Only through good communication can company policies and practices be formulated and administered. The success of all managerial functions depends on successful communication. Communication is a two-way channel. The manager should be able to transfer information and knowledge so that he is understood and results are achieved. He must also know how to receive knowledge and understanding in the messages sent to him by his subordinates and fellow managers.

Channels of Communication

Communication channels are official or formal and informal. Formal communication is the transmission of information or directive in the formal organisation structure. Where a superior directs his assistant to carry out some task, it is formal communication.

Informal communication is the communication between members of a group not on the basis of any formal relationship in the hierarchy but on the basis of informal relationships and understanding among people at the same or different levels. Middle and first-line managers are often associated with the planning and evaluation of data, informal channels

...pevine, as a natural outgrowth of informal organisation, is an informal communication. People like to communicate with each other. This desire must be regarded as a natural and normal activity. The grapevine fulfills the subordinate's need and desire to be "in the know" and to be kept posted on the latest information. It gives the members of the organisation an outlet for their imagination and an opportunity to relieve their apprehensions in the form of rumours. It also offers the superior insight into what the subordinates think and feel. An efficient manager will acknowledge the grapevine's presence and put it to good use.

Communication Media

The media of communication can be words, pictures and actions. Words are the most important symbols used in the communication by managers to subordinates and others and in the communication by subordinates and others and in the communication by subordinates and others to managers. It is, therefore, essential for managers to be able to use words effectively. Words can be transmitted orally and received by listening, or they can be transmitted in written form and received by reading.

Although oral communication is the most frequently used, a well-balanced communication system must pay attention to both written and oral media. Pictures are also powerful medium of communication and are important visual aids for conveying meaning and understanding to other people. They are particularly effective in connection with well-chosen words to complete the message.

Action is a third type of symbol used in communication. The manager must remember that what he does is interpreted as a symbol by his subordinates, and his actions often speak louder than his words. Purposeful silence, gestures, a hand shake, a shrug of the shoulder, a smile, all have meaning. For example, a frown on someone's face may at times mean more than ten times of oral discussion or a printed page. By the same token, the manager's inaction is a way of communication.

All those media are useful, and if the manager selects only one method inefficiency may result. Although written messages are indispensable at times, as they provide permanent record to which the receiver can refer as often as necessary, in most instances oral communications are superior to the written medium. Oral communications, because the superior and subordinate are face to face, normally achieve better ready understanding and save time. The greatest single advantage of oral communication is that it provides an immediate feed back. By merely looking at the receiver of the message the sender can judge how he is reacting to what is being said. Oral communication enables the recipient to ask questions there and then if the meaning is not clear, and the sender can explain his message and classify unexpected problems raised by the communication.

Interpersonal Communication Process

Managers spend between 50 and 80 per cent of their time at work communicating with other individuals; and most of the time prefer

INTERPERSONAL COMMUNICATION MODEL

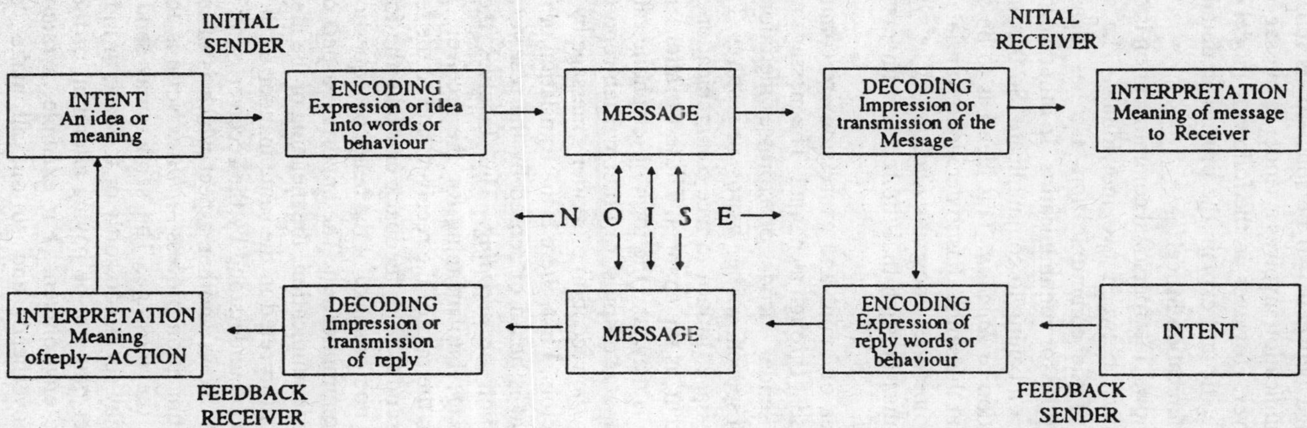

Adapted from Andrew D. Szilagyi—Management and Performance

face-to-face communication. This form of communication is referred to as *interpersonal* communication because it concerns the one-on-one information exchange between two persons. In its most basic form, interpersonal communication involves a sender, a message, a channel or medium and a receiver. However, as the following model illustrates, we need to be more specific and explain the process in detail.

Interpersonal Communication Model

As the model shows, interpersonal communication is quite simply a transfer of information between two individuals. The sender is the source or initiator of the communication. He has ideas, intentions, information and purpose for communicating. In other words, the sender has something with a meaning to communicate. So the first step is the sender's idea formation or *Ideation*. This idea has to be expressed. So the second step is that the sender has to decide to translate the idea into words or gestures, sometimes known as *Encoding*. The symbols, words or gestures chosen must be such that the receiver understands what is being communicated.

The senders idea or intent and expression are communicated by means of a message sent through a channel. The message is the physical form into which the sender encodes or expresses the information. This may take the form of speech, written words, or gestures. The channel is the carrier of the message. In face-to-face communication, air, in which certain vibrations occur, is the channel. These vibrations are the sound waves. Other channels may take the form of telephone-calls, meetings, written memos, computer outputs, or other written reports.

The next step is the reception of sender's message by the receiver. This involves two factors. First, there is the translation or *impression* of the message, or what is heard or sensed by the receiver. The second factor is interpretation or *decoding*. This involves the process of translating the message into meaning for the receiver. Then follows action or reaction on the part of the receiver, and so the feedback from the receiver to the sender. The feedback can take the form of verbal expression, a simple nod or shake of the head, or a question directed to clarify the original communication. The important aspect of the process is that for effective communication, the meaning of the message sent by the sender must be interpreted in the same manner by the receiver. In other words, it must be understood by the receiver.

The model also shows another aspect which is of importance to interpersonal communication process – *Noise*. Noise is any factor that disturbs or distorts the message. The sender may send a confusing memo, the sender may speak too softly or too fast, or indirectly to the receiver, the receiver may not be paying attention, or there are some other sounds in the environment. For example, a radio, telephone, aeroplane passing overhead, and so on, all make "noise". Any interfering sound waves are *noise,* even a beautiful and melodious (but interfering) song.

Barriers to Communication

As the sender and the receiver are two separate persons living in different worlds, there exist many barriers which tend to distort the messages that pass between them. As a result the meaning given to the message by one person may not be what the sender intended it to be. Misunderstandings frictions and inconveniences arise when communication network breaks down. A vast majority of the managerial problems are due to faulty communication. There are a number of barriers to communication, but more important of them are considered here.

Barriers due to organisation structure

The organisation structure of enterprises these days is complex and involves several layers of supervision, long communication lines, relations of staff to line and organisational distance of the worker from top management. This itself creates problems and barriers, because at any one level of supervision communication may break down due to faulty transmission. To check such a barrier from arising the management might reduce the number of levels of supervision, shorten the lines of authority and provide for more participative practices such as committees.

Badly Expressed Message

Lack of clarity in expression by use of empty words and phrases resulting in vagueness is a great barrier to communication. What is intended is not conveyed resulting in costing errors.

Barriers Due to Status and Position

The organisation structure creates a number of status levels among the members of the organisation. For example, the status and prestige of the manager at the plant are different from the worker's. When the worker listens to the message, he evaluates it in terms of his own position, background and experience. He very often adduces non-existent motives to the sender of the message and is suspicious of the manager. This stands in the way of understanding and there is no communication.

Inattention as a Barrier

Failure to read notices, bulletines, minutes, and reports is common. Similarly, non-listening of oral communication is quite common. Efforts to communicate with someone who is not listening will surely fail.

Resistance to change

Resistance to change is a chronic human failing. People prefer to preserve the status quo. This causes a strong communication barrier. The listener's receiving apparatus works like a filter, rejecting new ideas if they conflict with what he already believes

Insufficient Adjustment Period

Sometimes, communication announces change which seriously affects employees. Changes affect people in different ways, and it may take time to think through the full meaning of a message. It is therefore important to efficiency not to enforce change before people can adjust to its implications.

Distrust of communicator

The habit of modifying or countermanding messages, because of ill-considered judgments or non-logical decisions encourage subordinates to delay action or to act unenthusiastically. Inconsistency of the superior inhibits communication.

How to overcome communication barriers

Communication is one of the major keys to understanding people and how and why they act as they do. Effective communication is vital to successful management. Therefore, each manager should be familiar with several methods of over coming communication barriers and conductive to maximizing his success in communicating.

Feedback

Among the several methods of improving communication, feedback is probably the most important one. The manager must be ever alert to see whether or not he is understood. To make sure that the communication has resulted in mutual understanding it is important to observe the receiver and judge his responses by non-verbal clues such as expression of comprehension or bewilderment. The sender may even ask the receiver to repeat complex information in his own words. Receiving a perfunctory "yes" is not enough assurance.

Get Informed

If a manager does not know and understand, he cannot communicate. Therefore a manager must learn and clearly understand the information he is expected to communicate. He should normally be able to answer any questions raised by the subordinates. His span of information and understanding should be greater than his span of communication to his personnel.

Clarity. Messages should be couched in straight forward and simple language so that the message is understood by the recipient.

Consistency. Messages should be consistent with one another. Orders should be consistent with known objectives of the organisation and with its other activities.

Adequacy. The goal in communication is to ensure an optimum flow of information. It should be enough to cover the fields, but should not smother where directions are complicated, they may be repeated, probably in different ways.

Timing and Timeliness. The same massage will be received or responded to differently by different individuals and groups at the same time or by the same individuals and groups at different times. An effective communication looks to the situational psychological and technical aspects of timing. With respect to timeliness, a delayed report ceases to be a control medium and becomes a historical document.

Distribution. One of the most frequent causes of shortcomings in performance is the failure of information to reach the right position or person. *Who* is to be told is often as important as *what* is to be told. The person receiving a message should know its purpose, e.g., for action, information or other reason. A communication from top to bottom should pass through every stage of the line of authority.

Balance between Adaptability and Uniformity. The smooth working of an organisation depends in part upon uniformity. Yet adaptability should be resorted to when different situations and individuals are involved. Orders and reports may be communicated through systems that provide opportunity for adaptation to specific situations.

Interest and Acceptance. The purpose of communication is to secure a positive response. The person communicated to should be interested in and accept the message. Downward communication is more effective if morale is good, and upward communication gets through when the superior is a good listener.

It is important therefore for the manager to develop a positive communication attitude. He should see to it that the subordinates are properly informed and *feel* informed. The manager should also gain the confidence of others; for meaning is more effectively imported when the receiver understands the communicator's purpose. Furthermore, a manager must use informal organisation as a channel of communication, as most effective communication results when managers utilize informal organisation to supplement the communication channels of formal organisation.

Flow of Communication

Communication in any organisation moves in three directions: downward, upward and sideways or horizontally.

Communication downward in any organisation means that flow is from higher to lower authority. It is dominated by orders pertaining to policies and procedures and other instructions etc., issued by the superior to the subordinates.

The upward communication means the flow of information from the subordinates to the superior managers. It consists of reports dealing with statistics, financial items or narrative statements. Also, flowing upward are opinions and attitudes, ideas and suggestions, and complaints, grievances and rumours.

Horizontal or Sideways communication takes place between two subordinates or managers at the same level and under the same superior. It is especially important in large or decentralised organisations. Staff people, such as efficiency engineers, help to transmit information among positions and units at the same level.

To these three flows of communication may be added *Crosswise communication* which is very important at all levels to speed up information and improve understanding. *Crosswise* relationships exist between personnel in one division and personnel of equal, lower or superior status in other divisions. Direct communication between them substitutes for making a message follow the chain of command upward through one or more superiors, horizontally across level of organisation, and thence downward to the particular recipient. Enterprises simply cannot operate in such stilted fashion because the communication time would be excessively long and the quality of understanding would be inferior.

To make crosswise communication purposeful there should be an understanding between superiors that (1) crosswise relationships will be encouraged, (2) subordinates will refrain from making policy commitments beyond their authority, and (3) subordinates will keep their superiors informed of their important inter-departmental activities. Every manager should guide subordinates in their conduct of crosswise relationships.

However, the relationship between a superior and a subordinate does not exist in a vaccum, but in a particular cultural and organisational setting which helps to determine its character. The culture of the country, perhaps even of different parts of the country, as in India, provides the stage for the two roles. The degree of formality or of camaraderie between the two will be influenced by the cultural pattern, and so will be the type of leadership. In some countries a manager will be expected to be autocratic, because people pay respect to authority, in other a more democratic, participative approach will be the custom especially at the managerial level. For example, an Indian subordinate would be expected to be more deferential to his boss than would an American. In addition the national culture, the nature of formal organisation and personalities of individuals also affect the relationship. The question of leadership and leadership styles assumes importance in this connection.

LEADERSHIP

A traditional task of the manager, we have seen in earlier discussions, is that of getting people to do what he wants. According to Leavitt* there are three main ways of doing so, namely: (i) by the use of formal authority, (2) by manipulation, and (3) by influence. He suggests that a superior who relies on his formal authority is narrowing his effective range of control over others. He discusses the pros and cons of depending on authority. We will consider those under leadership style or types of leaders.

Meaning of Leadership. The word leadership has been widely used. Different disciplines have defined it in different ways, according to their particular approach. A definition in business situation. is one with which we are concerned. *In general terms leadership* may be defined *as the human factor which binds a group together and motivates it towards goals.*

Operationally, leadership has been defined as the process by which an executive or manager directs, guides and influences the work of others in choosing and attaining specified goals by mediating between the individual and the organisation in such a manner that both will obtain maximum satisfaction.[1] Leadership involves the way a manager behaves

* Harlod J. Leavitt. *Managerial Psychology,* Ch. 10.

in his man-to-man relationship with his subordinates. In leading, a manager strives to integrate the needs of people with the welfare of his company or department.

Conceptually, leadership is an interpersonal influence, exercised in situation and directed, through communication process towards the attainment of a specific goal or goals.[2] Leading involves reactions of individual personalities to each other, and is rooted in feelings and attitudes. Somehow, someway, each individual must desire to execute his duties effectively. The leader can provide motivation either by directive method or the cooperative method.

Leadership style, or Types of Leaders

According to the motivation they use leaders are either *Positive* or *Negative.* A *positive leader* motivates people by increasing their satisfaction, and the *negative leader* motivates through fear and insecurity by threatening to decrease satisfaction. The positive leader is employee-centered. He exercises power *through people* instead of power *over people.*

It is true that both positive and negative leaderships get results. The difference is that the former does so with satisfaction of those led, but the latter achieves results with their dissatisfaction; he is the "boss" and not the leader. The negative leader believe in what Douglas Mc Gregor calls Theory X and the positive leader follows Theory Y.

Douglas McGregor [3] developed his approach to direction and control based on certain assumptions, under traditional and integration approaches and called them Theory X and Theory Y. According to him, behind the beliefs and actions of negative and positive leaders are assumptions about human nature and human behaviour. He deals with these under the two theories, which are summarised here.

McGregor's Theory X. Under Theory X or traditional view of direction are found the following assumptions of human nature and human behaviour and the managerial policy and practice:

1. *The average human being has an inherent dislike of work and will avoid it if he can.*

Therefore, management must take steps to counteract this inherent human tendency to avoid work, by laying stress on productivity.

2. *Because of this human characteristic of dislike of work, most people must be coerced, controlled, directed, threatened with punishment to get them to put forth adequate effort towards the achievement of organisational objectives.*

The dislike of work is so strong that even a promise of reward is not generally enough to overcome it. People will accept the rewards and demand continually higher ones, but these alone will not produce the necessary effort. Only the threat of punishment will do the trick.

3. *The average human being prefers to be directed, wishes to avoid responsibility, has relatively little ambition, wants security above all.*

1. Theo Haimann, *Professional Management,* p. 440.
2. Tannenbaum, Weschler and Massarik, *Leadership and Organisation,* p. 24.
3. Douglas Mc Gregor, *The Human Side of Enterprise,* Chapters, 3, 4

This assumption of mediocrity prevails among many managers, although not always expressed openly. It can be seen reflected in policy and practice, and paternalism remains still a managerial philosophy in most cases. Although important progress has been made in the past two or three decades, and human side of enterprise has become a major pre-occupation of management, yet the assumptions of theory X remain predominant throughout our economy. A manager, it is argued, must take effective steps to direct the behaviour of his subordinates.

Theory Y. There have been a few breakthroughs in social science theory in recent years. Modern scientists argue that man by nature is not what Theory X assumes. On the contrary, it is the circumstances, the philosophy of getting things done and the work environment which make man behave the way the theory postulates. In other words, this behaviour is not the result of man's inherent nature. Accordingly, McGregor rejected theory X and proposed Theory Y or the integration of the individual and organisation goals' approach.

Theory Y makes the following assumptions:

1. *The expenditure of physical and mental effort in work is as natural as play or rest.*

The average human being does not inherently dislike work. Depending upon the controlable conditions, work may be a source of satisfaction (and will be voluntarily performed) or a source of punishment (and will be avoided if possible).

2. *External control and the threat of punishment are not the only means for bringing about effort towards organisational objectives.*

   Man will exercise self-direction and self control in the service of objectives to which he is committed.

Here, commitment to objectives is important. If the commitment is small, only a slight degree of self-direction and self control will be likely, and a substantial amount of external influence will be necessary. If it is large, many conventional external controls will be relatively superfluous, and to some extent self-defeating. Hence, managerial policies and practices materially affect this degree of commitment.

3. *Commitment to objectives is a function of the rewards associated with their achievement.*

The most significant of such rewards, e.g., the satisfaction of ego and self actualisation needs, can be direct products of effort directed towards organisational objectives.

4. *The average human being learns, under proper conditions, not only to accept but to seek responsibility.*

Avoidance of responsibility, lack of ambition, and emphasis on security are generally consequences of experience, not inherent human characteristics. Where management has failed to accept its responsibility to provide maximum possible satisfactions for workers, including human as well as economic factors, rejection of responsibility on the part of subordinates will result.

5. *The capacity to exercise a relatively high degree of imagination, ingenuity, and creativity in the solution of organisational problems is widely, not narrowly, distributed in the population.*

The organisation must foster a favourable climate for creativity to flourish. Such a climate requires creative management. A manager must himself continually create an environment in which originality is encouraged.

6. *Under the conditions of modern industrial life, the intellectual potentialities of the average human being are only partially utilised.*

There is substantial evidence for the statement that the potentialities of the average human being are farabove those which we typically realise in industry today. Each individual in the organisation should continuously be encouraged to develop and utilize voluntarily his capacities, his knowledge, his skill, his ingenuity in ways which contribute to the success of the enterprise.

The important difference between Theory X and Theory Y is that—

Theory X offers management an easy rationalisation for ineffective organisational performance. It finds causes of ineffectiveness in human resources. Theory Y, on the other hand, places the problems squarely in the lap of the management. If employees are lazy, indifferent, unwilling to take responsibility, uncreative and uncooperative, Theory Y implies that the causes lie in management's methods of organisation and control.

This does not, however, mean that the assumptions of Theory Y have been finally validated. But they are far more consistent with existing knowledge in the social sciences than the assumptions of Theory X. It may not be wrong to say that the Positive Leader applies Theory Y and the Negative Leader uses Theory X.

Theory Z. Recently, William G. Ouchi has developed Theory Z as an outgrowth of Japanese management. In Theory Z—

1. Individual responsibility is emphasised as a corevalue with concern for the whole person.
2. Management is people building, not problem solving.
3. Efforts are made to develop trust between employer and employee. Reciprocal loyalty is the norm.
4. Open communication is encouraged and there is sufficient involvement of employees in decision making, particularly in matters directly affecting them. Participative management is considered workable.
5. Patience and tolerance is required when dealing with people.
6. Organisation policies and procedures should be supportive; for example, life-time employment, slower rates of promotion, less formal control systems and extensive training and development programmes.
7. The management focus is on results after involving employees to obtain a commitment to equality.

Techniques of Direction or Leadership Practices

Different techniques of direction or leadership practices may classified according to the *philosophies of the leaders towards their followers as*—

1. Autocratic or Authoritarian or Leader-centered;
2. Democratic or Participative or Consultative or Employee-centered;
3. Bureaucratic or Rule-centered;
4. Free-rein or *Laissez-faire*.

1. *Autocratic or Authoritarian Leader* centralises authority and decision-making in himself. There is no participation by subordinates. They have to do simply what they are told. The leader takes full authority and assumes full responsibility. This type of leader is usually negative because followers are uninformed, insecure and afraid of the leader's authority.

The advantages of using authority are that it imposes orderliness and conformity. This simplifies the problem of coordination and control. It is simpler to use authority, because it is generally understood, whereas if one wants to use persuasion one must understand the motivations of the individual one is seeking to influence. Authority is faster, as time is not taken by explanations. Finally, some people enjoy exercising authority and like the demonstration of respect that it may produce.

The disadvantages of using authority are that: it may produce unintended reactions, such as a show of conformity without the reality, and an atmosphere of distrust and hostility. Also it may reduce the possibilities of future communication and hence superior's opportunity to influence the subordinate. The superior is usually disliked by his subordinates.

2. *Democratic or Participative Leader* decentralises authority. His decisions are not unilateral as with the autocrat. He invites his subordinates to participate in tackling problems so that the group and the leader are acting as a social unit. He holds consultations with his subordinates regarding all phases of his problems and adopts any suggestions made by them if they are worthwhile. Unlike the autocratic leader who controls through the authority he possesses, the democratic leader draws his authority from the participative forces within the group. For this reason the members of the group have great regard for him.

3. *Bureaucratic Leader* depends upon rules and so reduces the process of management to a series of routine actions. The rules specify the obligations of the subordinates, directing them to do particular things in definite ways. There is no participation or initiative on the part of the subordinates. This kind of leadership fosters worker apathy. The rules serve as a specification of a minimum level of acceptable performance. It is possible for the subordinate to remain indifferent to work, for he knows just how little he could do and still remain secure. Rules permit activity without participation. The rules also lead to red-tape, too much paper work and playing safe.

4. *Laissez-faire or Free Rein Leader* depends largely upon the group to establish its own goals and work out its own problems. Group

POWER BASE AND LEADERSHIP STYLES

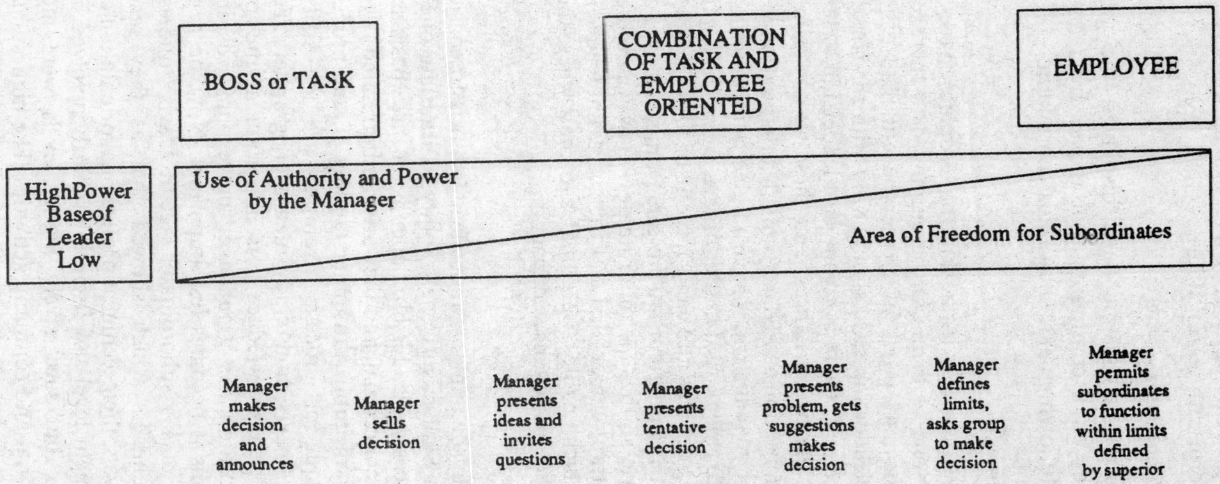

Adapted from Szilagyi, Management and Performance

members train themselves and provide their own motivation. The leader is more or less passive and the initiative is with the subordinates. This mode of direction can produce good and quick results if the subordinates are highly educated and brilliant people, who have a sincere desire to go ahead and perform with responsibility.

Leadership as Continuum

Tannenbaum and Schmit have displayed the wide range of leadership styles on a continuum that moves from authoritarian to free-rein. The following chart shows this continuum:

Situational Approach

All of the foregoing leadership philosophies have benefits and shortcomings. None of them can be employed to the exclusion of the others. Each one may prove of greater benefit than others in certain situations. The leadership style should vary with the situation and with the people concerned. There is no one best leadership style. What is best will depend on the circumstances, and these may vary in the different parts of the organisation as well as from one organisation to another. The most democratic manager may have to give autocratic directions when there is a need for them. As a matter of fact, a good leader is equally well versed in all the methods and can apply one or the other according to the situation. But it is important, at the same time, for a leader to have a recognisable style so that his subordinates know where they stand with him. One important characteristic of the successful leader is consistency of behaviour, which enables subordinates to know where they stand with him and to predict his actions and reactions.

Leadership Skills

Another way of thinking about leadership is to consider the skills the leader uses. Skill means one's ability to translate one's knowledge into action. Successful leadership depends on three basic skills—technical, human and conceptual, and they are all interrelated.

Technical skill implies an understanding of, and proficiency in, any type of technique or process. Examples are the skill learned by accountants, engineers, time study men. stenographers. Technical skill involves specialised knowledge. It is important at the lower level of supervisory position. As a manager moves upwards in the higher management jobs it becomes less important. Now, he depends on the technical skills of his subordinates. Keith Davis * quotes a study of engineering managers which showed that as they reached higher management levels, their technical professional orientation changed. The lowest management level saw itself as primarily involved in a technical engineering job, but successively higher levels were more oriented towards managerial and company activities. The highest managers were divorced from their technical speciality. This decreasing importance of

* Keith Davis, *Human Relations at work*, P. 116

technical skills in higher management jobs makes it possible for managers to transfer from one type of work to another, such as from marketing to production, while maintaining top leadership performance.

Human skill is the ability of the manager to work effectively as a group member and to build cooperative effort within the team he leads. Every manager at every level and in every type of work has to use human skill. In his day-to-day dealing with people human skill plays an important part. As technical skill is primarily concerned with working with "*things*", so human skill is concerned with working with "*people*". A manager with effective human skill accepts the existence of view point and beliefs which are different from his own and gives credit for them. He is equally skilful in communicating to others what he means by his behaviour. In this manner he generates goodwill and harmony and good response from the subordinates.

Conceptual skill involves the ability to see the enterprise as a whole. It deals with "*ideas*", while human skill deals with *people* and technical skill deals with *things*. Conceptual skill is used in establishing and carrying out policy decisions. It is important at all levels as is human skill, but it becomes increasingly more important in higher managerial jobs, because these leaders deal more with long-range plans, broad relationships and other abstractions.

Qualities of Leadership. A manager is essentially more effective if he is also a leader of his subordinates. His leadership transforms potential into reality. Most successful leaders work hard. They show a zeal for their work, backed up by great physical, mental and emotional energy. Since successful leadership calls for the highest psychological and physical traits, it is pertinent to note some of the essential characteristics or qualities of a leader. It should, however, be understood that the traits or qualities mentioned below do not guarantee good leadership. The most one can say is that there is better-than-chance probability that a leader will have more of the qualities than one of his followers. We can say, that, generally, the following characteristics or qualities have been found in successful leaders:

1. Intelligence, which is somewhat higher than possessed by the follower.
2. Broad interests and sound educational background.
3. Technical competence.
4. Power of judgment and ability to make prompt decisions.
5. Initiative and creative thinking.
6. Intellectual maturity and emotional steadiness including power of personality and scientific trend of mind.
7. Sense of responsibility.
8. Ability to understand and to get along with people.
9. A sense of social purpose and direction.
10. Alertness to and insight into situation.
11. Ability to inspire and integrate, teach and guide.

12. Verbal facility and ability to communicate with subordinates.
13. Enthusiasm and faith.
14. Physical and nervous energy.

The above list is not exhaustive of the leader's qualities, but it does indicate a co-relation between some qualities and success. It may be concluded by saying that effective leaders have a strong personal motivation to keep accomplishing something. Being emotionally mature and steady, they are neither crushed by defeat nor over-elated by victory. The Gita describes them as *Sthira Budhi*, who are even-minded with unbroken equanimity, who are the same in sorrow and happiness. They have high frustration tolerance. Successful leaders know that all administrative action is of no avail unless members of the enterprise are willing to contribute effort towards the fulfilment of their assigned tasks. They generate enthusiasm on the part of the subordinates to perform their tasks effectively. They motivate them.

PRINCIPLES OF DIRECTION

Koontze and O'Donnell suggest the following principles as foundation of sound and efficient direction :

1. *Principle of Individual Contribution to Objectives.* The manager should communicate effectively and motivate the subordinates for most effective performance.

2. *Principle of Efficiency of Direction.* Efficient direction results in the attainment of group objectives at minimum cost.

3. *Principle of Harmony of Objectives.* The manager should guide the subordinates so that their individual interests harmonize with group interests.

4. *Principle of Unity of Command.* For most effective direction. suordinates should be responsible to one superior.

5. *Principle of Direct Supervision.* The manager should supplement objective method of supervision and control with direct personal supervision to ensure personal contact.

6. *Principle of Appropriateness of Direction Technique.* The techniques of supervision should be appropriate to the person supervised and the task in hand for effective direction.

7. *Principle of Managerial Communication.* The manager, being the principal medium of communication, should keep lines of communication open.

8. *Principle of Comprehension.* The communication should ensure that the recipients of the information actually comprehend it.

9. *Principle of Information.* The direct flow of information is most effective for communication.

10. *Principle of Strategic use of Informal Organisation.* The managers should recognise and utilize informal organisation constructively.

11. *Principle of Leadership.* Ability to lead effectively is essential to effective direction.

Conclusion. In the directing phase of his job, the manager tells people what to do and sees that they do it. His objective here, of course, is to get everyone to do the best work he is capable of. This result has never been achieved merely by threats of dismissal. Financial incentives do produce some improvement, but optimum cannot be achieved by a system of financial rewards alone. Non-financial incentives play a very important role. If the work and environment can satisfy employee needs, there will be greater motivation to produce. But it has also been found that once a need is satisfied, it ceases to motivate a person any further. There are only two human needs that can never be completely satisfied—the need for self-esteem and status and the need for self-realisation or self-fulfilment or self-actualisation, through the continuing development of one's powers and skills. Hence, it held that jobs should be so designed that they afford an opportunity to work towards satisfaction of these two needs.

Managements who believe in Theory Y think that most people prefer to work, and want work that can give them some satisfaction in itself, and will work better at a job that provides some challenge. Some recent studies show that greater responsibility motivates people to work better. Job enrichment can be used as one of the methods of providing job satisfaction. Try to design jobs that encourage people to be productive.

Good leadership is undoubtedly an important factor. Besides possessing superior technical ability in the activities in which he is engaged, the leader shows consideration for his followers and appreciation of their needs and goals. Also, in many respects, he is democratic in his attitude towards them and allows them to contribute to his decisions. He is able to distinguish between different types of people and suit his type of supervision to his subordinates; his leadership is situational.

CHAPTER XXIV

CONTROL AND PUBLIC RELATIONS

In the series of managerial functions, planning is the first function and controlling is the last. The intermediary functions—organising, staffing and directing—act as the connecting link between planning and controlling. It may not be wrong to say that the twin concept of planning and control underlies all management. Success in business is very often proportionate to the astuteness of its planning and the skill with which it is controlled. Plans can be effectively achieved in most organisations only with good controls, and planning is always pre-requisite for controlling. Planning seeks to set goals and programmes and control seek to secure performance in accordance with plans.

Meaning of Control

In the words of Koontze and O'Donnell[1], "the managerial function of control is the measurement and correction of the performance of activities of subordinates in order to make sure that enterprise objectives and the plans devised to attain them are being accomplished. It is thus the function of every manager, from the chief executive to the foreman". Fayol[2] also clearly recognized decades ago when he stated: "In an undertaking, control consists in verifying whether everything occurs in conformity with the plan adopted, the instructions issued and principles established. It has for its object the pointing out weaknesses and errors in order to rectify them and prevent recurrence".

Thus, control is aimed at results and not at people as such. Its purpose is to assure that intended results occur and not that particular

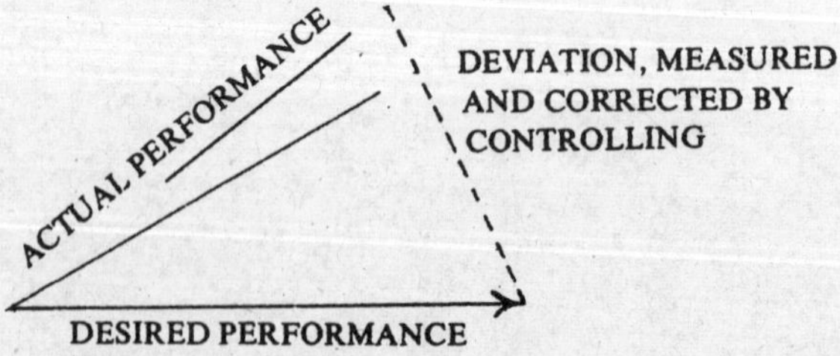

The broken line in the figure indicates the degree of deviation to be measured and corrected by controlling

1. *Management*, p. 639
2. Henry Fayol, *General and Industrial Management*. p. 107

workers are reprimanded. Control should try to prevent mistakes rather than seek to catch and punish those who have made mistakes. Accordingly, controlling is the part of the manager's job in which he checks upon assignments, sees what is being done, compares it with what ought to be done, and does something about it if the two are not the same.

"Controlling is the process by which management sees if what did happen was what was supposed to happen. If not, necessary adjustments are made[1]". Moore[2] sharply describes the controlling function: "There's many a slip between giving work assignments to men and carrying them out. Get reports of what is being done, compare it with what ought to be done, and do something about it if the two are not the same".

An analysis of the foregoing statements regarding control brings out the controlling function of management.

1. *Planning is the foundation of control.* Planning sets the course, control observes deviations from the course, and takes corrective action.

2. *Action is the essence of control.* Control terminates in taking corrective action where there is a deviation in performance from the desired goal.

3. *Delegation is the key to control.* Control is exercised by taking action and action can best be taken within the authority delegated. Accountability must be within the authority given to the manager,

4. *Information is the guide to control.* Control is exercised by a manager on the basis of the information and reports from those actually doing the job. Such reports, and information may be described as "feed-back" from subordinates. Feed-back enables the manager to determine how far the operations are proceeding in conformity with the plans and standards and where remedial action is called for.

The Control Process

The following three steps or phases are always present in control process:

1. *Setting standards that represent desired performance.* In order to be able to find out whether or not performance is as it should be, enterprise goals, objectives and targets etc., are set as standards of performance. The actual performance is then judged against them.

The standards may be tangible or intangible, although greater emphasis should be laid on tangible standards. The standards in tangible terms may be in terms of output, costs, profit, time, persons available for training etc. In intangible terms standards may be for the results to be expected from a training programme, or an advertising campaign or employee morale etc.

2. *A comparison of actual results against the standards—measurement of performance.* This is the second step in the process of control.

1. Hicks, *The Management of Organisations,* p. 205
2. Franklin G. Moore, *Management,* p. 122.

The evaluation must be either within the prior knowledge of the managers concerned or must be reported to them so that they can take the necessary corrective action, if needed.

Methods of Checking Performance. There are three methods of checking performance, namely:—

(a) *Prior approval.* The managers may insist on checking personally before the work is permitted to proceed. They may do so for two reasons: (1) to make sure that the work will be done as planned; (2) to be confident that the standards laid down will be maintained. However, this arrangement of prior approval is likely to cause delay in action.

(b) *Checking the unexpected.* As long as the operations are going on according to plans, there is no need to submit any report. Only when unexpected results occur, there is need for reports and corrective action.

(c) *Personal observation.* Many executives insist on making frequent visits to their plants.

3. *Taking Corrective action.* The third step is taking corrective action. As soon as the deviations are reported it is the duty of the manager concerned to take steps to correct the past action or at least to bring similar action closer to the standards in future.

Elements Involved in Controlling

Regardless of what is being controlled, these elements are always involved. The meaning and purpose of control, therefore is—

1. Knowing exactly what work is to be done as to (a) Quantity; (b) Quality; (c) Time available.
2. Knowing what resources are available for doing that work as to (a) Personnel, (b) Materials, (c) Other facilities.
3. Knowing that the work has been done or is being done (a) With the resources available; (b) Within the time available; (c) At a reasonable cost; (d) In accordance with required standard of quality.
4. Knowing immediately of any delays, hold ups, or variations as to (a) What happened; (b) Why it happened; (c) Remedial action.
5. Knowing what is being done to remove such hindrances as to (a) Who is doing it; (b) How is it being done; (c) What is it costing; (d) When will it be completed.
6. Knowing about the completed work as to (a) Time finished; (b) Quality; (c) Final Cost.
7. Knowing that recurrences are guarded against—(a) In what way; (b) By whom; (c) At what cost; (d) With what provision for periodic inspection.*

The first thing to do is to design the control system to cover these purposes of control and the three elements noted above. Control

* Adapted from Davis Stetson, *Office Administration.*

Standards should be set. The first step in doing that is to be clear about the results we desire. What shall we accept as satisfactory performance? What is the level of achievement or 'par'? The second step is the evaluation of performance. This involves measuring the work that is done in terms of the control standards, and communicating the appraisal to persons who can take corrective action. This control information must also be sent to the man whose work is being controlled. For instance it should go to the purchaser who decides how much to buy, to the foreman who decides when overtime work is necessary, or to the salesman who may be able to secure additional orders for slow-moving products.

Control reports call attention to deviations of performance from plans. The real thing happens when corrective action is taken. For instance, if the operation situation has shifted from what was planned-perhaps raw materials were defective or a machine breaks down—we will take steps to get the working conditions back to normal. If our subordinates are ineffective, we will clarify our directions to them, provide additional training where necessary, consider motivational lacks, and perhaps re-assign work. Control is a continuous process, and the manager should assure himself at every step that his enterprise or department is functioning in accordance with plans, and if it is not, revise plans to return his unit to the intended action. Action is implied in each case. Action is the essence of control. Control means action—action to correct a condition found to be in error, or action to prevent such a condition from arising.

Requisites of a Good Control System.

In order to be effective, a control system should fulfil the following conditions :

1. *Suitability.* Controls must reflect the nature and needs of the activity controlled. A system of control useful for the General Manager will certainly be different in scope and nature from that of the Sales Manager and of the latter from the Foreman. A small business will need different kinds of controls from a large business.

2. *Prompt reporting.* Controls must report deviations expeditiously. As the manager cannot do anything about the past, the best system of control is one which reports deviations as soon as, if not before they occur. This will ensure quick action to set things right.

3. *Flexibility.* Controls must be flexible. They must remain workable in the face of changed plans, unforeseen circumstances or outright-failures. To achieve flexibility, the manager should have alternative plans available for various probable situations.

4. *Reflection of organisation pattern.* Controls must reflect organisation pattern. Since events must be controlled through people, it is necessary that controls conform to the organisation pattern. The control should be acceptable on the psychological front. That is why management control should be decentralised. In this way, closer relationships

would become possible and greater interest in work would be generated because every one would see what he contributes and what his contribution means in the larger picture. The nearer you get to the specific operation, the more effective is your control and the more readily are control findings accepted.

5. *Economical.* Controls must be economical. A control must be worth its costs. For example, a small company cannot afford an extensive system of controls of a large company.

6. *Simplicity.* Controls must be simple and easily understandable. Too elaborate charts, mathematical formulas, complex break even charts, detailed analyses and statistical summaries which the manager cannot comprehend, are ineffective.

7. *Focus on strategic point.* A good system of control not only points out the deviations but also pin points them where they are important or strategic to his operation.

8. *Suggestive of corrective action.* Controls must ensure corrective action. An adequate system of controls should not only detect deviations but should disclose where they are occurring, who is responsible for them, and what should be done to correct them. Control is action; without corrective action control is not achieved.

9. *Acceptable.* Controls should be acceptable to people. Managerial controls will be a waste of effort unless they induce people to change their behaviour. Efforts must be made to attract response of people to standards, measurements, reports and other control devices by creating situations where they feel interested in them and the objectives behind the control. The manager should take positive steps to get response to controls, as they are essential. He should encourage subordinates to participate in setting standards, and be sensitive to personal needs and social pressures in the administration of controls.

Elements of Control. There are six Elements of Control, namely, authority and knowledge, guidance and direction, constraint and restraint. To be in a position to exercise control, the manager must

1. Know what the situation is,
2. Know what it should be;
3. Know how to correct it, and
4. Have the authority to take the appropriate action.

To bring about control, the manager must have his lines of communication established, open, and working. A department head must know what work is expected of his department and what facilities he has to accomplish the work. Then he must organise the workers and divide the work equitably among them. He must instruct them in the best methods of doing the work and must see that the work is carried out in accordance with his instructions.

How to secure control

A manager or department head can secure control of any operation, routine, or function by analysing the situation in the following order:

1. Outline the steps that take place in the performance of the work.
2. Indicate the points at which control is needed to prevent plans from going astray. Consider what might happen if control were not present, such as unauthorised action.
3. Establish control mechanisms at points where control is desired. A control mechanism is any device, means, or procedure that keeps the executive informed as to the activities for which he is responsible, and that ensures him that his plans and policies are being carried out according to schedule. Information is a guide to actions that control. Therefore, every executive should have information that is *timely* and *adequate.*
4. Assign to some individual the duty for seeing that control mechanisms work correctly, and make sure that he understands his responsibility.

But control action can be taken only by the individual executives who hold delegated authority and assume responsibility for the operation affected. Since control is exercised by taking action, the executive concerned must have the authority to take action. The only person who can directly control activities is the one directly responsible for them. He is in the best position to take action to correct condition found to be in error, or action to prevent such a condition from arising. Therefore, every key executive, in fulfilling his responsibilities, should be his own "controller".

HOW MANAGER EXERCISES CONTROL*

1. The purpose of a control mechanism is to assure the completion of all tasks:
   (a) In the order planned,
   (b) In the time schedule,
   (c) In the precise manner specified,
   (d) By the person or persons to whom assigned.
2. The manager must see that:
   (a) Flow of work is uninterrupted,
   (b) Each duty is performed in proper sequence,
   (c) Work is finished acording to schedule.
3. The manager must know :
   (a) How each activity is to be accounted for,
   (b) Who is accountable for each activity,
   (c) Available means to accomplish desired results,
   (d) If any department or part of the work is running behind schedule, in time to correct the situation.
4. Work running behind schedule may be due to:
   (a) Sudden and unexpected increase in volume of work,

* E.M.Robinson, *Business Organisation and Practice,* pp. 189–196 E.M.

(b) Absence of employees assigned to that work,
(c) Ineffective work,
(d) Ineffective supervision.

5. The manager should know daily for each department:
   (a) Volume of work received,
   (b) Quantity of work completed,
   (c) Amount of work left over, if any,
   (d) Reasons for work being left over.

Tools of Control

The tools of control available to modern management are as follows:

(a) Budgetary Control.
(b) Cost Control.
(c) Statistical Control.
(d) Work Measurement and Production Control.
(e) Quality Control.
(f) Financial Control, and
(g) Documentation.

We shall have much more to say about these in the following chapters. Single line notes on each are given here.

Budgetary control supplies quantitative data for various sections.

Cost control will permit you to determine the limits of expenditure and to see that they are not exceeded.

Statistical control ensures that the figures are supplied at the right time.

Work measurement and Production control enables you to check work values.

Quality control ensures that standards will be maintained.

Financial control will keep tight grip on money.

Documentation makes sure that you have the information as and when you want it and in usable form.

In conclusion it may be repeated that control function is performed by all levels of managers and supervisors. Management control reinforces the executive whom it serves. It multiplies his effectiveness. It tells him what kind of a job he really did. It helps uncover errors made while pursuing the plans or deviating from them. It gives information in clear-cut facts and figures. There is no hunch, no guess work, no opinions. It evaluates facts. It gauges actual performance against plans. It interprets results. It adds recommendations on how to prevent weak spots and avoid pit falls in the future. Finally, it supplies practical ideas on how to proceed to make an ever-better record of profit and service and it channels them back into the planning phase. Consequently, an effective control results in an efficiently run organisation, smooth flowing and trouble-free productive capacity, and a happy and contented staff.

PUBLIC RELATIONS

Public Relations is as good a management function as others

discussed so far, and when applied with intelligent planning, it will produce good results. Often, the right kind of public relations action is the fastest, most practical way to solve certain management problems. Sometimes public relations can economically replace techniques such as advertising. More often, public relations effort is strengthened when it is linked with equally well-planned actions in advertising, sales promotion, employee relations and so on.

What Public Relations Is. The simplest definition of public relations is : *educating people in favour of your company. Or,* public relations is the action of amlifying what you say about yourself through existing facilities of communication. Hence, public relations is a means of communication. It is used to convey, accurately and favourably, the facts and ideas that already exist. It is a means to project the "image" of your company to the public. Corporate image is the picture people have of your company. Public relations can create or strengthen that picture, or change it.

Public relations, however, should not be confused with publicity. Publicity is a specific part of public relations—the job of getting your company's name in the newspapers—but the entire function of public relations is much more than mere publicity. Public relations is an interaction of guiding and, in turn, being guided by public opinion. The public relations man of a company has one purpose, an established process, four functions, and unlimited media for activity. The purpose of public relations is to make the enterprise look good to all people in all its actions. The public relations process may be stated in a series of steps, from finding the facts and establishing a policy to planning a programme, and communicating the story to the business concern's internal and external publics. The process is constantly repeated as the publics, policies and facts evolve.

The four functions of public relations are:

1. To aid top executives to determine the overall purpose or goals of the enterprise.
2. To keep managers at all levels informed of the current status and of changes in the opinions of the various publics including internal publics—Key policy makers, supervisory personnel, employees and shareholders—and external publics—customers, suppliers and the general public.
3. To warn of unfavourable reaction which company action (or lack of action) may have and, conversely, to suggest desirable "good public relations" activity.
4. To communicate by way of all established media and means the company policy and actions.

The biggest problem in planning public relations programme lies in the fact that public relations encompasses a whole universe of varied activities, ranging from the simple distribution of news releases to the most imaginative kinds of promotion schemes. It is this unlimited nature of public relations that sometime causes its failure. Even a big public relations budget will produce relatively few results if time and money are sprinkled in all different directions. The first step in planning a public relations programme, therefore, should be to establish the limiting confines of the work to be done. The following four steps should be taken for good results.

Four Steps to Public Relations Results

When a programme is organised on the following four-steps procedure, favourable results are predictable:

1. *Set Specific Goals, Not General Goals.* If your goal is merely to create a better corporate image, most of your public relations budget will probably be wasted. But if it is something specific like company's good management and growth record, good results will follow.

2. *Make a Plan of Action Aimed Directly at Your Goal or Goals.* Limit your plan to those actions that you know you can afford and will move you towards the specific goals you have set. But be sure your plan includes several alternative actions. Success in public relations usually depends on selling your ideas to someone else. If you do not succeed with one action, rather than force the idea to work, it is generally wiser to shift to an alternative action that will produce equal or at least similar results.

3. *Measure Your Results against Your Plan at Regular Intervals.* A strong, well-planned public relations programme can become weak, if it is not appraised regularly. A formal appraisal should be built into the programme at least every six months, more frequently in many cases. In appraising the programme, look at both your successes and failures.

4. *Based on Appraisal and Analysis, Alter Your Goals, Your Plan, Your Actions.* Probe the validity of your public relations goals, and the validity of your public relations plan. Sharpen the goals and alter the plan as necessary, and continue the cycle over and over again.

For getting optimum results from a planned public relations programme follow the rules given below:

1. *Focus on the Pivotal Job First.* Try for multiple results from a single action if possible.

2. *Give people what they want, Not Just What you want.* The material must satisfy both the media man and the user or consumer.

3. *Have a Point of Distinction.* Every product has a unique selling proposition and all advertising should focus on it. The same applies to public relations; Every company has a distinctive quality, and all public relations effort should focus on it.

4. *Go Far Enough, Fast Enough—Then Stop.* Public relations results seldom, if ever, accrue overnight. Quitting too soon is as wasteful as continuing to race after you have crossed the finish line.

5. *Never substitute Words for Ideas and Honesty.* "Undersell, never oversell" is the watchword of professional public relations men. Do not make up facts, be honest, its worth it. Honesty pays off. Tricks are not worth the trouble.

In conclusion, it may be reiterated that public relations is the job of educating people in favour of your company. To get good results with public relations at low cost, adhere closely to these vital principles: Plan your public relations goals. Plan specific actions to meet these goals. Measure results against the plan at regular intervals. Alter the programme as soon as your analysis shows you can improve either goals or actions.

CHAPTER XXV

SCIENTIFIC MANAGEMENT

Meaning and Scope

Broadly speaking, scientific management is the art of knowing exactly what is to be done and the best way of doing it. Under this system the method of work is scientifically thought out, the workers scientifically selected and trained to perform the task, and the most efficient speed is scientifically determined. According to Person the term "scientific management" characterises that form of organisation and procedure .. which rests on principles or laws derived by the process of scientific investigation and analysis, instead of on tradition or policies determined by the process of trial and error. Indeed, it is a process of transference of skill from management to worker.

Scientific management is also knows as Taylorism, because Frederic Winslow Taylor, who is also known as the father of scientific management, was the first to introduce scientific method at the workshop level. As the Chief Engineer in a steel mill, Taylor noticed wastage of time and energy on the part of workers. He found that workers were deliberately slack in performing their work. Time-rate, being the basis of wage-payment, was not conducive to hard work. He was amazed at the employers who paid no attention to this wastage. The methods used for performing the task were crude and unscientific so that a worker could not produce to the maximum of his capaciy.

Taylor and other pioneers * came to the conclusion that, in comparison to what was possible with scientific control, the industries were working at about 50 per cent efficiency. Taylor demonstrated that proper method of work produced good results, and locating the proper method involved scientific investigation. Every employer should by scientific investigation, develop the best method of work and then teach it to workers who must follow it.

Another interesting fact discovered was that almost all workers were misfits : they were at wrong jobs. The workers were put by Taylor on jobs more suited to them, and their efficiency increased. The adjustment of tools and conditions was another phase of scientific management.

Gilbreth has also contributed considerably to the development of scientific management. Gilbreth was a building contractor. He noticed that the old and traditional methods of bricklaying were inefficient, because a bricklayer lost much time in examining and turning bricks in his hand and in making a number of movements to pick up the bricks and putting enough mortar on the wall etc. By introducing adjustable

* Taylor (1856-1915) was ably helped in his task by some other pioneers such as H.L. Gantt, H.K. Hathaway, H. Emerson, F.B. Gilbreth. Justice Brandies was the first person to use in 1910 the term Scientific Management.

scaffolding, Gilbreth arranged to reduce the number of movements required to lay a brick from 18 to 5, and the number of bricks laid per hour was raised from 120 to 350.

The two chief points in connection with Scientific Management made by Taylor have been :

1. Scientific Investigation as the basis of all decisions, and
2. Complete cooperation between employers and workers, or mental revolution.

Mental Revolution

In the words of Taylor, "scientific management involves a complete mental revolution on the part of workers and management, and without this complete mental revolution on both sides, scientific management does not exist". Both sides must aim for cooperation for maximising output and give up hostility and suspicion. Both sides should take their eyes off the division of the surplus as the all important matter and together turn their attention toward increasing the size of the surplus. Usually the workers try to keep output low for fear of creating unemployment. Again, due to payment on time basis, extra output or increased efficiency does not benefit the worker. Employers also do not take kindly to increase in workers' earnings. The net effect is mutual hostility and suspicion resulting in low profits and lower wages. Workers should realise that good work brings down cost and pulls up profits with a consequent rise in wages. The employers should also recognise that if output goet up cpst comes down, increased wages will still leave higher profits for them. Therefore, workers should welcome efforts to increase output and cooperate with the employers; employers should readily raise wages. Both must recognise that prosperity of both depends upon the prosperity of each and none should attempt to prosper at the cost of the other. Taylor never introduced scientific management without raising wages, for it is futile to expect workers' cooperation without material benefit to them.

Scientific Investigation

A management determined to make scientific management a success must make scientific investigation as its basis. It is necessary to investigate scientifically all factors relating to work and then perform the work according to the results indicated. The traditional rule-of-thumb methods, that is decisions based upon the whims of the managers, must be given up. Nobody should decide anything unless all the relevent information is collected and until experiments have been carried out to test the proposed line of action. The following sections deal with the various aspects of scientific investigation.

VARIOUS ASPECTS OF SCIENTIFIC INVESTIGATION

Time Study. One of the most important aspect of scientific management is Time and Motion Study. Time study and motion study move together; in fact they are complementary to one another. Motion study aims at eliminating unnecessary movements; Time study aims at determining the proper speed of movements made by the workers. When the standardisation of the shop, and of all the service agencies which work for it, has been laid so that the speed at which the machines shall be operated, and the way in which the work shall succeed one another, are known, the proper speed of human operation should be determined by means of time studies. Time study assumes that each job consists of so many elements or groups of elements and that a worker uses elements of movements in performing that job. Therefore time studies should be made by timing each element of a job. For element timing a stop watch is used and the snap back method is convenient. The watch is read when each element is completed, time noted down on a sheet of paper and the hand of the watch is snapped back to zero. A sufficient series of measurements of each elementary operation must be taken to make possible a sound opinion as to what the best time is. An appraisal of the effort expanded by the operator should be made during the study. The effort rating will reveal that effort varies from day to day, and even from morning until night. Some of the elements will be *constant*, i.e., time taken to perform them remain the same from operation to operation, or *variable*, which require different times. When the elements of a task are studied and timed separately, the standards computed are known as *element standards*, and the times recorded for each element are called actuals. The efficiency of the operator is rated and element standards are then computed as follows :

Actuals X Rating Factors plus Allowances = Element Standards

The rating of the operator is done with regard to his observed efficiency in performing the task. The rating will recognise continuity of speed, effort expected, and consistency of movements. On the basis of this information, the rating factor will be decided. This may be expressed in a percentage of the efficiency of the average or representative operator, which indicates how good an operator is in terms of the average run of his fellow workers. The allowances which are added are those for fatigue, personal requirements of the workers, variations in the qualities of materials or in the condition of equipment, and the fact that all men are not equal to the best man. Thereafter the standard time is computed on the basis of which rates of pay and bonus are fixed.

It may, however, be noted that time study as a means of determining fair days work is not one of hair-line accuracy; it only provides a practical and scientific method to supersede chaos of rumour and tradition. The workers, too, do not always like rates of pay based on time studies, as they believe them to be unfair. They are suspicious of "stop-watch technicians" and so-called specialists who are likely to set rates to please management rather than those which are fair to workers.

Motion Study. Human motions are made by parts of the body. These parts function most efficiently in doing particular tasks only when they have attained skill and learned to function with minimum fatigue.

Frank Gilbreth, the leading protagonist of motion-study defines it as follows :

"Motion study is the science of eliminating wastefulness resulting from using unnecessary, ill-directed, and inefficient motions. The aim of motion study is to find and perpetuate the scheme of least wasteful methods of labour". Motion study therefore aims to eliminate useless motions and save time and energy. It strives to link motions to each other in the most economical sequences, so that the end of one movement is as nearly as may be the starting point for the next creating rhythm. A few effective movements are substituted for a multiplicity of ineffectual ones, when a mason is instructed to lift a packet of 24 bricks to the wall instead of laboriously transferring each brick separately.

Fatigue study. Fatigue is "a diminished efficiency of the organism occurring after labour". It is diminution of the capacity for work which follows excess of work or lack of rest. It may be noted that fatigue is not so much over-work as it is a safety device which prevents over-work. When signs of fatigue appear work should be stopped to save the worker from over-strain, which if allowed would prove too costly for the worker, too costly for the employer, too costly for society. Among the causes of fatigue are long hours, the constant strain of working under wrongly-inspired supervision, and the strain of work carried on under conditions not allowing for physical recuperation. Among the effects of fatigue are a lessened output, a lower quality of work, an increase of accidents, bad temper and spoiled work.

Remedies and Control of Fatigue. Provide good working conditions for work and this will go a long way to improve the physique and fitness of the worker. Good physique is anti-fatigue. An abundance of well-diffused illumination, and a system of ventilaton which will keep the atmosphere fresh and invigorating are conducive to best work, minus fatigue. Noise and vibrations which distract the attention from the work exhaust the nervous system so that, fatigue symptoms being nervous symptoms, fatigue comes sooner. Check noise and you eliminate fatigue. Clothing should be comfortable but trim enough to offer fewest apportunities for entanglement in the moving parts of machinery. The pace of work set should be an average or a fair honest pace. As far as possible over-time should be avoided. Rest pauses should be provided. Change of posture also reduce chances of fatigue. Operatives who have to stand at their work should sit down on as comfortable a seat as possible, whilst those who sit at their work should stand up. A change to shorter ours will help check fatigue without reducing production, probably it would increase production.

Monotony. Closely connected with the question of fatigue is that of monotony. With the use of machinery, monotony cannot be avoided. The tending of machines working with bewildering rapidity must be monotonous. With a repetition of certain tasks one becomes "bored", and manifests a lessening desire to continue the performance, or one may have feeling of tiredness accompanied by a desire to do something else for a change. It is fatigue in the sense of a feeling of boredom. Periodic change of tasks has been adopted in some cases with good results. Shortening of working hours also helps to lessen monotony. More care in selection of workers also helps to check monotony. Some people like repetitive work, others do not. So selection of workers according to their physical and mental fitness to the tasks prevent monotony.

Tool Study. No worker can perform his task efficiently unless the tools and equipment which he uses are proficient. Uniformity and standardisation of units produced cannot be ensured unless the tools themselves are standardised. For every job there is a proper tool and it is the duty of management to make investigations to find out which tools will do the job well. Taylor, for instance, cut up 800,000 lbs of various types of steel to discover which tool would be best for cutting a particular variety of steel.

Machines are bigger and more complicated and require more detailed study. Efficiency in operation demands that productive capacities of various machines be in balance, and also uniform in performance. Proper machine balance will make for smooth flow of work from beginning to end there will be no accumulation at any point and no machine will be idle. For quality of work, proper speed of various machines should be discovered. Tools and machines should be available without delay for all the work to be done and there should be expert guidance for their use. Taylor advocated the setting up of a Tool Room, under the charge of an expert who knows how the tools work, what they can achieve and how best they can be used. From this room will issue, under expert supervision, well conditioned tools, each marked as the best for a particular job.

Personnel Matters. Contrary to the belief of some critics of scientific management that it was machine-oriented and Taylor and his associates concerned themselves only with the mechanical aspect of work, scientific management does include investigation into human aspect. Taylor believed that people should be carefully selected and trained and they should be given the work they could do best. He said that the interests of workers, managers and owners should be harmonised. Regard for the feelings and needs, the satisfactions and frustrations of men at work is necessary, and much is being done by Industrial Psychologists to bring to the forefront the human factor.

FUNDAMENTAL ASPECTS OF SCIENTIFIC MANAGEMENT

So far we have examined how different types of scientific investigations throw light on various aspects of work in a workshop. We will now discuss how the fruits of such investigations can be enjoyed: that is to say, how work can be done more efficiently.

However, before taking up the practical application of scientific management, it is pertinent to state the *fundamental principles* that

Taylor saw underlying the scientific approach to management. These have been summarised by Koontz and O'Donnel as follows :*

1. Replacing rules of thumb with science (organised knowledge)
2. Obtaining harmony in group action, rather than discord.
3. Achieving cooperation of human beings, rather than chaotic individualism.
4. Working for maximum output, rather than restricted output.
5. Developing all workers to the fullest extent possible for their own and their company's highest prosperity.

Planning Department. For any work to be done well, it must be planned in advance. No goal can be achieved efficiently and effectively without considerable planning as to how the desired end can be reached. Taylor suggested the establishment of a Planning Department where the entire work to be done in the workshop in a whole period should be planned. The work to be done by each person and each machine should be planned days before the work is actually due for execution. This involves complete information not only regarding the capacity of work a man or machine has but also the study of the exact time a job will take. In an efficient workshop, it will be known that, say, job No. 7 will be started on Machine No. 17 at 9 a,m, on May 9, 1979, and completed at 11 a.m. on June 10, 1979. Thus, no machine or worker will be overloaded with work and enough work will always be provided for each machine and worker.

Standardisation of Tools, Materials, etc. As a result of tool study and study of materials required, the planning department will determine the best tools and materials to be used for a particular type of work. Haphazard use of tools and materials is forbidden. Planning Department will keep the Tool Room and the Purchase Department informed continuously of the requirements so that action is taken to supply them at the required time.

Standardised Tasks. On the basis of motion study, the best method of doing work is determined. On the basis of time study the time required for doing a job is ascertained. This enables the management to determine how much work can be done in a given period of time.

It is a cardinal principle of scientific management that the exact amount of work that a worker can do in a period of time without injury to his health must be ascertained in advance. Arrangements must be made to see that the required quantum of work is turned out. Taylor has suggested numerous measures to do this. The essential features are detailed information and instructions, on the one hand, and incentives to workers, on the other. Provision of proper tools, materials, and machines is always understood.

The Planning Department determines —

1. the tasks to be performed by each section or each man in the workshop.

---

* *Management*, p. 36

2. the exact sequence of operations to be performed, together with the machines and tools to be used; and
3. The time allowed for completing each operation and task.

The Planning Department issues instructions for each task to be taken up. The men at the workshop level do not have to worry about the details and the order of work. The planning department supplies detailed instructions about what is to be done, when and how it is to be done. According to Taylor, the Planning Department does the planning and much other brain work through a few specialists and leaves the foremen and operatives to do their jobs more efficiently according to instructions.

Functional Foremanship. Taylor, in his anxiety to provide fullest information and instructions to workers recommended foremen according to functions instead of the traditional foremen according to number of workers to be supervised. In his view, having one foreman for so many workers was faulty, as one man could not be expected to know everything about all jobs to be done in a shop. Functional foremen, according to the instructions to be given, would, in his opinion, discharge their duties more efficiently and to the best advantage of the management and workers. Functional foremanship seeks to introduce the same kind of specialisation in the workshop as is usually found at the toplevels of management.

Taylor suggested a plan of functionalisation involving :

For a Typical Planning Room

1. *An order of work and route clerk* who, on the basis of instructions, prepares lists instructing the workers and all the bosses as to the order in which the work is to be done during the day and makes out the course of the work through the shop, i.e., he prepares the Route Sheet.

2. *An instruction card clerk* who, after studying the information in the route sheet, writes detailed directions for each job on an instruction card, indicating fully the manner and time in which the work is to be done.

3. *A time and cost clerk* who procures the time records from workers, calculates the wages and premiums earned and sends the various cost items to the cost accounting department.

4. *A shop disciplinarian* who deals with cases of insubordination, absenteeism, and exercises power of supervision and dismissal. He is a sort of an employment manager in embryo.

For the Shop

1. *A Gang Boss* who has charge of work until the material is set in the machine and directs men how to perform the necessary operations in the best way in the shortest possible time.

2. *A Speed Boss* who sees that proper tools and equipment are provided and that the best speeds and feeds are maintained in accordance with the instructions on the card.

3. *An Inspector* who is responsible for the quality of the product.

4. *A Repair Boss* who must see that machines are kept in good repair, that each worker keeps his machine clean, free from rust etc., and that he oils it regularly.

Wages And Incentives

Each worker must know what work and how much of it he has to do. All the facilities for efficient performance of his task must be provided to him. But more than that an incentive to complete the task in the given time should also be provided to the worker. It is a matter of common knowledge that the usual method of wage payment based on time rates gives no inducement to workers to work hard and finish the allotted task. The tendency under this system of wage-payment is for the efficiency to fall to the level of the least efficient worker.

Taylor, therefore, insisted that under scientific management the workers should be able to earn 30 per cent to 100 per cent higher wages than before and their earnings should strictly depend upon their output. He recommended the Differential Piece Rate System of wage payment. Under this system, the standard output per day is fixed, and two piece-rates are decided upon, one for those who achieve the standard output and the other (a lower rates) for those who fail to do so. This wage payment system and other systems under scientific management are discussed in the chapter on Method of Wage Payment.

Benefits of Scientific Management

1. By planning the entire work on the basis of results of scientific investigation and by ensuring that every one does his work in the given time and according to instructions, all types of wastages and losses are avoided, output is maximised and costs are lowered.

2. The detailed prescription of work methods and simplification of work-cycles have reduced the skill requirements for much industrial work. This shortens the period of learning or apprenticeship and renders individual workers more nearly inter-changeable in fact as well as in theory.

OPPOSITION TO SCIENTIFIC MANAGEMENT

Despite apparent advantages of the installation of scientific management in industry, "Taylorism", as it was at one time called, has been criticised on various grounds. Both the employers and workers oppose it, although its aim is to benefit both of them. The psychologist finds it wanting in psychological reactions. Below are detailed the major objections by the employers, workers and the industrial psychologist.

Employers' Objections

1. Most employers object to its installation on the ground of

cessive expense. The re-organisation involved in preliminary standardisation entails huge expenditure, as also the making of time and motion studies. In plants with constantly changing work and small jobs, the expense may be prohibitive.

2. Another objection is that the sudden change involved in the introduction of the system is bound to paralyse the existing arrangement of work and thus frustrate its own objective.

3. The third objection relates to the planning room and the paraphernalia associated with it. This is said to increase cost, particularly on account of the employment of "non-producers" whose salaries add to the overhead charges.

Workers' Objections

The leaders of organised labour have been most vocal with their objections to scientific management. The principal labour objections are as follows :

1. The leading objection is that scientific management, through sub-division and standardisation of processes destroys worker's initiative, kills his craft-skill, makes for montony, monopolises knowledge, and turns the worker into mechanical automaton

2. The second objection by labour leaders is that it is undemocratic, as it involves autocratic control by "functional bosses" and lessens the interest and responsibility of the worker. It is stated that scientific management "forces the worker to depend upon the employer's conception of fairness, and gives the worker no voice in hiring and discharge, in setting the task, in determining the wage rate or determining the general conditions of employment".

3. It is objected to on the ground of unfairness, for the major share of increased profits resulting from its application goes to capital, however much wages may be advanced. The system involves "speeding up" and "driving" and subjects the worker to nervous strain.

4. Another objection is based upon the fact that it renders workers unemployed as a consequence of the adoption of labour-saving devices, both in machinery and in arrangement of work.

5. The final and probably the real cause of opposition is that by providing conditions satisfactory to the workers in a plant, scientific management weakens to that extent, the hold of labour leaders over such employees. The satisfied workers do not need any assistance from their leaders.

Psychologists' View

"The main aim of scientific management has been to apply psychology so as to get the maximum quantity of production from the minimum expenditure of human energy". It is true that efficiency methods have eliminated physical fatigue and to that extent improved the worker's lot; but they have often been applied in such a way as to subject him to a greater nervous strain. Also, the rigid application of the "psychological" tests without making allowances for individual differences leads to inaccurate results.

The theories of scientific management are essentially non-psychological. They purport to specify the manner in which human activities shall be organised, without taking into account the nature of human beings. They assume that for any function which is to be performed in an organisation, there is one best method which can be prescribed and that it is the business of a management expert or a time-and-motion engineer to discover that method. It remains only to procure a worker, teach him the simplified motions of the best of all possible method, and then arrange for him to repeat those motions each hour of the day at the pace which time study sets as "normal" in physiological terms.

It follows from what is stated above that scientific management is non-psychological because it disregards the feelings and needs, the satisfactions and frustrations of men in the work situation. Indeed, it is almost a non-motivational system, in that only the motive to earn money is taken into account. The acceptance by the worker the wage offered to him makes him agree to do as he is told, and relinquish any aspirations of his own.

According to Professor Sargant Florence, scientific management has not given that attention to the efficiency of human factor in industry which has been lavished upon the efficiency of the material factors. Professor Florence concludes that scientific management is an improvement, yet as actually practised it fails to alter essentially autocratic control of industry, nor does it really introduce scientific research into the "labour problems" of industry.

In final analysis it may be stated that it is not so much scientific management that is objected to as the methods by which it has been carried out. The extent of the opposition to scientific management is justified by the considerable *mismanagement* conducted by incompetent persons in the field. Happily in recent years many of these objections have been overcome by the wiser application of the non-rigid methods of Taylorism by including human relations apporach. A better understanding of human factor in organisation will make scientific management more scientific. Productivity and satisfaction go together in a really "scientifically managed" plant.

[illegible] without making allowance for individual [illegible] general scale.

[illegible] cannot [illegible] organised [illegible] which [illegible] and which [illegible] the present [illegible] repeat [illegible] without each [illegible]

[illegible] the work [illegible] Indeed [illegible]

[illegible] Professor [illegible]

[illegible]

[illegible] methods of proof.

PART SIX

Production Function of Management

CHAPTER XXVI

PLANT LOCATION

One of the early decisions that an entrepreneur has to make is the choice of a location for his place of business. Although there are several factors which influence his choice, yet the choice of the location for building a factory may have been made by mere chance. There are many successful businesses that have no apparent reason for their location other than the fact that it was convenient when the business was founded. If a man has a better product for which there is a demand, he can build up a satisfactory business through persistent and well-directed advertising and sales efforts regardless of location. Few customers care where a product is made if it serves the purposes better than anything else, and if the price is right. There are, however, operating advantages and disadvantages that may affect economical manufacture and distribution of the product. *The governing principle is that the location of a plant should be fixed in such a manner that people interested in its success can sell goods most profitably and manufacture them with the least expense.*

Factors in Locating Business

The fundamental factors which have to be considered in determining the location of a plant for profitable working are as follows :

Buying

1. Nearness to raw materials.
2. Accessibility to raw materials.

Manufacturing

1. Proximity to large adaptive labour.
2. Nearness to sources of power.
3. Ready accessibility to repair shops.
4. Nearness to good banking and credit facilities.
5. Adequate transport and communication facilities
6. Ability to build and expand plant cheaply.
7. Government regulaton and subsidy.
8. Adequate fire fighting facilities.
9. State of organisation and development of learning.
10. Suitable soil, climate, and topography.

Association with Other Industries

1. Complementary industries.
2. Competing industries.
3. Momentum of an early start.

Selling

1. Nearness and accessibility to market.
2. Population.
3. Style movement.

BUYING

Nearness to Raw Materials. The cost of obtaining raw materials is an influence on location. The importance of nearness to raw materials varies greatly with the nature of the business. Two sub-divisions of this factor present themselves. One is the assurance of a constant and immediate supply, without dependence on transport or weather conditions. The other is the fact that the cost of transporting bulky raw materials a long distance may add so much to the cost of production as to make the business unprofitable. It is much better, for instance, to manufacture cement at the place where raw materials are than it would be to pay transport charges on them. The ideal location with reference to materials is the one where all factors combine to make the lowest possible raw materials cost per unit of completed product. The location of cotton textile in Bombay, jute in Calcutta, iron and steel in Jamshedpur, was influenced by this factor.

Accessibility to Raw Materials. The presence in abundance of any material is not sufficient in itself. It must also be easily accessible. If the region is inaccessible, it is unexploitable, for it is in effect bare of resources required to support life. The workers who have to work at getting the raw material should have supplies of food and water. There must also be present adequate transport facilities, fertile soil, and suitable climate.

MANUFACTURING

Availability of Labour. Labour supply means the number of skilled and unskilled persons who are available for the kinds of work to be done. Labour supply is perhaps the most important of all the factors, especially when skilled labour is required. This is demonstrated by the manufacturing centres such as Bombay, Jamshedpur, Madras, Kanpur, Nagpur and Ahmedabad where industrial labour is available.

Nearness to Source of Power. The sources of energy for turning the wheels of industry have had a very decisive influence in plant location and the development of industrial centres. The recent development of hydro-electric power with high tension lines to transport electric power to industrial areas has to some extent minimised the importance of power as a significant factor in plant location.

Ready Accessibility to Repair Shops. This factor is important mainly in the case of small-scale industries. Where orders are plentiful and a breakdown occurs at any point a firm loses business as well as prestige, if repairs are not carried out immediately and work completed at the stipulated time. In a large firm, repairs may be carried out in the factory itself.

Nearness to Good Banking and Credit Facilities. Industry cannot exist and grow with funds to be invested in its development. The funds are obtained from banks and other financial institutions. A small concern must be near banks, etc., although in the case of a large firm, which commands wide and good credit, location is not so important. There is an economic geography of the supply of loanable capital, and of the activity of financial institutions, as there is of raw material or labour supply. The rate of interest would be lower in remote corners than in cities, but it is available in abundance in large centres.

Transport and Communication. Of the economic factors governing plant location transport costs are very important. It is necessary to obtain raw materials and market finished goods. In the choice of a site, attention must be given to the availability and frequency of rail, water, road, air transport services. The term transport implies the existence also of storage, handling and service facilities, and industries are attached to those localities where these are readily available at reasonable cost.

Adequate Fire Fighting Facilities. Fire may orignate from within or without. Internal fire can be controlled with fire fighting appliances, but it is difficult to control agencies causing fire from outside. A site with adequate fire fighting facilities is therefore desirable.

State of Organisation and Development of Learning. New industries, as well as the development and expansion of those already established, hinge on research and investigation to develop products and improve methods. Moreover, the profitable operation of industry is dependent on a constant supply of educated and trained men. To provide both of these, educational institutions and research agencies are needed. These will be found where industry is successful.

Ability to Build and Expand Plant Cheaply. A plant has to be built in such a way that the manufacturing processes are carried on with minimum expenditure of time and material. Also, there must be ample scope for additions or re-arrangement, so that they can be carried out without stoppage of work. Low cost land will be most desirable for putting up a factory.

Political Stability. Governments influence the development of industry by maintaining political stability. and by means of subsidies. Lack of political stability stand in the way of establishment of factories or drive away those already established, as has been happening in West Bengal.

Suitable Soil, Climate and Topography. Soil and climate have direct bearing upon the type of activity which will be undertaken by any area in its early development. Climate has a great influence on the industrial activity. A cool invigorating climate develops the best type of industrial worker. Inhabitants of very warm climates are less efficient as industrial workers. Topography also exercises an important influence on location. For instance, mountain barriers, plateaus and large rivers have a retarding influence on industrial development.

Association with other Industries. Some manufacturers select locations which are near complementary or subsidiary industries, i.e., those which produce materials and supplies used in connection with their own manufacturing processes. From the plant location standpoint, this tends to encourage the centralisation of industry. On the other hand, competition between establishments may in many cases act as encouragement for decentralization. Industries tend to thrive best in groups for the following reasons :

(a) A number of similar concerns in a locality can usually secure materials to better advantage than any one can do singly.

(b) Concentration of establishments, even of a like kind and direct competitions, improves the labour market, both for employer and employee. in many ways.

(c) A group of plants can jointly produce such a demand as will cause a variety of repair plants and supply houses and industrial service industries to establish themselves nearby, such as foundries, machine shops, tool makers, etc.

(d) In specialised centres banks learn the standing of the firms in the trade, and can more readily and safely discount the special line of commercial paper.

(e) A group of similar or related manufacturers established in one place serves to perfect their local market. The reputation of each firm supplements that of others, until the name of the town becomes almost a trade mark, and a firm enjoys prestige from the mere fact of location in the noted place.

(f) A large specialised manufacturing centre is able to afford various commercial service industries such as packers, insurers, forwarders, professional graders and appraisers, advertising agencies, public warehouses, etc.

The Momentum of an Early Start. As a rule, people are likely to feel confidence in an industry that is being started in a locality where similar ventures have been successful. A certain amount of inertia attaches itself to industry where it has once been successful in a given place. The momentum of a great centre is so strong that it prevents other localities from lightly entering the ranks against it.

SELLING

Nearness and Accessibility to Market. The advantages of market consideration need to be compared with the advantages of locating near raw materials. Nearness to customers is as important as nearness to raw material. A manufacturer can keep in touch with the pulses of his markets when he is located near them. Sometimes industrial centres offer peculiar advantages because buyers gravitate towards them.

Characteristics of People. All manufacturers exist to supply markets with goods which people will buy. The market which a community affords for consumption goods depends upon the population, its wealth and its habits of life. Consumption goods can be sold only when the thinking and living habits of the people are such they can be persuaded to include these products in their pattern of living.

Style Movement. People will not buy style goods from a market which they believe to be one receiving new ideas later than themselves. The law of style movement is from larger cities to smaller ones, and from neighbourhood of abundant wealth to that of less wealth.

FACTORY SITES

Country, City or Suburb. The relative advantages of the three exact situations may be considered. Country (i.e., village) offers cheap land and so works can be spread out. This reduces fire hazards and one-storey buildings can be used. The rates, rents and taxes are low. More devoted labour disposed to teamwork is available. More healthy workers and hence more efficient. But highly skilled workers are hard to get in a village, and repair shops are not readily available.

The city offers abundant skilled labour, although the wage bill will be higher. City location is the best for women workers. It is near to the market, and a small plant will usually do well in a city, as auxiliary services are near at hand. But the land costs, rents, rates and taxes are high. Generally, village location is good for large plants and the city for small ones. In recent years, however, the tendency has been to locate plants in the suburbs of large cities. A suburb, being midway between the city and the rural area, offers advantages of both.

Decentralisation and Dispersal. The significance of location factors is not static but changing. Not only has human invention lessened the significance of some factors, but also by natural trends of events some have ceased to operate. For example, the introduction into textile mills of automatic humidifying equipment has lessened considerably the importance of climate in location problems of this industry.

Not infrequently, the original advantages sought are no longer of great significance in the achievement of profitable manufacturing operations. In recent years, large industries have tended to decentralise their activities, by placing subsidiary plants at a considerable distance from the parent plant. Or, in order to bring about lateral integration, subsidiary plants manufacturing complete products of allied nature are located at a distance to avoid congestion. This dispersal of plants has marked advantages in relation to material supplies, labour, and distribution of product. Dispersal of industries has become a universal phenomenon. In India a "Balanced Regional Development" has been advocated and followed.

Balanced Regional Development. With a view to bringing about regional balance in industrial location, as suggested by the Fiscal Commission, the Planning Commission has followed in the successive Five-Year Plans the balanced regional development policy. The Second Plan had the following programmes :

(a) provision of facilities such as power, water supply, transport and communications, training institutions, etc., in areas which were lagging behind industrially;

(b) programmes for the expansion of village and small industries;

(c) in the location of new enterprises whether public or private, consideration was given to the need for developing a balanced economy in different parts of the country.

While, in the selection of sites for basic capital and producer goods industries, proximity to raw materials and other economic considerations have naturally been important. in the wide range of consumer goods and processing industries regional pattern of development has been fostered. Typical examples are the establishment of the textile units in Rajasthan, Orissa, Assam and Punjab; sugar factories and distilleries in Andhra, Tamil Nadu, Mysore, Maharashtra; steel-rolling mills in Assam, Kerala, Madhya Pradesh and North Bihar. In the policy followed in licensing of new units, the same considerations have been kept in view.

The development of new processes and new uses of raw materials has assisted in the spread of industry. Thus, with the use of bagasse it is possible to set up paper factories in the sugarcane growing areas. Village and small industries are spread all over the country and various forms of assistance provided by the State are made available. Industrial estates have been set up in all States, and increasingly they are to be located in the smaller towns and rural areas.

With development on a scale larger and more comprehensive than in the earlier Plans, the Third Plan provided extensive opportunity for the development of different parts of the country. Greater dispersal of industries was continued and is being followed in the Fourth Plan too. In granting licences to industrial projects in the private sector, the claims of under-developed regions are kept in view and locations in such areas are suggested to prospective industrialists. As a result of this policy, the four important industries—cotton textile, sugar, cement and paper—have reached almost all the important regions and their concentration has been checked.

Optimum Plant Location. We began with our discussion of the problem of plant location with the governing principle that the location which results in the lowest unit cost in producing and distributing the product to the consumer would be the exact optimum location. As we have seen in previous sections, this optimum depends upon the interplay of various costs, such as freight charges on raw materials, cost of fuel, power and water, cost of plant site, cost of building, labour costs, and freight charges on finished products. The entrepreneur will have to work out the cost analysis on the basis of these costs to keep the cost of production as the lowest.

CHAPTER XXVII

FACTORY PLANNING

The planner's task is more satisfying when he has the job of planning a new factory or workshop at the outset than when he has to improve, as best he can, an already established "system". But it demands a great deal of thought and skill. Some of the most important factors are as follows

TYPE OF FACTORY BUILDING

Having selected a suitable site, the next problem is to make the most advantageous use of it, and, in particular, to choose the right type and size of building for the intended form of industry.

Building Structure. The structure of the building will depend upon a number of factors. The first factor in the choice of a building is its suitability to the nature, purposes and requirements of the business. The *unit stresses* to which the various floors will be subjected will determine the thickness of the walls, the cross-sections of the girders and pillars, and the style of construction. As a rule, heavy manufacturing calls for heavy construction; light manufacturing does not. The width of a building and the height of its ceiling are dimensions which must be determined with reference to each other. Unless there is roof lighting, the greater the width of a building, the higher the windows must be to give adequate illumination in the centre of the rooms. The length of a manufacturing building is influenced by fire hazards.

Single-storey or multi-storey Building. The single-storey building is generally more suitable for large constructional work and for housing heavy machinery, such as foundries, erection shops for engines, bridges, etc. The multi-storey building is usually favoured for lighter work.

Advantages of one-storey building. The advantages of a single-storey building over a multi-storey building are as follows :

1. One-storey building can be constructed for a lower cost per square foot than multi-storey structures meeting similar specifications. The multi-storey building requires expensive foundations and loses considerable areas to lifts, stairwells, and structural columns.

2. Flexibility of layout is generally greatest in a one-storey rectangular plant which provides a large production area that can be sub-divided to meet one's needs.

3. One-storey buildings admit of indefinite extension in any direction.

4. Erection time often can be minimised by selecting a one-storey structure.

5. Natural lighting can be made available throughout the plant.

whereas only on the top floor of a multi-storey building can equivalent use be made of natural light. However, one should realize that natural light is at best unreliable, and skylights require much maintenance.

6. Similarly, ventilation is much better in single-storey buildings; and such buildings are more easily heated and cooled.

7. In a one-storey building, the foundations for machinery are cheaper, and the machinery being set directly on the ground causes no vibration in the building.

8. One-storey buildings are exposed much less to the hazards of fire than multi-storey structures.

9. For most activities a one-storey plant lends itself to efficient supervision and operation.

On the other hand, the multi-storey building is not without its advantages for some enterprises.

Some of the *advantages of multi-storey* buildings are :

1. A multi-storey building facilitates the use of overhead storage and gravity feeds of materials.

2. For a specific amount of floor area, less land is required for a multi-storey building than for a one-storey structure.

3. Upper floors, being removed from dusty ground levels, may be considerably cleaner than lower floors and, of course, an entire one-storey structure.

Building design and fire prevention. Building should be so designed as to prevent fire. Selection of proper equipment and materials, as well as proper design of the plant and processes can prevent fire. Satisfactory detection and alarm systems should be provided, as also fire extinguishers, fire pails and hoses. Fire can be prevented from spreading through the installation of fire walls and doors, sprinklers and hose system . Adequate entrances for firemen and exits for employees should be provided, and the employees should be educated and trained in the need for fire prevention and emergency procedures.

Lighting. Good lighting is conducive to efficient working and high morale, reduction of eye strain and accident rates. The essentials of an adequate system of illumination are : (1) sufficient amount; (2) proper distribution and diffusion; (3) absence of glare; (4) freedom from fluctuations; and (5) freedom from injurious invisible radiations.

As the sense most employed in locating things is sight, scientific use of colours also will contribute to greater comfort and visibility. Colours seem to influence people's attitudes, green being cooling and relaxing, deep colours being oppressive, and red and yellow being warming and stimulating.

Ventilation. Many industrial studies have shown that the combined effect of high temperatures and humidity can reduce mental alertness and increase physical fatigue. Humidity must be maintained at proper level as provided by the rules under the Factories Act. Ideal heating and ventilation consists in distributing, without injurious drafts, an adequate supply of air of the proper temperature and degree of humidity, and free from dust and noxious gases. As a hot, humid and still atmosphere is bad, the air of the working place should be reasonably cool, moderately dry, and kept in motion.

Noise Control. Noise adversely affects one's co-ordination and ability to concentrate and causes one to be fatigued and irritable. Noise reduction methods must be adopted, such as the use of noise-absorbing materials or accoustics. Special attention must be paid to the accoustical treatment of vibration.

Machines and Equipment. Long before the new factory is nearing completion careful thought must be given to the ordering of new plant and equipment. Before purchase, the following points ought to be considered. As a first step, it will be necessary to decide which types of machine will be most suitable. The choice lies between (i) *general purpose* machines, which are not too highly specialised as regards the kind of work they are capable of undertaking, nor too restricted in respect of sizes; (ii) special-purpose machines, designed for a specific job, or for producing or dealing with a particular article or size of article.

Price must obviously be considered and the quotations of several suppliers ought to be compared, but other factors are equally, if not more important. Technical considerations, such as performance efficacy, simplicity of operation, reliability, modern design and techniques and uniformity of type and size, should be taken into account.

Plant and Equipment Maintenance. Effective maintenance of a plant and its equipment is pre-requisite to efficient plant operation as well as uninterrupted production. Plant buildings deteriorate because of (1) the effects of the weather—sun, rain, cold, heat, wind—and (2) wear and tear resulting from general use, vibration, fumes, etc. While deterioration cannot be stopped, it can be greatly retarded by maintenance.

Machines and equipment likewise are subject to wear and tear from use. They require maintenance, if only cleaning and lubrication, to keep them in good running order. Many require adjustment; some require more repairs than others. All maintenance work has to be scheduled to ensure regular attention. Inspection will anticipate and prevent many a breakdown. This is often called *Preventive Maintenance.* Preventive maintenance is more efficient than *Remedial Maintenance.* In other words, inspection before a breakdown enables the maintenance department to plan repairs and schedule them when the plant is inactive at nights or on Sundays, thus preventing a breakdown and disturbance of operations.

The *Maintenance Department* carries on the following activities: make emergency repairs; make routine repairs; inspect machines and equipment to detect misuse or needed repairs; make scheduled repairs and renewals in such a manner as to make maximum use of the available manpower and minimize the disturbance to operations. It keeps records of the various machines and equipment as a guide to the proper use and selection of new equipment for a given purpose. It supervises construction work carried out by an outside agency, if any. It arranges for the sharpening of production tools, and maintains cost records that are used by the accounting department and by management.

Equipment Replacement. The establishment of a sound programme for the replacement of equipment is essential for any concern interested in staying in business permanently. Any discussion of equipment replacement is concerned with depreciation and obsolescence. *Depreciation* is an annual charge reflecting the decline in value of an asset due to such causes as wear and tear, the action of the elements, obsolescence, and inadequacy and are influenced also by tax factors, the capital structure of the enterprise, and changing price levels. *Obsolescence* is the depreciation of existing equipment due to the invention of new and better processes or equipment. It is thus a measure in rupees and paise of the declining productivity and efficiency in relation to those of more recently developed equipment. A proper replacement policy must consider all cost factors for both present and proposed equipment. Whichever equipment will result in the lower over-all cost of manufacture generally should be purchased.

PLANT LAYOUT

Maximum productivity from plant buildings and equipment can be attained only where these facilities are so integrated as to provide a smooth flow of materials, parts, and products. Smooth flow is the result of a good plant layout.

Management can attain the desired objectives through an efficient plant layout. The objectives to be attained are as follows :

1. Economics in material and product handling.
2. Lower cost of useful areas.
3. Minimising of production delays.
4. Better production control and supervision.
5. Avoidance of bottlenecks.
6. Avoidance of unnecessary and costly changes once a layout is made.
7. Improvements in production processes and methods.
8. Provision of a layout that permits meeting of competitive costs; and
9. Incorporation of safety into the physical plant as part of the layout and organisation.

Plant layout ideally involves the allocation of space and the arrangement of equipmnt in such a way that over-all operating costs are minimised. A completed layout project represents the master plan for physically integrating the factors of production which are required on the premises. Poor layouts result in high materials handling costs, high labour requirements and costs, idle machinery, large in-process inventories, and excessive space requirements, to mention only a few of the consequent inefficiencies.

Definition. *Plant layout* is the technique of locating machines, processes and plant services, within the factory so as to achieve the greatest possible output of high quality at the lowest possible total cost of manufacturing. It aims at discovering an optimum plan by which each operation is performed at the point of greatest convenience, without permitting the point of 'greatest convenience' for one process to conflict with that appropriate to others.

Factors that influence the plant layout. The type of industry, the quantity of production, the type of product, the type of operations and the type of worker must be considered in determining the final plant layout. The industry may be either a continuous or an assembly type. A *continuous industry* is one in which all the material is received at one point, from which successive operations turn it into a finished product, as in yarn spinning and paper and pottery manufacture. *An assembly industry* is one in which the finished product can be produced only after various components have been made and then brought together for final operations, such as the manufacture of shoes and automobiles. In factory layout this difference is significant. Some continuous industries are *synthetic*; that is, the product is obtained by bringing together various ingredients which are combined in the manufacturing process, as paper manufacture or yarn spinning or paint making. Paint, for example, is a combination of white lead, oils and other pigments. Other continuous industries are *analytical*; that is, the product is obtained by successive processes that separate the final product from the mass of original material. All refining industries, such as oil and by-products of coke, are of this nature. Assembly industries are also of two types: (1) those in which the *components are similar* and go through similar operations, as, for instance, in clothing industry; and (2) those in which the *components are dissimilar* and go through unlike processes, as for instance, the automobile industry.

For continuous process industry, the layout decided upon should be such that successive processes will be carried through in shops that adjoin one another in the sequence the processes follow. Then the article being produced will pass in a continuous line from the first to the second, the second to the third and so on until the finished product is ready. For example, a synthetic process will usually be laid out to resemble a river. Just as a river's tributaries merge together as the river continues down-stream, so also do the various materials and parts of a synthetic process merge into the completed assembly as one follows the layout path through the plant. An analytic-process layout, on the other hand, takes the form of a tree as it starts out with a single material or substance (the trunk) and spreads out into a variety of resultant materials (the branches, leaves, and fruit). Where the product is constructed with parts assembled from the several shops in which they have been made, the erection of the complete machine takes place in an assembly department centrally situated in relation to the contributory workshop.

The type of worker is a fundamental consideration, where many decisions concerning factory layout must be changed because of the requirements of these employees. The type of product, that is, whether the product is heavy or light, large or small, liquid or solid, is another fundamental consideration in plant layout. Although the manufacture of spark plugs and locomotives both involve assembly work, layout problems differ materially. Layout problems in any plant in which the product can be flowed, either by gravity or by pumps, from one operation to another, as in flour or sugar manufacture, differ from those in which work in process must be handled by hand, conveyor, or truck in moving from one operation to the next.

The type of manufacture also markedly influences plant layout. The industry that manufactures in large quantities a relatively few standardised products may be laid out on the so-called *straightline* or *product* basis as well as *process* or *functional* basis, whereas the *job-lot-manufacturing* type of industry, in which many unlike operations of non-standard products are required, is almost of necessity largely on the *functional* basis.

Types of layout. Layout may be by product (line) or it may be by process (functional). It may also be by *stationary material.* A *product layout* is one in which each machine is located according to the operation sequence required in producing one product of a group of related products. Layout by products, therefore, implies that operations are performed in a sequence and that the product is assembled or worked upon as needed. For example, a firm having two products, A and B, might set up two different production lines. Line A, which produces product A, might have an oven, a lathe, a milling machine, and a surface grinder, in that order. Line B might start with a forge and have a heat-treating station, an inspection station, and two lathes following. The lathe for the A line could be in the north-east corner of the building, and those for the B line might be located diametrically opposite. The plan given above illustrates the product layout.

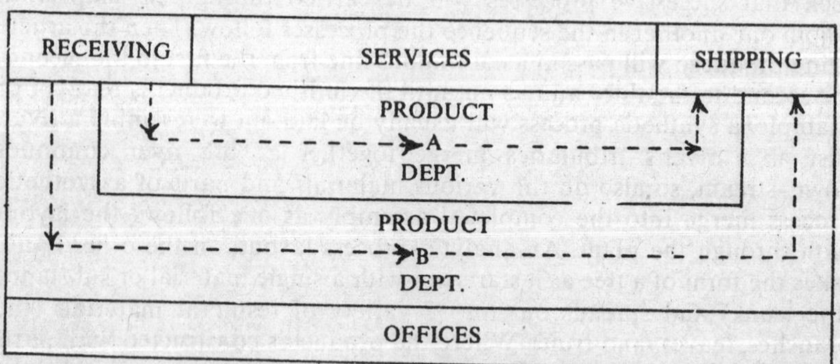

Fig. 1. A Product Layout.

Direct-line layout is applicable either to a single floor of the factory or to the building as a whole. The central idea behind layout of product is a continuous flow of materials in process towards the finished-product stage.

The *advantages* of layout by product are as follows :

1. It facilitates the use of materials-handling devices and conservation of floor space.

2. Internal transportation and back-hauling is minimised.

3. When properly adjusted, bottlenecks are eliminated.

4. Production control is facilitated, because once a product is started along the line, it is difficult for it to be side-tracked.

5. There is a considerable shortening of the manufacturing time from the first operation to the finished product.

6. There is a reduction of the work-in-process inventory.

7. There is also some reduction of the finished-product inventory, since production control is more complete and promises to customers from production are more reliable.

Some of the *disadvantages* of the product layout are : (1) Decreased flexibility; (2) increased investment in equipment; (3) frequently greater difficulty in expanding production beyond the capacities of the lines in layout by product than in functional layout; (4) greater difficulty in securing specialization in supervision.

Layout by process or *functional layout* is one in which machines are grouped according to their types, resulting in a lathe department, a milling-machine department, and an inspection department, among others. The functional layout is characterised by the assembling of

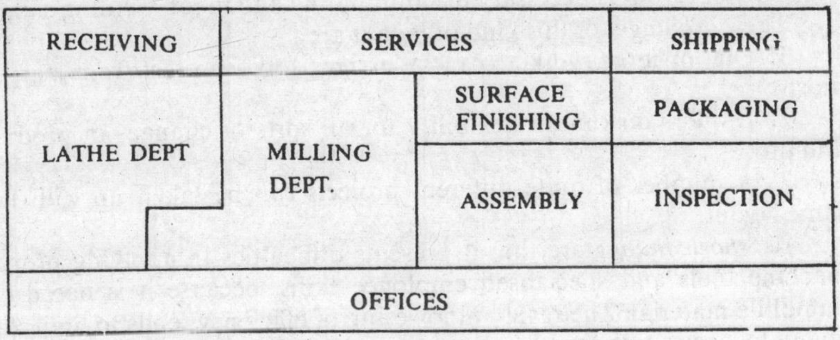

Fig. 2. Process Layout.

similar operations in one place; for instance, all drilling is performed in a drill-press department, and all electric welding is done in the electric-welding department. This type of layout carries out the functional idea of Frederick W. Taylor. It is useful for job-lot manufacturing or the manufacture of non-standardised products.

The *advantages* of layout by process are as follows :—

1. Greater flexibility, in that changes in operations and the sequence of operations seldom involve a change in layout.

2. Easier adjustment to changes in volume of production, especially when it is necessary to add equipment.

3. More ready adaptation to special needs arising from certain types of equipment, such as the protection of workers against exhausting fumes or the flashing of light in electric welding.

4. More complete utilisation of equipment, and hence a lower investment in equipment.

5. Better utilisation of the skill of the workers by following the principle of specialisation.

6. More effective use of the specialised abilities of supervisors.

The functional layout is strong where layout by product is weak, and weak where product layout is strong. It is seldom that an industrial enterprise of any magnitude is laid solely on either a product or a functional basis. Many organisations, however, are predominantly of one type or the other.

The *disadvantages* of functional layout are essentially the same as the advantages of the product type of layout. The *disadvantages* are : (1) Greater difficulty in automatic material handling and need for more floor space for the same volume of production; (2) excessive back-hauling of materials in process; (3) more time required to make the same product; (4) greater difficulty in production control; (5) excessive work-in-process inventory; (6) tendency to increase the finished-stock inventory if the same service to customers is given as is accomplished under product layout.

Layout by Stationary Material. This type of layout is designed primarily for manufacture of large parts and assemblies. Here the men and equipment are moved to the material, which remains in one place. This type of layout is necessary in shipbuilding and in job welding shops.

The *advantages* of this kind of layout are :

1. One or more workers can be assigned to a project from start to finish.

2. It offers maximum flexibility for all sorts of changes in product and process.

3. A number of quite different projects can be taken up with the same layout.

Its *shortcomings* are that it presents difficulties in applying proper machine tools and specialised employee skills, because it is based on immobile material. The resultant lowering of efficiency tends to limit this layout to large items made singly or in very small lots.

Sequences and Smooth Flow. In planning a layout care must be taken in allotting space to various workshops or departments, so that pressure here or there may not soon force these to burst their bounds. What space to allow to different departments will be decided on previous experience of the working of the business or, if that is not available, a careful estimate will have to be prepared for each room in relation to the equipment and operations it will have to house. Following this the relation of production centres with reference to the sequences of processes and the movements of materials in the course of manufacture must be determined. The aim must be to secure a smooth flow of work throughout the undertaking, avoiding both congestion because of bottlenecks, and the necessity of work-in-progress to retrace ground already covered. A crowded shop prevents employees from making rapid

The Layout of Shops. The elements of which manufacturing establishments are composed may be listed as: 1. Raw-materials

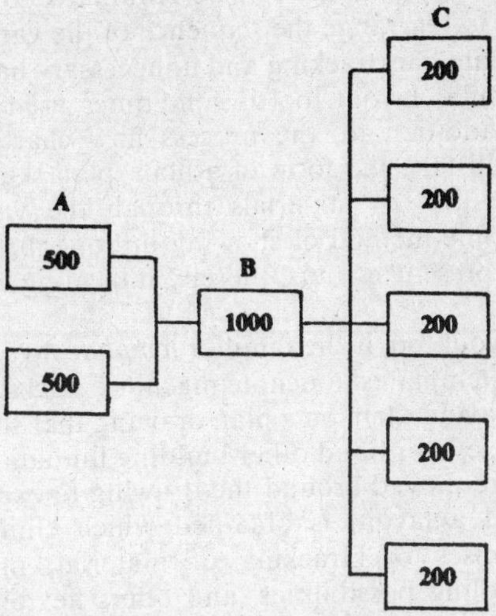

Fig. 6. Diagram of Co-ordination.

storage, and finished product storage. 2. Intermediate storage. 3. Manufacturing centres. 4. Assembling rooms and erecting floors. 5. Tool room, grinding room, and repair shops, 6. Stairways, beltways, lifts, and halls. 7. Toilets, lockers, and rest rooms. 8 Drafting room. 9. Planning room, 10. General offices, 11. Power plant. 12. Yard departments.

The arrangements of shops and other centres will depend upon the type of industry or process. In arranging these departments, care must be taken to see that the sequence of processes is maintained, co-ordination and internal transport are looked after and adequate provision for expansion is made. An actual ground layout plan will require any one of the following or a combination of two or more. These plans can be represented by capital letters, *I, L, U, C, H, F, E*. The simplest type is the *I* Plan, which can be enlarged to produce some sort of an *L* or *U* Plan. An *I* Plan can be duplicated by parallel arrangements of several buildings. The enlargement of duplicate *I* Plan may produce a quadrilateral, when connecting structures are thrown across between the original buildings.

Plant-layout Techniques. There are certain tools of plant layout in common use today which are a distinct aid in making or improving the layout of any plant. The first of these is the *process-flow chart.* It is a graphic map which follows material through its manufacturing cycle and records the sequence of the elements of that cycle as they occur. The process-flow chart enables a process to be visualised in such a compact form that possible improvements are usually readily discerned. Repeated static elements of storage, for example, indicate delays in production and unnecessary transport of material. The inefficiencies disclosed by such a chart will enable the management to rearrange the work stations. Analysis may disclose that some operations which add little or nothing to the final value of the product can be eliminated by minor changes. It may be possible to rearrange the sequence of the various elements in the process to eliminate backtracking and unnecessary handling.

Another similar layout tool is sometimes used in place of, and at other times in addition to, the process-flow chart is the *process-flow diagram.* This will take the form of a floor-plan sketch of the buildings upon which the flow of materials through the various operations is depicted. It is a fine method of showing up long material hauls and the backtracking of present layouts, thereby indicating how the layout may be improved.

The next layout tool is the familiar *template layout.* It is prepared by cutting out scale templates to denote machines, racks, benches, and other equipment and laying them on a plan drawing that shows building walls, columns, stairs, elevators, and other building limitations affecting layout. The templates are moved around the drawing to explore various layout possibilities until a layout is obtained which eliminates unnecessary handling, minimises backtracking of material, makes the most of mechanised handling possibilities, and offers flexibility to meet future changes in production requirements.

Another technique makes use of *scale-model layout.* The models are scaled reproductions of all pieces of equipment laid out on a plan drawing as above. It resembles a child's doll house. It aids in determining the amount of space and headroom required by equipment items. While it is a relatively expensive technique, it frequently pays off in laying out new processes. They are particularly useful where neither layout men nor plant supervisors have had much experience with the equipment and the flow of work. Models have been found particularly useful in laying out of refineries and chemical plants.

Revision of Layout Plans. Plant layouts are dynamic and must

LAYOUT OF AN ASSEMBLY SHOP

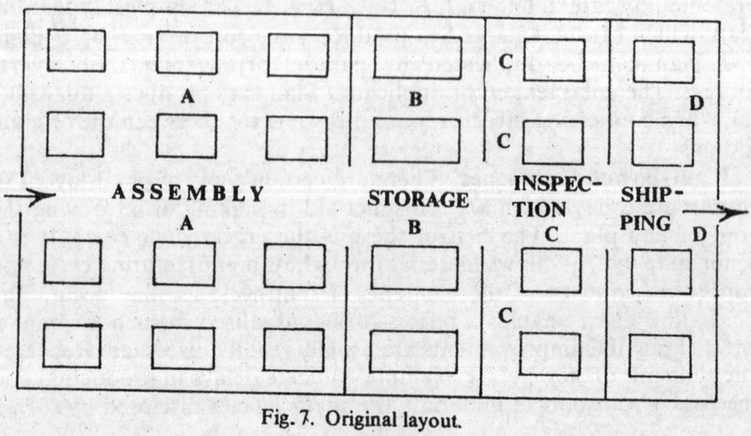

Fig. 7. Original layout.

change with conditions. Improvements in processes, altered methods, new or additional equipment, changes in production requirements, developments in materials-handling devices, better concepts of layout-any or all of these may necessitate a revision in an existing layout. This will be done to save costs and encourage savings. To facilitate revision, if need arises, layout must be *flexible.* They must be capable of incorporating without major change new equipment to meet technological progress or increased production requirements or to eliminate waste.

Good layouts are based on the principle of *flow.* This means regular movement of production, absence of bottleneck operations and minimisation of backtracking. The following diagrams illustrate the principle of flow and show how revision of layout ensures smooth flow.

In this small plant, small assemblies were made on semi-automatic machines in Department A. They were stored in Department B awaiting inspection. Only 10 per cent of the assemblies were inspected in Department C. Goods were packed for shipping in Department D. An excessive number of defects were left unchecked. It was decided to introduce 100 per cent inspection. This created a bottleneck as several days' work gathered in Department B awaiting inspection. Further congestion resulted as defective assemblies were repaired or scrapped.

To correct the position, the layout of departments was revised and conveyors in between work benches carrying goods to inspection tables were provided. This enabled the inspectors to give 100 per cent inspection immediately adjacent to assembly. Fig 8 shows the revised layout.

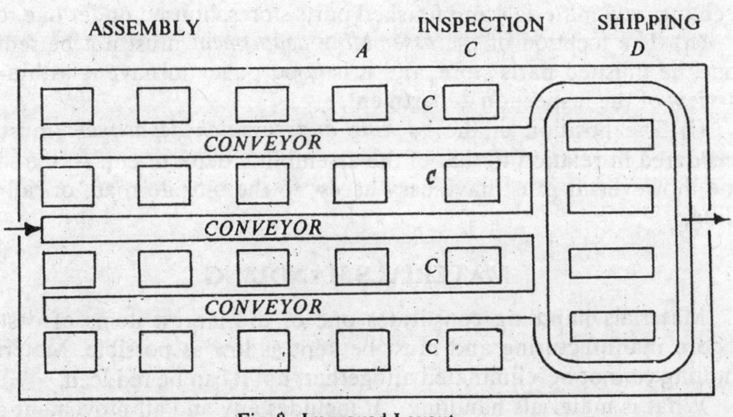

Fig. 8. Improved Layout.

The sequence has been changed, and inspection 100 per cent immediately adjacent to assembly is made. The revised layout resulted in the following improvements :

1. Bank of assemblies awaiting inspection were eliminated; there was no bottleneck at any stage.

2. The whole storage Department B was eliminated.

3. Rejects were discovered within a few minutes which afforded control before further "scrap" parts were made.

4. Congestion was removed and in fact more space was found for work benches and packing and shipping department.

Location of Departments. Departments must be located with many of the following factors in mind :

(a) *overlapping* must be avoided.

(b) *Obnoxious processes*, e.g., the vibrating of a heavy power press. the fumes and smells from the metal workers' section, must be isolated.

(c) The largest and the most easily accessible building ought to be utilised for the more important phase of production. For example, in an engineering works, the machining department occupies the premier position as a rule, and the allotment of other buildings is located in relation to it.

(d) The *receiving department* must be situated as close as possible to the raw material store, and the latter, being a "feeder" department, must not be too remote from the departments requiring raw materials.

(e) The *inspection department* must be closely associated with, and located either under the same roof as the machining department, or in an adjacent building, to ensure that rapid and continuous inspection can be arranged.

(f) *The finished parts store* should, if possible, adjoin the inspection department so that, after inspection, the parts can be taken direct to store, without further loading and transporting.

(g) It may be considered to have *all* sections of the *store*, i.e., receiving, raw materials and finished parts stores, housed under one roof.

(h) The location of the *assembling department* must not be remote from the finished parts store, and it is good policy to have it within the purview of the inspection department.

(i) The position of the *packing and despatch department* must be considered in relation to that of the assembling department. At the same time, however, it must have easy access to the outside road, or railway siding.

MATERIALS HANDLING

Materials handling constitutes one of the largest items of cost in modern manufacturing and must be kept as low as possible. Materials handling cannot be eliminated altogether, but it can be reduced.

What is materials handling ? It includes any and all movement and packaging of materials, parts, assemblies, and products. The handling of goods between plants, or internal transport, is also part of the materials handling function, as also the transfer of materials from one work place to another. A properly designed materials handling system has as its objective the reduction of overall production and distribution costs for a specific volume or range of output. To this end mechanical devices for handling materials have been extensively employed.

Advantages of mechanised handling. The advantages of mechanised handling properly integrated with processing may be summed up as follows :

1. The manufacturing-cycle time can be reduced by the elimination of much non-productive time in the manufacturing process.

2. Human fatigue in lifting and handling manually can be reduced and in some cases eliminated.

3. Idle machine and man time can be brought to a minimum especially intermittent delivery of materials is involved, as the special type of equipment ensures a steady, constant flow of materials.

4. The productivity of workers working on the product is increased by a reduction of the time they would otherwise spend in handling materials.

5. Increased safety of handling results where materials are not "manhandled". Mechanical equipment does not suffer back injuries, hernias, or toe accidents.

6. Storage space is conserved, particularly where mechanical equipment is used to stock materials vertically.

7. Non-productive, indirect labour can be released for more productive, direct-labour activities.

Some of the mechanical devices for handling materials are : chutes, trays, hangers, conveyors—roller, belt, bench, monorail, gravity conveyor, hand truck or power truck.

Rules for materials handling. For an efficient materials handling programme the following rules or principles should be followed :

1. Eliminate as much handling as possible. A sound plant layout can reduce or even eliminate the need for materials handling.

2. Remove handling tasks from among the duties of labour personnel, as materials handlers can he employed at lower rates and skilled workers' time is utilised more profitably.

3. Avoid using handling equipment below its capacity, and move materials at higher speeds as well as in larger groups.

4. Materials should be moved at constant rates of speed. Gravity should be used to full advantage.

5. Minimise transport distances, and avoid back tracking and rehandling of materials.

6. Move materials from their source to their destination in one continuous step, thereby eliminating unnecessary putting-down and picking-up operations.

7. Avoid congestion, as congestion breeds inefficiency.

8. Select the most flexible equipment, and use mechanical handling devices to eliminate or facilitate manual activity.

9. Combine the movement and storage of materials, and keep passageways lighted and unobstructed.

10. Avoid unnecessary mixing of materials, and assign the responsibility of promoting good materials handling to one individual.

11. Pay particular attention to packing and packaging. Remember

that materials handling job continues until the goods have reached the consumer.

WORK STUDY

All manufacturing processes require periodic study and changes in order to eliminate sporadic manufacturing difficulties and to bring about improvements in work. Entire processes must be re-evaluated from time to time in the light of new technological development and new concepts of manufacturing. Much of the success in achieving improvements in work rests with the management tool of *work study*.

Work Study is a technique of management whereby each job or operation is studied analytically with the prime objects of :

(a) Determining what the job or operation entails, e.g., method used, layout, equipment used, conditions in which work is done.

(b) Measuring the work content of the job, for the purposes of planning and control, costing, fixing wage payments and incentives.

Phases of Work Study. There are two distinct phases of work study; they are, however, interrelated :

(a) *Method Study:* The scientific approach towards the improvement of production methods by observing, recording, analysing and critically examining existing or proposed methods. It is sometimes described as methods analysis or methods engineering. Whatever the name, the object is *Work Improvement.*

(b) *Work Measurement:* The determination of the proper time to be allowed and of the effort required for the effective performance of a specified task.

Objectives of Method Study. The objectives of method study are :

(i) To improve processes and procedures.
(ii) To improve lay-out and design.
(iii) To improve working conditions.
(iv) To improve upon the utilization of man-power, machines and material.
(v) To effect economy in human effort and reduce unnecessary fatigue.

Objectives of Work Measurement. The objectives of work measurement are :

(i) To achieve more economic and effective manning of plant and equipment.
(ii) To improve production planning and control.
(iii) To provide reliable performance statistics.
(iv) To provide a rational basis for incentive schemes.
(v) To produce a reliable and realistic basis for labour costing and control.

The Prime Objective of Work Study, i.e., of the joint efforts of methods study and work measurement, is to provide a service for management which will help in increasing productivity.

Need for Work Study. The need for work study in industry may be explained as follows :

(a) Primarily, it is needed to increase production.

(b) Wasteful, unnecessary and ineffective work can be eliminated.

(c) A considerable saving in production costs can usually be effected.

(d) Information is provided for management, and inefficiency is revealed.

(e) Existing methods are improved, and delays and unnecessary effort are reduced.

(f) Unsatisfactory operating conditions are revealed.

(g) Operators on piece work or other methods of payment by results are protected; in particular :

(i) By ensuring that they are allowed adequate time for rest pauses and all personal needs considered to be justifiable.

(ii) By ensuring that there is equality of reward for equal skill and effort.

(iii) By stabilising a rate for the job, which has been based upon the time taken by an average worker working at normal speed under normal conditions.

Method Study Procedures. Method study procedures *to improve methods of production* are usually conducted on the following lines.

(i) First of all the work which it is considered can be studied with economic advantage is selected.

(ii) Then the scope of the study to be undertaken is defined.

(iii) Record is made of all relevant facts concerning the present (or proposed) method, using the appropriate recording techniques, such as process charting, flow diagrams, multiple activity charts and motion charts.

(iv) The next step is to examine critically the facts so recorded, and challenge, seek alternatives, eliminate or simplify wherever possible in order to produce a more effective method.

(v) Develop the improved method by recording it, and then re-examine the record until satisfied that the best method has been established to meet the prevailing circumstances.

(vi) Thereafter, define the new process or procedure, indicating the necessary layout, equipment, quality of materials and working conditions.

(vii) Install the new, improved method after careful planning and arrangement.

(viii) Maintain and verify that the new method is being fully implemented, and is achieving its intended objectives.

Work Measurement Procedures. Work measurement procedures *to assess human effectiveness* usually follow a set pattern as follows :

(i) The first step is to select the work to be measured.

(ii) The second step is to define the method to be used. Usually the job to be studied is broken down into its elements or individual movements.

(iii) The third step is to measure work involved, i.e., to accurately determine how long a job takes, by means of an accurate time recording instrument, usually a stop-watch. The technique employed in measuring work of a repetitive nature differs from that used in measuring work of a non-repetitive character, as the latter does not always lend itself to straight-forward timing, in which case some form of analytical estimating is used. The repetitive work is measured by *Time Study.*

(iv) Having made a detailed time study, decide upon the most appropriate work unit. Thereafter, after making justifiable allowances, e.g., an allowance for recuperation from fatigue and personal requirements, fix its value or *rating.*

(v) Finally, establish the *allowed time* for the work unit as the standard time for future costing, planning and calculation of bonus incentives.

Recording Techniques. Some of the techniques used, either separately or in combination, to record facts required concerning present or proposed operations are as follows :

(a) *Cyclograph.* This is a photograph of the work-place, upon which a continuous white line is traced, to show the path of movement of an operator's hand while it is performing an operation.

(b) *Chronocyclograph.* In this case the movement of the object is traced as an interrupted or dotted white line on a photograph of the work-place. The shape and spacing of the dots indicate the direction and speed of movement at any point along the path of the object—usually the operator's hand.

(c) *Flow diagrams.* These are used to show the location of the various activities being studied and the routes followed by personnel, material or equipment. The drawings are usually to scale.

(d) *Motion Charts.* These are used to record an operator's movements during the performance of his usual task, to enable the work study team to analyse them. As a result, it may be possible to reduce the time taken to do the job, and also to reduce the amount of physical effort by eliminating unnecessary motions.

(e) *Multiple activity time charts.* These are necessary when the activities of several subjects are to be compared, or when it is desired to show the relationship between the body movements of an operator in the course of his work.

(f) *Process charting.* In the course of producing a process chart, a variety of symbols may be used to save time and facilitate recognition of the activities recorded. There are many varieties of the symbols that are commonly used, but the following are adequate for most purposes :

Operation	○
Inspection	□
Transport	→
Storage	▽
Delay	D

(g) *Simo chart*, or simultaneous motion cycle chart. This is used for the purpose of recording simultaneously, on a common time scale, the movements of the two hands (or other parts) of the operator while he is performing a single cycle of any operation under investigation.

(h) *String diagram.* This is a variant of the flow diagram. It is used to show the paths of movement of operators, material, documents or equipment. A scale model of the location is made and each work position is marked by a pin. The distance travelled by the subject under investigation is measured by running a continuous thread from pin to pin. The total length of the thread used will represent the distance travelled in the time given to the observation.

(i) "*Therblings*" was the name concocted by Gilbreth, the pioneer of motion study, to the seventeen (subsequently increased to eighteen) basic movements, or groups of movements, into which he divided all types of human activity. These he reduced to a series of symbols and colours.

CHAPTER XXVIII

PRODUCTION AND COST CONTROL

Production Control. The organisation of the physical plant and management of labour force deal only with half of the problems of business organisation and management. Before the manager comes face to face with the problems of selling, he has to tackle problems which arise in connection with establishing and administering, operating and production controls. Nothing influences every factor—labour, material, equipment, and product—quite so much as does production control. To its lack or ineffectiveness much waste, much loss, and many failures in business can be traced. The problem of controlling production so that the required product shall be produced in the best and cheapest method, that it shall be of the required quality, and that it shall be produced at the required time is of vital importance to any manufacturing business.

Definition and Scope. The term "production control" has not been clearly defined, nor is there any clear-cut or definite limit to it. There is a great deal of confusion about its scope. Rightly esteemed, production includes all the processes of converting raw materials into a product ready for delivery to the purchaser. It is, in a broad sense, synonymous with manufacturing. Control in this sense means management. To control is to direct or restrain. So, used in this sense, production control might mean the management of manufacturing. This would, however, be too broad a definition, for it would include not only quality control, but also cost and methods control, which should be considered separately. Production control is concerned, primarily, with the *time* aspect of manufacture, and may combine with it the *place* aspect, and less often *quantity* or volume aspect, yet it should be allowed to concentrate only on those factors which involve the time element in manufacture. The British Standards Institute gives the following as principles which comprise production control : (1) the production plan or planning; (2) scheduling; (3) machine and labour utilisation or despatching; (4) stock control; (5) manufacturing order control or routing; and (6) progress. According to the Institute the aforesaid six principles or factors comprise production control—all taken together make up production control. Therefore, Production Control may be defined as a directive agency whose purpose, where production is divided into separate operations, is to co-ordinate those operations in the most effective fashion through the exercise of the functions of planning, scheduling inspecting, routing, despatching and observing, with the object of producing the desired quantity of goods of the right quality at the correct time and place.

Production control implies a dual problem. On the one hand, it requires a planning element to foresee each step in perhaps a long series of operations, and to arrange so that things may happen in the right place and at the right time with a minimum of effort and with maximum efficiency. On the other hand, a control technique is required to see that the plans that are made are actually put in hand. Planning aims to establish in advance *what* work shall be done, *how* the work shall be done, *where* the work shall be done, and *when* the work shall be done. The decisions reached as the result of this analysis are indicated in a manner so that routine arrangements will suffice to cause them to happen in the right place and at the right time. The function of the control technique is to put into effect these procedures determined in advance by planning, and to observe, inspect and record progress so as to keep up a continuous comparison between planned and actual results.

Planning. The production plan or Planning is the most important tool in industrial management. The idea behind it is to predetermine the work to be done throughout a factory. It is a definite time-table to which departments and people must work. It must be reduced to writing and work as a standard practice, and must be covered by Production Chart, Target Data Chart, and Time Cycle Chart. As a planning activity, therefore, production control is concerned with maximizing the employment of production facilities with the general purposes in view of minimizing operating costs and meeting delivery schedules. Consequently, this phase reflects needed planning in terms of material requirements, detailed equipment use, production runs, and other priority. The control phase is embodied in the follow up procedures. This is the technique of determining whether the production plans are working properly.

Routing. Production routing is one of the elements in planned production. It involves the planning of the exact sequence of work station to be used in processing a part of product. Once a layout has been established, the routing of an item is the determination of the path that item should follow as it is manufactured. This phase of production control is analogous to the initial planning of a personal rail journey. An individual wishing to reach London by air from Delhi could route himself through Bombay, Cairo, Rome, Geneva and Paris or through Bombay, Beirut, Zurich and Dusseldorf, to name only two of the many possibilities. Similarly, a part can be usually routed through a variety of combinations of machines capable of performing the operations required. In simple words, route is the path over which the part has to pass for execution of work. To determine the best route for a particular item, the planner must have a list of the operations required for processing the order, the probable time requirements for the work, and an availability schedule for various machines and works stations. A Route Card is prepared for this purpose in the planning section. But the routing should be done so that the machines in a plant are operated at their fullest capacity.For example, if a ten-ton press can perform a particular operation, one ordinarily should avoid using a twenty-ton press for the job. Of course, analysis might show that the larger press is idle for a period of time whereas the smaller presses are overloaded, in which case utilization of the heavier equipment might be the most economical alternative. Also for small lots one generally uses equipment with low set-up costs and high operating costs, whereas for large lots one usually uses machinery with considerable set-up expense but low operating costs. The most exacting routings reflect the experience and abilities of the personnel at the various work stations. When accuracy is paramount, work is routed through those work stations at which the most capable operators are situated.

Scheduling. Work scheduling consists of the assignment of starting and completion times for the various operations to be performed. Knowledge of the routing of an item and machine loading resulting from previously routed items are required for the scheduling of work. Strictly speaking, a schedule is a list. There are schedules of freight rates, schedule of ocean sailings, etc. When applied to manufacturing, the schedule is a list of parts to be made, often in a prescribed sequence, and sometimes within a specified period. It is the means by which the production plan is presented to all concerned to provide for the commencement and completion of work in all stages of manufacture. By it all jobs are filled into a logical time-table, so that the relative time at which each operation or event in connection with manufacturing will occur is determined. To return to the travel illustration, scheduling is like determining arrival and departure times at the different stops. At this stage of the planning there still may be several potential routes, the final selection being dependent on the time element and availability of facilities. The traveller might find that the shortest route creates scheduling difficulties and that the quickest route is the longest. He then will complete his scheduling activity by establishing the arrival and departure times for each stop along the way. For factory operations, in addition to individual route schedules, master schedules are prepared which record plantwise activity. On those schedules all the various products, together with their starting and completion dates, are shown.

Despatching. When the routing and scheduling of a product have been completed, there still remains the job of despatching. The despatching function involves the actual granting of permission to proceed according to plans already laid down. This is similar, in the case of the traveller, to his employer finally approving his vacation leave. In the industrial situation the despatcher provides an employee with a work ticket. This ticket indicates to the employee that he may proceed on work which has been planned for him, and it grants him authority to requisition the necessary tools and materials if this has not been done for him already. In its literal meaning despatching means starting something on its way, sending it along towards some destination. In factory parlance it usually indicates the method or process of assigning work to definite work places, and where necessary, accelerating or retarding its progress from point to point. It sees that the material is moved to the correct work place, that the tools are ready at the correct place for the particular operation; that the records of lines are made; that the work is moved according to routing instructions. It is the contact, between planning and operation. It carries out the physical work which has been planned by scheduling.

Progress or Expediting (Follow up). Progress is the means by which the execution of the production plan is co-ordinated so as to reveal, and as far as possible to eliminate or correct, any variations from the plan. Stated differently, progressing or expediting is the function of the management which is responsible for the movement of the work through the various processes as laid down in the Production Programme. It is an activity which owes its existence to the fact that actual progress often fails to match corresponding plans. In the case of the traveller, if the plane on which he is travelling should be delayed, he might have to revise his plans. A delay of several hours might cause him to miss proper connections. Similarly, in the industrial situation one might find that raw materials are delayed, in which case an expediter in either the purchasing or production control department would be assigned the job of investigating and remedying the difficulty as quickly as possible. He might have to trace a misrouted shipment or contact a vendor who has failed to ship on schedule. If the vendor's plight appears to be hopeless, the expediter might initiate action leading to a transfer of the order to an alternate supplier. But all follow up work is not initiated after something has gone wrong. Often expediters are assigned to spot check progress on randomly selected orders or to follow special orders throughout completion. If a particularly valuable customer is promised a quick delivery, a special expediter might be appointed to determine hourly that progress is being made as planned.

Production Control aims at giving the best service possible, consistent with available capacities, and at the same time to secure the lowest possible costs. It balances these two factors so well that one does not benefit at the cost of the other. But production control, to be effective, must be comprehensive, covering every factor that has any influence in the final results. There should be provided sufficient of the right kind of system, forms and clerical routine to (a) collect adequate detailed information needed for planning; (b) inaugurate work and give complete instructions and the detailed information needed in performance; and (c) provide records of current and past performance. The records should be prompt, adequate, and usable. Duplication and red-tape are to be watched and avoided. Moreover, competent personnel with sufficient authority should be employed. Finally, proper spirit should be inculcated throughout the organisation from the top boss to the workman.

Types of Production. Production may be defined as the organised activity of transforming raw materials into finished products. In this sense raw materials can include anything from rough ore to an electric motor. The finished product of one industry is frequently the raw material of another. Production, therefore, includes all manufacturing and extractive industries. In talking about production control, general principles, applicable to all types of production, have been stated. But these principles shall have to be modified according to the needs of each type of production. It is, therefore, necessary to note here the three types of production which may be found in each of the different groups of industries, such as mines and quarries, agriculture and fisheries, building and civil engineering , transport, dock and public utilities and manufacture. The three types and scales of production are :

1. Job Production, usually carried on small scale.
2. Batch Production, usually carried on medium scale.
3. Flow or Mass Production, usually carried on large scale.

Job Production is concerned with the manufacture of single product to a customer's individual requirements. Each job or order stands alone and is unlikely to be repeated. No two jobs are exactly alike and long runs on a single product are uncommon. Job production is carried on by quarries on special work for architecture, by building and civil engineering on bridges and individual houses, by manufacture on special purpose machines and Prototype work. The skill of all operatives must be very high.

Batch Production operates in those companies where a batch or quantity of products or parts is made at a time, but where production in a part or product is not continuous. This occurs when there is a variety of products manufactured to stock and when orders are diverse, but for farily large quantities. The most common reason for batch production is the use of standard components in different products and models. This type of production is typical of industry. It calls for general purpose equipment, and machine tools, flexibility in organisation, and a high standard of skill at the foreman and executive level. Whilst the skill of all operators may not be high as in factories in jobbing production, and tooling may not be so complex as in mass production, a high degree of skill is required in setting up tools and jobs and in deciding rapidly the most effective way to do a job. It is on this type of production in all industries that control is most difficult to secure. Normal mining, Public Works maintenance, poultry farming, all forms of transport and manufactured articles and most engineering and consumption industries make use of this type of production.

Flow or Mass Production is limited in general to large-scale units. In this type, product or parts of identical kind are in continuous production going through exactly the same sequence of operations, and all processing units (machine, plant, or operation) are always employed doing the same operation. Mass production has resulted in and depends on the development of the single-purpose type of machine. Frequently, only one product, and one or perhaps two or three models or grades only, are produced, and the production rate is high. Mass production reaches its most advanced stage in the large process industries like flour-milling sugar-refining, oil-refining and in factories making such standard articles as cars, vacuum cleaners, refrigerators, telephones, electric lamps, etc. Factories operating on mass-production scale are usually large and employ thousands of workers. Many of the problems of control arise from the very size of the units and the consequent lack of contact between the higher management and operators, and the de-skilling of jobs, resulting in lack of interest in them.

The development of a factory from job production to batch production occurs naturally, and creates as a rule no major problems. It is usually the logical result of a gradual increase in volume of turnover, or of application of standardisation of parts, as the business grows and the customers' needs become known. But it is the decision to apply mass production methods that is fraught with danger, particularly, if its application is premature. Change of fashion may upset all plans. The decision must be taken carefully by the Board as a matter of high policy.

QUALITY CONTROL

Quality Cont·ol is a statistical method of measuring deviation from standard quality by recording sample tests on a chart which immediately shows when work is being produced outside previously approved limits. It is applicable to all cases where limits can be worked to and is most suitable for continuous manufacture. It has the virtue of low cost and of early warning of a falling off in quality. It is a procedure which is used for the control of mass-produced articles by the application of the theory of probability to the results of examination of samples. A very important feature is that the examination is made close to the machine, and as soon as possible after the articles are produced, so that the results serve to give a direct indication of tendencies in the production process, and enables corrective action to be taken before excessive errors arise, thereby avoiding unnecessary scrap. Control may be based either on the percentage of defectives found in samples or on recorded measurement of the individual parts in the samples. In either case there is a considerable saving in the number of gauges required. It is claimed that the proper application of quality control can give as sure a result as 100 per cent gauging, when due regard is had to the possibilities of human error due to fatigue in continuous operation of the latter.[1]

It will be realised from what has been said that quality accuracy and finish are relative; there is, in a practical manufacturing sense, no absolute measurement. To an engineer dead size means as accurate as he can measure with his micrometer, e.g., to a ten-thousandth part of an inch (.00001"). In setting up any standard, therefore, it is not sufficient to state a single unit (of length, degree of heat, etc,), but to express the standard as a permissible variation between upper and lower limits, unless the accuracy obtainable with instrument normally in use is good enough, e.g., foot-rule, or commercial scales for weight. Standards should be laid down in writing in specifications or on drawings. The inspection should not be negative only, but it should control the quality

1. Institution of Mechanical Engineering Proceedings, 1947. vol. 157.

of production. The actual organisation of the work of inspecting, recording and taking a corrective action must obviously vary very widely with the type of product, process and scale of manufacture. With armaments and aeroplane manufacture, 100 per cent inspection at all stages and operations is usually called for. In the manufacture of barrows, agricultural machinery, etc., a much less rigid inspection is required. In the chemical process industries a different type of inspection altogether is required. Where precision is necessary, 100 per cent inspection will be required. In other cases sample inspection may be found to be adequate. The sample must be taken at a frequency to assure an adequate percentage check as indicated by experience, but there should also be random checks at irregular periods and of the batch.

The inspection may be either centralised or floor inspection. In the *former method* all work from a department is sent to the Inspection Department or made to pass through an inspection crib before passing on to the next operation. In the latter method inspectors go on to the floor and inspect work at the machine or bench. In deciding which to adopt the advantages of each should be borne in mind. Centralised inspection is easier and makes for better supervision. Division of labour is possible, permitting employment of less skilled labour. It is more thorough and less liable to interruption. The shops remain tidy and therefore it is easy to control the flow of work. More accurate checking for wage payment is possible and there is less chance of falsification. It is easier to progress, and losses from lost or stolen work and hidden scrap are at a minimum.

In floor inspection there is far less handling, and less delay due to time lag in Inspection Department. There is less work in progress and shorter production cycle time. Faults can often be rectified immediately and by the operator responsible. The inspector can act as adviser to operator, with an aim to preventing faulty work.

COST AND COST CONTROL

Average Cost. In a trading business where goods are sold practically in the same form as when purchased, the cost is a known factor; the selling price can be easily fixed by merely adding to the purchase price a percentage sufficient to cover establishment expenses which are more or less known and constant, and to leave a reasonable margin of profit. In a small manufacturing business also, a firm may only depend upon the yearly survey by comparing the total expenditure for the years with total earnings or revenue, and then estimate the actual financial position. In other words, it may be content with preparing a profit and loss account in order to determine the profits earned during the year. It may then prepare a balance-sheet showing the capital of the firm at the time and the total expenditure as representing the cost of supplying to total quantity of product manufactured. By dividing the total expenditure by the entire quantity of output the firm is able to find the Average Cost per unit. A bigger manufacturing firm may also stop at that. But this average cost does not help the firm, much less the bigger one, in its task of day-to-day policy determination or in respect of particular orders from customers. True, the average cost is of value, but it is known too late—after the expenditure has been incurred. What any firm of size must know is the cost actually incurred in making one unit of the product. But the task is very complicated. Some costs vary directly with the output, while others are more or less fixed and therefore difficult to be allocated to any unit of product. In order that proper allocation of different costs may be made it is necessary to build up an efficient system of costing and cost accounts. It must, however, be emphasized at the very outset that, contrary to the common belief, the use of costing is not to be confined to price fixing and price quotation, but should be extended to the provision of data which direct attention to where inefficiencies are occurring so that they can be corrected before it is too late.

Fundamentally, prices are determined by the interplay of supply and demand and should be established as the result of research into market conditions. Costing can point out the extent to which the firm is out of line with the general competitive set-up, and indicate the direction to be followed by any corrective action that may be necessary. Furthermore, business firms are concerned more with making profit or avoiding loss than with prices. Since profit is a function of both cost and price of an article, cost accounts will enable the firm to control its costs and measure its efficiency. In the absence of adequate information on market conditions, costs can legitimately be used in practice to regulate prices. Cost accounting aims at providing a system of analyses of the financial records in which all expenses are sub-divided and allocated to the individual jobs and processes upon which they have been incurred.

Costing Aims. The significance of costing varies widely in individual circumstances. There is no ready-made system of cost accounting, and each business must decide upon the particular plan it needs. Therefore, cost accounts should be adapted to the needs of the business, and not business to cost accounts. In broad terms, the aims of costing may be said to be : (1) the regulation of selling, subject to the conditions of demand and supply; (2) the introduction of accuracy in the framing of the estimate to avoid losses from unduly low quotations, or lost business from unnecessarily high quotations; (3) the ascertainment of the fact as to which groups of products pay or do not pay; (4) finding out whether any article costs more to produce than it would cost to buy; (5) the establishment of standards against which actual results can be compared to indicate waste of material and inefficient workmanship and management; (6) the determination of the degree of importance of each element of cost, or stage of process, with particular reference to the scope for economy; and (7) providing a definite collateral check on the financial records.

Main Elements of Cost. The various expenditures which are involved in holding a manufacturing plant ready for production, and in actually carrying on productive activities within it, can be divided into three main groups. The first of them includes the materials of which the product is composed, the second comprises the labour directly applied to those materials. The third group is composed of all those remaining items of outlay which do not attach themselves in a direct and definite way to the production of any individual unit of output. The first and second classes of expenditure are easily computed : when combined they form what is called Prime Cost. The third group is known as factory burden, or overhead, or supplementary cost, or simply as "expensive" The materials and labour directly employed in the manufacture of any product do not usually account for more than two-thirds of the total cost of running a business, and frequently do not amount to as much as 50 per cent of the total. The main problem then is how to divide up the remainder of the costs and expenses product by product, or products, or process by process, so as to arrive at an accurate figure for total costs.

Stated differently, expenditure may be divided into two main classes—direct and indirect. Direct expenses include (a) direct materials, (b) direct labour, and (c) direct expense. Indirect expenses are those which cannot be definitely identified with any particular jobs or processes. The benefit of such expenses is enjoyed by all the work that is going on. Indirect expenses include (a) works or factory expenses, or works or factory on cost, (b) office and administrative expenses, (c) selling and distributive expenses. The following chart shows the elements and division of costs :

COMPONENTS OF COST

Direct :	Materials Labour Expenses	Prime Cost or Flat Cost
	Work Expenses	Works or Factory Cost or Manufacturing Cost
Indirect :	Office and Administrative Expenses	Cost of Production or Works oncost
	Selling and Distributive Expenses Net profit and Net Loss	Cost of Sales Selling Price

The relation of cost elements to selling price can also be seen from the analytical chart:—

ANALYSIS OF SELLING PRICE

Direct or Productive Materials	+ Direct or Chargeable or Productive Labour Expenses	=	Prime Cost, Flat Cost or Basic Cost
Prime Cost Basic Cost or Flat Cost	+ Works Expenses or Factory Expenses or Works Oncost	=	Work Cost or Factory Cost
Factory Cost or Works Cost	+ Administrative Expenses	=	Cost of Production or Gross Cost or Office Cost
Cost of Production or Gross Cost or Office Cost	+ Selling and Distribution Expenses	=	Total Cost or Selling Cost
Total Cost or Selling Cost	Profit	=	Selling Price

The combination of these different types of cost which enter into the cost of production leading to the selling price may be given in a step-by-step build-up from prime cost to total cost as shown in the following figure :

COST BUILD UP

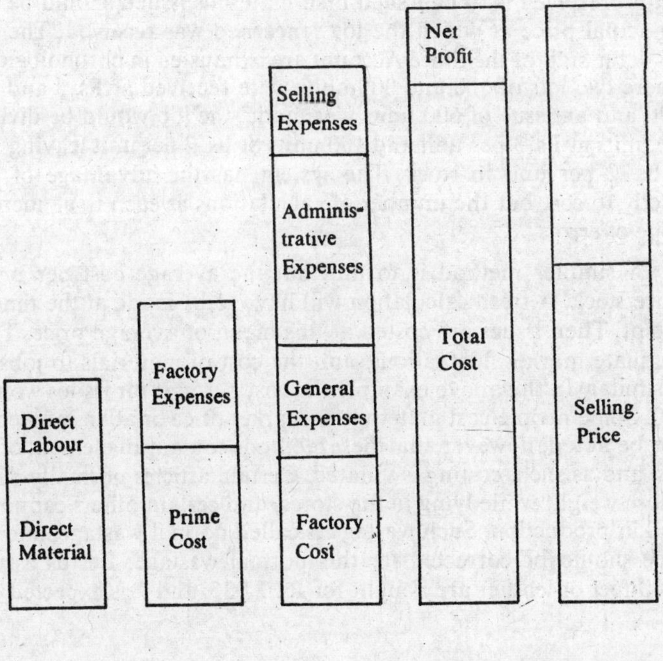

Direct Material Cost. The most tangible and specific beginning of cost is when raw materials are purchased, out of which a finished product is to be made. When materials are used exclusively for a particular job—a job being a series of productive steps ending in the completion of a unit or lot of product–and when it is easy to measure the amount of the material used in connection with each job, the cost of such materials may be charged directly as direct material cost. The original cost may be taken as the actual purchase price, or the last price, or the average price. Into the laid-down cost there enter other items such as freight, cartage, and the expenses of receiving, storing and issuing. These items will be difficult to sub-divide on to each batch of materials requisitioned for the job, and so will be treated as a part of factory expense. A proper system of purchasing and store-keeping must be set up for keeping a regular check over material cost. In most of the finished articles, the price of raw materials and other stores (indirect material) is substantial and any inefficiency in buying or storing will materially increase the cost of production. Efficiency in this respect consists of supplying the needs of the factory on demand without keeping too large stocks and without paying too high prices. Deterioration of product and material while they lie in the stores is to be avoided. An adequate routine for placing orders, receiving goods, storing them and issuing them and costing them is necessary. There should be maintained proper stores ledgers showing stocks in hand, on order, and under reservation, its value and the details of receipts and issues. While calculating the value of receipts, charges are to be added to the invoice price. Materials issued to various jobs are costed in various ways. According to the first method under which the first lot received is to be issued first, materials issued should be costed at the actual price at which the lot concerned was received. The items on the debit side of the Store Account are exhausted in chronological order. Where two lots of 500 and 300 units were received at Rs. 3 and Rs. 2 per unit, and an issue of 600 units was made, the job would be divided with 500 units at Rs. 3 per unit and 100 units at Rs. 2 per unit leaving 200 units at Rs. 2 per unit in stock. The system has the advantage of adhering strictly to cost but the number of calculations at each issue increases the scope of error.

A simpler method is to find out the average cost per unit of the entire stock. A fresh calculation will have to be made at the time of each receipt. Then issues are costed at this mean or average price. This tends to equate market fluctuations, and the cost of materials to jobs tends to be similar. In the above example the cost per unit for issues would be Rs. 2.50. Some people cost materials at market price or at an inflated price. It is to be noted, however, that these methods contain an element of profit or loss, and as such, costing is vitiated. Certain articles normally deteriorate or lose weight while lying in the stores, and certain others cannot be fully used in production. Such wastage is called normal wastage, and the issue price should be corrected for this normal wastage. Let us assume that 2,000 feet of leather are bought for Rs. 2,025, and it is expected that only

1,800 feet will be available for actual use; the issue price will be Rs. 2,025/1,800 or Rs. 1.12 per ft. But suppose due to some other cause actually only 1,600 feet are available for use; then the value of 200 feet, i.e., Rs. 225 (abnormal wastage) should be written off to Profit and Loss Account and not charged to production. The issue price should remain at Rs. 1.12 per ft. It is desirable, therefore, to differentiate between normal wastage and abnormal wastage. The former enters into the cost of production while the latter is a loss to be written off against Profit and Loss Account.

Materials used in running of machinery such as machine oil, cotton waste, belting, polishing substances, a few nails and screws used on a repair job, solder on sheet-metal work, cotter pins, and many similar items, though used in connection with manufacture, do not form part of the product manufactured, and which are not capable of being allocated to specific work are known as *indirect materials,* and their costs are *indirect material costs.* These costs are included in the indirect charges.

Direct Labour Cost. Under this head wages of only those workers who are engaged on definite jobs or processes or production articles are included. Such labour is called productive or direct labour, as it can be measured and directly charged to the separate products. The wages of those workmen who are engaged on general activity benefiting all jobs or processes (e.g., night watchman, crane handler, foundry helper, foreman) are included in indirect expenses and are so passed over into factory expense. The labour of these is called indirect or non-productive labour. The direct labour forms part of the Prime Cost of a product, and the indirect labour forms part of the Overhead Expenses of the factory.

In order to find out how much time a worker has spent on a particular job, each worker is provided with a Job Card for recording details of work done by him. The Jobs mentioned on the card are then debited with the wages of the worker for the time spent on the job. This applies only in case of "time workers." In case of "piece workers", labour charges in respect of each job or article are fixed. In case of time workers, "idle time" has to be accounted for. Each worker takes some time to go to his department from the factory gate in the morning. In the evening he leaves a little early to reach the factory gate "in time." The clocking in and clocking out takes some time. A worker also wastes a little time in taking up the next job after one in hand is finished. Such losses of time are known as "normal idle time"and the wages for this time are added to the cost of production. Abnormal idle time, abnormal wastage of materials, is not an item of cost, but is to be written off against Profit and Loss Account. Abnormal idle time may arise through breakdown of machinery or failure of electricity or shortage of raw materials, and so on.

Direct Expenses. In addition to the direct material and direct labour expenses discussed above, there are some other expenses which can be identified with individual jobs or processes. These expenses are usually : (a) hire of special machinery or plant; (b) trading expenses in connection with the job; (c) cost of special patterns or designs; (d) architects' and engineers' fees; (e) drawing office charges, if the amount is considerable; (f) experimental costs incurred for a particular job; and (g) cost of defective work, where several trials have to be made before work of suitable quality is obtained. If, as often happens, the management producing large quantities of repetitive work finds it necessary to change designs frequently and by so doing has to scrap the existing finished parts, the value of such scrapped parts will be an item cost for the production of the new set.

Indirect Expenses. As it is essential to compile cost of production even while production is going on, it is necessary to estimate the indirect expenses. Actual figures are available much later and for the purpose of costing quite valueless. After the indirect expenses are estimated, there is the further problem of equitably distributing these expenses over all the jobs that are undertaken in the factory. Obviously, this distribution cannot be made unless we also know the total production of the factory for the period concerned.

Prima facie it would be well to estimate output for the period and distribute the total of indirect expenses over the figure obtained. Thus entire expenses, say, during the year, would be debited to the cost of production. The system is, however, faulty when we have to deal with plants which for any reason (e.g., depression) remain idle or partly idle for any considerable period of time. The cost of production will rise from semi-idle periods because roughly the same amount of indirect expenses will be distributed over smaller output. The "value" of closing stock will rise, but during the depression or on account of it the price obtainable cannot be in conformity with this "value". Moreover, the accounts prepared on this basis will show the total loss, but not the reason for it. If, on the other hand, normal output basis is adopted, i.e., if indirect expenses are distributed on the assumption that plant will run to its normal capacity, then a certain portion of the indirect expenses will remain unrecovered in period of idleness. For example, if indirect expenses amount to Rs. 50,000, and if normal output is 25,000 articles, but the actual output is only 10,000 articles, then the cost of each individual unit will be debited with Rs. 2 for indirect expenses. This will mean that only Rs. 20,000 ($10,000 \times 2$) of the indirect expenses will be allocated to production. The balance of Rs. 30,000 will be a loss due to idle capacity. On this basis the cost of production does not change from period to period merely because of changing output. If there is any change in the cost of production, it will reflect duly the changing efficiency of the factory.

Works or Factory Expenses or Oncost. The works expenses, works or factory oncost, supplementary cost, standing charges, overhead charges are the various terms used for costs which are "fixed" relatively to that increase or decrease in output which is the subject of consideration. They cannot be allocated to specific units of output, for they would exist even if such units were not produced; but when produced; they would enter the cost of production. They also include expenses relating to works management and administration. Items usually included in works oncost or overhead charges are indirect material and indirect labour, which have been dealt with in the preceding section. Other items are steam and electric power, factory heating, lighting, rent and insurance, water, repairs and renewals, work stationery, depreciation of works building, plant and tools, wastage of material, works administration and management, etc, The task of estimating works or factory expenses or oncost becomes easier if well-defined departments are established so that these supplementary costs incurred for the whole factory can be apportioned to the various departments. Rent and rates should be allocated on the basis of floor space, lighting and power according to meter readings, oil waste, etc., according to number of machines, canteen expenses according to total number of workers in a department, and salary of the works manager according to approximate time occupied by each department.

Estimation, say for the month, can be made either on the basis of the previous month's working, or on the basis of the same month of the previous year, or on the basis of the average cost incurred so far. In making estimates, care should be taken to make allowance for new factors operating during the month. It should be noted that all the indirect expenses are not altogether "fixed", some of them may vary, more or less with the output. Fixed expenses, like salary of works manager or of the supervisory staff, or rent, rates and taxes remain constant, no matter whether the production during the month is up or down. But such expenses as power, depreciation, repair, etc., move to some extent with increase or decrease in production, and are known as "variable" expenses. Estimates should be based on considered judgement in addition to whatever factual information may be available. In addition to departmentalising the expenses, they must be allocated to different machines. Each machine shall have its own rate of depreciation, its own estimate of repairs and its own rate of power consumption. These variable expenses can be calculated and spread over the estimated run of the machine, during its entire life, and we can find out how much it costs to run the machine per hour.. We can also find out the proportion of the fixed expenses "chargeable" to the machine, say for a year. Dividing this sum by the estimated run of the machine for the year, we get "works expenses" (fixed) consumed by every hour's run of the machine. The total of the two hour-rates (fixed and variable) will give us the Machine Hour Rate. This will be different for each machine. By keeping the record of the time taken by a job on different machines, we can add to the cost of the job a sum by way of that job's proportion of works expenses. This proportion of works expenses debitable to a job is more correctly known as Works Oncost.

Machine Hour Rate method of charging works oncost to jobs is useful only in those departments where the major portion of the work is done by machines. Where hand labour is more predominant, we can calculate it in a manner similar to the Machine Hour Rate, or a Labour Hour Rate. The rate will be different from worker to worker according to his skill and requirement of power driven tools or otherwise costly tools. Where cost of materials is the dominant factor in the total cost, and where only one article is produced, a simple percentage on materials is enough for charging works oncost. But the total amount recovered as works expenses will depend upon the cost of materials. The method is useful only if the price of the materials does not fluctuate. If labour is the dominant factor in the total cost, and if there is only one product, a simple percentage on direct labour cost will be enough to charge works oncost to the cost of production.

Hourly Overhead Rates (Machine Hour Rates or Man Hour Rates) are a convenient means for approximating overhead costs for products at the time of their manufacture. The method of finding hourly overhead rates for a manufacturing department is as follows :

$$\frac{\text{Total overhead expenses for department}}{\text{Net operating time}} = \text{Hourly overhead rate (H.O.R.)}$$

Net operating time = N.U. × H.U.—I.T.A.

The mechanism of arriving at the net operating time follows:

Total productive hours (man or machine):	
Working days in period	300
Times hours' work per day	8
Total working time for each unit (man or machine) H.U.	2,400
Times number of units (man or machine) in the production centre of department N.U.	200
Total man hours or machine hours in department	480,000
Less idle time allowance I.T.A.	48,000
Net operating time (or total production time)	432,000

If a Rs. 150,000 overhead expense is estimated for the department having 432,000 man-hours or machine-hours, the hourly overhead rate (H.O.R.) will be 150,000/432,000 or Rs. 0.3472. The significance of this figure is that a product fabricated in this particular department will have added to its labour and material cost an overhead expense of Re. 0.3472 for each hour it is worked on in the department. The total factory cost (excluding selling and administrative expense) will be—

	Rs.	P
Raw materials cost (assumed)	3	0
Labour cost (assumed)	3	0
Overhead :		
8 hour @ Rs. 0.3472	2	78
Total department cost	8	78

Office Expenses are generally fixed in character and do not vary much from period to period. A percentage of the works cost is sufficient to charge office expenses to the cost of production.

Administrative and Selling Expenses. The so-called administrative overhead expenses, as distinguished from factory overhead expenses, do not comprise the part of the cost of operating the manufacturing departments of the plants, but are necessary for carrying on the business. They are the expenses of packing, shipping, showroom expenses. commissions, salesmen's salaries, advertising and overall general management. Commission depends on the selling price and is different from article to article. Packing also differs from product to product and the cost of packing per unit can be found out by calculating the cost of materials and labour involved. The average distance over which goods sold have to travel can also be found out and freight per unit calculated. Obviously packing, freight, and commission can be calculated for each unit, and should not be mixed with the other selling expenses which are common to all the products of the firm. These latter expenses include advertisement, salary and travelling expenses of the salesmen and the sales staff and showroom expenses. The total of these common expenses should be allocated to different products according to the effort involved in selling them, i.e., on the basis of past experience.

The selling and distributive expenses may appear in a cost sheet thus :

			Rs.	P.	
Works Costs		..	4	50	Per unit
Selling Expenses (common to all units)—					
Total Rs. 30,000 1/3 of this product or unit, or Rs. 10,000 divided by 10,000 units manufactured)		..	1	0	do
Packing per unit	0.25				
Freight per unit	0.30				
Commission 2½% of selling price	0.25	..	0	80	do
	Cost		6	30	

Marginal Costing. It has been seen before that some costs are fixed and others variable. In our calculations, however, we have included all expenses, variable as well as fixed. Variable cost, we have observed, increases or decreases in total as the production or output rises or falls; and the fixed cost remains unaffected or is affected only slightly by an increase or decrease in output. The fixed cost includes only that portion of indirect expense (selling, office and works) which has to be incurred whether or not production is going on. It would include salaries of the permanent staff, rent, rates taxes, advertisement, office expenses, etc. Some firms compile a cost sheet consisting only of variable expenses, i.e., the cost does not include fixed expenses. This type of costing is known as Marginal Costing. It shows how much more money will have to be spent if one more unit is produced. The difference between cost thus arrived at and the selling price is there, firstly, to meet the fixed indirect expenses, and secondly, to enable the firm to make a profit. If, for example, the variable cost is Rs. 7.50 per unit and the selling price Rs. 10 and the fixed expenses amount to Rs. 25,000, then 10,000 articles must be produced to enable the firm to meet all its fixed expenses (10,000 × Rs. 2.50 = 25,000). Every unit sold above 10,000 units will bring a net profit of Rs. 2.50.

This system is useful during depressions when prices have to be fixed below cost. As long as prices are above the variable cost, the firm will be able to make out its losses. Also, it enables a firm to know the idle time cost. In the above example, if the normal capacity of the firm is 20,000 articles, then it should normally earn a net profit of Rs. 25,000 (10,000 × 2.50; 10,000 being needed to meet fixed indirect expenses). If, due to any reason, production is only 8,000 units, then the firm will incur a loss of Rs. 5,000.

[(25,000—(8,000 × Rs. 2.50)]

The firm loses Rs. 30,000, i.e., Rs. 25,000 expected profit plus Rs. 5,000 actual loss. The system is, however, not useful for normal cases when it is desirable to know the total cost.

Normal Rate. In calculating the total cost, it is advisable to take machine-hour or man-hour totals or both that are based on operation extending over several manufacturing periods. The amount of productive work rises and falls from month to month, year to year, in keeping with changes in the business cycle and success in making sales. Consequently no particular period can be taken as normal or average for burden distribution. By using net operating or production times, which represent operations that are spread over several manufacturing periods, it becomes possible to arrive at hourly overhead rates that are useful in good times and bad-through the ups and downs of business. Since these rates are based on normal expectancy of business they are often called "**normal rates**". Normal Rates cannot be changed with ups and downs in production expenses. The overhead per hour that is charged to the product is kept at a constant figure during several periods. For example, if normal expectancy or productive time for a manufacturing department during any period is 10,000 hours and Rs. 5,000 is the overhead expense, the H.O.R. will be 50 P. per man or machine-hour. When the department operates 12,000 hours in a future period the overhead expense per productive hour is still charged to products manufactured at the same 50 Paise rate. Similarly, when productive time drops to 8,000 hours in still another period the same H.O.R. or 50 Paise is used. This is illustrated in the table on next page.

In the illustration the products made and sold in periods when operative time is above the normal, provide a plus balance in the overhead account which more than offsets the *minus* balance when the hours of production fall off. The use of the normal rates has three advantages: (1) it permits a uniformity of manufacturing cost as far as overhead expense is concerned; (2) it avoids the necessity of making repeated distributions of overhead expenses which are apt to be

	Actual Machine Hour 1	*Actual Overhead Expenses* 2	*Normal H.O.R.* 3	*Normal Overhead (cost 1×3)* 4	*Balance* 5
1	10,000	Rs. 5,000	50 Paise	Rs. 5,000	Normal
2	12,000	Rs. 5,500	50 Paise	Rs. 6,000	+ Rs. 500
3	8,000	Rs. 4,200	50 Paise	Rs. 4,000	− Rs. 200

*Based on actual expenditure. See Knowles and Thompson, p. 710.

compiled after the manufacturing operations involved are finished and are no help in pricing, (3) it lessens price fluctuations caused by wide variations in overhead expense from year to year.

Cost Accounting versus Ordinary Accounting. Cost accounting and book-keeping and accountancy (sometimes called proprietorship accounting) are two distinct activities. Accounting, by means of the balance sheet, discloses the property and the claims of proprietors to it. The trading, profit and loss and revenue accounts show, in a summary form, the receipts and expenditures for a period of time profit and loss and the disposition of profits. It also keeps records of financial relations with outside parties; it maintains a check on fraud, internal and external; and it constitutes one proof, among others, as to where ownership lies; it shows the proportional distribution of the capital fund between various forms of current and fixed assets; and establishes the condition of the business with reference to its soundness or otherwise. Cost accounting, on the other hand, aims at collecting all items of outlay, great or small, incident to the production of a unit of goods or services. It reveals the causes of fluctuations of expenditure, and indicates the true field of profit. It reflects the efficiency of the administrative and productive functions by detecting weak points in the organisation, and thus impels towards operative efficiency of the products. Accounting admits only original items, balances its data in the form of debit and credit, and when in perfect form, insists on the fine equilibrium of being balanced to a paisa. Cost accounting, on the contrary, freely uses estimates and averages, distributing sometimes more and sometimes less than it collects. Proprietorship accounting has had a long career, while cost accounting is of recent origin. One is the special instrument of the financier; the other is the daily working tool of the production engineer and works manager. In spite of these differences of aim and methods, the two are intimately interlinked, and in any organisation which aims at efficiency they should be thoroughly co-ordinated. Thus co-ordinated, one helps the other. The cost system serves as an intensified study of certain items in the proprietorship accounts, while the proprietorship accounts serve as comprehensive surveys which make certain that all proper items have been introduced into costs.[1]

1. D. Jones, *op.*, p. 359.

CHAPTER XXIX

BUDGETS AND BUDGETARY CONTROL

Financial control by means of a budget has long been employed in the sphere of governmental management, but the use of the idea as a tool in business administration is much more recent. Today, however, budgeting and records are found in practically every business organisation. Records give a detailed account of what has happened in the past. Budgeting plans future activities. Nothing is more important to sound management than systematic planning based on previous performance and business judgment.

Business Budget. One of the most used measures of management is profits. Usually the higher profits represent better management. An excellent method of determining profits and measuring managing performance in the company as a whole and in each department is by means of budgets. It should be emphasised that a budget is more than a financial instrument, for it relates also to quantities of product and to operations, and consequently serves as a complete programme of business activities in the period to which it relates. In a word, budgeting is planning the conduct of a business. As Professor Sanders[1] says : "The essence of a budget is a detailed plan of operations for some specified future period, followed by a system of records which will serve as a check upon the plan". This applies to the over-all planning of the whole business and the detailed planning of the operations in individual departments. In short, a budget defines the absolute annual expenditures (in terms of rupees, men, time, etc.) which will be permitted by a functional unit, with a possible refinement showing monthly breakdowns in those cases where costs are not expected to be constant throughout the budget period. The budget provides guideposts to point the way, and the actual steering of the vehicle is in the hands of the driver—the manager.

Budget planning starts with the setting up of an object to be achieved by a business during the next budget period, say, the next twelve months. This objective may be a given profit, or a total volume of sales, or a certain production. The next step, which may be taken by the executive, is to break up the chief aim into its component parts, divide the programme into a series of proposed accomplishments for each month, and assign to each department its particular part in the programme. The next step is the provision of a means whereby the objective can be achieved, and the results measured. These are recorded for comparison purposes.

The preparation of a budget is an intensive process of planning ahead for proper control. Past experience is examined to show what the

1. *Cost Accounting for Control*, p. 430.

normal rate of growth has been. And the future is studied by means of general and special business barometers. As the result of working to a forecast, stocks can better be controlled, for requirements can be anticipated by purchases during low price periods. The financing is made simpler because the period of liquidation is better known at the time of borrowing. The study of seasonal variations suggests the possibility of regularising, by producing for stock when current requirements are small. A more even operation of the plant cuts many costs, lessens unemployment, reduces labour turnover, attracts a better class of employees, and ensures more prompt and full shipments to customers. The analysis, incident to dividing a budget into its elements, serves also to divide into manageable parts the problem of carrying through the proposed plan. As the programme is divided into a series of brief periods, efforts are divided into short heats; and there is always an immediate and definite goal in sight. Each officer has the satisfying feeling that he knows exactly where he is in his work, and what remains to be done. There is a greater degree of delegation and more freedom in the use of initiative and judgment within the framework and scope of the budgets.

Classification of Budgets.[1] Most business organisations are too large to permit the detailed planning of the entire business in one budget. It becomes necessary to use a master budget that summarises all the plans and shows how they affect the business as a whole; and details are relegated to various specialised budgets. In other words, the budget for a business as a whole is constructed from estimates which are prepared by various departments. It is indeed the sum of the budgets for each of the main divisions of the business, and is very often supported by subsidiary budgets. The major classification of budgets is as follows :—

1. Sales Budget.
2. Production Budget.
3. Financial Budget.
4. Manufacturing Capacity Budget, made up of—
   (i) Physical property budget;
   (ii) Raw materials budget;
   (iii) Supplies budget;
   (iv) Labour budget;
   (v) Research budget.

The Departmental Budgets, which are subordinate to the major budgets given above, may contain parts of several different budgets. For example, a Production Department Budget would usually list labour, materials, supplies and research. Each of the major budgets is discussed in the following paragraphs.

Sales Budget. The starting point for any production planning is essentially an estimate of the market demand for what is to be produced. Upon this all else depends, such as the size of the plant which can be

1. For detailed figure-work, see the author's *Cost Accounts.*

employed, the requirements of labour, and the stock of materials. Also, as sales are the primary source of cash receipts, such sales estimate is the foundation-stone of financing planning. To be effective, however, sales estimate must satisfy certain basic requirements. It must be such as to achieve economic and balanced production in the factory departments. It must provide for a volume of sales sufficient to meet the minimum financial needs of the business. It must be such as will provide adequate stocks to meet the needs of consumers and distributors. In forming sales estimates, two sets of people would be consulted; the salesmen who perform the actual work of selling the products, and the sales manager and other executives who are responsible for framing and carrying into effect the marketing policies of the business. In finalising the sales estimates, and the trend of past results as revealed by records it should be analysed to act as a guide for building up a future potential. This will require a full scale programme of market research.[1]

Production Budget. The sales estimate will show the volume of each line of product which is expected to be required, period by period. The purpose of the production budget is to assure finished goods to meet the demands of the sales department. The production budget determines the quantity of such goods on hand which must be maintained at the proper size in relation to sales. If the stock on hand becomes too large, a financial loss results from many reason—deterioration, changes in style, spoilage, and storage charges. If the stock becomes too small, there is a danger of losing sales because no goods are available. The sales budget indicates the rate at which stock will be removed from the stock room, and the production budget must set a production quota that maintains the stock at its proper size. A detailed system must be worked out to obtain deliveries from the factory by the date on which the sales department requires the output.

Financial Budget. It is the financial aspect of the business which determines its success or failure. Fine performances in the different parts of the business will not be of much use if they are not co-ordinated so that the business makes money, or is at least able to keep enough cash on hand to meet its current obligations. The financial budget must provide an adequate cash balance at all times.

Manufacturing Capacity Budget. In order to manufacture goods it is necessary to have a factory building, plant and machinery, men, materials and supplies. The budgets for all of these fall into the general classification of manufacturing capacity, i.e., the ability and wherewithal with which to manufacture. The budgets aim at meeting the requirements of the production budget.

Physical Property Budget. Physical property includes the building, machinery and equipment which constitute a relatively permanent investment. The proposed programme as based upon the sales estimate may call for the installation of additional equipment. But anything in the

1. *Discussed fully in Chapter on Distribution. (supra).*

nature of permanent equipment can be justified only in the light of long term considerations. An increase in demand of permanent nature may justify further installation; but a temporary demand may have to be met by putting out work to sub-contractors during the peak period, or by overtime or double shift working or by the accumulation of stocks in slack periods against the time of peak demand.

Raw Materials Budget. Raw materials refer to the things from which the product is made. Material is prime or direct cost. Therefore, the control of raw material stocks presents a problem of considerable importance for every manufacturing business. There is, as said above, the direct cost of working capital which these stocks represent, and the indirect burden of deterioration, the provision of storage space, and of supervision. Closely associated with all this is the problem of where, how much and when to buy. On the basis of sales and production budgets, however, the buyer can take a longer view and plan his policy accordingly. The Materials budget is an instrument which enables the Purchasing Department to lay plans to secure materials by the time they are needed for the production. Advance planning of material stocks can be done easily in the case of mass production and continuous process industries. The relevant problems relating to materials are tackled in the following chapter.

Supplies Budget. Supplies are needed to carry on manufacturing, but they do not become part of the finished product. Supplies are consumed by the manufacturing operations in the factory, and new supplies must continuously be made available. A typical example is the oil necessary to lubricate machinery. The supplies budget makes necessary provision for regular supply.

Labour Budget. A manufacturer must have an adequate force of workmen in order to carry on his business. These men must be available at the time when they are needed; they must have the skills required to perform the work; and provision must be made to pay for their services. As a group they must be co-operative with the foreman and with each other. The labour budget is complicated by the fact that it is not always good policy to dismiss men when there is no work immediately available for them; and also that their very presence requires management to provide certain services for them, such as wash rooms, canteens, etc., where it is desirable to keep employees on the pay roll regardless of the volume of work to be done, productive and idle-time labour budgets can be used for control purposes. These budgets help in the comparison of relative costs of productive and idle-time of labour.

Research Budget. In order to keep the product design and manufacturing processes up-to-date it is necessary to devote part of the income to research. Research and development expenditure is in the nature of an insurance. The most important aspect of this expenditure is not the amount but the use made of the amount. Too many projects should not be taken in hand at one time.

Budget Co-ordination. Budget making is a co-operative affair involving the maintenance of proper balance between the different parts. A series of un-co-ordinated departmental budgets, which may be based on different assumptions, can be of little value. As said above, the size of any one part, or its performance, is no indication of success or failure. For example, a business with a large volume of orders cannot be said to be successful if goods are not available to meet the orders. Similarly, there must be a necessary balance between labour supply and material supply. Both must be available in the proper proportions at the same time. Therefore, in budgeting one of the principal objectives is the maintenance of proper relation between all the divisions of the business. It is not possible to make a budget for one part without making a budget for the remaining parts of the business also. For example, a sales budget cannot be made without budgeting the activities of the production department. A cash budget cannot be drawn up without also knowing the plans of the collection and purchasing departments. There must be co-ordination which may be the work of a specially delegated Budget Officer, reporting direct to the higher administration. Unless this is done, departmental heads may not appreciate the importance of the budget and fail to devote the requisite time and attention which the work demands. In the case of a large business, a Budget Committee will be set up; and its personnel will include the principal executives such as representatives of sales, production, accounting, research and finance. By means of such a round table conference, each executive who puts forward a departmental estimate has to face criticism and to justify his figures by rational argument. In fact, "budgeting co-ordinates the plans of several branches of a business—buying and selling, manufacturing and sales, development and capital requirement—and effects this co-ordination by a process of consultation between the various intelligence directing or substantially influencing the course of the business. Such consultations, moreover, are based not merely on judgment and impressions but on analysed facts and concretely expressed intentions developed from such facts."[1] The general relation between the budgets is shown in the diagram on next page.

The diagram has been made in a circle rather than a straight line, because it is impossible to start at any one point and make plans in which the planning to be done at other points is not a factor. As every departmental budget will both influence and be influenced by the others, it is necessary that each budget shown in the diagram should aim at keeping a balance between the parts on either side of it. For example, the production budget should maintain a balance between sales orders and finished goods. If any one of the budgets fails to maintain its own balance, the business is in danger in the same way as a person is in danger if any one part of his body, such as stomach or lungs, is either over-supplied or under-supplied with the things it needs. The major classifications of budgets, the things they control, and the things they

1. Bruere and Lazarus, quoted by Branton, *op. cit.*, p. 185.

must balance are explained below.[1] It will be noted that each budget must be a balance between the thing controlled by the budget above it, and that controlled by the budget below it.[1]

The Introduction of Budgets. The introduction of Budgetary control is usually a long-term job. Apart from the many problems connected with devising budgets, adaptations and modifications in accounting are required. Mr. Maddock[2] suggests the following steps in this direction :—

1. Relate budgets to established chart of organisation and established policies.
2. Draw up expense responsibility account classification accordingly.
3. Prepare schedule of performance responsibility.
4. Prepare budget programme.
5. Determine the form of account presentation necessary for budget comparisons.

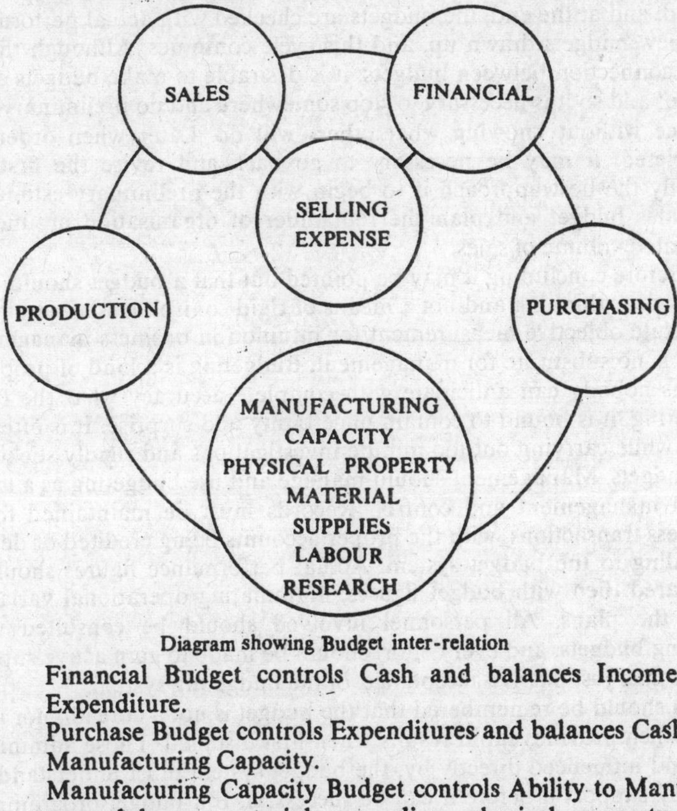

Diagram showing Budget inter-relation

Financial Budget controls Cash and balances Income and Expenditure.

Purchase Budget controls Expenditures and balances Cash and Manufacturing Capacity.

Manufacturing Capacity Budget controls Ability to Manufacture—labour, materials, supplies, physical property—and balances Purchase Orders and Production.

1. Adapted from Knowles and Thomson, *op. cit.*, pp. 16, 17.
2. *Op. cit.*, p. 580.

Production Budget controls Finished Goods Stock and balances Manufacturing Capacity and Sales.

Sales Budget controls Income and Balances Finished Goods and Cash.

In this, as in many other matters, the gradual approach is invariably the best. A period of re-education is required for the successful operation of budgetary control. The first reactions towards control of expenditure and performance are hardly likely to be encouraging. The gradual introduction of budgetary control will start with "block" of expenditure or of revenue. It is wiser to proceed slowly and not to endeavour to introduce too much control information at one time. There are no rigid rules which can be applied to all companies, but some routine should be established, keeping the budgets flexible. The budgets should not be so rigid as to stand in the way of making adjustments in the budget period. At the beginning of the budget period, the budgets are drawn up for the period, and at the end, the budgets are checked with actual performance and new budgets drawn up, and this cycle continues. Although there is close connection between budgets, it is desirable to make budgets one at a time; and so it is necessary to stop somewhere and do preliminary work on one without knowing what others will do. Later when orders are completed, it may be necessary to go back and revise the first one. Usually the best approach is to begin with the preliminary estimate of the sales budget and plan the remainder of organisation around this estimated volume of sales.

Before concluding it may be pointed out that a budget should be an aid to clear thinking and not a means of rigid control. It is an attempt to substitute objective measurement for intuition in business management, but it is no substitute for management. Budgeting is a kind of prophecy, and as nobody can anticipate with complete accuracy what the future will bring, it is bound to contain uncertainty and surprise. It is often not worthwhile carrying out too minute investigations and rigidly sticking to the budgets. Management should manage and use budgeting as a tool of sound management and control. Records must be maintained for all business transactions, with the proper accounts being credited or debited according to the budget system. Actual performance figures should be compared then with budget figures, illuminating operational variations from the plans. All personnel involved should be consulted when drafting budgets, and every effort should be made to gain active support, rather than just passive acceptance, of the budgeting system.

It should be remembered that the budget is not a cure all, nor is it a tool which provides rapid results when first installed. Those administering, and influenced directly by, the budget system must understand and actively support it before it can be successful. If a budget programme is not installed properly, those working under it are likely to view it as a rigorous control. Management personnel must actively participate in the analytic and development work which must go into a budget; otherwise budget padding and end-of-period spending may be resorted to, and these practices are not compatible with the purposes of budgeting.

A budget is a prediction. It tells how the financial accounts should look at some future date. Like any other prediction, it is subject to error because of unanticipated events. Strikes may occur, competitors may introduce a new product, prices may fall, or some other unmanageable influence may prevent the prediction from coming true. A budget is also used as a standard in the control process. Insofar as the budget is in error, because of these unmanageable influences, it loses its validity as a standard. A district sales manager, for example, cannot be held accountable for a drop in sales if a traders' strike prevents delivery of merchandise to his customers. Obviously, we need some means of adjusting budgets if we are to use them as standards of performance. The budgets should be flexible.

One way of introducing flexibility into budget standards is to compute in advance any adjustments for shifts in volume of work. If a plant supervisor is asked to step up output above the budgeted figure, his material and labour costs will also probably be over the budget. The question is, how much increase in expenses is justified? We need a revised chart to serve as a control standard. Variable budgets are a device for computing such expense standards for any volume of work within a broad range. The underlying approach is simple. A budget expense is set for both a high volume and a low volume, and a plan is prepared for interpolating between these figures. Then, at the end of the budget period, when the actual volume is known it is possible to compute the appropriate expense for this particular volume. But a variable budget deals only with changes in volume. No adjustment is made for other unmanageable varibles. Also, variable budgets are hard to apply when different products are handled. Standard costs are one way to deal with this difficulty.

In a standard cost system, budgeted costs for materials, labour and so on are computed per unit for each different product. Then, at the end of a given period, the number of units of products A, B, C and so forth, that were processed are multiplied by their respective costs. By adding these figures, we get a total for materials, a total for labour, and a total for overhead that altogether reflect the specific product-mix for this period. Such totals become control standards that can be used to evaluate performance for that period. Unfortunately, this flexibility for a product-mix carries with it some weaknesses. Most seriously, the cost per unit is assumed to be the same no matter what volume of work is processed. This assumption is not valid, especially for overhead costs. Therefore, when using control standards based on standard costs, we must still make some allowance for the level of activity.

Although variable budgets and standard costs do provide flexibility in some situations, by far the most common type of adjustment is periodic revision of the normal budget. A common practice is to prepare a budget for 12 months in advance, but to revise it for a particular month just before the beginning of that month. In this revision, we can adjust for volume, price, wage rates, or any other factor. This modified budget becomes the realistic statement of results that can and should be achieved.

Properly conceived and adequately applied budgeting results in many advantages. The greatest strength of budgeting is its use of a single common denominator—Rupees—for many diverse actions and things. Second, budgeting uses records and systems that are already in existence and new expenditure is to be incurred on new set of records. Finally, budgeting deals directly with one of the central objectives of a business enterprise—making a profit. What shows up in budgets is what affects recorded profit and loss. Budgeting often makes its greatest contribution as a stimulant to other good management practices.

The most serious risk in using budgets is an unbalanced emphasis on factors that happen to be the easiest to observe. For example, the operating expenses of the engineering or purchasing department stand out clearly in budget reports, and the supervising executives are under pressure to keep expenses within prescribed limits. But the services such departments perform are of even greater importance. Inadequate service, unfortunately, is reflected only indirectly in the profit-and-loss figures—perhaps in manufacturing costs or in low sales—and is difficult to trace back to the service division. There are some other drawbacks such as the danger of its opening the way for dictatorial action. For example, an executive, in order to conform to the objective figure of a budget, may order the cutting down of the expense by 30 per cent, which may be done by changing the budget without realizing the consequences of such an action. Sometimes, a company may go through the form of budgetary control without the substance, becuase some staff man has predicted what the accounts will look like several months in future, with little or no actual planning by operating executives. Sometimes, budgets are prepared routinely and mechanically, without giving much thought to the ways of improving operations. Later, the executives simply make excuses if performance compares unfavourably with the budget. In such circumstances, budgeting is a nuisance rather than an aid to management. Remember, budgetary control can be helpful only if key executives incorporate it as a dynamic part of their way of managing.

CHAPTER XXX

PURCHASING AND STOREKEEPING

Purchasing is an everyday function and occupies much of the time both of business houses and ultimate consumers. The ultimate consumer is proverbially an inexpert buyer; but even among business purchasers, skilled and experienced as they are, errors are not infrequent. Erroneous buying raises the cost of materials, stores, equipment and the finished product. It is not always appreciated that the Buyer is frequently responsible for by far the largest single item in the total cost, the average figure being something like 30–50 per cent of the total sales value. It is obviously important, therefore, that the activity of buying should be just as effectively performed as any other operation in the organisation.

There are four types of Buyers—

1. Industrial Buyers, those who buy raw materials, stores and equipment for manufacturers.
2. Buyers for wholesalers.
3. Buyers of merchandise for retail stores.
4. Ultimate consumers, buying from the retail stores.

Dr. Walters defines INDUSTRIAL PURCHASING as "the procurement by purchase of the proper materials, machinery, equipment and supplies or stores used in the manufacture of a product, adapted to marketing in the proper quantity and quality at the proper time and at the lowest price consistent with the quality desired."[1] A modern purchasing is exact buying based upon facts. It is indeed very much a specialist activity calling for the commercial rather than the technical training and outlook.

The objects of scientific purchasing may be stated as follows :—

1. Procurement of a given quality and quantity of materials at the 'best' price (not necessarily the lowest)
2. Procurement of materials which best suit the product and the purposes for which they are intended.
3. Purchasing for time utility, by a schedule sufficiently in advance of the demands of production departments, so that there shall be no delay for lack of materials to work upon.
4. Buying the quantity so that the stock at hand is not too much, involving locking up of capital, nor is it too little, militating against the regular supply for production.
5. Improvement of the product with reference to quality and distribution by means of selection of adequate material.

The basic task of the purchasing department is Buying, by which is meant going into the open market, finding the lowest price at which a standard item is offered, and selecting a supplier who offers it at that

1. *Modern Management*. p. 209.

price. This task is clerical. Scientific or effective purchasing is much more than "buying", it is an executive job, involving co-operation with other functions, e.g., production, distribution, etc. The purchaser therefore does not think solely in terms of buying. He thinks part of the time as if he were producing, part of the time as if he were financing, and great deal of the time as if he were managing the sales department. In all his varied thinking he works out ways in which purchasing can be most helpful to every phase of the business.

Effective purchasing may be carried out by the following steps :—

1. The ascertainment of an accurate statement of character and amount of material needed, preferably based upon exact specifications.
2. The selection and development of desirable and dependable sources of supply, negotiations with the sources, analysis of the proposals, the selection of the seller, and placing of the order.
3. Follow-up of the order, routing the order, receiving the goods, checking invoices and the inspection of goods.
4. Storage to protect the materials from deterioration, and to make them readily accessible when required for use.
5. A control system for stores, and stores accounting system to charge the cost of materials correctly to individual units of product for cost accounting and price fixing purposes.
6. An internal move system for regulating passage of materials to and from production centres, by means of hand trucks or movement.
7. Shipping, crating and packing, carting and consigning to customers.
8. Keeping under full documentary control all the above operations to facilitate supervision of higher officers.

Determining Quality. To a large degree, manufacturers determine the quality of goods purchased by the kind of product they make. Quality involves such considerations as materials, workmanship, grades, sizes, designs, colours and patterns. Although the finer product depends greatly upon the skill of craftsmen assigned to its production, minimum qualities of raw materials must be established. The first step in this direction is to prepare an accurate statement of the character and amount of material needed, which can be done in the Production Control Department. Exact and correct specifications for the material should be made for determining quality of the material and the product. It is essential that the materials which are best adapted to the product at the marketing end of manufacturing be procured at the start. Quality control of materials on strict lines serves to cut down the waste of raw materials, labour and overhead on account of spoiled work; facilitates uniform and high-speed manufacturing operations; lessens sales resistance and selling costs. An efficient process of purchasing is something very much more than the mere matter of buying at the lowest market rate; it is the selection of the suitable raw material at the "best" price.

Determining Quantities. The determination of proper quantities to be purchased rests upon planned sales. Where production is altogether or largely based on orders already placed and little or no production for stock is made, the purchase of raw materials may be deferred to the time when orders have been received. In practice, however, production for stock is made to avoid delay in delivery of the product. In such case the quantity to be purchased will be largely determined by the stock to be maintained.

Determining Sources of Supply. After the need for quality is ascertained and the specifications correctly stated and simplified, the next step is to locate the desirable sources of supply by means of (1) Purchasing Records, classified by products and suppliers, and subdivided according to price, quality, terms of sale, delivery dates, etc., Catalogues, classified and cross-indexed by products, and any other division which may be needed for the purchase of the required material. Old sources of material supply may be adequate, but it is usually thought wise in buying to consider constantly the development of new sources. Only reliable sources of supply based upon investigations should be approached and requested to give quotation. The quotations, so received, are then analysed to determine the "right" price for the product. The right price is the "fair", or "best" (not necessarily the lowest) price for the material.

The dates of delivery will influence the choice of the supplier, e.g., if business is very active and large volumes of orders are on hand, the buyers may even pay higher prices for early deliveries. Discounts and length of credit period granted may also aid in determining from whom to buy. The reliability and responsibility of the supplier is another important patronage motive. The reputation of the vendor for integrity in observing the terms of contracts, making prompt deliveries, and delivering goods in accordance with samples or established grades, may be most important in directing patronage. Distribution policies of suppliers may strongly influence buyers. Many manufacturers are reluctant, or refuse to place orders for materials with suppliers who will not accept cancellations at the option of buyers.

The Order. When the best price has been determined and other terms settled, the order is placed. The order is a legal contract and should be drawn with care and in the simplest terms which precisely define what is expected of the buyer and seller. Most contracts consist of a purchase order and its acceptance. The major parts of a purchase order are (1) serial number, (2) date of issue, (3) the names and addresses of the parties involved, (4) quality and description of the material ordered, (5) date of delivery, (6) shipping instructions, (7) prices, and (8) terms of payment. Where the order has been based upon detailed specifications, those specifications should be included or specially referred to in the contract or purchase order.

When the purchase order has been placed, the purchaser must follow it up to see that it is promptly filed, routed through the shortest or most economical route, and the delivery date maintained. A sufficient number of copies of the order should be prepared : two copies for the purchasing department, one for the stores department, one for the department originating requisition, and one for the receiving department. The copy for the receiving department may omit the quantities ordered, so that when the material is received the exact amounts and quantities are checked and accounted for correctly without reference to the amounts and quantities ordered. The amount received and amount ordered are then checked by the purchaser, and the order is approved for payment, if the two amounts agree in every detail.

Buying Policies. Among the important policies to be decided by the buyer is that relating to the size of the order the quantity of the material to be purchased at any one time. Total quantities to be purchased over any period of time are derived from the estimated sales for the period. In some cases the size of the individual order is fixed by terms of a special contract with the seller according to which a minimum limit is fixed below which an order is not accepted. However, in general, most manufacturers have the choice to determine the size of industrial orders and must balance the advantages of placing larger orders (Bulk Buying) against the disadvantages of such a practice or the advantages of small order (Small-Lot Buying).

There are certain marked advantages in quantity or bulk buying. Many sellers quote special prices on larger orders. Other advantages are : the assurance which an ample stock gives the factory will not be suspended by railway strike or interruptions of supply; the economy of large orders in the matter of freight, cartage and receiving expenses. Small and frequent orders may be made, because they mean small investment in stock, less chance of physical deterioration, style obsolescence, decreased risk of loading up at top price or of entering dull seasons with heavy stocks. The utmost advantage of buying on a large scale, consistent with high stocks and rapid turnover, is only obtainable by standardising consumption upon a few articles.

A buying policy is, of course, part of the production policy, or arises from it, and is dictated by the kind of prosecution programme adopted. For example, the programme may require much greater quantities at one time of the year than another but the buying policy may be to take regular supplies over the whole year to suit the suppliers, and to take advantage of lower prices, stocking during the period of lower demand.

Buying Practices. Continuity of supplies is as important as cost. Indeed, in large-scale production it is the essential prerequisite. Those connected with manufacturing industry in the period following the Partition have had frequent and bitter experience of this. Running out of raw materials meant danger of stoppage of work, to avoid which inflated prices had to be paid for supplies from alternative sources. In normal times, as in difficult times, regular supply of raw materials at a reasonable price is essential. Three broad lines of buying policy or procedure are usual.

1. *To buy against current market conditions.* To make current purchases is the usual practice. Buyers are given wide discretion to buy a part or all of the materials that are required from day to day, week to week, or month to month. Reliance is generally placed on purchases in the open market as the need appears, or on contracts for delivery in the immediate future. The success of this policy depends on the Buyer's knowledge of the market and on the goodwill of supply houses. The Buyer who has the goodwill of those from whom he buys, whether producer, broker, *arhtia*, or merchant, and who buys of the best houses without dividing his purchases among too many, is likely to find that in times of threatened shortage his suppliers will live up to their contracts, give him warning of advances in prices so that he may stock up, or in case of actual shortage see to it that he is kept stocked with necessary materials.

2. *To buy on contract.* An adequate supply of materials often assumes such importance that the Buyer cannot rely on his knowledge of the market or on the services of the supply houses. In such cases, he may contract for future delivery, buying a sufficient supply to cover his needs for a year, or for indefinite periods subject to review and cancellation with an appropriate period of notice. It has the advantage of avoiding the necessity for carrying stock by the user and of giving a measure of stability to suppliers. Flour mills often buy for future delivery, or buy early in the season, so as to protect themselves against advances in price of wheat. Semi-finished production goods, such as motor-car parts and accessories, are also commonly contracted for in advance. Contracts for Running Delivery are also common. Coal is often bought by contracts running for a year, or even longer, the supplier agreeing to deliver agreed quantities at regular intervals.

3. *To buy on a Bargain basis.* In this policy, a supply sufficient to cover the requirements for a considerable period of time is bought at one time and possession taken. This is usually done in the case of staple commodities and for the major process industries, such as cotton and woollen textile mills. It offers large profits, attendant upon bulk and assures against shortage, but involves large financial risks, where the company has no sales contracts at hand to cover the resulting product. The contract is essentially of a speculative nature. This risk is usually covered by "Hedging", if there is an organised market for future trading.

When the material is received at the factory it may be sent to the place where it is to be worked upon or placed in stores. If it is placed in stores, the amounts are entered on a perpetual store register supervised by the Purchasing or Production Department. These stores records maintain the amounts of material in stores at all times with a minimum expense and at the same time adequately serving production needs. When the material is correctly received, checked with the specifications and tested as to quality, the records are then completed and the material paid for as soon as possible in order to take advantage of purchase discounts. When the material is paid for, the purchaser still has to follow up this purchase to see that it fulfils the purpose for which it was intended, and a record is made of the finding. This completes the purchasing procedure.

Wholesale Buying Practice. Wholesalers act as the suppliers to retailers. They must buy goods which the retailers want and at prices permitting re-sale by retailers at levels to yield them profits. Wholesalers may purchase from a great many manufacturers. Since their profit margin is generally very small, mistakes in buying may be dangerous. As in the case of industrial purchase, a buyer for the wholesalers must be skilled. He must know what he wants, and at what price. But his problems are much more difficult of solution than that of an Industrial Buyer. He must think constantly of the vagaries of consumer demand which will be reflected through the purchase policy of retailers. Wholesalers must constantly examine the current purchases of retail stores to notice fashion trends, buying habits, consumer reactions to price levels, and the growth and decline in popularity of different types of goods.

One of the major problems of the wholesaler centres around inventory or stock control. Serving as the supply house for his retail customers, he must carry adequate stock of merchandise or cease to perform his function satisfactorily. If he permits his stocks to become too large, however, he assumes risk of price change, style shift and merchandise deterioration, which may endanger his normal profit. His determination of proper quantities to be purchased rests upon planned sales, based upon estimates of future sales. The sales estimate may be made directly in terms of number of units of merchandise to be sold, i.e., dozens, hundreds, quintals, kilograms, pounds, etc., or first in terms of money values. Expressing planned sales in money is a convenient common denominator for indicating total potential sales of a diverse and varied line of goods. The wholesaler has one safety outlet not possessed by the retail buyer. He is serving a great many retail stores. If he makes a mistake in buying he is reasonably sure of being able to dispose of that merchandise possibly at a price concession.

Retail Buying Practice. The fundamental function of the retailer is to assemble a variety of merchandise for the convenience of his customers. To buy correctly, he must analyse and determine consumer demand. The risk in buying goods to meet an existing demand is not great. But in selling fashion goods the retailer incurs an added risk. He must anticipate consumer demands. For example, the buyer for the ladies' saris and blouses pieces often faces this type of situation. Certain styles and designs are being offered by the mills for the coming season. The styles and designs are new and have not as yet appeared in the stores in his city. His customers are not yet wearing the new styles, but the manufacturers are showing them in their sample rooms. The buyer knows that not all the styles will be popular out of the hundreds of designs offered; only a few may ever achieve great popularity. Which of the styles offered should he buy? In each style or design, how many saris? How many of each colour? Worked up or plain? His records cannot tell him anything about the customer preferences. He shall have to base his selection to some extent on his own shrewd estimate of the potential popularity of the various styles. If he buys well, the right styles, in the right quantities, and the right colours, he will have a successful season. If his purchases are poorly, in wrong style, colour and quantities, he will have a disastrous season. He will be hard put to mark down his prices to dispose of the saris and the materials. The buyer for the retailer must cope with these risks. Continually he must watch his rivals, his own stocks to see that they are still popular and to get rid of them before the peak of their popularity is over. Yet he must be careful not to be out of stock when consumers ask for goods in popular demand.

Technique in Buying. With regard to the policy or practice of buying, nearly all the points that were discussed in connection with industrial purchasing apply to wholesale and retail buying. The technique of buying goods includes all the elements of a major business problem. Successful buying makes for successful marketing, failure in buying may make it impossible to earn profit. "Goods well bought are half sold" is an old adage, and still holds good to a large measure. Some of the aids to successful buying are as follows : the careful buyer for a retail store or for a wholesaler maintains sales records in rupees and units sold. For example, the buyer for a shoe shop has sales records which tell him as frequently as necessary how many pairs of shoes have been sold, at what prices, styles, colours, materials, and sizes. These records are maintained continuously so that the buyer is able to compare recent experience with the sales records of the most distant past.

A second aid to buying is the use of "want slip". The shop assistants are asked to make a note of customer's requests for goods of which the shop does not carry stock. By examining these "want slips", the buyer may ascertain consumer demand for goods he has not yet bought for his stores. Valuable adjunct to "want slips" are accurate stock statistics which tell the buyer at all times exactly what goods he has in stock. In this way he knows not only what customers are buying, but also what they are not buying. The wholesaler who handles thousands of different items must keep similar elaborate records to ensure rapid turnover. Budgeting already discussed in the previous chapter is an additional aid to skilful buying. Budgets, when intelligently used, serve as warning signals. With all these aids, buying still remains in large part a problem for individual judgment to solve. After all, consumer demand is a tenuous thing. It is flexible. The "aids" are helpful, but used alone without the guiding hand of a skilled buyer they will not produce successful purchasing.[1]

STOREKEEPING

The importance of storekeeping in modern industry is not always appreciated as it should be. Whilst the production departments are

1. *Modern Marketing(Barker and Anstein).*

well-equipped, the storekeepers are hidden away in quarters, ill-equipped and with poor lighting conditions, and are generally underpaid. No wonder that loss of stock, wrong issue, unexpected running out of stock, and incorrect vouchers are a continued source of delay to production and worry to production staff. For adequate and efficient handling the work of storekeeping should be entrusted to competent persons, few in number, who are tidy minded, neat, and have a good memory and a fund of commonsense. They should also be good at figures. Lately, card indexes, stock control 'systems' and goods bins have been employed for effective storekeeping. But card indexes are no substitutes for good storekeeping—they do not work for themselves, but must be used.

The *functions* of a stores department may be stated as follows :—

1. The receiving, storing and safeguarding of materials.
2. The issuing of correct amounts of stores as desired by the manufacturing and shipping departments.
3. The keeping of stores records which will show at all times what is on hand or expected, or what has been issued or reserved, classified according to items and order numbers.
4. The giving of timely notice when replenishment is required, by establishing minimum quantities for each item and issuing purchasing requisitions.

The materials, tools, supplies and equipment, which come to the works from outside by railway, lorries, messengers, or in any other way, are delivered to the Receiving Department, or if this is not possible owing to the weight or bulkness of the commodities, they have to be entered into the books of this department, which must be informed of their arrival. Generally, the Receiving Department has to count, weigh, or otherwise measure the quantity of goods as soon as they arrive and check their quantity and description with the advice and delivery notes. The system of advice and delivery notes is almost universal today. The advice note is sent by post by the supplier to advise the customer that he has despatched goods, and usually arrives long before the goods. The Receiving Depot should check the advice note as soon as it is received with the copy of the order sent by the Purchasing Department to the Receiving Depot when order is placed. Any discrepancy between order and advice note must be notified at once, without waiting for the receipt of the actual goods, either to the Purchasing Department, or, better still, direct to the supplier with a copy to the Purchasing Department. This check of the advice note is most important as much trouble, expense, and time can be saved if errors in despatch have been made. The delivery note, which should be attached to the goods, is usually a carbon copy in all essential particulars of the advice note and should be checked against the advice note and discrepancies notified, usually to the Purchasing Department, leaving them to take up the matter in this case direct with the suppliers.[1]

1. Mayenberg, *Industrial Administration and Management*, p. 153.

Under ideal conditions, materials would be manufactured into finished products directly after they have been received. But such conditions are almost impossible to attain, although they may be approached in some of the simple continuous industries. In most manufacturing industries the raw materials are used in varying amounts at varying times, and sales are likewise intermittent and varied. For these reasons, and also because purchasing and transportation are facilitated by quantity, provision must be made for these varying demands. Where sales are varying and product must be made in advance of sales, similar provision must be made for carrying the finished product, in order to ensure prompt delivery to customers. In shops that make product to order only, as a shipbuilding company, this last feature is not of much importance. Thus the reason for a system of storage between the Receiving Depot and the Production is that it is in most cases only by the establishment of an adequate store system that it is possible to buy material in bulk, consistent with the economic consideration that no loss on the investment in stores is incurred. Secondly, it is possible to make sure that the material is always available when needed by the manufacturing department. The ideal of storekeeping is to maintain the smallest possible inventory consistent with the needs of production. The same principle is involved with finished goods as with the unfinished material. The stock should be as low as possible, yet consistent with sales demand. The third reason why stores system is established is that it is possible to review thoroughly the economic situation in the works and establish effective production control. These three points—quantities, time, and costs—are highly important, and the greatest care must be taken by the management to avoid mistakes which may be detrimental to the whole concern.

From the standpoint of stores and stock keeping, the materials involved are (1) Raw Materials, directly transformed into goods by a manufacturing process and represent the finished goods; (2) Supplies or indirect materials which are used and consumed during production; (3) Tools and Equipment; and (4) Finished Product, or Saleable Goods. These distinctions are important and necessary for costing purposes. Unworked or raw material is usually known as "Stores", and the place where it is kept is known as the "Store Room". The place where supplies are housed is also called by the same name. This room acts as the reservoir between the incoming materials and supplies and the factory proper, equalising the varying supply and demand. Finished Products ready for shipment are called "Stock", and the place where it is stored is called a "Stock Room" or "Warehouse". The stock room acts as a reservoir between the factory and the selling department equalising the varying demand of the customers and the varying output of the shop.

The layout and organisation of the stores varies widely with the industry and size of factory, though principles are still generally applicable. In engineering, pig iron for the foundry and rough casting and rolled steel sections for the machine shops can be stored outside in the open, as they are unaffected by climatic conditions. In large factories a separate store for each material, or similar kind of material, is justified. In the textile mills, the different types of fabric are kept separate; in printing, the paper, sundries and inks are kept in different stores. In all cases, however, it is essential for smooth production flow, for the raw materials stores to be at the input end of the factory, and the finished stock next to the shipping department. When production flow is arranged in the form of a 'U', stores and stocks must be side by side. It is advisable to store supplies—consumable or indirect materials, those which do not go directly into the product—in separate store rooms. Oils, greases, paint, and rags are messy, and soon make a store dirty and untidy.

For proper storage, a store room should be systematically laid out and equipped with separate receptacles especially suited to facilitate access, identification, and storage for each item of stock. The location of any item will depend upon its size, weight, shape, quality, perishability or delicacy, quantity carried, and frequency of use. Accessibility is insured by storing as far as possible in issuable units, each lot of item distinct, and the greatest number of units showing. Identification is facilitated by marketing the article, or by tags or packages, and by identifying names and numbers on each bin or storage space. The most important principle of good storekeeping is the old maxim for good housekeeping, "a place for everything and everything in its place." To this should be added "and know where it is !" Nowhere else in factory is tidiness more important.

An indispensable rule, which may at first sight appear as "red tape" must be observed in all stores. When stores are drawn from the store room it should be considered the same as drawing money, because stores represent money, and a saving in stored materials represents saving in money. Nothing should be taken out of the stores without a regular requisition slip signed by the appropriate authority. Unless this rule is strictly enforced no survey of the economic situation of the works, no orderly book-keeping and correct profit and loss account, is possible. Where, however, the stores must deliver, for technical reasons, more than is asked for, the return of this excess with a return slip is equally important.

The next stage in treating these requisition slips is the valuing of the material, for which they are the vouchers. There are in use various methods of doing this and the most usual, as explained by Mayenberg,[1] are : (a) To take the actual value of this material, as shown by the invoice in cases where the material is delivered from outside, or by calculation when produced or transformed in the works; (b) to choose the market price; (c) to fix a standard value unchangeable for a certain period, perhaps the business year; or (d) to use the refund price. The first method seems to be the best, although other methods may be used with advantage in some cases. Whatever the method, for right results the

1. *Op. cit.*, p. 160

requisition and return slips should be correctly written out in the first place and forms properly used at later stages. In order to maintain small stock, consistent with need, and to keep turnovers of the materials at the highest number, the principal basic record from the viewpoint of management is the 'Balance of Stores' Record. This record gives the amount ordered, received, issued, balance on hand, the amount apportioned, and the amount available—a complete picture of the state of the stores. Another important stores record is the bin tag already referred to, which is maintained on the bin or shelf where the actual material is stored.

Organisation of the Stores. There are conflicting opinions with regard to the position of the stores in the organisation of the works, and a good deal of loose thinking as to what a storekeeper's duties should include and to whom he should be responsible. It is maintained by some that, in addition to looking after stores, the storekeeper should keep all stock records and be responsible for ordering material. It is also maintained that the Chief Store Keeper should be responsible to the Buyer, or the Secretary, or to the Accountant, or to Production Controller, or for sections of stores he should be responsible to departmental foremen, and all these arrangements can be met with in practice. A storekeeper's job is to keep stocks, to receive and issue them, and in between to store them tidily in a minimum space with the minimum of labour. It is a physical job. It is not his job to keep records that is part of stock recording which in turn is part of production planning. To function effectively, production planning must have up-to-date information of stocks, and must be able to refer to stock records immediately in building up production programmes. This can be done if the records are in the Production Planning Office. While the management of the stores should be independent of that of production proper close co-operation between the Chief Store Keeper and the Production or Works Manager is essential.

In order to better understand the organisation of stores and their day-to-day working, it will be profitable to discuss how the stores are connected with other departments of the works. Meyenberg gives an interesting example of the flow of a material into and out of a store and the clerical work that must be done.

Receipt of Material. When the material enters the works the office of the receiving Depot makes out seven copies of the receipt, using suitable printed forms. Copies 1, 2, 3 and 4 are called "preliminary receipt", copies 5, 6, and 7, "definite receipt". Copy 1 is sent to the Purchasing Department for quick information. This copy is then sent together with the supplier's invoice to the Accounts Department, which retains the invoice and returns copy 2 to Purchasing Department for filing. Copy 2 is sent to Stores Control for quick information of the Ordering Department. Copies 3 and 4 are sent to the Technical Inspection Department, which retains copy 3 for its files and sends copy 4 to the Purchasing Department, after having made the necessary test.

and entered the results on this copy. The Purchasing Department decides whether the material can be accepted, makes this decision on copy 4 and returns it to the Receiving Department. Here copies 4 and 5 are fastened together and sent to the Purchasing Department for comparison with the invoice of the supplier. Copies 1, 4 and 5 and the invoice are then sent to the Accounts Department, which returns the receipts 1, 4 and 5 to the files of the Purchasing Department. Copy 6 is sent with a copy of the invoice to Stores Control, Copy 7 to the Stores themselves.

Any Returns (goods returned by the buyers) are treated in the same way as new material. In these instances the intermediate storage in the Receiving Depot is very important, and if possible this practice should be adhered to so that close inspection of the return goods is possible before they are accepted by the stores.

Issue of Material from the Stores. The material requisitioned from the stores may be of two kinds : "Reserved" stock and "Available" stock, and may require to be separated in the stores book-keeping. Reserved stock is one for which orders have already been received and on which work has not begun. It is always 'direct' or 'raw' material. Available stock, as the name indicates, is not reserved and cannot be issued on requisition. It may be 'direct' or indirect' material. Both kinds of material are demanded from the stores by requisition slips of the same printed form, but of different colours. Requisition slips for direct material are generally made out by the Planning Department, those for indirect material by the Consuming Department; an original and one copy are provided, having the same number, so that all slips can be traced and controlled.

The Planning Department makes out the requisition slips and sends the original and the copy together to the workshop, which in turn forwards both to the stores. From the stores the copy of the requisition slip travels, together with the material in question, to the workshop, while the original is sent to Stores Control. In the Stores Control all necessary details are entered into a card-indexing system, which can be regarded as the key to the information about each material issued from the stores and must therefore be very carefully kept. After the valuation of the issued material and the entry of the value on the requisition slip as well as in the card-index, a summary is prepared and made out in duplicate. This may consist of a daily or a weekly summary, according to the number of items issued, and the originals of the requisition slips, with both copies of the summary, then travel to the Costing Department, where they are examined, mistakes corrected and failures rectified. The current numbers of the requisition slips provide for the latter purposes. When the copy of the summary is acknowledged as correct, it is returned as a receipt to the Stores Control and a short voucher informs the Accounts Department of the necessary figures to be taken from the summary. Thus the Accounts Department receives daily or weekly figures for entering into the accounts.

INVENTORY CONTROL

Before concluding, it may be reiterated that the stocks should never be allowed to run out completely before ordering a new supply. On the other hand, there should not be too much on hand and ahead that it will be deteriorated before it can be used. There are several methods of keeping a check on stock, such as fixing a minimum below which the stock on hand will be allowed to go before ordering new supply, or by keeping stock records which show quantities received and quantities issued, the difference being the balance of stock on hand. Whether it is accurate can be determined only by actually counting the stock. Such a count is called physical inventory. So we may notice only two methods of knowing and maintaining adequate stock—the minimum level and the inventory. An effective plan to prevent stock from running out is to set aside a *RESERVE* at regular intervals and used only when order is placed. This "Reserve" is wrapped or placed in a small box, bag, or envelope of the proper size and plainly labelled in red *RESERVE.* This reserve supply is placed at the back of the regular supply. When the regular supply is used up, it is necessary to open the reserve package and to place a new order at once. Under this plan, it is not necessary to keep stock records to maintain a sufficient supply on hand. Notification is automatically brought to the stock clerk's attention when the reserve package is opened. What quantity should be kept as Reserve will depend upon how much is used at a time and how long it takes to replenish the stock. Experience will decide the quantity.

Physical Inventory is taken by some firms once a year and by others monthly or weekly. But if the records are carefully kept, a complete physical inventory may not be necessary oftener than every six months or once a year. Some concerns keep a continuous check on their stock records by having the storekeeper take one section of the stock room each day and compare the actual amount on hand with the stock record, correcting the record if necessary In any case, items no longer used should be taken out of stock and disposed of, to make room for currently used items. Some concerns examine their stock record cards at intervals and investigate all cards on which there have been no issues since the last inspection. In this way, obsolete items are cleared off the shelves.

Perpetual Inventory. Some concerns keep a prepetual inventory which in its simplest form is a stock record card showing receipts, issues, and balances. Under a prepetual-inventory system, therefore, supplies are stocked, and requisitions for materials to meet specific production requirements are filled from inventories on hand. Sometimes, a perpetual-inventory record also shows quantities marked, scheduled, apportioned, allocated, or set aside for designated jobs or orders, so that the material thus indicated will not be used otherwise. Effective production control requires needed materials to be on hand before the manufacturing process is started, to avoid delays due to the lack of materials. To be of value, a prepetual inventory record should be kept strictly up-to-date at all times. Items received and issued must be entered on the cards the same day, every day. The perpetual-inventory record shows the minimum stock to be kept on hand, and as withdrawals are entered, the clerk compares the balances with the minimums. The stock requisitions from which withdrawals usually are posted to the stock records, may be sent to the accounting department for pricing and charging to the department concerned.

Sometimes, it is necessary to keep a perpetual inventory only of certain items. In such cases, it would be waste of time and money to operate a perpetual inventory of all items. Once the purpose of any record is clearly determined, it is relatively easy to select the type or combination of type of records necessary to accomplish the purpose. At any rate, with a prepetual inventory system, a company is able to make purchases in economic lots, maintain continuity of operations, avoid small, time-consuming orders, and guarantee prompt delivery of finished goods.

For any inventory-control system to be useful, it is necessary to reconcile its conflicting objectives. On the one hand. an inventory-control system should ensure adequate stocks for continuity of operations and sales; on the other, it should minimize inventories on hand. Obviously, the greatest insurance against running out of any item at a crucial moment is maintaining huge supplies of everything stored within the plant. This practice will, generally, prove to be costly, for it requires expensive storage areas and large investments in inventories. The use of such a system also tends to increase losses attributable to deterioration, obsolescence, or declining prices for the materials in storage. Even record keeping and accounting for materials becomes more costly as inventories rise. Minimisation of inventories is the obvious solution. Of course, this minimisation must be consistent with the costs of maintaining adequate stocks, and a compromise is in order. Reduced inventories may result in increased purchasing and handling costs because of smaller lots and may also increase the frequency of operational or sales delays. In other words, as the quantity of goods on hand rises, costs of maintaining inventories rise, and costs associated with not having adequate inventories fall. Optimum control is achieved when the total cost is at a minimum. It is the function of the inventory control personnel to see that the best level of inventories, from an overall point of view, is maintained.

It is also important for any inventory control system to ensure against undue losses from careless waste and outright theft of materials. This can be done by making it difficult for employees to gain unauthorised access to or possession of materials. Physical safeguards should be supplemented by accounting practices which point out the occurrence of wasteful or dishonest activity.

PART SEVEN

Personnel Function of Management

CHAPTER XXXI

PERSONNEL MANAGEMENT

Personnel Function of Management

Personnel function is the basic function of management which means getting effective results with people. It permeates all levels of management, since each executive must depend upon his subordinates for good results. Personnel management is the responsibility of line managers and the staff also performs this function by advising, counselling and providing service to line managers at all levels including the chief executive. Appley goes to the extent of describing all management as personnel management, so that every member of the management group, from the top down, is "personnel manager". A manager does not deal with men, money and materials. He deals with money and materials through people. His job is not a number of major activities, one of which is human relations. His job is human relations job that functions through several major activities. Although we cannot centralise human relations, in every organisation there has to be someone who is primarily concerned with helping to develop in operating officials the point of view and skill of personnel management. That person is the Personnel-Man, normally designated as Personnel Manager. His most important role is to create conditions where the line managers become their own personnel managers.

Definition of Personnel Management

Probably the best definition of personnel management is one given recently in its revised form by the British Institute of Personnel Management. According to that definition : "Personnel Management is that part of management concerned with people at work and with their relationships within an enterprise. Its aim is to bring together and develop into an effective organisation the men and women who make up an enterprise and, having regard for the well-being of the individual and of working groups to enable to make their best contribution of its success.....Personnel management is also concerned with the human and social implications of change in internal organisation and methods of working and of economic and social changes in the community".

Looking at the term in another way, personnel management may be said to be a method of developing the potentialities of employees so that they will get maximum satisfaction out of their work and give their best efforts to the organisation. The management must create a climate where individuals are encouraged for development. One of the ways to do this is for every manager to encourage self-development of his subordinates, and mutual confidence and understanding between employers and employees and between employees and employees.

Genesis of Personnel Function

The Personnel-Man in the Indian set-up has played a varying role in the past. By and large, he reflected the top management's own concept of personnel function and their methods of managerial control. He was, in retrospect, more of an instrument to fulfil the changing objectives of management at different times. The earliest role that the Personnel-Man played was that of a police-man when the management believed that an average employee disliked work, avoided responsibility and therefore, needed to be goaded, controlled and coerced. The authoritative do's and dont's were laid down and the Personnel-Man was required to be a watch-dog for enforcement of prescribed regulation. When State rules and regulations were enacted, he became the law-man. Legal knowledge and experience still remains one of the preferential attributes of the Personnel-Man in most industrial concerns. With the passing of labour legislation, the Trade Unions grew in strength and the Personnel-Man was required to deal and negotiate with them.

While laws were being enacted to grant benefits to employees and the Trade Unions were asking for more and more, there were managements who had a heart and a conscience of their own. They paid fairly good wages and did more than what the law required for the welfare of the workers. The Personnel-Man came handy to administer welfare activities, and so performed the function of welfare-catering. But in the case of majority of industrial houses the voluntary welfare was not at all adequate. Therefore, Section 49 of the Factories Act conscripted a Welfare-Man into industry and put on the employer's payroll. It was believed that because of the numerous duties assigned to him, the Welfare Officer would successfully perform the Personnel Function in Indian Industry. But by entrusting these responsibilities by statute to Welfare Officers, the Government has inadvertently done more harm than good. The personnel function is a line responsibility and a staff function. It cannot be performed by one man. This statutory provision has been a major handicap in the way of growth of the Personnel function. One can understand the regulation of working hours, physical conditions of work and provision of welfare activities under the law, but creating and spelling out a basic management function like the personnel function under a legal umbrella is patently inappropriate. Any man labelled and installed as a Welfare or Personnel Officer and tagged to the management would always work in a void and isolation.*

Another barrier to the development of personnel function in India has been the domination of the members of the family of the entrepreneur over the industrial concerns. These men, though endowed with business acumen, nave not been sold to the idea of sound personnel management, being largely production-orinted. Furthermore, the Industrial Legislation has resulted in a legalistic approach to personnel problems. Over the years, as stated earlier, personnel executives have

* Y.B. Bhonsle, *Personnel Management—The Indian Scene;*

been spending a large percentage of their working time in conciliation and adjudication proceedings. The resulting decisions and awards satisfy neither the workmen nor the managements.*

It is heartening, however, that some organisations have, in recent years, accorded personnel functions its rightful position. A greater awareness of the importance of personnel functions is noticeable among many others.

Role of Personnel Manager—to Advise or to Decide

Personnel Department comes into the picture as a service department to the management in recruitment, induction, placement, merit rating, promotions, transfers and training. The personnel manager is a staff officer whose function is to provide specialised services to the line officers and advise and counsel them on personnel problems. Looked at in this light, a personnel manager has to advise the line manager, the final decision resting with the latter. The classical or traditional view, therefore, is that the staff shall advise and the line shall decide. But the line of demarcation between line and staff functions, that is to say between deciding and advising is a thin one. When advice is accepted it becomes the basis of decision-making. The staff advisory authority really assumes the role of decision-making when the line has known from experience the sanctity and practicality of the advice. Most of the time the line executives have no time to decide on staff advice and generally accept it as decision in toto because of the staff advisers' technical competence in their specialities. In this manner, the personnel officer, by virtue of his sound and practical advice, acquires the status of a decision maker on behalf of the line officer concerned who will welcome such technical assistance. In organisations where the personnel function has established its technical competence and professional expertise, the advisory relationship at the plant and corporate levels has almost always resulted in decision-making authority on behalf of line management and general management of the organisation.

In studies at Princeton University by Helen Baker and Robert France and at MIT by Charles Myers and John Turnbull, it was found that personnel officers would define their capacity as one of giving advice, assistance and counsel to the line organisation, but when questioned about their specific actions, it became apparent that they were actually making the decisions.

When this is the situation in an advanced management setting such as the USA, it is much more relevant in our own developing management practice. Here, personnel function cannot afford to remain merely advisory but has to assume many diverse roles in working with the line according to the exigencies of the organisation, its management philosophy and the industrial environment. The activities of personnel department are thus directed towards making line control of the human

*Ibid.

element stronger and more effective. The personnel manager should rank equally with the other executives, operating under the supervision and directly responsible to the Chief executive.

Activities and Techniques of Personnel Department.

Traditionally, there are 3 areas of Personnel Management namely the areas of Recruitment, Retainment and Retirement. A purposeful personnel policy will be judged for its effectiveness in all the purposes of these three areas. All our personnel functions, such as manpower planning, selecting, inducting, developing, promoting etc., lose all their significance if our policy does not take into account the responsibility of retaining, developing, utilising and gracefully retiring our employees. Also, the purposeful personnel policy will begin at the pre-recruitment stage by taking responsibility for attracting potentially promising candidates for employment by the scouting process, campus visits and other means. It will also extend its jurisdiction by assuming some responsibility for ex-employees' health and housing.

In addition to the foregoing 3 Rs. of Personnel Management, there are some other functions that naturally belong to the personnel department. The activities and functions tabulated below are frequently found under the supervision of the personnel department :

1. Recruitment, Selection and Placement.
2. Training and Development.
3. Job Analysis and Job Evaluation.
4. Employee Rating, Promotion, Transfer, Demotion, Discharge and Separation.
5. Industrial Relations.
6. Health and Welfare
7. Collective Bargaining.
8. Wage and Salary Administration.

Recruitment, Selection and Placement.

Recruitment and selection of a new employee is an important personnel function. The selection involves two basic steps : (1) the tapping of sources of supply, and (2) the interviewing or picking out from among potential candidates. The sources of supply for procuring manpower is present and former employees, friends and colleagues, public and private employment agencies, advertising schools and colleges and casual applicants.

The establishment of the National Employment Service in 1945 has helped in improving the methods of recruitment. Employment Exchanges has been set up under this service. All fresh employments in Government, Quasi-Government and Local Bodies, as also private enterprise are required to make use of these Exchanges.

Interview. After a prospective candidate appears for employment, the second step, in selection by "sizing up" the candidate is taken by interviewing him and by reference to testimonials and recommendations, if any. Every interview should be conducted frankly in a straight forward manner. This applies to both parties. It should not be hurried, but should be sufficient in length to put the candidate at his ease, so that he may reveal himself in his natural state by talking of himself and his previous employment, if any. Sometimes a second interview may be necessary to properly appraise a candidate. The interview should also supply information about the job and the company for which the applicant is to work.

The interview will be followed by certain mental and trade tests for placing the worker in the organisation. The tests which have been used with profit for this purpose are: *Intelligence Tests* for measuring intelligence or scholastic aptitudes; *Interest tests* for finding out the candidate's likes and dislikes for different occupations; *Aptitude tests,* designed to measure a number of native abilities not concerned with "intelligence"; and *Personality tests* which relate to the subject's social life, relations with his family, emotional reactions, etc. A word of caution is called for. Too much reliance in selection should not be placed on psychological techniques and tests which seem to be fast growing; and the majority of which are of questionable value. It is not intended to imply that all the methods are useless, but they must not be regarded as anything like a complete and foolproof solution to the problem of selection. After a person is selected, he should be sent for medical examination. Medical examination is beneficial both to the employee and the employer.

It is axiomatic that selection should be on the basis of merit without any other consideration, but a number of pressures are often applied from within and outside the organisation. The task of matching the man to the requirements of the job becomes very difficult. The fundamental principle of selection that we must fit a man to the job and not the job to the man has been ignored. Very often, because of certain pressures, a man is appointed but then no one knows what to do with him. Perhaps a job is created or modified to fit him.

Another aspect of selection is the extent of participation of the Personnel and Line Officers in the selection procedure. It varies from organisation to organisation. The line officer may assess the suitability of the candidate from the functional angle. The personnel man plays a more important role to see that the person selected will fit in the group in which he is expected to work, has the ability to get along with others and to ensure that the rules and regulations prescribing the standards for recruitment are uniformly and meticulously observed

Guidance and Placement. Selection of right men for given tasks is only the first step in securing an efficient working force. After employment the new employee should be courteously and intelligently dealt with in the matter of placement. He has to be helped and guided in deciding what he can do best of all possible chances open to him. Modern industry is becoming increasingly aware of the importance of placing on every job an individual who is not only able to do the job well but who, in addition, is temperamentally adapted to the job in question. An individual is best adapted and is usually most satisfied, when he has found an outlet for whatever energy, drive and ability he may possess. Each position should be filled by one who wants it. One who knows he is "better off" in it than in any other place he can find. Misfit and dissatisfied men are burdens. It is better to have each position filled by a man who is barely competent to fill it than to have it filled by a man who should have a much better position.

Training and Development. Training is a corner-stone of sound management. Employees must be systematically trained if they are to do their jobs well. New workers must be taught to do the job correctly from the outset; channels ought to exist to teach old employees new methods as they are developed. A training programme gives management an opportunity to explain carefully and clearly its policies, rules and regulations. Tangible results of a training programme include reduction in labour turnover, less spoiled work, less damage to materials and equipment, and improvement in quality and quantity. Above all good will is generated, as in the final analysis, training programme is a reflection of management attitudes.

There are two general approaches to instruction.

1. *The Absorption Method and* 2. *Intentional Method.*

1. *Instruction by absorption* leaves men on their own to sink or swim. Sometimes an older employee may be assigned to take an interest in the new employee, but usually left to learn himself by trial and error, by watching others and asking questions.

2. *Instruction by intention* is the planned method of training new men. In the ideal situation every step in learning the job by the new employee has been planned in advance. The learner is given every opportunity to develop as rapidly as possible and is encouraged at every step.

The following training methods have enjoyed widespread use namely :—

1. On-the-job training.
2. Off-the job or training centre training.
3. Training by experienced workmen.
4. Training by supervisors.
5. Apprenticeship training.

On-the-job training takesplace in the departmenton the equipment where the employee will work. It is suited for teaching relatively simple production and clerical operations to new employees. It is also used when job methods are significantly changed or when an employee is transferred to a different job. When employees are trained on the job they get the feel of actual production conditions and requirements. The trainees learn rules and regulations and procedures by observing their day-to-day application. The management can size up trainees.

Off-the-job or Training-Centre training is providing by schools or centres (the Americans call the Vestibule Schools) established by the young persons in specified trades.

Training can also be provided by experienced fellow-workers. This type of training is particularly adaptable where experienced workmen need helpers. It fits in well also in departments where workmen advance through successive jobs to perform a series of operations.

Training by supervisors provides the trainees opportunities for getting acquainted with their bosses and the supervisors have good chances to judge the abilities and possibilities of trainees from the job performance point of view.

Apprenticeship training aims to develop all-round skilled craftsman. The major part of apprenticeship-training is done on the job doing productive work. Each apprentice is given a programme of assignment according to a pre-determined schedule. The well-balanced programmes provide for efficient training in trade skills and permits a sufficient amount of time for the training to the apprentice to mature as a responsible worker and then a supervisor.

Management Development. Management development is one of the most challenging personnel functions. The primary objective is the creation of a management team with shared objectives and cooperative attitudes. The basis of all management development programmes is performance appraisal. The appraisal has to be made to determine how an executive must be developed in order to do a better job, to prepare for himself for a bigger job and to provide competent successors for his. After having discovered the strong and weak points of the management people, the next step is to provide purposeful training in human relations, line management, decision making, organising and other aspects of management.

The following steps may be taken to ensure proper development of people in the management cadre.

Creating a climate for self-development. It is a well-recognised fact that self-development is the best form of development, because without inner urge to progress further no programme, however well-thoughtout it may be, can succeed. The Management has to create a climate where individuals are encouraged for development. It is the duty of every manager to develop his subordinates by helping them to apply their self-development efforts productively.

Development takes place in diverse ways. For example, it may be brought about by association. The junior executive is associated with a senior executive in number two position so that he learns the higher job while assisting the superior and in course of time may take over part of the job of the superior, or even act as an understudy to him.

Sometimes young executives with little or no previous experience are taken and they are made to go through all the aspects of job in a methodical manner thus enabling them to do the job after necessary training.

Formal outside management courses run by Management Institutes

Government or other public and private bodies for training prospective contribute considerably to the training of managers. Another very useful method of providing training is by delegation of authority. Since delegation means giving the subordinate authority to do something which the superior does not have the time to do, the subordinate gains by delegation, because he comes closer to his chief and is a true lieutenant, perhaps an understudy, ready for promotion.

Job Definition and Description. So far, attention in relation to employment process, has been paid to the study and training of the candidate in order to fit him to the job. But to match talent to task it is essential to know exactly what the position to be filled consists of. Each craft or sub-division of a craft must have an unambiguous name, or title, based upon standardised "Trade Specifications." This will avoid confusion. As the Employment Service is becoming more and more popular, a regular 'dictionary' with standard names should be prepared; without this, it is possible that a mechanical draftsman may be supplied for a task of a machine designer, or fitter or assembler may be sent where a semi-skilled machinist is required, and so on. After preparing the job definition, the next step is to analyse the job and, on the basis of such analysis, to prepare a skeleton specification of the nature of the work and the general conditions to which the employee will be subject. The original record which a job analyst makes often is quite voluminous. When this information is condensed, the record is known as a *job description,* in which one finds statements as to the job title; the job number; the function of the job and responsibilities involved; the machinery or equipment that is used, and an explanation of how and why it is used; the usual working hours involved; the working conditions; the method of compensation; the major operational relationships of the job with others in the organisation; the jobs just below and above it in the normal promotional sequence; and the qualifications which an individual must possess in order to fill the job satisfactorily. The emphasis placed upon each of these items varies according to the particular use to which the job description is to be put. Job descriptions should emphasise functional responsibilities rather than specifications. For example, instead of saying the holder of a job "types" or "works at a typewriter," it is perferable to say that he "must get out all typewritten materials accurately and on time." It is also important that the job description includes a statement such as "performs other duties as instructed by the supervisors." If this is done there should be less difficulty with union grievances in regard to whether a specific task is a part of some particular job. After this follows the process of job evaluation.

JOB EVALUATION

Job evaluation is the rating of jobs according to specific planned procedure in order to determine the relative worth of each job. It is a systematic method of appraising the worth or value of each job in relation to other jobs in the company. Job evaluation rates the *jobs,* not *men*, or *women* on the jobs, which is the task of *employee rating.* The principles of job evaluation can be applied to all kinds of employees, operatives as well as executives. They can be applied to businesses of all sizes. The sole purpose of job evaluation is to divide up any given pay roll so that all jobs are paid according to their relative difficulties. For example, the job of a machinist and that of an electrician may appear to be quite different, but if they are of the same relative difficulty, requiring similar skill, effort and intelligence, both would be paid at the same rate. Job evaluation is useful in many ways; and with a job evaluation plan in operation, inconsistency in rates is minimised and the entire wage structure becomes unified. According to Knowles and Thomson,[1] job evaluation is useful in eliminating many of the evils to which nearly all systems of wage and salary payments are subject. These are: (1) payment of high wages and salaries to persons who hold jobs and positions not requiring great amounts of skill, effort and responsibility; (2) paying beginners less money than they are entitled to receive in terms of what is required of them; (3) giving raises to persons whose performances do not justify them; (4) deciding rates of pay and increases in pay on the basis of seniority rather than ability; (5) payment of widely varied wages and salaries for the same or closely related jobs and positions; and (6) the payment of unequal wages and salaries because of race, sex, religion, and political differences.

Types of job evaluation. Job evaluation systems may be classified into 3 major groups, namely, (1) The Ranking, or Grading Method; (2) The Factor Comparison Plan, or the Weighted-in-money Method; and (3) The Various Point Methods. All types of job evaluation strive to eliminate personal whims and to introduce scientific procedures. Any type when carefully used will give satisfactory results.

The ranking, or grading system of job evaluation consists primarily in arranging the various jobs in the enterprise in an order from the simplest to the highest or the reverse, each successive job being either higher or lower than the previous one in the sequence. This system should be preceded by careful job analysis and the writing of accurate job descriptions before the rating process is undertaken. Another procedure, which is in reality merely a modification of the simple rating described above, is to establish a series of grades, or zones, and arrange all the jobs in the plant into groups within these classifications, or groups. A more common practice is to arrange all the jobs in the plant according to their requirements by rating them and then to establish the classifications, or groups. The detailed job description is particularly helpful when ranking of jobs is done by different individuals and there is a disagreement among them. It is desirable to associate workers in the construction of the job description and in rating the job. Usually a series

1. *Industrial Management,* p. 387

of key jobs that are well known throughout the plant are first rated and the other jobs roughly compared with these key jobs to establish a rough rating, after which each job is compared in greater detail to establish its exact rank in the scale.

In establishing the relative rank of a given job, as far as possible, the current wage being paid should be ignored, if we want the ranking to be serviceable in wage adjustments. Rating the jobs, by ranking method, should also ignore the qualifications of the person filling the jobs at the time, since the ranking is of the jobs and not of the workers. The particular worker may have qualifications that are higher than those required for the job. It is to be remembered that ranking of jobs requires infinite patience and attention to details. It usually results in a compromise or pooled judgement of the relative worth of a job. As an example of this method may be quoted the programme of a company which measured each job in comparison with other jobs in terms of the relative importance of the following six factors :

1. *Supervision and leadership of subordinates.*

2. *Co-operation with associates outside the line of authority :* exchange of opinion on controversial matters involving tact, diplomacy, appreciation of the other person's point of view; necessity for and degree of teamwork, exchange of information, etc.

3. *Probability and consequences of errors :* assuming that the occupation is filled by an experienced, conscientious employee, consider typical errors that are apt to be made and the consequences of each in terms of waste, damage to equipment, delays, complaints, confusion, spoilage of product, discrepancies.

4. *Initiative and resourcefulness.* Requirements concerning originality, creativeness, judgement, analysis of conditions and reaching independent decisions, planning, estimating, etc., extent to which supervision is received.

5. *Minimum experience requirements* including both preliminary experience and the experience in the occupations; estimated time required for inexperienced but otherwise qualified persons to reach a satisfactory degree of proficiency.

6. *Minimum education requirement :* amount of schooling or study absolutely necessary to fill successfully the occupation.

The **advantages** claimed for the Ranking or Classification system briefly are :

1. *Simplicity.* It is relatively easy to understand by the workers and supervisors. It is less mechanistic and theoretical than the point system. Each job is compared as an entity with each other job. One can write the title of each job on a card, with one card being used for each job, and then arrange the cards so that the top one holds the most important job title, the next holds the next most important job title, and so on. Grade groups then can be designated and salaries assigned.

2. *The time element.* Unless carried to the detailed point used by the company, it requires less time.

3. *Frankness.* It avoids the criticism of claiming to be scientific.

The **disadvantages** of the system are as follows :

1. Unless the same detailed analysis is pursued as that used in the various point systems, the analyst or committee cannot possibly be familiar with all the jobs. If the same details are followed, most of the advantages of this system, other than simplicity, do not exist.

2. The ranking system merely produces a job order and does not indicate to what degree a job is more important than the one below it. It gives the rank, or tells that a job is higher than another, but does not say how much higher.

3. The system tends to be used without adequate job descriptions having been made, thus the ranking is likely to be severely biased by general opinions and existing wage rates. Because of these limitations the ranking system is suitable for only the smallest enterprises.

Under the **Factor Comparison System of job evaluation** the analyst or evaluation committee selects key jobs for which there exist clearly understood job descriptions and counterparts in other organisations, and for which the money rates are considered satisfactory. Each of these jobs is analysed in terms of the following factors, and that portion of the money rate which is considered appropriate is assigned to the factor; (1) Mental requirements; (2) Skill requirements; (3) Physical requirements; (4) Responsibility; (5) Working conditions. For example, the prevailing wage for the filing clerk may be established at Rs. 1.25 per hour. The evaluation committee would then estimate what portion of the Rs. 1.25 is paid in consideration of each of the factors. In this case mental (intelligence) requirements might be credited with 40 P.; skill requirements, 10 P.; physical requirements, 50 P.; responsibility, 10 P.; and working conditions 15P. This process is followed for each key job with due attention being given to the factor rankings of the previous survey. If one job were ranked above another for the skill factor, it should also be ranked higher monetarily, or the differences should be reconciled.

At this point the analyst using the factor comparison system can begin evaluating the jobs of undermined value. Each job is considered factor by factor in the process, the factor being evaluated according to their positions along the pre-established scales. For example, the skill value of key job A might be 50 P. and that of key job B might be only 45 P. If the amount of skill required for job X is considered to be less than the requirement for job A but more than for job B, job X should be awarded some amount between 45 P. and 50 P. in consideration of the skill required. Each other factor is considered in the same manner, and the total base rate for the job is determined by summing the factor values. When one completes the same steps for every job in the organisation an overall wage structure has been established.

The **advantages** *of the Factor Comparison Plan* are as follows :

1. *Flexibility.* There are no limits to the value that may be assigned to each factor.

2. *Simplicity.* The Plan does not require a translation from points to

money. It involves a comparative process wherein jobs are priced against other jobs rather than against some established numerical scale.

3. The system lends itself admirably to the establishing of classification.

Disadvantages of the system are :

1. It is costly to install, and somewhat difficult for anyone who is not acquainted with the general nature of job evaluation techniques to grasp.

2. Wage levels change from time to time, and thus adjustments are required.

3. Money rates, when used as a basis for rating, tend to influence the actual rate more than abstract points.

The Point System of evaluating jobs consists of several plans using points for job evaluation as a basis of establishing relative job worth. All the point systems are based on the assumption that it is possible to assign points to the respective factors considered pertinent in evaluating the individual jobs and that the sum of these points will give an index of the relative significance of the jobs being rated. The difference in the various systems arises mainly from the number of characteristics used in establishing the relative requirements of the various jobs. One Plan uses three major divisions under which the various job characteristics are classified, namely, (1) Job conditions, (2) Physical ability required, and (3) Mental requirements. Under each of these three main headings are listed the various factors, with each factor clearly defined and under each factor a description of the degrees required, the number of points allotted to each degree. The factors used in the job rating in another plan are grouped under 4 headings, namely, (1) skill; (2) effort, (3) responsibility, and (4) job conditions. Each of these general heads has subheads as in the first plan. Most of the point systems include the following 5 items in evaluating jobs; (1) Mental requirements; (2) Physical requirements; (3) Skill; (4) Responsibility; and (5) Job or Working conditions.

The assignment of points to the major factors—skill required, effort required, responsibility of the job, and job conditions—is the next step. Each of these categories is then broken up into subgroups. For example, skill requirements are evaluated according to education required, experience required, and the necessary initiative and ingenuity of a satisfactory job holder. For each sub-factor 5 degrees of importance are defined, and a specified number of points is associated with each degree. For example, the first degree under education may be defined as "the ability to read, or add or subtract"—and be awarded 14 points. The fifth degree, on the other hand, carries 70 points and involves a high level of knowledge, such as technical university training. Points given to each degree of a sub-factor vary from one sub-factor to another according to the relative importance placed upon each. For example, experience may carry 14 points for the first degree and 110 points for the fifth degree. Therefore, experience is of greater significance than the education factor which carries a maximum of 70 points. This system, thus, permits management to place added weight upon those characteristics which are selected as the most important in the establishment of a suitable job hierarchy.

The point systems are too easy to use, and therefore permit managements to employ them without giving serious thought to the selection of factors to be utilised and the adding weights. It is necessary for their success that management should determine the purposes and objectives of the job hierarchy to be established and then select and weigh the factors accordingly. In selecting the factors, care should be taken to cover all phases of work with a few factors, without, of course, allowing overlapping of factors. Precise definition of degrees is of extreme importance to the success of the system. Such ambiguous words as "low", "medium", and "high" should be avoided, as they lend themselves to different interpretations by different analysts.

As an illustration of Factor Descriptions and Point Values in different levels of jobs such as (1) Labour, Trades and Operating Jobs; (2) Clerical, Technical and Supervisory Jobs; (3) Executive Positions, the following factors and points are given. The points are allotted arbitrarily but they obviously vary according to the type of industry in question.

Factor Descriptions and Point Values relating to Labour, Trades and Operating Jobs in Light Manufacturing Industries:

Factors	*Points*	*Total Points*	*Percentage*
1. Efforts		99	19.8%
1.1. Physical Demand	75		
1.2 Attention	24		
2. Skill		213	42.2%
2.1. Initiative and Ingenuity	45		
2.2 Schooling or Equivalent	60		
2.3. Experience	108		
3. Responsibility		93	18.7%
3.1 Responsibility for Materials and Equipment	19		
3.2. Responsibility for Materials or Products	19		
3.3 Responsibility for Safety of others	20		
3.4 Leadership	35		
4. Working Conditions		95	19.1%
4.1 Working conditions	75		
4.2 Accident Hazards	20		

The Physical Demand factor appraises the extent to which physical effort must be expanded in performing the job. The elements to consider are weight of material moved, the distance it is moved and the type of conveyance, the continuity of effort, and the resultant fatigue. The Attention Factor appraises the degree of mental or visual concentration required. Initiative and ingenuity appraise the independent action, exercise of judgement, the making of decisions or the amount of planning that the job requires. Schooling pertains to the educational requirements essential to satisfactory performance of the job. This factor should not be confused with experience or on-the-job training. The Experience factor pertains to the amount of job training necessary to gain satisfactory proficiency.

The Responsibility factor for different items measures responsibility for preventing damage to machinery or equipment which might result from error or negligence, and also to the probability of damage to materials, parts in process or finished goods. Responsibility for safety of others is an important factor, as it involves care to avoid or prevent injuries to fellow workers. Leadership is a factor which pertains to responsibility for the work of others. It is limited to instruction or direction and is not intended to appraise complete supervisory responsibility for results and matters.

The working conditions factor appraises the surroundings or physical conditions under which the job must be done and the extent to which such conditions make the job disagreeable. Consideration will be given to the presence, relative amount and continuity of exposure to dust, dirt, heat, fumes, cold, noise, vibration, wet, or other unpleasant conditions. The factor of accident hazards appraises the conditions which expose the employee to the possibility of accident.

A brief mention is made of the factor descriptions and point values relating to clerical, technical and supervisory jobs—

Factor	*Total Points*
Experience	100
Education	75
Initiative and Ingenuity	80
Attention and Concentration	60
Responsibility	60
Supervision	90
Working conditions	35

Factor Descriptions and Point Values relating to Executive Positions are summed up below:

Knowledge; Education; Experience; Ingenuity; Administrative Responsibility; and Operating Responsibility. The evaluation of the position in regard to different factors can be made by determining the minimum requirements of each factor.

MERIT RATING

In the foregoing discussion we were interested in the relative worth of jobs. In this section, we are concerned with the relative worth of men—as measured by certain specific techniques. These techniques, which are formalised procedures for differentiating among or assessing workers, are usually referred to as merit rating plans, employee-rating plans or performance rating. *Merit rating may be defined as a systematic evaluation of an employee's performance on the job in terms of the requirements of the job.* The merit-rating systems are used by firms primarily because each supervisor must differentiate among his subordinates. He has to decide which employee to recommend for promotion, for layoff, for wage increases, or for special training. Thus, his job involves making judgments about people. A good supervisor bases his judgment on a systematic approach—merit rating, rather than rely on rule of thumb, intuition and other less systematic procedures.

It is appropriate to recognise at the outset that employees are rated for a number of different reasons. Therefore, the subject of merit rating covers more than wage and salary administration. It is even regarded as a technique for improving communication and building *esprit de corps.* The specific uses of merit rating vary from firm to firm. Merit rating is used for the following purposes and reasons :

1. Merit rating is most commonly used to justify wage increases, but it has many other industrial-relations uses.

2. It is used as a part of the selection process itself in deciding whether employees on probation are to be confirmed or not.

3. It helps the supervisor in the task of job placement in line with the individual employee's personal peculiarities.

4. It helps in identifying employees who deserve promotion and those who should be transferred to some other job where he is likely to perform more efficiently.

5. It acts as a criterion to be used by the employment office to judge the effectiveness of its own selection.

6. It can be used as part of a seniority system for layoff purposes. Where ability and length of service are considered as a part of seniority, merit rating can be of great assistance.

7. Merit rating may be used as a part of the employee's disciplinary record to protect the employee, the supervisor and the company from discrimination, favouritism, or charges of such unfair practices.

Merit rating is, thus, used to give employees an idea of how they are doing, identify promotable employees, award wage adjustments, improve supervision, discover training needs, guide selection and placement, and comply with union contracts.

In spite of its usefulness, merit rating is opposed by many employees. A part of this opposition arises from a basic distrust of anyone in authority, and a part of it arises from a sincere questioning of the ability of the supervisor to judge accurately the abilities and performance of the employees. For this reason managements go to great lengths to secure uniformity among the various raters as well as objectivity as far as possible. Certain forms and certain procedures aid in securing uniformity in evaluation.

Types of Merit-Rating. Employees are rated by various companies in different ways. The simplest merit rating plan is *Straight Ranking*

Method. It involves ranking the men in a work group one against the other. For example, in a work group of 20 men, the foreman is required to list in terms of numeric rank the relative position of each man. It may also be done by ranking a person on his job performance against other members of a competitive group by placing him as number so and so in the total group.

Rank system does not, however, eliminate snap judgments, nor does it provide the rater with a systematic procedure for determining the relative ranks of his subordinates. A number of plans have been designed to remedy these weaknesses. The *Graphic Rating Plan,* as used by a company, is given here as an illustration.

Reference Guide

1.2		2.4		3.6		4.8		6.0		7.2		8.4		9.6		10.8		12.0

In rating a person in relation to various characteristics, the points in numeric terms are given ranging from 1.2 for the weakest going up to 12.0 for the best worker. For example, in terms of "accuracy of work", a worker would be rated as follows : where he makes many errors and spoils the work, or makes many mistakes in carrying out instructions and generally turns out poor quality of work, he will be rated as 1.2 to 2.4. Rating of 3.6 to 4.8 will indicate: careless. Inclined to make mistakes. Errors due to lack of interest rather than ignorance. Believes in just getting by. A man who produces average quality of work on repetitive jobs and requires comparatively little supervision is rated 6.0 to 7.2. The one who seldom makes mistakes, turns out high quality of work and carries out instructions accurately is placed between 8.4 and 9.6, and a man who is most accurate, checks and observes his work and reports errors, and whose quality of work can be rated upon is rated highest at 10.8 to 12.0.

Similarly, quantity of work can be made the basis of merit rating. The worker who is very slow, clumsy and does not care is rated 1.2 to 2.4. The one who is slow with low production, possesses insufficient knowledge of the job and lacks skill is rated 3.6 to 4.8. The man who works at moderate speed, needs encouragement and urging and has good output on repetitive work is rated 6.0 to 7.2. The worker who works fast and skilfully, uses good methods for turning out high quality work and does his share when working with others is rated 8.4 to 9.6. The exceptionally fast and skilful worker who does his work in the best and quickest way turning out best production and when working with others does more than his share is rated 10.8 to 12.0.

Under the *graphic rating plan,* rank-and-file factory workers are rated on ten characteristics, each of which is explicitly described for the rater in the manner stated above in relation to accuracy and quantity of

Merit Ability Evaluation Chart[1]

Department————
Name of Employee—'A'
Date of Employment————

Occupation to be rated on————

Characteristic	*Mark only with 'A'*										*Employees points*
1. Accuracy of work	1.2	2.4	3.6	4.8	6.0	7.2A	8.4	9.6	10.8	12.0	7.2
2. Quantity of work	1.2	2.4	3.6	4.8	6.0	7.2A	8.4	9.6	10.8	12.0	7.2
3. Use of working time	1.2	2.4	3.6	4.8	6.0	7.2	8.4A	9.6	10.8	12.0	8.4
4. Ability to work with others	1.2	2.4	3.6	4.8	6.0A	7.2	8.4	9.6	10.8	12.0	6.0
5. Ability to Learn	1.0	2.0	3.0	4.0	5.0	6.0	7.0	8.0A	9.0	10.0	8.0
6. Safety	1.0	2.0	3.0	4.0A	5.0	6.0	7.0	8.0	9.0	10.0	4.0
7. Initiative and acceptance of reponsibility	.8	1.6	2.4	3.2	4.0	4.8A	5.6	6.4	7.2	8.0	4.8
8. Conduct on the job	.8	1.6	2.4	3.2	4.0	4.8A	5.6	6.4	7.2	8.0	4.8
9. Care and use of equipment, tools, materials, power	.8	1.6	2.4	3.2	4.0	4.8	5.6A	6.4	7.2	8.0	5.6
10. Attendance and punctuality	.8	1.6	2.4	3.2	4.8	5.6	6.4A	6.4	7.2	8.0	6.4
Total Points				4.0	6.0	24.0	14.0	14.4			62.4

Rated by *Foreman X* Date————

Employee Interviewed by———— Date ————

plus or Minus Points
Ranking Points

1. Adapted from Wolf, *The Management of Personnel*, pp. 220-222.

work. For each characteristic, points are assigned to the employee on the basis of his performance and attitudes. Thus, if an employee is inclined to be careless, he will be ranked low on the accuracy of his work. If his accuracy is extremely poor, he is given 1.2 points. If it is extremely good, he gets 12 points. In this manner points are arrived at for each factor and a total point score is obtained. The Evaluation Chart given on page 525 shows the merit and ability evaluation of "Employee A". Similarly, other employees can be ranked and then compared.

It will be noticed that employee A received 7.2 points for accuracy of work; 7.2 points for quantity of work; 3.4 points for use of working time; and so forth. His total score is 62.4 points. Before the total score is used in comparing workers, it is adjusted for the systematic error of the rater (i.e.. the tendency to rate everyone either too high or too low). First, the average rating given by the rater is determined. Then each rating given by the rater is compared with his average rating, and the net difference between a specific rating and the average rating is added to or subtracted from a base score of 70. To illustrate : If Foreman X's average rating for all his employees is 72.4, we can obtain employee A's final rating by finding the difference between 72.4 and 62.4 (i.e., 10 points) and subtracting it from the base score of 70. Employee A's merit-rating score, then, is 60 points (70–60).

Descriptive or Essay type Merit Rating. In this plan, the supervisor writes an essay on his subordinates. The essay approach has advantages in evaluating supervisory employees. It forces the rater to think about his men and avoids a mechanistic approach to evaluation. The "Review' or 'Appraisal' should consider the following factors :

1. Relation with Fellow Supervisors and Personnel Assigned to him.
2. General Organisation and Planning Ability.
3. Understanding and Application of Company Policies and Procedures.
4. Job knowledge and Potential.
5. Production Quality and Cost Control.
6. Housekeeping and Safety.
7. Demonstrated Attitude and Personnel Characteristics.
8. Physical Condition.

After Reviews have been completed for all first level supervisors they should be examined by other reviewing supervisors in the same shop or group to obtain concurrence. The "Appraisal of Performance must clearly indicate how the supervisor is performing on his assigned job. Then "Suggestions for Development", if any, should be made i specific and helpful terms.

Forced-Distribution Method. This method is used to eliminate or minimize the rater's bias. The Forced-distribution plans require the rate to distribute his ratings to follow a predetermined distribution. Fo example, students are sometimes graded as A, B, C, D and E, accordin to their performance in the test. In a large under-graduate class, 5 to 1 per cent of the studens be given A's; 20 to 30 per cent, B's; 40 to 60 per cent. C's and 10 to 20 per cent, D grades. In the same manner, a normal group of workers doing the same job would fall into some such grouping as superior, above average, average, below average, and poor and the relative percentages would be approximately 10-20-40-20-10. Although this method does tend to eliminate or reduce bias, its use in wage administration leads to low morale and low productivity.

Forced-Choice Method. The forced-choice method attempts to correct a rater's tendency to give consistently high or consistently low ratings to all employees. The rater is asked to choose from several sets of phrases the one phrase that best describes the man being rated, and the phrase that least characterises him. The ratings are then scored by a key that has been worked out in great detail. The rater does not know what kind of score he is giving a person. He merely marks him as indicated above. This system has merit when properly worked out, but some raters do not like to use a form unless they know the results of their efforts. The four groups of statements given below are illustrative of the type of statements that are used :

Forced-Choice Blocks

☐ Makes little effort at individual instruction.
☐ Organises work well.
☐ Lacks the ability to make people feel at ease.
☐ Has a cool, even temperament.

☐ Has a high degree of initiative.
☐ Never makes excuses for his mistakes.
☐ Fails to work for the best interest of all.
☐ Slow in accomplishing his work.

☐ Possesses good health and vitality.
☐ Late for staff meetings.
☐ Co-operates with top management.
☐ Somewhat timid and retiring.

☐ Always gets the job done.
☐ Contradicts the words of other supervisors.
☐ Refuses to admit a mistake.
☐ Consistent in expectations of the workers.

Field-Review Method. This type of merit-rating is useful for large organisations, and appears to overcome a number of the weaknesses found in many of the other systems. It consists of having a trained employee from the personnel department interview line supervisors about their respective subordinates. The supervisor is asked to give his opinion about the progress of his subordinates, the level of performance of each subordinate, and possible plans of action in cases requiring further consideration. The representative of the personnel department takes detailed notes of the interview.These notes are approved by the supervisor and placed in the employee's personnel folder. The success of this system depends on the competency of the interview. If this man knows his business, he can contribute significantly to reasonably accurate appraisals. Moreover, he can help the supervisor think through his evaluations, so that bias and prejudice can be more readily minimised.

Critical-Incident System. This system is designed primarily to contribute to the *growth and development of supervisors and their subordinates.* The distinguishing feature of this type of plan is that it attempts to measure workers' performances in terms of *episodes.* The heart of the plan *involves training supervisors* (1) to recognise episodes of exceptionally good or bad performance; (2) to speak with the worker at a time relevant to dealing with the observed episode; (3) to keep a written record of the episodes so that they can be easily recalled and used during the periodic appraisal and coaching interview; and (4) to develop skill in handling the coaching and appraisal interview.

As a device for developing effective supervision, the plan has a number of advantages. First, its administration requires the supervisors to develop habits and skills that are essential to good supervision (i.e., they become aware of criteria for judging exceptional performance; they develop skill in interviewing and in handling episodes of unusually good or bad performance; they get to know their subordinates, and vice versa). Second, it avoids having the supervisor make direct comparisons between workers. The focus is on the concrete examples of performance. The third and major advantage of this type of plan is that it brings employees and supervisors together in a constructive environment. It directly attacks what appears to be a basic problem in all large organisations—namely, the workers' anxiety about where they stand. It enables the employee to discuss job performance with his supervisor through daily interaction as well as a periodic appraisal interview. The worker receives individual attention. He knows better where he stands and also where his supervisor stands.

In order that any merit rating system should prove effective, it should rate the employee in terms of his actual performance on the present job. A given employee might be rated C or D on performance, yet under the promotability side might be marked promotable to a higher job because of special qualifications for the higher job when he is average or even below average on his present job. Such a situation might easily arise in the case of a toolmaker by trade who is currently working on a production machine because there is no vacancy in toolmaking. A similar situation might arise in a department store or office or even among supervisors. It could readily arise in the case of a college teacher who was teaching statistics but who was primarily trained in accounting. Again, employees tend not to be rated but to be paid on an automatic basis of increments, or to be paid, in case of an incentive basis, solely on objective data, such as quantity of output, quality of output, attendance, and tardiness, etc. The employee should be encouraged to participate in the scheme.

PROMOTIONS AND TRANSFERS

The fundamental principle of employment, which every employer should keep in mind, is to put on a job the best possible man obtainable for the money he is prepared to spend, no matter where he comes from. Very frequently, however, the knowledge of the firm and its methods possessed by "insiders" will make them more suitable for the higher posts than any outsider could be. Therefore, every employer should make an efficient effort to produce his own skilled workers, and should plan to fill higher positions, as far as possible, by promotions and transfers. Undoubtedly, doors should not be barred to outsiders, who may bring valuable new ideas, and save the firm they join from going to sleep, but the "discards" of the other plants should be avoided. Ordinarily, the demand made upon the outside labour market should be for beginners only, unless some specially qualified outsider fits better than any of the insiders. After all, ambitious employees are anxious for promotional opportunities.

A promotion is the transfer of an employee to a job that pays more money or one that enjoys some preferred status. The job evaluation, by means of analysis as to their requirements, and merit rating showing capacities of individual workers, will open natural lines of transfers and promotions. Transfers enable the management to check up its own mistakes in the selection or placement of workers. Every man is good for something and the business of the employment department is to find what that something is. The proper remedy for a misfit is usually a transfer, and not a discharge. Transfers stimulate the labour force as much as promotions, for they are an evidence of regard for the individual worker. Promotions are transfers to higher pay and better work for the merit; the making of them stimulates employees to earn merit. Promotions are the proper answer to the argument that an employee must not do his present work conspicuously well or he will always be held upon it. A promotion by leaving a position vacant creates an opportunity for a stimulating series of promotions below it. This acts as a satisfying recognition of the logical claim that the opportunities within an establishment belong to those who are members of its labour family rather than to outsiders.

To facilitate promotion, positions should be arranged like the steps of a strairway or the rungs of a ladder, so that each place is a preparation for the next higher one. It was Frank Gilbreth who conceived what he called the Three-Position Plan according to which all the positions throughout an establishment are to be placed together by functions of teaching and learning. He described this plan thus "The three positions are as follows; first and lowest, the position that the man has last occupied in the organisation; second, the position that the man is occupying at present in the organisation; third, and highest, the position that the man will next occupy. In the first position the worker occupies the place of the teacher, this position being at the same time occupied by two other men, that is, by the worker doing the work who receives little or no instruction in the duties of that position except in an emergency, and by the worker below who is learning the work. In the second position the worker is actually in charge of the work, and is constantly also the teacher of the man next below him, who will next occupy the position. He is also, in emergencies, a learner of duties from the man above him. In the third position, the worker occupies the place of learner, and is being constantly instructed by the man in the duties of the position immediately above".[1] It is, however, not enough to construct stairways or ladders; they must be kept open. "An officer who stagnates, blocks a line below him, and leaves a place above without a candidate in reserve". Therefore, a promotion programme must be kept alive by promoting men for merit, and never for pull or favouritism. Seniority may at times be given weight, but seniority alone is as bad a basis as pull or favouritism. Promotions based upon merit awaken ambition; and each promoted person becomes a symbol of what may be attained by another. In such a system each subordinate is a sort of standing challenge to his superior.

Demotions. Opinions differ with regard to the demotion of an employee. Some managers hesitate to demote a man on the theory that he will not be satisfied to take the lower job and it is therefore better to discharge him than to have a disgruntled employee. This attitude is especially true with regard to executives. There is some merit to this way of thinking; yet many a worker, especially an executive, would be only too happy to be removed from a job that he recognises he is unable to fill as it should be filled, provided that this can be done without too much shock to his personal pride. Often, such men should be transferred to another job or section, where he may be a success. The man, who has failed, is not always solely responsible for his failures. His superiors have erred in judgment as well as he. If a man, who has reached a position, after successfully filling various positions over a period of 20 years, and finds himself incapable of handling the job fully successfully, he may ask to be permitted to revert to his old job; provided the situation is properly handled. Such adjustments require a high type of personnel administration. Discharge is the easy way but not necessarily the sound one. The management should prepare the men for stepping down and not merely handle the occurrence as a matter of course. Demoted workers or supervisors have a psychological adjustment to make. Attention to this matter is a mark of real leadership and pays dividends in helping people when they really need it. You may not be able to avoid altogether some heartaches in demoting an employee, but you can minimise them.

1. *The Three Position Plan of Promotion.*

Withdrawals and Dismissals. The Personnel Manager's part in dealing with (1) Retirements; (2) Terminations; (3) Redundancy at Retirement; (4) Dismissal: (i) for disorderly conduct, or (ii) for unsatisfactory work, is the complement of his tasks in recruitment, training and promotion.

Retirement of a worker is an important event in his life; and from the company's standpoint it turns on the morale value. At the time of parting the Personnel Manager (in a smaller firm, the owner) should arrange a special interview with the employee. The firm's policy makes this the occasion for a souvenir presentation. In any case, it should be made clear to the employee that the company is still interested in him and always ready to help him. All legal obligations to him may have ceased, but where a man has given a major portion of his working life to a firm, they have a moral duty to extend a considerate and helping hand to him. They undoubtedly draw benefit from this contribution, for such an attitude adds to the morale of all employees in the firm.

Termination of service of one employee or another for some reason may have to be made at one time or other— This involves a task with two distinct phases. There is the purely routine task of seeing that the departing employee is paid his dues, returns tools or equipment belonging to the firm, gets back his insurance card, and so on. But there is also the human side, the face-to-face contact with the employee by the Personnel Manager or his deputy. Not long ago, employees could be dismissed at a day's notice, or none at all, without regard to the personal damage done to the individual by the shattering of security, to the morale of the factory or office, or to the fabric of society. But today the existence of a personnel policy usually guarantees against unfair dismissal. The Personnel Manager sees that the guarantee is upheld and the employee is given fair chance to explain before he is asked to quit. He must also see that the employee leaves with a sense of justice done rather than injustice suffered, and that his former mates do not bear a self-justified resentment. On the other hand, an employee may want to leave either because he is dissatisfied with the conditions of service or unfair treatment, or because he is getting married and leaving the district or for some other genuine reason. Where a worker's leaving reflects discontentment, the Personnel Officer should see to it that the weakness in organisation or supervision is removed, and if possible, the good employee is retained.

Redundancy of operators may occur because of the completion or cancellation of contract or other outside economic factors and retrenchment of usually the last employees to join may become necessary. If retrenchment is to be on a considerable scale, the detailed work needs to be carefully planned beforehand. In every case, the employees should be given adequate notice or pay in lieu of notice, so that they have the opportunity of seeking another employment. The shop stewards (foremen or head jobbers) should be taken into confidence, and reasons for retirement explained at the outset. Ordinarily, the principle of "last come, first go" should be observed.

Dismissal for disorderly conduct must always be based on some definite evidence. It may be a breach of the rules, a brawl or fight between two employees, the merits of which must be gone into by the Personnel Manager, before discharge is ordered. Ample opportunity must be given to the employee to explain his side of the case. In highly emotional cases, including drunkenness, it is wise never to make a decision on the day the incident happens, but to wait until the next day. People who are giving an account of what has happened will give an entirely different story when they are cool, calm and collected, than they will when tempers are frayed.

Dismissal for unsatisfactory work may have to be made by the Personnel Officer on complaints received from a department. He usually handles this type of case by seeing the man to explain that his work has been unsatisfactory over a long period, and that he has had several warnings, despite these, no improvement has been shown, and finally it has been felt that he must go. But if the employee protests and challenges certain facts as incorrect, the person who made the allegations must be asked to repeat them in the presence of the employee. Hearing the facts on both sides, the Personnel Manager will have the final word, but it is much better to get agreement from the worker that he has been unsatisfactory and that it is a logical thing for him to be discharged as he has not improved. It is also a good policy to pay an employee who is discharged (whether from factory or office) wages in lieu of notice rather than ask him to work out the notice and be a misery to himself and everyone else. But when it comes to the end, try to discharge him in a friendly way; there is no need to be hostile, abrupt or unkind. The fact that he has not been successful in one company is no criterion that he will not be an outstanding success in the next. He may well be helped to obtain a suitable job elsewhere.

MORALE

One of the important activities of the personnel department is to keep line management informed about the attitudes of workers and the human problems of the organisation. Such information is the basis of sound policy and guide to constructive action. Inventories of employee attitudes (commonly known as morale surveys) are increasingly being used to measure morale. Since morale or attitude survey of employees supplements the labour audit in very much the same sense as the physical inventory aids in the financial audit; it is imperative to study the concept of morale.

Meaning of Morale. Morale has been recognised by military authorities as one of the most important factors in winning or losing wars. Napoleon rated morale so high as to say that morale conditions made up 75 per cent of the success or failure in a military situation. High morale leads to success and low morale brings defeat in its wake. In a military sense high morale means ;

> "The state of mind which makes a soldier contented with his surroundings; confident of himself, his comrades, and his leaders; and determined to execute all of his missions with effectiveness and efficiency. It relates to the condition of an individual or group with regard to courage, confidence, and enthusiasm in the performance of duty." [1]

For managerial purposes morale has been defined in many ways, although all the definitions revolve round the attitude and willingness to work to achieve the objectives. Aldrich defines morale as a readiness to co-operate warmly in the tasks and purposes of a given group or organisation. Industrial morale has also been defined as the possession of a feeling, on the part of the employee, of being accepted and belonging to a group of employees through adherence to common goals and confidence in the desirability of these goals. It is really a collection of employee attitudes, feelings, and sentiments towards his employer or company, his job relationship and his supervisor. It is also described as 'an attitude of satisfaction with desire to continue in, and willing to strive for, the goals of a particular group or organisation'. It is a by-product of satisfactory group relationships. It is a mental process, often subtle, but once started it permeates in the entire group, creating a mood which results in the formation of a common attitude.

High morale makes for effective work and economical operation. It results from job satisfaction and generates job enthusiasm. A clear conviction is present among all the workers of the rightness of everything in the organisation—the leaders or executives, their aims and themselves—generating a moral force, so that all work for the common good. It is indeed a manifestation of their strength, dependability, pride, confidence and devotion. All these qualities of mind and character taken together are summed up in the term Morale. In any organisation worth the name, high morale is essential.

Low morale of the workers indicates the presence of mental unrest. This mental tension does not only hamper the production but also leads to ill health of the working men. Industrial accidents, labour turnover, strikes, 'gheraoes' and lock-outs are some of the obvious consequences of industrial tension. These industrial troubles lead to mental strain of the workers. The effects of such strain do not remain limited within the factory but also affect the workers' normal personal and social behaviour. In extreme cases it may lead individuals to frustration and increase the susceptibility to indulge in anti-social activities.

On the other hand, high morale is associated with less industrial troubles, few mandays lost, improvement of quality and quantity of production, less complaint of disobedience. High morale also contributes to the reduction of accidents, elimination of fatigue and provides an

---

1. Beishlinte, John Robert, *Military Management for National Defence* p.229.

opportunity to the workers for better adjustment in the work situation. Whether in a group morale is high or not can best be judged from the attitude of the individuals. *When, for instance, a group of workers regard its leaders as capable and considerate, their methods as efficient, their policy as fair, and their ultimate aims as something right and worthwhile-—something with a thrill—morale of high order is present.* Emphasis is upon the drive to do good work rather than job satisfaction or contentment. High morale is the hallmark of good human relations in an organisation; yet it cannot be bought or ordered into existence.

Need for Morale Study. Since morale is fundamentally the result of good human relations, its promotion is the primary responsibility of the management. It should be remembered, however, that the work of morale promotion is not a new development in industry; it is only much more necessary than in handicraft days. Even in those days, the worker had to be encouraged to give the best value to the master, by applying his knowledge and skill to the making of the article which the employer hoped to sell to pay wages and make his profit. But there is a vast difference in the attitudes then and now. At that time the worker knew for whom he made the article; why he was making it; how much the master would charge; how much the material cost; where it would come from; there was a full chance for him to show his workmanship; it was his product, and he was proud of it. It gave him complete satisfaction and a sense of pride. his morale was high. In the factory of today the worker produces only a fraction of an article. He sees neither the preceding nor the subsequent processes of manufacture. The product is not his; he does not know the consumer; and it is only by chance that he might see the product rendering its service in use. He does not know who the proprietors are, behind the mask of the company; and he is likely to know but few of the executives. He is seldom told what the company's policies are; and more seldom yet what its financial condition is, although his risk, in case of failure of the company, is much greater than that of the shareholders. For him the modern process turns chiefly upon two bearings—arbitrary authority and wages. There is hardly any interest in accomplishment and resultant satisfaction which should impel him to work with a will.

Man, by nature, is co-operative, but modern industry has contrived a situation in which friction is chronic. This may, in part, be ascribed to the fact that the existing industrial organisation has shattered the personal bond between workers and employers. "The incentive to work, that is, willingness of the worker to increase or even maintain output at lowest cost," says Professor Sargant Florence,[1] "is checked at the outset as soon as he finds himself divided off as a mere employee, from ownership of the products of his labour." As a general rule, it is true that more a mere employee loses personal contact with the ownership the more indifferent he will become to the efficiency of the industrial

1. *The Logic of British and American Industry*, p. 237.

organisation and the more he will stick to habits, customs and conventions. The employee's sense of fraternity and social equality with his employer and the sense of his own dignity and self-respect tend to be lost as the size of the firm enlarges; he identifies himself less and less with the interests of the firm. In a large firm, the feeling of 'being in the same boat' is lost, and the ordinary employee can no longer regard his non-interests in the business as identical with his employer's. The incentive of identification of oneself with the firm is absent. Red-tape and bureaucracy undermine *esprit de corps,* and low morale supervenes.

The process of depersonalisation is usually complete in an organisation employing 1,000 workers; and management's responsibility for the eradication of psychological interest or for the promotion of morale becomes fundamentally great. The Personnel Manager faces the problem of discovering factors which contribute towards a happy and successful organisation.

Major Morale Factors. Although morale consists of an infinite number of separate attitudes in each person, recent researches have brought out certain morale factors or ingredients. The management should study these by means of morale surveys, interview and observation in order to appraise the quality of a company's morale. Following are the significant morale factors or determinants.[1]

1. *Adequacy of immediate supervision.* The supervisor is important because he is the point of contact between the organisation and its employees and he has the largest influence upon their day-to-day activities. He is the pivot around which many things revolve. He is the leader and the workers must have confidence in him and in his leadership. A supervisor, who is fair, helpful, socially minded and capable, will create confidence in employees. He should have a natural interest in people and he must be emotionally well adjusted. By being fair and impartial, he can instil in the men values and standards which will be respected. By welcoming ideas and praising men for their efforts whenever possible, he can make his men feel that they are part of the organisation. His patience and tolerance can set an example and create an atmosphere which will encourage mutual respect for the rights of others. The position of a supervisor as a driver is a thing of the past. The modern supervisor should function as a democratic leader. In this capacity he becomes responsible to the men as well as to management. His attitude should be that he is representing his men to management, rather than that he is management's stooge. He should be worker-oriented rather than management-oriented. By being so he can cause men to do the job as a co-ordinated and co-operative project, and the management will benefit.

2. *Satisfaction with the job itself.* Most people find certain intrinsic satisfaction in having a job they like, doing it well, and feeling that it

1. Adapted from Keith Davis, *Human Relations at Work*, p. 78, and Maier, *Psychology in Industry*, pp. 85-89.

gives them opportunity to use their talents and grow personally. The supervisor should encourage his employees to be proud of their work, help them to see where they fit in the general scheme of things, what their part in the finished product is and what the final article itself is like.

3. *Compatibility with fellow employees.* Man is a social being. He finds work more satisfying when he feels he has the acceptance and companionship of fellow workers. He should have confidence in fellow workers and faith in their loyalty. Confidence in fellow workers or feeling of togetherness generates high morale. When men work in fairly close quarters, it is desirable that those who are congenial be placed side by side. Congeniality and group spirit should be encouraged. Friendships within a department are to be encouraged, so that all workers pull in the same direction.

4. *Satisfactory Organisational purpose and effectiveness as a system.* Employees want to be part of an organisation which has a worthwhile purpose in which they can believe, and they want their company to be reasonably efficient in meeting that common purpose. During the nation-building campaign, as at present in our country, an undertaking may have been entrusted with an important work of production. The manager may impress upon his workers the importance of meeting the national need, and once awake to the national need, the workers will play their part. They will produce the most they can or do their work in the quickest or best way possible.

The manager says, "we are all working towards one goal winning the war against poverty." He talks things over with his employees, he appreciates their efforts and refers to them with pride. He listens to all of their problems, even personal ones. His employees feel important and their work shows it. Their morale is high. They get the same sort of satisfaction which players have by being members of a winning team.

5. *Reasonable satisfaction with economic and related rewards.* As a compensation for helping their team towards its goals, employees expect adequate reward compared to the rewards of others in the company and, to a lesser degree, outside the company. The group spirit remains high if the joint efforts result in progress. Advancements and promotions always have a stimulating effect. Public recognition of efforts serves to raise morale.

6. *Tolerance and freedom.* In order to develop co-operation and group spirit, tolerance and freedom are essential. The work atmosphere plays an important part in developing these conditions. Where everyone is under pressure and the atmosphere is authoritarian rather than democratic, tolerance and co-operation are rarely found. Fault-finding and nagging over minor details are signs of intolerance and they restrict the free behaviour of others. Where, on the other hand, each worker is not only allowed but is actively encouraged to participate in achieving a common goal, morale is the highest. Every person should be made to feel that his efforts are important, for when a person feels indispensable, he is most likely to co-operate.

7. *General physical and mental health.* Physical and mental health make for high morale or low morale. Of-the-job factors influence work satisfaction. For instance, trouble at home or ill health will bring down morale. Similarly, general emotional tone of the individual will influence morale. For example, one man may be very much satisfied with his home and community life, but he thinks his job is average. In this case his job morale is relatively low because it is below his other satisfactions. Another man may be loaded with home and community dissatisfaction, but he also feels that his job is average. This means that his job morale is relatively high and that his "effective morale" is probably higher than that of the first man.

It will be seen that most of these factors imply group relationships. This means that morale is largely a social phenomenon and is subject to social influences. When social situations are not involved and we are dealing with an isolated individual, we speak of high motivation, persistence and self-confidence. People will tolerate deprivation and hardship if all are subjected to the same conditions.

Signs of High Morale. Following are the signs or criteria of high morale of a group :

1. A tendency for the group to hold together not merely as a result of external pressures but rather through internal cohesiveness.

2. A lack of tendencies of its members to divide into smaller antagonistic groups.

3. An ability of the group to adapt itself to changing circumstances and to handle internal conflicts.

4. A feeling of belongingness and togetherness among the members of the group.

5. A commonality of goals among the members of the group.

6. A positive attitude of the members with respect to the objectives of the group and to its leaders.

7. A desire on the part of the members to retain the group and a regard for its positive value.

Administrative Measures for Promotion of Morale and Provision of Incentives to work. We have seen earlier that organisations are people. They are the life blood of the organisation. The supervisor at each level should therefore give greater emphasis to the people with their complex feelings, emotions, needs, wants and demands than to work flow. He must possess knowledge of human nature which is "the totality of motives that cause human actions." Man's needs are many; but the significant ones may be classified as (1) basic physiological or *primary* needs, and (2) social and psychological needs, called *secondary* needs. Some of the physiological needs are hunger, thirst, sex, sleep, air to breathe, and satisfactory temperature. These needs arise out of the basic physiology of life and are important to survival and preservation of the species. They are therefore virtually universal among people.

Secondary needs are those of the mind and spirit, rather than the physical body. Many of these needs are developed as one matures. Examples are rivalry, self-esteem, sense of duty, self-assertion, giving, belonging, and receiving affection. The secondary needs are the ones which complicate the motivational efforts of managers. Nearly any action management takes will affect secondary needs. Therefore management should take into consideration the effect of proposed action on the secondary needs of employees.

Secondary needs are also called secondary motives, because they motivate a person towards certain behaviour. They provide a stimulus to action and we call them incentives to work. The incentives are either pecuniary or non-pecuniary. Man works because work provides an opportunity to make money with which he can buy what he wants. But in addition to pecuniary incentives, there are a dozen psychological or non-pecuniary incentives or factors which the employees expect to be taken into consideration by the management and on which he bases his value of the job.

We know that no one ever does anything without an incentive. People generally carry on as far as they think it worth while and then stop, unless a further incentive appears. Money or the hope of a reward is a powerful incentive, but it is by no means the only one. Pride of accomplishment, the hope of praise or promotion, the satisfaction of working under pleasant conditions, and many other non-pecuniary incentives are often more effective where money alone is not. In summary, it may be stated that a worker wants :

1. Fair wages and hours of work.
2. Absence from fear.
3. Security of tenure.
4. Recognition as an individual.
5. An opportunity to advance himself.
6. Competent supervision (Leadership).
7. Justice or square deal.
8. Individual worthwhileness—status.
9. To know and understand—communication.
10. Getting the job done (creative impulse).
11. Pride of product, job and company.
12. A voice in the matters of mutual interest—joint consultation.

All these wants are related to morale and their fulfilment promotes morale. It is imperative for the management to take various administrative measures towards the achievements of these goals by the workers in the interest of high morale and harmony in the organisation.

The following **administrative measures** in relation to aforementioned wants are conducive to the promotion of morale and harmony :

1. *Good wages and short hours.* The desire for high wages and short hours is so strong that workers have a keen and rather precise feeling about what is a "fair day's work". The employee of today expects to be paid a just wage which will be sufficient to provide for his family a reasonable level of subsistence, including entertainment and a modicum of savings. A wage structure based upon sound incentive schemes coupled with bonus earnings is conducive to high morale. Good wages

are also an important contribution to a happy factory where harmony reigns.[1]

2. *Counselling and guidance to eliminate fear.* The oldest and the most universal incentive is fear. A threat will temporarily make a person work harder. Fear has in the past played a very large part in industry. It is true that under the influene of fear workmen work vigorously but not enthusiastically. It induces antagonism and is the basis of "enmity complex." Effort induced by fear lasts as long as the threat of punishment or dismissal lasts, but it tends to pass into resentment, resentment into revenge and revenge into agitation. Human fear is contagious. It engenders trouble and is the enemy of morale. The management should take steps to replace it with guidance and counselling which will raise the morale of the workers and they will perform task because they want to.

3. *Security.* One of the most important desires of an employee is to feel secure in his job. He wants to be sure that at the end of each month he will have a certain income, so that he can build his future around it and establish his home. It is for this reason that many employees prefer a steady job with regular income to intermittent earnings of high wages for a shorter period. The management should therefore follow a personnel policy which will assure perfect security of income and tenure to capable workers. Only then the morale of workers will be high.

---

1. It is, however, important to remember that money is not the only incentive for work although some employers still believe it to be so. According to them 'money incentive' is either positive, *i.e.*, pecuniary reward in the form of wages for the work done, or negative, *i.e.*, deductions in the form of penalties for failure to do work. The negative of penal incentive has been brought under control by legislation: *e.g.* the Payment of Wages Act, 1936, prohibits arbitrary reductions in the form of fines, etc. The positive financial incentive implies that human behaviour is simple and predictable in relationship such as "more money, more output", whereas no such simple relationship exists.Pay is merely one of a dozen factors of motivation. True, money acts as a very potent incentive but that is so because industry has "monetised" human motives and satisfaction. No one, except a Midas, wants money as such. People want it as a means to the satisfaction of their real wants—transpecuniary incentive. Money is a means and not an end. Therefore, when employers grumble about demands for higher wages, they forget that they are themselves responsible for such demands. They follow a contradictory policy. Because they wish to sell their goods, they are always trying to teach people to take their satisfaction in monetised form. This naturally evokes a demand for higher wages, which they then resist. People have been taught that money is the key to satisfaction, so that when they feel that something is wrong with their lives, they naturally ask for more money. But, unfortunately, while a demand for money indicates that they want something, it does not tell us what. Therefore, when an employer says: "All the men want is money, and if I prove that piece rates or time-rate will give them money, they should be satisfied," he is acting irrationally. He is trying to attribute behaviour to any single factor, whereas people constantly weigh up all the factors in their situation before deciding how they will act. Therefore, it is something more than a cash consideration which affects a person's output of energy

4. *Recognition.* A worker desires that his achievements should be recognised. The desire to possess, which every one has, is often changed in industry into desire for recognition. Thus a machine-tender thinks of *his* machine, an office worker of *his* desk, and so on. In many cases merely placing a nameplate on a machine or desk will greatly improve employer-employee relations. It is a big morale-booster. Another aspect of this same thing is the desire of the average employee to be recognised by the "big boss". A mere word from him will suffice.

5. *Sound promotion policy.* Everybody wants an opportunity to advance himself. Most employees are stimulated to work enthusiastically when they know that they will get an opportunity to grow in responsibility through adequate promotion. Their morale will be impaired if their chance of promotion is arbitrarily blocked. The awareness of the opportunities for advancement available in the concern increases the morale of the work people.

6. *Competent supervision—Leadership.* The desire for competent supervision has a two-fold aspect. There is first the well-recognised desire to have somebody to depend upon for decisions and advice, whose judgement is respected. Usually he is respected because of his competence and knowledge, but he may qualify also because of the example that he sets. The executive should exhibit a sense of respect for the employees, and take interest in their individual problems. A friendly word from him to the workers will improve the worker-employer relationships throughout the organisation. The leader should identify himself with the rank and file for high morale.

7. *Justice or square deal.* The modern worker demands justice and a fair deal. The management must work for mutual trust and respect. It must consider much more than the mere immediate search for profits at any price. For harmony the management should recognise the utility of a more tolerant attitude to alleged breaches of regulations or refusal to work according to instructions. Justice tempered with mercy heightens morale.

8. *Status.* Perhaps the thing that everybody desires most passionately is an individual sense of worthwhileness. Recognition of his expectation can be a valuable factor in morale. The more important an employee can be made to feel, the better work he is likely to do. The management should therefore follow a policy whereby every worker in the organisation enjoys a status according to his position and skill.

9. *Communication.* One of the characteristics of man is curiosity. He wants to know not only *what* but also *why* and *how*. Therefore, the communication of information by the management is one of the best ways of improving morale. Being "in the know" promotes co-operation both because it gives the employee an understanding of what is going on, and because it encourages a sense of participation. Hence, the workers should be kept well informed. Bulletins containing up-to-date information regarding the working of the unit may be issued at regular intervals.

10. *Encouraging creative impulse.* The creative impulse in man is

very strong. The creative impulse is often expressed in one's work. This impulse carries with it also an idea of perfection. The management, that wishes to have loyal, well satisfied employees with high morale, must create conditions in which his workers are able to show their ingenuity.

One of the ways to achieve this end is to organise exhibitions of products made by the workers. Another method is the introduction of suggestion schemes. The Workers' suggestions should be invited and they should be suitably rewarded for every suggestion accepted. This gives the workers a sense of participation and generates morale.

11. *Pride of job, product and company.* Fostering pride in the job is one of the most useful means of creating high morale, especially if it is backed up by the full information of a company's policy, plans, progress and problems. An employee likes to feel that the product he is producing is useful and the firm for which he works is a good one. It is the duty of the management to instil his pride by following a policy of reality and truth. One of the important results of this policy is that the worker will have a positive attitude towards his work and the company. He will avoid wasting material, switch off the light and fan when going out, return to the stores nails, screws and other small items at the completion of the job. Little things of this kind can mount up and make a useful contribution to the profits of the company. The larger consequences will be higher morale and productivity.

12. *Joint Consultation.* A voice in matters of mutual interest is what workers today desire. The wise executive is ready to listen and act. In this way he takes a positive step towards the workers' participation in management.

Before concluding the subject of morale, it may be pointed out that all the afore-mentioned administrative measures are conducive to the promotion of morale and cannot be expected to build it up in a day. Nor is morale something which can be bought or ordered, or even persuaded into existence. It can be created only by introducing into the work situation the conditions stated above which are favourable to its development.

MORALE AND PRODUCTIVITY

It is sometimes believed that high morale and high productivity always go together. Some managers think that as long as the morale of the workers is high, the output automatically would be high. Recent researches reveal that, although there is some correlation between morale and productivity, yet they are not absolutely related. That is, an increase of 10 per cent in morale does not guarantee a proportionate increase in productivity. There is a possibility of high morale and low productivity, low productivity and low morale, high morale and high productivity and so on. This indicates the lack of any clear-cut relationship. It should, however, be remembered that no research has shown that there is no relationship between the two so that morale can be ignored.

But regardless of whether or not there is a correlation between high morale and high productivity, it is the supervisor's function to try to maintain a high level of morale in his work group for other reasons. As we have already observed, a high level of morale makes work pleasant for all the members of the organisation and is conducive to cooperation towards the achievement of the enterprise objectives. The supervisor who works towards effective human relations through positive integration of goals so that people work together productively, cooperatively and with satisfaction will achieve the desirable high morale and high productivity. Productivity at the expense of morale may be efficient in a technical sense, but if it is not effective in a human sense, there is no "job enthusiasm". It is important, therefore, that the supervisor should possess the leadership qualities. He should have the ability to inspire confidence in his judgment and trust in his decisions. He must win the loyalty of his subordinates. To do these things he must know his own job and objectives. He must also make those objectives clear to employees so that they will be with him to reach them. Finally, since his main task is to get things done through people power, he has to make the fact that people actually like working at jobs that interest them pay off in productivity. Job enthusiasm and high morale can go together.

CHAPTER XXXII

INDUSTRIAL RELATIONS

The most human of all human relations in management is the problem of industrial relations.

Meaning of Industrial Relations

Industrial relations is the most broadly inclusive term. It describes relationship between management and individual employee, and in that light it is sometimes called "employer-employee" relations, or "personnel relations". It also embraces relationship between management and trade unions, and is named as "Labour Relations". In fact, the term Industrial Relations is used to refer to all types of relationships between all the parties concerned with industrial enterprises.

An industrial organisation is a social system made up of independent parts; the parts are the relations of people at all levels of the organisation to each other. Throughout history, cooperative effort has been the Key to human programmes. This has created some problems to be resolved. These may be said to be (i) the problem of discipline, (ii) the problem of industrial unrest, (iii) the problem of getting cooperation with trade unions, and (iv) the problem of establishing a state of democracy in industry by associating workers with the management of industry. These problems are discussed in the same order in the following pages :

INDUSTRIAL DISCIPLINE

Discipline refers to a condition in an enterprise in which there is orderliness and in which the members of the enterprise conduct themselves within the standard of the acceptable behaviour as expressed by the needs of the organisation. Discipline is said to be good when the members of the organisation willingly conduct themselves within the standards of acceptable behaviour and willingly follow the rules and regulations of the enterprise. Discipline is said to be bad when subordinates either do this reluctantly and unwillingly or actually disobey regulations and the standards of acceptable behaviour as promulgated by the needs of the enterprise.*

Although discipline is not the same as morale, yet the level of morale influences discipline. There are fewer problems of discipline whenever the morale is high. Low morale means many problems of discipline. Morale and discipline usually go together.

Types of Discipline. There are three types of discipline :

(1) The discipline associated with rigid control on the army pattern.

---

* Haimann, *Professional Management*, p.458

(2) The discipline which guides and instructs.

(3) The self imposed discipline.

The military type of discipline is neither necessary nor acceptable in industry. Rigid control creates the automaton and the automaton is not a lively thinker, neither is he likely to contribute anything more than is demanded of him. A good soldier is one who obeys orders unquestioningly. It may be necessary for a factory worker to obey orders without question from time to time, but to obey an order blindly whether it be wise or unwise is not the hall mark of good worker. Discipline obtained by fear is not a successful way of conducting affairs. Rules are necessary in any organisation, because they guide and instruct. They are important in helping to maintain discipline by establishing confidence, a sense of direction and orderliness. Most indiscipline can be traced to lack of confidence, insecurity, and the accompanying sense of grievance. Discipline, above all things should be instructive.

The following elementary principles of justice are conducive to the maintenance of discipline :

1. Discipline means securing normally consistent behaviour in accordance with accepted rules. Therefore, rules should be easily understood, and acceptable to those who have to keep them. For this reason the code of discipline must be decided in consultation with those who are to be under its jurisdiction or concerned in its application.

2. Penalties for non-observance should be imposed without personal prejudice and in such a way that will ultimately benefit the transgressor.

3. Arbitrary personal decisions are never a solution to a disciplinary problem and should always be discountenanced. A man has a right to be judged dispassionately. There should, therefore, be a right of appeal to a completely independent tribunal. This is fundamental justice.

The self-imposed discipline is the highest form of discipline and should be encouraged and desired. In it all are regulated (i.e. self-regulated). and are free. It is the result of inspired leadership, a leadership of example. It flourishes where there is a lively concern for justice and fair play and all those things which satisfy deep human needs. Discipline is fundamentally a matter of good human relations, the encouragement of self-respect, pride in one's work, the dignity of work and an unfailing sense of responsibility.

To sum up, the modern conception of discipline is not the discipline of fear and threats, or even authority, but self-discipline imposed by good leaders, by example. True discipline is educational. The intelligent approach to the matter is a conscious attempt to change the attitude of people towards the giving of an instruction.

Code of Discipline in Indian Industries. During 1956–57, an alarming number of cases of violence and intimidation, strikes and lockouts were recorded. There were numerous instances of gross breaches of discipline both by the workers and employers. To put a stop to such activities a Tripartite Sub-Committee of the Labour Conference was appointed in 1957 to draw up a code of discipline. The Code was ratified in March, 1958 by central organisations of employers and workers.

The Code binds the parties to settle all future disputes by mutual negotiations, consultation and volun ary arbitration. The parties are also required to encourage the growth of healthy trade unions and eliminate all forms of coercion, intimidation and violence in industrial relations.

The more important clauses of the Code are as follows :

(a) The Code prohibits strikes and lockouts without prior notice and recourse to coercion, intimidation, victimisation and the use of 'go-slow' methods by workers.

(b) No unilateral action can be taken by either party, and all industrial disputes must be settled through the machinery provided for the purpose.

(c) A common grievance procedure is to be established on a mutually agreed basis to ensure speedy and full investigation leading to a settlement.

(d) The employer must take prompt action for redress of grievances and implementation of settlements and awards.

(e) The employers will not increase the workloads without prior agreement with workers.

(f) The employers must discourage the use of unfair practices like victimisation of members of recognised trade unions, and encourage the healthy growth of trade unions.

(g) Prompt and appropriate actions should be taken by the management against any officers who are responsible to provoke workers to act in an indisciplined manner.

(h) The workers will not indulge in any trade union activity during working hours, nor will they engage in any activity or demonstration which is not peaceful.

(i) The unions will discourage unfair labour practices such as negligence of duty, careless operation, damage to property, disturbance of normal work and insubordination.

(j) The trade unions will implement promptly awards and settlements and take appropriate action against office-bearers and members indulging in actions in violation of the Code.

The Code had a sobering effect on industrial relations for some time, but breaches have been noticed from time to time.

Grievance Procedure. A well defined grievance procedure is an important element of a sound industrial relations machinery. Prompt and effective disposal of workers' grievances is the key to industrial peace. The grievance procedure set up by agreement with a union provides a medium for the worker to transmit his grievance to management in an orderly manner and get his answer in writing.

Broadly, grievance machinery in Indian industry is in an elementary stage; a formal grievance procedure is rather uncommon. But the Draft

Model Grievance Procedure, accepted by the Labour Conference, is as follows :

An aggrieved employee shall first present his grievance verbally in person to the officer designated by the management for this purpose. An answer shall be given within 48 hours. If he is dissatisfied with the answer, the worker will present his grievance to the Head of the Department, who will give his answer within 3 days. If the answer does not satisfy the worker, he may ask that his grievance should be referred to the Grievance Committee, which shall make its recommendation within 7 days to the manager. Unanimous recommendations of this Committee must be implemented by the management. A dissatisfied worker can apply to the management for a revision of its decision.

The Grievance Committee shall consist of 4 to 6 members and shall be constituted as follows :

1. Where the union is recognised, two representatives of management *plus* a union representative and the union departmental representative of the department in which the workman concerned works.

2. Where the union is not recognised or there is no union but there is Works Committee, two representatives of management *plus* the representative of the department of the workman concerned on the Works Committee *plus* either the secretary or vice-president of the Works Committee.

It is suggested that in the case of the management, their representatives should be the Departmental Head *plus* the official who dealt with the matter at the first stage, or the Personnel Officer should act as the adviser.

INDUSTRIAL UNREST

The proper study of management is man, the satisfaction of human wants being the principal aim of all economic enterprise. Whenever this is ignored industrial relations tend to be strained, ending up in industrial unrest or strife. Two categories of causes of industrial unrest are : (1) tangible causes, (2) intangible causes.

Intangible causes are closely connected with the study of human nature. Man seeks to satisfy his wants but the path that he follows in his search for satisfaction is a complex one, governed by reason, emotion and instinct. Very often the path may appear to be irrational and illogical to the outsider, but to the person himself it is perfectly rational and logical. Different people have different attitudes towards the same fact. Therefore, when dealing with human behaviour management must recognise that it is sentiments that are being dealt with.

Tangible Causes of Industrial Disputes. The possible causes of industrial disputes may be—

1. Demand for increase in Wages;
2. Demand for reduction in hours of work;
3. Demand for increase in over-time allowance;

4. Demand for payment of bonus:
5. Demand for re-instatement of any dismissed workers;
6. Demand for greater facilities in leave rules;
7. Demand for representation of labour on management;
8. Demand for recognition of a Trade Union;
9. Desire of the workers to share in the profits of industry;
10. Sympathy for strikers in other concerns or industries; and
11. Political causes leading to general agitation.

Soon after the end of World War II, there was an outburst of phenomenal unrest in the industrial sphere. Then following the partition of the country there was general turmoil and dislocation. Indian labour was in revolt. All over the country, discontent on the part of workers resulted in outbursts in the form of strikes. The country was deprived of goods which were already in short supply. This resulted in tremendous loss of mandays and national wealth. The situation continued to be serious in spite of a number of measures adopted. Only the declaration of emergency in June, 1975 put a stop to strikes and lockouts.

The following tables gives an idea of industrial unrest from 1946 to 1974.

Number of disputes, number of workers involved and number of mandays lost

Year	*No. of disputes*	*No. of workers involved*	*No. of mandays lost ('000)*	*Year*	*No. of disputes*	*No. of workers involved ('000)*	*No. of mandays lost ('000)*
1	2	3	4	1	2	3	4
1946	1,629	1.926	12.718	1961	1,357	512	1.919
1947	1,811	1,841	16.563	1962	1,491	705	6,121
1948	1,259	1,069	7,837	1963	1,471	563	3,269
1949	920	685	6.601	1964	2,151	1,003	7 725
1950	814	720	12.807	1965	1,835	991	6.470
1951	1,071	691	3.819	1966	2.556	1,410	13 846
1952	963	809	3.337	1967	2.815	1,490	17.148
1953	772	467	3,383	1968	2.776	1,669	17.244
1954	840	477	3.373	1969	2.627	1.827	19.048
1955	1.166	528	5,698	1970	2.889	1.828	20,563
1956	1.203	715	6,992	1971	2.752	1.615	16,546
1957	1.6[illegible]	889	6,429	1972	3.243	1.737	20,544
1958	1.524	929	7,798	1973	3.370	2.546	20.626
1959	1.431	694	5.633	1974	2,938	2,855	40.262
1960	1.583	986	6.537				

The figures in the table above and the table on next page include both strikes and lock-outs and include industrial disputes in all types of concerns—industrial, commercial, public and private.

With the declaration of emergency in June, 1975, the number of disputes and loss of mandays fell considerably. The lowest loss of

Percentage Distribution of Industrial Disputes

Cause	1965	1966	1967	1968	1969	1970	1971	1972	1973	1974
Wages and Allowances	33.5	35.8	39.9	38.4	36.0	37.1	34.3	31.8	34.1	36.1
Bonus	9.9	13.2	10.9	9.4	10.0	10.6	14.1	8.4	10.3	6.2
Personnel and Retrenchment	27.3	25.3	23.6	28.2	26.6	25.6	23.0	24.2	24.3	26.5
Leave and Hours of Work	2.5	2.4	1.0	1.9	2.2	2.1	1.4	1.4	1.5	1.6
Indiscipline and violence	—	—	—	3.2	3.8	3.8	3.6	5.1	5.7	6.2
Others	26.8	23.3	24.6	18.9	21.4	20.8	23.6	29.1	24.1	23.4
Total No. of Cases	1,825	2,536	2,760	2,717	2,609	2,843	2,723	3,153	3,296	2,863

mandays was in 1976, it being 12.8 million. With the lifting of the emergency in 1977 and the change of Government, the situation again became grave. In 1977, there were 3,117 strikes and lock-outs, involving 2.19 million workers and resulting in 25.3 million mandays lost. In 1978, there was a slight improvement. There were 2,728 strikes and lock-outs involving 1.47 million workers and resulting in a loss of 21.5 million mandays.

Position in the Post-emergency Period

Year	*No. of Disputes*	*No. of workers involved*	*No. of Mandays lost ('000)*	*Year*	*No. of Disputes*	*No. of workers involved*	*No. of Mandays lost ('000)*
1	2	3	4	1	2	3	4
1976	1459	736	12746	1982	2421	N.A.	33200
1977	3117	2193	25320	1983	1696	N.A.	21600
1978	3185	1916	28300	1984	2094	1949	56025
1979	3048	2873	43900	1986	1892	1545	32748
1980	2856	1900	21900	1987	1199	1250	30617
1981	3589	1588	36600				

Percentage Distribution of Disputes by Causes (Post-emergency period)

Cause	1976	1977	1980	1982	1985	1987
Wages and Allowances	23.4	31.2	28.4	27.3	22.5	26.1
Personnel and Retrenchment	29.9	23.0	24.3	24.4	23.1	15.4
Bonus	13.8	15.2	7.3	4.7	7.3	4.2
Leave and Hours of Work	2.3	2.2	2.2	1.9	1.8	0.2
Indiscipline and violence	9.9	8.8	8.9	12.0	16.1	15.7
Others	20.1	19.5	28.9	29.7	29.2	30.7

Machinery for Settling Disputes

Disputes can be settled either by voluntary agreement between the employers and employees or by means of adjudication under the provisions of a statute. Collective bargaining (Voluntary agreement) to be effective presupposes :—

(a) Strong trade union at the industry level or plant level;
(b) Recognition of such union by the employer for the purposes of bargaining;
(c) Readiness of the employer to meet the representatives of the union and discuss in good faith the problems or issues under consideration.

While collective bargaining on voluntary basis is most desirable, in majority of industries the unions are rather weak, and the management is not keen to open negotiations with the union. Therefore, it is imperative that some machinery should be created under the enabling provisions of law. The National Commission on Labour observed that "although a beginning has to be made in the move towards collective bargaining, the process has to be gradual".

Statutory provision for the settlement of disputes has been made in the form of the Industrial Disputes Act, 1947.

Works Committee. An industrial establishment employing 100 or more workers may be required to constitute a Works Committee consisting of an equal number of representatives of workmen and employer. The Committee is required to promote measures for securing and preserving amity and good relations between the employer and the workmen.

Conciliation Officer and Boards. The Conciliation Officer or the Conciliation Board is required to take appropriate steps to bring the parties together and help them settle their dispute amicably. But if no settlement is reached, the appropriate Government may refer the dispute to a Labour Court or an Industrial Tribunal for adjudication.

Labour Courts and Industrial Tribunals. The Labour Court or the Industrial Tribunal will consist of an independent person who is or has been a Judge of a High Court. It makes an award after hearing the parties to the dispute, and the award is binding on them.

The Labour Courts can adjudicate on a dispute relating to —

(a) the propriety or legality of an order passed by an employer under standing orders;
(b) the application and interpretation of standing orders;
(c) discharge or dismissal of workmen including re-instatement of, or grant of relief to workmen wrongfully dismissed;
(d) withdrawal of any customary concession or privilege;
(e) illegality or otherwise of a strike or lockout; and
(f) all matters other than those reserved for the Industrial Tribunal

Industrial Tribunals may adjudicate industrial disputes relating to any matters specified above as in the case of Labour Courts, or the following matters :—

(a) Wages, including the period and mode of payment;
(b) Compensatory and other allowances;
(c) Hours of work and rest intervals;
(d) Leave with Wages and holidays;
(e) Bonus, profit sharing, provident fund and gratuity;
(f) Shift working otherwise than in accordance with standing orders;
(g) Classification by grades;
(h) Rules of discipline;
(i) Rationalisation;
(j) Retrenchment of workmen and closure of establishment; and
(k) Any other matter that may be prescribed.

National Tribunal. The Central Government may appoint a National Tribunal where it is of opinion that an industrial dispute involves questions of national interest and importance or is of such a nature that establishments situated in more than one State are likely to be interested in, or affected by, such a dispute. The National Tribunal shall consist of an independent person who is or has been a judge of a High Court.

Arbitration. An industrial dispute can also be referred to an arbitrator appointed by the parties to the dispute. The arbitration award is binding upon the parties who referred the dispute to arbitration.

The Act prohibits strikes and lock outs during the pendency of conciliation and adjudication. Legislation alone is not enough to bring about the real harmony between management and workers. Joint consultation must take the place of autocratic conception of ownership. Day-to-day contact between labour and management provides an excellent opportunity to reconcile minor difficulties, so that they do not grow into disputes. Labour and management must meet half-way and steer a middle course. A very effective way of reviving "buoyancy" among workers is to provide non-monetary incentives in the form of welfare work.

Welfare Work

Welfare work in its accepted parlance means voluntary effort of employers to improve the conditions of their employees. It is this activity that puts the human factor in its true light. The most valuable possessions of a workman are his health, strength, and intelligence. The prolongation of working life and prevention of disease are problems which affect every employer. It is both in the interest of the employer himself and the workers that welfare activities are carried out by the employers. Because some employers do not follow the example of their enlightened brethren, the State provides for minimum requirements with respect to health and safety and makes special provision for specific welfare activities such as washing facilities, first-aid appliances, canteens, rest rooms, creches, etc.

Medical Aid. The incidence of illness among industrial workers is great resulting in loss of working time. Medical advice and medical aid are major welfare works for ensuring loyalty on the part of the workers. The medical aid, however, should not end in the factory, but should extend to the workers' home. The efficiency of a workman may be quite as much reduced by wrong conditions in the home as in the factory. A number of large factories in the country now provide medical aid and facilities, and some of them have even employed nurses and health visitors.

Accidents and their Prevention. Accidents are not only expensive but they also lower the morale of the workers and in addition result in lower production rates. Companies with good safety records have more satisfied workers than the companies with high accident severity and frequency. There is an interaction here. Just as accidents lower morale, poor morale appears to be a cause of accidents.

The rate of accidents among industrial workers has been rather high. The union Labour Minister, while speaking at the Sixth National Conference on Industrial Safety, pointed out that the rate of accidents per 1,000 workers in the country continued to increase till 1971 when it attained the peak figure of 75.67 compared to 51.33 in 1966. However, this rate started declining from 1972 right upto 1975 when the provisional figure came to 45.19.

While it was natural for the causes of accidents and the nature of hazards to differ from industry to industry, the common ones are carelessness, ignorance, dearth of experience, inadequate skill, improper handling of heavy weights and the effects of fatigue. The dangerous ages are 17 to 23 and over 50. Single men are more often injured than married men, and unskilled more often than skilled. The Minister underlined the need for legislative action to prevent industrial accidents. In the meantime, it is necessary to raise the level of safety consciousness "to that of an instinct or protective reflex". The National Safety Council should expand its network of activities.

Legal and Financial Aid. Arrangements for help to employees in legal and financial difficulties should be made to save them from harassment and complete upset. To maintain high morale and to save the worker from compulsory absence from works it is well worth a few rupees which it will cost the company for the matter to be dealt with by the company's legal adviser or some one specially instructed to act on his behalf.

The problem of lending money to employees is a difficult one and at the same time one which requires to be tackled with a good deal of flexibility. A worker can seldom put away anything out of his wages for a rainy day. When an emergency arises, the problem of finding a large sum of money is also one of great difficulty. Going to the money-lender may sometimes solve the problem but the cost is very high. The rate of interest is usually so high that the borrower is seldom able to pay back the principal. To save him from the clutches of the money lender the employer should make arrangements to lend to his employees money in times of need.

In addition to these matters, the personnel officer should give practical guidance and help on such matters as—

Facilities for transport to and from works. Facilities for education outside working hours through local adult education centres. evening classes, and lectures arranged by the firm.

Recreational and social facilities where there is a spontaneous demand.

Help to employees and their families in case of hardship. This can best be done by setting up mutual aid clubs

Industrial Housing. About housing conditions in India, the less said the better. Nearly all industrial concerns provided housing for certain portion of their workers. Although conditions are bound to differ according to different places, in general the tenements are hardly better, than hovels. The 'cheris' of Madras, 'Chawls' of Bombay, 'bastis' of Calcutta and 'ahatas' of Kanpur with single rooms measuring 10 × 10, housing a family with ten or more members, are a blot on civilization; and which, in the words of the late Prime Minister, Jawaharlal Nehru, should be burnt down. A good housing programme and living conditions will draw a better class of workers and make them contented and stable in their relation to the management.

The Government of India introduced in 1950 an industrial housing scheme. Under the Five-Year Plans provisions have been made for housing, and good progress has been made in this direction. In the private sector, too, there has been an increasing amount of construction. Yet much more remains to be done so far as industrial housing is concerned.

WORKERS' PARTICIPATION IN MANAGEMENT

Workers' participation in management is an important part of human relations because it offers an enormous potential for higher productivity, improved satisfaction, and creative thinking. What is Participation ? Keith Davis defines participation * as a "mental and emotional involvement of a person in a group situation which encourages him to contribute to group goals and share responsibility in them". This definition contains three ideas of importance to managers. *First*, participation means mental and emotional involvement, rather than mere muscular activity. A person's *self* is involved rather than his body. It is psychological rather than physical. Merely holding meetings, asking opinions, but doing only what the manager wants to do as an autocrat is not participation.

The second idea in participation is that it motivates persons to contribute to the situation. They are given an opportunity to exercise

* *Human Relations at Work*, p.427

initiative and make creative suggestions towards the achievement of common objectives. In this way participation differs from mere consent. The consenters do not contribute ideas; they merely approve the ideas brought by the manager to the group. Therefore, participation is more than getting consent for something already decided. It is a *two-way* psychological and social relationship among people, rather than a procedure for imposing ideas from above.

A third idea in participation is that it encourages people to accept responsibility in an activity. Because they are self-involved in an organisation, they want to see it work successfully. Participation helps them become responsible employee members of the group, rather than mere hands to do a job as told to do. It is not only their 'handpower', that is involved, but also their 'mindpower'. They are ready to work with the manager, instead of against him.

Scope of Participation. Workers' participation in management is used here in a restricted sense. It is confined to sharing information with the employees, consulting them in all matters which directly or immediately affect them and share administrative and executive powers and authority with the employees' representatives in certain non-critical areas like welfare, safety, training etc. It does not extend to matters which are subject to collective bargaining, such as wages, hours of work, bonus and so on.

Pre-requisites for Effective Participation. As in the organisational domain formal delegation of authority is essential so is *social delegation* necessary in the human relations domain. A participative manager does not hesitate to make both formal as well as social delegation. To him participation is not just a theory; he regards it an essential practice for achieving co-operation. For participation to succeed, however, certain conditions must be met. Keith Davis outlines these conditions as follows :

1. There must be time to participate before action is required. Participation is hardly appropriate in emergencies.

2. The financial cost of participation should not exceed the values, economic and otherwise, that come from it. Employees should not spend their full workday participating, to the exclusion of all other work.

3. The subject of participation must be relevant to the participant's organisation or something in which he is interested.

4. The participant should have the ability, such as intelligence and knowledge, to participate.

5. The participants must be able mutually to communicate in order to be able to exchange ideas.

6. Neither the management nor the workers should feel that their position is threatened by participation. For example, if a worker thinks his status will be adversely affected, he will not participate. If a manager feels that his authority is threatened, he will refuse participation.

7. Participation for deciding a course of action in an organisation should take place only within the group's area of job freedom, subject

only to a restriction for maintaining internal stability and subject to the overall policy of the unit.

Advantages of Participation. The principal advantages of participation are as follows :

General benefits—

1. It enourages better decisions.
2. It uses the creativity of all employees.
3. It restores a measure of human dignity, motivation, and mutual interest.
4. It encourages people to accept responsibility.
5. It improves morale and teamwork.
6. It encourages acceptance of change.

As a result of the foregoing general benefits, the following more specific production and economic benefits tend to occur :

Specific benefits—

1. Higher rate of output.
2. Improved quality of product.
3. Fewer grievances and conflicts because of mutual understanding.
4. Reduced turnover, absenteeism and tardiness.
5. Increased income for distribution to those involved in the enterprise.

Methods of Encouraging Employee Participation in Management. A number of plans to employee participation in management have been tried in recent years for getting teamwork in organisations. Before dealing with some of the more important methods of worker's participation, it is important to point out that no one plan is self-sufficient and all-inclusive. Better practice would be to use a workable combination of several plans according to situations with a view to integrating the worker into the whole industrial process.

Suggestions Scheme. One of the ways of encouraging worker-interest is the introduction of "suggestion scheme". Very often, in the daily performance of their task, workers get bright ideas about the way in which things would or could be done. Those ideas are often good ones and if there is an opportunity for putting them forward, valuable improvements may result. But even more important is the emotional influence on the employees themselves; to them the scheme means first and foremost that the company is aware of them and interested in their contribution. The usual way of conducting the scheme is through "Suggestion Boxes," installed in each department, with public announcement of awards for ideas which are original and which are usable or adopted. The scheme has been tried in India and abroad with remarkable success.

The suggestions scheme is usually supervised by a committee comprising 5 or 6 people who represent different parts of the organisation and competent to assess the ideas put forward and thus capable of recommending the award. For a scheme to succeed, the machinery must function promptly; for, ideas will be killed if months elapse between their submission and consideration. A badly run scheme will damage morale.

Joint Consultation. Joint consultation is one of the important schemes by which management endeavours to bring its employees into responsible and full participation in the activities and purposes of the enterprise. Joint committees consisting of the representatives of management and employees have been tried successfully for the mutual discussion of difficulties and problems. The function of such committees is usually advisory and consultative, although the advice is more often than not accepted being the outcome of the deliberations between the representatives of management and labour. As these committees are the means of exchanging views and information, and of promoting communications among the various sections or layers of the organisation, they do not deal with subjects like the wages, bonus, piece rates, hours of work, which are left to collective bargaining. The usual matters discussed by these committees include accident prevention, safety, first-aid, management of canteens and other matters relating to welfare, such as meals, drinking water, issue and revision of work rules, avoidance and elimination of waste of time and materials, absenteeism, and lateness, problems of discipline, training of apprentices, improvement in the production set-up, grievances and their removal, adjustment of national and festival holidays, administration of welfare and fine funds and so on. These committees are of the nature of "Whitley Councils" set up in Britain after World War I which discussed all sorts of questions.

Conditions for success. Since a joint committee is intended to 'weld the management and employees into a team', it bridges different functions and interests or aims. Therefore, for any scheme of joint consultation to succeed, it is essential that—

1. It should be worked with honesty of purpose, bearing in mind the sincerity behind the words "joint consultation."
2. The deliberations, even of roundtable pattern, must be free and frank, each person whether representing the management or the employees must be genuine and sincere.
3. The workers should not put forward ridiculous and extravagant demands, and the management should not make lame excuses for not meeting or for explaining away alleged deficiencies.
4. The management should try to win the confidence of the workers. For, where 'good intentions' are only superficial, a few meetings will do more harm than good. Time will be wasted, tempers will be frayed, frustration will be built up and suspicion will be created which may take many years to eradicate.
5. Functionally, joint committees should be recommendatory.
6. The decisions of the consultative committees should be widely publicised, perferably through supervisory staff.
7. The subject of joint consultation should not encroach upon the sphere of collective bargaining.

8. The workers' representatives on the joint committees should be employees of the concern and not outsiders.

9. Supervisory staff may, wherever possible, be associated with consultative committees.

Consultative Supervision. This team describes a manager's general efforts to develop informal participation, with minor emphasis on formal joint committees and procedures. Consultative supervision means that the manager consults with his employees on key problems which affect them, in order to get them to think about those problems and contribute their own ideas *before he makes decision.* The manager should be genuinely receptive to ideas of his men so that they perceive that their ideas are useful. He must have the humility to admit that he does not know more than all his men together and that his ideas are not always best.

Democratic Supervision. Democratic supervision moves more towards group decision making. In some cases the supervisor "delegates" decision-making authority to his group so completely that he does not proceed until group decision is reached on matters referred to it. If the group does not decide, this is the supervisor's cue that no action should be taken. Although he theoretically retains ultimate authority, in practice he shares it with his group. The difference between consultative supervision and democratic supervision lies in the fact that in the former the leader brings problems to his group so that their advice and decision will affect *his decision,* but in the latter the leader brings problems to the group for *their decision,* usually under his guidance. In both cases, he is the decision-leader, rather than the sole decision maker.

Multiple Management. Multiple management is a participative practice primarily for junior executives.[1] It uses formal advisory committees of junior executives for the purpose of creating ideas, screening ideas from committee members or other sources, giving junior executives more participation, developing their executive ability, and broadening their experience. Multiple management has been used successfully around the world in hundreds of companies. Its central core is a junior Board of Directors which is given the opportunity to study any problem and to recommend courses of action. Employer information is made freely available to them, and at their meetings no senior executive is present. Members set their own by-laws and rotate their membership. There are only two checks on them. First, all recommendations must be unanimous. Second, no recommendation becomes effective until the chief executive or the Board of Directors approves it, which is a means of retaining ultimate top-management control. In practice this second check or "brake" is seldom needed when the plan is working well.

Auto-Management. This form of participation virtually means workers' control. It is the most advanced form, practised in Yugoslavia, which virtually eliminates the management and gives the workers the sole right to manage the enterprise. It is a unique system as the workers

1. Charles P. McCormick, *Multiple Management. The Power of People.*

themselves constitute the management and there is no question of consultation or sharing of powers with some other party or person. The responsibility both for production and management and for decision-making regarding the apportionment of income from production rests with the workers themselves. It is a two-tier system and the workers manage the enterprises through Workers' Councils and Management Boards. The Workers' Council is the highest agency, representing the Workers' Collectives, but it cannot directly conduct everyday business affairs. It makes collectively general decisions outside its session it has no rights. Consisting of 15 to 120 members, depending upon the size of the undertaking, the Council is selected on yearly basis by the collectives directly from among the candidates sponsored by the union or individual groups of employees. Almost a similar pattern is being built up in Poland. This type of system can succeed only in single party dictatorship where all the means of production are owned by the State.

Co-partnership. Under the scheme of co-partnership the workers become the shareholders in the company for which they work. The idea is to make the workers part-owners and to give them opportunity to have some say in the control of the business. In this system, it is possible for the worker-shareholders to elect their representatives to the Board of Directors and through them participate in the management of the concern in which they are employed.

Employee Representatives on Board of Directors. Experiments have been made in many countries, with more or less success, with regard to the admission of workers' representatives on Board of Directors. The advocates of the workers' representation argue that it goes a long way to create good relations. Much may be gained both from the counsel which able workmen may contribute and also from the consciousness of operation, all with each and each with all, which will result from the sense of responsibility and participation. A worker will have more pleasure in work in the direction of which, in the sense of management, he has representatively some control.

It is true that full-fledged participation by workers in management should be the ultimate objective. But it should be ultimate objective or the end product of all the schemes of workers' participation in management. Some administrators and writers believe that the workers are not interested in the management of all the diverse affairs including production, finance and riskmanship, marketing. Employee participation, they say, should be confined to fields of their direct concern. The Study Team on Public Sector undertakings[1] feels that to include a labour representative on the Board of Directors is not a desirable step since it is difficult for the representative of labour to discharge at the same time the different responsibilities attaching to a Board member and a labour representative. The Team add that "such an arrangement

1. Administrative Reforms Commission, *Report of the Study Team on Public Sector Undertakings*, 1967, p. 161.

detracts from the constructiveness of discussions in the Board without bringing about any appreciable improvement in the transaction of business relating to industrial relations." A person having experience of trade union work could, of course, be appointed to the Board not in the capacity of a labour representative but as an expert on labour matters. The experience of some of the public sector undertakings, such as the Air Corporation, Sindri Fertilizers, Ship building Yard at Vishakhapatnam is not quite a happy one in this respect.

Employee Participation in India. In the Tata Iron and Steel Company at Jamshedpur there have been no strikes, no arbitration or adjudication for several years.[2] This is in contrast to struggle and strife, strikes and lock-out, arbitration and adjudication in the rest of industry in the country. Peace in TISCO has been the result of union management relation which has been one of mutual co-operation and of negotiation and mutual consultation, as well as joint action. The scheme of joint consultation was introduced in 1947 as a result of an agreement. Since 1948, when joint committees for joint consultation on various matters were set up, labour-management co-operation has worked to the mutual advantage of the workers and the management. Tata Workers' Union which has been recognised by the company as the sole bargaining agent of the employees has its representative on all joint committees.

The following Joint Committees are functioning at present :

(i) Works Committees;
(ii) Advisory Development and Production Committee;
(iii) Joint Rates Committee;
(iv) Job Evaluation Committee;
(v) Trade Tests Specification Committee;
(vi) Minimum Qualification Committee;
(vii) Safety Committee;
(viii) Safety Appliances Committee;
(ix) Canteen Managing Committee;
(x) Housing Allotment Committee.

The working of these committees has been quite satisfactory. A spirit of trust and cooperation rather than suspicion and rivalry governs the relationship of management and labour to one another. Others should emulate. But the scheme of labour participation through joint councils of management has not caught the imagination either of the workers or the managements.

As a positive measure for securing the participation of workers in management, Government had introduced the scheme of Joint Management Councils. The scheme, which is purely voluntary, envisages the setting up of joint councils of management. The scheme has been tried only in a few undertakings, in private and public sectors. The manage-

2. In May, 1958 a strike was declared which lasted for 12 days involving a loss of over 90,000 tons of steel valued at Rs. 1,25 crores.

ments of these undertakings have stated that joint councils of management have not been successful because of inter-union rivalries, lack of workers' co-operation and the fact that they were sometimes used for the purpose of collective bargaining.

In 1963, the working of the scheme was assessed by the Ministry of Labour and Employment and a report was circulated among public enterprises suggesting measures for strengthening the joint councils. The Ministry of Labour and Employment have also set up a special unit to assist managements in the public sector in setting up joint management councils and working out the relevant details. "We find, however, that the scheme has not made much headway for various reasons. We feel that public enterprise should take the lead in setting up joint consultative machinery. If such councils function with the spirit and perspective that should characterize such institutions and if they receive the requisite support from the top management of the undertakings, the public sector will really be able to set an example in harmony and co-operation."[1]

THE DRAFT MODEL AGREEMENT

The Draft Model Agreement for the setting up of Joint Councils of Management provides as follows :

"The Company and the Union appreciate that an increasing measure of association of employees with the management of the works would be desirable and would help (a) in promoting increased productivity for the general benefit of the enterprise, the employees and the country, (b) in giving employees a better understanding of their role and importance in the working of the industry and in the process of production, and (c) in satisfying the urge for self-expression. It is agreed therefore to set up the Council/Councils of Management consisting of representatives of management and the employees. The Council/Councils will endeavour (i) to improve the working and living conditions of the employees, (ii) to improve productivity, (iii) to encourage suggestions from the employees, (iv) to assist in the administration of laws and agreements, (v) to serve generally as an authentic channel of communication between the management and the employees, and (vi) to create in the employees a live sense of participation.

The Council would be *consulted* by the management on matters, such as—

(1) General administration of Standing Orders and their amendment when needed;

(2) Introduction of new methods of production and manufacture involving re-development of men and machinery;

(3) Closure, reduction in, or cessation of operations.

The Council/Councils will also have the right to receive information, discuss and give suggestions on—

1. Administrative *Undertakings*, p. 162.

(1) General economic situation of the concern;
(2) The state of the market, production and sales programme;
(3) Organisation and general running of the undertaking;
(4) Circumstances affecting the economic position of the undertaking;
(5) Methods of manufacture and work;
(6) The annual balance sheet and profit and loss statement and connected documents and explanations;
(7) Long-term plans for expansion, re-deployment, etc.;
(8) Such other matters as may be agreed to.

The Council/Councils would be entrusted with responsibility in respect of—

(1) Administration of welfare measures;
(2) Supervision of safety measures;
(3) Operation of vocational training and apprenticeship scheme;
(4) Preparation of schedules of working hours and breaks and of holidays;
(5) Payment of rewards for valuable suggestions received from the employees;
(6) Any other matter as may be agreed to by the Joint Council.

All matters, e.g., wages, bonus, etc., which are subjects for collective bargaining are excluded from the scope of the Council/Councils. Individual grievances are also excluded from its/their scope. In short, creation of new rights as between employers and workers should be outside the jurisdiction of the Joint Council.

New Scheme of Workers' Participation

The voluntary scheme of joint management councils did not meet with the desired result. The National Commission on Labour also recommended the enhancement of powers and scope of Works Committees to ensure a greater degree of consultation and cooperation between employers and workers. The subject of workers' participation in management both at shop floor level and plant level was also one of the items in the 20-point programme. Accordingly, the Government had brought forward a Resolution outlining the functions of the Shop Councils and joint councils to be set up in manufacturing and mining industrial establishments employing 50,000 more workers. The scheme is to be applicable to all such units in private, public and cooperative sectors, even to those which have joint management councils already functioning.

To begin with the scheme will be flexible so as to allow variations to suit local conditions and hence will be implemented through executive action. Legislation will be considered after adequate experience is gained.

Shop Councils

The main features of the Scheme of Participative Management through Shop Councils may be as follows :

(i) In every industrial unit employing 500 or more workmen, the employer shall constitute a shop council for each department or shop, considering the number of workmen employed in different departments or shops;

(ii) (a) Each council shall consist of an equal number of representatives of employers and workers.

(b) The employers' representatives shall be nominated by the management and must consist of persons from the unit concerned;

(c) All the representatives of workmen shall be from amongst the workers actually engaged in the department or the shop concerned;

(iii) The employer shall decide in consultation with the recognised union or the various registered trade unions, or with workers as the case may be, in the manner best suited to local conditions, the number of shop councils and departments to be attached to each council of the undertaking or the establishment;

(iv) The number of members of each council may be determined by the employer in consultation with the recognised union, registered unions, or workers in the manner best suited to local conditions obtaining in the unit, the total number of members may not generally exceed twelve;

(v) All decisions of a shop council shall be on the basis of consensus and not by a process of voting, provided that either party may refer the unsettled matters to the joint council for consideration;

(vi) Every decision of a shop council shall be implemented by the parties concerned within a period of one month unless otherwise stated in the decision itself and complete report shall be submitted to the joint council;

(vii) Such decisions of a shop council which have a bearing on another shop, of the undertaking or establishment as a whole will be referred to the joint council for consideration and decision;

(viii) A shop council once formed shall function for a period of two years. Any member nominated or elected to the council in the mid-term to fill a casual vacancy shall continue to be a member of the council for the unexpired portion of the term of the council;

(ix) The council shall meet as frequently as is necessary and at least once in a month;

(x) The Chairman of the shop council shall be a nominee of the management; the worker members of the council shall elect a Vice-Chairman from amongst themselves.

Functions of the Shop Councils

The Shop Council should, in the interest of increasing production.

productivity and overall efficiency of the shop or department attend to the following matters :

(i) Assist management in achieving monthly or yearly targets;

(ii) Improvement of production, productivity and efficiency, including elimination of wastage and optimum utilisation of machine capacity and manpower;

(iii) Specifically identify areas of low productivity and take necessary cooperative steps at shop level to eliminate relevant contributing factors;

(iv) To study absenteeism in the shop/department and recommend steps to reduce them;

(v) Safety measures;

(vi) Assist in maintaining general discipline in the shop/department;

(vii) Physical conditions of working, such as, lighting, ventiliation, noise, dust etc., and reduction of fatigue;

(viii) Welfare and health measures to be adopted for efficient running of the shop/department; and

(ix) Ensure proper flow of adequate two-way communications between the management and the workers, particularly on matters relating to production figures, production schedules and progress in achieving the targets.

Joint Council

In every industrial unit employing 500 or more workers, there shall be a Joint Council for the whole unit. The main features of the scheme of joint council may be as follows :

(i) Only such persons as are actually engaged in the unit shall be members of the joint council.

(ii) The council shall function for a period of 2 years;

(iii) The chief executive of the unit shall be the Chairman of the joint council; there shall be a Vice-Chairman who will be nominated by the worker-members of the council;

(iv) The joint council shall appoint one of the members of the Council as its Secretary. Necessary facilities for the efficient discharge of functions by the Secretary shall be provided within the premises of the undertaking establishment;

(v) The term of the council once formed, shall be for a period of 2 years; if, however, a member is nominated in the mid-term of the council to fill a casual vacancy, the member nominated in such vacancy shall continue in office for the remaining period of the term of the council;

(vi) The joint council shall meet at least once in a quarter;

(vii) Every decision of the joint council shall be on the basis of consensus and not by a process of voting and shall be binding on employers and workmen and shall be implemented within one month unless otherwise stated in the decision itself.

Functions of Joint Council

The Joint Council should deal with matters relating to:

(i) Optimum production, efficiency and fixation of productivity norms of man and machine for the unit as a whole;

(ii) Functions of a shop council which have a bearing on another shop or the unit as a whole;

(iii) Matters emanating from shop councils which remain unresolved;

(iv) Matters concerning the unit or the plant as a whole, in respect of matters relating to work planning and achieving production targets; more especially, tasks assigned to a shop council at the shop/department levels but relevant to the unit as a whole will be taken up by the joint council;

(v) The development of skills of workmen and adequate facilities for training;

(vi) The preparation of schedules of working hours and of holidays;

(vii) Awarding of rewards for valuable and creative suggestions received from workers;

(viii) Optimum use of raw materials and quality of finished products; and

(ix) General health, welfare and safety measures for the unit or the plant.

After indicating the main features and function of shop councils and joint councils, the Resolution once again emphasises the need for flexibility at present and the voluntary nature of the scheme. It states that there is a considerable diversity in the siuation prevailing from unit to unit in different industries. Even departmental undertakings and public enterprises under the same ministry of the Government of India, have had to adopt different systems depending upon the local conditions and their individual needs. Keeping this diversity in view, no uniform pattern is being laid down for the constitution for shop councils and joint councils, particularly relating to the representation of workers. The management in consultation with workers should evolve the most suitable pattern of representation so as to ensure that the representation of the workers results in effective, meaningful and broad-based participation of workers.

For any scheme of workers' participation to succeed, there must be an effective two-way communication and exchange of information between the workmen and management. It is only then that the workers would have a better appreciation of the problems and difficulties of the undertaking and its overall functioning with this end in view, each unit should devise a suitable system of communication within the undertaking.

As workers' participation will bring about workers' involvement in the effective functioning of the unit and in improving production and productivity, the Government has appealed to all the managements and workers and trade unions concerned to take speedy and effective steps for the early adoption of the scheme in their units and its continued healthy functioning. It may be observed here that quite a few undertakings, particularly in the public sector, have adopted the scheme. It should, however, be noted that the Works Committees as prescribed under the Industrial Disputes Act, 1947 shall continue to function in spite of the shop and joint councils.

It is proposed to make workers' participation a statutory requirement. A Bill is being drafted

TRADE UNIONISM

In a democratic country workers enjoy the right to combine themselves into an organisation for promoting and protecting their interests. Says N. Barou : "The right of the workers to combine and act in combination in their own interests is one of the essential freedoms of modern civilization." The organisations of workers are known as TRADE UNIONS. Sharp differences in outlook and opinion between the working class and management groups give rise to trade unions.

Definition. Trade unions have been defined differently by different writers and thinkers. The Webbs defined a Trade Union as a "continuous association of wage earners for the purpose of maintaining and improving the conditions of their working lives."[1] Cunnison defines it as "a monopolistic combination of wage earners who as individual producers are complementary to one another but who stand to the employers in a relation of dependence for the sale of their labour and even for its production; and that the general purpose of the association is in view of that dependence to strengthen their power to bargain with the employers.[2] Shvernik describes a Trade union as "an organisation, the chief aim of which is the regulation of mutual relations between the workers and the employers." The Indian Trade Union Act defines it as "any combination....formed primarily for the purpose of regulating the relations between workmen and employers...." We may define a Trade Union as an organisation of employees formed primarily for the purpose of the pursuit of the interests of its members.

Objects and Purposes of Trade Unions. Trade Unions are formed to act as an instrument for meeting some of the economic, political, social, and psychological problems of large-scale industry, machine technology, and mass production. They are a means of achieving working-class desires and goals.

On the economic side, trade unions through collective bargaining help to improve worker's wage and job security.

On the governmental side, they serve as an agency for industrial democracy, seeking to establish rights for workers to have a voice in the

1. Sydney and Beatrice Webb, *History of Trade Unionism*, p. 1.

2. *Labour Organisation*, p. 13.

determination of their "working conditions" and to afford them protection against arbitrary and unfair treatment on the job.

On psychological grounds, the worker, from a membership in a labour organisation, enjoys both a sense of power that helps to overcome feelings of inferiority and creates a sense of belonging to a group movement.

His self-respect and dignity are enhanced by winning objectives through his own organisation.

Unions may also help to fulfil the needs of members on the social side. Through such activities as educational, health-and-welfare, and community-service programmes they may develop new patterns of working-class life outside the plant and enable workers to participate in community affairs.

On the basis of the above functions of Trade Unions we may recount their *objectives* as follows :

1. *Better Wages.* Trade Unions Act to secure better wages for their members in keeping with the prevailing standards of life and cost of living in the country.

2. *Bonus.* They strive to obtain a part of the increased prosperity of industry for their members in the form of bonus.

3. *Better Working Conditions.* They work to attain better working conditions for the workers by procuring shorter working hours, leave with wages, social security benefits, and other welfare facilities.

4. *Enhancement of self-respect and dignity.* They foster a sense of self-respect and dignity among the workers.

5. *Fulfilment of social needs.* They help workers to fulfil their social needs through such activities as educational, health and welfare and group benefit schemes.

6. *Stable Employment.* They strive for securing stable employment for workers by working against retrenchment of workers or rationalization plans.

7. *Foster sense of security.* The Trade Union removes the sense of insecurity among the workers by granting a number of benefits such as sickness benefits, old age pensions, accident compensation and unemployment allowances.

8. *Political power.* They enable workers to participate in legislative activities by sending their representatives to Parliament and State Legislatures.

Trade Union Movement in India. Trade Union movement is coextensive with large-scale industries. The Trade Union movement goes back to the year 1875 under the leadership of Sorabji Shapurji who agitated to draw the attention of the Government to the appalling conditions in factories. This was followed by the establishment in 1890 of the Bombay Mill-hands Association through the efforts of N.M. Lokhande, himself a workman. In 1897 the Amalgamated Society of Railway Servants of India was formed, followed in 1903 by the Printers' Union, Calcutta and the Bombay Postal Union (1907). the Kamgar

Hitwardhak Sabha (1909) and the Social Service League in 1910. These associations were more of the nature of social service organisations than proper trade unions.

The First World War, the Russian Revolution, the Swaraj Movement and the establishment of the International Labour Organisation gave a new life to the Trade Union Movement in India. In the inter-war period a number of Trade Unions came into existence, the All-India Trade Union Congress, being the most important of all, having a membership of 10,000 workers. In 1942, the Indian Federation of Labour was established, but it did not last long. In 1947, the Indian National Trade Union Congress was formed as a labour wing of the Indian National Congress. In 1948, the Hind Mazdoor Sabha was established which is led by the Praja Socialist Party and the Samyukta Socialist Party.

The Trade Union movement in India is closely linked up with the growth of political parties. The recent additions to the All India Trade Unions are : (a) the United Trade Union Congress, (b) the Bhartiya Mazdoor Sangh, and (c) the Centre of Indian Trade Unions.

The Present Position. The total membership claimed by all the 11 trade union organisations in the country, each with a membership of more than one lakh, was 74, 32, 627 at the end of 1978, as against the verified total membership of 25, 50, 480 in four Central Organisations in the Year 1968.

In 1968, there were only four recognised Central or All India Trade Union Organisations. The norms then prescribed a minimum membership of one lakh for a trade union to be recognised as a Central or All-India Trade Union Organisation. These four were INTUC, AITUC, HMS and UTUC. The minimum membership norms were officially revised later to eight lakh members. Despite the upward revision, the number of All-India or Central Trade Unions Organisations as officially defined, has risen to five.

During the last decade, Bhartiya Mazdoor Sangh and Centre of Indian Trade Unions have come up, while the United Trade Union Congress has lost its status as a recognised All-India Union, as it could not measure upto the revised minimum membership. Although its memberships went up from 1,25,754 in 1968 to 1,73,571 by the end of 1978, it lost recognition as a Centrally recognised Trade Union. The INTUC continues to be the largest of the Central Trade Unions. The following is the ranking of the All-India or Central Trade Unions, in terms of membership :

1. *The Indian National Trade Union Congress* (INTUC). This union came into existence in May, 1947, as an adjunct of Congress Party. The aims of the union are to adopt peaceful means for settlement of labour disputes. The Government of India declared this union in 1948 as the most representative union in the country. It represented Indian labour organisations at the International Labour Organisation meets right upto 1978. But the Government of India has broken this monopoly and

nominated a member of the Hind Mazdoor Sangh to represent the working class at the world labour meet at Geneva on June 3, 1979. The membership of this union was claimed to be 23, 88, 451 at the end of 1978.

2. *The All-India Trade Union Congress* (AITUC). This union was formed in 1920 mainly on the pattern of the British Trade Unions. It is today dominated by the Communist Party and Radicals. Its membership at the end of 1978 was 13, 07, 471 members, and it occupies the second place.

3. *The Bhartiya Mazdoor Sangh* (BMS). This union was formed as an affiliate of Bhartiya Jan Sangh Party. During the last couple of years its membership has gone up, it being 8,59,200 as against 8,52,558 of the HMS. This gives it the third position and the BMS has been relegated to the fourth position.

4. *Hind Mazdoor Sangh.* (HMS). This union was formed by those socialists in the Congress Party who parted company with it. The Praja Socialist Party and Samyukta Socialist Party dominated this union. These parties are now constituents of the Janata Party.

5. *The Centre of Indian Trade Unions* (CITU). This union is backed by the Communist Party of India Marxist (CPI-M) and has come up during the decade, and has found a place as the fifth Central Trade Union organisation with a membership of 8,17,805 at the end of 1978.

6. *The United Trade Union Congress* (UTUC). This trade union is more radical than the HMS, but much less revolutionary in its objectives than the AITUC. As stated earlier, with its membership of only 1,73,571 at the end of 1978, it ceased to be recognised as a Central Trade Union.

Among the other labour organisations are the Hind Mazdoor Panchayat (2,21,522 members), the UTC (3,84,564 members), the National Labour Organisation (2,02,965 members), and the non-party National Federation of Indian Trade Unions, with a membership of 2,24,520 at the end of 1978*.

Weakness of Trade Union Movement. The Trade Union movement in India has not reached its state of maturity. It does not compare favourably with giant unions of the U.K. and the U.S.A. Some of the weaknesses of the movement in India are as follows :

1. *Domination of political parties.* The Trade Unions in India are dominated by political parties and leaders. The political aims overshadow the genuine objectives of the trade unions. In fact, the greatest obstacle to the growth of healthy trade union movement in India is the unhealthy influences of rival political parties.

2. *Absence of unity.* There are too many rival unions. This militates against cohesive and united action on the part of all the workers.

3. *Inadequacy of finances.* The finances of almost all the unions are very poor. Only the Indian National Trade Union Congress can claim good financial position. The paucity of funds stands in the way of the unions doing much for the welfare of the workers.

* Source: The Times of India, New Delhi, June 3, 1979

4. *Small number of members.* The trade unions do not command good membership. On top of this, the meagre membership is spread over a very large number of unions thereby weakening the position of individual unions.

5. *Lack of common goal.* For the success of any organised group the individual members of the group must have commonness of mind. There is absence of commonness of mind because of the domination of political parties with different ways of achieving ends, so the goals also differ.

6. *Absence of craft unions.* We have no craft unions in our country, all workers being unionised unit-wise or industry-wise. The workers following different crafts becoming members of the same union often create problems rather than meeting them.

The weak position of the Trade Unions in the country stands in the way of the healthy growth of the device of collective bargaining for the achievement of workers' aims. It is one of the principal reasons that adjudication rather than negotiation has to be applied for the settlement of industrial disputes. It is incumbent on the part of all concerned with the welfare of the workers to make the trade unions strong and effective for the purposes for which they are formed. A strong union is good both for the workers and the management, as well as for the community.

CHAPTER XXXIII

EMPLOYEE REMUNERATION

Introduction. Despite the importance of other issues in labour management negotiations wages remain the most vital matter at stake, the most controversial problem of industrial management. Upon the outcome of wage negotiations depends employer costs and worker income. A rational wage policy should give the worker the highest possible wage over the business cycle. It should give the enterprise a predictable wage burden that would combine flexibility of labour costs over the cycle with efficiency for each wage rupee spent. It should give the economy a maximum of stability. Wages cannot in the long run be set by pure power play. *The management should give with grace and the Union should accept with dignity.*

There are two clear stages in the determination of wages : one, the bargaining over the wage burden and of the factors relevant to it. *Secondly,* the setting of concrete wage rates.

Industry-wise determination gives us the wage burden and the individual unit gives us the wage rates. Ordinarily, all wage negotiations focus on wage rates. But wage rates per hour or per piece are not really what the enterprise is interested in. It is interested in wage costs per unit of production. Similarly, wage costs per hour or per piece are not what the worker is interested in. He is interested in income. Therefore, the major question for the community, the management and the unions is what the wage burden on production should be. How much of the total cost should go for labour costs ? How much of the total income should be the worker income?

Factors Affecting Wages. The price to be paid as wage or salary for the utilisation of services of an individual-worker or executive—is affected by a number of factors as follows :

(a) *Demand and Supply.* Demand for and supply of labour and its availability will have great influence on the determination of wage rates. If there is a shortage of labour, the wages demanded will be high. If, on the other hand, labour is plentiful, workers will be too willing to work at low rates of wages. But in recent years both management and labour has been becoming less and less dependent on this "law" as a basic factor. Payment of high wages at times when labour is scarce leads to difficulties in meeting cost standards, and reduction in wages is almost impossible. The payment of low wages when labour is abundant often causes resentment in the long run and so saving in wages is outweighed by a sense of dissatisfaction and low productivity.

(b) *"Goving Wages".* The goving wage is usually the ruling wage, in any locality, but some companies pay higher rates in order to foster the continued goodwill of workers in the community.

(c) *Cost of Living.* The cost of living or more precisely changes in the cost of living which affect the purchasing power of the wage, have been used with profit by many companies. Where, however, the employers are short sighted and ignore the changes in the cost of living, trade unions come out with a demand for a wage rate which takes into account the current cost of living index.

(d) *Union-management negotiations.* A well-organised labour which is directed by strong leadership is usually in a position to secure higher wage levels through union management negotiations. Collective bargaining can be a useful method if pursued rationally by both the managements and unions. It can give the enterprise a predictable wage burden, and the workers the pedictable income.

(e) *State of competition.* The wage level is also affected by the degree of competition in the market for the products of an industry. In a state of perfect competition (which is hardly ever present), the level of wages may be at par with the value of the net addition made by the workers to the total output. If there is imperfect competition in the product market, the wages are not likely to reach this level.

(f) *State Regulation.* Often it was found that the bargaining power of the workers was not strong enough to ensure fair wages. Consequently, the State found it necessary to step in. To ensure the payment of a minimum wage in certain specified industries and occupation the Minimum Wages Act was passed in 1948. Payment of bonus was made compulsory under the Payment of Bonus Act, 1965, and fringe benefits given under the Employees State Insurance Act, 1948, and Provident Fund Act, 1952 and so on.

(g) *Other Factors.* In addition to above factors, there are some others which influence actual wage levels in an organisation. These may be the firm's ability to pay, the level of national income and its distribution, the place of industry in the national economy, e.g., in a strategic industry wage level could be quite high.

SYSTEMS OF WAGE PAYMENT

The fundamental bases of wage payment are only two : (1) Payment by time worked, and (2) Payment for output. There are indeed all kinds of modifications and minglings of these two principles, but they are nonetheless fundamentally distinct.

In its simplest form, time wage system would adopt time as the basis of worker remuneration without taking into account the units produced. Similarly, in the simplest form of payment for output, wages are paid on the basis of the units produced regardless of the time taken to produce them. In actual practice, however, these systems in their simplest forms are seldom applied. A time-wage system is never wholly without relation to output; for the employer inevitably expects a certain amount of work from a worker whom he employs and if this amount is not forthcoming, he discharges him. Payment by output is never wholly without relation to a time standard; for prices are invariably determined to a great extent by the income which constitutes the normal standard of life for the workman concerned. Subject to this overriding consideration the two systems and their variations are distinct, and are examined below.

Time Wage System. In this system, time is made the basis of payment. It is the oldest of the wage systems and offers the workers a given sum of money for a fixed period of his time taking no account of the quantity of work done. The worker is guaranteed a definite sum, and the rate may be quoted as so much per hour, day, week, fortnight, or month. The payment of the wage may be made at the end of the day, the week, the fortnight or the month, according as is mutually agreed, provided that not more than one month must elapse between two wage periods (Sec. 4. Payment of Wages Act, 1936).

Advantages. Time wage system has the following advantages :

(a) Simplicity is the greatest merit of time wage system. The time which a man expends on a job is easy to measure.

(b) It gives the worker some security which is so important for sustaining his interest in work. There is no danger of the worker losing his remuneration or part of it due to temporary reduction in his efficiency resulting from unavoidable accident or sickness.

(c) A worker, being assured of a fixed income, can adjust his expenditure to his income and maintain a certain standard.

(d) Time rate favours careful work, for the workman can show his craftsmanship and enjoy the pleasure of a perfect product without any loss to him.

(e) The quality of the work is not degraded, as the workers are in no hurry to increase the output.

(f) As a corollary to this, there is no rough handling of machinery which is a distinct advantage to the employer.

(g) The system requires less administrative attention than others, and leaves men contented with delays and breakdowns.

(h) Since the calculations are simple, the Trade Unions favour this system. It also creates a solidarity of interest with each wage group as the standard wage is always paid and it can be made the basis of easily understood negotiations.

(i) Where the productivity of a worker cannot be accurately measured because the production is not standardised, time rate system is the only just method of wage payment.

Disadvantages: The time wage system suffers from the following weaknesses:

(a) The principal weakness of the system is that it does not discriminate between the efficient and inefficient worker and between the honest worker and the shirker.

(b) As both good and bad workers are paid alike, the system "represses the superior man", for there is no incentive to hard work.

(c) The time basis provides no basis to reward the good worker and punish the loafer. In fact, the system tends to place a premium on inefficiency.

(d) The system encourages "soldiering".

(e) Since it does not encourage men to work hard, it becomes the responsibility of foremen and supervisors to keep men working.

(f) The system permits many a man to work at a task for which he has neither taste nor ability, when he might make a mark in some other suitable job.

(g) The herding together of men into classes regardless of personal character and performance leads to employer-employee trouble.

(h) The result of all the above factors is that latent talent finds vent in antagonistic forms of activity rather than productivity for it produces a sense of personal injury in exceptional men.

Grading System. It is suggested that as a measure of improvement on the time rate system graded payments may be made, based on the normal or ordinary wages according to the skill and experience necessary to perform different tasks. This is done by what is called as Grading System. Each worker is graded according to his ability and placed in one of several different classes, for each of which a minimum wage is set by collective bargaining.

Piece—Wage System. In contrast to time wage, this system makes speed as the basis of payment. The piece rate plan of payment is based on the idea that men are hired to work, not to stand around, and so their pay is based on the quantity of work they complete satisfactorily during a specified period, called the pay-period. Thus, a worker is paid according to the speed at which he works, the amount of work per day, or per week, not merely the amount. Under this system the employee makes all the gain or loss of his own time. If he shortens the time used, i.e., works with greater speed, he receives no less for the job finished, and he gains time in which to make extra earnings at the same time. If he takes a longer period, the remuneration may fall below time wage. The employers also gain because through rapid performance the factory burden to be charged to each piece or job is decreased.

Employers favour piece—wage system where soldiering is difficult to detect, as in moulding, where speed is unusually important, as in railway repair shop; where work is done away from employers' place of business. The system is best suited for work of repetitive nature and for trades which "sell-then-make". It has been successfully followed in coal mining, textile industries, shoe factories, etc.

Advantages. The piece-wage system offers the following advantages :

(a) Since payment is based on results of efficiency, this system recognises merit. It is therefore more equitable than the time-rate system.

(b) It encourages voluntary effort as against a "drive" under time-rate, creating an atmosphere of willingness and zeal for work.

(c) The total costs are reduced, for which direct labour costs remain constant at all speeds of performance, the increase in the amount of work per hour decreases the hourly charge on account of plant and management. This illustrates the proposition that higher wages mean lower labour costs.

(d) The direct labour cost per unit of product or per job becomes a fixed amount reliable for use in cost calculations.

Disadvantages : The piece-wage system suffers from the following drawbacks :

(a) Straight piece rate does not guarantee day wages, so that a worker may at times earn below the subsistence level because of some factor beyond his control. The fluctuations in earnings are a source of constant worry and annoyance to the worker.

(b) While payment based on speed provides an incentive for greater volume, it discourages quality and judgement.

(c) It also becomes necessary for supervisors to inspect the work carefully, since the system encourages the sacrifice of quality for quantity.

(d) High speeds are injurious to the workers and also they are hard on machinery and equipment.

(e) It is objected to on ethical grounds as it encourages greed and unhealthy rivalries among the workers. Politically, piece-rate weakens trade unions, and higher earnings are likely to encourage absenteeism.

(f) The system can become a source of trouble between the management and workers. Where, for instance, piece wage is introduced in place of time rate, workers, have increased their output and income. The employers thinking that some employees are earning too much money, have often "cut" the rate, which the workers resent. This induces antagonism and economic warfare between management and men.

(g) As a result of this, the system encourages soldiering because to escape further cuts the workers begin to produce less, and also regard their employers as their enemies, to be opposed in everything they want.

Balance and Debt System. This system combines within itself the time-and piece-rate. Under this system a minimum weekly wage is guaranteed for a full week's work, with an alternative piece-rate determined by the rate fixed on the assumption that the worker would put in enough effort to earn his minimum wage. If the wages calculated on piece basis are in excess of the time rate, the worker earns the excess; if the piece-rate wages are less than the time-rate earnings, he would still get the weekly wage, but on the condition that he shall have to make good the excess paid to him out of the subsequent wage he would earn. Suppose a worker is expected to complete at least 10 pieces during the week in order to earn his minimum wage of Rs. 60, the piece rate has been fixed at Rs. 6 per unit. If the worker produces 12 units within the week his earning will be Rs. 72. If, on the other hand, he produces only 9 units, he will still be paid Rs. 60, his minimum weekly wage, but as on the basis of piece-rate, his earnings should amount to only Rs. 54\ Rs. 6 paid in excess will be debited to him to be deducted out of his subsequent earnings. Under this plan the whole of the benefit of extra pay as an inducement to increased output goes to the worker; and yet speed is not the only factor in the basis of pay. A man's wages are determined by both the number of hours he works and the speed at which he works.

INCENTIVE PLANS OF WAGE PAYMENT

We have observed above that time wage maintains quality but affects production, whereas piece rate affects quality but increases production. The incentive plans attempt to combine the good points of both the systems. In this way, both the employers and workers benefit and derive satisfaction. Thus, the chief objectives of an incentive wage plan may be said to be to realise : (1) increase in productivity, (2) reduction in labour cost, (3) improvement in efficiency, (4) rise in employees' earnings, (5) higher employee morale, and (6) harmonious labour-management relations.

Characteristics of a sound incentive wage plan. Since the underlying objective of an incentive wage plan is to encourage workers to perform with zeal and enthusiasm and earn good wages, an incentive plan should have the following characteristics of a sound incentive wage plan :

(a) The incentive plan should be simple and easily understandable by the employees.

(b) The plan should be evolved in such a manner that it is acceptable to all the interested parties. If the employee acceptance and support is lacking, the plan will not succeed.

(c) The reward under the plan should be as nearly related to effort as possible both in amount and in time of payment.

(d) The norm or standard upon which wage incentive is to be based should be fixed after careful work measurement devices, such as time and motion studies, work sampling, standard data, etc.

(e) The plan must be fair and just both to the employer and employees. It should not cast unwarranted burden on the employer nor should it deprive the worker of his due reward for an increase in output.

(f) Guaranteed basic or time rates should be established by job evaluation. This will give the workers a feeling of security about their earning.

(g) There should be no unwarranted rate cutting, otherwise the plan would fail and create resentment among the workers.

(h) The incentive scheme should be definite and should not be changed frequently. Changes should be made only if there is a substantial change in method of work. But the incentive should not be affected by matters outside the control of the workers, e.g., shortage of raw materials or power shortage.

(i) To avoid development of grievances among certain workers, the scheme should be made applicable to all jobs for which incentive plan can be profitably adopted.

Incentive Wage Plans. Some of the well known incentive plans of wage payment are discussed below.

Halsey Plan. The Halsey Plan is a simple combination of the time-speed basis of payment so that the workers are encouraged to work efficiently and are paid a guaranteed wage on time basis. First of all, the standard time required for a job is determined on the basis of time and motion studies or on the basis of average previous times of doing jobs. A worker who performs the job in less than the standard time and thus saves time is rewarded with a bonus, but the worker who takes longer than the standard time is paid wages on the time-wage system so that he does not suffer in any way. The bonus or compensation for time saved is a percentage (30 to 50 per cent) of the value of the time saved as measured by the hourly rate. Thus his total pay is the sum of the guaranteed hourly rate time hours worked plus a predetermined percentage of the hourly rate (30 to 50 per cent) multiplied by whatever time he has saved by working faster. Mr. Halsey indicates that the 50 per cent may be paid if the task is a difficult one which has been scientifically set, but that 30 per cent is enough when the records of past day-work or piece-work are used. If a job requiring 10 hours is done in 8 hours the worker will be paid wages for 8 hours plus wages of 50 per cent of the time saved namely one hour. In all therefore, he will get wages for 9 hours. In England, the Weir System which is on par with the Halsey Plan is more commonly used. It is called the Weir Plan because it was first used in Weir Engineering Works, Cathcart on the Clyde.

If a workman who is on an hourly rate of Re. 1 has ten-hour task given to him, and completes it in 8 hours and the bonus is 50 per cent of the time saved, his total earning will be Rs. 9 as explained below :

Time x Hourly Rate plus (Bonus x Time Saved x Hourly Rate)

8 x Re. 1 plus $\frac{1}{2}$ x 2 x Re.1 = Rs. 9

The premium is calculated on each job separately so that failure on one job does not sacrifice premium earned on another. The acceptance of the plan is voluntary with each workman.

Advantages. Halsey Plan has the following advantages :

1. It is easy to introduce as no preliminary study is necessary except the circulation of previous average times.

2. By dividing the profit of saved time between men and management, it makes for permanance of the bonus rate, as both parties benefit by it.

3. The psychology is adroit; an employee is satisfied with what he gains although part of the saved time is shared by the employer.

4. By assuring every workman a minimum hourly wage, the plan gives him a feeling of security, and by rewarding for saved time, the plan encourages efficiency.

5. The workers can very easy follow the method of calculating the bonus and so there is no room for any misunderstanding.

Disadvantages. The plan suffers from the following drawbacks :

1. It possesses the weakness of the straight piece-rate of taking an unscientifically determined standard time for its job. It depends upon past performances instead of making new standards.

2. The fairness of the plan dividing the profit of saved time between management and men has been questioned.

3. Since bonus is calculated on each job, the worker can spurt on certain jobs to capture a premium, and slow down on others to rest up, under the guarantee of day wages.

4. From the point of view of administration, the policy is one of drift as in this plan the worker is left alone to decide whether or not to produce more after a standard is reached.

Rowan Premium Plan. A slightly modified form of the Halsey System is the Rowan Plan introduced for the first time in 1901 by James Rowan of David Rowan and Sons of Glasgow. This plan is very popular in Britain. Under this plan, as under Halsey Plan, a standard time is determined beforehand based on past experience. A time-wage is guaranteed to those who fail to reach the standard and bonus is paid according to time saved. The Rowan Plan differs from the Halsey Plan in the method of bonus determination. Under this plan the wages of time taken shall be increased by the same percentage as that by which the time set for the job has been reduced. Thus, if a workman reduces the time by 25 per cent the wages are increased by 25 per cent. Algebrically, the bonus or premium can be computed as follows :

$$\text{Bonus} \quad \frac{\text{Time saved}}{\text{Standard Time}} \times \text{Time taken} \times \text{Rate per hour}$$

Taking the same example, where the standard time is ten hours and the hourly rate is Re. 1 and the workman completes the job in 8 hours, thus saving two hours, the bonus will be 2/10 x 8x 1 = 8/5 = Re. 1 and 60 p. and the total wage for an 8 hour day would be wage for time taken plus bonus, or Rs. 8 plus 1.60 = 9.60. Expressed differently, the amount of bonus bears the same relation the ordinary wages due for the time actually taken as the time allowed (standard time) bears to the full time allowed.

Evaluation. Rowan Plan is more liberal than the Halsey Plan upto $\frac{2}{3}$ time economy; but after that it is less liberal. The maximum a worker can earn is double the guaranteed wage, which is humanly impossible. Increase in effort is much less rewarded than in the Halsey Plan. The ordinary worker finds it difficult to understand the calculations to compute his earnings, and is no more very popular.

The Hour-for-Hour or 100 Percent Bonus Plan. The plan is based on estimates of production standards established by carefully analysed time studies. The main feature of the plan is that the workers receive 100 per cent of the bonus earned. It compares, in this way with straight piece work, and differs from Halsey Plan. But it differs from straight piece-rate in that the standards are expressed in time per unit of production rather than in money. The time saved is multiplied by the full value of the hourly rate, with the result that a rapid worker is paid a guaranteed hourly wage, plus the additional amount that a slower, standard worker would have eventually received on completing the same quantity of work. Thus, if the hourly rate is Re. 1; time is hours 8; standard time per piece, one hour, and number of pieces completed 10, then the total earnings will be :

Total Earnings = (Time x hourly Rate) plus (Time saved x Hourly Rate)
8 x Re. 1 plus 2 x Re 1 = 8 plus 2 = Rs. 10

The plan is most suitable from a cost accounting and budget standpoint, as well as, equity and justice point of view.

The Bedeaux or Points Plan. The two specialities of this Plan are that workers in all departments earn bonus or premium at the same rate and that the foreman also shares the bonus with the workers; in ratio of three-fourths to workers and one-fourth to the foreman. In this system, a point or Bedeaux or "B" is defined as the work which a man should be able to perform in one minute. The difficulty of the job is then measured in terms of its number of B's. A careful time study is made and normal standards for various jobs are fixed. The rate of pay is also reduced to the minute basis and the task is defined as 60 x B hours. Thus each 8 hour day contains 480 B's and a worker meets the standard if he completes 480 B's of work during the day. Below the standard he is paid a guaranteed hourly wage. Above the standard he receives a premium, usually 75 percent of the value of the time saved, the remaining 25 per cent going to the foreman. The number of points or B's produced by every worker and the amount of what he has earned are posted daily so that every worker can see what his earnings were for the previous day. The plan is further explained by an example.

Where the standard for 8 hour day is 480 B's (60 x 8), the standard rate per B is one paisa and a worker completes 600 B's during the day and the premium percentage is 75 per cent. his total pay will be :

Wage = (Standard x Rate) plus Bonus %, i.e. (Actual-Standard) x Rate

480 x lP plus 75% of 600-480 = 120 × IP
4.80 plus 90P = Rs. 5.70

The main weakness of this system of payment is that a worker may not understand how the standard time is determined because of the use of B's. Some workers might even resent that part of his saving of time is paid to the foreman.

Hayne's Plan. This is another variation of Bedeaux Point Plan. In this plan, the standard time of a job is fixed in terms of *Manits* which means man-minutes. The worker receives wages on time basis in any case, but the standard time of various jobs done by him exceeds the actual time, i.e., if there is a saving of time, the worker is paid a certain share of it. The saving is calculated in terms of *manits* (like B's in Bedeaux Plan). The resultant saving is divided by 60 to convert it into hours. These hours are then multiplied by the time rate to determine the total value of the time saved. The benefit of time saved is divided in this manner; (a) where the work is standardised, 5/6ths to the workman and 1/6th to the foreman, (b) where the work is not standardised, 5/10ths to the worker, 1/10th to the foreman and 4/10ths to the management. The bonus payable to the foreman is credited to a fund. If a worker loses time due to a fault of the foreman, the foreman loses his bonus to the extent the worker has to be paid wages for idle time. No *manits* are credited to the workman for a product that fails to pass inspection.

INCENTIVE PLANS UNDER SCIENTIFIC MANAGEMENT

Taylor's Differential Piece-Rate. This system is now almost out of use, but it is considered because of the principle involved and also because it was introduced by the man who is regarded as the father of scientific management. The underlying principle of the system is to pay a low piece-rate for low production and a higher piece-rate for a higher production. Taylor was against payment of wages on time basis, and so under his system there was no guaranteed wage. He was, however, convinced that through time study, the standard performance as a fair day's work could be fixed quite accurately. He fixed standard of output per hour or per day, and to encourage workers to reach the standard performance he fixed too piece rates. If a worker performs the standard task or in excess of it, he is paid a higher piece rate, and if he fails to attain the standard he gets lower piece rate. Thus, if the production has been fixed at 10 units per day, the piece rate for the output or beyond may be Rs. 1 per unit, but for any production below the standard of 10 units the rate might be 75 paise per unit, a worker producing 10 units will get Rs. 10, the one producing 11 units will get Rs. 11 and so on, but a worker producing 9 units will get at the rate of 75 paise per unit, or Rs. 7.75p and the one producing 8 units will get Rs. 6 and so on.

Evaluation. By rewarding for extra exertion or greater efficiency and by penalising slowness or inefficiency this system provides every incentive towards maximum production. It does not only enable a good worker to earn high wages, but the management also benefits through increased output and lower cost of production per unit.

The system suffers from its inherent limitations. It is difficult to apply, and fails to guarantee a minimum day wage. The change in the rate is too abrupt at the point where the standard task is determined, with the result that the man who just fails to reach the standard limit earns much lower wage that a man who just reaches it. This is likely to cause ill-feelings among workers. Since the management fixes the standard production, an unscrupulous employer might fix it at an unreasonably high level and so deprive even an efficient worker from earning higher wages which he deserves.

Merrick Multiple Piece-Rate Plan. This plan is a modification of Taylor's system. The defect of abrupt change in Taylor's Plan is attempted to be removed by grading the workers as beginners, developing or average and first class workers and so offering three graded piece rates instead of two. All the other considerations underlying Taylor's Plan are to be kept in mind. The three rates are : first 83 per cent of the standard task production, the second is at the task point or the standard, and the third is beyond the standard.

Gantt's Task and Bonus System. This Plan also assumes the establishment of standardised conditions by preliminary investigations and is based upon careful time study. Like the Halsey Plan, it provides hourly wages for slower workers and a piece rate for fast workers, and in addition, like the Taylor Plan makes a definite distinction between those who can attain the standard and those who cannot. Unlike Taylor Plan, it guarantees a day wage to all workers. Under this Plan, a definite task, representing first-class performance, is set as a standard. The wage of those who attain or excel the standard consists of the day rate for the time allowed as standard for the tasks accomplished, *plus* an agreed percentage-anywhere from 20 to 50 per cent of that time calculated at the day rate, added as a bonus.

Let us assume a case where the day rate is Re. 1 per hour and the bonus is 25 per cent of the standard time. If a worker completes an 8-hours job in 10 hours he will get the time rate for ten hours or Rs. 10 for the job. A worker who does the job in 8 hours will receive the day rate for 8 hours, plus 25 per cent of 8 hours or a total wage of Rs. 10 for the job. If a worker does the work in 6 hours, he will still get for 8 hours, that being the standard laid down to complete the task, plus 25 per cent of 8 hours, making a total wage of Rs. 10. Thus, every reduction in time means progressive increase in total earnings. For this reason, Gantt system is also described as *Progressive Rate System.* The system is day wage for substandard workers, and a piece rate for standard and super-standard workers.

Evaluation. The system has many strong points as follows :

1. It is simple, easily understood and can be easily introduced.
2. It guarantees time rate to all workers and bonus to those who reach or excel the standard, thus proving both security and incentive.
3. It encourages planning and better supervision. A supervisor is also given a bonus if a certain number of workers under him earn the bonus.
4. It satisfies the workers because the bonus is substantial and proves beneficial to employer by spreading overheads over larger units produced.
5. The day wage is a flat rate, however small the output. Beyond this the wage increases by piece-rate as it approaches the standard. When the standard is reached, a bonus is paid. Beyond the standard the piece rate is on a diminishing scale. This discourages unlimited speeding up.

The main drawback of the plan is that the marked leap upward in wages at standard point discriminates rather severely between say, the just efficient and the barely efficient worker. Again it may be that even the "living wage" may not be provided to a sub-standard worker inspite of guaranteed time wage.

Emerson's Efficiency Plan. Emerson's Efficiency Plan, like Taylor and Gantt Plans, demands the Standardisation of shop conditions and setting of tasks by careful time studies. This task represents a full and fair task for a first-class worker who is said to be 100 per cent efficient. For the attainment of this standard, a large bonus is offered as in the Gantt system, but smaller graded bonuses may be earned before reaching this standard. It guarantees day wages as long as a man is retained regardless of peroformance. The distinctive feature of this plan is the gradual nature of the transition effected from the day rate to the piece rate as performance improves. The remuneration is fixed on the basis of efficiency. A worker's efficiency is the ratio between time set and the time he has taken, i.e., the standard hours of his finished jobs and the clock hours he has consumed. The daily wage rate is paid without bonus to those who attain lower than 66.7 per cent efficiency. Above this there is a bonus payable on a graded scale in a fixed ratio to the increased output. For example, when efficiency is 80 per cent of the bonus payable is 4 per cent, and when it is 90 per cent, the bonus is 10 per cent and for 100 per cent efficiency the bonus added to the day wage is 20 per cent, thus giving a parallel increase in efficiency and bonus between 90 per cent and 100 per cent. For all efficiencies above 100 per cent the worker receives the wages of the time used and of the time saved, i.e., piece rate plus 20 per cent of wages of the time used. For example, where standard-output (100 per cent of Efficiency) is 800 units, a worker producing 400 units will have 50 per cent efficiency and will get daily wage rate. If he produces 600 units his efficiency will be 75 per cent and he will get his daily wage rate plus 10 per cent, if he produces 750 units his efficiency will be 93.75 per cent and he will get his daily wage plus 14 per cent, and for 800 units production his efficiency is 100 per cent and he will get his daily wage plus 20 per cent and if he produces 880 units his efficiency will be 110 per cent and he will get his day wage plus 30 per cent and so on.

The following curve shows the summary of the wages scheme under "Scientific Management."

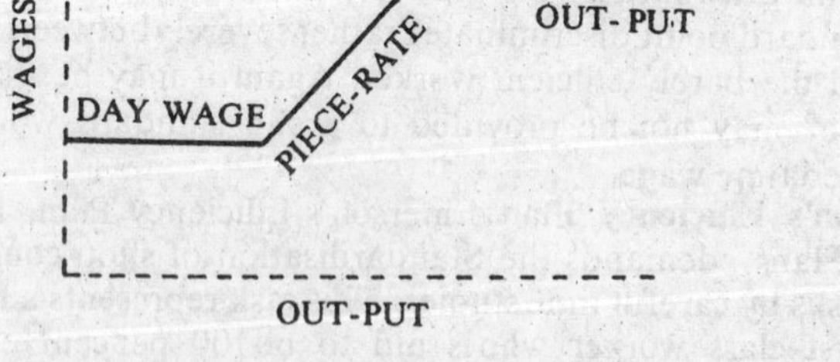

Co-operative Production Bonus Plans.

It is not always possible to determine the efficiency of individual workers and pay them bonus on individual basis. Some types of work can be performed by groups and so individual piece rates have to be sought on group basis. In some cases, collective bonus payment ensures greater union-management cooperation and encourages "participation" Four of such group bonus plans are considered here.

Group Piece Work. Under this plan a number of workers are asked to work together and are paid on a per unit basis. As the workers cooperate directly on the same job or piece of work, the total earnings of the group are divided equally at the end of a week or a month. The total price for the work done in excess of their weekly or monthly wages is divided among them according to some pre-determined basis which is satisfactory to all concerned.

Priestman Bonus System. Under this system productivity of all workers is taken into account. In case, during a year, the output rises either above the standard output or the output of the previous year, the wages of the workers are increased in the same ratio. Thus, if in 1978 the output per man hour came to 10 units, while in 1979 the hourly output per worker (man hour output) is, on the average, 11 units, the wages in 1979 would be 10 per cent higher than in 1978.

Overhead Piece-Work System. It is used for remunerating certain employees whose earnings are included in the overhead charges. Such employees receive, in addition to their ordinary time-rate earnings, increased amounts based on the excess of production over an ascertained normal output.

The chief advantages for these systems are cooperation among workers, and their ability to get better terms than are possible for an individual. As against this, there is always a danger of rivalry and bickering within the group if all the workers are not of equal ability.

Union-Management Productivity Scheme or Scanlon Plan. Joseph Scanlon, after whom the plan is named, believed in *participation* as a basic principle of organisation. According to this principle an average worker is *able* to make and, given the right kind of circumstances, *wants* to make important contributions to the solution of production problems. Under this plan, constructive cooperation,mental as well as physical, is solicited from every one-workers, foreman, top management. Each individual has the opportunity and feels the obligation to work for the best interests of the group. By group participation a means of rewarding labour for any increase in productivity is found. Under the plan, productivity being the labour's as well as management's interest, the labour force receives, as a bonus every month, all of the savings it can effect on its own cost for that month. At the same time, management profits from increased production with no corresponding increase in total overhead. Increased productivity is brought about chiefly by suggestions as to how time and effort can be saved. Many plants keep suggestion boxes, and where a suggestion is adopted, the reward for such suggestion goes to the entire shop. As a result of participation, dynamic working unity is achieved, the workers are not resentful and suspicious, they are enjoying their work. They are participating.

Sliding Scale. This is another of the schemes of wage payment for creating a feeling among workers that they are recognised as eligible to share in the prosperity of the enterprise and therefore they should work for its prosperity. The sliding scale system is usually based upon the results of collective bargaining by which the wages are so adjusted that they will automatically rise or fall with the average selling price of typical products connected with the industry. The basic idea is that when prices are good wages would be high and low wages should follow low prices. The standard wage and standard price, which are subject to periodical revision, are fixed.

The Advantages claimed for the system are :

(1) Prevention of disagreements about wages during definite periods;
(2) Promotion of feeling of co-partnership and mutual interest between employers and employees;
(3) It is possible to make a ready computation of wage element in cost of production, and as a result long contracts can be made with certain feeling of security;
(4) Changes in wage rates take place gradually, and by series of small graduations, instead of suddenly;
(5) The system furnishes to the workmen absolutely reliable information, usually extracted by an auditor appointed by themselves, from the books of the employer.

Inspite of many advantages and its long use, the system has not become very popular. Its inherent *disadvantages* are : It is not equitable that the wages should rise and fall with the prices of the products. If prices fluctuated widely, this method would be nothing better than speculation in wages. As the worker has no control over the prices, the employer may be tempted to sell at reduced prices during a period of depressed trade. Widely fluctuating wages are likely to lead to industrial unrest. Even the consumer can be exploited by a conspiracy between the worker and management.

Profit Sharing and Labour Co-partnership

Inspite of numerous incentive plans employer-employee differences have continued to exist. Profit sharing and labour co-partnership have been tried with more or less success as part of an effort to find techniques that might contribute in some way to lessening the vexation of present-day industrial strife. It is also hoped that they will help to build the cooperative spirit so vital for productive and successful enterprise. They are also expected to increase the employees' interest in the business and to create a feeling within their minds that they are partners and so should share in the profits.

Profit Sharing

Profit sharing is a method of industrial remuneration under which an employee agrees to pay his employees a share in the annual net profits of the enterprise, as fixed in advance. This share is in addition to wages based on incentive plans or otherwise, and is not based on time or output. It should, however, be noted that profit sharing is not a system of wage payment. It is only an adjunct added to any of the fundamental wage plans. Again the fixation of the share in advance is an essential feature of profit sharing schemes. Any profit sharing plan to succeed must attempt to cover, as far as possible, all employees without any imposition of restrictions with regard to length of service.

Basis of Sharing. Some of the bases of profit sharing are :

(a) *Individual Basis.* Each worker is paid that share of the profit which has been earned through his effort.

(b) *Departmental Basis.* In some cases, each department would have its own profit sharing plan. Therefore, the profits earned by a particular department will be distributed among the workers of that department.

(c) *Unit-wise.* Profits are shared by the workers employed in each industrial unit.

(d) *Industry Basis.* The profits earned by all the units in a particular industry in a particular locality are pooled and then divided among all the workers of that industry and also the employers.

Methods of determining portion of profit for distribution. There appear to be three basic methods for determining the portion of the profits to be distributed.

(1) The plan may provide for a predetermined percentage of profits to be computed before or after taxes or after a fair return on capital investment payment or dividend has been deducted.

(2) Another method is the discretionary or arbitrary method under which management determines annually, the amount of profits to be distributed to the employees.

(3) The third basic method provides that the share of profits shall bear a relationship to the employee's contribution for savings.

Methods of Distribution. When the total share to be received by labour has been decided upon, the next step is to distribute it to the individual workman. The most commonly employed method is to distribute on the basis of the wages earned. Some companies reward long service by weighing the individual's share by his years of service. Some companies encourage saving by increasing the share in proportion to the individual's savings.

Methods of actual payment. Having determined the share of the profits to be distributed among the workers the actual payment may be made—

(a) *Cash payment.* Each worker may be paid in cash the amount of the share of profit. This method of distribution of profit is most commonly adopted as the workers prefer it.

(b) *The savings or deposit account* may be credited with the share of profit payable to each worker.

(c) *Transfer to pension or provident fund.* The share of profit due to each worker or employee may be credited to his provident fund or his pension fund. This should be in addition to the pension or provident fund which the worker is otherwise entitled to.

(d) *Investment in capital.* Another method of payment of share of profit is to issue bonus shares to the workers. This is, of course, a form of co-partnership.

(e) *Combination of different methods.* Payment may be made partly in cash and partly by issue of bonus shares. Or it may be done by transferring a part to provident fund and pension account and the rest by issue of bonus shares.

Advantages. It is claimed that profit sharing leads to the following benefits or advantages :

(a) *Improved industrial relations.* Labour management relationship are considerably improved resulting is high morale. It contributes to the building up and development of loyalty in the personnel.

(b) *Better team work.* A joint aim for management and men makes for greater cooperation and solidarity of interest and conducive to better team work.

(c) *Increased interest in company welfare.* The sharing of profits being on collective basis, steady work on the part of all workers is encouraged. The workers feel a sense of responsibility as they are interested in the prosperityof the company. Idlers become unpopular.

(d) *Increased productivity and greater efficiency.* The worker is motivated to greater effort by pecuniary interest in the profits which go up through his sustained exertion.

(e) *Saving in cost of supervision.* As the elimination of waste and spoilage means larger profits, the worker takes care of tools, machinery and materials, so that there is a saving in the cost of supervision and control.

(f) *Reduction in labour turnover.* Profit sharing aims to provide greater economic security for workers. An employer can be sure of a dependable and consistent workers, as the latter is sure of getting a share of profit.

(g) *Reduction in labour disputes.* All in all profit sharing overcomes wage demands, labour unrest, and increases production and wages, all of which are ultimately good for the community.

(h) *Better relationship between company's financial position and employee compensation.* In recent years, profit sharing plans have been made with the object of tying the total employee compensation to the fate of the business rather than raising and lowering the basic wage as profits rise or fall.

Disadvantages. As against these benefits, many shortcomings and failings of profit sharing have been voiced. It is stated by some that profit sharing is fine in principle and very unsatisfacory in practice.

1. Profit sharing plans by their very nature depend on profits and thus tend to be fair weather plans.

2. The plan is appropriate only for well established and prosperous businesses which can reasonably anticipate regular profits.

3. Another defect is that it provides no direct relationship between effort and reward. The payment is based on individual efficiency but it is made collectively to the labour force.

4. As payments are made six-monthly or yearly they do not appear to provide a stimulus as the reward is too remote to effort. The uncertainty and remoteness act as dampers to the enthusiasm of the workers.

5. Profit shares are often allocated on an arbitrary basis (usually a percentage of pay) and offers no encouragement to the good employees.

6. Plans tend to be too complicated, and are established without the solicitations of the employees, or union's attitude and suggestions.

7. The shares under the plan come to be regarded as a matter of custom and right and any curtailment or failure in payment is bound to be resented.

8. Trade unions oppose profit sharing on the ground that it creates disunity among workers. Says Taussig, "It tends to make the workman interested chiefly in the welfare of his immediate fellow employees, not in that of all workmen of the trade or industry".

Conclusion. Profit sharing is not an end in itself, and cannot create good relations in industry between workers or management. It can only be an adjunct, a contributory factor in raising industrial morale but not a generator of morale. As a means of securing workers' loyalty and as an incentive it is likely to prove a failure because it concentrates the worker's attention at the wrong point, To be of real value, profit sharing should be only the last tier of the three-fold wage structure, which consists of—

(a) a fixed minimum time wage for every worker;
(b) an incentive or piece-work bonus; and
(c) a share in company's annual profits.

Because profit sharing alone suffers from so many weaknesses and because, without capital investment, it misleads and gives a false sense of value to employees, it is recommended that profit sharing and labour co-partnership should go together.

Labour Co-partnership

As suggested above, the profit sharing plan succeeds only when coupled with share holding arrangement. Co-partnership claims for all workers that they shall share to some extent in the profits, capital and control of the business in which they are employed. As such the worker shall receive, in addition to the standard wages of the trade, a share in the final profits of the business. He shall accumulate his share of profits in the capital of the business employing him, and he shall also acquire some share in the control of the business either by acquiring share capital and thus gaining the ordinary rights and responsibilities of a shareholder, or by the formation of a co-partnership committee of workers, having a voice in the internal management.

As a result of this system the workers become part owners of the business, receiving their share of the capital and also return on the capital, and thus are induced to put forth their efforts to secure the prosperity of the undertaking. The plan, however, suffers from the same drawback of speculation as does profit sharing. It is an axiom that speculation is unsuited for small investors. Business profits are speculative and the worker with small income cannot adjust his expenditure to this fluctuating income.

Profit Sharing Plan in India. The Tripartite Conference held in December, 1947, resolved to work for better industrial relations in the country. The Government appointed an Export Committee to study and suggest ways for determining fair wages to labour, fair return on capital, labours' share of surplus profits, etc. The Committee on Profit Sharing recommended that an experiment on profit sharing should be tried in some industries, such as cotton textiles, jute, steel, cement, tyre manufacturing and cigarette making. This Committee, while rejecting slide scale for determining labours' share in profits recommended labours' share at 50 per cent of the surplus profits of the undertaking. The individual worker's share of profit was suggested to be in proportion to his total earnings during the preceding 12 months minus dearness allowance and any other bonuses received by him. If an individual worker's share exceeds 25 per cent of his basic wages, the cash payment is to be limited to this 25 per cent and the rest to be held on his account either in his provident fund or otherwise.

The Committee further recommended that profit sharing should be unit-wise so that the workers may have a direct interest in the fortunes of the undertaking. Although profit sharing has been tried (1) as an incentive to production, (2) as a method of securing industrial place, and (3) as a step in the participation of labour in management, it has had a chequered history in almost all countries. The experience of the Tata Iron & Steel Company has not been a very happy one in spite of a handsome bonus of 22½ per cent of net profits; the productivity for workers has declined instead of going up. There may be many reasons for this decline, but one is forced to the conclusion that profit sharing has at best failed in its avowed aim of increasing productivity.

Bonus Commission and Payment of Bonus Act. Bonus has been a controversial subject for long-time. In December, 1961, therefore, the Government of India set up a Bonus Commission under the Chairmanship of Mr. M.R. Meher. The Commission was required (a) to examine the extent to which bonus should be influenced by the current rates of wages, (b) to consider the question of payment of bonus based on profit, (c) to recommend the principle for computation of such bonus, and (d) to suggest the methods of payment of bonus.

The Commission submitted its report in January, 1964 and made the following recommendations :

(a) A minimum of 4 per cent of a worker's total annual wages or Rs. 40 whichever is higher should be paid as bonus.

(b) The maximum limit of bonus should be fixed at 20 per cent of the total annual earnings of the workers.

(c) The bonus should be calculated after providing for depreciation and taxes, 7 per cent return on paid up capital and 4 per cent on reserves.

(d) Sixty per cent of the available surplus should be earmarked for the payment of bonus to workers and employees and the balance of 40 per cent should go to the employers.

(e) All employees drawing upto Rs. 1,600 p.m. and have been in employment for at least 30 days in a particular year are entitled to bonus.

(f) The quantum of bonus payable to employees drawing more than Rs.750 will be the same as for those drawing Rs. 750 p.m.

(g) The bonus must be paid within 8 months after the close of the year.

The Government accepted these recommendations and the Bonus Act was passed in 1965. The provisions of the Act apply to every factory regardless of the number of employees and to other establishments employing not less than 20 persons in India except the State of Jammu and Kashmir. The Act was amended in 1969 for increasing the amount of surplus. In 1972, a Review Committee under the Chairmanship of Dr. B.K.Madan was appointed, and the minimum rate of bonus was raised to 8.33 per cent irrespective of the fact whether the concerns were making profit or not. In September, 1975, however, The Payment of Bonus (Amendment) ordinance was promulgated. It provided that bonus was payable only on the basis of profits or on the basis of production or productivity. The minimum rate of bonus payable for the accounting year 1974 was fixed at 4 per cent.

The Janta Government restored the minimum rate of bonus of 8.33 per cent in 1977 by the Payment of Bonus (Amendment) Act, 1977. This bonus is payable whether there is allocable surplus or not.

WAGE POLICY

A rational wage policy is essential both on social and economic grounds. Without it there is a danger of unreasonable exploitation of workers leading to discontent which must result in disharmony between workers and management. Therefore, a sound wage policy is needed in the interest of workers, employers, the Government and the country.

Three Concepts of Wages. Three concepts of wages are commonly used in discussions on wage policy, and the same concepts were also explained by the Fair Wages Committee, namely: (1) Minimum wage, (2) Fair wage, and (3) Living Wage. These are broadly based on the needs of the workers and the capacity of employers to pay, as also on the general economic conditions prevailing in a country.

Minimum Wage. A minimum wage is said to be a wage which is sufficient to satisfy at least the minimum needs, of at least a frugal and steady workers. According to the Committee on Fair Wages, the minimum wage is an irreducible or minimum amount regarded necessary for the bare sustenance of the worker and his family and for the preservation of his efficiency at work. In most countries, like ours, Minimum Wages Legislation has fixed minimum wages for specified occupations, especially where sweating and exploitation of labour had been prevalent. In fixing a minimum wage both the need of the workers and the capacity of the industry to pay are taken into account. From the social point of view, an industry which cannot even afford to pay a basic minimum wage has no justification for existence in the long-run.

Living Wage. It is a wage which should offer an employee incentive to work and produce enough in quantity, without sacrificing quality, so that the payment of such a wage is justifiable by the industry. The living wage for a worker should be such as to include not merely the cost of maintenance for himself but also for supporting his family. As such, living wage should include provision for the following:

(a) Bare necessaries such as food, clothing and shelter;

(b) A measure of frugal comfort including (i) education for children, (ii) protection against ill-health, (iii) requirements of essential social needs, and (iv) a measure of insurance against the more important misfortunes including old age.

(c) Some margin for self-development and recreation.

The concept of living wage, to be realistic, should be linked with economic conditions and the size of the family. While determining expenditure under various heads, attention should be paid to the changes in the cost of living as prices fluctuate from time to time.

Fair Wage. While living wage is the cherished goal and the ultimate aim or target, a fair wage is a step towards a living wage. In the narrow sense, a wage rate is fair if it is equal to the rate prevailing in the same area and industry. In the wider sense, fair wage is the predominant rate available for similar jobs and occupations throughout the country or in all industries. The demand for a fair wage is also reflected in the slogan 'equal pay for equal work' In simple terms, it is the wage equal to that received by employees performing equal work, demanding equal skill, equal difficulty and equal unpleasantness. Equal work is considered not only in the same job but also work in similar and comparable jobs. Fair wage is positively higher than the minimum wage, but it may be lower than the living wage. The actual fixation of a fair wage depends upon the productivity of labour, prevailing rates of wages, level of national income, capacity of the industry to pay, wage differentials in corresponding places and the importance of industry in relation to the national economy.

Wage Policy in India. Recent wage practices in India in the organised sector are such that dearness allowances are paid to neutralise at least partially, price increases, bonus paid as per the Bonus Act, and fringe benefits given under the Employees' State Insurance Act and the Employers' Provident Fund Act. Wage Boards have attempted to settle wage disputes, taking into account the principle of fair wages first set forth by the Report of Committee on Fair Wages.

The Fair Wages Committee recommended that the "minimum wage should represent the lower limit of the fair wage, the upper limit being the capacity of industry to pay". Between these two limits, the Committee suggested that the fair wage should depend upon (a) productivity of labour; (b) prevailing rates of wages in the same and similar occupations in the same neighbouring localities; (c) level of the national income and its distribution, and (d) place of the industry concerned in the economy of the country. The Committees' recommendations are similar to the requirements laid down above.

The Minimum Wages Act, 1948. The Act empowers the Central and State Governments to fix minimum rates of wages and to revise such wages from time to time in respect of schedule employments. The State Governments are required to appoint Advisory Board for fixing minimum wages and there is to be a Central Advisory Board to advise on the wage-fixation matters in general and for the coordination of the work of the State Advisory Boards. All these bodies are to consist of an equal number of employers' and employees' representatives, and of independent persons not exceeding one-third of the total number of members.

Fringe Benefits. In almost all industrial organisations, the employees receive several employee benefits, commonly known as fringe benefits. In India, fringe benefits for the labour personnel in common use may be categorised as; Dearness allowance; overtime pay; shift allowance; conveyance allowance; city compensatory allowance and special housing assistance allowance. To these may be added cleaning charges for uniform, travelling allowance, canteen subsidy, food subsidy, special financial assistance to worker's educational schemes, leave with wages for attending basic education schools etc. Discount on purchases from the employees' cooperative societies, supply of uniforms and scholarships for higher education, as also financial assistance to workers' club and supply of newspapers, magazines and books to the workers' reading rooms. Free medical aid, contributions to workers' welfare fund, different kinds of bonus, besides the statutory bonus, and many other benefits.

Mechanics of Wage Fixation in India. Collective bargaining can be used for negotiating wages and hours of work. Unfortunately the trade unions lack solidarity. The multiplicity of unions often makes workers. bargaining power rather weak. The state, therefore, has provided conciliation and adjudication machinery. The Industrial Tribunals usually attempt to fix a reasonable rate of wage. Very often, however, a tribunal's award was not found satisfactory either by the employer or the workers. The Government, therefore, set up a number of Wage Boards as envisaged by the First and the Second Five Year Plans.

Wage Boards. A Wage Board is a tripartite body with representatives of management, and workmen, presided over by an independent person nominated by the Government. The Board is required to fix wages in accordance with the principles of wage fixation as discussed earlier. The Wage Boards help to resolve the disputes in a democratic manner by bringing the parties together, without compulsion on either side. It may, however, be pointed out that a Wage Board can only make recommendations, as there is no legal sanction behind it. But for all practical purposes, a Board's recommendations are regarded as awards, and if unanimous, are made binding on the parties. The first wage board was set up in 1957 in the Cotton Textile Industry. Following this, Wage Boards were set up for working journalists, sugar, cement, jute, tea plantation, rubber and coffee, coal mining, iron and steel, road transportation and electricity undertakings.

The wage boards have, however, been criticised on the following counts :

1. The recommendations of the Boards have no legal sanction so that the parties are not bound to accept them.

2. Very often the recommendations of the Boards are results of compromise decisions and cannot therefore become consistent long range wage policy.

3. When the Government has to legislate for giving effect to the recommendations of a Board, as it happened in the case of the Textile Board award, the element of compulsion is brought back, and that militates against the very spirit of such boards.

4. Since the members of the Boards are not always the true representatives of the employers and workers, individual units are led to doubt the bona fides of the members.

5. The Boards often make recommendations on all-India basis, with the result that at times the special problems relating to any particular region may be ignored.

6. The time lag between the making of the recommendations and their implementation is generally very great.

Some people have suggested that Wage Boards should be made statutory bodies. They can probably be used as potent agency for collective bargaining in units which are in favour of this method of wage fixation.

PART EIGHT
Financial Function of Management

CHAPTER XXXIV

FINANCIAL PLANNING

Need for Finance. Within the present basis of society it is impossible to escape from Finance in one form or another. To live we must have money, without money we cannot live. Thus, money may be the root of all evils, but the need for money is certainly the root of all industrial and trading activity. Money is needed when the business is started. It is required to keep the business going, and it is needed when the business expands. Availability of money and its use whenever required therefore is Finance. By Industrial Finance, we mean the finance for industries whether the industrial unit is established by an individual proprietor or partnership or an incorporated company. The phrase Corporate Finance has narrower meaning and is applied to the study of Finance for companies.

But where does the money come from the financing business enterprises ? There is only one original source of money. That source is savings. An individual may invest his savings to set up his own business. Or he may purchase securities, such as shares and debentures of a company. With technological developments necessitating the use of large amount of capital, the company form is being relied upon more and more. The company is indeed the most important form of business organisation from the point of view of capital investment. In a large business enterprise the time lag between production and consumption is very great. Finance is required to keep the industrial unit going. Since large industries are owned by companies or what is known as the corporate sector, the problem of industrial finance has become the problem of Corporate Finance. In the case of other forms of organisation, the problems of finance are not so complicated, as the proprietors themselves are able to solve them. Even their borrowings are on personal level and they are personally liable to repay the loans. Hence, our discussion is confined to the problems relating to Corporate Finance.

What is Financial Planning ? The planning process includes the selection of the objective and the selection of policies, programmes and producers to achieve the objective. The basic purposes of financial planning are to make sure that adequate funds are raised at the minimum cost (optimal financing) and that they are used wisely. Thus, the persons concerned with financial planning and policies must see that the concern has the proper amount of capital, because an inadequate supply will hamper operations and will lead to difficulties. Too much capital, on the other hand, means that the earning will have to spread over an unnecessarily large amount of capital. Moreover, the ready availability of funds may lead management to make unwise investments in inventory, fixed assets, or in other assets that have no direct connection with the operation of the company. A proper financial planning is therefore necessary. The financial plan should be set up to provide for the present needs and future developments. The various considerations relating to present capital need, requirements of investors and possibilities of expansion, resolve themselves into a present determination of :[1]

1. The amount of capital to be raised.
2. The form and proportionate amount of securities to be issued.
3. Policies as to the administration of capital.

It is not too much to emphasise the correct estimates of present and future needs of capital, a sound capital structure and proper use and protection of capital will lead to success of the company.

Calculation of Total Capital to be raised. In calculating the total capital needed for putting the project into operation, six main costs are to be considered. They are :—

1. Promotion expenses, which include the incorporation fee, office expenses, lawyers' fees and other preliminary expenses.

2. The cost of the fixed assets necessary for the business to begin with such as land, buildings, machinery, tools and equipment. The amount invested in these items is called Fixed Capital.

3. The working capital, i.e., the amount of cash or liquid capital which is advisable for the business to have on hand.

4. The cost of financing. This includes the total cash needed to be raised and the cost of raising this money, e.g., brokerage and commissions.

5. The costs of getting the business well established. These include operating losses which are usual in the initial stages of production.

6. Cost of intangible assets such as goodwill, patents, etc.

There are two methods of calculating total capital needed. The first is the *Estimating Method* and the second is the *Comparison Method.* Under the first method an estimate is made of the various costs. By the comparison method an attempt is made to find a number of concerns similar in size and condition to the proposed company. On the basis of the statistics of these concerns, probable requirements in the way of capital for the new concern are estimated. The use of both methods will yield better results.

As of the various items listed above only some are important for our consideration, they may be condensed to (1) financing of fixed assets; (2) financing of current assets or working capital; and (3) financing of improvements and extensions. A brief description of these is given in the following paragraphs :

Fixed or Block Capital. The capital which is invested in fixed or more or less permanent assets like land and buildings, plant and machinery, tools and equipment, patents, etc., is called "Fixed Capital". In other words, it is the capital which is used to procure assets without

1. Gilbert, Harold: *Corporation Finance,* p. 84.

which the business of the company cannot be carried on, or which cannot be disposed of without breaking up the business. In term of time, it is the capital which is used to meet the long-term needs of the business.

The amount of the fixed capital required depends upon (i) the nature of industry, (ii) the size of the business unit, and (iii) the technique of production. A heavy industry like iron and steel, or a public utility or railway, will require a heavy amount of capital for equipment and property. A light industry such as the textile or pharmaceutical industry will need a smaller amount of block capital. A trading concern will need very little fixed capital. Of course, in all cases the size will have influence on the fixed capital investment. The larger the scale the heavier the investment in fixed assets.

Working Capital. The working capital is invested in raw materials, in stock of partly finished products, in meeting current or day-to-day expenditure on salaries, wages, rents, rates, advertising, and in cash. In other words, it is the capital which is utilised in meeting current liabilities by cash payments in the ordinary course of business. It is also defined as "the excess of current assets over current liabilities", or current assets *minus* current liabilities are equal to working capital. Therefore, the capital required to finance the current assets (working capital) is short-term capital.

The following diagram adapted from Practical Commercial Self-Educator, Odham's Press shows the liquid capital needed to start up the circulation in a new business and keep the business in operation.

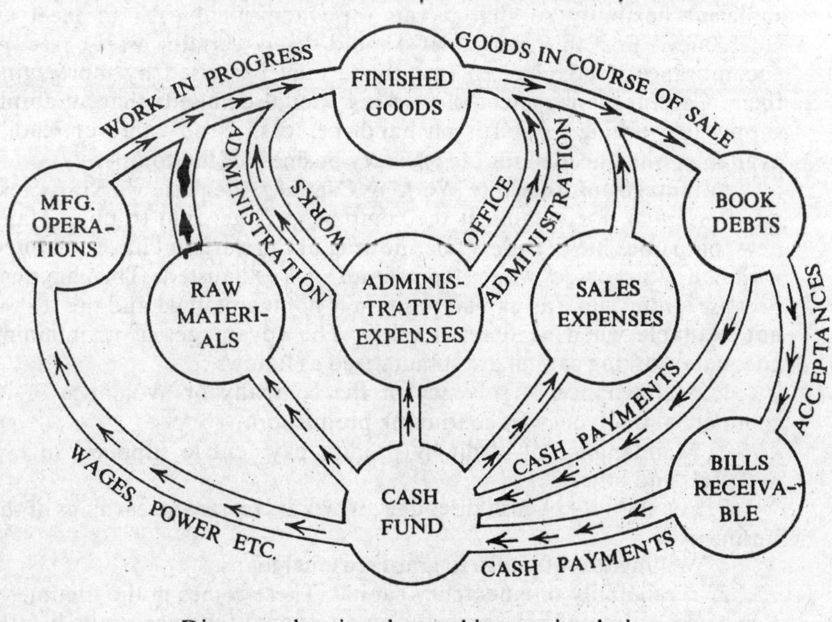

Diagram showing the working or circulating capital of a manufacturing business.

It should be noted that current assets are continuously changing. In the simplest form, some time must pass between the time taken in production and the time when the goods so produced are sold. During this time cash is being used to buy raw materials, to pay wages and to store goods. The cash to meet these charges must be at hand. When goods are sold for cash at a profit, the cash is used to meet further charges regarding raw materials and wages, etc. In this manner a circle is formed and the capital revolves or circulates constantly from cash to current assets and then to cash and so on. Since it is repeatedly invested, recovered and re-invested as long as the concern is functioning, or is being "turned over", it is often called "circulating" or "revolving" capital. As there is a constant need of working capital in the case of a going concern, a certain amount of it must always be at hand or permanently held. This is usually described as 'permanent', 'regular' or 'fixed' working capital, and is the minimum with which the company can manage in 'normal' times. There are also variable or fluctuating funds, i.e., the amount of ready cash, in excess of the permanent working capital, needed to meet heavy seasonal payments. If, after these payments are made, the cash is replenished quickly by corresponding seasonal sales, these funds may be acquired by bank loans. If, however, the cash is realised slowly or after a long interval, or if seasonal needs arise several times during each year, then the seasonal need may well be merged in a large permanent working capital. The excess may bring in interest when the seasonal need falls off. A company should try to retain sufficient flexibility so that it can raise additional cash to meet an emergency. For this reason it should keep certain assets free of encumbrance if possible, so that funds may be raised by mortgaging them. Careful management of working capital demands that an ample supply of working capital is on hand, i.e., cash is on hand, or readily available, when needed for the ordinary business of the company.

Advantages of Adequate Working Capital. Adequate working capital is essential, for without it the company will get into trouble. Many new companies have made a fine showing at the start, but have collapsed within a year or so when their funds got exhausted. This happens because strong working capital position is not maintained and the cash is not available when need for it arises. The advantages of maintaining adequate working capital are summarised as follows :

1. Maintenance of solvency of the company or avoidance of its commercial insolvency by continuing production.

2. Maintenance of credit by prompt payment to suppliers of raw materials and others.

3. Availability of cash discounts, which increases the earnings of the business.

4. Willingness of banks to grant seasonal loans.

5. Availability of emergency capital. There comes in the lifetime of a business a time of emergency when additional funds can save it from ruin. These additional-funds will be readily available because of the security in the form of adequate working capital.

6. Regular payment of dividends is assured, for the profits need not be retained in the business, if the working capital is adequate. It will also help to raise money for future operations.

7. Efficiency in the conduct of business is maintained, for with ample working capital, supply of raw materials is assured, steady work becomes the rule, with the rise in the morale and efficiency of workers and reduction of cost of production. The company also enjoys goodwill in the community.

Factors Affecting Working Capital. It follows from what has been said above that a company, in order to keep on the safe side, should have adequate amount of working capital, neither too small nor too large. There is, however, no standard formula which can be applied to fix the amount of working capital. It will vary from industry to industry and from company to company. The Nature of Business and the Volume of Business are two fundamental factors affecting working capital. For example, if the business consists of providing transport facilities, or supplying electricity, the working capital required will be very small. In such cases almost all of the investment will be in the fixed form. If the business is manufacturing, then a relatively small proportion will consist of working capital. If it is a trading concern or a banking company, the chief requirements will be for working capital. Different degrees of mechanisation in different companies will influence their working capital needs. Subject to these general remarks, the following factors are of practical importance in determining the working capital requirements of an individual concern.

1. *Length of Period of Manufacture.* The average length of the period of manufacture, i.e., the time which elapses between the commencement and end of the manufacturing process, is an important factor in determining the amount of the working capital. If it takes long to make the finished product, the working capital required will be very large and kept invested in the form of work in progress at all stages. If the period of manufacture is short, the working capital needed will be very little. Two examples will illustrate the point. To build and equip a large ship may require three or four years, and the outlay may amount to several crores of rupees. So an enormous amount of capital will be necessarily tied up in raw materials, wages paid to workers and other expenses incident to manufacture and for a long time. On the other hand, a baker needs very little working capital, for only one night is required to bake the bread which he sells in the morning. Between these two cases may fall other businesses with varying periods of manufacture requiring different amounts of working capital.

2. *The Nature and Value of the Product.* Where the cost of the raw materials to be used in the manufacture of a product is very large in proportion to its total cost and so its final value, working capital required will be very large. In a sugar or cotton textile mill raw materials are of prime importance necessitating the availability of huge amount of working capital. A building contractor also needs huge working capital for this reason.

3. *Use of Manual Labour or Mechanisation.* In labour intensive industries larger working capital will be required than in the highly mechanised ones. The latter will have a large proportion of fixed capital.

4. *Need for keeping large stock of raw materials and finished goods.* The necessity for stockpiling of raw materials and finished goods increases the amount of funds tied up in stocks and stores. In certain lines of business, such as where the materials are bulky and should be purchased in large quantities, as in cement business, stockpiling of raw material is usual. Similarly, in public utilities, which must have adequate supplies of coal to assure regular service, stockpiling of coal is necessary. In seasonal industries finished goods stocks have to be stored during off seasons. All these require large working capital.

5. *Turnover.* The rapidity of turnover of working capital is an important factor. By turnover is meant the ratio of annual gross sales to average working assets. In simple words, it means the number of times the amount invested in working assets has been recovered in cash by sale of the finished production and re-invested in the working assets during a year. The faster the sales are made the larger the turnover. Conversely, the greater the turnover, the larger the volume of business that can be done with a given working capital. In spite of large sales, the amount of working capital required will be small, because of quick sales. Where the sales take place slowly, the working capital shall have to be larger. Two examples of extreme cases will illustrate the point. A News Agent starting business by selling only daily papers will have a very rapid turnover, for the capital invested in the papers plus profits are "turned over" once a day. If he adds magazines which sell slowly, his turnover will decrease and the need for working capital will increase. When he adds books which sell more slowly, the turnover will decrease still further and there will be the need for greater amount of working capital. On the other end of the scale is a great jewellery store, which must stock valuable goods of different varieties from which the customers may choose. The sales in this case are infrequent and irregular; so the turnover is very slow necessitating the provision of very large amount of working capital.

6. *Terms of purchase and sales.* If an enterprise is paying cash for everything it buys and is selling on credit, it will obviously need a working capital sufficient to buy outright its entire stock of goods, and also for everything that has been sold on credit. On the other hand, if the enterprise is able to buy on credit and sell for cash, it can have whole stock without making immediate payment, and pay its bills as they mature out of the receipts from its own sales. The length of the period of credit has a bearing on working capital.

7. *Conversion of working assets into cash.* The need to have cash on hand to meet various requirements, e.g., payment of salaries, rents, rates, etc., has an effect on the working capital. The greater the cash requirement, the higher will be the working capital needs of the company. But if the company has a good amount of quick or liquid

working assets, it need have no working capital. The rule in this respect is the nearer the company approaches the condition of cash being the working assets (because they can be cashed quickly), the smaller are its requirements of working capital.

8. *Seasonal Variations.* A great many companies have to carry on seasonal business. Sugar mills, oil mills and ginning factories produce all their stocks within a limited period, and have to keep the goods for off season. Therefore, much larger sums of money must be tied up in working assets during a certain period which are reduced as the sales are made.

FINANCING OF MAINTENANCE AND BETTERMENTS

In addition to the provision of adequate working capital, a successful concern provides for maintenance and betterments. The company's assets must be taken care of. A well-oiled and well-cleaned machine will not deteriorate and lose its efficiency as quickly as one that gets no care. Maintenance involves inspection and repairs and in some renewals. Maintenance costs are essential, for a properly maintained plant may require lower maintenance costs. Therefore, the plant must be kept in repair if the business is to survive. Skimping on maintenance is not permitted by a good management.

It should be remembered, however, that maintenance costs are not uniform for different industries, or for companies in the same industry, or within the same company during different periods. Sound management procedures call for a maintenance budget somewhat related to the volume of operations. Necessary repairs should be carried out as and when the need arises. Postponement might cause unnecessary loss and additional expenditure.

Relative Proportion of Block Capital and Working Capital. The proportion between fixed and working capital depends on the nature of the industry and the length of time required for manufacturing the product. The more roundabout the processes of production, the greater is the amount of fixed capital in relation to working capital. In the producer goods' industries, the fixed capital predominates over working capital. In the 'consumer goods' industries working capital scores over the block capital. For example, in the cotton textile industry the amount of working capital often exceeds the fixed capital, owing to the cost of raw cotton and stores, and the length of the period during which these and the finished goods have held. The proportion between working capital and block capital is 3 to 1. In iron and steel industry and heavy engineering, both the fixed and working capital required is very large. The proportion between fixed and working capital is about 3 to 2.

CAPITALISATION AND CAPITAL STRUCTURE

The term "capitalisation" has been differently defined by different writers, each authority giving his own interpretation of the concept. For instance, Dewing takes it to mean[1] "the sum total of the par value of all shares". In legal sense, capitalisation usually refers to the total par value of the authorised share capital of the company. As used in business and financial circles, "Capitalisation" is generally understood to refer to either of the following concepts :

1. The total par value of all the securities—shares and debentures—outstanding at a given time.
2. The total par value of all the securities outstanding at a given time plus the valuation of all other long-term obligations.[2]

All of the above definitions refer to the quantity or *amount* at which a company's business can be valued. Some writers take a broader view of the concept and regard "Capitalisation" and "financial planning" as interchangeable terms. According to them capitalisation includes the amount of capital to be raised, the securities through which it is to be raised, and the relative proportions of the various classes of securities to be issued, as also the administration of the capital.

The narrower view, which refers to the amount of securities to be issued, or the amount of capitalisation, is the view that we shall keep in mind while discussing the concept of "capitalisation". The kinds of securities to be issued for raising the necessary capital will be discussed under "Capital Structure" or "Capital Gearing".

We may now attempt a definition of Capitalisation as derived from our discussion of the concept. Thus *Capitalisation is the sum total of all kinds of long-term securities issued by a company as well as the surpluses which are not meant to be distributed.* If we spell out the securities and surpluses mentioned in the definition, we will find that Capitalisation comprises—

(a) the value of shares of different classes;
(b) the value of 'creditorship securities', i.e., the value of bonds and debentures issued by a company and still not redeemed;
(c) the amount of long-term loans secured by a company; and
(d) the value of surpluses, whether earned surpluses or capital surpluses.

The reader may be reminded that earned surpluses consist of undistributed profits which have been accumulated over a period of time in the form of reserves, for utilising them to meet the company's longterm requirements. Capital surpluses arise from other sources. For example, if an asset of the company is sold at a profit the surplus resulting from this transaction is capital surplus. Such surplus is also meant for long-term use in the concern.

It should also be remembered that the term capitalisation is used only in relation to companies and not in respect of sole proprietorships or partnership firms. It is to be distinguished from 'capital' which represents total investment or resources of a company, or its total wealth. It should

1. Arthur S. Dewing, *Corporation Finance,* p. 4.
2. Gilbert, Harold, *Corporation Finance,* p. 83.

also be distinguished from 'share capital' which refers only to the paid-up value of the shares issued by a company. Capitalisation, on the contrary, refers only to the par value or face value of the long-term securities, shares and debentures plus reserves meant to be used to meet long-term and permanent needs of a company.

Sometimes capitalisation refers to certain *action* on the part of the company's organisers or managers. In this sense, "capitalisation is the act or process of fixing the value of an enterprise for the purpose of determining the capital liabilities which the company may assume in exchange for the property".[2]

Theories of Capitalisation. There are two well recognised theories of capitalisation, viz., Earnings Theory and Cost Theory.

Earnings Theory. The earnings theory assumes that an enterprise is expected to make profit and states that its true value depends upon its earnings and earning capacity. Accordingly, the capitalisation of a company, or its value, is equal to the capitalised value of its estimated earnings. To find out this value, a company, while estimating its initial capital needs, should also prepare an estimated profit and loss account for the first few years. To make the earnings estimate, the manager will have to arrange for making a sales forecast and work out the probable costs. These probable costs can be worked out by him by applying his knowledge of material and labour costs and other operating expenses. Having arrived at the estimated earnings figures, he will compare them with the actual earnings of other companies of similar size and engaged in the same business, making necessary adjustments. After this the rate at which other companies in the same industry and similarly situated are making an earning on their capital will be studied. This rate is then applied to the company's estimated earnings for determining its capitalisation. A simple example will make the point more clear. Let us suppose, the estimated net profit or earnings per year during the first few years is Rs. 50,000 and 10 per cent is a fair rate of return for this kind of business; that is to say, the other companies, similarly situated and carrying on the same business, are earning a return of 10 per cent on their capital, the capitalisation of the company based on earnings will be

$$\frac{50{,}000 \times 100}{10} = \text{Rs. } 5{,}00{,}000.$$

It will be observed that two factors enter into the determination of capitalisation. One, how much the business is capable of earning, and second, what is a fair rate of return for capital invested in a particular enterprise. These two factors bring out the merit of valuing or capitalising a company on the earnings basis, for the amount is directly related to the company's earning capacity. It is therefore possible to find out the worth of the company. After all a *company is worth what it will earn.* But a new company may find it risky

1. Bonnevill and Dewey, *Organizing and Finance of Business*, p. 108.
2. Gerstenberg, *Financial Organisation and Management of Business*, p. 167.

to depend only on the estimates of its earnings as the expected return; for even the most experienced promoters can make mistakes in their estimates. It may be desirable to adopt the cost basis of capitalisation, or better still, adopt both the bases.

The Cost Theory. Under the cost theory of capitalisation, a company's value, worth or capitalisation is worked out by aggregating, the cost of fixed assets, such as plants, machinery, patents and the like, the working capital regularly required to run the business, the cost of establishing the business and other costs like promotion expenses. The total original outlays on all the above-mentioned items obviously becomes the basis of company's capitalisation. This method is quite useful in the case of a new company, as capital estimates so made give a clear indication to the promoters of the amount of the capital to be raised. There is a close relation between the amount of capital needed and capitalisation and the promoters determine both together with a view to persuading prospective investors to invest their savings. The basis, however, is not quite satisfactory in capitalising a company whose earnings are not steady and are rather irregular. For example, in the case of a manufacturing or commercial enterprise, the earnings may change with the passage of time whereas the amount for establishing and starting business remains unchanged. It may happen that some of the machines are idle or are not fully employed. In that case the earnings will be low and company will not be in a position to pay a fair return on the capital invested. But the value of the investment made in the company's business will not fall. The result will be over-capitalisation.

Over-Capitalisation. A company is said to be over-capitalised when its earnings are not large enough to yield a fair return on the amount of shares and debentures that have been issued, or where the amount of securities outstanding exceeds the current value of the assets. In other words, the amount of the shares issued is much in excess of actual requirements, and this is more than real assets, so that the dividend rate is too low to allow the shares to sell at par value. In simpler terms, a company is over-capitalised when its earning power is so low that it has not at its command sufficient profits to pay dividends and interest at proper rates. This, of course, does not indicate that there is an excess of capital. What it means is that in an over-capitalised company the funds invested therein are not effectively or profitably employed with the result that there is a drop in the earning capacity and in the rate of dividend payable to equity shareholders, as well as a fall in the market value of the shares. The concern may be said to have grown beyond the financial optimum.

The reader is warned against the danger of believing that a company should be regarded as over-capitalised because over a few years it has not been able to pay a proper rate of dividend. The phenomenon occurs as a result of persistent inability to earn the prevailing rate of return on its outstanding securities and so failure to pay adequate rate of dividend.

Over-capitalisation may result in any of the following ways :

1. *Where an enterprise raises more money by the issue of shares and debentures than can be profitably used in it.* A larger capital than necessary may be issued intentionally or un-intentionally. It is issued intentionally to take advantage of a favourable sentiment in the market. The issue of too large a number of shares will leave very large funds idle or unemployed with the company.

2. *Where the promoters over-estimate future earnings at the time of promotion, or under-estimate the capitalisation rate although earnings were correctly estimated.* In either case the result will be the same. The shares will fall below the purchase price, in the first case (over-estimate of future earnings) because the shareholders will not receive the dividends they had been promised, and in second case because the rate of return is less than what money invested in such a company should bring.

3. *Where a company borrows large sums of money and has to pay a very high rate of interest,* a rate definitely higher than its rate of earning. This will result in a very big portion of the profits being given away as interest to the creditors, leaving little or nothing for the shareholders. With the fall in the rate of dividend the value of the shares will also decline.

4. *Where a company incurs high establishment or promotion expenses.* This has been a potent cause of over-capitalisation. Very often excessive amount is paid for goodwill, patent rights, and for fixed assets acquired from the transferor company or from promoters and others associated with the company. All these amounts paid usually have no relation to the earning capacity of the assets.

5. *Acquisition by a company of plant, machinery and building during the boom period makes the company over-capitalised.* During a boom, the prices are very high, with the result that the amount of capital is very large. On the setting in of depression the value of these assets decline although their book value is maintained at the original figures. In the result some of the capital is actually lost. The earning capacity of the company has declined, while the amount of the capital is very large, causing a sharp drop in dividend and a consequent fall in the share value.

6. *Where a company does not make adequate provision for depreciation, replacement or obsolescence of assets.* Failure to make such provision may be due to the fact that the company is distributing higher rates of dividend to shareholders. After some time the company will discover that, although the book value of the assets is still high, the real value is very low. In the result, the efficiency of the company is adversely affected. Its earning capacity falls causing a drop in the value of the shares. The company suffers from the malady of over-capitalisation.

7. *Where a company spends too much on elaborate establishments, costly machines and devices,* while the production is not enough to justify such a huge expenditure. This raises the operating costs with the result that profits available to the shareholders are inadequate.

8. *Where a company follows a liberal dividend policy, instead of ploughing back a good portion of profits.* Such a company may find after some years that the book value of its shares is higher than the real value and that it is over-capitalised.

9. *High rates of taxation may cause over-capitalisation of a company.* Excessive taxes may leave very little with the company to provide for depreciation and replacement and to pay dividend to shareholders. This is likely to bring down the earning capacity of the company and causes a fall in the real value of its shares, leading to over-capitalisation.

Watered Capital. Water in the capital is that part of the capital which is not represented by assets, or which does not help directly in the profitable working of the business. It is like water mixed in milk. Where a company, taking over an existing business as a going concern, pays by means of shares a far heavier price for the goodwill of that business than ordinary prudence would approve, the major part of that capital being represented by this intangible asset, the capital is said to be watered. The share capital is not represented by assets of equal value. If a company pays Rs. 2,00,000 as the price of goodwill which, if valued prudently, would be worth Rs. 75,000 only, the capital has water to the tune of Rs. 1,25,000.

'Watered capital' and 'over-capitalisation' are not necessarily synonymous terms and must be distinguished. Water usually goes into capital at the time of the promotion of a concern. Over-capitalisation is discovered after the company has worked for some years. Water in capital may or may not result in over-capitalisation. A company may start with water in its capital, but its working may be very efficient and it may make high earnings resulting in its shares selling above par. The company will not be over-capitalised in spite of the fact that part of its capital is watered. On the other hand, the company may receive full payment for its shares and yet be over-capitalised because it is unable to develop sufficient earning power and so its shares sell below par.

Evils of Over-capitalisation. Over-capitalisation has evil effects on the company, the shareholders and the society.

Effects on the company. (1) In an over-capitalised company, with its reduced earning capacity resulting in fall of the market price of the shares, the investors' confidence is shaken.

(2) A company whose shares sell below par suffers from a fall in its credit, so that it may find it hard to raise further capital for extension and improvements.

(3) Questionable devices may be adopted to inflate profits or to cover up lack of profits. Accounts may be manipulated and "unearned dividends" paid to keep up the show of prosperity by "window-dressing".

(4) To make up the deficiency of the decreased earnings, provisions for depreciation, replacements and renewals will not be made. This will lead to decline in efficiency still further, and fall in profits.

(5) An over-capitalised company more often than not has to go into

liquidation, unless drastic steps are taken to re-organise its share capital. But re-organisation in such circumstances will involve heavy loss of goodwill of the company.

Effects on Shareholders. (1) As a result of over-capitalisation, the shareholders suffer a loss in capital through depreciation of investment. The shares of an over-capitalised company sell below par in the market, while the shareholders had originally paid for them a higher price. If they sell now, they will suffer a heavy loss on account of the fall in the value of the shares.

(2) The shareholders also suffer in the loss of income because of a low return on their investment which is usually uncertain and irregular. If they hold these shares, they will hardly get any dividend.

(3) The shares held in an over-capitalised concern have small value as collateral security. In case the shareholders wish to borrow on their security.

(4) The price of shares in an over-capitalised company is invariably unstable and lends itself to speculative manipulation or gambling. The real investors suffer because of this manipulation.

(5) The burden of re-organisation, which is more or less certain in the case of an over-capitalised company, if it has to survive, will fall heaviest on the shareholders. It is possible that they have received no returns on their investments. For the purpose of re-organisation the share capital is usually reduced to write off lost capital. This results in the reduction of the par value of the shares which is a clear loss to the shareholders.

Effects on Society. (1) Over-capitalisation spells decline in efficiency. This leads to reduction in the quality of the products, but rise in their price. The consumer is the sufferer, as he has to pay more for poorer quality.

(2) In an over-capitalised company, the workers are also likely to suffer. It may either try to effect economy or raise its profits by cutting on wages and welfare facilities on the pretext of "low profits".

(3) An over-capitalised concern may not be able to stand the competition from other concerns and may have to close down. The collapse of a few over-capitalised companies may cause panic, which would injure the interests of the creditors. The workers will also suffer on account of the loss of their jobs.

(4) Over-capitalisation also leads to the misapplication of the resources of the community. The capital lying idle could have been better and more profitably employed by other concerns in need of funds.

(5) Over-capitalisation generally creates a bad ethical atmosphere in industry. Speculation and gambling in shares of an over-capitalised concern is encouraged.

(6) The industry as a whole may suffer a great setback. Even legitimate enterprises may not be able to obtain adequate capital. Public confidence in industrial investment is bound to be shaken.

Remedial Measures to Correct Over-capitalisation. As the disease of over-capitalisation is diagnosed after it has taken root, it is not easily cured. An operation in the form of an outright re-organisation will be the most suitable remedy for the malady. One or more of the following corrective measures may be tried with advantage :

1. *Reduction of long-term debt.* The debentures and bonds should be redeemed to restore parity between the book value of the company and its real value. Redemption of debentures can be made with cash received by issuing more shares, but that will do more damage than good. This remedy will not reduce total capitalisation, for the capital reduced by redeeming debentures will be replenished by the cash received by issue of new shares. Total reorganisation and the utilisation of the accumulated earnings for the purpose is the proper remedy to bring down the capital.

2. *Reduction of interest on debentures.* The existing debenture-holders may be persuaded to accept new debentures at lower rate of interest to remedy the malady. But to induce them to accept the new low interest rate debentures, the company shall have to allow them some premium. This would not result in the reduction of over-capitalisation.

3. *Redemption of Preference Shares.* Where preference shares, particularly cumulative preference shares, carry high dividend rate, they may be redeemed.

4. *Reduction of par value of shares.* If the equity shareholders can be persuaded to agree to the reduction of the par value, this is a fairly good method.

5. *Reduction in number of equity shares.* The equity shareholders may agree to accept one share in exchange for several shares, if they are convinced that this procedure does not decrease their proportionate interest in the equity. The method is quite good.

Under-Capitalisation. Under-capitalisation is the reverse of over-capitalisation. It means insufficiency of capital required to meet the *total needs* of the concern. A company will also be under-capitalised 'when the rate of profits it is making on the total capital is exceptionally high in relation to the return enjoyed by similarly situated companies in the same industry'. It is a condition where the real value of the company is more than the book value. Where a company has inadequate funds to meet long-term needs, it will not be able to function efficiently. To meet its long-term needs, it may have to use its short-term funds. This may mean borrowing for short periods at very high rates of interest; and such funds may be called back when needed most urgently. Excessive borrowing acts as a deterrent to industrial growth.

Causes of under-capitalisation. Under-capitalisation may occur for any of the following reasons :

1. *Under-estimation of future earnings.* The promoters, while preparing the financial plan, may anticipate future earnings at a lower figure and capitalise on the basis of that estimate. If the earnings prove to be higher than the estimated figure, the company will become under-capitalised.

2. *An unforeseeable increase in earnings.* A company floated during depression will usually find itself under-capitalised during boom period. This may happen because during boom the earnings would often increase proportionately more than the increase in the amount of capital employed.

3. *Conservative dividend policy.* A company may follow a conservative and commendable policy of paying moderate rate of dividend and creating adequate reasons for depreciation, renewals and replacements and plough back the earnings. This policy would result in high earnings and the increase in the real value of the company's share will be more as compared with its book value.

4. *Maintenance of high efficiency.* A company may maintain and improve its efficiency by financing out of its savings new schemes and processes of production. As a result of efficient production, the profits of the concern will go up, and the real value of the company is likely to exceed its book value.

5. *Under-stating earnings.* A company may under-state its earnings or build up secret reserves for keeping the price of shares down. This sometimes permits 'insiders' to acquire the shares at low prices, and thus exploit the 'outside' shareholders. Secret reserves are now prohibited by law.

Evils of under-capitalisation. (1) An under-capitalised enterprise is constantly faced with the danger of going out of business. Although an under-capitalised company can show a high rate of earnings on equity shares, yet their high price may act as a deterrent to their marketability.

(2) If the shares fail to find ready market, their market price will be lower than what the earnings of the company justify.

(3) The high rate of earnings per share may encourage potential competitors to enter the market with obvious consequences. The workers will demand higher wages. Failure to pay them will create dissatisfaction among them resulting in lowering of efficiency and so fall of production or higher costs.

(4) High rates of earnings are also likely to create an impression among the consumers that they are being overcharged.

(5) In case of the levy of excess profits taxes, the company may lose by under-capitalisation.

Remedial Measures. Under-capitalisation can be more easily remedied than over-capitalisation. It can be corrected by any of the following methods:

1. *Sub-division of shares.* The company may offer several shares of smaller value in exchange for every share held by the shareholder. By this method the capital remains the same and the rate of earnings is not changed. But the amount paid per share as dividend will be much less.

2. *Increase in par value of shares.* The assets of the company may be revalued so as to assign them higher values. The existing shareholders may be given shares carrying higher face (par) value for the old shares. This procedure will bring down the rate of earnings per rupee of share value but will not affect the amount of dividend per share.

3. *Capitalisation of profits.* The most commonly used and effective method is to capitalise the profits kept as reserved and issue bonus shares. This will easily increase the capitalisation and number of shares. The dividend rate per share and the rate of earnings will be reduced.

Over and under-capitalisation compared. Sometimes a question is asked : "which is better, over-capitalisation or under-capitalisation"? The answer is simple:"neither"! Judging from the evils or disadvantages of the two, the question should be : "which is the lesser evil"? Since both are undesirable, we can make a general statement that a company should neither be over-capitalised nor under-capitalised. It is true, though, that over-capitalisation can prove more dangerous to the company, the shareholders and the society than under-capitalisation. Also, over-capitalisation occurs more often than under-capitalisation. It can be remedied only after the shareholders have paid a high cost in the form of sacrificing their interests in the company or by bringing still more capital into it. Under-capitalisation encourages competition on the part of rivals, characterised as it is by high share values and high rates of dividend. It can be remedied by capitalisation of reserves. To conclude, it may be emphasised that proper capitalisation should be the aim; it should be related to the earning capacity.

CAPITAL STRUCTURE OR CAPITAL GEARING

We have so far discussed the problems relating to capitalisation, which comprises a company's ownership capital or share capital and its borrowed capital, as represented by its long-term indebtedness, usually in the form of debentures. The other phase of corporation finance is the capital structure of a company. By capital structure we mean the kinds of securities and their proportionate amounts that make up the capitalisation.[1] Decisions about the amount of securities to be issued relate to *capitalisation,* and decisions as to the kinds of securities to be issued relate to the *capital structure.* In what proportion will the various kinds of securities be issued is the question of *gearing of capital. Thus, capital gearing may be defined as the fixation of a proper ratio between two or more types of securities and the ratio which each type of security will bear to the total capitalisation.* A company would be *highly geared* when the proportion of equity capital to the total capital is small or when the proportion of preference shares and/or debentures bearing fixed rate of dividend and/or interest is large. On the other hand, a company which raises a very large proportion of its funds by the issue of equity shares which do not bear any fixed rate of dividend *is low geared.* In simpler terms, a company which has raised its funds mainly by the issue of equity shares is *low geared,* and a company which has secured substantial proportion of its long-term funds by the issue of preference shares, bonds and debentures is *highly geared.* A company which has obtained

1. Gerstenberg, *Financial Organisation and Management of Business,* p. 166.

funds amounting to Rs. 5,00,000 by the issue of equity shares and Rs. 2,00,000 by the issue of preference shares and debentures is low geared, and the one which raises Rs. 4,00,000 by the issue of debentures and preference shares and Rs. 1,50,000 by the issue of equity shares is geared high.

The capital structure of a company, in relation to the prospects of earning, should be built up on the fundamental principles of safety and economy. In general a company in choosing the different securities may follow these principles : (1) It may issue only equity shares when regular earning or income is not quite certain. (2) When the average earnings are rather good, even though annual earnings may not be quite certain, preference shares (preferably cumulative) may be issued. (3) A company which expects to have a stable and reasonably good income to pay the fixed interest may issue debentures. These general principles do not in practice become operative, because a company usually resorts to the issue of all the three types of securities. It is the gearing that is really of importance in capital structure, and, we will do well to consider the factors which influence capital gearing.

Factors Governing Proper Capital Gearing. The following factors determine the proportion of securities or govern the capital gearing of a company:

1. *Trading on the equity.* The term "equity" refers to the "stock" or ownership of a company and "trading" means "taking advantage of". Hence, 'trading on equity' means taking advantage of equity share capital to borrow funds on reasonable basis. It refers to the additional profit which equity shares make at the expense of other forms of securities. It is based on the theory that there is a difference among the rates of returns on the different types of securities issued by a company. On borrowed capital as also on preference capital, the company pays only a fixed rate of interest or dividend. If this fixed rate is lower than the general rate of company's earnings, the equity shareholders will enjoy an advantage in the form of additional profit; and this amounts to trading on the equity. Thus, trading on the equity is an arrangement under which a company makes use of borrowed funds carrying a fixed rate of interest in such a way as to increase the rate of return on the equity shares. A company, by issuing debentures and preference shares, can substantially increase the dividend rate for the equity shareholders. On the other hand, the dividend rate cannot go beyond the general earning, if the entire capital is raised by the issue of equity shares. This can be explained by an illustration.

Suppose a company has a total investment of Rs. 10,00,000 and earns a profit at the rate of 10 per cent on it. If the company had raised the entire capital by the issue of equity shares, it cannot pay more than 10 per cent as dividend, or more than Rs. 1,00,000. If the company decides to trade on equity it may raise funds in the following way:—

(i) By issuing debentures carrying 6 per cent interest—Rs. 5,00,000;

(ii) By issuing preference shares carrying dividend at the rate of 9 per cent—Rs. 2,00,000;

(iii) By issuing equity shares—Rs. 3,00,000.

In this case, the company will have to pay, out of the profits of Rs. 1,00,000 earned by it, a sum of Rs. 30,000 as interest on debentures and Rs. 18,000 as dividends on preference shares. A sum of Rs. 52,000 will be available for paying dividends to the equity shareholders. As the amount of equity capital is now only Rs. 3,00,000, the dividend will be at the rate of 17.33%. In this way, by issuing debentures and preference shares. the rate of dividend to equity shareholders is considerably increased. There is another advantage in the saving of income tax, as the interest paid on debentures is deductible expense. This double advantage may tempt the management to trade on equity, but the concept also suffers from certain limitations.

Limitations on policy of trading on equity. The policy can succeed only if the company is sure of stable and regular income without any fluctuations. With fluctuating income, the company, saddled with large amount of indebtedness, may not be able to pay its interest during lean years and suffers the consequences following an inability to pay interest to its creditors. A company whose products have very low elasticity of demand and which has non-speculative field of operation and so stable and certain income can derive real benefit from trading on equity Therefore, too much dependence on borrowed funds should be avoided. Mead suggests[1] that only so much loans should be raised as will absorb not more than 20% of the gross earnings of the company by way of interest. Let us suppose that the profits of the company amount to Rs. 1,00,000. Twenty per cent of this amount is Rs. 20,000. Therefore, the amount to be borrowed must not be more than a figure on which the interest will add up to Rs. 20,000. If the rate of interest is 10% the amount of the borrowed funds should not exceed Rs. 2,00,000, for if they exceed this figure the interest will exceed Rs. 20,000.

Secondly, if the rate of earning of the company is less than the rate of interest, borrowing will depress the rate of dividend on equity shares below the rate of earning rather than accelerate it. If the rate of earning of a company is 5% it will make a profit of Rs. 50,000 on its total investment of Rs. 10,00,000. If it issues 6% debentures for Rs. 5,00,000 and equity shares for the remaining amount of Rs. 5,00,000, it will have to pay Rs. 30,000 as interest and only Rs. 20,000 will be left which will yield 4% dividend on equity shares, which is lower than the rate of earning of the company.

The *third limitation* on trading on equity is that every successive borrowing can ordinarily be made at a higher rate of interest, because every new lender runs a greater risk. In the result, raising funds by borrowing becomes more costly and any advantage to the equity shareholder is reduced.

Lastly, to successfully resort to borrowing on large scale the

1. *Corporation Finance,* p. 117.

company must have huge investments in fixed assets which can be offered as security to the lenders.

2. *Retention of control of the company.* Different types of securities are included in the financial plan, because the promoters want the public to invest their savings without getting control of the affairs of the company. Accordingly, the promoters, with a view to retaining control of the company, will raise large proportion of the funds by issuing debentures and preference shares. It is the equity shareholders who exercise control as they enjoy the voting powers, and the debenture holders and holders of preference shares have no voting rights. In this way, the company is able to raise vast funds from the public, and the promoters or existing management can control the affairs of the company by holding equity shares.

3. *Elasticity of capital structure.* The capital structure should be as elastic as possible so as to provide for expansion and raising of future capital. Too much dependence upon debentures and preference shares makes the capital structure rigid as this requires the payment of fixed charges. As a general practice, debentures are not issued in the initial stages and are resorted to in case of emergency or for the expansion purpose. In their stead preference shares are issued at the commencement.

4. *According to the nature of the business.* The nature of the business shall have to be taken into account while preparing the financial plan and determining the basic capital structure. Thus, a manufacturing company will have a different capital structure from merchandising, financing, extractive or public utility business. These enterprises differ with regard to the amount of investment, risk of failure involved and trade cycles as well as freedom from competition. Consequently, one type of business may find it profitable to issue securities which may not be suitable for the others. For instance, public utilities and railway companies will be financed through fixed interest securities such as bonds and debentures because of their monopoly condition and stability of income. Manufacturing businesses are usually subject to competitive conditions, and rely to a large extent on equity share capital.

5. *Period for which funds are required.* Funds needed for short periods are usually borrowed from banks as short period loans or received as public deposits for a year or two. Such loans can be paid back as soon as the company has raised its own funds. Long-term finance can be raised by the issue of shares and debentures.

6. *Cost of financing.* The cost of financing has an important influence on the choice of securities, as the funds can be collected at varying costs through different kinds of securities. In raising capital a company must incur the lowest cost in terms of interest, dividends and the relationship of earnings to the price of the shares. In general, a company would raise funds by borrowing when interest rates are low and by issuing equity shares when the earnings-price relationship of shares is high. Bonds can always be issued more cheaply than shares, for the

buyer of bonds looks more for safety than the size of the income. As stated earlier, the company can deduct the interest paid on bonds or debentures as a business expense in arriving at its income tax, thus further reducing the cost of capital. Such deduction can be made for dividends paid on shares. Yet, debentures should never be issued if there is any doubt about the regular payment of interest.

7. *Market conditions.* The 'capital-gearing' is also influenced by the prevailing conditions of the money market and the security market. The investor is very often influenced by the general mood or sentiment of the capital market, although his own mood and prejudices may also guide him in investing his savings in one type of security or the other. The phase of the trade cycle will have great influence on the choice of a security. For example, in times of depression investors will look more to safety than to income, and will be willing to invest in debentures and not in equity shares. During boom period, the investors will go in for shares. The management, looking for more funds, must therefore watch the mood of the market and adjust its financial plan to it for successful capital-gearing.

8. *Needs and requirements of the investors.* From the point of view of the investor, the time and amount of investment will very largely depend upon the nature of the security, as also on his own way of thinking. A security to be attractive must possess the fundamental characteristics. The principal invested in it must be sure, it must yield a fairly good return and provide stable income. In addition, it must command a ready market and value as a collateral, should be of an acceptable denomination and duration, and should enjoy potential appreciation. However, to meet the needs of different kinds of investors, it is necessary to issue different kinds of securities. The investors who want the security of the principal and stability of income will go in for debentures. Preference shares will be bought by those who are for higher and stable income, as well as safety of the capital invested. Equity shares will be taken up by those who are ready to take risk for higher income and capital appreciation. They may also like to acquire control over the affairs of the company. It is also desirable to issue securities with different face values in order to secure subscriptions from people in the different strata of society—rich, middle and lower classes.

9. *Legal restrictions.* In certain types of businesses it may not be permissible to issue all kinds of securities. Therefore, hands of the management are tied by the restrictions that may be imposed by the law. For example, the Indian Banking Regulation Act, 1949 does not allow any banking company in India to issue any securities except equity shares.

TIME OF FLOATATION

The selection of the proper time for floatation of a company is an important factor in financial management and capital gearing. Business

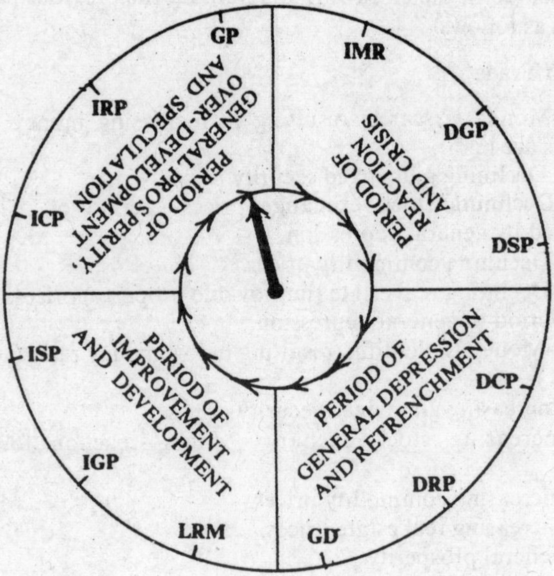

Diagram showing Cycle of Trade

in all countries where there is a recognised system of financial machinery and modern credit, passes concurrently through a succession of phases or cycles of uncertain duration, the complete cycle usually occupying a period of three to five years. These cycles of trade or economic "ups" and "downs" which represent the tendency of certain conditions of trade to repeat themselves over and over again in the same order although not necessarily in the same manner, may be grouped into four phases of period:

1. Period of improvement and development.
2. Period of general prosperity, over-development and speculation.
3. Period of reaction and crisis.
4. Period of general depression and retrenchment, followed again by period of improvement.

The periods of trade activity, or general business prosperity, are reasonably well heralded in advance by the conditions of the money market and the stock market. And they proceed in a logical way, by first involving the more basic lines of manufacturing, and subsequently spreading to industries dealing with complex products and consumers' goods. It may be noted that the trade cycle is the result of the reactions of three markets—the money market, the stock market and the market for industrial, mining and agricultural products. The order of changes in a cycle is presented in the clockwork diagram on the previous page, which is explained as follows:

The Cycle of Trade

IMR—Money is scarce, resulting in increasing money rates (i.e., interest rates are high).

DGP—Declining gilt-edged security prices.

DSP—Declining stock exchange prices—period of reaction and crisis followed by general depression.

DCP—Declining commodity prices.

DRP—Declining real estate (immovable property) prices.

GD—Period of general depression.

LRM—Money is plentiful, resulting in low money rates (i.e., interest rates are low).

IGP—Increasing gilt-edged security prices.

ISP—Increasing stock exchange prices—reaction followed by prosperity.

ICP—Increasing commodity prices.

IRP—Increasing real estate prices.

GP—General prosperity.

Period of Improvement. During this period new enterprise and courage are manifested. Quiet industries become active again, and there is a ready output of capital for development purposes. Commodities which have realised relatively low prices begin to advance. Failures are less frequent and business, although not large, is promising and from a state of depression comes back to a more normal condition. At this period deposits are at the maximum limit and loans are small in proportion to deposits. Interest rates remain relatively low. There is an anticipation of increased earnings in the future which causes the price of securities, that have previously been quoted at a low figure, to advance to normal or even somewhat above it.

Period of Over-development. Following the above conditions there is a more intense business activity and a period of over-development. Factories and workshops are now fully employed. There is a strain put upon banking resources, loans have increased rapidly and overrun deposits. Interest rate rises. The banks begin to restrict facilities. The stocks having reached top, prices begin to decline owing to the fear of future trouble. The market is top heavy owing to persons having bought on rising prices, actuated by the hope of big profits on bill market.

Period of Reaction. This is always a difficult period. Commodity prices and those for securities must be brought into harmony with producing and consuming power. A check must be imposed upon unrestricted expansion which has been engendered by the preceding period of improvement. Great strain is thrown on the banking world which is busily engaged in saving fixed assets from being altogether destroyed by forced liquidation on a panic-stricken market. Deposits are relatively low, but increase as liquidation is proceeded with. Loans are in great demand, and interest rate rises to a high figure. Towards the end of the period, banking resources become easy owing to strain being released. Now is the opportunity to pick up good class securities, which have fallen from a high price.

Period of Depression. The pendulum has now swung far back and points to the period of calmer stagnation, which inevitably follows crises and storms, such as have shaken the business world to its foundations. Business becomes normal and is carried on sound lines and with manifest restrictions. Prices for commodities are at low level, traffic is small and bank earnings are much reduced in value. Failures are above the average, business is generally steady at a low level with perhaps a slight improvement towards the end. Interest rates are extremely low and banking reserves increase rapidly. On the stock market the demand for securities brings increased business and prices rise.

In view of this trade cycle, the financing of new enterprises or of extension of old ones may be most advantageously carried out during phases ISP and ICP, falling within the periods of improvement and general prosperity, while securities are still being absorbed freely at high prices, and long before a panic breaks. The money so raised can then be applied in providing equipment during the ensuing depression while the prices of materials and labour are low. "An enterprise launched according to this plan would be in a position to prepare for business slowly and thoroughly, to try out processes, to select the cream of the labour market, to establish discipline, and to settle all factors into a smooth working order so as to be ready to take advantage of the first recovery in demand."[1] On the other hand, if, as Matheson[2] has pointed out, "capitalists begin to build new works at a time of high prices, it will often be found that by the time they are ready prices have fallen, probably because new factories have increased the productive power, or even because the mere prospect of new factories induces demands. It is in a time of deep depression that a prudent purchaser will often find the best opportunity for buying or building a factory." Therefore, the work of collection of funds should be done during boom period and during the period of depression should be carried out the work of construction or purchasing of buildings and machinery so as to be ready with the product when the first rays of recovery are visible.

1. Jones, *op. cit.*, p. 30.
2. *The Depreciation of Factories* (3rd ed.), pp. 114-15.

CHAPTER XXXV

SOURCES OF FINANCE

The sources of finance for an enterprise can be many and diverse. In the case of individual proprietorship, the main source of finance is the individual proprietor. In partnership, the various partners contribute the funds. A joint Hindu family business obtains its capital from the family funds. This may be supplemented in each case by borrowed money in varying amounts according as the credit of the concern is good or poor. Since the capital requirements are comparatively small, there are hardly any financial problems confronting these enterprises. But major or large industries, which are run by companies, require vast amounts of capital, and must therefore resort to all sorts of methods for raising the necessary funds and tap all kinds of sources for the purpose. The main sources of finance in India may be classfied as—

1. Individual investment, only in the case of individualistic concerns.
2. Issue of shares of different kinds.
3. Issue of bonds and debentures.
4. Public deposits.
5. Loans from joint stock banks and indigenous bankers.
6. Gradual development methods of using profits to increase capital, i.e., "ploughing back" of earnings.
7. The State:
   (a) Life Insurance Corporation;
   (b) Financial Institutions;
   (c) Development Corporations;
   (d) Unit Trust of India.

METHODS OF RAISING FINANCE

We have considered at length the theory of financing and financial planning. The list of sources noted here may be re-classified according as one or the other is a suitable source of financing fixed and working capitals and extensions and improvements.

Financing of fixed capital The finance for fixed capital by our major or large-scale industries is raised through (1) share capital; (2) Debentures; (3) public deposits; (4) managing agents; (5) the State—loans from financial and development corporations.

Financing of working capital. The working capital of industries may be raised in three ways, namely, (1) by resorting to borrowing; (2) by issue of additional securities; (3) by re-investment of earnings. Indian industries have in the past raised their working capital mainly by borrowing. At present the main sources of working capital in India are (1) managing agents, (2) public deposits, (3) issue of shares and debentures, (4) loans from commercial banks, (5) loans from indigenous bankers and big financiers.

Financing of extensions and improvements. The financing of extensions and improvements is very important in the case of Indian industries, because of the need for development. The sources of finance for these are— (1) re-investment or ploughing back of profits, (2) issue of securities, either shares or debentures or both, (3) managing agents, (4) public deposits, (5) the State—loans from the Financial and Development Institutions.

The following pages deal with the several sources of finance, and discuss their relative merits and defects. Some suggestions are also made for improving methods of financing of industry in our country.

Broadly speaking, there are two chief or basic models of raising funds by a company, namely, (i) issuing of 'ownership securities' or shares and (ii) 'creditorship securities' or bonds and debentures. The money collected by the issue of shares is termed as 'owned capital' and that raised by the issue of bonds and debentures is called 'borrowed capital', which may also include loans from the public, the managing agents and specialised finance institutions. The citizen wish to find a profitable use for their money. That money they may utilise in buying ownership securities or shares in a company, or they may buy creditorship securities or debentures, or lend it otherwise to the company. We shall begin our discussion with shares passing on to other methods as we proceed.

SHARES

A company's capital, or 'owned capital', as it is sometimes called, is divided into equal portions which are bought by persons, called the shareholders, who wish to acquire an interest in the company. Stated differently shares represent equal portions into which the capital of a company is divided, each shareholder being entitled to a portion of a company's profits corresponding to the number of shares he holds. For example, the capital of a company may be Rs. 50,00,000 divided into 50,000 equal portions or shares of Rs. 100 each. If a person holds 100 shares and a 10% dividend is declared by the company, he will get Rs. 1,000 as his share of the profit being 10% of Rs. 10,000, the value of his shares. The aggregate ownership interest in the company is Rs. 50,00,000 and his interest in it, as measured by the sum of money, amounts to Rs. 10,000. As stated earlier, share capital is most suitable for meeting long-term requirements of a company, in particular fixed capital needs, as it is not paid back to the shareholders as long as the company is a going concern.

Kinds of Shares. Before the passing of the Companies Act, 1956, a company could issue any or all types of shares, such as preference shares, ordinary shares, deferred shares or founders' shares, possessing different rights. The Act, however, allows a public company to issue only two types of shares, namely, Preference Shares and Equity Shares. A private company may issue any class of shares.

Preference shares. Preference shares are those shares which carry preferential right in respect of dividends and also the preferential right in regard to repayment of capital in case of winding up of the company. The rate of dividend on these shares is fixed. But this dividend on preference shares must be paid before any dividend is paid on other shares. The directors have the right to decide whether dividend should be paid or not even if the company has made some profit during the year. Preference shares are themselves divided into different classes. There are **Cumulative Preference Shares and Non-cumulative Preference Shares.** *Cumulative* preference shares enjoy the right to receive, when profits permit, the dividends missed in years when profits were nil or inadequate. In the case of *non-cumulative preference* shares, arrears of dividends do not accumulate, so that any unpaid dividend in any year will not be paid in future. For example, a company had no profits in 1966 and paid no dividends, but in 1967, it made good profits. The non-cumulative preference shareholders will get dividends only for 1967, and the cumuiative preference shareholders will get dividends for both 1966 and 1967.

The Guaranteed Preference Shares are usually issued where a private concern is converted into a limited liability company or where one company is sold to another company. The seller or any other interested party, in these cases, guarantees the payment of a specified rate of dividend for a certain number of years.

A company may issue *Participating Preference Shares,* which have a right to something over and above their fixed dividend. The holders of such shares will get their fixed dividend and a share of dividend after dividend at a certain rate has been paid on equity shares.

Redeemable Preference shares can also be issued by a company, where it undertakes to return the amount paid on such shares under certain conditions, making it clear at the time of their issue that the money is intended to be returned. These shares can be redeemed only if they are fully paid up, and out of the profits which would be available for dividend or out of the proceeds of the issue of new shares made with the object of redemption. These shares cannot be redeemed out of the sale proceeds of any property of the company. In order that the redemption of the shares should be convenient and systematic, the Companies Act provides that where the redemption is to be made out of profits, a Capital Redemption Reserve Fund must be created by transferring to it an amount out of profits equal to the nominal value of the shares to be redeemed. Redeemable preference shares are a very good source for long and medium-term funds, and play an important role in corporate finance. Their redemption helps to remedy over-capitalisation.

Sub-section (5A) added to section 80 by the Companies (Amendment) Act, 1988 prohibits the issue, by any company of

irredeemable preference shares or any shares redeemable after the expiry of a period of 10 years from the date of their issue.

Convertible Preference Shares. If the holders of preference shares are given a right to convert these shares into equity shares within a specified period of time, such shares are known as convertible preference shares. A company may also issue partially convertible preference shares. Under this plan, only a portion of preference shares can be converted into equity shares.

Advantages of Preference Shares. Preference shares have certain merits and may be issued to achieve certain objectives.

(a) Although dividend payable on preference shares is fixed, they are susceptible to capital appreciation. Cautious and conservative investors who do not want to take risks regarding capital but would like to get higher income than what can be earned on debentures usually go in for preference shares.

(b) The promoters and the existing management can retain control over the affairs of the company by issuing preference shares to 'outsiders', as these shareholders can vote only on resolutions directly affecting their rights.

(c) Preference shares may be issued as a bonus for the buyers of equity shares and debentures, thereby increasing their sale.

(d) The amount of redeemble preference shares can be paid back after the company has built up a capital reserve fund out of its profits.

(e) These shares can be issued to finance capital expenditure involved in expansion programmes and to strengthen the present equity base with a view to future expansion.

(f) Some companies may issue preference shares with the object of liquidating their public deposits in excess of the limit prescribed by the Reserve Bank of India. Under a directive issued by the Reserve Bank of India no non-banking company can accept public deposits of an amount which aggregates to more than 25% of its paid up capital and free reserves. Tata Mills issued preference shares in August, 1967 for this purpose.

(g) The equity shareholders are able to earn higher dividends because of the fixed rate payable to preference shareholders.

(h) These shares do not prove a burden on the finances as do debentures because dividends are paid only if profits are available. The issue of preference shares rather than bonds and debentures, leaves the company with a stronger balance sheet and hence greater leeway for future borrowing. These shares are especially useful if its assets cannot be given as sufficient collateral security for borrowing on debentures. By the issue of preference shares, a company can save itself from paying higher interest which it must pay on fresh debentures against assets which are already mortgaged. A company can reserve its strength by the issue of these shares rather than the issue of debentures which would require adequate security in the form of a mortgage on its assets.

(i) It costs less to finance with preference shares than with equity shares.

Disadvantages of Preference Shares. Despite so many merits of preference shares, there are some important disadvantages also, as given below:

(a) It usually costs more to finance with preference shares than with bonds and debentures. They have to be given a higher dividend than the prevailing rate of interest on debentures. Also, most of the preference shares are cumulative which means that all the arrears of preference dividends must be paid before anything can be paid to the equity shareholders.

(b) The issue of preference shares involves dilution of equity shareholders' claim over the assets of the company.

(c) The issue of preference shares may limit the flexibility of company because of restrictive covenants. For example, very often consent of preference shareholders is necessary to incur further indebtedness.

(d) The existence of preference shares may pave the way to insolvency. Where business activity is falling but before serious strains are felt the Board of Directors may (and very often it does) decide to continue paying dividends on preference shares to preserve their attractiveness though subsequent events may prove that cash so used should have been put to more productive use.

(e) The existence of preference shares may adversely affect the creditworthiness of the company. The creditors may anticipate that the continuance of dividend on preference shares even after the suspension of dividends on equity shares and the use of funds for the retirement of preference shares may deprive them of the chance of getting back their principal in full in the event of the winding up of the company.

(f) The most serious disadvantage of preference shares is the non-deductibility of preference dividend for income-tax purposes. As a result, a company has to earn not only the percentage dividend to which the preference shareholders are entitled but also the tax related thereon. For example, the current rate of dividend on preference shares in India is 9.5 per cent. To be able to pay this rate, the company should earn not 9.5% but at least 21.1%, assuming the tax rate to be 55%, the rate applicable to most of the companies in India. If the company is not able to earn this much, the earnings available to the equity shareholders will be adversely affected.

Equity Shares. As per the Companies Act, shares which are not preference shares are equity shares (sometimes called ordinary shares). Dividend on them is paid after the fixed dividend on preference shares has been paid. The rate of dividend on them varies according to the amount of profits available and the intention of the Board of Directors. In the event of the winding up of the company, equity capital can be paid back only after all the other claims, including those of the preference shareholders for the refund of their capital, have been settled. The equity shareholders control the affairs of the company, as they are entitled to vote at the general meeting of the company. The preference shareholders can vote only if their rights and interests are affected. These shares earn very good dividends, but they also run the risk of earning nothing. While the preference shareholder is cautious and prefers security to return, the equity shareholder is venturesome and goes in for higher income in preference to security. He is really the risk bearer. The equity share capital, or venture capital as it is sometimes called, is subscribed by the public in larger proportion than preferred capital.

Advantages of equity shares. The advantages of issuing equity shares are many:

(a) The equity shareholders are not entitled to any return as dividend unless sufficient profits are available for the purpose, and unless the Board of directors decides to recommend the payment of dividend. As such these shares do not cast any burden on the resources of the company.

(b) Directors enjoy the discretion in setting dividend policies. Generally, dividend payment are apt to be more stable and also more liberal.

(c) With an equity shares base, the company can raise funds easily in the future, either by issuing preference shares or debentures, as equity shares have no charge on the assets.

(d) These shares are a very good source of long-term finance, as their value is paid back only in case of company's winding up and that too, after preference shareholders have been paid back their capital.

(e) The company runs no risk of magnifying losses in bad periods through trading on equity.

(f) Equity shares provide a company with the requisite flexibility in the disbursement of its income and avoids the rigidity of fixed payments.

Disadvantages of equity shares. Equity shares have the following disadvantages:

(a) It costs more to finance with equity shares than with preference shares or debentures.

(b) Raising of capital only by equity shares may bring about dilution of control, as certain groups of equity shareholders may manipulate control to the detriment of the company.

(c) If equity shares alone are issued, the company cannot trade on equity, with the result that it loses the opportunity to obtain capital at low rate, as well as the opportunity to increase profits in prosperous periods.

(d)Excessive issue of equity shares is likely to result in over-capitalisation.

Deferred Shares. Deferred shares can now be issued only by private companies and not by public companies. These shares used to be of small nominal value and were frequently taken by the promoters of a company with a special purpose, namely, keeping control in their hands. As each share gave the holder one vote; these shares enabled the promoters to control the working of the company with a very small investment. Only after preference and equity shareholders have been staisfied do they receive a dividend. As voting right has now to be strictly in proportion to the amount paid up on shares, they cannot be used as a means of acquiring control over public companies, and have lost all their attraction.

Shares of No Par Value. In India and England a share in the share capital of a company has a certain nominal, face or par value, which indicates the extent of interest in and liability to the company of the holder of the share. In the U.S.A. and Canada, shares which have no face or par value are issued by many companies. The capital of a company issuing shares of "No Par Value" is divided into a certain number of shares having no specified denomination. The share certificate merely states the number of shares held by a shareholder without mentioning the face value of the shares. The dividends on those shares are paid at the rate of a given amount per share and not as a percentage of the par value of each share, as there is no par nominal value to be used as the base of a percentage. Such shares are not allowed to be issued in India. In the U.K. the Gedge Committee had recommended in 1954 that companies should be allowed to issue ordinary shares of no par value. The Jenkins Committee in 1962 not only endorsed the recommendation of the Gedge Committee but went a step further and recommended the issue also of preference shares of no par value.

Advantages of no-par shares. The following advantages are claimed for shares of no par value.

(a) The balance sheet shows a true and correct position with no par value shares, as the capital is equal to the net worth. Where par value shares are issued the equities side of the balance sheet is written up first and then assets are valued to balance equities, usually by way of exaggeration.

(b) The shareholders always know the real value of their shares, as the value of these shares is in direct relation to the earnings of the company.

(c) The shareholders are not liable to pay anything on these shares at a further date, as the full value of the shares is collected in the beginning. Being fully paid up no-par value shares may be sold at any price later on.

(d) Additional capital can be raised with great facility, as no-par shares can be issued at a price which is commensurate with the conditions of the capital market. There is no question of issuing of shares at a discount, as there is no minimum par value of these shares. This provides relief from legal formalities relating to discount or commission on shares.

(e) As the value of the shares is automatically adjusted to the earning capacity, there is no need for reduction of share capital.

Disadvantages of no par value shares. The no par value shares suffer from the following drawbacks:

(a) Since no-par value shares have no face value, it is difficult to have a standard on the basis of which valuation of assets may be compared with capitalisation. These shares may be used to deceive ignorant investors.

(b) Mere chance being the governing factor there cannot be any planning for financing need, and this might result in over-capitalisation or under-capitalisation.

(c) There is no basis on which the value of the shares could be regarded high or low, nor is there any standard for judging the fairness of return on the investment.

(d) These shares render the balance sheet unduly complex and difficult to be understood by investors, creditors and tax authorities.

(e) Dishonest management will be in a position to manipulate the sale proceeds of shares and pay dividend out of capital.

(f) The creditors do not get the additional security of uncalled capital which is available to them in the case of partly paid share with par value.

(g) Because of the fluctuating nature of the capital account, it may become convenient for promoters to pay themselves unduly high remuneration.

DEBENTURES

So far we have dealt with 'owned capital'. But a company may wish to borrow money from persons who are willing to lend instead of buying shares. Money received as a loan is called "Borrowed Capital", and we shall now deal with it. The money lent to the company must be recorded and acknowledged. The document which the lender receives is called a debenture or creditorship security.

Definition. A debenture is an acknowledgement under seal of a debt by a company. It is also an instrument executed by a company under its common seal acknowledging indebtedness to some person or persons to secure the sum advanced. As shares are the equal parts of share capital, debentures are equal parts of a loan raised by a company. Like shares, they are also offered to the public by means of a prospectus The terms and conditions on which they are issued are endorsed on the back of the instrument. As in the case of the issue of shares, certain formalities required by the law must be carried out.

Distinction between shareholder and debenture-holder. (1) A debenture-holder is a creditor of the company, while the shareholder is one of the proprietors of the capital of the company and so responsible for its liabilities. The debenture-holder is one of the liabilities for which the shareholder is responsible as a proprietor. For this reason, a debenture is called a creditorship security and a share is known as 'ownership security'.

(2) As a creditor, a debenture-holder is entitled to receive the interest due to him whether the company makes any profit or not. A shareholder, on the other hand, can get dividend only if the company

makes a profit, and the Board of directors decides to recommend payment of a certain rate of dividend.

(3) The amount of debentures, being a debt, must be repaid by the company according to the terms of issue, but the share capital, except in case of redeemable preference shares, cannot be repaid unless legal formalities regarding reduction of share capital are observed.

(4) In the event of winding up of the company the amount due to debenture-holder must be paid before anything is paid to the shareholders.

(5) A lender of money (debenture-holder) can procure debentures at a discount, if the company finds it necessary to issue them and the law does not impose any restrictions. But shares can be issued at a discount subject only to certain stringent conditions as laid down in Section 79 of the Companies Act.

(6) An unlimited company cannot issue debentures and so cannot have debenture-holders, but it can have a share capital and shareholders.

(7) A debenture-holder has no right of voting at any meeting of the company, as a company cannot issue any debentures carrying such voting rights. A shareholder, as a member of the company, is entitled to attend and vote at the company's general meetings.

Classes of Debentures. Debentures can be classified into different types on the basis of the terms and conditions of issue.

As regards security. (a) Naked, unsecured or simple debentures are issued with merely a promise of payment, without any security by way of charge on the assets of the company for the payment of interest or capital; (b) *Secured or mortgage* debentures are those debentures which are issued with a charge on the undertaking and assets of the company as security. The charge may be fixed, i.e., on a particular asset, or it may be floating, when it does not fasten on any asset until it crystallises.

As regards registration or records. (a) *Registered debentures* are payable to a holder whose name, address and particulars of the holdings are entered in the register of debenture-holders maintained by the company. They can be transferred by a regular transfer deed and the transfer must be registered with the company; (b) *Bearer debentures* are payable to the bearer and are transferable by mere delivery. They are negotiable instruments, and the company keeps no records in respect of them. Interest coupons are attached to them and interest is paid to a person who produces the coupons.

As regards repayment or redemption. (a) *Redeemable debentures* are those the repayment of the principal by the company on which is to be made on a specified date, or by instalments either at company's option or at fixed intervals as long as the company is a going concern; (b) *Irredeemable debentures or perpetual debentures* are those in respect of which no time is fixed in which the company is bound to pay, although it may pay back at any time it chooses. The debenture-holders cannot demand payment as long as the company is a going concern and does not make default in payment of interest. But all debentures, whether redeemable or irredeemable, become payable on the company going into liquidation.

As regards status. (a) *Equitable debentures* are those which are secured by deposit of little deeds of the property with a memorandum in writing creating a charge; (b) *Legal debentures* are those in which the legal ownership of the property of the company is transferred by a deed to the debenture-holders as security for the loans.

As regards rank or priority. (a) *Preferred or First debentures* are those which are, in the event of winding up of the company, paid *first.*

Ordinary or Second debentures are paid after the preferred, or first debentures have been redeemed.

As to conversion. (a) *Convertible debentures* are those in which an option is given to the debenture-holders to exchange their debentures for shares in the company under certain conditions and limitations imposed regarding the period during which the option may be exercised; (b)*Non-convertible debentures* cannot be exchanged for shares, and the debenture-holder cannot change his status to a shareholder.

Merits of Debenture Issue. Debentures as the source of capital have many advantages. *From the point of view of the investors,* they offer a definite security and so appeal to the cautious investors. For example, a mortgage debenture-holder knows exactly what his security is, and generally, there are trustees to protect his interest. The better the security, the greater will be the chance of successful debenture issue. The debentures of sound and stable concerns are good investment from the point of view of the class of investors who do not want to risk their savings too much and yet wish to earn an income higher than what can be earned on gilt-edged or Government securities. Regular fixed rate of interest payable by the company to the debenture-holders even out of capital if profits are not available adds to the merits of debentures.

From the point of view of the company. (i) Debentures enable the company to raise finance without giving any control to the debenture holders, (ii) the rate of interest payable on them is fixed, as well as lower than the rates of dividend paid on shares; (iii) debentures being issued for a fairly long period, there is a certainty of finance for that specific period and the company is in a position to adjust its financial plan accordingly; (iv) the company is able to trade on equity, and consequently pay better rates of dividend to equity shareholders.

Limitations of Debenture Issue. It is no doubt desirable to raise part of the permanent finance by debentures, as it ensures economy, but all companies cannot usually issue debentures. Like preference shares, debentures constitute a financial burden on the concern. The companies suffering from the following weakness should not issue debentures; (i) companies with fluctuating earnings; (ii) small concerns with insufficient security to offer; (iii) companies manufacturing and supplying products with highly elastic demand such as luxury goods; (iv) companies which are unable to earn a rate of profits greater than the rate of interest payable on debentures. Therefore, debentures can be issued more easily and gainfully by those companies which have ample immov... property and a fairly stable earning capacity than one with little real estate and ever-fluctuating earnings.

A company would generally issue debentures to secure long-term finance for its initial needs and more often to supplement its share capital for extensions, improvements and developments. Only successful companies should resort to debenture issue, and even they should not depend too much on them, as very large borrowed funds adversely affect the interest of the shareholders even in the normal times.

To conclude our discussion on the question of devising the capital structure of a company, we may state here certain broad principles enunciated by authorities on Business Finance.[1]

1. In the field of public utility sector, a new company may collect a fairly large amount through debentures, as its future earnings will be liberal and reasonably constant.

2. In the case of basic and manufacturing industries, equity shares should be issued and no debt should be contracted in the beginning.

3. When fresh capital is required by an existing concern whose previous earnings have been unstable, only equity shares should be issued.

4. When a company has become well established and the earnings have stabilised, cheap borrowed funds may be used for expansion purposes, but when debentures are issued to obtain these funds, it should be seen that at least twice the interest charges are earned by public utility concern and four times by other industries. In case of preference shares, the amount should be one and a half times and two and a half times respectively.

5. When funds are obtained on the basis of mortgage issues, the total amount thus collected should not exceed half the depreciated value of the assets covered by the mortgage.

6. Industries having large fixed assets may issue irredeemable debentures or long-term redeemable debentures.

7. Preference shares may be issued when the earnings are irregular but when average over a period of years give a fair margin over preference share dividend.

PLACE OF DEBENTURES IN COMPANY FINANCE

For a long time, debentures were unpopular in India. Only 7 to 11 per cent of the total capital was raised by the issue of debentures. The reasons for this unpopularity were many and varied. Some of the main causes of their unpopularity were:

1. The heavy stamp duty (at Rs. 7.50 per Rs. 1,000 for registered debentures and Rs. 15 per Rs. 1,000 for bearer debentures) on debentures made them too costly as a source of finance.

2. The banks and other institutions regarded, though fallac...

[1] ...ewing, A.S., Bonneville, J. H. and Dewey, L.E., quoted by Mehrotra, H. C., in the *Indian Journal of Commerce*, December, 1967, p. 36.

the security of a company weakened after it had issued debentures. In fact banks in India never relished debentures.

3. The managing agents usually discouraged the issue of debentures for fear of losing their financial importance.

4. The debentures were usually issued with high face value, e.g., Rs. 1,000 each. so that people with moderate means could not invest in them.

5. Their limited marketability because of the lack of a developed capital market, made debentures unpopular. Cautious investors therefore went in for preference shares.

6. The presence of Government securities proved a great handicap, because conservative investors preferred them to debentures. Moreover, the banking and insurance companies, which were the main institutional investors, were required to invest a major part of their funds in Government securities under statutory provisions.

7. The terms of issue of debentures were not as attractive as in industrially advanced countries.

Recent trends. In recent years debentures have been used more and more for raising finance. The investors have subscribed for them more readily than before and the companies have taken steps to make them popular. Some of the conditions and factors which have been contributing to the popularity of debentures may be summed up as follows:

1. The companies have been issuing debentures with more attractive terms, e.g., by making them convertible.

2. The banks do not any more regard credit-worthiness of a company which issues debentures as lowered.

3. Trustee services are being made available to investors in debentures.

4. Institutional investors are now permitted to invest in company debentures and they are doing so at an appreciable rate.

5. The provision recently made to permit institutional investors, e.g., Industrial Finance Corporation, L.I.C., to convert debentures held by them into shares whenever they find it necessary, will encourage them to invest in debentures.

6. The development of underwriting facilities for the issue and sale of debentures.

7. Payment of debentures is allowed as a charge against taxable profits. The prospect of saving tax has acted as a spur to companies to issue debentures.

In short, debentures are no more unpopular.

INVESTMENT BANKS AND TRUSTS

The investment banks and investment trusts play a very important part as financial intermediaries between the investor and the industry. These institutions and similar others are discussed in the following chapter which deals with Finance and Development Corporation.

PUBLIC DEPOSITS

The cotton textile industry of Bombay and Ahmedabad and the tea gardens of Bengal and Assam depended in a large measure on deposits from the public. The practice has spread to almost all manufacturing and service industries and throughout the country. the period of which deposits have been accepted ranged from 6 months to 7 years and at fairly high rates of interest. In recent years, however, many companies failed to repay the money received on deposit. To protect the interests of depositers, the Reserve Bank of India was empowered in 1963 to exercise control over the acceptance of deposits by non-banking companies. The Companies Amendment Act, 1974 inserted section 58A which empowered the Central Government to frame Rules to regulate the acceptance of deposits. The Rules were framed in Feburary,

The Rules were framed in February, 1975 and have been amended a few times. The amended Rules provide as follows:

1. While inviting deposits the company must issue an advertisement including in it, its financial position in a leading English language newspaper and also in a vernacular newspaper. But, where a company intends to accept deposits without inviting such deposits it must deliver to the Registrar a statement in lieu of advertisement.

2. No company shall accept any deposit which is repayable on demand.

3. The minimum period for acceptance of deposits is normally 6 months and the maximum period 36 months. But for meeting short–term requirement of funds a company may accept deposits for a period not less than 3 months, but the amount must not exceed 10 per cent of the aggregate of paid up share capital and free reserves.

4. Deposits against unsecured debentures or from shareholders by a public company or guaranteed by the directors of the company, and those accepted for not less than 3 months to meet current needs, all put togther must not exceed 10 percent of the paid-up share capital and free reserves.

5. Others, i.e. deposits from the general public must not exceed 25 per cent of the aggregate of the paid-up share capital and free reserves.

6. It is further provided that in order that part of the assets are maintained in a liquid state, every company must before the 30th day of April of each year deposit or invest a sum which shall not be less than 10 per cent of the deposits maturing during the year ending on March 31 next following in a scheduled bank or Government securities or trust securities. This amount shall be used only for repayment of deposits maturing during the year.

7. Companies accepting public deposits must regularly file returns giving detailed information regarding such deposits.

8. Every deposit accepted on or after June 15, 1988 shall, unless renewed, be paid in accordance with the terms and conditions of such deposit. Where a company has failed to repay any deposit or part thereof, the Company Law Board may, either on its own motion or on the application of the depositor direct by order the company to make the repayment forthwith or within a specified time. Whoever fails to comply with the order of the Company Law Board shall be punishable with imprisonment upto 3 years and shall also be liable to pay a fine of not less than Rs.50 for every day during which such non-compliance continues.

Merits of Public Deposits. The method of borrowing by public deposits has the following advantages :

1. The method is very simple and does not involve any formalities. An application from the depositor and a deposit receipt to him are all that is necessary.

2. It is a cheap method of raising working capital, as the interest on such deposits is usually lower than charged by banks and financial institutions.

3. Further, the cost of collecting deposits from the public is much less.

4. Again, the loans advanced by financial institutions and banks are hedged in with numerous cumbersome conditions, such as imposition of convertibility clause, appointment of directors on the Board.

5. It helps companies to pay higher dividends than would be possible if the entire money were raised in the form of share capital.

6. The assets of the company remain unencumbered, as public deposits are mostly unsecured debts.

Demerits of Public Deposits. The method of public deposits has some inherent weaknesses:

1. The method is dangerous during period of depression when the industry is on the down grade. It is unreliable, because it is at such a time that the industry needs more money and the depositors become panicky and withdraw their funds. As a method of finance the system is like a "fair weather friend". When industry is flourishing, deposits are pouring in. but with a depression this source dries up. Hence, it is an unreliable source of finance.

2. The method has unduly narrowed the investment market by restricting the supply of good securities, such as shares, debentures to an ordinary investor.

3. From the point of view of the depositor, in spite of so many safeguards, there is a danger of his losing his money to the mismanaged companies.

Yet, despite legal limitations as noted above, public deposits with companies are estimated to be approximately Rs. 2,000 crores. This clearly shows that public deposits with companies serve a genuine economic purpose, by providing the badly needed funds to the companies and at the same time providing a good return to the public

MANAGING AGENTS

The managing agent has been the central figure in the promotion, financing and management of industrial concerns in India. In the field of industrial finance managing agents are a unique form of institutional agency. They have not only provided block and working capital themselves but have been instrumental in obtaining it from other sources. They have in the past done valuable service to the development of industrial enterprise in India, by promoting industrial concerns, and taking large blocks of their shares themselves or otherwise using their influence to place the shares amongst their friends and relatives and then amongst the general public. They have also supplied additional capital whenever the concerns under their control have needed it. Besides directly supplying finance, the managing agents have attracted funds in the form of debentures, bank loans and public deposits. By placing securities of the companies on the market they perform the functions of the underwriters or issueshouses of the West or "industrial banks" of the Continent, and in this manner bring together the investor and the company. In Ahmedabad, for instance, managing agents have at times held as much as 60 per cent of the share capital in cotton mills, and cases are not wanting where 85 to 90 per cent of the shares were owned by them. In Bombay, too, they are generally the majority shareholders. Their activity of initially holding a large number of shares but later unloading them on to the public is very similar to the function of the German industrial banks in the investment field. Also, during the development period or during depression when banks would not advance money or public would neither take up debentures nor make deposits, the managing agents have rendered considerable financial assistance.

Although the managing agency system has rendered a yeoman service to Indian industry by furnishing the necessary finances directly or indirectly, the system had many failings. Dr. Lokanathan points out three defects, viz., (a) domination of industry by financial rather than industrial consideration; (b) too much dependence on managing agents for finance; and (c) enormous speculation in the shares of the companies under their control. To these may be added the deterioration in recent years of their financial position and private fortunes which should be disclosed. We can no more depend upon managing agents as a source of finance for industries, as managing agency system has been abolished.

JOINT STOCK BANKS
(Commercial Banks)

Much has been said and written about the reluctance of banks in India to supply the block and working capital needs of the country's industries. It is argued that, like the German banks, the Indian banks should foster industry by taking shares and debentures of newly created companies. But the critics of the Indian banks fail to realise that when the German banks performed this function during a short period of 40 years from 1870 to 1913, they were purely industrial banks, receiving no deposits. But after 1913, they started receiving deposits and concentrated more and more on commercial banking business. Now they are commercial banks like the banks in England and India.

The Indian banks are deposit banks and their liabilities are short term, they can make advances only for short periods. They cannot tie up their funds in long-term loans as the deposits can be withdrawn either on demand or a short notice. In order to maintain liquidity of assets, Indian banks have not participated in the financing of block capital requirement of industry. After all long-term investment cannot be financed out of short-term deposits.

Commercial Banks and Short-term Capital. The commercial banks have rendered great service to Indian business in meeting its needs of current financial and short-term or working capital requirements. They have met the needs of companies by :—

(i) discounting bills and other commercial papers;

(ii) granting cash credits and advancing loans.

The most common method of lending is by means of granting a cash credit. A cash credit, which permits the borrower to withdraw from the bank up to a stipulated amount by cheques, is opened on the execution of a promissory note with two signatures, or on the pledge of stock of raw material, or its hypothecation. The banks insist upon the full backing of tangible and easily realisable assets. They also keep a high margin as regards hypothecation of stock. With regard to small units and for rural development the banks have been asked by the Government to be more lenient and advance loans on easier terms.

Bank advances to Industry. In the past, the banks have made advances mainly to large enterprises. But in recent years, particularly during the last two years, small units have also benefitted. According to a study prepared by the planning division of the Industrial Financial Department of the Reserve Bank of India the number of small units assisted by the scheduled commercial banks had reached 5.13 lakhs as at the end of June, 1978 with a balance outstanding at Rs. 1,927.8 crores. The share of small scale industries in the total outstanding bank credit has touched a level of 14.1 per cent. The public sector banks continued to account for about 90 per cent of the total outstanding bank credit to small scale industries. There was a significant spurt in the credit limits including term loans and advances granted to craftsmen and other qualified entrepreneurs. The credit limit touched a level of Rs. 2,404 crores as against Rs. 2,081 crores in June, 1977.

According to another study by the Reserve Bank of India published in the January, 1979 issue of the RBI Bulletin there has been substantial increase in loans and advances to large scale sector both in the southern and northern regions.

Commercial Paper — In the field of corporate finance, the year 1990 heralded the announcement of detailed guidelines by the Reserve

Bank of India for the issue of Commercial Paper by reputed companies. This short term instrument consists of an unsecured promissory note, negotiable by endorsement and delivery, typically with a fixed maturity between 2 months and 6 months and is to be issued on a discount basis. Top rated corporate clients of commercial banks who would satisfy the following six preconditions could explore the possibility of tapping the short-term money market through the medium of this tradeable instrument:

(i) the net tangible worth to exced Rs.10 crores as per the latest audited balance sheet;
(ii) the fund–based working capital limits to exceed Rs.25 crores;
(iii) the shares of the company to be listed with one or more recognised stock exchanges (for the other than those in the public sector);
(iv) company to have P1 + rating from (CRISIL) which is not older than 2 months;
(v) the Health Code assigned by the banker/s to be No.1; and
(vi) the current ratio of the company to be not less than 1.33:1.

This paper is likely to be more attractive to the investors, because the discount rate at which it could be issued could be anywhere between 12.5% and the lending rate of commercial banks for top class borrowers, viz. 16%.

FINANCING OF LONG-TERM REQUIREMENTS

The banks have not done much to finance long-term capital requirements. An experiment of long-term financing was unsuccessfully tried by establishing "Industrial banks", the Tata Industrial Bank being the largest of them. Their objective was to finance the development of new and existing industries by holding a considerable portion of shares and debentures in the companies and also underwriting such securities. As the experiment proved a failure, the Tata Bank, to escape complete collapse merged with the Central Bank. The other "industrial banks" just disappeared one after the other. As a result of this failure, the banks have stuck to commercial banking functions. The plan of mixed banking has not found favour with our banks. They have, however, begun to make small investments in the shares and debentures of companies. But they are underwriting capital issues on a fairly large scale.

The Shroff Committee on Finance for the Private Sector had recommended the formation of a *Consortium* by the leading banks for subscribing to new issues of shares and debentures of industrial companies and/or underwriting them. The recommendation has not been implemented. But the Industrial Development Bank enables the banks to advance medium-term loans to industrial concerns.

INDIGENOUS BANKS

Joint stock banks are not the only or even the principal suppliers of working capital. The indigenous bankers and loan offices have also rendered useful service to industry, especially when they have come forward at times of difficulty. They have supplied long-term capital, and the tea industry of Bengal and Assam is a notable example. Their charges however, have always been high. One of the reasons of the high rate of interest is that only small or medium sized industries have to go to them as they cannot receive public or private deposits or advances from banks. The small industralist is prepared to pay high interest and borrow on the quiet. If he went to a joint stock bank he would have to expose himself to inquiries and regularised procedure. He would also have to pledge valuable, or at least a substantial party's signature. The indigenous banker lends on personal knowledge, and often on simple personal bond. But the importance of indigenous bankers in the realm of industrial finance is fast diminishing, and the joint stock banks are competing them out.

PLOUGHING BACK OF EARNINGS

Every growing concern requires capital for extensions and improvement. Ploughing back or re-investment of a part of the profits is an ideal method of financing expansions and improvements. Ploughing back is an adjunct of sound financial management, it raises no problems or complications as does borrowing either from the banks or from the public. The reserves which have been built up during a continuous spell of prosperous period, and by following a conservative dividend policy can be used as working capital. This policy of creating reserve funds to build up reserves can help individual units to escape the crushing effects of depressions, however severe. On the contrary, such reserves can be used with great advantage for expansion and betterment during periods of dull business, when materials are cheap, labour is abundant and betterment work can be done with the least disturbance to operation. The method of ploughing back is cheaper and also has the effect of dispensing with the finance supplied by managing agents.

Also, from any national standpoint, the method of accumulation of capital out of earnings for expansion and re-organisation that may become necessary is more logical than the plan of distributing every year large sums in the form of dividends to individuals as income. The latter course is followed because it is expected, believing in the implied but illogical condition, that the recipients of this income will not spend them but will invest them in order to provide new capital for development. There are clear signs in industrially advanced countries of this time-honoured method of individual saving out of income becoming obsolete as the chief method of providing new capital for the expansion of industry. The State can be in a position to determine not only the necessary amount of the national saving, but also its allocation to different industries and services. The ploughing back of earnings has been a great factor in building and expansion of British and American companies. There is no reason why this method should not prove useful in India, too. In fact, it should prove of greater service in our country where the need for abundant capital formation and direction of capital is urgent and pressing.

The method of ploughing back or self-financing has its shortcomings, and if carried too far, might prove dangerous. In the hands of over-zealous directors it might lead to over-investment in the industry causing over-expansion with the inevitable result—one-sided consumption. Again, the shareholders who have little individual interest in the company and who are ever changing, want as high a dividend as possible. If in the pursuit of a policy of building up reserves, the directors, though unwittingly, lead the shareholders to believe that they are inconsiderate to the interest of the latter, there is great danger of the available capital being distributed in an ill-balanced manner, so far as the whole industry is concerned. On the contrary the system will as said above, get the shareholders out of the clutches of the managing agents who leave very much less for the shareholders than would be possible by putting something out of profits to be ploughed back. Therefore, if a cautious but bold policy of self-investment is followed, Indian industry can develop a system of internal finance without depending on the managing agents who, judging from the course of events, shall have to go eventually.

FINANCING OF DEPRECIATION

"Well managed business enterprises," says Mead, "make provisions out of their income for impairment in the value of their physical assets" or for depreciation. The provision for depreciation is indeed of supreme importance for the safety of any concern. But in India, however, very little attention is given to this item in the ramifications of company finance. Webster defines depreciation as "the act or state of lessening worth". According to this definition all lessening of worth, whether due to age, wear and tear, lack of proper maintenance, decrepitude, inadequacy, or obsolescence, can be termed depreciation, although from a accounting standpoint, depreciation is only that deterioration of an object that cannot be made good by repairs, but requires a complete renewal. It follows from this that the life of every tool, building, machine or structure which a company may own, with the exception of permanent structure, is limited, and is subject to deterioration, although the pace of deterioration can be controlled by constant vigilance and proper care. The termination of the active life of a machine may also be due to the discovery of some better machine for doing the same work faster and cheaper. The new inventions or changes in the art may render the plant or any part of its equipment uneconomical of use as compared with new types available of greater efficiency and used by rivals. This going out of use is called depreciation due to obsclescence; and depreciation from lescence is spicially prominent during the early stages of an industry n improvements are taking place at quick pace.

Depreciation, then, is made up of two prime factors, deterioration and obsolescence, and they do not run concurrently in any given case, for whichever of the two is the operating factor, governs. A given type of standard machine tool may last fifty years at its present usage rate before it can be no longer commercially repaired. That would be depreciation at the rate of 2 per cent a year. It may, however, become obsolete two years after it is purchased for the purpose for which it was secured, and the rate, if such it can be called, would be 50 per cent a year. It is essential to make provisions for replacement continually, for if it is not done, the whole burden may fall upon the business as to crush it. When the plant is new, repairs are light and no replacement is necessary, the management should make adequate provision for replacements in the future. It is a sound policy to be conservative in dividend distribution and liberal in reserve creation out of current earnings which may be kept apart in readily available investment or mingled with general assets where they can be used most advantageously. It is a sound practice to so apportion the depreciation charge as to recover through the current operation accounts the original investment in the asset, as and when the asset is replaced, and it is more or less immaterial how this charge is determined, i.e., straight lines, reducing balance, sinking fund, or any other method; provided that it represents the facts as nearly as possible and provided furthermore that fluctuations in value and the fact of obsolescence are cared for by suitable appropriations of surplus or by some form of insurance.

DIVIDEND POLICY

The investors are particularly interested in earning the maximum returns on their investments in the shares of a company, but in no case less than the rate of interest that they may get in the money market. A successful company, on the other hand, while recognising the need of distributing part of its net profits as dividends, must make provision for meeting the fixed charges, e.g., taxes, rentals, interest payments on the funded obligations and for additions to surplus. Assuming that, after meeting the fixed charges, the profits are sufficient for dividends and surplus, the apportionment of this balance between dividends and surplus is the function of the Board of directors. It is in the directors' discretion to determine the rate of dividend and fix the amount to be added to surplus. The officers or shareholders cannot increase or decrease the rate, nor can they demand payment of dividend, if the directors decide not to distribute profits in this form. With the legal restrictions that dividend cannot be paid out of capital and must only be paid out of profits the directors are left free to determine whether or not to pay or the rate at which to pay. This discretion casts a duty on the directors to be careful and conservative, while fixing dividend rates. There are some fundamental rules of corporation finance relating to dividend policy which must be followed by the directors if they wish to save the concern they direct from collapse.

As a preliminary to fixing a rate the directors will look to the cash or liquid assets of the company from which dividends can be taken. Then they will examine the prospects of business for the early future , as also the ability of the company to obtain funds which may be necessary for new construction by the sale of shares and debentures. These considerations are important because a company may be exceptionally prosperous without being able, on account of the rapid growth in its business which has locked up its cash assets in the forms of accounts receivable, materials, etc., to pay out any portion of the profits in dividends. In these circumstances a dividend can be declared by raising funds through the sale of shares and debentures. This is, however, not a good practice, and should be avoided.

The second thing that an honest and conservative Board of directors sets before it is to establish a dividend rate which can be maintained under all conditions of earnings. It is in the interest of both the shareholders and the company that the rate once established shall be maintained. The regularity of dividends is of highest importance to the shareholders, as some of them, at least, count upon these returns as a fixed portion of their income to meet certain living expenses of dependants. The directors should see that the needs of such shareholders are met with a permanent rate of dividend with the fewest possible changes. As a rule, this rate of dividend should not vary except when it is increased, and it must not be increased until after the directors have assured themselves that in all human probability a later decrease will not become necessary. The dividend, in addition to being a permanent source of income to the shareholder increases the value of his shares. For example, the value of shares whose dividends run 6, 6, 2, 2 and 4 averaging 4% for the 5 years, but irregularly distributed, will command a lower price than shares on which 4% is paid every year.

Shares with regular dividends are worth more to sell and also more valuable as collateral security. The company also enjoys considerable benefit from a stable rate of dividend with its resultant advantage of higher and permanent value. In the eyes of the bankers such a company enjoys high credit, and borrowing becomes cheaper and easier. Also new issues of shares and debentures can be made more readily with a steady rate of dividend and high value of the existing securities. Thus a successful company will always follow the policy of declaring low but regular rate of dividends so that in times of lower earnings the rate can be maintained. During exceptionally prosperous years, bigger amounts should be transferred to reserve to be made available in lean years to make up the fixed rate of dividend. Even at the risk of repetition, it may be stated that dividends must not be allowed to rise, even in the most prosperous periods, above a conservative estimate of the minimum earnings of the company.

The above discussion on the desirability of maintaining regularity in dividend rate may be summed up in the words of Mead, who says,[1] "In

1. Corporation Finance, P. 217.

order to maintain an even rate of distribution on its stock, the directors of well-balanced companies are governed by the following rules:—

"*First,* to pay no dividends for a considerable period after the company begins operation.

"*Second,* to manage the expense accounts of the company in such a way as to reduce the fluctuations in surplus profits to the minimum.

"*Third,* to pay out, in any one year, only a portion of profits in dividends."

Before concluding, it may be observed that, as far as possible, dividends not earned during a given period should not be paid and charged against the surplus that has been accumulated in previous periods. Surplus is as much a part of the permanent capital of a company as is the capital stock itself. It is understood as a matter of course by the creditors that it represents a permanent investment. Also, dividend payments should be dependent not only upon profits, but also on the company's cash position if embarrassment is to be avoided a short time later. For to attempt to do a large volume of business with a small working capital is one of the quickest and surest methods of financial suicide. Yet this is precisely the course that is followed by those concerns which. on the strength of a showing of profits, declare dividends, the payment of which seriously depletes their working capital. Under these conditions the only prudent course is to withhold dividends until in the normal course of the company's business cash is accumulated beyond the requirements of the business. An illustration will make this point clear.

Where a company with a share capital of Rs.10,00,000 reports net profits available for dividend amounting to Rs. 91,462 and declares dividend of Rs. 30,000. i.e., 3% leaving an addition to the surplus of Rs. 61,462; appears to have followed a very conservative dividend policy. But a reference to the balance sheet discloses a secured overdraft at the bank of Rs. 1,91,000. The cash on hand is less than Rs. 6,000, and cash and bills receivable together are less than its current liabilities. Only a glance at this balance sheet shows that payment of dividend was not merely unwise but a thoroughly reckless and dangerous proceeding. The only possible reasons which may lead directors to adopt such a course of action can be ignorance, a false belief in the immediate return of prosperity, a desire to give the company a higher standing in the stock market, or with creditors, than its earning warrants.

Legal Rules for Payment of Dividends. The Companies Act lays down the following rules for the payment of dividends:

1. Dividends must only be paid out of profits, and not out of capital. Dividends may, however, be paid out of funds provided for the purpose by the Government pursuant to a guarantee regarding dividend.

2. Dividend must be paid in cash, except where profits are capitalised with the object of issuing fully paid-up "Bonus" shares.

3. Dividends can be declared or paid for any financial year after providing for depreciation and also after transferring to reserves of the company of such percentage of its profits for the year, not exceeding 10 per cent, as may be prescribed.

4. A company may, if authorised by its articles, pay dividends in proportion to the amount paid up on each share where a larger amount is paid up on some shares than on others.

5. Where a dividend has been declared, it must be paid or the dividend warrant must be posted to the registered shareholder within 42 days of the declaration.

6. Any dividends remaining unpaid or unclaimed after the expiry of 42 days must be transferred within 7 days after the expiry of such 42 days to a special account known as "Unpaid Dividend Account of.....Co.....Ltd./Co. Private Ltd".

7. Any money transferred to the unpaid Dividend Account of a company which remains unpaid or unclaimed for 3 years from the date of such transfer shall be transferred to the general revenue account of the Central Government and any claim after such transfer must be preferred to the Central Government and that Government will pay to the claimant.

8. Dividend shall be paid to the registered shareholder or to his order or to his bankers. In case of share warrant, it is to be paid to the bearer of such share warrant.

9. Dividend on shares pending registration of transfer shall be held in obeyance by transfer to the special unpaid Dividend Account, unless the transferer of such shares authorises the company to pay it to the transferee.

Capitalisation of Profits. A company may, if authorised by its articles, capitalise its profits instead of paying them as dividends. In such a case, the company declares dividend or "Bonus" out of its undistributed profits and issues at the same time a corresponding number of new shares and then applies the dividend or bonus which belongs to the shareholders in full payment of amount due on the shares. The effect of capitalisation is that the company does not part with any of its assets, and is enabled to increase the capital, and the shareholders get their dividends, in the shape of further shares which are called "Bonus Shares." Capitalisation of undistributed profits is made by issuing fully paid-up shares to the members. thereby transferring the sum capitalised from the profit and loss account and reserve account via the bonus to the share capital. The reason why bonus is first paid out of reserve and taken back for payment on the newly issued shares is that direct transfer from reserve to capital for payment of fully paid-up shares will be payment by the company to itself, which is illegal. These bonus shares are not income but capital and so not liable to surtax.

CHAPTER XXXVI

INSTITUTIONS OF INDUSTRIAL FINANCE

State Aid. The necessity of financial aid by the State has long been recognised all over the world. But in India, a World War had to impel the Government to stir in its slumber of *laissezfaire* and give up its misconceived notion that "interference by the State in the economic life of the country is injurious to its well-being." As early as 1918 the Industrial Commission had recommended that the State should play a definite role in financing industry. In compliance with this recommendation, several Provinces had introduced schemes for providing financial assistance to industrial concerns. Unfortunately, these schemes did not succeed for various reasons. The most important reasons were bureaucratic delays in disbursement of loans and the absence of suitable machinery for disbursement of loans to deserving business units.

Because of the failure of that Scheme and many of the "industrial banks" that had been set up for financing industrial enterprises, and with a view to making State aid to industry a reality, the Central Government decided to set up Industrial Finance Corporation. This was followed by other specialised finance and development corporations. In the present chapter each one of these corporations is discussed at some length.

INDUSTRIAL FINANCE CORPORATION

The Industrial Finance Corporation was established in 1948 under the Industrial Finance Corporation Act, 1948, with the object of "making medium and long-term credits more readily available to industrial concerns in India."

Financial Resources. The main sources of funds of the I.F.C. are its capital, retained earnings, repayment of loans and sale of investments, borrowings from the market by the issue of bonds, loans from the Central Government and foreign credits. Money is also borrowed from the Reserve Bank of India for temporary periods, when found necessary.

1. **Share Capital** The authorised capital of the Corporation is Rs. 20 crores divided into 40,000 shares of Rs. 5,000 each. The issued, subscribed and paid up capital of the Corporation stood at Rs. 10 crores as on 30 June, 1978.

2. **Bonds.** The Corporation is authorised to issue bonds and debentures. These, together with the loans guaranteed by the Corporation, should not exceed ten times its paid-up capital and reserves. The bonds have been issued from time to time beginning with the year 1949-50, and on June 30, 1978, the aggregate amount of the Bonds outstanding was Rs. 285.42 crores.

3. **Borrowings from the Central Government.** As on 30 June 1978

Distribution of Shares

Shareholder	*No. of Shares held*	*Percentage in the total*
Industrial Development Bank of India	10,000	50
Scheduled Banks	4,067	20
L.I.C. & Insurance Concern etc.	4,314	22
Co-operative Banks	1,619	8
Total	20,000	100

loans outstanding from the Central Government stood at Rs. 66.06 crores. During 1975, a sum of Rs. 2.09 crores was borrowed, while a sum of Rs. 6.55 crores was repaid, so that the balance outstanding on 30 June, 1978, stood at Rs. 44.85 crores. As in the previous 4 years, no budgetary allocation of funds was made for the Corporation this year.

4. **Borrowings from the Reserve Bank of India.** As in the past borrowings from R.B.I. were availed of for temporary periods during the year. As on 30 June 1978, there were no outstandings under this head.

5. **Borrowings in foreign currencies.** In 1978 further loan of DM 15 million, being the 16th line of credit, was allocated to the Corporation. As at the close of the year, the total amount of West German Credit made available to the Corporation including the above line of credit amounted to DM 192.50 million, against which the Corporation had sanctioned sub-loans to the extent of DM 180.54 million. The credit is now fully convertible that is, it can be utilised for the import of capital goods, engineering know-how and services from countries such as the U.S.A., U.K., Italy, France, Norway, Sweden, Denmark, Spain, Japan, etc., in addition to West Germany.

A further allocation of U.K. credit to the extent of £4.00 million was made available to the Corporation by the Government of India under U.K./India Capital Investment Grants, 1977, 1978. With this allocation the total U.K. credit amounted to £9.50 million against which sub-loans for the aggregate amount of £4.50 million have been sanctioned up to 30 June, 1978,. The total value of the French credit available to the Corporation from Banque Francaise Du Commerce Exterieur, Paris amounted to FF 15 million and sub-loans sanctioned three—against totalled FF 14.89 million.

6. **Reserve Fund.** The aggregate amount of reserves held by the Corporation as on June 30, 1978 was Rs. 30.66 crores.

The total resources out of which disbursements on loans and amounts paid on shares and debentures, up to 30 June, 1978 aggregated Rs. 783.25 crores. The following table gives the break-up of the sources of finance and disbursements at 30 June, 1978.

Sources and uses of Funds as on 30th June, 1978

SOURCES OF FUNDS	Rs. Crores	USES OF FUNDS	Rs. Crores
Paid up Capital	10.00	Disbursement assistance	
Profits before tax	73.19	Rupee loans	447.58
Repayment of loans by borrowers	205.38	Foreign Currency loans	58.48
Sale/Redemption of investments	15.99	Underwriting obligations and direct subscription	37.73
Recoveries under guarantees	4.76	Amount met under guarantees	10.09
Borrowings from market by issue of bonds	285.42	Loan amount converted into Shares	1.86
Borrowings from Central Govt.	114.28	Repayment of borrowings	146.58
Borrowings from IDBI	10.00	Other uses	59.83
By transfer of interest	9.98	Closing cash and bank balances	21.10
Foreign Credits	52.52		
Specific grants by Govts.	1.73		
Total	783.25	Total	783.25

Functions and Lending Policies. A public limited company or co-operative society incorporated and registered in India which is engaged, or proposes to engage itself, in the manufacture, preservation or processing of goods, or in the shipping, mining or hotel industry or in the generation or distribution of electricity or any other form of power, is eligible for financial assistance. Public sector projects, which are set up as public limited companies, can also receive assistance from the I.F.C. on the same basis as industrial projects in private sector. Financial assistance, on concessional terms, is available for setting up industrial projects in certain districts in less developed States notified by the Central Government.

The assistance given by the I.F.C. may take the following form or shape:

(1) Guaranteeing loans raised by industrial concerns which are repayable within a period of 25 years.

(2) Underwriting the issue of stock, shares, bonds or debentures by industrial concerns, but must dispose of such securities within 7 years.

(3) Granting loans or advances to or subscribing to debentures of industrial concerns, repayable within 25 years.

(4) Acting as agent for the Central Government and for the World Bank in respect of loans sanctioned by them to industrial concerns.

(5) Granting loans to industrial concerns.

(6) Guaranteeing deferred payments by importers of capital goods who are able to obtain this concession from foreign manufacturers.

(7) Guaranteeing loans raised by industrial concerns from scheduled banks or State Co-operative Banks.

(8) Guaranteeing, with the prior approval of the Central Government, loans raised from, and credit arrangements made with. any bank or financial institution in any country outside India by industrial concerns in foreign currency.

(9) The Corporation is empowered to subscribe directly to the stocks and shares of an industrial concern, and also to convert, at its option, the loans granted or debentures subscribed to by it into stocks or shares of the concern.

It will be noticed that the Corporation combines mortgage lending with the business of underwriting. It acts, in a way, as an issue house, underwriting the issues of securities of limited companies as well as a lending institution, guranteeing and granting loans. It is now permitted to subscribe to the shares of companies. The Corporation has been treated as a company for the purposes of the Income Tax Act and is required to pay income-tax and super-tax on its income, profits and gains.

Consideration in Sanctioning Assistance. As the Corporation is keen on financing projects which will make a useful contribution to the industrial development of the country, it is very careful in judging and evaluating each project before granting assistance. In making decisions, the Board of Directors keep in view the following considerations:

1. The kind and quality of the contribution which the project will make to the industrial development of the country;
2. The technical and commercial viability of the project;
3. Its profit earning capacity;
4. The integrity and experience of the management;
5. Availability of adequate supplies of raw materials;
7. The cost of the scheme in relation to the resources of the company seeking financial assistance;
8. The extent to which the assistance is likely to help in increasing the efficiency of the company;
9. The profit earning capacity of the company;
10. The security offered by the company;
11. The economic prospects of the industry and its importance in the country.

Special attention is paid to projects in relatively under-developed areas and consideration is given, wherever necessary, to relaxation of normal terms and conditions to enable new units to operate sucessfully in such areas. Sugar and textile co-operatives are given priority treatment in granting assistance.

The purposes for which loans are granted are : (1) establishment of new industrial undertakings, (2) expansion, modernisation or diversification into other lines of production by existing units. The total cumulative assistance sanctioned upto June 30, 1978, amounted to Rs. 763.84 crores for 1029 projects of 893 industrial concerns spread all over the country.

The total cost of these projects was Rs. 5208.03 crores. This cumulative assistance included assistance of Rs. 157.42 crores for 165 projects in the cooperative sector. The balance of Rs. 606.42 crores was sanctioned for 864 projects in the corporate sector. In this was included assistance to the extent of Rs. 57.85 crores for 58 public sector projects and Rs. 66.43 crores for 68 joint sector projects. Disbursement amounted to Rs. 605.97 crores which represented 79.3 per cent of the sanctions. The total assistance outstanding as on June 30, 1978 amounted to Rs. 357.10 crores.

Procedure for obtaining assistance. A company seeking financial assistance from the Corporation has to adopt the following procedure :

(a) *Application.* The first step is the submission of an application for the loan. Before submitting the application the company should make sure that it is eligible for assistance. The application should be accompanied by a detailed financial and technical statement of the proposed project.

(b) *Scrutiny.* On receipt of the application the Corporation will arrange for it to be scrutinised by its technical and financial staff to ascertain the soundness of the project. After this the views of the appropriate Advisory Committee, which consists of experts drawn from the public and private sectors having specialised knowledge of the particular industry, are invited.

(c) *Sanction.* The Board of Directors of the Corporation then takes a decision by taking into account the recommendations of the Advisory Committee, and sanctions the loan if it is favourable.

(d) *Letter of Intent.* After financial assistance is sanctioned by the Board, a Letter of Intent is issued to the applicant communicating the sanction and also indicating the terms and conditions governing the same.

(e) *Loan Agreement.* Thereafter, the borrower is required to execute a Loan Agreement and other documents of security, which have been standardised and printed.

(f) *Disbursement.* Disbursements start only after completion of legal formalities and on compliance with conditions precedent to disbursement of loans as incorporated in the Loan Agreement. Further disbursements are made according to the requirements of the project after verification of the progress.

(g) *Follow-up and Progress Reports.* Both during the construction period of a project and after its implementation, the Corporation maintains proper follow-up. An assisted concern is required to submit regular progress reports in prescribed forms as also its audited balance sheet. The officers of the Corporation inspect the project from time to time to verify its physical and financial progress, and to offer guidance that may be required.

After the project has gone on stream, inspections at regular intervals by the technical and financial officers of the Corporation continue. Where considered necessary, the Corporation also nominates directors on the Boards of assisted concerns to have a closer watch over their affairs.

Assistance to New Entrepreneurs and Technocrats. The abolition of managing agency system has set in a transformation of the industrial organisation in the country. Increasing emphasis is being placed on the need for having technocrats or professionally qualified managers to be at the helm of industrial enterprises. It has also been accepted as an objective of national policy to encourage new entrepreneurs in the industrial field. The financial institutions like the Corporation have to play an important part in this context.

Though the Corporation is meant to assist medium and large-scale units in the organised sector, it has been encouraging the growth of new entrepreneurship and has always accorded special consideration to applications for financial assistance from technocrats and professionally qualified persons promoting new projects. The Corporation has already assisted quite substantial projects promoted by new entrepreneurs and technocrats in industries, such as engineering, textiles, chemicals, sugar, cement, paper and paper boards, rubber products, glass, hotels, etc.

Assistance Sanctioned

The financial assistance sanctioned by the Corporation increasing over the years. In 1949-50 it sanctioned assistance to the tune of Rs. 2.71 crores and if went up to Rs. 150.58 crores in 1979-80 and the Rs. 853.02 crores in 1986-87. In 1986-87, the amount of Rs. 853.02 crores was sanctioned for 556 projects and the actual amount disbursed was Rs. 506.85 crores. The Corporations' cumulative assistance upto June, 1987 stood at Rs. 4,042 crores to finance 2,541 projects of 2,077 industrial concerns, and cumulative disbursement was Rs. 2,886 crores. In addition to financial assistance to industry, the Industrial Finance Corporation has played a vital role in industrial development, through resorce mobilisation to a substantial figure of Rs. 32,559 crores.

MANAGEMENT DEVELOPMENT INSTITUTE

The Corporation has sponsored the Management Development Institute which was inaugurated in March 1973. The main objective for which the Institute has been set is to provide training in modern management techniques to the Corporation's clients, particularly to new entrepreneurs and technologists, who, for the first time, promote an industrial project with financial assistance from the Corporation and also to impart training in development banking to the staff of the Corporation as also to the staff of the financial institutions at the State and all-India levels.

The Institute has made a promising beginning and has already held a number of seminars and courses in various areas of management. It is expected to contribute to a large measure to the executive development in private and public sectors.

Evaluation. The Corporation has rendered a very useful service in relation to industrial development in the country during the 30 years of its existence. Yet, it has been criticised by politicians and businessmen. In the first place, it is said that the rate of interest at $8\frac{1}{2}$% with $\frac{1}{2}$% rebate for prompt and regular payment of instalment is very high. This is not a valid criticism, because the Corporation's rate compares favourably with the prevailing rates on debentures. Second criticism is that there is great delay in sanctioning loans and making the amount of the loan available. When it is remembered that the Corporation is required to function on business principles and make sure that the loan granted would be gainfully employed by the applicants; it is not meant to dole out money without making sure that it will not be squandered away. In many cases, the delay takes place because the applications do not contain the detailed information about the project.

The third criticism is that there has been uneven distribution of assistance over the various States, and less developed areas have not received adequate attention. It is true that more developed States have received nearly 70% of the aid and the relatively less developed areas have not received as much as the Corporation would like to give. The main reason for this state of affairs is that not many acceptable applications are received from less developed areas. Despite this the Corporation has in recent years extended sizeable assistance to industrial concerns in relatively less developed areas. Special concessions are given to applicants from these areas in form of lower rate of interest, 3 years moratorium for the first repayment, repayment of total loan within 15 or 20 years instead of the regular 10 or 12 years, margin of security at 30% instead of 50%, and reduction in Corporation's charges besides other concessions. It should be noted in this connection that the Corporation is willing to extend financial assistance on liberal terms, but there has to be in existence adequate infrastructure for industrial development in the areas concerned, availability of local entrepreneurial and industrial skills and drive or initiative of the State or other local authorities.

The charge that the Corporation has not sufficiently assisted capital goods industries may have been true in the past. Now, however, it has been guaranteeing deferred payments on machinery purchased from abroad. Moreover, the Corporation can give assistance only to those who apply for it. If more consumers' goods industries apply than the others, the Corporation is not to be blamed.

It is creditable on the part of the Corporation that it has always taken note of criticism and tried to improve its working and remove all the defects. It has made positive contribution to the development of industries. A commendable service of the Corporation is in the direction of extending assistance to co-operatives. It has taken up the task of assisting new entrepreneurs and technocrats or professionally qualified persons. It has also extended its activities to public sector undertakings The Corporation has shown commendable results and is rendering useful service.

STATE FINANCIAL CORPORATIONS

Since a single Corporation could not be expected to shoulder the responsibilities of meeting the financial requirements of Indian industry, and since the Industrial Finance Corporation was established to advance loans only to large concerns owned by public limited companies or to co-operatives, it was found necessary to establish similar corporations in the various States. Accordingly, the State Financial Corporation Act, 1951 was passed by Parliament, which empowered State Governments to establish Financial Corporations for their respective States. All the States have established these Corporations and there are (in 1968) a total number of 18 State Financial Corporations in the country. These Corporations are expected to be complementary to the Central Corporation, and may grant accommodation to all kinds of industries, big or small. But in practice, they are required to concentrate on small, medium and cottage industries. They also advance loans to private limited companies, partnerships and sole proprietorships. Thus, the scope of the activities of a State Financial Corporation is wider than that of the Industrial Finance Corporation.

Functions. The State Financial Corporations are authorised by the Act to—

1. grant loans or advances to industrial concerns repayable within a period not exceeding 20 years;
2. guarantee loans raised by industrial concerns repayable within a period not exceeding 20 years and floated in the public market;
3. subscribe to the debentures of industrial concerns repayable within a period not exceeding 20 years;
4. subscribe to the share capital of the borrower company in the event of their raising additional capital;
5. underwrite the issues of stocks, shares, bonds or debentures of industrial concerns;
6. guarantee deferred payments due from industrial concerns in connection with their purchases of capital goods within India;
7. convert loans into share capital, if the terms of the transaction permit such conversion.
8. act as agent of the Central Government or State Government or the Industrial Finance Corporation of India in the transaction of any business with an industrial concern in respect of loans or advances granted or debentures subscribed to by them.

An SFC is permitted to charge commission for the services rendered by it in connection with the guaranteeing of loans and advances and underwriting of issues. Where it has to retain any shares or debentures under an underwriting agreement, it must dispose of them within a period of 7 years from the date of acquisition.

The State Financial Corporations perform more or less the same functions as performed by the IFC. The overlapping that results from similar functions is avoided not only by dividing the size of the industries assisted, but also by close co-operation between the IFC and SFCs in matters of policy in regard to finance and industry as a whole It has been agreed between the IFC and SFCs that assistance of Rs. 10 lakhs or 10 per cent of the paid-up capital of the Corporation granting the assistance, whichever is less, would be granted only by the State Financial Corporations. For public limited companies and industrial co-operatives, the limit has been raised to Rs. 20 lakhs.

Working. The SFCs mostly give assistance by way of loans. The loans are granted on the borrower furnishing adequate security by way of pledge, mortgage, hypothecation of Government securities, stocks or movable or immovable property. The margin of 50% on the security is kept while granting loans, and the interest rates vary between 8.5% and 9.5.%.

The State Financial Corporations are functioning in all the 18 States.* All of them have each a paid-up capital of Rs. 1 crore except Andhra Pradesh, Tamil Nadu and Jammu and Kashmir which have capitals of Rs. 1.5 crores, Rs. 1.32 crores and Rs. 76.62 lakhs respectively.

As regards financial assistance, there has been a step-up of assistance in 1969-70 to small-scale sector of industry. The total assistance given by all the 18 corporations went up to Rs. 149.9 crores in 1969-70 as compared to 1968-69, when it was Rs. 132.3 crores. The performance of the SFCs in Andhra Pradesh, Gujarat, Maharashtra, Rajasthan and Uttar Pradesh was particularly commendable. The total assistance sanctioned by all the SFCs in 1969-70 was Rs. 33 crores, while in 1968-69 it was only Rs. 19.6 crores, and actual disbursals during these periods were Rs. 22.3 crores and Rs. 18.4 crores. In 1983-84, disbursed Rs. 434 crores and in 1984-85, they disbursed Rs. 494 crores.

THE INDUSTRIAL CREDIT AND INVESTMENT CORPORATION OF INDIA LTD.

The Industrial Credit and Investment Corporation of India Ltd., was sponsored by a mission from the World Bank for developing, in the main, small and medium scale industries in the private sector, was set up in January, 1955, with a capital of Rs. 25 crores. Its subscribed and paid-up capital is Rs. 8.75 crores. Its share capital is subscribed both by Indian and foreign investors from the U.K. and the U.S.A., the L.I.C. being the largest Indian shareholder.

The Corporation aims to stimulate the promotion of new industries, the expansion and modernisation of existing ones and to furnish technical and managerial aid so as to increase production and afford employment opportunities.

Scope of its activities. The Corporation is authorised to—

(a) provide finance in the form of long or medium term loans or equity participation;

*In Tamil Nadu there is an Industrial Investment Corporation Ltd. registered under Companies Act, but functions on the lines of a State Financial Corporation.

(b) sponsor and underwrite new issues of shares;
(c) guarantee loans from other private investment sources;
(d) make funds available for re-investment by revolving investments as rapidly as prudent:
(e) furnish managerial, technical and administrative services and assist in obtaining these services to Indian industries.

Financial Resources. The net resources of the Corporation as on December 31, 1971, amounted to Rs. 231.29 crores, comprising approximately—

(A) In Rupees. 73.34 crores, made up of—

	(Rs. in crores)
(i) Share Capital	8.75
(ii) Reserves	9.76
(iii) Loans from the Government of India	29.73
(iv) Advances from Industrial Development Bank	14.10
(v) Debentures issued by the Corporation	11.00

(B) In Foreign Currencies. Rs. 308.47 crores, consisting of loans from (i) the World Bank, (ii) Agency for International Development, (iii) the U.K. Government, and DM 74.58 million.

Working. The Corporation has rendered invaluable service to large industrial units in the form of loans, direct subscription and underwriting. Since its inception to the end of December, 1986, the cumulative disbursement were Rs. 3,611 crores. Foreign currency loans accounted for the largest share, followed by rupee loans, underwriting and guarantee assistance. During 1986, the sanctions amount led to Rs. 1,082 crores and disbursal to Rs. 603 crores. The Corporation took of leasing in 1984 and did leasing business to the tune of Rs. 20 crore in the first year and of Rs. 35 crore in the following year.

THE NATIONAL INDUSTRIAL DEVELOPMENT CORPORATION

The corporation was set up in 1954 in the public sector with an authorised share capital of Rs. one crore and paid-up capital of Rs. 10 lakhs which rose to Rs. 50 lakhs by the end of 1963, and was entirely subscribed by the President of India and his nominees. The capital is supplemented by annual grants and loans from the Central Government.

Objects. The primary object of the Corporation is the development of those industries which are necessary to fill up gaps in the industrial structure and which require intensive capital employment, and are not considered attractive by private enterprise because of low return. Although it provides financial assistance by making loans, the main emphasis is on its development function. It gives priority to establishments for the manufacture of capital goods, machinery and equipment for other industries. It takes up study and investigation of industrial projects and schemes, and implementing them, tries to secure, wherever possible, the maximum use of industrial equipment, experience and skill available in the private and public sector. It may also set up industries, which may, in their turn, lead to the growth of ancillary industries in the private sector.

Working. Besides granting long-term loans, the corporation, assists in the promotion of consultancy services in the country. For this purpose, it has set up a Technological Consultancy Bureau. The Bureau performs the function of making preliminary studies for industrial units, collection, analysis and compilation of basic engineering and economic data, investigation of sites including soil problems, transport and water and power supply, preparation of plant projects, reports and designing of structure including mechanical and electrical services.

NATIONAL SMALL INDUSTRIES CORPORATION

The Corporation was set up in Feburary, 1955, with the object of providing marketing service, facilities of hire-purchase system of machineries, and for the general promotion of small industries by setting up of industrial estates. The main functions and divisions to which these functions are assigned may be classified as follows: (See page 654)

The activities of the Corporation are classified as Promotional and Commercial. The former activities comprise the functions performed by Government Purchase Division, Works Division and Project Division. Among its commercial activities are included those functions which are performed by Hire-Purchase and Marketing Divisions.

Division	*Functions*
1. Government Purchase Division	Assistance to small units in securing Government orders. Development of small-scale industrial units as ancillaries to large units.
2. Hire Purchase Division	Supply of machines under Hire-Purchase Scheme.
3. Marketing Division	Marketing assistance including export promotion.
4. Industrial Estates Division	Construction and management of industrial estates.
5. Project Division	Setting up and running of Prototype Production-cum-Training Centres.

Financial Resources. The Corporation was started with an authorised capital of Rs. 10 lakhs, out of which Rs. 2 lakhs were paid up during 1955-56, and Rs. 8 lakhs in 1956-57. Because of the heavy load of work assigned to it, the Government has increased its authorised and paid-up capital from time to time. The paid-up capital stood in 1968-69 at Rs. 50 lakhs, but it was increased to Rs. 350 lakhs in 1969-70. The Reserves and Surplus stood at Rs. 194.37 lakhs on March 31, 1970. In 1987-88, the paid up capital stood at Rs. 7.5 crores. The entire capital is supplied by the Government. The capital is supplemented by borrowings from the Government and foreign agencies. The amount of the loans taken from the Government of India outstanding as on 31st March, 1970 was Rs. 1,127.07 lakhs. Two foreign loans outstanding on the same date were Rs. 189.14 lakhs from the Agency for International Development, and Rs. 419.19 lakhs from Kreditanstalt, West Germany. Both of these loans are guaranteed by the Government of India.

ACTIVITIES

Government Purchase. The Corporation acts as a liaison agency between the small units and the Director-General of Supplies and Disposal, Government of India, for making purchases from the smaller units to supply the order of the Government. The trend of contracts secured by small units with the assistance of the Corporation from the Government has been encouraging. The benefits of the scheme are available only to those units which are enlisted with the Small Industries Institute, and only technically sound units competent to execute Government contracts are so registered.

Credit Guarantee. The Corporation has a credit guarantee arrangement with the State Bank of India. Under this scheme the State Bank advances money to such small units as are recommended by the Corporation to the full value of the raw materials against pledge, without maintaining the usual margin and the Corporation guarantees the margin money usually kept by the Bank.

Hire-Purchase Scheme. Working in close co-operation with the Small Industries Service Institute, the Corporation provides machineries and equipment on hire-purchase system to small industrial concerns. Though the scheme is supposed to be a commercial activity; it is heavily promotion-oriented to achieve socio-economic objectives laid down by the Government. With a view to assisting small entrepreneurs, the Corporation supplies machines without securities and other safeguards which are generally taken for ensuring repayments by banking institutions.

Marketing. The marketing division was set up by the Corporation with two objectives: Sales Promotion and Publicity for products of small industrial units. The turnover in the Marketing Division has been increasing over the years. The Corporation's efforts in securing scarce raw materials have been successful. During 1969-70, the Marketing activities achieved sizeable turnover and earned a profit. The sales turnover during this period was Rs. 205 lakhs against Rs. 160 lakhs in 1968-69. The profit earned during this year was Rs. 0.95 lakhs as against a loss of Rs. 1.10 lakhs suffered in 1968-69. The value of marketing activity was Rs. 22.77 crores and in 1987-88, it was Rs. 27.88 crores.

Promotional Activities. The Corporation has set up Prototype Production and Training Centres at Okhla, Rajkot and Howrah with the object of producing and developing prototype of those machines and machine tools which are imported from Germany and the U.S.A., the two collaborating countries and also to impart training to the workers and executives of industries and Government. The value of production in these centres in 1986-87 was Rs. 2.07 crores and it rose to Rs. 2.71 crores in 1987-88. The Corporation has set up two model industrial estates at Okhla and Naini. The Okhla Estate has been handed over to Delhi Administration while the Naini Estate is still being managed by it.

INDUSTRIAL DEVELOPMENT BANK OF INDIA

Objects. The establishment of the Industrial Development Bank of India in July, 1964, marks a great step forward in the field of industrial finance in India. The Bank has been set up to fill the gap and provide much greater financial assistance to developing and emerging industries. It is intended to act as the reservoir on which the existing financial institutions can draw. Normally, it is to act as a residual lender. As its operations are freed from restrictions, the Bank is able to assist all sound projects both in the private and public sectors. Since its working is flexible, it is in a position to promote the establishment of new enterprises, especially key industries.

Resources. The authorised capital of the Bank is Rs. 1000 crores and the paid up capital is Rs. 475 crores subscribed by the Central Government and the Reserve Bank of India. In addition, the Government has been granting loans to the Bank on liberal terms. The Bank is also authorised to borrow from the market on its own bonds. It may accept public deposits.

Two funds — Central Fund and Development Fund — are demarcated. The letter is used for financing projects which other financial institutions do not finance. The former is made up of paid up capital, bonds and debentures, public deposits, borrowings from the Central Government, the Reserve Bank of India and foreign currency loans, and are used for all financial assistance operations.

Management. Originally, the Bank was set up as a subsidiary of the Reserve Bank of India with a common Board of directors. But in November, 1976, it was reorganised and was delinked from the Reserve Bank of India and placed directly under the Central Government. The Board of directors consisting of 22 members and nominated by the Central Government manages the Bank, The Reserve Bank of India and other financial institutions are given representation on the Board.

Functions. The Bank combines commercial, promotion and refinancing activities. It conducts the following business to carry out these activities:—

(a) granting loans and advances to—

(i) the IFC, and SFC or any other financial institutions, by way of refinance of any long-term loans repayable between 3 and 25 years granted by such Corporation or financial institution to industrial concerns:

(ii) any scheduled bank, or State co-operative bank, by way of refinance of any loans or advances granted to industrial concerns by such bank which are repayable between 3 and 10 years;

(iii) export loans, by way of refinance, repayable between 6 months and 10 years given by any scheduled bank or State co-operative bank or the IFC or any SFC or any other financial institution notified by the Central Government.

(b) accepting, discounting or rediscounting bills of exchange and promissory notes of industrial concerns;

(c) subscribing to or purchasing stocks, shares, bonds or debentures of the IFC, any SFC or any other notified financial institution;

(d) granting loans and advances to any industrial concern or subscribing to, or purchasing, or underwriting the issue of, stocks, shares, bonds or debentures by any industrial concern,

subject to the right of the Bank to convert the loans, advances or debentures into equity stocks and shares of that concern;

(e) guaranteeing deferred payments due from any industrial concern;

(f) guaranteeing

(i) loans raised by industrial concerns which are floated in the public market;

(ii) loans raised from scheduled banks, co-operative banks or the IFC or SFC or any other financial institution;

(g) underwriting obligations of banks or any finance institution;

(h) underwriting research and surveys for evaluating or dealing with marketing of investments;

(i) providing technical and administrative assistance to any industrial concern or any person for promotion, management or expansion of any industry;

(j) planning, promoting and developing industries to fill up gaps in the industrial structure in India;

(k) forming or conducting subsidiaries for carrying out its functions;

(l) doing any other kind of business which the Central Government, on the recommendation of the Reserve Bank, may authorise.

Operations During the 26 years of its existence the Industrial Development Bank has played a significant role in the field of industrial finance in the country both as a guide to the financial institutions and as a purveyor of financial assistance. By virtue of its flexible policy, it has been progressively modifying and liberalising its terms and conditions with a view to providing assistance in the largest measure possible.

During 1969-70, the Bank made a beginning in undertaking the developmental and promotional work of developing backward regions and encouraging small and new entrepreneurs. As a first step it initiated regional surveys to identify industrial potential in the backward areas. The first two surveys covering the State of Assam and the Union Territory of Tripura were completed in June, 1970, and the action is being initiated. Surveys relating to Jammu and Kashmir, Bihar, U.P.and Rajasthan are going on. Similar surveys will be taken up for other backward areas also.

Regional offices were opened during 1970 in Calcutta, Madras and New Delhi. These offices will help in establishing the necessary local contacts.

In the sphere of refinance, the Bank has offered concessions and incentives to State Financial Corporations and banks to enable them to provide assistance to entrepreneurs in backward areas on softer terms. Loans are being granted on concessional terms

Industrial Reconstruction Bank of India.

Originally, the Industrial Reconstruction Corporation of India was set up as a public limited company in April,1917, as an adjunct to the development institutions already functioning in the country. The Reserve Bank of India had at the instance of the Central Government, set up that corporation with the object of reviving and revitalising the sick and closed industrial units. The corporation functioned not only as a lending institution, but also as a reconstruction agency by helping in the restructuring of management and by providing technical and managerial guidance. It continued to function by granting reconstruction loans and by issuing guarantees to banks in respect of margin money for working capital. However, the corporation was not able to meet the needs of all the applicants, and is no more in existence. It was taken over by the Industrial Reconstruction Bank of India in March, 1985.

The Industrial Reconstruction Bank of India was established as a statutory corporation on March 19,1985, on all India basis as the principal credit and reconstruction agency for industrial revival. As stated above, it took over the whole of the undertaking of the Industrial Reconstruction corporation of India, including its assets, liabilities, rights, privileges and activities.

The Bank performs all those functions which its predecessor corporaton performed. Its main objective is to revive and/or revitalise industrial units already closed down or likely to be closed, which appear to be viable. Bulk/of the assistance provided is in the form of term loans. The other forms of assistance include line of credit, equipment leasing and hirepurchase. Term loans are sanctioned for modernisation, diversification, expansion, renovation and for bridging liquidity gap as well as for providing margin money for working capital. In addition to acting as the principal credit and reconstruction agency, the Bank may also purchase or underwrite issues of shares, bonds, debentures of any institution providing credit to any state level agency. The Bank sanctioned assistance of Rs.108.26 crores and disbursed Rs.73.48 crores in 1985-86. In 1986-87, the respective figures were Rs.148.9 crores and Rs.94.7 crores. Additionally, the bank acts as consultant to banks and financial institutions.

Life Insurance Corporation of India

As distinguished from Development Banks, the Life Insurance Corporation is an *investment institution,* and the largest investment institution at that, and provides long-term finance to industrial undertakings except those owned by private limited companies. It extends support to industrial concerns by way of subscription to or underwriting of shares, bonds and debentures of public limited companies.

The investment policy of the LIC is based on the following principles: (i) to invest funds in socially useful schemes; (ii) to invest in safe securities and avoid risky and speculative ventures; (iii) to diversify investments, both in terms of types of securities and number and types of enterprises to be assisted; (iv) to assist in the development of backward areas. Its investments are spread over various classes of securities, industries and regions. The modified Section 27A of the Insurance Act, 1938 lays down the categories and proportions in which the Corporation may invest its funds as follows:

(a) In Central and State Government Securities – 50 per cent;
(b) in approved investments 35 per cent; and
(c) in unapproved investments – 15 per cent.

The approved investment include shares and secured debentures of companies, first mortgage on immovable property, loan on life interests or on life insurance policies, fixed deposits with scheduled or cooperative societies, and debentures or shares of cooperative societies. The Corporation may hold up to 30 per cent of the equity capital of any company, althogh it may exceed this limit with the prior approval the Central Government.

The Life Insurance Corporation sanctioned Rs.1077.46 crores and disbursed Rs.816.17 crores in 1984. It disbursed Rs.196.87 crores, in the form of loans and Rs.89.61 crores in the form of underwriting and direct subscription. In 1985, the Corporation underwrote and subscribed to 120 new issues for an amount of Rs.153.52 crores. In 1986-87, the Corporation underwrote 36 new issues for an amount of Rs.199 crores and subscribed to 31 new issues of an amount of Rs.191.35 crores.

In addition to the Life Insurance Corporation of India, General Insurance Corporation of India and the Employees' State Insurance Corporation have been investing their funds in the securities of Companies.

Convertibility of Loans into Equity

The loan agreement between a financial institution and the borrower company is required to provide for a clause that the loan shall be convertible into equity shares in the company under certain conditions. Therefore, where the lending institution excercises this option of conversion it becomes a shareholder of the company to the extent of the conversion. The idea behind this policy of the Government is that the loan should be converted into equity shares where a more positive say in the management of the company is desirable or where it is profitable to be a shareholder than to be a lender.

The guidelines issued by the Central Government and, as revised in 1984, are as follows:

1. Convertibility clause in the agreement will be mandatory in cases where the aggregate financial assistance exceeds Rs.5 crores.

2. Regardless of the equity holdings, the convertibility clause will be operative in the event of default in repayment of instiutional dues or mismanagement of the affairs of the company.

3. In case of sick units, convertibility clause must be stipulated regardless of the amount of assistance and the/level of shareholding in the assisted company.

4. No convertibility clause will be stipulated in an agreement granting loans under Soft Loan Scheme or modernisation.

5. Conversion option may be exercised, if necessary, on more than one occasion, within a period of three years from commencement of commercial production except in the case of sick units where there is no time limit for conversion.

6. The investment institutions are free to buy shares in the market as part of their normal investment operations, even if the combined holdings exceed percentage limit aforesaid.

Policy on Nominee Directors

The policy of the Government on the appointment and role of nominee directors is as follows:

1. The financial institutions should have a separate Department/Cell at the level of General Manager and Deputy General Manager, whose whole-time function will be to represent the institutions on the Boards of directors of companies. Outsiders may be appointed as nominee directors only as additional directors on Boards when the institution wishes to have more than one nominee director.

2. Nominee directors must be appointed on Boards of MRTP companies assisted by the financial institutions. As regards non-MRTP companies, nominee directors should be appointed on a selective basis, especially in cases where one or more of the following conditions obtain:

(a) the unit is running into problems and is likely to become sick;
(b) institutional holding is more than 25 per cent;
(c) where the institutional stake by way of loans or investment exceeds Rs. 5 crore;

3. Nominee directors should be given clear, identified responsibilities in a few areas which are important for policy. The illustrative list is –

(a) financial performance of the company;
(b) payment of dues to the institutions;
(c) payment of Government dues such as excise and customs duties and statutory dues;
(d) intercorporate investments and loans, where the promoter group has significant interest;
(e) transactions in shares;
(f) managerial remuneration; and
(g) policies relating to the awards of contracts and purchase and sale of raw materials, finished goods, machinery, etc.

4. The nominee directors must ensure that the tendencies of the companies towards extravagance, unwarranted expenditure and diversion of funds are curbed. The institution should constitute a small Audit sub-committee of the Board of directors for this purpose, where the paid up capital of the company is Rs. 5 crore or more.

The Small Industries Development Bank of India

The Small Industries Development Bank of India Bill was passed by Parliament to establish an apex institution to strengthen and broadbase the existing institutional arrangements to meet the requirements of industries in the tiny and small scale sector. The SIDBI is to function as a principal financial institution for the promotion, financing or development of industry in the small scale sector and to coordinate the functions of the institutions engaged in the promotion, financing and development of industries in that sector.

The SIDBI will also give special attention to the expert-oriented industrial units in the small scale sector. It commenced operations on April 2, 1990.

The Bank will have an authorised capital of Rs. 250 crore which can be increased upto Rs. 1,000 crore. The issued capital at the intitial stage shall be fully subscribed by the Industrial Development Bank of India and SIDBI will be a fully owned subsidiary of IDBI. Apart from share capital contribution of IDBI, the sources of funds of this bank will comprise loans from IDBI, short-term and long-term funds from the Reserve Bank of India loans from the Government of India, etc. It is also proposed to transfer the business assets and liabilities of the IDBI relating to the Small Industries Development Fund and the National Equity Fund.

The SIDBI will be refinancing National Industries Corporation State Financial Corporations, State Industrial Development Corporations, State Small Industries Corporations, Scheduled banks, State Cooperative Banks, etc.

It can also subscribe to or purchase shares, bonds or debentures of any State Financial Corporation.

UNIT TRUST OF INDIA

The Unit Trust of India was established under the Unit Trust of India Act, 1963. It was inaugurated on July 1, 1964, from which date it started the sale of its units. The Trust has been organised mainly on the same lines as are followed by the British Unit Trusts, which are those of a flexible unit trust. The basic principles underlying the Unit Scheme is to augment the Small Savings plan of the Government by enabling small investors a means of acquiring a share in the widening prosperity through industrial growth. The overalll investment objectives of the Trust are *safety of capital and regular and growing income*. The Trust is also meant to strengthen the capital market, both the new issue and the stock exchanges. In order to implement the objectives, the Trust has its portfoiio, a balanced proportion of safe and liquid securities as well as growth stocks offering prospects of capital appreciation and reasonable return on capital.

Capital. The Unit Trust was set up in the public sector with an initial capital of Rs. 5 crores contributed as follows:

The Reserve Bank of India	Rs. 2.5 crores
The Life Insurance Corporation	Rs. 75 lakhs
The State Bank of India	Rs. 75 lakhs
The Scheduled Banks and other financial institutions	Rs. 1 crore.

It also acquired unit capital of Rs. 330 crores through sale of units from July 1, 1864 to June 30, 1979.

Management. The management of the business of the Trust is vested in a Board of Trustees. The chairman and four other trustees are appointed by the Reserve Bank of India from among persons with special knowledge or experience in commerce, industry, banking, finance or investment. One trustee each is nominated by the Life Insurance Corporation and the State Bank of India, and two trustees are elected by the institutions contributing to the initial capital of the Trust. In addition to these, the Reserve Bank of India appoints an Executive Trustee. There is an Executive Committee consisting of the Chairman of the Board, the Executive Trustees and two other trustees nominated in this behalf by the Reserve Bank. This committee functions in all matters subject to the direction of the Board. The Board is required to act on business principles with due regard to the interest of the unit holders.

Investment policy. In making investments, the Board of Trustees must keep in mind the two broad principles and objectives of the Scheme, namely, (i) security of capital or safety of investment, and (ii) reasonable return, including capital appreciation, on investment. It is specifically provided in this regard that (i) investment by the Trust in any one company should not exceed 5% of the value of the total investible funds of the Trust or 10% of the value of the securities issued and outstanding of such company, whichever is lower; and (ii) not more than 5% of the investible funds should be invested in the initial issues of securities of new undertakings.

Unit Scheme. The Unit Scheme of the Unit Trust of India was prepared by the Board of Trustees in 1964, which came into operation on and from July 1, 1964. The salient features of the Scheme are as follows:

1. The face value of a unit is Rs. 10.
2. A person can buy any number of units, as long as they are a multiple of ten.
3. The units can be sold back by unit holders to the Trust at prices to be fixed from time to time by the trust.
4. A unit holder may transfer his units to a bank for securing loans and advances.
5. A unit holder may re-invest his dividend on the units under the Re-investment Plan, introduced in 1966.

Tax exemption. The Act provides for significant tax concessions to the Unit Trust and the unit holders.

1. The Trust is exempted from payment of income-tax, super-tax and other taxes on its income.
2. **Income up to Rs. 3,000 received by an individual unit-holder from the Trust is exempt from income-tax. As a result, the Trust distributes income to individual unit-holders without deducting income-tax at source. This exemption is in addition to the general exemption of Rs. 3,000 as interest.**

t is an intermediary institution which pools the savings of the community, and invests in the various types of securities and then returns to the unit holder a reasonable and regular income on his investment. The unit holder shares the assets of the Trust and prosperity of the country. As the management of the Trust is in expert hands who make prudent investments, the risk of loss is eliminated, or at least considerably minimised, and the unit holder gets the benefits of equity investment. The Unit Scheme is, undoubtedly, most suitable medium of investment by small savers; for it offers to them security of capital, safety of investments and reasonable but regular return, as well as exemption from tax

Unit Scheme, 1971. The Unit Trust of India Act was amended in 1966 with a view to permitting the Trust to formulate more than one scheme as well as plans, including the Savings-cum-Insurance Plan in cooperation with the Life Insurance Corporation of India. Accordingly, the Unit Scheme of 1971 began operating with effect from October 1, 1971. This Scheme provided for a 10 year Contractual Savings Plan with a life insurance cover. Under this Plan, the investors, particularly those with Small and Medium incomes are able to regularly save and invest in the units of the Trust and also enjoy the advantage of life insurance cover during the currency of the plan. The plan is applicable to persons who are between the ages of 18 and 45 years at the time of joining the plan.

Capital units Scheme, 1976. This scheme was made applicable from January 1, 1976 and is oriented towards capital growth. The funds raised under this scheme are invested by the Trust in the equity shares of companies with good growth potential. The Trust aims to double the initial investment in about five years. The value of the unit is Rs. 100 and units are sold in multiple of five.

Children's Gift Growth Fund, 1986. Under this scheme, a gift in the form of units can be made to a child under the age of 15 years. The gift matures when the child reaches the age of 21 years. There is an option to withdraw from the scheme when the child reaches the age of 18 years. A dividend of 12.5 per cent is guaranteed and is invested in the units so that the gift grows from year to year at a compound rate. Besides, there is a bonus dividend which is also invested in units.

Mutual Fund Unit Scheme, 1986 – Mastershares. In collaboration with Merrill Lynch the Trust set up a £75 million India Fund. The mutual Funds is the domestic version of the India Fund. The Fund makes investments in the shares in well-managed and growing companies. The individual investors in the fund are given 'Mastershares', which are redeemable after 19th October, 1993. The Mastershare has been performing very well and there has been capital appreciation. The Net Assets value moved in 1988-89 from low of 12.78 to a high of Rs. 27.04 cum-rights. The initial capital of Rs. 150.43 crore went up to Rs. 232.91 crore after rights issue and was valued at 498.67 crore in 1989.

Encouraged by the response from overseas investors to the first off-shore country fund – the India Fund – listed on the London Stock Exchange and in the context of increasing interest shown by the US investors, the Trust launched the second offshore fund listed on the New York Stock Exchange. The India Growth Fund of US $60 million was open to subscription in August, 1988 in association with Merrill Lynch Capital Markets. This Fund, which provided yet another vehicle for participation in the Indian Capital market by investors in U.S.A., Canada, U.K., Japan and other countries, was well received. These funds have helped to increase the visibility of Indian Capital market among the global investors.

In 1988, the eleventh series of the popular Monthly Income Unit Scheme with Extra Bonus – plus growth opened for sale during November and December, 1988. The dividend and minimum capital appreciation were kept at 12 per cent and 2 per cent respectively as in the previous series. The response has been encouraging. The Growing Income Unit Scheme providing for a progressive rate of dividend from 12.5% to 14% per annum was on sale in January, 1989. The investors are given the option either to receive dividend at half yearly rests or cumulation of the dividend leading to doubling of the investment in a period of 5½ years. One more scheme known as the Monthly Income Unit Scheme with extra Bonus plus Growth was launched in May, 1989. The Scheme assures payment of dividend at 12% per annum, 2% capital appreciation at the end of the 5th year and provides for payment of bonus dividend in the fourth year. The scheme has already netted more than Rs. 200 crore.

Evaluation. The Unit Trust of India is playing an important role in mobilising the savings of the people, particularly those with moderate means. Through its numerous schemes, it is acting as an intermediary institution which pools the savings of the community, and invests in the various types of securities and then returns to the unit-holders a reasonable and regular income on their investments. In this way, the unit holder shares the assets of the Trust and prosperity of the country.

The Trust completed its 25 years service to the community in 1989, and showed a tremendous progress in all directions. The Trust crossed the landmark of Rs. 10,000 crore in its investible resources and achieved a new high of over of Rs. 3,700 crore in unit sales while adding 9.21 lakh unit holding accounts which have by now reached the figure of 5 million.

The Trust is in the process of establishing a training college as an institute of capital markets to serve as a catalyst organisation in the professional development of the Indian Capital Markets. The institute will offer professional training and research for the securities industries in India. In fine, the Trust has emerged as one of the largest institutional investors in the capital market. Investment operations of the Trust both in the new issues market and in the secondary market have been helping a broad based and orderly development of the market.

CHAPTER XXXVII

THE SECURITIES MARKET

(Including Stock Exchange)

The pattern of financing varies from industry to industry and firm to firm. Different types of business find it advisable to use different combinations of credit and capital resources, depending upon the degree of risk and scale.

The Scope of Capital Market. The capital and money markets, including securities market, are best reviewed as a whole to begin with. In seeking sources of capital, one finds a vast unified market which provides short-term credit at one end and permanent risk capital at the other. For example, a company may be able to meet its cash requirements for the purchase of machinery with the help of a bank advance. Although the bank advance is a temporary form of finance, it provides an alternative source of capital to shareholders' funds. Again, business generates most of its capital requirements from its own savings. We have already discussed the relative merits of the different sources of finance. Here we are concerned with that part of the Capital market which is concerned with securities of a company, and so designate it as Securities Market.

Securities Market. The expression 'securities market' is a composite term embracing buyers and sellers of securities and constituting all the agencies and institutions which assist the sale and resale of company securities, viz., shares and debentures. According to Wheeler,[1] securities market includes

1. All the activities relating to distributing and trading in securities.
2. Organisations which facilitate the various activities in the securities market.
3. Buyers and sellers of securities—both individual and institutional.
4. Rules, regulations, customs and practices that control of the organisation and conduct of business in the securities market.

A newly organised company issues securities for the first time, and a company which is a going concern and needs additional capital may either issue further capital or borrow from certain financial institutions. Such newly issued shares and debentures and the people who buy them out of their current savings may be termed as the New Issues Market. The market is also engaged in buying and selling 'second-hand' securities. They had originated at some earlier time for financing some new investment, but are now nothing more than claims to future interest

1. Bayard O. Wheeler, *Business—An Introductory Analysis*, p. 428.

or dividends and/or repayment of a fixed capital sum. For example, Mr. A may have spent Rs. 1,000 years ago on 100 Rs. 10 shares, issued at par, in Company XYZ Ltd. (New issue market). The company has used this money along with other money as well, and the shares are today worth Rs. 1,500. Mr. A decides to sell them, and instructs his broker to do so. One Mr. B, who wishes to buy shares in XYZ Ltd., instructs his broker to buy 100 shares for him. The transaction is completed by the brokers on behalf of their clients. Mr. A gets back his money and Mr. B makes an investment in the shares of XYZ Ltd. in a transaction in second-hand shares. Mr. B's 'investment' has been balanced by Mr. A's 'disinvestment' without in any way disturbing the capital or working of XYZ Ltd. The whole transaction was facilitated by an organised securities market, viz., the Stock Exchange.

The securities market may therefore be studied under two heads:
(a) The New Issues Market.
(b) The Stock Exchange.

As stated above, the new issues market is concerned with the disposal of new issues of shares and debentures through their allotment by the company to individuals and institutions. In simple terms this part of the securities market consists of buyers and dealers of new issues of securities. The Stock Exchange, which is the other part of the securities market, is concerned with re-sale of second-hand securities. In other words, it is the market where shares and debentures are bought and sold either for investment or for speculative purposes.

A. THE NEW ISSUES MARKET

The securities of a company are bought by different classes of customers, such as businessmen, potential customers of the company, creditors of the company, its employees, institutional investors, and in the case of an established company the present holders of equity shares. Since the prospective buyers have different considerations in investing their savings in company securities, the selling methods used must conform to the needs and way of thinking of the various types of investors. The marketing of securities is a specialised activity, and a company wishing to raise money from the public should enlist the aid of one or more of the financial houses specialising in public issues. The new issues market is now virtually monopolised by a small number of firms who are experts in this type of transaction.

Techniques or methods of selling securities. A public company may employ any of the following methods for raising funds by the issue of shares and debentures:

1. Direct sale to the Public.
2. Sale through intermediaries:
   (a) Offer for sale;
   (b) By placing;
   (c) Through sundry intermediaries.

3. Managing brokers.
4. Underwriting.

1. *By direct invitation to the public through a prospectus.* This is the most obvious method by which a public company will seek to raise capital. It will do so by publishing a prospectus inviting members of the public to subscribe for its shares or debentures. The prospectus sets out the prospects of the company and the purposes for which the capital is required. The investor reads the prospectus and applies for shares on the strength of it.

This is the cheapest method of disposing of securities to the general public. But it has its pitfalls. The company itself bears the risk of the issue being unsuccessful. In the case of a new company, there is a further danger that even the minimum subscription may not be forthcoming within the 120 days after the first issue of the prospectus. The company will have to insure by negotiating contracts whereby financial houses agree to take up such part of the securities as are not taken up by the public.

2. *By offers for sale.* The second method, usually adopted in the case of large original issue, is by an offer for sale under Section 64 (1) of the Companies Act. Here the company allots or agrees to allot shares or debentures at a price to a financial institution or an issue house. The issue house or the financial institution publishes a document called an 'offer for sale' with an application form attached offering to the public shares or debentures for sale at a price higher than what it paid for them. This document is regarded as a prospectus. On an application by a member of the public the issuing house renounces the allotment of the number of shares mentioned in the application in favour of the applicant purchaser who becomes a direct allottee of the shares or debentures.

This procedure saves stamp duty which would be payable on a transfer of shares. As far as the company is concerned, this procedure relieves it from the administrative work of a new issue, and at the same time ensures that the whole issue is sold. The issuing house receives its remuneration by the virtue of the profits it makes on the sale by charging higher price than it has paid to the company.

3. *By placing of shares or debentures.* Another method commonly adopted is for the company to arrange for the issuing house, broker or underwriter to purchase the securities and to "place" them with its clients or associates. Alternatively, the shareholders or issuing houses may, without purchasing the shares of the company, merely act as agents of the company for the disposal of the securities to their clients which is done privately and not by public offer, and placing is described as "Private Placing."

If the first alternative is adopted the effect is identical with an offer for sale, and the offer is a prospectus and must comply with the requirements relating to a prospectus. This method is, of course, very much cheaper than prospectus issues or offers for sale, but it is only feasible if the issue can be absorbed by a few selected institutions.

4. *Through sundry intermediaries.* Company's agents, salesmen or shareholders are also employed to secure suitable market for its securities. Commercial banks, investment trusts and other institutions may also lend assistance in disposing of the securities. But the brokers, agents and other intermediaries do not guarantee the sale. This method also suffers from the drawback of uncertainty of market. The pace of sale may also be as slow as in the case of direct sale.

The company will in all probability get its securities listed with a stock exchange. The rules of the recognised stock exchanges require that, before the shares of a company can be allowed to be quoted on a stock exchange, at least 49 per cent of the issued capital must have been offered to the public for subscription. The balance can be taken up by the promoters, their friends and relatives and institutional investors. This method also suffers from the drawback of uncertainty of market.

5. *Managing brokers.* Managing brokers have been assisting companies in the task of marketing securities. They advise companies about the terms and proper time of the issue of securities so that there is no clash between rival issues. They assist companies getting stock exchange listing and in securing loans from financial institutions. They also advise on pre-issue publicity, capital structure and the form it should take. They help in the drafting and getting up of the prospectus and in raising debenture loans at reasonably low rate of interest. By maintaining constant touch with various details relating to the issue they enlist the support and co-operation of sharebrokers.

6. *Issue to existing shareholders, including 'rights issue' and 'bonus issues.'* When an existing company requires funds for further expansion, it has two additional methods available to it, namely: (1) Rights Issue, and (2) Conversion, Capitalisation or Bonus Issue. In both cases, shares are offered or allotted to existing shareholders *pro rata* their holdings. In the case of rights issue new capital is raised and the new shares are first offered to the existing shareholders in a fixed proportion, *e.g.*, three new shares for every Rs. 10 of old shares. In the case of bonus shares, the bonus is provided out of the credit balance of the profit and loss account, out of reserves, or out of the quasi-capital funds, so that the shareholders to whom the shares are allotted have to pay nothing. A bonus issue cannot be used for the purpose of raising new capital, its purpose is to capitalise profits which may be available for distribution.

7. *Underwriting.* This method is probably the most important one by which a company may sell its shares and debentures. The arrangement for underwriting is made by the promoters by getting in touch with persons and institutions that are willing to act as guarantors of the success of a public issue of shares or debentures. Large issues are frequently underwritten, but in India underwriting has begun to play significant role only recently, and even now nothing much as compared with western countries.

Meaning of underwriting. Underwriting may be defined as a contract made by the promoters of the company acting on its behalf with persons like brokers, or institutions like banks, insurance companies, financial institutions such as Industrial Finance Corporation, or the Industrial Development Bank, or other large investors, called underwriters, who undertake, in consideration of a stipulated commission, which must not be more than 5 per cent of the issue price of the shares, or 2½ per cent of the issue price of the debentures, to take the whole or a portion of such of the offered shares or debentures as may not be subscribed by the public. The definition shows that the underwriter insures or guarantees the sale of securities within a certain period of time; and whatever is not taken up by the public is taken up by him and paid for. In this way the company is not to worry, as the necessary money is provided at once by the underwriters.

Importance of Underwriting. The company and investors in its shares derive many advantages from underwriting. The services of underwriters to the company are well worth the money paid as commission. Some of the principal advantages of underwriting may be listed here.

1. In the first place, an issue once underwritten is an assured success. The underwriters guarantee the company against the uncertainty and risk of selling the securities. The company gets from the underwriters a large sum of cash at once or at agreed times whether or not the underwritten shares are sold to the public. As a result the company can at once proceed with its projects which are intended to be financed by the fresh issue. It does not have to wait till the shares have been actualy subscribed to buy fixed assets. Where time is an important element, *e.g.*, new plant is being set up to handle a contract, or effort is being made to forestall competition, underwriting serves a very useful purpose.

2. The second, though incidental, advantage is that the company gets benefit of expert advice. The underwriters with their specialised experience and judgment save the company promoters from making serious error in the form or in the price of the new security.

3. Thirdly, the underwriters, being men or firms of financial integrity and established reputation, help to raise the issue they underwrite in public estimation. The public take such security very readily.

4. The fourth advantage to the company is that underwriting helps in the geographical dispersal of the securities, and underwriters maintain working arrangements with other brokers throughout the country.

5. To the buyers of securities, too, the underwriters render very useful service. The fact that the issue has been underwritten by a reputed firm acts as a guarantee that the security is sound. An investor, therefore, runs little risk when he buys shares or debentures which have been underwritten.

Underwriting in India. In spite of so many advantages of underwriting, it has not fully developed in India. It made an insignificant beginning in 1912 when M/s. O. Batliwala and Karni underwrote the shares of the Central India Spinning and Weaving Co., Ltd. After the

First World War, a few firms took up underwriting, but it was only in the middle of 1950's that some progress in this direction began, especially with the setting up of the Industrial Credit and Investment Corporation of India in 1955.

Causes of slow growth. The slow growth of underwriting in India may be traced to the following circumstances:

1. As India's industrial development began rather late, the capital market remained underdeveloped. This proved a handicap in the way of development of underwriting.

2. The commercial banks followed the policy of staying away from investing their funds in industry and underwriting of securities.

3. As a result of underdevelopment, India did not have specialised financial institutions such as the issue houses of the U.K. or investment bankers of the U.S.A.

4. The managing agency system indirectly stood in the way of the growth of the underwriting institutions. The managing agents used to buy the securities themselves of the companies they managed and then sold gradually to the public. They also arranged to sell the securities to their relatives, friends and acquaintances. In this way, they performed the underwriting function.

As stated above, that underwriting by finance institutions, following the lead of the ICICI, began underwriting securities. Besides some firms in the private sector (e.g., Messrs. Place, Siddous and Gough, Batliwala and Karni, Kothari and Co., Dalal and Co., etc.) the following financial and development corporations among others are the most important underwriters: Industrial Credit and Investment Corporation of India, Industrial Finance Corporation, State Financial Corporations, Life Insurance Corporation, Industrial Development Bank of India, Unit Trust of India. The Commercial banks also underwrite to a significant extent.

B. STOCK EXCHANGE

Meaning. The stock exchange, we have observed in the earlier part of this chapter, is concerned with the sale and purchase of second-hand securities. It is in simple terms a highly organised market for the purchase and sale of shares and debentures as well as financial securities. It is a market through which shareholdings in public companies, for example, can be bought and sold. As seen earlier, such a market enables an investor to dispose of his shares easily and conveniently, as he will find a buyer readily when his shares are admitted on the official list of a stock exchange.

The Securities Contracts (Regulation) Act, 1956 defines a stock exchange as "an association, organisation or body of individuals, whether incorporate or not, established for the purposes of assisting, regulating and controlling business in buying, selling and dealing in securities." This means that a stock exchange is a market which provides necessary facilities for the transfer of all kinds of securities at competitive rates and without undue delay. To repeat, *a stock exchange is an open market for the sale and purchase of securities.*

Economic Functions. The stock exchange performs very important economic functions in relation to the proper working of the corporate sector. The main economic functions are listed below.

1. *Ready market.* The stock exchange provides a market for the resale of existing securities. It facilitates the marketability of shares and debentures and enables investors to realise quickly and with the least possible loss. Persons with cash can convert it into securities and those with securities can readily obtain cash for them. This easy marketability of shares and other securities increases their liquidity (i.e., makes them more easily encashable). The liquidity in its turn increases the value of securities and facilitates their use as collateral security for loan. The creditor constantly knows the worth of his security on the basis of the price quotations of securities on the stock exchange.

2. *Proper appraisal of securities.* Under the stock exchange rules all transactions on the exchange are required to be recorded and made public, so that the prices paid and received become the official market quotations. On the basis of these quotations every holder of a security knows its worth at any one time. In this way, the stock exchange assists in evaluating the prices of different securities. The market quotation also helps a lender on the security of shares to know the value of the security.

3. *Protection of investors.* Through the strict enforcement of their regulations the stock exchanges protect the interests of the investors in securities. For any malpractice or unfair dealing on the part of a member broker while dealing with his client is severely dealt with by the stock exchange and may result in his suspension, fine or expulsion. Thus, the stock exchange provides a reasonable measure of safety and fair dealing in the purchase and sale of securities.

4. *Proper canalisation of capital.* It gives mobility to capital particularly in the direction of profitable avenues. People like to invest their savings in securities of companies yielding good profits. The moment it ceases to be profitable, capital begins to leave it and move towards profitable enterprises. Thus the savings of peope are canalised into industry yielding good return through well-organised stock exchanges. But for the stock exchange, such savings are either likely to be wasted or pushed to less useful channels.

5. *Aid to capital formation.* Stock exchange contributes considerably to the capital formation in the country. The publicity which the stock exchange gives to various securities and their prices induce people to invest their savings in useful projects. The steady and continuous facilities provided by the stock exchange for the purchase and sale of securities encourage people to save and invest. In this manner, it maintains a steady and regular flow of capital into new enterprises which need it the most. Even the dividends and interests earned on investments are invested in industrial enterprises or Government projects.

6. *Facilities for speculation.* The stock exchange enables shrewd businessmen (genuine speculators) to speculate and secure substantial gains through fluctuations in security prices. Speculation is really an integral part of stock exchange operations. As a result of speculation the supply of securities at different places would be equalised with demand. Similarly, the price movements are rendered smoother by the activities of the speculators.

Because of the important functions performed by stock exchanges, and because of the pitfalls that are likely to be encountered by some, they have been endowed with different epithets.. Some people regard it as 'Ali Baba's Treasure,' or a place to 'get rich quick,' while others regard it just a place for gambling. Some have found it a bottomless pit,—worse than all the hells. It is also described as the *mart of the world,* because the securities dealt in on it represent property in every part of the world. As the stock exchange is the market for business for securities of business enterprises, it has been referred to as the market where business of businesses is carried on. Thus, its business is business of businesses. It is also known as a business of all businesses, as indirectly it provides the capital for commerce and industry. The investor with an idea to develop, the trader with a business to expand, the pioneer with a country to explore, the investor with his savings to invest, the banker with his funds to earn profits over a short period, the Government with a scheme to finance, all take themselves eventually to the stock exchange. It is in this sense that it is a business of all businesses. Stock exchanges also act as barometers of the industrial atmosphere and indicators of investment in sound businesses. A slight change in the economic policy of the Government is immediately reflected in the dealings on the stock exchange.

Benefits of stock exchange. A well-organised stock exchange is of great benefit to the country and community, the company and the investor. These benefits are summarised under the three heads.

1. *Benefits to the community.*

(a) The stock exchange generates economic growth by encouraging investors to invest their savings through its facilities for their free flow into productive enterprises.

(b) By encouraging marketability of securities, the stock exchange upholds the position of efficiently run companies.

(c) As a result of the foregoing benefit, a well-managed enterprise can easily raise further funds.

(d) It encourages capital formation.

(e) It helps the Government to borrow from the public and thus enables it to undertake projects of national importance and social value.

2. *Benefits to the Company*

(a) A company whose shares are dealt in on a stock exchange enjoys greater reputation in the credit market.

(b) The marketability of its shares is ensured and in consequence enjoys a wide market for its shares.

(c) Because of their being bought and sold on the stock exchange, the market value of the shares of a company is prone to be higher in relation to earnings, dividends and property values. This enables the company to command better bargaining power in case of an amalgamation or merger.

3. *Benefits to the investor*

(a) The liquidity of his investments is increased.

(b) He enjoys much greater security in respect of his investments because of strict rules and regulations of the stock exchage.

(c) As the values of securities are determined by expert and well-informed judgment, the true worth of the security becomes known to the investor. The prices being known in advance, he can buy or sell and reap a good profit.

(d) The stock exchange provides a reasonable measure of safety and fair dealing and the investors can invest their savings with confidence.

(e) The fact that a security is dealt in on the stock exchange makes it a good cover for loans.

(f) The facility of ready marketability of securities provides a great incentive to people to invest their spare savings, as they can be realised easily and promptly when required.

History of Stock Exchanges. The stock exchange is of comparatively recent growth. Two centuries ago there were no stock exchanges in the world; and the London Stock Exchange, the first of its kind, was founded in 1773. It soon became the financial nerve centre of the world. During the space of a century, France followed the example of London, and soon after Germany and the U.S.A. came into the field. In India, however, the stock exchange in the modern sense was unknown before 1840, and the Native Share and Stock Brokers' Association of Bombay, better known as Bombay Stock Exchange was formally constituted in 1887. The Calcutta Stock Exchange was founded in 1908. The first stock exchange in Madras came into being in 1920, but due to paucity of business, it closed down in 1923. It was revived in 1937 under the name of the Madras Stock Exchange Limited. A new stock exchange under the name of the Indian Stock Exchange Limited was set up in Bombay in 1938 with a powerful Board of directors.

Stock exchanges were opened at other places in the course of the next years in the following order : at Ahmedabad in 1939, at Kanpur in 1940, at Hyderabad in 1943, and at Delhi in 1947. Indore and Bangalore also set up stock exchanges.

In 1956, the Securities Contract (Regulation) Act was passed to regulate the functioning of stock exchanges and centralise control over them. Under the Act, only recognised stock exchanges are permitted to deal in securities. Only eight stock exchanges have so far been recognised by the Government. They are: (i) The Stock Exchange, Bombay, (ii) The Calcutta Stock Exchange Association, Calcutta, (iii) The Ahmedabad Share and Stock Brokers' Association, Ahmedabad, (iv) The Madras Stock Exchange Ltd., Madras, (v) The Delhi Stock Exchange Association

Ltd., (vi) The Hyderabad Stock Exchange Ltd., Hyderabad, (vii) The Stock Exchange, Indore, (viii) The Stock Exchange, Bangalore. Bombay is the only stock exchange enjoying permanent recognition. The other exchanges are granted recognition for 5 years at a time. All the stock exchanges excepting Bombay and Indore, are incorporated as limited companies under the Companies Act.

Management. The administration of the affairs of a stock exchange is entrusted to a Committee of Management that functions like a Board of directors of a company. The Committee is vested with the general powers of supervision and management, but the day-to-day management is delegated to sub-committees such as the Arbitration Committee, Defaulters Committee, Listing Committee, etc.

Membership. Only members are permitted to do business on a stock exchange, and a stock broker cannot do any other business. Only financially sound persons are admitted as members. To become a member, say of Bombay Stock Exchange, it is necessary for a person to be recommended by at least two members of standing. If no member raises any objection and the Managing Committee is satisfied with regard to his financial stability and experience of the market, he is declared elected. To become a member of a stock exchange which is registered as a company, the holding of one share is sufficient.

Normally, only members who enjoy "full" rights and privileges of doing business on the "floor" are allowed to enter the building. For reasons of convenience, however, some other persons with limited rights are allowed to enter the House and act on behalf of members They are:

(a) *Remisiers.* At the Bombay Stock Exchange, remisiers are engaged by the full members to secure business for them. He can only act as an agent of a full member, and not entitled to do business on his own account. He is for all practical purposes a sub-broker, and is subject to all rules and regulations. His remuneration is paid out of the commission received by the member on the business procured by him. The remisiers are often described as "half commission men" because their commission cannot exceed 40 per cent of the commission received on the business secured by them.

(b) *Authorised Clerks.* Members of all stock exchanges are permitted to employ a certain number of clerks or member assistants who are authorised to transact business on behalf of their employers on the floor of the house. They cannot do business in their own names. Bombay and London Exchanges permit 5 clerks, Calcutta Exchange allows a maximum number of 8, and Madras Exchange allows three.

BROKERS AND JOBBERS

The members of the London Stock Exchange are divided into two sections: (i) Brokers, and (ii) Jobbers. This division into jobbers and brokers is strictly adhered to. So far as the status goes, both brokers and jobbers are exactly on the same footing as members of the stock exchange. But at the outset a member has to declare whether he wants to work as a broker or jobber. He cannot work as both, and no partnership between a broker and a jobber is allowed. No member can change over from a broker to a jobber or from a jobber to a broker during the course of the year.

As no member of the public can directly deal on the stock exchange, he must buy or sell securities through a broker. A broker therefore is an intermediary or agent for his non-member clients and transacts business of buying and selling of securities on their behalf with the jobber who cannot deal with non-members. A jobber deals in securities and works "inside the House" buying and selling as principal. Thus, a broker is a commission agent who brings together his outside client and the inside jobber who is a dealer in securities. The broker works for commission and does not ordinarily deal for himself, while the jobber trades for profit which he makes on sales and purchases as a dealer. The broker as agent of numerous clients is ready to deal in a variety of securities, but the jobber usually specialises in a certain group of securities. As a jobber acts as principal, he must be prepared to carry any stock he buys and to find any stocks he sells. Although not a wholesaler or retailer in the strict sense, he is in the nature of a wholesale dealer in stocks and shares.

The transaction of business at the London Stock Exchange, because of the clear distinction between the brokers and jobbers, is conducted a little differently than at the Indian Stock Exchanges. When a broker wishes to buy or sell on behalf of a client, he asks a jobber for a quotation. The broker does not tell the jobber whether he wants to buy or sell. The jobber, therefore, names two prices (two-way or double-barrelled price), one at which he is willing to sell and the other at which he is ready to buy. The former will be slightly higher than the latter. For example, if a broker asks for a price in "Imps", i.e., Imperial Tobacco Company shares, and the jobber replies £4.90 to £5 in a thousand, it means that the jobber will buy at the first price and sell at the second up to a thousand shares either way. If the broker is not satisfied, he may either go to another jobber or he may say "make it closer", i.e., reduce the margin between the buying and selling prices. The jobber may improve his quotation, and broker having the buying order from his client will then say, "take five hundred" meaning that he is buying 500 shares from the jobber. Each party then enters the deal in his dealing book.

Both the jobber and the broker perform useful functions. But the separation appears to be of greater advantage to the public as it provides a certain amount of protection against the expert dealer, the jobber. The broker, who acts as an agent of his client, becomes a shield against the professional dealer, and as a fiduciary, is bound to protect the interests of his clients against the expert jobber. The dealer also renders useful service by executing the orders promptly and this narrows down price fluctuations. His expert knowledge plays an important role in the fixation of prices for various securities so that the investors are ensured of reasonably adequate prices.

Tarawaniwala and Brokers. Members on the Bombay Stock Exchange are classified (unofficially though) as *Tarawaniwala* (i.e., those who take away the cream of the business) and *Commission Brokers* who transact business on behalf of non-members or other members on commission basis. A tarawaniwala deals on his own account and, in this respect, resembles a jobber on the London Stock Exchange. But unlike a jobber he can also act as a commission agent. This practice is objectionable as he can with his inside knowledge sell to his clients at higher prices and buy from them at lower prices. His sole object is to make profit arising from his purchase and sale prices. He gambles in differences. The Securities Contracts (Regulation) Act, 1956, provides that a member of a recognised stock exchange cannot buy or sell securities as principal from or to anyone except another member of a recognised stock exchange. If he wants to deal with a non-member as principal he must disclose this fact to the non-member and get his consent.

LISTING OF SECURITIES

No company is entitled automatically to have its shares to be dealt in on a stock exchange. It has to apply for permission and the Stock exchange will have to decide whether to list the securities of the company or not. If permission is granted, then the securities of the company are said to have been listed. i.e., they have been included in the official list of the stock exchange for the purpose of trading.

Before the securities are listed at any stock exchange the company has to furnish details about its organisation and working to the stock exchange and comply with its rules and regulations. By listing the securities of a company the stock exchange does not guarantee its financial soundness, or recommend its securities to the public. All that it does is that at the time of listing the company was legally incorporated and was solvent as a going concern. All the same the listing does create a favourable climate for the securities and the investor makes his investment with confidence. Listing therefore proves of advantage to the company as well as the investor. Listing enhances the credit of the company and widens the market for its securities. To the investor it provides safety of dealing and facility of quick disposal in times of need.

Although stock exchanges are empowered to refuse listing, an appeal to the Government lies against their decision. The government has framed the following rules under the Securities Contracts (Regulation) Act, 1956, for the listing of securities:

A company wishing its securities to be listed must apply in the prescribed form supported by the documentary evidence as under:

(a) Copies of the memorandum and articles, prospectus or the statement in lieu of prospectus, directors' report, balance sheet, and agreements with underwriters.

(b) Specimen copies of shares and debenture certificates, letters of allotment, acceptance, renunciation, etc.
(c) Particulars as to its capital structure.
(d) A statement showing distribution of shares.
(e) Particulars of dividends and cash bonuses during the last 10 years (only in the case of old companies).
(f) Particulars of shares or debentures for which permission to deal is applied for.
(g) A brief history of the company's activities since its incorporation.

Criteria for listing. While scrutinising the application of a company the stock exchange concerned will pay special attention to see

(a) Whether the articles of association contain the following regulations:

(i) a common form of transfer shall be used (No restrictions on the transfer of shares);
(ii) Fully paid shares shall not be subject to company's lien;
(iii) Calls paid in advance may carry interest, but shall not confer a right to dividend;
(iv) Unclaimed dividends have been paid into the unpaid Dividend Account;
(v) option to call on shares shall be given only after sanction by the general meeting.

(b) Whether at least 49 per cent of each class of securities issued was offered to the public for subscription through newspapers for not less than three days.

(c) Whether the company is of a fair size, has a broadbased capital structure and there is a sufficient public interest in its securities.

After the application has been scrutinised, the stock exchange authorities, if satisfied, will normally call upon the company to execute a listing agreement which contains the obligations on the part of the company as follows:

1. The company must be fair to all applicants for shares while making allotments. In the event of over-subscription, the stock exchange will usually advise the company about the basis to be adopted for making allotments. It will endeavour to make sure that applicants for large blocks of shares are not given undue preference over others.

2. The company must keep the stock exchange fully informed about matters affecting the company, such as:

(a) to notify the stock exchange of the Board meeting at which decision about dividend is taken;
(b) to inform the stock exchange about the details of dividend distribution after the meeting of the Board of directors;
(c) to forward forthwith to the stock exchange copies of its annual accounts (duly audited) after they have been issued;
(d) to notify the stock exchange of any material change in the general nature or character of company's business;

(e) to notify the stock exchange of any change in company's capital; and

(f) to inform the stock exchange of the issue of any new shares, whether rights or otherwise, as also of any bonus issues.

3. The company must undertake

(a) to comply with all the conditions on the basis of which the listing has been obtained and not to commit any breach thereof;

(b) to notify the stock exchange of any occasion which will result in the redemption, cancellation or retirement of any listed securities;

(c) to avoid as far as possible the establishment of a false market for the company's shares; and

(d) to supply to the stock exchange any other information necessary to enable the shareholders to appraise the company's position.

Section 73 of the Companies Act. 1956, provides for the listing of securities. It states that where a company has made a statement in its prospectus that an application has been or will be made to a recognised stock exchange for permission for its securities to be dealt in on it, such permission must be applied for before the tenth day after the first issue of the prospectus. The permission is to be obtained within ten weeks from the date of the closing of the subscription list. No allotment of shares can be made in violation of these provisions, and if so made, it shall be void and the company shall have to repay forthwith all money received from the applicants.

The Central Government is empowered to compel any public company to get its securities listed on a recognised stock exchange.

BUYERS AND SELLERS

The stock exchange, we have observed earlier, is an organised market for the sale and purchase of securities or scrips. The buyers and sellers of scrips may be either investors or speculators. The investors buy securities with the object of making investments for earning an income. The speculators would buy on the hope of selling later on at a profit or sell hoping to be able to buy at a lower price and so make a profit. They do not take or give delivery of the scrips but make their profit through price differences.

The investor is concerned with the safety of investment and the security and regularity of income. The speculator, on the other hand, is interested in the appreciation of his capital and quick profit. Thus, an investor seeks income from his investment, and a speculator is after profit arising out of his sales and purchases. In practice, however, there are no genuine investors or pure speculators. Both are at times investors as well as speculators; the difference between the two in such cases being of degree and not of nature.

Types of Speculators. The terms used to describe the different kinds of speculators who make up the Stock Exchange Menagerie are taken from animal kingdom. The name given to each kind is probably based on the behaviour of the animal chosen for him. They are Bulls, Bears, Stags and Lame Ducks. A short description of each one is given below.

Bull. In the simplest terms a "bull" is a person who buys a certain security in the expectation of a rise in its price. He buys shares which he does not want; in the hope that he will be able to sell them at a higher price, before the time to take delivery arrives, and pocket the difference. He is an optimist, believing as he does that the price will rise. Since he does not intend to permanently acquire the security, but hopes to be able to sell at a profit before the time comes when it has to be paid for, he is a potential seller. On the Indian stock exchanges, a bull is also known as a *Tejiwala*—one who buys securities for a rise. He is said to be "on the long side of the market." He is called a bull because of the bull's practice to throw its victim with its horns up in the air. He often tries to raise the price of the security in the share market. For instance, a bull may buy shares at Rs. 25 per share at the beginning of a stock exchange Account. On the Bombay Stock Exchange, a month (on London Stock Exchange a fortnight) will elapse before he has to pay for them. If meanwhile the price has gone up to Rs. 30 per share, he sells and takes his profit of Rs. 5 per share, less commission and charges. At the end of the Account he will receive a cheque for the difference between Rs. 25 and Rs. 30 less charges, although he has parted with no money.

Bear. A bear is essentially a speculator. He is a person who has sold short. That is to say he has sold shares which he does not possess, in the hope that he may be able to buy it back more cheaply, and make his profit on the deal. The bear is a pessimist; he believes the price will fall. He is also known as *Mandiwala.* A bear usually presses his victim to the ground, and the bear speculator works for pushing the prices in the securities market down. He hopes and works for the fall in prices so that he may buy by the settlement day at a lower price and make his profit. He is therefore a potential buyer. Suppose a bear, believing a share is likely to fall in price, may sell a number of shares at Rs. 30. They are not in his possession, but he hopes that the price will fall sufficiently for him to acquire at a lower figure before he has to deliver them to the buyer. If all goes well for him, the shares fall in price to Rs. 25. He buys at this level, and clears a profit of Rs. 5 per share, less commission and charges, and receives a cheque which is all profit.

The illustrations have been given in the simplest form for the sake of clearness, but in practice, the battle between the bulls and bears may take Homeric proportions. One group of speculators sells heavily with the object of depressing the price of a share and then buying back at a cheaper rate. An opposing group may take the opposite view and buy all available shares, so as to clear the market. When the time comes for the first group (bears) to buy the shares for delivery, they are at the mercy of their opponents (bulls), who are in the position to demand what price they like. This is known as "bear squeeze", and has brought about the ruin of many big operators. When the operators for the fall in price of shares find that the price is not declining as they wish, they resort to "bear covering", i.e., they are buying shares either to close the deal or to avoid loss. The effect is to cause a rally in the price of the shares.

Lame Duck. A bear struggling against the immediate difficulties of meeting his engagements is called a lame duck. This would happen, as explained above, when he has been 'cornered' because he cannot buy back at any price as no share are obtainable; and he cannot make terms with the person to whom he has sold the shares, or with some one else who would let him have the shares so that he may deliver them to the buyer.

Stag. Another familiar animal is the "Stag." A stag is a speculator, who applies for shares of a new issue, with the only intention of snatching a quick profit if the issue goes to a premium, that is the shares are now selling at a price higher than their issue price. As he has no intention of becoming the actual holder of shares, he sells the allotment at a premium, if the shares have gone to a premium. The difference between the application money paid by him and the price at which he sells the allotment is his profit. As he is only a 'premium hunter,' the stag is usually cautious although always bullish, for he always hopes for a rise in price. When the issue is very popular and likely to go to a premium, the enthusiastic stag will often send in a number of applications under different names, in the hope that one or more of them will get an allotment. Sometimes the stag is badly caught, as he may get a full allotment which he mav not be able to pav for and must sell at loss.

The existence of the stag explains the apparent anomaly of a steady decline in the price of an issue soon after it is made, although at the time of issue the demand was enormously in excess of the supply. The fall is caused by the selling of the stags who created the fictitous demand. Their activities are looked at with disfavour by the Government and the recognised stock exchanges.

Effect of Battle Between Bulls and Bears. The bulls and bears are important speculators to the stock exchange and affect the prices considerably. The very existence of a big bull account, or of a big bear account has a most important effect upon the market. The bull weakens it and the bear strengthens it because every bull is a potential seller and every bear is a potential buyer. While bulls are buying the prices may rise, and while bears are selling they may fall; but a time comes that their operations, however successful, have to be completed and the movement in the opposite direction sets in . Good news is frequently followed by a sharp relapse in prices because of the selling by bulls anxious to take advantage of it. Bad news is frequently without effect, or is followed by a rise, because the bears see their opportunity of buying back the securities they have sold, and thus support the market.

In their battle with the bears, the bulls may have their own way, and by concerted action, called a "Bull Campaign," by spreading stories ourably affecting the security—true, half true, or untrue—bring about artificial rise in the prices and thus "Rig the Market." This artificial e is likely to prove of great harm to the bulls who have bought in large ıantities unless they manage the position with extreme skill. For, when ıe time for selling comes and "unloading"is made, there will be left a ırge number of "Stale bulls," i.e., bulls who are unable to take delivery ınd pay for the securities they had got and thus close their accounts at a oss.

On the other hand, the bears may have it all their own way. By concerted action they may "Bang the Market," indulge in a "Bear Raid," and bring prices down to a level much lower than is warranted by the intrinsic merits of the securities which they have thrown on the market in such large quantities. At the end of the raid, however, the position of the bear is an exceedingly dangerous one. Having sold, he has undertaken to deliver. But prices begin to rise again, and "Bear Covering" or buying back only enhances upward movement. At times it may become impossible to buy back at any price, as there is no stock obtainable. In such a situation, the bears are "cornered". Unless a bear so situated can make terms with the party to whom he has sold the securities, he stands in the position of one who cannot meet his engagements. To revert to the stock exchange of zoology applied to all members struggling against difficulties, the bear is now a lame duck.

Outside Dealers. There are some other persons and firms dealing in securities, but they are outside brokers. They can function only after obtaining a licence from the Government, and in places where no recognised exchange exists. Many of the outside firms do legitimate business, and are in fact of highest standing possessing business superior in magnitude and status to those of many of the stock exchange firms. But there are a large number of rogues who swindle the public as they deal directly with them. They are known by many names such as "share-purchasers", "bucket shops", "unloading shops" and "gambling shops"

HOW TO DEAL WITH THE BROKER

We have already observed that the rules of the stock exchange do not permit any outsiders to transact business on it without the agency of member brokers. Anyone wishing to buy or sell at a stock exchange must engage a broker who is a member of the stock exchange to conduct this business for him. From the client's point of view; the first step is the choice of a broker, then engaging a broker, placing an order, making the contract, preparation of the contract note and finally the settlement. A brief description of each step is given below.

Choosing a Broker. A person wishing to buy and sell shares on the stock exchange may either act through his banker who has his brokers to do business, or deal directly with a broker of repute. The latter course, of course, ensures prompt action which may prove profitable. The choice of the broker may be made on the advice of the banker.

Engaging the Broker. Having decided upon a broker, the next step is to find out whether he would be willing to transact business on your behalf. The broker will ask for a bank or other references regarding the financial position of the prospective client and honesty and integrity. If he is satisfied, the client will be asked to open an account with him.

Placing the Order. The client now selects the security, preferably in consultation with the broker, in which he would like to invest his savings. Having done that he places an order with the broker by letter, telegram or on the telephone. While placing an order, it is essential that the instructions are absolutely clear. They should take the form of "Please buy....,"or "Please sell...." Ambiguity may cause delay or even serious loss. Hence, the instructions should read like this: "Please sell 100 Century 8 per cent cumulative preference shares at Rs. 135 or best." Here best means the best or the highest price obtainable. There are some other methods of placing the order and are summarised here.

(a) *Fixed Price Order.* It is an order which must be executed at the price indicated by the client, or below it, if it is for buying, or above it, if it is a sale. A fixed order may say "buy 10 Tatas at 155" or "sell 10 Tatas at 157." The broker is to buy at Rs. 155 or below; or sell at Rs. 157 or above. The brokers, however, do not encourage fixed price orders; they prefer a variation of this type, namely, At Limit Orders.

(b) *At Limit Order.* This type of order fixes definite limits beyond which the broker is not to go. A Limit Order would read: "buy not over 155" or "sell not under 157." As the broker is his client's agent, he is expected to, and usually does, buy at the lowest price and sell at the highest price possible.

(c) *Immediate or Cancel Order.* This is an order which must be executed at once at the best possible price. If it cannot be executed immediately because prices are not favourable, the broker will cancel and report to the client. Such an order would read: "buy (or sell) 10 Tatas 155 immediate or cancel."

(d) *Stop-loss Order.* The client places this kind of order in order to protect himself against a heavy fall or rise in prices. It would read: "buy 10 Tatas at 155 Stop." On receipt of the order, the broker will act only when the market price is below 155, but when it reaches this figure he must act. When a customer who bought 10 Tatas at 155 is required to sell, he may place an order to "sell 10 Tatas 153 stop," therefore limiting his loss to Rs. 2 per share. As soon as the price reaches 153 or begins to decline, the broker will *sell the shares.*

(e) *Discretion order* is an order which leaves the broker free to buy or sell certain inactive securities and has full confidence in his broker.

(f) *At Best Order.* This order does not specify any price and must be executed immediately at the best price obtainable at the time. The broker has no discretion. These orders are the most frequent. In an At Best Order the instructions would read "buy (or sell) 10 Tatas at best."

(g) *Open Order.* Where the client does not place any limit on the time during which his order has to be executed, it is called an open order.

After receiving the order, the broker notes it down in a rough note book from where it is transferred to the Order Book. Normally, big brokers transact business through their authorised clerks, although small brokers will execute the order personally.

Making the Contract. The floor of the stock exchange is divided into recognised 'markets' or 'pitches' and the name of a particular scrip is mentioned there. The broker or his authorised clerk approaches a broker in the appropriate 'market' or 'pit' and asks for a quotation or quotes his own price and when the bargain, which is always by word of mouth, is closed, both the parties make short notes in pencil on a pad of handy size. This pad is divided into two parts, one for purchases, or the debit side, and the other for sales on the credit side. The number, description of securities and the name of the party from whom bought or to whom sold are recorded. The broker may 'mark' the bargain by entering brief details on a slip of paper which is put in a box officially provided for the purpose and which ensures that the price at which the deal was done shall appear under the heading of "business done" in the Official List of prices published by the Managing Committee, known as the Stock Exchange Daily Official List.

Preparing the Contract Note. At the end of the day's work, the authorised clerks return to their offices and enter the details of the transaction in the '*Kacha Sauda Book*' from the rough notes in the pad. From this book the details are recorded into the '*Pucca Sauda Book*' maintained separately for Cash or ready delivery transactions and Forward delivery contracts. After this the broker makes out a regulation form of contract note, which he sends to his client, giving details of the security dealt in, the price, the broker's regulation commission, the cost of the revenue stamp, together with the fee charged by the issuing body, and the date on which the settlement is to be made unless the bargain is "for cash". The contract note is signed by the broker, and a copy of this note is sent to the other party. The next day the clerks from each firm meet each other to compare the contract notes and sign in each other's books as a token of correctness of the contract notes. Any losses due to genuine errors in recording are usually shared equally by the parties, and the clients do not suffer on this account.

SETTLEMENT

Some transactions are made on cash basis for ready delivery and others for forward delivery. The procedure for the settlement of each is different from the other, and is detailed below:

Settlement of Cash or Ready Delivery Contracts. A cash or ready delivery contract is one in which the parties intend to deliver the securities forthwith and pay for them. The settlement of this type of contract is either made on the same day (spot delivery and payment) or within the next few days as fixed by the Stock Exchange. For example, the Bombay and Madras Stock Exchanges allow the settlement to be made within seven days, and the Calcutta Exchange allows only three days for the purpose. In special circumstances extension of time for settlement may be granted.

The cash list securities are either cleared or Non-cleared securities. Cleared securities are settled through the Clearing House, while others in either of the following ways without the intervention of the Clearing House.

Settlement of non-cleared securities. A ready delivery contract in respect of non-cleared securities may be settled in either of the following ways:

(i) The broker may make "hand delivery" of the securities that he has sold and receive payment of the price on behalf of his client. Conversely, he may receive actual delivery of the securities purchased by him and pay the price on behalf of his client.

(ii) The second method involves squaring up of the original transaction by means of a fresh sale or purchase at the time of settlement. For example, if the broker had contracted to buy 100 shares at Rs. 30 each, he may contract to sell them at Rs. 25 each, which is the prevailing price on the settlement day. In this way, he will have squared up the transaction and his client will have suffered a loss of Rs. 500.

Settlement through Clearing House. Cleared list securities are cleared through the Clearing House. Clearing houses have been set up by the following stock exchanges, namely:—Bombay, Calcutta, Madras, Ahmedabad and Delhi. The clearing house serves a similar purpose as the banks' clearing house; it acts as a useful link between the buyers and sellers of securities. It enables the parties to pay or receive only the net dues instead of the total amounts of their contacts. A bargain in cleared securities made on any business day is to be settled on Thursday the following week and the day is known as the Day of Clearing. Bargains made on Saturday are deemed to have been made on Monday following. On Monday the seller makes out a Seller's Clearance Ticket in duplicate and sends it to the buyer who retains the original and returns the duplicate duly signed. On Wednesday preceding the day of clearing the seller will submit to the Clearing House a Clearing Sheet, showing details of the security purchased and the value to be paid on the debit side and the account of each security sold and the money to be received on the credit side, and also the net balance. In case of a net debit balance, the member also sends a cheque for the amount and in case of credit balance a draft on the Clearing House is attached. On the Clearance Day, the securities sold, together with the necessary transfer deed, are delivered to the Clearing House by the seller. The buying member receives the securities from the Clearing House on the day following the clearing and signs a receipt personally or through his clerk.

Settlement of Forward Delivery Contracts. For Forward contracts the year is divided into 12 settlements, so that we have monthly settlements in India, while on the London Stock Exchange they have fortnightly settlements. The settlement days are fixed by the Managing Committee, and they are usually in the last week of the month. The parties can by agreement postpone the settlement to the next settlement period. Technically, such postponements is called 'Carryover' or 'Budla'. Forward dealings are allowed only in those securities which have been placed on the forward list of an exchange. Indore and Hyderabad Stock Exchange do not have any security on the forward list. In law, all contracts, including forward transactions are made with the intention of taking and giving delivery of securities on cash payment of their prices. In practice, forward business is done with the object of making profit by settlement of differences. On the day of settlement either (i) the delivery is taken (a rare occurrence), or (ii) the transaction is reversed through a neutralising purchase or sale in the same way as under Ready Delivery Contracts, or (iii) the transactions is 'carried over' to the next settlement day.

The settlement of forward delivery contracts normally extends over a period of four days as under:

(i) The first day is called Contango or Carry-over Day, and the brokers as buyers and sellers compare their memorandum slips and carry over the transactions on this day

(ii) The second day of the settlement is called the 'Ticket Day' or 'Name Day' and is meant for the preparation of a ticket for the securities which is endorsed back until it reaches the original owner of the securities in question.

(iii) On the third-day, which is known as the 'Intermediate' or 'Making up Day,' the securities are actually delivered to the Clearing House.

(iv) The last day is known as the 'Account Day' or 'Pay Day.' This is the actual day of settlement when each member submits a balance sheet and a statement of differences to the Clearing House. Any balance shown in the statement is debited or credited to the account of a member with the Clearing House. If a member fails to pay up the balance before noon, the next day after the Pay Day is declared a 'defaulter.' On this day the market is closed for forward business.

Forward trading in securities was banned by an order of the Government of India in 1969.

Carrying over or Budla. Every speculator tries to foresee the future trend of prices with the object of making profit from the fluctuations in prices. If his forecast favours he makes a profit. If the prices do not move according to his expectations, he is faced with the prospect of a loss. He is, however, given an opportunity to avoid or at least postpone this loss by means of a postponement of the final settlement. This facility of postponing the transaction to the next settlement is called 'Carry over' or 'Budla'. For this concession the party making it charges, *budla* brokerage from the other party.

Budla or carry over is effected by means of two new bargains. A bull transaction is carried over by a sale for current settlement and re-purchase for the next settlement. A bear transaction is made a *budla* or carried over by a purchase for the current settlement and re-sale for the next settlement. The result is that the original bargain is completed for the current settlement and a new transaction at a new price is opened up for the next settlement. The party effecting the *budla* is in the same position, but to complete the transaction he requires finance. The bull operator, who is unable to pay for the delivery of securities, approaches a Budliwala or a "taker-in" who advances money at a high rate of interest or *contango.* But instead of securing finance for buying, it may be arranged between the buyer and seller (bull and bear) to carry over the bargain to the next settlement on payment of interest to the party permitting the carry over or *budla.* This is the common practice, because bulls buy without any intention of taking delivery and bears sell what they have not got. If no rise has taken place, or if the bull looks for a further rise, he will carry over the bargain and pay to the bear interest known as *contango* or *budliwala* or *budla* charge which varies according to the security dealt in. When the market becomes oversold in a particular scrip, i.e., there are more bears than bulls in the settlement of the scrip, the bear will be anxious to carry over and will pay to the bull for this privilege interest known as *Backwardation.* This happens when the security is so short, and therefore not obtainable, that instead of receiving *contango* rate from the bull or buyer, the bear or seller is prepared to give some consideration for the accommodation. If the demand of the buyers for loans to pay for the security they have bought is balanced by the demand of the sellers for the same security which they have undertaken to deliver, there is neither a contango rate nor a backwardation rate. There is an even rate as neither buyers nor sellers of that security have to pay anything for carry over.

PURELY SPECULATIVE TRANSACTIONS

There are several specialised methods of conducting speculative transactions. The following are some of the important ones:

Option Dealings. There is a class of business in which some indulge on the stock exchanges as well as commodity exchanges, and facilities are provided by these exchanges to bulls and bears to enter into speculation freely. This kind of business, if transacted cautiously, results in the limitation of losses and great deal of fascination to a skilful operator. This business is called "option dealing," i.e., right to buy or sell certain securities at a certain price by a certain date. Options are of three kinds, and an operator may obtain any one or all of them. They are "Put Option", "Call Option", and "Put-and-call Option" or "Double Option". In the case of Put Option, the operator buys the right to sell so many shares on or before a certain day at a certain price. In the case of Call Option, the operator buys the right to buy so many shares on or before a certain day at a certain price. In Put-and-Call or Double

Option, the operator buys the right either to buy or to sell so many shares on or before a certain day at a certain price. The operator pays the person granting the option a certain amount per share for the option, and this option money or premium must be allowed for in calculating the price at which the operation must be closed out in order to make a profit. Put Options are bought when it is believed that the prices are likely to fall and Call Options are bought when it is believed that the prices would rise. Put-and-Call Options are bought in shares of a widely fluctuating nature, and the operation partakes more of a gamble, a mere betting upon chance, than do either Put Options or Call Options. When the time for the exercise of option arrives, the buyer of the option has to declare whether he will exercise it or not. If he exercises a call option, he has to pay the money and receive the shares, and if it is a put option, he has to deliver the shares and receive the money. *Option business on the Stock Exchanges in India is now illegal and a cognisable offence punishable by imprisonment or fine or with both.*

The Cover System. The cover is a deposit of an amount per share or per cent given to a broker by his client with instructions to buy or sell on his behalf with the implied condition that in case the market moves against the dealer and the loss swallows up the cover the transaction has to be closed without the amount of the cover. If, on the other hand, the transaction proves profitable, the client receives the profit plus the cover money. There is a difference between cover money and option money. Cover money is returnable with the profits, while option money, being a premium given to the party granting the option in consideration of his giving option to buy or sell, is retained by him, whether the option is exercised or not. The cover system is based on the same principle as the horse race betting.

Margin Trading. Margin trading is a system of purchasing securities with funds borrowed from brokers. It resembles dealings to purchase with funds borrowed from banks and financial institutions, but there the resemblance ends. Margin trading is a by-product of speculation, for in a cash transaction the necessity for a margin does not arise. It is only when traders deal on account and wait for appreciation in the value of securities that they make a purchase on margin. A client wishing to trade on margin opens an account with his broker by making an initial deposit of a certain amount in cash or securities, and agrees to maintain it at a certain level. The system of margin trading enables a private operator to deal in amounts which would be quite beyond his means, if he had to find them in full. A broker is always prepared to finance, or to find finance for a client who can "put up a margin" and, as the margin is needed only to cover a possible difference in the price at which the shares are bought and eventually sold, a deposit of Rs. 500 with a broker would normally suffice to permit of the purchase or sale of shares worth nearly Rs. 10,000.

Arbitrage. The dictionary meaning of the word arbitrage is "traffic in bills of exchange or stocks and securities to profit by different prices in different countries or markets." Arbitrage in securities consists in the simultaneous buying and selling of the same stock in two different centres at prices which show a profit to the operator. This may be illustrated by taking an example of an arbitrage transaction between the London and the Amsterdam Stock Exchanges. If Royal Dutch Petroleum shares are quoted at 360 florins per share, sellers in Amsterdam, and at £30 per share buyers in London, and the exchange between London and Amsterdam is 12.10 florins per pound sellers, any operator could buy the shares in Amsterdam at about £29/15/- per share and sell them in London for £30 per share, which would show a profit, unless the margin was swallowed by the expenses. Such dealings are highly technical and are undertaken only by professional operators working for large firms.

Wash Sales. Where a broker-speculator wishes to create a false situation to raise the price of a security in order to unload his holdings at a high price thereby making profit, he is said to make a wash sale. This is an objectionable practice and all recognised stock exchanges provide for heavy penalties for such sales.

Cornering. A corner is a word of American origin used for a speculation in a stock exchange in which the entire supply of a particular security is held by a broker or a group of brokers. In such a situation, the bears, who are short sellers, and have contract to sell the security without actually possessing it, are unable to deliver it to the buyers who have formed the corner or cornered the market. This enables the buyers to compel sellers to buy the security at their own price. The short-sellers are said to be "squeezed." A corner is generally brought off in a new security when by false dealing stock-brokers are persuaded to sell speculatively shares which are really in the hands of the set of people who cornered the market.

Blank Transfer. The holding of shares on 'blank transfer' is a common practice in India. The practice is most widely used for speculative dealings and all stock exchanges recognise a blank transfer as a valid delivery. When a shareholder signs the transfer form without filling in the name of the transferee and the date of execution and hands it over with the share certificate to the transferee thereby enabling him to deal with the shares, he is said to have made a transfer "in blank" or a "blank transfer." Such a transfer is particularly useful and convenient when shares are to be delivered as a part of a carry over.

The practice of blank transfers for legitimate purposes is not objectionable. But it has also led to certain abuses, such as (i) encouragement of unhealthy speculation, the securities being easily negotiable, (ii) concealment of the identity of the real beneficial owner behind the nominee. This leads to evasion of income-tax, giving control of the company to the transferee, window-dressing of the balance sheet by reshuffling of shares held in blank transfers between associated companies and bringing into existence of fictitious or ante-dated transactions in the books of companies in order to create fictitious losses in investments for the purposes of reducing taxable profits.

In order to curb these abuses the Companies Act was amended in 1965. It is now provided that every instrument of transfer of shares shall be in the prescribed form and presented to the prescribed authority (Registrar of Companies) before it is signed by the transferor. The Registrar will stamp the date on which it is presented. Then the transfer form duly executed must be presented to the company for registration of transfer in the case of listed securities at any time before the first closure of register of members after the date of transfer or within 2 months of the date of presentation whichever is later, and in the case of non-listed securities, within 2 months of the date of such presentation. This means that a blank transfer can now remain in circulation for not more than 2 months.

Failures. When any member of the stock exchange finds himself unable to meet his engagements, he must at once inform the Managing Committee, who may declare him to be a defaulter and cause him to be "hammered." The person or firm in question immediately ceases to be a member of the House and his affairs are wound up by the Official Assignee. After a member has been declared a defaulter, all bargains with other members are immediately reversed at the price ruling at the time of the declaration of the default. A defaulter may be re-admitted if he satisfies certain conditions. Upon his application for re-admission, the Defaulters Committee will investigate his conduct and accounts and report to the Managing Committee. The Committee may, subject to such conditions as they think fit, re-admit the defaulter only if, in their opinion, he had kept his operation within a reasonable proportion of his means, or resources and had been irreproachable in his general conduct. On the Bombay Stock Exchange, a defaulter shall not be re-admitted unless he has made a bona fide payment of not less than 40 paise in the rupee of the amount of the loss he has incurred. But if his default has been contributed by his reckless dealings, he will not be re-admitted.

CAUSES OF PRICE FLUCTUATIONS

Broadly, the following factors influence the prices of stocks and shares and cause fluctuations in them on the stock exchange:

(a) *Demand and supply.* Competition prevails on the stock exchange and so forces of demand and supply interact to determine price of a security. If a particular security is in abundant supply at a particular moment it will fetch low price. If there are more buyers than sellers, the price will tend to rise. Normally, the demand for certain equity shares will go up if the actual yield from them is higher, say 10 per cent, than the general expectation about the return in the industry as a whole, say 8 per cent, and the supply being limited, because no one would like to sell such shares, their price will rise. If the actual yield is less than the general expectation, the price will fall, because there will be more sellers than buyers.

(b) *Financial Position of the Company.* The financial position of the company directly affects the dividend payment. That in turn influences the price of the shares, the higher the rate of dividend the higher the price of the share. Sometimes the speculators may depress the price even when dividend is high. For instance, they may, anticipating a high rate of dividend, buy up shares and so raise the price. When the price has gone high enough they would sell out and reap their profits. Their selling will push down the price.

(c) *Action of underwriters.* The underwriters of shares are also responsible for causing fluctuations in share values. In order to create a good demand for shares underwritten by them, the underwriters make artificial purchases of the shares. This action of theirs tends to raise the price of shares.

(d) *Actions of financial institutions.* The financial institutions like banks, Life Insurance Corporation, other insurance companies, Industrial Finance Corporation, Industrial Credit and Investment Corporation invest their funds in good income-yielding securities. Large scale buying or selling of shares by these institutions will influence the general public to follow their lead and so raise or depress the prices.

(e) *Bank rate.* This is a rate at which the Central Bank of a country is ready to rediscount approved bills of exchange. A raise in the Bank rate puts a check on investment and this in turn causes the prices of securities to fall. When the Bank rate is lowered the prices of shares go up.

(f) *Changes in the constitution of the Board.* The personnel of the Board of directors also influence the price of the shares of the company. For example, if an influential and reputed director resigns from the Board, the public gets nervous which adversely affects the price of shares. Also, where on the death of a director who held a large number of shares, such shares have to be disposed of, the price is bound to come down causing depression in the market.

(g) *Trade Cycle.* During the boom period in trade the prices of shares go up and during slump conditions, the prices come down.

(h) *Speculative pressures.* The battle between the bulls and bears are both the cause and effect of fluctuations in security prices. The activities of the bears who always make contracts for the sale of shares they do not possess tend to force the prices down. Similarly, the activities of the bulls who buy without any intention of paying for them tend to raise the prices.

(i) *Sympathetic fluctuations.* Where the shares of a company are listed with more than one stock exchange, the change of prices at one exchange will be reflected on the other so that the price will tend to be uniform on all exchanges.

(j) *Politicial factors.* Political upset even of a minor kind is likely to have an adverse reaction on stock exchanges. Disturbances even in foreign countries may affect the market which is extremely sensitive.

(k) *Miscellaneous factors.* The stock exchange is so sensitive to actions and happenings that it reacts sharply even to remotely connected events with it. Personal health of the head of the Government, sudden rainfall, strike, rumours of various kinds all affect the market.

SPECULATION AND GAMBLING

We have seen, while dealing with 'bulls' and bears' as well as with options dealings, that a certain amount of speculative business is transacted on the stock exchanges as in other markets. A large number of dealers, buying and selling securities on their own account, give the stock market a breadth of business and continuity that cannot exist otherwise. This cannot be provided by genuine investors alone. Speculators are necessary for this purpose. Speculation is thus an integral part of stock exchange business. Speculation may, however, be scientific or genuine or it may be unscientific or in the nature of gambling. Since genuine speculation performs an important economic function and unscientific or illegitimate speculation is highly injurious to the interests of all concerned, it is appropriate at this stage to say something about speculation and gambling.

Speculation. The term 'speculation' is derived from the Latin word *speculare,* meaning look at from afar. It, therefore, implies the visualisation of future events and occurrences. In relation to market transactions it means the buying or selling of commodities or securities at one time with the object of making profit by selling or buying at another time, usually in the same market. It involves the making of profit from the difference between present and future prices of the goods the speculator buys or sells. A speculator differs from an investor insofar as he buys or sells in the hope of a profit from anticipated changes of value, while an investor purchases any property for earning an annual income. A speculator thus assumes greater risks of capital loss and at the same time expects greater profits. Speculative business may include any or some of the following.

Legitimate enterprise, undertaken by a man conversant with the business, with the object of making profits by producing in anticipation of a carefully estimated demand. The element of risk is limited and may be reduced to a minimum by the highly-skilled entrepreneur.

Speculator proper, which involves the investment of money in an enterprise, the risk and details of which cannot be known to any man. Dealers on the produce exchanges and those on the stock exchanges speculate on the probability of a rise or fall in the prices of commodities or securities respectively. In the case of commodities if crops are likely to be abundant they sell their rights to supplies in anticipation of a future fall in prices; if crops are likely to be poor they buy as much as possible in anticipation of a future scarcity and high prices. The dealer has expert technical and general information at his disposal, and he speculates according to his own judgment of the future course of events. So many factors, however, may intervene to upset his calculations that his business is essentially speculative; whilst his profit may be very great, his losses may reduce him to ruin.

Gambling or Illegitimate Speculation (Satta), signifying in the main operations undertaken blindly and ignorantly by speculators in the hope that they will reap rich rewards therefrom. These transactions include deliberate manipulation of the market, e.g., corners, which are operated by highly skilled but unscrupulous operators. The risk of loss is considerable, frequently the whole of the invested capital may disappear. But the evil lies chiefly in the fact that such operators actually risk little, inasmuch as they operate largely on borrowed capital or without capital at all. Thus, on the stock exchanges, bull and bear operators may endeavour to manipulate prices with the object of influencing public demand for stock and shares. When prices have sufficiently risen, or have been sufficiently depressed such oppressors "unload" their holdings at the high prices or buy inasmuch as possible at the low figures. This form of operation is harmful to the community generally inasmuch as private investors are frequently victimised and violent fluctuations in price are engineered. Legitimate speculation tends to smooth out fluctuation in price: gambling serves only to accentuate these price fluctuations.

The Economics of Speculation. The fundamental effect of legitimate or mercantile or organised speculation is to promote the establishment of the equilibrium of supply and demand. It tends to make daily market prices conform to the seasonal market price, and to make the seasonal market prices such that the whole season's supply is disposed of. The risks of loss are much greater in some industries than in others, and particularly in those industries which utilise large quantities or raw material, such as cotton, wool and wheat. The quantity and quality of crops are always uncertain factors beyond the control of man, while there is an absence of regularity and continuity in the supply of raw produce which is harvested at periodical intervals. In distinct contrast to the irregularity of supply is the steadiness of demand: cotton, wool and wheat are required everywhere and at all times for industrial purposes. Fluctuation in prices would tend therefore to extreme limits in such departments of production unless other forces were at work tending to minimise the movements. These forces make their influence felt on the highly organised produce markets and in the case of securities on the stock markets. The buyers and sellers consist of expert middlemen, who make a living by forecasting for profit. They do not actually touch the raw material, but act as intermediaries between producers on the one hand and manufacturers on the other. Their mode of operating is determined by their estimation of the future course of events; if they anticipate a fall in prices, they proceed to sell for future delivery; on the other hand, if in their judgment a rise may be expected, they buy supplies for future delivery. Present sales tend to send down prices now, therefore to reduce the "steepness" of the anticipated fall. Similarly, present purchases tend to raise prices immediately, and thus obviate too rapid an appreciation in the near future. If the judgment of the speculator is correct, his operations tend to steady prices and to prevent violent fluctuations. In this respect he renders a valuable economic service, and the community benefits as a whole.

The skilled speculators help in the equalised distribution of supply. The specialised information possessed by them is of great assistance to the producers. It makes possible a steadiness of production and of employment and tends to co-ordinate the supply of goods and the demand for them. The organised markets in various countries permit also of a more economic distribution of necessary commodities between the various nations. Scarcity in one place is hardly possible if generous supplies are available elsewhere. For, the professional speculator not only buys when prices are relatively low and sells when prices are relatively high, but he also buys where prices are relatively low in order to sell where prices are relatively high, thus tending to eliminate differences in prices as between one place and another. Speculation is a struggle of intelligence against chance and in so far as the speculator minimises the uncertainty which must exist in regard to the prices and supplies of necessary commodities, he performs a valuable service to his fellow men.

The development of cold storage in recent times has led to further equalised distribution of supply, under the influence of dealings that are essentially speculative. Fruit, meat, fish, eggs no longer come on the market in spasmodic and irregular amounts. Supplies that are heavy at one time are bought by dealers, put in storage, and held for sale at a later period of scantier supply. Prices are more equable and on the whole the profits of the dealers are probably less. There is less risk to them and the community gets its supplies at a smaller charge for the middle-men's services as a result of sound speculation.

Speculation also encourages standardising and grading of the articles dealt in, particularly on the exchanges. This process puts an end to all disputes regarding the quality of the thing contracted for. Speculation is centred chiefly on the stock markets and in the produce exchanges, where is made available the most accurate information it is possible to obtain concerning price, supplies, demand and the many influences which may affect the market. The organisation of exchanges is exceedingly specialised and highly technical. The arrangements are such that by various systems of dealing the chief of which is that of *futures*, producers are enabled to relieve themselves of much of the risk of the market fluctuation. Such risks are not only transferred, but by means of hedging contracts they are eliminated by the off-setting of risks in one direction by risks in another. The hedging transactions are not gambling but are in the nature of insurance. The manufacturer who purchases raw materials covers himself so that he neither loses nor gains by a change in prices. By being thus absolved of the risk of fluctuating prices, he can concentrate on his main work.

Against the advantages which professional speculative dealings bring are to be set serious evils. These evils are made possible and are enhanced by the very facilities which enable speculation to work out its good effects. In the first place, once a commodity has been standardised, anybody and everybody can deal in it. Therefore, besides the cool-headed and well-informed dealers who are qualified to gauge the market influences, a multitude of ignorant and excitable persons, alternately reckless and timorous, begin to speculate. These "outside" speculators or the "ignorant public", like all amateur gamblers, are losers as a class and most of them are in the long run losers individually. Much of such speculation is done on the stock exchanges because of the homogeneous nature of the securities dealt in. One share of a given company is precisely as good as any other share. There are economic losses in another direction more serious and reaching farther. Widespread speculation, especially in stocks and shares, tends to increase the intensity of industrial fluctuations and crises.

CONTROL OF SPECULATION AND REGULATION OF STOCK EXCHANGES

We have seen above that the aim of speculation is to promote the establishment of equilibrium of demand and supply. This is possible only if speculation is legitimate and regulated. Conversely, widespread and illegitimate speculation by means of deliberate manipulations, bordering on to gambling, increases the intensity of industrial fluctuations and crises. Therefore, with a view to preventing undesirable speculation it is necessary for the State to regulate stock exchanges and transactions in securities dealt in on them. It is also necessary to regulate the buying and selling of securities outside the limit of stock exchanges through the licensing of security dealers. In 1922, a committee was appointed to look into the affairs of the Bombay Stock Exchange, and to recommend ways and means to control, direct and regulate the Exchange. The Bombay Securities Contracts Control Act, 1925, declared all transactions outside a recognised exchange as void but not illegal. This, however, did not check unauthorised markets from functioning. In 1936, another Committee known as the Morrison Committee was appointed which made detailed recommendations in respect of the power of the Board to intervene for the minimisation of unhealthy speculation and the improvement of the administrative machinery of the Exchange. But it was the post-war boom in the stock exchanges between 1945 and 1946 and its aftermath that emphasised for the first time the urgency of stock exchange reform on all India basis. Accordingly, Dr. P. J. Thomas, the then Economic Adviser to the Ministry of Finance, was appointed to undertake a comprehensive study on the subject. Dr. Thomas reported towards the close of the year and made many useful recommendations for the stock exchange reform. These recommendations were examined by a high-powered official committee in 1948. On the basis of its recommendations a bill was prepared which was referred to another committee with a predominantly non-official membership, under the chairmanship of Mr. A. D. Gorwala. The Gorwala Committee submitted its report along with a revised Draft Bill in August, 1951, and on the basis of this report and draft the Securities Contracts (Regulation)

Bill was introduced in the Lok Sabha in December, 1954, and was enacted in 1956. The evils which were sought to be eradicated by this Act may be summarised as follows: (1) there was no uniformity in the rules, regulations and working of the stock exchanges; (2) there was no restriction on the membership of the stock exchanges and, as a result, many undesirable persons gained admittance as members; (3) unhealthy and excessive speculation was a common feature of the stock exchange transactions, and Kerb-trading by bucket shops was freely carried on. Option dealings were permitted and there was no check on blank transfers; (4) there was no limit to the number of stock exchanges at a place; (5) no margin was required to be deposited with the management of a stock exchange which encouraged speculators to exceed their limits; (6) the listing of securities was not subject to any control by the Government so that companies without sound capital structure managed to get their shares quoted on the stock exchanges, and the public was very often deceived.

SECURITIES CONTRACTS (REGULATION) ACT, 1956

The Act came into force with effect from 20th Feburary, 1957 and seeks to regulate stock exchanges in India with the object of preventing undesirable transactions in securities. The more important provisions of the Act are summarised here:

1. *Recognition of Stock Exchanges.* Only such stock exchanges as are recognised by the Central Government can deal in securities. Non-recognised exchanges are illegal and prohibited from functioning. The Central Government grants recognition on an application of an exchange on the Government being satisfied with the following conditions: (i) that the rules and by-laws of the exchange ensure fair dealings to investors and protect their interests; (ii) that the exchange is willing to act in accordance with any conditions which the Government may impose on it from time to time; (iii) that it would be in the interest of the trade and the public at large to recognise the exchange.

Refusal to grant recognition will be finalised after an opportunity to be heard has been given to the stock exchange. The Government also reserves the right to withdraw recognition in public interest. Eight stock exchanges, as we already know, have been so far recognised.

2. *Government Control.* The Act places the stock exchanges under the control of the Central Government. The recognised stock exchanges are required to supply such information and explanations as the Central Government may demand, to furnish periodical returns about their affairs, and to submit a copy of its annual report. The Central Government is empowered to order an enquiry into the conduct and affairs of stock exchanges as and when it thinks it necessary. It can direct a stock exchange to adopt a rule, or to amend any rule relating to its administration and its constitution. Government may also prohibit trading in any or all securities or to suspend the Board of directors of any

recognised stock exchange. The Government can appoint its own nominees on the govering board of an exchange provided the total number of such nominees on an exchange does not exceed three. The Government can suspend business on an exchange in an emergency for a period of seven days at a time.

Additionally, the Government can compel certain public companies to comply with the listing requirements of an exchange and get their securities listed. It can grant licences to certain individuals to deal in securities outside the stock exchanges.

The Act applies to all dealings in securities whether forward or ready though spot or across the counter transactions are exempted. But even in the case of spot transactions the Government is empowered to regulate in the interest of trade or in public interest. The members of the stock exchange can be compelled by the Government to keep proper accounts and have them audited by Chartered Accountants.

3. *Regulation of Working of Stock Exchanges.* The Act empowers the Central Government to regulate the following important matters relating to stock exchanges: (i) the hours of trade at a stock exchange; (ii) the maintenance of a clearance house for all business transacted at the exchange; (iii) the regulation, limitation or abolition of blank transfers and carry over facilities; (iv) determination and declaration of market rates; (v) regulation of *tarawani* business; (iv) settlement of claims and disputes by arbitration; (vii) the limitation of business done by individual members; and (viii) the fixation of the scale of brokerage, fines, fees and the margin requirements.

4. *Curbs on Speculation.* All option dealings have been made illegal. *Kerb trading,* i.e., dealings in securities outside the stock exchanges. Prior to the passing of the Act, the Katni Market of Calcutta and the Grey Market of Bombay were important Kerb markets

Directorate of Stock Exchanges. In order to ensure a proper administration and enforcement of the Act the Government of India has set up a Directorate of Stock Exchanges with headquarters at Bombay and branches at Calcutta and Delhi. The Directorate is required to keep a close watch over the activities of the stock exchanges and advise authorities whenever market shows untoward developments. The Directorate studies the returns that the members of the stock exchanges are required to submit daily containing statements of their dealings. If it finds from such returns that any brokers are overtrading, it suggests suitable action against them. In areas outside the jurisdiction of stock exchanges, the Act empowers the Directorate to issue licences to dealers and brokers in securities. In this manner it acts as a link between the Central Government and the leading stock exchanges of the country. If the Directorate considers it necessary, it may require public companies to comply with the listing requirements of recognised stock exchanges, and also ensures that no exchange discriminates against any company.

Appraisal of the Act. The Act has made a bold attempt "to prevent undesirable transactions in securities," yet it has been criticised on many counts as follows:

1. The first criticism is that the Act does not clearly define what 'undesirable transactions in securities' are. The result is that the very purpose of the Act is defeated by those who are clever enough to bypass the obvious undesirable practices.

2. Secondly, and because of the lack of precise meaning of 'undesirable transactions' the Act is not able to exercise an effective check against undesirable speculative transactions and unfair practices. Thus, it does not deal effectively with corners, wash sales, poor operations, etc.

3. The Act does not abolish *Futka* trading, i.e., Forward trading which is in reality at the root of overtrading by speculators. But, as indicated earlier, this criticism does not hold good any more, because the Government has by an order issued in 1969 banned Forward trading in securities.

4. The Act does not make any positive distinction between brokers and *tarawaniwallas,* with the result that the evil following the latter's transactions continues on the stock exchanges. As we have seen earlier the tarawaniwallas take away the cream of the business by acting both as a principal and an agent and more often than not backing out of their word.

5. On the other hand, advocates of uncontrolled economy feel that the Act seeks to cut at the root of the internal autonomy of stock exchanges by imposing too many stringent regulations. But the argument seems to run against the very object of the Act. The regulation became necessary because the stock exchanges did not function properly when left alone.

Conclusion. It follows from the discussion about the nature and functioning of the stock exchange that it is one of the most vital parts of the capital market. In a country like India that is endeavouring to develop industrially at a fast rate, stock exchanges lend a helping hand. It is an instrument by which the Government has been able to canalise the savings of the community into the most important channels. Indirectly the stock exchange provides the capital for commerce and industry. The inventor with an idea to develop, the trader with a business to expand, the pioneer with a country to explore, the investor with his savings to invest, the banker with his funds to earn profits over a short period, the Government with a scheme to finance, all take themselves eventually to the stock exchange. No wonder it is said to be the business of all businesses.

undesirable transactions in securities" and has been criticised on many counts as follows:

1. The first criticism is that the Act does not clearly define what undesirable transactions in securities are. The result is that the very purpose of the Act is defeated by those who are clever enough to bypass the [illegible] inadequate [illegible].

2. Secondly, and because of the lack of precise meaning of undesirable transactions, the Act is not able to exercise an effective check against undesirable speculation [illegible] and [illegible] practices. [illegible] not deal effectively with [illegible] over [illegible].

3. The Act does no [illegible] which is [illegible] the root of [illegible] by [illegible] as [illegible] its [illegible] in [illegible] in 1969 [illegible] in [illegible].

4. The Act does not make any [illegible] distinction between [illegible] and [illegible], with the result that the [illegible] the [illegible] or [illegible] as we have seen earlier the [illegible] take [illegible] the [illegible] in [illegible] of [illegible].

5. [illegible] the Act [illegible] at the root of the [illegible] of [illegible] in [illegible] the Act. The [illegible] for [illegible] 1956.

Commenting [illegible] the [illegible] of the [illegible] market [illegible] on [illegible] of [illegible] by which the [illegible] has been able to [illegible] the [illegible] another [illegible] the [illegible] with a [illegible] to [illegible] and [illegible] with a [illegible] to [illegible] the [illegible] to [illegible].

PART NINE

Marketing Function of Management

CHAPTER XXXVIII

MARKETING AND ITS FUNCTIONS

Marketing as a business function. Marketing as a business function is charged with the movement of products and services from the producer to the user. Ability to produce does not guarantee success. Ability to sell at a profit is the critical test. In this traditional sense marketing is said to "consist of those efforts which effect transfers in ownership of goods and care for their physical distribution."[1] In economic terms marketing is concerned with the creation of time, place and possession utilities.

Total Marketing Concept. Marketing is something more than a business function. It is a view of the entire business process—a new philosophy of being "marketing mindedness." Under this concept the company objectives are established and the business managed with the sole purpose of making and selling what the customer wants, in the way he wants it, when and where he wants it, and at a price he is willing to pay. Therefore, your company's entire operation must be oriented towards discovering the customer's total needs and problems and towards attempting to satisfy them. Instead of being "product" oriented, you should be "customer" oriented. In other words, instead of merely by various devices to get the customer to buy what you have, you should try to have what the customer wants.

The effective application of the marketing concept starts with a "state of mind" on the part of the owners and managers of a business—taking the customer out of the role of simple sales target and making him the constant focal point for all basic business planning and decision making.

The leadership of a business stems from the top, so it is necessary to get the Board of Directors marketing oriented for advantageous decisions on such fundamentals as the objectives of the business, the guiding policies, capital expenses for facilities, budgets involving advertising, selling, product development, research and the like, evaluation of the performance of management and many other matters. Only the marketing oriented management can select appropriate personnel and provide leadership to them. Again, only such management can determine the proper balance between the marketing function, production, finance, and research and development.

The marketing oriented top management should orient the company's second and third line executives on the overall corporate marketing philosophy and the way each major part of the business should work together. Production, engineering, financial and research

1. F.E. Clark: *Principles of Marketing*, p. 1.

personnel are not normally marketing oriented. Substantial amount of management leadership, patience and direction are required to weld them, along with the marketing function, into smooth working team under the total marketing concept. In this way total "marketing mindedness' is achieved throughout the entire organisation.

Integration of the Marketing Function. If the top management of a business has accepted the marketing concept, its implemenation for maximum success results from the integration of the marketing function. By integration is meant the combining of all activities related to the effective carrying out o. the marketing function under the responsibility and authority of a single executive. Typically, such activities include:

1. Field sales and sales management.
2. Product service.
3. Sales administration (order handling and so on).
4. Marketing personnel (recruiting, sales training).
5. Marketing research.
6. Advertising and promotion.
7. Product planning.
8. Dealer relations and distribution planning.
9. Customer or consumer relations.
10. Public relations.
11. Production scheduling.

Advantages of total marketing concept. Adoption of the total marketing concept can have a fundamental effect on the course of business as follows:

1. The executives and key personnel have a much better team attitude and understanding of the importance of marketing to the entire business.

2. There is a broader orientation to customer wants throughout the organisation, including the Board of Directors.

3. Decisions are made more promptly, and there are fewer costly errors since the application of marketing concept throughout the business.

4. Product and profit planning is vastly improved.

5. A better balance to marketing programme can be set up. It becomes easier to determine the proper roles (and budgets) for selling, advertising and promotion, market research, and physical distribution as well as customer service.

6. With the adoption of marketing concept a tremendous improvement can be made in the way the product is introduced to the market.

7. The marketing concept helps the entire executive group to understand the need for good planning, and the elimination of snap judgments which very often prove very costly.

Despite so many benefits which follow the adoption of marketing concept, it should not be regarded as a panacea for all corporate problems. Yet, when applied in conjunction with other good management principles and techniques, it can be a force of great benefit to both the short and long-term success of a business.

VARIOUS DEFINITIONS OF MARKETING

The word marketing has been defined by many people and in many ways. Paul Mazur[1] defined marketing as the delivery of a standard of living to society.." Professor McNair of Harvard added an important concept when he amended Mazur's definition to read that "marketing is the creation and delivery of a standard of living to society."

The American Marketing Association gives us a factual or descriptive definition when it says: "Marketing is the performance of business activities that direct the flow of goods and services from producer to consumer or user." The legislative definition would be as follows: "Marketing includes all activities which are connected with the transfer of ownership and possession of goods and services."

According to Harry Hansen,[2] "Marketing involves the design of the products acceptable to the consumers and the conduct of those activities which facilitate the transfer of ownership between seller and buyer." This definition no doubt, attempts to combine the modern marketing concept with the traditional view of marketing, but it is not truly a managerial definition.

Managerial definition of Marketing. In the words of William Stanton,[3] "Marketing is a total system of interacting business activities designed to plan, price, promote, and distribute want-satisfying products and services to present and potential customers."

This definition has several important implications.

First, it is a managerial definition rather than legalistic or economic one.

Second, the entire system of business action should be market oriented or customer oriented. Customers' wants must be recognised and satisfied effectively.

Third, the definition suggests that marketing is a dynamic business process. *Marketing is not any one activity, nor is it exactly the sum of several: rather, it is the result of the interaction of many activities.*

Fourth, the marketing programme starts with the product and does not end until the customer's wants are completely satisfied, which may be some time after the sale is made.

Finally, market programming should be done with a maximum of effectiveness and a minimum of cost; and marketing must maximize profitable sales over the long run.

Above all the customers must be satisfied in order for a company to get the repeat business which ordinarily is so vital to success.

Marketing, Selling and Distribution. It follows from the foregoing discussion of the 'customer-oriented' concept of marketing that marketing is not just "selling", "merchandising", or "distribution". When used

1. *Fortune Magazine,* November, 1957, p. 138.
2. *Marketing—Text, Cases, and Readings,* p. 208.
3. *Fundamentals of Marketing,* p. 5.

in the ordinary sense, marketing is the comprehensive term. The other terms are each only one part of the marketi: ystem.

Merchandising may be defined as product planning. It includes the internal planning needed to get the right product or service to the market at the right time, at the right price, and in the proper colours, quantities and sizes.

Selling is concerned with the plans and tactics of trying to get the customer to exchange his money for the goods or services. It is one method of promotion, and promotion is only a part of the total marketing programme. As a management concept, marketing is concerned with trying to *have* what the customer will want, while selling is concerned with passing on what the seller has got. Selling focuses on the needs of the seller, marketing on the needs of the buyer.

The term "*distribution*" is here used in the sense of physical distribution. It means transporting the goods from factories to consumers' homes with intermediate stop at warehouses and retail shops and stores.

Marketing as a philosophy and a policy confirms the view that an industry is a customer-satisfying process, not a goods-producing process. An industry begins with the customer and his needs, not with a patent, a raw material, or a selling skill. Given the customer's needs, the industry develops backward, first concerning itself with the physical delivery of customer satisfactions. Then it moves back further to creating the things by which these satisfactions are in part achieved. Finally, the industry moves back still further to finding the raw materials necessary for making its products. In this sense, marketing views the entire business process as consisting of a tightly integrated effort to discover, create, arouse, and satisfy customer needs.

The Concept of Marketing Mix. Marketing is still an art; and the marketing manager must creatively marshall all his marketing activities to advance both the short-term and long-term interests of his firm. To this end he must design a "marketing mix", by mixing the various marketing activities. Each marketing manager may build his own list with some variation from any lists prepared by others. But the general "mix" is likely to conform to a pattern. Professor Neil H. Borden[1] suggests the following elements of marketing mix of manufacturers:

ELEMENTS OF THE MARKETING MIX OF MANUFACTURERS

1. *Product Planning*—policies and procedures relating to:
   (a) Product lines to be offered—quaities, designs, etc.
   (b) Markets to sell; whom, where, when and in what quantity.
   (c) New product policy: research and development programme.
2. *Pricing*—policies and procedure relating to:
   (a) Price level to adopt.

1. In *Marketing Management and Administrative Action*, p. 34.

(b) Specific prices to adopt.
(c) Price policy, e.g., one price or varying price, price maintenance, etc.
(d) Margins to adopt—for company; for the trade.

3. *Branding*—policies and procedures relating to:
(a) Selection of trade mark.
(b) Brand policy—individualized or family brand.
(c) Sale under private label or unbranded.

4. *Channels of Distribution*—policies and procedures relating to:
(a) Channels to use between plant and consumer.
(b) Degree of selectivity among wholesalers and retailers.
(c) Efforts to gain co-operation of the trade.

5. *Personal Selling*—policies and procedures relating to:
(a) Burden to be placed on personal selling and methods to be employed in:
(i) Manufacturer's organisation.
(ii) Wholesale segment of the trade.
(iii) Retail segment of the trade.

6. *Advertising*—policies and procedures relating to:
(a) Amount to be spent—i.e., the burden to be placed on Advertising.
(b) Copy platform to adopt:
(i) Product image desired.
(ii) Corporate image desired.
(c) Mix of advertising: to the trade; through the trade; to consumers.

7. *Promotions*—policies and procedures relating to:
(a) Burden to place on special selling plans or devices directed at or through the trade.
(b) Form of these devices for consumer promotions, for trade promotions.

8. *Packaging*—policies and procedures relating to:
(a) Formulation of package and label.

9. *Display*—policies and procedures relating to:
(a) Burden to be put on display to help effect sale.
(b) Methods to adopt to secure display.

10. *Servicing*—policies and procedures relating to:
(a) Providing service needed.

11. *Physical Handling*—policies and procedures relating to
(a) Warehousing.
(b) Transporting.
(c) Inventories.

12. *Fact Finding and Analysis*—policies and procedures relating to:
(a) Securing, analysis, and use of facts in marketing operations.

Market Forces Bearing on the Marketing Mix

The forces which managements must weigh when formulating their marketing mix may be classified under the following *four* heads, namely the behaviour of consumers, the trade, competitors, and government.

The outline below gives these four behavioural forces along with the determining factors in each case. If the marketer studies these and formulates his marketing mix in terms of these behavioural forces, he will be able to build a well-knit marketing programme, and succeed in achieving the maximum benefit from the various marketing functions.

Below is given the outline of forces which govern the mixing of marketing elements.

Marketing Forces Governing Market Mix

1. *Consumers' Buying Behaviour,* as determined by their:
   (a) Motivation in purchasing.
   (b) Buying habits.
   (c) Living habits.
   (d) Environment (as revealed by consumers' attitudes towards products and their uses).
   (e) Buying power.
   (f) Number (i.e., how many).

2. *The Traders' Behaviour*—wholesalers' and retailers' behaviour, as influenced by:
   (a) Their motivation.
   (b) Their structure, practices, and attitudes.
   (c) Trends in structure and procedures that portend change.

3. *Competitors' Position and Behaviour*—as influenced by:
   (a) Industry structure and the firm's relation thereto.
      (i) Size and strength of competitors.
      (ii) Number of competitors and degree of industry concentration.
      (iii) Indirect competition—i.e., from other products.
   (b) Relation of supply to demand—over-supply or under-supply.
   (c) Product choices offered consumers by the industry—i.e., quantity, price, service.
   (d) Degree to which competitors compete on price vs. non-price bases.
   (e) Competitors' motivations and attitudes—their likely response to the actions of other firms.
   (f) Trends, technological and social, portending changes in supply and demand.

4. *Governmental Behaviour—Controls over Marketing:*
   (a) Regulations over products.
   (b) Regulations over pricing.
   (c) Regulations over competitive practices.
   (d) Regulations over restrictive practices.
   (e) Regulations over advertising and promotion.

When building a marketing programme to fit the needs of the firm, the marketing manager has to weigh the aforesaid behavioural forces and then juggle marketing elements in his mix with a keen eye on the resources with which he has to work. His firm is only a part of an industry which is competing with many other industries. He has to know what his firm has in terms of money, product line, organisation, and reputation. He will then devise a mix of procedures that fit these resources. If he has large resources at his command, he may rely on heavy campaigns of advertising in rapid succession in select areas for introducing his product in a market already covered by a similar product. *Limca* outdoor advertising campaign vigorously followed has captured a substantial market within a short period of three months.

FUNCTIONS OF MARKETING

Adam Smith stated long ago, 'Consumption is the sole end and purpose of all production.' Today also, as has been explained above, the task of marketing system is to adjust the production of goods and services to the needs of customers. Having decided upon the marketing strategy the marketer has to consider the question of the journey that his product has to cover and pass through many operations and hands before it reaches the ultimate consumer. All the various activities and operations are usually termed as marketing functions.

Broadly speaking, marketing functions comprise two processes: *one,*concentration, and *second,* dispersal or dispersion. The process of concentration consists of gathering and putting together into large qualities of raw materials or finished goods at central points or market places. Dispersion means distribution of goods from market places to the ultimate consumers. These processes also involve a number of other marketing functions of auxiliary nature which facilitate the total marketing of goods. The Marketing Functions may be grouped as follows:

Merchandising Functions–

1. Buying—(a) determining needs; (b) finding a seller or seeking out source of supply; (c) negotiating price and other terms; (d) transfer of title; (e) payment, or arranging for credit.
2. Assembling or its converse Disbursing.
3. Standardizing and Grading.
4. Storing or Warehousing—Creation of time utility.
5. Transporting—creation of place utility.
6. Dividing, Packing, Packaging and Processing.

Auxiliary or General Business Functions—

7. Financing.
8. Risk Taking—Insurance or Futures Trading.
9. Recording.

Sales Function—

10. Selling—(a) creating demand; (b) finding a buyer; (c) advice to

buyer as to the use of product; (d) negotiating price and other terms; (e) transfer of title; (f) collection, or extension of credit.

All these functions are discussed in the following sections.

BUYING

The Buying activities of marketing are complementary to selling efforts. Buying includes the determination of one's needs, the seeking out of sources of supply, the negotiating of prices and other terms, and the transfer of title from the seller to the buyer. Buying is an important function, and occupies much of the time of both business concerns and ultimate consumers. The ultimate purpose of buying is to bring commodities together where they are wanted for immediate use in production or in personal consumption.

Modes of Purchasing. Goods may be purchased in any of the four ways, namely,—

(i) by Inspection; (ii) by Sample; (iii) by Description; or (iv) by Grading.

1. *Purchasing by inspection* means buying after the buyer has examined the goods to determine their quality and their adaptability to his needs. This is the oldest type of purchase and is still widely used in retail and wholesale transactions.
2. *A purchase by Sample* is made after the buyer examines a sample of the goods, it being understood that the entire quantity is to be of as good a quality as the sample.
3. *A purchase by description or brand* is made when the buyer examines a catalogue or obtains description of the goods by some other means, e.g., a brand or trade name. The bulk supplied is required to correspond with the description.
4. *A purchase by Grade* is made when the buyer buys a stated quantity of a given grade of a specified product as strict middling cotton, grade A milk, special grade eggs, etc. Purchases by grade are used largely as a basis of futures trading.

ASSEMBLING

Assembling is not buying; it is merely putting together of goods to secure larger lots for shipment, for sale, or for manufacture. Assembling plays an important part in the marketing of agricultural goods which are normally grown in small quantities by large number of producers in territories spread over vast areas. Concentration of raw materials is necessary, because they are used in large quantities by manufacturers, and who require a regular supply of standardized materials. Assembling assures this.

STANDARDIZING AND GRADING

To grade is to assort goods into lots which are approximately alike in variety, size and quality. To standardize is to give permanence to grades by means of inspection of commodities. When goods, as produced, are not standardised, and when the standard to which they conform is unknown, grading or classification is necessary. The object of these efforts is to prepare goods so that a common standardised nomenclature or grade can be utilised in bringing about an understanding between buyer and seller. Grading may be based on size, colour, appearance, chemical contents, strength, shape, specific gravity, amount of foreign matter, amount of moisture, ripeness, sweetness or length of fibre, etc. A grade carries the idea of uniformity. Therefore, a standard or grade often means that the goods are of certain quality regardless of the producer.

BRANDING

Besides general gradations, individual producers establish their own standards, commonly known as Brands. Branding is the process of identifying the name of the producer with the product. This is usually done by affixing to the product or its container the trade name or brand represented by words or designs. Branding is very common with consumption goods and with equipment. A brand conveys an idea of permanence, subject to the possibility of change for improvement in quality.

As a rule, in selecting a brand name or design consideration should be given to the following points:

1. The name or word should be simple and easy to pronounce so that it can be remembered.
2. The name or design should possess its own distinctive feature to avoid its being confused with some other name or design.
3. It should not lend itself to easy imitation.
4. It should be suggestive of good quality.
5. It should not be frequently changed.

Advantages of Grading and Branding

There are numerous advantages of grading. They are listed below.

1. Purchase and sale are simplified when they are made on the basis of sample, grade, description, or symbol.

2. Grading according to definite standards decreases marketing costs and often means higher prices to the producers and lower prices to the consumers.

3. Graded products can be marketed more cheaply owing to lessening of risk, and increase in the case of financing the necessary transactions; a reduction in transport and storage costs; a decrease in the cost of demand creation; and saving in the time of buyers and sellers in making purchases and sales.

4. Standard goods command wider market than the non-standardised goods.

5. Grading makes possible dealings for future delivery so that hedging transactions can be easily made.

6. Since standardized goods are of known quality and price the

owner desiring to borrow money on them may store them in public warehouses and deposit the warehouse receipts at the bank as collaterals for loans. Banks will often lend almost the full market value of such goods.

7. This facility enables owners to carry their goods until they can obtain higher prices for them. Most eggs in cold storage are carried in this way for a number of months.

8. Transport and storage costs are lessened by grading. Inferior or unmarketable goods may be discarded so that no transport or storage expenses are incurred on goods not wanted by the consumers.

9. Development of grading widens the market and facilitates dissemination of accurate market knowledge.

10. Grading leads to greater uniformity of production types and tends to eliminate or at least reduce the heterogeneous number of varieties and trade descriptions.

11. Pooling is made possible by resorting to grading and standardisation. As selling of lots is uneconomical, goods of one grade can be pooled together to reap the benefits of large-scale selling.

12. Grading introduces greater equity or justice. A farmer who sells the commodity which is not standardised does not realize the exact price. But by grading all cultivators can get full price for the quality they sell.

The advantages of Branding may be stated in the words of Whitehead:[1] "Branding, in the eyes of the consumer, may spell reliability, standardisation, quality and other abstractions about which he desires to be assured before he purchases, but its economic significance is that it gives definition to competition. If to the consumer the brand assures a standard, to the merchant it represents a standard in an older and different sense; it is the flag by which he knows his own forces and the flag by which he recognises his competitors....Branding is more than a service and a safeguard to the consumer....the essential mechanism through which competition can most easily function and employ the increasing effective force of advertising."

PACKING AND PACKAGING

Packing refers to the wrapping and crating necessary for the transport or storage of goods. Many goods must be packed in order to be preserved or delivered to the buyers. Liquids must be placed in barrels, bottles or cans. Bulky fabrics are compressed into bales. Heavy goods are often crated for handling or protection during transportation. Goods must be placed in boxes for delivery to dealers, while the retailers often wrap goods or place them in bags for delivery to ultimate consumers. Fragile goods must often be packed in special containers.

Packaging means placing the product in small packages—boxes, cartons, bottles or cans—for sale to the ultimate consumers. It is

1. *The Administration of Marketing and Selling*, pp. 14-15.

axiomatic that the job of packaging is to sell; and the major purpose of any package is to influence or control the location of product storage within the marketing channel right to the ultimate consumer.

The *Functions* of the Product's *Package* are:

1. Protecting the product.
2. Adapting to production line speeds.
3. Promoting the product.
4. Increasing product density, i.e., increasing the ratio of product volume to package volume.
5. Facilitating the use of the product.
6. Having re-use value for the consumer.

The successful package is not the one with an intriguing shape or design, but the one whose over-all design, shape, colour, and printed message delivered an impact that resulted in a personal relationship between the consumer and the package on the shelf. Today the package must come alive at the point of the purchase. The salesman has now stepped inside the package. The manufacturer can create and control the salesman in the package. A poorly designed package tells the consumer that the maker of the product does not care. Like an impatient salesman at five minutes before closing time, he is saying "take it or leave it". But a well designed package is proof that the manufacturer really cares about both the customer and the product and is willing to make an extra effort to please. He is employing a friendly, interested salesman.

But what is a well designed package? The consumer himself is the measure of a good package. Through his emotional needs, the consumer sets up very demanding standards of good packaging. They may be listed as follows:

1. *Convenience.* Does the package hold enough of the product to satisfy his needs without being too bulky or too heavy?
2. *Adaptability.* How well does the package fit into his cupboard, refrigerator, drawer, or glove compartment of his car?
3. *Security.* Does he feel assured that you have given him quality? Does the package make him feel it?
4. *Status of prestige.* Does he feel that by buying your package he is expressing something about himself?
5. *Dependability.* Does the package let him feel that he can rely upon you, the manufacturer?
6. *Aesthetic Satisfaction.* Is he pleased and satisfied by the impact of the design?

Actually these six criteria can be described as combining *utility, security* and *aesthetic appearance.* A good package expresses personality of a product in a dramatic, easily recognisable way. A bad package, on the other hand, contradicts, underplays, or undermines a product's personality. Therefore, a tasteful design, high in status value will always give a product prestige and the consumer will like to possess it.

But like people, packages also grow old and tired. Yet unlike people, they can be renewed. A tired package communicates the personality of a tired product. Today's consumer demands that his favourite product be full of freshness and youth. This calls for a constant renewal of design.

A sale does not end with the purchase of a product. Advertising and promotion continually strive to renew the relationship between consumer and product so as to create an uninterrupted flow of sales. The package must resell itself to the consumer every time he sees it.

WAREHOUSING

Warehousing or *storage* creates time utility. Many goods are not produced regularly at the point where they are wanted for consumption, and they must be stored from the time of production until they are wanted by the consumer, if they are to be used in satisfying human wants. Goods produced at a distance from the consumer must be transported to the consumers. In order to ensure an even supply, a stock of such goods must be maintained near the consumers as protection against delays and uncertainties of transport and to permit transport in economical units. Many agricultural goods produced seasonally are supplied to consumers more or less evenly throughout the year. Grains, cotton, tobacco and sugar furnish examples. They can be stored for a fairly long time without any deterioration. Cold storage further enables many perishables such as butter, eggs and fruits, to be stored for regular supplies.

Again, demand for some products is irregular. In such cases storage can be called into use so that production can be more regular. Most jewellery, fancy goods, utensils, toys are bought at special occasions, such as Diwali or Christmas. Such goods produced in "off months" must be stored until they are wanted by the consumers.

Storage Facilities. In order that goods can be marketed efficiently, it is important that adequate storing facilities should be available. Sufficient space, proper location, adequate equipment to give protection to goods against heat, cold, moisture, dryness, vermin, fire and thieves should be available. A warehouse should be so located and constructed that goods can be received and shipped at minimum expense. It is generally desirable that a warehouse, where large quantities of goods are stored, should be located on railway siding or on the harbour according to need. It should have adequate space for the trucks to load and unload and should be situated near the arterial streets or highways. Facilities for handling goods are important.

Types of Warehouses. Storage facilities are provided by three types of warehouses: (i) Private Warehouses; (ii) Public Warehouses, and (iii) Bonded Warehouses.

Private Warehouses. A private warehouse belongs to the owner of goods, usually a wholesaler, who stores his goods there. Such a warehouse is maintained by the owner of goods stored. Private warehouses have limited value and utility as business units cannot make use of them.

Public Warehouses. A public warehouse may be owned by a dock authority, wharfingers or any member of the public. Such a warehouse is operated in accordance with law for the purpose of storing goods belonging to other people for a charge. Many times a consignment of goods arrives from upcountry at the docks at a time when it is difficult to find tonnage on an outgoing steamer. Sometimes a cargo arrives in a port when it is not convenient for the importer to take it into his custody. During such periods these goods are stored in public warehouses.

In law, the relationship of a public warehouseman to the owner of the goods is that of an agent on the one hand and landlord on the other, i.e., he is a Bailee of the goods. He must give goods in his possession the same care as would a prudent man if they were his own. As his responsibility is no more than this, the goods are usually insured by the owner.

Public Warehouses render many useful *Services* to the trade

1. They are well constructed and are watched by attendants 24 hours a day. This makes low insurance rates possible.
2. They have excellent transport facilities for receiving and shipping goods by both rail and road.
3. The manufacturer who uses these is relieved of the necessity of providing capital for erecting his own buildings, or of going to the trouble of leasing buildings owned by others. He pays only for the space used.
4. Goods stored in public warehouses are more easily financed than goods stored in private warehouses. The public warehouse receipts are excellent collateral securities for borrowing from banks or finance companies.
5. A public warehouse is particularly adapted to the needs of the person who wishes to carry regional stocks and who does not have enough goods in various storage centres to justify keeping his own warehouse and maintaining his own employees.
6. A public warehouse enables smaller sellers to carry regional stocks. This factor is very important in competitive markets.

Bonded Warehouses. A Bonded Warehouse is one which is licensed to accept imported goods for storage before payment of customs duties. By storing his goods in a bonded warehouse the importer gains some control without paying the duty. He can make delivery of small quantities of the goods as he sells them merely by paying duty on those portions which he desires to remove thereby saving paying the full duty.

In the case of re-exporting, the goods are allowed to be stored in licensed warehouses because that saves the double work of payment of duty and its refund on re-export and hence locking up of big amounts till refund.

Certain operations which are necessary to make goods suitable for consumption or re-export are allowed to be performed in these warehouses. For instance, tea can be blended and packaged, liquid articles can be bottled or put in other containers, etc.

Even home manufactured goods which are subject to Excise Duties, e.g., beer, matches, cigarettes, patent medicines, etc., may be stored in bonded warehouses until they are required.

In all the above cases the payment of duties is deferred. The warehouse man is required to give a "Bond" that he will not allow the goods to be removed without the consent of the Customs Authorities. The goods in bonded warehouses are under the strict supervision of Customs Officers, and before the owner can interfere with them, previous permission is necessary.

INSURANCE

In business, as in private life, there are risks of every kind. Fortunately, most business risks are comparatively remote, but that does not lessen the loss they involve when they do occur. All prudent men will always catalogue most carefully every possible risk which the business they own or control may be running and consider how best they can prevent each risk materialising, or minimise and provide against its effects.

The word "risk", as used here, means uncertainty of loss where the loss is caused by accidental and unexpected circumstances beyond the control of the management. Such risks have to be guarded against, and one of the ways to cover them is to take insurance. Every prudent businessman resorts to insurance. Insurance is really an element of business; without it no vehicle of transport on sea or land or in the air is allowed to move, nothing is built, and no wheel turns.

Insurance may be described as the provision which a prudent man makes against fortuitous or inevitable loss or misfortune. It is a commercialised form of spreading risk. The risk of loss is spread over a number of persons, each of whom is prepared to bear a fraction of the loss should the eventuality against which the owner of the property wishes to protect himself actually take place. The person who assumes this risk is called the insurer, and he does so in consideration of the payment of a sum of money called premium, so that those entering into contracts of insurance called the assured, who suffered damage, are compensated from a common fund to which they and others have contributed. Insurance is, therefore, sometimes described as a cooperative way of spreading risk.

Fundamental Principles of Insurance. Insurance transactions are conducted upon certain fundamental principles which must all be strictly followed.

1. The first of these principles is good faith. The assured must exercise the utmost good faith and disclose all material facts truthfully about the subject of the insurance and all circumstances surrounding it. Any misstatement or concealment of material facts will enable the insurer to declare the contract void so that he will not be liable to pay anything.

2. The assured must have an insurable interest in the subject of the insurance. Either he must own part or whole of it or he must be in such a position that injury to it would affect him adversely.

3. The contract of insurance is essentially a contract of indemnity. The insurer undertakes to make good the actual loss caused by events insured against. Because of this principle the assured can never make a profit of his loss.

4. In the event of mishap causing loss to the assured, it is his duty to do everything in his power to mitigate the loss and to save what is left.

5. Where a result has been brought about by two or more causes, the insurer will be liable to make good the loss if it is caused by the proximate event insured against and not the remote cause.

The contract of Insurance is incorporated in a document known as the Policy, in which are set out clearly and accurately the names of the policy holder and insurer, a description and value of the insured property, the risk or risks covered, the period or duration for which the insurance is effected, and all conditions relevant to the contract.

Marine Insurance. Marine insurance protects merchants from losses due to sea perils, and the importance of a country's overseas trade is largely to be ascribed to the high degree of security given by those specialising in this class of business. Marine insurance has moved hand in hand with the overseas trade during the past two centuries, and the tremendous increase in the volume of this trade has led to a corresponding increase in the importance of marine insurance.

The principal losses which may be made good under a marine policy are: (i) Actual Total Loss; (ii) Constructive Total Loss, (iii) Partial Loss which may be Particular Average Loss, (iv) Partial Loss which may be General Average Loss.

An actual total loss occurs where the subject insured is destroyed, or is so damaged as to cease to be a thing of the kind insured, or where the assured is irretrievely deprived thereof.

A constructive total loss occurs where the subject insured is reasonably abandoned on account of its actual loss appearing to be unavoidable, or it could not be preserved from actual loss without an expenditure which would exceed its value when the expenditure has been incurred.

Particular average is partial loss or damage sustained accidentally from a peril insured against. Where the damage or loss is incurred voluntarily on an occasion when the vessel and cargo are in peril, it is termed General Average. Also general average expenses are those which are incurred for the benefit of the whole venture, i.e., ship, cargo, and/or freight at a time of peril. Where cargo is thrown overboard with the object of making the ship more seaworthy, it is called jettison.

Fire Insurance. Fire insurance, which has been described as the "handmaid of commerce", is concerned with the protection of capital. Factories, stores, shops are invariably exposed to fire hazards. To protect these the organisation of fire insurance is an absolute necessity. Fire insurance not only provides for the actual loss of capital, but it also helps appreciably to reduce the possibility of loss, thereby preserving capital. This is done by penalising those who expose their property to unnecessary risks and encouraging those who take every precaution to guard against loss. Also, it is done by transferring a proportionate loss on to the insured in case of undervaluation of property by inserting the average clause in the policy.

In order to make a successful claim in case of any fire loss, immediate notification of a fire loss is essential, so that the insurers may take prompt steps to safeguard their interest, and to verify the fact of the loss and its extent.

Life Insurance or Assurance. Life insurance is a contract in which the insurer, in consideration of a certain premium, agrees to pay to the assured, or to the person for whose benefit the policy is taken, a stated sum of money on the happening of a particular event contingent on the duration of human life. For instance, under a Whole Life Insurance, the policy money is payable at the death of the assured, and under an Endowment Policy, the money is payable on the assurd's surviving a stated period of years or at his death should that occur previously.

The most important uses of life assurance are to provide for dependants and old age; for the repayment of capital on a partner's death; collateral security for a loan; creation of a fund for educating children or establishing them in profession or business; marriage of daughter, etc., and payment of taxes and duties at death. It may also be resorted to for obtaining protection against monetary loss through the death of a Managing Director, or other expert, or the debtor.

Life Insurance differs from other forms of insurance protection in that the probabilities on which it is dependent can be accurately calculated, and in that the contingency of human death is one which must ultimately arise. The only uncertainty in the case of life insurance is the time of death. Consequently, a life insurance policy is a contract with an increasing value, as its determination grows near. It is not a contract of indemnity.

Surrender Value. The surrender value of a life policy is the amount which the insurer is prepared to pay in total discharge of the contract, in case the assured wishes to surrender his policy and extinguish his claim upon it. The surrender values are based on the actual premium paid and values increase with each payment of premium.

Loans on Policies. Where a policy has a surrender value, it also has a loan value, and assurance companies usually lend 95% of the surrender value, keeping the balance of 5% as margin for year's arrears of interest. Granting of loan by the insurance companies on the security of the life policies is the best investment, as there is never any danger of the money being lost.

Paid-up Policy Value. The paid-up value of a policy is the amount to which the sum assured would be reduced at any time if the assured requested a re-arrangement of his contract so that no further premiums should be payable. The amount on the paid-up policy is payable on the appending of the event assured against.

Assignment. Life assurance policies are freely assignable as an actionable claim. They may be sold, mortgaged, or settled, provided that a written notice to the insurance company is given of such assignment, so as to make the assignee's title effective against the company. If no written notice is given and the company makes some payment to the assignor after the assignment, with the knowledge of the assignee, the company would be protected.

Claims. Claims may arise by death or at maturity of the policy, and are payable on proof of the event and subject to verification of the title of the claimant to policy moneys.

Nominee. The mainspring of life assurance is the laudable desire on the part of a person to provide a sum of money for his dependants in the event of his death. Since he takes out the life policy for the benefit of someone, he usually mentions his name in the policy or endorses it thereon, so as to enable him to get the sum assured after the death of the policyholder. The person so named is called the nominee or beneficiary. The assured may cancel or change the nomination before the policy matures. The policy money is to be paid to the policy holder if it matures during his lifetime, but on his death the money is payable to the nominee.

FINANCING OF TRADE

Methods of financing internal trade in different countries are different. Bulk of the Indian trade is financed by the indigenous system, and a little by the modern or Western system of banking. The financing agents or the constituents of the money market in India are: (1) the numerous and heterogeneous group of indigenous bankers and brokers, called by different names in different parts of the country, such as Shroffs, Banias, Mahajans, Sahukars, Marwaris and Chettis, whose operations are almost entirely confined to the interior of India; (2) the co-operative banks, which advance mainly to member-cultivators; (3) the Indian joint-stock banks run on European lines, which advance for a short-term on collateral securities, by discounting trade bills, and against commodity security; (4) the exchange banks, which mainly finance external trade; (5) the State Bank of India; and (6) the Reserve Bank of India.

In the import trade the source of finance for the merchant is the Commission Agent, who functions as an intermediary to the buyers and sellers of goods in an upcountry market. He advances money to several merchants. The purpose of this agent in advancing money is to secure substantial business for his own loan. He advances loans to cultivators also so that the cultivators are under obligation to sell their commodities through this agent. In this way commission agents act as financing agencies for getting business for themselves. It is no exaggeration to say that 80 to 90 per cent of the total business is done by the native Shroffs or

Mahajans; and Hundi is the instrument in the hands of these indigenous bankers. Hundis are drawn for three purposes: (i) for raising loan (hand bill) ; (ii) for financing trade (bill of exchange) ; and (iii) for remittance of money from place to place (draft or cheque).

The joint-stock banks follow different methods of financing trade. The most common method of short-term lending is through discounting the concern's promissory note or *hundi*. There are unsecured time loans with a definite date of maturity ranging from one month to six months. A small concern would borrow from local banks, for they can render frequent advice, and can be relied upon to take a personal interest in the concern's welfare. Another method is bankers' acceptances, although they are used primarily in financing export and import trade and in financing domestic shipments where the buyers and sellers are unknown to each other, when because of distance or other reasons the seller finds it difficult to investigate the credit-standing of the buyer. Another method is commodity loans. Business concerns often obtain their short-term funds by borrowing from banks against commodity collateral. By this means the business concern can obtain a relatively greater advance than its own financial standing and credit rating would entitle it to obtain on unsecured *hundis*. Borrowing on bills of lading against shipments is another means of securing funds for short periods of time. Specific merchandise in the concern's profession at times may be used as security for loans. A floating charge may be created on the stock. The banks allow overdrafts and open cash credit accounts against suitable security. Occasionally, in order to secure the necessary funds with which to postpone or forestall financial insolvency, companies sell their open book accounts. This is referred to as "assigning", "hypothecating" or "pledging" accounts receivable. Loans of this type can seldom be obtained from the ordinary commercial banks but must be secured from finance companies at a higher charge than the customary rate of interest.

Methods of Inland Remittances. Five main types of inland remittances may be distinguished: (1) remittance by *hundi* or cheque; (2) transfers through the Reserve Bank and the State Bank, including bank drafts; (3) transfers through Government treasuries; (4) transfers of cash by rail, road and air; (5) remittances through the Post Office. All these methods help in increasing the fluidity of money and prevent the rates for it at different places from being uneven. In India, *hundis* have been a popular method of remitting money from place to place. The creditor or holder of the *hundi* can obtain payment from the agent of the drawee, or from a banker by having it discounted, or by selling it to the banker for its face value, less interest or discount for the period it has to run. Cheques are also becoming quite popular these days. The Reserve Bank provides cheap facilities by issuing and paying telegraphic transfers. The State Bank purchases demand drafts and pays drafts and telegraphic transfers. The joint-stock banks issue bankers' drafts. Instead of the creditor himself drawing a *hundi* on the debtor, it is possible for the debtor to purchase a draft from his Banker, and to send it to the creditor in settlement of the debt owing. Such a draft takes the form of a *hundi* or a bill of exchange drawn by the issuing bank upon a branch or correspondent in the creditor's town, from whom the creditor can collect payment of the amount. Although the above methods have considerably superseded sending of cash by rail or road, large sums are still sent to cotton and jute areas for purchasing cotton and jute, for the cultivators still prefer cash payment.

Remittances of small amounts are made through the Post Office. Postal Orders are a convenient form of order for payment to a named person, drawn on the Post Office itself, on payment of a charge known as poundage, varying with the value of the order, and are issued for amounts of 0.50 P. and multiples thereof up to Rs. 10. They can be made available for intermediate amounts by the affixing of stamps not exceeding forty-four paise in value. A Postal Order can be made safe by filling in the name of payee and the name of the Post Office at which the order is to be payable, and also by crossing like a cheque. With these precautions the Postal Order is a cheap and fairly safe form of remittance as it is not negotiable. Money Order is another method which is more commonly used in India than the Postal Order. It is an order addressed by one Post Office to another requiring the latter to pay a sum of money to a specified person. The sender of the money has to pay a commission varying with the amount to be remitted.

Functions of a Modern Bank. Like insurance and transport, banks render very useful services to trade and industry. The part played by commercial banks in the financing of industry in India was discussed in a previous chapter. Space does not permit of a detailed examination of their functions. It will suffice only to outline the principal functions of a modern joint-stock bank, which may be grouped as follows:

(a) *The receipt of deposits*

1. On Current Account, in which case the money is returnable on demand, and is usually withdrawn by means of cheques drawn by the customer on the account, either in favour of himself or in favour of some third party. No interest is usually paid on such an account:
2. On Fixed Deposit Account, where the money is returnable only on the expiration of an agreed period of the deposit. Interest is paid on such accounts at rates varying with the Bank Rate and with the period for which the funds are deposited. The funds cannot be withdrawn before the agreed period, but a loan can be taken on their security.
3. On Savings Bank Account, which cater for the needs of the people with small incomes, and are run on the lines of Post Office Savings Bank Accounts. Ordinarily, an account can be opened with Rs. 5, and money can be withdrawn once or twice a week up to a limited amount, usually not more than Rs. 250 at a time and not more than Rs. 500 in all;
4. On Home Safe Account. "Home Safes" for small cash saving

are issued free to any customer, and the contents can be paid in as desired for the credit of the Savings Account.

(b) *The granting of loans and overdrafts on approved lines.*

(c) *The indirect granting of accommodation by the purchase of credit instrument, e.g., discounting of bills of exchange.*

(d) *Agency services.*

In addition to the main functions described above, the modern bank will undertake many services for the convenience of its customers. The functions which arise out of the ordinary business of a bank (agency services) are grouped hereunder:—

1. The collection and payment of cheques, bills, dividends and other instruments;
2. Purchase and sale of stocks, shares and other securities;
3. Acting as trustee or executor;
4. Assisting companies to raise capital,
5. Executive standing order, such as periodical payment of subscription, insurance premiums and similar payments of a regularly recurring nature, on behalf of customers;
6. Transfers from one branch or bank to another. Customer may pay in, or have paid in by a third party, money for his credit at a particular office of a bank, or at any other office of the same bank, or at the office of any agent bank. By arrangement he can also draw cheques on his account at the particular office of a bank and have them cashed at other offices or agencies.

(e) *Miscellaneous services and the financing of foreign trade.*

Other business undertaken by a bank includes—

1. Safe custody of valuables, etc.;
2. Management of securities lodged for safe custody;
3. Maintaining night safes;
4. Acceptance of bills of exchange on behalf of customers;
5. The issue of personal and commercial Letters of Credit;
6. Assisting foreign trade by transacting foreign exchange business;
7. Acting as reference supplying trade information statistics, etc.

(f) *The issue of Notes.*

In India this right is given to the Reserve Bank of India alone. No other bank can issue notes.

CHAPTER XXXIX

TRANSPORT

Transport in its widest import, is the conveyance of persons, goods and ideas. Effective transport is indispensable to economic progress. No nation can reach an advanced stage of development without adequate facilities for moving goods and people. It is said that if agriculture and industry are the body and bones of a national organism, transport and communications are its nerves. In a large country such as India, transport is especially important. All the means of transport collectively constitute a large portion of our wealth, give employment directly or indirectly to lakhs of people, and contribute substantially to the national income.

The history of civilisation is the history of transport. Indeed, transport is civilization. The road-makers carry the torch of light. They lead and civilization follows. Homesteads, hamlets, villages, towns and cities follow in their wake, one after the other. Trade develops unifying the world. In fact the progress of man corresponds with the evolution of the means of transport. Not only are goods carried by their means, but the cultural, social and moral advancement of a country directly depends upon them. They diffuse knowledge, remove prejudices and destroy ignorance.

Effects of Improved Transport. Improvement of transport has moved mainly in two directions, namely, reduction in the unit cost and the increase in speed, safety and flexibility. The results of this improvement can be set fourth conveniently under three heads—economic, social and political. The economic effects revolve round the reduction in the unit cost of transport, which makes it possible for passengers and goods to move a given distance at less expense. With regard to passengers, it facilitates travel wanted for its own sake as well as travel necessary in the production of goods. With respect to goods, there are at least four important results.

Economic Effects. The consumers today enjoy the benefits of many goods that could not be produced in the immediate vicinity on account of the various limiting factors. Such goods are acquired by means of an exchange of things that can be produced locally and the exchange is made possible by cheap transport. Communities without cheap transport must be largely self-sufficing: and since the means of producing many important commodities are evenly distributed, the people of such a community are denied the benefits of diversified consumption. A corollary of the diffusion of goods is equalisation of their supply in different markets. Goods tend to move from points where the supply is large in relation to demand to places where it is small in relation to demand. The cheaper the transport the easier the shift; hence, more nearly the supply equalised. In agriculture where output is difficult to control, cheap transport is therefore particularly advantageous. Here it minimises famines and reduces the waste from over-production. It also equalises and stabilises prices; for the lower the cost of transport the broader the market and the broader the market, less extreme the fluctuations in price.

The most important effect of cheap transport is that it reduces the cost of goods to consumers. The reduction may arise from the intensification of competition that is sometimes caused by an improvement in transport but the chief way it is brought about is by lessening the cost of producing goods. By encouraging large-scale production, improved transport may in the long run promote monopoly rather than competition. But some industries are not well adapted to large-scale production, and in such instances the tendency is towards the increase in number of buyers and sellers in the market. The lowering of price is the result of lower cost of production which in turn is made possible by cheap and adequate transport. Improved transport helps to lower cost of production in two ways: by facilitating geographical division of labour and by encouraging large-scale production; hence specialisation and localisation.

Transport exerts greater influence upon industrial location than any other factor. For transport cost is not only an independent factor affecting the location of productive activity but it is also an element in other locational factors such as nearness to market, raw materials and fuel or power. Hand in hand with division of labour is large-scale production. Large-scale production, like specialisation, depends upon the extent of the market and therefore upon efficient transport. It is probably true that broadening of the market through improved transport facilities is the fundamental cause of the movement towards large-scale production. The demand in the immediate neighbourhood of a large plant is seldom sufficient to absorb the entire output of the plant. Neither is the local supply of raw materials likely to be adequate. For example, the automobile industry of the U.S.A. or Great Britain markets its products in foreign countries and obtains its raw materials from all corners of the earth. Efficient transport makes it easier to manage large enterprises because it promotes the movement of goods and facilitates cheap and rapid communication either through travel or by mail.

Finally improved transport affects not only the production of income, but also its functional distribution. The relation to economic rent and therefore to land values, is especially significant. Since location is an important factor determining rent, and as distance is primarily a matter of the cost and time of movement rather than of miles, it is clear that improvements in transport influence that share of the total income of society which goes to landowners, by readjusting the distribution of rent. Except when it is impossible to increase the output of a product, the rent from some lands is decreased while that from others is increased. Those owners of natural agents who enjoy the advantages of better locations with respect to the market and therefore higher rents before the improvements are made, see their returns reduced after the improvements; and those individuals farther from the market find their former low rents increased. The coming of the automobiles has enhanced suburban rents and land values.

Social Effects. Improved transport has profound social effects. First, it largely determines the concentration and spread of population. The automobile and the bus have facilitated the movement of people into suburban communities, where life is generally said to be more attractive than in the city proper. Secondly, better transport raises the standard and changes the mode of living. Our housing, clothing, recreation, even the food we eat are improved. Occupations, habits and thinking are readily affected. The tempo of life has been quickened since the perfection of the automobile, the aeroplane, and the streamlined train. The spanning of continents in a few hours has brought about a new concept of time and distance. Thirdly, efficient transport promotes culture and intelligence. The enlargement of the surplus above the minimum of subsistence increases leisure; and the wide distribution of the mails together with the establishment of personal contacts over broad area furthers education and the incentive to progress. In social contacts the contribution of the automobile is especially outstanding. It has given to citizens in practically all classes of population a freedom in travel never before known. It has virtually destroyed rural isolation. In short, transport has increased welfare.

Political Effects. Efficient transport has at least two very significant political effects. First, it promotes national unity. Countries like India, the U.S.A. or U.S.S.R. could not be held together without an adequate system of transport and communications. An effective transport system creates a need for national unity. In making the different sections of the country economically interdependent through promoting the geographical division of labour, transport makes political unity essential in order to guarantee freedom of trade and effective control of industry. Then, transport makes it easier to maintain national unity by fostering social homogeneity. The second political effect of efficient transport is a strengthening of national defence. Transport also brings about unification of nations. Institutions and customs, laws and languages, make rapid progress in assimilation.

Modern transport is divisible into three main types: Land. Water, Air. Inland transport is of three kinds: Road, Inland Waterways, Railways. The transport of material goods or persons implies two factors, a vehicle or unit of conveyance and medium in which or upon which to move. The choice of medium determines the type and design of the vehicle. The medium includes two factors: Public highway or Private highway. Air transport and sea transport have public, natural and free highways. The road and inland highways occupy an intermediate state.

RELATIVE ADVANTAGES OF VARIOUS MEANS OF TRANSPORT

Railways. In providing general transport over broad land areas in large volumes the railway knows no superior. Given the condition of an adequate volume of business, no means of transport except certain waterways can handle traffic so economically as railways; and no method of land transport is potentially so fast for distances. Even where waterways are more economical, their services are restricted to few kinds of traffic. The railway has four marked advantages: First, it can be constructed to practically any point usually at far less cost than a waterway, though at a greater cost than an ordinary highway. Second, the railway is less hampered by variations in the weather than any other means of transport. Neither highways nor airways are so dependable and safe. Third, the railway requires comparatively little tractive power at high speed, because it utilises the principle of the smooth rail. Fourth, the railway is well-adapted to handling traffic in large volumes. Long trains of heavily loaded wagons can be operated with safety.

The advantages of the railway tend to be neutralised by the time and cost of terminal operations. Wagons must be loaded and assembled at origin, re-assembled at intermediate points, and disassembled and unloaded at destination. The goods train is in fact generally slower than the truck or lorry, and the rail express is slower than lorry for distances under 100 miles, although the railway is potentially faster for distances exceeding 150 miles. As regards cost, although wagon-load shipment is generally cheaper by rail except for distances less than 20 miles, less-than-wagon load transport is inherently more economical by truck for distances under 60 miles and possibly under 110 miles. Actual charges for less than wagon load traffic are generally less by highway for all distances. Moreover, the railway lacks the flexibility of the motor vehicle, as well as its capacity to extend service from door to door. In moving bulk freight at low speed from port to port, railways are also at a disadvantage in competing with carriers operating on natural waterways.

Water Transport. The great advantage of water transport is the relatively little tractive power required to move large floating equipment, provided movement is slow. One ordinary power unit can propel in a single tow of barges more freight than can be carried by several goods trains. On natural waterways relatively small capital or maintenance costs are involved in providing the way. These make transport by water cheaper than by rail. On canal, however, the cost of transport is higher, with the result that a substantial part of the real cost of transport by artificial waterways is borne by taxpayers.

Road Transport. Motor transport is highly varied. Passenger carriers may be classified as private cars, taxis, and buses Goods trucks fall into three classes: owner-operated, contract, and common carrier. Some of the carriers are in operation over regular routes, while others go "anywhere for hire." Some carry practically all kinds of commodities while others are engaged in specialised service. In the field of passenger transport, probably more traffic moves by highways than by all other means of transport combined. Most of the road goods traffic moves in small units relatively short distances, although fresh fruits and vegetables move longer distances. The advantages of the motor vehicle rest fundamentally upon two factors: first, the unit of carriage is small; second, the vehicle is not confined to its own fixed roadway. It can supply service in small loads over public highways to or from practically any point in the country, if necessary, from door to door, up the steep grades, or over poor roads. The motor vehicle can thus function in an exceptionally flexible and diversified manner, rounding out the other means of transport, opening up areas untouched by the latter, and offering new services.

The bus finds its greatest field of service where traffic is light, or where flexibility is required. Here it is cheaper than the steam train, is able to change its route more readily, can provide more frequent service, and can load and unload largely according to the convenience of the passengers. In hauls of moderate length the bus is therefore an effective competitor of the steam and inter- urban electric railway. The bus is at a disadvantage where traffic is heavy both in cost and in speed. Here it must yield to the railway which operates at a low unit cost when the volume of travel is large and which is ordinarily less obstructed by traffic congestion. On long journeys rail is more comfortable than the bus. Moreover, bus is subject to interruptions and dangers growing out of changes in the weather. The truck has at least five outstanding advantages: First, carriage of goods by truck is frequently cheaper than by rail, either because railway rates, loaded with terminal charge, are relatively high for short distances, or because the cost of carriage must be added to the railway charges. Second, the truck is speedy on the short haul because it eliminates much rehandling and can take the quickest route, especially where the carriage is on a contract or private basis. Third, the truck can operate more readily from door to door than other agencies of transport. Fourth, the truck can supply a comparatively frequent service; it is well adapted to light and short hauls. Fifth, packing requirements are generally less burdensome in trucking than in rail or water shipment, because of differences in handling. This advantage is of great significance in transporting such goods as fresh fruits, vegetables and household effects.

Airways. Air transport is the least important as regards volume of traffic of all forms of inland transport. The tonnage of freight carried is negligible, although all cargo has been established. Airway passenger traffic is more significant, yet the number of scheduled airline passengers is insignificant at present. Also, internal air transport is possible only in countries with vast areas and important commercial towns, such as India, the U.S.A., the U.S.S.R. The primary advantage of air transport is speed. A second advantage is its freedom from topographical obstructions.

Though landing fields and market routes are necessary, the air carrier is spared the expense of a track, can fly on direct line, and can reach inaccessible places. A third advantage of air service is its convenience. The aeroplane is a small unit in comparison with a train or a ship, thus making it easier to schedule trips as needed.

The great disadvantage in air transport is that not much weight can be carried per vehicle. This means that the unit cost of service is high. A second disadvantage of air transport is its high degree of risk. Though the safety record has steadily improved, weather, terrain, defects of vehicles, and mistakes by personnel offer great obstacles to safe navigation. A third disadvantage of air transport—a corollary of the second—is lack of reliability. On the average about ten per cent of the scheduled trips are never begun, and of those begun a considerable number are not completed, usually because of unfavourable weather. A fourth disadvantage is lack of comfort, either because of restricted space, or air sickness. These defects have been remedied to some extent, but the possibility of removal appears to be less than for surface carriers.

TRANSPORT COSTS

Monopoly and Competition

Railways. The capital outlay in railway is huge both in the aggregate and in proportion to the volume business. Huge fixed investment gives to railway expenses in the short run two characteristics. First, the expenses are largely independent of the actual traffic. Second, the expenses cannot all be scientifically allocated to particular hauls. Only the cost that varies with a given haul is caused thereby and can be assigned thereto. This means that railway expenses are in the most part fixed or constant as contrasted with variable. These fixed expenses are two-thirds of the aggregate regardless of the traffic; only the variable costs vary as they are affected by the traffic.

The second feature of railway expenses relates to the apportionment of costs. Costs may be "common" or "Special", i.e., Direct, Prime, or out-of-pocket. The costs are common when incurred on behalf of the business as a whole, and they are special when incurred on behalf of a particular service or class of service. Because railways find it profitable to carry all types of traffic, and because costs cannot be allocated to particular traffic or service, the railway costs are "Common Costs," though sometimes described as "joint costs", which is wrong. As such railway costs are constant, those independent of traffic; and common, those incurred on behalf of the business as a whole. These facts are significant in relation to railway rates.

Again, railway is usually a partial monopoly. Where one line operates at a profit, two can fail to meet operating expenses. Usually the Government would not deem it in public interest to permit competition between two railway lines. Potential competition is thus largely ineffective. Even with regard to other means of transport railways occupy a semi-monopolistic position with respect to long distance traffic of basic commodities. Being a monopoly a railway aims at maximum net revenue which it does by charging differential rates and fares. This is made possible by the nature of railway expenditure which enables it to run under increasing returns or decreasing costs.

Airways. As regards property investment, utilised productive capacity and constancy of cost, air carriers appear to be between the railways, on the one hand, and the trucking industry, on the other. No outlay is required for the track, but capital is needed for the making, landing fields and aerodromes. And the investment in land, buildings, and similar equipment is fairly large, and is of considerable importance in relation to the volume of business. Planes can be varied in number and capacity more or less according to the traffic; but large purchases mean lower initial costs, and more expensive machines reduce operating expenses. Air-lines costs may be divided between ground expenses and flying expenses. The former are relatively constant, at least for short periods. The latter, especially the fuel, are largely variable even in the short run, although there is a considerable degree of constancy even in those.

Water and Highways. Most characteristics of water and highway carriers are similar. and the two modes may be considered together. There are, however, important differences in the nature of the service. One difference is that water transport is far more limited geographically than highway transport. Another difference is that water transport tends to be confined to the bulk movement of a smaller variety of commodities. Still another difference is that the carrying unit is larger in the waterway industry.

In comparison with railways, waterways and road carriers need little capital. As to the way, no carrier investment at all is necessary for the way is provided by nature or by the government. The principal capital outlays that the carriers need make are for vessels or vehicles. These modes are generally conducted on a relatively small-scale. The capacity of vessels and vehicles can be easily adjusted to the demand. Since unutilised capacity is very small, the expenses of water and highway carriers are for the most part variable.

RATE TECHNIQUE

Railway Rates. Freight rates produce about four-fifths of the annual operating revenues of railways. They have to be constructed in a highly complex manner, because of multiplicity of items carried, stations and routes. For the purpose of simplification and to avoid discrimination thousands of varieties of goods are classified by the Indian railways into 16 classes, and same rates are quoted for opposite directions, or for two or more routes. The effect of classification is to reduce the number of rates, as all items within class or sub-class take one and the same charge. But not all shipments take class rates. Some traffic moves at lower than rates and in some cases station to station rates, which are special reduced rates, are charged, usually to meet road competition. To encourage long distance booking, tapering or telescopic rates are quoted, according to which the rate decreases with the increase in the distance covered.

Water carriers. The rate structures of water carriers, although relatively simple, are similar in general to the structure of railways. But only the Liners publish the rates in full. The Tramps or contract carriers quote minimum rates only, although even these change according to demand and supply. The charges of Liners tends to be based upon railway rates, while contract carriers reflect more closely the cost and character of waterway service. Contract rates are therefore generally lower and vary with the size of the shipment subject to a minimum quantity, say, three hundred tonnes. The Liners publish class rates as well as commodity rates.

Motor-Carrier Rates. In the early period motor rates were matters of individual bargaining but with the development of government regulation, rates have assumed a semblance of a rate structure. The elements of the structure are similar to those in railway business, but there is not much of classification. Usually, the truck-load rates are similar to railway scheduled rates. Motor rates are generally more closely related to distance than either rail or water rates. Carrier costs are largely variable and depend primarily upon the length of haul.

Air-carrier Rates. Local and international or joint passenger fares, including rules and regulations, are published in the "Air Tariffs." Like railway fares, they are based primarily on distance. Rate scales are determined largely by first class rail fares, plus certain other charges making the air fare higher than the first class fares. Because of the saving of time and some other factors, the air carriers have been able to compete with railways without equalising rates.

PRINCIPLES UNDERLYING RAILWAY RATES.

Objectives. There are three rational objectives in fixing rates, namely:—

1. Each rate should contribute towards the total cost of service.
2. Each rate should stimulate the maximum economic amount of traffic.
3. Each rate should bear its fair share of cost in comparison with other rates.

In addition to these direct objectives there are some other considerations which must be given weight while fixing particular rates. These considerations relate to the furtherance of *non-transport objectives:*

(a) promotion of prosperity in an industry other than transport, such as agriculture;
(b) relief of urban congestion;
(c) stimulation of foreign trade;

(d) control of traffic in given commodity; and
(e) encouragement of market competition.

THEORIES OF RAILWAY RATES

Basis of Rate. Broadly speaking, that basis of railway rates is the best which will stimulate all the traffic that will pay to handle. For, additional traffic reduces the average unit cost of transport, thereby making possible a low level of rates and increasing the availability of service. Average unit decreases (i) because of the economies of fuller utilisation of plant, (ii) because of economies of large-scale production. It is on account of those economies that railway industry is said to be characterised by increasing returns or decreasing costs. Keeping this fact in mind we discuss below the different theories or bases of railway rates.

Cost of Service Theory

The cost of service theory implies that railway charges should be based on the cost incurred by the railway in rendering the service. Prima facie it is simple and appears to be reasonable, but in practice the principle is unsound.

There are peculiar difficulties in the way of analysing "cost of production" of transport services. Transport services are provided under various conditions in which the expenses differ from one condition to another. In case of a factory, one unit of output is similar to the other unit of output. In railway services, it is not easy to determine a unit of output or work done. A 'Ton mile' might be taken as a unit, but expenditure incurred in constructing different miles of railway track differ. A mile of track over the hills will cost considerably more than a mile of track laid across flat land. Then the cost of carriage will differ according to the size of the consignment or its packing. Bulk, fragility, explosiveness and structure will affect cost of handling. The phrase 'cost of service' is itself ambiguous. Does it mean additional cost incurred in carrying on particular item of particular traffic, or additional cost plus a proportionate share of fixed charges. It is well nigh impossible to determine exactly the share of fixed charges due to a particular item of traffic.

A further difficulty arises if charges are fixed on the basis of cost of service. Cost of carriage can only be known after the service has been rendered, whereas the charges have to be fixed in advance. This difficulty is further aggravated by the fact that railway services are common or joint in nature. Common costs arise as one train may carry both goods and passengers, and then goods of different varieties and bulks and values. It is therefore practically impossible to have charges only on the cost of service principle. The only thing that can be done is to treat the out-of-pocket or special cost as the lower limit of the rate and do not ordinarily fix below this minimum.

Value of Service Theory

This theory means charging a rate which the traffic can afford to pay, e.g., if coal at Raniganj coal-mines is worth Rs. 10 per tonne and Rs. 20 at the railway wharf at Bombay, evidently the coal merchant could not afford to pay a railway rate of more than Rs. 10. The rates on this basis are fixed according to the principle of discrimination. Some goods can afford to pay more than others, e.g., a kgm. of gold is worth thousands of rupees and can afford to pay much more than a tonne of coal which is worth a few rupees.

Value of service refers to the pecuniary worth of a particular service with individual shipper. It is what the shipper would pay, if required rather than forego transportation. Measured objectively the value of service is equivalent to the maximum demand price, or the highest rate that can be charged without destroying traffic. In our coal example, the maximum that the railways can charge is Rs. 10 for carrying coal from Raniganj to Bombay. Thus, value of service principle lays down the upper limit beyond which the traffic will not pay. If the maximum is charged it would amount to extortion. Any rate between the maximum determined by the value of service principle and the minimum set by the cost of service may be fair and attract traffic.

Charging What the Traffic will bear

As the railway rates cannot be based entirely on the cost of service nor only on the value of service, the railways follow the practice of "charging what the traffic will bear". As stated above, cost of service determines the minimum rate and the value of service to the shipper makes the maximum of a reasonable rate of charge. Charging what the traffic will bear in the monopoly sense signifies rates that will provide the largest net returns. This does not mean exacting the maximum possible revenue from every customer. On the contrary, rates applying between specified points are quoted for particular commodities or classes thereof, not for individuals. By changing different rates according to ability to pay, the railways assist both high-rated and low-rated goods. As long as the rate is kept on the lower side, the traffic will move and generate more revenue.

CHAPTER XL

SELLING OR DISTRIBUTION OF GOODS

Selling is one of the most important and expensive functions of marketing in the present economic system. More sales at less cost is the norm, for without sales production is useless. Selling involves distribution of goods, and that means incurring costs. Distribution costs comprise:

(1) the cost of physical removal of goods from the point of manufacture to the point of consumption;

(2) the cost of financing stocks and collecting;

(3) the actual cost of selling which includes the cost of sales control, advertising, sales promotion, salesmen and their training, market investigation, keeping of records and service to consumers.

It has been estimated that all these costs account for about 50 per cent of what the consumer pays for goods. Selling includes creating demand, finding buyers and keeping them, supplying value-satisfying goods and services, negotiating price and other terms of sale.

Keeping in mind what has been stated in the previous chapter that marketing (and selling is part of marketing) is concerned with satisfying the needs of the customer by supplying what the customer wants. Selling activities set the stage for goods and services so that people will buy them. Setting the stage includes designing goods which people want.

Selling is, therefore, the planning of the strategy to get—

(i) the right product;

(ii) in the right quantity;

(iii) at the right price;

(iv) at the right time;

(v) to the right place;

(vi) under the right impressions.

The six 'rights' need some explanation. The right product is a product which the customers will readily buy because it fills their needs and wants. The right quantity is that quantity of the right goods that the customers can absorb during the right time without necessitating cutting down of the price. It is also the quantity that provides efficient use of the merchandise investment.

The right price is a price that will accomplish two ends: (i) move the right goods promptly, and (ii) assure a profit for the seller after costs and expenses of operation are paid. The right time is the day, week or season when customers want goods of the type in question. Everyday is the right time for staples; festival season (Diwali, Christmas) is the best time for toys and other goods for presentation.

The right place will depend upon the type of seller, e.g., the right place for the retailer is the most satisfactory location of his store from the point of view of his customers. The right impressions involve winning customers and retaining them. All these involve planning, coordinating and timing the market effort, or Sales Administration.

A. SALES ADMINISTRATION

Sales administration [1] is the direction of those activities and functions which are concerned with the distribution of products and services. It embraces the sales research and planning, demand creation, sales costs and budgets, price fixing, development of products, development of sales policies, co-ordination of sales, finance and production, conduct and control of personal selling, recruiting, training, remunerating, supervising salesmen, establishing sales territories, advertising and sales promotion.

Importance of Sales Management. The need for improved methods of distribution to keep pace with our expanding productive capacity and to stay in business in a competitive world has made sales administration or sales management one of the most important functions of business. Several other factors are responsible for the growing importance of sales management.

1. Increased productive capacity and the introduction of new products as the result of technical and scientific innovations and planned development. For these new products markets must be found.

2. Sound sales management has to make sales at lower prices so that more people can enjoy more of the products.

3. The increasing per capita income of consumers has created new markets and opportunities for the sales manager.

4. Never before has there been a greater need for exporting goods to foreign countries for earning foreign exchange for economic development. Sales opportunities in foreign markets have broadened the scope of sales management.

5. Rapid advances in transport communications have opened new markets for goods both at home and abroad.

6. The consumer habits are different and often unpredictable in free enterprise. He is free to buy or not to buy, and free to buy what he likes. Consumption being uncontrolled, sales management assumes great importance.

In view of such an importance attached to distribution of goods, sales management must be conducted on scientific lines. Very often in our country sales managers are guided mainly by personal experiences and observations, and not by any scientific standards or methods. This lack of scientific method in sales management is due to the fact that the sales manager is dealing specially with the human element in controlling his organisation as well as in developing the market. Recently, however, efforts have been made to apply scientific method and psychology to sales and selling.

1. Confield: *Sales Administration,* p. 3.

Functions of Sales Manager. The functions of sales managers vary widely according to the type of product, method of distribution, size of organisation, and the personal abilities and inclinations of the men themselves. In general, the functions of a sales manager may be grouped into two phases:

1. Administrative or Planning; and
2. Executive or Operating.

The Administrative functions of the sales manager include—

1. Research of markets;
2. Study of distribution trends;
3. Development of policies;
4. Investigation of sales methods;
5. Analysis of operations;
6. Creation of plans and programmes.

The Executive functions of a sales manager include—

1. Sales promotion, including assisting salesmen and distributors with advertising;
2. Sales operation, involving departmental organisation, recruitment, selection, training, compensating, and supervising salesmen;
3. Dealing with distributors and dealers;
4. Sales control, which includes setting up of sales territory, routing, transporting, quotas, etc.

To carry out all these functions, an organisation of the sales department on sound lines is necessary. The sales organisation should be created in such a manner that it is able to perform its functions efficiently. These functions fall logically into two divisions, namely, (1) Sales Planning Function, and (2) Sales Operating Function.

Sales Planning. While dealing with the functions of the sales manager, we divided his functions under planning and operating. Similarly, the functions of the sales organisation are grouped into planning and operating. Sales planning is a most important function of marketing. It includes: (1) Product analysis; (2) Market analysis; (3) Distribution research; (4) Co-ordination with other executives and departments in the business and outside distributive organisations; (5) Policy development on price, credit and service; (6) Sales statistics, budgets, quota establishment.

Sales Operating. This is a much more highly developed function of sales organisation than sales planning. The principal Sales Operating Functions are: (1) locating, selecting and training salesmen; (2) stimulating and supervising salesmen; (3) paying salesmen; (4) maintaining relations with distributors; (5) controlling branch houses; (6) co-ordinating sales and advertising when these functions are not performed by an advertising or sales promotion department; (7) transporting, including warehousing.

CREATION OF DEMAND

By creation of demand we mean arousing desire, or making people want things. Desire must be accompanied by ability to pay, if desire is to be effective. Thus desire *plus* ability to buy makes demand. Desire alone will not sell goods; and yet it may sell one brand over another and may lead to the purchase of one product in preference to another.

There are many producers in the field, and the individual seller must exert himself to make the consumer prefer his goods to those of others. Demand can be created by personal salesmanship, advertising, display of the goods, demonstrations, and general educational work or publicity. But before actual sales can be started it is essential to understand the market situation, because misfit sales may be forced for a time by high pressure salesmanship and misleading publicity but they will not be maintained for long, for each sale gives in the possession of the buyer an article which begins to educate him as to the error he made in acquiring it. Thus a force of negative advertising and negative salesmanship comes into existence in the community which automatically introduces a check to the sales.

To avoid this kind of veto, a thorough study of the factors which determine the success or failure of a marketing programme has to be made. The seller should know thoroughly the properties of the products and the needs, wants and demands of the people. He should chalk out a plan of preliminary investigation for discovering the latent demand, customer tastes, habits and ability to pay for the goods. This is termed Marketing Research or Preliminary Investigation.

B. MARKETING RESEARCH

Marketing Research is the disciplined collection, array, and evaluation of facts relating to the marketing process. Its primary purpose is to solve or forestall marketing problems and thus to increase the efficiency and lower the costs of marketing through the development, selection, and improvement of the best products and marketing methods.

The more progressive companies implement the marketing concept properly. This means that the marketing man is introduced at the beginning rather than at the end of the production cycle. Marketing assumes responsibility for guiding the engineer and the manufacturing man towards products the customer wants at prices he is willing to pay.

It is inherent in the marketing concept that all business functions (production, financing, designing) must look beyond the plant and office walls out into the market-place for guidance in the planning of their activities. In more progressive companies, marketing has become not only a full partner but the dominant partner with production, engineering, and finance in planning for growth of the entire business. With the implementation of this marketing concept, it is clear that the gathering of accurate, reliable information about the market place is essential for planning for profitable growth.

Nature of Marketing Research

A company selling a product or a service needs information about market—its customers, prospective customers, and in many cases, the ultimate consumers of its products, to determine what it should produce, to whom it should offer what it produces, and the way in which it should offer its product. The company should make a systematic and impartial marketing research and evaluate the results without bias.

There are some basic differences between research in industrial and consumer markets. In industrial markets, purchasing decisions are made in quite a different atmosphere compared with the consumer. Products sold to industry tend to be technical in nature, and are subject to technical evaluation by the buyer. In industrial markets, the researcher must be able to talk the buyer's own language. He must be experienced in the general practices of business and must be able to interpret as well as observe and inquire.

In the consumer-goods market, it is necessary to gather information at various levels to assist management in planning for the future. Information can be gathered by interviews conducted in personal visits to the home, by mail, on the street, in stores, by telephone, or in public groups. Surveys may be made of a neighbourhood, a city, a region or the nation and may cover the public as a whole or be limited to specific types of people.

In both industrial and consumer research, additional information is available from government sources and other outside agencies which can be used in conjunction with information collected directly from the market by the researchers to formulate plans for management.

Functions of Marketing Research. The principal functions of marketing research are describing, evaluating, explaining, predicting, and assisting in making decisions.

1. *Describing* includes a description of events or activities that have occurred or are taking place.

2. *Evaluating* includes the evaluation of products, sales performance, competition and the like.

3. *Explaining* includes explaining why certain things have happened or are happening, such as declining sales volume in a certain sales territory or why competition is a leader in a certain product.

4. *Predicting* includes prediction of what might, will, or should happen in terms of sales volume, product needs, distribution, pricing and the like.

5. *Assisting in making decisions* implies the requirement that marketing research evaluate its information carefully in an unbiased manner and make recommendations to management that can be acted upon.

Marketing Research Methodology

To ensure that the recommendations emanating from marketing

research are acceptable and will be acted upon, it is essential that marketing research (i) understand the problem to be researched, (ii) establish specific objectives, (iii) develop a research plan, (iv) choose the proper sample, (v) determine information needs, (vi) analyze the information gathered, (vii) develop conclusions and recommendations, and (viii) prepare a report to management.

1. *Understanding the problem to be researched.* If the user of the research is to receive full benefit from the researcher, he must define the problem to be researched carefully before the researcher can undertake the development of a research plan which will ultimately assist the user in making decisions.

2. *Establishing specific objectives.* The next step is to establish the specific objectives to be achieved by the research plan. The problem may be as narrow as what the share of market is in a given area; or it may be as broad as an extensive study of the market place to build a five-year growth plan for the company. The objectives of the study should be clearly stated and agreed upon between the users and the researchers.

3. *Developing the research plan.* This requires a determination of how to obtain the information required to meet the objectives of the study. This includes all sources of data readily available in printed form within the company and outside the company, such as government statistics, trade association data, and the like.

4. *Choosing the proper sample.* The next step is to determine specifically where it will be necessary to go to obtain the remaining information, and the number of persons to be contacted. In the case of research on consumer products, the selection of the sample depends on the nature of the problem.

Sampling applies to research in both consumer products and industrial products. If a product is sold directly to automobile manufacturers, the sample is not difficult to choose. If a product is sold through retail outlets, the sample will be larger, but again, it is not difficult to choose, because retail stores are well known. The more complex sampling problems typically occur when the study involves the public at large. In that case, carefully designed mathematical techniques must be used to select a representative sample of the population to be measured.

5. *Determining information needs.* Having designed the sample, it is necessary to determine what information is required from each unit and person in the sample. When a large sample is drawn to measure a certain segment of the public at large, a carefully structured questionnaire is usually developed. Each interviewer must use the same questionnaire and stick to it. The questions should be carefully worded to avoid any bias on the part of individual interviewers in recording the answers.

6. *Analysing the information gathered.* Having completed the interviewing among whatever population was chosen, the information so obtained must be analysed carefully and put into an orderly form. The analysis can be done either by data-processing equipment or by hand and then tabulated.

7. *Developing conclusions and recommendations.* Following the tabulation of results or the making of a summary analysis, it will then be necessary to develop specific conclusions and recommendations. Here the researcher is called upon to exercise marketing management judgement, and make actionable recommendation to the users of the research.

8. *Preparing the report to management.* All research projects should be presented to the user of the research in the form of a written report. This report should contain a statement of the objectives of the research, its scope, and the approach used. It should set forth the information obtained in factual form and the interpretive analysis of the information in the form of conclusion and recommendations.

AREAS OF ACTIVITY OF MARKETING RESEARCH

The purpose of marketing research is the solving or forestalling of marketing problems, thus helping to increase the efficiency of the marketing function and the profitability of the enterprise. To play this role successfully, it must concern itself with all aspects of the marketing function. The various aspects or areas of activity of marketing research include:

1. Products or services.
2. Markets.
3. Distribution.
4. Pricing.
5. Sales organisation.
6. Service.
7. Advertising and Sales promotion.
8. Packaging.
9. Brand
10. Acquisition.

Products or services. Because of keen competition the development of new or improved products or services becomes a vital part of management planning. In this area, marketing research can make a very important contribution. It should evaluate existing products to determine the extent to which they are fulfilling the needs of customers, and at the same time, look for possible modifications which can provide the basis for gaining competitive advantage. The area of new products is particularly important if a company has to build and maintain position of leadership in its industry. Marketing research must play an important role in defining product needs, otherwise the product may fail.

2. *Markets.* The study of market is equally important. There is a great correlation between the product and the kind of consumer. The market potential should be determined by knowing whether the possible user has money or not; whether it is worthwhile selling to a particular class. Effort must be made to find out possibilities of changes in demand for the article, or modified product.

3. *Distribution.* Drastic changes are constantly taking place in distribution methods and techniques. Studies should be made at frequent intervals to determine the most efficient means of getting a company's product to its customer or ultimate user. Marketing research can make recommendations for changes in distribution methods and techniques to meet the changing needs of the market place and changing needs of those intermediaries within the market place who serve their customers. Distribution costs are an important element of these studies of distribution. In a number of industries, the role of the middleman is being seriously questioned, it is even suggested to eliminate him. Marketing research can assist distributors and other kinds of middlemen to improve the efficiency of their operations.

4. *Pricing.* Projects in the area of pricing existing products, and new products as they relate to channels of distribution and competitive activities, are also important marketing research activities. Continuing review of competitive pricing is an important activity to help management make pricing decisions.

5. *Sales organisation.* Marketing research assists the sales department in making sales forecasts, establishing quotas for sales territories, analysing salesmen's activities, measuring salesmen's effectiveness, and measuring territorial yield.

6. *Advertising and sales promotion.* Marketing research can be used to measure the effectiveness of advertising, for both the company and its competition. Appraisal can be made of media, copy, and amount of advertising. Another important contribution is its assistance in establishing the objectives of the advertising programme.

7. *Service.* In most companies making industrial goods and many companies producing consumer goods, service can be a very important factor in customer relationships. It should be the duty of marketing research to analyse and review periodically the content, facilities, and effectiveness of the service function of the company and its competitors.

8. *Packaging.* Packaging should be appraised from two points of view: (i) functional and (ii) the merchanding aspects of the packaging. Packaging should be studied for both existing and new, because particularly in the consumer-goods field, packaging is becoming more and more important not only as regards the material used and the protection of contents, but also regarding appearance on shelf. Good packaging can move the goods from the retailer's shelf to the customer at a good speed. The quick turnover helps the retailer save space on the shelf.

9. *Brand names.* Brand-name policy should be appraised by marketing research in terms of treatment of the corporate name, product names, and other factors as they relate to the organisation structure of the company. Marketing research should appraise the strengths and weaknesses of the company's existing brand compared with competition.

10. *Acquisitions.* If the acquisition of another company is the most

feasible method of achieving penetration in a new market, broadening a product line, or achieving diversification, marketing should play an important role in appraising the acquisition. It is a relatively straightforward task for an accountant to check the financial records and for an engineer to appraise its physical assets. The intangibles which are the most important, however, are the marketing strengths and weaknesses of the other company, and this is the area in which marketing research can play a significant role.

C. PRICE FIXING AND PRICING POLICY

Prices are a basic and critical factor in generating the return on capital invested in a business enterprise. They not only determine how resources are to be used, but they are also the means by which products and services that are in limited supply are distributed among buyers. Pricing methods and policies contribute directly to the success or failure of a business irrespective of any other single profit activity.

What is Price? If we were to ask a group of individuals selected at random to define "price", many would reply that price is an amount of money paid by the buyer to the seller of a product or service, or, in other words, that price is the money value of a product or service as agreed upon in a market transaction. This definition is, of course, valid as far as it goes. For a complete understanding of a price in any particular transaction, much more than the amount of money involved must be known. Both the buyer and the seller should be familiar with not only the money amount, but with the amount and quality of the product to be exchanged, the time and place at which the exchange will take place and payment will be made, the form of money to be used, the credit terms, and discount that apply to the transaction, guarantees of the product delivery terms, return privileges, and other factors, In other words, both buyer and seller should be fully aware of all the factors that comprise the total "package" being exchanged for the asked-for money in order that they may evaluate a given price.

The "true" price of a product or service changes whenever any of the associated elements in the package change, as well as when the money amount to be exchanged is altered. For example, if a department store discontinues return privilege on certain articles, or if a manufacturer of industrial machinery reduces the period during which interest will not be charged on credit transactions, the true price has been changed. The money price has not changed, but the package has.

Similarly, the "published", "quoted", or "list" price of a product or service may, in reality, not be the price actually paid. Various kinds of concealed price concessions may be given to some or all buyers. In such cases, the quoted price is not the "true" price.

Factors Affecting Price Policy. It follows that many factors underlie price fixation and the sales manager must weigh all of them while making a pricing policy and when putting a price on products. The various factors are as follows:

1. The cost of the goods to the consumer, allowance having been made for all items and expense and reasonable profit. As a rule, no concern is justified in selling at a loss although in certain circumstances it may become necessary. The selling price of a product must cover the cost of manufacture, including material, labour and overhead, as well as administrative and selling expenses. Ample provision must be made for depreciation, taxes, interest and the like. There should then be a sufficient margin to yield the seller a "reasonable" profit, which should cover not only a "fair return" on the owner's capital, but also an additional amount as compensation for the risks which have been assumed by the owners in the capacity of entrepreneurs.

2. The next point is to know the charges made by the competitors for similar goods, and what it costs them to produce. That obviously means knowing the conditions of production under which the commodity is made. If production is carried on under conditions of increasing cost or diminishing return, it will be foolish to attempt to increase sales by keeping the price as low as possible. On the other hand, when production is carried on under conditions of decreasing cost or increasing returns, it would be possible to gain definite advantage in increasing value of sales by means of a decrease in prices. The considerations of these factors will enable the seller to know whether he can afford to do business.

3. The nature and conditions of demand, which have already been studied, should be kept in mind when fixing price. Can a sufficient amount of the goods be sold at a price necessary to enable the business to be carried on? It will be most important to study the demand not only in a general way as to its elasticity or inelasticity, but also with specific reference to the peculiarities of prospective purchasers, the prevailing psychology, standard of living, customs and prejudices. Many a hopeful business has been wrecked by neglecting some of these psychological and social factors which have no relation whatever with questions of cost of production or of the abstract theories of demand and supply.

4. Closely related to the foregoing considerations is the question of quality and service. Quality may be tangible or intangible as far as it relates to the sale of a particular commodity. What people can be made to think of a product is frequently far more effective in influencing its selling price than the real quality as measured in terms of usefulness or durability. The appeal to the imagination is frequently the most effective appeal to the pocket. Particular individual services rendered in connection with the sale of the goods may enable a price to be secured which is very much out of line with the actual cost of production.[1] It should be remembered that with most people price in itself is not a buying motive. A normal person only buys something he wants, so that low price in itself will not persuade him to buy an article which cannot serve any purpose he has in mind. Price is no attraction without service-value. If, however, a man sees an article for which he has a possible (but not immediate) use, the price of that article may influence his decision to buy it, but it will be

1. Lincoln in *Handbook of Business Administration*, ed. Donald.

a limiting and not a deciding factor. Too much weight should not be attached to the importance of price. Customers do recognise that a low priced article which is also of low quality is not, in the long run, likely to prove cheap. Very low prices are often suspect among customers. A consumer would very often pay a high price to satisfy his vanity; desire for prestige is the motive, to satisfy which he pays extra. It should be remembered that, up to a point, the more a certain type of person (snobbish or one influenced by social consideration) pays for an article, the more pleasure it gives him.

5. To the aforesaid considerations may be added three more points which should be borne in mind while determining price policy. Certain types of seasonal goods can be sold at a price which is apparently very high as compared with the actual cost of production, due to unusual risk undertaken by the seller. Very highly "fashional" articles may also be governed by similar considerations. Sometimes the customary or possible rate of turnover will affect the price. Similarly, if the terms of sale are long, the price must be increased to cover up interest on capital locked and the risk.

Price of Product in Relation to Market Prices. After the analyses mentioned above have been made, the sales manager will be in a position to determine whether he wishes to sell (i) below the market, (ii) at the market, or (iii) above the market. In the former case his aim will be to undercut competitors and make larger net returns through a small margin of profit on a large volume of units sold. If the second course is adopted, the manager shall have to depend upon energetic selling by vigorous advertising, and careful scrutiny of his costs of production and distribution. It will also be necessary to adopt some methods of differentiating the product from similar ones already on the market. When conscious attempt is made to sell goods at a higher price than is commanded by those of a similar quality now on the market, the manufacturer or distributor must emphasize some distinctive feature so as to persuade his customers that his article offers additional use-value. Since this means that he is asking for a larger share of the consumer's spending power, he must convince the latter that the increased use-value of the product will compensate for having to do without some other product. In such cases advertising must be extensively used. On the whole, therefore, a businessman in attempting to arrive at the most profitable price for his goods thinks more of 'consumer's surplus' than of the mere interplay of demand and supply. He knows that there are many buyers who can, and will, pay a much higher price than could be secured from the mere marginal purchaser. He would, very often, find it much more advantageous to appeal to these "intramarginal" customers until competition forces his prices downwards.

Quotation of Prices. Another very interesting question to be answered is whether uniform or differential prices may be charged. Uniform prices may mean any of these things—uniformity to all customers irrespective of their status or of the quantity purchased. It may extend only to all buyers within a given class or group. For example, all wholesalers are quoted one price, usually lower, and all retailers another price. This uniformity results in differential prices between the two groups. Uniformity as to territory supplied may be arrived at; but if transport costs are different for different territories, differential charges are made. In the latter case, uniformity can be secured by quoting prices F.O.B. the factory. The terms of sale may be kept uniform for all buyers, so that either all are required to pay cash, or all are granted credit on the same terms. Differential prices may be charged by giving concessions for the purchase of the full line of the seller instead of buying only one product. Also, special prices can be quoted to dealers who undertake not to handle the goods of a competing producer. Special off-season prices break the uniformity and introduce differential charges. The problems of uniformity of differential prices have been attempted to be solved by various methods, some of which are outlined below.

List-and-Discount Price. The most common method in the case of convenience and luxury goods, such as automobiles, radio sets, typewriters, gramophones, drugs, is to quote prices by means of a nominal or list price, modified by various combinations of percentage discounts, commonly known as trade discounts. A *trade discount* is a device used primarily in order to conceal the actual purchase price of goods from the ultimate customer. It makes possible a uniform selling price of the product without actually fixing that price to the consumers, but rather gives a definite range of price discretion to salesmen or dealers. It is also useful when sales are made at different prices to wholesalers and retailers. The second method is that of *cash discounts.* Discounts are frequently given for prompt payment. This system really is not a discount given for cash payment but a premium charged for slow payment. The price quoted includes interest and charges to cover risk, if cash is paid; they are not included in the price. The psychology is adroit, for the customer feels he has paid less than the price. *Quantity discounts* are often allowed on the assumption that large orders can be more profitably handled than small ones. The actual discount should be carefully determined, because any slackness is likely to lead to disastrous results, as terms offered may be abused. When prices vary according to the quantity sold, chain stores or other retailers, by co-operative purchasing may be able to offer to the consumer a price which is as low as that which the wholesaler or manufacturer can offer to the retailer. The offer of quantity discounts to retailers also leads to over-buying with very disastrous consequences. In order to avoid mutual misunderstanding and unjust discrimination it is perhaps better to refuse to allow quantity discounts.

Resale Price Maintenance. Manufacturers very often place restrictions upon the price at which a buyer (wholesaler or retailer) may resell a product which is identified by some brand, copyright, trade-mark, or the like. This control by the manufacturer of the resale price is known as resale price maintenance. From the point of view of the manufacturer, the practice is significant. The branded articles are widely advertised so that the utility and the customary prices are known to most customers. Where these products are offered at cut prices, they definitely create an impression of cheapness. This injures the business of the producer. Also, fixing of a uniform price to be charged to the ultimate customer prevents over-charging and much ill-will.

TECHNIQUE OF SELLING AND SALES PROMOTION

The sales campaign will succeed if properly administered. The sales manager must secure cooperation of the designing and the manufacturing departments or produce a product suited to the market demands, of reliable quality, and in sufficient quantity and variety to give a workable trade assortment. The co-ordination between the sales department and other departments is provided by committees of the departmental heads or by a special official entrusted with this particular work. This task may easily be achieved. But difficulties arise in establishing proper relations between the sales department and other sections of the business, and the indoor and outdoor staffs. Different sections may give conflicting instructions. Anything that may cause friction between the customer and salesman will make selling difficult, and antagonise the salesman or the customer. For example, the collection department might write a sharp letter to a customer asking for immediate payment, although another section had received a complaint in respect of the goods supplied. Some firms seek to obtain closer co-operation by bringing salesmen into the office for a time, and by sending for short periods, members of the inside staff on the road. A good plan is to have sales clerks to deal with all communications for salesmen and customers within certain geographical areas. Every salesman and every customer can thus look to a single individual at head quarters for assistance and hold him responsible for mistakes.

Another important thing that the sales manager has to decide, relates to the part to be played by dealers, agents, salesmen, demonstrators, canvassers, samples, window displays, direct mail, press and other types of advertising in building up the means to be employed. In practice, in most sales these all play important roles; and they all should be dovetailed one into the other so that each receives added force. To successfully achieve the object, a Sales Promotion Department is established as an integral part of the Sales Department. In addition to the task of establishing contact with the customer through salesmen by supplementing the voice or personality of the salesman, i.e., by advertising and by direct or mail-order selling (all of which are discussed in a subsequent chapter) the manufacturer has to decide his policy with regard to credit, and make arrangements for collection of accounts. This is outlined in the following section.

CREDIT AND COLLECTION

Credit is agency through which goods and services may be transferred in the present while payment is deferred to some future time.

In essence credit rests upon faith or confidence which is engendered between two persons, and which results in "sale on trust". Thus, in commercial terms, credit means the sale of goods or services on the promise of future payment.

Since credit involves an exchange of values usually represented by goods and expressed in terms of money, the seller of goods on credit makes a short-term investment in the buyer's business. Credit permits those who have more property than opportunity to aid those who have more opportunity than property. "It is one of the greatest of economic agencies by which capable men are selected out from among their less competent competitors, are furnished with resources, are given enlarged opportunity, and are aided to perform a larger service for themselves, their backers, and the community at large.... To give credit with care means to encourage honest and capable men as proprietors of business, and to discourage those who are dishonest or incapable."

Terms of Credit. Credit is influenced by the terms of sale. The time and general conditions of payment are specified by the terms of credit. A very wide divergence is found in the length of the credit under which goods are sold. The period may extend to six months or one year, but the recent tendency is to shorten the period, so that most common terms range from 30 to 60 days. Among other factors having an influence on terms of credit are:

1. Purpose to which goods will be put;
2. The nature of the product, e.g., perishable goods can command short credit;
3. The buyer's ability and willingness to pay;
4. The location of customers, as more distant customers may get longer terms than near customers;
5. The business cycles, as terms have a tendency to shorten or lengthen with changes in the business cycle.

Sources of credit information. To extend credit, we have observed earlier, implies trust. Most trust is based upon familiarity as a result of one's own prior experience or upon information obtained from other sources who have had experience. Credit information can be obtained from several sources, the most common of which are:

1. Your own files and ledger cards.
2. Credit reporting agencies that specialise in this work.
3. Other creditors and suppliers.
4. Banks.
5. Trade organisations.
6. Directly from potential account.

Categories of credit information. The various kinds of information that can be obtained for use in determining a line of credit may be broken down into three main categories:

1. *Antecedent information.* The history and background of a business and its principles are revealing. The integrity and honesty of the account are two of the most important factors to be considered before extending credit.

2. *Trade information.* Trade information consists of a record of recent payments to other suppliers that includes high credit, previous amounts owing, terms, amount past due and general ledger experience. Trade information is often considered by many credit managers as the true test of the credit worthiness of an account.

3. *Financial information.* Financial information is often the most difficult to obtain and undoubtedly is the most difficult to analyse, because of the many factors that determine the financial strength or weakness of an account.

Other Influencing Factors. The actual decision on whether or not to approve a line of credit and for what amount depends upon more than just the plain, bare facts revealed by the information gathered. Aside from the worthiness of the potential account, there are often other important considerations that a credit manager must weigh. The financial condition and credit policy of his own firm are of primary importance. A general credit policy is decided upon by management, and the credit manager acts according to that policy. For example, does management wish to carry slow-paying accounts, and if so to what extend? How much in accounts receivable does management wish to carry and for what length of time? What is the percentage of bad debt losses a company can absorb, and what is the largest amount of credit it wishes to grant to any one debtor? All of these questions and more must be answered before a credit manager can make an intelligent decision.

The financial condition of the creditor firm and the general economic condition of the industry and of the country as a whole are important factors. There is usually a more liberal attitude in so-called good times and more conservative outlook in depressed times. Again, a firm looking to promote a new product or build a new territory will take greater credit risks.

Collection of Accounts. The collection of accounts forms one of the most important phases of business organisation. Business consists of a multitude of individual transactions each of which consists of a series of steps—production, selling and collection. Collection is the ultimate aim of each transaction. Therefore good business requires that collections shall not only be made but that they shall be made promptly and without any damage to the concern's market. It is this latter requirement, viz., to retain the customer's goodwill, which makes the collection problem a difficult one, and which makes skill and tact essentials of those handling the collection. In the majority of cases collection can be made promptly, if the collector is willing to sacrifice goodwill, but goodwill is to be sacrificed only as a last resort. Stated in the order of their importance, the three objectives of the collection department are: first, to collect the debt; second, to collect the debt and retain the customer's goodwill; and third, to collect the debt promptly, retaining the goodwill of the customer. If these three objectives cannot all be attained, they are usually abandoned in reverse order, and, as a last resort, goodwill is sacrificed to the main objective which is to obtain payment.

Stages of a Collection. Collection procedure begins with the mailing of the invoice which informs the purchaser of the exact amount of the indebtedness and the day it becomes due. At the same time the bill of goods is charged against the customer on the ledger, which fact puts the credit and collection on the alert to compile information which may be of use at any stage in the life of the account. Usually the next step in the collection effort consists of mailing a maturity statement to the customer. If the statement has failed to bring in the payment a firm and candid letter should promptly follow. Prompt action and follow-up aid both the creditor and the debtor. Promptness saves trouble to look after accounts and also interest and business profit of he funds otherwise locked up. Chances of unfavourable changes in debtor's business are kept within limit. The debtor is kept in liquid position to buy more goods. If a customer has bought and is owing as much as the seller cares to sell him, subsequent sales to that customer may be delayed so long as his account is unpaid. Even though the creditor might be willing to accept further orders in spite of the delinquent account, the buyer will often avoid the house where his account is overdue and place his orders with a rival. Debts long postponed are notoriously hard to pay. During the delay the debtor enjoys the use of the property of another and this false situation gradually breaks down his value sense. Insistence on prompt payment is cheaper in the end.

The hundi, sight draft of promissory note mark another step in collection procedure. In some cases the credit man strives to obtain this instrument, but the use of hundis is very common in India, and, therefore, buyers do not mind them. Hundis are more often than not honoured. If the hundi is dishonoured, collection reaches a critical stage, where thorough investigation must be made before taking further steps. The investigation may lead to (a) an extension of time, coupled, if possible with part payment and, in some cases, better security. The usual method is to split up the hundi into three or four hundis of smaller amounts arranged to fall due at intervals; (b) an account may be transferred to a collection agency, if any available; (c) papers may be handed over to a legal adviser for legal action; or (d) account may be charged to Profit and Loss account as bad debt. The entrance of a lawyer ends amicable relations. All collection efforts short of a suit should, therefore, be made before papers are handed over to him.

CHAPTER XLI

CHANNELS OF DISTRIBUTION

Planned or Free Consumption. Different methods of selling goods have been adopted in capitalist countries, because consumers are different from one another, both in their tastes and in their residences, and, therefore, it is difficult for any producer to have a "circle of customers". If the manufacturer is a large-scale firm it would have planned its production; but it would find it almost impossible, unless it is a monopolist, to plan consumption, as might be done in an authoritarian system of organisation. For example, in the USSR it is not planned production that is so important as planned consumption.

Under capitalism goods are supplied at a price that will yield profit to the supplier; under the Soviet system of industrial production prices and profits are not the ultimate test. The Soviet system does not have to take account of changes in styles and fashions. Goods and services are provided as the Supreme Council of National Economy thinks fit. Production is organised without being guided by the desires of the consumers as manifested on the market; prices of goods are fixed independently of the market; and there is no question of equilibrium between demand and supply. The authoritarian consumption, therefore, puts an end to the free satisfaction of needs. Such a distribution means that a man must eat the food—and it may be excellent enough—which is set before him by the communal food centre; that he is not entitled to choose the sort of furniture he likes; that a woman is not permitted to wear the hat which suits her best. "Eat what you get, and wear what you are supplied" is the rule. Obviously, this consumption, planned as it is by the producers, simplifies the organisation of production, eliminates the "need for marketing" and minimises the problems of distribution, with hardly any 'distributive' or 'middle-men' costs.

In free or mixed economy, however, where there is competition, the problem of bringing the product to the market has to be solved. This involves establishing distribution policies and strategies, including selecting channels of distribution or middlemen.

Where goods are not sold direct to consumers, they are distributed through middlemen. Direct sales are made through salesmen, advertising, and by the mail order system. The sale through middle-men is made either through wholesalers and retailers, or through retailers alone.

Who is a middleman?

A middleman is an independent business concern standing between the producer and the ultimate consumer or industrial user. It is through him that title to or control of a product or service is transferred from producers to consumers or business users.

According to the nature of their customers middlemen may be classified as:

1. wholesale middlemen,
2. retailers.

According to whether or not they take title middlemen may be classified as :

1. merchant middlemen;
2. agent (functional) middlemen.

The merchants not only take title to the goods but perform most or all of the distributing functions. They include wholesalers and retailers.

Agents negotiate transactions without taking title. They include commission agents and brokers.

Whatever the type, middlemen are those firms which set policy and instigate marketing action with respect to someone else's goods. The essence of a middleman's operation is his active and prominent role in negotiations involving the buying and selling of goods; his income arises directly from the proceeds of these transactions. It is his part in *transfer of ownership* which differentiates a middleman from other institutions, such as banks, insurance companies, and transport firms, which help in marketing process but do not take title and are not actively involved in purchase and sales negotiations.

A *Channel of Distribution* for a product is the route taken via the marketing institutions (agents, brokers, wholesalers, retailers) by the *title* to the goods as they move from the producer to the ultimate consumer or industrial user. A channel always includes both the producer and the final customer for the product, as well as all agents and merchant middlemen involved in the title transfer.

Importance of Middlemen

The habit, and in most cases, the necessity of petty purchasing, makes it essential to use the services of middlemen. Indeed, it is not economically feasible or convenient for a producer to deal directly with an ultimate consumer. Think for a moment how inconvenient and complicated our daily existence would be if there were no retail middlemen.

Concentration, equalisation, dispersion. Frequently the quantity and assortment of goods produced by a firm are out of balance with the variety and amounts wanted by consumers or industrial users. A businessman needs paper, pencil, typewriters, and desks. A householder wants grass seed, fertilizer, a rake, a spade, and eventually he hopes to need a lawn-mower. No single firm produces all of the items either of these users wants and no producer can afford to sell the small quantity the user desires. Obviously, there is a need for someone to perform the function of balancing or equalising what various producers turn out with what the final customers want.

The job to be done involves (1) collecting or concentrating the output of various producers, (2) subdividing these quantities into amounts desired by the customers and gathering the various items together in the assortment or variety wanted, and (3) dispersing this assortment to consumers or industrial buyers. In some cases, the task of concentrating, equalising, and dispersing is simple enough to be done by the producer and final customer working together. In most cases, however, the producer and consumer are not able to work out the proper quantity and assortment. A specialist in concentration, equalisation, and dispersion is needed, and this is the role of the middleman.

Creation of Utility. Middlemen aid in the creation of time, place and possession utilities. The product is more easily available as and when required and at the location, as well as, in the form it is required.

In spite of the utility of the middlemen, both to the manufacturer and the customer, there has been persistent demand by the consumers, labour representatives, and legislators that middlemen should be eliminated. Their demand, of course relates to the elimination of wholesale middlemen alone. Ordinarily, they realize that they cannot get along without retailers. Yet wholesale middlemen also continue to be an important force in the distribution system. In many cases they are the dominant figures in the channels of distribution used by manufacturers. Efforts, no doubt, have been made to eliminate the wholesaler from the distribution channel, but wholesalers are very much there as a link in the marketing system.

MAJOR CHANNELS OF DISTRIBUTION

There are several alternative channels of distribution to choose from. The proper selection of a distribution channel or several distribution channels depends on such factors as the nature of the product involved, market, sales volume for each outlet, relative distribution costs, and how much of the marketing function the manufacturer wants to assume.

It may, however, be mentioned here that the choice of channels does not rest entirely with the manufacturer. The middleman has considerable freedom and power to make his own choices in establishing channels for products. The names of some big stores or middlemen, e.g., WEST END, mean more to the consumers than the Swissmakers of the watches. Nevertheless, the most frequently used channels are outlined here for the two major classes of markets-the CONSUMER MARKET and the INDUSTRIAL MARKET. These channels are illustrated in the following diagrams (page 752).

In each channel, a manufacturer or producer may use his own sales branches or personnel to reach the next institution. The channel leading directly from the producer to the consumer at the upper left of the diagram represents door-to-door selling and direct mail. In any channel, two levels of merchant wholesalers may be involved—one wholesaler sells the product to another wholesaler.

DISTRIBUTION OF CONSUMER GOODS

Five channels are widely used in the marketing of consumer products. In each, the manufacturer may in addition use sales branches or sales depots. Furthermore, whenever wholesalers are used, goods may be distributed from one large wholesaler to several sub-jobbers and then to retailers. But for the sake of simplicity we will discuss this unwieldy subject in a few paragraphs:

Producer—Consumer. The shortest, simplest channel of distribution for consumer products is from the producer to the consumer, with no middlemen involved. The producer may sell house-to-house, or may sell by mail.

Producer—retailer—consumer. Many large retailers buy directly from manufacturers and agricultural producers. Also, some manufacturers have established their own retail stores, e.g., Delhi Cloth and General Mills Co., Bata Shoe Co., Jay Engineering Company for the sale of Usha Sewing Machines and fans.

Producer—wholesaler—retailer—consumer. This is the "traditional"

Charts showing Channels of Distribution

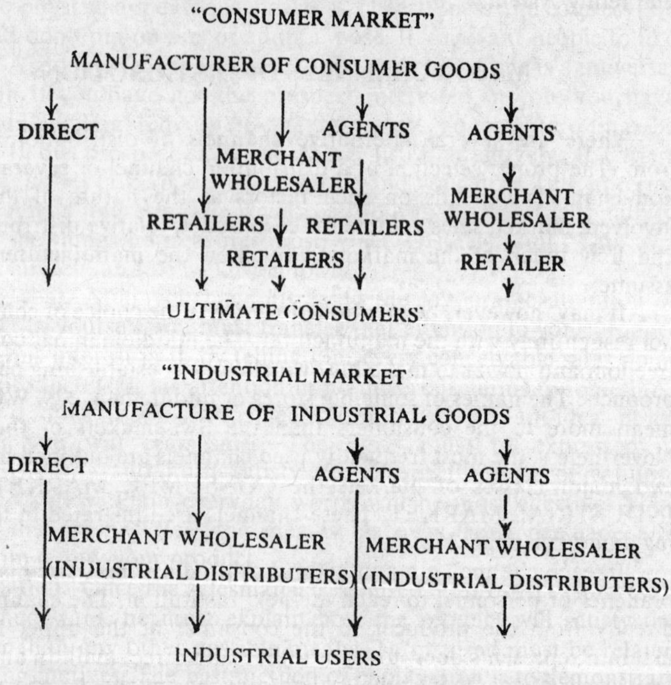

1. Stanton: *Fundamentals of Marketing*, p. 339.

channel for consumer goods. Small retailers and small manufacturers by the thousands, find this channel the only economically feasible choice.

Producer—agent—retailer—consumer. Instead of using whole-salers, many producers prefer to use a manufacturers' agent, selling agent, broker or another agent middleman to reach the retail market, especially *large scale* retailers.

Producer—agent—wholesaler—retailer—consumer. When trying to reach small retailers, producers very often use agent middlemen, who in turn go to wholesalers who sell to small stores.

DISTRIBUTION OF INDUSTRIAL GOODS

Four general types of channels are widely used in reaching industrial users. Here again, a manufacturer may use a sales branch or a sales depot to reach next institution in the channel. As in the distribution of consumer goods, two levels of wholesalers are used in some cases.

Producer—industrial user. This direct channel accounts for a greater money volume of industrial products than any other distribution structure. Manufacturers of large installations, such as locomotives, generators, etc. usually sell directly to users.

Producer—industrial distributor—user. Producers of operating supplies and small accessory equipment frequently use industrial distributors to reach their markets. Manufacturers, building materials, construction equipment, and air-conditioning equipment make heavy use the industrial distributor.

Producer—agent—user. Firms without their own marketing departments find this a desirable channel. Also, a company which wants to introduce a new product or enter a new market may prefer to use agents rather than its own sales force.

Producer—agent—industrial distributor—user. This channel is similar to the preceding one, except that for some reason it is not feasible to go through agents directly to the industrial user. Probably the unit sale is too small to sell directly, or perhaps decentralised inventories are needed to supply the users rapidly. In such cases, the storage services of the industrial distributor are required.

FACTORS AFFECTING CHOICE OF CHANNELS

The major classes of factors that influence decisions regarding choice of channels of distribution are: (i) the nature of product, (ii) the nature of market, (iii) number and types of middlemen, (iv) competition, (v) legal constraints, (vi) nature and size of the company.

The nature of the Product. The physical characteristics of a product and other product considerations have a strong influence on the choice of distribution channels.

(a) *Perishability.* Products subject to physical or fashion perishability are usually distributed through relatively short channels so that they are speeded through to avoid dangers associated with delays and repeated handling.

(b) *Standardisation.* Unstandardized goods also usually pass through short channels because of the need of direct contact between producers and users. Standardised products, e.g., machine tools, are commonly handled by wholesale distributors. If a product is custom-built it will normally be distributed directly from producer to ultimate consumer or industrial user.

(c) *Technical nature of product.* An industrial product which is highly technical often will be distributed directly to the industrial user. The manufacturer must have salesmen and servicemen who can explain the product to potential customers and who can provide pre-sale and post-sale service. Wholesalers normally cannot do this. Consumer products of a technical nature will be sold to retailers, but servicing may have to be done by the manufacturer.

(d) *Product bulk and weight.* A producer of a heavy, bulky item, where freight is a significant part of the total value, will seek to minimize the physical handling of the product and will prefer to ship in wagonload or truckload quantities. For instance coal is shipped directly to the industrial user or retailer, even little passes through middlemen.

(e) *Unit Value.* Usually, the lower the unit value of a product, the longer the channels of distribution. Fur coats (with high unit value) can be sold directly from the manufacturer to the department store whereas small items, such as housewares (with low unit value) may have to go through a wholesaler before reaching the retailer. This is one reason why industrial installations are sold direct, while small accessory equipment items usually go through industrial distributors or agents.

The Nature of the Market. The nature of the market is probably the most important factor influencing the choice of channels of distribution, because the choice really depends upon the number and types of ultimate customers who comprise the market.

(a) *Consumer or industrial market.* The first question to consider is whether the product is intended for consumer or industrial market. If it is going to the industrial market, retailers will not be included in the channel. If it is going to both markes, the company will want to use more than one channel.

(b) *Number of potential customers.* A large potential market is likely to necessitate the use of middlemen. If the market is relatively small, the company may be able to use its own sales force to sell direct. If the products are to be sold to many different industries and to many firms in each industry, the manufacturer will make extensive use of middlemen.

(c) *Geographic concentration of market.* Where the buyers are concentrated in a few geographic areas, direct sale is more feasible than if the market were spread over the entire nation. In densely populated markets, a seller may establish sales depots or branches, but he will use middlemen in markets where the numbers of potential customers are less heavily concentrated.

(d) *Size of Order.* The volume of sales which may be made to individual firms will influence the channels used to reach these companies. A food products manufacturer will sell directly to large grocery stores because the total volume of business makes his channel economically desirable. To reach small grocery stores, he will have to use wholesalers who will buy in large quantities.

(e) *Customer buying habits.* The buying habits of ultimate consumers and industrial users, the amount of effort the consumer is willing to expend, the desire for credit, and the desire for the services of a personal salesman significantly affect channel policies.

Number and types of middlemen. Middlemen are particularly important because so often middlemen control the channel for a given producer's product.

(a) *Service provided by middlemen.* A producer should select middlemen who will provide the marketing services he himself either is unable to provide or cannot economically perform. If a product needs aggressive promotion to enter a new market, manufacturers' agent can usually provide the service better than a wholesaler. If a product requires special storage facilities, a wholesaler may provide these facilities best. If a producer is financially weak, he must seek middlemen who can remedy this deficiency.

(b) *Availability of desired middlemen.* The marketing manager should recognise that the middlemen he desires may not be available. They may be carrying competitive products and may not wish to add another line. One maker of industrial machinery who could not secure desirable distributors in a metropolitan market opened a sales depot in that city. It proved so successful that eventually he opened branches or depots in several other markets and discontinued his use of industrial distributors in those cities.

(c) *Attitude of middlemen towards manufacturer's policies.* It may sometimes happen that the marketing policies of the manufacturer are not acceptable to certain types of middlemen. For example, the producer's unwillingness to guarantee the product against a price decline will eliminate many middlemen from consideration. Some wholesalers and retailers are willing to carry goods if they get sole agency for a particular territory.

(d) *Sales volume possibilities.* A point for careful study is the determination of which channel offers opportunities for maximum sales volume. All other factors being equal, a producer will select a channel offering the greatest potential volume over the long run.

(e) *Cost requirements.* The cost of selling through alternative channels will influence choice. If the expenses are in consonance with services performed by the middleman, he would be chosen.

Competition. The nature and extent of competition in an industry may have an important bearing on marketing channels. When several manufacturers offer very similar products to the same markets, it is natural that all of them should seek to employ essentially the same channels. Where competitive products are stocked by retailers it is profitable to have your products also carried by them.

Legal constraints. The channels for some products are affected by governmental regulations, such as inspection requirements, special taxes, or restrictions on markets where the product can be sold. Durgs and alcoholic beverages are examples of products subject to these limitations. A distiller has to market through prescribed outlets, such as licensed liquor stores.

Nature and size of the company. Size of the company has great influence on the selection of channel. Given comparable market and product considerations, a large firm is more apt to have shorter channels than is a small enterprise.

(a) *Reputation.* Well-known companies with good reputations are in a better position to acquire channels and middlemen of their choice than are unknown businesses.

(b) *Financial resources.* A firm's reputation can affect its channels. A financially strong company needs middlemen less than one which is financially weak. A business with adequate finances can establish its own sales force and even branch organisation. It can also grant credit or warehouse its own products, whereas a weak firm would have to use middlemen to obtain these services.

(c) *Experience and ability of management.* Channel decisions are affected by the marketing experience and ability of the management. Many companies lacking marketing know-how prefer to turn the job over to middlemen.

(d) *Desire for control of channel.* A manufacturer may establish as short a channel as possible simply because he wants to control the distribution of his product, even though the cost of the more direct channel is higher. He may feel that he can give his product more aggressive promotion by controlling the channel. Moving closer to the final customer affords the manufacturer a greater opportunity to gather current market information.

(e) *Services provided by seller.* Often a producer's channel decision is influenced by the quantity and quality of marketing services he can provide in relation to those demanded by the middlemen. Frequently, manufacturers can sell their products to retail chains only if the goods are presold through heavy advertising. Other middlemen may demand that the manufacturer build in-store displays or send missionary salesmen to call on retailers and industrial users.

WHOLESALER

There is a considerable disagreement as to what can be included in wholesaling. The broad usage includes in wholesaling all sales transactions and incidental activity where the buyer is to resell the goods or use them in the conduct of his business rather than in ultimate consumption. The narrow usage defines wholesaling as the function performed by wholesalers, namely, the merchant middlemen, excluding the work of agent middle-men. A wholesaler may, however, be defined as a trader who purchases goods in large quantities from producers and growers and resells them to retailers in small lots, and thus acts as a link between the producer or the grower and the retailer. The wholesaler's place in the stream of production and distribution lies between the maker of goods or the grower of produce on the one hand and the retailer from whom the goods pass on to the user or consumer on the other hand.

Functions of Wholesaler. From the foregoing it is clear that the wholesaler performs useful services to the manufacturer the retailer and the consumer. The wholesaler renders to the manufacturer a four-fold service: (a) economy of mass production; (b) making up big orders; (c) relieving the manufacturer from holding stock; (d) permitting manufacturer to specialise. Manufacturers cannot produce small quantities of goods cheaply, and mass production is the most economical method, as in this processes are standardised, the planning part of the operations is done once for all. This is made possible, as the wholesaler is willing to buy in larger quantities. The wholesaler helps the manufacturer by placing large orders for each kind of goods to be made. In supplying numerous retail dealers over a wide area, he has a big outlet for his wares. Further, he interprets and stimulates the desires of his customers. He helps the manufacturer in getting market. He forecasts and thus helps the manufacturer in determining the quantity and quality to be produced. In the absence of the wholesaler, the manufacturer will have to seek orders from the retailer, which will entail great trouble and expense, and distribution will involve large transport charges. Moreover, the wholesaler maintains warehouse to store goods. He acts as an importer and exporter, and helps to keep prices steady, as he buys when prices are low and sell from his warehouse when prices again rise. Goods in general demand have to be produced before they are wanted for use. The supply must be ready when the demand occurs, as the buyers cannot wait. This means that somewhere large stocks must be held ready. The shopkeeper can afford to hold very little stock, just sufficient to meet short-period demands. It is the wholesale warehouse-man who takes upon himself to hold this second line reserve of stock and keep it continuously replenished. Thus he relieves the manufacturer from holding constantly stock of finished goods, and thus helps him to concentrate on his own particular share of the work of supply with much less capital than would be required if he had to hold large stocks to meet the day-to-day demand. In general, the manufacturer is able to collect orders in bigger bulk from the wholesaler and in less variety of types than he would if the orders came from the retailers direct. The wholesaler sorts out in advance into big orders the small and varied requirements of the retail shops. Such an arrangement enables the manufacturer to specialise in the kinds of goods he can produce best. This method permits the wholesaler, on his part, to select for each order a manufacturer who has executed that kind of order most satisfactorily in the past.

The wholesaler helps the retailer (a) by holding a varied stock; (b)

by offering a ready supply; (c) by allowing a period of credit; (d) by offering expert advice. To the retail shopkeeper it is a convenience to be able to find in the warehouse of the wholesaler many kinds of goods and many varieties of each kind drawn from many makers. The demands of public are very varied, the retailer needs a very varied supply, if he is to serve more than a narrow section only of these demands. The retailer cannot get in small lots of goods from a large number of manufacturers, and he must turn to the wholesaler. The wholesaler saves the retailer from storage expense and also from the risk of carrying large quantities. He helps to keep prices steady. A retailer with only small capital cannot successfully load his stocks with large quantities, each of one kind. The capital put into such stocks would lie idle too long waiting for each kind to sell out. The policy of the successful retailer is to turn his stocks over quickly, to hold at one time so much only of one kind of goods as will serve to meet his customers' wants for a short period, and to renew without delay any class of goods, that he finds running out. The wholesale warehouse, with a ready supply of many kinds of goods, held at the retailer's instant disposal, gives the retailer the means of renewing his stocks as often and as quickly as his trade allows. The manufacturer may not be willing to allow credit to the retailer, or even may not be in a position to do so. The wholesaler is ready to allow a fairly good credit to the retailer. Obviously, a shopkeeper, who sells on cash and buys on three or four months' credit terms, is given the opportunity of converting his purchases into cash before he is called upon to pay. This means that his wholesaler helps him to the extent of finding him, year in and year out, the capital he needs to carry three months' stock. Furthermore, being a specialist he can give valuable assistance to the retailer. By watching the market he can advise the retailer as to what goods can sell best and in what quantities it would be best to buy and when.

The Wholesalers' Organisation. The wholesaler merchants buy goods in large quantities, and they necessarily run their undertakings on large scales. A wholesale warehouse resembles in many respects a big departmental store, the business being divided into different departments, each of which forms a separate unit under the charge of departmental manager. The departments fall into two divisions, namely, Administrative and Executive. The administrative staff is concerned with such duties as finance and accounts, correspondence, records, filing and general administration. The number and extent of the executive departments vary with the size and type of business, but generally they include the Selling Departments, the managers of which are also the buyers, the Publicity Department, the Warehouse, where the goods are stored, the Despatch Department, which includes also the Invoice Department and the Packing Sections. As the wholesale merchant deals almost exclusively with a retail trade, the question of premises is not very important. The main consideration is that they should be reasonably accessible to trade customers, and conveniently situated for the delivery and despatch of the goods stocked by the wholesaler. The large wholesale concerns generally concentrate their business in the business centres of the large cities and port towns.

The amount of capital required by the wholesaler is usually much greater than that required by the retailer. This is so because (1) a good deal of capital is tied up in the stock which a wholesaler is bound to carry; (2) sometimes the producers whose goods the wholesaler stocks are men of small means, and not infrequently the wholesaler has to advance them sums of money to enable them to carry on their work; (3) the wholesaler, as a rule, has to give the retailer long credit, while he himself has to pay soon after delivery for the stock he obtains. The amount of capital will depend partly upon the size of his stock and partly upon the amount of credit granted to retailers on the one hand and producers on the other. We should, therefore, expect to find a marked difference in the amounts of trading capital employed by different kinds of wholesalers. For example, a wholesale draper would be expected to have more capital locked in credit than a wholesale tobacconist.

RETAIL TRADE

The retailer is the last link in the economic chain whereby our wants are catered for smoothly and efficiently. It is his duty to study the requirements of the consumer and accordingly inform the wholesaler. The position of the retailer in the field of distribution is important and strategic. From the point of view of the manufacturer, he is a specialist in selling, and from the point of view of the consumer, he is a purchasing and supply agent. The retailer, by assembling at convenient places, from numerous sources, various types of products, which consumers demand, enables the consumer to purchase a variety of goods in small quantities, on short notice, and with a minimum trouble. He saves the manufacturer from the upkeep of stores for retaining goods. He normally performs all the marketing functions, namely, buying, selling, transporting, storing, grading, financing and risk-taking. The functions of retailer are that he sells goods in small quantities; holds stocks of goods at convenient centres; displays the goods; studies the tastes and habits of consumers and endeavours to satisfy them; meets the daily demands for necessaries; procures goods to suit individual requirements; supplies local needs of the district and the special needs of different classes and individuals; and often grants credit to consumers.

The Art of Buying and Selling. The success of a retail trader depends primarily on the number of customers he can attract and the quantity of goods he can sell at a profit. But the true basis of retail business is not only good selling but good buying. To sell successfully he should meet the demands of the customers as exactly as possible, in quantity, quality and price. This requires knowledge of the customers and the source of supply. He must constantly exercise judgment as to what to buy and from whom to buy and when to buy and what price to pay. He must also be able to forecast changes in fashion and taste. Since the buyer for a retail business has to depend upon his own judgment, he must have complete knowledge of the sources of supply and the general market conditions. In addition, he must be able to deal with a large number of salesmen who wish to persuade him to buy "novelty" lines which may be failures, but on the other hand, may, if rejected, be great success in the hands of some rival. Assuming that he has performed his buying functions successfully, it is evident that his ultimate success depends on his ability to sell. He comes into direct contact with the consumer and can exercise great influence on the demand for goods and services. He should be able to attract prospective purchasers and then induce them to buy his goods. He should be able to interest people in his goods before he can strike a bargain. His methods of advertising, window display, adequate service and arrangement in an attractive manner of his store will go a long way to make his business a success.

The size and nature of the business will determine the amount of the capital to be invested. If the shop is to be conducted on a cash basis, less capital will be needed than would be required to finance a similar business on credit lines. All the same the retailer must find sufficient cash to carry adequate stocks of goods, although he may be able to obtain trade credit from his wholesale suppliers. The retailer's capital consists of his stock, premises, furniture and fittings, cash in his till and in the bank and credit allowed to him by suppliers. Many a time a retail firm may be conducted on borrowed capital but since this means that the trader, in fixing his prices, has to make provision for payment of interest, it cannot be considered a thoroughly sound mode of finance. The questions of locality and position are vital to a retail house. The locality must be suited to the nature of the proposed business.

Profits and Selling Price. The profit gained by a retailer must be sufficient to remunerate him for his capital and labour, and his selling prices must be fixed at a figure which will bring in a reasonable rate of profit, regard being had at the same time to the prices charged by competitors. Selling prices are fixed on a different basis in each trade. Where the turnover is rapid, as in the case of perishable goods, the selling price will be lower in comparison with cost price than in a business such as a jeweller's or furnisher's where the turnover is slow The trader must also consider from time to time whether he would benefit by lowering his selling price a little, thereby making a smaller profit on each article, but increasing total profits by reason of larger turnover induced by lower prices. In other cases, it may be more profitable to fix the selling price at a higher level and be content with smaller turnover, but this can succeed only where no suitable substitute is being marketed at a lower price. The majority of the goods sold retail are disposed of at standard prices, fixed very often by the manufacturer, and where this is the case there is no reason why the retailer should not mark the selling prices distinctly on the goods so that the customers may be able to see at a glance what they are required to pay. Usually the price is marked so that it may be easily removed or obliterated, for buyers would not like the prices of their possessions published to the world at large, while articles commonly sold for gifts or presents would never sell if prices were marked on them indelibly. Consequently, the prices on such articles are usually marked in cyphers. Various methods are followed in cypher devices. They are frequently made up of numerals or alphabets. Whatever the method, cyphers must be concise, legible and unmistakable so that they can be distinguished immediately by any of a number of assistants. Apart from the question of secrecy, the cypher system is often used in connection with goods whose price is elastic.

Kinds of Retail Houses. Like any other business, retailing of goods may be done either on small scale or on a large scale. In our country retailing is mostly done on small scale, while in countries like the U.S.A. and England, there has been a tendency in recent years towards large-scale retailing, although small retailers still remain dominant even in those countries. Small-scale retailing may consist of (1) peddlers, (2) stall-holders, (3) independent or unit retail shops. Large-scale retailing is done by (i) Multiple Shops, (ii) Chain Stores, (iii) Departmental Stores, (iv) Fixed Price Chain Stores, (v) Mail Order Houses, (vi) Consumers' Cooperative Stores, (vii) the Combination Stores or "Supermarket", (viii) direct selling by the manufacturer.

Independent Retail Shop. It has often been said and remains true that retailing is, from the point of view of the total number of shops, the province of the small man. Small independent retail stores are the oldest and remain the most common type of retail units. Such a unit is independently owned by an individual, a partnership, or a joint Hindu family. It is generally run by the moderate capital of the individual and is managed by family members. These stores are sometimes located in residential quarters. The stocks are limited because of the limited capital and also because of the limited number of customers. Being able to come into direct touch with his customers the individual retailer is more easily able to study the habits of his customers and so supply their day-to-day needs. He is in a position to give personal and detailed attention to the wants of his customers, which the large-scale stores are unable to do. A small store may be Single Line Store, specialising in one line, e.g., jewellery, paints, stationery; or it may be a General Store, carrying a wide variety of merchandise, e.g., groceries, drugs, hardware, dry goods, without having any departmental organisation; or it may be Intensive General Store selling almost everything. The last type is generally found in villages in India.

Large-scale Retailing. In recent years the retail units have tended to expand. If the development goes on with the same rapidity, it is quite likely that they may outnumber the small retailers. As the manufacturing concerns develop into large units by means of integration, so do the retail houses. The various methods of integration, namely, horizontal, vertical, lateral and diagonal, have been used for expansion in this line. The horizontal integration takes place where a concern buys its stock in bulk ready for sale and does not, as a rule, manufacture the goods or deal in any way with raw materials. Two or more shops may get together and form themselves into a single large unit by merger or any other method of consolidation. The vertical development occurs when a concern not only distributes its goods to the consumers but also manufactures goods, and possibly controls raw material sources. For example, Liptons own plantations, prepare tea ready for sale and finally distribute it. In India, Batas own tanneries, make shoes and distribute them through a chain of stores. The multiple shop system is the best example of vertical integration. The lateral development takes place where a store deals in allied goods in order to render complementary services to the customers. The best example of this kind of integration are drug stores. It may happen that a drug store with patent medicines is started to begin with, which may also take up dispensing medicines. This line may be supplemented with toilet goods, cosmetics, and patent foods, etc. The diagonal integration takes place where with the sale of the articles other facilities are provided by the retailer, such as free delivery, information bureau, writing and reading rooms, repairs, banking facilities, resting rooms, etc. Diagonal integration is most common in departmental stores.

Multiple Shop. The multiple shop method of retail trading is of quite recent growth. A multiple shop consists of a number of similar shops owned by a single business firm. Thus, it is essentially a horizontal combination of like selling units specialising in one or two definite kinds of merchandise. Every multiple shop business has a head office from which the branches are controlled. The head office is the nucleus of the business around which the branches are grouped. From the head office there pass out instructions and less definite influences that unify the branches into one organisation, with the same policy and the practice followed in all its shops. The head office is usually also the supply depot from which goods are despatched to branches as required. Where the branches are very widely spread, district supply depots may be set up. The head office may be situated at the factory, where all the goods that the branches sell are made. This kind of multiple shop is called the Manufacturer's Retail Store. The Batas are the best example of this type in India. It may be only a central office from which supplies are ordered up from outside manufacturers to be delivered direct to local depots or to the branches themselves. This kind is called Middlemen Multiple Shop. Again, the head office may be a warehouse that collects and distributes the supplies. Or again, part of the goods for the branches may be manufactured at the head office, the remainder being bought outside.

Where the branches are spread over distant areas, an efficient system of branch inspection must be kept in operation, each inspector having a district with a number of branches to look after. He will supervise the condition of the shops, the window displays, the stocks and the services, and will deal with irregularities and difficulties that crop up. His visits to the shops should be timed irregularly so that branch managers will never know when to expect him. Occasionally, the inspector will count the cash in hand to see that it is intact, and once in a while he will superintend a stock-taking of each branch. Where the branches are not widespread and therefore no inspectors are needed, the branch manager in charge of his branch is required to submit reports daily or weekly to the head office. The internal organisation of a branch is the responsibility of the branch manager, but the general policy for all the branches is framed by the head office. With regard to locality, a multiple shop can open a branch in any fairly populous place or district, and in this respect it enjoys a clear advantage over a department store. Locality is not of any great importance as long as customers are readily available. Cash sales or ready money is the rule with customers. The cash taken each day is banked at a local bank by the manager of the shop and the account is sent to the head office along with the daily report and the requisitions for any supplies that may be required.

Advantages. The multiple shop system enjoys all the advantages which normally accrue to a large-scale enterprise, namely, economies of buying in large quantities, centralised and highly efficient control, and the expert advertising of firm's special lines. In addition to these there are the following advantages peculiar to the multiple shop: (1) Shortage of stock at any branch can be made up by transfer from one branch to another. (2) A speedy turnover of stock is attained and can be accentuated by studying sales figures to discover which goods have a large sale and which are slow sellers; and then concentrating advertising effort on the slow sellers only. (3) As a result of speedy turnover, multiple shops are able to run their business at a slightly lower cost than the other types. (4) As sales are made on cash basis there are no bad debts and no expenses of maintaining a large clerical staff. (5) The multiple shop benefits also from the fact that its numerous branches can cater easily and efficiently for customers at a comparatively short distance from their homes. The total number of its customers is larger than of single store or departmental store. (6) Each branch of the firm is in itself an advertisement for the other branches, and so long as the goods sold are of good quality in relation to the price, there is no limit to the number of branches that an efficient concern may control.

Limitations. Multiple shops suffer from two important limitations: They have heavy expenses to meet. Much of the difference between their buying and selling prices is absorbed by high rents on big premises in busy streets, with rates proportionately high and by provisions for writing off the initial cost of new shop fronts and new equipment and by the maintenance of poorly paying branches in places where the trade to be done is not enough for all the shops. Secondly, many managers and staff, without constant supervision, do not evince the same interest in their duties as the proprietors would do.

Chain Stores. A chain store is one of a group of retail stores of essentially the same type centrally owned and with some degree of uniformity of operation. It represents centralised buying combined with decentralised selling: one firm owns and operates on very similar lines a number of retail shops combining the economies of large-scale ordering and standardised methods, with a wide distribution of retail outlets. A chain store may be "variety" store, dealing in a wide range of goods, or those specialising in a restricted range of goods, like the multiple store. The third variety is the Fixed Price Chain Store. The chain store, like the independent store, depends for its success upon the adherence to fundamental retailing principles, namely (a) scientific training of the entire personnel, (b) intelligent buying, (c) rapid turnover, (d) favourable location, (e) knowledge of the merchandise needs of the community, (f) a satisfactory and well-trained store personnel, and (g) elimination of all unnecessary operating expenses. The chain store system is of economic value to the community to the extent that it provides better values, assures sound credit, seeks to serve an ever-widening trade area for the national type of merchandise that it needs, and educates and trains its working personnel in community service and in the best methods of merchandising procedure.

The chief *advantage* of the chain store is that the *central* management has the authority to insist that all units adopt and adhere to enlightened policies and efficient and standardised methods of operation. The second advantage is in buying. Markets may be thoroughly covered before purchases and quantity orders are placed. This method results in the obtaining of the lowest price. Thirdly, the chain store policy of selling is to specialise in goods most in demand and to eliminate slow selling lines. The system has its *limitations.* The first of these is its inflexibility in adjusting each unit to local conditions. It is difficult to obtain first class store managers and keep expenses down at the same time. The advantages of centralisation are almost incompatible with those of freedom of managers to adjust merchandise and service to varying shades of demand.

Fixed Price Chain Stores. The fixed price or one price-chain stores or multiple departmental stores appear to have reached the highest point in the U.S.A. It is still developing in England, but we have nothing of this kind in our country. Woolworths' "3d. and 6d. Stores" in England and "5 cent and 10 cent Stores" in America are the best examples. Before the War every branch of Woolworths had printed in large letters over the shop front, the price limit of 6d. and in America, customers still speak of the "Five and Ten." During the War, as prices rose and the universal scarcity of consumables increased, the price limit for a single article was raised to a maximum of two shillings and six pence. The fixed price has great attractions for the shopper. He knows that nothing in Woolworths will cost him more than two shillings and six pence and nothing in Marks and Spencers will cost him more than ten shillings. He avoids the embarrassment of being confronted with merchandise which he cannot afford to buy. He knows where he is. The principle followed in such stores is that of mass production applied to distribution. The goods are standardised to enable economies to be made by buying on a large scale at prices which cannot otherwise be obtained. The prices are fixed at levels which produce the maximum demand and the articles sold are always those which are readily acceptable to all kinds of customers, but more particularly to people with small and medium incomes. The organisation is very simple. Severe simplicity in layout and decoration is observed. Being run on an open store system, it calls for practically no salesmanship on the part of the assistants. Cash payment, no free delivery, no advertising, and large variety of goods at very low price make it possible to run the store very cheaply and make high profits in the aggregate.

Department Stores. Like the chain store types, a departmental or department store achieves the economies of large-scale distribution notably those of centralised purchase. But whereas the chain store extends its field of operations over a number of shopping districts, the department store sells a wide variety of merchandise under one roof. A departmental or department store may thus be described as a large retail establishment having in the same building a number of departments each of which confines its activities to one particular kind of trade, and forms a complete unit in itself and is centrally controlled. A retail business of this description may be looked upon as a number of single shops under one roof and one management. Each department normally has a "buyer" at the head who is responsible both for the buying for his department and for its selling policy. Each department operates as a separate unit with regard to purchases, merchandise control, selling activities and in the determination of profit and loss. This arrangement, however, fails to make the most of the possible economies of centralised purchase, and while it provides a certain discipline insofar as the man who buys the goods for his department is also responsible for selling them, it is contrary to the fullest application of the principle of the division of labour. To get over this weakness of the general policy, some stores now employ single buyers who control the buying of merchandise for all its departments.

The department store is based on the principle that it is easier to sell more goods to the same customer by providing a wide range of merchandise both with regard to type and price-range, than to find more customers in a given locality to purchase the same kind of merchandise. Originally, department stores were started to cater for the better class of customers who require commodities of good quality and who look for service and facilities which small retailers cannot supply. In the inter-war-period, department stores felt the competition of the chain stores very keenly, and in order to increase their turnover they extended their services to meet the needs of the people with lower incomes, so that now a large department store will be found to sell nearly everything. In Western countries such stores are increasing in number and size. To take one example, Selfridges in London have over 300 different departments in one building. In India we have no large department stores but the Army and Navy Stores, and (now no more) Whiteways and Laidlaw may be quoted as examples of small size stores. Since a department store depends on attracting customers from all quarters of the town, it must occupy a central position. The premises are of extensive description, luxuriously appointed, and provided with every conceivable comfort, including writing rooms, resting rooms, information bureaus, etc. The department store development is a very good example of horizontal, lateral and diagonal integration. It is usually constituted as a limited company, the control resting in the Board of Dirctors. The Managing Director, if any, or the General Manager is in supreme charge of the concern, and under him are the managers. In a store with a large number of departments there may be section managers immediately below the Managing Director or the General Manager. A section manager is in charge of a section which is a division of the business comprising several allied departments, e.g., merchandise section, hardware section, staff manager. It is the duty of the section manager to correlate the activities of the various departments in his section, and he is directly responsible to the Managing Director or General Manager for this part of the work. The section managers form a Board of Management with a Managing Director or General Manager as its Chairman. They meet about once a week when broad questions of management are discussed, and important decisions taken as to the conduct of the business as a whole.

A section is divided into various departments each of which is under the charge of a manager. In the selling department he is called a buyer and in the non-selling department he is described as a departmental manager or staff manager. Each buyer has under him a certain number of salesmen or shop assistants. It is his duty to see that these assistants are efficient and courteous to customers. He is also in charge of expert window dressing. He occupies a position of the greatest importance in the store, and it is largely upon his skill and discretion in buying that the prosperity of the store must ultimately turn. Salesmanship in the great stores has been reduced to a fine art. The departmental manager is solely responsible for his department for earning good profits. Most of the goods sold by departmental stores are paid for at the time of the purchase, cash sales being the general practice. In some stores, however, credit is allowed to approved customers on a monthly or other periodic account. Most of the large departmental stores now sell goods on the Instalment Plan, whereby a customer takes immediate possession of the goods and pays for them over a period by periodical payments or instalments. Broadly speaking, there are two forms of payment by instalments : (1) hire purchase, and (2) deferred payment. These will be discussed in a later section.

Advantages and Disadvantages. The department store is perhaps the most notable development in large-scale retail enterprise and is subject to all the merits and defects of any large-scale organisation but the following apply particularly to it; The chief advantage is convenience in shopping. It is pre-eminently the shopping store. Many lines are found under one roof and the shopper can complete his purchases without leaving the store. The possession of a central site gives it certain advantages over other retail houses in less prominent positions, in attracting large number of customers. The variety of goods attract customers, and courtesy and fair treatment are the rule rather than the exception. Service is the motto of this kind of store. Most people pass through more than one department and are therefore induced to make purchases in the same building which they might have made outside or not at all. Each department advertises the other. On the contrary, the elaborate services provided tend to increase overhead expenses, and therefore prices. The position of such concerns, which are away from residential areas, gives an advantage, to the smaller concerns who are more favourably situated "near the market".

Mail Order Business. Mail order business may briefly be described from the buyer's point of view as "shopping by post", and it appeals to the public largely on the score of "convenience". The customer is enabled, as it were, to make his purchases at his own "fireside", and is thus saved the trouble of a journey to the retailer. A mail-order house is that type of retail institution which solicits patronage by means of catalogues sent through the mail and containing detailed description of merchandise offered for sale, and supplemented by general publicity. Orders for such merchandise are filled by mail, express, or goods train. There is no personal contact between the seller and the buyer, and all transactions are consummated through the mails. A "mail-order", "post-order", "letter-order", or "country-order" section is attached to most of the big departmental stores. There are in existence businesses which do nothing else but post-order trade, working from warehouses or factories without providing shop windows or counters for personal trade.

There are three types of mail-order houses : (1) The Manufacturing Type, where the makers and manufacturers sell their products direct to the public without the intervention of middle-men. (2) The Departmental Type, which are run by large departmental stores and supply goods by mail in addition to selling in the departmental store. (3) The Middle-Man Type, i.e., a business concerned only with mail order selling where goods are brought from manufacturers in the required quantities and stored pending the receipt of orders by post from the public. He may also buy on receipt of orders. This type is the true mail-order business.

The orders are obtained by a mail-order house by means of publicity in the form of advertisements in newspapers or periodicals, or by sending out price lists and catalogues, or by submitting patterns and samples to prospective buyers. The follow-up system is extensively used; as advertising and publicity are the main anchors to fall back upon. It is a common practice to "key" advertisements by a number or a letter introduced into the address. The readers of advertisements are asked to write to say "Department A-35". Then, the answers received can be counted and divided into the price of the advertisement, so that the cost of each answer is obtained. A more accurate method is to advertise an article in one medium only, and to note against the cost of the advertising how many of the articles are sold. The organisation of this type of business has its own peculiarities. Where the business is solely concerned with mail orders, buying is comparatively simple, for goods are ordered according to a pre-arranged plan. Thus, in winter an extensive campaign for the sale of blankets may be initiated in which case a quantity of blankets will be ordered from the manufacturers and stored pending the receipt of orders. In some cases the goods will be "parcelled" in varying quantities so that when orders are received it is necessary only to affix the address of the buyer. The organisation is very much simpler than that of other types of retail stores. There is no need to have a big shop or a store; no shop assistants are necessary, just a few clerks and packers can carry on the work.

The payments are received either in the form of remittances along with the orders, or by getting some advance and the balance on delivery of the goods. The V.P.P. method or receiving payment through the bank is also resorted to. In the case of some approved customers goods are supplied in advance of payment. Credits are generally not allowed. It is to be remembered that all goods are not suitable for this type of business. Generally speaking, for the success of mail-order business the following conditions are necessary, namely, the goods must satisfy a well-defined need, i.e., it must not be necessary to "educate" the people in their use; they must lend themselves to pictorial representation and forceful descriptive writing, there must be a wide margin of gross profit. It may be stated as a maxim that branded goods lend themselves most adequately to this method of sale.

Advantages. (1) Salesmen's salaries and expensive shop fronts, etc., are eliminated, although against this must be set higher office costs, especially follow-up expenses. (2) The sale department is in direct touch with the buyer, and therefore it is generally possible to know the demands of the customers more easily. (3) Advertising can be more effectively carried out, since the results can be checked with fair accuracy. (4) The actual selling is reduced to routine, the work being performed by low grade and hence cheap labour. (5) The sales appeal can be designed by experts and is not dependent upon the capacity of individual salesman. (6) The customer buys sitting in his home, and, therefore, saves himself a journey to the retailer.

Limitations. (1) The small retailer is still able to compete with the mail-order house in most lines as he has "convenience appeal" in his varied stock. (2) All retail shops have the advantage of enabling the customer to see and examine goods which definitely lacks in this type of business. (3) The expenses of advertising tend to increase the cost to the consumer as compared with shops, retailers, even slightly higher than the departmental stores. (4) The advertisement of mail order houses often gives false idea of the quality of goods offered. The wording is usually made attractive and may in many cases be even misleading. (5) The sales appeal is stereotyped and cannot easily be altered. (6) It is not easy to find causes of failure to effect sales or get orders.

Combination Store or Super-Market. The competition between different types of retailing units gave rise in America during the inter-war period to a new type of retail trading unit, the "Combination Store" or "Super-market", trading typically in groceries and meats. In 1929 the super-market accounted for 36% of the total food business and by 1929 for as much as 54%. It is typically a large cash-and-carry food store with a turnover of more than $100,000 per annum. The main feature is the exercise of individual selection without sales assistants; the customer goes into the shop through a grill and he is free to select his own merchandise from open shelves (except where cutting is required) entirely without the service of sales people. Conveyances on wheels are available to the customer on which he can place his purchases as he buys them. Finally when he has completed his purchases, he detaches the tray upon which he has placed his accumulated purchases, puts it on a counter by the next grill, whereupon the total expenditure is computed by a clerk and payment is made in cash. If services are made available an extra charge is usually made for them. These stores are of great advantage to both the sellers and the buyers. Paying cash, the customer saves credit charges. Waiting on himself and taking his purchases home, the customer saves clerk and delivery expenses. Buying in large quantities, the customer shares the super-market's savings from big volume purchase. In this way there is easily a saving of at least 10 per cent in the cost of goods. And price is not the only attraction. The customer likes the store's astounding variety. As compared with a big department store, which may carry 600 to 1,000 items, super-markets run well over 2,000; and really an outsize specimen may carry 10,000. What is more, the customer likes the absence of sales pressure, the feeling that he can take as long as he pleases in making his selection. The success of the super-market has prompted quite a number of departmental stores to resort to such devices. Recently food wholesalers have joined the super-market.

Direct or House-to-House Selling. Direct Selling by canvassers, or house-to house salesmen, is the oldest type of retailing. Today direct selling of this type is significant. House-to-house canvassers seem to thrive best in periods of early recovery after a depression. This is probably due to the fact that when incomes are first augmented, customers respond to the salesman who calls on them even before they renew their former habits of shopping at stores. Direct selling methods are not economical. From the angle of delivery, merchandise sold from a store can be delivered with much less expense than that sold by direct selling methods. An article of equal quality, if sold rightly, can be sold at less expense over the counter than by house-to-house canvassing. This method is probably the most difficult type of retail salesmanship. A special sales technique is needed not only securing interview but also in displaying the merchandise and in closing the sale. At best the fertile fields for house-to-house canvassing are the medium-sized and small towns. It is difficult to built up a permanent clientele.

INSTALMENT SELLING

In recent years large stores have taken to selling goods on instalment basis. An instalment plan may take the form either of hire-purchase or deferred payment. In hire-purchase system, the customer takes possession of the goods at once and agrees to pay a certain sum at stated intervals. The ownership still vests in the seller, who, if the customer fails to pay any instalment, can retake possession of the whole of the goods, as well as keep by way of forfeit the instalments already paid. In law, the periodical payments are treated as hire charges, and if the payments are made regularly, the hirer gets the option of purchasing the goods on making the full payment. Until this option is exercised, the hirer may return the goods hired. The essence of hire-purchase agreement is that there is no agreement to buy, but only an option is given to the hirer to buy under certain conditions, i.e., on payment of the full price. The hire-purchase system has been modified by enterprising retailers who, in order to offer further inducement to purchasers, allow payment after a time on their making the first deposit of a certain sum. Goods become the property of the buyer when he takes possession. The seller may take away parts of the goods for which instalment is not paid, but the customer keeps that part for which he has paid the instalments. The arrangement can, however, be altered by mutual agreement.

Merits and Demerits of Instalment System. The method of buying by instalment has its advantages, and is economically sound provided that it is not abused. To furnish a home, or even to buy a house, under this system, is distinctly advantageous and tends towards thrift. But the buyer has to pay for the convenience of early possession, and the seller requires a consideration for granting the convenience and for taking the extra risk. The supplier, in this system, does for the individual consumer what the wholesaler does for the retailer with scanty capital at his demand. He makes good to the consumer his present deficiency of funds by supplying the goods on terms that permit of the buyer's saving out of future income the money with which to pay. The seller charges a higher price for the goods, either by marking all prices higher and allowing a discount for cash, or by adding a percentage to the cost prices. In the latter case, the percentage usually varies according to the period over which the instalment payments are spread—the longer the period the greater the percentage. The advantage of the system is that it encourages trade. People with small incomes find it almost impossible to pay cash down for the purchase of expensive articles. Also it sets the buyers to save up for the purpose of payment for what they have got. The period of waiting to have sufficient funds to buy on cash payment would be so long in most cases that they would probably fritter away their money in the meantime. The disadvantage of the system, however, is that it frequently induces a person to purchase more than what he can afford to pay for. It induces him to mortgage his future income to an unhealthy extent. Therefore, moderation should be the keynote of instalment buying.

The system has been criticised on the grounds that it amounts to anticipating future trade, and that depression, when it comes, is accentuated by the existence of a burden of hire-purchase contracts made in good times and relating to goods which may already be worn out. It is probable, however, that the dangers of the system have been over-emphasised. The proportion of bad debts in hire-purchase finance proves to be less than the proportion suffered by bankers. Moreover, mass production needs mass consumption, and one of the surest ways of obtaining this is by an extension of consumer's credit. It has been truly said that it is better business to lend money to a man to purchase goods that have been produced for sale than to lend money for the erection of factories that will turn out goods for which there is doubtful market, and which may prove difficult even impossible, to sell profitably. Whatever the merits or defects of the system, it has come to stay. The real test seems to be the nature of the article to which the system is applied. Where an article is of lasting quality and utility, the system is fairly beneficial. But goods which are of temporary use, or which are consumed before the payments are completed, are not suitable for hire-purchase. From the point of view of the buyer buying on this system articles of necessity is commendable, and those of convenience practicable.

Consumers' Co-operative Stores. The consumers' co-operatives are voluntary organisations controlled by the consumers. They aim at engaging in the production, wholesaling and retailing of consumption goods. It is at the retail level that the co-operatives have had their most spectacular success. For detailed discussion reference should be made to the chapter on "Co-operative Undertakings."

CHAPTER XLII

SALESMANSHIP

Importance of Effective Selling. Production, and more production is the slogan of the day. But supply without demand is of no value; output that cannot be sold profitably is not an asset but a liability; making without selling spells insolvency. The only profit in a business is in sales. Everything else is expense. The need for creating demand for ever-increasing production is a vital one; and without a continuous demand production declines. Of course, the business cycle is subject to other forces than that of the failure or success of selling, but demand creation is an important element. It is immaterial how well the producer of raw materials does his job, or how well the manufacturer produces his articles, or how economically the dealer or retailer can buy them. Unless you can successfully, economically and profitably pass that merchandise over the counter to the consuming public, all that has gone before breaks down. We must face the facts and recognise that "Better Selling is the key to Better Business." This is very important, because so far there has been hardly any selling in our country. Anything that has been produced has just got sold, as a result of the presence of the seller's market. In fact, a generation has grown up which has never had to think of ways and means of making the consumer buy. Now that the seller's market is over, our businessmen must polish up their merchandising and try to learn from others the good lessons instead of just grumbling at the industrial policy of the Government.

Now that we are fast developing our industrial production, we must find an outlet not only in the home market but also in other countries, where we have to compete with those who are far advanced in the art of merchandising. For instance, we can learn much from the U.S.A. in this field, for there they have made a fine art of selling and salesmanship. Their methods are different. They have long discarded "blind selling", which we still practise, and employ creative salesmanship, aggressive sales promotion and adequate advertising to overcome sales resistance. How amazingly successful their methods are, even in conditions very different from those in their own country, can be seen from the marketing of Coca-Cola, and very recently of Pepsi-Cola, in our country. It is fascinating to see how these companies have had the courage to launch products completely new to Indian consumer, and how they have tackled with success the distribution problem in making Coca-Cola available throughout the country by improvising refrigeration facilities so essential for the retailing of this product. Their distribution feat has been probably more remarkable in Egypt, a country which is weak in communications, lacking in suitable retail outlets and lacking in refrigeration facilities. The sizes of our two countries are similar, and we can learn much from their merchandising methods. Henceforth our selling should grow in strength, and then supported by the reconnaissance of market research and barrage of advertising, we should go into the selling battle. Today the great need in our country is sales-minded management engaging and training salesmen who are willing to study and profit by the sales teaching of others.

Meaning of Selling and Salesmanship. What is this Selling ? What is Salesmanship ? Are they something new ? Taking the last question first, it may be stated that selling or salesmanship is not a new art. It has existed throughout the history of civilisation; indeed, it is as old as man himself. When man first began to exchange ideas he began to sell. Selling has been demonstrated in the form of exchanging ideas, products, plans or services. Almost everyone, from the labourer selling his labour to the capitalist selling the use of his money, practises the art of selling in a greater or less degree, and everyone has something to sell to his fellow beings. What is new in selling is the realisation of the truth that successful selling or salesmanship is no longer a hit-or-miss business. It is the art of influencing people, and the knowledge that to influence a man it is necessary to please him.

In a broad sense, the word 'selling' may be regarded as synonymous with the word 'persuading'. But strictly speaking the words do not mean the same thing. Selling in the business world refers to the transfer of ownership of goods or services to a buyer in exchange for money. Salesmanship is the process of persuading a person to buy goods or services. It is in this commercial sense that salesmanship will be treated in this chapter. A superficial observer would conclude from this meaning of salesmanship that the primary function of a salesman is to sell his wares, but this is not true salesmanship. To attempt to sell something that the 'prospect' neither wants nor needs, or a quantity of something in excess of real requirement, is not only ethically wrong but also very poor business. The 'high-pressure' sale or 'over-selling' can be achieved only once. In the long run, it reacts to the detriment of the reputation of the salesman and his firm. Nevertheless, the line between over-selling and legitimate persuasion is a fine one, and whoever keeps on the right side of it wins. To succeed in this task of persuading a prospect to go in for his firm's product, a salesman requires, not only the specialised knowledge of the line he is selling, but also the art of selling—the psychology of salesmanship. From the foregoing emerges a definition which has been stated variously. Salesmanship has been defined as "the art of so presenting and offering that the prospect appreciates the need for it and then mutually satisfactory sale follows". "Salesmanship", says Garfield Blake, "consists of winning the buyer's confidence for the seller's house and goods, thereby winning a regular and permanent customer". It is a method of arriving at a common point of view with the prospect in regard to the desirability of some article, service or idea. Indeed, the act of sales (salesmanship) consists of 'one human mind influencing another human mind.' The definition is fundamental; it shows the act of sale in its grand simplicity. Be it an idea, a religion, typewriter, or a box of chocolates, if the sale has been made, then one human mind has influenced another human mind, by this simple act. Simple ? Yes—if you know how !

It is a well-known maxim that any one to be successful in any walk of life must 'sell' his point of view to those around him and to those with whom he comes in contact. A salesman also sells his point of view; but he starts with the point of view of the prospect and leads his mind to the point where he will accept the salesman's theory. Henry Ford told his salesmen that they were not selling automobiles but transportation. Another executive of a company selling paints and varnishes addressed his salesmen in the following words: "First, it is your business to sell. But what is it you are to sell? Why, you are to sell paints, varnishes, and so on. But these things are merely instruments. The fundamental thing is that you are to sell ideas: ideas of beauty, of health, of economy, of prosperity, of service." Therefore, a salesman must have knowledge of human nature in order to lead the minds of his prospective customers to accept his point of view, his ideas.

Attributes of a Real Salesman. Probably the most essential ingredient for success as a salesman is a capacity for hard work. No matter what the product, this is fundamental. Among the other essentials of character is dependability, both from the point of view of the firm and the customer. The good name of the firm is in the salesman's hands. He is the firm to the customer, and the reliance the customer places on his integrity and dependability are the measures of confidence he will have in his employer, the goods he makes and which the salesman sells. Be loyal to your firm and its executives and to its products by being truthful. Cheerfulness and sympathy are further characteristics which must be developed. An understanding of the real needs of the customers he meets must be developed as a sixth sense. Patience and persistence must be blended into the correct balance, so that the pressure on the potential customer does not turn him away, nor on the other hand, should the order be lost through giving up just as the customer's resistance is weakening. The final qualification, without which no one should consider a career as a salesman, is enthusiasm for his product, for an unsettled life,. and for long hours, and for the people he is going to meet. Then the knowledge of the product, knowledge of the organisation of the firm and knowledge of the prospect with enthusiasm and you have an unbeatable combination. Remember, more races are won, more businesses built, more obstacles overcome by cheerful, energetic enthusiasm than by any other human attributes.

To make your success doubly sure, add the following: *Personality*—the ability to mix easily with one's fellow men, to be able to impress one's own ideas on another person, and do so with charm; *determination*—to go on and on and try again and again in the face of disappointments; *ambition*—the desire to do well, to be better and to do better than your colleagues. But don't try to be the 'personality-plus' type of man, ruthlessly ramming unwanted goods on to intimidated buyers. Remember that each prospect you approach is a human being who is unconsciously striving to preserve a sense of happiness and well-being, and it is your business to act and speak in such a manner as to help the customer to succeed. Be a real salesman—the influencer of human minds. That takes very little time to write, it takes years to learn—but those who have learned it, know its power! Training of the selected person is essential; for contrary to popular belief, salesmen are made, they are not born.

In order to get a purview of a salesman's composite personality, we give a list of the eleven "Characteristics of successful Salesmen" as commonly indicated by psychologists:—

1. Emotional Stability.
2. Self-Sufficiency.
3. Objective-mindedness.
4. Dominance.
5. Self-confidence.
6. Social-mixing qualities.
7. Tact and diplomacy.
8. Sizing up people.
9. Sense of humour.
10. Sales aptitude.
11. Mental ability.

If one were to attempt to give the several desirable qualities of personality and character, one would come by the following:—

Good health, intelligence or capacity to exercise mental faculties fully; open-mindedness; pleasing voice; power to express clearly and accurately; clean habits and dress; cheerfulness; enthusiasm; power to observe; courtesy; honesty; good reputation; sincerity; tactfulness; sociability; thoroughness; good memory; sound reasoning; systematic and orderly habit; loyalty; punctuality; courage; self-confidence; perseverance; adaptability; thrift; tolerance; imagination; ambition; faith.

Training for Salesmanship. There is no 'born' salesman; he is made by an organised and definite training. The so-called 'born' salesman may be born the possessor of some fundamental characteristics which will make it easier for him to become a salesman—but he has to learn salesmanship. Whatever the qualities innate in a man, they must be developed, no matter how well endowed he may be. Knowledge of the goods he is trying to sell can only be acquired by study and concentration. The ideal condition would be for the salesman to work in the factory where the article is produced. He should be there long enough to learn the whole process of production, so that he can answer customer's queries satisfactorily. Inside training will enable him to speak with authority because he will have been steeped in the traditions and atmosphere of the firm. Many firms in the Western countries today pass their salesmen through special selling courses.

Having mastered the basic drill for the sale of the product, the next step in the training should be to see a salesman in action. A period should be spent going the rounds with an experienced colleague, with no other responsibility than to watch and learn from him. Older colleagues will give their best at such times, and countless tips will be passed on by word of mouth, anecdote, and demonstration. How to manipulate the order book, the best method of handling the samples, the right way to approach the buyer, how to treat the General Manager and the shop assistant. It is good thing to make the first attempt with the senior colleague standing by.

Having tried his wings, like a baby bird, under close supervision, one of the best ways of training a salesman is to send him out to take over a ground for a spell, say a fortnight, while the regular man is away on holiday. This will teach him the complexity of the whole job, show him that the planning he has so far taken for granted requires careful thought and work so that the day goes through smoothly. In the very beginning, a novice may make mistakes : but learning from mistakes can be among the best ways of learning the art of salesmanship, providing, of course, that a desire to go on learning exists. The training can be continued by careful observation of the activities not only of the competitors, but also of other firms in quite unrelated groups of products. The study of the advertising messages and techniques being employed by the major industries can give a clue to a live salesman. Customers, too, have much to teach, by direct criticism of the product or the method of its presentation. By carefully noting why a sales approach made one way fails, a slight variation may bring success. But the training of a salesman, whatever his sphere of activity, is never finished. This leads us to consider the different types of salesmen one encounters in the business world.

Types of Salesmen. Dr. William A. Nielander[1] divides salesmen into two principal types: *Creative* and *Service* salesmen. He defines *creative* salesman as one who is seeking to introduce a new product or a new brand into the market and create a demand for it. He is also described as a missionary or a crusader. The *service* salesman is one who sells to those who already want to buy or at least are familiar with the product being sold. The creative salesman creates or expands a business. The service salesman maintains or carries on a business.

Another method of classifying salesmen is on the basis of the goods or services they sell. In general, there are two principal classifications on this basis: *Tangible or Intangible.* The first includes all those who sell products that can be seen or felt or tested. The second includes those who sell things not subject to sensory perception, such as the *pleasure* one derives from entertainment, the *security* that results from a safe investment, or the *profit* that will arise *in the future* from an advertising campaign.

A third method is to classify salesmen on the basis of the type of

1. Quoted by Breen, Thompson and West in *Effective Selling*, p. 30.

customer to whom they sell, such as consumers, retailers, wholesalers, industrial firms and professional men. The task of the salesman does not depend, however, on the type of customer as much as one might at first suppose. In every case he deals with a person and people are similar regardless of profession.

Salesmen are also classified as follows: *(1) Retail salesman or shop assistant* who sells goods over the counter in a retail store. *(2) Wholesaler's salesman* who calls on his customers and must be familiar with a wide range of merchandise. He usually calls upon retail traders. *(3) Manufacturer's representative* who sells a limited line regardless of whether he calls on other manufacturers, wholesalers, retailers, professional men or even consumers. He must know a great deal about the uses and features of the few products he sells. *(4) Direct salesman* is one who sells some speciality product, not regularly purchased by his prospects. He may sell new or unusual types of equipment to manufacturers, transport companies, etc. He may sell office machines to merchants. (5) *A salesman of intangibles* sells service or utility, e.g., Life Assurance. But all these classifications may be grouped into three broad types, based on the difficulty of the selling task, viz., (1) Shop Assistants or Retail Salesmen; (2) Commercial Travellers, who combine the functions of wholesalers' salesmen and manufacturers' representatives; and (3) Speciality or Master Salesmen, who perform the duties of direct salesmen and salesmen of intangibles. Before we deal with these types, it may be reiterated that whatever the class to which a salesman belongs, the one who works hard to improve his methods will be rewarded with greater sales. Therefore, salesmen are also described as follows:

The tired salesman—when he decides to make a call, he does it in a half-hearted way and can hardly find time to talk about his good.

The artificial salesman—who tries to come to 'big stuff', is over-impressive, and forgets to sell.

The ideal salesman—who knows how to handle a man and a sale. He knows how to start a sale and when to close it. He is the influencer of human minds.

Before we deal with the Shop assistants, the Commercial travellers and the speciality salesmen and their methods it is advisable to first consider the buying motives.

Buying Motives. A good salesman should ask himself why a prospect buys, and why ought he to buy his product. Many students of psychology have listed buying motives in different ways. From the point of view of the salesman the most useful arrangement of a list of buying motives is according to the nature of their origin. On this basis they may be *Primary, Selective* or *Patronage*. *Primary* buying motives grow out of the nature of the buyer and they determine what kind of product or service will be bought to satisfy a want. These may be subdivided into Physiological and Social. Thus the Primary Physiological motives may satisfy appetite, thirst, sex, comforts, safety, activity, rest. The Primary Social motives may be devotion, approval, mastery, prize, emulation.

Selective buying motives grow out of the *nature of the product* and determine which of the several varieties or brands will be purchased. These motives are healthfulness, efficiency, economy, dependability, durability, convenience in use, curiosity. *Patronage* motives are those that grow out of the *nature of the seller* and determine from whom the goods or service will be bought. They may be stated as reputation of seller, services offered, convenience of location, personality of salesman. Obviously, no such classification is hard and fast. It is only suggestive.

Another method of classifying buying motives is on the basis of whether they arise from the *emotions* or from *reasoning*. The motives listed under 'primary social' are emotional, while most of those listed under 'selective' are more rational. In general, consumers are motivated by emotional buying motives, while professional buyers prompted by rational motives.

Buying motives may be classified by analysing the acts of the prospect as controlled by his interests and the benefits he hopes to derive from his purchases. An analysis of his motives shows that a prospect is motivated by the following reasons. *First:* he has desire and a desire is an unfulfilled want, seeking satisfaction. *Second:* The prospect has an urge, and the urge stimulates and incites him to buy. *Third:* The prospect has a reason, and the reason is based on definite knowledge of an established need. Man has three interests in life, and on these three interests are based most of his reasons for buying. The first interest is his family. He buys things to aid them and to give them comfort and good living. The second interest is his vocation or business. He buys things to re-sell, things to use in his own operations, or things that help him to be more efficient in his activities. The third interest of a prospect is to satisfy his own personal wants. If we analyse these causes and interests we will discover that they may be influenced by certain advantages and the effects they have on the life of the prospect. The first advantage the prospect desires is happiness or peace of mind. He derives great satisfaction from what he buys. His purchases buoy him up. He feels he is doing something worthwhile. The second advantage that he desires is the gain of health. He places great value on this because it is his greatest and most important asset, and he will buy almost anything if he is convinced that it will improve and safeguard his own health or his family's. The third advantage he desires is a gain of money or wealth.The prospect realises that it is necessary to spend money to earn money. Therefore he will buy those things on which he can make money or those that he can resell and make a profit. For the sake of simplicity, however, all these motives, reasons, interests and advantages may be reduced to the following seven reasons or motives or buying:—

1. Gain of money;
2. Satisfaction of caution;
3. Utility value;
4. Satisfaction of pride;
5. Sentiment;

6. Satisfaction of pleasure;
7. Benefit to health.

Now analyse closely the product you are selling and you will discover the reasons why the prospect will benefit by buying from you. You can then take each step in turn, going through the buying reasons and the analysed points of your product, and evolving a selling sentence to deal with each step. By analysing an average sale, we can discover the buying and selling steps. The manner of application, however, is slightly different in selling over the counter and by approaching prospective buyers. We shall, therefore, consider the different steps to be followed byshop assistants and commercial travellers and specially salesmen separately.

Retail Seller or Shop Assistant. Selling at the retail level in our country is done mainly by proprietors with the help of the members of their families, although in a few cases paid shop assistants are also employed. It is generally contended that the work of a person who sells goods in a retail store is the easiest. The customer who comes to the store has alreadv decided to buy a certain article. Courtesy and quick service, coupled with efficiency, are all that is required to make a sale and profit. This may be true to some extent where trained sellers, whether owners or paid servants, retail goods. But experience shows that most of the proprietors are much too conscious of their wealth and make the customer feel uncomfortable. Unless the attitude of mind is changed, retailing in our country cannot be a success that it is in other countries. It should be borne in mind that "Better Retail Selling is the key to Better Business." It is the key to better service, better opportunity, and therefore the key to greater net profit. In many cases customers are lost because of poor salesmanship, errors and delay in service, unwillingness to exchange goods. tricky methods employed by sales people to sell goods, discourteous behaviour and indifference. More than 70 per cent customers may be lost due to human element. It is necessary for every retailer to 'streamline his retailing', i.e., adopt efficient methods to remove resistance that may have been built up through indifference and carelessness. This can be done if the following seven steps are followed.

Seven Steps in Retail Salesmanship. Remember, a sale is not getting a piece of merchandise a customer asks for when he comes into the shop, wrapping it up, taking his money, and saying "Good day". A sale is not a sale until the customer gets what he or she thinks he or she wants and leaves the store with a feeling in his or her heart because of something he or she received, *plus* that for which he or she has paid. He leaves the store with a feeling that is comparable to the feeling which I have in my heart when I leave your home after having been invited to come and spend the evening with you, with a feeling of gratitude, a feeling of appreciation for something that you have done for me voluntarily, and that I want to come back again and again because of these added things you have given me and that money cannot buy. There are seven vital steps which must be taken before a sale is really completed.

The first step is "greeting", sometimes called the approach. At this point you can build up or break down resistance, depending largely on your reception or attitude to the customer.When a customer walks into a store, he should be made to feel at home. If he is only 'shopping', i.e., looking round, let him be, without of course ignoring him altogether. If he raises his head inquiringly, you should be available to him. Remember, no one would come into your store or to your shop without wanting something. Not long ago I went to a bookshop to buy a few school books. I had to wait for full three minutes before the shop-keeper condescended to put down his newspaper and attend to me, and that, too, after I had attempted several times to attract his attention. In the meantime his partner arrived and apologised in the following words: "I am very sorry for the poor service you have got at the hands of my partner." To this I replied: "Please don't apologise for the service—I have got no service at all", and walked off. Attend to your customer, even if you are a millionaire. Your customer is your guest for the time being, invited through some form of advertising, and like a guest he should be treated if you want him to buy. Welcome the people coming into your store with a smile, because they are contributing directly to the success of your store through their purchases. You should smile at them, because they have chosen your store of all the stores in the town to spend their money. Do not ever forget the Chinese proverb: "A man without a smiling face must not open a shop." If you know the name of the customer, say a hearty 'Good morning" calling him by name. Calling customers by name flatters them. And he should be known, the same as a guest coming to your home is known by name. If for any reason you don't know the customer, a "Good morning, Sir" or "Good afternoon, Madam" will suffice.

Let your welcome be genuine and sincere. Let it be uniform, regardless of the position in life the customer of the store occupies, financially, socially, politically, or otherwise. Treat them all alike.

The second step is "Learning what the customer wants". Generally they volunteer this information. They may not always be able to name it. Sometimes they describe it very poorly, and you have to use your imagination and knowledge to get the correct piece of merchandise. The third step is "Showing the Merchandise the customer is interested in"—if you can find it. Sometimes the customer goes elsewhere because the salesman through lack of full knowledge of the stock informs him that the article asked for is out of stock. The salesman must know his stock. The dull moments of the day can be utilised in going over the stock, rearranging it, replacing it. The fourth step is "Giving the Selling Points of the Merchandise." By that is meant, the reasons for its creation, what it was made with, its quality, how it can be used, how it will solve the problem that is confronting the customer. Talk about your merchandise and not the price. Create in the customer's mind and heart a desire for quality goods. Show, from your knowledge of it, the economy in the possession and use of better grade goods. Knowledge creates confidence. Confidence begets enthusiasm. As you know your goods, you will have confidence in them. And if you have confidence in your merchandise, you are bound to become enthusiastic about it, and enthusiasm is contagious.

In the fifth step, you complete the sale of the article asked for, but the great opportunity in merchandising comes in the sixth step—making suggestions—trying to sell second item, other merchandise, It is true that some people object to what may be called suggestive-item selling. but suggestive-item selling, or selling the second article, is not objectionable if the salesman genuinely and sincerely believes the customer ought to have that article. When one is sincere and genuine in his proposal, there is an entirely different mental reaction on the part of the customer. The seventh step is the step in which the store's interest is the greatest. When the customer finally says, "I will take it", or "That is all", his interest is elsewhere, in some other activity, and he is in a hurry to get to that place. But the store must make a record of this sale; and while speed should enter into the transaction at this point, accuracy is of greatest importance. Now when the record is made, voucher prepared and payment received, the goods are wrapped. And always remember that a well-wrapped package is a good advertisement for any store. Wrap your merchandise neatly and securely without wasting paper, boxes, twine or tape. Now when the package is wrapped, hand it to the customer. Don't lay it on the counter. Hand it to him with a "Thank you; good bye".

Window Display. In retail selling window display is of vital importance, particularly during the gift buying seasons such as Diwali and Christmas. It is important to remember that nearly everything sells through the year. If merchandise is to be sold it must be seen in a favourable light. As much merchandise as possible should be placed in the window, preferably related items—items that suggest each other—but without creating a crowded or heterogeneous effect. Window display is the cheapest and the most valuable form of advertising. Its results are traceable, because people are continually entering the store and asking for articles displayed in the windows. Here a few fundamental facts of window display may be stated. More persons look towards the floor sections of the window than any other part. The next largest group looks at the middle. The right side is slightly preferable to the left, and only a comparatively few persons look above the eye level. Between 4 and 5 feet is the proper height for displays. But most of all, in the selection of merchandise to be placed in the windows, give window shoppers a chance to see what they want. They may not know what they want until they see it, but when they do discover an item that appeals, the sale is practically made. Windows should be changed and rearranged as often as circumstances require. In a big store in a big city weekly change may be appropriate, while in a small town where so many people see the windows more often, the changes may be oftener.

Principles of Window Display. The more important principles of window display may be summarised as follows:—

1. Cleaniliness and a well finished appearance are essential to creating a good window. Glass, floor, woodwork, and fixtures should be

clean and free from dust. Scaly or scruffy paint and lack of varnish are inexcusable and can kill the attractiveness of the display.

2. Adequate lighting is necessary for the most efficient use of a window. See the lights are large enough and bright.

3. An adequate stock of pedestals, plateaux, tables, glass shelves, etc., are important for variety of display.

4. Do not fill up the window with a miscellany of small objects. The fewer the items in the window the stronger each can be made to stand out.

5. High narrow windows can be given a wider appearance by the use of horizontal lining in the decorations. Likewise, long, low windows can be made to look higher by the use of vertical lining.

6. Be careful in the selection of the goods for the window. They should not be soiled or damaged in any way as this naturally gives a bad impression.

7. Plan the centre panel of the background first and build the display around it.

8. At least one show card should be used to carry your message to those who are a bit slow on the "up-take". The price should also be shown.

9. Make your windows timely and seasonal. Try to be the first to display for the season.

10. Make effective use of colour.

11. Change your window displays regularly. Don't allow the goods to get dirty, look dirty or faded.

Commercial Travellers. The second class of salesmen include salesmen who sell necessities or staple goods. They call upon wholesalers and retailers who re-sell. Staples have always a steady demand and the apparent duties of a commercial traveller appear to be simply order taking. But a successful salesman acts as the representative of his firm in every sense of the word. A person who has mastered the requisites of a good salesman ceases to be a traveller. He follows the technique of sales sequence in dealing with prospects. His work is much more difficult than that of the shop assistant. He needs to follow the selling steps to meet the needs of the buyer. Therefore, to be successful he must follow the sales sequence technique.

Sales Sequence. If we analyse an average sale, we find it inevitably covers the following five selling steps: The first selling step is the *approach,* by which the salesman creates pleasant atmosphere to obtain *favourable attention* and *interest* on the part of the prospect. The second selling step is an *appeal* to buying motive made to cause recognition of *need or want* on the part of the prospect. The third selling step is *explanation* of the features or benefits of the product so that the prospect can *investigate its ability* to satisfy his want. The fourth selling step is *persuasion* to establish *conviction* of the desirability of the product and *creating the desire to buy.* The last step is to *close the sale* by getting the prospects to buy. When thus expressed the process of selling seems almost mechanical. But the selling steps cannot be taken mechanically because of the human element involved and because of the natural resistance of prospects.

Sales resistance is the hardest nut to crack before a sale can be made. Everyone desires to be the master of his life and fortune, to exercise his right of pursuit of happiness. Consequently, everyone resents being told how to conduct himself and his business. Every consumer has had contacts with poor salesmen, who crudely tried to force him to accept advice without properly motivating him. As a result most people are suspicious of salesmen and set up a barrier of resistance at once. Furthermore, many salesmen are not beyond reproach for their ethics. By misrepresenting their wares they have left a feeling of antagonism in the mind of the buyer who was thus cheated. Every new salesman who comes along must first of all break down the fear that his purpose is dishonourable. Sales resistance is overcome by the salesman who skilfully relates the value of his product to the buying motives and self-interest of the prospect. He must lead the prospect to the point where he—not the salesman—makes the decision. He feels he is buying—not being sold. And when a man buys, he stays sold. This is the essence of successful salesmanship.

Preparing for a Sale. To be able to present an accurate picture of the utility of his product, he must know all the facts. We have seen before that knowledge breeds enthusiasm. If we know we can meet any question the prospect may ask, we look forward to the interview. As the salesman sells satisfaction primarily, he must know everything about the product, and should be able to describe its main features, such as construction, performance, and operation. For example, a cloth-bound book is more durable than one covered with paper. The dealer who buys goods for re-sale wants to know the distribution policies. The company behind the product may enjoy great reputation in the industry, its sales policy may attract buyers. It is necessary to know how his product stacks up relative to the others to meet prospects' objections who may be dealing in rival's goods. This is necessary because to 'knock' the products of another you are not to criticise them or their makers; for it is considered unethical and poor selling to do that.

Having studied your product thoroughly you are now in a position to prepare a sales presentation. The simplest method to do that is to review in your mind, or even on a piece of paper, the selling steps and think of the things you will say to accomplish each one. This plan permits of the utmost flexibility in dealing with different prospects. The next step before the actual-approach is *prospecting*. As a salesman's time is limited he must spend it most effectively. Prospecting to find out prospects who are potential 'leads' will save waste of time and energy. Having located the prospect, the salesman will analyse the individual's characteristics to qualify him as buyer. His willingness and ability to buy should be studied.

The Pre-approach. Even after a salesman has completed a list of prospects, he does not rush to meet them. He learns the prospect's name, its correct spelling and pronunciation. Shakespeare may well have said: "What's in a name?" But a man's name is his chief mark of distinction, it is his symbol, and he loves it. If the salesman shows that he knows it he creates a good impression and is well on the road to an order. The next thing to do is to find out personal characteristics of the prospect and his hobbies. Most people are flattered, though they may deny it, when a complete stranger, like a salesman, inquiries about the progress of a son at college, or the health of an ailing member of his family. Another pre-approach task for the salesman is to plan his time and work so as to use the bulk of that time talking to prospects and not in travelling to see customers who are not at home. A salesman's job is to sell—travelling should be left to travellers. Making advance appointments will often result in saving of time, and it adds to the prestige of the salesman. It is always best to be expected.

PERFORMING THE SELLING STEPS

The Approach. The first selling step is to approach the prospective customer and gain his favourable attention—by a pleasant approach. You can do that by developing an attractive personality with special reference to physical appearance, neatness, cheerfulness and courtesy. Be natural, and don't put on airs or adopt a pose. If you want people to like you, smile. A gloomy face is a barrier to success and a smile is a universal introduction. If you have got the prospect interested in you, you have succeeded in leading him up to the first step. To be interesting, be interested. If the prospect says something, listen attentively; it flatters him. Do not as yet talk about your product and your firm. Talk in terms of the customer's interests. The royal road to a man's heart is to talk to him about the things he treasures most. Once Disraeli said: "Talk to a man about himself, and he will listen for hours."

The Appeal. After you have attracted the favourable attention of the prospect to yourself you must transfer that attention to your product and arouse his interest in it, by telling him every conceivable sales point about the product. Call his attention in no uncertain terms to something that will add to his happiness, his health or his wealth. Plant ideas in his mind, and you will reap sales. The ideas must be expressed in well-chosen words and must satisfy the prospect's sense of caution, security and safety. Plain everyday words will be most effective. They will make the prospect feel the idea is his own. They persuade and convince him to buy your product.

Explanation. Once the salesman has aroused the prospect's interest in an unsatisfied want, he must explain how the product will satisfy the want better than any other possible means. Terms used must be related to his buying motives. The best method of explanation is to demonstrate the product itself in as dramatic a way as possible. Remember, one salesman demonstrating is worth a dozen who just rely on sales talk. The successful explanation is one which enables the buyer to make a thorough and complete investigation of the ability of the product to meet his needs and wants.

Conviction. Before he will buy, a prospect must be convinced that his need for the product is pressing and that the particular brand being sold will best fill that need. But to convince is not so easy. First of all the salesman must convince himself about his ability to perform the task, based on his faith in himself, faith in others, and faith in the product. If you are convinced of the suitability of your products for the prospect's needs, you will make that whatever you are selling speak with dynamic authority and ring with the spirit of sincerity. It infuses in you an unfaltering trust and an unbounded faith. Its influence is instantaneous and the prospect is invariably convinced, nay, inspired and persuaded to buy from you. One method of convincing is to reason with the prospect, but except for technical buyers most people do not respond to an appeal to reason. There is another danger. If you are not careful it may develop into an acute angle. Therefore, suggest but never argue. For there is only one way to get the best of an argument—and that is to avoid it. You can never win an argument. You cannot because if you lose it, you lose it; and if you win you lose it as well as the customer. A man convinced against his will is of the same opinion still, *minus* the goodwill. Another method is that of persuasion. The essence of persuasion lies in proof. One proof is demonstration. Another proof is testimony of experts. Testimonials of users of products are another tool of conviction. But conviction is not obtained unless all objections are met. Objections are either real or excuses. New salesmen usually dread objections, but experienced salesmen turn objections into sales. There are different kinds of buyers and they raise all manners of objections. These buyers may be divided into five sets of pairs.

First, we have the buyer who never stops talking, and his opposite number is the man who won't talk at all. There is only one way to deal with Mr. Talker. Don't interrupt him; but when he stops to take breath, assert yourself politely but firmly. Being timid is no use. Link up what he says with your own goods and *sell* as forcefully as you can. With Mr. Silent, however, the problem is to get him to talk. It is no use carrying on a monologue. Ask him questions to which he must say either yes or no. If his answer is yes, you can carry on, because if he agrees often enough, he will eventually buy. If he replies in the negative, then you use the well-known stand by a salesman. 'Why?' His answer will enable you to develop your talk and work your way to the close.

The second pair are the over-effusive, friendly type and the sneering, sarcastic buyer. Mr. Friendly is a snare and a delusion. By being nice he may make you forget your story. Be on your guard and make him so interested that he gets down to business. The sarcastic type just love to make you feel small. The poor souls are suffering from inferiority complex and they try to overcome it by adopting a superior attitude. When dealing with such buyers, don't lose your temper. Keep smiling, let them feel superior, and help them to feel important, and they will think you are a fine fellow. They will buy.

Next we have the timid, wavering buyer and the boastful bluffer. The former worries, and is scared stiff of doing the wrong thing. He is often afraid that if he makes a mistake in making the purchase he will lose his job. You have to put every ounce of enthusiasm in your sales story to show him what he will lose if he does not buy. Make him more frightened of not having your goods than of buying them. With the bluffer, however, you have to do just the opposite. He will, in order to satisfy his vanity, talk big. He is never interested in small quantities. He is the case for under-selling. Tell him you appreciate his kindness and will be happy to supply him with a large order when he is ready. But pin him down to a small order on the spot, and don't leave without it.

The fourth couple consists of the old gentleman who has been in business since before you were born, who does not like either new ideas or new salesmen; and the young man has, perhaps, just come down from university and wants to show that he knows everything. The thing to remember when dealing with the irritable old man, is the fact that he has been dealing with salesmen for years, and has probably heard everything you are going to tell him many many times before.All right, get him to help you. Treat him with respect that is his due and ask him advice. Point out to him that you are sure that he has always taken advantage of everything which can prove an asset to his business, as witness, for example, his use of the telephone and typewriter, neither of which he used in his early days. He will feel flattered, his vanity will be tickled, and he will be interested in your product. Strangely enough, similar methods are necessary in dealing with the young man. His worry is that he is young, probably looks young, too, and he is afraid he will be made to look foolish. He wants to show how clever he really is and may, in fact, be. As the good salesman tries to learn from everybody, give the youngster a chance to teach you something. Ask his opinion about certain aspects of your job or product, and he will be glad to talk when he feels you respect him. Don't look down upon him; show him courtesy and he will reciprocate—and what is more, he will buy.

Finally, we come to that troublesome individual, the person who won't listen to what you say, and with him we link the careful buyer, who does listen, but just won't be rushed into placing an order. How irritating that non-listener can be. He never looks at you, appears to be miles away, and spoils your most brilliant utterances by his complete lack of attention. You have to treat him like Mr. Silent of the first group. Ask him questions, make him talk to you, get his agreement on every point before you continue with your sales talk, and gradually he will listen and buy. The careful buyer is often a slower thinking and talking type than most and although he may listen closely to what you say, you must be sure that he is following your remarks. Many salesmen in their enthusiasm speak rather quickly and use technical or trade terms freely during their sales talk. It is important to make sure that your prospect understands you, and make him sell *himself* on your product.

It follows that every customer is an individual. The salesman must attempt to discover customer's feeling and then adjust his attitude to that of the customer's to win his goodwill. Since every customer is different from the rest, and may be stated as follows:

Nervous Customers

For Customers who are:	*You will need:*
Tired and cross	Patience
Fussy and nervous	Consideration
Excitable	Quiet manner

For Customers who are:	*You will need*
Impatient	Despatch
Unreasonable	Calmness

Dependent Customers

For Customers who are:	*You will need:*
Timid and Sensitive	Gentleness
Undecided	Decision
Old and deaf people	Sympathy
Children	Power to think for them
Foreigners	Helpfulness

Disagreeable Customers

For Customers who are:	*You will need:*
Sceptical	Candid manner
Inquisitive	Knowledge
Talkative	Courteous brevity
Insulting	Self-control

Trying Customers

For Customers who are:	*You will need:*
Critical	Knowledge of goods
Indifferent	Tact
Silent	Perseverance
Bargain hunters	Convincing manner

Commonsense Customers

For Customers who are:	*You will need:*
Pleasant	What they expect
Intelligent	Efficient service

Handling Objections. The second problem relates to the type of objections likely to be raised, and the best method of dealing with them. At the very outset it may be pointed out that when a prospect raises an objection, he is probably asking for more information. After all, unless a prospect asks questions it is very difficult to sell to him. But an objection may be real or an excuse. A real objection very often means prospect's interest. Real objections should be answered directly, but without antagonising the prospect. Excuses indicate the salesman has failed to build in the prospect's mind an adequate picture of his need or of the ability of the product to satisfy his need. Objections should be anticipated as far as possible and points brought out in the sales presentation. For example, a prospect might say that he is not familiar with the reputation of the company because it is a new one. You can reply by pointing out that in spite of the firm's very recent formation, its officers are all men of repute and vast experience. Don't counter his statement with "No, you are wrong". No one relishes a direct contradiction. The proper reply would seem to be: "It is true, Mr. Prospect. Our firm was organised just last year. However, here is a list of the officers of the company and a brief history of their past experience. Notice that for over 15 years the General Manager was the Sales Manager of X Co., and so on. The prospect may say, "No, I think your goods are too dear." In such a case, don't bark back, "Oh no. they are not" The better method is to admit the higher price but justify it by mentioning features which less expensive competitive products do not have. Sell to him the benefits which outweight the cost. In the case of valid objections, therefore, *always* start your answer to any objection by apparently agreeing with the prospect. Then by using the word 'but', tell your side of the story. By your apparent agreement, you make the prospect relax, and then you bring home your sales point. This method is sometimes referred to as the "Yes. but" method of meeting objections and is always a good one, because of its respect for the feelings of the prospect.

When you feel quite sure that your prospect is seeking to make excuses for not buying there are many things you can do to handle the situation. One is the so-called "boomerang" method. This means that you turn the excuse offered into a reason for buying. If the prospect says, "I am too busy to talk with you", you might reply like this: "I realise you are a busy man, Mr. Prospect. This is undoubtedly one reason why you are successful. You know that your success is worth protecting against contingencies. Therefore, I feel sure you are not too busy to consider how my proposition will aid your plans for safeguarding your future financial security." If the prospect says, "Come and see me next week," or, "I should like to think it over", the reply could be as follows; "Thank you, sir, for telling me to come again but without wishing to be too persistent do you really think you will know any more about my goods than you do now? After all, we have discussed them thoroughly, and you have agreed with what I have said about them. Every proposition is either a good one, or a bad one. If this is a bad proposition, then you won't want to see me again next week, or any other time. But as we have agreed it is good, then I am sure you, as a businessman, will want to avail yourself of the benefits as soon as possible...." If the prospect says, "I am not interested," the reply would be: "Of course, you are not interested. No interest, because you have not heard how our plan will cut your operating costs in half. This is what I would like to explain to you today...." To the excuse of being "fully stocked" one might say: "Every successful merchant keeps a complete line of goods on hand at all times, I know, Mr. Merchant. That is why he is successful. It is because you do plan your inventories carefully that I feel sure you will want to include our new Rayon Shirts. Customers of better dealers everywhere are asking for them." Another method of handling an excuse is to ignore it. If it is brought up again, it may be dealt with as a real objection. If it is simply an excuse, the prospect will try some other statement the next time.

The Close. The close of a sale is the last step in the sale. If the other steps are completed successfully, the close will naturally follow. After all the close of a sale is only the logical and natural conclusion of an interview that has been properly conducted from the moment it began. There is, however, no special time when, judged to a split second, the order form is presented and the prospect signs without a murmur. It may be stated as a rule that the right time to close a sale occurs when you feel the prospect yielding and know you can take an order. If the right time arrives in five minutes seize your opportunity by closing the sale. If it arrives in an hour, two hours or three hours, follow the same procedure. Do not linger and overstay your time. Do not become over-excited when you find the prospect is going to buy. The prospect notices this and begins to withdraw. The prospect argues: "This man is so thrilled to get an order, it must be an unusual occurrence. I had better go slow". Be calm and collected, and make up your mind that you are going to get the order. Alway be surprised if you do not get it. Never, when you do. One sure way to close the order is to speak as if the prospect will buy. Don't say: "When you instal this...." This plants the motivating idea in the sub-conscious mind. There are different closing techniques and different types of closes.

Trial Close. Throughout all stages of your progress, you must try to lead your prospect making certain that his thoughts are in step with your selling. At the completion of each phase or demonstration, ask your prospect's opinion. This will help you to appreciate his reaction. Use it at every possible point. Keep on asking questions. Then ask for an order. If it does not materialise, try again. Remember, the trial close is rather the experimental approach.

Alternative Close. If your trial close shows that you are on the way to that order, a further closing stage can be developed quite simply. Buyers do not like to be sold—they prefer to buy. The alternative close allows a prospect to make the choice. For example, you may proceed something like this. "This shirt is an excellent line—made in rayon as good as pure silk, with two trubenised collars of the latest style. It is hard wearing and will have a long life. Which colour do you prefer, sir—the grey or the blue?"

Summary Close. Having discussed the various points of your proposition, summarise them and express them in terms of your prospect's needs. Bring out your order book, letting the prospect appreciate that he is going to buy something, and then write down each article mentioning them as you set them down. Price them and, having completed the list, add it up and hand it over to your prospect, asking him to check it. Then ask him to verify the order and hand him your pen. The world 'verify' implies so much less than a request for a signature.

Fighting Close. Some prospects are going to resist automatically any effort to be sold—irrespective of how good the proposition. They adopt a dogmatic attitude and curtly answer "No" to all your sales arguments. If you go down under this barrage, you are finished. Don't be intimidated, but appease the fiery onslaught. Agree with almost everything they say, but don't lose a chance to bring in your sales arguments whenever possible. Listen attentively and almost apologise, when you say: "We pay the freight....we can allow you 30 days"...."To get the material to you in time will mean a special journey, but I can arrange for that straightaway!" "Our normal delivery is 4 weeks, but I think I can persuade Head Office to let you have it after 2 weeks. If we take your order it will mean overtime in the factory to deliver to your requirements but with a firm of your standing...." Make your prospect feel that his order is most important and the desire to serve him makes the inconvenience a very minor point. You will almost certainly find he will repent, and you will get your order. You will be told not to take any particular trouble—the normal conditions will be accepted.

Service Close. Don't give all your information away, even when trying to close your order. If you get a 'No' you are left without anything more to say—like a gun without ammunication, you are silent. Save something as a final persuader. Nearly every organisation or product has something to offer? The Service? Advertising? Sole Agency? But be sure it is something that your prospect will be interested in and wants. It is like giving away a bonus with every order. We all like to feel that we are getting something for nothing.

Whatever the type of close you use, in closing a sale *insist* with tact, *plead* with earnestness, and *persuade* with diplomacy.

SPECIALTY SALESMEN

Specialty salesmen have the hardest but the most paying job. They sell insurance policies, typewriters, adding machines, cash registers, scales and other inventions and specialties for which there is no active demand. Specialty selling is no field for the lively amateur, however enthusiastic he may be. It can be covered by the highly trained man with enthusiasm, intelligence, and agility of mind, who is prepared to go on training, and who has the strength, determination, and charm of character. A specialty salesman is not invited. He is not expected; he is seldom welcomed. He fights for each order, and does not lose heart after a series of rebuffs. He analyses his failures and then fights harder. Staying power is a vital ingredient of his success. By cold canvass, careful planning and charm of manner he 'sells himself' as well as his product at each call. He does not sell the product, he sells its advantages. His task is not easy, but if he possesses all the attributes of a good salesman and the ones mentioned here in abundance he can succeed and his income can exceed many of those who are at the top of their profession.

Of all the specialty products, life assurance policy is the toughest thing to sell. Life insurance is an intangible product, and requires the highest form of creative selling. It is sometimes said that anyone who can sell life assurance can sell anything. The buying motive in this category is the satisfaction of his caution. A man wants to assure himself for the security of his family. He wants to make certain that his own wants in time of need will be provided for. Old age is looming up; when it comes he wants to be financially independent. The purchase of a life policy contributes to his peace of mind and adds substantially to the welfare, happiness, and comfort of himself and his family. Every person over 18 and under 65 is a possible prospect, and that includes women, who are fast becoming more insurance conscious than ever before. Moreover, everyone believes in life assurance, and wishes to get down to buying a policy but they never do. Your job as a salesman is to persuade them to action.

The sales plan of life assurance requires great deal of thought. When you approach a prospect visualise to him what life assurance will do for him. Centre his attention on an estate for himself and his family. Call his attention to the fact that this estate has many advantagdes. Point out to him that this plan would set up a savings account, which is readily available in case of need or emergency. Point out to him that your plan will take care of the premium if he should become totally incapacitated by any kind of sickness or accident, and that this estate and savings would remain intact. Don't start telling him what you know about life assurance. Only tell him what it will do for him. The plan affords the prospect an opportunity to invest money where it will be compound and grow and be there when he gets there. It sets up an income for him when he retires. Another very difficult problem today for the man who has a large estate is to have the cash to meet Death Duties. Often, his assets are not easily realisable, and cash at death is a very serious problem for his dependents. Life Assurance provides cash at death.

The specialty salesman's success depends upon his ability to use words and paint word-pictures, and if he can paint a future in glowing colours, he will get an ever-increasing market.

SALES LETTERS

You have learned just how to handle an interview. You know the selling point of your goods or service. You know your customers and prospective customers and have studied them individually so that you know how to anticipate and meet each individual's probable objections and use them to your advantage. You know which is the best way to attract each individual's favourable attention; the best way to arouse *his* interest; the best way to make *him* desire your product or service, and just when and how to close by making it easy for *him* to take the desired *action.* No one knows better than you how much one individual differs from another and how necessary it is to adapt your sales talk accordingly. But if you cannot get an interview, because your customer or prospect is too busy or ill, or on holiday, or cannot or will not see you for any of the many reasons then the next best thing to personal interview is a personal letter. A skilfully written letter can bind your customers to you with ever strengthening ties of friendship, and result in your getting a good welcome from prospects and customers instead of a 'Not today, thank you'.

Remember, everybody likes receiving letters; and no matter how big or small a business may be, the first thing to claim the attention of every businessman every morning is the post. A letter can very often get much better result than a personal interview. The prospect is alert and respective, he is at business to do business, ready to be attracted and interested by any proposition that may make his business more efficient, more successful, and more profitable. You could not find a customer or prospective customer in a more favourable frame of mind to consider your proposition. Take full advantage of it. Write him a good sales letter. No one else is so well placed as you to do this.

There are many different kinds of letters, and many books have been written on the subject, but we shall confine our thoughts to letters that pertain to selling. What is a letter ? A letter is written communication expressing your feelings or conveying information to a particular person, about a particular proposition, at a particular time. A letter is a record of your thoughts. A letter on which you have spent some time and thought gives your prospect something on which to ponder. Design your letter to sell advantages, and not product. Make a practice of reading all the letters you can get hold of, and you will find that very few of them contain the slightest touch of real salesmanship: Most of the letters written by business houses are staid and stolid, with leaden thoughts and wooden expression. Most of them are colourless and tasteless, and are the antithesis of what a good letter should be. Use them as a guide and do the opposite, and you will learn to write a good sales letter.

How to construct a good letter. A letter might be divided into five parts:

First: The salutation. A letter should always individualise the person to whom it is addressed. Instead of saying "Dear Sir", say "Dear Mr.....", or even "My dear Mr......" "Dear Sir" can refer to anyone, but when you insert the name of the person, the letter takes on warmth and cordiality. In this way you personalise your message.

Second: The opening sentence. The first sentence of a letter should express interest.Be warm and hearty, and eliminate a selfish and haughty attitude. Indicate your interest by saying "You instead of "I". Start the letter with "your kind letter", not "I received your letter." Another effective way to open a letter is to ask a question. "Have you ever thought....? It shows interest in the person to whom you are writing.

Third: The heart of the letter. A letter, to be effective, must be direct and to the point. Organise the knowledge or information that you want to incorporate in the letter. Every word, every thought, and every sentence must have its place. Therefore, before you start to write, make up your mind exactly what it is you want your reader to do, and stick to the point. He will never know if you don't. Remember that people are moved by appeal to the emotions rather than by appeal to the intellect. Sobase your letter on an appeal to such primary emotions as love, gain, duty, pride, self indulgence, self-preservation. Make your letters 'newsy'. Give a man news and you secure his interest. Millions of newspapers sell every day, and they sell for news and not for the editorials or the advertisements. Then suggest—don't argue. Help the reader to build up in his mind such a vivid picture of the advantages he will obtain that your proposition will be irresistibly attractive to him. Paint pictures with words which your reader can understand. Give your reader a reason to do *at once* what you have succeeded in making him want to do. Many a man makes up his mind to do something, but in fact never does it because of the absence of any reason for doing it at once. Thousands of sales are lost every day simply because salesmen fail to give the customer a good and sufficient reason to place his order as soon as he has made up his mind. Be definite in your reason and leave no room for doubt, otherwise you will leave reason for delay. Having helped the reader to make up his mind that he has decided (entirely of his own free will) to do what you want him to do, and having offered him a worth-while reward to do it at once, make it easy for him to do it. This is the critical moment. All his instincts are urging him to hold back. You goad him to action through the close.

Fourth: The close. The close of any letter should be a brief summary of the main points and advantages set fourth in the heart of the letter. Use short sentences, make them crisp and pungent. Inject a feeling of kindness and respect into every line and by no means fail to include it in the close of the letter. Use kind words in a letter; they make the prospect feel friendly towards you. Close your letter as follows: "With kindest regards and all the good wishes, I am, Sincerely yours,"

Fifth: Signature. Always sign your letter in a natural way with your customary signature.

A letter, like a person-to-person call, is a meeting of two minds. Therefore, the letter should convey the facts and circumstances in a manner that will influence, persuade, and convince. Cut out all useless words, words which add nothing to your meaning. Padding has no place in business letters. Use short words; there is strength and force in short words. When you make a call but fail to obtain an interview, try to find time to write a personal letter. Stereotyped letters, whether sent from the head office or posted by you, saying something like "We beg to advise you that Mr. So and So hopes to call on you at such a time and on such a day, and we trust that you will favour him with an interview" are about as effective as cold rice pudding, and suffer the fate they richly deserve. Write a warm, friendly, personal letter which should let your man know how much he may be missing by refusing to consider your offer. Let him see how others have gained by dealing with you. Here is a letter that has been used with great advantage: "Dear Mr.—*Increased output of 35%*— That is exctly what we did for one of our recent clients, who previously was having difficulty in showing reasonable 'profits' on orders booked. *How is your profit picture?* Are your profits smaller than they should be, due to rising costs of materials and labour or inadequate controls of production and costs ? In today's business economy, outside help for inside problems is one successful way by which progressive managements have been able to increase the size of their 'profits'. It is quite possible that we may be able to serve you to advantage as we have our other clients. We should like an opportunity to outline our methods to you in person, without obligation of course...."

Notice this letter says just enough to arouse the interest of the prospect and to make him wonder what it is all about. The following letter will always arouse curiosity of the prospect'": "Dear Mr.—, An important situation now confronts your company that can easily affect its entire future operation. You should know about this situation, and I am coming in on Wednesday morning around 10-30 a.m. to give you the facts. Thanking you for your co-operation, and with kind regards and all good wishes, I am, Sincerely yours...."

These letters are just good patterns to follow. You can construct your own letters, bearing in mind the rules, but use them after you have written your letter to find out whether your letter conforms to the rules. Use these rules as yardsticks rather than recipes. Your letter when read aloud would sound like you giving the sales talk. Avoid all the old fashioned business jargon. Leave out all the 'ultimos', 'instants', 'favours', 'commands', 'esteemed', 'beggings', 'respectfully', and 'submittings'. Just imagine your prospect is sitting opposite you and construct your letter as if you were talking to him.

The whole matter in relation to sales letters may be summed up as follows:

1. Your spelling must be correct, as also grammar and punctuation. Your reader will assume that your poor spellings, grammar and punctuation result from ignorance or carelessness. You cannot afford to give him reason to accuse you of either one.

2. Be careful about the construction. Use short and simple sentences. Let your letter invite reading. Try to confine to one or two subjects. Make short paragraphs. Make your signature readable. Do not use too many superlatives. Avoid them, if possible. Do not use obsolete, time-worn and out-of-date words and expressions.

3. Make your letter concise, complete and courteous.

4. The tone of your letter must be natural and friendly. Be sympathetic and human. Be calm and reasonable. Be customer-minded; and carefully size up the needs of your prospect, and answer his inquiry in terms of advantages to him of your product.

5. Finally, be sales-minded in your correspondence. You do not have to ask for an order in every letter, but every letter should be a means of easing the way to secure business for your product.

Remuneration of Salesmen. The remuneration of salesmen is a question of great complexity and one where there has been much experiment. No one method seems to fit every situation. Whatever the method of combination of methods employed, the objects should be to (1) attract and keep the right type of man; and (2) to reward him according to the value of his services. The problem bristles with difficulties. Even with the same business, some things are easier to sell than others, and some yield a bigger gross profit than others. It is easier to sell in a boom than in a slump; in season than out of season. Some territories are much easier and cheaper to work than others. Again it is difficult to measure and reward that work which is intended to build up future sales rather than to bring immediate results. The two principal methods of remunerating salesmen are either by straight methods oı relating their earnings in some way with results. The latter plan, in its various forms, seeks two objectives: (1) to supply a direct incentive to increase the volume of sales, and (2) to establish a definite percentage of relationship of selling expenses to volume of sales.

The principal systems of payment in use are: (1) Fixed salary; (2) Commission on a fixed basis; (3) Commission at a varying rate according to the volume of sale; (4) Salary and Commission; (5) Pooled Commission, when a group of salesmen work together and commission is paid to each on the total results of the group. Payment of a fixed salary is simple, but fails to provide an incentive to hard work. Nevertheless it is the only suitable method where a large amount of development work must be carried out; where orders vary considerably in size; or where they are infrequent. There is, however, a danger that the salesman will be less enterprising than one whose income is more quickly related to results. The second method is payment of a percentage commission on sales or payment by results, as it is sometimes termed, though erroneously. It is intended to give incentive to obtain more and large orders, and also to be a fair system of payment. But sales may be obtained to the detriment of future business. A salesman paid in this basis alone will be able to earn when he is in the presence of a prospective customer—'a bird in the hand is worth two in the bush' is his maxim. He will resist reductions of his territory or transfer to under-developed areas, however desirable that may be in the interest of the firm. He is tempted to ignore the danger of over-selling.

The use of basic salary in combination with commission has certain advantages for both employers and salesmen. Selling cost fluctuates to a certain extent in accordance with the volume of sales. The salesman is relieved from immediate financial worry. But the system is equitable as between territories of differing degrees of development or productivity. Pooled commission is adopted to get over this difficulty. Salesmen working in a certain area are regarded as a team. The total commission earned on the sales of the group as a whole is divided amongst the salesmen. The division may be equal, or it may be partly on the individual sales and the remainder equally distributed. By making each man partly responsible for the earnings of each member of the group, a certain influence is brought to bear which is expected to give stimulus to hard work. Recourse is also had to Sales Quotas. Each salesman is allotted a certain volume of sale depending on the relative prosperity of his territory, the degree of development and the difficulty of coverage. Point system is adopted by some firms which realise that a salesman's work comprises many tasks each of which must be evaluated for proper appraisal of his worth. Marks or points are allotted to such factors as value of orders, numbers of orders, number of calls made, new accounts secured and demonstrations booked. The number of bad debts incurred and complaints received are given negative marks. The salesman's activities are valued in accordance with this schedule and payment is made on the basis of the total points secured. Sometimes the profits contributed by each salesman are made the basis of payment, but the plan is difficult and is impossible to function if there are losses. From the foregoing it is clear that much of the success or failure of any sales campaign will depend upon the ability or otherwise of the salesmen to drive home the message. Therefore, personal salesmanship is being more and more supplemented, and in many cases eliminated, by scientifically planned advertising. Firms of any size and magnitude do not now depend upon one or the other, they count on publicity for success.

CHAPTER XLIII

ADVERTISING

Definition. Advertising is one of the most powerful tools available to corporate management in its drive to build a profitable business operation, and to compete successfully with other comparable businessses. The term advertising has been differently defined by different people. It is said to be salesmanship in print. It is also said to be a sort of machine made, mass-production, method of selling. In its basic meaning, Advertising is a form of communication, but a special type of communication. We would, therefore, define Advertising as mass, commercial or paid communication, the ultimate purpose of which is to import information, develop attitude and induce action beneficial to the advertiser — generally the sale of a product or service. It is paid for by a sponsor who expects to induce some kind of action on the part of the reader or listener, resulting in a sale. It is essentially controlled communication about a product or service or the company. It is, in effect, a substitute for sampling. Through, symbols of language, written or spoken, and pictorial presentation, advertising conveys a sense of what a product or a service or a company, is, and can do.

Advertising is a function, and basically a supportive activity, which enlarges the possibility of production and makes the selling process more efficient. It does not produce direct sales, by physically impelling the consumer towards the purchase of goods. Its purpose is to create a state of mind conducive to purchase. In fact, advertising is, one of several communication forces, known as "total market mix", leading to consumption of the product. These forces, as we have discussed in the previous chapter, include the product itself, its distribution, styling, packaging, pricing, publicity, availability, display, personal selling and performance. Thus, the purpose of advertising is not to build sales, or establish brand preference or create a market for the product. Advertising can contribute to those desiderate, but cannot by itself, bring them about. Advertising cannot for example, for very long, build sales for an inferior product, or a product over-priced in comparison with a competitive product. In fact, the most successful advertising is that which stems directly from the product itself. It tells people about new products, seeks to attract their attention to benefits which they may not be aware of or may have forgotton, urges them to try the product for the first time, if they have not yet done so; urges them to buy it again, if it satisfied them.

Preliminary Investigation

Because all the factors or forces comprising marketing mix, including advertising impel the consumer towards the purchase of goods, it is vital for a manufacturer to carry out preliminary investigation before launching an advertising campaign. He should start by finding where his product stands in the market place vis-a-vis competitve products where he would like it to be, what will be required to get it there, how expensive will it be, and how much he can afford to spend to reach the goal. All this requires a careful assembling of facts which will determine the advertising strategy. The investigation will also bring home to the advertiser the fact that no product has a universal market. Accordingly, he will find it more economical to communicate with the logical market for his product than to advertise to all and sundry.

Economics and Benefits of Advertising. Advertising is now an accepted power in the business world. It has become a great social force. While it involves expenditure, businessmen all over the world have found that advertising helps manufacturers, whole-salers and retailers to increase sales, and insofar as it does this, it helps to increase production. Advertising helps to increase distribution. It brings before the public the advantages of buying the goods and services offered. It awakens new desires and inspires consumers to work harder to earn more money to satisfy these new desires. It spreads information speedily about new products and helps to enrich our lives.

But who pays the cost of advertising? The consumer, of course. In fact, he pays everything. Who else is there to pay? He pays the manufacturing cost, Central and State taxes, overhead, salesman's remuneration, manfucturers', whole-salers and retailers profits, transport charges and all other costs, including advertising. Therefore, what the consumer (and we are all consumers) would really be interested to know is, "Could I have bought my commodities more cheaply had they not been advertised"? Judged from the experience of everyone, the answer obviously is "No, Certainly not"! Advertising is an important factor which sets the *virtuous* circle in motion. The advertiser invests his money to tell you about his products. If what he tells you is helpful, you respond, and he prospers. But he gets his reward only to the extent he benefits you, the consumer. By spreading knowledge far and wide, advertising helps the manufacturer to increase his sale and reduce his cost of production through larger production per unit and lower price to the consumer. In addition to those direct benefits, there are several incidental benefits of advertising. It subsidises newspaper and magazines and this makes them cheaper for the reading public. It makes the country brighter.

Distrust of Advertising. Until recent times, advertising was looked upon with suspicion. This is because the patent medicine people, who were the first to advertise, sold 'rivers of tonics and mountains of pills, good, bad and indifferent. Some of these people were dishonest men and advertising got a bad start, and came to be adversely criticised. We give below the main criticisms and try to answer them. It is alleged —

1. That advertising is unnecessary and wasteful. But if it were so, businessmen would have given it up in favour of some other selling aid

2. That through it people are induced to buy worthless products, and it promotes quackery, particularly in the sale of patent medicines and cosmetics. Now, the law takes care of such people under the MRTP Act relating to unfair trade practices.

3. That much advertising is misleading and untruthful. But this does not last long because of the MRTP Act.

4. That advertising causes people to want things they cannot afford. At times this accusation is true. But if we want civilisation to progress, then we must enable the succeeding generations to have more comforts, new forms of recreation and finer emotional experiences in life. New desires can best be met with the help of advertising.

5. That advertising just takes business from one concern and gives it to another. This criticism is based on the fallacious assumption that purchasing power is a static quantity like seats in a cinema hall. Actually, the quantity of goods and services that people can buy in a year depends not only on the quantity of purchasing power but also on the rapidity of turnover. Advertising speeds up the turnover of trade, and the result is a greater annual volume of individual purchases.

6. That advertising increases the cost of goods to the consumer. This allegation is not correct. The contrary is more true; effective advertising tends to lower the prices to the consumer.

7. That advertising tends to create semi-monopoly for branded goods. This criticism is baseless, because monopoly through advertising is not possible in a competitive market. Advertising, on the contrary, stimulates competition.

8. That the large sums of money spent for advertising are appalling. Although the total amount of money spent on advertising may be very large, the advertising expenditure as percentage of sales price is hardly more than one percent.

Advertising can be justified economically and socially. It needs defence only to those who do not appreciate its contributions and to those who do not understand many of the problems the advertiser is facing and sincerely trying to solve. The old code of business of *caveat emptor* does not govern advertising today. *Caveat emptor* has been replaced by *Caveat Vendor,* and the seller must beware of making promises in his advertising which he cannot fulfil. Today, the right thinking advertisers are constantly striving to make the message truthful and believable. Advertising these days is made factual, informative and educative with a view to rendering maximum helpful service.

Functions of Advertising

Advertising aims at fulfilling a variety of different purposes which depend upon the needs of the particular enterprise as determined by a painstaking analysis. These purposes or functions may be classified as **Primary** and **Secondary.**

Primary Functions. Among the primary functions the following purposes are more important —

1. *To help increase sales.* The chief aim of advertising is to make its contribution to the consummation of a sale of the advertiser's product.

2. *To secure dealers.* More dealers can be persuaded to stock the goods by advertising in trade press. This makes far wider distribution of goods.

3. *To help the dealer.* Dealers are materially assisted by the manufacturer's advertising. The very advertising which is designed to help the manufacturer also seem to assist the retailer by clearing his shelves and increasing his turnover.

4. *To increase use per capita.* Constant repetition of the darable features of a product tends to increase the consumption per capita, and advertising if effectively used to increase the consumption per capita by describing the uses for articles of which the consumer is unaware.

5. *To relate new products to existing ones.* Advertising aims to relate a new product, or a new model or form of a familiar product to a name for which prestige has been firmly established.

6. *To create insurance.* Advertising creates insurance for the manufacturer's business. Through advertising of trade names or the general appearance of the package and so goodwill is established, and a kind of trade insurance is effected. This makes the manufacturer more independent of wholesalers and retailers.

7. *To create confidence in quality.* The buyer of nationally advertising goods believes, because of his past experience, that if the manufacturer advertises that his goods are of a certain quality, they will be found as advertised. Advertising also cultivates brand and company image.

8. *To eliminate seasonal fluctuations.* Advertising has, in many instances, eliminated or lessend seasonal fluctuations.

9. *To keep the customer sold.* One who is satisfied with a particular product is kept "sold" by advertising so that when the time comes to replace it, he will most likely go in for the same make or brand.

10. *To create more business for all.* Competitive advertising of two or more manufacturers in the same field expands market; and creates more business for all. This is exemplified by the fact that not only the use of a particular brand of an article, say, a portable typewriter, is recommended but the use of the article is, vigorously suggested, with the result that more typewriters of different makes are being sold.

11. *To raise the standard of living.* In the raising of standard of living advertising deserves some credit. It is helping to stimulate desire for better things. Many of the so-called luxuries of yesterday are today's necessities, and the things enjoyed today exclusively by the wealthy may tomorrow be enjoyed by those of smaller incomes. Advertising, in spreading the news and increasing the desire for better things and, in many cases, decreasing costs, has rendered great service to humanity.

Secondary Functions. In addition to the primary functions detailed above, many advertisers have come to attach importance to certain other functions which are classed as secondary although at times some of those may assume primary role. The secondary functions are as follows:

1. *To encourage salesmen and lend them moral support.* Very often advertising supply the necessary encouragement to a salesman who finds himself face to face with a difficult buyer. It is much easier for a salesman to sell advertised goods, because part of the selling has already been done for him. Also, manufacturers who advertise can usually get salesmen of better calibre than those who do not.

2. *To furnish information to salesmen and dealers.* Advertisements usually are mines of information for salesmen and dealers and many times serve as a check upon erroneous or extravagant claims. The printed word is the manufacturer's guarantee.

3. *To impress executives.* The effect on the executives and adminstrative staff of company may become important. While dealing with the public, the executives become more enthusiastic over the product every time they read one of the advertisements.

4. *To impress factory workers.* There is often a good effect on workers who work in the factory producing advertised goods. The workers consciously or unconsciously take pride in helping to produce something that is known far and wide. The knowledge that what they produce has wide acceptance tends to make the work less grinding and monotonous.

5. *To create a feeling of security.* Goodwill gained by advertising is a present asset and an insurance for the future. It means steady work and consequent prosperity. There is a feeling that the job is permanent and that as the business grows the chances of promotion will be much greater.

6. *To secure better employees.* Advertising tend to make it possible

for manufacturers to secure better executives, better salesmen and even better factory workers. It is natural to be identified with a widely known company whose advertising is alert and aggresive.

To sum up, advertising at committing the producer, educating the consumer, supplement the salesman, converting the dealer to eliminate the competitor, but above all, it is a link between the producer and the consumer. Properly used, advertising can perform the following functions:

1. It can bring down selling expenses by reaching large number of prospects at the same time and at low cost;
2. It will go to prospects who usually refuse to see salesman;
3. It makes the product known widely;
4. It helps to create new markets;
5. It helps to keep up a steady demand;
6. It helps to build up company's reputation and give it an image;
7. It helps manufacturers to recruit the best available talent;
8. Advertising is a powerful weapon in the hands of a new manufacturer to establish himself in a market dominated by large, long-established firms who are too complacent to undertake systematic advertising.

The very essence of advertising is that it is an instrument of competition. Competition and advertising move together.

THE ADVERTISEMENT

Purpose of an advertisement. While the underlying purpose of all business is eventually to increase business and profits, an advertiser may advertise to sell goods and services either immediately or at some future time. Accordingly, the purpose of any particular advertisement may be either –

1. to cause the reader to act leading to an immediate sale or inquiry; or
2. to establish an attitude of mind that will result in an ultimate sale at some future date when a need for the article arises or when the salesman calls to solicit order.

The copy to produce the first of these effect may be termed *present action* copy and the latter *future action* copy. The present action advertisement or copy is intended to perform all the functions of the complete sales process as performed by a salesman or by a sales letter. It must attract reader's attention, arouse his interest, develop that interest into desire, lead him to decide that the advertised product will satisfy his desire, and so prompt him to go in for the product. The greater part of all advertising is of this type, as its purpose is to persuade customers to take immediate action, by entering the store and making a purchase.

Future Action copy aims at creating familiarity with the product. Familiarity creates goodwill which is very valuable to the advertiser. For example, a customer asks for summer suiting and is shown cloth of various mills. He selects Raymond's terricot material, because he had heard Raymonds' as one of the best makers of cloth. Future action copy does not perform all the functions of selling process, but only the preliminary steps. Its duty is to interest and educate.

Appeal: The use of appeals in advertising is of great importance. The appeals primarily are 'rational' and 'emotional'. The advertising strategists consider emotional appeal more effective, except in certain situations, such as advertising of expensive appliances. But the communication researchers, do not find it more effective than the rational appeal. In fact, recent thinking and research have led to the belief that most effective appeal may be one which is both highly emotional and highly rational. Many advertisements are so written as to appeal to different instincts or desires or motives. The sex or romantic appeal is frequently used by makers of cosmetics, scents and perfumes and toilet soaps with the help of illustration, e.g. 'something wonderful happens when you change to Caline Snow—it is healthy — it protects — it beutifies'. "Evening in Paris scent lingers lovingly — it is worne by more women than any other perfume". "Palmolive — keeps that school girl complexion". The desire to impress others is often responsible for the purchase of a more expensive car. Whatever the kind of appeal, it will be effective if it functions to *reinforce* existing attitudes and behaviours, or to *stimulate* or *active* people who are already predisposed to act to the desired manner. It is also vital to remember that some people are more predisposed than others to be influenced by advertising for a particular product or brand.

Another factor of great importance that affect advertising is the presence of different varieties of people in the total market. There are people who have never heard of your product or company. The messages about the product have not penetrated to the point where consumer recognises the brand or company name. The advertising has to strive for achieving consumer Awareness. The next step is comprehension. In this state the consumer not only is aware of the product or service, but knows the brand name and recognises the package or trade mark and possesses some degree of comprehension of what the product is and does. This is followed by Conviction, and this can be illustrated by a consumer who says, 'Brand B is name for a polyester fibre made by X Company. Garments made of this fibre dry faster, wear longer and hold their shape better. I intend to buy this product in the future'. Finally, there is Action, in which the consumer has made some overt move towards the purchase of the product. He may have visited a store and made the purchase. It can also happen that the actual sale is beyond the power of advertising; the store did not have the brand in stock, the price was considered too high, or the product lacked appeal when physically examined. However, the advertising induced action. It is the inhibitary factors that stood in the way of consummation of the sale.

Let us suppose that the market consists of an equal number of people at each level; those who are unaware of the product, those who are aware of the product but do not know of its advantage, those who comprehend the product, but are not convinced, those who are convinced but have not gotten around to buying and finally those who are present users of the product. The advertising in this situation has been designed to work at all levels at the same time, moving some people from unawareness to awareness, others to comprehension, conviction and action.

Suggestion. In addition to an appeal to instinct, there are three approaches to secure what the advertiser desires: *Suggestion, appeal to reason* and *rationalisation.* Suggestive advertisements aim ultimately to secure action by display of name, illustrations of various kinds and surroundings that impart distinction, or sometimes by direct command. Suggestive advertising tends to get ideas into the mind, largely through repetition, impressive size, illustration and short phrases. In one of the Videocon TV advertisement a lion is shown sitting on the word Videocon and underneath is the Command – Statement : "Bring Home The Leader" "Sugar Free Sets You Free" – free from bitter Saccharine taste. Free from Weight – inducing Calories "Says YES to SUGAR FREE".

Reason. In advertisements which appeal to reason, logical arguments and facts are presented that will enable the reader to decide after due deliberation. Articles bought by businessmen for business purposes, such as data processing machines, cash registers, factory machinery, trucks, etc. are usually advertised by reason appeal. The prospective customer wants the question: "What will it do to help me"? "What has been the experience of other users"? Weliel Telematik adapts high-tech from Siemens". "The new T1200 is the World's most advanced teleprinter — because it is based on a 140 year old idea. Little wonder that T1200 is already finding important buyers".

Rationalisation. Some advertisements begin with an appeal to instinct and close with an appeal to reason. When instinct and reason are in conflict, rationalisation appeal seeks to resolve this conflict. For example, your instinct say, "Buy a new suit". Your reason says, Don't buy, you cannot afford it". The rationalisation appeal in the advertisement says, "To succeed in business you must be well dressed.

You need that suit for the sake of your business". Rationalisation is really a process of finding apparently logical reasons for an illogical act; and it is because of this appeal that advertising is accused of inducing people to buy things they cannot afford.

An appeal to be effective should be presented in concrete form. Abstractions such as 'comfort', 'durability', etc., should be shown in application or by illustration. For example, durability of shoes is shown in the phrase, "You get the Wear of an Extra-Pair". "Discover the joy of being pampered in a million way" — Hotel Sofitel Surya. Selling a car superbly built: Your creative strategy should be demand advertising that shows how the car performs and not how beautiful it is.

Give your product a distinctive personality; that will build "brand image". Advertise what is important not what is obvious. Direct the appeal towards the interests of the buyer, not those of seller. A product should be advertised as a means to an end rather an end in itself. One does not buy books out the joys of knowledge; not things but benefits. The *You* attitude of selling should enter the copy. Think ahead – Being first in the market is best. Keep your strategy upto date. The world changes so does your market and your consumer. People who try new products are younger, better educated, richer and more venturesome than the average. But don't change your strategy without good reason. Above all, have a better product. Better advertising starts with a better product.

Copy. When the appeal to be used in an advertisement has been decided upon, the question arises what importance should be given to copy or illustration. This will depend upon circumstances. Illustration alone will serve the purpose if it is merely to flash a message upon the consciousness of the reader, to remind him of the product. If the advertisement has to carry the large portion of the selling load, the sufficient printed salesmanship shall be necessary. Copy is the means by which the advertiser's ideas are given expression to in a message to the reader.

Requisites of a good copy. (1) The psychological aims of an advertisment are that the public must be made to Look; (2) Like; (3) Learn; (4) Buy. In other words, a scientifically drafted copy should (1) attract primary initial attention; (2) hold attention in an interesting way, awaken and stimulate interest; (3) bring about an association or impression which will have permanence, or memory value; (4) convince, persuade or induce; (5) suggest and lead to specific response to encourage the decision to act — determination to buy. The following are the essentials of a good copy:

You must make people see it
You must make people read it
You must make people comprehend it

You must make people believe it

You must make people want your product.

Mental steps. The foregoing essentials of a good copy are discussed here in the form of mental steps:

1. The first step is to catch or attract attention, which means that the readers' mind as-well-as his eye must be captured. Attention can be secured by a variety of devices — size, large littering, brilliant colours, striking illustrations, layout copy, novelty, humour, and so on.

2. The next step is to create interest and hold it. The copy must be so interesting that, once the attention has been captured, the prospect wants to read it to the exclusion of other items. This may be done by exciting the curiosity of the individual, by embodying in the advertisement some matter of particular relevance to the reader's needs.

3. The next point to bear in mind is that people must understand what you say. Clearness is a matter of words, or the manner in which you use them. Words are the tools to describe, define, explain, illustrate and visualise the ideas of the product to the reader. Words are the wings to thought — choose words that make thought fly. Use plain words that the reader can understand.

4. The next step is to make people believe your copy. This means not only the truth, but also restraint and moderation in copy. Don't make extravagant claims, nor use superlatives. Get read; above all, get believed.

5. The final step is to stimulate action; to make people like your product so much as to cause them to jump out of their chairs and rush to buy it or inquire about it. Or, if you are advertising for future action response, the copy should build up memory and arouse enthusiasm in their minds for your product so that when the need arises they buy it rather than some other product.

Action-attracting devices. The first device is the use of the *headline*. Hero Honda – "Fill it Forget it". Headline should be as short as possible. "Thirty Plus – Energy Rechargers" – tonic capsules. Bring home, happiness. Bring home Kelvinator". More Flashes of Genius from Canon" – Camera. The ideal headline does three things: (1) arouses curiosity, (2) contains new value, (3) appeals to self-interest of the reader.

Slogans are used to attract and hold attention. To be effective, a slogan should be short, simple, easily remembered and filled with a pleasing suggestion of the product. "Better buy Capstan – they are blended better". "Glaxo Builds Bonny Babies". "Good to the last drop" – coffee "when you need it Bad, we 've got it good". "Works while you sleep".

Illustration helps the advertisement to perform any or all the mental steps of A.I.D.A., but usually it does more for attention and interest. An illustration, to be effective should be not only relevant but also be free from technical errors, such as milking a cow from the wrong side, or smoke going in wrong direction of a ship. The package also plays a vital role as an identifying characteristic of the brand as in "Buy the film in the Yellow box", Green, Yellow, Red Label Lipton Tea. Where products are not sold in packages, or where the appearance of the package is not important the product itself may be shown in any of the various ways. Showing the product in use is a popular and efficient way of employing illustration. Automobiles, telephones, typewriters, soaps, cleaning powders, shaving creams, razors are frequently pictured in use. A favourite way is to show the result obtained by using the product, e.g. in a Surf advertisement, "Why is his shirt whiter than Mine", or "Rin Washes Whitest", by displaying washed garments.

Colour is often used to attract attention and to introduce memory value. Colour can bring about emotional reactions that no word description can do. Bright colour is the easiest way to attract attention. Red attracts most eyes. The second best is green, and the third best is black. *Contrast* is closely allied to colour brightness. Black on white is the oldest combination of contrasting colours; others are Blue on Yellow, red on green, but never white on black.

To conclude, an advertisement next to reading matter is twice as effective as when surrounded by other advertising. To be successful an advertisement should completely satisfy these three questions: (1) Will it increase sales? (2) Will it add prestige? (3) Will it help build price line?

Advertising Media. Media is one of the most important studies of the advertising man. They are the means by which the pre-determined aim has to be achieved, and the right choice of media is, therefore, vital to the success of a selected advertising campaign. Sound appeal presented through the right medium constitutes the ideal advertisement. If the medium is unsuited to the aim of commodity, the appeal, however, sound, will miss the mark. An *advertising medium* may be defined as any publication, poster, sign, radio, television or any other of the various forms of advertising service designated to convey the message which the advertiser expects to reach his buying public, with the ultimate aim of inducing them to purchase his goods or service. It acts as an intermediary between the producer and the consumer. There are a great many kinds and classes of media in general use in present day advertising. All have their particular values and uses, and the advertiser's business is to choose the one or more best suited to his needs.

The media in current use may be classified as follows:-

1. Press
   (a) Newspaper — city, small-town, Sunday, daily, weekly, English or Vernacular.

(b) Magazine	General or class, illustrated or otherwise, English or Vernacular.
(c) Trade and Technical Journals	Also Industrial Year Books, Commercial Industrial and Telephone Directories.
2. Direct Mail	circulars, catalogues, leaflets, booklets, folders and other printed matter.
3. Outdoor	Posters and bills or hoardings on railway station walls, outside commercial buildings, bases, printed and electric signs on buildings or sky-writing.
4. Radio and Television	Spot, Sectional or national broadcasts.
5. Publicity	Movie slides and films, metal signs attached to trees, fences, electricity poles, or other prominent places, store cards, calendars, blotters, diaries, theatres, schools, plants, tours, exhibitions.
6. House-to-house	Sampling, couponing.
7. Industrial and Cinematograph films.	

Press. No two media are alike. Each must be studied for its suitability to the task. Press and now television are, the most patent forces in advertising. However, the value of any press media depends upon its circulation, in terms of figures as well as quality and several other factors such as periodicity of issue and flexibility. Similarly, television message will reach those who watch the television. Quality shows the class of people who read and those who view the television. Quality often yield better results than quantity. The dominant idea of the newspaper is news. The reading is hurried. The advertisement must, therefore be striking, informal and timely. The newspaper is of great importance as an advertising medium in India. It reaches all classes of the population. Its timeliness is another advantage. A campaign can be started or stopped quickly. Selectivity of markets is possible, as campaigns can be limited to a select area. Newspapers offer great opportunity for repetition and classified advertisement.

Magazine advertising aims to give wide publicity to firms' name and brands and to create prestige for a product by the impression of extensive and permanent connection with a respectable company. There is great chance of picture advertising in a magazine. High class goods, luxuries and conveniences can be profitably advertised in them. The Technical and Trade Press is dominated by professional or vocational interest. The audience is usually small but select, technically well informed, in earnest, and influential e.g. medical men, consulting engineers, architects. The nature of appeal to them should be informative on the highest plane of accuracy as to facts.

Circulars and Catalogues. An important adjunct to the press is circulating or direct advertising or mailing. The circulating material can be used for supply and gathering information. A short letter, worded in attractive language may work wonders with a busy man. It is a personal communication to an individual and is thus superior to a newspaper or a magazine. A catalogue aims at supplying all information needed to place an order. It is a silent but effective salesman for the house. Mailing cards act as a form of business insurance rather than as means of actually making sale. It acts as a reminder. Folders usually have perforated reply cards attached or separate reply cards inserted. Booklets are used to present the talking points of the product in detail.

Posters and Bill Boards. For the sale of articles of common utility poster is one of the most suitable types of media. Posters must be pasted on walls or on boards set up in thoroughfares. A bill board of a hoarding is an extension of a poster. It is bigger, more elaborate and attractive. A poster or a bill board is, at most, a picture in colours, with an epigram, reduced to its lowest terms. It is a name or a symbol printed large. Seen but for a moment, it must convey the message in a flash.

Electric Signs. Electric signs are either still or moving. The still signs have the attraction of light and colour, while the latter also have the attribute of movement. The main objection against electric signs is their heavy cost, especially in case of mammoth signs. They can be used only by very large firms of repute which wish to keep the product constantly in public mind.

Radio. Radio advertising is well established now. Messages are broadcast from the Vibhid Bharti Channel or Commercial Service of All India Radio. These are mainly broadcast along with popular programme of music, mostly film songs. Radio advertisements reach a vast section of the population. People can listen to them even when they are busy in other activities.

Television. Television is the youngest but fast growing medium of advertisment. It makes its appeal, both to the eye and ear. Demonstration is the common feature of television commercial. Only well established companies with vast funds can make use of it as it is very costly.

Films and Exhibitions. Large firms make extensive use of films, either in two minute films is the Cinema house, or an industrial film exhibition in industrial exhibitions and other suitable places. The film incorporates the history of the firm and a trip to all the sections of the works, and the technical processes involved from the raw material stage to the finished product ready for sale.

In addition to those principle media, there are many more methods of publicity which have been used with advantage by numerous firms. Gift schemes for increasing sales are already on the market. The prize schème by means of competitiòn for a solgan or a name. Display advertising is also very important. It helps the dealer to move the goods from the shelves in to the hands of the consumers. Lastly, we come to the advertising medium afforded by Direct Mail which helps sell goods of the mail order advertiser.

Television Commercial. Ever since the television medium began accepting advertising commercials in January, 1976, there has been progressive use of television. In 1983, the share of TV in total advertising business of Rs. 375 crore was a mere 5 per cent. In 1987, this share rose to 21 per cent out of a total business of Rs. 700 crore in spite of a steep 200 per cent hike in TV Tariff rates in March, 1987. In the current year (1990), the TV's share is expected to be 30 per cent of Rs. 1000 crore advertising business.

The biggest loser has been the Cinema from a share of over 9 per cent of the total advertising business in 1983, it fell to 2 per cent and it is expected to come down to one per cent in 1990. The share of advertising business of Press slipped from 77 per cent in 1983 to about 70 per cent in 1987, and estimates place the figure at about 64 per cent in 1990. In spite of the TV commercial being very costly, TV, which has already achieved a big success in consumer goods advertising, is going to grow faster in advertising earnings.

How to make Effective Use of Different Media[1].

It is said that the advertising should not only charm the consumer, but it should also persuade him/her to buy. In the following pages are given some of the ways to use various media to achieve this objective.

Starting with television, the "story beared" in it has three elements: the picture that indicates the main action of the commercial and a written description of what the viewers will see and hear. The picture must tell the story. Television is a visual medium. The viewers remember what they see, not what they hear. So get the viewer's attention. Be single-minded and make the commercial simple and direct for immediate effect. Also take extra pains to implant your product name in the viewer's mind. Show people, not objects. People are interested in people. Show that your product does what you said it will a moment ago.

Demonstrate when you can show your product does something well, or better than competition, show it. Show the viewer what your

1. Adapted from Kennoth Romen and Jane Mass, How to Advertise.

product does. Secondly, get a celebrity endorse the claim to make it believable. Construct your commercial on a single product benefit. When product differences are small, focus attention on the user, rather than on the product. For special communication purpose, use animation, more especially to talk, to children. They enjoy and remember cartoon characters. Look for a human quality in your commercial, put warmth in it. Emotional commercials can be used for Final Touch. Food cooked in Rath Vanaspati shows husband praising his wife for delicious food.

Printed Media. Newspapers and magazine advertisements carry out similar strategy as television commercial. If you are supporting a television campaign with print as a secondary media, that advertising should carry out the same theme as the television commercials. In order to get more effective print-advertising, do the following:

(a) Get your message in the head line, which should tell the whole story.
(b) Use your headline to reach your prospect. Single out the prospect. Great news for matters of growing children—"Horlicks builds bones".
(c) Offer benefit in the headline to sell more.
(d) Inject news in your headline. If you have a new product or an improvement of an existing product, announce it.
(e) Avoid negative headlines. People are literal minded and may remember only the negatives. Sell the positive benefits in your product.
(f) Look for story appeal in the illustration. Next to the headline, illustration is the most effective way of getting reader's attention.
(g) Use simple layouts. One big picture works better than several small ones. Avoid cluttered pages.
(h) If you have a photograph, put a caption under it.
(i) Give facts and not adjectives, and be specific.
(j) Do not print copy in reverse type, i.e. white or black.
(k) In corporate advertising, offer service.
(l) Make each advertisement a complete sale.

You must get your message in the headline. What works best in Radio? Radio has the unique power to stir the imagination. It is also the most flexible medium. You can get on or off the air quickly. It is a personal medium. You can talk directly to the listener. To get better radio commercial, stretch the listeners imagination. Present one idea and be direct and clear. Mention the brand name and your promise early. Ask listeners' to take action.

All outdoor advertising sells to an audience in motion. People driving past your poster cannot stop for a second look, even if they want to. So give only one idea on a billboard. Keep it simple, but use bold lettering. Use colours for readibility, and look for human and emotional content for memorability. Personalise when you can.

In all types of advertising media, make sure your offer is right. More than any other element, what you offer the consumer — in terms of product, price or premium — will make the difference. Free gift is the most powerful offer you can make.

Testing the Advertisement. There is necessarily a great amount of inefficiency in advertising. So many things are unknown and many cannot be found. Still the advertiser wants to known how far his advertising has been effective. Over the years a variety of measures have been developed and used for testing the effectiveness before and after publication. There are indeed four stages of copy research, namely, –

(a) Research prior to the development of the advertising;
(b) Research during the development of the advertising;
(c) Pre-testing of advertisements;
(d) Posts testing of advertisements.

The research prior to the development of the advertising concerns both the development of the advertising ideas and the evaluation of these ideas. There is continuous analysis of past experience in the search for guiding principles.

Secondly, the research during the development of the advertising essentially is the evaluation of the advertising idea in rough form. Scientifically planned consumer surveys make it possible to obtain advertising guidance through consumer contacts.

Thirdly, the pretesting of the advertising consists of research on a print advertisement or a commercial before it is run. This includes measurement of various consumer responses after new advertisement are prepared, but before money has been spent to circulate them. It is important to discover if there are any weaknesses and to make revisions in advance.

Fourthly, the post-testing of advertising is research on the effectiveness of the advertisement or commercial, or campaign, after it has run. Various techniques are used to check up on the effectiveness of current advertisements and to enlarge the rules to be applied to similar future advertising situations. Too many businessmen think that comparative sales results are the only check on advertising effectiveness. If sales during and after a campaign are higher than before it is easy to assume that advertising had an effect on the increase in sales – and vice versa. But this does not distinguish between the success of advertising in different media or of different approaches used in campaign or of other variables affecting sales.

Post-testing of advertisement may be in the following ways: Direct

Mail test, where large number of mailing pieces are to be sent out, only a small number is sent out first as a trial. If sales are satisfactory it is reasonable to suppose that they will be so for a large number. In Testing by window Display, the article is displayed in the windows of several stores for some time and sales are recorded. Then the advertisement appears in the press or commercial and is tied up with the article in the window and on the counter. If the sales go up, the advertisement is successful. Another method is 'split run' test. Some magazines and newspapers allow the publication of different advertisements for the same product in different number of copies. In all split run tests, keyed coupons are used so that the advertiser can tell which advertisement pulled best. Keying up is a good method in mail order selling.

SALES PROMOTION

Sales promotion, as part of the total distribution system, plays a vital role in inducing the consumer to buy your product. Sales promotion covers so many activities that it is difficult to define it precisely. The American Marketing Association defines it as follows:

"Sales Promotion, consists of those marketing activities other than advertising, publicity and personal selling, that stimulate consumer purchasing and dealer effectiveness, such as displays, shows, and exhibitions, demonstrations and various other non-recurring selling efforts not in the ordinary routine". In short, Sales Promotion is any activity which supplements or improves the effectiveness of personal selling and advertising.

Sales promotion devices can include premiums, coupons, contests temporary price reduction, free goods, letters to trade, literature, educational material, displays and trade shows. Sales promotion takes into consideration the communication gaps that always exist between the producer and the consumer. Sales Promotion should therefore be closely coordinated with advertising and personal selling. The sales promotion programmes are often designed to accomplish the following objectives:

1. To introduce a new product.
2. To increase the inventories of middlemen and consumers.
3. To increase a products rate of use among existing consumers.
4. To attract new customers.
5. To counter a competitors sales promotion and other activities.
6. To reduce the extent of a seasonal decline in sales.
7. To make it easier for salesmen to secure more orders and arrange displays in retail stores.

Promotions Planning. In order to achieve the foregoing objectives, it is but necessary to have a proper promotion plan. Planning before launching a sales promotion is emphasised because companies very often make no plans for sales promotion until sales begin to fall in the market place, when it is difficult to revive a falling product. The manager responsible for sales promotion has to be a professional, for every time he writes a letter, he is engaged in some form of sales promotion. He must remember that both he and his product are judged by the written words coming out of his office. It is becoming more and more important that printed pieces be well conceived, be printed on good paper and use photographs that truly depict the product or the image the company wishes to project. Above all, the product that is being promoted must be good in all respects, otherwise the promotion effort may be considered frivolous and will not receive cooperation of the trade.

Approach to Sales Promotion. There are five different market categories in which sales promotion is used, namely,—

1. Industrial Selling;
2. Selling to wholesalers;
3. Selling to retailers;
4. Selling to consumers;
5. The Selling of Services.

The industrial field comprises a relatively small number of rather important customers. Sales promotion should approach them with adequate and descriptive literature giving accurate and full information about the product and the service the supplier will provide.

Those manufacturers who sell through wholesalers must gear their sales promotion to the needs of the wholesaler and his salesmen. In this field sales promotion and sales training are very close. It may pay to entertain wholesaler's sales force and provide training at the same time. Sometimes factory salesmen may work on the dealer's sales floor by demonstrating their own product, and kill two birds with one stone. They are directly promoting their products and lending support to a sales promotion effort at the point of sales.

The various kinds of envelope stuffers which are used either as mailing pieces such as bill inserts or straight give-away pieces for those customers who want to know more about the product will be the best kind of sales promotion for the retailer. The catalogues, which should be in the proper size and give accurate description of the products. Dealers usually prefer price lists that give only the retail price so that confusion does not arise between the dealer's cost and his selling price. Sometimes, displays, which do not take up too much space, are welcomed by the retailers.

Selling to customers, of course, is the field that belongs to the retail dealer, the mail order house, and house to house specialist. All three use sales aids furnished by the manufacturer in addition to their own sales promotion.

Material used in Sales Promotion. The following items are used in sales promotion efforts under different conditions:

Advance Premium is a gift given before the sale, usually in return for a promise to buy later or to become a regular customer.

Bill enclosures are small pieces that are mailed in the same envelope with the monthly statement. Brochure is book bound or stitched or stapled in semipermanent form carrying a complete presentation. Usually more detailed than a catalogue, it gives useful information relating to skills and services. Catalogue is a complete and current listing of all products information necessary to place an order. Circular is an inexpensive hand bill that may be distributed freely.

Counter display covers a wide variety and quality of top-of-the-counter displays, usually made to accommodate one or more of the actual products.

Demonstration means public use of the product, such as making and serving coffee from a coffee maker. Envelope Stuffers are small pieces of give away literature used either as bill enclosures or for hand out pieces.

Free offers are free gifts to attract customers in anticipation that a sale of the product will be made.

Giveaways are items of small value packed together with the merchandise such as a measuring spoon given with Chavanprash, or a tooth brush given with toothpaste, or a mug given away with Bournevita tin.

Handbills are printed pieces usually distributed by hand to passersby or within a certain marketing area.

Inserts are printed pieces inserted in the daily newspapers.

Pamphlets are small booklets often used for educational or instructional purposes. Point-of-Purchase Displays are displays which help the customer make a selection without help from the salesperson. This is particularly useful for impluse merchanside.

Permium is an article of merchandise used as an extra inducement to buy another product. Sampling involves distributing merchandise to the trade or to the public in anticipation that further purchase will result from a free trial.

Trade Fairs are exhibitions open to trade only for a certain period of the day, while open to the public at a different time of the day. Visual aids is that part of the sales presentation which demonstrates by being seen, such as charts, slides, and the like.

In conclusion, it may be stated that sales promotion, just as all other phases of marketing, should be inter-related and compatible with the entire distribution system of the company. The manufacturer must keep the needs of the consumer in mind. The consumer is said to be the king or queen.

CHAPTER XLIV

THE TRAFFIC DEPARTMENT AND FOREIGN TRADE

A—THE TRAFFIC DEPARTMENT

Organisation of the Traffic Department. The central management must provide a suitable organisation for the safe, rapid, and economical transport of goods and materials, whether outgoing or incoming. In a manufacturing concern of size, there is generally a separate department known as the Traffic Department. In charge of this department and all traffiic matters is the Traffic Manager, who is an expert on everything connected with his function. Not only is he responsible for the proper operation of the department, but he also conducts negotiations with the carriers and attends to matters raised before the Ministry of Transport. In a large concern, there may be an Assistant Traffic Manager or chief clerk who looks after the details of the department management, leaving the Manager free for general supervision and outside conferences. Other members of the traffic department may include rate clerks, tracers, packers, checkers, record clerks, file clerks, stenographers, etc. Each of these has specific duties to perform, but one person may handle more duties than one, or in a large concern, there may be many persons performing one duty.

Many concerns of comparatively small size do not have a separate traffic department. Instead, a shipping clerk is entrusted with the traffic function and his department is called the shipping room. Many concerns have receiving rooms, which receive all goods delivered to them. In some others, the stock clerk may handle the receiving work, or he may handle both receiving and despatching, acting as both shipping clerk and receiving clerk. Sometimes the receiving room is a part of the purchasing department, since the 'buyer' buys what is received. Where there is a traffic department, both shipping and receiving are a part of this department. Whatever the organisation set-up, the functions are there in all sizes of concerns.

Functions of Traffic Department. It has been observed that upon the Traffic Manager rests the responsibility of safe, rapid, and economical transport of outgoing goods and incoming materials. He has to ascertain the transport rates applicable to his company's products. He must also determine the best routes, to secure speed, diminish risk of breakage and give the most convenient destinations. For outbound shipments, he will select the best means of transport, notify the carrier selected, deliver the goods to the carrier and frequently follow the shipment to its destination with a view to ensuring that there are no delays in delivery. For incoming shipments, he will specify the method of transport and follow the shipment to ensure its safe and prompt arrival.

These are the main functions or duties of the Traffic Manager and his department, but the following outline will give a better idea of the chief as well as subsidiary and ancillary functions.

Functions relating to incoming shipment. Incoming shipments are concerned with goods which have been bought, and are shipped as per purchase order sent to the supplier by the purchasing department. The supplier may ship the goods in any of several ways. If he is located at a distant place and there is no special hurry for the goods, or if the goods are bulky but not costly, they will probably be shipped by goods train. If the goods are wanted immediately, they may be shipped by passenger or express train which is more expensive than goods train but much quicker. If the distance is not very great, motor truck may be used. In an emergency, such as broken machine standing idle, the parts for repairing it may be shipped by air, but this method is very expensive. Packages up to a certain size and weight may be sent by parcel post. Local deliveries may be made by van, bullock-cart, hand cart, or by a messenger, either on foot, bicycle, or motor cycle.

The Traffic Manager determines the type of transport—railway, motor truck, air, or parcel post. In case of railway whether to ship by goods trains or passenger train. He checks the rates to see whether they are class, tariff or special. He sees to the expeditious arrival of the shipment. On their arrival, he arranges to receive the goods, and in that connection attends to the following matters: notice from purchasing department that gave the order for the goods, recepit for delivery, unloading of goods, weighing contents, if necessary, checking contents, noting loss or damage, sending the goods to the store room.

The job of the traffic department is that of checking the bills, especially freight bills. This work involves seeing (1) that the quantities are right, (2) that the weights are correct, (3) that the routing is the proper one, (4) that the classification is the right one (especially in case of railway transport), and (5) that the correct rate is applied. Any discrepancies are taken up with the carrier for adjustment. If there is any shortage or damage, the traffic department prepares a claim, presents it to the carrier and follows it up.

Functions relating to outbound shipment. While goods arrive as a result of purchase orders, they are despatched in execution of sale orders placed by customers or taken by salesmen. In short, a firm's purchase orders are its suppliers' sale orders, and customers' purchase orders are a firm's sale orders. This is indicated on the diagram on the next page.

As in the case of inward goods, the selection of the route may devolve on the traffic department. Ordinarily, a customer, when placing an order, indicates the route and the method of shipment. To many customers, however, it does not make much difference so long as they get their goods promptly and economically. In such cases, the traffic department has to select the route and method of shipment. In making the choice same considerations apply as are stated above for incoming shipments, due regard being given to speed cost and safety of transport.

In case of a foreign order, shipping company shall have to be contacted and shipment by rail and transhipment into the ship shall have to be arranged if the firm is located upcountry at a distance from the port. In case of delays, delayed shipments shall have to be traced; and in case of loss or damage, claim shall be prepared, filed and followed up.

In addition to the direct work of despatching and receiving goods, there shall be maintained full and up-to-date correspondence, files, records and tariffs, for both inward and outward shipments. In a large concern, considerable correspondence passes through the traffic department, and the department files are important in keeping track of all the papers concerning the movement of goods. Another very important duty cast upon the traffic department is to keep in close contact with the sales department, inasmuch as the delivery to a carrier is an act more closely connected with selling than with manufacturing. Goods are shipped

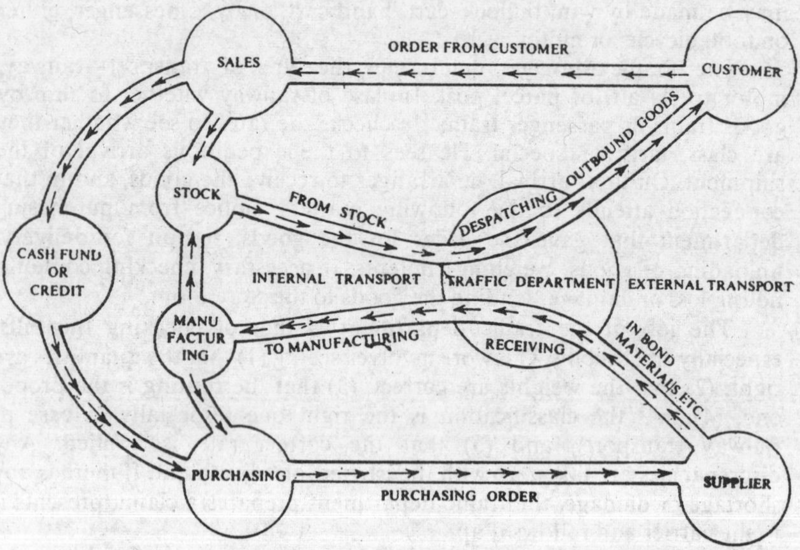

where, when and in the quantities ordered by the selling department. The cost of delivery is often absorbed as a part of selling price, and so becomes an item the limits of which must be controlled by the same factors which control the general process of price setting. The selling department finds its field determined, in part, by the speed and cost of shipment. Errors in shipment, or delays, bring complaints to the sales department for adjustment, and may even require the sending out of duplicate merchandise. Similarly, the traffic department should furnish to all buying officers, on request, information as to the length of time required to secure supplies from designated places and as to the relative freight rates from rival supplying points. It will ship merchandise or order bills of lading or railway receipts when instructed to do so by the credit department; and on the motion of the creditman it will exercise the right of stoppage in transit.

Freight rates and classification. Most of the long distance, generally more than 100 miles, traffic in our country is handled by railways. Therefore, railway rates influence considerably the movement of goods. In view of this, the traffic department of every concern should compile information regarding freight rates applying to the good of the house. We have seen in an earlier chapter that the chief factors which enter into the determination of railway rates are: (1) the value of the service to the shipper, or the ability to pay; (2) the cost of performing the service; (3) competition with other carriers; (4) protection of vested interests; and (5) compliance with the requirements of law. Since railway undertakings are joint concerns for all practical purposes, and since they must charge both according to value and cost of service, they charge different rates on different goods. To charge different rates on each of the lakhs of articles that may be shipped would be an impossibility. Therefore, the railways group all the known articles into a few classes, so that a correspondingly small number of class rates will provide a determination of the charge to be made in any individual case. Some of the important factors which influence classification may be summed up here; for the traffic department is much concerned with classification of products and its effect on freight rates. In the first place, the bulk of the article in proportion to its weight is taken into consideration. A bulky article occupies large space, and must pay higher rate. If the same thing is pressed, and packed well, it may be placed in a lower class and so pay lower rate. The liability to damage of an article is the next point. Glassware, china, porcelain or clay models require careful handling and are placed in a higher class.

The size of the consignment also influences classification. The "smalls" demand almost as much attention as large consignments. The "smalls" therefore usually pay higher rates. Similarly, wagon loads are charged lower rates, e.g., if apples are of the weight of one ton per wagon, they are placed in Class I, the lowest class, otherwise in Class II. The time within which goods have to be carried to their destination also plays an important part in determining the class to which they are assigned. Articles to be conveyed within a short time are placed in a higher class because they have to be carried by faster trains. Perishable and fresh goods all fall in this category. Regularity of shipment of certain goods helps in classification. If the Manager knows that certain goods are regularly shipped he may place them in a lower class or charge a 'special' rate on them. The type of wagon to be used also influences classification. If goods can be carried in an open truck, they will be placed in a lower class, while those requiring closed wagon will go to the higher class. For a special wagon, such as the one for carrying horses, cattle, etc., still higher rate will be charged. Articles which are substitutes for one another are usually placed in the same class irrespective of other considerations. For example, all those raw materials and articles which are used in paper making, like esparto grass, wood pulp, and rags, are placed in the class subject to certain conditions.

Obviously every company wants to get the lowest freight rate possible; therefore, the rate clerk with traffic department keeps abreast of the rates as applicable to its products. There are also special rates for some special commodities, e.g., coal, which is lower than the class rates. Station to station rates also prevail especially between stations where railway has to compete with road transport. All those rates should be taken advantage of. The tariffs giving the rates are available and they should be kept handy. Where a concern has customers or cities to which it makes frequent shipment of the same articles, it is helpful to prepare a statement of rates to different localities, instead of looking up in the tariffs every time a shipment is made. Of course, the statement must be kept up-to-date.

Packing. Proper packing is very important, for it is often possible to save not only unnecessary breakage in transit, but also freight charges if the best method of packing is adopted. The nature of the package and the method of packing exert a decisive influence upon the freight rate charged. In a company of small or medium size, the shipping clerk will look to the packing. In the large concern, however, where large quantities of goods are shipped, a special method of packing is standardised by the traffic department. Proper packing means that the goods are packed so as to minimise the chances of loss, theft, breakage, and deterioration from weather. As goods are packed, they are also checked against a copy of the sales order. The packer and checker should initial the packing slip to fix their responsibility. This slip should be placed in the shipment to enable the customer to compare the contents with it.

Marking. Next comes the marking of the package. Each package should be legibly marked with the name of the consignee and the destination. The marking should be done in such a way that it will not become obliterated or separated from the merchandise. Care should be taken to see that the marks on the packages agree with the shipping instructions. The shipping instructions and the bill of lading should be made out with care, legibly, with full names and addresses, with accurate descriptions, with the numbers and marks of all packages, and with full instructions. The railway receipt, bill of lading, air consignment note or motor truck receipt are all documents of title to goods so as to enable the holder to take delivery of the consignment.

Delivery to Carrier. If the sales order indicates that either the price has been received or credit is given, the packages are delivered to the carrier or taken to the post office. If in some places the railways have pick-up and house delivery service, they will call for the shipment and deliver it for a nominal charge. Parcel post packages must be delivered to the post office. The motor freight carriers pick up goods at the company's place of business and deliver them there.

As soon as a shipment has been delivered to the carrier the shipping clerk notifies the sales department, which then notifies the customer. This notification usually consists of the bill of lading, railway receipt, air consignment note, etc., and invoices or bill and a covering letter.

Sometimes a letter is sent, and in urgent cases a telegram so that the customer may know his goods are on the way. If the goods arrive safely at the destination the traffic department has no further responsibility. But any one or more of a number of things may happen.

Claims for loss or damages. In India the liability of railways is that of a common carrier. When goods are carried at railway risk and therefore at a higher charge, and have been properly packed, the railway is responsible for the loss. If they are carried at owner's risk, the railway administration is liable for loss or damage caused by misconduct or negligence on the part of the railway administration or its servants. If the goods arrive at their destination in a damaged condition, or are lost, the liability will rest on carrier in accordance with terms of the contract and the law. The receiving clerk should note the damage or loss and also see that the carrier or his agent notes it down. Where the consignment is lost, the carrier is liable to pay the price of the goods unless he is exempted by law, e.g., loss by act of God, or by contract. The shipper has to prove that he shipped the goods and also what the shipment contained. The bill of lading or the railway receipt or air consignment note or way-bill is a sufficient proof of shipment, and a certified copy of the invoice is proof of the contents. A comparison of the weight when shipped with the weight when received by the consignee will often show up any discrepancy, since a decrease in weight would indicate that a shortage occurred while the carrier had the shipment.

When the shipment is damaged or lost the traffic department prefers to the carrier a claim for such loss or damage. The claim must be accompanied by supporting papers such as the railway receipt and the invoice. As the law requires the filing of claims within a certain time, the traffic department should get together all the evidence required to support the claim and file it promptly. The authorities are usually slow in looking into and settling the claims. They should be followed up to avoid the claims being side-tracked.

Where a shipment has been delayed, the tracing clerk in the traffic department, on being informed of the delay, should take out the file copy of the bill of lading or the railway receipt and telephone, wire or write to the station master of the place where the shipment was made. He should also ask the consignee to make inquiries at the destination. The railway authorities are alerted to locate the consignment and deliver to the consignee immediately on being traced. If the shipment is not delivered within a reasonable time, a claim should be filed.

It usually happens that the officers, department heads, salesmen and other employees have to travel on business by train, aeroplane or steamship. It is usual to ask the Traffic Manager to arrange for the booking for such accommodation. Very often last-minute decisions are made for travelling, and it may in the ordinary course be difficult to arrange for accommodation by the person wishing to travel. A good Traffic Manager will be in much better position to arrange for the last minute demand.

B—FOREIGN TRADE

Export and Import Trade. In spite of modern complications and the use of money, trade, especially foreign trade, is fundamentally still the barter of the old. Just as an individual offers a fair return for what he receives, so a nation cannot in the long run import more than it exports. It is, however, not necessary for imports of goods to balance export of goods. Export, for instance, may take the form of services such as those of shipping or insurance or accommodation of holiday visitors—'invisible exports',—but for the present purposes it is necessary only to consider transfer of tangible goods and not of services.

Until recent times, the importer was mainly a merchant who specialised in brining into his country goods which he could sell at a profit. He usually had his own ships like those of Antonio in "The Merchant of Venice". Such were also the other merchants who went abroad with their ships loaded with merchandise which they sold in exchange for foreign goods. Such merchantmen had to go armed and be prepared to fight. Foreign customs and languages presented real difficulties, so the trading abroad was restricted to those who specialised in it. Nowadays, however, commercial methods in different countries approximate more to each other. Standard of commercial honesty has improved considerably during the last two centuries, information about goods available abroad is more easily obtainable through trade catalogues, journals and trade papers, so that now even private individuals can make enquiries of the foreign manufacturer and ask for samples and estimates. Transport facilities have improved immeasurably. It has, therefore, become possible and convenient to carry on import and export trade quite freely and widely.

Controls. While improvements in transport and communications have considerably removed the obstacles of time and distance, foreign exchange machinery has been devised to facilitate settlement of payments in foreign currencies, fresh controls on imports and exports have had to be introduced, especially during the War, although Hitler had imposed very rigid controls on foreign trade in the early 'thirties. During the War, the Allied countries were faced with the three-fold problem of (1) conserving supplies of essential commodities, (2) carrying at the same time the maximum possible foreign exchange, (3) utilising the available foreign exchange in the best manner. The proper solution of the problem made it necessary that the available surplus of any commodity should be directed towards those countries whose currencies were needed. It was also necessary to make sure that all the available foreign exchange was utilised for the prosecution of the War and not frittered away on non-essential consumer goods.

After the war difficulties of balance of payments in respect of certain currencies, especially the dollar, led to the continuance of the controls. It was essential for us to direct export to countries whose currencies were hard to obtain and it was also found necessary that the foreign exchange earned by the exports should be utilised in the interest of the country and not for individual gain. Control on exports were therefore designed to ensure that all the foreign exchange earned was surrendered to the Central Bank—the Reserve Bank of India, in our case. Imports were similarly licensed with a view to checking the import of non-essential goods at the expense of the essential raw materials and equipment. Controls on imports have also been utilised to help the development of new industries in the country. Now, however, with the improvement in world situation, there has been a general relaxation of the control. More and more goods have been put on the O.G.L.—Open General Licence. The Government of India announces its import policy for six months in advance and the Chief Controller of Imports grants licences in accordance with that policy. Goods are not permitted to be landed, nor does the Reserve Bank of India release foreign exchange to pay for them, unless the necessary licence is produced. Since the middle of 1957, however, stringent restrictions have been placed on imports, particularly of consumer goods, as a result of foreign exchange shortage. O.G.L. has been suspended for the time being to preserve foreign exchange.

To understand clearly the mechanism of export trade let us follow the journey an article travels from the place of its market to its final destination, the consumer abroad. "Polycurene", an all-purpose drug, manufactured by a British firm, has been recommended to a man by his doctor. It is very unlikely that he will go home and write to the manufacturer for the supply of the drug. There are many reasons why he cannot be expected to do that. First, he probably does not know the address of the maker; second, the manufacturer, even if located, will not take the trouble of supplying such a small quantity to an occassional customer overseas, in consideration of all the formalities involved in connection with this order; third, an import licence may not be granted to him. Last, but not least, he will not be inclined to wait eight or ten weeks, he wants his medicine now. Obviously, he will call at his usual chemist and will be glad to learn that the chemist stocks the wonder drug. Being gifted with an inquiring mind, the customer wants to know how the drug got there. Two answers to this question are possible. Either there has been previous demand for Polycurene and the chemist considered it necessary to obtain and maintain a stock; or the manufacturer, anticipating a demand in this country, saw to it that this chemist and others stocked the drug. In the first case the initiative came from the chemist and the import machinery was moved, and in the second case from the manufacturer who arranged for its export to India and other foreign countries, a more up-to-date method. This distinction should be kept in mind, as the journey from the producer of the drug to the consumer is different in each case.

Turning first to the case where the chemist notices regular demand for Polycurene and wishes to obtain supplies. Most probably he informed a wholesaler of his requirements and eventually received the goods. The wholesaler, an importer himself, with similar orders from various retailers, has three ways open to obtain the drug from England:

(1) He contacts the manufacturer direct and orders a large quantity of Polycurene, partly to satisfy the immediate needs of his customers and partly for stock.

(2) He approaches an export merchant in the United Kingdom, his regular supplier of British goods. This export merchant supplies the drug as principal whether he has it in stock or buys it from the manufacturer for the purpose.

(3) He sends an "indent", i.e., a buying order, to his commission buying agent appointed by him to do all his buying in Great Britain. The drug will then be supplied by the manufacturer's export department direct to the Indian importer under the supervision of the commission buying agent. This is the most common method employed by importers in India. One reason for this is that an importer of merchandise and other consumer goods rarely requires goods manufactured by a single firm, and the commission buying agent who specialises in handling orders from abroad, buys the goods from various manufacturers, arranges for their proper packing and shipment. Remuneration is by way of commission on the value of the goods purchased.

The term "indent" comes from the ancient legal practice of cutting or indenting edges of duplicated deeds so that identity with each other could be assured on comparison. There is no set form for an indent. It may be a mere bill-heading or it may consist of several foolscap sheets carefully embossed on the front pages like a legal document. An indent may be 'closed or 'open'. If it signifies the source from which goods are to be purchased and the price to be paid for them, as well as brands, it is a "closed indent". If, however, the matter is left to the discretion of the commission house, so that the buying agent invites quotations and places the order at the best price, it will be an "open indent." The importer enjoys the advantage of the expert knowledge of the export routine that the commission house possesses. The work of buying, as we already know, is a serious matter, calling for careful judgment and knowledge. Not only have prices and quality to be considered, but the suitability of designs and patterns for the market for which they are required are also to be taken carefully into account. Further, there is the question of the reliability of the manufacturer in regard to punctual delivery and experience in packing and preparing for shipment.

Since goods have to travel over long distances and have to overcome many hurdles involving expense of time and money, the indent must not be vague or ambiguous. The goods wanted should be precisely stated. The indent should also clarify matters regarding packing, preparing consular and other invoices, insurance, the route to be followed unless these matters are left to the shipper at the other end. At any rate, the manufacturer should get the fullest instructions in all matters. It is also usual for the indent to specify the special marks that the packages should bear so as to obviate the possibility of these being mixed with other packages. The merchant shipper, as distinct from the commission buying agent, would also probably insist on the absence of all labels and marks by which the manufacturer could be discovered, and would give instructions for delivery to his own warehouse or packing firm in suitable form for making up into combined consignment.

Having bought the goods, the next step would be to confirm the orders placed by sending a purchase note to each of the manufacturers concerned. This must be complete and precise in the details it contains, specifying exactly the qualities, prices, markings, time and place for delivery, and terms of payment, discounts, etc. The following is a very generally used form of purchase note[1] —

London, 10th June, 1969.

Messrs.................Smith & Co............

We now confirm our instructions to you for the supply of the under-noted goods.

OR

We have this day purchased from you the undernoted goods.

Please invoice for Order No.......

....(Goods as description)......

Marking......

Price.........

Terms........

Delivery.......

N.B. Please note delivery date as above is final, and if exceeded we may be compelled to cancel this order.

The supervision of the packing, shipping and insurance of the goods is an important duty the export merchant or indent house has to perform before he can be satisfied that the indent is successfully completed. As he often deals on his own account he can be held responsible for any mistakes made in these respects. That is the reason why only large firms undertake this part of the transaction themselves. The more common arrangement, however, and the only one possible for small firms, is to use the services of a firm of packers and also of shipping and insurance agents. Before we deal with this part of the procedure, let us first turn to the manufacturer of Polycurene who takes the initiative.

The manufacturer of 'Polycurene', foreseeing a demand for the drug created by local advertising to the public, a notice or a report in a medical journal or by other reasons, has three means of inducing this particular chemist to stock his product—

(1) The export manager of the manufacturer circulates to all medical practitioners, hospitals and chemists of the locality information about the drug. The forthcoming advertising

1. Croner—*How to Export Goods*, p. 20

campaign and potential recommendation by the medical profession will encourage him to stock it.

(2) The manufacturer's export agent, who holds the sole selling rights of such goods for India, or what is more usual, the sole export rights for all foreign markets, influences the importers to introduce the drug to local chemists by offering good terms, etc.

(3) The manufacturer sends his own travelling representatives to the overseas country with a view to achieving better results by personal contacts, than the Export Manager or the export agent can expect by correspondence, samples, etc.

Before continuing the story beyond the acceptance of the order and its compliance, stress must be laid on the need for advertising in the foreign market by the manufacturer, the export agent or the export merchant. Goods that are exported without a sound, trustworthy introduction might easily be treated with reserve, or even be ignored. In an effort to effect export advertising, the first thing to do is to carry out preliminary investigation of the type already discussed in connection with the marketing of goods. But much greater care has to be exercised when advertising in a foreign land, because habits of people in a distant land and their customs may require special study. In planning his advertising for overseas the exporter must bear in mind that he may be appealing to more than one community. For example, a figure dressed as a Hindu with 'Abdullah' as its name will be ridiculed in India. Keeping this point in mind, the exporter must facilitate the importer's work by advertising and corresponding in his native language.

Quotations. In quoting prices for export, not only the cost of the goods and the profit to be added must be considered but also all those expenses which occur in connection with the shipment. The amount of these expenses depends upon the terms offered in the quotation. It will be nil if the goods are offered "Loco", that is to say, where they lie without packing, carriage, freight, or insurance; it will be considerable if the goods are offered "Free Domicile", i.e., all costs paid to the consignee's doorstep. Every quotation must, therefore, contain a clause stating clearly the stage of the journey up to which the expenses are included in the price. There are a score of standard terms in common use, each with a legally confirmed interpretation, and it will be advisable to employ these terms with strict care and accuracy on every occasion to avoid costly disputes.

F.O.B. terms are among the simplest and most commonly used. The literal meaning is Free on Board, and covers costs of the goods, packing, transport to the docks, lighterage in case where the ship is not lying at the quayside, and the charges for loading and stowing. Freight and insurance are not included. Importers usually prefer through rates, or else C.I.F. (Cost, Insurance, and Freight) as a near approach to through rates. A C.I.F. quotation carries the goods to the port of delivery, but does not cover import dues, railway charges, cartage, etc., after unloading. After all the costs of freight and insurance are easier for the shipper to ascertain than for the importer, who may be thousands of miles away, and the convenience to the latter of a C.I.F. quotation is so obvious that no shipper can doubt that he scores a direct selling point when quoting on this basis against a less obliging competitor's F.O.B.

There are several variants of C.I.F., the principal being C.I.F.C.I. (Cost, Insurance, Freight, Commission, and Interest); C.I.F.C. which does not include Interest; and C.F. which covers Cost and Freight only, omitting insurance. Franco and Free Domicile are terms covering the charges right to the consignee's door; Franco Delivered Custom House includes C.I.F. and landing charges, etc; and Free Duty Custom House includes the payment of Customs duty in addition. Free Harbour is a term used mainly in the Bombay trade, and covers all charges to port of destination.

There are also numerous terms which are either variations of F.O.B. or do not cover the goods so far as F.O.B. For example:—

F.A.S. (Free Alongside Ship) is the equivalent of F.O.B., less loading charges.

F.O.R. (Free On Rail) covers cost, packing, collection, and transport to the railway at the shipper's end, or a point specified, but does not include the railway charges.

D.D. (Delivered Docks) or (Free Docks) covers all charges until the goods are placed in the docks.

Free Port of Departure is a term of somewhat elastic interpretation, and therefore to be avoided. It does not make it clear whether the goods are to be charged as far as the railhead, docks, or actually on board ship at the port of departure.

Loco means simply cost of goods where they lie, without packing or carriage of any kind.

Freight Forward means that freight is to be paid by the consignee.

Packing.—An exporter of goods must give very careful consideration to the packing of goods for shipment. Not only is he responsible to his overseas customer for the safe arrival of the goods, he also endangers his future business if the goods arrive in an unsatisfactory condition at their destination. Export merchants and commission buying agents who have no control over the packing of the goods, as well as manufacturers who are not doing their own packing, should at least inspect the packing and make sure that the instructions of the consignee are strictly observed. Before an exporter passes the packed goods for shipment he must also satisfy himself of the plain marking of all packages in bold stencilled letters on at least two faces with the consignee's name and address, the port of destination, and identifying letters and numbers. Any special warning or instruction to stevedores, such as 'this side up", "breakable", etc., must be clearly indicated.

If the packing is done at the exporter's premises the job should be entrusted to an expert packer who is acquainted with the many customs requirements and the rules of shipping companies. A few methods of packing are given here as illustrations. Soft goods are either baled or packed in cases lined with tin or oil-paper. Wood casing is more costly than baling, but it is safer, and also better preserves the appearance of goods. Therefore, it is used for the more expensive goods. Large machinery has to have the case built up around it, the weight being carefully supported at the correct points of strain. Small pieces, screws, bolts and other spare parts are boxed separately, and boxes firmly fixed inside the main case. Hardware usually travels better in barrels lined with quilted straw and sacking. Twisted wire for binding is less likely to "jump" than metal strips. China and glassware travel best in kegs or barrels.

When preparing the packing of certain goods, e.g., cloth, for shipment the "making-up" must no be overlooked. For example, the law in India compels the stamping of the length on every piece of cotton print and also the number of parts in cut pieces. The "making-up" consists of method of folding, ticketing, stamping, stitching, wrapping in paper or cloth etc. Long cloth is made-up with 36'' fold, dhotis and mulls, "square-fold" according to width, but most commonly 12'' by 12'' or 18'' by 21''. Brocades, sateens, and Italians are folded round boards and wrapped in yellow paper or white "tillot". While some goods are "made-up" there are others which have to be "knocked down" for shipment. This term is used mainly in reference to furniture, which is disjointed in such a manner that an unskilled man with a glue pot can put together on arrival at destination and it is packed flat for shipment in rectangular cases. So with cycles, which are crated in half-dozens, with handle bars and pedals removed and fastened firmly to the frames.

Shipping. When the party accepts the order and agrees to supply the goods ordered, the first part, i.e., legal transfer, is over. The second stage is the actual physical transfer, which is achieved by making use of shipping services. The shipping of goods, however, requires a thorough and specialised knowledge, and it is desirable to employ an experienced shipping clerk, if the exporter wishes to ship goods himself or to appoint a shipping or forwarding agent. It is usually profitable to make use of the services of a good shipping agent who spends all his life in overcoming the constantly changing difficulties connected with the movements of goods from one country to another. As soon as the shipping agent receives word that the goods are packed ready for shipment he books space on the most convenient steamer and either transports the goods to the steamer or gives the exporter suitable despatch instructions. In cases where consular documents are needed, the shipping agent prepares and legalises them. He also covers marine and war insurance, if required, at the official tariff rates without any extra charge, and obtains the policies before the ship sails. Finally, the shipping agent clears the goods through customs and sends the bill of lading, either on the ship to the consignee, or promptly to the exporter's bankers, together with the insurance policy, Consular invoices, etc.

The first step in shipping is to select the ship by which the goods are to be carried. Normally, shipping lines issue announcements of forthcoming sailings, which are published in sailing lists or shipping journals. By consulting these the forwarding agent or the shipping clerk will be able to choose a vessel scheduled to arrive at a time giving a reasonable margin before the contract date of delivery. If the goods are of small bulk and high value, or needed very urgently (general goods), a "Liner" (mail and passenger boat, which also carries a certain amount of cargo) will be selected; otherwise an "intermediate" or cargo steamer, a "Tramp", particularly if bulk cargo is to be shipped, will be engaged to save freight. Before sending the goods, the shipper must inform the company of his intention to ship goods. Thereupon the shipping company will issue a "shipping note" which contains a full statement of the number of packages, their nature and contents, making value, consignee's name, and instructions for effecting insurance. Having completed and returned the shipping note the exporter will receive from the shipping company "Freight note" and "Bill of Lading". The former is simply a debit note for the freight charges; the latter is a detailed certificate of shipment, and three copies are usually provided, one being retained by the shipowners, while the shipper also keeps one and sends the third to the consignee with a full set of invoices, customs declaration, certificate of origin, and other necessary documents for obtaining delivery on arrival of the goods. It should be added that when the goods are placed on board the ship a "mate's receipt" is given for them, and is later exchanged for the complete Bill of Lading.

The *Bill of Lading* is the essential document in making shipment and constitutes a list of, and receipt for, the goods shipped, a recital of the terms of the freight contract, and a document of title or a certificate of ownership. It is signed by the master of ship or some other duly authorised person on behalf of the shipowner. Bills of lading are made out in "sets" and any number may constitute the set according to requirements of the particular trade, three being the usual number. At least one stamped bill of lading must be supplied to the consignee and the unstamped copy may be retained by the master for the purposes of record. The master of the ship would deliver the goods to any person who produces the stamped bill of lading, and thereupon the other "parts" will be void. There are two types of bills of lading in use. The first type is the "Received for Shipment" bill of lading, which states that the goods have been received for shipment on board the vessel. This type is more useful and is used more commonly. If the goods are received on board the ship in good order and condition, a "clean" bill of lading is issued. A special importance attaches to the bill of lading in its character of a quasi-negotiable instrument, and in its usefulness as a means of arranging payment while safeguarding the interests of the shipper. For example, if the exporter has arranged for "payment against documents" he does not send the bill of lading to the consignee but to a bank at the port of destination with the necessary instructions. The consignee can get the bill of lading from the bank in exchange for payment for the goods.

If the exporter desires to raise money on shipment before payment is due, the bill of lading is an essential item of the documents which he hypothecates. The bill of lading, being a document of title, is the security offered with the draft which he requires to be discounted. The quasi-negotiable character of the bill of lading consists in the fact that ownership in it and the goods it refers to can be transferred by its endorsement and delivery by the transferor to the transferee, the latter's title, however, being limited to that of the transferor. Since a bill of lading is not a negotiable instrument, its tranferor cannot give a better title to the transferee than he himself has. When a bill of lading is made out "to order" instead of to the customer's name, the shipper must endorse it or it will be invalid and useless to the consignee when he desires to take delivery of goods.

A carrier must be employed to get the goods to the docks, and a consignment note for him must be prepared. This is an instruction to forward the goods, and gives a detailed list of them, with marks, name of consignee, and the persons responsible for paying carriage. On arrival at the docks the goods are weighed, and weight note is handed over to the carrier. This note serves as the basis of charging carriage. In the Bombay trade, it is necessary to obtain a carrier's receipt, which is a certificate of delivery signed by the wharfinger, and is eventually forwarded with the bill of lading and other documents as legal proof. The forwarding charges will include such incidentals as dock dues cranage, master porterage, special labour, and customs entries, and are generally described as F.O.B. When despatching goods to the docks it is essential to ascertain whether an "alongside date" has been announced for the vessel, otherwise the goods may arrive before the vessel is prepared to accept the cargo and demurrage charges will become due.

The Customs authorities in most countries require Certificate of Origin and Consular Invoices, i.e., invoices for goods shipped certified by the Consul of the country to which goods are going. Consuls are officers appointed by a country in foreign countries to look after the home country's trade interests. The purpose of Consular Invoices is to establish the value of the goods consigned. The Consular Invoices are used for the purposes of charging import duties, and the Certificates of Origin for making preferential allowances. For most part of the Commonwealth combined certificates of value and origin are required. All values given in these documents should be actual cost of manufacture, and not F.O.B. or C.I.F. except where specially required.

While the Consular documents and the certificates of value and origin are required to satisfy the Customs authorities overseas, a Customs specification in respect of every consignment has to be completed for the use of the home Customs authorities. Before goods are taken on board, the master of the ship must lodge with the Customs an "inward clearing note" of the vessel's last voyage, and an "entry outwards" for the vessel. All export documents must be in accordance with the approved forms. On the exportation of any goods for which no bond is required the master or owner of the ship should deliver within six days after clearance of the ship a "manifest" of shipped goods of every kind, setting out the marks, numbers, and descriptions of packages and the name of the consignee according to the relative bill of lading, and make a declaration that the manifest contains a true account of all the cargo of the ship.

Freight. Freight charges are usually made either by weight or by size at the shipowner's option. As a rule he prefers ton measurement based on a standard of 40 cubic feet, which makes 2 cubic feet equivalent of 1 cwt. for the purpose of calculating freight, primage being added. For fixing freight rates on regular routes the goods are divided into several broad classifications by most shipping companies, with a "special" detailed list in addition. Others issue detailed lists, and give special quotations for goods not included in the lists. Included in freight quotations will be found the term "Primage". This is a charge by the shipowners for the use of the ship's cargo-handling appliances when loading and unloading. When the phrase "Primage and Average Accustomed" occurs in bills of lading, it means that the consignors of goods will each pay a pro rata share of the total primage with other such dues as wharf charges, pilotage, etc. Commissions, or "Rebates", usually deferred, being a percentage of the freight money (usually 10 per cent), are returned by the shipowner to the shipper if, after a certain period (usually six months), the latter has not shipped goods by a competing line or vessel. Most customary now is the Shipping Conference System, under which member-shipping companies charge a uniform freight rate to all shippers alike. For shipments to destinations to which no regular liner service exists and tramp steamers have to be used, the freight rates depend on the movement of the open freight market; the rates therefore fluctuate according to supply and demand for shipping space. The freight becomes payable on the arrival of the ship at its destination except if otherwise contracted. The exporter is liable for it, though, in case of F.O.B. sale, he can recover the freight from the consignee.

Sometimes the shipper may require the use of an entire ship or a definite part of it for the carriage of his goods. The shipper will then "charter" a ship, and will be known as the "charterer". This will involve the preparation of a voyage "charter-party", i.e., for a particular voyage, or a time "charter-party", or a hiring agreement, i.e., for a specified period of time. Unless a demise charter-party is prepared the possession and control of the ship remain with the shipowner and the charter is only allowed to have his goods carried by a particular ship. The principal provisions of a charter-party are that the ship hired shall be seaworthy and properly equipped, ready at the specified port on the date agreed, and will make the specified voyage without undue delay and deviation. The charter engages to have his cargo ready for prompt loading and to pay all charges due to the shipowner. The charterer is usually required to load a "full and complete cargo', in which case the charterer, if his original cargo does not occupy the full space available, must supply additional cargo, known as "broken stowage", or pay compensation for the deficiency of cargo, which is known as "dead freight". Even in the case of a charter, a bill of lading is issued in addition to the charter-party. But in this case the bill of lading is merely a receipt for the goods and is not a document of title, nor a contract of affreightment.

Whether shipping is under charter or bill of lading, the shipper must ship his goods promptly and take delivery of them without delay at the port of destination. Failure to do this renders him liable to payment of demurrage. Usually, definite periods are contracted for loading and unloading and they are known as "lay days", which commence as soon as the ship arrives.

Insurance. In spite of so many modern innovations, goods are still exposed to the perils of the sea, and should be insured against the risks of loss and damage. This will be done by the exporter in the name of, and on behalf of, the client to whom the goods are consigned. The subject of marine insurance has already been discussed elsewhere.

Payment. At the time of the sales transaction the exporter wants to be satisfied that payment for the goods will be forthcoming, and the importer wants to be sure that when he pays the goods or the title to the goods will be delivered to him. There are various methods of obtaining payment of exports. Draft terms are usually preferred, but other forms of payment, such as payment by remittance, cash against documents, telegraphic transfers, etc., are often used.

If draft terms are prescribed in the sales contract the exporter draws a Bill of Exchange for the amount, including interest to cover time of maturing, sight and return, on the overseas customer, who accepts it, if his credit is good; otherwise his banker accepts the bill before documents of title are delivered. The documents of title are delivered to the importer either against acceptance (D/A), or against payment (D/P) of the relative bill of exchange. The exporter can get the bill discounted by his bank and thus get the payment immediately. Security, has, of course, to be provided by the shipper who desires to discount the bill and this he accomplishes by a process known as the "Hypothecation" of shipping documents. In addition to the bill of exchange, he hands to the bank the full set of bill of lading, insurance policy, and invoice with a letter of hypothecation. The latter simply sets forth the terms of the bill of exchange, and a description of the other documents, with an authorisation to dispose of the goods for the benefit of the shipper in the event of the bill of exchange being dishonoured, and to deduct the amount discounted, in return for which an advance of the sum required is requested. The banker then credits the shipper with the amount, and forwards the documents to his bank or agent at the port of destination, who hands them over to the consignee on receiving from the latter payment of the amount of the bill. On completion of the transaction the banker advises the shipper, and at the same time credits him with the remaining percentage of the amount of the bill which was not originally advanced.

Lately, the Letter of Credit has acquired a greater popularity as a method of payment. The importer is required to ask his banker to place at the disposal of the exporter's bank or at the disposal of the exporter himself a certain sum of money to be actually drawn against the surrender of documents proving the despatch of goods. A Letter of Credit is revocable, if it can be withdrawn at any time, and it is irrevocable, if it cannot be cancelled without the previous permission of the person in whose favour the credit is opened.

The exporter should prepare the shipping documents strictly in accordance with the terms of the credit. A specimen[1] of a Letter of Credit is given below.

THE BRITISH BANK LTD.

London, E.C.2.
17th June, 1969.

In replying please quote credit number and initials.

A.B. Co.,
London.

Dear Sirs,

Revocable Credit No. 47742/167784

We beg to inform you that a revocable credit has been established with us in your favour for an amount of £370 10s. 6d. (Say three hundred and seventy pounds, ten shillings and six pence) on account of Messrs. X, Y. & Co., Bombay................

This credit is available by your drafts drawn on us........at sight.........marked as relating to credit No. 47742/67784 supported by the following documents:

Commercial invoice in triplicate
Marine Insurance Policy or Certificate in the currency of the Credit
Consular Invoice

Full set of bills of lading to order of X.Y.& Co., Bombay........
covering..............200 Fibre Rugs...........

The bills of lading must evidence shipment of the goods actually on board the vessel, not merely received for shipment, and must be manually signed.

Provided the credit is not previously cancelled drafts must be drawn and presented to us on or before the 24th December, 1969.

Kindly note that this advice does not constitute a confirmation of the credit, which is subject to modification or withdrawal at any time.

Please sign and return the enclosed acknowledgement.

Your's faithfully,
G. Brown,
Manager.

1. Adapted from Sladen, *Modern Commerce*, p. 94

It will not be out of place to mention here that foreign exchange transactions in India are mostly handled by the Exchange Banks which are either the branches of foreign banks established in India or are foreign banks specially floated to handle transactions in foreign currencies. Recently, however, Indian banks have also begun handling foreign exchange business.

Another method is "Payment by Remittance", which is the rule in the Chinese trade, and is practised to some extent in all markets. This method leaves the shipper too much at the mercy of customers who may be unscrupulous enough to delay payment on such excuses as that exchange is against them, or that money is temporarily tight. "Cash against Documents" is the most satisfactory form of payment, for it involves no credit at all. Under this system the bills of lading and other documents are forwarded to a bank at the port of destination with instructions to hand them over to the consignee in exchange for payment of the amount due on the consignment. Another method of cash payment very largely used is by "Telegraphic Transfer." The importer pays into his local branch bank which later cables the fact to the head office of the bank in the exporting country; where the shipper is at once credited with the amount The bank charges a small commission and the cost of cabling for renedering this service.

Having obtained the bill of lading and other documents from the bank, the importer will endorse it in favour of a Clearing Agent for clearing the goods and their transmission upcountry The Clearing Agent will file three copies of a "Bill of Entry" containing full and correct particulars of the goods with the Customs authorities, who will charge customs duty on the goods imported. Two copies are returned to the clearing agent who gets the goods unloaded from the ship and inspects them thoroughly. If there is any damage or defect in the goods, the matter is immediately reported to the agent of the shipping company who arranges for the survey of the damage so that compensation can be claimed from the insurance company. If the necessary shipping documents are not available, and therefore the clearing agent is not able to file the bill of entry, another document known as "Bill of Sight" is presented. A provisional customs duty is charged on the goods subject to final adjustment, and goods are allowed to be unloaded. Having cleared the goods, the clearing agent will despatch them upcountry and forward to his principal the Railway Receipt, together with the receipts issued by the Customs and Port authorities.

If the importer of dutiable goods does not wish to take delivery of them immediately, either because the duty is heavy and he does not wish to pay the whole amount at once, or because he hopes to sell the goods immediately, so that the buyer will pay the price inclusive of the duty, then he will place the goods in a Bonded Warehouse. This is a warehouse owned by a firm who has given a Bond to the Government that all dealings in respect of dutiable goods will be carried out in a lawful manner; that no goods will be allowed to be taken out of the warehouse unless the necessary duty is paid first. The importer who places his goods in the Bonded Warehouse has to pay a small charge. He can repack the goods or arrange them into smaller lots for selling purposes. On the basis of the receipt issued by the warehouse-keeper, the importer can sell the goods, and duty is charged only on the portion sold.

Sometimes goods are imported only for the purpose of re-export to other countries (entrepot trade), usually subject to a "drawback". A drawback is the relief or rebate which can be obtained by an exporter on manufactured or finished goods for export in the manufacture of which duty-paid articles were used. The drawback system is based on the general principle that Customs duties are intended to fall only on goods for use or consumption in the importing country. Therefore, where raw materials or semi-finished goods are imported into a country rebate will be allowed to the extent of the import duty paid on the raw material used.

In the case of exports from India the services of forwarding agents are utlised. Most of the goods are free from any export restrictions; but the Government has powers to impose them. For example, exports of cotton cloth were not permitted above a certain figure determined from time to time. Today, however, the country wants the maximum exports. Some goods are liable to export duty and hence a customs declaration similar to the one made for import has to be made, and goods have to be insured against marine risks.

It may be added that in the foreign markets certain complaints have been made against Indian goods. Some unscrupulous exporters have sent goods different from the samples on the basis of which orders were received. This has discredited Indian trade. Now, however, a system of inspection exists at various ports to see that spurious goods are not exported. Our packing is also far from satisfactory, resulting in damage to goods. Those who would like to have substantial and effective export business should see to it that their foreign buyers are satisfied in all respects.

On the recommendation of a Committee appointed by the Government of India, the State Trading Corporation was set up in 1956 for conducting trade with the Communist countries. The Corporation is striving to increase India's exports with countries having controlled economies in order to secure from them such commodities as steel, cement and industrial equipment without straining country's sterling reserves. It has already dealt in commodities like cement, soda ash, caustic soda, raw silk, fertilisers and gypsum. The Corporation has exported mineral ores, shoes, handicrafts, etc. The Corporation has shown good profit, e.g., Rs. 5 crores on the sale of cement only.

Office Organisation. The export of goods is a complicated and specialised trade, and therefore men with complete understanding of the various activities, such as marketing, shipping, financial operation, should be employed to handle it. The cashier must have an expert acquaintance with many financial instruments other than ordinary cheques. Bankers' drafts, bill of exchange, bill broking, discounting and protesting, letters of hypothecation, letters of credit, guarantee accounts, remittances, rate of exchange, etc., are some items which he must thoroughly understand, and he must be able to handle the complicated machinery of the export finance with sureness and ease.

The next work is that of general book-keeping, invoicing and preparation of shipping, insurance, and forwarding documents, and must be entrusted to specialists. The invoice clerk, for example, must possess a high degree of accuracy and knowledge of shipping procedure. In addition to preparing a usual commercial shipping invoice, he may have to prepare Consular invoices and Customs declarations in correct form and have them certified by proper authority. He must pay special attention to a comprehensive item of "charges" which includes such items as bank commission for discounting bills and other services, brokerage, bill stamps, postage, cables, buying commission, reference patterns, etc.

The accountant or book-keeper will have to see to the proper keeping of the following principal books: Ledger, ruled for double entry; Purchase Book, showing the amounts of invoices received for goods purchased or for expenses incurred. The entries will be posted to the credit side of the ledger account of the shipping firm; Sales Journal, which is a record of goods sold and shipped, into which are copied all invoices sent out, for ready reference in calculating C.I.F. prices, insurance, etc. Postings from this book will be to the debit side of the account of the customers supplied; Cash Book, showing money received or paid out; Bills Receivable Book giving details of all bills on which money is to be received by the holders; Bills Payable Book, giving details of all bills in which money is to be paid away by the holder; Consignments Outward Book, recording all details of shipments "on consignment."

The correspondence relating to the trade must be in the hands of a competent person, well-versed not only in English, but an adept in selling ideas and winning customers. The typist should, in addition to being accurate, be skilled in tabulation and other special work. For all other matters in relation to office organisation, the reader is referred to Chapter XII.

CHAPTER XLV

PRODUCE EXCHANGES

A Produce Exchange is a specialised organised market (like the Stock Exchange) which provides a place where its members buy and sell certain commodities or contract for future trading. Therefore, like a Stock Exchange, a Commodity or Produce Exchange provides a market place where its members meet at specific timing and enter into transactions according to its rules and regulations.

Characteristics of Commodities Handled. All types of commodities do not lend themselves to be dealt in on an organised market. To be suitable for handling there, a commodity must possess the following characteristics:

1. *Homogeneity.* The commodity must be homogeneous, i.e., all units of a lot of a particular commodity must be identical in quality so that it will mean the same thing to different persons and at different times and places.

2. *Durability.* It must be durable so that it does not deteriorate during the period of a 'futures' contract which may extend to a year or more.

3. *Gradability.* The commodity must be capable of being graded, weighted, measured or numbered so that dealing can be effected by sample or description, and it can be acceptable to all concerned as an identical article without being subjected to quality determination every time a transaction is made.

4. *Large Volume of Trading.* The trading in the commodity must be frequent and in sufficiently large volume to justify the cost of facilities to be provided by the produce exchange. In other words, there must be a regular and steady demand for the commodity.

5. *Price Fluctuation.* There must be frequent fluctuations in the price of the commodity so that the speculators may have inducement to deal in it on the produce exchange. In other words, it must lend itself to organised speculative dealings. The fluctuation in demand should be so large that the supply cannot be adjusted immediately to demand by rapid changes in the rate of production.

6. *Open Supply.* The supply of the commodity must be free and open, and should not be controlled or monopolised by one or a group of persons. Also, the supply must not be controlled by the Government nor should its price be regulated by the governmental action.

The following commodities possess these characteristics and are handled on the organised produce exchanges:

(i) Natural products of the soil, e.g., grain, cotton, jute, oilseeds, tea, coffee, pepper, etc;

(ii) Mineral products e.g., lead,, copper, and other non-ferrous metals.

(iii) Certain manufactured products, e.g., cotton goods, jute bags, sugar, hides and skins, etc.

Functions and Objects. Produce exchanges provide facilities for bulk transactions in commodities and regularise the business dealings in them. The main functions and services of produce exchanges are as follows:

1. They provide a convenient place for the members to meet for the purpose of trading and of exchanging views.

2. They collect and disseminate market information. The buyers and sellers enter into transactions after assessing the trends of prices and the prospects of their rise or fall. The market report published daily in newspapers and the statistical data assist the dealers in making their decisions to buy or sell.

3. They establish and enforce rules and regulations which are intended to facilitate trade on sound lines. These rules define the duties of members and lay down the methods of transacting business.

4. They establish and maintain grades. As we have seen before, commodities which are dealt in on the produce exchanges have to be graded according to quality and description so that there is no confusion or misunderstanding between the dealers in respect of their agreements.

5. They provide machinery for the arbitration and settlement of trade disputes. Almost all the produce exchanges have their arbitration committees which decide cases of disputes between the members relating to dealings in commodities. This is provided to save time and money which would be spent in litigation.

6 They help to crystallise market values by bringing about an interplay of the forces of demand and supply. The dealers, on the basis of the information they gather from the produce exchanges in different parts of the country, are able to determine the prices at which they would transact business. In the process of price-making, the produce exchanges indicate the general trend of the market and thus serve as "barometers" of market conditions.

Services. In their efforts to perform their functions and to subserve their aims and objects, the produce exchanges render the following valuable services to the producers, traders, consumers and others in the community:

1. The produce exchanges provide a ready and continuous market for the purchase and sale of commodities. The producer is made independent of the middleman. The commodity acquires the quality of liquidity. The buyers of raw materials are able to estimate their cost and budget properly.

2. The produce exchanges help in absorbing risks of probable fluctuations in prices due to parallel markets. The manufacturer usually buys raw material in large quantities and stores them. To avoid losses arising from falling prices, he sells the goods in the forward market at a

higher price. This enables him to retain his margin of profit.

3. They provide an opportunity to traders to shift or transfer their risks to professional risk bearers, i.e., speculators.

4. The produce exchanges provide continuity in commodity trading which induces bankers and financiers to make advances against commodities.

5. They afford a useful method of insurance or protection by means of hedging transactions. Hedging will be dealt with in the latter part of this chapter.

6. The produce exchanges provide facilities for transferring hedges from one market to another market or for "arbitraging" or "straddling" and thus equalise the price levels of commodities at various centres.

Types and Constitution of Produce Exchanges. The produce exchanges are usually classified either on the basis of the variety of commodities handled or on the basis of the sharing of profits. Under the former kind are: (1) General Exchanges, which provide facilities for dealings in a wide variety of products; (2) Special Exchanges, which handle only a particular or specified commodity. From the point of view of profits, a produce exchange may be either (1) Profit sharing, or (2) Non-profit sharing.

As a rule, produce exchanges all over the world are incorporated bodies. In India, the majority of them are registered as companies under the Companies Act, and have been formed mainly for dealing in "futures". Only a few of such exchanges control spot trading also. All the produce exchanges in India fall into two main classes: (1) Profit sharing, or (2) Non-profit sharing. Almost all the non-profit sharing associations are located at the ports. The East India Cotton Association and the Marwari Chamber of Commerce, both of Bombay, may be cited as typical examples. The profit sharing associations are found in upcountry only. The Indian Exchange Limited, Amritsar, is one of the most outstanding examples of this class. It is significant that the non-profit sharing associations enjoy a greater degree of stability and influence than the majority of profit sharing associations. The former also provide for their members greater amenities than the latter. The management of both classes of associations is vested in Boards of Directors or Committees and the composition of which varies with the different institutions, as does their capital. TheCommittees might take the form of a Survey Committee, Clearing House Committee, Rates Committee, etc.

Membership. The membership of a produce exchange is acquired by purchasing a share and enrolling as a member by paying the prescribed fees. Only members are permitted to enter a futures market and transact business there. The members of a produce exchange may be classified on the basis of the nature of functions they discharge or on the basis of the transactions they make. According to functions, a member may be (1) Broker, (2) Jobber, (3) Wholesaler, (4) Retailer, (5) Importer, or (6) Exporter. According to the transactions they make, members are either "hedgers" or "speculators"

TYPES OF TRANSACTIONS

There are two classes of transactions on the produce exchanges: (1) Spot or cash transactions, and (2) Futures contracts. Accordingly, a produce exchange may be a Cash or Spot Market or a Futures Market or may combine both.

Cash Transactions. As in the stock exchange, a spot or cash transaction on a commodity exchange is purchase or sale of a commodity or of a specific grade of it by paying cash on the spot or within a short period as prescribed by the rules of the produce exchange and delivery is taken either on the spot or usually within 8 days. A spot transaction is an executed contract, a sale, and cannot be rescinded for the purpose of taking away the margin if the price rises, as is possible in a forward transaction, which is only an agreement to sell.

Futures Transactions. A futures transaction or "Futures" is an agreement between the parties to buy or sell a particular commodity or grade thereof, according to the rules and regulations of the produce exchanges, on the understanding that the delivery may be taken on a stipulated future date. A futures transaction may be made for the purpose of speculating on price changes or for hedging against price fluctuations. The price of the commodity is fixed on the basis of recognised grades. For example, cotton futures in Bombay Cotton Market were graded into three varieties, namely, (1) Broach (Fully good); Ormra (Fine); and (3) Bengal (Fully good).

There are some special features of futures contracts, which deserve mention here, and are enumerated hereunder:

1. Futures contracts can be made only in the 'ring' of the commodity exchanges, and not outside.
2. As only members of a produce exchange can make futures contracts, no outsider can be a party to a futures contract.
3. These contracts can be made in multiples of a fixed unit of trading, say 50 or 100 quintals, as specified in the rules of the exchange.
4. These contracts are settled only in what are called trading months, as adopted by each produce exchange. The seller is free to deliver or settle on any day of the trading month for which the delivery was fixed.
5. The rules of every exchange require each contracting party to deposit a certain percentage of the contract price with the exchange as 'margin money' every time a futures contract is made.
6. All disputes relating to futures transactions must be referred to the arbitration machinery provided by the exchange concerned.

Speculative Transactions may be (1) Forward or Waida, (2) Options, (3) Straddle, and (4) Budla. Speculative transactions have already been discussed in Chapter XIV on Stock Exchange, and the reader is referred to that chapter. Only a brief mention of each is made here.

Forward or *Waida* transactions are those in which a speculator buys at the current price with the hope of selling in future at a higher price or vice versa.

Options, which may be put option, or call option, or put and call option, are dealings of the same nature as on the Stock Exchange and the reader is referred to Chapter XIV for their study.

Straddle and Arbitrage. These terms indicate trade between one market and another, a common feature of speculation. In the securities market (Stock Exchange), the term used is arbitrage or arbitraging, and in commodity or produce exchanges, it is designated 'Spreading' in grains market and 'Straddling' in cotton market. According to Todd, "a Straddle means an operation which aims at bringing the gap or covering the 'Spread' between two values, by buying the one which seems low at the moment; and selling the other which is relatively high." Under Straddle transactions the commodities purchased in one market and the commodities sold in another market need not be the same and such purchases and sales need not therefore be subject to one set of rules.

Budla transactions are those transactions which are carried from one 'waida' to the next. This is done in the same way as the bulls and bears do on the stock exchanges.

Hedging. The produce exchange affords a useful method of risk transference or insurance by means of hedging transactions. Hedging may be defined as the practice of entering simultaneously into two contracts of an opposite though corresponding nature, one in the spot or cash market and the other in futures market. The contracts are opposite in nature insofar as one involves purchase and the other sale, but they correspond in respect of the quantity of merchandise covered. The practice involves the making of contra sales and purchases of equal amounts, one in the stock market where the actual physical commodity is handled, and the other in the future market. If prices in the two markets move exactly parallel, losses from price change in one market will be offset by profits in the other. When so made, futures trading provides a form of insurance or protection in which the body of speculators constitutes the insurers and the body of hedgers the insured. Hedging operations may be conducted in different trades such as cotton, grain, seeds, etc., and by different functionaries, viz., growers, dealers, importers, exporters, stockists, manufacturers to protect themselves against losses which might result due to price fluctuations.

As an example we will consider the case of a flour millowner who buys wheat at the current price as a raw material for his mill. If the price of wheat falls before his flour is marketed, he may have to sell the flour at a reduced price, since the price of flour usually falls in sympathy with the price of wheat. In order to cover this risk, therefore, the flour mill-owner "hedges" his purchase of "spot" wheat (i.e., grain for immediate delivery) by making another contract to sell wheat "in the future", in other words, he effects a forward sale. If, as he feared, the price of wheat falls before his flour is ready for the market, he will lose on his product, the flour, because he will have paid more than subsequent prices warrant, but he makes a profit on his "futures" contract, for when the time comes for completion of the contract by delivery he is able to buy "spot" wheat at a price lower than which he receives for his forward sale. Thus he is able to set off the gain on his futures contract against the loss on his flour transaction. If the price goes up, then he will be able to set off his loss on his flour transaction. If the price goes up, then he will be able to set off his loss on his futures contract against his spot transaction. The effect of hedging is to ensure to the trader his normal trading profit and to eliminate any speculative profit or loss due to price changes.

Let us illustrate this by assuming that the miller buys wheat at Rs. 80 per quintal on July 1, and that by August 1 he has processed the wheat into flour. If it costs him Rs. 1 per quintal to process the wheat, he must sell the flour at Rs. 81 in order to break even. However, if by August 1, the price of wheat has fallen 25 P., the miller will be unable to get Rs. 81 for each quintal processed, for competitors will have depressed the price of flour to Rs. 80.75. The miller will suffer a loss of 25 P. per quintal of flour. He will protect himself from _ such a loss by opening a hedge at the same time as he bought the wheat to be processed. The cash transaction stated above was as follows:

July :	Purchase wheat at	Rs. 81.00	per quintal of wheat
August 1 :	Sell flour at	Rs. 79.75	per maund of wheat plus processing cost and conversion profit
	Loss :	Rs. .25	per quintal of wheat

This loss could have been offset in the future market as follows:

July 1 :	Sell wheat for December delivery at quintal plus possession costs	Rs. 80.00 per
August 1:	Buy wheat for December delivery at quintal plus possession cost	Rs.79.75 per
	Gain :	Re. .25 per maund of wheat

The above process of selling future at the time one buys a commodity and of buying futures to close the hedge when the actual materials are subsequently sold is summarised as shown below:

	In Spot or Cash Market ↓	Future Market ↓
Now →	Buy	Sell
Later →	Sell	Buy

REGULATION OF PRODUCE EXCHANGES

It was during the Second World War that regulation of produce exchanges in India was taken up to meet the exigencies of the war. The Government of India made use of the Defence of India Rules and banned forward trading in oilseeds, vegetable oils, foodgrains, spices, sugar, raw cotton, cotton cloth and yarn. At the end of the war, the ban on the forward trade in these commodities was sought to be continued by passing the Essential Supplies (temporary) Act in 1946. The Forward Contracts (Regulation) Act, 1952, however, introduced a more comprehensive control of futures trading in commodities. The Act was amended in 1960. Under the Act, a Forward Markets Commission has been set up to maintain control over and regulate trading in produce exchanges.

The Act does not apply to such contracts as call for actual delivery and payment of price by the original sellers and buyers respectively. These contracts are known as non-transferable spot contracts because the parties to them cannot transfer their rights and obligations to others.

Subject to the above exception, the Act covers all kinds of contracts. All the contracts have been divided into two classes: (1) Ready delivery contracts, i.e., those contracts which require the delivery of the goods to be made and price to be paid within a period not exceeding eleven days from the date of the transaction, (2) Forward delivery contracts including forward deals, futures transactions and transferable spot contracts. Transferable spot contracts are those which are transferable from hand to hand so that the delivery is to be given by the first dealer to the last buyer in accordance with the detailed specifications relating to goods set out in the contract.

The provisions relating to control and regulation of forward contracts are as follows:

1. As in the case of Stock Exchanges, the produce exchanges for forward contracts are to be recognised by the Central Government on the recommendation of Forward Markets Commission. Only recognised exchanges can permit dealings in forward contract.

2. The Central Government is empowered to nominate a maximum of four representatives and to require the reorganised commodity exchange to give representation to outside interests subject to a maximum of three representatives on its governing body.

3. The Central Government can alter the rules, regulations and bye-laws of a recognised commodity exchange and can withdraw recognition, supersede the governing body and suspend the working of the exchange for a maximum of seven days. It can also call for periodical returns or reports relating to the affairs of a recognised commodity exchange or of the members of an exchange.

4. The bye-laws of a recognised produce exchange are required to provide for the (a) establishment of a Clearing House, (b) fortnightly clearing of transactions, (c) fixation of market rates. (d) provision for margins to cover futures trading, (e) fixation of contract grades and

tenderable grades, (f) fixation of scale of brokerage, (g) prevention of corners and squeezes, (h) provision for penalty for contravention of the bye-laws.

5. Options dealings in commodities have been declared illegal.

6. Kerb dealing beyond official hours has also been made illegal with effect from December 28, 1960.

7. *Dabha* trading and other similar undesirable trading has been declared illegal.

8. The Central Government has the power of regulating even the non-transferable specific delivery contract by notification.

9. Penalties of fine and imprisonment are provided for contravention of the provisions of the Act.

SOME IMPORTANT RECOGNISED PRODUCE EXCHANGES

East India Cotton Association, Limited. The East India Cotton Association, Limited, Bombay, as reorganised after the passing of the Forward Contracts (Regulation) Act, was permitted to carry on future trading with effect from June, 1956. Two contracts Jarilla 25/32″ fine and Vijay 27/32″ fine are recognised.

The Board of Directors of the Exchange consists of 22 members. 14 of whom are elected by panels of buyers (4), sellers (4), brokers (4), and associate members (2) , seven members are nominated to represent the cotton growers (4) by Indian Central Cotton Committee and 3 by Forward Market Commission and one is co-opted by the 14 elected members to represent the general body of members. The following sub-committees assist the Board in the conduct of the business of the exchange.

1. Daily Rates Committee, which fixes market rates for different grades;
2. Survey Committee, which settles disputes relating to quality of cotton:
3. Standards Committee, which fixes different standards of cotton;
4. Ring Committee, which is entrusted with the task of looking after the conduct of trading within the ring;
5. Clearing House Committee regulates payments and settlements.

Trading is done in the ring of the Association between 12 noon and 5 p.m. All offers and acceptances are recorded by the staff in the ring. The months of delivery are February, May and August.

East India Jute and Hessian Exchange, Calcutta. At one time forward trading in jute goods was prohibited; but the Government of India granted a licence to the East India Jute and Hessian Exchange of Calcutta in March, 1958, for futures trading in raw jute and jute goods. The permission to do this business applies only to Calcutta, and in the rest of India forward trading in jute and jute goods is not allowed.

A member is required to make an initial security deposit of Rs. 10,000 for trading in raw jute, Rs. 10,000 for trading in jute goods, and

Rs. 20,000, if he wants to trade in both. Margin requirements have to be complied with as fixed in respect of each commodity. Transactions have to be cleared every week. In case of disputes between members, the arbitration machinery of Bengal Chamber of Commerce is to be used.

The Bombay Oilseeds and Oil Exchanges, Ltd. The exchange was accorded recognition for futures trading in cotton seeds in October, 1956. It is also recognised for futures trading in castor seeds. The unit of trading is 100 *khandies* and the commodity dealt in is small cotton seed. One *khandi* is equal to 784 lbs. or 355.62 kilograms. Delivery or settlement months are February, May and September.

CLEARING HOUSE

Commodity Exchange Clearing House is a place in which the adjustment and clearing of commodities takes place at the close of the business session. Each commodity exchange usually has its own clearing house, which is governed by the rules of the exchange, and members of the exchange are the members of the clearing house. Both the buyers and sellers are required to deposit a certain percentage of margin or some fixed amount with the exchange officials or some approved bank or with the clearing house. Every member submits to the clearing house a statement showing the number of contracts bought and the price and also the number of contracts sold and the price at which they have been sold. If the net balance shows a loss, a cheque for the amount of the loss will be attached. If there is a profit, he will attach a bill for the amount due to him.

The settlement in a clearing house may take place daily, weekly, fortnightly or monthly. Pending final settlement and the delivery of the commodity, the clearing house helps in the settlement of partial payment. The clearing house helps parties to settle amounts and to avert defaults. The clearing house also protects the interests of the contracting parties and lessens complications.

SELECT BIBLIOGRAPHY

oks

HARYA· Business Organisation and Management in India.
BU. Sales and Sales Management.
NDERSON. Management Practice.
NSTEY, VERA. The Economic Development of India.
PLEY. Management in Action.
ADGER AND GUTHMANN. Investment Principles and Practice.
LKRISHNA. Regional Planning in India.
ASU. Industrial Finance in India.
ATLIBOI. Works Organisation, Management and Cost Control.
ATTY. Industrial Administration and Management.
ECKERATH, VON. Industrial Organisation.
ERCE. Cartels.
ERGSON. Socialist Economics.
ERN. Collective Economic Planning.
ETHEL, ATWATER. Essentials of Industrial Management.
MITH, STACKMAN. Industrial Organisation and Management.
EVERIDGE. Full Employment in Free Society.
HONSLE (ed.)—Personnel Management
BIGG. Cost Accounts.
BISHOP. The Economics of Advertising.
BLOOM AND NORTHRUP. Economics of Labour and Industrial Relations.
BRANTON. Administration of Business Enterprise.
BRECH. The Principles and Practice of Management.
BREEN, THOMPSON AND WEST. Effective Selling.
BRITT AND BOYD. Marketing Management and Administrative Action.
BROOM. Production Management.
BROWN. The Machine and the Worker.
BROWN AND SMITH. The Director Looks At His Job.
BRAYANT. English Saga.
BULL. The Directors' Handbook.
BURNHAM. The Managerial Revolution.
CAMPBELL. Wholesale and Retail Trade.
CONFIELD. Sales Administration.
CHAPIN. Credit and Collection, Principles and Practice.
CHAMPMAN (ED.). Modern Business.
CLARKE. Principles of Marketing.
COLE. Modern Theories and Forms of Industrial Organisation. Principles of Economic Planning.
CONDLIFEE. Technological Progress and Economic Development.
CONVERSE. Elements of Marketing.
CRIPPS. Towards Christian Democracy.
CURIE. Work Study.
DALE. Industrial Management.
DALE AND URWICK. Staff in Organisation.
DAS, N. Industrial Enterprise in India. Industrial Planning, Why and How?
DAVIES. National Enterprise.

Books

DAVIS, K. The Population of India and Pakistan. Human Relations at Work.
DAVIS AND SCOTT. Readings in Human Relations.
DAVIS AND STETSON. Office Administration.
DICKSEE. Business Organisation.
DOBB. Political Economy and Capitalism. Wages.
DONALD (ED.). Handbook of Business Administration.
DRUCKER. The New Society. The Practice of Management. Management By Results.
ELBOURNE. Fundamentals of Industrial Administration.
EUCKEN. The Unsuccessful Age.
FIELD. Corporation Finance.
FLORENCE. Economics of Fatigue and Unrest. Logic of Industrial Organisation. Investment, Location and Size of Plant. Logic of British and American Industry. Industry and the State.
GALBRAITH. The New Industrial State.
GARG. Stock Exchanges in India.
GERSTENBERG. Financial Organisation and Management.
GHOSH AND OM PRAKASH. Principles and Problems of Industrial Organisation.
GILRRETH. The Three Position Plan of Promotion.
GIRI, V.V. Labour Problems in Indian Industry.
GORDON. Business Leadership in the Large Corporation.
HAIMANN. Professional Management.
HALL. Distributive Trading.
HALL, L. Business Administration.
HANEY. Business Organisation and Combination.
HARDING. Production Management
HARRIS. Economic Planning.
HAYEK. The Road to Serfdom.
HEPNER. Effective Advertising.
HICKS. The Management of Organisations.
HICKS AND PLACE. Office Management.
HOBSON. Evolution of Modern Capitalism.
HOOVER. Economic Life of Soviet Russia.
HUGH JONES. Human Relations and Modern Management.
HUMBLE. Improving Business Results.
HURLEY. Business Administration.
HURFF. Social Aspects of Enterprise in the Corporation.
HUXLEY, ALDUOUS. Science, Liberty and Peace.
JENKINS. Psychology in Business and Industry.
JEWKES. Ordeal of Planning.
JONES, D. Administration of Industrial Enterprises.
JONES, H. Economics of Private Enterprise.
KAPP. The Social Costs of Private Enterprise.
KEYNES. Treatise on Money, Vol. 2.
KIMBALL AND KIMBALL. Principles of Industrial Organisation.
KIRKALDY. Spirit of Industrial Relations.
KNOWLES AND THOMSON. Industrial Management.
KOLASA. Introduction to Behavioral Science for Business.

Books

KOONTZ AND O'DONNELL. Management.
LANDAVER. Theory of National Economic Planning.
LEMKE AND EDWARDS. Administrative Control and Executive Action.
LESTER. Labour and Industrial Relations.
LEWIS (ED) Essentials of Selling.
LIFFMANN. Cartels, Concerns and Trusts.
LIKERT. New Patterns of Management.
LOKANATHAN. Industrial Organisation in India.
LOUDEN. Wage Incentives.
LOUGH. Corporation Finance.
LUNDY. Effective Industrial Management.
MAIER. Psychology in Industry.
MALLYA. Public Enterprises in India.
MARLING AND MACDONAL. (ED). Management and its People.
MAYNARD. Handbook of Business Administration.
MARSHALL, A. Industry and Trade. Principles of Economics.
MARSHALL, L.C. Business Administration.
MASSIE. Essentials of Management.
MATHEWS, ETC. Marketing.
MAURER. Great Enterprise.
MAUSER. Modern Marketing Management.
MAYNARD. Top Management Handbook.
MCGREGOR. The Human Side of Enterprise.
MEAD. Corporation Finance.
MEHTA, ASHOK. India Comes of Age, 1940.
METHESON. Depreciation of Factories.
MILES. Problems of Incentives in Industry.
MILLER. Problems of Labour.
MILLER AND BLOOD. Modern Maintenance Management.
MILWARD. Large Scale Organisation.
MOND. Industry and Politics.
MULKY. The New Capital Issue Market in India.
MULLA. Principles of Hindu Law.
MYERS. Business Rationalisation. Industrial Psychology.
MYERS, C.A. MYERS. Industrial Relations in India.
NEUNER AND HAYNES. Office Management and Practice.
NEWMAN. Administrative Action. Business Politics and Management.
NEWMAN AND SUMMER. The Process of Management.
OWEN. Business Organisation and Combination.
PAISH. Business Finance.
PIGORS AND MYERS. Personnel Administration.
PIGOU. Economics of Welfare.
PREVETTE. The Power of Effective Selling.
RALLAN. Secretarial Work.
RAO, V.K.R.V. Values and Economic Development.
RATENSTRAUCH. Principles of Modern Industrial Organisation.
ROBBINS. Economic Planning and International Order.
RORETSON. Control of Industry.
ROBINSON, E.T.G. The Structure of Competitive Industry. Monopoly.
ROBINSON. W. Fundamentals of Business Organisation.

Books

ROPKE. The Social Crisis of Our Time.
ROSEMARY STEWART. Reality of Organizations.
ROTH. Professional Salesmanship.
SALVI. Commodity Exchanges.
SCOTT, CLOTHIER. Personnel Management.
SEAGER. Principles of Economics.
SHARMA. Indian Industries.
SHIELDS. The Evolution of Industrial Organisation.
SHUKLA. A Manual of Mercantile Law. Industrial Law. Administrative Problems of Public Enterprises in India. Company Law.
SMITH. Economic Planning and the Tariff.
SMITH, J.G. Organised Produce Exchanges.
SMITH. Retail Distribution.
SMITH, STACKMAN. Industrial Organisation and Management.
SPRIEGAL. Industrial Management.
SPRIEGAL AND SHULZ. Element of Supervision.
STANTON. Fundamentals of Marketing.
STRAND. Salesmanship.
SUTTON. The Technique of Selling.
TAUSSIG. Principles of Economics.
TAYLOR, G.R. Are Workers Human?
TAYLOR, F.W. Principles of Scientific Management. Shop Management.
TEAD AND METCALF. Personnel Administration.
THOMAS. Commerce, Its Theory and Practice.
THOMPSON AND SMITH. Public Utility Economics.
TIFFIN. Industrial Psychology.
TIRANTI AND WALKER. Introduction to Production Control.
TROXEL. Economics of Public Utilities.
URWICK. The Elements of Administration.
VROOM. Management and Motivation.
WADIA AND MERCHANT. Our Economic Problem.
WALPOLE. Management of Men.
WHITEHEAD. The Administration of Marketing and Selling.
WILLSMORE. Modern Production Control.
WILSON. Method of Remuneration.
WOLF. The Management of Personnel.
WOOTTON, BARBARA. Freedom under Planning.
WRIGHT. Business Organisation.
YODER. Personnel Principles and Practices.
ZELKO. The Business Conference.

Periodicals and Memoranda

Advanced Management.
Business Weekly.
Capital.
Chartered Secretary.
Commerce.
Company News and Notes.
Economic Review.

riodicals and Memoranda

conomic Weekly.
astern Economist.
nance and Commerce.
arvard Business Review.
dian Economic Journal.
dian Finance.
Ianager.
eaders' Digest.
he Indian Journal of Agricultural Economics
he Indian Journal of Commerce.
he Indian Journal of Public Administration.
Iemorandum of the Bombay Shareholders' Association, 1949.
Iemorandum of the Bombay Shareholders' Association, 1936.

iovernment Publications and Reports

A Draft Outline—The First, Second, Third, Fourth and Fifth Plans.
ndia 1974.
ndian Labour Gazette (now Journal).
Large Industrial Establishments in India.
Manufacturing Industries for India.
The Indian Labour Year Book.
Report of the Advisory Planning Board of the Government of India
Report of the Coal Enquiry Committee, 1937.
Report on Currency and Finance, Reserve Bank of India.
Report on Fairs, Markets and Produce Exchanges in India.
Report on Fiscal Commission, 1949-50.
Report (Gorwala) on the Efficient Conduct of State Enterprises.
Reports of Indian Tariff Boards.
Reports (Annual) of Industrial Finance Corporation of India.
Reports of the various Labour Enquiry Committee, 1946-48.
Reports and Proceedings of the 4th Congress of the Labour and Social International, Vienna, 1931.
Report of Panels on Different Industries.
Reports of Millowners' Association, Bombay and Ahmedabad.
Reports of the National Planning Committee.
Report of the Taxation Inquiry Committee, 1955.
Companies Act, 1956, as amended.
Labour Management Consultation and Co-operation in TISCO.
Report of the Companies Act Amendment Committee.

APPENDIX

TEST QUESTIONS

CHAPTER I

The Nature of Business

1. What do you mean by Business? What are its objectives? Can profit be regarded as the sole objective of business?
2. In what way does business differ from profession?.
3. Briefly explain the various divisions or components of business.
4. Explain the true field of Business Organisation, and state the requisites of a successful business.
5. What qualities make a businessman a success in business?

CHAPTER II

Evolution of Business

1. Define Commerce. Sketch the evolution of Commerce and enumerate the principal occupations which may be described as commercial.
2. Trace the various stages in the evolution of business. To what extent is the modern industrial structure capitalistic?
3. Explain the main points of distinction between the present-day structure of industry and that before the Industrial Revolution.
4. 'The term "Industrial Revolution" is used not because of a sudden change, but when accomplished the change was fundamental.' Elucidate.
5. Indicate the factors which gave Great Britain the lead in Industrial Revolution. State briefly the social problems created by the change.
6. Trace the evolution of industrial development in India.

CHAPTER III

Forms of Legal Ownership

1. Discuss the factors that affect the choice of a form of business organisation or legal ownership.
2. What are the advantages and disadvantages of a single entrepreneur business? Discuss the prospects of such a form of business organisation in India.
3. What limitations is a sole trader likely to face as his business continues to expand? Explain how he may overcome them.
4. A successful sole trader wishes to expand his business. What steps would you advise him to take to do that?
5. 'The one-man control is the best in the world if that one man is big enough to manage everything.' Comment.
6. Why is the single proprietorship not in danger of being crowded out by large corporations?
7. What do you consider to be the essence of partnership? If you want to start a business in partnership with certain other people, what precautions ought you to take so as to avoid future disputes and consequent litigation?

8. What are the requisites of an ideal partnership?

9. What is the position of a partner in relation to (i) his co-partners, the creditors of the firm?

10. What is a limited partnership and how does it differ from a private limited company?

11. Discuss the various points of distinction between a Partnership Firm and a Joint Hindu Family Firm.

12. Evaluate Partnership as a form of business organisation.

13. The proprietor of a big general store wants to expand his business and consults you as to the type of business organisation he should choose. What advice will you give him and why?

CHAPTER IV

Company Form of Organisation

1. Explain the meaning of a joint stock company and state its characteristics.

2. Indicate the chief features of company form of organisation.

3. Account for the extension of a joint stock principle in modern times and for the change in economic opinion regarding its usefulness.

4. Discuss the circumstances in which limited company constitutes to be the most desirable form of business organisation and state the chief difference between private and public company.

5. In many instances it has been noticed that a sole proprietorship or partnership, after some years of its existence, has been converted into a limited company. Explain the various reasons which might have prompted this conversion.

6. "From the social point of view the joint stock organisation has great potentialities both for good and evil." Discuss the statement bringing out clearly the merits and evils of joint stock company method of organising business.

7. Set out the principal features and indicate the differences in the organisation of a sole trading concern, a partnership and a joint stock company.

8. Briefly examine the advantages and disadvantages of the company form of organisation.

9. Indicate the steps that are taken in the promotion of a company.

10. What do you understand by a Memorandum of Association? How does it differ from Articles of Association?

11. What is a Prospectus and what is its object?

12. What precautions should an intending investor take before parting with his money? What safeguards are provided by the law to protect him?

CHAPTER V

The Cooperative Organisation

1. What is cooperation? What motives lie behind its rise and growth?

2. Briefly explain the meaning, principles and characteristics of co-operative organisation.

3. Give a brief account of the various classes of cooperative societies.

4. Distinguish between cooperatives and joint stock enterprises, bringing out clearly the business principles underlying each. Give the advantages and limitations of cooperatives.

5. Discuss the future of cooperation as a form of business organisation in ur country.

6. Write a critical note on Consumers' Cooperative Stores.

7. Distinguish between the main types of business undertakings as regards a) the method of formation, (b) liability of owners, (c) method of raising apital, (d) direction and management.

8. Who precisely obtains the profit and suffers the loss arising from ndustrial enterprise in (i) private business, (ii) public joint stock company, (iii) ooperative retail society, (iv) Government company. Do you consider this uestion important in determining the probable efficiency of the enterprise?

CHAPTER VI

Entrepreneurial Decisions

1. Indicate the fundamental problems in starting a new business.

2. Summarise the entrepreneurial decisions in connection with the launching of a new enterprise.

3. What major factors may influence the choice of a particular type or organisation in specific kinds of business?

4. Mention the problems that a firm will face as it expands? State how changing the form of organisation may help solve these problems.

5. The proprietor of a retail store wishes to open a branch in another locality of a big city. Would you advise him to take a partner or employ a manager to run the branch?

CHAPTER VII

The Scale of Operation and Size of Firm

1. How would you define (a) a firm, (b) an establishment or plant, (c) an industry? What is the relationship between them?

2. Critically examine the different standards employed to measure the size of a business unit.

3. Explain clearly what is meant by (a) an optimum firm, (b) a representative firm, (c) an equilibrium firm.

4. Explain the term 'optimum firm'. Explain the factors that determine the size of such a unit. How can the various optima be reconciled?

5. What is meant by large-scale production? What are the various methods of effecting large-scale operation? Outline the advantages of conducting business on a large scale.

6. Describe the salient features of different methods of integration.

7. State the relative advantages of Big Business and Small. Also indicate the social effects of Big Business.

8. Why is efficiency of management greater in large-scale firms than in small ones? If large-scale operation is more efficient, how do you account for the existence of a large number of small firms?

9. What factors operate in favour of enlarging the size of the representative unit in industry? Show the force of the factors you mention in a number of industries.

10. State the factors that impose a limit on the size of a business unit. Give illustrations in support of the factors you mention.

11. "There are logical reasons for supposing that large-scale operati results in maximum efficiency.' Do you agree? Give reasons.

12. Account for the simultaneous existence of small and large busin units in modern times.

CHAPTER VIII

Structure of Company Management

1. 'The company is an instrument that unites the efforts of great numb of people.' Explain and mention the principal organs of company manageme in India.

2. Show how the structure of modern business tends more and more separation of ownership and management.

3. In what ways do shareholders exercise control over the affairs of the company, and to what extent is their control real?

4. What are the statutory and managerial functions of the Board Directors of a company?

5. What is meant by saying that the Board of Directors is the highe executive organ of a company? Explain fully.

6. What do you understand by 'inside directors' and 'outside directors What is meant by a balanced Board?

7. 'The Board of Directors stands between the shareholders and th Chief Executive'. Elucidate. Also state the position and functions of the Chi Executive.

8. Distinguish between Managing Director and Manager of a company.

CHAPTER IX

Pattern and Problems of Company Management

1. "Although company organisation gives the impression of democracy yet in practice it exhibits the worst form of oligarchy in business management." Do you agree? Discuss.

2. "Company management in India is a glaring example of economic oligarchy." Comment on this statement, showing how far the Directors' contro over management is effective and to what extent their responsibility to shareholders is real.

3. "Shareholders' democracy has signally failed in this country."Commen on this statement.

4. "The company is the only form of organisation in which a permanen opposition of interests can exist." Examine the truth of this statement. How ha the Companies Act, 1956 attempted to remove this position?

5. "The Executive Machinery of a company as represented by the Board of Directors and the Chief Executive has been made more answerable to the wishes of the shareholders by the Companies Act, 1956." Do you subscribe to this view? Why?

6. "The managing agency system had outlived its utility, and was rightly abolished." Comment.

7. Explain the role of shareholders' associations in fostering the control by shareholders of company's affairs.

CHAPTER X

Company Meetings and Resolutions

1. Discuss the position of a secretary in the organisation and working of a company. What qualification should he possess in order to perform his duties efficiently?

2. "The Secretary is no doubt the servant of the company but he is also the servant of law." Amplify this statement and examine fully his more important duties and the manner of their discharge.

3. Explain the different resolutions, and enumerate the cases in which each is required. Draft each to illustrate one of the cases covered by it.

4. Explain the scope and nature of different meetings and state how each is convened. Describe the law and procedure of voting at a meeting.

5. Discuss the powers and responsibilities of the Chairman at the Annual General Meeting of a company.

6. Write explanatory notes on: (i) voting by proxy, (ii) amendments, (iii) closure, (iv) next business, (v) postponement and adjournment.

CHAPTER XI

Company Office—Its Organisation and Management

1. What is an office? What are its basic functions?

2. Give a brief description of any modern office with which you are acquainted. Mention at least five of the labour-saving devices used in an office and explain the functions of each.

3. Give an account of the activities of an office and the office manager.

4. Briefly indicate the principles on which the internal organisation, layout of office furniture and equipment, stationery and forms are based.

5. Give an account of office services and their principal purpose.

6. What is filing? What are the essentials of a good-filing system? Briefly examine the various methods of filing and indexing.

7. Under what conditions should office appliances be used?

8. What is card index? What are its advantages, and what are the uses to which card index can be put?

CHAPTER XII

Business Combinations

1. What circumstances contribute to the formation of industrial combinations? Illustrate your answer from Indian experience.

2. What are the different forms of combination in business? Deal with any two of the forms of combination which have helped modern industries.

3. Discuss the nature, economies and limitations of different types of combinations.

4. Indicate the chief reasons for the modern tendency towards combination of business undertakings. Point out the effects of such combinations.

5. Quote two industries for each case where you consider economies could be obtained by an increase in (a) horizontal, (b) vertical, (c) lateral integration. Has the combinations of firms in fact followed these lines of integration?

6. What are the chief functions of Chambers of Commerce and Trade Associations? Illustrate your answer with an example from each type.

7. Distinguish the holding Company and the Amalgamation as method of large-scale control. In what sense is the control of modern industr capitalistic?

8. Distinguish between:
   (a) Holding Company and Interlocked Directorate;
   (b) Holding Company and Trust;
   (c) Cartel and Trust;
   (d) Cartel and Consolidation?
   (e) Pool and Cartel.

Comment upon the social and economic consequences of these types of busines organisation.

9. What is a pool? Describe the various types of pools in operation. D you agree with the view that pools are economically inefficient?

10. The cartel is essentially less efficient than the amalgamation. In fact, possesses no advantage except that of easier formation. Discuss.

11. How far did the managing agency system enable concerns to tak advantage of the vertical and horizontal combination characteristic of highl industrialised countries?

12. Discuss the merits and demerits of business combinations.

13. What are the evils that are associated with industrial combinations What measures would you suggest to check them?

14. "Combinations by giving rise to monopoly harm the interests of th consumers." "Combinations by reducing costs offer goods and services at lowe price to consumers." Reconcile these statements.

15. What is 'big business' and why do businesses tend to become big? It i said that 'some business are born great, some achieve greatness and others hav greatness thrust upon them.' Discuss this statement in Indian conditions.

16. Discuss fully the combination movement in India paying particula attention to the types most predominant. Give examples. Also account for th scanty progress in this direction.

17. Distinguish the economies that constitute the advantages of large scal production and those that are dependent upon the existence of monopolisti control.

18. 'In the sphere of private enterprise, complete consolidation complete the cycle in the evolution of Business organisation.' Explain and trace th evolution referred to therein.

CHAPTER XIII

Rationalisation

1. Explain clearly the meaning of 'Rationalisation of Industry'. an discuss its effects on personnel. Can it be used as an effective method fo increasing efficiency in India?

2. 'Rationalisation is not an unmixed blessing.' Explain and bring out th advantages and dangers of rationalisation.

3. 'Rationalisation without the co-operation of labour results in straine relations between labour and management leading to breach of industria peace.' Comment.

4. Distinguish scientific management and rationalisation. How are the related to industrial psychology?

5. 'The greatest opposition to rationalisation has been from the side o

our.' What measures should be taken to get the support of labour in any eme of rationalisation?

6. Make out a case for the rationalisation of Indian industry. Mention the ficulties in the way of implementing rationalisation measures in Indian lustries.

7. Distingurish between—

(a) Rationalisaton and Nationalisation.

(b) Rationalisation and Combination.

8. Since rationalisation in its true sense has not made much headway in dia, do you consider nationalisation would help re-orient our industry?

CHAPTER XIV

Public Utilities

1. What is a Public Utility? State its essential characteristics which istinguish it from a non-utility form.

2. Distinguish the principles underlying tariff, making it a public utility nterprise.

3. State the case for and against public ownership and autonomous nanagement of public utility undertakings.

4 What are the special features of a public utility undertaking which istinguish it from other business undertakings?

5. Discuss the various aspects of the price policy of public utilities.

CHAPTER XV

Government and Business

1. 'The old concept of non-interference in business and industry of a country has outlived today.' Elucidate.

2. Illustrate from Indian experience how *laissez-faire* economy has been replaced by mixed economy.

3. Under what conditions and to what extent is state intervention justified in the economic life of the nation?

4. Tracc the events leading to the concept of 'Welfare State'. Indicate how the State in India has tried to control and regulate private enterprise to this end.

5. Briefly deal with the various types of control exercised by government.

6. State the important features embodied in the Industrial Policy of Government of India.

7. What are the main provisions of the Industries (Development and Regulation) Act? Discuss the advantages of this measure in relation to existing industrial organisation of the country. Explain the meaning and functions of Development Councils.

8. Write a note on government as a promoter of various interests through promotional activities.

CHAPTER XVI

Public Enterprise
(Government in Business)

1. Make a case for nationalisation or public ownership and management of business. Is public ownership necessarily better than private enterprise?

2. Indicate the weaknesses and limitations of public undertakings.

3. Outline the principal characteristics of the following forms of organisation employed to run public undertakings:

(a) Government Department;

(b) Public Corporation;

(c) Government Company

4. Discuss the reasons for which—

(a) the departmental type of management of state enterprises is being given up in India.

(b) the government company is being adopted in preference to public corporation.

5. Write a reasoned note on the different kinds of Boards of Directors usually appointed for administering public enterprises.

6. What types of Boards are prevalent in India and with what effects? Would you suggest any change to improve the working of public enterprises here?

7. 'A proper balance between autonomy of a public enterprise and Parliamentary control over it is conducive to efficient administration.' Explain this statement and briefly examine the different ways in which Parliament may exercise control, indicating your preference.

8. Show how corporate independence and responsibility are compatible with ministerial guidance and control in the case of public undertakings. How does government exercise control over public undertakings?

9. Explain the meaning of 'Public Corporation'. Justify or controvert the assertion that public corporation is the best administrative machinery for state enterprises.

10. How far has the working of public undertakings in India been successful? What measures would you recommend to improve it?

11. 'While there is a place for Government in business, there is a real place for "business" in Government'. Examine the implications in this statement.

CHAPTER XVII

Social Responsibilities of Business

1. What are the social responsibilities of business?

2. Briefly examine the economic and social objectives of business?

3. Summarise the obligations of business to itself, to shareholders, to workers, to consumers, and to society.

4. Can management run a business for profit and still have due regard for fair play for workers, consumers and the community?

5. Discuss the responsibilities of management to society.

6. 'The business of business is to do business and thus serve social and economic ends.' Explain this statement.

7. 'Business is an economic institution operating in a socio-political environment'. Discuss.

CHAPTER XVIII

Nature and Importance of Management

1. What is the true field of (a) management, (b) administration? Distinguish between them.

2. Discuss management as a function and management as a process.
3. Comment on the true nature of management. Is it a science or an art?
4. To what extent, in your opinion, is management a profession?
5. 'Management is getting things done through people.' Amplify.
6. 'Management is the development of people and not the direction of ngs'. Elucidate.
7. Trace the development of modern management theory.
8. Evaluate the contribution made by F.W. Taylor, Henry Fayol, Elton ayo, and Mary Parker Follet to the growth of management thought.
9. Why are Behavioural Sciences important in management?

CHAPTER XIX

Functions of Management

1. 'It is good management that produces sound business'. Discuss.
2. 'All managers, by whatever name called, manage'. Discuss, bringing out e universality of management functions.
3. Outline the various management or managerial functions.
4. What is decision-making? Assess its importance in management process.
5. Explain the various phases in decision making.
6. What steps should a manager take, and in what order, to arrive at the est possible decision?
7. Explain co-ordination as a function of management, and state its rinciples and techniques.
8. Illustrate the need for co-ordinating, purchasing, design, production nd sales policy.
9. 'An organisation needs new ideas to keep it healthy'. Discuss, and point ut the value of promoting innovation and creativity.

CHAPTER XX

Planning

1. 'Planning is the essence of management; it is management function'. Elucidate.
2. 'All managers plan whether they are at the top, middle, or bottom of the organisation structure.' Explain and illustrate.
3. Is it feasible to divorce the planning phase of management almost completely from directing and controlling on the theory that planners, directors and controllers will all prove more efficient with thorough-going specialisation of functions?
4. Explain business forecasting and discuss the various methods of forecasting.
5. Discuss the concept of 'management by objectives'. How does it differ from traditional management?
6. Briefly explain the important elements that are included in any comprehensive planning activity.

CHAPTER XXI

Organisation

1. Discuss the various theories of organisation.

2. Distinguish organisation as a structure and as an administrative proce
3. Define the concept of organisation and state the principles of organis tion.
4. What is departmentation and what are its methods?
5. What are the different bases in grouping activities?
6. What is an organisation chart? Should the organisation structure built around people, or people be adapted to the structure?
7. Why has business departed to a large extent from the use of the li type of organisation in its pure form?
8. Give a critical analysis of Line and Staff organisation, and show how combines the advantages of line as well as functional organisation.
9. State the relative merits and demerits of line, line and staff a functional organisations.
10. What are the causes of conflict between line and staff? What measur would you suggest to make line and staff relations successful?
11. 'Inadequate working relationships between line and staff departmen are the most potent sources of friction and inefficiency'. Explain and illustrate.
12. Explain in general terms how organisation structure causes huma relations problems.
13. Explain the advantages and disadvantages of management by Commi tees.
14. How would you make effective use of committees?
15. How would you distinguish between formal and informal organisa tions? Do you think we need both in an organisation?

CHAPTER XXII

Authority and Responsibility

1. Define the levels of authority and responsibility normally found in th organisation of a modern industrial undertaking.
2. Give the meaning of delegation of authority, and mention the source of authority.
3. Establish a relationship between authority, power, responsibility an accountability.
4. Give your views on the concept of delegation of authority. State th principles of delegation of authority, and the obstacles to delegation.
5. What is the relationship between the exception principle and delegatio of authority?
6. What steps would you take to make delegation effective at variou levels? What test would you apply to judge the effectiveness of delegation?
7. What do you understand by 'span of control in business management Examine the factors that determine the span of control.
8. 'It is of great importance to smooth working that at all levels authorit and responsibility should be co-terminous and co-terminous'. Examine th statement.
9. Discuss the need for decentralisation in business organisation. How may managerial decentralisation help human relations?
10. It is generally conceived that authority to command and power t enforce should be fully decentralised.
11. Bring out clearly the benefits of decentralisation.

2. What characteristics distinguish informal from formal organisation? a manager weaken informal organisation by making formal organisation ıger and stricter?

CHAPTER XXIII

Staffing and Directing

1. What do you understand by staffing? Indicate the steps that a manager ıld take in performing this function.

2. 'Directing is the process around which all performance revolves lain and state the methods of directing subordinates to achieve objectives.

3. Briefly explain the principles of direction.

4. What do you understand by motivation? Discuss the part played by the der in promoting motivation.

5. What is management communication? State the importance of communication, and mention its guiding principles.

6. Explain the principal barriers to managerial communication and ggest measures for improvement.

7. 'A common reason for friction within an organisation is faulty nmunications.' Explain and illustrate.

8. 'The manager must have his lines of communication established, open d working.' Why?

9. Management has been defined as the technique of providing group adership in order to achieve some purpose or goal. Discuss.

10. 'Good leadership is an integral part of effective direction.' Elucidate.

11. Classify business leaders and point out some important qualities that ıakc for successful leadership. Discuss how leaders influence others.

12. 'Management is executive leadership; it makes things happen and gets ıings done through others.' Discuss.

13. Explain the assumptions under McGregor's theories X and Y, bringing ut the important distinction between the two.

CHAPTER XXIV

Control and Public Relations

1. What precisely is meant by control? How can it be secured? How does a nanager exercise it?

2. State the various steps involved in exercising control and the elements of control.

3. Discuss the requisites of a good control system, and mention the tools of control.

4. 'Planning is the basis of control, action its essence, delegation its key and information its guide.' Elucidate.

5. 'Management control should free rather than restrict; it should be dynamic rather than bureaucratic'. Explain and illustrate.

6 'Planning and control are complementary to each other.' Do you agree?

7. Understanding control really means understanding three principal things about it. What is control? Who is controlled? And who controls? Discuss.

8. 'Effective control depends upon the fixing of responsibilities, and so control cannot be really effective beyond the extent to which specific employees are charged with definite responsibilities, and are so informed.' Examine the statement.

9. Define Public Relations. Explain the various functions of pub relations and its benefits.

10. Explain how you would set about obtaining favourable results of pub relations.

CHAPTER XXV

Scientific Management

1. Briefly explain the main principles of Scientific Management and sh why organised labour opposes its application.

2. Suggest a criticism of the assumptions of Scientific Management fro the point of view of an industrial psychologist.

3. What parts of the programme of Scientific Management would y apply in (a) a large, (b) a small, Indian factory? If you would not apply Scienti Management at all, give your reasons.

4. 'Scientific Management is an improvement, but it fails to alter th essentially autocratic control of industry, nor does it really induce scienti research into the labour problem of industry.' Comment.

5. 'Scientific Management involves in its essence a complete ment revolution on the part of the workman and the management'. Comment. Sho how Scientific Management renders a useful service both the employer and th employee.

6. 'To work according to scientific laws the management must take ove and perform much of the work that is now left to the man." Comment.

CHAPTER XXVI

Plant Location

1. Discuss the various factors that affect the location of a plant.

2. 'The governing principle is that a location of a plant should be fixed i such a manner that the people interested in its success can sell goods mos profitably and manufacture them with the least expense.' Explain and show hov this object can be achieved.

3. Discuss the relation between location, size and profits of an industria concern.

4. In deciding location of an industry, would you attach importance t sources of raw materials or market? Why?

5. As an industrial promoter where in India and why will you locate (i) an iron and steel mill, (ii) an automobile factory, (iii) a woollen mill, (iv) a cement factory, (v) a cotton textile mill?

6. What considerations should be borne in mind while deciding upon a site of a plant?

CHAPTER XXVII

Factory Planning

1. What factors should be considered in deciding on a business building? Contrast the advantages and disadvantages of a one-storey versus a multi-storey building.

2. What factors enter into the selection of machinery and equipment?

3. What is meant by efficiency in plant layout? Differentiate between process and product layouts and give the merits of each.

4. Outline the approach which should be taken in plant layout problems.

5. Describe the characteristics of a theoretically perfect plant layout. How are machines and equipment arranged in manufacturing? Why?

6. What is materials handling? State the rules for materials handling, and indicate the advantages of mechanised handling.

7. What is meant by work study? Discuss its two phases-method study and work measurement bringing out clearly their respective objectives.

8. Why is it necessary to make work study? Outline the procedures for method study and for work measurement.

9. What useful purpose do work study and work measurement serve in effective control?

CHAPTER XXVIII

Production and Cost Control

1. Explain what is meant by 'Production Control'. What are the fundamental principles underlying it?

2. Explain the important facets of production planning.

3. "Production control involves planning, routing, scheduling and follow up." Discuss.

4. What special points must a Production Manager keep in view so that maximum efficiency can be achieved?

5. Examine the relative advantages of the various types of production, and state when each is useful.

6. What do you understand by Quality Control? State in what direction quality control is useful in industrial management.

7. Briefly examine the various techniques and methods of quality control in manufacturing industries.

8. What are the objectives of Production Planning and Control? What connection, if any, is there between the sales department and production department?

9. Analyse the selling price of an article and briefly examine the various elements of cost that compromise the cost build-up.

10. "An efficient system of costing is essential for adequate industrial control." Elucidate this statement bringing out clearly the role of costing as an aid to efficiency.

11. Assess the importance of production and cost control in promoting industrial efficiency.

CHAPTER XXIX

Budgets and Budgetary Control

1. Explain the term 'budgets' and 'budgetary control' and show how they are used for effective financial control in governmental and business management.

2. Discuss fully the importance of budgetary control in big business and trace the steps in its application.

3. Classify budgets, and show with the help of a diagram how different budgets are co-ordinated for effective control.

4. "Budgetary control is really a technique for planning and direction well as for control." Explain this statement.

5. What is budgetary control? Show how it enables the business administrator to implement the business policy throughout the organisation.

6. What is budgetary control? Examine the human problems involved making the budgetary control effective.

CHAPTER XXX

Purchasing and Storekeeping

1. Explain the term 'Scientific Purchasing.' and state the objects scientific buying.

2. State and explain the various steps necessary for effective purchasing.

3. Comment upon the buying policies and detail out the current buyi practices as followed by (i) manufacturers, (ii) wholesalers, and (iii) retailers.

4. What is the importance of efficient stock-taking? Indicate the functic of a stores department and briefly discuss them.

5. Describe the procedure for the receipt of materials into the stores a their issue therefrom.

6. State and explain the precise position of the stores department in t organisation of the works.

7. Distinguish between 'Stores' and 'Stock'. Describe a system of sto control which facilitates stock-taking.

8. State the importance of inventory control and the methods of exercisi it.

CHAPTER XXXI

Personnel Management

1. Define Personnel Management. What are the principal responsibilit of a Personnel Manager?

2. 'Management is people'. Explain, bringing out clearly the role human factor in worker-management relationship.

3. Argue the case for and against seniority as a major consideration regard to promotion decisions.

4. Define Industrial Psychology. How can it help to tackle the 'labo problem' created by the factory system?

5. Distinguish between (a) vocational selection, (b) vocational guidan (c) vocational training. What importance do you attach to each? Explain h they can be applied in practice.

6. Describe the various methods recently adopted in industry for (a) selection, (b) the training of workers and administrative personnel, and estim the value of these methods.

7. What do you understand by 'job evaluation' and 'merit rating?' In w ways may higher wages and shorter hours be expected to increase efficiency?

8. Explain what is meant by saying that since high wages often mean l labour costs, there may be an economy in high wages. Do you think there is a an economy of short hours?

9. What precisely is meant by efficiency? How is it measured?

10. What are the factors of labour efficiency? Trace the trend of labo efficiency in India.

11. Examine the different methods of job evaluation and merit rating.
12. 'Management is Personnel Administration'. Discuss.

CHAPTER XXXII

Industrial Relations

1. Is it true to say that in the typical business firm the workman is deprived of all incentive to work except the receipt of wages? What would you do about it, if put in charge of labour management in such a firm?

2. "The Trade Union movement exists to obtain out of Capitalism the best possible bargain for Labour." Do you think the present policies and methods of Trade Unions in India are best calculated to attain this object?

3. What do you understand by 'Welfare Work?' What circumstances make it easy or difficult to establish 'Welfare' arrangements in industrial establishment. Do you think workers are justified in objecting on principle or on certain conditions to such arrangement? Would you advise an extension of welfare work even in times of industrial depression?

4. What are the causes of labour unrest in India? Account for the phenomenal unrest in India after World War II. What remedial measures have been taken and what others would you suggest?

5. Make constructive suggestions for the minimisation and settlement of industrial disputes and for the establishment of better industrial relations in our country.

6. "In the highest form of discipline all are regulated, and all are free." Explain with special reference to morale.

7. Discuss the suggestion that some measure of compulsory arbitration or conciliation is desirable. Refer to experiments that have been made under the Disputes Act, 1947.

8. It has been often remarked that Indian labour is cheap and inefficient. Trace some of the causes of low efficiency and suggest ways and means to stimulate production and to improve efficiency.

9. What administrative measures are conducive to the promotion of morale and harmony in industrial relations?

10. What is meant by collective bargaining and compulsory adjudication? State the merits and weaknesses of each as a method of settlement of industrial disputes.

11. Explain the term human factor in industry. Discuss the various social relationships and inter-relationships in a factory organisation.

12. Discuss the merits and demerits of the present-day trend of providing participation in management to labour in our country.

13. 'Benefit accruing from labour legislation cannot be measured by the number of laws on Statute Book but by the method and spirit of enforcement'. Discuss.

14. 'The greatest obstacle to the growth of healthy Trade Union Movement in India is the unhealthy influences of rival political parties'. Elucidate.

CHAPTER XXXIII

Methods of Wage Payment

1. "Despite the importance of other issues in labour-management negotiations wages still remain the most controversial problem of industrial management." Comment, bringing out clearly the factors affecting wages.

2. Define basis of pay, rate of pay. Examine the various 'incentive plan of wage payment.

3. State the various methods of wage payment. Discuss the metho employed under scientific management.

4. Recommend a system of wage payment which may stimulate industri productivity at the present juncture. Do you think that profit sharing will most effective to that end? Discuss.

5. "Both the Halsey and Rowan systems have primarily in view reduction in the labour cost of the article manufactured." Do you agree? Justi your opinion.

6. "Until the workers are given a share and a direct share in the profits the industry there will be no inducement for them to regard their work anything but a daily task." Examine this view, with particular reference methods which have been adopted to give workers a share in profits.

7. "Instincts, conventional habits and calculations all influence the supp priceof labour." Explain and illustrate.

8. Women are, on the average, paid 55 to 65 per cent the wages of men f similar occupations. What economic and other grounds are there for th differentiation?

9. Enumerate the principal methods of wage payment based on resul Examine one of them in detail and show how far it can serve to meet t present-day labour crisis.

10. Profit sharing has been recommended as a panacea for the curre industrial ills in India. Show how far it can serve to:

(a) promote industrial efficiency;
(b) provide security of employment to the worker;
(c) quell the prevailing labour unrest.

11. What is 'Minimum Wage'? How would you calculate it? What are t likely effects of the enforcement of such a wage? What types of industries a suitable for the application of the principle?

CHAPTER XXXIV

Financial Planning

1. What is meant by financial planning in business? What are determinants?

2. How would you calculate in advance the working capital needs different kinds of business enterprises of various sizes?

3. Distinguish between working capital and fixed capital. How would y calculate the total capital required to put a project into operation?

4. "The basic problem in financing an enterprise is to maintain a sou capital structure." Discuss this statement, and explain how the problem can met and pitfalls avoided.

5. What do you understand by 'financial forecasting'? Indicate functions of a business administrator in regard to the preparation and execut of financial forecasting.

6. State briefly the principles which should guide the directors of a pub limited company in determining (a) the adequacy of working capital, (b) rate of dividend, and (c) the adequacy of reserves.

7. Define over-capitalisation. Give examples of circumstances in whic may arise. What remedies, if any, should be adopted, and why?

8. State the dangers and disadvantages of over-capitalisation and explain ıy they are greater than those of under-capitalisation.

9. Define 'Working Capital'. To what extent would the advantages of nple working capital' be set off by the disadvantages of redundant working pital?

10. Explain fully (a) capitalisation, (b) over-capitalisation, (c) under-pitalisation and indicate the dangers of (b) and (c).

11. What points would you bear in mind while devising the capital ucture of a proposed public limited company?

12. Discuss the extent to which the following factors condition the financial an for capital structure of a public limited company;

(a) Initial requirement of funds.
(b) Rate of return on investment.
(c) Stability of earnings.
(d) Prevailing rates in the capital market.
(e) Income taxation.

13. What do you understand by financial planning in business? What ctors would you consider in devising it?

14. What are the factors that should be taken into consideration in stributing the capital of a limited company into different categories of shares? xplain fully.

15. What do you understand by the term 'capital gearing'? When will a mpany be said to be 'high-geared' and 'low-geared'?

16. Write an explanatory note on 'trading on equity', pointing out the nitations of this principle.

17. "The selection of the proper time for floatation of a company, is an portant factor in financial management and capital gearing." Discuss, inting out clearly the proper time for floatation of a company.

CHAPTER XXXV

Sources of Finance

1. Briefly examine the methods employed in India for raising funds to eet (a) fixed capital, (b) working capital, needs of a joint stock enterprise. How e extensions and improvements financed?

2. As the head of a business corporation how would you finance the urchase of new equipment? Consider the various alternatives that are open to ou.

3. Describe the procedure you would follow to secure funds sufficient to) finance a fresh venture, and (b) to expand a going concern.

4. Discuss the advantages of issuing different classes of shares and ebentures by a company from the point of view of (i) the company, (ii) the vestor.

5. Discuss the relative merits and demerits of deposits, debentures and oughing back as methods of business finance.

6. Discuss the role of commercial banks in the financing of industries. Is it niform in all countries? What is the position in India?

7. In what ways and on what security can a company borrow money? lustrate your answer from Indian experience.

8. Describe the various ways in which reorganisation (reconstruction and nalgamation) may take place, and state the circumstances in which it may ecome necessary.

9. "The main weakness of the financing of industrial enterprises in India is that they depend too much on outside agencies." Discuss this statement.

CHAPTER XXXVI

Institutions of Industrial Finance

1. Write a note on the Constitution and scope of the Industrial Finance Corporation of India and state how it functions.

2. Review the working of the I.F.C. How far has it succeded in financing Indian industry?

3. Comment on the part played by the following institutions in financing Indian industry:

(a) Industrial Credit and Investment Corporation of India.

(b) The National Industrial Development Corporation.

(c) National Small Industries Corporation.

4. Briefly describe the constitution and scope of the Industrial Development Bank. Also discuss the part played by it as the apex organisation in the industrial finance structure in India.

5. It is alleged that the existence of so many finance and development corporations results in wasteful duplication of effort. Do you agree with this allegation? Give reasons in support of your answer.

6. Write a comparative note on the working of State Financial Corporations.

7. Explain clearly the constitution and functions of (a) Investment Trust, (b) Finance Company, and discuss the relative merits of the various types of investment trusts.

8. Write a short note on the Unit Trust of India, and say what principles underlie the setting up of this trust.

CHAPTER XXXVII

The Securities Market

1. "The Stock Exchange is a legalised gambling den." "The Stock Exchange is the pulse of economy." How would you reconcile these views regarding the stock exchange?

2. How do operations on the Stock Exchange affect the economic life of a country? Is it necessary to control stock exchanges? If so, how?

3. Mention and explain some of the factors that rule the fluctuations in prices on a stock exchange.

4. How is business transacted on a stock exchange and settlement made?

5. Discuss the part played by the Stock Exchange in the economic development of a country, with special reference to its importance in the money market.

6. Explain the various methods that a company may adopt for selling its securities. In what ways can a stock exchange assist it in this task?

7. Examine fully the functions and services of the brokers and jobbers on the London Stock Exchange. Is it possible to have this division of functions on Indian stock exchanges?

8. Bring out the points of difference between a bull and a bear on a stock exchange. How may each carry over his commitments?

9. What is meant by 'Options Dealings' and 'Blank Transfer of Shares'? Mention the evils associated with each.

10. Explain the essential functions of a stock exchange.

11. Indicate the drawbacks and defects in the working of the stock xchanges in India. How far has the Securities Contracts (Regulation) Act, 1956, ucceeded in removing them?

12. Discuss the economics of speculation and distinguish speculation and ambling.

CHAPTER XXXVIII

Marketing and its Functions

1. Define marketing and explain what is meant by marketing concept.
2. Distinguish between marketing, selling and distribution.
3. Marketing is an art; and the marketing manager must design a narketing mix'. What do you understand by 'marketing mix' and what are the ements of the marketing mix of manufacturers.
4. State the marketing forces which have a bearing on the marketing mix id govern it.
5. Briefly explain the function of marketing.
6. Illustrate the advantages of assembling, grading and branding.
7. Describe the functions of different kinds of warehouses. How is wnership in warehoused goods transferred? Outline the procedure for taking oods out of bond.
8. State how trade and industry are helped by insurance and banking.
9. Describe the methods used in financing internal trade in India. What e the methods of inland remittances?

CHAPTER XXXIX

Transport

1. Explain in what way transport is an essential function of marketing.
2. Discuss the economic importance of transport.
3. Examine the relative advantages of various means of transport regard-g cost, speed, flexibility and regularity of service.
4. Write short notes on the present position and future prospects of (a) vil aviation, (b) shipping in India.

CHAPTER XL

Selling or Distribution of Goods

1. Selling is the planning of 'Six rights'. Mention the six rights and explain em.
2. What is meant by sales management and what is its importance in odern industry?
3. Briefly explain the administrative and executive functions of sales anager.
4. Show the importance to the seller of an article of knowing its demand rve. What are the main factors determining whether the demand curve for the oduct of (a) an individual firm, (b) the whole trade, is elastic or inelastic?
5. What is meant by marketing research, and what are its functions.
6. Describe the marketing methodology for successful results.

7. Discuss the various areas of activity of marketing research, paying special attention to market research area.

8. Examine the various factors that must be weighed by the Sales Manager while fixing the price of the product.

9. How is the market price likely to be determined when conditions of (a) complete monopoly, (b) perfect competition prevail? To what extent are these conditions found in any industry to-day ?

10. Write a note on the policy of resale price maintenance.

11. Discuss the importance and functions of the credit collection department of a business.

12. Show how by extending credit, a producer can help himself, the dealer and the consumer.

CHAPTER XLI

Channels of Distribution

1. Assess the value of the part played by the consumer in a society with a system of (a) free consumption, (b) planned consumption.

2. Who is a middleman? What is his importance in the distribution of goods?

3. In what sense is it possible to say that 'there are too many middlemen? How would you remedy such a situation?

4. Briefly discuss the factors that affect the choice of channels of distribution of goods.

5. Distinguish carefully between wholesale trade and retail trade. Indicate the services rendered by wholesalers and retailers in the distribution of goods.

6. Outline the main features in the organisation of a wholesale warehouse. To what extent is it possible to dispense with the services of wholesaler, and with what results?

7. Explain the meaning and organisation of (a) multiple shops, (b) departmental stores, (c) mail order houses. Give the advantages and shortcomings of each.

8. Enumerate the principal channels and institutions for handling the distribution of goods from producers to consumers. What factors would influence a producer's choice of distribution channel?

9. Explain the different forms of instalment selling, bringing out clearly their merits and demerits.

CHAPTER XLII

Salesmanship

1. What are the essential qualities which a salesman should possess in order to be successful? Discuss fully the points that a salesman should bear in mind while dealing with a prospect.

2. What are the buying motives? How should a salesman match these with selling steps?

3. Discuss fully the selling steps leading to the close of a sale.

4. What is aggressive salesmanship? Is it characteristics of imperfect competition? Discuss the administrative problems involved in aggressive sales promotion.

5. Do you think that modern industrial management is more concerned

with salesmanship than with production efficiency? Illustrate your answer from any industry you are familiar with.

6. Examine the various methods of remunerating salesmen.

7. You are considering the appointment of a salesman. What personal qualities would you look for?

8. 'Selling is a contest in which two protagonists—the buyer and the seller—aim to overcome one another's arguments.' How can the salesman prepare himself?

9. There are seven steps in retail salesmanship. What are they? Explain them briefly.

10. Briefly explain the more important principles of window-dressing.

11. What factors, if any, may influence a passer-by in his decision to enter a shop or not?

CHAPTER XLIII

Advertising

1. Consider advertising as a business method, and discuss its relation to competition.

2. 'Advertising is a sort of machine-made, mass-production method of selling.' Comment.

3. What are the functions, aims and benefits of advertising?

4. Who pays the cost of advertising? How can this cost be economically justified?

5. What are the principal causes of waste in advertising?

6. How would you combat the argument that advertising is un-necessary and wasteful and that it is untruthful?

7. What do you understand by scientific advertising? Explain clearly the essentials of a scientifically drafted copy of an advertisement.

8. "Smith in effect announces that his product is superior to Brown's and Brown announces to the contrary. The announcements cancel each other out, and are sheer waste......." Comment on this description of advertising.

9. Consumers are faced with a wide range of choice in satisfying their needs. In what manner does advertising assist them in choosing the right goods?

10. How would you determine the essential role of advertising?

11. Analyse with the help of suitable examples, the various advertising media.

12. Illustrate the characteristics of a good headline, slogan and illustration.

13. How may advertisement copy be tested (i) in advance, (ii) after publication? Who is the final judge of the success of an advertisement? Why?

CHAPTER XLIV

The Traffic Department and Foreign Trade

1. Briefly describe the organisation of the Traffic Department, and explain its functions relating to inbound and outbound shipments.

2. What is the position of Traffic Manager in the organisation setup of a large concern? Enumerate his powers and duties.

3. Discuss the importance of proper packing and packaging in securing economical freight rates.

4. 'Outline the various stages in the import trade, commencing with the

placing of an order till the arrival of the shipment. Name and explain the documents employed in the trade.

5. Explain the different methods by which an Indian exporter may obtain payment for goods shipped abroad. State the merits of each method.

6. Write short notes on: Letter of Credit; Liners and Tramps; Letter of Hypothecation; Bill of Lading; Charter Party.

7. Outline the procedure for exporting goods from India. What documents constitute the shipping documents?

8. What is meant by Indent Business? How is it carried on in India?

CHAPTER XLV

Organised Commodity Markets

1. What do you understand by an organised commodity market? Examine the characteristics which make a commodity suitable for handling on an organised market.

2. What is a Produce Exchange? Describe the contributions and objects of produce exchanges in India.

3. Examine the working of any Produce Exchange in India.

4. What types of transactions are conducted on a Produce Exchange? Describe Hedging and state its advantages.

5. Distinguish between a produce exchange and an ordinary market and a regulated market.

6. Distinguish speculation and gambling. Discuss the uses and abuses of speculation in commodity futures market.

OTHER IMPORTANT BOOKS ON COMMERCE AND MANAGEMENT

MODERN MARKETING
(Principles and Practices)
R.S.N. Pillai & Bagavathi

This serviral and enlarged edition of the book is suitable for students of Marketing in college in India. The book consists of 38 chapters and is presented in a systematic manner.

CONTENTS: Market and Marketing • Modern Marketing Concept • Marketing System, Marketing Mix, Marketing Function • Buying, Assembling and Selling • Transportation • Storage and Warehouses • Standardisation and Grading • Marketing Finance • Marketing Risk • Marketing Information and Research • Marketing Management • Marketing Startegy & Planning • Product • Pricing • Branching and Packaging • Promotional Programme • Sales Promotion • Advertising • Personal Selling • Sales Organisation • Sales Forcast Management • Control of Sales Force • Sales Process • Remuneration to Salesmen • Consumer Behaviour • Consumerism • Law Relating to Sale of Goods • Channels of Distributional • Channels of Distribution-II • Market- ing of Consu- mer Goods • Marketing of Industrial Goods • Marketing of Securities • Marketing of Agricultural Goods • Regulated Markets • Organised Markets • Co-operative Marketing • International Marketing • Marketing & Society.

07 301 ISBN : 81-219-1697-6 pp. 400

ISO 9000
A MANUAL FOR TOTAL QUALITY MANAGEMENT
Suresh Dalela & Saurabh

The basic objective of the book is to provide the students of Engineering Discipline and Quality Professionals of business sectors, a survey of different Standards of Quality Assurance & Quality Management Systems.

CONTENTS: Introduction to Quality Concepts & ISO 9000 Series of Quality Systems • Quality Management System • Key Elements of ISO 9001 & Its Requirements (July 1994 version) • Defects Prevention & Quality Improvement Techniques • Documentation of Quality Management System • Quality Planning & Quality Programmes • Sample of a Quality Manual (form and Structure) • Assessment or Audit (Internal & External) • Implementing ISO 9000 Quality Systems & Certification • Quality Costs • Quality Management (Some relevant Topics) • Total Quality Control (Through Statistical Means) • Quality Awareness, Education & Training •

07 278 2nd Edn.1999 ISBN : 81-219-1483-3 (H.B.)pp. 448

HUMAN RESPONSE DEVELOPMENT

G.D. Maheshwari

Everybody is not a job hopper or a high jumper but even then he can reach the top of the ladder step by step. This book lays stress for creation of work environment in such a way that the individual is treated as an important component of the whole infrastructure and not just a cog in the wheel. This book describes even those who can never boast of a position or rank is their academic career, have acheived spectacular success in life.

CONTENTS: Time Management • Making meetings effecive • How to be a good boss? • Communication–The Key to Success • Motivation • Leadership How to Make a Mark as a Manager • Are you a Supervisor Stress Management • Conflict Management • Acheiving Improved Performances Towards Higher Administrative Efficiency • Delegation in Principle 'Yes' and in Practice? • The Art of Looking Busy and Doing Nothing Creativity and Brain Storming • Managing Success Successfully, Cutpieces • of TACT.

07 306 1st Edn. 1998 ISBN : 81-219-0431-5 pp. 742

PROFESSIONAL MANAGEMENT IN INDIA

Problems and Prospects

M.V. Pylee

K.C. Sankaranarayanan

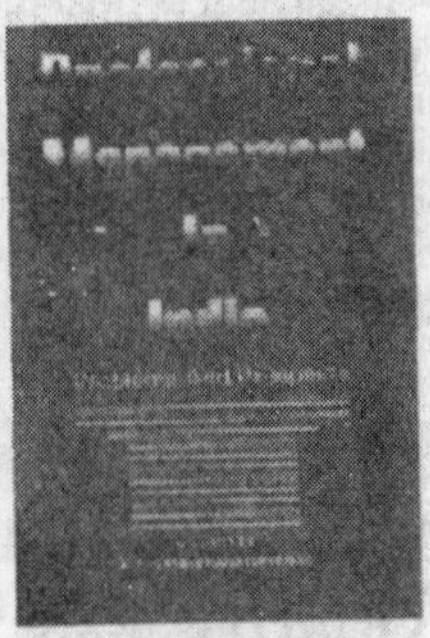

The book, gives a detailed account of the Problems, that professional Management body in India faces with. these and related questions are, dealt with in this volume which consists in all thirty-nine. Papers by Knowledge able persons, practising managers as well as management teachers.

07303 2nd. Edn. 1998 ISBN:81-219-1772-7 pp. 304

ENTREPRENEURIAL DEVELOPMENT

S.S. Khanka

The book has been written in a simple and self-learning style. Clarity has been given top priority throughtout the book. It is intended as an indepth knowledge source for an intending practitioner/entrepreneur in the field of entrepreneurship development.

CONTENTS : Entrepreneur • Women Entrepreneurship • Enterpreneurship• Factors Affecting Entrepreneurial Growth • Entrepreneurial Motivation Entrepreneurial Competencies • Entrepreneurial Mobility • Entrepreneurship Development Programmes (ED Ps) •Small Enterprises: An Introductory Framework • Project Identification and Selection

(PIS) • Project Formulation • Project Appraisal • Financing of Enterprise • Institutional Finance to Entrepreneurs • Lease Financing and Hire-Purchase • Institutional Support to Entrepreneurs • Taxation Benefits to Small-Scale Industry • Ownership Structures • The Business: Its Nature and Scope • Fundamentals of Management • Working Capital Management • Inventory Management • Production and Operation Management • Marketing Management • Human Resource Management • Accounting for Small Enterprises • Growth Strategies in Small Business • Government Policy for Small-Scale Enterprises • Small Enterprises in International Business.

07 307 1st. Edn. 1998 ISBN : 81-219-1801-4 pp. 330

प्रबंध लेखांकन

योगेन्द्र प्रसाद वर्मा, विजय बहादुर सिंह एवं अजेय वर्मा

प्रस्तुत पुस्तक में, विषय की प्रकृति को सही रूप में समझने से सम्बन्धित सभी बातों का समावेश तथा इसकी सरल भाषा में पूर्ण व्याख्या की गयी है। साथ ही इसमें प्रबंण लेखांकन का क्षेत्र क्यों और कैसे लेखांकन के अन्य प्रारूपों से व्यापक है आदि का सविस्तार विश्लेषण किया गया है जो बी.कॉम (प्रतिष्ठा) और एम.कॉम के विद्यार्थियों के लिए उपयोगी सिद्ध होगी।

विषय सूची-प्रबंध लेखांकनः एक परिचय • वित्तीय विवरण : प्रकृति एवं महत्त्व • वित्तीय विवरणों का विश्लेषण एवं निर्वचन • तुलनात्मक एवं समानाकार विवरण • प्रवृत्ति विश्लेषण • अनुपात विश्लेषण • कोष प्रवाह विवरण • रोकड़ प्रवाह विवरण • स्कंध नियंत्रण • मुद्रा-स्फीति लेखांकन.

07311 1st Edn. 1999 ISBN:81-219-1854-5 pp. 504

HUMAN RESOURCE DEVELOPMENT AND MANAGEMENT

A.M. Sheikh

CONTENTS : Introduction • Human Resource Planning • Job Analysis • Acquisition of Human Resource • Training and Development • Human Resource Motivation • Organisation Development and Change • Group Behaviour • Working Life and its Quality - Communication • Leadership • Workers Participation in Management • Job Evaluation • Merit Rating • Managing Stress & Conflict at Work Place • Industrial Disputes • Time Management • Computer Applications in HRM • HRM Scenario in 21st Century • Manpower Statistics in India.

07309 1st Edn. 1999 ISBN : 81-219-1805-7 pp. 312

THEORY AND PRACTICE OF COST ACCOUNTING

Sk. Sahajahan Ali,
Subir Datta,
Ashit Baran Saha

The book goes into details of the principles and techniques of Cost Accounting. It presents a sound theoretical exposition and numerous illustrative problems have been worket out and charts are given to enrich to sit for University and professional examinations both as private and collegiate student.

CONTENTS : Introduction • Concept, Analysis and Classification of Cost • Materials • Labour Overhead • Specific Order Costing • Process-Costing.

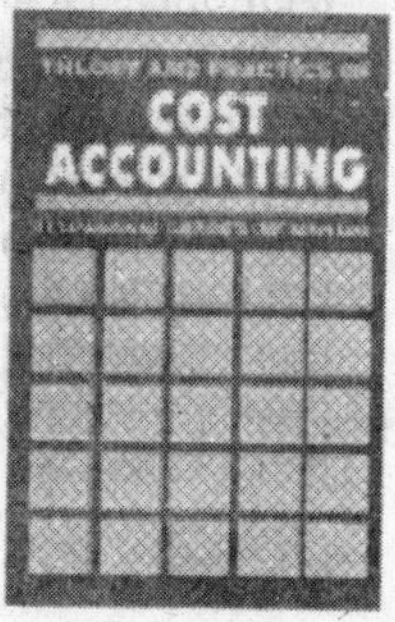

07274 ISBN : 81-219-1446-9pp. 440

PERSONNEL MANAGEMENT AND INDUSTRIAL RELATIONS

N.G. Nair

The book Consists of 23 chapters divided into five parts. Part I deals with development of perception and Part II deals with Acquistion and Absorption. Part III deals with Development Utilisation, Part IV deals with Maintenance with Motivation and Empowerment..

CONTENTS : H.R. DEVELOPMENT OF PRECEPTION • Introduction • Evelution And Environment • Theories of H.R.M. • ACQUISITION AND ABSORPTION • Human Resources Planning • Recruitment • Selection Placement, Induction and Socialisation • DEVELOPMENT AND UTILISATION • Theories of Training and Development • Employee Training • Management / Executive Development • Career Development • Promotion, Transfer and Separation • MAINTENANCE, AND RETENTION • Wages and Salaries Administration • Discipline and Grievances • Industrial and Labour Relations • Trade Unionism • Collective Bargaining • Rewards and Labour Welfare • Industrial Health and Safety • Performance Appraisal & Merit Rating • MOTIVATION AND EMPOWERMENT • Theories of Human Relation and Motivation • Vocational Guidance, Job Satisfaction and Morale • Steps to Promote Intrinsic Motivation •Organisation Structure Design and Development • Empowerment and Future of H.R.M.

07295 1st Edn. 1999 ISBN :81-219-1808-1 pp. 536

ACCOUNTING THEORY & MANAGEMENT ACCOUNTING

Sujit Kumar Roy

Sisir Kumar Bhattacharya

The book bears the testimony of being lucid in its expression and brevity in its expression and brevity in its exposition. Numerous problems of various nature have been worked out so that the users may find it useful to achieve their end and to have clear understinding of the subject.

07 270 1st Edn. 1999 ISBN : 81-219-1882-0 pp. 620

PROFESSIONAL HOTEL MANAGEMENT

Jagmohan Negi

The book provides a comprehensive description about the principles, concepts and techniques required for successful operation and management of hotels. Emphasis is on policies and strategies, planning and designing, organisational and departmental structure like, Room Division (Front Office and House-keeping), Food and Beverage Division (Kitchen and Restaurant), Sales and Marketing Techniques, Administration and Human Resource Management, Finance, etc.

07 298 Ist Edn. 1997 ISBN : 81-219-1518-X pp. 768
07 299 Hardbound ISBN : 81-219-1548-1 pp. 768